FINANCIAL ACCOUNTING

JAMIE PRATT

University of Washington

SCOTT, FORESMAN / LITTLE, BROWN HIGHER EDUCATION
A Division of Scott, Foresman and Company
Glenview, Illinois   London, England

To all my family, especially Mom and Dad

Cover illustration showing doors of the Federal Reserve Bank, Chicago, by Rudy Ohrning

Illustration acknowledgements

Page 1, Photography by Jean-Blaise Hall; page 247, © Karen Halverson; page 793, © Nocholar Foster/Image Bank.

Acknowledgments

Page 15, Figure 1–6, "The Accounting Policymaking Process." Reprinted with permission from *Journal of Accounting Education,* Volume 5, Jamie Pratt, "The Economics of External Reporting: Three Frameworks for the Classroom," Copyright, 1987, Pergamon Press plc.

Page 36, Figure 1–10, "The Role of Financial Accounting Statements." Reprinted with permission from *Journal of Accounting Education,* Volume 5, Jamie Pratt, "The Economics of External Reporting: Three Frameworks for the Classroom," Copyright, 1987, Pergamon Press plc.

Page 256, Table 6–3, from *Accounting Trends and Techniques,* 1987. Reprinted by permission of the American Institute of Certified Public Accountants.

Page 273, Table 6–5, From "Black Monday Casts Shadow Over Profits," in *The Wall Street Journal,* January 26, 1988. Reprinted by permission of the Wall Street Journal, © Dow Jones & Company, Inc. 1988. All Rights Reserved Worldwide.

Page 408, Table 9–3, from *Accounting Trends and Techniques,* 1987. Reprinted by permission of the American Institute of Certified Public Accountants.

Page 432, Table 9A–1, from *Accounting Trends and Techniques,* 1987. Reprinted by permission of the American Institute of Certified Public Accountants.

Page D–1, Appendix D, From *K Mart Corporation's 1988 Annual Report.* Used with the permission of K Mart Corporation, Troy, Michigan.

Library of Congress Cataloging-in-Publication Data

Pratt, Jamie.
   Financial accounting/Jamie Pratt.
     p.   cm.
   ISBN 0-673-16634-1 :
   1. Accounting.   I. Title.
HF5635.P916   1990
657'.48—dc20   89-29574
                             CIP

Artwork, illustrations, and other materials supplied by the publisher.
Copyright © 1990 Scott, Foresman and Company.

2   3   4   5   6-RRW-95 94 93 92 91 90

Preface

≡ *Financial Accounting* is intended for a first course in financial accounting. It can be used at the undergraduate or graduate level by both majors and nonmajors and requires no previous knowledge about accounting or business. The coverage is comprehensive and flexible, allowing its use in courses of one quarter, one semester, or two quarters.

The goal of this text is to provide a balanced coverage of (1) the procedures used to prepare financial statements, (2) the measurement theories underlying the procedures, and (3) the economic environment in which accounting operates. The essential feature distinguishing this text from other introductory accounting texts is its **economic perspective.** Financial accounting statements result from a dynamic process that reflects a demand for information that is used for evaluation and control—information that affects the economic wealth of investors, creditors, managers, auditors, and consumers. The economic environment gives meaning and interest to financial accounting.

In 1980, Professor Stephen A. Zeff, then editor of *The Accounting Review,* called for more coverage of economic consequences in financial accounting textbooks.[1] In response to concerns over shrinking enrollments in accounting programs and reports of a decline in the quality of accounting graduates, Professor Gerhard G. Mueller, president of the American Accounting Association, made the following statement in 1989, almost ten years later:

> *Our present textbooks and pedagogy haven't changed since the 1950s and are quite obsolete. There has developed a huge schism between what's taught in the classroom and what the real world is like. In most colleges, you get the bright, bushy-tailed students into the first-year accounting class, and within the first two weeks, they're totally turned off. They think that accounting is nothing but number-crunching.[2]*

This textbook meets these concerns by demonstrating that financial accounting is more than journals and ledgers. It is an information system that affects students' lives in significant ways, a system that can prepare them better for the challenges awaiting in the world of business.

While the text describes the economic context of financial accounting, it does not ignore important **procedural issues.** Complete chapters are devoted to the accounting cycle (including an appendix on special journals and subsidiary ledgers) and adjusting journal entries. Furthermore, journal and ledger entries throughout the text illustrate accounting methods and concepts. Teaching financial accounting from an economic perspective is meaningless unless the student understands how transactions affect the financial statements. Accounting procedures define such effects and are a necessary and important component of this text.

---

1. Stephen A. Zeff, " 'Intermediate' and 'Advanced' Accounting: The Role of Economic Consequences," *The Accounting Review* (October, 1980), pp. 658–63.

2. Jean Evangelauf, "Accounting Educators Plan to Update Curriculum, Debate Tighter Entrance Requirements for CPAs," *The Chronicle of Higher Education* (May 10, 1989), p. A31.

THREE LEVELS OF FINANCIAL ACCOUNTING

Figure P-1 illustrates the three interrelated levels from which to view financial accounting—economics, measurement theory, and mechanics. The **economic relationships** among investors, creditors, managers, and auditors give rise to a demand for relevant and reliable measures of earning power and solvency. This demand introduces **measurement theory,** the second level from which to view financial accounting. This level provides measures of earning power and solvency, the conceptual or theoretical foundation of financial accounting and underlies the procedures that lead to the financial statements. The **mechanical level** consists of the procedures used to prepare financial statements. These procedures maintain the basic accounting equation and specify how transactions affect a company's financial statements.

The arrow in Figure P-1 linking the mechanical level to the economic level illustrates that the financial statements, which result from the underlying theory and mechanics of accounting, fulfill an economic need. Investors and creditors use these statements to evaluate and control the actions of managers; managers use them to attract capital from investors and creditors; independent auditors, who are hired by managers, examine them to attest to their fairness. The financial accounting system cannot be understood unless all three levels of financial accounting are understood from the perspectives of investors, creditors, managers, and auditors. Introductory accounting students will pursue a wide range of careers, and it is important that they appreciate the multidimensional nature of financial accounting.

CHAPTER COVERAGE

The text is divided into three parts. Part 1 (Chapters 1 through 5) establishes the foundations at the economic, measurement theory, and mechanical levels that will enable students to understand and appreciate the more detailed chapters in Parts 2 and 3. In a sense Part 1 represents a mini-course in financial accounting. Its general coverage of the financial statements provides a balance of mechanics, measurement theory, and economics.

Chapter 1 focuses primarily on the economic level, illustrating first the economic relationships among investors, creditors, managers, and auditors and then discussing the environment and institutional structure within which accounting operates.

Chapter 2 begins to link the economic, measurement theory, and mechanical levels. It introduces the basic accounting equation and the financial statements; it defines each account and discusses each statement in terms of earning power and solvency. Students see how investors and creditors use the numbers in these statements to evaluate and control management.

Chapters 3 and 4 focus on the mechanical level and its link to measurement theory. Chapter 3 is devoted exclusively to mechanics. It covers the accounting cycle (excluding adjusting journal entries) and contains additional sections on computerized accounting systems, special journals and ledgers (Appendix 3A), and internal control (Appendix 3B). Chapter 4 completes the discussion of the accounting cycle and introduces important issues of measurement theory. It begins by distinguishing cash from accrual accounting and then explains how to prepare

Figure P–1   The three levels of financial accounting

Economics

Macroeconomics: The relationships among accounting numbers and macroeconomic variables (e.g., stock prices, interest rates, inflation rates).

Microeconomics: The relationships among accounting numbers and the decisions and wealth levels of investors, creditors, managers, and auditors.

Demand for financial accounting

Measurement Theory

Measures of earning power and solvency

Alternative valuation bases (net present value, exit value, replacement cost, historical cost)

Assumptions (entity, stable dollar, fiscal period, going concern)

Principles (objectivity, matching, revenue recognition, consistency)

Exceptions (materiality, conservatism)

Mechanics

The basic accounting equation: Assets = Liabilities + Stockholders' Equity

The effects of transactions on the financial statements

The accounting cycle (journals, ledgers, worksheets)

The Financial Statements

Accrual-based statements (balance sheet, income statement, statement of retained earnings)

Cash-based statement (statement of cash flows)

the statement of cash flows from the entries to the cash account in the ledger. The remainder of the chapter covers adjusting journal entries and how they implement accrual accounting and the matching principle. Appendix 4A describes how to convert revenues and expenses to cash inflows and outflows, and introduces the fundamentals of preparing the statement of cash flows from accrual-based information.

Chapter 5 integrates the four previous chapters. It explains the assumptions, principles, and exceptions of financial accounting using a framework that links accounting measurement theory to both the economic and mechanical levels. This chapter provides a capstone to Part 1.

Part 2 (Chapters 6 through 15) and Part 3 (Chapters 16 and 17) provide more in-depth coverage of the financial statement accounts in a way that balances mechanics, measurement theory, and economics. Part 2 covers the Current Asset Classification, Cash, and Marketable Securities (Chapter 6), Short-Term Receivables (Chapter 7), Merchandise Inventory (Chapter 8), Long-Lived Assets (Chapter 9), Current Liabilities, Contingencies, Pensions, and Deferred Income Taxes (Chapter 10), Long-Term Liabilities: Notes, Bonds, and Leases (Chapter 11), Stockholders' Equity (Chapter 12), Long-Term Investments (Chapter 13), the Complete Income Statement (Chapter 14), and the Statement of Cash Flows (Chapter 15). Part 3 includes chapters on Consolidated Financial Statements and International Operations (Chapter 16) and Using Financial Statement Information (Chapter 17).

These chapters clearly and precisely describe the methods of accounting and the underlying measurement theories. Easy-to-follow numerical examples support and illustrate the methods and theories. Each chapter also contains a section on economic consequences, tables containing industry and company comparisons, integrated discussions relating financial accounting to significant and timely events (e.g., "Black Monday," problems in the savings and loan industry), numerous quotes from business publications, and frequent excerpts from current corporate annual reports.

The remainder of the text contains special appendixes on the Time Value of Money, including compound interest and present value tables (Appendix A), Correcting Accounting Errors (Appendix B), Accounting for Changing Prices: Inflation and Market Values (Appendix C), and the 1989 annual report of K mart Corporation (Appendix D). A page-referenced glossary and an index are provided at the end of the text.

SPECIAL REAL-WORLD FEATURES

The economic perspective followed in this text requires that the material be up-to-date and reflect important contemporary economic issues. Several text features were designed specifically for this purpose.

Industry Data

Many of the chapters contain tables that compare accounting practices and show the importance of accounting numbers and ratios across different industries and well-known companies. These tables illustrate that the financial accounting issues faced by retailers, manufacturers, service enterprises, and financial institutions are quite different. A brief explanation of the operations of companies in different industries and how these operations give rise to different financial accounting concerns follows each table.

Excerpts from Business Publications and Professional Journals

Excerpts from various business publications (*The Wall Street Journal, Forbes,* and other professional and academic journals) are integrated throughout the text. In addition to documenting and clarifying important points, these excerpts provide a real-world flavor to the text presentation.

Excerpts from Current Corporate Annual Reports

Actual disclosures and quotes from the annual reports of well known corporations are integrated throughout the text. These excerpts provide actual examples of the accounting and disclosure practices of major U.S. corporations and, in many cases, indicate the issues foremost in the minds of management when it reports to the stockholders. To impress students with the variety of disclosure and presentation practices of major U.S. corporations, these excerpts have not been modified to conform to the financial statement presentation style used throughout the text. While this approach results in certain inconsistencies, it is an unavoidable characteristic of a text designed to capture real-world accounting practices.

K Mart's Annual Report

The 1989 annual report of K mart Corporation appears in Appendix D at the end of the text. Each chapter contains a section relating the report to accounting issues covered in the chapter. This feature provides students with another opportunity to relate the text material to the real world. The end of Chapter 17 presents a complete and comparative ratio analysis of K mart Corporation and Wal-mart Stores, Inc.

Real-World Cases

Each chapter is followed by cases for analysis and discussion. These cases are based on current, real-world situations. Some require that the student analyze and/or interpret actual corporate disclosures, while others ask for commentaries on relevant quotes from well known business publications and business leaders. Once again, the student has the opportunity to relate the chapter material to current events in the business environment.

SPECIAL PEDAGOGICAL FEATURES

The text contains a number of features designed specifically to aid the student's learning process. These features are discussed below.

From Simple to Complex

The text develops broad and relatively simple concepts first, followed by gradually increased detail and complexity. Such a strategy helps students to understand better the fundamental concepts without getting lost in the detail that characterizes much of financial accounting. It also enables students to see more easily how relatively few concepts underlie most of financial accounting measurement. This strategy is used within and across chapters of the text.

The presentation of the statement of cash flows provides an example of gradually building from broad and simple to detailed and complex. The statement is introduced in Chapters 1 and 2 where it is discussed in general terms and where its relationship with the other financial statements in the measure of solvency is emphasized. The mechanics of preparing the statement are introduced in Chapter 3 where the statement is prepared directly from the cash account in the ledger. In Chapter 4 a more complex form of the statement of cash flows is prepared from the cash account in the ledger, and throughout the chapter, the differences between accrual and cash-basis accounting are examined. Appendix 4A demonstrates how the revenues and expenses on a relatively simple income statement can be adjusted to compute net cash flow from operating activities. The notion of accrual versus cash flow is mentioned many times in the subsequent chapters, but it is not until Chapter 15 that a comprehensive coverage of the statement of cash flows appears. This chapter covers how the statement is used and, using a relatively complex example, illustrates how it can be prepared from the information contained in two balance sheets and an income statement.

Presenting the statement of cash flows in the above manner allows the text to give balanced coverage to the three major financial statements from the beginning, highlighting the fact that no statement is more or less important than the others. At the same time, presenting the material in this way allows the student gradually to work up to the level of understanding required to prepare and appreciate the statement of cash flows in its complete form.

Visual Frameworks

Many visual frameworks illustrate and describe complex procedural processes, measurement theories, and economic relationships. Figure P-1 is a typical example. Such frameworks aid the learning process by enabling students to see relationships that otherwise would be obscure. Instructors may also find these frameworks useful in organizing lectures and discussions.

Simple and Relevant Examples

Numerical examples, both simple and relevant, appear throughout the text. Some illustrate basic accounting procedures, others compare the financial statement effects of alternative accounting methods, and still others demonstrate how operating decisions and accounting methods and estimates relate to the terms of contracts. The mathematical operations involved in these examples are always simple, and in each case, the example demonstrates a point developed in the text. In cases where examples are used to compare different accounting methods, the methods are normally presented side-by-side on a single figure. This type of presentation is not only efficient, but it also enhances comparability.

Chapter Materials and End-of-Chapter Materials

Learning Objectives and Chapter Summaries. Each chapter is preceded by a list of learning objectives designed to highlight the important issues in the chapter. These objectives guide the student through the material, indicating those areas needing additional attention. The chapter summary restates the learning objectives and includes a summary answer of each, providing both a concise statement of the basic issues addressed by each objective and an efficient summary of the chapter material.

Review Problems. Each chapter (except Chapter 1) is followed by a comprehensive review problem that tests the student on the mechanics underlying the essential accounting methods covered in the chapter. A solution follows each problem. These problems not only test a student's knowledge, but also serve as a reminder that procedural issues are at the heart of understanding important accounting concepts.

Key Terms and Glossary. An important objective of this course is to establish an understanding of the relevant terminology. Accordingly, several features are designed to help students learn key financial accounting terms. The important terms in each chapter are printed in bold face type when they are first defined in the text. A list of these terms appears at the end of each chapter, and a glossary of key terms is provided in the back of the text. Each term in both the end-of-chapter lists and the glossary is referenced by the page in the text where it is first defined.

Questions, Exercises, Problems, and Cases. The review material at the end of each chapter is comprehensive and complete. Twenty or more questions, which follow the order of topics covered in the text and provide a systematic review of the chapter material, are provided at the end of each chapter.

The procedures and concepts discussed and illustrated in a given chapter are each covered by at least one exercise and one problem. The exercises and problems have been arranged by degree of difficulty, moving from simpler to more complex within each type. Chapters typically contain ten to fifteen exercises and ten to fifteen problems. The exercises are relatively simple and require fewer and less complicated computations than do the problems. In addition, most exercises deal with only one concept, while the problems often consider several concepts simultaneously. The exercises and problems, each of which is accompanied by a brief description of the concepts or procedures being covered, can be classified into three categories requiring the student to (1) perform straightforward accounting procedures or classify various financial statement accounts, (2) determine the effects of different accounting methods on important financial statement numbers (e.g., net income, current ratio, debt/equity ratio), or (3) assess the impact of different accounting methods on contracts such as debt covenants and compensation contracts. As mentioned earlier, each chapter is also followed by at least five cases, each of which is based on a real-world situation.

FLEXIBLE ORGANIZATION

The text can be adapted to different course formats at either the undergraduate or graduate level. A number of chapters, for example, are followed by appendixes that the instructor may choose to cover. Chapters 13 (Long-Term Investments), 14 (The Complete Income Statement), 16 (Consolidated Financial Statements and International Operations), 17 (Used Financial Accounting Information), and Appendixes A (Time Value of Money), B (Correcting Accounting Errors), and C (Accounting for Changing Prices: Inflation and Market Values) at the end of the text represent topics that, depending on time considerations and the interests of the instructor, may or may not be assigned. Many chapters are organized so that certain topics can be omitted without losing continuity. Contingencies, pensions, and deferred income taxes, for example, can easily be deleted from Chapter 10, while capital leases can be deleted from Chapter 11. As a result, instructors can develop courses to fit almost any format by selectively choosing from the available material.

The traditional one-quarter introductory accounting course at the undergraduate level, for example, could include Chapters 1 through 12, deleting contingencies, pensions, deferred income taxes, and capital leases and using Appendix 4A to cover the statement of cash flows. A more procedural approach could cover the same topics, but spend more time with Chapter 3 and Appendix 3A and less time with Chapter 5.

A one-quarter course at the graduate level might include Chapters 1 through 12 and Chapter 15 without deleting one or more of the topics mentioned above, while a one-quarter course designed for nonaccounting majors could consist of Chapters 1 through 5, 14, 15, and 17, and Appendixes A and C at the end of the text.

A semester course at either the graduate or undergraduate level could cover Chapters 1 through 12, and Chapter 15, and some combination of Chapters 14, 16, and 17, and Appendixes A, B, and C at the end of the text. Virtually the entire textbook could be covered in a two-quarter course.

These course strategies are merely suggestions designed to highlight the fact that the text can be used in a variety of circumstances. It is sufficiently comprehensive to provide the material for a conceptually oriented, two-quarter graduate level course and, at the same time, can be adapted to a one-quarter undergraduate course with an emphasis on procedures. In any case, one aspect about the text is certain—the coverage will provide an interesting balance of mechanics, measurement theory, and economics.

ACCURATE PRESENTATION

Throughout the development and production of this book, accuracy has been a primary concern. The manuscript was extensively reviewed over several drafts by accounting faculty from a variety of universities, and was also class tested a number of times. All exercises, problems, and cases were solved completely by independent reviewers. The attention to accuracy continued as the manuscript was typeset. All chapters were reviewed once again by accounting faculty, with some concentrating on textual content, some on illustration material, and others on the exercises, problems, and cases. Extreme care has been taken to ensure that the text is consistent, accurate, and clearly written.

STUDENT LEARNING AIDS

Study Guide. Prepared by S. Sam Sedki (St. Mary's University). Designed to have a procedural flavor that complements the text, this invaluable study aid includes the following elements for each chapter: chapter overview; review of key terms, including definitions; matching, fill-in-the-blank, and multiple-choice questions; and short procedure-specific exercises, all of which highlight important concepts and relationships introduced in the text.

Working Papers. This supplement contains a sufficient number of appropriate blank forms for all exercises and problems in the text. Each form is identified by exercise/problem number.

Practice Set. Created by Mark Friedman (University of Miami), "Byte of Accounting, Inc." is an effective computerized practice set that uses the general ledger component of DacEasy Accounting™, one of the most popular commercial accounting packages on the market, to demonstrate the value of the computer as a tool of the accountant. By using a real general ledger, students are able to acquire a more meaningful experience with the computer and the monthly accounting cycle of a corporation. "Byte of Accounting, Inc." gives students the opportunity to complete the accounting cycle manually prior to using the computer, an exercise that allows them to build upon work already completed. The package is available for student purchase and is intended for use with the IBM-PC and compatibles.

Financial Accounting Simulation Analysis. Developed by Jamie Pratt to be used on either Lotus 1-2-3 or Excell, this flexible simulation provides the student with the ultimate form of role playing. Step-by-step instructions allow the student to build a set of financial statements and assess the effects of a variety of managerial decisions on these statements and related financial ratios over a three-year period. The decisions include (1) issuing stock and long-term debt under various terms, (2) purchasing and selling marketable securities, inventory, land, and equipment at various prices (3) selling goods at various prices, (4) declaring cash and stock dividends, (5) employing different collection and payment strategies, and (6) choosing from among the different methods of accounting for uncollectibles, inventory, depreciation, and amortizing debt premiums and discounts. This unique simulation will bring to life the economic consequences of financial accounting.

SUPPLEMENTS FOR THE INSTRUCTOR

Instructor's Manual. Prepared by James R. Frederickson. This instructor's resource includes suggested syllabi for courses for various lengths and approaches. Each chapter includes a synopsis that highlights general chapter topics; chapter learning objectives; a list of key terms; a text/lecture outline that summarizes the chapter in detail; lecture tips for areas in which students commonly have difficulty; an annotated bibliography relevant to chapter topics; answers to chapter questions; and an assignment classification table on difficulty level, approximate completion time, and relation to chapter learning objectives for each exercise and problem. The manual also contains a checklist of key figures.

Text Bank. Prepared by Steven Reimer (University of Iowa). This bank of more than 1500 questions features chapter tests comprised of questions that are categorized by learning objectives and by question orientation (i.e., whether the question tests procedures, measurement concepts, or economic concepts). Also included are four comprehensive exams, each of which include questions over four to five chapters.

Solutions Manual. Developed by James R. Frederickson. This supplement provides complete solutions to all exercises, problems, and cases in the text.

Solutions Transparencies. This package includes over 750 acetates that illustrate the solutions for each exercise, problem, and case in the text.

Teaching Transparencies. Fifty carefully developed two-color acetates focus on the key concepts of the text, concepts that lend themselves to illustration and classroom discussion. Each acetate was selected by a special review panel that included the author.

ACKNOWLEDGEMENTS

This text benefited significantly from the constructive and insightful comments provided by the individuals listed below. Their painstaking review of the text resulted in suggestions that helped to focus and integrate the ideas presented into a text that now can serve as a source of great pride for us all.

Hobart W. Adams
University of Akron
Ashraf ElNaggar
University of Kentucky
Peter E. Battelle
University of Vermont
Thomas A. Buchman
University of Colorado at Boulder
Roberta J. Cable
Sacred Heart University
Janet Cunningham
University of Oklahoma
Edwin A. Doty, Jr.
University of South Carolina
Mark Friedman
University of Miami
David Gotlob
University of Wisconsin, Oshkosh
David W. Harvey
Tulane University
Elizabeth Jenkins
San Jose State University
Charles A. Konkol
University of Wisconsin, Milwaukee
William C. Lins
Rutgers University

David J. Marcinko
State University of New York at Albany
Alan G. Mayper
University of North Texas
Dennis Murphy
California State University, Los Angeles
Virginia L. Parks
Seattle University
Patrick M. Premo
Saint Bonaventure University
Steven C. Reimer
University of Iowa
Philip Shane
University of Arizona
Brian B. Stanko
University of Kentucky
James Stanley
University of Oklahoma
Earl K. Stice
University of Arizona
T. Sterling Wetzel
Oklahoma State University
Beth A. Yerington
University of Northern Iowa
David Ziebart,
University of Illinois

Many other people deserve thanks and recognition for the contributions they have made to this text. I appreciate the efforts of all those who prepared ancillary material, but I especially want to mention the people at the University of Washington. James Frederickson developed the majority of the exercises and problems, class tested earlier versions of the manuscript on several occasions, and prepared the instructor's and solutions manual. His interest and consistent attention to this text improved it immeasurably. Marilyn Johnson, Ruth Kgosi, and Ken McGhee also class tested earlier versions and provided helpful comments. Tom Porter developed most of the cases and the case solutions, and Jim Stice wrote a number of the exercises and problems in Part 1.

The editorial, design, and marketing staffs, including Jim Boyd, David Brake, Patricia Schmelling, Nick Murray, John Young, Jeanne Schwaba, Paula Meyers, and Don Grainger represent a first-rate group of professionals. Their high quality work helped to ensure that the manuscript was comprehensive, coherent, and completed in a timely and orderly fashion.

Special thanks go to my wife, Kathy, and children, Jason and Ryan. Their support and understanding were consistent through the seemingly endless development and production processes. Now that the text is complete, it will be nice to turn more attention to being a husband and father.

Jamie Pratt

Contents

P A R T   2

A Closer Look at the Financial Statements   *247*

PART 1

An Overview of Financial Accounting

Financial Accounting and Its Economic Context

Learning Objectives

1 Identify and briefly describe the four basic components of the financial accounting process.

2 Name the four financial statements, and briefly explain the kind of financial information that each provides.

3 Briefly describe the contents of the audit report, the management letter, and the footnotes to the financial statements.

4 Describe the two basic forms of investment, and explain how the information on the financial statements is related to them.

5 Explain the role of financial accounting statements in terms of the business relationships among investors and creditors, managers, and auditors.

6 Explain why ethics is important in the accounting process.

7 Provide a general definition of financial accounting and briefly elaborate on its components.

8 List the four different kinds of accounting and briefly describe each.

9 Briefly explain the nature of the accounting profession and the different employment positions held by accountants.

10 Describe the Securities and Exchange Commission and the Financial Accounting Standards Board and their respective roles in the development of generally accepted accounting principles.

11 Explain how and why economic consequences are important to financial accounting standard-setting.

≣ This text concerns the **financial accounting** process, which consists of four basic components. Each component is briefly introduced below, and the remainder of the chapter develops these ideas more completely.

1. The financial accounting process is initiated when managers of profit-seeking companies prepare reports containing financial information for the owners of these companies. In addition to other information, these reports contain four basic financial statements: the balance sheet, the income statement, the statement of retained earnings, and the statement of cash flows.

2. Although prepared primarily for the owners of the company, these financial reports are available to the public and are read by a variety of interested parties, who use them to assess the financial condition and performance of the company as well as the performance of its managers. Such interested parties include, for example, potential investors, bankers, government agencies, and the company's customers and suppliers.

3. These parties obtain information from the financial reports that helps them to assess the company's past performance, predict its future performance, and control the activities of its managers. Financial reports, therefore, help them to make better business decisions. Investors, for example, use financial reports to choose companies in which to invest their funds; bankers use them to decide where to loan their funds and what interest rates to charge.

4. The decisions these parties make affect the financial condition and performance of the company and the economic well-being of its managers. For example, a banker may use the information contained in a financial report to decide not to loan a certain company much-needed funds. Such a decision may cause the company to fail and cost its managers their jobs.

Figure 1–1 illustrates the four basic components of the financial accounting process. Note, in particular, the dynamic nature of the process: the financial infor-

Figure 1–1   The financial accounting process

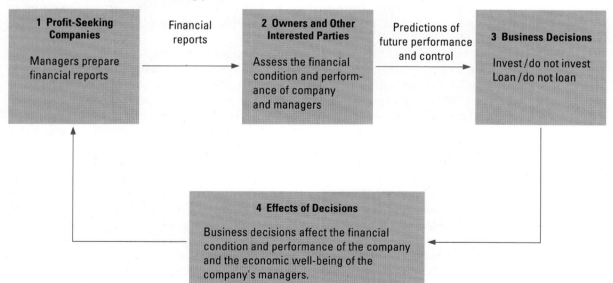

mation provided by a company's managers is used by interested parties to make business decisions which, in turn, affect the company's financial condition and the economic well-being of its managers. In short, the managers of profit-seeking companies are required to provide financial information that the owners of these companies and others use to evaluate the managers' performance.

The next section develops a scenario designed to highlight the important general issues that arise in the financial accounting process. Then, in terms of those issues, we discuss the objectives of the text, the basic role of financial accounting statements in the business environment, and the general definition of financial accounting. The remaining sections describe the four different kinds of accounting, the different employment positions held by accountants, and the evolution and establishment of **generally accepted accounting principles (GAAP),** the standards that guide the preparation of the financial accounting statements.

THE DEMAND FOR FINANCIAL INFORMATION: AN EXAMPLE

Suppose for the moment that you recently received notice that a long-lost relative died and left you a large sum of money. You are not particularly knowledgeable about financial matters, so you consult Mary Jordan, a financial advisor, to help you decide what to do with the funds. She tells you that you have two basic choices: you can consume it or you can invest it.

By consuming your new fortune, Mary simply means that you spend the money on goods and services; for example, a trip around the world, expensive meals, a lavish wardrobe, or any other expenses that bring about immediate gratification. Consumption expenditures, by definition, are enjoyed immediately and have no future value.

By investing the fortune, she means that you spend the money on items that provide little in the way of immediate gratification. Rather, they generate returns of additional money at later dates. In essence, investments trade off current consumption for more consumption at a later date. Examples include investing in stocks and bonds, real estate, rare art objects, or simply placing the money in the bank.

You decide to invest the money and with a little direction from Mary, you begin to explore investment alternatives. You find that investments come in a number of different forms, however, and you quickly become overwhelmed, confused, and frustrated. Just as you are about to give up your search and put all your money in the bank, a man by the name of Martin Wagner knocks at your door. Through a mutual friend, Martin has heard of your recent windfall and states that he has an interesting offer for you.

Martin claims that he manages a very successsful research company, called Microline, owned by a group of European investors. In its short, two-year history the company has earned a reputation for innovation in software development. As Martin describes it, Microline's research staff is on the verge of designing a voice-activated word-processing system that will revolutionize word-processing in the future.

Martin has come to you for capital, $1 million to be exact. The company's research and development efforts have run short of funds, and money is still needed to complete the design. With your money, Martin asserts that the software system can be completed and sold, producing millions of dollars of income, some of which will provide you with a handsome return on your investment. Without your capital, on the other hand, Martin believes that the project may have to be abandoned.

The Demand for Documentation

You have listened to Martin's story and now must decide what to do. Your first thought is that you cannot simply accept his word without some documented evidence. How do you really know that he has successfully managed this business for the past two years and that $1 million will enable the company to turn this design into a fortune in the future? Martin is likeable and very intelligent but, at the same time, his presentation seems to be a little too smooth, and there is no doubt that he is certainly asking you for a lot of money.

After careful consideration, you decide that you need to see some proof before making a final decision. You ask specifically for documents to show that Microline has been run successfully for the past two years, is presently in reasonably good financial condition, and has the potential to generate income of the magnitude Martin suggests. He agrees to provide you with such documentation because he knows that if he does not, you will invest your money elsewhere, and both he and Microline will suffer.

Several days later Martin returns with a set of financial statements prepared by Microline's accountants. He explains the meanings of the numbers on the statements and further claims that the records at his office can be used to verify them. Taken at face value, the figures look promising, but somehow Martin's explanation is not convincing. It occurs to you that Martin might fabricate or at least bias the figures. After all, Microline needs money, and who would blame Martin for only showing you the figures that make Microline's situation look attractive to a potential investor?

The Demand for an Independent Audit

You decide to demand that Martin go one step further: he must return again with financial statements that have been checked and verified by an independent outsider who is an expert in such matters. You insist that the person not be employed by Microline or have any interest whatsoever in the company and have the appropriate credentials to perform such a task. In essence, you demand that Martin hire a **certified public accountant (CPA)** to verify Microline's financial statements. You require, in other words, that Microline subject itself to an **independent audit.** Martin agrees because, once again, if he does not, you will take your money and invest it elsewhere. At the same time, however, Martin is somewhat troubled. He knows that hiring and working with a CPA can be very costly and time-consuming.

Martin and the CPA: Different Perspectives

Time passes and you become concerned that Martin has taken too long to return with the financial statements. You have thought of several questions since Martin's last visit and decide to call on him in person. You arrive at Microline's well-kept but modestly furnished office and are seated by Martin's secretary. As you are waiting, you chance to hear Martin's voice through the partly open door to his office. He seems to be discussing Microline's financial statements with the CPA. While you cannot understand exactly what is being said, it is clear that they are not in complete agreement and that they are both strong in their convictions.

You wonder why Martin and the CPA might view the financial statements from different perspectives and speculate that perhaps the CPA recommended presenting Microline's financial condition in a way that was unsatisfactory to Martin. You reason that Martin should probably follow the CPA's recommendation because, after all, the CPA is the expert in financial reporting. You realize, however, that Martin wants the statements to be as attractive as possible and that he may have some influence over the CPA. Indeed, Martin did hire the CPA and does pay the CPA's fee.

Before long, the CPA leaves and Martin invites you into his office. During your short discussion, you mention nothing of what you think you have heard. Martin answers your questions confidently and assures you that the statements will be ready within the week. Satisfied, you return home.

The Auditor's Report, the Management Letter, and the Financial Statements

Soon thereafter, Martin arrives at your home with seven official-looking documents: (1) an **auditor's report,** a short letter written by the auditor that describes the activities of the audit and comments on the financial position and operations of Microline. (2) a **management letter,** signed by Martin, which accepts responsibility for the figures on the statements, (3) a balance sheet, (4) an income statement, (5) a statement of retained earnings, (6) a statement of cash flows, and (7) a comprehensive set of footnotes, which more fully explain certain items on the four statements listed above. You briefly review the documents and tell Martin that you will have a decision for him soon.

The Auditor's Report
You decide to begin your examination by reviewing the auditor's report, from which you hope to learn how credible the financial statements actually are (see Figure 1−2).

Overall, you are reassured by the auditor's report. It indicates that the auditor reviewed Microline's records thoroughly and concluded that the statements (1) were prepared in conformity with generally accepted accounting principles and (2) present fairly Microline's financial condition and operations. You suspect that the auditor could have rendered a much less favorable report, such as that the statements were not prepared in conformance with generally accepted accounting principles, or that no opinion could be reached because Microline's accounting system was so poorly designed, or that Microline was in danger of failure. You also realize, however, that you know very little about either generally accepted auditing standards or generally accepted accounting principles, and that Microline's management made a number of significant estimates when preparing the statements. This discovery is somewhat troubling because, even with the audit, it seems that Microline's management may have had some subjective influence on the financial statements.

Figure 1–2 The audit report

> To the Board of Directors and Shareholders of Microline:
>
> We have audited the accompanying balance sheet of Microline as of December 31, 1989 and 1988, and the related statements of income, retained earnings, and cash flows for the years then ended. These financial statements are the responsibility of the Company's management. Our responsibility is to express an opinion on these financial statements based on our audit.
>
> We conducted our audit in accordance with generally accepted auditing standards. Those standards require that we plan and perform the audit to obtain reasonable assurance about whether the financial statements are free of material misstatement. An audit includes examining, on a test basis, evidence supporting the amounts and disclosures in the financial statements. An audit also includes assessing the accounting principles used and significant estimates made by management, as well as evaluating the overall financial statement presentation. We believe that our audit provides a reasonable basis for our opinion.
>
> In our opinion, the financial statements referred to above present fairly, in all material respects, the financial position of Microline as of December 31, 1988 and 1989, and the results of its operations, and its cash flows for the years then ended in conformity with generally accepted accounting principles.
>
> *Arthur Price*
>
> Arthur Price, Certified Public Accountant
> March 12, 1990

The Management Letter

You next move to the management letter, hoping to learn more about how the financial statements were prepared and audited (see Figure 1–3).

Once again, you are both reassured and troubled. It is comforting to know that Microline's management is accepting responsibility for the integrity of the statements, which have been prepared in conformance with generally accepted accounting principles, and that the company has an **internal control system** that safeguards the assets and reasonably ensures that transactions are properly recorded and reported. It is also nice to know that Microline's policies prescribe that its employees maintain high ethical standards. However, you still do not understand generally accepted accounting principles, are still concerned that the statements reflect management's estimates and judgments, and have very little idea about the function of Microline's Board of Directors and Audit Committee.

The Financial Statements

You briefly review the four financial statements (see Figure 1–4) and note first that dollar amounts are listed for both 1988 and 1989. This discovery is somewhat discouraging because only information about the past is included on the statements and subject to the auditor's report and management letter. Nothing at all about Microline's future prospects is included in the financial statements—but the future is what interests you most. Whether Microline is able to provide an

Figure 1–3 Management's letter

Management's Responsibilities:

Management is responsible for the preparation and integrity of the financial statements and the financial comments appearing in this financial report. The financial statements were prepared in accordance with generally accepted accounting principles and include certain amounts based on management's best estimates and judgments. Other financial information presented in this financial report is consistent with the financial statements.

The Company maintains a system of internal controls designed to provide reasonable assurance that the assets are safeguarded and that transactions are executed as authorized and are recorded and reported properly. The system of controls is based upon written policies and procedures, appropriate divisions of responsibility and authority, careful selection and training of personnel, and a comprehensive internal audit program. The Company's policies and procedures prescribe that the Company and all employees are to maintain the highest ethical standards and that its business practices are to be conducted in a manner which is above reproach.

Arthur Price, an independent certified public accountant, has examined the Company's financial statements, and the audit report is present herein. The Board of Directors has an Audit Committee composed entirely of outside directors. Arthur Price has direct access to the Audit Committee and meets with the committee to discuss accounting, auditing, and financial reporting matters.

Martin Wagner

Martin Wagner, Chief Executive Officer
March 12, 1990

---

acceptable return on your $1 million investment depends primarily on what happens in the future. The past is often a poor indicator of the future.

You also observe that each statement emphasizes a different aspect of Microline's financial condition and performance. The balance sheet, for example, lists the company's assets, liabilities, and stockholders' equity. On the income statement, expenses are subtracted from revenues to produce a number called net income. The statement of retained earnings includes (1) the beginning and ending retained earnings balance, which can be found on the 1988 and 1989 balance sheets, (2) net income, which is the bottom line on the income statement, and (3) dividends. The statement of cash flows includes the beginning and ending balance of cash, which can be found on the 1988 and 1989 balance sheets, and net cash flows from operating, investing, and financing activities. It becomes clear quite quickly that you do not understand these terms, that you know very little about the information conveyed by these statements and, therefore, cannot begin to assess whether Microline would be a good company in which to invest.

The Footnotes

At this point you decide to examine the **footnotes**, hoping that they will clear up some of your uncertainty about the financial statements (Figure 1-5). They state that many of the numbers on the statements are the result of assumptions and

Figure 1–4   Financial statements for Microline

Microline Financial Statements For the Years Ended Dec. 31, 1988 and 1989		
Balance Sheet	**1989**	**1988**
Assets		
Cash	$ 100,000	$ 60,000
Accounts receivable	80,000	90,000
Equipment	330,000	300,000
Land	500,000	500,000
Total assets	$1,010,000	$ 950,000
Liabilities and Stockholders' Equity		
Short-term payables	$ 50,000	$ 30,000
Long-term payables	420,000	450,000
Common stock	400,000	400,000
Retained earnings	140,000	70,000
Total liabilities and stockholders' equity	$1,010,000	$ 950,000
Income Statement		
Revenues	$1,650,000	$1,500,000
Expenses	1,450,000	1,350,000
Net income	$ 200,000	$ 150,000
Statement of Retained Earnings		
Beginning retained earnings balance	$ 70,000	$ 0
Plus: Net income	200,000	150,000
Less: Dividends	130,000	80,000
Ending retained earnings balance	$ 140,000	$ 70,000
Statement of Cash Flows		
Net cash flow from operating activities	$ 250,000	$ 120,000
Net cash flow from investing activities	(50,000)	(340,000)
Net cash flow from financing activities	(160,000)	280,000
Net increase (decrease) in cash	$ 40,000	$ 60,000
Beginning cash balance	60,000	0
Ending cash balance	$ 100,000	$ 60,000

estimates made by Microline's management, which does not surprise you because similar statements were made in both the audit report and the management letter. It is also clear from the footnotes that Microline was able to choose from a number of different acceptable accounting methods. While you know little about generally accepted accounting principles, you confidently conclude that they do not ensure exact and unbiased statements. Alternative accounting methods as well as assumptions and estimates by Microline's management are very evident.

After your initial examination you decide that Microline may be a reasonable investment, but your lack of knowledge and understanding renders you incapable

Figure 1–5   Notes to the financial statements

Cash. Cash consists of cash on hand and cash in a bank checking account.

Accounts Receivable. The balance in accounts receivable has been adjusted for an estimate of future uncollectibles.

Equipment. Equipment is carried at a cost and includes expenditures for new additions and those which substantially increase its useful life. The cost of the equipment is depreciated using the straight-line method over an estimated useful life of ten years.

Land. Land is carried at cost.

Short-Term Payables. Short-term payables consist of wages payable, salaries payable, short-term borrowings, interest payable, taxes payable, and an estimate of future warranty costs.

Long-Term Payables. Long-term payables consist primarily of notes that must be paid back after one year.

Common Stock. Common stock represents the contributions of the company's stockholders.

Revenue Recognition. Revenues from sales are reflected in the income statement when products are shipped. Revenues from services are estimated in proportion to the completion of the service.

Expenses. Expenses include selling and administrative expenses and estimates of uncollectible receivables and depreciation on the equipment.

---

of making a confident choice. You decide to return to Mary Jordan, your financial advisor, for help. Perhaps she can explain the nature of the financial statements and improve your understanding of the decision that faces you.

The Financial Statements: Definitions and Preliminary Analysis

Mary begins by defining some of the fundamental terms used on the financial statements. The **balance sheet,** for example, which lists Microline's assets, liabilities, and stockholders' equity, is a statement of the company's financial position as of a certain date. **Assets** include Microline's cash balance, the dollar amounts due from Microline's customers (accounts receivable), and the original cost of the equipment and land purchased by the company. **Liabilities** consist of the amounts presently owed by Microline to its **creditors.** Satisfying these liabilities will generally require cash payments in the future. Common stock and retained earnings comprise the **stockholders' equity** section. **Common stock** represents the initial investments by Microline's owners, and **retained earnings** is a measure of Microline's past profits that have been retained in the business.

The **income statement** is divided into two components: **revenues,** a measure of the assets generated from the products and services sold, and **expenses,** a measure of the asset outflows (costs) associated with selling these products and services. The difference between these two amounts is a number called **net income (profit),** which measures the success of Microline's operations over a particular period of time.

The **statement of retained earnings** describes the increases and decreases to retained earnings, which is a measure of Microline's past profits over a period of time. The net income, or profit, amount from the income statement is first added to the beginning balance of retained earnings. **Dividends,** the assets paid to Microline's owners as a return for their initial investment, are then subtracted from this amount to compute ending retained earnings. The ending retained earnings amount appears on the balance sheet and becomes the beginning balance of the following period.

The **statement of cash flows** summarizes the increases and decreases in cash over a period of time. The beginning cash balance is adjusted for the *net cash flows* (cash inflows less cash outflows) associated with Microline's operating, investing, and financing activities. **Operating activities** are associated with the actual products and services provided by Microline for its customers. **Investing activities** include the purchase and sale of assets, such as equipment and land. **Financing activities** refers to the cash collections and payments related to Microline's *capital sources*. Examples include cash borrowings and loan payments as well as collections from owners' contributions and the payment of dividends.

After defining the terms on the financial statements, Mary notes that Microline appears to be in reasonably strong financial shape. She focuses first on the statement of cash flows, pointing out that the company's cash position has been increasing and that operating activities have contributed $120,000 and $250,000 in cash in the last two years. She also notes that Microline has invested heavily in new assets since its inception, and that $160,000 was paid during 1989 for dividends and to reduce outstanding debts. In short, Microline has demonstrated the ability to generate cash, which Mary believes is very important because in order to remain **solvent,** the company must be able to generate enough cash to meet its debts as they come due.

Mary then moves to the income statement and statement of retained earnings, noting that Microline has shown profits of $150,000 and $200,000 over the past two years and, at the same time, has paid significant dividends to its owners, specifically $80,000 in 1988 and $130,000 in 1989. These numbers show that Microline has demonstrated **earning power,** the ability to grow, over the past two years. Moreover, the company seems to have provided a substantial return to its owners.

Finally, Mary notes that the balance sheets indicate Microline's assets have increased during the past year from $950,000 to $1,010,000, while its liabilities have decreased from $480,000 to $470,000. She indicates that such a trend is promising.

What Form of Investment?

The definitions and analysis provided by Mary are encouraging, and you decide that Microline is a good investment. However, Mary cautions you not to move too quickly and states that now you must decide what form your investment should take. Should it be in the form of a loan, or should you purchase ownership (equity) in Microline? She explains that the risks you face and the potential returns associated with these two forms of investment are really quite different. Moreover, the relative importance to you of the different kinds of information disclosed on the financial statements depends on the kind of investment you make.

A Debt Investment
You would make a **debt investment** if you loaned the $1 million to Microline. You would then become one of the company's creditors and would require that Microline's management sign a **loan contract** prepared by a lawyer. The contract would specify (1) the *maturity date,* the date when the loan is to be paid back; (2)

the **annual interest** payment, the amount of interest to be paid each year; (3) *collateral*, assets to be passed to you in case the principal or the interest on the loan is in *default* (not paid back); and (4) any other **debt restrictions** you feel you should impose on Microline to protect your investment. The contract might specify, for example, that Microline maintain a certain cash balance throughout the period of the loan, or that dividends during that period be limited to a certain amount.

As one of Microline's creditors, your first concern would be Microline's ability to meet the loan's interest and principal payments as they come due. Since such payments are made in cash, you would be especially interested in Microline's cash management record and its ability to generate cash over the period of the loan. Thus, the information in the statement of cash flows would be very relevant. You would also be interested in the selling prices of assets that could be used as collateral, and in the amounts of the loans and other liabilities owed by Microline to other creditors. The balance sheet, therefore, which lists Microline's assets and liabilities, would also contain some useful information.

Mary reminds you, however, that many of Microline's assets are valued on the balance sheet at **historical cost,** the dollar amount paid when the assets were acquired, which, in many cases, was two years ago. This discovery is worrisome, because the historical cost of an asset is rarely the same as its current selling price, the relevant amount if an asset is to be considered as collateral for a loan.

An Equity Investment

Rather than loaning Microline the $1 million, you may wish to puchase **equity** in the company. As an equity investor you would become one of the owners, or **stockholders,** of Microline.

Equity investments give rise to considerations that are somewhat different from those of debt investments. As a stockholder, for example, your return would be primarily in the form of dividends, which would tend to be large if Microline performed well and small, or nonexistent, if the company performed poorly. Unlike a loan investment, for which interest and principal payments are specified by contract, dividend payments are at the discretion of Microline's **board of directors,** which is elected annually by the stockholders to represent their interests. Such representation involves quarterly meetings where company policies are set, dividends are declared, and the performance and compensation of the company's upper management is reviewed. The board of directors has the power to hire and fire upper management as well as determine the form and amount of their compensation.

As a stockholder who could vote in the election of the board of directors, your primary concern would be the performance of Microline's management—specifically, its ability to generate and maintain earnings in the future. To achieve such an objective, management must both ensure that cash is available to meet debts as they come due and invest in assets that produce a satisfactory return in the long run. Consequently, stockholders are interested in the information contained in all four of the financial statements: the balance sheet because it indicates Microline's assets and liabilities, the income statement and statement of retained earnings because they indicate Microline's earning power and dividend payments, and the statement of cash flows because it provides a report of Microline's past cash management policies. As a stockholder, however, you would be especially interested in the income statement, since the board of directors often sets dividends as a percentage of income, which is generally considered to be the overall measure of management's performance and the company's earning power.

You would also be interested in the methods used to compensate Microline's upper management. You may wish, for example, to encourage the board of directors to institute a system of compensation that paid upper management on the basis of its performance. One way to implement such a system would be to set compensation levels at amounts expressed as percentages of net income. This would motivate Microline's management to increase net income and, accordingly, their compensation. Such a result should also mean increased earning power and greater dividend payments in the future.

A Decision Is Made but Important Questions Still Remain

After a lengthy discussion with Mary, you decide to invest in the equity of Microline. From the information contained in the audit report, the management letter, the financial statement, and the footnotes, you have concluded that Microline is a legitimate operation that is solvent, has shown significant earning power, and has provided a reasonable return to its stockholders. You reason further that if Martin is correct in his prediction that their new voice-activated word-processing system will revolutionize the industry, there is a distinct possibility of large returns in the future. Stockholders would receive such returns in the form of larger dividends, while payments to creditors would be limited to the contractual interest and principal payments.

You thank Mary for her advice and feel satisfied with your decision. You realize, however, that the future is uncertain and that your investment involves risks. Furthermore, a number of troubling questions still remain unanswered:

• What is the nature of the relationship among a company's owners, creditors, and managers, and how can the owners and creditors ensure that their investments are managed effectively?

• What is the nature of the relationship between a company's management and its independent auditor, and why would there be disagreements between Martin and the CPA?

• What are generally accepted accounting principles and why do they allow the manager's subjective biases, assumptions, and estimates to enter into the preparation of the financial statements?

• Why do financial statements report only on the past, and why are many of the assets on the balance sheet valued in terms of historical cost?

THE MAIN OBJECTIVE: UNDERSTANDING THE ECONOMIC CONTEXT, THEORY, AND PROCEDURES OF FINANCIAL ACCOUNTING

The discussions, illustrations, and problems in this text are designed to enrich your understanding of the isssues illustrated in the scenario described above. They do not, however, provide definite and clear-cut answers. Financial accounting statements provide no simple solutions to the problems that face creditors, stockholders, managers, and auditors. Yet, as your understanding of financial accounting matures, you will increasingly appreciate what financial statements do provide for each of these parties and, perhaps more importantly, you will also come to realize what they are unable to provide.

The Microline scenario introduces in a general way the role of accounting statements in the business relationships among creditors, stockholders, managers, and auditors. Each of these parties views financial statements from a different perspective and benefits from them in a different way. Creditors and stockholders, for example, demand that managers provide financial statements because such information helps them decide among alternative investments and can be used in contracts (e.g., debt contracts and compensation contracts) to ensure that management's business decisions are made in their interests. Managers are willing to incur the costs of preparing such statements and having them audited because financial statements (1) attract capital from potential creditors and investors; (2) provide public measures of their performance, which can be used to increase their compensation levels and their values in the employment market; and (3) provide information that helps them in their day-to-day operating decisions. Independent auditors benefit from the demand for financial statements because it creates a demand for their services.

The main point is that the roles and functions of financial statements are different for different parties. Many of you are already creditors (do you have a savings account at a bank, or do you own bonds?) and stockholders (do you own life insurance or stocks, or are you covered by a pension plan?), and many of you will undoubtedly be managers and auditors in the future. In fact, many of you will find yourselves in each of these roles. It is important, therefore, that when you study financial accounting, you do so from a number of different perspectives: that of the creditor, the stockholder, the manager, and the auditor.

This text takes such a multiple perspective. It presents not only the mechanics involved in preparing a set of financial statements and the underlying theories involved in measuring assets, liabilities, revenues, and expenses, but also many of the economic issues that surround the preparation, presentation, auditing, and use of financial statements. For example, why is there a demand for audited financial accounting statements, and what role do generally accepted accounting principles play in their preparation and auditing? What incentives do managers have to manipulate the information contained within them? How do investors and creditors use financial statements, and why and how do they use the numbers they contain to control the business decisions of managers? An appreciation of such questions is a prerequisite for a meaningful understanding of financial accounting and, accordingly, should accompany discussions of the mechanics and underlying measurement theory involved in preparing financial statements. Therefore, we devote the remainder of this chapter and a considerable amount of the remainder of the text to economic issues and the environment surrounding the financial accounting process.

THE ECONOMIC ROLE OF FINANCIAL ACCOUNTING REPORTS

Figure 1–6 depicts financial accounting statements in terms of the relationships among providers of capital, managers, and auditors. Take a few minutes to review it. You may find it useful to refer to this chart frequently as you read through the text.

Figure 1–6 The role of financial accounting statements

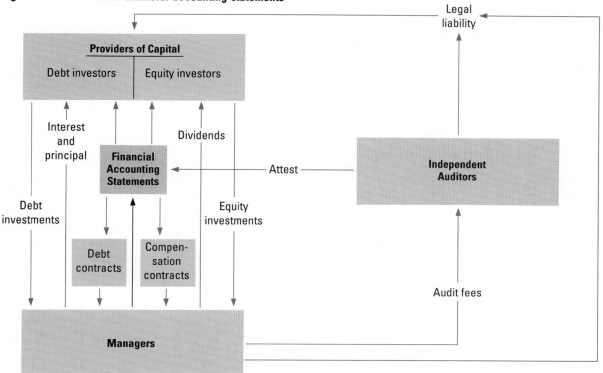

Source: Jamie Pratt, "The Economics of External Reporting: Three Frameworks for the Classroom," *Journal of Accounting Education* (1987): 177.

Providers of Capital: Investors and Creditors

Focus first on the top part of the illustration, the section referred to as *providers of capital,* which represents those people or organizations who have cash beyond what they need for current consumption. They seek ways to invest their extra funds so that they can increase their future levels of wealth and consumption.

Providers of capital include both current and potential investors and creditors: individuals and entities who provide companies with the capital they need to conduct operations. Investors purchase ownership interests with the expectation of future dividends; creditors loan funds in exchange for interest and principal payments.[1] The U.S. stock markets, such as the New York Stock Exchange, the American Stock Exchange, and the *over-the-counter* market, provide a forum for the buying and selling of the equity interests, called *shares of stock,* of major companies in both the United States and foreign countries. The U.S. bond markets provide a forum for the buying and selling of debt securities issued by a number of major U.S. and foreign companies. Banks are also important debt investors in the United States and other countries. In the Microline scenario you represented a potential provider of capital who decided to become an equity investor.

---

1. Owners of equity securities also hope that the market values of their securities increase, but keep in mind that such increases typically occur because future dividends are expected to increase.

Managers

Focus now on the lower portion of Figure 1–6, where you see **managers:** those individuals who are talented and resourceful, but lack the capital to use their talents fully. They compete with each other for capital, attempting to convince investors and creditors that they offer the best potential return at the lowest level of risk. In 1987, for example, Chrysler Corporation collected over $1.5 billion from creditors and investors, two-thirds of it from long-term loans and the remainder from selling equity interests to shareholders. In the Microline scenario Martin was a manager who competed with other investment alternatives for your capital.

Contracts

Convincing investors and creditors that investment opportunities are attractive is a difficult and costly task for managers. They must first provide assurance that the funds will be managed so that providers of capital receive satisfactory returns. Management (i.e., companies) must enter into contracts with creditors and investors so that some legal influence can be exerted over its activities. Loan contracts and management **compensation contracts** are common examples. In 1987, for example, the Pillsbury Company entered into a contract with a group of banks that limited the dividends it could pay to its stockholders. Exxon Corporation has a management incentive program that pays upper management a percentage of the company's annual net income. Recall that a loan contract and a management compensation system were each discussed in the Microline scenario, as you decided how to structure your investment.

Financial Accounting Statements

Managers must also convince investors and creditors that their investments will bring high returns at low levels of risk. Management must, therefore, publish periodic reports of its activities that include measures of financial performance. Thus as indicated in Figure 1–6, managers provide financial statements to stockholders, and these statements are available to the public. In summary, investors and creditors demand financial reports for two reasons: they need financial numbers to monitor and enforce the contracts written with management, and they need financial information to guide their investment decisions.

Independent Auditors

Investors and creditors are understandably concerned that managers may bias the financial statements they provide. After all, managers compete with each other for the capital they need to conduct operations. Investors and creditors, therefore, demand that managers incur the costs of hiring independent auditors, and they agree because they need the capital. All major U.S. companies incur considerable expense to have their financial statements audited by independent public accounting firms. For example, in 1987 the U.S. public accounting firm, Arthur Andersen & Co., collected in excess of $1.5 billion, mostly from auditing services. Note the independent auditor in Figure 1–6, and recall that Martin quickly agreed to hire a CPA because Microline needed your money, and without audited statements you would have taken it elsewhere.

The Relationship Between Management and the Independent Auditor

Since investors and creditors demand the independent audit, it seems reasonable that they would choose the auditor and make sure that the audit was conducted in an independent manner. Such a solution is impractical, however, because stockholders and creditors are often too widely separated and removed from the business to agree on an auditor and monitor the audit. As Figure 1–7 shows, in all major U.S. companies the stockholders elect a board of directors, which appoints a subcommittee of outside directors, called the **audit committee.** This committee, which is part of the board of directors and therefore represents the interests of the stockholders, works with management to choose an auditor. The committee monitors the audit to make sure that it is thorough, objective, and independent.

In spite of these controls, management still pays the audit fee and has considerable influence over whether the auditing firm is hired again. Such influence can threaten the auditor's independence. *Forbes* magazine, for example, reports that

Figure 1–7   The role of the board of directors and the audit committee

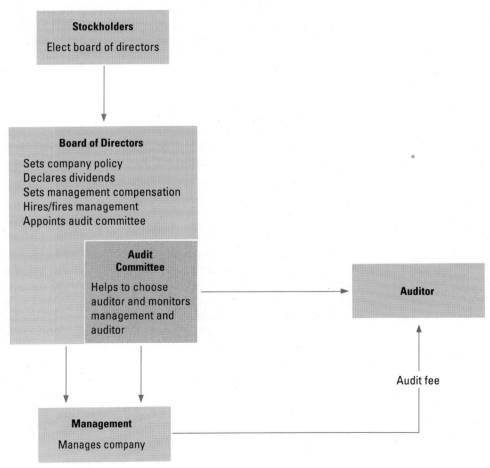

"there is little doubt that the pursuit of ever-increasing revenues and profits [by company management] puts continuing pressure on auditors to be sympathetic, if not malleable."[2] Some managers have been known to "shop around" for favorable audit opinions. For example, when Broadview Financial Corporation, a large company in Ohio, switched auditors, it was revealed later that the switch was due to disagreements about proper methods of accounting. In the Microline scenario Martin could have pressured the auditor to revise the audit report by threatening to find another auditor.

While pressure from management can threaten an auditor's independence, it is important to realize that there are federal regulations against "opinion shopping" and that auditors have a responsibility to the public to conduct a thorough and independent audit. Such responsibility gives rise to legal liability, which provides an economic incentive for auditors to conduct their work in a diligent and ethical manner.

Suppose in the Microline scenario that the company was not a legitimate operation and, for whatever reason, the auditor conducted an incomplete and careless audit and was influenced by Martin to write a favorable audit report. Trusting the report and the financial statements, you decide to invest your $1 million. In a short time the company goes bankrupt, and it is revealed later that the statements were in error as of the time of the audit. In such a situation you would have a strong case for suits against both Martin and the auditor. Such suits are common and very costly in the United States and the auditor's legal liability seems to be increasing with each passing year. For example, *Time* magazine reported that 2000 liability suits, asking for $10 billion in worldwide damages, faced public accounting firms in 1985. Arthur Andersen alone paid more than $180 million to settle lawsuits between 1980 and 1985.[3]

Consequently, as indicated by the liability arrow linking capital providers and independent auditors in Figure 1−6, auditors have strong economic incentives to maintain their independence and not allow themselves to be influenced by pressures from managers. Similarly, the legal liability faced by managers encourages them to refrain from pressuring auditors too strongly.

THE IMPORTANCE OF ETHICS
IN THE ACCOUNTING PROCESS

Financial accounting statements are one of several mechanisms designed to control management's business decisions and protect the interest of the shareholders. They serve this purpose by enabling an evaluation of management's performance and providing numbers that can be used to establish and monitor contracts. Other control mechanisms include the board of directors, which represents the interests of the shareholders and can hire and fire management, and the audit committee, which helps to ensure that management does not exploit its influence over the independent auditor.

All these control devices make it appear that a large amount of mistrust exists among shareholders, managers, and auditors. It is difficult to question such a conjecture when you realize that cases of management fraud and embezzlement have risen significantly in recent years and that audit firms have increasingly been

---

2. Richard Greene, "If I Don't Cross the t..." *Forbes*, 11 February 1985, pp. 134−135.
3. George Russell, "All Eyes on Accountants," *Time*, 21 April 1986, p. 61.

found guilty of accounting improprieties. Some have suggested that the United States is suffering from an ethics crisis. Indeed, businesspeople in general are often viewed as greedy, driven, and unscrupulous.

Notwithstanding these developments, there is little doubt that ethics is a major business asset, and that ethical behavior is in the long-run best interest of managers, shareholders, and auditors. In recognition of the value of ethics, major U.S. companies, such as Boeing, General Mills, and Johnson & Johnson, have instituted special programs designed specifically to instill ethical behavior in their employees. Harvard Business School and other well-known universities are implementing courses in business ethics. The **American Institute of Certified Public Accountants (AICPA),** the professional organization of CPAs, has recently rewritten and strengthened its professional code of ethics, largely to instill higher ethical standards in the members of the accounting profession.

Such efforts are not only moral, they are driven by sound economic logic. Companies like IBM with reputations for quality, service, and ethical business practices are valued highly by investors and creditors partially because their financial statements can be trusted. Such companies and their managers are sued less frequently. As noted in *The Wall Street Journal,*

> *There can be little doubt that most corporate chief executives place a high value on the reputations of their companies and employees. Aside from the general market benefits, a good reputation makes companies less vulnerable to the legal and political attacks launched against business by "public interest" groups and the like in this contentious and litigious age. Also, a code of conduct may help discourage an unscrupulous employee from trying to take advantage of the company.[4]*

Auditors also benefit from ethical behavior and strong reputations. Independent and respectable auditors face fewer liability suits and can generally charge client companies higher fees, primarily because their audit reports are trusted by the public. Consequently, it is important to realize that while the financial accounting process is a system of control, and manager and auditor fraud will continue to occur, it is best to be ethical, from both a moral and an economic standpoint. Not surprisingly, the most successful companies and audit firms enjoy the best reputations for high ethical standards.

A GENERAL DEFINITION OF FINANCIAL ACCOUNTING

This section summarizes and expands on much of what we have already covered. We begin by providing a definition of financial accounting:

> Financial accounting is a *system* through which *managers* report *financial information* about an *economic entity* to a variety of *individuals* who use this information in a variety of different *decisions*. These decisions affect the *economic wealth* of the reporting entity and its management.

The seven items in italic type—(1) system, (2) managers, (3) financial information, (4) economic entity, (5) individuals, (6) decisions, and (7) economic wealth—are the main components of the definition of financial accounting, and each is explained more fully in the following sections.

---

4. George Melloan, "Business Ethics and the Competitive Urge," *The Wall Street Journal,* 9 August 1988, p. 27.

System: A Series of Procedures

Financial accounting is a system, or series of procedures, designed to convert measurable economic events (e. g., transactions) into financial accounting statements. This system consists primarily of a variety of categories, or "storage units," called *accounts,* where changes in the dollar values assigned to the separate assets, liabilities, stockholders' equities, revenues, expenses, and dividends of a business are recorded. The number of separate accounts may be small and easily managed, as in a small company selling a single product or service, or there may be a large number of separate accounts arranged in a complex hierarchy of categories and subcategories, as in a large corporation. Periodically, the accounts are summed to produce the financial statements in the manner described in Chapter 3.

This system produces the financial accounting statements, which report to the shareholders and other interested parties the results of the company's operations and its financial position. Generally accepted accounting principles (GAAP) represent the standards of financial accounting. They prescribe the information that should be disclosed by the system as well as how the system should attach dollar values to the asset, liability, stockholders' equity, revenue, expense, and dividend accounts. Most of this text is devoted to preparing, understanding, and using financial statements produced under GAAP.

Managers: Responsible for the Financial Statements

The ultimate responsibility both for producing financial statements and having them audited by an independent certified public accountant rests with management. Managers, however, are not required by law to follow GAAP, and only companies that have their securities traded on the U.S. public security exchanges (e. g., New York Stock Exchange and American Stock Exchange) are required to have their financial statements audited. Most managers are free to choose whether to have their statements audited as well as whether to follow GAAP.

Nevertheless, economic pressures encourage managers to hire auditors and follow GAAP. Managers wishing to raise capital from outside investors, for example, may find it difficult to do so without audited financial statements. In many companies the board of directors and audit committee help to ensure that the financial statements are audited by an independent CPA. Banks often require audited statements when considering loan applications, and equity investors typically pay less for equity securities when the financial statements are not audited. In addition, an unfavorable auditor's report indicating, for example, that the financial statements are not consistent with GAAP can be quite costly to management. Such statements are generally viewed as less credible by stockholders and outside investors and creditors, which in turn reduces management's market value and makes it more difficult for management to attract outside capital. An article appearing in *The Wall Street Journal* in 1988, for example, stated that an unfavorable audit opinion can raise the cost of borrowing.[5]

Most U.S. companies, however, especially small and medium-sized ones, do not rely heavily on outside sources of capital. For these companies the economic consequences of unaudited statements are not significant, accordingly, they nor-

---

5. Robert Taylor, "U.S. Home Loan Bank of Dallas Releases 1987 Report Without Auditor's Opinion," *The Wall Street Journal,* 12 April 1988, p. 10.

mally choose not to incur the costs associated with having their statements audited. Indeed, most companies in the United States neither hire auditors nor follow GAAP because the costs of doing so exceed the benefits realized.

Financial Information: More than the Financial Statements

The financial accounting system provides more information than is contained in the four financial statements, the accompanying footnotes, the auditor's report, and the management letter. For example, **annual reports,** which are published each year by major U.S. companies, and the *Form 10-K,* which must be completed and filed annually with a government agency (the Securities and Exchange Commission) by companies whose securities are traded on the major U.S. stock exchanges, contain a wealth of information beyond what is contained in the financial statements alone.

Generally accepted accounting principles, for example, require that annual reports furnished to stockholders include audited balance sheets for the two most recent years and audited statements of income, retained earnings, and cash flows for the three most recent years. GAAP also require the following:

• Selected quarterly financial data
• Descriptions of disagreements with auditors on accounting and financial disclosure
• Summaries of selected financial data for the last five years
• Descriptions of business activities
• Separate information about each of a company's major segments
• A listing of the members of the board of directors and the executive officers
• Market prices of a company's stock for each quarterly period for the two most recent years
• Management's discussion and analysis of the company's financial condition and results of operations.

The annual report of K mart Corporation for the twelve months ended January 25, 1989 is provided in Appendix D at the end of the text. Take a few minutes now to briefly review it, especially the sections mentioned in the preceding paragraph. Table 1–1 may aid you in your search.

Table 1–1   Key to the K mart annual report

Section	Annual Report Page Number
11-Year Financial Summary	14–15
Management Discussion and Analysis of Operations	16–28
Quarterly Stock Prices	27
Reports by Management and Independent Accountants	30
Consolidated Financial Statements	31–34
Notes to Consolidated Financial Statements	35–49
Business Group Information (major segments)	45
Quarterly Financial Information (unaudited)	49
Directors, Committees of the Board, Officers, and Corporate Data	50–52

While annual report format and content vary somewhat across major U.S. companies, K mart's report is a representative example. At the end of each chapter of the text, we review K mart's report and discuss it in terms of the material covered in the chapter.

Economic Entities: Different Kinds

Financial accounting statements refer to a specific and definable *economic entity.* In this text we call this entity a *company* or *business* and limit our coverage to entities established primarily to generate profits. Such profit-seeking entities may be subdivided into segments and subsidiaries, each of which provides its own financial statements. For example, in the annual report of PepsiCo, Inc., the financial statements are referred to as **consolidated financial statements,** which means that the total dollar amounts in the accounts on PepsiCo's financial statements include those of other companies, such as Kentucky Fried Chicken, Pizza Hut, and Taco Bell, which PepsiCo owns. These companies, called *subsidiaries,* publish their own separate financial statements. Furthermore, PepsiCo is divided into three segments: soft drinks, snack foods, and restaurants, and financial reports on each of these segments can be compiled.

Accounting reports are also prepared for entities that are not established to make profits. Counties, cities, school districts, and other municipalities as well as charitable organizations and foundations are examples of **nonprofit entities.** The methods used to prepare accounting statements for such organizations are not covered in this text; they are usually the focus of courses devoted exclusively to not-for-profit accounting.

Individuals and Their Decisions: A Wide Variety

Annual financial reports are designed primarily to report a company's financial condition and the results of its operations to its stockholders, but these reports and the Form 10-K are also available to the general public and can be obtained by virtually anyone interested in a company's financial condition and performance. In addition to the company's stockholders, the company's creditors, customers, suppliers, and employees, as well as governmental bodies and public enterprises, often find these reports useful. Indeed, many different parties are interested in financial accounting information.

However, as you probably noticed when you reviewed K mart's annual report, financial accounting information can be complex, confusing, and intimidating. Consequently, many interested parties delegate the task of analyzing financial statement information to more knowledgeable representatives. *Financial and security analysts,* for example, use financial information to evaluate equity and debt investments for individuals, companies, and other institutions. *Stockbrokers* use it to buy and sell securities for their clients. *Bank loan officers* and *credit analysts* use it when deciding whether to loan money to individuals or businesses.

While investors, creditors, and their representatives are the largest group of financial information users, there are many others. A company's customers, suppliers, and competitors, for example, have obvious interests in its financial condition and may use financial reports to assess it. Government bodies, like the Federal

Trade Commission, often base regulatory decisions on information disclosed in annual reports, and public utilities normally base their rates (the prices they charge their customers) on financial accounting numbers such as net income. Labor unions often use accounting numbers to argue for more wages or other benefits, and company management and the board of directors use financial accounting information to determine dividend payments, set company policies, and in general to help guide operating business decisions. Indeed, financial accounting reports provide information to a wide variety of users, each with specific needs.

Economic Wealth: Consequences for the Company and Management

Financial accounting information is used to evaluate the past performance of a company and its management, assess its future potential, and control and direct its business decisions. Thus, the preparation, auditing, and public disclosure of financial accounting information can have significant effects on the economic wealth of the reporting entity and its management. In this text such effects are referred to as **economic consequences.** Consider the following examples.

• *The Wall Street Journal* recently reported that an unfavorable opinion from the auditors on the financial statements of Federal Home Loan Bank of Dallas would substantially raise the cost of the bank's debt.[6]

• A well-known investor service lowered the credit rating of Summit Health, Ltd., a Los Angeles-based health care company, because the company experienced significant reductions in net income. Such a move was expected to substantially increase the interest costs of Summit's borrowings.

• *Forbes* magazine reported that a partner at a New York law firm indicated that recent decisions to extend auditor liability have resulted in massive increases in the liability-insurance premiums paid by major accounting firms and a drastic reduction in insurance coverage. This development is expected to substantially increase the fees auditors charge their clients.[7]

• In response to a proposal by the accounting profession to increase a certain reporting requirement, the senior vice-president and chief accountant of Chemical New York Corporation commented: "It is questionable whether the cost of this proposal is worth the benefit . . . the cost to our company of complying with this proposal will be well in excess of $250,000 per year. To implement such a requirement we would virtually have to revamp all our financial reporting systems."[8]

• In 1988 Arthur Andersen & Co., the independent auditors of First Republic-Bank Corporation, which at the time was Texas's largest banking concern, noted that if the numbers reported on the bank's financial statements continued to worsen, the bank might violate the terms of its debt contracts and be forced to immediately pay over $550 million in long-term debt. If this occurs, the bank may be forced to discontinue operations.[9]

---

6. Robert Taylor, "U.S. Home Loan Bank of Dallas Releases 1987 Report Without Auditor's Opinion," *The Wall Street Journal,* 12 April 1988, p. 100.

7. Jill Andresky, "A Matter of Privity," *Forbes,* 23 September 1985, p. 122.

8. Lee Berton, "Accounting Board Proposes that Firms Disclose Risk of All Financial Instruments," *The Wall Street Journal,* 1 December 1987, p. 14.

9. Leonard M. Apcar, "String of Losses Seen by First RepublicBank," *The Wall Street Journal,* 31 March 1988, p. 3.

In each of these examples the preparation, auditing, or use of financial accounting information was associated with a potential cost that would be borne primarily by the reporting entity, its stockholders, its management, or its auditors. Economic consequences include, for example, the costs of producing and auditing the accounting information, changes in the values of the company's equity and debt securities listed on the security markets, the costs of borrowing and raising equity capital, changes in management's compensation and stockholder dividends, and even the costs of avoiding or going through bankruptcy. Such economic effects are important in general because they represent the costs associated with the financial accounting process. More specifically, they provide management with incentives to prepare accounting reports in ways that depict them as successful managers. These incentives may cause company officials, for example, to pursue operating strategies that make the financial statements look attractive, to choose accounting methods or subjective estimates that boost net income or defer the recognition of losses, to pressure auditors for favorable audit reports, or to intentionally misstate the financial statements.

As noted earlier, the most successful companies are managed in a manner that is above reproach, and the great majority of managers are ethical. Yet fraud still exists, and even within the guidelines of generally accepted accounting principles, managers are given much lattitude, and use much discretion, in preparing their financial reports. Indeed, in February 1987 the front pages of newspapers related how four officials at Wedtech Corporation, a Bronx-based defense contractor, pleaded guilty to a scheme that increased the company's net income through false invoices and flagrant accounting gimmicks, and in 1988 *Forbes* reported that "many . . . young companies . . . use accounting rules to maximize income and minimize expenses where they can."[10] Consequently, it is important that students of accounting understand the economic consequences associated with the financial accounting process.

THREE OTHER KINDS OF ACCOUNTING

This text is devoted almost exclusively to financial accounting. However, you should be aware of the three other kinds of accounting usually covered in other accounting courses: not-for-profit accounting, managerial accounting, and tax accounting.

Not-for-Profit Accounting

As mentioned earlier, many economic entities do not have profit as an objective. Municipalities, such as cities, simply receive money from taxes, service fees, and debt investors and allocate it to address public needs. For example, a city allocates funds to a police department to ensure public safety. The process of recording these fund inflows and outflows and reporting them to the public is quite logically called *not-for-profit accounting.*

---

10. Gretchen Morgenson, "They Won't Wait Forever," *Forbes,* 16 May 1988, pp. 66, 68.

Managerial Accounting

Managers need *internal information systems* to generate timely and accurate information that helps them plan and operate efficiently on a day-to-day basis. To guide their decisions, managers rely to some extent on the information produced by the financial accounting system. However, more important to such decisions is information that is not available to the public and is produced strictly for management's own use. Such information is referred to as *managerial accounting information,* and managerial accounting is usually covered in a separate course.

Tax Accounting

The area of accounting devoted to understanding and applying the tax law is known as *tax accounting.* Our complicated and constantly changing tax structure requires that thousands of accountants specialize in this area. Furthermore, tax law is extremely detailed and complicated; even a moderate coverage of tax accounting requires a number of separate accounting or law courses.

An important distinction should be made at this point between the income number resulting from applying income tax laws (called **taxable income**) and the income number which results from financial accounting (called net income). The **Internal Revenue Code** specifies the rules to be followed to calculate taxable income. An entity's tax obligation is then computed as a percentage of this taxable income. Financial accounting income, or *net income,* is determined by applying financial accounting principles and procedures, which differ in many ways from the tax laws stated in the Internal Revenue Code. As a result, net income is not necessarily equal to taxable income. Tax laws are enacted for purposes quite different from those which drive the development of financial accounting principles. Accounting students often confuse these two sets of rules.

Comparing the Four Kinds of Accounting

Figure 1–8 compares the four kinds of accounting. Note that the comparisons illustrated in the chart are based on the first six main components of the definition of financial accounting.

At the top of the figure, these components are represented by boxes linked by arrows. This format depicts a sequential process in which the managers of an economic entity follow certain accounting processes that convert financial facts about the entity to a set of financial statements. Interested parties then use this information for a variety of business decisions. The remainder of Figure 1–8 compares the four kinds of accounting on each of the six components.

THE ACCOUNTING PROFESSION

Accountants are employed in all types of business and nonprofit entities. In the United States alone well over one million individuals currently work as accountants, and an even larger number are employed in accounting-related computer

Figure 1–8 Four kinds of accounting

Economic Entity	Managers	System	Financial Information	Individuals	Decisions
Financial Accounting Profit-making companies	Finance or accounting department	Generally accepted accounting principles	Income statement Balance sheet Statement of retained earnings Statement of cash flows Other disclosures Auditor report	*External* Investors Creditors Suppliers Employees Managers Government General public	Equity and debt investments Contract negotiations Regulation Dividend payments
Not-for-Profit Accounting Nonprofit entities	Finance or accounting department	Fund accounting principles	Balance sheet Funds flow statements	*External* Creditors Government General public	Debt investments Budget allocations
Managerial Accounting All entities	Internal accounting department	Company information system	Manager reports Production costs Performance evaluation, etc.	*Internal* Managers	Operating decisions
Tax Accounting All entities	Finance or accounting department	Internal Revenue Code	Official tax forms: 1040 for individuals 1020 for corporations	Internal Revenue Service	Collection of government revenues

and clerical positions. From the largest multinational company and government organization to the smallest specialty shop, accountants play a very important role in the functioning of the economy.

Accountants can be placed into three different categories: (1) accountants in nonprofit organizations, (2) accountants in industry, and (3) accountants in public practice. More than half of the total number of accountants presently employed are in industry, while accountants in public practice make up about two-thirds of the remainder. The following sections describe the nature of each category and its professional organizations and credentials.

Accountants in Nonprofit Organizations

Nonprofit organizations include governments, educational institutions, churches, charities, museums, foundations, and hospitals. Profits are not the goal of these organizations, but they must still be run efficiently. This requires relevant and timely information as well as proper control over the use and distribution of the organization's resources. Accountants play an important role in helping to achieve these ends.

The Federal Government

Governments at all levels employ accountants and accounting-related personnel. Not surprisingly, the federal government employs more than any other single nonprofit entity, most acting as accountants, auditors, or budgetary officers. The Internal Revenue Service (IRS), the Federal Bureau of Investigation (FBI), the Central Intelligence Agency (CIA), and the General Accounting Office (GAO), which audits the operations of the federal government and reports to Congress, are several well-known federal organizations that employ a high percentage of accountants. Their principal organization is the Association of Government Accountants.

State and Local Governments

State and local governments also employ large numbers of accountants. Their principal professional organization is the Municipal Finance Officers Association (MFOA). The accounting profession, in cooperation with the MFOA and other interested groups, recently established the Government Accounting Standards Board (GASB), a private-sector agency that establishes guidelines for accounting in government organizations.

Education

Accounting educators, including accounting professors, lecturers and instructors, also make up a large portion of the accountants employed in nonprofit organizations. Many devote considerable effort to developing curricula, school administration, research, and textbook writing. Accounting academics publish the results of their research in professional and academic journals like the *Journal of Accountancy, The Accounting Review* and the *Journal of Accounting Research*. The major association of accounting educators is the American Accounting Association.

Accountants in Industry

Accountants in industry are employed by individual profit-seeking companies. They are involved primarily in two accounting functions: (1) managerial accounting, which entails gathering, verifying, and reporting the information required for the decisions made inside a company, and (2) financial accounting, which entails preparing financial statements for stockholders, creditors, and other users of financial statements.

Managerial Accountants

The functions of managerial, or management, accountants include tax planning, budgeting, performance measurement and evaluation, and providing information for a variety of operating and investment decisions. Three specific positions within the company are usually held by management accountants: controller, treasurer, and internal auditor.

The *controller* is the chief management accounting officer of the company, whose responsibility is often to coordinate the functions listed above. Most controllers are trained as accountants and often have public accounting experience. The *treasurer* oversees the financial resources of the company and is responsible for cash management. *Internal auditors* are company employees who examine and evaluate the accounting system to ensure that it operates efficiently.

Financial Accountants in Industry

The financial vice-president, or *chief financial officer*, is normally responsible for preparing the periodic financial statements for the shareholders, which includes choosing the appropriate accounting methods and providing the necessary estimates. Accountants in this area must make a special effort to stay up-to-date with changes in generally accepted accounting principles because they must often analyze the effects of potential transactions on the financial statements and on any relevant contracts. The chief financial officer often works closely with the controller and the internal auditors because there is much overlap between the information system that produces the external financial statements and the one that produces internal financial reports.

Organizations for Industry Accountants

The National Association of Accountants (NAA) is the principal organization of management accountants. It publishes *Management Accounting*, a monthly journal, and other professional research studies and educational aids. The NAA also oversees the certification of management accountants, which involves passing a three-day examination offered in a number of major cities throughout the United States in June and December of each year. Those who pass the exam are known as *Certified Management Accountants (CMAs)*.

The Financial Executive Institute (FEI) and the Institute of Internal Auditors (IIA) are two other organizations composed primarily of industry accountants. The FEI consists mostly of chief financial officers, controllers and treasurers. In addition to a number of other activities, it publishes a monthly journal called *The Financial Executive*. The IIA administers a professional examination and confers the designation of *Certified Internal Auditor (CIA)* on those who pass the exam and have the requisite amount of experience.

Accountants in Public Practice

Accountants who offer their services to the general public are called *public accountants*. They are hired by individuals, profit-seeking companies, and nonprofit organizations.

Public Accounting Services

Public accountants perform three kinds of services: (1) audits, (2) tax services, and (3) management consulting services. The result of the audit is the auditor's report (see Figure 1–2). Tax services include advice on structuring transactions to minimize the payment of tax as well as the actual preparation of a client's tax returns. Management consulting is a fast-growing aspect of public accounting services that consists of working with company management on a wide range of business problems and often involves the design and operation of the company's computer-based accounting system.

Public Accounting Firms

Public accounting firms range in size from individually-run operations to large international organizations. A relatively small number of large firms account for most of the total billings, but there are many successful small public accounting

Table 1–2   The twenty largest U.S. accounting firms

Firm (home office)	Professionals	CPAs	Partners	Revenues*	Offices
Arthur Andersen (Chicago)	15,206	4693	1207	$1513	81
Coopers & Lybrand (New York)	14,493	3996	1176	1100	98
Peat Marwick Main (Montvale, NJ)	13,107	8189	1922	1640	135
Ernst & Whinney (New York)	10,650	6144	1240	1030	117
Price Waterhouse (New York)	9360	3120	805	845	112
Arthur Young (New York)	7500	N/A	850	738	95
Touche Ross (New York)	7100	3100	780	820	80
Deloitte, Haskins & Sells (New York)	6717	4600	817	701	111
Laventhol & Horwath (Philadelphia)	3310	1090	460	306	50
Grant Thornton (Chicago)	2100	1200	350	206	53
Seidman & Seidman (New York)	1629	943	316	160	48
McGladery & Pullen (Des Moines)	1531	1031	391	141	70
Pannell Kerr Forster(Los Angeles)	1014	453	150	93	35
Spicer & Oppenheim (New York)	670	275	106	67	9
Kenneth Leventhol (Los Angeles)	658	335	63	109	13
Clifton Gunderson & Co. (Peoria)	448	270	80	34	30
Crowe Chizek & Co. (South Bend)	435	165	67	34	7
Baird Kurtz & Dobson (Springfield, Mo.)	401	308	104	39	20
Plante & Moran (Southfield, Mich.)	330	270	72	43	11
Moss Adams (Seattle)	312	196	61	30	16

Source: *Accounting Today,* 12 September 1988.
*Revenues in millions of dollars
Note: See footnote 11 below.

firms. The eight largest firms, usually referred to as the *Big 8,* maintain offices in most major cities throughout the world and audit the financial statements of the majority of publicly owned companies in the United States.[11] Auditing is the major service provided by the large public accounting firms, but management consulting is becoming increasingly more.important. The smaller public accounting firms tend to specialize in tax planning and preparation, but they also provide a variety of other financial services.

Most accounting firms are organized as *partnerships*—the owners (partners) share profits and are legally responsible for the actions of the firm—although a few are corporations. Graduates in accounting typically enter public accounting as staff accountants and after several years, if they perform well, they are promoted to the position of senior accountant. Senior accountants are then promoted to managers and successful managers become partners. The time required for an individual to move from staff to partner is relatively short (10–15 years) but very few remain in public accounting long enough to achieve the rank of partner. Many accept positions along the way in industry as controllers and financial executives. Table 1–2 lists the twenty largest U.S. accounting firms and some additional information.

---

11. Ernst & Whinney and Arthur Young, two of the Big 8 firms, have recently merged and at the time of this writing, Arthur Andersen is considering a merger with Price Waterhouse, and Deloitte, Haskins & Sells is negotiating a merger with Touche Ross. As a result, the Big 8 may now have been reduced to the Big 5.

Professional Certification and Organizations

Public accountants who render opinions on the financial statements of their clients are required by state law to be licensed as certified public accountants (CPAs). CPAs are licensed to practice on a state-by-state basis. All states require that candidates pass a uniform national examination (the CPA examination), pass a professional ethics exam, and acquire a certain amount of experience, which varies from state to state. The CPA examination requires two and one-half days and is given in most major U.S. cities in May and November of each year.

The American Institute of Certified Public Accountants (AICPA) is the principal professional organization of public accountants in the United States. The AICPA prepares and grades the uniform CPA examination and, among other activities, establishes standards of ethical and technical performance for public accountants and auditors. It also conducts research, administers continuing educational programs, and publishes the *Journal of Accountancy*. Individual states also maintain societies of CPAs, which publish journals, provide continuing education courses, and perform other services for accounting professionals.

THE EVOLUTION OF GENERALLY ACCEPTED ACCOUNTING PRINCIPLES

Generally accepted accounting principles (GAAP) play a critical role in the financial accounting process. They define the standards for external reporting, which produces greater uniformity in the accounting methods used by the variety of profit-seeking entities in the economy. Defining general reporting practices by a single set of standards facilitates meaningful comparisons of the financial performance of different companies. In addition, the level of credibility in the financial statements is largely determined by the extent to which their preparation follows GAAP. For example, if neither Exxon nor Amoco, two major oil companies, followed GAAP in the preparation of their financial statements, not only would it be virtually impossible to compare their levels of performance, because their measures of profit would be computed in different ways, but neither measure of profit would be very credible.

The financial accounting process has evolved over time in response to changes in the business environment. Specifically, the nature of financial accounting has been driven by the demands of outside investors and creditors for external reporting information. The following discussion shows that as the conditions of the business environment have changed, so have the demands of investors and creditors, and so has the nature of financial accounting information. This process of change will undoubtedly continue; the financial accounting process is truly a dynamic phenomenon.

Although the development of financial accounting can be traced back to the beginnings of record-keeping, we begin with the late nineteenth century in the United States. At this time the U.S. economy comprised primarily small companies. Their managers were often also their owners, and they could usually meet their relatively small capital needs through personal funds or profitable operations. In such cases external reporting and auditors were not necessary; no outside stockholders or creditors demanded audited financial statements. Managers may have prepared some financial reports for their own use, but they were certainly very informal and never audited.

The Importance of Bank Capital

As companies grew, their capital needs began to exceed the amounts available from personal funds or other internal sources. They began to seek outside sources of capital, and local banks were the logical alternative. A visit to the bank in search of a business loan usually entailed a meeting with a loan officer, who demanded some evidence of a company's ability to meet interest and principal payments.

The bankers' demands gave rise to a form of external reporting, often consisting solely of the loan application forms, that usually provided information about both the company's and the manager's personal ability to meet the loan obligations as they came due. Once again, these reports were not generally subject to formal review by an independent outsider, they rarely made a clear distinction between the manager's personal assets and those of the company, and they varied widely in format and content from one situation to another.

The Rise of Stock Markets

In the early 1900s business in the United States began to boom. The industrial revolution brought great growth to many companies, and their managers began to seek different ways to meet the capital needs of their fast-growing operations. The banking system alone no longer satisfied the demand for capital, and many owner/managers began to raise funds by selling equity interests to outside investors in the form of shares of stock. The **corporate form of business,** which legally separated the owner's personal assets from those of the company, evolved at this time, and **stock markets,** which provided a marketplace for the buying and selling of these ownership interests, emerged.

This business environment placed new demands on the financial information management was required to provide. Stockholders, most of whom were not involved in the business operations, required information that allowed them to assess whether their investments were being managed judiciously. Potential investors, who bought and sold shares on the stock markets, required information to help them assess the potential of alternative investments. Since managers were now competing with one another for the capital of these outside investors, they were compelled to provide financial information that met these demands. Thus, early forms of financial accounting statements were prepared for the stockholders and made available to the investing public.

No Reporting Standards: Lack of Credibility and Uniformity

The financial accounting information available at this time met many of the demands of the business environment, but the lack of generally accepted reporting standards left a number of problems. Reporting practices were largely at the discretion of management, which reduced the credibility of the reports and gave rise to wide variations in their contents and formats. Audits did not eliminate this problem because auditors had no reporting standards upon which to base their opinions. As a result, the quality of the information available to stockholders and the investing public at this time was questionable.

In 1929 the U.S. capital markets collapsed, and the Great Depression followed. Many factors contributed to this dramatic economic downturn, and the lack of both credibility and uniformity in the financial accounting information available to investors and creditors did little to help the situation. In 1930 the AICPA, the official organization of professional CPAs, and the New York Stock Exchange responded by developing a few uniform accounting principles. These standards, however, were largely ineffective, primarily because they lacked any power of enforcement and were extremely general.

The Securities and Exchange Commission

In response to demands from the investing community for uniform and credible financial accounting information, in 1934 the U.S. Congress created the **Securities and Exchange Commission (SEC).** An agency of the federal government, the SEC was commissioned to implement and enforce the Securities Act of 1933 and the Securities Exchange Act of 1934. The Securities Act of 1933 requires that companies issuing securities on the public security markets file a registration statement (Form S-1) with the SEC prior to the issuance. The SEC Act of 1934 states, among other requirements, that companies with securities listed on the public security markets *(listed companies)* must (1) annually file audited financial reports with the SEC (Form 10-K), (2) file quarterly financial statements with the SEC (Form 10-Q), and (3) provide audited financial reports annually to the stockholders.

The SEC Act of 1934 established the SEC as the governmental body responsible for ensuring that listed companies prepare and file registration statements, the Form 10-K, the Form 10-Q, and annual stockholder reports. The SEC was also given broad powers by Congress to prescribe, in whatever detail it desires, the accounting practices and standards to be used by companies within its jurisdiction.

The Role of the Accounting Profession

The SEC did not, and to this day has not, assumed total responsibility for determining appropriate accounting practices and standards. Instead, it has allowed and encouraged the AICPA, a nongovernment body, to take an active role. The AICPA has responded by establishing several standard-setting bodies since 1939: the Committtee on Accounting Procedures (1939–59), the Accounting Principles Board (1959–71), and the Financial Accounting Standards Board (1973–present).

Early Rule-Making Bodies: CAP and APB
The AICPA's first attempt to develop uniform accounting practices was to create the Committee on Accounting Procedures (CAP), a group of practicing CPAs. From 1939 to 1959 this committee issued 51 Accounting Research Bulletins, which recommended certain reporting methods and served to narrow somewhat the range of accounting practices used at the time. These bulletins considered the methods of accounting for such items as taxes, compensation, leases, and pension plans. Like the early attempts by the AICPA, however, they were very general, and the SEC never officially granted them authoritative support. Almost all of

these bulletins have either been amended or superseded by subsequent accounting standards.

In an effort to establish a well-defined and more structured body of accounting standards, the AICPA created the Accounting Principles Board (APB), which operated from 1959 to 1971 and issued 31 Accounting Opinions. The APB, a group of part-time and volunteer CPAs, led a stormy and controversial thirteen-year existence. It received some support from the SEC, but came under constant fire from a variety of interest groups for lack of productivity, failing to act promptly to correct alleged accounting abuses, failing to encourage input from outside parties, and addressing accounting issues in an uncoordinated manner. Nonetheless, during the APB's existence the first definition of what are still referred to as generally accepted accounting principles (GAAP) was created. As of 1971, the year of the demise of the APB, GAAP consisted of the 51 Accounting Research Bulletins and the 31 Opinions from the APB. However, only five of the APB Opinions have not been amended or superseded by subsequent standards.

The Financial Accounting Standards Board

In 1971 the AICPA, responding to warnings from the SEC that it might take over accounting standard-setting, appointed a study group (The Wheat Committee) to examine the organization and operations of the APB and determine what changes were necessary. The result of this committee's efforts was the **Financial Accounting Standards Board (FASB),** which assumed the responsibility for establishing accounting standards in 1973. The expectations of success for this new, seven-member board were based on three essential differences between it and the APB.

• *Fewer, full-time, well-compensated members.* The FASB is composed of seven members, who work full-time for annual salaries in excess of $100,000. The APB was composed of eighteen to twenty-one members who volunteered their efforts on a part-time basis.

• *Greater independence from industry, public accounting, and the AICPA.* The members of the FASB are required to sever all ties from their previous employment. The APB members retained their employment positions.

• *Broader representation.* The members of the APB were all CPAs, while the members of the FASB come from a wide variety of business backgrounds.

The FASB began its tenure by making changes in two areas where the APB had received much criticism. First, many complained that the APB did not allow sufficient public input in the process of developing GAAP. In response, the FASB opened its activities to the public and made a number of specific changes designed specifically to invite public participation. The process of establishing an accounting standard now includes several points at which letters and personal presentations from the public are invited and encouraged.

Another criticism often leveled at the APB was that it handled accounting issues on an ad hoc, problem-by-problem basis rather than in a systematic, integrated, and consistent way. The FASB responded to this criticism by writing a **Conceptual Framework,** which consists of a number of essays that provide a structure for a comprehensive and coherent set of interrelated objectives and fundamentals for financial accounting. General subject areas such as the objectives of financial reporting, the qualitative characteristics of accounting information, and the exact definitions of essential accounting terms are addressed in the conceptual framework.[12] Using this framework as a kind of constitution, the FASB is presumably better able to address accounting and reporting issues in a more organized and consistent way.

Since 1973 the FASB has enjoyed the full authoritative support of the SEC and has issued well over one hundred standards, many of which amend or supersede the bulletins and opinions passed by the CAP and the APB. These standards constitute the bulk of what are currently known as GAAP.

THE CURRENT PROCEDURE FOR ESTABLISHING GAAP

The FASB follows a nine-step procedure when setting an accounting standard (see Figure 1–9).

Areas of financial reporting that need consideration are usually brought to the attention of the FASB by such groups as the SEC, industry, auditing firms, government, report users, and academics. As these topics create enough interest, they are placed on the FASB's public agenda some six to twelve months before they are actually reviewed.

The FASB then assigns a task force to study the topic, which usually consists of several experts in the area under consideration. The task force prepares a discussion memorandum, a lengthy document discussing the pros and cons of various alternative accounting treatments. It is typically written in very general terms and rarely recommends a particular treatment.

The discussion memorandum is then made public, and after sixty days a public hearing is conducted where interested parties can make formal comments in person on the discussion memorandum to the FASB members. Individuals representing industry, auditing firms, government, report users, academics, and other groups present their positions at these hearings.

After considering the various viewpoints expressed at a public hearing, the FASB prepares an exposure draft, which is considerably more specific than the discussion memorandum and typically advocates one or more specific accounting treatments. The exposure draft is published, and after a thirty-day period, during which many letters from the same interested parties are reviewed by the FASB, the final **financial accounting standard** is issued.

The most important feature of this process is that the FASB members do not simply dream up what they believe to be the appropriate accounting treatment for the issues under consideration. Outside parties actually initiate the policymaking process and continually provide input that has a significant impact on the final standards. It is not unusual, for example, that certain accounting issues fail to make it beyond the discussion memorandum stage, or that exposure drafts are rejected or significantly changed before they become financial accounting standards. In fact, a number of the accounting standards established by the FASB have been revised and rewritten in response to public input. Indeed, the development of GAAP is a joint effort among specialized experts, industry interests, government representatives, report users, the auditing profession, academics, and the FASB—

---

12. See "Objectives of Financial Reporting by Business Enterprises," *Statement of Financial Concepts No. 1* (Stamford, Conn.: FASB, November 1978); "Qualitative Characteristics of Accounting Information," *Statement of Financial Concepts No. 2* (Stamford, Conn.: FASB, May 1980); "Elements of Financial Statements of Business Enterprises," *Statement of Financial Accounting Concepts No. 3* (Stamford, Conn.: FASB, December 1980).

Figure 1–9   The procedures of the Financial Accounting Standards Board

1. Place item to be considered on FASB's **public agenda.**
2. **Task force** of experts prepares discussion memorandum.
3. Publish **discussion memorandum.**
4. Sixty-day **waiting period.**
5. **Public hearing** on discussion memorandum.
6. **FASB** prepares exposure draft.
7. Publish **exposure draft.**
8. Thirty-day **waiting period**/possible revision.
9. **Financial accounting standard** is issued.

not to mention the influential role played by the SEC, which is constantly working with the FASB and at any time has the constitutional authority to overturn what the FASB has done.

ACCOUNTING STANDARD-SETTING: A POLITICAL PROCESS

Figure 1–10 illustrates the political nature of the financial accounting standard-setting process, summarizing much of what has been described in this section. It is divided into five major segments: (1) policymakers—the procedures followed by the FASB as overseen by the SEC; (2) generally accepted accounting principles—the current standards of financial reporting; (3) actual accounting practices—the accounting practices actually used by companies; (4) economic consequences—the costs and benefits associated with the production, auditing, and use of accounting information; and (5) public input—the efforts by outside parties to influence the establishment of GAAP.

Figure 1–10 depicts GAAP as the result of a joint effort by the FASB and the SEC that is subject to a number of direct influences from the public: the influence of Congress, of the White House and other government agencies, and of those who attend the FASB's public hearings and write letters in response to discussion memoranda and exposure drafts. GAAP, in turn, define the standards of financial reporting, upon which actual accounting practices are based. Note in Figure 1–10 that actual accounting practices are separate from GAAP, which illustrates the fact that the accounting practices used by companies are not always consistent with GAAP.

Actual accounting practices impose costs on and create benefits for managers, stockholders, investors, creditors, auditors, and the general public. Managers, for example, must pay to have financial accounting statements produced, processed, and audited. At the same time, however, they benefit because these statements enable them to attract capital from investors and creditors. Investors benefit from financial accounting information because it helps them to choose among alternative investments and to control the actions of managers, but investors must incur the costs of analyzing the information. Auditors benefit from financial accounting information because it creates a demand for their services. Yet, auditors must bear the significant costs associated with conducting audits and the liability that comes from providing the audit report. These costs and benefits, which are passed on to the general public, are represented in Figure 1–10 as economic consequences.

Figure 1–10   The accounting policymaking process

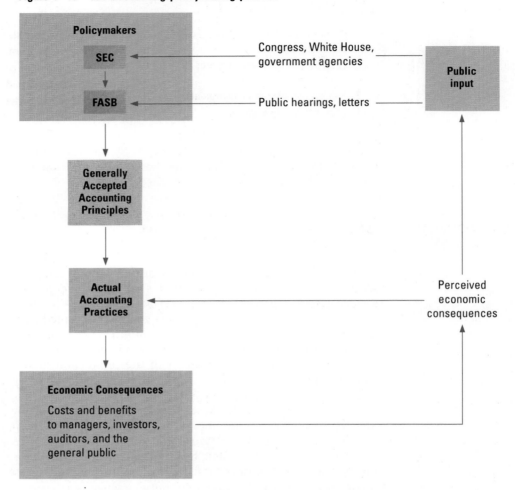

Source: Jamie Pratt, "The Economics of External Reporting: Three Frameworks for the Classroom," *Journal of Accounting Education* (1987): 182.

As shown by the arrow linking perceived economic consequences to actual accounting practices, managers consider these costs and benefits when choosing accounting methods. Understandably, they choose those methods that best enable them to achieve their goals. Moreover, as shown by the arrow linking perceived economic consequences to public input, economic consequences create incentives for managers, investors, auditors, and others to influence policymakers. Recently, for example, the FASB rescinded a standard on accounting for inflation in the face of significant pressure from a strong industry lobby, which claimed essentially that the costs of implementing the standard were too high.

The political process described above is crucial if GAAP are to continue to serve the business community because it allows those who are affected by GAAP to influence their development. If this political process continues to operate efficiently, accounting standards will continue to reflect the costs and benefits experienced by those whom they serve.

SUMMARY OF LEARNING OBJECTIVES

1 Identify and briefly describe the four basic components of the financial accounting process.

The financial accounting process consists of four components. (1) It is initiated when managers of profit-seeking companies prepare reports containing financial information for the owners of these companies. (2) In addition to the company's owners, these reports are made available to a wide variety of interested parties, who use them to assess the company's financial condition and the performance of its managers. (3) Financial accounting reports enable these parties to improve their business decisions by helping them to predict the future performance of the company and control the activities of management. (4) The decisions these parties make affect the financial condition and performance of the company and the economic well-being of its managers.

2 Name the four financial statements, and briefly explain the kind of financial information that each provides.

The four basic financial statements are (1) the balance sheet, (2) the income statement, (3) the statement of retained earnings, and (4) the statement of cash flows. The balance sheet lists the assets, liabilities, and stockholders' equity of a company at a given point in time. The income statement contains the revenues earned and expenses incurred by a company over a period of time. Revenues less expenses equal net income. The statement of retained earnings reconciles the retained earnings amount from one period to the next. Beginning retained earnings, plus net income, less dividends, equal ending retained earnings. The statement of cash flows reconciles the cash amount from one period to the next. It lists net cash flows from operating activities, investing activities, and financing activities.

3 Briefly describe the contents of the audit report, the management letter, and the footnotes to the financial statements.

The auditor's report is divided into three paragraphs. The first paragraph states that the financial statements are the responsibility of management, have been audited, and that the auditor's responsibility is to express an opinion on them. The second indicates that the examination of the company's records was made in accordance with generally accepted auditing standards and that the auditor has obtained reasonable assurance that the financial statements are free of material misstatement. It also notes that the audit includes (1) examining evidence that supports the amounts and disclosures on the financial statements and (2) assessing the accounting principles used and significant estimates made by management. The final paragraph states that the financial statements present fairly the financial position of the company, the results of operations, and its cash flows in conformity with generally accepted accounting principles (and notes any exceptions).

The management letter normally states that the company's management is responsible for the preparation and integrity of the statements, that the statements were prepared in accordance with generally accepted accounting principles, and that certain amounts were based on management's best estimates and judgments. It further indicates that the company maintains a system of internal controls designed to safeguard its assets and ensure that all transactions are recorded and reported properly, pointing out in addition that the company's employees maintain the highest ethical standards and that its business practices are conducted in a manner that is above reproach. Finally, the management letter refers to the respective roles of the auditor, the board of directors, and the audit committee.

The footnotes provide additional information about the dollar amounts on the financial statements. They indicate which accounting methods were used and suggest that many of the numbers on the statements are the result of assumptions and estimates made by management.

4 Describe the two basic forms of investment, and explain how the information on the financial statements is related to them.

There are two basic forms of investment: debt and equity. A debt investment is a loan, and debt investors are called *creditors*. When debt investments are made, management is normally required to sign a loan contract, which specifies (1) the maturity date, (2) the annual interest payment, (3) collateral, and (4) any other restrictions the creditor imposes. Creditors are primarily concerned that the interest and principal payments are met on a timely basis. Since such payments are made in cash, creditors are especially interested in the statement of cash flows. They are also interested in the selling prices of assets that could be used as collateral and in the company's other outstanding liabilities. Consequently, the balance sheet, which lists the company's assets and liabilities, also provides useful information. However, most balance sheet assets are carried at historical cost, not selling price.

Equity investments involve purchasing ownership interests in a company. Equity owners of corporations are called stockholders. Their returns come in the form of dividends (or *stock price appreciation*), which tend to be large if the company performs well and small, or nonexistent, if it performs poorly. The primary concern of stockholders is the performance of the company's management—specifically, its ability to generate and maintain earning power in the future. To achieve this objective, management must both ensure that cash is available to meet debts as they come due and also to invest in assets that produce satisfactory returns in the long run. Consequently, stockholders are interested in the information contained in all four of the financial statements. Since dividends are often set as a percentage of net income, and net income is generally considered to be the overall measure of management's performance and the company's earning power, stockholders are especially interested in the income statement.

5 Explain the role of financial accounting statements in terms of the business relationships among investors and creditors, managers, and auditors.

Investors and creditors demand that management provide financial accounting information for two fundamental reasons. First, they need financial numbers to monitor and enforce the debt and compensation contracts written with management. Second, they need financial information to decide where to invest their funds. Managers incur the costs of providing the statements and having them audited because they need to attract capital from investors and creditors and they want to maintain their levels of compensation and value in the employment market. Management hires auditors who must act independently because they face high levels of legal liability and must maintain their professional ethical standards.

6 Explain why ethics is important in the accounting process.

The financial statements, debt and compensation contracts, the board of directors, auditors, and the audit committee all represent methods of controlling the business decisions of management in an effort to protect the investments of stockholders and creditors. While management and auditors have incentives to misrepresent the financial statements or exploit the system, there are compelling moral and economic reasons to act ethically. Ethical managers and auditors face less legal liability and are able to charge higher fees for their services than those whose behavior has been questioned. Accordingly, companies, universities, and the accounting profession have recently pursued efforts to enhance the ethical behavior of businesspeople.

7 Provide a general definition of financial accounting and briefly elaborate on its components.

Financial accounting is a system through which managers report financial information about an economic entity to a variety of individuals who use it in a variety of different decisions. These decisions affect the economic wealth of the reporting entity and its management.

The system, or series of procedures, is designed to convert measurable economic events into financial statements. This system consists primarily of accounts in which changes in the dollar values assigned to the separate assets, liabilities, stockholders' equities, revenues, expenses, and dividends of a business are recorded. Generally accepted accounting principles (GAAP) represent the standards for this system.

The responsibility for producing the financial statements and having them audited rests with management. However, only listed companies are required by law to follow GAAP and have their financial statements audited. Other companies may do so, but many, especially small companies that do not rely on outside capital, choose not to because the costs of being audited often exceed the benefits.

Financial information includes the financial statements, the footnotes, the audit report, the management letter, and the rest of the information contained in the annual report. *Economic entity* refers to the reporting unit under analysis. Financial accounting information is produced by profit-seeking entities, which may consist of separate segments and subsidiaries. In a consolidated financial statement the total dollar amounts include the accounts of a company's subsidiaries.

Annual financial reports are designed primarily to report a company's financial condition and the results of its operations to stockholders, but they are also available to the general public. Other interested parties include potential investors, creditors, customers, suppliers, employees, government enterprises, and public enterprises, who use the information contained in these reports to decide, for example, whether to invest in the company, loan the company funds (and what terms to attach to the loans), do business with the company, argue for higher wages, or impose regulations.

Preparing, auditing, and publicly disclosing financial accounting information can have significant effects on the economic wealth of the reporting entity and its management. Such effects are called *economic consequences* and result directly from the decisions of the interested parties mentioned. Examples include the costs of producing and auditing the accounting information, changes in the values of the company's equity and debt securities as listed on the security markets, the costs of borrowing and raising equity capital, changes in management's compensation and stockholder dividends, and even the costs of bankruptcy. Such costs provide management with incentives to prepare financial accounting reports in a manner that depicts them as successful.

8   List the four different kinds of accounting and briefly describe each.

The four kinds of accounting are financial accounting, not-for-profit accounting, management accounting, and tax accounting. Financial accounting refers to the preparation of financial reports that are used by parties outside the company. Not-for-profit accounting refers to the methods used to account for the fund flows of nonprofit entities. Management accounting refers to the preparation and reporting of internally generated and used information, which is designed to improve management's planning and control decisions. Tax accounting refers to understanding and applying tax law.

9   Briefly explain the nature of the accounting profession and the different employment positions held by accountants.

Accountants can be placed into three different categories: (1) nonprofit organizations, (2) industry, and (3) public practice. Nonprofit organizations include governments, educational institutions, and churches. The federal government employs more than any other nonprofit entity, most acting as accountants, auditors or budgetary officers. Many accountants are also employed by state and local governments. Accounting educators also compose a large portion of the accountants employed in nonprofit organizations. Accountants in industry are involved primarily in two functions: management accounting and financial accounting.

   Public accountants perform three kinds of services: (1) audits, (2) tax services, and (3) management consulting services. Public accounting firms range in size from individually-run operations to large international organizations. Auditing is the major service provided by the large public accounting firms, but management consulting is becoming increasingly more important. The smaller public accounting firms tend to specialize in tax planning and preparation but also provide a variety of other financial services.

10 Describe the Securities and Exchange Commission and the Financial Accounting Standards Board and what their respective roles are in the development of generally accepted accounting principles.

The SEC Act of 1934 established the Securities and Exchange Commission as the governmental body responsible for ensuring that listed companies prepare and file registration statements before they issue new securities, submit the annual Form 10-K, and prepare quarterly and annual reports for stockholders. The SEC also has broad powers to prescribe, in whatever detail it desires, the accounting practices and standards to be employed by companies within its jurisdiction.

   The SEC has not assumed total responsibility for determining appropriate accounting practices and standards. Instead, it has allowed and encouraged the AICPA, a nongovernmental body, to take an active role. In 1973 the Financial Accounting Standards Board was established by a committee of the AICPA to assume responsibility for developing financial accounting standards. Since that time, the FASB, the third private body to develop standards of financial accounting, has issued over 100 standards and has received the full support of the SEC.

11 Explain how and why economic consequences are important to financial accounting standard-setting.

Economic consequences are important because standard setting is a political process that encourages input from interested parties who may have differing views about the consequences of proposed standards. The SEC is a government agency that represents the interests of the public, and the FASB publishes discussion memoranda and exposure drafts that are subjected to critical evaluation and review by outside parties. Such a political process must be followed if the SEC and FASB are to develop financial accounting standards and reporting requirements that provide useful information at a reasonable cost.

KEY TERMS

American Institute of Certified Public Accountants (AICPA) (p. 19)
Annual interest (p. 12)
Annual reports (p. 21)
Assets (p. 10)
Audit committee (p. 17)
Auditor's report (p. 6)
Balance sheet (p. 10)
Board of directors (p. 12)
Certified public accountant (CPA) (p. 5)
Common stock (p. 10)
Compensation contracts (p. 16)
Conceptual Framework (p. 33)
Consolidated financial statements (p. 22)
Corporate form of business (p. 31)
Creditors (p. 10)
Debt investment (p. 11)
Debt restrictions (p. 12)
Dividends (p. 10)
Earning power (p. 11)
Economic consequences (p. 23)
Equity (p. 12)
Expenses (p. 10)
Financial accounting (p. 3)
Financial accounting standard (p. 34)
Financial Accounting Standards Board (FASB) (p. 33)
Financing activities (p. 11)

Footnotes (p. 8)
Generally accepted accounting principles (GAAP) (p. 4)
Historical cost (p.12)
Income statement (p. 10)
Independent audit (p. 5)
Internal control system (p. 7)
Internal Revenue Code (p. 25)
Investing activities (p. 11)
Liabilities (p. 10)
Loan contract (p. 11)
Management letter (p. 6)
Managers (p. 16)
Net income (profit) (p. 10)
Nonprofit entities (p. 22)
Operating activities (p. 11)
Profit (p. 10)
Retained earnings (p. 10)
Revenues (p. 10)
Securities and Exchange Commission (SEC) (p. 32)
Solvent (p. 11)
Statement of cash flows (p. 11)
Statement of retained earnings (p. 10)
Stockholders (p. 12)
Stockholders' equity (p. 10)
Stock markets (p. 31)
Taxable income (p. 25)

QUESTIONS FOR DISCUSSION AND REVIEW

1. Define the accounting process and briefly explain how it is a dynamic phenomenon.

2. List and describe the seven components of the definition of financial accounting. Refer to Figure 1–8 and compare the four kinds of accounting with regard to the first six components of the definition.

3. Critique the following statement: Generally accepted accounting principles represent a precise and narrowly-defined set of laws that are set by a council of accounting experts who insulate themselves from political pressures. Failure to follow these laws can result in heavy fines and sometimes jail sentences for managers.

4. Capital providers include both equity and debt investors. Purchasing 100 shares of IBM common stock is an example of an equity investment. Bank loans and extensions of credit represent debt investments.

    a. What are the basic differences between equity and debt investments? Which kind of investment entails greater risk? Which has the potential for greater returns? Why?

    b. What kind of financial information would you consider when deciding whether or not to purchase IBM common stock? Would you consider the same kind of information if you were a banker considering a loan to IBM?

5. Financial accounting statements are used by many parties. Describe how each of the parties listed below might use them.

    a. Security analysts

    b. Stockbrokers

    c. Bank loan officers

    d. A company's customers or suppliers

    e. Public utilities

    f. Labor unions

    g. A company's managers

6. What does it mean to be solvent? What kind of financial information would be useful in assessing solvency? Would debt or equity investors be more likely to take a greater interest in assessing a company's solvency position? Why?

7. W. T. Grant, a large department store chain, reported profits on its income statement almost all the way up to its financial collapse. How could this happen? What kind of information could have provided an earlier warning signal than profits? How is it that profitable companies sometimes go bankrupt?

8. What is the purpose of the audit and the auditor's report? What benefits do audits provide for managers and investors? Under what conditions might managers choose not to have audited financial statements? Under what conditions might they choose to have audited financial statements but still choose not to follow generally accepted accounting principles? In such a situation, what would the manager's auditor be likely to do?

9. What is meant by independent when describing auditors? Why is it important that they be independent? What economic incentives do they have to be independent? Are there pressures on auditors not to be independent? If so, from where?

10. Recently, Touche Ross, a major accounting firm, conducted and published an extensive survey on ethics in American business. (See Touche Ross & Co., *Ethics in American Business: A Special Report [1988].*) The results indicate that intense concentration on short-term profits is a major threat to American business ethics. Briefly explain how this could be so.

11. The same study referred to in Question 10 also discovered that ethical standards are perceived by businesspeople to strengthen a company's competitive position. Briefly explain how this could be so.

12. Consider the following scenario. Mary Howard, a CPA, has completed the audit of Galaxy Enterprise and has signed an opinion letter stating that Galaxy's books have been prepared "in conformance with generally accepted accounting principles" and "present fairly" the company's financial position and the results of its operations. The financial statements look good to a group of twenty investors and, relying on Mary's opinion letter, they decide to invest $50,000 each in the equity (i.e., purchase common stock) of Galaxy. Soon thereafter, Galaxy is forced to declare bankruptcy; all twenty

investors lose their entire investments. It is later revealed that Galaxy's financial statements were in error at the time of the audit.

    a. What recourse do the investors have to recover their investments?

    b. What arguments would you expect Mary to make in an effort to defend herself in court?

    c. Would you expect Mary to carry liability insurance to protect herself in the event of a lawsuit?

13. Equity and debt investors are very interested in the future prospects of the companies in which they invest. Since the form and content of financial reports are ultimately driven by the demands of these investors, would you not expect to see audited financial statements that contain future projections? If not, why? Would the need for verifiable and objective numbers as well as legal liability have anything to do with it? If so, how?

14. A number of recent articles in publications like *The Wall Street Journal, Forbes,* and *Time* have noted that auditors are facing increasing levels of legal liability. At the same time, some business professionals advocate that future-oriented information (e.g., future earnings projections) be included in the financial statements and subject to the auditor's report. Comment on the problems that could arise in view of these seemingly opposing trends.

15. We have stated that financial statements must contain objective and verifiable numbers if they are to be useful. Yet, we have also pointed out that many estimates and subjective assumptions are required for the preparation of these reports. Can you reconcile these apparently inconsistent statements?

16. You have closely analyzed the financial statements of two companies in the same industry. Company A's profits and total assets have consistently exceeded those of Company B. According to the audit reports, the financial statements of both companies have been prepared in conformance with generally accepted accounting principles. Even though Company A's financial statements appear to look better, you note that the common shares of the two companies are presently selling at the same price. Does this mean that Company A's stock is necessarily a better buy than Company B's stock? What might account for the difference in reported profits and assets?

17. What incentives might managers have to manipulate the numbers on the financial statements by choosing various estimates, assumptions, and accounting methods? Are generally accepted accounting principles broad enough to allow for such manipulation? How does this present problems for financial statement users?

18. This chapter mentioned that investors require managers to provide financial information so that they can (1) assess the levels of risk and potential returns offered by alternative investments and (2) control the actions of managers through the creation of contracts. Refer to the list below and explain how each of the following items relates to this statement.

    a. The managers of many U.S. companies receive bonuses at the end of each year that are determined by a percentage of that year's net income.

    b. The profits of XYZ company over the past five years have far exceeded the average profit of the companies in the industry in which XYZ is a member.

    c. Leverage, Inc. has recently borrowed $1 million from First National Bank. The loan contract states that the dividends Leverage pays to its shareholders in any one year cannot exceed 50 percent of that year's net income. It also specifies that Leverage's ratio of total liabilities to total assets cannot exceed .75 at any time during the period of the loan. Net income, total liabilities, and total assets must be measured in conformance with generally accepted accounting principles.

    d. Tarpley and Sons has doubled its outstanding debt in the past year.

    e. Dun and Bradstreet, a financial rating service, determines IBM's credit rating to be AAA.

19. Why might an equity investor insist that a manager be paid a bonus expressed as a percentage of income? Suppose that Elmer Smith is a manager of a company in its first year of operations who will be paid a bonus at year end that is equal to 1 percent of the company's net income for that year. The bonus contract states that net income for the purposes of the bonus must be audited and measured in conformance with generally accepted accounting principles. Suppose that either of two accounting methods for reporting inventory values are allowed under generally accepted accounting principles. One of the methods, FIFO, gives rise to net income equal to $100,000. The other method, LIFO, results in a $70,000 net income. Based on the bonus contract, which inventory method would Elmer be likely to choose? What other considerations might Elmer make in the choice of inventory accounting methods?

20. Why would a debt investor (e.g., a bank) insist on a loan contract specifying that total liabilities divided by total assets cannot exceed a certain percentage, or that dividends paid to stockholders cannot exceed a certain percentage of net income? Suppose that Acme Custom Design is in danger of violating a loan contract stating that total liabilities divided by total assets (as measured by generally accepted accounting principles) cannot exceed 50 percent. If FIFO, an acceptable method for valuing inventory assets, results in a higher asset valuation than LIFO, another acceptable method, which of the two methods would Acme's management be likely to prefer?

21. According to generally accepted accounting principles, many of the assets on the balance sheet are valued at historical cost: the cost incurred when the assets were originally purchased.

    a. How useful are historical costs to equity and debt investors in their efforts to assess the solvency position and long-run earning power of a company?

    b. How useful are historical costs in providing numbers that can be objectively verified and therefore used in the legal contracts that exist between capital providers and managers?

    c. How might the fact that auditors and managers face high levels of legal liability lead to financial statements that rely heavily on historical costs?

22. In preparing financial statements to accompany a loan application for a local bank, Mary Jones was unsure about the proper reporting of a piece of land purchased by the company ten years ago. The land was purchased for $10,000, but recently, similar parcels of land in the area sold for between $25,000 and $40,000.

    a. If you were a CPA auditing Mary's books, what amount would you insist that she disclose for the land value?

    b. What amount would Mary probably prefer?

    c. What amount would the bank find to be most useful?

23. Distinguish financial statements from financial reports. Are both subject to the auditor's report?

24. What is the role of the management letter? Why would investors, creditors, and auditors benefit from it?

25. The AICPA's list of red flags, alerting auditors to possible management fraud, includes "a domineering management coupled with a weak board of directors." Briefly explain the role of the board of directors and how such a situation could indicate management fraud. Why are auditors concerned with management fraud?

26. Explain the function of the audit committee and describe why it is important that it consist of outside (nonmanagement) directors.

27. E. W. Hauser and Associates showed $38,000 of net income on this past year's income statement. Yet the tax form filed with the Internal Revenue Service indicated only $25,000 of taxable income. Can you suggest several reasons and cite several examples that might explain this difference?

28. Why were external financial statements and auditors virtually unnecessary in the United States in the late nineteenth century?

29. Trace the development of financial accounting statements in response to changes in the business environment from the nineteenth century until today.

30. What government agency was formed shortly after the Great Depression to regulate the flow of information in the public security markets? How and to what extent has this body continued to influence accounting standard-setting and GAAP in the United States?

31. What body sets financial accounting standards today? How is this body structured? Is it a private body, a government body, or some combination of the two? In what two areas has this body attempted to improve upon its predecessor's efforts?

32. We have stated that financial accounting has evolved and continues to evolve in response to the demands for external reports from the business environment. What do we mean by this statement and can you provide some examples of how it has been true over time?

33. List and describe the steps followed by the FASB when issuing a financial accounting standard. What is the most important feature of this process?

34. What are economic consequences and how do they affect the setting of financial accounting standards?

35. Why should investors, creditors, managers, and consumers be concerned if auditors must charge higher fees due to increasing levels of legal liability and increasing liability insurance rates?

36. Suppose an accounting standard, which requires companies to report projections of earnings two years in the future, is presently being considered by the FASB. The FASB has just issued an exposure draft and is now receiving letters from interested parties. What kind of comments would you expect the FASB to receive from auditing firms? Do you believe that auditors would be willing to audit such projections? Why?

37. Differentiate among government accountants, industry accountants, and public accountants. What are the differences in the work generally performed by a controller and a chief financial officer?

38. For years many individuals have claimed that public accounting firms should not be allowed to offer management advisory services to the same companies they audit. What is the rationale behind such claims?

39. Accountants have long recognized that although the FASB issues reporting standards, there is often much leeway in their application, which managers can use to boost or depress profits or hide debt off the balance sheet. Explain why managers might wish to hide debt off the balance sheet.

40. Moody's Investor Service, Standard & Poors Corporation, and Dun & Bradstreet are well-known services that use publicly available financial information to provide ratings on the outstanding debt securities of many U.S. companies. High ratings indicate less risky debt than low ratings. IBM, for example has the highest AAA rating. Briefly explain why a company would desire a high debt rating and how such a desire may encourage management to manipulate the financial statements.

The Four Financial Statements

Learning Objectives

1 State the accounting equation and demonstrate how it is used to organize business transactions.

2 Describe how the accounting equation is related to the balance sheet, income statement, statement of retained earnings, and statement of cash flows.

3 Describe the format and basic divisions of the balance sheet, income statement, statement of retained earnings, and statement of cash flows.

4 Explain the difference between a capital and an operating transaction.

5 Identify the general ways in which the financial statements are used and some of the incentives that influence how they are prepared.

≡ This chapter focuses on the information contained in and relationships among the four basic financial statements: the balance sheet, the income statement, the statement of retained earnings, and the statement of cash flows.[1] It describes in detail the nature of each statement, how the information they contain is related, and how this information can be used. Chapters 3 and 4 cover the specific procedures used to prepare the financial statements.

As you read this chapter, consider the following questions. What information on the financial statements can be used to assess a company's solvency position and earning power? How might investors and creditors use the dollar values shown on the financial statements to control and monitor the business decisions of managers? How can management influence the preparation of these statements so that they depict its solvency position and earning power as attractively as possible? What kind of economic incentives underlie management's reporting decisions? Under what conditions should management follow GAAP in the preparation of these statements and have them audited by an independent CPA? How are the statements audited, and are some kinds of information more difficult to audit than others? Such questions give economic meaning to financial statements and must be considered as you begin to understand the role they play in the business environment.

THE FUNDAMENTAL ACCOUNTING EQUATION

The four financial statements are all based on a mathematical equation which states that the dollar value of a company's assets equals the dollar value of its liabilities plus the dollar value of its stockholders' equity.

$$\$Assets = \$Liabilities + \$Stockholders' \ Equity$$

Accounting procedures are structured so that this equality is always maintained. If the two sides of this equation are unequal, the books do not balance, and an error has been made in the accounting procedures. However, maintaining this equality does not ensure that the financial statements are correct; errors can exist even if the accounting equation balances. The equality of this equation is a necessary but not sufficient condition for accurately kept accounting records.

Assets

Assets are items and rights that a company acquires through objectively measurable transactions that can be used in the future to generate economic benefits (i.e., more assets). Such acquisitions are usually made by purchase: the asset is received in exchange for another asset (often cash) or a payable. Assets include cash, securities, receivables from customers, land, buildings, machinery, equipment, and rights such as patents, copyrights, and trademarks. Simply, the left side of the accounting equation represents the dollar values of the items and rights that have been acquired by a company and are expected to benefit the company in the future.

---

1. Major U.S. corporations are also required to prepare a statement of stockholders' equity that includes information in addition to that in the statement of retained earnings. Due to its complexity, we do not cover the statement of stockholders' equity until Chapter 12. The earlier chapters refer only to the statement of retained earnings.

Assets come from three sources: (1) they are borrowed, (2) they are contributed by stockholders (owners), and (3) they are generated by a company's operating activities. The right side of the equation, liabilities and stockholders' equity, represents the dollar values attached to these three sources. For each dollar amount on the asset side of the equation, a corresponding dollar amount is reflected on the liability and stockholders' equity side.

Liabilities

Liabilities consist primarily of a company's debts or payables. They are existing obligations for which assets must be used in the future. The dollar amount of the total liabilities on the balance sheet represents the portion of the assets that a company has borrowed and must repay.

Stockholders' Equity

Stockholders' equity consists of two components: **contributed capital,** the dollar value of the assets contributed by stockholders, and **retained earnings**, the dollar value of the assets generated by operating activities and retained in the business (i.e., not paid to the stockholders in the form of dividends). Operating activities are those transactions directly associated with the acquisition and sale of a company's products or services. Dividing stockholders' equity into its components, the fundamental accounting equation appears as follows:

$$\$Assets = \$Liabilities + \$Contributed\ Capital + \$Retained\ Earnings$$

That is, the dollar value of the assets is equal to the sum of the dollar amounts owed, the dollar amount of stockholders' contributions, and the dollar amount retained from profitable operations.

BUSINESS TRANSACTIONS, THE ACCOUNTING EQUATION, AND THE FINANCIAL STATEMENTS

Companies conduct operations by exchanging assets and liabilities with other entities (e.g., individuals and businesses). These exchanges are referred to as **business transactions.** Exchanging cash for a piece of equipment, for example, is a transaction that represents the purchase of equipment. Borrowing money is a transaction in which a promise to pay in the future (i.e., note payable) is exchanged for cash. The sale of a service on account is a transaction in which the service is exchanged for a receivable. In each of these exchanges, and in all business transactions, something is received and something is given up. These receipts and disbursements affect the financial condition of a company in a way that always maintains the equality of the fundamental accounting equation. That is, each business transaction is recorded in the books so that the dollar values of a company's assets always equal the dollar values of its liabilities and stockholders' equity.

The following sections demonstrate the mechanics of the accounting equation by showing how it can be used to record business transactions and to produce the four basic financial statements.

Figure 2-1 Business transactions and the accounting equation

Transaction	Assets	=	Liabilities	+	Contributed Capital	+	Retained Earnings
(1)	+10,000	=			+10,000		
(2)	+ 3,000	=	+3,000				
(3)	+ 5,000	=					
	(5,000)						
(4)	+ 8,000						
	+ 4,000	=					+12,000
(5)	(9,000)	=					(9,000)
(6)	(1,000)	=					(1,000)
End-of-year balance	15,000	=	3,000	+	10,000	+	2,000

Transactions and the Accounting Equation

The six transactions below were entered into by Joe's Landscaping Service during 1990, its first year of operations. Figure 2–1 shows how each transaction affects the accounting equation. Study it carefully and read the following discussion of each transaction.

Transaction (1).   Joe, the owner of the company, contributes $10,000. This dollar amount increases the company's cash balance, an asset, by $10,000 and is also recorded on the right side of the accounting equation under contributed capital. Note that both sides of the accounting equation are increased by $10,000, so its equality is maintained.

Transaction (2). $3000 is borrowed from a bank. The dollar amount of this exchange also increases the company's cash balance, but in this case liabilities are also increased: the company now owes $3000 to the bank.

Transaction (3).   The company purchases equipment for $5000 cash. This exchange both increases and decreases the company's assets. It now has an asset called *equipment*, and its cash balance is reduced by $5000. Still, the equality of the accounting equation is maintained because the asset side was both increased and decreased by $5000.

Transaction (4).   The company performs a service for $12,000. This transaction increases the company's cash balance by $8000 and creates a receivable of $4000. Thus, total assets increase by $12,000. The corresponding $12,000 adjustment on the right side of the equation, which maintains its equality, is reflected in Retained Earnings because the company generated this $12,000 through its own operations.

Transaction (5).   The company pays $9000 for expenses—wages, interest, and maintenance. This transaction decreases the company's cash balance by $9000 and maintains the equality of the equation by decreasing Retained Earnings in the amount of $9000. Retained Earnings is decreased because, as in Transaction 4, these expenses are associated with the company's operating activities.

Transaction (6). Joe pays himself a $1000 dividend as a return on his original investment. The dollar amount of the dividend reduces the company's cash balance by $1000 and is also reflected on the right side of the equation by a $1000 reduction in Retained Earnings. Retained Earnings is reduced because the fundamental objective of the company's operating activities is to provide a return for the owner, and Retained Earnings is the measure of the assets that have been accumulated through operations.

The Accounting Equation and the Basic Financial Statements

This section introduces and defines the concept of an account and describes the preparation of simplified versions of the balance sheet, statement of cash flows, income statement, and statement of retained earnings for Joe's Landscaping Service. Spend enough time with this section to make sure that you understand the meaning of an account, how accounts are compiled in preparing the financial statements, and how the accounts and the financial statements relate to the accounting equation. Diligent effort now will be repaid later in the chapter as we explain each of the four statements more completely.

Accounts and the Accounting Equation

For purposes of recording transactions and preparing financial statements, the main components of the accounting equation (assets, liabilities, and stockholders' equity) can be further subdivided into separate categories called accounts. The general category of assets is normally divided into a number of accounts including, for example, a cash account, a receivables account, and an equipment account. Liabilities normally consist of various payable accounts, and as mentioned earlier, stockholders' equity can be divided into a contributed capital account and a retained earnings account. Accounts serve as "storage units," where the dollar values of business transactions are initially recorded and later compiled into the financial statements.

In Figure 2–2 the main components of the accounting equation are divided into separate accounts for the purpose of recording the six transactions entered into by Joe's Landscaping Service. Note that Figure 2–2 is very similar to Figure

Figure 2–2 Accounts and the accounting equation

Transaction	Cash	+	Receivables	+	Equipment	=	Loan Payable	+	Contributed Capital	+	Retained Earnings
(1)	+10,000					=			+10,000		
(2)	+ 3,000					=	+3,000				
(3)	(5,000)				+5,000	=					
(4)	+ 8,000		+4,000			=					+12,000
(5)	(9,000)					=					(9,000)
(6)	(1,000)					=					(1,000)
Total	6,000	+	4,000	+	5,000	=	3,000	+	10,000	+	2,000

Column group headers: **Assets** = **Liabilities** + **Stockholders' Equity**

Figure 2-3 Balance sheet for Joe's Landscaping

Joe's Landscaping Service			
Balance Sheet			
December 31, 1990			

Assets		Liabilities and Stockholders' Equity	
Cash	$ 6,000	Loan payable	$ 3,000
Receivable	4,000	Contributed capital	10,000
Equipment	5,000	Retained earnings	2,000
		Total liabilities and	
Total assets	$15,000	stockholders' equity	$15,000

2-1. It differs only in that it records the transactions in more specific categories, which represent the accounts that eventually appear on the financial statements.

Note that total assets ($15,000 = $6000 + $4000 + $5000) equal total assets in Figure 2-1 as well as total liabilities plus stockholders' equity ($15,000 = $3,000 + $10,000 + $2,000). The components of the accounting equation have simply been divided into more specific "storage units." In the next sections the information contained in Figure 2-2 is used to prepare the financial statements.

The Balance Sheet

The balance sheet is the statement of the basic accounting equation as of a particular date: in this case, the end of 1990. It is called a *balance sheet* because assets are always in balance with liabilities plus stockholders' equity. That is, there is a source for each asset the company has acquired. Figure 2-3 shows the balance sheet for Joe's Landscaping Service at the end of its first year of operations.

This balance sheet was prepared by simply listing and grouping the totals of the individual asset, liability, and stockholders' equity accounts, which appear at the bottom of Figure 2-2. Total assets ($15,000) equal total liabilities and stockholders' equity ($15,000), and the equality of the accounting equation is maintained. Indeed, the balance sheet is a statement of the accounting equation.

At the end of the year, Joe's Landscaping Service has three different assets, each represented by a separate account: Cash, Receivable, and Equipment. These three accounts are disclosed on the left side of the balance sheet and the dollar value associated with each represents the accumulated dollar amount of the transactions recorded in it. The Receivable account, for example, is valued at $4000, and the Equipment account is valued at $5000, the dollar amounts of Transactions (4) and (3), respectively. Similarly, the $6000 balance in the Cash account represents the amount of cash accumulated by Joe's Landscaping Service from all cash transactions entered into during the year.

The dollar values on the right side of the balance sheet also can be traced to the original transactions and to Figure 2-2. The $3000 in the Loan Payable account was recorded from Transaction (2), the $10,000 in the Contributed Capital account was recorded from Transaction (1), and the $2000 in Retained Earnings represents the accumulated balance of Transactions (4), (5), and (6), which were recorded in the Retained Earnings account.

Figure 2–4   Statement of cash flows for Joe's Landscaping

Joe's Landscaping Service		
Statement of Cash Flows		
For the Year Ended December 31, 1990		
Beginning cash balance		$ 0
Cash inflows		
Owner contribution (1)	$10,000	
Sale of service (4)	8,000	
Bank loan (2)	3,000	
Total cash inflows		21,000
Cash outflows		
Purchase of equipment (3)	5,000	
Operating expenses (5)	9,000	
Dividend to stockholder (6)	1,000	
Total cash outflows		(15,000)
Ending cash balance		$ 6,000

Note: The colored numbers indicate the specific transactions leading to each cash inflow or outflow. Dollar amounts in parentheses indicate subtraction in the computation of the ending cash balance.

Statement of Cash Flows

The statement of cash flows in Figure 2–4 was prepared directly from the activity recorded in the cash account in Figure 2–2. Each dollar value on the statement of cash flows corresponds to an increase or decrease in the cash account indicated in Figure 2–2. Note also that the ending cash balance of $6000 on the statement of cash flows equals the balance in the Cash account on the balance sheet. While the statement of cash flows in Figure 2–4 is somewhat simplified (the format does not conform exactly with generally accepted accounting principles), it does illustrate that this statement is nothing more than a record of the activity in the company's cash account. A more complete statement of cash flows is illustrated and discussed later in the chapter.

Income Statement

The income statement is a measure of the assets generated from the company's operating activities (i.e., the transactions directly associated with the acquisition and sale of the company's products or services) during a period of time. It compares *revenues,* the asset inflows due to operating activities, to *expenses,* the asset outflows required to generate the revenues. The difference between revenues and expenses is called *net income* or *net loss.* If revenues exceed expenses, there is net income or profit, if expenses exceed revenues, there is a net loss.

In terms of the accounting equation, revenues, expenses, and dividends are reflected in the retained earnings account. Like the general categories of assets, liabilities, and stockholders' equity, retained earnings can be further subdivided into revenue accounts, expense accounts, and dividend accounts. Recording a transaction in a revenue account increases retained earnings; recording a transaction in an expense or dividend account decreases retained earnings.

Figure 2–5   Income statement for Joe's Landscaping

Joe's Landscaping Service Income Statement For the Year Ended December 31, 1990	
Revenues: Fees earned for services	$12,000
Expenses: Wages, interest, maintenance	9,000
Net income	$ 3,000

In the example of Joe's Landscaping Service, revenues in the form of cash and a receivable were generated in Transaction (4), the sale of landscaping services for $12,000. Expenses were recognized in Transaction (5), which reflects payments made for wages, interest, and equipment maintenance. The dollar amounts of these two transactions are recorded in the Retained Earnings account in Figure 2–2, but in practice they would be recorded in separate revenue and expense accounts, which are components of retained earnings. An income statement can be prepared by disclosing Revenues and Expenses in the manner shown in Figure 2–5.

Statement of Retained Earnings
The statement of retained earnings is similar to the statement of cash flows, in that it is a record of the activity in a single balance sheet account over a period of time. Rather than explaining the activity in the Cash account, however, it explains the activity in the Retained Earnings account. The statement of retained earnings in Figure 2–6 was prepared directly from the activity in the Retained Earnings account in Figure 2–2.

As indicated earlier, revenues, expenses, and dividends are reflected in the Retained Earnings account. On the statement of retained earnings, the dollar amount of revenues less expenses (i.e., net income) and the dollar amount of dividends are disclosed separately. Note that net income is also reported on the income statement and that the ending balance of retained earnings in Figure 2–6 is equal to the balance in the Retained Earnings account on the balance sheet in Figure 2–3.

Figure 2–6   Statement of retained earnings

Joe's Landscaping Service Statement of Retained Earnings For the Year Ended December 31, 1990	
Beginning retained earnings balance	$ 0
Plus: Net income	3000
Less: Dividend to stockholder	1000
Ending retained earnings balance	$2000

THE CLASSIFIED BALANCE SHEET

We now turn to more in-depth discussions of the four financial statements. The balance sheet is discussed first because it is a statement of the basic accounting equation, the formula upon which the other three statements are based. We discuss the income statement, the statement of retained earnings, and the statement of cash flows after the balance sheet because all three statements explain the activity in one or more of the balance sheet accounts.

Figure 2−7 shows the balance sheet for Harbour Island Company as of December 31, 1990. It is entitled a **classified balance sheet** because the asset and liability accounts are grouped into classifications: current assets; long-term investments; property, plant, and equipment; intangible assets; current liabilities; and long-term liabilities.

Think of the balance sheet as a photograph of the business at a specific point in time. The title includes a specific date (December 31, 1990). As of this date, the balance sheet measures the financial condition of Harbour Island Company. In fact, some companies refer to the balance sheet as the *statement of financial condition*. This "photograph" of financial condition shows that as of December 31, 1990 Harbour Island has $220 in cash, total assets of $18,615, contributed capital of $9550, retained earnings of $1385, and total liabilities plus stockholders' equity of $18,615.

The balance sheet in Figure 2−7 lists Harbour Island's assets and their sources as of December 31, 1990. The company's total assets (valued at $18,615) came from three separate sources: (1) $7680 (41 percent) came from various forms of borrowing (total liabilities) and must be repaid in the future, (2) $9550 (51 percent) came from investments by stockholders (contributed capital), who expect some form of return in the future, and (3) $1385 (8 percent), the dollar amount in the Retained Earnings account, was generated through the company's operating activities and not returned to the stockholders in the form of dividends.

Like the balance sheet of Joe's Landscaping Service in Figure 2−3, Harbour Island's balance sheet is divided into two major sections: assets ($18,615) and liabilities plus stockholders' equity ($18,615). Similarly, stockholders' equity is divided into contributed capital ($9550) and retained earnings ($1385). However, the classified balance sheet in Figure 2−7 differs in that it classifies the assets and liabilities into additional categories.

Assets are divided into current assets ($1415), long-term investments ($4000); property, plant, and equipment ($11,500); and intangible assets ($1700). These categories and the order of the accounts within them are listed in order of **liquidity,** closeness to cash. That is, the assets listed near the top of the balance sheet (e.g., current assets) are expected to be converted into cash within a shorter time period than those listed at or near the bottom. They are, therefore, considered to be more liquid. The assets in the current asset category are also listed in order of liquidity. Cash, the most liquid of all assets, is understandably listed at the top.

Liabilities are divided into current liabilities ($740) and long-term liabilities ($6940). These two categories, and the accounts within them, are also listed in order of liquidity. Those near the top of the balance sheet (e.g., current liabilities) are expected to require the payment of cash within a shorter time period than those at or near the bottom. Study these categories and the order of the accounts contained within them. This is the general format required under generally accepted accounting principles, and it is important that you be familiar with it.

Figure 2–7 Classified balance sheet for Harbour Island Company

<table>
<tr><td colspan="4" align="center">**Harbour Island Company**
Classified Balance Sheet
December 31, 1990</td></tr>
<tr><td>Assets</td><td></td><td></td><td></td></tr>
<tr><td>Current assets</td><td></td><td></td><td></td></tr>
<tr><td> Cash</td><td></td><td>$ 220</td><td></td></tr>
<tr><td> Marketable securities</td><td></td><td>150</td><td></td></tr>
<tr><td> Accounts receivable</td><td>$ 350</td><td></td><td></td></tr>
<tr><td> Less: Uncollectibles</td><td>5</td><td>345</td><td></td></tr>
<tr><td> Inventory</td><td></td><td>600</td><td></td></tr>
<tr><td> Prepaid expenses</td><td></td><td>100</td><td></td></tr>
<tr><td>   Total current assets</td><td></td><td></td><td>$ 1,415</td></tr>
<tr><td>Long-term investments</td><td></td><td></td><td></td></tr>
<tr><td> Long-term note receivable</td><td></td><td>1,000</td><td></td></tr>
<tr><td> Land</td><td></td><td>500</td><td></td></tr>
<tr><td> Securities</td><td></td><td>2,500</td><td></td></tr>
<tr><td>   Total long-term investments</td><td></td><td></td><td>4,000</td></tr>
<tr><td>Property, plant, and equipment</td><td></td><td></td><td></td></tr>
<tr><td> Property</td><td></td><td>6,000</td><td></td></tr>
<tr><td> Plant</td><td>4,000</td><td></td><td></td></tr>
<tr><td> Less: Accumulated depreciation</td><td>1,100</td><td>2,900</td><td></td></tr>
<tr><td> Equipment</td><td>3,500</td><td></td><td></td></tr>
<tr><td> Less: Accumulated depreciation</td><td>900</td><td>2,600</td><td></td></tr>
<tr><td>   Total property, plant, and equipment</td><td></td><td></td><td>11,500</td></tr>
<tr><td>Intangible assets</td><td></td><td></td><td></td></tr>
<tr><td> Goodwill</td><td></td><td>800</td><td></td></tr>
<tr><td> Patent</td><td></td><td>200</td><td></td></tr>
<tr><td> Trademark</td><td></td><td>700</td><td></td></tr>
<tr><td>   Total intangible assets</td><td></td><td></td><td>1,700</td></tr>
<tr><td>Total assets</td><td></td><td></td><td>$18,615</td></tr>
<tr><td>Liabilities and stockholders' equity</td><td></td><td></td><td></td></tr>
<tr><td>Current liabilities</td><td></td><td></td><td></td></tr>
<tr><td> Accounts payable</td><td></td><td>$ 250</td><td></td></tr>
<tr><td> Wages payable</td><td></td><td>25</td><td></td></tr>
<tr><td> Interest payable</td><td></td><td>155</td><td></td></tr>
<tr><td> Short-term notes payable</td><td></td><td>75</td><td></td></tr>
<tr><td> Current maturities of long-term debts</td><td></td><td>60</td><td></td></tr>
<tr><td> Deferred revenues</td><td></td><td>75</td><td></td></tr>
<tr><td> Other payables</td><td></td><td>100</td><td></td></tr>
<tr><td>   Total current liabilities</td><td></td><td></td><td>$ 740</td></tr>
<tr><td>Long-term liabilities</td><td></td><td></td><td></td></tr>
<tr><td> Long-term notes payable</td><td></td><td>1,500</td><td></td></tr>
<tr><td> Bonds payable</td><td></td><td>3,500</td><td></td></tr>
<tr><td> Mortgage payable</td><td></td><td>1,940</td><td></td></tr>
<tr><td>   Total long-term liabilities</td><td></td><td></td><td>6,940</td></tr>
<tr><td>Stockholders' equity</td><td></td><td></td><td></td></tr>
<tr><td> Contributed capital</td><td></td><td>9,550</td><td></td></tr>
<tr><td> Retained earnings</td><td></td><td>1,385</td><td></td></tr>
<tr><td>   Total stockholders' equity</td><td></td><td></td><td>10,935</td></tr>
<tr><td>Total liabilities and stockholders' equity</td><td></td><td></td><td>$18,615</td></tr>
</table>

Assets

Having covered the balance sheet in general, we now discuss the individual balance sheet accounts. This section reviews current assets; long-term investments; property, plant, and equipment; and intangible assets.

Current Assets

Assets categorized as current are expected to be realized or, in most cases, converted into cash in the near future, usually within one year. They are grouped into a separate category because they are considered to be highly liquid. The amount of highly liquid assets held by a company can be an indication of its ability to meet debt payments as they come due. Consequently, the current asset category is often reviewed by financial statement users who are interested in assessing a company's solvency position. **Current assets** include cash, marketable securities, accounts receivable, inventory, and prepaid expenses, and they often represent a significant portion of a company's total assets. For example, current assets of new and used car dealers, who typically carry large inventories of automobiles, represent on average 86 percent of total assets.[2]

Cash. Cash represents the currency a company has access to as of the balance sheet date. It may be in a bank savings account, a checking account, or perhaps on the company premises in the form of petty cash. Cash amounts that a company can use immediately should be separated on the balance sheet from cash that is restricted. As a condition of granting a loan, for example, banks often require that the borrowing company maintain a certain cash balance with the bank while the loan is outstanding. Cash amounts of this nature, called *compensating balances,* are normally described in the footnotes to the financial statements so that readers can draw a distinction between available cash and restricted cash. In 1987, for example, the financial report of Atlantic Richfield noted that "the company maintains compensating balances for some of its various banking services and products."

Marketable Securities. **Marketable securities** include stocks (equity investments in other companies), bonds (debt investments in the government or other companies), and similar investments. These securities are both *readily marketable* (i.e., able to be sold immediately) and intended by management to be sold within a short period of time, usually less than one year. A company often purchases these kinds of securities to earn income with cash that would otherwise be idle for a short time. The dollar value of this account is the total purchase cost of securities held by a company or their total selling price as of the balance sheet date, whichever is lower.

Many companies invest in marketable securities, but this account is especially important for financial institutions, like banks and insurance companies. Safeco Insurance Company, for example, reported almost $5 billion in marketable debt and equity securities on its 1987 balance sheet, which represented almost 70 percent of the company's total assets.

---

2. Dun & Bradstreet, *Industry Norms and Key Business Ratios* (Dun & Bradstreet, 1987).

Accounts Receivable. The **accounts receivable** account represents the amount of money a company expects to collect from its customers. Such receivables arise from sales of products or services for which customers have not yet paid. These sales are often referred to as *credit sales* or *sales on account.* The dollar amount appearing on the balance sheet for this account is computed by taking the total dollar amount of the receivables owed and subtracting an estimate for *uncollectibles,* those accounts not expected to be received.

The dollar value of accounts receivable is very significant for large retailing companies, such as Sears and J. C. Penney, whose sales are primarily on a credit basis. J. C. Penney, for example, reported net accounts receivable of $4.5 billion on its 1987 balance sheet, which was almost 65 percent of current assets and approximately 42 percent of total assets.

Inventory. Inventory represents items or products on hand that a company intends to sell to its customers. It is often called **merchandise inventory.** The dollar value in this account is very important because a company's success often depends on its ability to sell these items. The balance-sheet value of inventory is usually the cost of acquiring (purchasing or producing) it or the cost of replacing it as of the balance sheet date, whichever is lower.

Major retailers (e.g., K mart) and manufacturers (e.g., McDonnell Douglas) carry significant inventory balances on their balance sheets, while financial institutions (e.g., American Express Company) and companies in the service industry (e.g., H & R Block) carry very little. McDonnell Douglas, for example, on its 1987 balance sheet reported a dollar amount for inventory of almost $4 billion, which equaled 44 percent of total assets. That same year the American Express Company and H & R Block reported no inventories.

A second kind of inventory account is called *supplies inventory.* It represents items used to support a company's operations: office supplies and spare parts are two common examples. The dollar amount of this account on the balance sheet is usually the cost of acquiring the items. Major manufacturers often carry a substantial inventory of spare parts. In 1987 McDonnell Douglas reported materials and spare parts inventories of approximately $1.4 billion.

Prepaid Expenses. **Prepaid expenses** are exactly what the name suggests: expenses that have been paid by a company before the corresponding service or right is actually used. Insurance premiums, for example, are normally paid prior to the period of coverage. Similarly, rent is usually paid before the rental period. A prepaid expense, therefore, is considered an asset because it represents a benefit to be enjoyed by the company in the future. Prepaid expenses are originally recorded on the balance sheet at the cost of acquiring them. For most companies, prepaid expenses are a very small, often insignificant, part of total assets.

Long-term Investments

Long-term investments are acquired by companies to provide benefits for periods of time usually extending beyond one year. Examples include long-term notes receivable and investments in land, debt and equity securities, life insurance, and special funds for specific purposes.

The Notes Receivable account includes company receivables that are evidenced by promissory notes. *Promissory notes* are contracts (formal, legally enforceable documents) that state the face value of the receivable, the date when the face value is due, and the periodic interest payments to be made while the note is outstanding. The date when the receivable is due, called the *maturity date,* is often beyond one year, so this account is often listed in the long-term investment section of the balance sheet. However, if the maturity date of a note receivable is within one year, it should be disclosed as a current asset.

Notes receivable often arise because companies receive notes in exchange for the sale of expensive items. For example, the Boeing Company, a major aircraft manufacturer, often receives notes in payment for sold aircraft. As of December 31, 1987, it reported $392 million in long-term notes receivable. Alternatively, such notes can result from direct company loans to employees and others. It also happens that customers with large, overdue accounts are asked to sign promissory notes.

In addition to notes receivable, the long-term investment section of the balance sheet can include a number of other investments. Land, for example, may be purchased and held as a long-term investment. Investments in debt and equity securities that are not intended to be sold in the near future represent other common examples. Most major U.S. companies have made significant investments in the equity securities of other, usually smaller, companies, intending to exert long-term influence over their management. As of the end of 1987, for example, Chrysler Corporation reported an investment of $242 million in Mitsubishi Corporation in the long-term investment section of its balance sheet.

The *cash value of life insurance,* the amount for which ordinary insurance policies held on the lives of company officers can be cashed in, and the assets of investment funds designed to finance future events, like plant expansions and debt payments, also appear in this section of the balance sheet. The dollar amounts in these accounts, which are relatively small for most major U.S. companies, normally equal the costs of acquiring them.

Property, Plant, and Equipment

The property, plant, and equipment section of the balance sheet includes assets acquired for use in the day-to-day operations of the business. For many companies, especially manufacturers, this is the largest asset category on the balance sheet. For example, the property, plant, and equipment account for ARCO, a major oil company, is valued at over $14 billion, which represents approximately 65 percent of its total assets.

The **Property** account represents the land on which the company conducts its operations. It is carried on the balance sheet at the original price for the land, which is not adjusted as the value of the property appreciates (i.e., increases). Be sure not to confuse this account with land in the long-term investment section. The property referred to in this account is used in the operations of the business, while land is held for investment purposes only.

Plant and equipment represent the physical structures owned by a company that are involved in its operations. The Plant account, for example, includes the value of factory and office buildings and warehouses, while the Equipment account includes machinery, vehicles, furniture, and similar items. The dollar amount in these accounts on the balance sheet is the original cost at the time the assets were purchased, reduced by an amount that loosely approximates the asset's lost usefulness or deterioration over time. This dollar amount is called *accumulated depreciation.* Subtracting accumulated depreciation from the acquisition cost results in the *net value* or **net book value** of the assets. The excerpt below, which illustrates the methods used to disclose property, plant, and equipment, was taken from the 1987 balance sheet of General Motors (dollars in millions).

	1987	1986
Real estate, plants, and equipment—at cost	$59,809	$55,241
Less: Accumulated depreciation	30,976	27,658
Net real estate, plants, and equipment	$28,833	$27,583

Intangible Assets

Intangible assets are so named because they have no physical substance. In most cases they represent legal rights to the use or sale of valuable names, items, processes, or information. Many companies, such as Coca Cola, have patents on certain formulas that grant them the sole legal right to produce and sell certain products. In a similar way, a company's trademark (e.g., the golden arches of McDonald's) or its name (e.g., Goodyear Tire & Rubber) can also be valuable. Perhaps the most common intangible asset, called *goodwill,* represents the cost of purchasing another company over and above the total market price of that company's individual assets and liabilities. The Goodwill account is prominent on the balance sheets of many major U.S. companies because they often purchase other companies, called *subsidiaries.* In 1986, for example, when General Electric purchased RCA Corporation, it recognized $3.7 billion of goodwill on the transaction.

Like the Plant and Equipment accounts, intangible assets are carried on the balance sheet at net book value, which is equal to the cost of acquiring an intangible asset reduced by a dollar amount, called *accumulated amortization,* which loosely approximates the asset's reduction in usefulness over time. However, unlike accumulated depreciation on plant and equipment, accumulated amortization is usually not disclosed in a special account on the balance sheet; only the net book value of the intangible asset is disclosed. The excerpt below, which illustrates the method of disclosing intangible assets, was taken from the 1987 financial report of General Electric Company (dollars in millions).

	1987	1986
Goodwill	$3820	$2793
Other intangibles	610	788
Total	$4430	$3581

Liabilities

This section covers current and long-term liabilities. The dollar amounts disclosed in these sections of the balance sheet are very important to those who are interested in the timing of a company's future cash obligations. Total liabilities, as a percentage of total assets, varies signifiantly across companies in different industries. Department stores, for example, normally carry liabilities of approximately 40 percent of total assets, while the dollar values of liabilities reported by accident and health insurance companies average about 60 percent of total assets.[3]

---

3. Dun & Bradstreet, *Industry Norms and Key Business Ratios* (Dun & Bradstreet, 1987).

Current Liabilities

Current liabilities are obligations that are expected to be paid (or services expected to be performed) with the use of assets that are listed in the current asset section of the balance sheet. Examples include Accounts Payable, Wages Payable, Interest Payable, Short-Term Notes Payable, Income Taxes Payable, Current Maturities on Long-Term Debts, and Deferred Revenues.

Accounts Payable are usually obligations to a company's suppliers for merchandise purchases made on account. Wages Payable are obligations to a company's employees for earned but unpaid wages as of the balance sheet date. Interest Payable and Short-Term Notes Payable are dollar amounts owed to creditors, often banks and other financial institutions. Income Taxes Payable are amounts owed to the government for taxes assessed on a company's income. **Current Maturities of Long-Term Debts** are portions of long-term liabilities that are due in the current period. They often arise when the principal amounts of long-term liabilities are due in installments over time. Deferred Revenues represent services yet to be performed by a company for which cash payments have already been collected. (Think of them as the "flip side" of the prepaid expense account on the asset side of the balance sheet.)

Financial statement users often closely examine a company's current liabilities as they assess a company's solvency position because most current liabilities require cash payments in the short-term future. For many companies, current liabilities represent the largest source of financing. For example, the 1987 dollar balance in current liabilities for McDonnell Douglas was $4.8 billion, which represents 56 percent of the company's total assets. The company's long-term liabilities and stockholders' equity represented only 9 percent and 35 percent of total assets, respectively.

Long-Term Liabilities

Long-term liabilities are obligations expected to require payment over a period of time beyond the current year. These obligations are usually evidenced by formal contracts that state their principal amounts, the periodic interest payments, and maturity dates. The form of these debt contracts, however, can vary widely. Common examples include accounts like Long-Term Notes Payable, Bonds Payable, and Mortgage Payables.

Long-Term **Notes Payable** refer to obligations on loans that are normally due more than one year beyond the balance sheet date. They usually involve either direct borrowings from financial institutions or arrangements to finance the purchase of assets. **Bonds Payable** represent notes that have been issued for cash to a large number of debt investors (called *bondholders*). Issuing bonds is a common form of financing for many major U.S. companies, which often use the funds to expand operations. In 1987, for example, Coca Cola Enterprises collected approximately $263 million by issuing bonds. The proceeds were used primarily to purchase property, plant, and equipment and to acquire several bottling companies. **Mortgage Payables** are obligations that are secured by real estate and are usually owed to financial institutions.

Stockholders' Equity

The stockholders' equity section of the balance sheet is basically divided into two parts: contributed capital and retained earnings. Note in Figure 2−7 that the total amount of stockholders' equity ($10,935) is equal to total assets ($18,615) less total liabilities ($7680). This dollar amount is called the *net book value* of the company.

Contributed Capital

Contributed capital is a measure of the assets that have been contributed to a company by its owners. Such contributions are made by purchasing the equity securities issued by the company, contributing cash or other noncash assets, or providing services. Whatever the form, the investor's contribution is exchanged for ownership interests (e.g., shares of stock) in the company. Such interests usually carry with them the right to have a voice in the management of the company (e.g., vote for the board of directors) as well as the right to receive assets (e.g., dividends), if they are distributed. In many cases these ownership interests can be purchased and sold freely (e.g., through public stock markets), but such transactions have no effects on the company's balance sheet.

Issuing stock is a common method used by major U.S. companies to raise capital for expansion. In 1987, for example, Chrysler Corporation issued over 15 million shares of stock, collecting approximately $518 million dollars. These funds were used primarily to finance the acquisition of American Motors Corporation.

Retained Earnings

Retained earnings is a measure of the assets that have been generated through a company's operating activities but not paid out to stockholders in the form of dividends. This account is particularly troublesome to accounting students who tend to visualize it as a tangible pool of cash. Nothing could be farther from the truth. The $1385 in Harbour Island's retained earnings account in Figure 2−7 is not in the form of cash in the company treasurer's office or in the bank. In fact, it is not associated with any specific asset or group of assets. It is simply a measure of the amount of the assets appearing on the balance sheet that have been provided by profitable operations. All we know from the balance sheet in Figure 2−7 is that $1385 of the $18,615 total in the asset account has been provided by the company's profitable operations.

The relative size of retained earnings on the balance sheets of major U.S. companies varies significantly across industries. BankAmerica, for example, reported retained earnings at the end of 1987 of only 2 percent of total assets, while Microsoft, a fast growing computer software developer, reported retained earnings of 56 percent of total assets. We return to the Retained Earnings account when we discuss the statement of retained earnings.

Organizational Form and the Equity Section

A business entity in the United States can be legally organized in either of two basic ways: as a corporation or as a partnership (called a *proprietorship* if there is only one partner). A *corporation* is a legal entity that is separate and distinct from its owners. It can be taxed or sued, and the owners, called *stockholders* or *shareholders*, are legally liable only for the amount of their original contributions to the corporation. Stockholders acquire ownership interests by purchasing shares of stock in the corporation, and their interests give them the right to vote for its board of directors at annual stockholders' meetings as well as the right to receive dividends, which are distributed on a per-share basis, if declared by the board.

A *partnership*, or *proprietorship*, on the other hand, is not a legal entity. It can neither be taxed nor sued, and the legal liability of the owners, called *partners* or

Figure 2–8   Owners' equity: corporation vs. partnership

Corporation		Partnership	
Stockholders' Equity		Owners' Equity	
Contributed capital	$20,000	Capital account, Ms. A	$12,000
Retained earnings	14,000	Capital account, Mr. B	15,000
Total stockholders' equity	$34,000	Total owners' equity	$27,000

proprietors, is not limited to their original contributions. Asset distributions to partners are called *withdrawals.*

The differences between corporations and partnerships are reflected in differences in the equity sections of their balance sheets. The stockholders' equity section of a corporate balance sheet, as illustrated in Figure 2–7, draws a distinction between contributed capital, the measure of the assets contributed by the stockholders, and retained earnings, the assets generated through the company's operating activities and not returned to stockholders in the form of dividends.

On the other hand, the equity section on a partnership's balance sheet, called **owners' equity,** makes no distinction between contributed capital and retained earnings. Instead, it consists of separate accounts for each partner, which show the status of each partner's personal capital balance, reflecting all contributions and withdrawals. Figure 2–8 illustrates the differences between the stockholders' equity section of a corporation and the owner's equity section of a partnership with two partners.

Throughout most of the text, the discussions and illustrations assume the corporate form of organization. The appendix to Chapter 12, which examines the equity section of the balance sheet more completely, also covers the fundamentals of accounting for partnerships.

Transactions That Affect the Balance Sheet Only

This section demonstrates how transactions involving balance sheet accounts affect only the balance sheet. The transactions of Pink Sands Resort during 1990 are described following Figure 2–9, which illustrates the impact of each transaction on the balance sheet.

Figure 2–9   Transactions that affect the balance sheet of Pink Sands Resort

	Assets					=	Liabilities		+	Stockholders' Equity	
Transaction	Cash	Accounts Receivable	Land	Equipment	Patent		Accounts Payable	Note Payable		Contributed Capital	Retained Earnings
(1)	+100	(100)				=					
(2)	(300)					=	(300)				
(3)	(5000)		+5000			=					
(4)				+10,000		=				+10,000	
(5)					+8000	=		+8000			
(6)	(2000)					=		(2000)			

Transaction (1). Received $100 cash in payment of one of its customer accounts.

Transaction (2). Sent $300 cash to a supplier in payment of an account payable.

Transaction (3). Purchased land to be held as an investment for $5000 cash.

Transaction (4). Purchased a piece of equipment (list price: $10,000) and in exchange issued shares of stock.

Transaction (5). Purchased a patent in exchange for a note payable in the amount of $8000.

Transaction (6). Paid $2000 cash on a loan outstanding at the bank.

Review each of the six transactions illustrated in Figure 2–9 and note that the main components of the basic accounting equation (assets, liabilities, and stockholders' equity) have been divided into specific accounts. Also note how each exchange increases or decreases the dollar amounts of the related accounts. In each case at least two accounts are affected, and the equality of the basic accounting equation is always maintained.

THE STATEMENT OF RETAINED EARNINGS

None of the six transactions in Figure 2–9 affect the Retained Earnings account; their effects are limited exclusively to asset accounts, liability accounts, or contributed capital. To illustrate the concept of retained earnings, consider the three transactions listed below, which were also entered into by Pink Sands.

Transaction (a). Provided a service for which a client was billed $1000.

Transaction (b). Owed salaries in the amount of $500 to employees.

Transaction (c). Declared and paid an $800 cash dividend to stockholders.

Each transaction affects the Retained Earnings account. Transactions (a) and (b) are operating transactions, and Transaction (c) is the payment of a dividend. Transaction (a) creates an asset, called a *receivable,* and a revenue, which increases retained earnings. Transaction (b) creates a payable and an expense, which reduces retained earnings. Transaction (c) reduces both cash and retained earnings. Figure 2–10 summarizes the effects of these three transactions on the Retained Earnings account and the other balance sheet accounts.

Since revenues increase retained earnings, and expenses and dividends decrease retained earnings, it follows that the Retained Earnings account is nothing more than the accumulation of a company's past revenues less expenses, less dividends. Revenues less expenses define net income, so retained earnings is simply a measure of the company's past net incomes, or earnings, that have been retained (i.e., not paid out to the stockholders in the form of dividends).

Figure 2–10   Transactions that affect the retained earnings of Pink Sands Resort

		Assets		=	Liabilities		+	Stockholders' Equity	
Transaction	Cash	Accounts Receivable	Other Assets		Salaries Payable	Other Liabilities		Contributed Capital	Retained Earnings
(a)		+1,000		=					+1,000
(b)				=	+500				(500)
(c)	(800)			=					(800)

Retained earnings, therefore, is nothing in and of itself: it is a measure of something else. In Transaction (a), that "something else" is the receivable earned through the operations of Pink Sands. In Transaction (b) it is a liability for salaries owed. In Transaction (c) it is the reduction of cash. Retained earnings is like an inch, a gallon, or a pound, which are nothing in and of themselves: they are measures of something else. An inch reflects the length of rope, the width of a table, or the height of a person. The Retained Earnings account reflects the accumulated inflows and outflows of assets and liabilities due to the past operating activities and dividend disbursements of a company.

Figure 2–11 is the statement of retained earnings for Harbour Island Company for the year ended December 31, 1990. Note the basic format. The balance of Retained Earnings at the beginning of the period is adjusted for net income (or loss) and dividends to the stockholders to compute the balance at the end of the period. This end-of-period balance is the Retained Earnings dollar amount that appears on Harbour Island's balance sheet as of the end of 1990 (see Figure 2–7).

THE INCOME STATEMENT

The operations of a company over a period of time are important enough to the users of accounting information to warrant a special financial statement that categorizes revenues earned and expenses incurred during a particular period. It is not sufficient simply to provide a statement of retained earnings, which discloses only the resulting net income (or loss) number. The revenues and expenses of each period, therefore, are brought together in a separate financial statement called the *income statement*.

Figure 2–11   Statement of retained earnings for Harbour Island Company

Harbour Island Company Statement of Retained Earnings For the Year Ended December 31, 1990	
Beginning retained earnings balance (December 31, 1989)	$ 500
Plus: Net income	1085
Less: Dividends	200
Ending retained earnings balance (December 31, 1990)	$1385

Figure 2–12 Income statement for Harbour Island Company

Harbour Island Company			
Income Statement			
For the Year Ended December 31, 1990			
Revenues			
Sales		$4000	
Fees earned		1000	
Other revenues		880	
Total revenues			$5880
Expenses			
Cost of goods sold		1500	
Operating expenses			
Wage expense	$1000		
Rent expense	295		
Selling expense	300		
Depreciation expense	500		
Amortization expense	300		
Total operating expenses		2395	
Other expenses		900	
Total expenses			4795
Net income			$1085

The income statement of Harbour Island Company for the year ended December 31, 1990 (Figure 2–12) consists of two categories: revenues ($5880) and expenses ($4795). Subtracting expenses from revenues yields a number called *net income* or *loss, net earnings,* or *profits* ($1085). Net income is a very common and useful measure of a company's operating performance over a period of time. Indeed, many businesspeople agree that net income is the most important number disclosed on the financial statements.

However, it is important to remember that net income is not a separate account; it is merely the result of subtracting expense accounts from revenue accounts. Moreover, as part of retained earnings, net income is nothing in and of itself. It is a measure of something else: the asset and liability inflows and outflows due to the operating activities of the period. Note in Figure 2–12 that several different kinds of revenue and expense accounts enter into the net income computation.

Revenues

Revenues represent the inflow of assets (or decrease in liabilities) due to a company's operating activities over a period of time. Examples include sales, fees earned, and a number of other miscellaneous revenues. The ability to generate revenues is often viewed as one of the important keys to success for a company. For example, the chairman of the board of directors of Sears, Roebuck and Company opened the company's 1987 financial report with the following statement: "1987 was an excellent year for Sears, Roebuck and Company with records established in revenues and net income. Total revenues increased 9.4 percent to $48.44 billion, surpassing 1986 revenues of $44.28 billion. Each business group reported record revenues for the year."

Sales and Fees Earned

Sales is perhaps the most common revenue account. It represents a measure of asset increases (usually in the form of cash or accounts receivable) due to selling a company's products or inventories. If a company provides a service (e.g., a law firm or accounting firm) instead of selling a product, the revenue account reflecting such activity is called **fees earned** or **service revenue.** For example, H & R Block, Inc., which provides tax preparation services, reported service revenues of $625 million in 1987.

Other Revenues

The category called *Other Revenues* can include a number of items. It usually contains revenues generated from activities that are not central to a company's operations; therefore, the dollar amount of this category is usually comparatively small. This section often includes interest income on bank savings accounts, rent collected on the rental of excess warehouse space, and book gains recognized when assets other than inventory are sold for amounts that exceed their original costs. During 1987, in addition to the service revenues mentioned above, H & R Block reported royalties of $61 million, investment income of $9.6 million, and other income of $14.3 million, most of which was recognized when the company sold one of its subsidiaries to Hyatt Legal Services.

Expenses

Expenses represent the outflow of assets (or creation of liabilities) required to generate revenues. Examples include cost of goods sold, operating expenses, and other miscellaneous expenses. As important as generating revenues, controlling expenses is a barometer of a company's success. Monsanto, a large chemical company, noted in its 1987 financial report, for example, that record levels of income were achieved largely because of "aggressive cost-reduction actions."

Cost of Goods Sold

The **Cost of Goods Sold** account represents the original cost of the inventory items (purchase price or cost of manufacturing) that are sold to generate sales revenue. For retail and manufacturing companies, this *inventory expense* is normally separated from other operating expenses because it is comparatively large, and it is often expressed as a percentage of sales revenue to indicate the relationship between the selling price of the inventory and its cost. Cost of Goods Sold as a percentage of sales for J. C. Penney, a large retailer, and Monsanto, a large manufacturer, are normally around 65 percent. On the other hand, H & R Block, a service firm, reports no Cost of Goods Sold on its income statement.

Operating Expenses

Operating Expenses are those periodic and usual expenses that a company incurs to generate revenues. For retailing companies, which simply purchase finished goods and then sell them (e.g., K mart), this expense category contains accounts

Figure 2–13   Income statement for The Quaker Oats Company

The Quaker Oats Company Income Statement For the Year Ended December 31, 1988	
	1988
Sales	$5330*
Cost of goods sold	2907
Gross profit	2423
Selling, general, and administrative expenses	1905
Interest expense	48
Other expense	56
Income before taxes	414
Provision for income taxes	158
Net income	$ 256
*Dollars in millions.	

reflecting the decrease in assets (or creation of liabilities) due to such items as commissions to salespersons, salaries, wages, insurance, advertising, rentals, utilities, property taxes, equipment maintenance, depreciation of plant and equipment, and amortization of intangible assets. Manufacturing companies, on the other hand (e.g., General Motors), typically include only selling and administrative expenses in this category. Note from the expenses listed on the income statement in Figure 2–12 that Harbour Island is a retailer.

Other Expenses

Like the category Other Revenues, *Other Expenses* can include a number of items. It usually contains expenses incurred from activities that are not central to a company's operations, therefore, the dollar amount of this category is also usually small. Interest expense on outstanding loans and book losses recognized when assets other than inventory are sold for amounts that are less than their original costs are often found in this section of the income statement. The income statement in Figure 2–13 is from the 1988 financial report of The Quaker Oats Company, a major manufacturer of grocery products.

THE STATEMENT OF CASH FLOWS

Students often believe the statement of cash flows to be more complicated than it actually is. Fundamentally, it is nothing more than a summary of the activity in a company's cash account over a period of time. Preparing a statement of cash flows is simply a matter of recognizing that certain transactions entered into by a company during a given period increase the Cash account, while others decrease it. The statement summarizes these transactions and in the process explains how the cash balance at the beginning of the period came to be the cash balance at the end of the period. The statement of cash flows for Harbour Island Company for the year ended December 31, 1990, appears in Figure 2–14.

Figure 2–14   Statement of cash flows for Harbour Island Company

Harbour Island Company Statement of Cash Flows For the Year Ended December 31, 1990			
Operating activities			
Cash collections from sales	$4800		
Cash collections from rent	800		
Cash collections from interest	10		
Cash provided by operating activities		$5610	
Cash paid to suppliers	(1800)		
Cash paid to employees	(1050)		
Cash paid for rent	(290)		
Cash paid for selling activities	(300)		
Cash paid for interest and taxes	(700)		
Cash disbursed for operating activities		(4140)	
Net cash increase (decrease) from operating activities			$1470
Investing activities			
Purchase of long-term investment securities	(100)		
Purchase of property	(4500)		
Proceeds from sale of long-term investment securities	500		
Net cash increase (decrease) from investing activities			(4100)
Financing activities			
Proceeds from issuing of equity	3000		
Payments on short-term notes	(100)		
Payments on long-term debt	(50)		
Cash dividends to stockholders	(100)		
Net cash increase (decrease) from financing activities			2750
Increase (decrease) in cash balance			120
Beginning cash balance (December 31, 1989)			100
Ending cash balance (December 31, 1990)			$ 220

The statement of cash flows is divided into three basic categories: (1) operating activities, (2) investing activities, and (3) financing activities. The transactions summarized within each of these three categories either increased or (decreased) cash during the period, and the net result of the three totals explains the change in a company's overall cash balance. For example, on Harbour Island's cash flow statement, operating activities increased cash by $1470, investment activities decreased cash by $4100, and financing activities increased cash by $2750. The net result is $120 (1470 − 4100 + 2750), the increase in the cash balance during 1990.

The statement of cash flows provides important information to investors and creditors, especially those who are interested in assessing a company's solvency position. Dennis Beresford, current chairman of the FASB and former partner in charge of accounting standards at the accounting firm of Ernst & Whinney (now Ernst & Young), was quoted in *Forbes* as saying, "Many people feel that cash flow information is important and in some cases even more important than net income."[4]

---

4. Richard Greene, "The Missing Number," *Forbes*, 18 June 1984, p. 123.

Cash Flows from Operating Activities

Cash flows from **operating activities** include those cash inflows and outflows associated with the acquisition and sale of a company's products and services. The items found in this section of the statement of cash flows are closely related to those found on the income statement because both measure operating inflows and outflows. However, the dollar amounts of these items on the statement of cash flows do not necessarily agree with the dollar amounts appearing for these items on the income statement. The statement of cash flows records only *cash* inflows and outflows; the income statement consists of revenues and expenses, which reflect more general *asset* and *liability* inflows and outflows. Cash is just one of a company's many assets.

Consider, for example, the sale of a service in exchange for a receivable. This transaction produces no cash; therefore, it has no effect on the statement of cash flows. It does, however, appear as a revenue on the income statement because an asset in the form of a receivable has been created. Consequently, net cash flow from operating activities on the statement of cash flows is rarely equal to net income on the income statement. In the case of Harbour Island, for example, net cash flow from operating activities in Figure 2−14 is equal to $1470, while net income for the same period (see Figures 2−11 and 2−12) is equal to $1085.

For many major U.S. companies, net cash flow from operating activities is the primary source of cash. In its 1988 financial report, for example, The Quaker Oats Company noted that the company's operations were characterized by "strong positive cash flows." In support of this statement, the company reported $469.5 million of cash inflow from operating activities on its statement of cash flows. This amount exceeded net income for the year by $214 million.

Cash Flows from Investing Activities

Cash flows from **investing activities** include the cash inflows and outflows associated with the purchase and sale of a company's noncurrent assets. Cash effects from the purchase or sale of a company's investments or property, plant, and equipment are common examples. Note in Figure 2−14 that Harbour Island used $100 and $4500 to purchase long-term investment securities and property, respectively. It also generated $500 in cash by selling long-term investments. These transactions in total reduced Harbour Island's cash balance by $4100.

Net cash flow from investing activities is normally a negative number because, as companies grow, they typically purchase more long-term assets than they sell. In 1988, for example, The Quaker Oats Company spent $207.5 million and $5.9 million in cash for additional property, plant, and equipment and long-term investments, respectively. The company collected only $32.4 million from disposals of property, plant, and equipment. Consequently, net cash flow from investing activities was a negative $181 million.

Cash Flows from Financing Activities

Cash flows from **financing activities** include the cash inflows and outflows associated with a company's two sources of outside capital: liabilities and contributed capital. Cash proceeds from and cash principal payments on short- and long-term liabilities are reflected in this section of the statement of cash flows. As indicated in Figure 2–14, while Harbour Island borrowed no additional funds during 1990, it made cash principal payments on both short-term notes ($100) and long-term debt ($50). Cash proceeds from stockholder contributions, or equity issuances, and cash dividends to stockholders are also included in this section. Note that Harbour Island collected $3000 in cash from issuing equity, and paid cash dividends of $100.

The main financing cash outflows of The Quaker Oats Company during 1988 consisted of principal payments on short- and long-term debt of $484 million and cash dividends of $80 million. Cash collections from financing activities included long-term borrowings and stock issuances of $25.3 million and $33.4 million, respectively.

RELATIONSHIPS AMONG THE FINANCIAL STATEMENTS

Having discussed each of the four financial statements, we now illustrate and discuss their relationships. Figure 2–15 presents a general overview of the four basic financial accounting statements and shows how they relate to each other. Take some time to study it.

Note the four basic statements indicated by the numbers: (1) balance sheet, (2) income statement, (3) statement of retained earnings, and (4) statement of cash flows. Note also that an additional balance sheet, prepared at the end of the period, is included on the right side of the figure. The account balances on this balance sheet are different from those on the balance sheet on the left. To explain how the balance sheet accounts changed during the year, examine the other three financial statements: the statement of cash flows, the statement of retained earnings, and the income statement.

The statement of cash flows explains the activity during the year in the company's Cash account. At the beginning of 1990 the balance in the Cash account was $100. During the year, operating, investing, and financing transactions affected the cash balance, and the end result was $220. Note how the statement of cash flows ties into the Cash accounts listed on the balance sheet at the beginning and end of 1990.

The statement of retained earnings, like the statement of cash flows, also explains the activity in a balance sheet account during 1990—the Retained Earnings account, which appears in the lower right-hand corner of each balance sheet. Note how the beginning and ending balances of Retained Earnings tie directly into the Retained Earnings accounts listed on the balance sheets for the beginning and end of 1990.

The income statement contains Revenues and Expenses, which are reflected in the statement of retained earnings through the net income number. The income statement, therefore, is depicted in Figure 2–15 as tying in directly to the statement of retained earnings, which in turn ties directly into the two balance sheets.

As a result of these interrelationships, every transaction affecting the income statement affects the balance sheet in at least two places. Revenues and expenses are components of retained earnings and increase or decrease the Retained Earnings balance accordingly. In addition, each account on the income statement has a related account in either the asset or liability section of the balance sheet. Recognizing a sale, for example, can affect cash and accounts receivable. Recognizing

Figure 2–15 Relationships among the financial statements

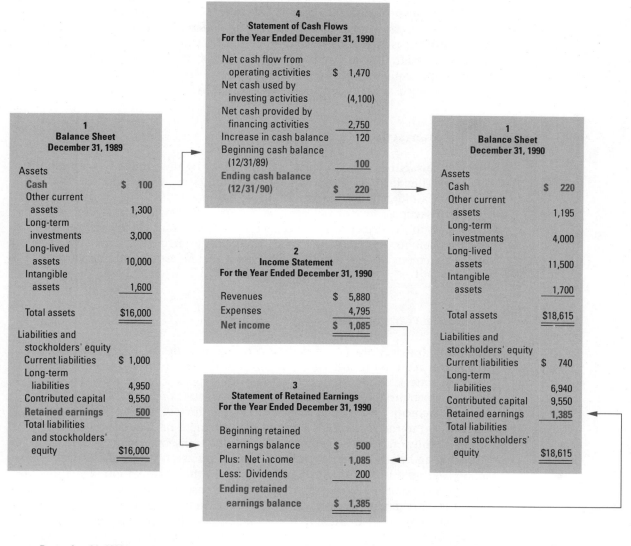

an expense, such as wage expense, can affect Cash and Wages Payable. Thus, the balance sheet and the income statement are inextricably related. As you work through this text, it is important that you understand these relationships well.

CAPITAL AND OPERATING TRANSACTIONS

We have completed an overview of the financial statements but have yet to consider directly one very important question: How are capital transactions distinguished from operating transactions? For example, if a company receives $100 for services rendered, a revenue is recognized. The Cash account and the Retained Earnings account are increased, and a revenue of $100 appears on the income statement, which in turn increases net income. If, on the other hand, this same company borrows $100 from a bank, Cash is increased and a liability account (Notes Payable) is increased. Revenues, net income, and retained earnings are unaffected by this transaction. In both cases Cash is increased and the equality of the accounting equation is maintained, but these two transactions (services rendered and borrowings) are handled very differently. Why?

Capital Transactions

Capital transactions concern building and financing the productive capacity of a company. They include, for example, purchasing assets, exchanging assets, taking out loans, issuing equity, paying off loans, and paying dividends to stockholders. These transactions are not reflected on the income statement and, therefore, do not enter into the calculation of net income. Capital transactions always affect at least two balance sheet accounts, and when cash is affected, they are represented on the statement of cash flows in the sections for investing and financing activities.

Operating Transactions

Operating transactions concern the operating activities of a company, in other words, the acquisition and sale of its inventories or services. Operating activities give rise to asset and liability flows that are represented by revenues and expenses, which are found on the income statement as components of the Retained Earnings account. When operating transactions involve the Cash account, they are reflected in the operating section of the statement of cash flows.

The distinction between capital and operating transactions is very important in preparing and understanding the financial statements. It determines which transactions are reflected on the income statement in the computation of net income. This distinction also determines which transactions are reflected in the operating, investing, and financing sections of the statement of cash flows. As a result, choosing to treat an exchange as a capital transaction instead of an operating transaction (or vice versa) can have significant effects on the financial statements.

For example, in 1987 McDonnell Douglas spent $648 million dollars on research and development for new aircraft. Under generally accepted accounting principles, the company was required to treat these costs as operating transactions and, accordingly, they were accounted for as expenses and appeared on the income statement. Had the company been allowed to treat these costs as capital transactions and include them as an asset on the balance sheet, a treatment many accountants support,[5] its 1987 net income would have increased the $313 million reported to almost $1 billion. Furthermore, treating these costs as capital transactions would have increased net cash flows from operating activities, which is disclosed on the statement of cash flows, by over $600 million dollars.

---

5. See, for example, Harold Bierman and Roland Dukes, "Accounting for Research and Development Costs," *The Journal of Accountancy* (April 1975), 48–55.

USING THE INFORMATION IN THE FINANCIAL STATEMENTS

We have noted that investors, creditors, and other interested parties use financial information to assess a company's past performance, predict its future performance, and control the business decisions of its managers. Reported financial information, therefore, must provide measures of the company's solvency and earning power. This section briefly discusses how such measures are assessed and used.

Assessing and Using Measures of Solvency

Assessing solvency involves evaluating a company's ability to meet its debt payments as they come due. Debt payments require cash at various points in time, so assessing solvency involves estimating the timing of a company's future cash inflows and outflows. Such information comes primarily from two of the financial statements: the balance sheet and the statement of cash flows. The balance sheet includes a statement of a company's present asset and liability position, and the statement of cash flows indicates the activity in a company's cash account over the past period.

The Balance Sheet

The right side of the balance sheet lists a company's outstanding liabilities and therefore provides information about future cash outflows. The footnotes to the financial statements, which provide further information about the dollar values reported, are often helpful in this regard because they describe the terms (e.g., interest rates and maturity dates) of the company's outstanding debt agreements. The asset side of the balance sheet provides information about the timing of the company's cash inflows. Since the assets are listed in order of liquidity, the company's ability to generate cash can be evaluated by comparing the portion of liquid to nonliquid assets.

Comparing the dollar values of certain balance sheet accounts to the dollar values of other balance sheet accounts, usually in the form of ratios, is a common method of analyzing the financial statements. Three popular comparisons, two of which are ratios, that are used to evaluate a company's ability to meet its debts are the current ratio, working capital, and the debt/equity ratio. The **current ratio** is computed by dividing current assets by current liabilities, **working capital** is computed by subtracting current liabilities from current assets, and the **debt/equity ratio** is computed by dividing total liabilities by stockholders' equity.

The current ratio and working capital provide indications of a company's ability to meet current obligations with current assets. In general, the higher these two numbers are, the more assurance exists that current obligations can be met. Typical current ratios range from slightly under 1.0 for companies in the motion picture industry to as high as 4.0 for family clothing stores. The current ratio and working capital of Harbour Island Company (see Figure 2–7) as of December 31, 1990 are 1.91 ($1415 ÷ $740) and $675 ($1415 − $740), respectively.

The debt/equity ratio indicates the relative importance of debt in a company's capital structure. The higher this ratio, the greater a company's future cash obligations, and the riskier its financial condition. Normal debt/equity ratios for major

Table 2–1   Financial ratios used to assess solvency

Current ratio	Current assets ÷ current liabilities
Working capital	Current assets − current liabilities
Debt/equity ratio	Total liabilities ÷ stockholders' equity

U.S. companies range from approximately .4 to 3.0. Harbour Island's debt/equity ratio (see Figure 2–7) as of December 31, 1990 is .7 ([\$740 + \$6940] ÷ \$10,935). Table 2–1 summarizes these ratios.

In addition to their use by individual investors and creditors to assess solvency, the current ratio, working capital, and the debt/equity ratio are also used by services, such as Dun & Bradstreet, Moody's Investors Service, and Standard & Poor's, which compute and publish **credit ratings** on many companies. Dun & Bradstreet, for example, includes both the current ratio and the debt/equity ratio in its fourteen key business ratios, all of which are very important in determining a company's credit rating. These ratings are used by banks and other lenders to assess the risks associated with loaning funds. A low credit rating on a company often results in denied loans or high interest payments.

The current ratio, working capital, and the debt/equity ratio can also be found in debt contracts, where they are used to control the business decisions of managers and protect the loan investments of creditors. In 1987, for example, Alcoa entered into a loan agreement that required it to maintain a current ratio of at least 1 : 1 during the period of the loan. Similarly, Nordstrom, a specialty clothing retail store operating mostly in the western United States, has signed restrictive debt contracts requiring that, while certain loans are outstanding, working capital must be at least \$50 million or 25 percent of current liabilities, whichever is greater.

Statement of Cash Flows

The statement of cash flows can be used to assess a company's performance in two basic areas: (1) its ability to generate cash and (2) the effectiveness of its cash management policies. Information about these two areas of performance can indicate whether a company can meet its debts as they come due. Specifically, the statement provides information about the net cash flows associated with operating, investing, and financing activities. Thus, the statement of cash flows is very useful to those who wish to assess a company's solvency.

The magnitude and behavior of a company's cash flows are often associated with its credit rating and its ability to borrow, as illustrated by the following quote from the 1987 financial report of Marriott Corporation, which maintains a superior credit rating: "The company's cash flow growth has been steady and predictable. This stability enables Marriott to utilize higher debt levels than would be appropriate for an enterprise with more volatile cash flows."

Assessing and Using Measures of Earning Power

The income statement and the amount of net income represent the accountant's measure of a company's ability to continue to generate assets in the future. Net income results from matching expenses against revenues: to the extent that revenues exceed expenses, a company has produced assets through its operations. By definition, assets reflect future economic benefits and earning power.

Table 2-2   Financial ratios used to assess earning power

Earnings per share	Net income ÷ Number of shares outstanding
Price/earnings ratio	Per share market price ÷ earnings per share
Return on equity	Net income ÷ stockholders' equity

Financial ratios involving income numbers are very popular in assessing earning power. Three such ratios include earnings per share, the price/earnings ratio, and return on equity. **Earnings per share** is computed by dividing net income by the number of common shares held by the stockholders, the **price/earnings ratio** is computed by dividing the market price of a company's common shares by earnings per share, and **return on equity** is computed by dividing net income by stockholders' equity. Table 2-2 summarizes these financial ratios.

Earnings per share is well known because it is often treated by the financial press as the primary measure of a company's performance and it varies considerably across companies. In the past few years, for example, AT&T, Chrysler, and Polaroid have reported earnings per share amounts of $2.00 or less, while RJR Nabisco, GTE Corporation, and J. C. Penney have reported amounts in the range of $3.00–$5.00, and McDonnell Douglas has consistently reported values of $7.00–$8.00.

The price/earnings ratio is used by many financial analysts to assess the investment potential of common stocks. The values of this ratio normally range from 10:1 to 25:1, but some companies have ratios as low as 4:1 and as high as 70:1. Return on equity compares the profits earned by a company to the investment made by the company's stockholders. Average returns range from approximately 10 percent to 30 percent. Like the current ratio and the debt/equity ratio, return on equity is included as one of Dun & Bradstreet's fourteen key business ratios.

Net income and retained earnings, which are the accumulation of previous net income amounts (less dividends), are both used in contracts to control and direct the business decisions of managers. Management incentive plans, which are usually administered by the board of directors, often base a portion of management's compensation on net income to encourage managers to act in the interest of the company's stockholders. Texas Instruments, for example, has an incentive compensation plan that pays key employees 10 percent of the amount by which net income in a given year exceeds 6 percent of stockholders' equity.

Furthermore, loan contracts often limit dividends to a percentage of retained earnings. Such limitations protect the interests of the creditors by helping to ensure that the company has adequate cash to meets its interest and principal payments. As of December 31, 1987, for example, Nordstrom reported $387 million of retained earnings, which the payment of dividends, due to a debt contract, could not reduce below $247 million.

FINANCIAL INFORMATION AND MANAGEMENT'S INCENTIVES

The use of financial accounting information to evaluate, control, and monitor the business decisions of managers creates an incentive for managers to manipulate the numbers reported on the financial statements, or at least choose those reporting methods, assumptions, and estimates that serve their individual interests, which may or may not be in line with those of the stockholders. Managers know that accounting numbers such as net income, earnings per share, the price/earnings ratio, and return on assets, are used to evaluate their performance and that such evaluations have a bearing on their levels of compensation and their value in the employment market. They also know that accounting numbers such as the current ratio, working capital, the debt/equity ratio, and retained earnings, are used to determine credit ratings as well as to limit their activities through contracts. Consequently, managers have incentives to make decisions that yield the most desirable accounting numbers. Such decisions might include the timing of cash payments, the decision to buy or lease a piece of equipment, the choice of a certain method of financing, or the choice of a certain accounting method, estimate, or judgment.

For example, managers have been known to structure financing transactions and choose certain accounting methods so that debt need not be reported on the balance sheet. By avoiding the recognition of debt, such activities, called **off-balance-sheet financing,** may produce more favorable values for the current ratio, working capital, and the debt/equity ratio. It may not be clear whether such activities are in the interests of the stockholders, but it is important that those who use financial statements be aware that managers have much discretion over the numbers reported in them. As noted in *Forbes,* "One of the great business myths is that accounting rules are fixed and clear-cut."[6]

It is also important to realize, however, that there are economic incentives for managers to report truthfully. Truthful managers are sued less often, and investors, creditors, and other interested parties value financial statements that they can trust. In the long run, therefore, managers who manipulate the financial statements may hamper their abilities to attract capital and reduce their economic well-being. *Forbes* has also reported that "companies which consistently employ liberal accounting methods deserve close scrutiny."[7]

THE ANNUAL REPORT OF K MART CORPORATION

Turn now to K mart's annual report located in Appendix D. Find the Statements of Income (page 31), Balance Sheets (page 32), Statements of Cash Flows (page 33), and the Statements of Retained Earnings, which are part of the Statements of Shareholders' Equity (page 34). The Statement of Shareholders' Equity, which will be discussed in Chapter 12, explains the changes during the year in the shareholders' equity accounts, one of which is retained earnings. Note that Income Statements, Statements of Cash Flows, and Statements of Shareholders' Equity are provided for each of three years while Balance Sheets are provided for each of two years. Such disclosure allows and encourages comparisons across time.

These financial statements are more involved and complex than those discussed in the chapter, but a number of familiar and important items can still be identified. The Statement of Income, for example, reports that net income for the year ended January 25, 1989 was $803 million, representing a $111 million (16

---

6. Walecia Konrad, "Take Your Fees and Come Out Fighting," *Forbes,* 18 July 1983, p. 98.
7. Jill Andresky, "Hidden Rocks," *Forbes* 15 August 1983, p. 111.

Table 2-3 Selected financial ratios K mart corporation

Financial Ratios	1989	1988
Solvency Ratios		
Current ratio (current assets ÷ current liabilities)	2.05	1.89
Working capital (current assets − current liabilities) (dollars in billions)	$3.65	$3.00
Debt/equity ratio (total debt ÷ stockholders' equity)	1.42	1.52
Earning Power Ratios		
Earnings per share (net income ÷ weighted average shares)	$4.00	$3.40
Price/earnings ratio (stock price ÷ earnings per share)		
High	9.9	14.2
Low	7.2	6.4
Return on equity (net income ÷ beginning stockholders' equity)	18.2%	17.6%

percent) increase over the previous year and a $221 million (38 percent) increase over 1987.

The Balance Sheet reports total assets as of January 25, 1989 to be $12.126 billion, composed of current assets ($7.146 billion), Investments in Affiliate Retail Companies ($506 million), Property and Equipment ($3.896 billion), and Other Assets and Deferred Charges ($578 million). Total liabilities and shareholders' equity ($12.126 billion) consists of current liabilities ($3.492 billion), long-term liabilities of $3.625 billion (1.588 + 1.358 + .459 + .220), and Shareholders' Equity of $5.009 billion (including Retained Earnings of $4.345 billion). In other words, the total assets reported by K mart as of January 25, 1989 came from three sources: current and long-term borrowings ($7.117 billion - 59 percent), shareholder contributions ($664 million - 5 percent), and retained earnings ($4.345 billion - 36 percent). Note also that during the year the dollar amounts of almost all accounts on the balance sheet increased.

The Statement of Cash Flows is divided into Net cash provided by operations ($1.211 billion), Net cash used for investing ($505 million), and Net cash used for financing ($207 million). Note that cash proceeds from operations ($1.211 billion), the sale of property ($117 million), and long-term debt issuances ($346 million) were used primarily to purchase additional property ($570 million), pay dividends ($256 million), reduce long-term debt ($184), and increase the year-end cash balance by $499 million.

The financial ratios discussed in this chapter have been calculated and appear in Table 2-3. Refer also to the 11-Year Financial Summary on pages 14 and 15 of the annual report. Note that K mart refers to the current ratio as the working capital ratio and that it discloses neither the debt/equity nor the price/earnings ratio.

It appears from these calculations that K mart is strong from both an earning power and solvency standpoint. Net income, earnings per share, and return on equity have generally increased over the past eleven years. In addition, operations have provided large amounts of cash over the past three years, which have been used primarily to invest in new assets, reduce long-term debt, and pay dividends. The price of the company's stock, however, has fluctuated substantially in the past two years: from a low of $21 ⅝ to a high of $48 ⅜ (page 27). This fluctuation has caused the price/earnings ratio to vary from 6.4 to 14.2. K mart has also carried a large portion of debt in its capital structure.

REVIEW PROBLEM

The following problem records the transactions executed by Ed's Delivery Service during 1989, its first year of operations. The transactions are first described, their effects on the basic accounting equation are then illustrated (Figure 2–16) and, finally, the balance sheet (Figure 2–17), income statement (Figure 2–18), statement of retained earnings (Figure 2–19), and statement of cash flows (Figure 2–20) are prepared.

Transaction (1).   The stockholders contributed $20,000 cash.

Transaction (2).   A delivery truck was purchased for $12,000. Five thousand dollars were paid in cash, and a note payable was signed for the remaining $7000.

Transaction (3).   Delivery services for $18,000 were performed. The clients paid $7000 in cash, and accounts receivable were recognized for $11,000.

Transaction (4).   Wages totaling $9000 were paid in cash.

Transaction (5).   Miscellaneous expenses totaling $6000 were incurred during the year. Two thousand dollars were still payable as of the end of the year.

Transaction (6).   Land was purchased in the amount of $1000.

Transaction (7).   Half of the land was sold for $700.

Transaction (8).   Payments of $3000 were received on the outstanding accounts receivable.

Figure 2–16   Accounting equation worksheet

		Assets			=	Liabilities		+	Stockholders' Equity	
	Cash	Accounts Receivable	Land	Equipment		Misc. Payable	Note Payable		Contributed Capital	Retained Earnings
(1)	+20,000				=				+20,000	
(2)	(5,000)			+12,000	=		+7,000			
(3)	+7,000	+11,000			=					+18,000*
(4)	(9,000)				=					(9,000)*
(5)	(4,000)				=	+2,000				(6,000)*
(6)	(1,000)		+1,000		=					
(7)	+700		(500)		=					+200*
(8)	+3,000	(3,000)			=					
(9)	(2,200)				=		(2,000)			(200)*
(10)	(1,000)				=					(1,000)
	8,500	8,000	500	12,000	=	$2,000	$5,000		$20,000	$2,000

*Operating transactions

Transaction (9). Payments of $2000 were made on the outstanding notes payable, and $200 were paid on interest.

Transaction (10). One thousand dollars were distributed to the stockholders at the end of the year.

Figure 2–17 Balance sheet for Ed's Delivery Service

Ed's Delivery Service			
Balance Sheet			
December 31, 1989			
Assets		Liabilities and Stockholders' Equity	
Cash	$ 8,500	Miscellaneous payable	$ 2,000
Accounts receivable	8,000	Notes payable	5,000
Land	500	Contributed capital	20,000
Equipment	12,000	Retained earnings	2,000
		Total liabilities and	
Total assets	$29,000	stockholder's equity	$29,000

Figure 2–18 Income statement for Ed's Delivery Service

Ed's Delivery Service		
Income Statement		
For the Year Ended December 31, 1989		
Revenues		
Fees earned	$18,000	
Gain on sale of land	200	
Total revenues		$18,200
Expenses		
Wages	9,000	
Miscellaneous	6,000	
Interest	200	
Total expenses		15,200
Net income		$ 3,000

Figure 2–19 Statement of retained earnings for Ed's Delivery Service

Ed's Delivery Service	
Statement of Retained Earnings	
For the Year Ended December 31, 1989	
Beginning retained earnings balance	$ 0
Plus: Net income	3000
Less: Dividends	1000
Ending retained earnings balance	$2000

Figure 2–20   Statement of cash flows for Ed's Delivery Service

Ed's Delivery Service **Statement of Cash Flows** **For the Year Ended December 31, 1989**			
Operating activities			
Cash collections from services	$ 7,000		
Cash collections from accounts receivable	3,000		
Cash provided by operating activities		$10,000	
Cash paid for wages	(9,000)		
Cash paid for miscellaneous expenses	(4,000)		
Cash paid for interest	(200)		
Cash disbursed from operating activities		(13,200)	
Net cash increase (decrease) from operating activities			($ 3,200)
Investing activities			
Purchase of equipment	(5,000)		
Purchase of land	(1,000)		
Proceeds from sale of land	700		
Net cash increase (decrease) from investing activities			(5,300)
Financing activities			
Contributions from stockholders	20,000		
Payment on note payable	(2,000)		
Distribution to stockholders	(1,000)		
Net cash increase (decrease) from financing activities			17,000
Increase (decrease) in cash balance			8,500
Beginning cash balance (December 31, 1988)			0
Ending cash balance (December 31, 1989)			$ 8,500

SUMMARY OF LEARNING OBJECTIVES

1 State the accounting equation and demonstrate how it is used to organize business transactions.

The accounting equation states that assets equal liabilities plus stockholders' equity. Business transactions represent exchanges between entities in which assets, liabilities, or stockholder equities are traded for one another. That is, an asset, liability, or equity is received, and at the same time an asset, liability, or equity is given up. Companies record these exchanges in their books so that the equality of the accounting equation is always maintained. For example, every time an asset is received, either an asset is given up or a liability or equity is created.

2 Describe how the accounting equation is related to the balance sheet, income statement, statement of retained earnings, and statement of cash flows.

The main components of the accounting equation (assets, liabilities, and stockholders' equity) are divided into subcategories, called *accounts*, in which transactions are recorded and from which the financial statements are compiled. When a business transaction occurs, two or more accounts are increased or decreased in such a way as to maintain the equality of the accounting equation. For example, when a company borrows $5000, Cash, an asset, is increased by $5000 and Notes Payable, a liability, is increased by $5000. Over a period of time a number of such transactions will give rise to cumulative balances in the asset, liability, and stockholders' equity accounts. Increases and decreases in the Cash account, for example, over a period of time may give rise to an ending balance of $10,000.

The balance sheet contains the balances as of a given point in time of all the asset, liability, and stockholders' equity accounts. It is a statement of the accounting equation because total assets always equal total liabilities plus stockholders' equity (contributed capital and retained earnings). Each of the assets held by a company came from one of three sources: (1) borrowings (liabilities), (2) contributions by stockholders (contributed capital), or (3) operating activities (retained earnings—not returned to the stockholders in the form of dividends).

The income statement contains a summary of the operating transactions entered into by a company during a period of time. Operating transactions directly involve the acquisition or sale of a company's products or services. They affect asset or liability accounts and always either increase or decrease retained earnings in the stockholders' equity section of the accounting equation. Revenues are operating transactions that increase retained earnings and expenses are operating transactions that decrease retained earnings.

The statement of retained earnings and the statement of cash flows summarize the transactions that affect the Retained Earnings and Cash accounts, respectively. The statement of retained earnings includes the net effect of the operating transactions mentioned above (net income) as well as asset distributions to stockholders (dividends). The statement of cash flows is basically composed of cash inflows and outflows and explains the change in the Cash account during the period.

3 **Describe the format and basic divisions of the balance sheet, income statement, statement of retained earnings, and statement of cash flows.**

The asset accounts reported on the balance sheet are listed in order of liquidity and are divided into four categories: (1) current assets, which include cash, marketable securities, accounts receivable, inventory, and prepaid expenses, (2) long-term investments, which include long-term notes receivable, land, securities, the cash value of life insurance, and special investment funds, (3) property, plant, and equipment and (4) intangible assets, which include patents, trademarks, and other intangibles, such as goodwill.

Liabilities are divided into two categories: (1) current liabilities, which primarily include short-term payables, and (2) long-term liabilities, which include items such as long-term notes, bonds, and mortgages payable. The stockholders' equity section for a corporation contains contributed capital and retained earnings; the owners' equity section for a partnership contains an account for each partner that records the cumulative balance of the partner's contributions less withdrawals.

The income statement consists of two basic categories: revenues and expenses. Revenues, which represent asset inflows (or liability decreases) associated with operating transactions during a given period, include sales, fees earned, service revenues, and other revenues (e.g., interest, book gains). Expenses, which represent the asset outflows (or liability increases) required to generate the revenues, include cost of goods sold, operating expenses (e.g, wages, rent) and other expenses (e.g., interest, book losses). Revenues less expenses equal net income.

The statement of retained earnings has four components: (1) the balance in Retained Earnings at the beginning of the period, (2) net income (or loss), (3) distributions to stockholders, and (4) the balance in Retained Earnings at the end of the period. The statement of cash flows contains three categories: (1) cash flows from operating activities, (2) cash flows from investing activities, and (3) cash flows from financing activities.

4   Explain the difference between a capital and an operating transaction.

Capital transactions involve building and financing the productive capacity of a company. They are not reflected on the income statement and therefore do not enter into the calculation of net income. Capital transactions always affect at least two balance sheet accounts and, when Cash is affected, they are represented on the statement of cash flows in the sections that list the company's investing and financing activities.

Operating transactions concern the operating activities of a company; they are transactions that directly involve the sale of the company's inventories or services. Operating activities give rise to asset and liability flows that are represented by revenues and expenses, which are found on the income statement and are also components of the Retained Earnings account. When operating transactions affect the Cash account, they are reflected in the operating section of the statement of cash flows.

5   Identify the general ways in which the financial statements are used and some of the incentives that influence how they are prepared.

Financial statements are useful because they provide objective and verifiable information that managers use to attract the capital of investors and creditors. These and other interested parties require financial information to assess a company's past performance, predict its future performance, and control and monitor the business decisions of managers. To meet these requirements financial accounting numbers and ratios must provide reasonably objective and reliable measures of a company's solvency position and earning power.

Assessing solvency involves evaluating a company's ability to meet its debt payments as they come due. Such information comes primarily from two of the financial statements: the balance sheet and the statement of cash flows. The balance sheet provides information about a company's available cash and its outstanding cash obligations; the statement of cash flows provides a record of how the company's cash has been managed. Certain balance sheet numbers and ratios are also used to assess solvency. The current ratio (current assets divided by current liabilities), working capital (current assets less current liabilities), and the debt/equity ratio (total debt divided by total stockholders' equity) are three common examples.

Earning power is usually assessed by examining the income statement, which provides information about a company's ability to continue generating assets in the future. Net income is a measure of the net assets produced by the company during a given period of time. Ratios involving income numbers are also very popular in assessing earning power. For example, earnings per share (net income divided by the number of equity shares outstanding), the price/earnings ratio (market price of a company's common shares divided by earnings per share), and return on equity (net income divided by stockholders' equity) are often used in this regard.

To control, monitor, and direct the business decisions of managers, investors and creditors insist that managers enter into contracts, which are written in terms of financial accounting numbers. Stockholders, for example, use financial numbers, such as net income, in management compensation contracts, and creditors use financial numbers and ratios, such as the current ratio, working capital, the debt/equity ratio, and retained earnings, in debt contracts. Such agreements encourage managers to act in the interests of the stockholders and protect the interests of creditors.

Managers know that accounting numbers are used to evaluate their performance and control their business decisions and thus influence their future wages and overall levels of wealth. Accordingly, they have incentives to choose business decisions, accounting methods, estimates, and assumptions that make the financial statements appear as attractive as possible. However, managers who manipulate the statements or choose to report untruthfully are hurting themselves economically in the long run because ethical managers are sued less frequently and investors and creditors place additional value on companies that provide credible financial statements.

KEY TERMS

Accounts payable (p. 60)
Accounts receivable (p. 57)
Bonds payable (p. 60)
Business transactions (p. 48)
Capital transactions (p. 72)
Classified balance sheet (p. 54)
Contributed capital (p. 48)
Cost of goods sold (p. 66)
Credit ratings (p. 74)
Current assets (p. 56)
Current liabilities (p. 60)
Current maturities of long-term
  debts (p. 60)
Current ratio (p. 73)
Debt/equity ratio (p. 73)
Earnings per share (p. 75)
Fees earned (p. 66)
Financing activities (p. 69)
Intangible assets (p. 59)
Investing activities (p. 69)
Liquidity (p. 54)

Long-term investments (p. 57)
Marketable securities (p. 56)
Merchandise inventory (p. 57)
Mortgage payable (p. 60)
Net book value (p. 59)
Notes payable (p. 60)
Off-balance-sheet financing (p. 76)
Operating activities (p. 69)
Operating expenses (p. 66)
Operating transactions (p. 72)
Owners' equity (p. 62)
Plant and equipment (p. 58)
Prepaid expenses (p. 57)
Price/earnings ratio (p. 75)
Property (p. 58)
Retained earnings (p. 48)
Return on equity (p. 75)
Sales (p. 66)
Service revenue (p. 66)
Stockholders' equity (p. 48)
Working capital (p. 73)

QUESTIONS FOR DISCUSSION AND REVIEW

1. What are the differences between debt and equity investments? What are the characteristics of each? Give three examples of debt investments. What kind of financial information would interest a debt investor (creditor)? How does it differ from the information that would interest an equity investor?

2. If financial statements are to encourage the exchange of capital between investors, creditors, and managers, of what two general concepts must they provide measures? Explain the similarities and differences between these two concepts.

3. State the fundamental accounting equation. What financial statement is a statement of this equation?

4. What characterizes business transactions and how are they reported in the financial records of a company so that the equality of the accounting equation is maintained? Choose five different transactions, and explain how proper accounting for them maintains the equality of the accounting equation.

5. The balance sheet is associated with a specific date. The income statement, statement of retained earnings, and statement of cash flows are each associated with a period of time. What does this mean in terms of the kind of information each statement provides, and how is each statement related to the accounting equation?

6. What is an asset? List the asset accounts on the balance sheet. In what order are they listed? Why?

7. From what three sources do a company's assets come? Define each source, and explain how the right side of the balance sheet provides a summary of them.

8. What asset accounts are usually considered to be current? Why is the current description useful?

9. What is a prepaid expense and what liability account represents the reverse of a prepaid expense?

10. What is a revenue? How are revenues related to assets, liabilities, and retained earnings?

11. What is an expense? How are expenses related to assets, liabilities, and retained earnings?

12. Retained Earnings is an account that appears in the stockholders' equity section of the balance sheet, yet it consists primarily of revenues and expenses, which are both found on the income statement. How can this be?

13. What two statements explain the changes in balance sheet accounts during a period of time? How are the formats of these two statements similar?

14. What is the difference between a capital transaction and an operating transaction? What financial statement(s) do capital transactions affect? What financial statement(s) do operating transactions affect?

15. The statement of cash flows is divided into three different categories. Name them, describe what transactions are contained within them, and explain how these categories are related to the idea of operating and capital transactions.

16. Are all balance sheet accounts valued in the same way? Provide several examples.

17. What is the difference between marketable securities, listed on the asset side of the balance sheet, and capital stock, which can be found in the contributed capital portion of the balance sheet?

18. What income statement account is closely related to plant and equipment on the balance sheet?

19. What two asset accounts are closely related to the income statement account, Sales? Can you name a liability account that relates to sales? Go down the income statement and relate each income statement account to one or more balance sheet accounts.

20. "Net cash flow from operating activities" is listed on the statement of cash flows. This number is similar to, yet different from, net income, which appears on the income statement. Explain the similarities and differences between these two numbers.

21. What specific accounts and numbers on the financial statements would be particularly useful in assessing a company's solvency position and earning power?

22. Name and define some of the ratios that are commonly used to assess a company's solvency position and earning power.

23. How are the numbers in the financial statements used to control the business decisions of managers? Why is this necessary?

24. Financial statements that are prepared in conformance with generally accepted accounting principles can still be biased. Why?

25. Suppose you are a manager who has signed a debt contract (covenant) requiring that the current ratio (current assets divided by current liabilities) be kept above 2:1. How might this affect the methods you choose to account for certain transactions? Provide several other examples of contracts between investors, creditors, and managers that might influence the accounting methods chosen by managers.

26. How might managers who manipulate the financial statements through the use of biased estimates or assumptions be hurting themselves economically?

EXERCISES

E2-1

(Effects of transactions on the accounting equation)   On a separate piece of paper, complete the following chart to show the effect of each transaction on the accounting equation.

Transaction	Assets = Liabilities + Stockholders' Equity
(1) Owners contribute $10,000 cash.	
(2) Equipment is purchased for $2000 cash.	
(3) $3000 cash is borrowed from a bank.	
(4) Services are sold for $4000 on account.	
(5) $4500 cash is paid for expenses.	
(6) A $500 cash dividend is paid to the owners.	

E2-2

(Effects of transactions on accounts)   Consider the same transactions as in E2–1, but this time complete the following chart, using a separate sheet of paper.

	Assets			=	Liabilities	Stockholders' Equity	
Trans.	Cash	Accounts Receivable	Equipment	=	Notes Payable	Contributed Capital	Retained Earnings
(1)							
(2)							
(3)							
(4)							
(5)							
(6)							

E2-3

(Preparing the financial statements from the accounts)   Total each asset, liability, and stockholders' equity account in E2–2, and prepare a balance sheet, an income statement, a statement of retained earnings, and a statement of cash flows. Assume that the current year is the company's first year of operations.

E2-4

(Balance sheet or income statement account?)   Listed below are accounts that may appear on either the balance sheet or the income statement.

a. Equipment

b. Fees Earned

c. Retained Earnings

d. Wage Expense

e. Patent

f. Cost of Goods Sold

g. Common Stock

h. Dividend Payable

i. Accumulated Depreciation

j. Prepaid Expense

k. Gain on Sale of Marketable Securities   o. Land

l. Rent Revenue   p. Insurance Expense

m. Supplies Inventory   q. Interest Payable

n. Accounts Receivable   r. Deferred Revenue

Required: For each account, indicate whether a company would ordinarily disclose the account on the balance sheet or the income statement.

E2–5   *(Relationship between retained earnings and revenues and expenses across three years)* Berne, Incorporated began operations in 1988. At the end of 1990 Berne's Retained Earnings account had a balance of $100. Compute the missing amounts in the following table.

	1990	1989	1988
Beginning retained earnings	$ 70	$ 50	$ 0
Revenues for the period	700	?	550
Expenses for the period	565	525	?
Dividends declared	?	30	10

E2–6   *(The statement of cash flows across three years)* Rogers and Company began operations on January 1, 1989. As of the end of 1989 Rogers had a cash balance of $10,000. Compute the missing amounts in the following table.

	1991	1990	1989
Beginning cash balance	3000	?	0
Net cash flow from operating activities	3000	?	2000
Net cash flow from investing activities	(4000)	1000	?
Net cash flow from financing activities	?	(4000)	14000
Ending cash balance	9000	?	10,000

E2–7   *(Preparing a statement of cash flows)* From the following transactions, prepare a statement of cash flows for Tara and Sons in the proper form. Assume that this is Tara's first year of operations.

(1) The stockholders contributed $5000 cash.

(2) Performed services for $5000, receiving $3000 in cash and a $2000 receivable.

(3) Incurred expenses of $6000. Paid $3000 in cash and $3000 are still payable.

(4) Purchased machinery for $10,000. Paid $2000 in cash and signed a long-term note for the remainder.

(5) Paid the stockholders $2000 in the form of a dividend.

E2–8   *(Preparing the balance sheet, income statement, and statement of retained earnings)* Show how the five transactions in E2-7 affect the accounting equation, and prepare a balance sheet, income statement, and statement of retained earnings.

E2–9   *(Using working capital to assess solvency)* A retailing company's recent balance sheets showed the following information. Accounts payable is the only current liability.

	12/31/90	12/31/89
Cash	$ 4,500	$ 7,000
Accounts receivable	6,000	9,000
Inventory	13,000	10,000
Total current assets	$23,500	$26,000
Accounts payable	11,000	9,000
Current assets minus current liabilities	$12,500	$17,000

Required: Briefly discuss how this information might be used to assess the company's solvency position. What drawbacks are associated with using this information in this way?

E2-10   *(The effects of different forms of financing on the current ratio and debt contracts)*   Suppose the retailing company in E2–9 signed a debt covenant specifying that its current ratio (current assets divided by current liabilities) must be kept above 2:1. Assume further that early in January of 1991 the company plans to purchase $4000 worth of inventory and has three possible methods of paying for it: (1) cash, (2) account payable or (3) long-term note payable. Compute the effect of each of the three alternatives on the current ratio of the company, and discuss which method seems to be the most feasible.

PROBLEMS

P2-1   *(Effects of transactions on the accounting equation)*   Seven transactions entered into by a corporation are listed below. Using the same format as in Figure 2–1, show how each transaction affects the accounting equation.

(1) Issues ownership shares in exchange for $1000 cash.
(2) Borrows $1500 from a bank.
(3) Pays $300 for a piece of equipment.
(4) Pays $200 in wages to its employees.
(5) Provides a service for which it bills a customer $500.
(6) Declares (but does not yet pay) a dividend to its shareholders in the amount of $100.
(7) Pays $50 interest on a loan taken out earlier.

P2-2   *(Effects of transactions on the accounts of the accounting equation)*   Divide a separate sheet of paper into four columns with the headings "Accounts Affected", "Assets", "Liabilities" and "Stockholders' Equity." For each of the ten transactions listed, identify the accounts involved and the effect on the accounting equation: assets = liabilities + stockholders' equity. After each transaction, total the accounts to ensure that the equality of the accounting equation is maintained. The first transaction has been completed for you and is illustrated below.

(1) Four hundred ownership shares are issued at $2.50 per share.
(2) Supplies are purchased for $150.
(3) Machinery costing $1500 is purchased; $500 is paid in cash, and the remainder is financed with a long-term note.
(4) Salaries totaling $250 are paid to employees.
(5) Services are sold for $1350 on account.
(6) Marketable securities costing $1100 are purchased for cash.
(7) Cash of $500 is received from customers.
(8) The marketable securities purchased earlier are sold for $1600 cash.
(9) Five hundred ownership shares are issued in payment of a long-term liability with a book value of $1500.
(10) At the end of the period, one-half of the supplies purchased earlier have been used up.

Accounts Affected	Assets	=	Liabilities + Stockholders' Equity
1. Cash	+1000		
Contributed Capital			+1000
Total	1000	=	1000

P2-3   *(Effects of transactions on the income statement and statement of cash flows)*   Ten transactions are listed below. For each one, indicate what specific accounts are affected as well as the direction (increase or decrease) of the effect. Also indicate whether the transaction would increase or decrease both net income (revenues minus expenses) on the income statement and net cash flow from operations (operating cash inflows minus operating cash outflows) on the statement of cash flows. Use the following key: increase (+), decrease (−) and no effect (NE). The first one has been completed for you.

Transaction	Accounts	Direction	Net Income	Net Cash Flow
(1) Issue ownership securities for cash.	Cash	+		
	Contributed			
	Capital	+	NE	NE
(2) Purchase inventory on account.				
(3) Sell a service on account. *(not income)*				
(4) Record depreciation of fixed assets.				
(5) Receive cash payments from customers on previously recorded sales.				
(6) Purchase equipment for cash.				
(7) Pay cash to reduce the Wages Payable account.				
(8) Sell a service for cash. *(affects net income)*				
(9) Pay off a long-term loan.				
(10) Make a cash interest payment.				

P2–4   *(Classifying balance sheet accounts)*   Presented below are the main section headings of the balance sheet:

a. Current assets
b. Long-term investments
c. Property, plant and equipment
d. Intangible assets

e. Current liabilities
f. Long-term liabilities
g. Contributed capital
h. Retained earnings

Required: Classify the following accounts under the appropriate headings, and prepare a balance sheet in proper form without account balances.

1. Dividend Payable
2. Payments Received in Advance
3. Allowance for Uncollectible Accounts
4. Inventories
5. Capital Stock
6. Accumulated Depreciation (Building)
7. Bonds Payable
8. Machinery and Equipment
9. Accounts Receivable
10. Marketable Securities
11. Buildings
12. Patents

13. Property
14. Investment Fund for Plant Expansion
15. Wages Payable
16. Cash
17. Accumulated Depreciation (Equipment)
18. Prepaid Rent
19. Trademarks
20. Land Held for Investment
21. Current Portion Due of Long-Term Debt
22. Accounts Payable
23. Short-Term Notes Payable

P2–5   *(Classifying income statement accounts)*   Presented below are the main section headings of the income statement:

a. Sales
b. Fees earned
c. Other revenues

d. Cost of goods sold
e. Operating expenses
f. Other expenses

Required: Classify the following descriptions under the appropriate headings and prepare an income statement in proper form without account balances.

1. Office salary expense
2. Sales of services provided
3. Insurance expense
4. Sales of inventories
5. Salesmen commission expense
6. Depreciation expense
7. Office supplies expense
8. Loss on sale of equipment
9. Income from interest on savings account
10. Income from dividends on investments
11. Advertising expense
12. Loss on sale of building
13. Interest expense on outstanding loans
14. Cost of sold inventories
15. Gain on sale of marketable securities

P2-6

(Preparing a balance sheet in proper form) The following information is available relating to the activities of Johnson Co. as of December 31, 1989.

Cash balance on 12/31/89 is $5500.

Marketable securities costing $35,000 have a fair market value on 12/31/89 of $42,000.

Accounts Receivable balance of $125,000 on 12/31/89 includes $2400 that are not likely to be collected.

Inventory costing $165,000 has a replacement cost (market value) on 12/31/89 of $162,000.

Buildings having a fair market value of $63,500 were purchased for $35,000 and have accumulated depreciation of $8000.

Accounts Payable at year end total $119,500.

Taxes Payable at year end total $23,400.

Balance in the Long-Term Notes Payable account at the end of the period is $69,100.

Fair market value of the Johnson Co. stock on 12/31/89 is $10 per share. When originally issued, 12,500 shares were sold for $8 per share.

The total amount of net income earned by Johnson Co. since its inception several years ago is $60,000. Over that same period, Johnson Co. has paid $19,900 in dividends.

Required: Prepare a balance sheet as of 12/31/89 in proper form for Johnson Co.

P2-7

(Balance sheet and income statement relationships across five years) Compute the missing values for the chart below. The first year of operations is 1988.

	1991	1990	1989	1988
Assets				
Cash	$500	$200	$ 300	$100
Accounts receivable	700	?	300	200
Inventory	400	500	?	400
Land	400	400	300	100
Property, plant, and equipment	700	800	600	700
Liabilities and Stockholders' Equity				
Accounts payable	?	500	400	200
Bonds payable	700	800	600	500
Contributed capital	600	600	400	?
Retained earnings	600	300	800	400
Sales	?	700	1000	900
Expenses	(600)	?	?	(400)
Net income	?	(100)	400	?
Dividends	100	?	?	?

P2-8   *(Preparing the financial statements from transactions)*   Gordon and Gray, Unlimited, began operations January 1, 1989. During 1989 the following transactions took place.

(1) The owners invested $125,000 in exchange for ownership shares.

(2) Fees earned during the year amounted to $235,000, of which $50,000 had not been collected as of 12/31/89.

(3) Operating expenses totaled $200,000, of which $25,000 had not yet been paid.

(4) Gordon and Gray borrowed $35,000 from the bank on 12/31/89. The loan is due on 6/30/90.

(5) Property in the amount of $75,000 was purchased during December of 1989; $25,000 was paid in cash, and the remainder was covered with a ten-year mortgage.

(6) During December a $15,000 dividend was declared, to be paid to the stockholders on January 15, 1990.

(7) During the year, Gordon and Gray invested $50,000 cash in rental property. Rent revenue earned on this investment amounted to $5000, of which $4000 were received in cash.

Required: As done in the review problem at the end of the chapter, show how each transaction affects the accounting equation. Compute the totals for each account, and prepare a balance sheet, income statement, statement of retained earnings, and statement of cash flows.

P2-9   *(Effects of different forms of financing on the financial statements)*   The following condensed balance sheet for December 31, 1989 comes from the records of Krohn and Associates.

Assets		Liabilities and Stockholders' Equity	
Cash	$ 10,000	Current liabilities	$ 20,000
Other current assets	40,000	Long-term notes payable	20,000
Property, plant, and equipment	70,000	Contributed capital	30,000
		Retained earnings	50,000
		Total liabilities and	
Total assets	$120,000	stockholders' equity	$120,000

Krohn and Associates is considering the purchase of a new piece of equipment for $30,000. They do not have enough cash to purchase it outright so they are considering alternative ways of financing. As management sees it, they basically have three options:(1) issue 3000 ownership shares for $10 per share, (2) take out a long-term loan (12 percent annual interest) for $30,000 from the bank, or (3) purchase the equipment on open account (must be paid in full in thirty days). Presently Krohn has 12,000 ownership shares outstanding.

Required

a. Compute the present current ratio, the debt/equity ratio, and the book value of Krohn's outstanding ownership shares: (assets minus liablities) ÷ number of shares outstanding.

b. Compute the current ratio, debt/equity ratio, and book value per share under each of the three financing alternatives and express your answers in the following format.

Financing Alternative	Current Ratio	Debt/Equity Ratio	Book Value per Share
1. Issue stock			
2. Long-term note			
3. Open account			

c. Discuss some of the pros and cons associated with each of the three financing options.

d. The chairman of the board of directors commented at a recent board meeting that with $50,000 in Retained Earnings, the company should be able to purchase the $30,000 piece of equipment outright as well as pay a dividend of at least $1.50 per share ($1.50 × 12,000 shares = $18,000). Comment on the chairman's claim.

P2-10 *(The effects of transactions on financial ratios)* The balance sheet of Evert and Company as of December 31, 1989 appears as shown.

Assets			Liabilities and Stockholders' Equity	
Cash		$ 5,000	Accounts payable	$10,000
Accounts receivable		8,000	Wages payable	3,000
Inventory		15,000	Long-term notes payable	20,000
Equipment	50,000		Contributed capital	10,000
Less: Accumulated depreciation	(10,000)	40,000	Retained earnings	25,000
			Total liabilities and	
Total assets		$68,000	stockholders' equity	$68,000

Required: Nine transactions that occurred during 1990 follow. Indicate the effect of each transaction on net income (revenues minus expenses), the current ratio (current assets divided by current liabilities), working capital (current assets minus current liabilities), and the debt/equity ratio (total debt divided by total stockholders' equity) of Evert and Company. Use the following key: increase (+), decrease (−), no effect (NE). Treat each transaction independently.

Transaction	Net Income	Current Ratio	Working Capital	Debt/Equity Ratio
(1) Ownership shares were issued for $10,000 cash.				
(2) Equipment costing $7000 was purchased for cash.				
(3) A $500 long-term note payable was paid off.				
(4) Services were sold for $9000.				
(5) A $1000 dividend was declared but not paid.				
(6) $3000 in wages payable were paid.				
(7) $6000 was received from customers on account.				
(8) $1800 in interest was incurred and paid on notes payable.				
(9) Depreciation of $1000 on equipment was recognized.				

P2-11 *(Balance-sheet value and the fair market values of the assets)* Because of consistent losses in the past several years Eat and Run, a fast-food franchise, is in danger of bankruptcy. Its most current balance sheet follows.

Assets		Liabilities and Stockholders' Equity	
Cash	$ 25,000	Accounts payable	$ 42,000
Marketable securities	15,000	Wages payable	20,000
Accounts receivable	35,000	Other short-term payables	34,000
Inventory	42,000	Long-term notes	75,000
Prepaid insurance	10,000	Mortgage payable	25,000
Property, plant, and equipment	82,000	Contributed capital	50,000
Other assets	50,000	Retained earnings	13,000
		Total liabilities and	
Total assets	$259,000	stockholders' equity	$259,000

Additional Information

The fair market value of the marketable securities portfolio is $19,000.

The sale of the accounts receivable to a local bank would produce about $25,000 cash.

A portion of the inventory originally costing $21,000 is now obsolete and can be sold for $3000 scrap value. The remaining inventory is worth approximately $30,000.

Prepaid insurance is nonrefundable.

In the event of bankruptcy, the property, plant, and equipment owned by Eat and Run would be divided up and sold separately. It has been estimated that these sales would bring approximately $100,000 cash.

Other assets (primarily organizational costs) cannot be recovered.

Required:

a. The book value (balance sheet assets less liabilities) of Eat and Run is $63,000. Comment on why this balance sheet value may not be a good indication of the value of the company in the case of bankruptcy.

b. If Eat and Run goes bankrupt, what would you consider the value of the company to be?

c. When a company goes bankrupt, the creditors are usually paid off first with the existing assets, and then, if assets remain, the stockholders are paid. If Eat and Run goes bankrupt, would the stockholders receive anything? If so, how much?

P2–12   *(Effects of transactions and changing account balances)*   The balance sheets below come from the records of Ryan and Brothers, a retail clothing store.

	12/31/90		12/31/89	
Assets				
Current assets				
Cash	$ 25,000		$ 32,000	
Accounts receivable	73,000		45,000	
Inventory	31,000		42,000	
Prepaid insurance	4,000	$133,000	3,000	$122,000
Noncurrent assets				
Land	$ 42,000		$ 61,000	
Buildings (net)	157,000		165,000	
Equipment (net)	36,000	235,000	18,000	244,000
Total Assets		$368,000		$366,000
Liabilities and stockholders' equity				
Current liabilities				
Accounts payable	$ 62,000		$ 75,000	
Salaries payable	6,000		8,000	
Interest payable	4,000	$ 72,000	4,000	$ 87,000
Noncurrent liabilities				
Notes payable		82,000		72,000
Stockholders' equity				
Contributed capital	180,000		180,000	
Retained earnings	34,000	$214,000	27,000	$207,000
Total liabilities and				
stockholders' equity		$368,000		$366,000

Additional Information

a. Net income for 1990 was $12,000. The company paid a cash dividend of $5000.

b. Depeciation during 1990 on the building and the equipment was $8000 and $4000, respectively.

c. A piece of equipment was purchased during 1990 for $22,000; $12,000 was paid in cash, and a $10,000 long-term note was exchanged for the remainder.

d. Land with an original cost of $19,000 was sold for $25,000.

Required:

a. Prepare the statement of retained earnings for the year ending December 31, 1990.
b. Compute the change (increase or decrease) in Cash that occurred during 1990.
c. Compute the change in each balance sheet account during the year, and in each case briefly explain what occurred to bring about the change.

CASES

C2-1

(Why might profits triple?)   Nike, Inc., maker of sports shoes and apparel, reported that for 1988, profits nearly tripled to $101.7 million from $35.9 million. Revenues rose 37 percent to $1.2 billion. The company noted it had trimmed its selling and administrative expenses and also enjoyed a lower tax rate due to changes in the tax law in 1986.

Required:

a. Explain how profits could triple even though revenues only rose 37 percent.
b. Would you expect that net cash flows from operating activities would necessarily triple during 1988. Why or why not?
c. Would the stockholders of Nike reasonably expect to receive a higher dividend in light of the increased profits? Why or why not?

C2-2

(Debt contract restrictions)   The following excerpt was taken from the 1987 financial report of Cummins Engine Company, a manufacturer of heavy-duty truck engines.

> *Loan agreements contain covenants which impose restrictions on the payment of dividends and distributions of stock, require maintenance of a 1.25:1 current ratio, and limit the amount of future borrowings. Under the most restrictive covenants, retained earnings of approximately $351 million were available for payment of dividends.*

Required:

a. Briefly explain the meaning of the above excerpt.
b. Why would a bank or other creditor impose such restrictions on a borrowing company?
c. Explain the role of financial accounting numbers in the restrictions described above.

C2-3

(Negative cash flows, positive net income, and dividends)   For over a year, Center Energy Corporation, a utility company in Ohio, had negative cash flow from operating activities caused primarily by the escalating costs of one of its nuclear plants outside Cleveland. Yet, the company reported earnings per share of $2.82 and paid a dividend to its stockholders of $2.56 per share.

Required:

a. Briefly explain how a company could have negative cash flow from operating activities, positive net income, and still pay dividends.
b. Could a company continue such a strategy over an extended period of time? Why or why not?

C2-4

("Liberal"accounting practices)   Like many young companies, Continuum, a software manufacturer, uses what might be called "liberal" accounting practices. For example, in 1987 Continuum treated as capital transactions $1.6 million in costs for the development of new

software products. In 1988 the company capitalized over $2.9 million of such costs. These accounting practices are in line with generally accepted accounting principles.

Required:

a. Explain why treating these costs as capital transactions might be referred to as a "liberal" accounting practice.
b. Provide several reasons why a company like Continuum would use such practices.
c. How could such practices lead to problems in the future for Continuum?

C2-5   *(Unqualified opinions and accurate financial statements)* In 1984 a major accounting firm commissioned an extensive poll to find out how people understand various business terms. According to the study, 34 percent of the shareholders questioned thought that the phrase *unqualified opinion,* which is used to describe an auditor's report, meant that every number on the financial statements was "totally accurate."

Required: Do you agree with 34 percent of the shareholders? Why or why not?

The Accounting Cycle

Learning Objectives

1 List the sixteen steps of the accounting cycle. *FOCAL POINT IS FLOW (not steps)*

2 State and describe the two criteria necessary for entering an economic event in the accounting cycle.

3 Name the three important components of a transaction, and explain how each is represented in a journal entry.

4 Describe how the form of a journal entry reflects the basic accounting equation.

5 Describe the roles of the journal, ledger, and worksheet in the accounting cycle.

6 Explain why the closing process is necessary, and describe the procedures involved.

7 Explain how the income statement, statement of retained earnings, balance sheet, and statement of cash flows are prepared at the end of the accounting cycle.

8 (Appendix 3A) Describe the nature and function of special-purpose journals and subsidiary ledgers.

9 (Appendix 3B) Describe the nature and importance of internal control, and list the five principles of effective internal control.

≡ Chapter 2 presented the general nature and format of the balance sheet, income statement, statement of retained earnings, and statement of cash flows. It also explained how each statement is related to the fundamental accounting equation. We now turn to the specific procedures for preparing these statements.

This chapter is devoted entirely to the **accounting cycle,** the sixteen-step process leading from an exchange transaction to the preparation of the financial statements. Included in this process are the journal entry, the journal, the ledger, the closing process, and the worksheet, which constitute the procedural foundation for creating the financial statements.

Most of this chapter concerns bookkeeping, which is primarily mechanical but can get very involved. We make a special effort, however, not to get too immersed in specific procedural details. Bookkeeping procedures vary among companies and computerization has done much to shift the concerns of today's accountants away from procedures and toward analysis and decision making. Many of today's journals and ledgers, for example, are actually maintained on electronic storage media, such as computer disks. Consequently, the study aids and illustrations in this chapter emphasize concepts rather than specific mechanics.

Bookkeeping may be procedural, but it is very important. This chapter presents the fundamentals that underlie virtually all accounting systems. Trying to understand the remainder of this book without a thorough understanding of these fundamentals is like trying to read without learning the alphabet. It simply cannot be done. So spend some extra time on this chapter—read through the material closely and work through the illustrations diligently. A little extra effort now is a worthwhile investment.

THE ACCOUNTING CYCLE: AN OVERVIEW

Figure 3–1 illustrates the complete accounting cycle. It consists of sixteen steps that lead from (1) the recognition of an economic event (i.e., a relevant and objectively measurable exchange transaction) to (13) the preparation of the income statement, (14) statement of retained earnings, (15) balance sheet, and (16) statement of cash flows.

The accounting cycle begins when a relevant and measurable (1) economic event is (2) interpreted and (3) converted to a journal entry. Journal entries, the fundamental units of the accounting system, are recorded in the original book of record, (4) the journal, and are then posted in (5) the ledger. The process of recording journal entries and posting them to the ledger continues until it is time to prepare financial statements (monthly, quarterly, or annually).

At this time, denoted by *End of Period* in Figure 3–1, a worksheet is prepared. Completing the worksheet encompasses Steps 6 through 10 in the accounting cycle. First, the account balances in the ledger are transferred to the worksheet. The list of the account balances on the worksheet is called the (6) unadjusted trial balance. The unadjusted trial balance is then adjusted for certain events that are not captured in the daily recording process (e.g., depreciation and earning interest). These (7) adjusting entries (or adjustments) are entered on the worksheet and added to the unadjusted trial balance, giving rise to (8) the adjusted trial balance. (9) Closing entries are then entered on the worksheet to transfer the balances in the income statement (Revenue and Expense) and Dividend accounts to the Re-

Figure 3-1 The accounting cycle

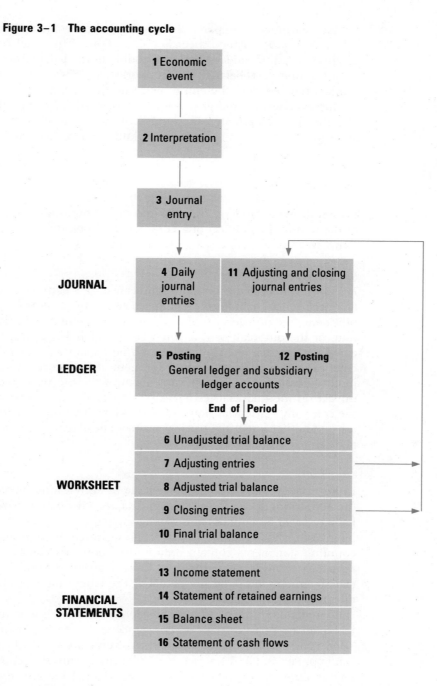

tained Earnings account. They are added to the adjusted trial balance, resulting in (10) the final trial balance, which completes the worksheet.

The adjusting and closing entries from the worksheet are now (11) recorded in the journal and (12) posted to the ledger. At the completion of Step 12, the financial statements are prepared. The (13) income statement can be prepared from the closing entries from either the worksheet or the journal. The (14) statement of retained earnings is prepared directly from the Retained Earnings account in the ledger. The (15) balance sheet is a collection of the final balances in the asset, liability, and stockholders' equity accounts in the ledger and can simply be taken from the final trial balance on the worksheet. The (16) statement of cash flows can be prepared from the entries listed on the cash account in the ledger.

This overview should give you a general feeling for the process. The following sections present each step thoroughly. As you read through the discussion, refer often to Figure 3–1, so that you will know where each step fits into the process.

Economic Events

Economic events that are entered into the accounting cycle must be both relevant to the financial condition of a company and objectively measurable in monetary terms. We discuss these two criteria below.

Relevance

Relevant events have economic significance to a particular company and include any occurrence that affects its financial condition. Events of general economic significance, like the election of a new U.S. president, the passage of federal legislation, or the outbreak of war could be considered relevant. Events that are more company-specific, like the signing of a new labor agreement, the hiring of a new chief executive officer, the sale of an item of inventory, or simply the payment of monthly wages, are also relevant. Each of these events could have a significant impact on the financial resources of a particular company. Anyone interested in the company's financial status (stockholders, investors, creditors, managers, auditors, and other interested parties) wants to be able to assess the financial impact of all such events.

Objectivity

Unfortunately, only a small percentage of all relevant events can be recorded in the accounting cycle. Recall that in Chapter 1 we pointed out the extensive legal liability faced by auditors and managers, and the demand for reliable information by investors and creditors. These economic forces help to insure that financial accounting statements contain only information that can be *objectively measured* in monetary terms. That is, the dollar values assigned to the accounts on the financial statements must be the result of exchange transactions that are backed by documented evidence.

In general, a dollar value is considered objective if it results from an exchange in which two parties with differing incentives reach agreement. To illustrate, in 1986 PepsiCo, Inc. offered to purchase Kentucky Fried Chicken (KFC) from RJR Nabisco. PepsiCo and Nabisco had differing incentives because PepsiCo wanted to pay as little as possible, while Nabisco wanted to receive as much as possible. When they reached agreement on the value of KFC, a transaction took place. KFC passed to PepsiCo for a price of $841 million. The price represented an objective valuation of KFC because two parties with differing incentives reached agreement on it. The transaction was accompanied by documented evidence (e.g., receipts, cancelled checks, vouchers, bill of sale), that could be used to verify its entry into PepsiCo's financial records, and after the purchase an investment of $841 million was reflected on PepsiCo's balance sheet.

In sum, economic events that are recorded in the accounting cycle and reflected on the financial statements must be both relevant and objectively measured in monetary terms. They must be relevant to be significant in evaluating the financial condition of a company. They must be objectively measurable so that they can be audited and viewed as credible by financial statement users.

As we will point out many times, the most relevant information unfortunately is not always the most objective. King World Productions Inc., for example, is a television syndicator with the rights to *Jeopardy, Wheel of Fortune,* and *Oprah Winfrey,* which are expected to generate over $700 million in licensing fees over the next several years. Yet, as of December 31, 1988, these rights were valued on the balance sheet at their purchase costs, less accumulated amortization, which totaled less than $3 million (the rights to *Wheel of Fortune* were valued at zero). Similarly, a partner at Coopers & Lybrand, a major accounting firm, noted: "Coca-Cola is one the the the best-recognized trademarks in the world, but it is not on their books. It got that recognition through advertising, but you don't book advertising as an asset, because you don't know if it will have future value."[1]

Interpreting Economic Events

Interpreting a relevant and objectively measurable economic event or, in other words, entering an exchange transaction into the accounting cycle, involves answering three questions:

1. What *accounts* on the financial statements are affected?
2. What is the *direction* of the effect?
3. What is the *dollar amount* of the transaction?

These questions were addressed implicitly in Chapter 2 as it discussed and illustrated how transactions affect the accounting equation: Assets = Liabilities + Stockholders' Equity. We will see now how each of these three questions relates to the accounting equation.

What Accounts Are Affected?

All exchange transactions affect at least two financial statement accounts. The first step in entering a transaction in the accounting cycle is to identify which accounts are affected.

Three different kinds of accounts compose the basic accounting equation: (1) assets, (2) liabilities, and (3) stockholders' equities. Asset accounts include Cash, Marketable Securities, Accounts Receivable, Inventories, Prepaid Expenses, Long-Term Investments, Property, Plant, Equipment, and Intangibles. Liability accounts consist primarily of Short- and Long-Term Payables. Stockholders' equity accounts include contributed capital, which we will refer to as Common Stock,[2] and Retained Earnings. All these accounts appear on the balance sheet (Figure 2−7).

As described earlier, Retained Earnings, a stockholders' equity account, is the net result of combining the income statement accounts (Revenues and Expenses)

---

1. Richard Greene, "Inequitable Equity," *Forbes* 1988 July 11, p. 83.

2. In Chapter 12, which covers the stockholders' equity section of the balance sheet, we point out that contributed capital is composed of a number of different accounts. For the time being, however, we will refer to only one account, Common Stock.

Figure 3–2 Accounts and the accounting equation

(1) Assets	=	(2) Liabilities	+	(3) Stockholders' equity:
				Common stock
				+ Retained earnings
				+ (4) Revenues
				− (5) Expenses
				− (6) Dividends

and the dividend account. The financial statements, therefore, can be viewed as containing six different kinds of accounts: (1) assets, (2) liabilities, (3) stockholders' equity, (4) revenues, (5) expenses, and (6) dividends. Figure 3–2 shows how these six kinds of accounts relate to the accounting equation.

What Is the Direction of the Effect?

Once the affected accounts in the six categories described are identified, the direction of the effect must be determined. That is, are the balances in the accounts increased or decreased? In all transactions assets, obligations, or rights, which are represented by the accounts, are exchanged; some are received, and others are given up. These exchanges change the balances of the accounts, which are recorded so that the equality of the accounting equation is maintained.

What Is the Dollar Value of the Transaction?

The dollar value of the transaction is the money value attached to the exchange and represents the amount of the change in the account balance. It is an objective valuation agreed upon by the transacting parties. It is therefore measurable in money terms and can be verified by supporting documentation.

Interpreting Exchange Transactions: A Few Examples

We now illustrate how answering these three questions provides the information necessary to record exchange transactions in a way that maintains the equality of the accounting equation.

Transaction (1) Burlington Northern purchases a piece of equipment for a cash amount of $5000.

What accounts are affected?
  Equipment, a long-term asset account
  Cash, a current asset account

What is the direction of the effect?
  Equipment is increased (the company received equipment).
  Cash is decreased (the company gave up cash).

What is the dollar value of the transaction?
  $5000—the agreed value of the equipment

Accounting Equation

Assets	=	Liabilities	+	Stockholders' Equity
+$5000 Equipment				
($5000) Cash				
$0	=	$0	+	$0

Transaction (2) H & R Block provides a tax service and bills its client for $1000.

What accounts are affected?
Fees Earned, a revenue account
Accounts Receivable, a current asset account

What is the direction of the effect?
Fees Earned is increased (the company provided a service).
Accounts Receivable is increased (the company received a receivable).

What is the dollar value of the transaction?
$1000—the agreed value of the service

Accounting Equation

Assets	=	Liabilities	+	Stockholders' Equity
+$1000 Accounts Receivable				+$1000 Retained Earnings via Fees Earned
+$1000	=	$0	+	+$1000

Transaction (3) Ed's Delivery Service pays its monthly payroll of $2000.

What accounts are affected?
Wage Expense, an expense account
Cash, a current asset account

What is the direction of the effect?
Wage Expense is increased (the company received employee services).
Cash is decreased (the company gave up cash).

What is the dollar value of the transaction?
$2000—the agreed value of the employee services

Accounting Equation

Assets	=	Liabilities	+	Stockholders' Equity
($2000) Cash				($2000) Retained Earnings via Wage Expense
($2000)	=	$0	+	($2000)

Transaction (4) Wendy's International borrows $10,000 from a bank.

What accounts are affected?
Notes Payable, a liability account
Cash, a current asset account

What is the direction of the effect?
Notes Payable is increased (the company created an obligation).
Cash is increased (the company received cash).

What is the dollar value of the transaction?
$10,000—the agreed value of the exchange

Accounting Equation

Assets	=	Liabilities	+	Stockholders' Equity
+$10,000 cash		+$10,000 note payable		
+$10,000	=	$10,000	+	$0

Described below are five transactions entered into by a corporation. Answer the three questions required when interpreting transactions, and relate each transaction to the accounting equation. Try this without looking at the solution in Figure 3–3.

Transaction (1)   Issues 100 ownership shares for $25 per share.

Transaction (2)   Purchases machinery, paying $1000 down and signing a one-year, $4000 note payable.

Transaction (3)   Provides services and receives $3000 in cash and $2000 in accounts receivable.

Transaction (4)   Incurs $2000 in miscellaneous expenses, paying $1500 in cash. Five hundred dollars are still to be paid.

Transaction (5)   Declares, but does not pay, a $700 dividend.

The Journal Entry

A **journal entry** is recorded in the journal, the original book of record, to represent each transaction entered into by a company. Journal entries have a particular structure that indicates and quantifies the important elements of exchange transactions, so that they can be incorporated into the financial statements.

All journal entries have three components: (1) the accounts affected (2) the direction of the effect, and (3) the dollar value of the transaction. Note that they correspond exactly to the three questions that we must answer when interpreting economic events. Once we answer these questions, we can prepare a journal entry and enter the transaction into the books. The form of a typical journal entry follows.

	Debit	Credit
Equipment	5000	
Cash		5000
To record the purchase of equipment for cash.		

The affected accounts in this entry are Equipment and Cash, and the dollar amount of the transaction is $5000. Placing the $5000 assigned to Equipment on the left side of the entry indicates that the Equipment account has been increased by $5000. That account is said to have been *debited*. In the terminology of financial accounting, to **debit** an account simply means to place the dollar amount assigned to it on the left side of the journal entry. The debit is always placed on the top of the entry.

Placing the $5000 assigned to the Cash account on the right side of the entry, or *crediting* it, indicates that the Cash account has been decreased by $5000. To **credit** an account means to place it on the right side of the journal entry. The sample entry indicates that equipment was purchased for $5000 cash.

Compound journal entries are treated in exactly the same way, but they involve more than two accounts. For example, if equipment is purchased for $5000

Figure 3–3 Solution to example

Transaction	Accounts	Direction	Amount (in $)
(1)	Cash	Increase	2,500
	Common Stock	Increase	2,500
(2)	Machinery	Increase	5,000
	Cash	Decrease	1,000
	Note Payable	Increase	4,000
(3)	Cash	Increase	3,000
	Accounts Receivable	Increase	2,000
	Fees Earned	Increase	5,000
(4)	Miscellaneous Expenses	Increase	2,000
	Cash	Decrease	1,500
	Miscellaneous Payables	Increase	500
(5)	Dividend	Increase	700
	Dividend Payable	Increase	700

Accounting Equation

	Assets			=	Liabilities			+	Stockholders' Equity	
Cash +	Accounts Receivable +	Machinery	=	Miscellaneous Payables +	Dividend Payables +	Note Payable	+	Common Stock +	Retained Earnings
(1) +2,500			=					+2,500	
(2) (1,000)		+5,000	=			+4,000			
(3) +3,000	+2,000								+5,000
									Fees earned
(4) (1,500)			=	+500					(2,000)
									Expenses
(5)			=		+700				(700)
									Dividends
3,000 +	2,000 +	5,000	=	500 +	700 +	4,000	+	2,500 +	2,300
	$10,000		=			$10,000			

cash and a $10,000 note payable, we would record the following compound journal entry.

	Debit	Credit
Equipment	15,000	
Cash		5,000
Notes Payable		10,000

To record the purchase of equipment for cash and a note payable.

The Double Entry System

Note in the preceding journal entries that the total dollar value on the debit side is always equal to the total dollar value on the credit side and that at least two different accounts were affected. Both characteristics are true of all journal entries and illustrate the **double entry system** of bookkeeping, which is the cornerstone of financial accounting. The equality of the debit and credit sides maintains the equality of the accounting equation (assets = liabilities + stockholders' equity), and the fact that at least two different accounts are affected indicates that in all exchange transactions, something is received and something is given up.

The Journal Entry Box

A useful way to learn journal entries is to view them as shown in Figure 3–4. We call this a *journal entry box*. It provides a systematic way of converting exchange transactions to journal entries by answering the three basic questions already discussed.

Each question has a particular place in relation to the journal entry box. Note that the top of the box is an expression of the accounting equation and that each cell contains a T that is associated with a group of accounts and has a left and a right side. Answer the three questions, and the journal entry box indicates the form of the journal entry, which in turn insures that the equality of the accounting equation is maintained.

For example, increases in asset accounts (Cell 1) and decreases in liability and stockholder's equity accounts (Cell 4) are always represented on the debit (left) side of the journal entry. Decreases in asset accounts (Cell 3) and increases in liability and stockholders' equity accounts (Cell 2) are always recorded on the

Figure 3–4   The journal entry box

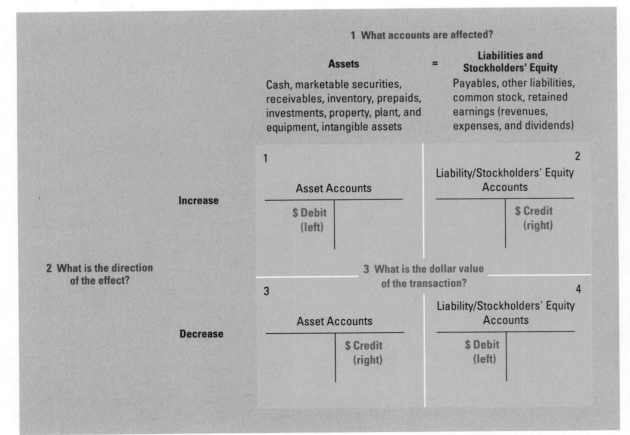

credit (right) side of the journal entry. It is important to recall that revenue, expense, and dividend accounts are all part of the stockholder's equity account, Retained Earnings. Thus, revenues, which increase Retained Earnings, are recorded on the credit side of the journal entry. Expenses and dividends, which decrease Retained Earnings, are recorded on the debit side of the journal entry.

The accounting equation at the top axis of the journal entry box shows that journal entries have been devised so that transactions are recorded in the journal in a way that always maintains the equality of the accounting equation. Debits always equal credits and, accordingly, assets always equal liabilities plus stockholder's equity.

You will not need to rely on the journal entry box for long, but until journal entries become second nature, we suggest that you diligently follow the steps indicated above by identifying (1) the affected accounts, (2) the direction of the effect, and (3) the dollar amount of the transaction for each transaction you examine. This procedure will establish good fundamental habits that will make it much easier for you as more complex topics are covered in later chapters. Remember, journal entries represent the alphabet of financial accounting, and if you fail to understand them well, you will never master the language of financial accounting.

Journal Entries and the Accounting Equation: Examples

The seven examples in Figure 3–5 should be self explanatory. The transactions give rise to seven different journal entries, affecting the accounting equation in seven different ways. Note that the equality of the accounting equation is always maintained, and the debit side of each journal entry is exactly equal to the credit side. Note especially Transactions 5, 6 and 7, where the equality of the accounting equation is maintained through the effect of a revenue, an expense, and a dividend on retained earnings. The explanations on the right side of the chart indicate how the journal entry box was used to construct each journal entry.

Look back at Figure 3–1 and note that we have only covered through Step 3 in the accounting cycle. Yet, we have covered by far the most important and difficult steps. If the journal entries are correct, the remaining steps lead directly to correct financial statements. If the journal entries are incorrect, the remaining steps lead directly to misstated financial statements. Journal entries are indeed the heart of the financial statements.

The Journal

The **journal** is a chronological record of the transactions, in journal entry form, entered into by a company. It is often referred to as the *book of original entry* because it is where transactions are first recorded. The process of recording transactions is called **journalizing.** As we mentioned earlier, journals can take many forms depending upon a company's accounting system. While many companies use several different kinds of journals, for the purposes of this chapter we assume that only one, called the **general journal,** is maintained. We do so because all journals play essentially the same role in the accounting cycle, and the addition of special journals makes the mechanical procedures somewhat involved. Special journals are briefly described and illustrated in Appendix 3A at the end of this chapter.

Figure 3-5 Journal entries and the accounting cycle

Transaction	Assets		=	Liabilities and Stockholders' Equity		Journal Entry	Debit	Credit	Explanation*
(1) Company receives $100 cash in payment of one of its customer accounts.	Cash Accts. Rec.	+100 (100) 0	=		0	Cash Accts. Rec.	100	100	Cash, an asset, is increased and debited. Accts. Rec., an asset, is decreased and credited.
(2) Company borrows $500 from a bank in exchange for a short-term note pay.	Cash	+500 +500	=	Note Pay.	+500 +500	Cash Note Pay.	500	500	Cash, an asset, is increased and debited. Note Pay., a liability, is increased and credited.
(3) Company pays $300 cash in payment of an accounts pay.	Cash	(300) (300)	=	Accts. Pay.	(300) (300)	Accts. Pay. Cash	300	300	Cash, an asset, is decreased and credited. Accts. Pay., a liability, is decreased and debited.
(4) Company issues com. stk. in exchange for an outstanding note pay.		0	=	Note Pay. Com. Stk.	(1000) +1000 0	Note Pay. Com. Stk.	1000	1000	Note pay., a liability, is decreased and debited. Com. Stk., an equity, is increased and credited.
(5) Company provides a service for which it bills its clients $2000.	Accts. Rec.	+2000 +2000	=	Ret. Earn. via Fees Earned	+2000 +2000	Accts. Rec. Fees Earned	2000	2000	Accts. Rec., an asset, is debited. Fees Earned, a Revenue, which increases Ret. Earn., is credited.
(6) Company pays salaries to its employees of $500.	Cash	(500) (500)	=	Ret. Earn. via Salary Expense	(500) (500)	Salary Exp. Cash	500	500	Cash, an asset, is decreased and credited. Salary Exp. decreases Ret. Earn. and is debited.
(7) Company declares an $800 dividend to be paid later to its owners.		0	=	Dividends Pay. Ret. Earn. via Dividends	+800 (800) 0	Dividend Dividend Pay.	800	800	Dividends Pay., a liability, is increased and credited. Dividend reduces Ret. Earn. and is debited.

*See journal entry in Figure 3-4.

Note: Accts. Rec. = Accounts Receivable; Accts. Pay. = Accounts Payable; Com. Stk. = Common Stock; Dividend Pay. = Dividend Payable; Note Pay. = Note Payable; Ret. Earn. = Retained Earnings; Salary Exp. = Salary Expense.

Figure 3–6 The general journal

General Journal					Page 1
Date		**Description**	**Post. Ref.**	**Debit**	**Credit**
1990 Feb.	8	Cash		300	
		Accounts Receivable		500	
		Fees earned			800
		Sale of a service.			
	10	Office Supplies		200	
		Accounts Payable			200
		Purchase of office supplies on credit.			

For each transaction the following information is recorded in the general journal: (1) the date, (2) the accounts that are debited and credited, (3) the dollar amounts of the debits and credits, (4) a brief explanation of the transaction, and (5) a posting reference, so that each journal entry can be traced to the ledger. Figure 3–6 shows an exerpt from a general journal. The first entry describes the provision of a service for which $300 in cash and a $500 receivable were received. The second entry describes the purchase on credit of $200 of office supplies.

The Ledger

Immediately after the transactions are recorded in the journal, they are posted in the **ledger,** where a running balance for each asset, liability, stockholders' equity, revenue, expense, and dividend account is maintained. The ledger can be viewed, therefore, as a "scoreboard" that keeps track of the "score" in each account during the period.

It is useful to think of the ledger as containing a **T-account** for each account on the financial statements. T-accounts are so named because they are in the form of a **T**. The left side of the **T** represents the debit side of the entry, and the right side corresponds to the credit side. Since journal entries also have a debit and a credit side, the debited and credited dollar amounts are easily transferred (posted) to their respective T-accounts. Figure 3–7 shows how the debits and credits in two journal entries are posted to their respective T-accounts.

In the first entry a service was exchanged for $200 cash and a $300 accounts receivable. Note that in the ledger the Cash T-account is increased (debited) by $200, the Accounts Receivable T-account is increased (debited) by $300, and the Fees Earned T-account is increased (credited) by $500. In the second entry $100 cash is received on an outstanding account receivable. Accordingly, the Cash balance in the ledger is increased (debited) by $100, and the Accounts Receivable balance is decreased (credited) by that amount. Note how the final balances in each account in the ledger have been computed.

Figure 3–7 Posting journal entries

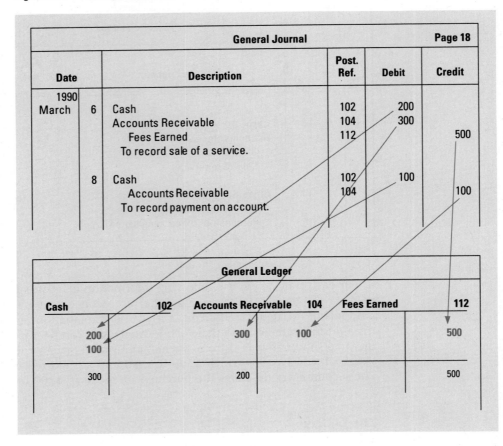

If every journal entry is immediately entered in the ledger, at any point in time the balance for a given account can be computed directly from its T-account. The balance is simply equal to the difference between the total dollar amount debited to the T-account and the total dollar amount credited. Having a convenient way to compute the account balances is particularly useful when it comes time to prepare the financial statements at the end of the accounting period. Without an up-to-date ledger, computing the account balances and preparing the financial statements would involve tracing back through the journal to find each transaction that affected each account. For most companies this would be time-consuming and tedious and could give rise to a number of recording errors.

The General Ledger and Subsidiary Ledgers

We have described the ledger as containing one T-account for each account on the financial statements, which is actually a description of the **general ledger.** Companies also commonly use **subsidiary ledgers,** which contain T-accounts that relate to certain specific accounts in the general ledger. A $110 balance in an accounts receivable general ledger T-account, for example, may comprise a number of accounts associated with individual customers. Cindy Jones may owe $35 to

Figure 3–8   Ledger account form

General Ledger							
Accounts Receivable							**Account No. 104**
						Balance	
Date		**Item**	**Post. Ref.**	**Debit**	**Credit**	**Debit**	**Credit**
1990 Mar.	6		18	300		300	
Mar.	8		18		100	200	

the company, Jason Smith may owe $50, and Heather Johnson, $25. T-accounts for each individual would be kept in a subsidiary ledger, which is tied directly to the $110 (35 + 50 + 25) Accounts Receivable balance in the general ledger. We discuss and illustrate the use of subsidiary ledgers more fully in Appendix 3A at the end of this chapter.

The Ledger Account Form

For the sake of simplicity and to avoid getting into the specific details of book-keeping we have shown ledger accounts in the form of a **T**. While this is true in concept, in practice a different form, called the **ledger account form,** is needed to record more information. An example of such an account appears in Figure 3–8.

The account title and number appear at the top, and the form contains columns for the date, a description of the entry, a posting reference, and four columns for the dollar amounts. The date is in the first column as it is in the journal. The description column is rarely used because the related transaction is already described in the journal. The posting reference gives the journal page number of the related entry. The first two debit and credit columns contain the debited and credited dollar amounts of the journal entry; the last two debit and credit columns carry the accumulated balance in the account. Figure 3–9 uses the first transaction from Figure 3–7 to show how the general journal and the ledger accounts form are cross-referenced.

Journal Entries and Posting: An Example

The following example illustrates what we have covered so far. We will also use it to illustrate the remaining steps of the accounting cycle (i.e., the unadjusted trial balance, the adjusted trial balance, the closing process, and the preparation of the financial statements). Take time to study it thoroughly.

The December 31, 1989 balance sheet of Maple Services Company appears in Figure 3–10. The company's journal, showing the transactions recorded during

Figure 3–9 General journal and general ledger cross-referencing system

General Journal — Page 18

Date		Description	Post. Ref.	Debit	Credit
1990 March	6	Cash	102	200	
		Accounts Receivable	104	300	
		Fees Earned	112		500
		To record sale of a service.			

General Ledger

Cash — Account No. 102

Date		Item	Post. Ref.	Debit	Credit	Balance Debit	Balance Credit
1990 March	6		18	200		200	

Accounts Receivable — Account No. 104

Date		Item	Post. Ref.	Debit	Credit	Balance Debit	Balance Credit
1990 March	6		18	300		300	

Fees Earned — Account No. 112

Date		Item	Post. Ref.	Debit	Credit	Balance Debit	Balance Credit
1990 March	6		18		500		500

1990, and the ledger, which has a T-account for each financial statement account, appear in Figure 3–11. Note first that the account balances from the balance sheet are the beginning balances in the ledger accounts. Note also that the journal entries, numbered 1–12 are posted in the ledger. Review each journal entry and trace the dollar amounts of the debits and credits in the ledger.

The Worksheet

The process of recording journal entries and posting them to the appropriate ledger accounts continues throughout the **accounting period,** the time between the

Figure 3–10   Maple Services balance sheet

Maple Services Company
Balance Sheet
December 31, 1989

Assets		Liabilities and Stockholders' Equity	
Cash	$12,000	Salaries payable	$ 4,000
Accounts receivable	9,000	Note payable	6,000
Land	15,000	Common stock	21,000
		Retained earnings	5,000
		Total liabilities and	
Total assets	$36,000	stockholder's equity	$36,000

preparation of financial statements, which is usually a month, a quarter (three months), or a year.

At the end of the accounting period, when the time comes to summarize the accounts and prepare financial statements, a worksheet is often prepared. A **worksheet** is simply a piece of paper divided into a number of columns. It is used to transfer the account balances in the general ledger to the income statement, statement of retained earnings, and balance sheet in a systematic fashion.

A worksheet is certainly useful in preparing these three financial statements, but it is not necessary. As we show later, we can prepare the financial statements without it. Nevertheless, you should use one at this point, because they make it much easier to trace your work and check for possible errors. Furthermore, worksheets of many kinds are important in the everyday practice of accounting.

The Unadjusted Trial Balance

Transferring the ledger account balances to the financial statements begins by simply copying the general ledger account names in the column at the far left of the worksheet. Asset account names are usually listed first, followed by liability and stockholders' equity accounts, dividend accounts, revenue accounts, and expense accounts, in that order. The account balances from the ledger are then copied next to the account names in the adjoining two columns: debit balances on the left and credit balances on the right. The result (Step 6 in the accounting cycle) is called the **unadjusted trial balance.** Figure 3–12 shows the unadjusted trial balance for Maple Services Company on an incomplete worksheet.

Note the order of the accounts in the unadjusted trial balance and that asset, dividend, and expense accounts have debit balances, while liability, stockholders' equity, and revenue accounts have credit balances. Refer to the balances in the ledger T-accounts in Figure 3–11 for an explanation of the dollar amount of each entry and why each account has a debit or credit balance. Note also that total debits ($42,000) on the unadjusted trial balance are equal to total credits ($42,000). If they are not equal, an error has occurred somewhere in the cycle.

Adjusting Entries

In Step 7 of the accounting cycle, the unadjusted trial balance is adjusted to capture certain relevant events that are not normally recorded as they occur during

112

Chapter 3 / The Accounting Cycle

Figure 3–11   Maple Services journal and ledger

**Maple Services Company
Journal and Ledger**

General Journal

(1) Cash	5,000	
Common Stock		5,000
To record the issuance of common stock.		
(2) Land	7,000	
Cash		7,000
To record the purchase of land.		
(3) Salaries Payable	4,000	
Cash		4,000
To record the payment of salaries owed at the end of 1989.		
(4) Cash	6,000	
Accounts Receivable		6,000
To record the receipt of cash on outstanding accounts receivable.		
(5) Cash	7,000	
Service Revenue		7,000
To record the receipt of cash for services performed.		

(6) Rent Expenses	500	
Cash		500
To record the payment for rent.		
(7) Insurance Expense	100	
Cash		100
To record the payment for insurance coverage.		
(8) Salary Expense	3,000	
Cash		3,000
To record the payment for salaries.		
(9) Interest Expense	500	
Notes Payable	2,000	
Cash		2,500
(10) Dividends	1,000	
Cash		1,000
To record the payment of a dividend.		

General Ledger

Cash

	12,000	7,000	(2)
(1)	5,000	4,000	(3)
(4)	6,000	500	(6)
(5)	7,000	100	(7)
		3,000	(8)
		2,500	(9)
		1,000	(10)
	11,900		

Accounts Receivable

9,000			
		6,000	(4)
3,000			

Land

	15,000	
(2)	7,000	
	22,000	

Salaries Payable

		4,000
(3)	4,000	
		0

Notes Payable

		6,000
(9)	2,000	
		4,000

Common Stock

		21,000
		5,000	(1)
		6,000

Retained Earnings

	5,000

Service Revenue

	7,000	(5)

Salary Expense

(8)	3,000

Rent Expense

(6)	500

Insurance Expense

(7)	100

Interest Expense

(9)	500

Dividends

(10)	1,000

Figure 3–12   Unadjusted trial balance for Maple Services (incomplete worksheet)

Accounts	Unadjusted Trial Balance Dr.	Unadjusted Trial Balance Cr.	Adjusting Entries Dr.	Adjusting Entries Cr.	Adjusted Trial Balance Dr.	Adjusted Trial Balance Cr.	Closing Entries Dr.	Closing Entries Cr.	Final Trial Balance Dr.	Final Trial Balance Cr.
Maple Services Company Worksheet For the Year Ended December 31, 1990										
Assets:										
Cash	11,900									
Accounts Receivable	3,000									
Land	22,000									
Liabilities:										
Notes Payable		4,000								
Stockholders' Equity:										
Common Stock		26,000								
Retained Earnings		5,000								
Dividends	1,000									
Revenues:										
Service Revenue		7,000								
Expenses:										
Salary Expense	3,000									
Rent Expense	500									
Insurance Expense	100									
Interest Expense	500									
Total	42,000	42,000								

an accounting period. Machinery and equipment, for example, are subject to wear and tear as they are used, and interest is earned continually on bank accounts. These events are both relevant and objectively measurable, but they are not reflected in the ledger or on the unadjusted trial balance because they do not result directly from exchange transactions during the accounting period. Consequently, certain accounts on the worksheet must be debited or credited to reflect the extent of the adjustment. These debits and credits are recorded in the two columns that adjoin the columns of the unadjusted trial balance. Adjusting entries are also recorded in the journal and, like all journal entries, posted to the ledger. It is common practice to record and post (Steps 11 and 12) the adjusting entries after completing the worksheet.

A full appreciation of the different kinds of adjustments requires an understanding of several important financial accounting measurement issues. Since we discuss these issues in the next chapter, we cover adjusting entries in detail at that time. As a result, we assume that no adjusting entries are required to prepare Maple Services Company's financial statements. Remember, however, that adjusting entries are an important part of financial accounting, and note their placement in the accounting cycle.

Figure 3–13   Adjusted trial balance for Maple Services (incomplete worksheet)

Accounts	Unadjusted Trial Balance		Adjusting Entries		Adjusted Trial Balance		Closing Entries		Final Trial Balance	
	Dr.	Cr.	Dr.	Cr.	Dr.	Cr.	Dr.	Cr.	Dr.	Cr.
Assets:										
Cash	11,900				11,900					
Accounts Receivable	3,000				3,000					
Land	22,000				22,000					
Liabilities:										
Notes Payable		4,000				4,000				
Stockholders' Equity:										
Common Stock		26,000				26,000				
Retained Earnings		5,000				5,000				
Dividends	1,000				1,000					
Revenues:										
Service Revenue		7,000				7,000				
Expenses:										
Salary Expense	3,000				3,000					
Rent Expense	500				500					
Insurance Expense	100				100					
Interest Expense	500				500					
Total	42,000	42,000	0	0	42,000	42,000				

Maple Services Company
Worksheet
For the Year Ended December 31, 1990

Adjusted Trial Balance

After entering the adjusting entries on the worksheet, the **adjusted trial balance** (Step 8) can be prepared. This is simply the result of adding the debits and credits from the adjusting entries to the debit and credit balances from the unadjusted trial balance. The resulting balance for each account is carried over to the two columns to the right of the adjusting entries. Once again, the total dollar amount in the debit column equals the total dollar amount in the credit column. Figure 3–13 shows adjusted trial balance, which is the same as the unadjusted trial balance because we assumed that no adjusting entries were necessary.

Closing Entries and the Closing Process

In the closing process (Step 9) the dollar balances in the Revenue, Expense, and Dividend accounts are transferred, or *closed*, to the Retained Earnings account. Since this process is often difficult for students to understand, we first explain why closing is necessary, then distinguish permanent from temporary accounts, and finally describe and illustrate the actual procedures involved.

Why Closing Is Necessary. Assume that Jenotech, Inc. (1) sold services for $500 cash, (2) paid $300 cash for miscellaneous expenses, and (3) paid a $100 cash dividend. Recall the journal entry box in Figure 3–4, and note that these transactions would be recorded in the journal as follows.

1.	Cash	500	
	Fees Earned		500
	To record the receipt of cash in exchange for services.		
2.	Miscellaneous Expenses	300	
	Cash		300
	To record the payment of cash for expenses.		
3.	Dividend	100	
	Cash		100
	To record the payment of a cash dividend.		

Consider how these transactions affect the balance sheet and the accounting equation: assets = liabilities + stockholders' equity. Each involves cash and, accordingly, either increases or decreases assets. The accounts named *Fees Earned, Miscellaneous Expenses,* and *Dividends,* however, do not appear on the balance sheet. How are they handled so that the equality of the balance sheet and the accounting equation are maintained?

Until now we have answered this question by simply stating that retained earnings, which is part of stockholders' equity, is the net accumulation of past revenues, expenses, and dividends and is, therefore, adjusted when revenues, expenses, and dividends are recognized: revenues increase retained earnings, while expenses and dividends decrease retained earnings. These three transactions, therefore, would affect the accounting equation and the balance sheet as shown in Figure 3–14.

From a procedural standpoint, if revenues, expenses, and dividends are to be reflected on the balance sheet and, in the process, maintain the equality of the accounting equation, we need a method of transferring the end-of-period balances in the Revenue, Expense, and Dividend accounts to the Retained Earnings account. This method is known as the *closing process.*

Permanent and Temporary Accounts. The need to transfer revenues, expenses, and dividends to retained earnings introduces an important distinction among the accounts on the financial statements. The balance sheet accounts (assets, liabilities, and stockholders' equities) are called *permanent accounts;* the income statement and dividend accounts (revenues, expenses, and dividends) are called *temporary accounts.* **Permanent accounts** have balances that accumulate from one accounting period to the next. The balance sheet, which consists of permanent accounts, reflects transactions that have occurred since a company's inception. It is a statement of a company's accumulated financial condition as of a particular point in time.

Figure 3–14 Revenues, expenses, dividends, and the accounting equation

	Assets	=	Liabilities	+	Common stock	+	Retained Earnings
(1)	+500	=					+500
(2)	(300)	=					(300)
(3)	(100)	=			•		(100)

Temporary accounts accumulate only throughout a single period. At the end of that period their balances are reduced to zero, where they begin the next accounting period. For example, the income statement, which consists of temporary accounts, only reflects transactions from a single period.

The distinction between permanent and temporary accounts is at the heart of the closing process, in which a series of journal entries transfers the balances in the Revenue, Expense, and Dividend accounts to the Retained Earnings account. The balances in the temporary accounts are zeroed out and transferred to a permanent balance sheet account, where they are accumulated.

The Procedures of the Closing Process. The closing process consists of four basic steps:

1. *Create an Income Summary Account.*
   A ledger T-account, called **Income Summary,** is created solely to execute the closing process.
2. *Close the Revenue and Expense accounts into Income Summary.*
   A series of **closing entries** transfers the balances in the Revenue and Expense accounts to the income summary account and sets the new balances in the Revenue and Expense accounts to zero.
3. *Close the Income Summary account into Retained Earnings.*
   A single journal entry closes the Income Summary account to Retained Earnings. As in the previous step, this entry simply transfers the balance in the income summary account to the Retained Earnings account, and brings the Income Summary balance to zero.
4. *Close the Dividend account into Retained Earnings.*
   A single entry closes the Dividend account directly to retained earnings. Once again, the entry sets the Dividend account to zero by transferring its balance to the Retained Earnings account.

Figure 3–15 shows the procedures to close the Revenue, Expense, and Dividend accounts for Maple Services at the end of 1990. The balances in the Revenue, Expense, Dividend, and Retained Earnings accounts from the adjusted trial balance are indicated by *italics*. In Step 1 an Income Summary account is created. In Step 2 closing journal entry (1) debits service revenue for $7000 and credits each expense account (Salary, Rent, Insurance, and Interest) for the amount of expense recognized during the year. When this entry is posted in the ledger, it brings the balances in the revenue and expense accounts to zero. In addition, this entry requires a credit of $2900 to make the total credits equal the $7000 debit. This amount is recorded in the Income Summary account and represents the dollar amount of the difference between the revenues and expenses recognized during the year, which incidentally is Maple Services' net income for 1990.

In Step 3, closing journal entry (2) is prepared, which, when posted to the ledger, brings the balance in the Income Summary account to zero and transfers $2900 to Retained Earnings. Thus it transfers the net amount of revenues and expenses (net income) to the Retained Earnings account. In Step 4, closing journal entry (3) is prepared which, when posted, brings the balance in the Dividend account to zero and reduces Retained Earnings by $1000. Note that the ending balance in the Retained Earnings T-account ($6900) is computed by adding net income ($2900) to the beginning balance of Retained Earnings ($5000), and

Figure 3-15   Maple Services Company: The closing process

Step 1: Create Income Summary account.

Step 2: Close revenue and expense accounts into Income Summary account.

Journal entry: (1)	Service Revenue	7,000	
	Salary Expense		3,000
	Rent Expense		500
	Insurance Expense		100
	Interest Expense		500
	Income Summary (plug)		2,900
	To close revenues and expenses		
	to Income Summary.		

Step 3: Close Income Summary account into Retained Earnings account.

Journal entry: (2)	Income summary	2,900	
	Retained Earnings		2,900
	To close Income Summary to		
	Retained Earnings.		

Step 4: Close Dividends account into Retained Earnings account.

Journal entry: (3)	Retained Earnings	1,000	
	Dividends		1,000
	To close Dividends to Retained		
	Earnings.		

General Ledger

Service Revenue		Salary Expense		Rent Expense		Insurance Expense	
(1) 7,000	7,000	3,000	3,000 (1)	500	500 (1)	100	100 (1)
	0	0		0		0	

Interest Expense		Income Summary		Dividends		Retained Earnings	
500	500 (1)	(2) 2,900	2,900 (1)	1,000	1,000 (3)		5,000
0			0	0		(3) 1,000	2,900 (2)
							6,900

subtracting the dividend ($1000). This computation is exactly what appears on the statement of retained earnings.

Figure 3–15 shows only the closing entries recorded in the journal and ledger. However, as the accounting cycle in Figure 3–1 indicates, these entries are recorded first on the worksheet in the debit and credit columns to the right of the adjusted trial balance. When the worksheet is complete, these entries are recorded in the journal and posted to the ledger. The completed worksheet for Maple Services appears in Figure 3–16.

Figure 3–16 Completed worksheet for Maple Services

	Maple Services Company Worksheet For the Year Ended December 31, 1990									
Accounts	**Unadjusted Trial Balance**		**Adjusting Entries**		**Adjusted Trial Balance**		**Closing Entries**		**Final Trial Balance**	
	Dr.	Cr.	Dr.	Cr.	Dr.	Cr.	Dr.	Cr.	Dr.	Cr.
Assets:										
Cash	11,900				11,900				11,900	
Accounts Receivable	3,000				3,000				3,000	
Land	22,000				22,000				22,000	
Liabilities:										
Notes Payable		4,000				4,000				4,000
Stockholders' Equity:										
Common Stock		26,000				26,000				26,000
Retained Earnings		5,000				5,000	(3) 1,000	(2) 2,900		6,900
Dividends	1,000				1,000			(3) 1,000	0	
Revenues:										
Service Revenue		7,000				7,000	(1) 7,000			0
Expenses:										
Salary Expense	3,000				3,000			(1) 3,000	0	
Rent Expense	500				500			(1) 500	0	
Insurance Expense	100				100			(1) 100	0	
Interest Expense	500				500			(1) 500	0	
Income Summary							(2) 2,900	(1) 2,900	0	
Total	42,000	42,000	0	0	42,000	42,000	10,900	10,900	36,900	36,900

The Final Trial Balance

After the closing entries have been recorded on the worksheet and all the temporary accounts have zero balances, the only remaining balances are in the permanent asset, liability, and stockholders' equity accounts. In Figure 3–16 these balances are carried to the **final trial balance** (Step 10). Asset accounts typically carry debit balances in the final trial balance, while liability and stockholders' equity accounts normally carry credit balances. Total debits ($36,900) will equal total credits ($36,900) if the entries have been recorded correctly.

Preparation of the Financial Statements

Preparing the income statement, statement of retained earnings, balance sheet, and statement of cash flows (Steps 13 to 16) at this point is a very straightforward procedure. Each statement comes directly from a segment of the accounting cycle.

The Income Statement

The income statement can be prepared directly from either the journal entry that closes the Revenue and Expense accounts (Fig. 3–15, journal entry [1]) or the closing entries on the completed worksheet (Fig. 3–16). These entries correspond

Figure 3-17 Income statement for Maple Services

Maple Services Company Income Statement For the Year Ended December 31, 1990		
Service revenue		$7,000
Expenses		
Salaries	$3,000	
Rent	500	
Insurance	100	
Interest	500	
Total expenses		4,100
Net income		$2,900

to those on the income statement. The dollar amount initially recorded in the Income Summary account is equal to net income. Figure 3–17 presents the income statement of Maple Services Company.

The Statement of Retained Earnings

The statement of retained earnings can be prepared directly from the Retained Earnings T-account in the General Ledger (Fig. 3–15). Recall the reconciliation format of this statement: beginning balance, plus (minus) net income (net loss), less dividends, equals ending balance. The beginning balance of Retained Earnings for the current period is the dollar amount of retained earnings that appears on the previous balance sheet ($5000). The entry to close the Income Summary into Retained Earnings represents the adjustment for net income ($2900). The entry to close the Dividend account into Retained Earnings reduces Retained Earnings in the amount of the dividend ($1000). The ending balance in the Retained Earnings T-account, which also appears in the end-of-period balance sheet, is the net result of these adjustments. The statement of retained earnings for Maple Services appears in Figure 3–18.

The Balance Sheet

The balance sheet is prepared from the ending balances in the permanent asset, liability, and stockholders' equity accounts. These balances appear in the ledger and in the final trial balance on the worksheet. Figure 3–19 shows the balance sheet of Maple Services.

Figure 3-18 Statement of retained earnings for Maple Services

Maple Services Company Statement of Retained Earnings For the Year Ended December 31, 1990	
Beginning retained earnings balance	$5,000
Plus: Net income	2,900
Less: Dividends	1,000
Ending retained earnings balance	$6,900

Figure 3–19   Maple Services balance sheet

Maple Services Company Balance Sheet December 31, 1990			
Assets		**Liabilities and Stockholders' Equity**	
Cash	$11,900	Notes payable	$ 4,000
Accounts receivable	3,000	Common stock	26,000
Land	22,000	Retained earnings	6,900
		Total liabilities and	
Total assets	$36,900	stockholder's equity	$36,900

The Statement of Cash Flows

The statement of cash flows can be prepared from the Cash account in the ledger (Fig. 3–11). Entries on the left of the Cash T-account (debits) indicate cash inflows; entries on the right (credits) indicate cash outflows. Recall that the statement of cash flows is organized into three categories: cash flows from operating activities, from investing activities, and from financing activities. To prepare the statement, each of the cash inflows and outflows in the ledger must be placed in one of the three categories.

Cash flows from operating activities include inflows and outflows associated with the acquisition and sale of a company's products and services. For Maple Services, cash flows from operating activities come from transactions (3) and (8) cash payments for salaries ($7000), (4) cash receipts from outstanding accounts receivable ($6000), (5) cash receipts from providing services ($7000), and cash payments for (6) rent ($500), (7) insurance ($100), and (9) interest ($500). Note that each of these acccounts also appears on the income statement, which is another statement of operating activities.

Cash flows from investing activities include inflows and outflows from the purchase and sales of noncurrent assets. For Maple Services, cash flows from investing activities come from transaction (2), the purchase of land ($7000). Cash flows from financing activities include inflows and outflows associated with a company's two sources of outside capital: liabilities and stockholders' equity. For Maple Services cash flows from financing activities include transactions (1), the issuance of stock for cash ($5000), (9) the principal payment on the loan payable ($2000), and (10) the payment of a dividend ($1000). Figure 3–20 shows the statement of cash flows for Maple Services.

THE ACCOUNTING CYCLE: A SHORT EXAMPLE

The example in Figure 3–21 depicts a company's first month of operations. It is intentionally short, allowing you to follow each transaction from journal, to ledger, to closing, to the financial statements. We do not use a worksheet in this illustration in order to show as clearly as possible the link between the journal and ledger entries and the financial statements. A comprehensive problem at the end of the chapter illustrates the entire accounting cycle and includes a worksheet.

Figure 3–20   Statement of Cash Flows for Maple Services

Maple Services Company Statement of Cash Flows For the Year Ended December 31, 1990		
Operating activities		
Cash receipts for services	$7,000	
Cash receipts from accounts receivable	6,000	
Cash payments for salaries	(7,000)	
Cash payments for rent	(500)	
Cash payments for insurance	(100)	
Cash payments for interest	(500)	
Cash increase (decrease) due to operating activities		$ 4,900
Investing activities		
Cash payment for purchase of land	(7,000)	
Cash increase (decrease) due to investing activities		(7,000)
Financing activities		
Cash receipt from issuing stock	5,000	
Cash payment for loan principal	(2,000)	
Cash payment for dividends	(1,000)	
Cash increase (decrease) due to financing activities		2,000
Increase (decrease) in cash balance		(100)
Beginning cash balance		12,000
Ending cash balance		$11,900

INTERNAL CONTROLS AND THE ACCOUNTING CYCLE

Throughout the discussion of the accounting cycle, we have implicitly assumed that employees faithfully and accurately record all relevant and measurable transactions in the journal, post them to the ledger, and follow the procedures necessary to reflect them on the financial statements. Unfortunately, this assumption is not always realistic. Errors are sometimes made in the accounting cycle, and a company's assets must be safeguarded from loss and from the occasional dishonest employee. An important responsibility of a company's accountants is to help management ensure that errors in the recording process are minimized and that assets are not lost or stolen. To achieve this goal, accountants are usually responsible for the design and management of the company's internal control system. The importance and principles of effective internal control are discussed in Appendix 3B at the end of this chapter.

COMPUTERIZED ACCOUNTING SYSTEMS

We have assumed so far that the accounting cycle is implemented manually. Each transaction is recorded manually in the appropriate journal and each debit and credit is posted manually in the correct ledger account. A worksheet is then manually prepared to produce the financial statements. While describing an accounting system as a manual process is a useful way to explain basic bookkeeping pro-

Figure 3–21   Short example of the accounting cycle

General Journal Activity During January

(1) Cash	5,000	
Common Stock		5,000
Issue stock for cash.		
(2) Equipment	2,000	
S-T Pay.		1,000
Cash		1,000
Purchase equipment.		
(3) Cash	3,000	
Accts. Rec.	1,000	
Fees Earned		4,000
For services performed.		

(4) Salary Expense	1,200	
Cash		1,200
Payment of salaries.		
(5) Cash	2,000	
Notes Payable		2,000
Borrowed $2,000.		
(6) Other Expenses	1,500	
Cash		1,500
Payment of other expenses.		
(7) Dividends	500	
Cash		500
Payment of dividends.		

Closing entries

(8) Fees Earned	4,000	
Other expenses		1,500
Salary Expense		1,200
Income Summary		1,300
Close expenses and revenues.		
(9) Income Summary	1,300	
Retained Earnings		1,300
Close income summary.		
(10) Retained Earnings	500	
Dividends		500
Close dividends.		

General Ledger

Cash

(1)	5,000	1,000	(2)
(3)	3,000	1,200	(4)
(5)	2,000	1,500	(6)
		500	(7)
	5,800		

Accounts Receivable

(3)	1,000		
	1,000		

Equipment

(2)	2,000		
	2,000		

Short-Term Payables

		1,000	(2)
		1,000	

Notes Payable

		2,000	(5)
		2,000	

Common Stock

		5,000	(1)
		5,000	

Income Summary

(9)	1,300	1,300	(8)
		0	

Retained Earnings

		1,300	(9)
(10)	500		
		800	

Dividends

(7)	500	500	(10)
	0		

Fees Earned

(8)	4,000	4,000	(3)
		0	

Salary Expense

(4)	1,200	1,200	(8)
	0		

Other Expenses

(6)	1,500	1,500	(8)
	0		

Note: Accts. Rec. = Accounts Receivable
S-T Pay. = Short-Term Payable

cedures, manual systems are used only by relatively small companies. Larger companies usually rely upon computer systems.

In computerized accounting systems the steps of the accounting cycle, which are the same as those in a manual system, are performed with the aid of a computer, and the journal and general and subsidiary ledgers are stored on files in the computer system. These systems consist of both hardware and software and the

Figure 3–21   (continued)

Income Statement (See closing entry (8).)

Fees earned	$4,000
Salary expense	1,200
Other expenses	1,500
Net income	1,300

Statement of Retained Earnings (See Retained Earnings T-account.)

Beginning retained earnings balance	$ 0
Plus: Net income	1,300
Less: Dividends	500
Ending retained earnings balance	$ 800

Balance Sheet (See final balances in asset, liability, and stockholders' equity accounts.)

Assets		Liabilities and Stockholders' Equity	
Cash	$5,800	Short-term payables	$1,000
Accounts receivable	1,000	Notes payable	2,000
Equipment	2,000	Common stock	5,000
		Retained earnings	800
Total assets	$8,800	Total liabilities and stockholders' equity	$8,800

Statement of Cash Flows (See Cash T-account.)

Operating activities		
Cash collections from fees earned	$3,000	
Cash payments for salaries	(1,200)	
Cash payments for other expenses	(1,500)	
Net cash increase (decrease) from operating activities		$ 300
Investing activities		
Cash payments for equipment	(1,000)	
Net cash increase (decrease) from investing activities		(1,000)
Financing activities		
Cash collections from issuing stock	5,000	
Cash collections from borrowing	2,000	
Cash payments for dividends	(500)	
Net Cash increase (decrease) from financing activities		6,500
Net increase (decrease) in cash balance		$5,800
Beginning cash balance		0
Ending cash balance		$5,800

actual processing of the accounting data involves three phases: (1) input, (2) processing, and (3) output.

Hardware is the equipment needed for the operation of the system and it is involved in all three phases of data processing. Transactions can be input to the system with optical scanners, cards or tape readers, console typewriters, on-line keyboards, voice terminals, or other hardware devices. The central processor, the heart of the computer system, is the actual processor of the data. It directs the internal processes of the computer, including arithmetic computations, logic, and memory storage. Processors range in size and power from mainframes, which make up the complex computer networks of major US corporations, to mini and microcomputers, which are normally used by medium-sized corporations and individuals, respectively. Output hardware normally includes printers and video display terminals.

Software consists of the programs, routines, and sets of instructions that guide the hardware of the computer system in performing its varied operations and functions. Software programs, which must be written in a language the computer can understand, instruct the central processor on how to process the transactions which have been fed into the system through the input hardware. Instructions for the posting and closing processes, required mathematical computations, trial balance preparation, and financial statement format are all included in the software programs. Software is often written and programmed by particular companies to meet their individual data processing needs, but a number of predesigned packages developed by software firms are also available.

There are two basic approaches to processing transactions in computer-based accounting systems: (1) batch processing and (2) real-time processing. **Batch processing** involves the periodic processing of data in similar groups. Source documents representing transactions are collected and stored temporarily until a sufficiently large batch is accumulated or until a designated time arrives. The documents are grouped together and a batch total is computed which is entered into the computer system. The sales receipts of a given week, for example, may be totaled and entered into the computer system at the end of each week. The processing total is compared to the batch total to ensure that all transactions have been entered correctly. The processing system updates the subsidiary and general ledgers, which are stored in the computer on master files. From this process a variety of outputs can then be generated including, for example, the transaction journal, account balances from the general ledger, a trial balance, and a set of financial statements.

Real-time processing consists of processing each transaction at the time it is executed. Data entry involves a device such as a terminal, optical scanner, or voice input unit and source documents underlying the transactions may or may not be involved. As soon as a transaction is entered, the relevant subsidiary and general ledgers are updated and the journal, general ledger, trial balance, and financial statements can be provided as output if desired.

The main advantage of a real-time system over a batch system is that transactions are entered immediately and up-to-date information is available in a timely manner. Such systems also require fewer steps which reduces the likelihood of recording errors. Real-time systems, on the other hand, require more costly and complex hardware and software. Moreover, it is certainly more difficult to trace transactions in these systems because there tend to be fewer supporting documents.

In this section we have simply introduced and defined some of the important terms used in computerized accounting systems. More complete coverages of such systems are found in textbooks dealing specifically with management information systems. However, keep in mind that all computer systems, regardless of the level of sophistication or complexity, are based on the same fundamentals which underlie manual accounting systems.

THE ANNUAL REPORT OF K MART CORPORATION

Turn now to K mart's annual report located in Appendix D. In management's discussion and analysis of general merchandising operations, at the bottom of page 17, it describes point-of-sale (POS) systems which are being installed in domestic K mart stores. The installation of these systems has been part of a continuing retail automation program which has improved expense control. Such systems represent an example of online processing, where transactions are entered with optical scanners and the relevant accounts are immediately updated.

The management letter (page 30) describes the role and importance of K mart's system of internal accounting control. It states that "a system of internal accounting controls . . . provides for the integrity of information for purposes of preparing financial statements and to assure that assets are properly accounted for and safeguarded. This concept of reasonable assurance is based on the recognition that the cost of the system must be related to the benefits derived. Management believes its system provides this appropriate balance." Note also that "an Internal Audit Department is maintained to evaluate, test and report on the application of internal accounting controls," and that "the Board of Directors appoints the independent accountant to perform an examination of the financial statements [which] includes . . . a review of the system of internal controls as required by generally accepted auditing standards."

In the section on Corporate Responsibility (page 29) the company mentions the importance of corporate ethics. It states "the reputation of the company is one of our most valuable assets. To preserve and protect that asset, K mart prepared a booklet setting forth a general statement of the standards by which the company conducts its business. The booklet, entitled Standards of Business Conduct, is available to employees, customers, suppliers and shareholders."

A COMPREHENSIVE EXAMPLE OF THE ACCOUNTING CYCLE

In this comprehensive example of the entire accounting cycle, Figure 3−22 represents the journal, containing ten entries recorded during the accounting period (1990) and three closing entries recorded at the end of 1990. Figure 3−23 represents the ledger, which contains a T-account for each financial statement account. Figure 3−24 shows the worksheet. Figure 3−25 shows the income statement, statement of retained earnings, balance sheet, and statement of cash flows.

The ledger indicates that ABC company began operations in 1990 with beginning balances in its asset, liability, and stockholders' equity accounts. For example, $600 was in the Cash account, $300 in Accounts Receivable, and a $400 (credit) balance in Retained Earnings. The beginning balances in the Revenue, Expense, and Dividend accounts are zero because they were closed at the end of the previous accounting period (1989).

The journal entries numbered (1)–(10) represent the exchange transactions entered into by ABC during the month of January. Note that each entry has been posted in the ledger and is coded by an entry number. At the end of January the ledger balances are totaled and transferred to the worksheet in the form of an un-

Figure 3–22 Comprehensive example: journal entries

General Journal

Entry	Date	Journal Entry			Description of Transaction
(1)	1/4/90	Accounts Receivable	300		Sales of services on account.
		Service Revenue		300	
(2)	1/7/90	Misc. Payable	50		Payment of misc. payable.
		Cash		50	
(3)	1/8/90	Cash	500		Sale of service for cash.
		Service Revenue		500	
(4)	1/18/90	Cash	200		Receive payment on
		Accounts Receivable		200	outstanding receivable.
(5)	1/20/90	Notes Payable	100		Payment on outstanding notes
		Cash		100	payable.
(6)	1/22/90	Land	700		Purchase land for cash and
		Cash		300	sign a note payable for the
		Notes Payable		400	remainder.
(7)	1/26/90	Interest Expense	40		Payment of interest on notes
		Cash		40	payable.
(8)	1/27/90	Cash	1,000		Issue stock for cash.
		Common Stock		1,000	
(9)	1/29/90	Salary Expense	350		Pay salaries and other
		Other Expenses	200		expenses.
		Cash		550	
(10)	1/30/90	Dividends	100		Declare dividends to be paid in
		Dividends Payable		100	February.

Closing Entries

Entry	Date	Journal Entry			Description of Transaction
(11)	1/31/90	Service Revenue	800		Closed revenues and expenses
		Interest Expense		40	into Income Summary.
		Salary Expense		350	
		Other Expenses		200	
		Income Summary		210	
(12)	1/31/90	Income Summary	210		Closed Income Summary into
		Retained Earnings		210	Retained Earnings.
(13)	1/31/90	Retained Earnings	100		Closed dividends into Retained
		Dividends		100	Earnings.

adjusted trial balance. We assume no adjustments, so the adjusted trial balance is the same as the unadjusted trial balance.

The journal entries to close the temporary accounts (Revenues, Expenses, and Dividends) are numbered (11), (12) and (13) in the journal. These entries have been posted to the ledger and are also indicated on the worksheet. In Entry (11) the Revenue and Expense accounts are closed to the Income Summary. Entry (12) closes the Income Summary to Retained Earnings, and entry (13) closes Dividends to Retained Earnings.

The income statement comes directly from Journal Entry (11), where the Revenue and Expense accounts are closed to the Income Summary. The statement of retained earnings is simply a statement of the Retained Earnings T-account, and

Figure 3–23   Comprehensive example: general ledger

General Ledger

Asset Accounts

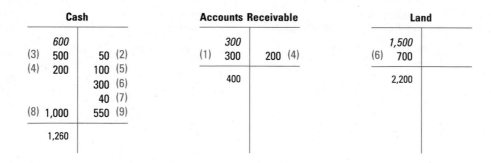

Cash			
	600		
(3)	500	50	(2)
(4)	200	100	(5)
		300	(6)
		40	(7)
(8)	1,000	550	(9)
	1,260		

Accounts Receivable			
	300		
(1)	300	200	(4)
	400		

Land		
	1,500	
(6)	700	
	2,200	

Liability and Stockholders' Equity Accounts

Miscellaneous Payable			
		100	
(2)	50		
		50	

Dividends Payable		
	100	(10)
	100	

Notes Payable			
		400	
(5)	100	400	(6)
		700	

Common Stock			
		1,500	
		1,000	(8)
		2,500	

Retained Earnings			
		400	
		210	(12)
(13)	100		
		510	

Temporary Accounts

Service Revenue			
		300	(1)
		500	(3)
(11)	800		
		0	

Interest Expense			
(7)	40		
		40	(11)
	0		

Salary Expense			
(9)	350		
		350	(11)
	0		

Other Expenses			
(9)	200		
		200	(11)
	0		

Dividends			
(10)	100		
		100	(13)
	0		

Income Summary			
		210	(11)
(12)	210		
	0		

the final trial balance on the worksheet provides the data needed for the balance sheet. The statement of cash flows was prepared by categorizing the entries to the Cash T-account as operating, investing, and financing.

It may be helpful at this point to return to Figure 3–1, the accounting cycle, and attempt to trace each of the sixteen steps in this comprehensive example. Also, make doubly sure that you are comfortable with the construction of journal entries. As this example illustrates, an error in a journal entry carries through the entire accounting cycle and is reflected in the financial statements.

Figure 3–24   Comprehensive example: worksheet

ABC Company
Worksheet
For the Period Ended January 31, 1990

Accounts	Unadjusted Trial Balance Dr.	Cr.	Adjusting Entries Dr.	Cr.	Adjusted Trial Balance Dr.	Cr.	Closing Entries Dr.	Cr.	Final Trial Balance Dr.	Cr.
Assets:										
Cash	1,260				1,260				1,260	
Accounts Receivable	400				400				400	
Land	2,200				2,200				2,200	
Liabilities:										
Misc. Payable		50				50				50
Dividends Payable		100				100				100
Notes Payable		700				700				700
Stockholders' Equity:										
Common Stock		2,500				2,500				2,500
Retained Earnings		400				400	(13) 100	(12) 210		510
Dividends	100				100			(13) 100		
Revenues:										
Service Revenue		800				800	(11) 800			
Expenses:										
Interest Expense	40				40			(11) 40		
Salary Expense	350				350			(11) 350		
Other Expense	200				200			(11) 200		
Income Summary							(12) 210	(11) 210		
Total	4,550	4,550	0	0	4,550	4,550	1,110	1,110	3,860	3,860

Figure 3–25   Comprehensive example: The financial statements

Income Statement (See closing entry (11).)

Service Revenues	$ 800
Salary expense	350
Interest expense	40
Other Expenses	200
Net income	$ 210

Statement of Retained Earnings (See Ret. Earn. T-account.)

Beginning retained earnings balance	$ 400
Plus: Net income	210
Less: Dividends	100
Ending retained earnings balance	$ 510

Balance Sheet (See final balances in asset, liability, and stockholders' equity accounts and final trial balance.)

Assets		Liabilities and Stockholders' Equity	
Cash	$1,260	Miscellaneous payables	$ 50
Accounts receivable	400	Dividends payable	100
Land	2,200	Notes payable	700
		Common stock	2,500
		Retained earnings	510
Total assets	$3,860	Total liabilities and stockholders' equity	$3,860

Figure 3-25   (continued)

Statement of Cash Flows (See Cash T-account.)

Operating activities

Cash collections from services	$ 500	
Cash from receivables	200	
Cash payments on misc. payables	(50)	
Cash payments for interest	(40)	
Cash payments for salaries	(350)	
Cash payments for other expenses	(200)	
Net cash increase (decrease) from operating activities		$ 60

Investing activities

Cash payments for land	(300)	
Net cash increase (decrease) from investing activities		(300)

Financing activities

Cash collections from issuing stock	1,000	
Cash payments on notes payable	(100)	
Net cash increase (decrease) from financing activities		900
Net increase (decrease) in cash balance		$ 660
Beginning cash balance		600
Ending cash balance		$1,260

SUMMARY OF LEARNING OBJECTIVES

1   List the sixteen steps of the accounting cycle.

During the accounting period:

1. Identify relevant and measurable economic events.
2. Interpret relevant and measurable events by identifying accounts affected, direction of effect, and dollar value of effect.
3. Prepare journal entry.
4. Enter journal entry in journal.
5. Post journal entry to ledger.

At the end of the accounting period:

6. Prepare worksheet and unadjusted trial balance.
7. Enter adjusting entries on worksheet.
8. Prepare unadjusted trial balance on worksheet.
9. Enter closing entries on worksheet.
10. Prepare final trial balance on worksheet.
11. Record adjusting and closing entries in journal.
12. Post adjusting and closing entries to ledger.

13. Prepare income statement from journal entry to close Revenue and Expense accounts.

14. Prepare statement of retained earnings from Retained Earnings account in ledger.

15. Prepare balance sheet from final trial balance on worksheet.

16. Prepare statement of cash flows from the Cash account in the ledger.

See Figure 3–1 for a summary of the accounting cycle.

2 State and describe the two criteria necessary for entering an economic event in the accounting cycle.

Economic events must be both relevant and objectively measurable in monetary terms if they are to be entered into the accounting cycle and ultimately reflected on the financial statements. Relevant events have economic significance to the company. Objectively measurable events result from exchange transactions where the dollar value is backed by documented evidence. Economic events must be relevant so that they can be used by investors to evaluate the financial condition of the company; they must be objectively measurable so that they can be audited and viewed as credible by investors.

3 Name the three important components of a transaction and how each is represented in the journal entry.

From a financial accounting standpoint, all transactions have three important components, expressed in the following questions:

1. What assets, liabilities, or stockholder equities are exchanged?
2. Are assets, liabilities, or stockholders' equities increased or decreased?
3. What is the dollar amount of the exchange?

Journal entries are designed to answer each of these questions by showing which financial statement accounts are affected, the direction of the effect (increase or decrease), and the dollar amount of the transaction. The debit, the left side of the journal entry, indicates increases in asset accounts and decreases in liability and stockholders' equity accounts. The credit, the right side of the journal entry, indicates increases in liability and stockholders' equity accounts and decreases in asset accounts. Revenues are credited because they increase Retained Earnings, a stockholders' equity account. Expenses and dividends are debited because they decrease Retained Earnings. See Figure 3–4 for a summary of the structure and meaning of journal entries.

4 Describe how the form of a journal entry reflects the basic accounting equation.

Journal entries are designed to record transactions in a way that maintains the equality of the basic accounting equation: assets = liabilities + stockholders' equity. The debit side of the journal entry is always equal to the credit side. For example, a debit to an asset account is always balanced by a credit to either another asset account or a liability or stockholders' equity account. See Figure 3–5 for examples of how the structure of journal entries maintains the equality of the accounting equation.

5   Describe the roles of the journal, ledger and worksheet in the accounting cycle.

The journal contains a chronological record of the transactions entered into by a company. It is called the *original book of record* because it is where transactions are first recorded.

The ledger contains a running balance for each asset, liability, stockholders' equity, revenue, expense, and dividend account. Immediately after transactions are recorded in the journal, they are posted to the ledger.

The worksheet is divided into a number of columns, which are used to transfer the account balances in the general ledger to the income statement, statement of retained earnings, and balance sheet. It is prepared at the end of each accounting period and contains an unadjusted trial balance, adjustments, an adjusted trial balance, closing entries, and a final trial balance.

6   Explain why the closing process is necessary, and describe the procedures involved.

In the closing process, the end-of-period dollar balances in the temporary (revenue, expense, and dividend) accounts are transferred, or *closed*, to Retained Earnings, a permanent account. Closing is necessary because the dollar balances in the revenue, expense, and dividend accounts must be transferred to Retained Earnings to maintain the equality of the accounting equation. The temporary accounts are thereby zeroed out and begin the subsequent period with a zero balance.

There are four steps to the closing process:

1. An Income Summary account is created.
2. Revenues and Expenses are closed to the Income Summary.
3. The Income Summary account is closed to Retained Earnings.
4. The Dividend account is closed to Retained Earnings.

See Figure 3–15 for an example of the closing process.

7   Explain how the income statement, statement of retained earnings, balance sheet, and statement of cash flows are prepared at the end of the accounting cycle.

The income statement contains Revenue and Expense accounts and, therefore, can be prepared directly from the journal entry to close those accounts to the Income Summary.

The statement of retained earnings can be prepared directly from the Retained Earnings account in the ledger. The beginning Retained Earnings balance is the ending balance of the previous period. The net income (loss) number comes from the journal entry to close the Income Summary to Retained Earnings. The dividend number comes from the entry to close Dividends to Retained Earnings.

The balance sheet consists of assets, liabilities, and stockholders' equity accounts and can be prepared directly from the final trial balance on the worksheet, which contains the end-of-period balances for all the permanent accounts. These balances also appear in the ledger.

The statement of cash flows can be prepared from the entries recorded in the Cash account in the ledger. The cash inflows and outflows during the period are categorized as operating, investing, or financing on the statement of cash flows.

A P P E N D I X   3 A

Special-Purpose Journals and Subsidiary Ledgers

Chapter 3 states that all transactions are entered into the journal, the original book of record and describes the accounting cycle as though only one journal existed for all transactions. In practice, companies typically group common transactions into separate categories and record them in **special-purpose journals.** A large percentage of the business transactions of most companies, for example, fall into one of four categories: (1) sales on account, (2) inventory purchases on account, (3) receipts of cash, and (4) disbursements of cash. Special-purpose journals are often kept for these four kinds of transactions. A fifth journal, the *general journal,* is used to record transactions that do not fall into any of the special categories.

Most of the discussion devoted to the ledger in Chapter 3 referred only to the general ledger. We described it as containing one T-account for each of the accounts that appear on the financial statements. Many companies, however, also use subsidiary ledgers. These ledgers tie directly to certain accounts in the general ledger, called *control accounts,* and are designed to provide further breakdowns of the balances in those general ledger accounts.

For example, the balance in the Accounts Receivable general ledger account usually represents a number of individual customer accounts. If management wants more information than is provided by the overall Accounts Receivable balance, subsidiary ledger accounts, which keep track of each customer's outstanding balance, can be maintained. The total dollar amount of the subsidiary accounts equals the overall dollar balance in the Accounts Receivable general ledger account.

It is possible to use a subsidiary ledger for almost any account in the general ledger for which management wants to set up specific accounts to record individual balances. In addition to Accounts Receivable, subsidiary ledgers are frequently used for Accounts Payable, Notes Receivable, Marketable Securities, and Equipment.

THE SALES JOURNAL AND RELATED LEDGER ACCOUNTS

The sales journal is a special-purpose journal specifically designed to keep a record of credit sales. Figure 3A–1 illustrates a sales journal and the related general and subsidiary ledger accounts. Three sales transactions involving two customers during the month of January have been recorded.

Note that each credit sale is entered in the sales journal and posted to the individual customer accounts in the subsidiary ledger at the time of the sale. Periodically, the dollar balance in the sales journal is computed and posted to the Accounts Receivable and Sales accounts in the general ledger. The total Accounts Receivable balance in the general ledger should be equal to the summed balances of the accounts in the accounts receivable subsidiary ledger.

Figure 3A–1 The sales journal and related subsidiary and general ledger accounts

Sales Journal				Page 4
Date	**Account Debited**	**Invoice Number**	**Post. Ref.**	**Amount**
Aug. 4	Hitzel Company	211	✓	400
9	ABC services	212	✓	700
15	Hitzel Company	213	✓	1,600
				2,700
				(113/411)

} Post daily to subsidiary ledger accounts.
} Post monthly total to general ledger accounts.

Accounts Receivable Subsidiary Ledger

ABC Services

Date	Post. Ref.	Debit	Credit	Balance
Aug. 9	S4	700		700

Hitzel Company

Date	Post. Ref.	Debit	Credit	Balance
Aug. 4	S4	400		400
15	S4	1,600		2,000

General Ledger

Accounts Receivable — 113

Date	Post. Ref.	Debit	Credit	Balance Debit	Balance Credit
Aug. 31	S4	2,700		2,700	

Sales — 411

Date	Post. Ref.	Debit	Credit	Balance Debit	Balance Credit
Aug. 31	S4		2,700		2,700

THE PURCHASE JOURNAL AND RELATED LEDGER ACCOUNTS

The purchase journal is specifically designed to keep a record of inventory purchases made on credit. It is maintained in exactly the same way as the sales journal, except that Purchases and Accounts Payable are involved instead of Sales and Accounts Receivable. Figure 3A–2 illustrates the relationships among the purchase journal, the Accounts Payable and Purchases control accounts, and the accounts payable subsidiary ledger.

THE CASH RECEIPTS JOURNAL AND RELATED LEDGER ACCOUNTS

The cash receipts journal is designed specifically to keep a record of cash receipts. Because cash receipts result from a number of different transactions, the cash receipts journal ties directly to a number of general and subsidiary ledger accounts.

Figure 3A–2 The purchase journal and related subsidiary and general ledger accounts

Purchase Journal					Page 5
Date		**Account Debited**	**Post. Ref.**	**Invoice Date**	**Amount**
Sept.	3	Acme Suppliers	✓	9/2	350
	20	Reynolds and Co.	✓	9/20	500
	25	Acme Suppliers	✓	9/23	650
					1,500
					(512/211)

Post daily to subsidiary ledger accounts.

Post monthly total to general ledger accounts.

Accounts Payable Subsidiary Ledger

Acme Suppliers

Date		Post. Ref.	Debit	Credit	Balance
Sept.	3	P5		350	350
	25	P5		650	1,000

Reynolds and Co.

Date		Post. Ref.	Debit	Credit	Balance
Sept.	20	P5		500	500

General Ledger

Accounts Payable 211

Date		Post. Ref.	Debit	Credit	Balance Debit	Balance Credit
Sept.	30	P5		1,500		1,500

Purchases 512

Date		Post. Ref.	Debit	Credit	Balance Debit	Balance Credit
Sept.	30	P5	1,500		1,500	

For example, cash receipts may result from cash sales, accounts receivable receipts, sales of marketable securities, borrowings, and equity issuances. Consequently, the cash receipts journal ties directly to the Cash, Sales, Accounts Receivable, Marketable Securities, Notes Payable, and Common Stock accounts in the general ledger as well as the accounts receivable subsidiary ledger accounts. The relationships among the cash receipts journal, several general ledger accounts and the accounts receivable subsidiary accounts are illustrated in Figure 3A–3. The following four transactions have been recorded.

Date	Description
January 5	Common stock is issued for $10,000 cash.
January 12	Cash sales of $4000 are recorded.
January 23	Five hundred dollars is received from Mr. Jones, a customer.
January 30	Marketable securities costing $1000 are sold for $1000.

Figure 3A–3 The cash receipts journal and related subsidiary and general ledger accounts

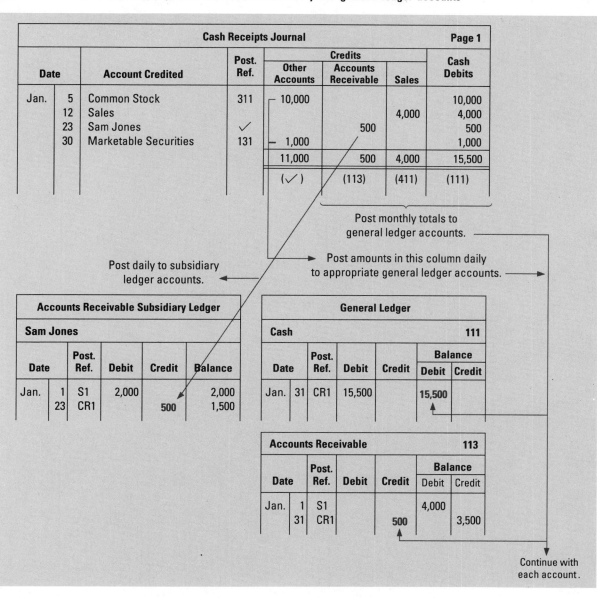

Note that the cash receipts journal contains a debit column for cash receipts and credit columns for Sales, Accounts Receivable and other accounts. The debit column ties to the Cash account in the general ledger, and the credit columns tie to Sales, Accounts Receivable and the remaining (other) ledger accounts. The transactions affecting the accounts receivable subsidiary ledger and the other general ledger accounts are posted daily. The totals in the Cash, Accounts Receivable, and credit columns are posted in the general ledger monthly.

Figure 3A–4   The cash disbursements journal and related subsidiary and general ledger accounts

THE CASH DISBURSEMENTS JOURNAL
AND RELATED LEDGER ACCOUNTS

The cash disbursements journal is designed to keep a record of cash payments. It is designed much like the cash receipts journal, except that it ties directly to the ledger accounts related to cash payments (e.g., Purchases, Wage Expense, Equipment) instead of the accounts related to cash receipts (e.g., Receivables and Sales). The credit column lists the cash payments and ties directly to the cash account in the general ledger. The debit column is divided between Accounts Payable and other accounts and ties directly to the related general ledger and subsidiary accounts. Cash payment transactions affecting the accounts payable subsidiary ledger and the other general ledger accounts are posted daily, while the cash (credits) and Accounts Payable totals are posted monthly. A cash disbursements journal is illustrated in Figure 3A−4, which shows the following three transactions.

Date	Description
January 14	Inventory is purchased for $500 cash.
January 26	Cash payments for previously purchased merchandise in the amount of $200 are sent to Harrison Supply.
January 27	Wages are paid in the amount of $800.

SUMMARY OF LEARNING OBJECTIVE

8   Describe the nature and function of special-purpose journals and subsidiary ledgers.

Companies typically group common transactions into special categories and record them in special-purpose journals. Such journals are often kept for credit sales, inventory purchases on account, cash receipts, and cash disbursements. Organizing transactions in this way allows companies to maintain better control over the activities in these accounts.

    The general ledger consists of an account for each item in the balance sheet, income statement, and statement of retained earnings. Subsidiary ledger accounts tie directly into a particular general ledger account and explain more completely the individual balances that make up that account. The balance in the accounts receivable general ledger account, for example, usually represents a number of individual accounts that are maintained as subsidiary ledger accounts.

A P P E N D I X   3 B

The Importance and Characteristics of Effective Internal Control

An **internal control system** consists of procedures and records designed to ensure that (1) a company's assets are adequately protected from loss or misappropriation, and (2) all relevant and measurable economic events are accurately reflected on its financial statements. Effective internal control is obviously very important to all companies, and financial reports often emphasize the quality of a company's internal control system. The excerpt following, taken from the Management Letter in IBM's 1987 financial report, is representative of such concerns.

IBM maintains an effective system of internal accounting control. It consists, in part, of organizational arrangements with clearly defined lines of responsibility and delegation of authority. We believe this system provides reasonable assurance that transactions are executed in accordance with management authorization, and that they are appropriately recorded, in order to permit preparation of financial statements in conformity with generally accepted accounting principles and to adequately safeguard, verify and maintain accountability of assets. An important element of the system is an ongoing internal audit program.

To assure the effective administration of internal control, we carefully select and train our employees, develop and disseminate written policies and procedures, provide appropriate communication channels, and foster an environment conducive to the effective functioning of controls. We continue to believe that it is essential for the company to conduct its business affairs in accordance with the highest ethical standards, as set forth in the IBM Business Conduct Guidelines. These guidelines, translated into numerous languages, are distributed to employees throughout the world, and reemphasized through internal programs to assure that they are understood and followed.

In 1977, Congress emphasized the importance of internal control when it passed the Foreign Corrupt Practices Act, which requires that companies have sufficient internal controls to ensure that their accounting records accurately and fairly represent their financial activities. The primary goal of this Act was to discourage U.S. companies from making improper payments (bribes) to overseas officials, and Congress reasoned that improving internal controls would be one way for companies to discover and control such payments.

GENERAL PRINCIPLES OF EFFECTIVE INTERNAL CONTROL

While the specific procedures for implementing internal control vary from one company to the next, all effective control systems have the following general characteristics in common.

1. **Competent and trustworthy employees.** Internal control systems can be no better than the people who implement them. Employees must be both efficient and honest because they execute the tasks required by the system and are often entrusted with company assets. High ethical standards are important.

2. **Clearly defined authority and responsibility.** Specific individuals should be given the authority to perform important tasks and be held responsible for their efficient execution. They should be evaluated on their performance and rewarded accordingly. Clear lines of authority and responsibility often motivate employees and help to identify when and where to take corrective action.

3. **Segregation of duties.** Record keeping should be separated from the administration of operations, transactions, and assets. Accounting for transactions should be done by employees who are not administrators. The same employee, for example, should not be responsible for both receiving the cash from sales and recording the sales in the books. A dishonest employee could simply keep some of the cash and adjust the records so that it was never missed. Good internal control would designate one employee to receive the cash and another to record the sale. Separation of duties reduces the likelihood of unintentional

recordkeeping errors, makes it harder for employees to execute misappropriations, and increases the likelihood that any misappropriations will be discovered.

4. **Sufficient records and documentation.** It is important that all exchanges, both within a company and between a company and outside parties, be recorded and backed by adequate documentation, such as cancelled checks, purchase orders, requisition forms, and receipts. Documentation not only provides the basis for preparing the financial statements but also underlies the reports designed to control and evaluate a company's internal operations.

5. **Physical control of assets and records.** The company's assets and records must be safe from theft, unauthorized tampering, and physical destruction. Fireproof vaults, safe deposit boxes, locked storage facilities, and duplicate copies can help to provide such protection.

AN EXAMPLE OF INTERNAL CONTROL

As you read the following example, note where the characteristics of effective internal control are evident. Companies that make frequent cash sales often use an electronic system to ensure that (1) all sales are recorded accurately, (2) cash payments are for the correct amount, and (3) cash payments are received by the company and not retained by an employee.

Consider a movie theater where cash is collected at the entrance for a ticket, with the price printed on it. In most modern theaters, when the customer pays, the employee at the ticket booth activates a machine that releases a ticket and also records the correct dollar amount of the sale. This dollar amount should correspond to the cash received by the employee. Periodically, the cash should be moved to a safe, or taken to a bank, and the amount of cash should be reconciled with the dollar sales recorded by the ticket machine. The employee is normally held responsible for discrepancies between the amount of cash collected and the amount of sales registered in the ticket machine.

This internal control system helps ensure that all sales are recorded accurately because the ticket machine releases a ticket only as a sale is being recorded. Customer cash payments should be correct because the amount of cash received should match the price written on the ticket, which is recorded in the machine. The theater can be reasonably sure that cash receipts are not retained by employees because they must account for differences between the total cash received and the sales registered in the machine.

BENEFITS AND COSTS OF INTERNAL CONTROL

Effective internal control not only safeguards assets and ensures that financial statements are prepared in accordance with generally accepted accounting principles, it characterizes well-run corporations. As noted in *Forbes*, effective internal control systems "do far more than keep employees honest. Tight accounting is essential to good management. When Osborne Computers filed [for bankruptcy] in September of 1983, for example, it became clear that corporate officers had little idea where their inventories were. Similar stories swirled around Texas Instruments [in 1983], when it reported big sudden losses involving its home computer business."[3]

While many business failings can be attributed to weak internal controls, it is also true that implementing and maintaining effective controls can be expensive. Many corporations, for example, realize that spending $1 million on a system to keep track of $500,000 worth of inventory makes little economic sense. Furthermore, companies are also concerned that tight internal control may constrain managerial talent. *Forbes* reports, for example, that "at General Electric managers are wary of controlling executives to the point where they can't get anything done . . . controls must be tight enough to keep the crooks out, but loose enough to encourage creativity. Such balancing is difficult."[4]

SUMMARY OF LEARNING OBJECTIVE

9   Describe the nature and importance of internal control, and list the five principles of effective internal control.

An internal control system consists of procedures and records designed to ensure that (1) a company's assets are adequately protected from loss or misappropriation, and (2) all relevant and measurable economic events are accurately reflected on its financial statements. Effective internal control is important because errors can be made in implementing the accounting cycle, and the company's assets must be safeguarded from loss or theft. It is also a prerequisite for effective management. Implementing internal controls, however, can be costly and may restrict management's talents and creativity. There are five principles of effective internal control:

1. Competent and trustworthy employees.
2. Clearly defined authority and responsibility.
3. Segregation of duties.
4. Sufficient records and documentation.
5. Physical control of assets and records.

KEY TERMS

Accounting cycle (p. 96)   Double entry system (p. 103)
Accounting period (p. 110)   Economic event (p. 98)
Adjusted trial balance (p. 114)   Final trial balance (p. 118)
Batch processing system (p. 124)   General journal (p. 105)
Closing entries (p. 116)   General ledger (p. 108)
Compound journal entry (p. 102)   Income summary (p. 116)
Credit (p. 102)   Internal control system (p. 137)
Debit (p. 102)   Journal (p. 105)

---

3. Richard Greene, "Internal Bleeding," *Forbes*, 1984 February 27, pp. 121–122.
4. Ibid.,

QUESTIONS FOR DISCUSSION AND REVIEW

1. List the sixteen steps of the accounting cycle. Why is it so important that journal entries be recorded correctly?

2. Distinguish the journal from the ledger. Why is the ledger referred to as a *scoreboard?*

3. What is an economic event? What two criteria must be met before an economic event can be recorded in the journal?

4. Define objectivity as it is defined in the chapter. What kind of economic events meet this definition of objectivity? What economic forces combine to ensure that accounting statements reflect only objective information?

5. Interpreting a recordable economic event (ie., an exchange transaction) consists of answering three questions. What are they? Assume that a company issued 1000 shares of capital stock for $10 cash per share. Answer the three questions for this particular transaction.

6. Assume that a company purchases a piece of equipment for $5000. What accounts are affected? What is the direction of the effect? What is the dollar value of the transaction? How do the answers to these three questions provide the information necessary for a journal entry? Convert this transaction to a journal entry.

7. Refer to Figure 3–4, the journal entry box, and prepare journal entries for the following transactions: (1) purchase of machinery for $5000 cash, (2) payment of $500 cash for an outstanding account payable, (3) completion of a service billed for $300, and (4) payment of $800 cash wages.

8. Show how each of the four transactions in (7) above affect the basic accounting equation, assets = liabilities + stockholders' equity. What stockholders' equity account does the completion of a service and the payment of cash wages affect? How do these four transactions affect the income statement and balance sheet?

9. Explain why ledgers contain accounts in the form of a T. How do T-accounts relate to journal entries? Why are T-accounts useful? Many of the general ledger accounts are comprised of subsidiary ledgers. Provide an example.

10. Explain the function of a worksheet. Is it an official book of record like the journal? Why or why not?

11. What is placed in the first two columns of the worksheet following the account names? From where do these balances come?

12. Where do adjusting journal entries come in the accounting cycle? Adding the adjusting entries to the unadjusted trial balance gives rise to what?

13. Distinguish temporary accounts from permanent accounts. There are six basic categories of accounts: assets, liabilities, stockholders' equities, revenues, expenses, and dividends. Which are temporary and which are permanent? Of what use is such a distinction?

14. Describe the closing process and list its four basic steps.

15. Is the Income Summary a temporary or permanent account? What role does it play in the closing process?

16. Why is the Dividend account closed directly to the Retained Earnings account instead of through the Income Summary account?

17. Is it possible for the Retained Earnings account to have a negative (debit) balance? What conditions could give rise to such a result?

18. In general terms, describe how the balance sheet is related to the income statement. Give several journal entries to illustrate this relationship, and demonstrate it through the closing process. What is the role of the Retained Earnings account in this relationship?

19. In terms of the accounting cycle, where can one find the numbers to be placed on the income statement, the statement of retained earnings, the balance sheet, and the statement of cash flows?

20. What is a computerized accounting system and how does it differ from a manual accounting system?

21. Explain the difference between computer hardware and software and describe how each is involved in the input, processing, and output of a computerized accounting system.

22. Explain the difference between a batch processing system and a real-time system. Many grocery chains are currently using bar code sensors at the check-out counter. Does this indicate a batch processing or real-time system?

23. (Appendix 3A) What is a special-purpose journal? How do special-purpose journals differ from the general journal? Name four special-purpose journals.

24. (Appendix 3A) What is the purpose of a subsidiary ledger, and how do such ledgers relate to the general ledger control accounts?

25. (Appendix 3A) Assume that Acme Co. uses a cash receipts journal and keeps subsidiary ledgers for all its customers. On January 19, 1991 Acme received $500 cash from Billy Brooks for merchandise purchased previously. Explain how this transaction would be recorded in Acme's records.

26. (Appendix 3B) What is internal control, and how does it relate to the accounting cycle? List and describe the five principles of effective internal control.

27. (Appendix 3B) Why would a company's board of directors be interested in its internal control system?

28. (Appendix 3B) Why would a company's auditors be interested in its internal control system?

29. (Appendix 3B) Why would a company's management be interested in its internal control system?

30. (Appendix 3B) What is the role of ethics in internal control?

EXERCISES

E3–1

(The effects of debiting or crediting accounts)   Indicate the effect (increase or decrease) of debiting and crediting each of the following accounts.

Account	Debit	Credit
Cash		
Fees Earned		
Notes Payable		
Common Stock		
Interest Expense		
Office Equipment		

Account	Debit	Credit
Unearned Rent Revenue		
Interest Payable		
Prepaid Rent		
Insurance Expense		
Rent Revenue		
Accounts Receivable		
Inventory		
Interest Receivable		
Dividends		

E3-2

(Normal account balances and financial statements) Indicate whether the following accounts normally have debit or credit balances and on which financial statement (income statement, statement of retained earnings, or balance sheet) each account appears.

Account	Debit	Credit	Financial Statement
Sales Revenue			
Cash			
Dividends Payable			
Retained Earnings			
Depreciation Expense			
Deferred Revenues			
Inventory			
Equipment			
Common Stock			
Marketable Securities			
Fees Earned			
Wage Expense			
Cost of Goods Sold			
Dividends			
Accounts Receivable			
Accounts Payable			
Patent			
Interest Expense			
Rent Revenue			

E3-3

(Which economic events are relevant and objectively measurable?) The Brown Corporation experienced the following financial events on October 10, 1990.

(1) The company entered into a new contract with the employees' union that calls for a $2.00 hour increase in wages, a longer lunch break, and cost-of-living adjustments, effective January 1, 1991.

(2) The company issued $200,000 in bonds that mature on October 10, 2000. The terms of the bond issuance stipulate that interest is to be paid semiannually at an annual rate of 10 percent.

(3) The company president retired and was replaced by the vice-president of finance.

(4) The company received $10,000 from a customer in settlement of an open account receivable.

(5) The company paid $1000 interest on an outstanding loan. The interest is applicable to September 1990 and is included on the books as a liability "Accrued Interest Payable".

(6) The market value of all the company's long-lived assets is $275,000. They are currently reported on the balance sheet at $250,000.

(7) The company purchased a fire insurance policy for $1500 that will pay the Brown Corporation $1,000,000 if its primary production plant is destroyed. The policy ensures the company from November 1, 1990 through October 31, 1991.

(8) The company placed an order to have $10,000 of inventory shipped on October 17, 1990.

Required: Indicate whether each of these economic events has accounting significance (i.e., would the company prepare a journal entry for the event?). In each case explain why or why not.

E3–4   *(Interpreting economic events and preparing journal entries)*   Hathaway, Inc. entered into the following transactions during 1990. Unless otherwise noted, transactions involve cash.

(1) Purchased equipment at a cost of $10,000.
(2) Purchased marketable securities for $2500.
(3) Provided services for $800, receiving $300 in cash.
(4) Issued 2000 shares of common stock for $20 per share.
(5) Collected $200 owed by its customers.
(6) Incurred and paid wages of $700.
(7) Paid $1000 on an outstanding note payable: $800 on interest and $200 on principal.
(8) Declared, but did not pay, a $700 dividend. The dividend becomes a liability at the date of declaration.

Required:

a. For each transaction, answer the following questions:
   1. What accounts are affected?
   2. What is the direction (increase or decrease) of the effect?
   3. What is the dollar value of the transaction?
b. Prepare journal entries for each of the transactions.

E3–5   *(Trial balance and the financial statements)*   The following accounts and balances were taken from the ledger of Pratt Printing Company.

Equipment	$30,000
Fees Earned	35,000
Retained Earnings	10,000
Notes Payable	24,000
Interest Expense	2,000
Accounts Receivable	32,000
Dividends	4,000
Prepaid Expenses	9,000
Accounts Payable	15,000
Common Stock	20,000
Advertising Expense	10,000
Other Revenues	8,000
Marketable Securities	10,000
Miscellaneous Expenses	15,000

Required:

a. Prepare a trial balance in proper form. Assume that all accounts have normal balances.
b. Prepare an income statement, statement of retained earnings, and balance sheet.

E3–6   *(Effects of transactions on the accounting cycle)*   M&T Enterprises was involved in the following transactions during the current year. Unless otherwise noted, all transactions involve cash.

(1) Issued 1000 shares of stock for $50 per share.
(2) Borrowed $5000 from a bank in exchange for a long-term note payable.

(3) Purchased equipment for cash.

(4) Purchased equipment in exchange for a long-term note.

(5) Provided services for $3000 cash.

(6) Paid miscellaneous expenses of $2000.

(7) Paid some of the principal on the loan established in (2) above.

(8) Declared and paid cash dividends.

(9) Received cash on outstanding accounts receivable.

(10) Received $500 cash interest payments on outstanding notes receivable.

(11) Paid $800 cash for interest on outstanding notes payable.

Required:

a. In a table like the one shown, enter debits and credits in the appropriate columns for each transaction. The first transaction has been done as an example.

Transaction	Assets	=	Liabilities	+	Stockholders' Equity
Issue stock	Debit				Credit

b. For the transactions that affect the stockholders' equity section, complete a table like the following by indicating whether the account is a debit or a credit. The first transaction has been done as an example.

Transaction	Common stock	+	Retained earnings	+	Revenues	−	Expenses	−	Dividends
Issue stock	Credit								

E3–7   *(Preparing a statement of cash flows from the cash ledger)*   The following Cash T-account summarizes all the transactions affecting cash during 1990 for Miller Manufacturing.

Cash

Beginning Balance	10,000	Equipment Purchases	25,000
Sales of Services	40,000	Rent Payable Payments	9,000
Receivables Collections	50,000	Bank Loan Principal	10,000
Sale of Land	7,500	Loan Interest	3,000
Issuance of Common Stock	15,000	Salaries	27,500
Long-term borrowings	10,000	Dividend Payments	4,000
		Miscellaneous Expenses	14,000
		Long-Term Investment Purchases	12,000

Required:

a. Compute the ending cash balance.

b. Prepare a statement of cash flows.

E3–8   *(Relationships among financial statements across three years)*   The following data pertain to St. Clair industries. Assuming 1989 was the first year of operations, compute the missing amounts.

	1991	1990	1989
As of December 31			
Assets	$1,100,000	?	$700,000
Liabilities	120,000	$150,000	?
Common stock	?	280,000	200,000
Retained earnings	700,000	675,000	?

	1991	1990	1989
During the year			
Revenues	900,000	850,000	900,000
Expenses	475,000	?	450,000
Dividends	?	75,000	75,000

E3–9   *(Preparing closing entries from a worksheet)*   Zachary Harris, the controller of Trump, Inc., has supplied you with the following adjusted trial balance as of December 31, 1990. Prepare the necessary closing entries for 1990.

	Debit	Credit
Cash	$ 100,000	
Accounts Receivable	200,000	
Inventory	200,000	
Prepaid Insurance	35,000	
Supplies Inventory	95,000	
Equipment	575,000	
Accumulated Depreciation		$ 100,000
Accounts Payable		100,000
Notes Payable		250,000
Common Stock		300,000
Retained Earnings		505,000
Dividends	100,000	
Sales		450,000
Rent Revenue		30,000
Cost of Goods Sold	200,000	
Depreciation Expense	25,000	
Insurance Expense	80,000	
Wage Expense	125,000	
	$1,735,000	$1,735,000

E3–10   *(Closing entries and the statement of retained earnings)*   The following entries appear in the journal of Lake Forest Real Estate during 1990.

(1)	Accounts Receivable	350	
	Cash	200	
	Fees Earned		550
(2)	Equipment	7000	
	Note Payable		2000
	Cash		5000
(3)	Interest Expense	70	
	Cash		70
(4)	Dividends	800	
	Dividends Payable		800
(5)	Commission Expense	450	
	Cash		450
(6)	Cash	900	
	Rent Revenue		900
(7)	Advertising Expense	300	
	Cash		300
(8)	Cash	3000	
	Common Stock		3000

Required:

a. Prepare a set of closing journal entries for the transactions above.

b. Assume that the beginning balance in retained earnings is $4000, and prepare a statement of retained earnings as of December 31, 1990.

E3–11

(Preparing a statement of cash flows from journal entries)   Butler and Associates, a small manufacturing firm, entered into the following cash transactions during January of 1990.

(1) Issued 500 shares of stock for $20 each.

(2) Sold services for $2400.

(3) Paid wages of $500.

(4) Purchased land as a long-term investment for $8000 cash.

(5) Paid a $5000 dividend.

(6) Sold a piece of equipment with a book value of $3000 for $3000 cash. The equipment had no accumulated depreciation.

(7) Paid $1500 to the bank: $900 to reduce the principal on an outstanding loan and $600 as an interest payment.

(8) Paid miscellaneous expenses of $1400.

Required:

a. Prepare journal entries for each transaction.

b. Prepare a cash ledger, and compute Butler's cash balance as of the end of January. Assume a beginning balance of $5000. (Use T-account format.)

c. Prepare a statement of cash flows for the month of January.

E3–12

(Effects of transactions on the accounting equation)   The following summary balance sheet is available for J & S Corporation on December 31, 1990.

Total assets	$750,000	Total liabilities	$205,000
		Common stock	300,000
		Retained earnings	245,000

J & S Corporation entered into the following transactions during 1991.

(1) Provided consulting services for $150,000.

(2) Collected $88,000 from customers on account.

(3) Paid miscellaneous expenses of $55,000.

(4) Incurred interest charges of $10,000, which were paid in cash.

(5) Declared and paid dividends of $8000.

(6) Purchased machinery for $175,000 on December 31, 1991. Paid $100,000 cash and signed a long-term note payable for the remainder.

(7) Incurred $30,000 in salary and wage expense during the year: $25,000 was paid in cash and $5000 is still owed as of December 31, 1991.

Required:

a. Prepare a sheet of paper with seven columns and label them with the following headings, which represent terms in the accounting equation.

  Assets = Liabilities + Common stock + Retained Earnings + Revenues − Expenses − Dividends

b. Record beginning balances in the appropriate columns on the sheet.

c. For each transaction indicate on the sheet its effect on the accounting equation. Subtotal the columns after each transaction to ensure that the equation is in balance.

d. Compute net income for 1991.

e. Compute retained earnings on December 31, 1991 after closing entries have been recorded.

PROBLEMS

P3-1   *(Accounts, debits, credits, and the financial statements)*   For each of the accounts below indicate the following:

a. Whether the account normally has a debit or a credit balance
b. Whether the account appears on the balance sheet as an asset, liability or stockholders' equity account, or on the income statement as a revenue or an expense
c. Whether a debit to the account increases or decreases the account balance

(1) Cash	(6) Sales
(2) Marketable Securities	(7) Prepaid Rent
(3) Deferred Rent Revenue	(8) Bonds Payable
(4) Common Stock	(9) Retained Earnings
(5) Office Equipment	(10) Accounts Receivable

P3-2   *(Preparing journal entries and identifying accounts to be closed)*   Below are several transactions entered into by Vulcan Metal Corporation during 1991. Unless otherwise noted, all transactions involve cash.

(1) Purchased equipment for $200,000.
(2) Paid employees $25,000 in wages.
(3) Collected $25,000 from customers as payments on open accounts.
(4) Provided services for $24,000: $15,000 received in cash and the remainder on open account.
(5) Paid $45,000 on an outstanding note payable: $8000 for interest and $37,000 to reduce the principal.
(6) Purchased a one-month ad in the local newspaper for $5000.
(7) Purchased a building valued at $250,000 in exchange for $100,000 cash and a long-term note payable.

Required:

a. Prepare journal entries for each transaction.
b. Indicate which accounts would have to be closed at the end of 1990.

P3-3   *(Preparing journal entries from the ledger)*   The following T-accounts reflect seven different transactions that Cummings Container Company entered into during 1990. For each transaction, prepare a journal entry including a description of the transaction.

Cash			Accounts Receivable			Rent Expense	
(a) 5,000	(c) 2,000		(a) 20,000	(f) 6,000		(e) 1,000	
(f) 6,000	(d) 20,000						
(g) 18,000	(e) 1,000						

Accounts Payable			Inventory			Sales Revenue	
(c) 2,000	(b) 10,000		(b) 10,000				(a) 25,000

Equipment	Notes Payable	Common Stock
(d) 50,000	(d) 30,000	(g) 18,000

P3–4

(Preparing the four financial statements) The December 31, 1990 balance sheet for Alexander Baseball Scouting is summarized below.

Assets		Liabilities and Stockholders' Equity	
Cash	$ 5,000	Liabilities	$ 4,000
Receivables	7,000	Common stock	10,000
Long-term assets	10,000	Retained earnings	8,000
		Total liabilities and	
Total assets	$22,000	stockholders' equity	$22,000

During January of 1991 the following transactions were entered into:

(1) Services were performed for $5000 cash.

(2) $2000 cash was received from customers on outstanding accounts receivable.

(3) $1000 cash was paid for outstanding liabilities.

(4) Long-term assets were purchased in exchange for a $5000 note payable.

(5) Expenses of $3000 were paid in cash.

(6) A dividend of $500 was issued to the owners.

Required:

a. Describe the effect of each transaction on the basic accounting equation.

b. For each transaction indicate: (1) the accounts affected, (2) whether each account is increased or decreased, and (3) the dollar value of the increase or decrease.

c. Provide a journal entry for each transaction.

d. Provide the closing journal entries required if financial statements are prepared at the end of January.

e. Prepare the income statement, statement of retained earnings, and statement of cash flows for January and the January 31 balance sheet.

P3–5

(T-accounts and closing entries from the worksheet) The preclosing (adjusted) trial balance of Irish Enterprises as of December 31, 1990 is as follows:

	Debits	Credits
Cash	$ 25,000	
Accounts Receivable	112,000	
Inventory	88,000	
Plant and Equipment	249,000	
Accounts Payable		$ 51,000
Notes Payable		100,000
Common Stock		200,000
Retained Earnings		148,000
Dividends	8,000	
Fees Earned		75,000
Wage and Salary Expense	50,000	
Rent Expense	12,000	
Other Expenses	30,000	
Total	$574,000	$574,000

Required:

a. Establish T-accounts for Retained Earnings, Income Summary, and all temporary accounts
b. Enter all preclosing account balances for these accounts.
c. Prepare all necessary closing journal entries.
d. Post the closing entries to the T-accounts.
e. Compute the ending balance in the Retained Earnings account.

P3-6   *(Journal entries and preparing the four financial statements)*   Earl Rix, controller of Rix, Inc., provides you with the following information concerning Rix during 1990. (Rix, Inc. began operations on January 1, 1990.)

(1) Issued 1000 shares of common stock at $100 per share.
(2) Paid $3000 per month to rent office and warehouse space. The rent was paid on the last day of each month.
(3) Made total sales for services of $190,000: $40,000 for cash and $150,000 on account.
(4) Purchased land for $35,000.
(5) Borrowed $75,000 on December 31. The note payable matures in two years.
(6) Salaries totaling $90,000 were paid during the year.
(7) Other expenses totaling $35,000 were paid during the year.
(8) $60,000 was received from customers as payment on account.
(9) Declared and paid a dividend of $20,000.

Required:

a. Prepare journal entries for these transactions.
b. Establish T-accounts for each account, and post the journal entries to those T-accounts.
c. Prepare closing journal entries, and post the closing entries to the T-accounts.
d. Prepare an income statement, statement of retained earnings, and statement of cash flows for 1990 and a December 31, 1990 balance sheet.

P3-7   *(Preparing a trial balance and closing entries from the financial statements)*   The balance sheet, income statement, and statement of retained earnings for Ed Hauser Consulting are provided below.

Balance Sheet (December 31, 1990)

Assets		Liabilities and Stockholders' equity	
Cash	10,000	Accounts payable	3,000
Accounts receivable	12,000	Wages payable	4,000
Land	5,000	Notes payable	15,000
Equipment	20,000	Common stock	20,000
		Retained earnings	5,000
		Total liabilities and	
Total assets	$47,000	stockholders' equity	$47,000

Income Statement 1990		Statement of Retained Earnings 1990	
Fees earned	$45,000	Beginning balance	$ 5,000
Selling expenses	25,000	Plus: Net Income	2,000
Administrative expenses	18,000	Less: Dividends	2,000
Net income	$ 2,000	Ending balance	$ 5,000

Required:

a. Prepare the adjusted trial balance that was used to prepare these financial statements.
b. Prepare the closing journal entries that were used to prepare these financial statements.

P3-8

(Preparing journal entries and the financial statements)   Refer to P3-7 and assume that Ed Hauser entered into the following transactions during the month of January, 1991.

(1) Paid the wages that were owed as of December 31.

(2) Provided consulting services, receiving in return $10,000 cash and $3000 in accounts receivable.

(3) Paid additional wages of $3000 (considered selling expenses).

(4) Received $6000 from customers.

(5) Paid $5000 to the bank on the note payable: $1000 in interest and $4000 on the principal.

(6) Sold the land for $5000.

(7) Paid the accounts payable outstanding as of December 31, 1990.

(8) Purchased equipment in exchange for a $3000 note payable.

(9) Paid administrative expenses of $3500.

(10) Declared, but did not pay, a $1000 dividend.

Required:

a. Prepare journal entries for each transaction.

b. Prepare a T-account for each account on the financial statements. Post the January transactions to the T-accounts.

c. Prepare a trial balance as of the end of January.

d. Prepare closing journal entries. Post the entries to the T-accounts.

e. Prepare a final trial balance.

f. Prepare the income statement, statement of retained earnings, and statement of cash flows for the month of January.

g. Prepare the balance sheet as of January 31, 1991.

P3-9

(Completing the worksheet)   The following adjusted trial balance was taken from the records of Ness Construction. Prepare and complete the worksheet.

	Debits	Credits
Cash	23,000	
Accounts Receivable	14,000	
Inventory	9,000	
Prepaid Expenses	2,000	
Long-Term Investments	15,000	
Machinery	35,000	
Buildings	54,000	
Accounts Payable		25,000
Interest Payable		4,000
Wages Payable		5,000
Short-Term Notes Payable		32,000
Long-Term Notes Payable		25,000
Common Stock		55,000
Retained Earnings		18,000
Sales		85,000
Cost of Goods Sold	35,000	
Wage Expense	22,000	
Advertising Expense	5,000	
Insurance Expense	4,000	
Miscellaneous Expenses	24,000	
Dividends	7,000	
Total	$249,000	$249,000

P3–10

(Journalizing economic events and preparing the financial statements)   Powell Rafting Company began operations on January 1, 1989. Listed below is a summary of events experienced by Powell Rafting during 1989.

(1) The company issued 10,000 shares of common stock for $50 per share.

(2) The company purchased six whitewater rafts for $12,000 each. It paid $10,000 in cash and for the balance signed a one-year note with an 8 percent annual interest rate.

(3) The company accepted bids from Foodworks and Candy's Catering Company to provide the food on all rafting trips.

(4) The company sold 200 rafting trips at $750 per trip. Cash in the amount of $45,000 was collected and the remainder has yet to be received.

(5) The company entered negotiations to build its own office building. The current estimate for the building is $250,000.

(6) The company paid $75,000 in cash for wages.

(7) The company paid $12,000 in cash for rent.

(8) The company paid interest on the note payable in the amount of $4000 cash.

(9) The company declared and paid cash dividends of $22,000.

Required:

a. Prepare the journal entries for each event that requires one.

b. Prepare a ledger (use T-account format) and post the entries to the ledger accounts.

c. Prepare and complete a worksheet.

d. Prepare closing entries and post them to the ledger T-accounts.

e. Prepare an income statement, statement of retained earnings, statement of cash flows, and balance sheet.

P3–11

(Reconstructing journal entries, completing a worksheet, and preparing the financial statements) The following T-accounts represent the general ledger of Crozier Company as of December 31, 1989. Beginning balances in the permanent accounts are in italics.

Cash		Accounts Receivable		Inventory	
20,000	5,000	*35,000*	10,000	*50,000*	115,000
10,000	7,000	100,000		125,000	
45,000	12,000				
	8,000				
	14,000				

Machinery		Accounts Payable		Common Stock	
200,000		7,000	*90,000*		*105,000*
12,000			125,000		45,000
8,000					

Retained Earnings		Sales		Rent Expense	
	110,000		100,000	14,000	

Cost of Goods Sold		Wage Expense	
115,000		5,000	

Required:

a. Reconstruct the journal entries recorded by Crozier during 1989.

b. Prepare and complete a worksheet.

c. Prepare the income statement, statement of retained earnings, statement of cash flows, and balance sheet.

P3–12   *(Appendix 3A: Special journals and subsidiary ledgers)*   J. R. Ewing and Sons sells high-fashion clothes. As of July 31, the Accounts Receivable control account for this company totaled $3000 and was made up of three accounts: Donna Smith, $875; Jimmy Johnston, $1100, and Loretta Jones, $1025. During the month of August, the following transactions took place.

(1) Donna Smith paid $500 on her account.

(2) Jimmy Johnston purchased merchandise on account for $300.

(3) Loretta Jones paid her account in full.

(4) Jimmy Johnston paid $700 on his account.

Required: Prepare a cash receipt journal, a sales journal, an Accounts Receivable control account, and Accounts Receivable subsidiary accounts for each customer. Record each transaction in the appropriate journal or ledger and post the end-of-month dollar amounts. (Use T-account format.)

P3–13   *(Appendix 3A: Special journals and subsidiary ledgers)*   Schlee and Company purchases inventory from a number of suppliers. As of January 31, 1990 the Accounts Payable control account had a balance of $5000 and was comprised of the following three accounts: M & S Supply, $2700; Ellery Industries, $1500; Thompson, Inc. $800. The following transactions took place during the month of February.

(1) M & S Supply was paid in full.

(2) Ellery Industries was paid $1000.

(3) $700 worth of merchandise was purchased from M & S Supply on account.

(4) $200 worth of merchandise was purchased from Thompson, Inc., and a $500 check was sent as payment.

Required: Prepare a cash disbursements journal, a purchase journal, an Accounts Payable control account, and an accounts payable subsidiary ledger for each customer. Record each transaction in the appropriate journal or ledger and post the end-of-month dollar amounts. (Use T-account format.)

CASES

C3–1   *(Journalizing a transaction and its effect on the accounting equation and balance sheet)*   In 1986, MCI Communications Corporation purchased Satellite Business Systems (SBS) from International Business Machines Corporation (IBM). In the transaction, MCI issued common stock to IBM valued at $376 million and signed a note payable for $104 million. MCI received miscellaneous assets valued at $52 million and the SBS system.

Required: Respond to the following.

a. At what dollar amount was the SBS system recorded on MCI's balance sheet?

b. Describe how this transaction affected the accounting equation from MCI's point of view.

c. Describe how this transaction affected MCI's balance sheet.

d. Identify the financial statement accounts affected, the direction of the effect, and the dollar amount of the effect on each account.

e. Prepare the journal entry MCI recorded when the transaction took place.

C3–2   *(Recording and closing sales on account)*   In its 1987 annual report, Black and Decker, a marketer and manufacturer of products for the home, reported sales of $1,934,799 on its income statement.

Required: Assume that all sales during the year were on account and were recorded with a single journal entry.

a. Describe how this journal entry would affect the accounting equation.

b. Identify the accounts affected, the direction of the effect, and the dollar value of the effect on each account.

c. Prepare the journal entry.

d. Prepare the journal entry recorded by Black and Decker to close the sales account at the end of 1987.

e. Assume that 1987 sales were all for cash. Prepare the journal entry recorded to close the sales account at the end of 1987.

C3–3   *(Closing revenue and expense accounts)*   Nordstrom, Inc. is principally a retail store operation with national outlets. In its 1986 annual report, it reported net income of $92,733 on sales of $1,850,231, and expenses of $1,757,498 (all dollars in thousands).

Required:

a. When the individual revenue and expense accounts are closed, into what account are the balances transferred?

b. After the Sales account is closed, does the dollar amount appear as a debit or credit in the account named in *(a)* above?

c. Prepare the journal entry to close the revenue and expense accounts into this account.

d. Prepare the journal entry to close this account.

C3–4   *(Inferring the worksheet from the financial statements)*   In its 1987 annual report, Aluminum Company of America (Alcoa) reported the following (dollars in thousands):

Assets	$9,901,900
Liabilities	5,131,200
Stockholders' equity	4,770,700
Revenues	7,838,200
Expenses	7,638,100
Net Income	200,100

Required:

a. What was the total dollar amount in the debit and credit columns on the year-end adjusted trial balance?

b. Prepare the closing entries recorded on Alcoa's worksheet. Assume no dividends.

c. What was the total dollar amount in the debit and credit columns of the year-end final trial balance?

C3-5   *(Appendix 3B: The characteristics and importance of internal control)*   In the annual report of the Chase Manhattan Corporation, one of the largest financial institutions in New York City, the Report of Management contains the following:

> *[Management] has developed a system of internal accounting control . . . designed to provide reasonable assurance that assets are safeguarded and that transactions are executed in accordance with management's authorization and recorded properly.*

Required:

a. Why would Chase Manhattan include this statement in its financial report?
b. List and briefly describe the characteristics of an effective internal control system.
c. Why would the following parties be interested in the internal control system of Chase Manhattan: the company's auditors, stockholders, creditors, and managers?

CHAPTER 4

Cash Flows, Accruals, and Adjusting Journal Entries

Learning Objectives

1   Describe the basic difference between the cash and accrual systems of accounting and the type of information that each provides about the financial condition of a company.

2   Explain the role of adjusting journal entries and why they are necessary for the accrual system of accounting.

3   Identify and define the two kinds of adjusting journal entries, and provide several examples of each.

4   Explain the matching process, and describe how accrual and cost-expiration adjusting journal entries help to apply it.

5   (Appendix 4A) Prepare the statement of cash flows under the indirect method and explain how net income is converted to net cash flow from operating activities.

≣ Several times in this text we have noted that two aspects of a company's operating performance are relevant to investors, creditors, and other interested parties: (1) solvency, a company's ability to meet its debt payments as they come due and (2) earning power, a company's ability to generate assets in the future. The statement of cash flows and the income statement are specifically designed to provide information that is useful in assessing these two aspects of performance. The statement of cash flows provides information that is primarily used to assess solvency, while the income statement is designed to provide information about earning power.

This chapter first compares and contrasts the measurement systems underlying these two financial statements and then more fully explains the measure of net income. The first section begins with a simple example designed to highlight the differences between cash flow accounting, which underlies the statement of cash flows, and accrual accounting, which underlies the income statement. In short, **cash flow accounting** measures performance by comparing the cash inflows of a certain time period to the cash outflows of that period. **Accrual accounting,** on the other hand, measures performance by comparing revenues, which are recognized when the earning process is complete and assets are created (or liabilities are discharged), with expenses, which are recognized when assets are used up (or liabilities are created). We then provide a brief review of a method used to prepare the statement of cash flows, called the *direct method,* and the procedures involved in preparing an income statement.

In the second section of the chapter, adjusting journal entries, which are essential to the accrual system, are discussed and illustrated. Recall from Chapter 3 that adjusting journal entries, Step 7 in the accounting cycle, were only briefly described because fully appreciating them requires an understanding of important measurement issues, which had not yet been covered. This chapter presents those issues and demonstrates how adjusting journal entries are necessary if an accrual accounting system is to be maintained.

This chapter completes the discussion of the accounting cycle. A comprehensive review problem at the end of the chapter illustrates the entire cycle, including adjusting journal entries, closing entries, and the preparation of the income statement, statement of retained earnings, balance sheet, and statement of cash flows. The Appendix to this chapter discusses a second method of preparing and presenting the statement of cash flows, called the *indirect method,* and in so doing illustrates how net income can be adjusted to equal net cash flow from operating activities. Many accounting students find these adjustments to be difficult, but it is important to master them, because knowledge of the accrual and cash systems is at the heart of your ability to understand and appropriately use financial statements.

This chapter covers information that is fundamental to an understanding of present-day accounting systems. We suggest that you work through it slowly. Make certain at first that you understand the cash system and the statement of cash flows, which are fairly straightforward and should present no major problems. Learn the accrual system next, noting how it departs from and extends the more fundamental cash system. Pay special attention to why adjusting journal entries are required when implementing the accrual system. Finally, from the Appendix, learn how to reconcile these two systems or, in other words, how to prepare the adjustments required to convert the accrual system to the cash system.

CASH FLOW AND ACCRUAL ACCOUNTING: TWO SYSTEMS OF MEASURING OPERATING PERFORMANCE

Financial accounting statements have evolved in response to demands from the business community for measures of operating performance. Stockholders, company creditors, and other interested parties require measures, such as net income and cash flows from operating activities, that they can use to monitor the efficiency with which company assets are being managed and to control and direct the actions of management. Potential investors and creditors require measures of operating performance in their assessments of earning power and solvency so that they can identify attractive investment and loan opportunities.

Operating performance is normally measured by viewing an entity as constantly expending effort (expending resources) in an attempt to generate benefits (resource inflows). Over a given time period, operating performance is defined as the difference between the benefits of that period and the resources expended to generate them. Consequently, two steps are involved when assessing operating performance: (1) the benefits and efforts of a period must be measured, and (2) the two measures must be compared.

These two steps represent a simple expression of the **matching principle,** which states that operating performance in a particular time period is the result of matching the dollar value of the efforts expended in that time period against the dollar value of the benefits realized. Thus, operating performance during a given year, 1990 for example, would be defined as follows:

$$\$ \text{ Operating Performance (1990)} = \$\text{Benefits (1990)} - \$\text{Efforts (1990)}$$

The next logical question is "How are the benefits and efforts of a particular time period to be measured?" The next section compares and contrasts two measurement systems: (1) cash flow accounting, which measures benefits and efforts in terms of cash inflows and cash outflows, and (2) accrual accounting, which measures benefits and efforts in terms of revenues and expenses.

Differences Between Cash and Accrual Accounting: A Matter of Timing

Suppose you operate a neighborhood odd-job service and are hired to till a neighbor's garden. You agree to perform the service for $200. You rent a tiller and quickly and efficiently complete the task. You then bill your neighbor, and when you return the tiller, the rental company bills you for $50. Imagine further that these activities occur within one week, and at the end of the week you prepare financial statements. During the second week, your neighbor pays you the $200, you pay $50 to the rental company. At the end of the second week you prepare a second set of financial statements. The following sections compare the financial statements under both the cash and accrual systems for both Week 1 and Week 2.

Cash Accounting

What do cash flow statements reveal about your performance in Weeks 1 and 2? If we look at the activity in the cash account, we see nothing during Week 1: no cash inflows, no cash outflows, and no change in the cash balance. In Week 2, when you receive cash from your neighbor and pay the bill for the tiller, the statement of cash flows appears as in Figure 4–1.

Figure 4–1   Cash flow statements: Weeks 1 and 2

Odd Jobs Co. Statement of Cash Flows For Weeks 1 and 2			
Week 1		**Week 2**	
Cash inflows	$ 0	Cash inflows	$200
Cash outflows	0	Cash outflows	(50)
Net cash flow	$ 0	Net cash flow	$150

Accrual Accounting

Under accrual accounting you would recognize that during Week 1 your wealth had been affected because both an asset and a liability had been created. As soon as you finished the tilling job, you had earned your fee and your neighbor owed you $200. Thus, at that point you would have recorded the following journal entry, which recognizes the creation of both an asset and a revenue.

Accounts Receivable	200	
Fees Earned		200
To record the provision of a service.		

A liability was also created that enabled you to generate this revenue; that is, you needed to rent the tiller. Therefore, under the accrual system the following journal entry, which recognizes both a liability and an expense, would also have been recorded.

Rental Expense	50	
Accounts Payable		50
To recognize an expense and a liability.		

Under the accrual system, the matching principle states that you must match the expense of the tiller against the revenue it helped to produce. As a result, your financial statements on an accrual basis at the end of Week 1 appear in Figure 4–2.

During Week 2 you received the $200 from your neighbor and paid $50 to the rental company. The journal entries under the accrual system for Week 2 are provided below and the financial statements as of the end of Week 2 would be as shown in Figure 4–3.

Cash	200	
Accounts Receivable		200
To record the receipt of the receivable.		

Accounts Payable	50	
Cash		50
To record the payment of the payable.		

Note in these accrual statements that net income of $150 is recognized during Week 1 when the asset and the liability are created. During Week 2 no net income is recognized because no new assets or liabilities were created. The assets and liabilities simply changed form in the second week. The account receivable was converted to cash, and the account payable was discharged with a cash

Figure 4–2   Accrual financial statements: Week 1

Odd Jobs Co.			
Financial Statements			
For Week 1			

Income Statement		**Statement of Retained Earnings**	
Fees earned	$200	Beginning balance	$ 0
Rent expense	50	+ Net income	150
Net income	$150	− Dividends	0
		Ending balance	$150

Balance Sheet			
Assets		Liabilities and Stockholders' Equity	
Accounts receivable	$200	Accounts payable	$ 50
		Retained earnings	150
		Total liabilities and	
Total assets	$200	stockholders' equity	$200

payment. Both the accounts receivable asset and the accounts payable liability, which were created in Week 1, gave rise to a cash flow, which was realized during Week 2.

Figure 4–4 compares the cash and accrual performance measures across Weeks 1 and 2. Note first that the total performance measured by the two systems is equivalent ($150). The important difference lies in the timing of the performance recognition. The accrual system recognizes the $150 in Week 1, when the asset and liability are created; the cash system does not recognize the $150 income until the second week, when the actual cash inflow and outflow occurred.

Figure 4–3   Accrual financial statements: Week 2

Odd Jobs Co.			
Financial Statements			
For Week 2			

Income Statement		**Statement of Retained Earnings**	
Fees earned	$ 0	Beginning balance	$150
Rent expense	0	+ Net income	0
Net income	$ 0	− Dividends	0
		Ending balance	$150

Balance Sheet			
Assets		Liabilities and Stockholders' Equity	
Cash	$150	Retained earnings	$150
		Total liabilities and	
Total assets	$150	stockholders' equity	$150

Figure 4–4   Comparison of cash flow and accrual measures of performance

System	Week 1	Week 2	Total
Cash	$0	$150	$150
Accrual	$150	0	$150

Cash Flow Accounting, the Statement of Cash Flows, and Operating Performance

The statement of cash flows, which is based on cash flow accounting, summarizes the cash transactions entered into by a company over a period of time. As illustrated in Chapter 3, it can be prepared from the entries in the Cash account in the ledger. Recall that preparing the statement requires placing each entry into one of three categories: (1) cash flows from operating activities, (2) cash flows from investing activities, or (3) cash flows from financing activities.

Cash flows from operating activities include cash inflows and outflows associated directly with the acquisition and sale of a company's inventories and services. This category primarily includes the cash receipts from sales and accounts receivable as well as cash payments for the purchase of inventories, the payment of accounts payable, selling and administrative expenses, interest, and taxes.

Cash flows from investing activities include cash inflows and outflows associated with the purchase and sale of a company's noncurrent assets. This category primarily includes the cash effects from the purchase and sale of investments in other companies' debt and equity securities; other long-term investments; property, plant, and equipment; and intangible assets.

Cash flows from financing activities include cash inflows and outflows associated with a company's two sources of outside capital: liabilities and contributions from the stockholders. This category primarily includes the cash inflows associated with borrowings and equity issuances as well as the cash outflows associated with debt repayments and dividends.

Figure 4–5 contains the journal, cash ledger account, and statement of cash flows for Baiman Services, which just completed its first year of operations (1990). Trace the cash effect of each numbered journal entry to the Cash account in the ledger, and then trace each ledger entry to the statement of cash flows.

Journal entries (3), (7), (8), and (10) involve cash flows due to operating activities: (3) the provision of a service, (7) the payment of selling and administrative expenses, (8) the payment of salaries, and (10) the payment of interest. Note that the statement of cash flows was prepared using the **direct method,** which means that the dollar amounts under "Operating activities" can be linked *directly* to the Cash T-account. A second method, called the *indirect method,* is discussed and illustrated in Appendix 4A. Note also that net cash flow from operating activities is negative $8000.

Journal entries (5), (6), and (9) involve cash flows due to investing activities: (5) the purchase of land, (6) the sale of land, and (9) the purchase of equipment. Note that net cash increase from investing activities is negative $6000.

Journal entries (1), (4), (10), and (11) involve cash flows due to financing activities: (1) the issuance of stock, (4) a borrowing and the establishment of a note payable, (10) a principal payment on a note payable, and (11) the payment of a dividend. Net cash flow from financing activities is $22,500, which brings Baiman's cash balance at the end of 1990 to $8500.

Figure 4–5   Baiman Services: general journal, cash account, and statement of cash flows

Journal Transactions during 1990

(1) Cash   20,000
      Common Stock   20,000
    Issue common stock.

(2) Accounts Receivable   10,000
      Fees Earned   10,000
    Provide a service on account.

(3) Accounts Receivable   2,000
    Cash   7,000
      Fees Earned   9,000
    Provide a service for cash and on account.

(4) Cash   5,000
      Notes Payable   5,000
    Borrowed cash from a bank.

(5) Land   9,000
      Cash   9,000
    Purchased land for cash.

(6) Cash   6,000
      Land   4,500
      Gain on Sale of Land   1,500
    Sold one-half of land purchased in (5).

(7) Selling and Admin. Exp.   8,000
      Cash   8,000
    Paid cash for selling and administrative exp.

(8) Salary Expense   6,000
      Cash   6,000
    Paid cash for salaries.

(9) Equipment   8,000
      Note Payable   5,000
      Cash   3,000
    Purchased equipment for cash and a note.

(10) Interest Expense   1,000
    Note Payable   500
      Cash   1,500
    Cash payment for interest and principle on
    outstanding note payable.

(11) Dividends   2,000
      Cash   2,000
    Paid dividends in cash.

General Ledger

	Cash		
	0		
(1)	20,000		
(3)	7,000		
(4)	5,000		
		9,000	(5)
(6)	6,000		
		8,000	(7)
		6,000	(8)
		3,000	(9)
		1,500	(10)
		2,000	(11)
	8,500		

While all three categories on the statement of cash flows provide useful information, net cash flow from operating activities provides a direct measure of the company's operating performance. It can be expressed in the following way:

Net cash flow from operating activities (1990) = Operating cash inflows (1990)
        − Operating cash outflows (1990)

Figure 4–5 (continued)

Baiman Services Statement of Cash Flows: Direct Method For the Year Ended December 31, 1990		
Operating activities		
Cash receipts from sales of services	$ 7,000	
Payments for selling and admin. expenses	(8,000)	
Payments for salaries	(6,000)	
Payments for interest	(1,000)	
Net cash increase (decrease) from operating activities		($ 8,000)
Investing activities		
Sale of land	6,000	
Purchase of land	(9,000)	
Purchase of equipment	(3,000)	
Net cash increase (decrease) from investing activities		(6,000)
Financing activities		
Issuance of common stock	20,000	
Long-term borrowings	5,000	
Principal payments on long-term notes	(500)	
Payments for dividends	(2,000)	
Net cash increase (decrease) due to financing activities		22,500
Net cash increase (decrease) during 1990		8,500
Cash balance at beginning of year		0
Cash balance at end of year		$ 8,500

Net cash flow from operating activities indicates how much cash the company produced through its normal and recurring operations. Indeed, many companies view operations as their primary source of cash. For example, Dupont, which relies on operations as its main source of financing, noted in its 1987 annual report.

> *Cash provided by operations in 1987 was $4.1 billion. These funds were used to finance the company's capital expenditures, pay dividends, repurchase 1.9 million [shares] of the company's common stock, and reduce borrowings.*

Professor Loyd Heath, in an article published in the *Journal of Accountancy* has further emphasized the importance to creditors of net cash flow from operating activities.

> *The central question in credit analysis today is . . . whether the cash expected to be received within a given time period will equal or exceed required cash payments within that same time period. . . . A company's principal sources of cash are from sale of its products or services to its customers.*[1]

---

1. Loyd Heath, "Let's Scrap the Funds Statement," *Journal of Accountancy* (October 1978): 94–103.

Accrual Accounting, the Income Statement, and Operating Performance

As indicated earlier, the system of accrual accounting is another method of measuring the benefits and efforts associated with a particular time period, which defines benefits in terms of revenues and efforts in terms of expenses. Revenues represent the inflow of assets (or discharge of liabilities) due to the operating activities of a company in a given period. Revenues are recognized in the books (i.e., a journal entry is recorded) when the earning process involved in providing a good or service is complete. Expenses represent the outflow of assets (or creation of liabilities) leading to the generation of these revenues. Matching expenses and revenues in a given period produces net income.

$$\text{Net income (1990)} = \text{Revenues (1990)} - \text{Expenses (1990)}$$

Note immediately one important difference between accrual and cash accounting. Revenues and expenses in the accrual system are defined in terms of assets and liability flows; the cash system recognizes only cash inflows and outflows. The asset and liability flows of a particular period include, but are not limited to, cash flows. For example, selling a service in exchange for an account receivable creates an asset but does not immediately create cash. Similarly, purchasing inventory on account creates a liability but not an immediate cash outflow. As a result, net cash flows from operating activities and net income can be two very different dollar amounts.

Consider, for example, the 1990 income statement of Baiman Services, which appears in Figure 4–6 and was prepared from the journal entries in Figure 4–5. Note that revenues were recognized in journal entries (2), (3), and (6), and expenses were recorded in journal entries (7), (8), and (10). Net income for 1990 equals $5500, which is $13,500 higher than net cash flow from operating activities for the same year (−$8000).

In this case the $13,500 difference between net income and net cash flow from operating activities can be explained by journal entries (2), (3), and (6). In those entries, revenues of $10,000, $9000, and $1500 were recognized and reported on the income statement, while cash receipts of only $7000 were reported in the operating section of the statement of cash flows.[2] Thus, total revenues of $20,500 exceeded cash receipts from operations ($7000) by $13,500.

Net income is probably the most popular measure of a company's operating performance. It is referred to frequently in the financial press and on radio and television financial news programs, and companies often view net income as *the* measure of performance. For example, J. C. Penney's 1987 financial report opened with the following statement.

For J. C. Penney, 1987 was a year of record sales and earnings. Net income rose 27% to $608 million from the previous high of $478 million in 1986. Earnings per share amounted to $4.11, as compared with $3.19 in the prior year.

Moreover, the Financial Accounting Standards Board (FASB) has stated explicitly

---

2. Journal entry (6) reported a cash receipt of $6000, but this amount was reported in the investing section of the statement of cash flows.

Figure 4–6 Income statement for Baiman Services

Baiman Services Income Statement For the Year Ended December 31, 1990		
Revenues		
Fees earned	$19,000	
Gain on sale of land	1,500	
Total revenues		$20,500
Expenses		
Selling and administrative expenses	8,000	
Salary expenses	6,000	
Interest Expenses	1,000	
Total expenses		15,000
Net income		$ 5,500

that "accrual accounting is superior to cash flow accounting as a means of reflecting a company's future cash flow generating ability."[3]

Net income is certainly an important and useful measure of financial performance, but the FASB's statement should not be interpreted to mean that accrual accounting is superior to cash flow accounting in producing measures of all important aspects of performance. As indicated in *Forbes*, "The two figures [income and cash flow] measure different things—and one isn't necessarily better, or more accurate, than the other."[4]

As the example at the beginning of the chapter demonstrated, the basic difference between cash flow and accrual measures of performance is timing. Note in the Baiman Services example that accounts receivable in the amount of $12,000 ($10,000 + $2000) were recognized in journal entries (2) and (3). This $12,000 was immediately recorded as revenue and therefore increased net income. As of the end of 1990, however, these receivables had not yet produced a cash receipt; accordingly, they were not reflected on the statement of cash flows. In 1991 these receivables will probably be collected, and the $12,000 will appear on the statement of cash flows for that year, while the income statement for 1991 will be unaffected by the cash receipt.

In general, cash accounting recognizes performance only when cash is received or paid. As a result, net cash flow from operating activities provides a relatively short-run measure of operating performance, indicating how much cash a company was able to generate from operating activities in a given period. Accrual accounting, on the other hand, recognizes performance when an asset or liability is created or discharged, thereby providing a longer-run measure of performance and earning power. Both measures are important to investors and creditors because a company must meet its debt payments in the short-run to take advantage of its long-run earning power.

---

3. Financial Accounting Standards Board, *Objectives of Financial Reporting by Business Enterprises* Concepts Statement no. 1 (Stamford, Conn.: FASB, 1978).

4. Richard Greene, "The Missing Number," *Forbes*, 18 June 1984 p. 123.

ADJUSTING JOURNAL ENTRIES

The discussion of the accounting cycle in Chapter 3 focused primarily on recording exchange transactions—transactions backed by documented evidence, in which assets and/or liabilities are transferred between parties. Assets and liabilities, however, are often created or discharged without the occurrence of a visible, documentable exchange transaction. They sometimes build up or expire as time passes. Interest, for example, is earned continually on a bank savings account. Machinery depreciates as it is used in a company's operations. Such phenomena are not evidenced by exchange transactions and, therefore, are not captured in the day-to-day recording process.

As stated earlier, the accrual system measures revenues and expenses in terms of the creation or discharge of assets and liabilities. Consequently, to prepare accrual-based financial statements (i.e., the income statement, the statement of retained earnings, and the balance sheet) items like interest and depreciation must be recognized in the financial records. In practice, adjustments for such items are recorded at the end of the accounting period before the financial statements are prepared through a series of entries, called **adjusting journal entries.** Take a moment now to look back at Chapter 3, especially Figure 3–1, to reacquaint yourself with the placement of adjusting journal entries in the accounting cycle.

The adjusting journal entries that we discuss and illustrate in this chapter all share the following three characteristics:

1. they are entered in the books to achieve a matching of revenues and expenses in the appropriate time period,
2. they always involve at least one temporary (revenue, expense, or dividend) account and at least one permanent (asset or liability) account, and
3. they never involve the cash account.

In discussing the various kinds of adjusting journal entries, we point out how they all reflect these three characteristics. In the future when you prepare adjusting journal entries, you should make certain that they have these same characteristics.

The adjusting journal entries covered in this chapter can be placed into one of two categories: (1) accruals, or (2) cost expirations. The following sections explain these two kinds of adjustments.

Accruals

Accruals refer to amounts in asset and liability accounts that build up over time. The term *accrue* simply means to build up gradually.[5] Two very common examples are accrued wages and accrued interest.

Accrued Wages

Suppose that employees of Taylor Motor are paid at the end of each week. The total weekly payroll is $10,000, which is earned at a rate of $2000 per day for each of the five working days. Assume that December 31 falls on a Tuesday, and

---

5. Note that the term *accrual* refers to a system of accounting, which recognizes revenues and expenses as assets and liabilities are created or discharged, as well as one of the two kinds of adjusting journal entries. The double meaning of this term can be a source of confusion, and it is important that you be aware of the context in which it is used.

Figure 4–7   Accrued wages

	Period 1 →		Period 2 →		
	Monday (12/30)	Tuesday (12/31)	Wednesday (1/1)	Thursday (1/2)	Friday (1/3)
Wages Earned:	$2,000	$2,000	$2,000	$2,000	$2,000

Adjusting journal entry (Tuesday, 12/31):

```
Wage Expense        4,000
   Wages Payable          4,000
To record
   accrued wages.
```

Friday (1/3):

```
Wages Payable       4,000
Wage Expense        6,000
   Cash                  10,000
To record the
   payment of wages.
```

the books are closed (financial statements are prepared) on that day. Figure 4–7 illustrates these facts and the journal entries that would be recorded under accrual accounting.

In applying the accrual system, Taylor's accountant must recognize that although no cash has been paid as of December 31, a liability has been created. The company owes its employees two days' worth of wages, or $4000. This liability is recognized with an adjusting journal entry of the form indicated in Figure 4–7: Wage Expense (an expense account) is debited for $4000, and Wages Payable (a liability account) is credited for $4000. Wage Expense of $4000 is reflected on the income statement of the period ending on December 31 (Period 1) and is closed to retained earnings, which would appear on the December 31 balance sheet. Wages Payable of $4000 appear in the liability section of the December 31 balance sheet and the amount is carried into Period 2. Note that on Friday, when the $10,000 cash payment for wages is made, $4000 serves to remove the Wages Payable (the liability is discharged) and $6000 is charged to Wage Expense of Period 2 and thus will appear on the income statement of Period 2.

The adjusting entry (debit to Wage Expense, credit to Wages Payable) in this example shares the three characteristics discussed earlier. First, it achieves matching, in that it matches the cost of the effort expended by the employees in Period 1 with the revenues generated in Period 1. Wage expense of $4000 is subtracted from Period 1 revenues in the computation of Period 1 net income. Similarly, the cost of the effort expended by the employees in Period 2 ($6000) is matched against Period 2 revenues on the Period 2 income statement. Note also that the adjusting journal entry involves a temporary (Wage Expense) and a permanent (Wages Payable) account, and that Cash is unaffected.

It is also important to realize that Taylor would prepare statements of cash flow for Periods 1 and 2 and the entire $10,000 cash payment would be reflected in the second period. None of it would appear on the statement of cash flows of Period 1. As Figure 4–8 indicates, the total resource expenditure recognized under the accrual system is the same as that recognized under the cash system. The difference lies in the timing of the recognition. Due to the adjusting journal entry, the accrual system recognizes $4000 in Period 1 and $6000 in Period 2.

Figure 4–8   Expenditure recognition

Accounting System/Financial Statement	Period 1	Period 2	Total
Accrual/Income statement	$4,000	$ 6,000	$10,000
Cash/Statement of cash flows	0	10,000	10,000

Accrued Interest

Suppose that on December 1, BankAmerica Corporation loans $12,000 to Exxon Oil Company at an annual interest rate of 10 percent. Assume that the books are closed on December 31 and that Exxon pays BankAmerica in full (principal and interest) on January 31 of the next year. Figure 4–9 illustrates these facts and the journal entries that would be recorded under accrual accounting.

BankAmerica prepares an adjusting journal entry on December 31, when the books are closed, to reflect the fact that an asset, Interest Receivable, has been created. The company has earned $100 ([$12,000 × 10%]/12 months) in interest during the month of December. Interest Receivable in that amount is recognized (debited) and Interest Revenue is credited. When the $12,200 cash payment is received on January 31, $12,000 serves to reduce the outstanding note receivable, $100 is charged against the Interest Receivable account, and the remaining $100 is recognized as Interest Revenue.

As in the example of accrued wages, the adjusting entry here helps to achieve a matching of revenues and expenses in the appropriate time period. It does so by dividing the total interest earned on the loan ($200) into two components, based on the periods in which it was earned and the time when the asset, Interest Receivable, was created. Half of the $200 interest payment was earned in Period 1 and therefore should appear as a revenue on the income statement of Period 1. The remaining $100 should appear as a revenue on the income statement of Period 2 because the loan was outstanding during one month of Period 2. Note also that the adjusting entry involves a temporary (Interest Revenue) and a permanent (Interest Receivable) account and does not affect Cash.

Consider again the effect of these transactions on the statements of cash flows for Periods 1 and 2. No cash inflow is recorded in Period 1, and therefore nothing

Figure 4–9   Accrued interest revenue

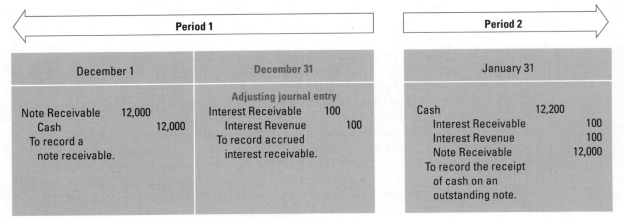

Figure 4–10 Accrued interest expense

Period 1		Period 2
December 1	**December 31**	**January 31**

December 1	December 31	January 31

Cash   12,000
   Note Payable   12,000
To record
  a borrowing.
	Adjusting journal entry
	Interest Expense 100
	   Interest Payable 100
	To record accrued
	  interest payable.
		Note Payable 12,000
		Interest Payable 100
		Interest Expense 100
		   Cash 12,200
		To record payment
		  on an outstanding note.

would be reflected on the statement of cash flows for that period. Instead, all $200 would appear on the statement of cash flows in Period 2, when the cash is actually received. Once again, the total interest recognized across the two periods under the cash system ($200) is the same as that recognized under the accrual system, but the timing of the recognition is different. The adjusting journal entry prepared under the accrual system ensures that $100 is recognized on the income statement of Period 1, with the remaining $100 appearing on the income statement of Period 2.

Figure 4–10, using the same facts as Figure 4–9, considers the borrowers' (Exxon's) point of view. Examine the journal entries, and note especially the characteristics and role of the adjusting journal entry. It matches revenues and expenses in the appropriate time period, it involves a temporary and a permanent account, and it gives rise to expense recognition in a time period when no cash payment is made.

Cost Expirations

The second type of adjusting journal entry is called a **cost expiration.** Like accruals, these adjusting entries (1) are recorded in the books in an effort to achieve a matching of revenues and expenses in the appropriate time period, (2) always involve at least one temporary and at least one permanent account, and (3) do not involve the Cash account. However, rather than building up an account over time, as is done with an accrual, these adjusting entries serve to *write down* an already-established account. In a sense, cost expirations represent the "flip side" of accruals.

Asset Capitalization and the Matching Principle
Before studying cost expirations, you should understand one very important concept in financial accounting measurement: that is, *asset capitalization* and how it relates to the matching principle. This concept is fundamental to accrual accounting, and understanding it is a prerequisite to understanding cost expiration adjusting journal entries.

Figure 4–11   The matching process

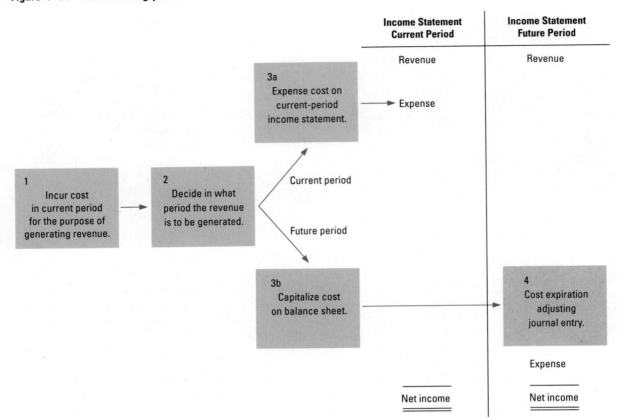

The four-step process depicted in Figure 4–11 provides a general view of how the matching principle is applied. The process begins at Step 1 with the recognition that all resource expenditures by a company in a given period of time are made to generate revenues. Recall from the previous discussion that companies are constantly expending effort (investing resources) for the purpose of generating benefits (revenues). Wages are paid, interest payments are made, and inventories, securities, and property, plant, and equipment are acquired, all in an effort to generate revenues.

Recall also that the matching principle states that, if income is to be measured on an accrual basis, these resource expenditures must be matched against the revenues they help to generate during the time period in which those revenues are generated. Thus, Step 2 in the matching process asks the question: "In what period is the revenue from the expenditure expected to be generated?"

If the answer to this question is "the current period," Step 3a indicates that the cost of the resource expenditure should immediately be matched against revenue or, in accounting terminology, **expensed.** In other words, the cost of the expenditure should be placed on the income statement of the current period as an expense. The following journal entry is an example of a $2000 expenditure on salaries that is immediately expensed and would appear on the income statement of the current period.

Salary Expense	2000	
Cash		2000
To record the payment of salaries.		

If the expenditure is expected to generate revenues in a future period or, in other words, if the answer to the question posed in Step 2 is "in a future period," Step 3b specifies that the cost of the resource expenditure be **capitalized** (i.e., placed on the balance sheet). Consequently, most assets on the balance sheet (i.e., inventory, prepaid expenses, long-term investments, property, plant, and equipment, and intangibles) represent expenditures made by a company that are expected to generate revenues in the future. The following journal entry is an example of a $5000 machinery purchase that has been capitalized and would appear on the balance sheet.

Machinery	5000	
Cash		5000
To record the purchase of machinery.		

Note in Figure 4–11 that capitalized assets are further subject to Step 4 in the matching process. In the future, when the revenue from the balance sheet asset is generated, the matching principle states that the cost of the asset must be converted into an expense and placed on the income statement of that future period. This conversion is achieved through a cost expiration adjusting journal entry. The following journal entries depict the initial purchase and capitalization of office supplies in Period 1, and the cost expiration adjusting journal entry required at the end of Period 2 when the supplies are used up (expired).

Period 1: Capitalization of supplies			**Period 2: Cost expiration adjusting journal entry**		
Supplies Inventory	100		Supplies Expense	100	
Cash		100	Supplies Inventory		100
To record the purchase of office supplies.			To record the use of office supplies.		

As in the accrual examples discussed earlier, the expense associated with the purchase of the supplies is recognized in a period other than the period in which the cash is paid. In this case the expense is recognized in Period 2 when the supplies are used, even though the cash payment is made in Period 1. Consequently, the income statement, which is prepared on an accrual basis, would show the effect of the expenditure in Period 2, while the statement of cash flows would show the effect of the cash outflow in Period 1.

In certain cases, as in the supplies example above, it is fairly easy to see when the asset is used up or the benefit from the expenditure is realized. In such situations it is not difficult to determine the dollar amount and the timing of the cost expiration adjusting journal entry. However, in many other cases the association between the expiration of the capitalized asset and the generation of the related benefit is vague. For example, Monsanto, a major manufacturer of chemical and agricultural products, recently acquired and implemented a computerized manufacturing and information system at a cost of nearly $1 billion, which was designed to "improve communication with customers and suppliers, increase the efficiency of plant operations, improve product quality, and reduce product costs."[6]

---

6. Monsanto, 1987 Annual Report.

The cost of this expenditure was capitalized by Monsanto, and undoubtedly the computerized system will produce benefits in the future. However, the benefits will be realized in many different, and often subtle, ways and in many different time periods. Consequently, devising a method of matching the costs of the system with the benefits it produces, in the time periods when they are produced, is a very subjective and difficult process.

In such cases the useful life of the capitalized asset must be estimated when the asset is acquired, and its cost must be periodically converted to an expense over this time period. The process of periodically converting the cost of an asset to an expense is referred to as **amortization,** and it is implemented by preparing a cost expiration adjusting journal entry at the end of each period of the estimated life. **Depreciation** is the amortization of the cost of buildings, machinery, or equipment.

Expense or Capitalize and Amortize: Examples

Figure 4–12 illustrates the basic procedures used to account for expensed and capitalized costs. It is divided into two sections. The upper section is a smaller version of Figure 4–11. The lower section consists of nine different transactions, each carried through the four steps involved in applying the matching principle.

Current Expenses. The first three transactions (salaries, interest, and utilities) represent resources expenditures, either through the creation of a liability or the payment of cash, for which the benefit is assumed to be realized in the current period. Salaries and interest in this case are accrued at the end of the current period with an accrual adjusting journal entry, and the associated cash payment is expected to follow in a future period. The utility expense is both recognized and paid in the current period. Since the benefit from each of these three expenditures is assumed to be realized in the current period, all are expensed, regardless of the timing of the cash payment. These expenditures have not been capitalized and, therefore, Step 4 in the matching process, a cost expiration adjusting journal entry, is not necessary.

Supplies Inventory. The fourth transaction in Figure 4–12, the purchase of supplies, is capitalized because supplies are normally expected to be useful beyond the current period. Typically, at the end of each period, an inventory of the remaining supplies is taken, and a cost expiration adjusting journal entry is entered in the books to reflect the cost of the supplies that were used (expired) during the period. This entry also restates the Supplies Inventory account on the balance sheet to reflect the supplies actually on hand at the end of the period.

To illustrate, assume that during 1987 McDonnell Douglas purchased supplies in the form of spare parts to support the manufacture of new aircraft at a total cost of $700. On December 31 a count revealed that supplies in the amount of $300 remained on hand. If the company began the year with $500 in the Supplies account, the cost of the supplies used during 1987 would be computed as shown below, and the following journal entries would have been recorded to reflect these facts.

$$\text{Supplies used} = \text{Beginning inventory} + \text{Purchases} - \text{Ending inventory}$$
$$\$900 \quad = \quad \$500 \quad + \quad \$700 \quad - \quad \$300$$

Figure 4–12   Expense or capitalize?

1 Incur cost in current period for the purpose of generating revenue.	2 Decide in what period the revenue is to be generated.	3a Current: Expense on income statement. / 3b Future: Capitalize on balance sheet.	4 Cost Expiration: as revenue is generated, convert asset to expense via an adjusting journal entry.
Salaries	Current period (expense)	Salary Expense XX Salary Payable XX	None required
Interest	Current period (expense)	Interest Expense XX Interest Payable XX	None required
Utilities	Current period (expense)	Utility Expense XX Cash XX	None required

Purchase of supplies	Future period (asset)	Supplies Inventory XX
		    Cash XX
			Supplies Expense XX
			    Supplies Inventory XX
			 (To adjust as supplies are used up.)

Purchase merchandise inventory	Future period (asset)	Inventory XX
		    Accounts Payable XX
			Cost of Goods Sold XX
			    Inventory XX
			 (To adjust as inventory is sold.)

Prepaid expenses (e.g., insurance, interest, rent)	Future period (asset)	Prepaid Rent XX
		    Cash XX
			Rent Expense XX
			    Prepaid Rent XX
			 (To adjust as rent period expires.)

Payments received in advance	Future period (liability)	Cash XX
		    Unearned Revenue XX
			Unearned Revenue XX
			    Earned Revenue XX
			 (To adjust as service is performed.)

Purchase property, plant, or equipment	Future period (asset)	Equipment XX
		    Cash XX
		    Note Payable XX
			Depreciation Expense XX
			    Accumulated Deprec. XX
			 (To adjust as useful life expires.)

Purchase intangible asset (e.g., patent, trademark)	Future period (asset)	Trademark XX
		    Cash XX
			Amortization Expense XX
			    Trademark XX
			 (To adjust as useful life expires.)

Consistency!

1987: Purchase of supplies			Dec. 31: Cost expiration adjusting journal entry		
Supplies Inventory	700		Supplies Expense	900	
Cash		700	Supplies Inventory		900
To record the purchase of supplies.			To record the use of supplies.		

In this situation, supplies in the amount of $300 would be reported on the company's December 31 balance sheet. In reality, McDonnell Douglas reported $1.3 billion of supplies in the form of spare parts on its 1987 balance sheet.

The events in this example could have been accounted for in a different manner with the same result. McDonnell Douglas, for example, could have expensed the $700 purchase of supplies and then at the end of the period, with a cost expiration adjusting journal entry, recorded an additional $200 of supplies expense and reduced the supplies on hand by $200. The following journal entries would have been recorded had McDonnell Douglas used this method.

1987: Purchase of supplies			Dec. 31: Cost expiration adjusting journal entry		
Supplies Expense	700		Supplies Expense	200	
Cash		700	Supplies Inventory		200
To record the purchase of supplies.			To record the use of supplies.		

While this second method may appear to be inconsistent with the matching principle because it initially expenses what should be a capitalized cost, it actually is not. The cost expiration adjusting journal entry, which is recorded at the end of the period *before* the financial statements are prepared, ensures that (1) the Supplies Inventory account reflects the supplies on hand at the end of the period, and (2) the Supplies Expense account reflects the supplies used during the period. Note that under both methods, the ending balances in the Supplies Inventory and Supplies Expense accounts are $300 and $900, respectively.

Merchandise Inventory. The purchase of merchandise inventory is capitalized because inventories are expected to generate revenues in the future when they are sold. According to the matching principle, the cost of the merchandise should be converted to an expense, cost of goods sold, in the period when the inventories are sold. As with supplies, the end-of-period expiration adjusting journal entry reflects the cost of the inventories that were used (sold) during the period. It also serves to restate the Inventory account on the balance sheet to reflect the merchandise that is actually on hand at the end of the period.[7]

To illustrate, assume that Toys "Я" Us, the world's largest toy specialty retail chain, purchased $5000 of merchandise inventory during 1988 and that a year-end inventory count revealed that inventories in the amount of $3000 remained on hand. Assuming that the company began the year with inventories valued at $2000, cost of goods sold would be computed as follows and the following journal entries would be recorded to reflect these facts.

---

7. This chapter assumes that Cost of Goods Sold is determined at the end of the year with a cost expiration adjusting journal entry. This procedure describes the periodic inventory method. The perpetual inventory method, which recognizes Cost of Goods Sold each time inventory is sold, is discussed in Chapter 8, which covers inventories more completely.

$$\text{Cost of goods sold} = \text{Beginning inventory} + \text{Purchases} - \text{Ending inventory}$$
$$\$4000 \quad = \quad \$2000 \quad + \quad \$5000 \quad - \quad \$3000$$

1988: Purchase of merchandise

Merchandise Inventory	5000	
Cash		5000
To record the purchase of merchandise inventory.		

Dec. 31: Cost expiration adjusting journal entry

Cost of Goods Sold	4000	
Merchandise Inventory		4000
To record the sale of merchandise inventory.		

In this example, Toys "Я" Us would report merchandise inventory of $3000 on its 1988 balance sheet and cost of goods sold on its income statement of $4000. In reality, Toys "Я" Us reported merchandise inventories of $773 million and cost of goods sold of $2.1 billion on its 1988 financial statements.

Prepaid Expenses. Prepaid expenses represent costs like insurance, interest, and rent that are paid in advance, before the associated benefit is realized. Insurance premiums, for example, are paid in advance and usually cover an entire year or more. Similarly, interest on loans is sometimes paid before the funds are used. In applying the matching principle, such prepayments are capitalized and then converted to expenses as the time period expires and benefits are realized. This periodic conversion is achieved through cost expiration adjusting journal entries.

To illustrate, assume that on January 1, 1987 General Motors (GM) purchased a $1000 insurance premium for a two-year period. The following journal entries would be made on the books of GM over the life of the insurance coverage.

Jan. 1, 1987: Purchase of insurance

Prepaid Insurance	1000	
Cash		1000
To record the purchase of insurance.		

Dec. 31, 1987 and 1988: Cost expiration adjusting journal entry

Insurance Expense	500	
Prepaid Insurance		500
To record the expiration of insurance.		

In this example GM reported in the current asset section of its 1987 balance sheet $500 of prepaid (unexpired) insurance, which was converted to an expense at the end of 1988. GM's actual 1987 balance sheet showed prepaid expenses of $3.2 billion, which represented 8 percent of current assets and 4 percent of total assets.

As in the case of supplies, a second series of journal entries can be used to apply the matching principle to prepaid expenses. That is, the initial payment can be expensed, and the cost expiration adjusting journal entry, which is recorded at the end of each period, can be recorded so that it (1) reinstates the dollar amount of the prepaid asset yet to be realized on the balance sheet and (2) reflects the amount of insurance expired during the period on the income statement. Using the same information, the following journal entries would have been recorded on January 1 and December 31 if GM used this method.

Jan. 1: Purchase of insurance

Insurance Expense	1000	
Cash		1000
To record the purchase of insurance.		

Dec. 31: Cost expiration adjusting journal entry

Prepaid Insurance	500	
Insurance Expense		500
To record the expiration of insurance.		

Unearned (Deferred) Revenues. Unearned revenues are the reverse of prepaid expenses. For every entity that prepays an expense before the associated benefit is realized, another entity receives a payment before it performs the required service. When applying the matching principle to the entity that receives payment and has yet to provide the service, a liability account, called **Unearned Revenues,** is credited when the cash is initially collected. This account is then converted to a revenue as the service is performed with an end-of-period adjusting journal entry.[8]

To illustrate, suppose that Time, Inc., the publisher of *Time, Sports Illustrated,* and other well-known magazines, received $5000 during 1987 for magazine subscriptions to be fulfilled during 1987 and 1988. Time's Cash account would immediately increase by $5000, but the company would not recognize revenue at that time because it had not yet performed the contracted service. Instead, Time would recognize a $5000 liability, indicating that it owed services in the form of magazines to its subscribers. Assume that as of the end of 1987 Time had fulfilled 60 percent of the subscriptions. At that time, therefore, an adjusting journal entry would be recorded to remove 60 percent of the liability for Time's balance sheet and, at the same time, recognize 60 percent of the revenue. The following journal entries reflect these facts.

Receipt of advance payment			**Cost expiration adjusting journal entry**		
Cash	5000		Unearned Revenue	3000	
Unearned Revenue		5000	Fees Earned		3000
To record the receipt of cash			To record the revenue from		
prior to a service.			providing a service.		

This sequence of journal entries would leave a liability for Unearned Revenues on Time's 1987 balance sheet of $2000, representing subscriptions that Time still had to fulfill. In 1987 Time actually reported unearned revenues of $404 million in the liability section of its balance sheet.

Once again, a second method can be used to apply the matching process in the case of payments received in advance. A revenue can be recognized when the cash is initially collected, followed by an end-of-period adjusting journal entry that makes the appropriate adjustments to both the Unearned Revenues and Fees Earned Accounts. The following journal entries use the preceding information to illustrate how this method is applied.

Receipt of advance payment			**Cost expiration adjusting journal entry**		
Cash	5000		Fees Earned	2000	
Fees Earned		5000	Unearned Revenues		2000
To record the receipt of cash			To restate the revenue from		
prior to a service			providing a service.		

Property, Plant, and Equipment. Transaction 8 in Figure 4–12 considers the costs of purchasing property, plant, and equipment. Since these assets are expected to help generate revenues beyond the current time period, the matching principle specifies that the acquisition costs be capitalized and amortized over the

---

8. Technically, an unearned revenue does not represent a capitalized cost because it is not an asset and, therefore, the adjusting journal entry to convert it to a revenue is not a cost expiration adjusting journal entry. However, we have chosen to categorize it as such because the concept of deferring the recognition of a revenue until the service is performed is the same as deferring the recognition of an expense until the associated benefit is realized. Both are essential to implementing the matching principle.

estimated useful lives of the assets. At the end of each period of the estimated useful life, a cost expiration adjusting journal entry is recorded to amortize a portion of the capitalized cost. As indicated earlier, the process of amortizing the cost of property, plant, and equipment is called *depreciation.*

To illustrate, assume that Delta Airlines invested $10,000 in flight equipment on January 1, 1987. At the time of the purchase, Delta's management subjectively estimated that the equipment would have a useful life of ten years, and they chose to depreciate an equal amount of the capitalized cost ($1000 = $10,000/10 years) at the end of each of the ten one-year periods. The following journal entries would have been recorded in Delta's books.

Jan. 1, 1987: Purchase of equipment		**Dec. 31, 1987, 1988, 1989, . . ., 1996:** **Cost expiration adjusting journal entry**	
Equipment	10,000	Depreciation Expense	1000
Cash	10,000	Accumulated Depreciation	1000
To record the purchase		To record depreciation	
of equipment.		on equipment.	

Note that the cost expiration adjusting journal entry involves a debit to depreciation expense that appears on the income statement for each of the ten years. It also involves a credit to an account called Accumulated Depreciation, instead of a credit to the Equipment account itself. Accumulated Depreciation is a special permanent account that appears on the asset side of the balance sheet. It offsets the asset account to which it applies (i.e., Equipment), maintaining an accumulated balance of the amount of depreciation taken on the asset up to the date of the balance sheet. Balance sheet accounts like Accumulated Depreciation, which are used to offset other balance sheet accounts, are called **contra accounts.** Subtracting the balance in the Accumulated Depreciation account from the original cost of the equipment gives rise to a number referred to as **net book value.**

Using the same information as in the preceding example, at the end of the second year (December 31, 1988) the Equipment account would appear on Delta's balance sheet as follows. The original cost of the equipment is $10,000, the accumulated depreciation is $2000, and the net book value is $8000.

Equipment	$10,000	
Less: Accumulated depreciation	2,000	$8,000

In reality, Delta purchased over $1 billion dollars of flight equipment in 1987, and the related portion of the company's 1987 balance sheet appeared as follows (dollars in billions).

Flight equipment	$4.485	
Less: Accumulated depreciation	1.915	$2.57

We commented earlier that estimating the useful life of property, plant, and equipment and choosing a method of allocating the capitalized cost to future periods is a subjective and difficult task for management. These choices can also have a significant effect on the amount of net income recognized each year because they have a direct bearing on the amount of depreciation expense that appears on the income statement. To illustrate the importance of such estimates, Delta Airlines recently decided to change the useful life estimate of its flight equipment from ten years to fifteen years. The company disclosed in its 1987 financial report that the change decreased the depreciation expense of that year by $130 million.

Intangible Assets. The final transaction in Figure 4–12 is the purchase of an intangible asset, such as a patent, trademark, or goodwill. The cost of this purchase is, once again, capitalized because the benefit of the purchase is expected to extend beyond the current period. Many intangibles have definable lives (often determined by law) over which the capitalized cost is typically amortized. The cost expiration adjusting journal entry consists of a debit to Amortization Expense and usually a credit directly to the Intangible Asset account. The contra account, Accumulated Amortization, however, is sometimes credited.

To illustrate, assume that Johnson & Johnson, a leading manufacturer of consumer health care products, purchased a patent for $34,000, which was determined by law to have a seventeen-year life. The following journal entries would be recorded by Johnson & Johnson's accountants over the patent's legal life.

Purchase of Patent			**End of each of seventeen subsequent years:** **Cost expiration adjusting journal entry**		
Patent	34,000		Amortization Expense	2000	
Cash		34,000	Patent		2000
To record the acquisition of a patent.			To record the amortization of an intangible asset.		

On its 1987 balance sheet Johnson & Johnson actually reported intangible assets in the manner illustrated below. The company's 1987 financial report indicated that these assets, which are amortized evenly over their useful lives, consist primarily of patents and goodwill. The useful life of a patent is normally seventeen years, and goodwill is amortized over a 40-year period.

	1987*	1986*
Intangible assets	$707	$449
Less: Accumulated amortization	85	56
Net book value	$622	$393

*Dollars in millions

Capitalizing and Matching: Examples

Figure 4–13 contains several examples where cost expiration adjusting journal entries are used to apply the matching principle. Such entries are designed to convert capitalized costs to expenses in future time periods as the benefits (revenues) from the initial expenditures are recognized. The transactions illustrated in Figure 4–13 consider supplies, merchandise inventory, prepaid insurance, unearned revenue, equipment, and a patent.

The $100 capitalized cost of supplies is converted to supplies expense as the supplies are used. The $600 capitalized cost of inventory is converted to cost of goods sold as the inventories are sold. The $300 capitalized costs of prepaid insurance, equipment, and the patent are amortized over the determinable, estimated, or legal life of each of these assets. These costs are allocated to future time periods by converting them to insurance expense, depreciation expense, and amortization expense, respectively, as their useful lives expire. The $240 received in advance is recorded as unearned revenue (a liability) and converted to fees earned (a revenue) as the contracted service is performed.

Note in Figure 4–13 that equal amounts of the cost of the equipment and the patent are depreciated, or amortized, in each of the three time periods. For exam-

Figure 4–13   Capitalize and match

Capitalize	Adjusting Entries during Cost Expiration Period			Explanation
	1	**2**	**3**	
Supplies 100 Cash 100 (To purchase supplies.)	Supplies Exp. 30 Supplies 30 (Supplies costing $70 on hand.)	Supplies Exp. 50 Supplies 50 (Supplies costing $20 on hand.)	Supplies Exp. 20 Supplies 20 (No supplies on hand.)	The cost of supplies is converted to expense as the supplies are used up.
Inventory 600 Accts. Pay. 600 (To purchase 6 items at $100 per item.)	COGS 100 Inventory 100 (One item sold.)	COGS 200 Inventory 200 (Two items sold.)	COGS 300 Inventory 300 (Three items sold.)	The cost of inventory is converted to expense (Cost of Goods Sold) as the inventory is sold.
Prepaid Ins. 300 Cash 300 (To purchase 3 years of insurance coverage in advance.)	Ins. Exp. 100 Prepaid Ins. 100 (The first year of insurance coverage expires.)	Ins. Exp. 100 Prepaid Ins. 100 (The second year of insurance coverage expires.)	Ins. Exp. 100 Prepaid Ins. 100 (The third year of insurance coverage expires.)	The cost of prepaid insurance is converted to expense as the insurance coverage expires.
Cash 240 Unearned Rev. 240 (Received $240 for services to be performed later.)	Unearned Rev. 120 Fees Earned 120 (Half of the service is performed.)	Unearned Rev. 60 Fees Earned 60 (One quarter of the service is performed.)	Unearned Rev. 60 Fees Earned 60 (One quarter of the service is performed.)	Revenue is recognized as the service is completed.
Equipment 9000 Note Pay. 9000 (Purchase of machinery with an estimated 3-year life and no salvage value.)	Deprec. Exp. 3000 Acc. Deprec. 3000 (First year passes assuming straight-line depreciation rate.)	Deprec. Exp. 3000 Acc. Deprec. 3000 (Second year passes.)	Deprec. Exp. 3000 Acc. Deprec. 3000 (Third year passes.)	The cost of machinery is converted to expense (Depreciation Expense) as the estimated useful life passes.
Patent 900 Cash 900 (Purchase patent with 3-year legal life.)	Amort. Exp. 300 Patent 300 (First year passes assuming straight-line amortization rate.)	Amort. Exp. 300 Patent 300 (Second year passes.)	Amort. Exp. 300 Patent 300 (Third year passes.)	The cost of obtaining the patent is converted to an expense (Amortization Expense) as the legal life passes.

ple, the $9000 equipment cost is depreciated at a rate of $3000 per period. This method is referred to as **straight-line**. It is almost always used to amortize intangible assets, but it is only one of several methods that can be used to depreciate the capitalized costs of property, plant, and equipment. We discuss these other methods in Chapter 9, where property, plant, and equipment are more completely covered.

As you study Figure 4–13, note that the cost expiration adjusting journal entries display the same three features that characterize accrual adjusting journal entries: (1) they achieve matching by allocating the cost of the asset to the period in which the benefit is realized, (2) they involve both a temporary account and a permanent account and (3) they do not involve the Cash account.

Revaluation Adjustments

At various points in the remainder of this text, we cover adjusting journal entries that are recorded at the end of the period but do not fall into the categories of accruals or cost expirations. Such adjustments serve to restate certain accounts to keep their reported values in line with existing facts. For example, the book balance of a company's Cash account is often different from the end-of-period cash balance indicated on the bank statement. When this situation arises, an adjusting journal entry must be recorded to restate the cash amount reported on the balance sheet. Similarly, the balance sheet dollar amounts of marketable securities, accounts receivable, and inventories are sometimes adjusted when the market values of these assets change.

The end-of-period adjusting journal entries required in such situations are called **revaluation adjustments.** We cover these kinds of adjustments as they arise in future chapters.

THE ANNUAL REPORT OF K MART CORPORATION

Turn now to K mart's annual report located in Appendix D. Note first that Net Cash Provided by Operations on the Statement of Cash Flows (page 33) for 1989 ($1.211 billion), 1988 ($908 million), and 1987 ($770 million) differs significantly from Net Income for 1989 ($803 million), 1988 ($692 million), and 1987 ($582 million), which is reported on the Statement of Income (page 31). In all cases Net Cash Provided by Operations is greater than Net Income, primarily because depreciation and amortization charges, which reduce Net Income, do not represent a cash outflow. Note on the Statements of Cash Flows that Depreciation and Amortization of $437 million, $401 million, and $377 were added to income in the computation of Net Cash Provided by Operations for 1989, 1988, and 1987, respectively. For a more complete explanation of the differences between Net Cash Provided by Operations and Net Income see Appendix 4A.

Refer now to merchandise Inventory ($5.671 billion), Prepaid Expense (part of $527 million), Property and Equipment ($3.896 billion), Other Assets and Deferred Charges ($578 million), Accounts Payable ($2.334 billion), and Accrued Payrolls and other Liabilities (650 million) on K mart's 1989 balance sheet (page 32). The dollar amount of Merchandise Inventory represents the capitalized cost of acquiring the inventories on hand as of the balance sheet date and the reported value of Accounts Payable is the year end amount owed due to inventory purchases on account. Cost of Merchandise Sold on the Statement of Income ($19.914 billion) represents the costs of inventories which were sold during the year. These costs were matched against sales revenues of $27.301 billion on the Statement of Income.

The dollar amount of Prepaid Expenses, which is included in Other Current Assets, represents the capitalized cost of insurance, rent, advertising, and other items expected to provide benefits during the following year. The expenses resulting from the adjusting entries to amortize these items are included on the Statement of Income in either Selling, General, and Administrative Expenses or Advertising.

The dollar amounts of Property and Equipment and Other Assets and Deferred Charges represent the capitalized costs of fixed assets and intangibles. The depre-

ciation and amortization adjusting entries, which match such costs against
nues, are also included on the Statement of Income in the category of Se
General, and Administrative Expenses. The dollar amounts of these charges can
be found on the Statement of Cash Flows. Note also that Property and Equipment, including Accumulated Depreciation, is more completely described in the
footnotes (page 37) and that the company uses principally the straight-line
method of depreciation for financial reporting purposes (page 35).

Included in the dollar amount of Accrued Payrolls and Other Liabilities are
wages, salary, and interest payable. These amounts were accrued as of January
25, 1989 with an adjusting journal entry and the related expenses are included on
the Statement of Income in the appropriate expense accounts.

REVIEW PROBLEM

This review problem illustrates the concepts developed in Chapters 3 and 4. It begins with the balance sheet of a small retail company, Kelly Supply, as of December 31, 1990 (Figure 4−14). Exchange transactions that occurred during 1991 are
then recorded in the journal (Figure 4−15) and posted in the ledger (Figure 4−
16). A worksheet (Figure 4−17) is prepared at the end of the year. Using the
worksheet, the remainder of the accounting cycle is completed, including adjusting and closing entries and the preparation of the income statement, statement of
retained earnings, and balance sheet (Figure 4−18). The statement of cash flows
is then prepared directly from entries to the Cash account in the ledger (Figure
4−19).

This illustration is intended to "tie it all together" for you. We suggest, therefore, that you spend considerable time with it. As you work through it, you may
find it helpful to refer back to the descriptions of the relevant procedures provided
in Chapters 3 and 4.

The December 31, 1990 balance sheet accounts are reflected in the ledger as
beginning balances. The journal includes the day-to-day transactions for the year
1991. These transactions are numbered (1)−(11). Each transaction is described
and has been posted in the ledger. The numbered entries in the ledger correspond
to the numbers assigned to the transactions in the journal.

At year end, the adjusting and closing journal entries are recorded in the journal and posted to the ledger. Adjusting entries are numbered (12)−(19) and closing entries have been assigned (20)−(22). Adjusting entries (14), (17) and (18)
are accruals, and adjusting entries (12), (13), (15), (16) and (19) are cost expirations.

Following the journal and the ledger is a worksheet for Kelly Supply for the
year ended December 31, 1991, that includes the unadjusted trial balance, adjusting entries, closing entries, and the final trial balance. Locate the account balances
on the worksheet in the ledger. Note also that the adjusting and closing entries in
the worksheet are numbered.

The income statement has been prepared from closing entry (20), the entry
that closed the revenue and expense accounts into the Income Summary account.
The statement of retained earnings can be traced to the Retained Earnings account
in the ledger. The balance sheet consists of the remaining balances in the permanent accounts, which can also be found in the final trial balance on the worksheet.

The statement of cash flows was prepared directly from the entries to the Cash T-account in the ledger. Transactions (1), (2), (3), (4), (5), and (6) are considered operating activities and the cash effects can be found in the operating section of the statement. Transaction (10) represents an investing activity. Transactions (7), (8), and (9) are considered financing activities.

After reviewing this example you may also wish to refer to Appendix 4A, where a statement of cash flows is prepared using the indirect method. In the process of preparing this statement, net income, which appears on the income statement (Figure 4–18), is reconciled with net cash flows from operating activities, which appears on the statement of cash flows (Figure 4–19). As indicated earlier, understanding the adjustments required to make such a reconciliation is important for understanding the difference between the accrual and cash systems.

Figure 4–14   Balance sheet for Kelly Supply

Kelly Supply				
Balance Sheet				
December 31, 1990				
Assets			Liabilities and Stockholders' Equity	
Cash		$12,000	Accounts payable	$ 8,000
Accounts receivable		15,000	Wages payable	3,000
Merchandise inventory		12,000	Interest payable	1,000
Prepaid rent		3,000	Dividends payable	2,000
			Unearned revenue	3,000
			Short-term note payable	5,000
Machinery	25,000		Long-term note payable	10,000
Less: Accumulated depreciation	5,000	20,000		
Patent		5,000	Common stock	30,000
			Retained earnings	5,000
			Total liabilities and	
Total assets		$67,000	stockholders' equity	$67,000

Figure 4–15   General journal for Kelly Supply

Daily Journal Entries

(1)	Cash	10,000	
	Accounts Receivable	15,000	
	Sales		25,000
	Sales of merchandise inventory.		
(2)	Cash	8,000	
	Accounts Receivable		8,000
	Receipt of cash on accounts receivable.		
(3)	Merchandise Inventory	10,000	
	Cash		3,000
	Accounts Payable		7,000
	Purchase of merchandise inventory.		
(4)	Accounts Payable	10,000	
	Cash		10,000
	Payment of accounts payable.		
(5)	Wages Payable	3,000	
	Wage Expense	7,000	
	Cash		10,000
	Payment of wages.		
(6)	Interest Payable	1,000	
	Interest Expense	1,000	
	Cash		2,000
	Payment of interest.		
(7)	Short-Term Note Payable	2,500	
	Cash		2,500
	Payment of short-term note payable.		
(8)	Cash	10,000	
	Long-Term Note Payable		10,000
	Issuance of long-term note payable.		
(9)	Dividend Payable	2,000	
	Cash		2,000
	Payment of dividend.		
(10)	Machinery	1,000	
	Cash		1,000
	Purchase of machinery.		
(11)	Dividends	1,000	
	Dividends, Payable		1,000
	Declaration of dividends.		

Adjusting Journal Entries

(12)	Cost of Goods Sold	9,000	
	Merchandise Inventory		9,000
	$13,000 of inventory on hand.		
(13)	Unearned Revenue	2,000	
	Sales		2,000
	⅔ of goods delivered.		
(14)	Interest Receivable	50	
	Interest Revenue		50
	Accrued interest on savings account.		
(15)	Depreciation Expense	3,000	
	Accumulated Deprec.		3,000
	Depreciation on machinery.		
(16)	Amortization Expense	500	
	Patent		500
	Amortization of patent.		
(17)	Wage Expense	1,000	
	Wages Payable		1,000
	Accrued wages.		
(18)	Interest Expense	2,000	
	Interest Payable		2,000
	Accrued interest on long-term note.		
(19)	Rent Expense	1,000	
	Prepaid Rent		1,000
	⅓ of rent period expired.		

Closing Journal Entries

(20)	Sales	27,000	
	Interest Revenue	50	
	Cost of Goods Sold		9,000
	Wage Expense		8,000
	Rent Expense		1,000
	Interest Expense		3,000
	Depreciation Expense		3,000
	Amortization Expense		500
	Income Summary		2,550
	To close revenue and expense accounts.		
(21)	Income Summary	2,550	
	Retained Earnings		2,550
	To close income summary.		
(22)	Retained Earnings	1,000	
	Dividends		1,000
	To close dividends.		

Figure 4-16   General ledger for Kelly Supply

Cash

	Debit	Credit	
	12,000		
(1)	10,000		
(2)	8,000		
		3,000	(3)
		10,000	(4)
		10,000	(5)
		2,000	(6)
		2,500	(7)
(8)	10,000	2,000	(9)
		1,000	(10)
	9,500		

Accounts Receivable

	Debit	Credit	
	15,000		
(1)	15,000		
		8,000	(2)
	22,000		

Interest Receivable

	Debit	Credit	
(14)	50		
	50		

Merchandise Inventory

	Debit	Credit	
	12,000		
(3)	10,000		
		9,000	(12)
	13,000		

Prepaid Rent

	Debit	Credit	
	3,000	1,000	(19)
	2,000		

Machinery

	Debit	Credit	
	25,000		
(10)	1,000		
	26,000		

Accumulated Depreciation

	Debit	Credit	
		5,000	
		3,000	(15)
		8,000	

Patent

	Debit	Credit	
	5,000	500	(16)
	4,500		

Accounts Payable

	Debit	Credit	
		8,000	
		7,000	(3)
(4)	10,000		
		5,000	

Wages Payable

	Debit	Credit	
		3,000	
(5)	3,000	1,000	(17)
		1,000	

Interest Payable

	Debit	Credit	
		1,000	
(6)	1,000	2,000	(18)
		2,000	

Dividends Payable

	Debit	Credit	
		2,000	
(9)	2,000	1,000	(11)
		1,000	

Unearned Revenue

	Debit	Credit	
		3,000	
(13)	2,000		
		1,000	

Short-Term Note Payable

	Debit	Credit	
		5,000	
(7)	2,500		
		2,500	

Long-Term Note Payable

	Debit	Credit	
		10,000	
		10,000	(8)
		20,000	

Common Stock

	Debit	Credit	
		30,000	
		30,000	

Retained Earnings

	Debit	Credit	
		5,000	
		2,550	(21)
(22)	1,000		
		6,550	

Sales

	Debit	Credit	
		25,000	(1)
		2,000	(13)
(20)	27,000		
		0	

Interest Revenue

	Debit	Credit	
		50	(14)
(20)	50		
		0	

Cost of Goods Sold

	Debit	Credit	
(12)	9,000		
		9,000	(20)
	0		

Wage Expense

	Debit	Credit	
(5)	7,000		
(17)	1,000		
		8,000	(20)
	0		

Rent Expense

	Debit	Credit	
(19)	1,000		
		1,000	(20)
	0		

Interest Expense

	Debit	Credit	
(6)	1,000		
(18)	2,000		
		3,000	(20)
	0		

Figure 4-16 (continued)

Depreciation Expense	Amortization Expense	Dividends	Income Summary
(15) 3,000	(16) 500	(11) 1,000	(21) 2,550
3,000 (20)	500 (20)	1,000 (22)	2,550 (20)
0	0	0	0

Figure 4-17   Worksheet for Kelly Supply

Kelly Supply
Worksheet
For the Year Ended December 31, 1991

Accounts	Unadjusted Trial Balance Dr.	Cr.	Adjusting Entries Dr.	Cr.	Adjusted Trial Balance Dr.	Cr.	Closing Entries Dr.	Cr.	Final Trial Balance Dr.	Cr.
Cash	9,500				9,500				9,500	
Accts. Receivable	22,000				22,000				22,000	
Interest Receivable			(14) 50		50				50	
Mer. Inventory	22,000			(12) 9,000	13,000				13,000	
Prepaid Rent	3,000			(19) 1,000	2,000				2,000	
Machinery	26,000				26,000				26,000	
Accum. Dep.		5,000		(15) 3,000		8,000				8,000
Patent	5,000			(16) 500	4,500				4,500	
Accounts Payable		5,000				5,000				5,000
Wages Payable				(17) 1,000		1,000				1,000
Interest Payable				(18) 2,000		2,000				2,000
Dividends Payable		1,000				1,000				1,000
Unearned Revenue		3,000	(13) 2,000			1,000				1,000
Sht. Term Note Pay.		2,500				2,500				2,500
Long-Term Note Pay.		20,000				20,000				20,000
Common Stock		30,000				30,000				30,000
Retained Earnings		5,000				5,000	(22) 1,000	(21) 2,550		6,550
Sales		25,000		(13) 2,000		27,000	(20) 27,000			
Interest Revenue				(14) 50		50	(20) 50			
COGS			(12) 9,000		9,000			(20) 9,000		
Wage Expense	7,000		(17) 1,000		8,000			(20) 8,000		
Rent Expense			(19) 1,000		1,000			(20) 1,000		
Interest Expense	1,000		(18) 2,000		3,000			(20) 3,000		
Deprec. Exp.			(15) 3,000		3,000			(20) 3,000		
Amort. Exp.			(16) 500		500			(20) 500		
Dividends	1,000				1,000			(22) 1,000		
Income Summary							(21) 2,550	(20) 2,550		
	96,500	96,500	18,550	18,550	102,550	102,550	30,600	30,600	77,050	77,050

Figure 4–18 Financial statements for Kelly Supply

Kelly Supply
Income Statement
For the Year Ended December 31, 1991

Revenues		
Sales	$27,000	
Interest revenue	50	
Total revenues		$27,050
Expenses		
Cost of goods sold	9,000	
Wage expense	8,000	
Rent expense	1,000	
Interest expense	3,000	
Depreciation expense	3,000	
Amortization expense	500	
Total expenses		24,500
Net income		$2,550

Kelly Supply
Statement of Retained Earnings
For the Year Ended December 31, 1991

Beginning balance	$5,000
Plus: Net income	2,550
Less: Dividends	1,000
Ending balance	$6,550

Kelly Supply
Balance Sheet
December 31, 1991

Assets			Liabilities and Stockholders' Equity	
Cash		$9,500	Accounts payable	$5,000
Accounts receivable		22,000	Wages payable	1,000
Interest receivable		50	Interest payable	2,000
Merchandise inventory		13,000	Dividends payable	1,000
Prepaid rent		2,000	Unearned revenues	1,000
Machinery	$26,000		Short-term note payable	2,500
Less: Accumulated			Long-term note payable	20,000
depreciation	8,000	18,000	Common stock	30,000
Patent		4,500	Retained earnings	6,550
			Total liabilities and	
Total assets		$69,050	stockholders' equity	$69,050

Figure 4–19   Statement of cash flows for Kelly Supply

Kelly Supply Statement of Cash Flows For the Year Ended December 31, 1991		
Operating activities		
Collections from sales	$10,000	
Collections of accounts receivable	8,000	
Payments for inventory purchases	(3,000)	
Payments on accounts payable	(10,000)	
Payments for wages	(10,000)	
Payments for interest	(2,000)	
Net cash increase (decrease) from operating activities		($ 7,000)
Investing activities		
Purchase of machinery	(1,000)	
Net cash increase (decrease) from investing activities		(1,000)
Financing activities		
Issuance of long-term note payable	10,000	
Payment of dividend	(2,000)	
Principal payments on short-term note payable	(2,500)	
Net cash increase (decrease) from financing activities		5,500
Net cash increase (decrease) during 1991		($ 2,500)
Beginning cash balance (December 31, 1990)		12,000
Ending cash balance (December 31, 1991)		$ 9,500

SUMMARY OF LEARNING OBJECTIVES

1   Describe the basic difference between the cash and accrual systems of accounting and the type of information that each provides about the financial condition of a company.

Across time the accrual and the cash systems recognize the same amount of performance. The basic difference lies in the timing of the performance recognition. The accrual system recognizes performance (net income) when a company's overall level of wealth (assets less liabilities) changes. The cash system recognizes performance (net cash flow) when there is a change in the cash balance.

Stockholders and potential investors place a special emphasis on the dollar amount of net income, which results from the accrual system, because they are interested in assessing the earning power and growth potential of companies. Creditors place a special emphasis on cash flow numbers because they are interested in assessing a company's ability to service outstanding and future debts. Both accrual and cash flow numbers are important, because cash must be managed in the short run for a company to realize its long-run earning power.

2   Explain the role of adjusting journal entries and why they are necessary for the accrual system of accounting.

The adjusting journal entries discussed in this chapter are recorded in the books for either of two primary reasons: (1) so that revenues are recognized when operating transactions create assets or discharge liabilities, or (2) expenses are recognized when operating transactions reduce assets or create liabilities. These adjusting entries give rise to a performance measure (net income) that reflects changes in a company's wealth, rather than changes in its cash balance. Such a performance measure is the objective of the accrual system of accounting. Thus, adjusting journal entries are necessary for implementing the accrual system of accounting.

3 Identify and define the two kinds of adjusting journal entries, and provide several examples of each.

The two kinds of adjusting journal entries are: (1) accruals, and (2) cost expirations. Accruals refer to asset and liability accounts that build up over time. Examples include Accrued Wages and Accrued Interest. The adjusting journal entries associated with accruals recognize the increase of either an asset or a liability.

Cost expirations refer to previously capitalized costs that are *written down* over time. Examples include the use of supplies, the sale of inventories, the expiration of prepaid expenses and unearned revenues, depreciation on fixed assets, and the amortization of intangible assets. The adjusting journal entries associated with cost expirations reduce a previously recognized asset or liability.

4 Explain the matching process and describe how accrual and cost expiration adjusting journal entries help to apply it.

The matching process consists of four separate steps:

1. A resource is expended.
2. The question is asked, "In what period is the benefit to be realized?"
3. If the benefit is realized in the current period, the expenditure is expensed. If the benefit is realized in a future period, the expenditure is capitalized.
4. Capitalized expenditures are converted to expenses as the future benefits are realized.

Accrual adjusting journal entries are designed to ensure that assets or liabilities that are created or discharged in the current period are recognized in that period. Accruals help to apply Step 3 in the description of the matching process above.

Cost expiration adjusting journal entries are designed primarily to convert previously capitalized assets to expenses as the benefits associated with the assets are realized. Such entries help to apply Step 4 in the description of the matching process above.

APPENDIX 4A

The Statement of Cash Flows: The Indirect Method

Another common way to prepare the statement of cash flows is called the **indirect method.** This procedure is identical to the direct method except for one important difference: the operating section of the statement of cash flows does not

Figure 4A-1   Statement of cash flows: indirect method

Kelly Supply Statement of Cash Flows For the Year Ended December 31, 1991		
Operating activities		
Net income (from income statement)	$ 2,550	
Less: Increase in accounts receivable	(7,000))	
Less: Increase in interest receivable	(50)	
Less: Increase in merchandise inventory	(1,000)	
Plus: Decrease in prepaid rent	1,000	
Less: Decrease in accounts payable	(3,000)	
Less: Decrease in wages payable	(2,000)	
Less: Decrease in unearned revenue	(2,000)	
Plus: Increase in interest payable	1,000	
Plus: Depreciation	3,000	
Plus: Amortization	500	
Net cash increase (decrease) from operating activities		$ (7,000)
Investing activities		
Purchase of machinery	(1,000)	
Net cash increase (decrease) from investing activities		(1,000)
Financing activities		
Issuance of long-term note payable	10,000	
Payment of dividend	(2,000)	
Principal payments on short-term note payable	(2,500)	
Net increase (decrease) from financing activities		5,500
Net cash increase (decrease) during 1991		($ 2,500)
Beginning cash balance (December 31, 1990)		12,000
Ending cash balance (December 31, 1991)		$ 9,500

consist of entries that can be linked to the Cash T-account. Instead, it consists of the adjustments required to convert net income to net cash increase (decrease) due to operating activities. The indirect method is so named because it computes net cash increase (decrease) due to operating activities in an *indirect* manner. Using the information provided in the review problem at the end of the chapter, Figure 4A–1 shows the statement of cash flows for Kelly Supply prepared under the indirect method.[9]

Note that this statement of cash flows is exactly the same as the one in Figure 4–19 except for the manner in which net cash increase (decrease) due to operating activities is computed. In this statement, net income, which is taken from the income statement (Figure 4–18), is adjusted to reflect the differences between accrual and cash accounting. These adjustments are described in Figure 4A–2.

An income statement can be converted to a cash basis by recognizing first that each income statement account is related to one or more balance sheet accounts. The chart in Figure 4A–3 summarizes these relationships. It includes each ac-

---

9. Professional pronouncements require that the adjustments required to get from net income to net cash increase (decrease) due to operating activities must also be disclosed in a separate section on the face of a statement of cash flows prepared under the direct method. Also, the format of the statement in Figure 4A-1 does not exactly conform to that prescribed. These provisions are discussed more completely in Chapter 15.

Figure 4A-2   Accrual: cash reconciliation

Income Statement		Activity in Related Balance Sheet Account		Statement of Cash Flows
Sales revenue	$27,000	Less: Increase in accounts receivable (22,000 − 15,000 = 7,000) Less: Decrease in unearned revenue (3,000 − 1,000 = 2,000)	$18,000	Cash inflow from sales
Interest revenue	50	Less: Increase in interest receivable (50 − 0 = 50)	0	Cash inflow from interest
Cost of goods sold	(9,000)	Less: Increase in merch. inventory (13,000 − 12,000 = 1,000) Less: Decrease in accounts payable (8,000 − 5,000 = 3,000)	(13,000)	Cash outflow from inventory
Wage expense	(8,000)	Less: Decrease in wages payable (3,000 − 1,000 = 2,000)	(10,000)	Cash outflow from wages
Rent expense	(1,000)	Plus: Decrease in prepaid rent (3,000 − 2,000 = 1,000)	0	Cash outflow from rent
Interest expense	(3,000)	Plus: Increase in interest payable (2,000 − 1,000 = 1,000)	(2,000)	Cash outflow from interest
Depreciation expense	(3,000)	Plus: Increase in accumulated depreciation (8,000 − 5,000 = 3,000)	0	Cash outflow from depreciation
Amortization expense	(500)	Plus: Decrease in patent (5,000 − 4,500 = 500)	0	Cash outflow from amortization
Net income	$ 2,550		($7,000)	Net cash increase (decrease) from operating activities

count appearing on the income statement, the related balance sheet accounts, and the numbers of the related journal entries recorded in Kelly Supply's journal (Figure 4–15).

Using this chart as a guide, the cash effect of each transaction affecting the income statement can be traced. For example, sales revenue on the income statement can be explained in part by changes in the Cash account (Entries 1 and 2), in part by changes in the Accounts Receivable account (Entries 1 and 2), and in part by changes in the Unearned Revenues account (Entry 13). To determine the cash receipts during the period due to sales activities, the dollar amount of Sales Revenue must be adjusted for changes in Accounts Receivable and Unearned Revenues.

In the review problem, Accounts Receivable of Kelly Supply increased from $15,000 to $22,000 during 1991. Increases in the Accounts Receivable balance suggest that cash receipts from Kelly's customers during 1991 were less than the dollar amount of sales recorded during that period. The increase of $7000 in the Accounts Receivable balance, therefore, must be subtracted from Sales Revenue in the computation of cash inflow from sales. The decrease of $2000 in the Unearned Revenues account also indicates that cash receipts were less than recorded sales during 1991, and also should be subtracted from Sales Revenue in the computation of cash inflow from sales. As a result, the following computation of cash inflow from sales is indicated on Figure 4A–2: Sales ($27,000), less the increase in Accounts Receivable ($7000), less the decrease in Unearned Revenues ($2000), equals cash inflow from sales ($18,000).

Note that on the statement of cash flows prepared under the indirect method (Figure 4A–1), net income is reduced by the $7000 increase in Accounts Receiv-

Figure 4A–3 Related income statement and balance sheet accounts

Income Statement Account	Balance Sheet Accounts	Journal Entry
Sales	Cash, accounts receivable, unearned revenues	(1) (2) (13)
Interest revenue	Cash, interest receivable	(14)
Cost of goods sold	Cash, inventory, accounts payable	(3) (4) (12)
Wage expense	Cash, wages payable	(5) (17)
Rent expense	Cash, prepaid rent	(19)
Interest expense	Cash, interest payable	(6) (18)
Depreciation expense	Accumulated depreciation	(15)
Amortization expense	Patent	(16)

able and the $2000 decrease is Unearned Revenues. Such adjustments are required because the dollar amount of sales, which increased net income, is $9000 greater than the cash received from customers, which represents the amount that should be reflected on the statement of cash flows.

A similar set of adjustments is required when computing cash payments for merchandise purchases from the dollar amount in Cost of Goods Sold. Cash, Merchandise Inventory, and Accounts Payable are the balance sheet accounts related to Cost of Goods Sold. To compute cash payments from merchandise purchases, the changes in the Merchandise Inventory account (Entries 3 and 12) and the Accounts Payable account (Entries 3 and 4) must be considered. In this case both the $1000 increase in Merchandise Inventory and the $3000 decrease in Accounts Payable are added to Cost of Goods Sold ($9000) in arriving at the $13,000 cash outflow from inventory purchases. These adjustments are added to Cost of Goods Sold because an increase in inventory and a reduction in accounts payable indicate that inventory purchases and, especially, the cash payments on those purchases exceed the cost of the inventories sold. In other words, cash payments due to inventory purchases exceed the dollar amount of Cost of Goods Sold. On the statement of cash flows, therefore, net income must be reduced both by the $1000 increase in inventory and the $3000 decrease in accounts payable when computing the cash increase (decrease) due to operating activities.

Wage, rent, and interest expense are adjusted in much the same way as the sales and cost of goods sold examples above. However, they are somewhat less complicated because the adjustments involve examining the changes in only one balance sheet account. Wages Payable decreased from $3000 to $1000 during 1991, which indicates that cash payments for wages exceeded by $2000 the amount of wage expense recognized. Thus, the cash payments for wages were $10,000, and on the statement of cash flows, net income must be reduced by $2000 in the computation of net cash increase (decrease) due to operating activities.

Prepaid rent decreased from $3000 to $2000 during 1991, indicating that the dollar amount of rent expense exceeded the cash payments for rent by $1000. Cash payments for rent, therefore, were $0, and on the statement of cash flows, net income, which was reduced by rent expense, must be increased by $1000 in the computation of cash increase (decrease) due to operating activities.

Interest payable increased from $1000 to $2000, indicating that the dollar amount of the interest expense recognized during 1991 exceeded the cash payments for interest by $1000. Cash payments for interest, therefore, were $2000,

Figure 4A–4   Formula to convert accrual numbers to cash numbers

Income Statement	Adjustment	Operating Section of Statement of Cash Flows
Accrual revenue	Plus: Increase in related liability Less: Decrease in related liability Less: Increase in related asset Plus: Decrease in related asset	Equals: operating cash inflows
(Accrual expense)	Less: Increase in related asset Plus: Decrease in related asset Plus: Increase in related liability Less: Decrease in related liability	Equals: (operating cash outflows)
Book gains (Book losses) (Depreciation) (Amortization)	No cash effect	
Accrual net income		Net cash flow from operating activities

and on the statement of cash flows, net income, which was reduced by interest expense, must be increased by $1000 in the computation of cash increase (decrease) due to operating activities.

The cash flows associated with depreciation and amortization expense can be determined by referring to Kelly Supply's journal (Figure 4–15) and, specifically, the adjusting journal entries that recognize depreciation on the machinery (15) and amortization of the patent (16). Note that they involve no cash payments; they are both cost expiration adjusting journal entries. On the statement of cash flows, therefore, the dollar amount of depreciation and amortization expense must be added back to net income, which they reduced, in the computation of net cash increase (decrease) due to operating activities.

The adjustments for depreciation and amortization often explain why net cash flow from operating activities normally exceeds net income, especially for companies with large amounts of property, plant, and equipment subject to depreciation. Consider, for example, the Statement of Cash Flows in K mart's annual report, which was prepared under the indirect method (page 33). For 1989, the difference between Net Income and Net Cash provided by Operations was $413 million, while depreciation and amortization charges for the year were $437 million.

Figure 4A–4 is a general formula for converting an accrual income statement to a cash basis. You may find it useful in explaining the adjustments on Figures 4A–1 and 4A–2. However, you should aim to understand the reasoning underlying each adjustment. Blindly applying formulas like the one in Figure 4A–4 can hinder the learning process as much as aid it.

SUMMARY OF LEARNING OBJECTIVE

5 Prepare the statement of cash flows under the indirect method and explain how net income is converted to net cash flow from operating activities.

Preparing the statement of cash flows under the indirect method is identical to using the direct method except for one important difference. The operating section of the statement of cash flows does not consist of entries taken *directly* from the cash T-account. Instead, it consists of the adjustments required to convert net income to net cash increase (decrease) due to operating activities. These adjustments, which involve analyzing changes in the balance sheet accounts that relate to each income statement item, reflect the differences between accrual and cash accounting. A formula that summarizes these adjustments is contained in Figure 4A−4.

KEY TERMS

Accrual accounting (p. 157)
Accruals (p. 166)
Adjusting journal entry (p. 166)
Amortization (p. 172)
Capitalize (p. 171)
Cash flow accounting (p. 157)
Contra account (p. 177)
Cost expiration (p. 169)
Depreciation (p. 172)

Direct method (p. 161)
Expensed (p. 170)
Indirect method (p. 188)
Matching principle (p. 158)
Net book value (p. 177)
Revaluation adjustment (p. 180)
Straight-line depreciation (p. 179)
Unearned Revenues (p. 176)

QUESTIONS FOR DISCUSSION AND REVIEW

1. Briefly describe how the statement of cash flows can be prepared from the Cash account in the ledger.

2. Define and differentiate among operating activities, investing activities, and financing activities. Why is the statement of cash flows divided into these three sections?

3. Distinguish between a capital transaction and an operating transaction. Provide four examples of each. Why is such a distinction important to the financial statements, and how is it related to the statement of cash flows?

4. Of what significance is net cash increase (decrease) due to operating activities? Is this number likely to differ from the net income number found on the income statement? Why or why not?

5. Briefly describe accrual accounting. Construct an example to show that the primary difference between accrual and cash accounting is the timing of the performance recognition.

6. Which of the two systems, accrual or cash accounting, provides the most useful information? What kind of investors (equity or debt?) tend to be most interested in accrual-

based accounting numbers and why? What kind of investors tend to be most interested in cash accounting numbers and why?

7. Define the matching principle, and explain how it relates to the accrual system of measuring performance.

8. What are adjusting journal entries and how do they relate to the accrual system of accounting? Why are they recorded in the books? Where do they fit in the accounting cycle, and when are they recorded?

9. What are the three categories of adjusting journal entries, and what three characteristics do all adjusting entries have in common?

10. Accruals represent one of the categories of adjusting journal entries. Provide two examples, journalize them, and show how they share the three characteristics common to all adjusting journal entries.

11. Differentiate a cost expiration from an accrual.

12. Explain the difference between *capitalizing* a cost and *expensing* it. How do these two accounting treatments affect the balance sheet and income statement? Which of the two treatments has the more negative effect on net income of the current period? Which of the two treatments recognizes the greatest amount of total expense?

13. Explain how the choice of capitalizing or expensing a given cost relates to the matching principle, and discuss how this decision reflects the distinction between a capital transaction and an operating transaction.

14. Explain how a cost expiration adjusting journal entry helps to apply the matching principle appropriately. Provide three examples of cost expiration adjusting journal entries.

15. When is the cost of purchasing inventory matched against the benefit the inventory produces for a company? How and why is this done on the books? Provide an example.

16. When is the cost of paying salaries matched against the benefit it produces for a company? How and why is this done on the books? Provide an example.

17. When a cash payment is received before a service is provided, how is this accounted for in the books? How is this accounting treatment an application of the matching principle? Compare this treatment to the methods used to account for a prepaid expense.

18. Suppose that Mr. Gizmo, chief executive officer of Galaxy Enterprises, purchased a piece of machinery at the beginning of 1990 and wants net income on the income statement of that year to be as high as possible. He has the choice of depreciating the machinery over five or ten years. Which of the two choices will he take? Is it clear which of the two choices is a better application of the matching principle? Why or why not?

19. Explain how a prepayment for a three-year insurance policy is treated on the books, and compare this treatment to the method used to account for the purchase of a piece of equipment. You will note that both treatments involve capitalizing and amortizing. Which of the two is a more straightforward application of the matching principle? Why? Which of the two involves more uncertain estimates, giving the manager greater discretion over the presentation of the financial statements?

20. When accounting for supplies inventory, prepaid expenses, or payments received in advance, it is not unusual to expense, instead of capitalize, the initial expenditure. Is this necessarily a violation of the matching principle? Why or why not? Construct an example to support your answer.

21. *(Appendix 4A)* What is the difference between the direct method of preparing the statement of cash flows and the indirect method?

22. *(Appendix 4A)* For each account on the income statement, identify the balance sheet accounts that are related to it. For example, Sales is related to Cash, Accounts Receivable, and Unearned Revenues.

23. *(Appendix 4A)* How can the related balance sheet accounts identified in (22) be used to convert net income to net cash increase (decrease) due to operating activities?

24. *(Appendix 4A)* What effect do the income statement accounts for Depreciation Expense and Amortization Expense have on the statement of cash flows?

EXERCISES

E4–1

(Preparing the statement of cash flows from the cash account in the ledger)   The following Cash T-account summarizes all the transactions affecting cash during 1990 for Miller Manufacturing.

Cash

Beginning balance	10,000	Inventory purchases	25,000
Sales of inventories	40,000	Accounts payable payments	9,000
Receivables collections	35,000	Bank loan principal payments	10,000
Sales of long-term investments	12,500	Loan interest	3,000
Issuance of common stock	15,000	Wages	17,500
Long-term borrowings	10,000	Dividend payments	4,000
		Administrative expenses	14,000
		Equipment purchases	12,000

Required:

a. Compute the ending cash balance.

b. Prepare a statement of cash flows (direct method).

E4–2

(Classifying adjusting journal entries)   Eaton Enterprises made the following adjusting journal entries on December 31, 1990. Journal entry explanations have been omitted.

(1) Rent Expense	1200		(4) Interest Receivable	1500	
Rent Payable		1200	Interest Revenue		1500
(2) Insurance Expense	5000		(5) Fees Earned	200	
Prepaid Insurance		5000	Unearned Revenue		200
(3) Depreciation Expense	20,000				
Accum. Dep		20,000			

Required:

a. Give a brief explanation for each of the above entries.

b. Classify each of the above entries as either a cost expiration adjusting entry or an accrual adjusting entry.

E4–3

(Classifying transactions)   Hog Heaven Rib Joint made the following journal entries on December 31, 1990. Journal entry explanations have been omitted.

(1) Wage Expense	5,000		(7) Equipment	5,000	
Wage Payable		5,000	Cash		5,000
(2) Interest Expense	1,000		(8) Supplies Expense	12,000	
Cash		1,000	Supplies Inventory		12,000
(3) Cash	10,000		(9) Accounts Payable	8,000	
Note Payable		10,000	Cash		8,000
(4) Rent Expense	1,500		(10) Depreciation Expense	14,000	
Prepaid Rent		1,500	Accum. Dep.		14,000
(5) Prepaid Insurance	2,500		(11) Advertising expense	8,000	
Insurance Expense		2,500	Cash		8,000
(6) Cash	3,000		(12) Prepaid Advertising	3,000	
Unearned Revenue		3,000	Advertising Exp.		3,000

Required: Place each of the transactions above in one of the following five categories: (1) operating cash flow, (2) investing cash flow, (3) financing cash flow, (4) accrual adjusting journal entry, (5) cost expiration adjusting journal entry.

E4–4 *(Recognizing accrued wages)* The Hurst Corporation pays its employees every Friday for the week just ended. On January 2, 1990 the company paid its employees $25,000 for the week beginning Monday, December 29.

Required:

a. Assuming that the employees earned wages evenly throughout the week, prepare any adjusting journal entries that were necessary on December 31, 1989.
b. Prepare the journal entry that would be recorded on Friday, January 2 when the wages are paid.
c. Complete a chart like the following.

	1989	1990	Total
Wage expense			
Cash outflow associated with wages			

d. What is the purpose of the adjusting journal entry on December 31?

E4–5 *(Depreciating a fixed asset)* Briland Manufacturing purchased a printing press on January 1, 1990 for $6000 cash. Using the straight-line method, the company depreciated the press over a three-year useful life.

Required:

a. Prepare the adjusting journal entries required over the three-year period related to the printing press. Compute the book value of the printing press at the end of each of the three years.
b. Complete a chart like the following.

	1990	1991	1992	Total
Depreciation expense				
Cash outflow associated with the purchase of the press				

c. What is the purpose of the adjusting journal entries at the end of each period?

E4–6 *(The difference between accrual and cash accounting)* Oregon Forest Products began operations on January 1, 1990. On December 31, 1990 the company's accountant ascertains that the following amounts should be reported as expenses on the income statement.

Insurance expense	$24,000
Supplies expense	$11,000
Rent expense	$12,000

A review of the company's cash disbursements indicates that the company made related cash payments during 1990 as follows.

Insurance	$30,000
Supplies	$25,000
Rent	$7,000

Required:

a. Explain why the amounts shown as expenses do not equal the cash paid.

b. For each expense account, compute the amount that should be in the related balance sheet account as of December 31, 1990. *Hint:* Note that Forest products began operations on January 1, 1990.

E4–7

(Notes receivable and accrued interest)   Security Financial Corporation loaned $250,000 to a customer on September 30, 1989 at an annual interest rate of 12 percent. Both the principal and interest are due on September 30, 1991.

Required: On the books of Security Financial Corporation, prepare the journal entries to record the following:

a. The loan on September 30, 1989

b. Accrued interest on December 31, 1989

c. Accrued interest on December 31, 1990

d. The principal and interest collection on September 30, 1991

E4–8

(The difference between net income and net cash flow from operations)   The following journal entries were recorded in the journal of Kelly Retailing during the month of July. Journal entry explanations have been omitted.

(1)	Cash	5000	
	Accounts Receivable	2000	
	Sales		7000
(2)	Cash	4000	
	Accounts Receivable		4000
(3)	Inventory	5500	
	Accounts Payable		5500
(4)	Accounts Payable	3000	
	Cash		3000
(5)	Cost of Goods Sold	2500	
	Inventory		2500
(6)	Accrued Expenses	3000	
	Accrued Payables		3000

Required:

a. From the journal entries above prepare an income statement and the operating section of a statement of cash flows.

b. Explain why net income is not equal to net cash flow from operations, and reconcile the two numbers.

E4–9

(Preparing a statement of cash flows from original transactions)   Rahal and Watson, a small manufacturing company, entered into the following cash transactions during January of 1990.

(1) Issued 700 shares of common stock for $25 each.

(2) Collected $3600 on outstanding accounts receivable.

(3) Paid wages for the months of January of $900.

(4) Purchased land as a long-term investment for $9000 cash.

(5) Paid a $4000 dividend.

(6) Sold a piece of equipment with a book value of $5000 for $5000 cash.

(7) Paid $2000 to the bank; $900 to reduce the principal on an outstanding loan, and $1100 as an interest payment.

(8) Paid miscellaneous expenses of $2500.

Required:

a. Prepare journal entries for each transaction.

b. Prepare a cash ledger account, and compute the company's cash balance as of the end of January. Assume a beginning balance of $4000.

c. Prepare a statement of cash flows (direct method) for the month of January.

E4–10   *(Cash and accrual accounting: comparison of performance measures)*   Ephemeral Company was in business for two years, during which it entered into the following transactions.

Year 1

(1) The owners contributed $10,000 cash.

(2) At the beginning of the year, rented a warehouse for two years with a prepaid rent payment of $4000.

(3) Purchased $6000 of inventory on account.

(4) Sold half the inventory for $12,000, receiving $10,000 in cash and an account receivable of $2000.

(5) Paid wages of $3000 and also accrued wages payable of $2000.

Year 2

(1) Paid the outstanding balance for the inventory purchased in Year 1.

(2) Paid the outstanding wages payable balance.

(3) Sold the remaining inventory for $16,000 cash.

(4) Received payment on the outstanding accounts receivable.

(5) Incurred and paid wages of $5000.

(6) Returned the cash balance to the owners and shut down operations.

Required:

a. Prepare an income statement and a statement of cash flows (direct method) for both Year 1 and Year 2.

b. Complete a chart like the following.

Performance Measure	Year 1	Year 2	Total
Net income			
Net cash flow due to operating activities			

E4–11   *(Appendix 4A: Preparing the operating section of the statement of cash flows using the indirect method)*   The information below is from the adjusted trial balance of J. M. F. Corporation.

	December 31, 1990		December 31, 1989	
	Dr.	Cr.	Dr.	Cr.
Accounts Receivable	10,000		12,000	
Inventory	15,000		14,000	
Prepaid Insurance	7,500		8,000	
Accounts Payable		12,500		15,000
Interest Payable		1,000		1,200
Sales		40,000		40,000
Cost of Goods Sold	27,500		24,000	
Insurance Expense	5,000		4,000	
Interest Expense	2,500		3,000	

Required:

a. Prepare an income statement for the year ended December 31, 1990.

b. Prepare the operating section of the statement of cash flows (indirect method) for the period ended December 31, 1990.

E4–12   *(Appendix 4A: Complete a worksheet and prepare a statement of cash flows)*   Balmer and Associates has operated for one year. Its unadjusted trial balance follows.

Accounts	Unadjusted Trial Balance	
	Dr.	Cr.
Cash	3,200	
Accounts Receivable	15,800	
Rent Receivable		
Inventory	18,000	
Prepaid Insurance	1,200	
Office Equipment	43,500	
Accumulated Depreciation		0
Accounts Payable		8,500
Wages Payable		
Bonds Payable		20,000
Common Stock		40,000
Retained Earnings		
Sales		30,600
Rent Revenue		1,100
Cost of Goods Sold	11,000	
Wage Expense	7,500	
Depreciation Expense		
Insurance Expense		
Income Summary		
	100,200	100,200

The following adjusting journal entries were recorded on December 31, 1990. Journal entry explanations have been omitted.

(1) Rent Receivable	500	
Rent Revenue		500
(2) Insurance Expense	600	
Prepaid Insurance		600
(3) Wage Expense	1200	
Wages Payable		1200
(4) Depreciation Expense	1000	
Accumulated Depreciation		1000

Required:

a. Transfer the adjusting journal entries to the worksheet.

b. Complete the worksheet and prepare the financial statements, including the statement of cash flows (indirect method).

PROBLEMS

P4–1

(The effects of adjusting journal entries on the accounting equation)   Anderson Alloys made the following adjusting journal entries on December 31, 1990. Journal entry explanations have been omitted.

(1) Wage Expense	10,000		(5) Depreciation Expense	20,000	
Wages Payable		10,000	Accum. Deprec.		20,000
(2) Insurance Expense	5,000		(6) Supplies Inventory	8,000	
Insurance Payable		5,000	Supplies Expense		8,000
(3) Interest Receivable	1,000		(7) Subscription Revenue	2,000	
Interest Revenue		1,000	Unearn. Sub. Rev.		2,000
(4) Unearned Rent Rev.	6,000				
Rent Revenue		6,000			

Required: Classify each adjusting entry as either an accrual adjustment *(A)* or a cost expiration adjustment *(C)*, and indicate whether each entry increases (+), decreases (−) or has no effect (NE) on assets, liabilities, stockholders' equity, revenues, and expenses. Organize your answer in the following way. The first journal entry has been done for you.

Entry Classification	Assets	Liabilities	Stockholders' Equity	Revenues	Expenses
A	NE	+	−	NE	+

P4–2

(Preparing adjusting journal entries)   The following information is available for M & M Johnson, Inc. Prepare the adjusting journal entries necessary on December 31, 1990.

a. The December 31, 1990 Supplies Inventory balance is $120,000. A count of supplies reveals that the company actually has $30,000 of supplies on hand.

b. As of December 31, 1990 Johnson, Inc. had not paid the rent for December. The monthly rent is $1500.

c. On December 20, 1990 Johnson collected $15,000 in customer advances for the subsequent performance of a service. Johnson recorded the $15,000 as service revenue, but as of December 31 had not yet performed the service.

d. The total cost of Johnson's fixed assets is $500,000. Johnson estimates that the assets have a useful life of ten years and uses the straight-line method of depreciation.

e. Johnson borrowed $10,000 at an annual rate of 10 percent on July 1, 1990. The first interest payment will be made on January 1, 1991.

f. Johnson placed several ads in local newspapers during December. On December 28 the company received a $25,000 bill for the ads, which was not recorded at that time.

g. On July 1, 1990 Johnson paid the premium for a one-year life insurance policy. The $250 cost of the premium was capitalized when paid.

P4–3

(Inferring adjusting journal entries from changes in the trial balance)   The following information is available for McKey Company. Prepare the adjusting journal entries that gave rise to the changes indicated.

Account	Unadjusted Trial Balance	Adjusted Trial Balance
Prepaid Rent	13,500	12,700
Prepaid Insurance	7,500	8,000
Accumulated Depreciation	37,000	39,200
Salaries Payable	1,500	2,300
Unearned Revenues	1,300	600
Fees Earned	87,600	88,300
Rent Expense	6,400	7,200
Insurance Expense	5,500	5,000
Depreciation Expense	0	2,200
Salary Expense	3,900	4,700

P4–4

(Reconciling accrual and cash flow dollar amounts) Burkholder Corporation borrowed $24,000 from its bank on January 1, 1988, at an annual interest rate of 10 percent. The $24,000 principal is to be paid as a lump sum at the end of the period of the loan which is after December 31, 1989. This is the only interest-bearing debt held by Burkholder.

Required: The chart below contains six *independent* cases, each related to the Burkholder Corporation. Compute the missing amount in each case, assuming that the loan described is Burkholder's only outstanding loan.

	Case 1	Case 2	Case 3	Case 4	Case 5	Case 6
12/31/88 interest payable balance	600	800	400	?	200	?
Cash interest payments during 1989	3000	?	2400	2600	?	2800
12/31/89 interest payable balance	?	400	?	200	400	0

P4–5

(Two ways to account for prepaid expenses and unearned revenues) Morrissey Real Estate rents a warehouse to the Hill Dance Group. On November 1, 1990 the Group pays Morrissey $1500 for the rental period November and December 1990, and January 1991.

Required:

a. Assume Morrissey Real Estate initially records all such collections as liabilities. Prepare both the original journal entry and the appropriate December 31, 1990 adjusting journal entry for Morrissey.

b. Assume Morrissey Real Estate initially records all such collections as revenue. Prepare both the original journal entry and the appropriate December 31, 1990 adjusting journal entry for Morrissey.

c. Assume that the Hill Dance Group initially capitalizes the $1500 payment. Prepare both the original journal entry and the appropriate December 31, 1990 adjusting journal entry for the dance group.

d. Assume that the Hill Dance Group initially expenses the $1500 payment. Prepare both the original journal entry and the appropriate December 31, 1990 adjusting journal entry for the dance group.

P4–6

(Revenue recognition, cost expiration, and cash flows) Prustate Insurance Company collected $240,000 from Jacobs Printing Corporation for a two-year fire insurance policy on May 31, 1989. The policy is in effect from June 1, 1989, to May 31, 1991.

Required:

a. Assume that Prustate Insurance Company recorded the $240,000 cash collection as a liability on May 31, 1989.

(1) Prepare the entry to record the cash collection.

(2) Prepare the adjusting entry necessary on December 31, 1989.

(3) What was the purpose of the adjusting journal entry on December 31, 1989?

(4) Complete a chart like the following.

	1989	1990	1991	Total
Insurance revenue				
Cash receipts associated with insurance				

b. Assume that Jacob's Printing Corporation recorded the $240,000 cash payment as an asset on May 31, 1989.

(1) Prepare the entry to record the cash payment.

(2) Prepare the adjusting entry necessary on December 31, 1989.

(3) What was the purpose of the adjusting journal entry on December 31, 1989?

(4) Complete a chart like the following.

	1989	1990	1991	Total
Insurance expense				
Cash payments associated with insurance				

P4–7 *(Two ways to account for prepaid insurance and unearned revenue)*   Opus Enterprises sold a one-year insurance policy to the Binkley Anxiety Support Group for $24,000 on September 30, 1990.

Required:

a. Assume that Opus Enterprises initially records all such collections as liabilities. Prepare both the original entry and the appropriate December 31, 1990 adjusting journal entry for Opus.

b. Assume that Opus Enterprises initially records all such collections as revenues. Prepare both the original entry and the appropriate December 31, 1990 adjusting journal entry for Opus.

c. Assume that the Binkley Anxiety Support group initially records the $24,000 payment as an asset. Prepare both the original entry and the appropriate December 31, 1990 adjusting journal entry for Binkley.

d. Assume that the Binkley Anxiety Support group initially records the $24,000 payment as an expense. Prepare both the original entry and the appropriate December 31, 1990 adjusting journal entry for Binkley.

P4–8 *(Two ways to account for prepaid insurance)*   Trudeau Graphics has a number of insurance policies to cover its employees, customers, and buildings. The following list shows the insurance policies organized by type.

Policy	Purchase Date	Length of Coverage	Purchase Amount
Customer liability	1/1/90	1 year	$ 50,000
Employee health	6/30/90	1 year	120,000
Storm damage	4/1/90	1 year	80,000
	4/1/90	1 year	100,000
Fire	1/1/90	3 years	300,000
	6/30/90	2 years	220,000
	9/30/90	1 year	90,000

Required:

a. Assume that Trudeau capitalizes the cost of insurance policies when acquired, and prepare the adjusting journal entries necessary on December 31, 1990. Prepare a separate entry for each policy.

b. Assume that Trudeau expenses the cost of insurance policies when acquired, and prepare the adjusting journal entries necessary on December 31, 1990. Prepare a separate entry for each policy.

P4–9 *(Completing the worksheet and preparing the financial statements)* The following unadjusted trial balance is presented for J. Feeney, Inc. as of December 31, 1990.

Account	Debit	Credit
Cash	$ 92,000	
Accounts Receivable	178,000	
Merchandise Inventory	200,000	
Prepaid Rent	14,000	
Supplies Inventory	75,000	
Plant and Equipment	550,000	
Accumulated Depreciation		149,000
Accounts Payable		104,000
Notes Payable		50,000
Common Stock		300,000
Retained Earnings		501,000
Sales		900,000
Cost of Goods Sold	650,000	
Supplies Expense	33,000	
Insurance Expense	49,000	
Wage Expense	143,000	
Dividends	20,000	
	$2,004,000	$2,004,000

J. Feeney used the following information to prepare adjusting journal entries on December 31, 1990.

(1) Depreciation expense in the amount of $40,000 is recorded each year.

(2) A physical count of the merchandise inventory indicates that $120,000 is on hand at the end of the year.

(3) The company makes a $14,000 rent payment on July 1 of each year, which covers the subsequent twelve-month period.

(4) A physical count on December 31, 1990 indicates that $58,000 of supplies are on hand. The balance in Supplies Expense represents all expenditures made during 1990 for supplies.

(5) The company will pay employees $30,000 for wages earned for the thirty-day period ending January 15, 1991. Assume that the $30,000 is earned at a rate of $1000 per day.

(6) On November 1, 1990 the company began renting office space to a small insurance agency. The contract calls for rent payments of $5000 per month. No rental payments have been received as of the end of the year.

(7) The $50,000 note payable was issued on August 1, 1990. It matures on January 1, 1991 and has a stated annual interest rate of 12 percent.

Required:

a. Prepare the adjusting journal entries necessary on December 31, 1990.

b. Prepare closing journal entries.

c. Prepare the 1990 income statement and balance sheet as of December 31, 1990.

P4–10 *(Comprehensive problem)* The following balance sheet is presented for J. D. F. Company as of December 31, 1989.

J. D. F. Company
Balance Sheet
December 31, 1989

Assets		
Cash		$ 96,000
Accounts receivable		178,000
Merchandise Inventory		210,000
Prepaid insurance		68,000
Supplies inventory		50,000
Long-term investments		150,000
Equipment	$480,000	
Less: Accumulated depreciation	98,000	382,000
Machinery	950,000	
Less: Accumulated depreciation	230,000	720,000
Patent		75,000
Total assets		$1,929,000
Liabilities and Stockholders' Equity		
Accounts payable		225,000
Wages payable		68,000
Mortgage payable		300,000
Bonds payable		500,000
Common stock		500,000
Retained earnings		336,000
Total liabilities and stockholders' equity		$1,929,000

During 1990, J.D.F. entered into the following transactions.

(1) Made credit sales of $1,250,000 and cash sales of $350,000. The cost of the inventory sold was $800,000.

(2) Purchased $788,000 of inventory on account.

(3) Made cash payments of $425,000 to employees for salaries. This amount includes the wages due employees as of December 31, 1989.

(4) Purchased $110,000 of supplies inventory by issuing a six-month note that matures on March 12, 1991.

(5) Collected $892,000 from customers in payment of open accounts receivable.

(6) Paid suppliers $820,000 for payment of open accounts payable.

(7) Sold a long-term investment for $34,000. The investment had been purchased for $30,000.

(8) Paid $60,000 cash for advertising, $36,000 cash for rent, and $52,000 cash for maintenance. It is company policy to expense all such payments.

(9) Issued additional common stock for $180,000 cash.

(10) On September 30, 1990 a customer gave the company a note due on May 1, 1991 in payment of a $72,000 account receivable.

(11) The company declared and paid a cash dividend of $40,000.

(12) The company purchased stock in Microsoft as a long-term investment for $65,000.

J.D.F. used the following information to prepare adjusting journal entries on December 31, 1990.

(a) 40 percent of the prepaid insurance on January 1 was still in effect as of December 31, 1990.

(b) A physical count of the supplies inventory indicated that the company had $34,000 on hand as of December 31, 1990.

(c) A review of the company's advertising campaign indicates that of the expenditures made during 1990 for advertising, $25,000 applies to promotions to be undertaken during 1991.

(d) The company is charged at a rate of $3500 per month for its rental contracts.

(e) The company owes employees $43,000 for wages as of December 31, 1990.

(f) The $72,000 note receivable accepted in payment of an accounts receivable (see [10] above) specifies an annual interest rate of 9 percent.

(g) Equipment has an estimated useful life of ten years, and machinery has an estimated useful life of twenty years. The patent originally cost $125,000 and had an estimated useful life of ten years. The company uses the straight-line method to depreciate and amortize all property, plant, equipment, and intangibles.

(h) The note issued by the company (see [4] above) has a stated rate of 9 percent and was issued on September 12, 1990.

Required:

a. Open T-accounts for all balance sheet accounts as of January 1, 1990. Post beginning balances. Leave room for twenty-two additional T-accounts with nine lines per account.

b. Prepare journal entries for the activity during 1990. Post the entries to the ledger.

c. Prepare a worksheet and an unadjusted trial balance.

d. Prepare adjusting journal entries. Post these entries to the appropriate T-accounts and to the worksheet.

e. Prepare closing entries and complete the worksheet. Post these entries to the appropriate T-accounts.

f. Prepare an income statement, a statement of retained earnings, a balance sheet, and a statement of cash flows (direct method).

g. *(Appendix 4A)* Prepare a statement of cash flows (indirect method).

P4–11   *(Appendix 4A: Adjusting accruals to a cash basis)*   The following income statement and balance sheet account balances were taken from the records of Russo and Brothers.

Income Statement

Sales	$54,000
Gain on the sale of investment	3,000
Less:	
Cost of goods sold	21,000
Wage expense	12,000
Rent expense	8,000
Miscellaneous expenses	5,400
Depreciation expense	3,500
Loss on sale of machinery	1,500
Net income	$ 5,600

Balance Sheet

Accounts	12/31/90	12/31/89
Accounts receivable	37,000	43,000
Unearned revenue	3,000	5,000
Inventory	25,000	32,500
Accounts payable	17,000	19,800
Wages payable	2,600	4,600
Prepaid rent	4,900	5,100
Miscellaneous payables	3,200	1,700
Investments	13,000	15,000
Machinery	28,000	33,000
Accumulated depreciation	19,500	18,000

Required:

a. Convert the dollar balance in each income statement account to cash flow.

b. Prepare the operating section of the statement of cash flows under the indirect method for Russo and Brothers. Assume that accounts payable are used exclusively for purchases of inventory on account.

c. Compute the cash inflow associated with the sale of the investment.

d. Prepare the journal entry that recorded the sale of the machinery.

CASES

C4–1

(Amortization and depreciation and the effects of useful-life estimates on net income)   The following excerpt was taken from the 1987 annual report of RJR Nabisco, Inc.

Depreciation
Property, plant, and equipment are depreciated principally by the straight-line method.

Goodwill and Trademarks
Goodwill and trademarks are generally amortized on a straight-line basis over a forty-year period.

Required:

a. Briefly describe the difference between amortization and depreciation. How do they relate to the matching process?

b. Goodwill and trademarks were reported on Nabisco's 1986 balance sheet at $4,603 million. Approximately how much amortization was recorded by Nabisco at the end of 1987? Prepare the cost expiration adjusting journal entry.

c. If Nabisco amortized goodwill and trademarks over twenty years instead of forty years, by how much and in what direction would the company's 1987 net income be different?

C4–2

(Differences between net income and net cash flow due to operating activities)   During 1980 The Boeing Company reported profit increases in each quarter over the previous year and showed a profit increase for the total year of about 18 percent. Net cash flows due to operating activities, on the other hand, dropped from a negative $34.6 million in the second quarter of 1980 to a negative $680.1 million in the fourth quarter.

Required:

a. Boeing reported depreciation of approximately $300 million during 1980. Would this account for the fact that net cash flows due to operating activities were far below earnings? Why or why not?

b. What other explanations might account for the difference?

c. From the end of 1980 to September of 1982, the market price of Boeing stock fell from $44 ⅛ to $19 ¾, a drop of approximately 55 percent. Provide several reasons why this stock price decline may have occurred.

C4–3

(Cash collections, revenues, and the statement of cash flows)   Mary Ann Lombard is the founder of a new business, Lombard Marketing, which manufactures puzzles. A short story on the puzzle box describes a mystery that can be solved by completing the puzzle. The product has been very successful and is sold in stores such as Macy's and Harrod's. Lombard "raided her family's savings accounts and drummed up bank loans for $60,000" to get the business started. In their first year on the market, Lombard Marketing's puzzles registered sales of $750,000.

Required:

a. Would the $60,000 received from family members and bank loans be listed on the statement of cash flows as an operating, investing, or financing activity?

b. If the first-year revenues were all in the form of cash, would they be classified on the statement of cash flows as an operating, investing, or financing activity?

c. If the revenues were composed of $300,000 cash sales with the remainder on account, what dollar amounts would appear on the income statement, the statement of cash flows, and in the year-end Accounts Receivable account for Mary Ann Lombard's fledgling company?

C4–4

(Accrued liabilities and net income)   Weyerhaeuser is a company that produces forest-related products. In its 1987 annual report the company reported the following current liabilities (dollars in thousands).

Notes payable	$ 5,609
Accounts payable	292,604
Wages and salaries payable	195,299
Interest payable	51,497
Accrued income taxes payable	52,010

Net income reported in 1987 totaled $446,623.

Required:

a. Which liabilities are the result of adjusting journal entries classified as accruals?

b. For each accrual, prepare the year-end journal entry recorded by Weyerhaeuser, and describe how each entry affected the accounting equation.

c. Had these accruals been overlooked at the end of 1987, what net income would have been reported by the company for 1987?

C4–5

(Appendix 4A: Reconciling net income with net cash flows due to operating activities)   The operating section of the 1988 statement of cash flows for Nordstrom, Inc. is provided below.

Net income	$92,733
Adjustments to reconcile net income to net cash provided by operating activities.	
Depreciation	50,090
Change in	
Accounts receivable	(51,953)
Merchandise inventories	(55,362)
Prepaid expenses	(879)
Accounts payable	49,265
Accrued salaries, wages, and taxes	15,050
Accrued expenses	283
Income tax liabilities	(11,552)
Net cash provided by (used in) operating activities	$87,675

Required:

a. Was Nordstrom's statement of cash flows prepared using the direct or indirect method? Briefly describe the difference between the two methods.

b. Why is depreciation added back to net income? Is it a source of cash from operating activities?

c. For each balance sheet account showing a change above, indicate whether the dollar amount in the account increased or decreased during 1988.

The Economic and Measurement Fundamentals of Financial Accounting

Learning Objectives

1   Identify, define, and relate the four basic assumptions of financial accounting.

2   Identify the two markets in which business entities operate, express the four alternate valuation bases in terms of these two markets, and briefly describe how the valuation bases are used on the financial statements.

3   Identify and define the principles of financial accounting measurement.

4   Explain how the principle of objectivity determines the dollar values that appear on the financial statements.

5   Explain how the principles of matching and revenue recognition relate to the measure of performance.

6   Identify and describe two exceptions to the principles of financial accounting measurement and explain the economic rationale behind them.

≣ This chapter reviews the economic and measurement fundamentals of financial accounting and is intended to serve a dual purpose: it provides a conceptual summary and economic explanation of the financial accounting process covered in Chapters 1 through 4, and it also serves as a general framework that relates the more specific issues covered in the remaining chapters.

Chapter 1 is devoted to the economic context of financial accounting. It explains why investors, creditors, and other parties require objective and reliable information about the solvency and earning power of companies, so that they can evaluate, control, and direct the decisions of management. It also describes how financial accounting standards result from a political process, which is driven by the economic needs of those who provide, audit, and use financial accounting information.

Chapters 2, 3, and 4 concern the nature and preparation of the four basic financial statements. Chapter 2 consists of an overview of the balance sheet, income statement, statement of retained earnings, and statement of cash flows, emphasizing in particular the relationships among these statements and the specific accounts that compose them. Chapter 3 describes the mechanics of the accounting cycle, from the recognition of a relevant, measurable exchange transaction to the preparation of the financial statements. Chapter 4 explains the difference between cash and accrual accounting and discusses adjusting journal entries.

The present chapter takes a broader perspective and explains the measurement and economic foundation that underlies the existing financial accounting process. This foundation consists primarily of the basic assumptions, valuation issues, principles, and exceptions of financial accounting. Understanding these ideas is essential to understanding current accounting practices, and more importantly, it can help accounting students anticipate and prepare for the accounting systems of the future. After all, in this dynamic world, you will not be working with the accounting systems of today; the systems of tomorrow will be your greatest concern.

You have already seen that investors, creditors, and other interested parties require information about a company's performance and financial position. To maintain its market value and ability to attract equity and debt capital, management responds to this demand by hiring auditors and providing audited financial statements, which contain measures like net income, net cash flows from operating activities, the current ratio, and the debt/equity ratio. These measures help interested parties assess the company's ability (1) to meet its debts as they come due (solvency) and (2) to generate assets in the future (earning power). Such measures also appear in management compensation contracts and debt covenants, where they help to control and direct management decisions. The assumptions, valuation issues, principles, and exceptions of financial accounting all play an important role in determining the nature and economic function of these measures of performance and financial position.

ASSUMPTIONS OF FINANCIAL ACCOUNTING

There are four basic assumptions of financial accounting: (1) economic entity, (2) fiscal period, (3) going concern, and (4) stable dollar. Some of these assumptions are reasonable representations of the real world and others are not. As each assumption is discussed, try to understand why it has evolved, and be especially aware of those that fail to capture the world as it really is. These relatively unrealistic assumptions define important limitations that are inherent in the financial statement measures of performance and financial position. Investors, creditors, managers, and auditors must thoroughly understand these limitations if they are to use financial statements appropriately.

Economic Entity Assumption

The most fundamental assumption of financial accounting involves the object of the performance measure. Should the accounting system provide performance information about countries, states, cities, industries, individual companies, or segments of individual companies? While it is important that each of these entities operate efficiently, financial accounting has evolved in response to a demand for company-specific measures of performance and financial position. Consequently, financial accounting reports provide information about individual, profit-seeking companies.

The process of providing information about profit-seeking entities implicitly assumes that they can be identified and measured. Individual companies must be entities in and of themselves, separate and distinct from both their owners and all other entities. This statement represents the **economic entity assumption,** the first basic assumption of financial accounting. Although this assumption may appear obvious on the surface, it nonetheless provides an important foundation upon which the financial accounting system is built. Moreover, in certain situations this assumption plays a critical role in determining the scope of financial statements.

For example, after General Electric Company acquired the common stock of RCA Corporation for $6.4 billion in 1986, it included all of RCA's assets and liabilities on its consolidated balance sheet. For financial reporting purposes, therefore, RCA, which operates as an independent entity and publishes its own separate financial statements, is included within the economic entity referred to as the General Electric Company. In fact, the consolidated balance sheet of General Electric includes the assets and liabilities of many other companies, called *subsidiaries,* each of which prepares its own financial statements. The National Broadcasting Company (NBC) is a well-known subsidiary of General Electric.

Fiscal Period Assumption

Once the object of measurement has been identified (i.e., the economic entity), we must recognize that to be useful, measures of performance and financial position must be available on a timely basis. Investors, creditors, and other users of financial information need periodic feedback if they are to monitor the performance of management as well as control and direct its decisions.

The need for timely performance measures underlies the **fiscal period assumption,** which states that the operating life of an economic entity can be divided into time periods over which such measures can be developed and applied. Most corporations, for example, prepare annual financial statements, providing yearly feedback and performance measures to their stockholders. The Securities and Exchange Commission requires that publicly-traded companies provide financial statements (called *Form 10-Q*) to their stockholders on a quarterly basis.

Timely vs. Objective Financial Information

It is important to realize that the fiscal period assumption introduces a trade-off between the timeliness of accounting information and its objectivity. Users need timely information, and thus they generally prefer fiscal periods that are relatively short. However, as the fiscal period becomes shorter, the applications of certain accounting methods become more arbitrary and subjective.

Assume, for example, that a company purchases a piece of equipment that is expected to have a ten-year useful life, for $10,000. If financial statements are prepared every ten years, it is fairly clear that the entire $10,000 should be matched (depreciated) against the revenue generated over the ten-year period. On the other hand, if financial statements are prepared every quarter, it is much less clear how much of the $10,000 should be depreciated in each individual quarter. Depreciating an equal dollar amount each quarter may not match the benefits provided by the equipment in each quarter. Thus, interested parties who demand more timely feedback (e.g., monthly or quarterly) must be willing to accept increasingly subjective measures of performance and financial position.

The quarterly accounting reports published by major U.S. corporations, for example, are not audited and are generally more subjective than the audited annual reports. To illustrate, the unaudited Form 10-Q report published by BankAmerica Corporation for the first quarter of 1988 contained the following statement:

> *This document serves . . . as the quarterly report on Form 10–Q of BankAmerica Corporation to the Securities and Exchange Commission, which has taken no action to approve or disapprove the report or to pass upon its accuracy or adequacy.*

A Calendar or Fiscal Year?

Another consequence of the fiscal period assumption is that companies must choose the dates of their reporting cycles. Most major U.S. corporations report on the calendar year. That is, they publish an annual report each year as of December 31, and their quarterly statements cover periods ending March 31, June 30, September 30, and December 31. However, a number of companies report on twelve-month periods, called **fiscal years,** that end on dates other than December 31.[1] In most cases a company chooses a fiscal reporting cycle because its operations are seasonal, and the financial statements are more meaningful if the reporting period includes the entire season.

Large retailers, like Federated Department Stores, K-mart, and Toys "Я" Us, for example, often end their fiscal years on January 31 after the completion of the Christmas season. Many companies in the food industry, such as Pillsbury, General Mills, and Quaker Oats, prepare annual financial statements in May or June, just after the winter grain crops are harvested. Companies in the automobile and farm machinery industries, such as Firestone and John Deere & Co. close their books in September or October, following the summer season when sales are heaviest. Universal Leaf Tobacco, a major processor in the tobacco industry, ends its fiscal year on June 30, immediately after the previous year's tobacco crop has cured.

---

1. According to a survey conducted by the American Institute of Certified Public Accountants, 37 percent of the merchandising and industrial companies in the United States close their books on dates other than December 31. (Christopher Power, "Let's Get Fiscal," *Forbes,* 30 April 1984, pp. 102, 104.)

Going Concern Assumption

A second assumption also results from the demand for timely information and follows logically from the fiscal period assumption. If we assume that an entity's life can be divided into fiscal periods, we must further assume that its life extends beyond the current period. In other words, we assume the entity will not discontinue operations at the end of the current period over which its performance is being measured. Taken to the extreme, this assumption, called the **going concern assumption,** states that the life of the entity will continue indefinitely.

The role of the going concern assumption in financial accounting is as fundamental as the definition of an asset. Recall that assets are defined to have *future* economic benefit: that is, benefits that extend beyond the current period. The cost of equipment, for example, is capitalized and placed on the balance sheet because the equipment is expected to provide benefits in the future. The matching principle states that such costs should be allocated to the income statement as the benefits are realized in future periods. The entire matching process, which is at the heart of the accrual system of accounting, is unworkable without an assumption that the entity's life extends beyond the current period. Thus, the going concern assumption is fundamental to financial accounting measurement. Indeed, the Financial Accounting Standards Board recently invoked the going concern assumption when, in Statement of Financial Concepts No. 3, it defined assets as "probable *future* economic benefits obtained or controlled by a particular entity as a result of past transactions or events."[2]

Stable Dollar Assumption

To measure the dimensions, quantity, or capacity of anything requires a unit of measurement. Height and distance, for example, can be measured in terms of inches, feet, centimeters, or meters; volume can be measured in gallons or liters; and weight can be measured in pounds or kilograms. Mathematical operations, such as addition or subtraction, on any such measure require that the unit of measurement must maintain a constant definition.

To illustrate, suppose you weighed yourself at the beginning of 1989 and found that your weight was 120 pounds. At the end of the year you weighed yourself again and noted that your weight was 128 pounds. You conclude that you gained 8 pounds during the year, but implicit in this conclusion is the assumption that the definition of a pound was the same at the beginning and the end of the year. Had a pound at the beginning of the year equaled 16 ounces and 15 ounces at the end of the year, for example, you would actually have gained no weight at all. You would have weighed 1920 ounces at both points in time.

The logical unit of measurement for the financial performance and condition of a company is the monetary unit used in the economic transactions entered into by that company. In the United States, for example, the monetary unit is the dollar. Consequently, the financial statements of U.S. companies are expressed in terms of dollars.

---

2. Financial Accounting Standards Board, "Elements of Financial Statements of Business Enterprises," *Statement of Financial Concepts No. 3* (Stamford, Conn.: FASB, December 1980), xi and xii.

The measures of financial performance and position on the financial statements all involve the addition, subtraction, or division of dollar amounts. Total assets on the balance sheet, for example, represent the addition of the dollar values of all the individual assets held by a company at a particular point in time. The current ratio and the debt/equity ratio involve dividing certain balance sheet dollar amounts by other balance sheet dollar amounts. As with the measures discussed previously, valid use of these mathematical operations requires that the definition of the dollar must be constant. Thus, a **stable dollar assumption** is implicit in the measures of performance and financial condition used to evaluate and control management's decisions.

A dollar is defined in terms of its **purchasing power,** the amount of goods and services it can buy at a given point in time. During inflation, which has come to be a fact of life, the purchasing power of the dollar decreases steadily. Therefore, financial statements, which are based on the assumption that the purchasing power of the dollar is constant (i.e., no inflation), can be seriously misstated.

Suppose, for example, that on January 1 you have $1000, and at that time the cost of rice is $1 per bag. You could purchase 1000 bags of rice, but you decide instead to use the money to purchase (invest in) a small tract of land. During the year the inflation rate is 10 percent, and at year end the price of the rice is $1.10 per bag, and the value of the land is $1100. You decide to sell the land, and on your income statement you recognize a gain on the sale of $100 ($1100−$1000). You read your income statement and count the cash in your hand and conclude that your economic wealth has increased by $100. However, you use the $1100 to buy rice and you are surprised to learn that it only buys you 1000 bags, the exact amount you could have purchased at the beginning of the year, even though your income statement indicates otherwise.

The stable dollar assumption is one instance in which the financial statements are based on an unrealistic assumption. Financial accounting standard-setting bodies have recognized this problem for many years and have attempted to solve it many times. The most recent effort occurred in 1979, when the FASB required certain large U.S. companies to provide information about the effects of inflation in their annual reports. However, this requirement was recently rescinded. Companies complained that the disclosures were costly, and financial statement users showed little interest in them, probably because they believed them to be unreliable. It is important that financial statement users at least recognize that this limitation exists and in some cases learn how to adjust financial statements for the effects of inflation. This topic is covered in some detail in Appendix C at the end of the text.

Our discussion of the basic assumptions of financial accounting is now complete. In summary, we have assumed the existence of a separate, measurable business entity (economic entity), whose infinite life (going concern) can be broken down into fiscal periods (fiscal period), and whose transactions can be measured in stable dollars (stable dollar). Each of these assumptions is briefly defined in Figure 5−1.

Now that the basic assumptions of financial accounting have been established, we can explain how dollar amounts are attached to the assets, liabilities, equities, revenues, expenses, and dividends of economic entities. In the course of this explanation we consider (1) valuation and the financial statements and (2) the principles of financial accounting measurement.

Figure 5–1   The basic assumptions of financial accounting

Assumption	Definition
Economic entity	Profit-seeking entities, which are separate and distinct from their owners and other entities, can be identified and measured.
Fiscal period	The life of the economic entity can be divided into fiscal periods, and the performance and financial position of the entity can be measured during each of those periods
Going concern	The life of the economic entity will extend beyond the current fiscal period.
Stable dollar	The performance and financial position of the entity can be measured in terms of a monetary unit that maintains constant purchasing power across fiscal periods.

VALUATION AND THE FINANCIAL STATEMENTS

The dollar values attached to the accounts on a company's financial statements are largely determined by the markets in which the company operates. To understand these markets, it is helpful to view a business entity in the following way.

INPUTS ⟶ ENTITY OPERATIONS ⟶ OUTPUTS
(Purchase Prices)   (Sales Prices)

A business entity operates in two general markets: an **input market,** where it purchases inputs (materials, labor, overhead) for its operations, and an **output market,** where it sells its outputs (services or inventories). Input market values (prices) are normally less than output market values (prices). For example, local automobile dealers purchase automobiles from manufacturers, such as General Motors, Chrysler Corporation, and Ford Motor Company, and sell them to consumers. The prices paid for automobiles by dealers in their input market are generally less than the prices paid by consumers in the output market. A new Chevrolet, for example, may cost a dealer $15,000 in the input market and sell for $17,000 in the output market.

Moreover, input and output markets are defined in terms of specific entities: one entity's output market may be another entity's input market. DuPont, for example, supplies complete front and back assemblies for the General Motors cars produced at a GM plant near Kansas City, Mo. When GM purchases these assemblies, the transaction takes place in the output market of DuPont and the input market of GM.

Viewing a business entity in terms of both its input and output markets introduces a number of different ways to value the accounts on the financial statements. Should assets, for example, be valued on the balance sheet in terms of prices from the input market, or prices from the output market—or is there a way to reflect both input and output prices in their valuations? For example, should the value of the Chevrolet on the dealer's balance sheet be expressed in terms of the dealer's input cost ($15,000) or the selling price in the output market ($17,000)?

Four Alternative Valuation Bases

Four different **valuation bases** are used to determine the dollar amounts attached to the accounts on the financial statements. They are: (1) present value, (2) fair market value, (3) replacement cost, and (4) historical cost. **Present value,** the computation of which is discussed and illustrated in Appendix A at the end of the text, represents the discounted future cash flows associated with a particular financial statement item. The present value of a note receivable, for example, is calculated by determining the amount and timing of its future cash inflows and then adjusting the dollar amounts for the time value of money. **Fair market value,** or sales price, represents the value of goods and services in the output market. **Replacement costs,** or current costs, are the current prices paid in the input market. **Historical costs** represent the input prices paid when inputs were originally purchased. Figure 5−2 depicts these four valuation bases in terms of an entity's input and output markets.

To illustrate, assume that during 1987 Watson Land Developers purchased an apartment building for $20,000, which an outsider recently offered to buy for $28,000. Watson estimates that if it continues to manage the apartment, it would produce net cash flows for the next ten years at a rate of $5000 per year. The company also recently investigated replacing the apartment building with a comparable structure and learned that it would cost $35,000. The present value, fair market value, replacement cost, and historical cost of the apartment building are provided below.

Present value	=	$30,723 ($5000 × 6.14457*)
Fair market value	=	$28,000
Replacement cost	=	$35,000
Historical cost	=	$20,000

*Present value factor (ten-year ordinary annuity, 10 percent discount rate)

Valuation Bases Used on the Financial Statements

All four of the valuation bases described in the previous section are evident in financial statements prepared under generally accepted accounting principles. This point is illustrated in Figure 5−3, which contains a balance sheet with the valuation base for each account indicated in parenthesis. Note that the code for each valuation base is located below the balance sheet.

Cash and all current liabilities are valued at **face value.** This valuation reflects the cash expected to be received or paid in the near future. For these current accounts, face value is essentially equivalent to fair market value or present value because the time period until cash receipt or payment is very short (usually less than one year). The statement of cash flows, which explains changes in the cash account, is completely expressed in terms of face value.

Marketable securities are valued at their historical cost or their fair market value, whichever is lower. This valuation is based on the **lower-of-cost-or-market rule,** which ensures that the dollar value of this account is not overstated. This rule represents an example of conservative reporting, which is discussed later in this chapter.

Accounts receivable are valued at **net realizable value,** the amount of cash expected to be collected from the outstanding accounts. This dollar amount closely

Figure 5–2   Markets and valuation bases

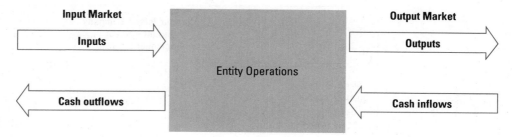

Valuation Bases

1. Present value—discounted future cash inflows and outflows

2. Fair market value—current cash inflows (output market)

3. Replacement cost—current cash outflow (input market)

4. Historical cost—past cash outflow (input market)

approximates fair market value and present value because the time period until collection is normally quite short (thirty to sixty days).

Inventories are valued at historical cost or replacement cost, whichever is lower. This second example of the conservative lower-of-cost or market rule illustrates that under certain circumstances, replacement costs are found on the balance sheet.

Land, securities held as long-term investments,[3] and property used in a company's operations are all valued at historical cost, unadjusted for amortization or depreciation. Prepaid expenses, plant and equipment, and all intangible assets are carried on the balance sheet at their historical costs, reduced by accumulated amortization or depreciation. Note that historical cost is the primary valuation base used for these assets.

Long-term notes receivable and long-term liabilities are valued at present value. The dollar amount attached to each of these accounts is calculated by determining the amount and timing of the future cash flows associated with the account and adjusting the dollar amounts for the time value of money.

Technically, the stockholders' equity section of the balance sheet is not valued in terms of any valuation base. It represents the residual interests of the stockholders or the book value of the company. In other words, the stockholders' equity section can simply be viewed as the difference between the total balance sheet value of the company's assets and the total balance sheet value of the company's liabilities. The accounts that compose this section are discussed in Chapter 12.

You may wonder why the valuation bases of the revenues and expenses, which appear on the income statement, are not discussed in this section. The in-

---

3. A special method, called the *equity method,* is used to value certain long-term equity investments on the balance sheet. This method is based on the historical cost of the investment, but certain additional adjustments to historical cost are made periodically. The method is discussed and illustrated in Chapter 13, which covers long-term investments.

Figure 5–3   Valuation bases on the balance sheet

Harbour Island Company Balance Sheet December 31, 1990			
Assets			
Current assets			
Cash	$ 220	(FV)	
Marketable securities	150	(LCM)	
Accounts receivable	345	(NRV)	
Inventory	600	(LCM)	
Prepaid expenses	100	(HC)	
Total current assets			$ 1,415
Long-term investments			
Long-term note receivable	1,000	(PV)	
Land	500	(HC)	
Securities	2,500	(HC)	
Total long-term investments			4,000
Property, plant, and equipment			
Property	6,000	(HC)	
Plant	2,900	(HC)	
Equipment	2,600	(HC)	
Total property, plant, and equipment			11,500
Intangible assets			
Patent	1,000	(HC)	
Trademark	700	(HC)	
Total intangible assets			1,700
Total assets			$18,615
Liabilities and Stockholders' Equity			
Current liabilities			
Accounts payable	$ 200	(FV)	
Wages payable	150	(FV)	
Interest payable	30	(FV)	
Short-term notes payable	200	(FV)	
Other payables	60	(FV)	
Unearned revenues	30	(FV)	
Dividends payable	70	(FV)	
Total current liabilities			$ 740
Long-term liabilities			
Long-term notes payable	1,500	(PV)	
Bonds payable	3,500	(PV)	
Mortgage payable	1,940	(PV)	
Total long-term liabilities			6,940
Stockholders' equity			10,935
Total liabilities and stockholders' equity			$18,615

Valuation base code: FV = face value   LCM = lower-of-cost-or-market   NRV = net realizable value   HC = historical cost   PV = present value

come statement accounts are not discussed separately because each one is related to one or more balance sheet accounts, and changes in the dollar amounts of the balance sheet accounts are reflected as revenues or expenses on the income statement. Increases in accounts receivable, for example, are reflected in the revenue accounts, Sales or Fees Earned, while adjustments for depreciating the cost of equipment are reflected in the expense account, Depreciation Expense. Consequently, by discussing the valuation bases used on the balance sheet, we have implicitly discussed the valuation bases used on the income statement.

So far we have assumed that economic entities can be identified and measured, their infinite lives can be divided into fiscal periods, and their performance and financial position can be measured in terms of stable dollars. We have also observed that a number of different valuation bases (face value, present value, fair market value, replacement cost, and historical cost) are used to determine the dollar amounts of the accounts in the financial statements. The next section presents the principles of financial accounting measurement, which explain why particular valuation bases are used for some accounts and not for others.

THE PRINCIPLES OF FINANCIAL ACCOUNTING MEASUREMENT

There are four basic principles of financial accounting measurement: (1) objectivity, (2) matching, (3) revenue recognition, and (4) consistency. The following discussion relates each of them to the financial accounting framework developed thus far.

The Principle of Objectivity

Financial accounting information provides useful measures of performance and financial position. In order to do so, financial accounting statements must provide information about value: the value of entire companies, the value of company assets and liabilities, and the value of the specific transactions entered into by companies.

The economic value of an entity, an asset, or a liability is its present value, which reflects both the future cash flows associated with the entity, asset, or liability and the time value of money.[4] Since financial accounting systems are concerned with measuring such value, the basic objective of financial reporting is to provide information that allows all interested parties to construct performance measures that reflect the present value of the company, its assets, and its liabilities. In other words, present value is the goal of financial accounting measurement.

There is, however, one critical problem with the present value calculation: it assumes that future interest rates and future cash flows are perfectly predictable. This assumption presents no problems in theory, but users of accounting mea-

---

4. The following discussion assumes that you understand the present value calculation. If not, refer to Appendix A at the end of the text, where present value is thoroughly discussed and illustrated.

sures of performance and financial position need reliable measures that can be audited at reasonable costs.

In 1987, for example, Colgate-Palmolive Company invested $49 million to build a major new facility that manufactures liquid detergents. Reporting this plant investment on the company's balance sheet at present value would require an estimate of the net future cash flows generated by the new facility as well as an estimate of future interest rates. Such estimates, which would be the responsibility of the company's management, are simply too subjective for the financial statements. Auditors would be unwilling and unable to verify such subjective judgments, and the legal liability faced by both managers and auditors would make such verification potentially very costly. In sum, it is not economical for financial information users to base transactions on measures that rely on highly subjective, uncertain, and unreliable predictions.

The principle of **objectivity,** which is perhaps the most important and pervasive principle of accounting measurement, states that financial accounting information must be verifiable and reliable. It requires that the values of transactions and of the assets and liabilities created by them be objectively determined and backed by documented evidence. Although it ensures that the dollar amounts disclosed on the financial statements are reasonably reliable, the principle of objectivity also precludes much relevant and useful information from ever appearing on the financial statements. The following sections discuss how the principle of objectivity determines the valuation bases used on the financial statements.

Present Value and the Financial Statements

The principle of objectivity means that present value, the goal of financial accounting measurement, cannot be used as the valuation base for all assets and liabilities. In some cases, however, the future cash flows associated with certain assets and liabilities are predictable enough to allow for sufficiently objective present value calculations. Suppose, for example, that on December 31 The Boeing Company received payment from United Airlines for an order of jumbo jets in the form of a note receivable. The note states that United will pay Boeing $1 million at the end of each year for the next two years. Certainly, this note should appear as an asset (receivable) on Boeing's December 31 balance sheet and as a payable on the balance sheet of United, but at what dollar amount should they be reported?

If we assume a discount rate of 10 percent and realize that the note is actually a two-period $1 million cash flow, we can use the present value calculation to place a value on the note ($1.735 million = $1 million × 1.735 [Table 5, at the end of Appendix A: $n = 2$, $i = 10\%$]). Further, the auditors of Boeing and United would be willing to attest to this valuation because the future cash flows are objectively determined in a legal contract, entered into and signed by both Boeing and United in an *arm's-length transaction*. The auditors for the most part are protected from legal liability because the responsibility to provide the contractual payments rests with United. The result is that a $1.735 million note receivable would appear on Boeing's balance sheet and a $1.735 million note payable would appear on United's balance sheet. In this case present value would be used to provide a balance sheet value for both an asset and a liability.

In general, present value is used on the financial statements only in those cases where future cash flows can be objectively determined. As illustrated, contractual agreements like notes receivable and payable represent cases that meet this criterion. Mortgages, bonds, leases, and pensions are other examples of contracts that underlie cash flows and remove much of the subjectivity associated with cash flow prediction.

Refer again to the balance sheet in Figure 5−3, and note that present value is used as the valuation base for long-term notes receivable, long-term notes payable, bonds payable, and mortgages payable. Recall also that all the accounts valued at face value (i.e., cash and current liabilities) are essentially equivalent to present value.

Market Value and the Financial Statements

Using market value (i.e., fair market value or replacement cost) as a valuation base for the accounts on the financial statements can be attractive because in many cases market value represents the best estimate of present value. If, for example, buyers and sellers in a given market use their individual estimates of present value when bidding on an asset, the resulting market price of the asset should approximate its actual present value. In addition, fair market value is often more objective than present value. Market prices for the equity securities of major U.S. companies, for example, are listed on public stock exchanges and can therefore be objectively verified. The market price of Johnson & Johnson common stock, for example, as of the end of May 24, 1989, was exactly $109½.[5]

Market values, however, suffer from two important deficiencies. While they are sometimes objectively determinable, in most situations they are not objective enough for use in the financial statements. For example, the market values of securities that are not traded on the major stock exchanges, most inventories, long-term investments, property, plant, and equipment, and intangible assets are not easily determined. The market values of such items may be very informative, but they fail to meet the principle of objectivity.

Second, valuing an entity, or one of its assets, at fair market value (output market price) assumes that the entity or the asset is being sold. This assumption is inconsistent with the going concern assumption, which states that an entity will exist beyond the current accounting period. Indeed, many of a company's assets are not intended for sale. Property, plant, and equipment, for example, are acquired for use in operations. To value these kinds of assets on the balance sheet at fair market value could give rise to irrelevant performance measures.

Refer again to the balance sheet in Figure 5−3 and note that market values are used in the valuation of relatively few accounts. Accounts Receivable are valued at net realizable value, which approximates fair market value, and Marketable Securities and Inventories are valued at historical cost or market value, whichever is lower.

Historical Cost and the Financial Statements

Note also in Figure 5−3 that the remaining accounts on the balance sheet (Prepaid Expenses, Land, Securities, Property, Plant, and Equipment, and Intangible Assets) are valued at historical cost, the price paid when the asset was originally acquired. Historical costs can be objectively verified and supported by documented evidence; they are reliable, can be audited at reasonable cost, and do not violate the principle of objectivity. However, historical costs are not particularly useful for the decisions made by users of financial information.

---

5. *The Wall Street Journal* (24 May 1989).

Goodwill and the Financial Statements

The principle of objectivity also precludes one very important asset from appearing on the balance sheet: *accrued goodwill.* A company may have a number of established and valuable clients or customers, and a strong reputation earned by providing years of high-quality products or services. It may have developed an extremely efficient system of managing personnel, inventories, or sales. Such items, called *goodwill,* can be very valuable to an entity. The reputation for quality and service and the systems used by industry giants such as IBM, Coca-Cola, and McDonald's, for example, are very valuable to these companies and, in some cases, may represent their greatest asset.

While accrued goodwill can be very valuable, no account on the balance sheet directly reflects it. Determining the value of goodwill is obviously very subjective, and to accrue it at the end of each accounting period with an adjusting journal entry would be a direct violation of the principle of objectivity. Considering that it can be an entity's most valuable asset, the absence of accrued goodwill represents a distinct and significant limitation of present-day financial statements.

This text has discussed an account, called Goodwill, that appears as an asset on the balance sheets of many companies. This account, however, does not represent goodwill that they have periodically accrued on their financial statements because they have good relationships with their customers, suppliers, and others. Instead, the Goodwill account is recognized when companies purchase other entities for prices that exceed the net value of the purchased entities' assets and liabilities. In such cases goodwill is recognized on the balance sheet of the purchasing company because it has been acquired in an arm's-length transaction for an amount that can be objectively determined and verified with documented evidence.

In 1987, for example, The Quaker Oats Company purchased Golden Grain Macaroni Company and Anderson, Clayton & Company, the manufacturer of Gaines pet food products, for a combined price of $1.08 billion. The purchase price exceeded the fair market values of the two companies' net assets (assets − liabilities) by $358 million. Presumably, Quaker Oats was willing to pay $358 million over and above the value of the individual assets and liabilities of these companies because they had developed significant goodwill since their inceptions. The Quaker Oats Company, therefore, recognized $358 million of goodwill on its 1987 balance sheet. The journal entry below was recorded by Quaker Oats at the time of the acquisition.

Net Assets*	722	
Goodwill	358	
Cash		1080

To record the purchase of Golden Grain Macaroni Company and Anderson, Clayton & Company (dollars in millions).

*Assets less liabilities

Objectivity is the most pervasive principle of financial accounting. It affects all areas of measurement, including operating performance, which is the focus of the principles discussed in the next section: matching and revenue recognition.

The Principles of Matching and Revenue Recognition

The **matching** principle, which states that the efforts of a given period should be matched against the benefits that result from them, underlies the financial accounting measures of operating performance. As noted in Chapter 4, applying this

Figure 5–4 The matching process

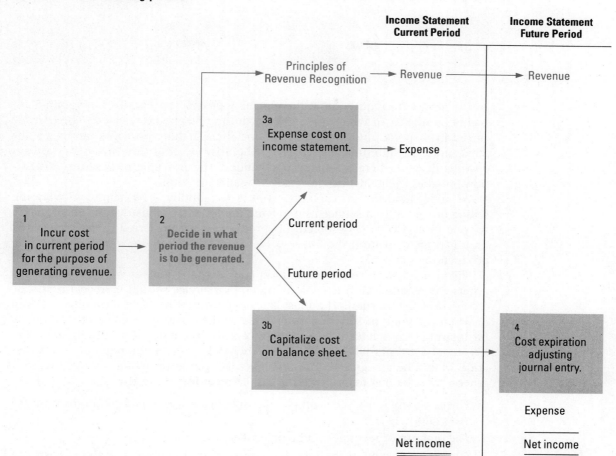

principle to the measure of net cash flow due to operating activities is relatively straightforward. It consists simply of matching the cash inflows and outflows that result from the operating activities of a given period. Applying the matching principle to revenues and expenses, however, in the measure of net income is somewhat more involved, as described below.

Our discussion of the process of matching in Chapter 4 included an illustration much like Figure 5–4. Recall that the matching process is initiated when a company incurs a cost (e.g., pays wages, purchases equipment, invests in a security) to generate benefits, normally in the form of revenues.[6] If the revenues are generated immediately, the cost is treated as an expense and appears on the income statement of the current period. If the revenues are expected to be realized in future periods, the cost is initially capitalized and appears on the balance sheet. In future periods, as the revenues are realized, the capitalized cost is converted to an expense, via an adusting journal entry, and appears on the income statements of the future periods. Thus, costs incurred to generate revenues are matched against those revenues in the time periods when the revenues are realized.

---

6. Benefits can also be in the form of cost savings.

Figure 5–5   The production sales cycle

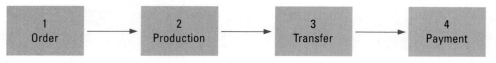

The most critical question in the matching process, as described in Figure 5–4, occurs at Step 2: In what time period will the revenue be realized? The cost incurred in Step 1 cannot be expensed, and the matching principle cannot be applied, until this question is answered. The answer, unfortunately, is not always obvious because there are many possibilities. The principle of **revenue recognition** provides the guidelines for answering this question.

To understand the principle of revenue recognition, it is helpful to view the selling of a good or a service as involving the four steps illustrated in Figure 5–5. A good or service is (1) ordered, (2) produced, (3) transferred to the buyer, and then (4) payment from the buyer is received. These four steps make a complete production/sales cycle.

The principle of revenue recognition helps to determine at which of these four points the revenue from the sale of a good or service should be recognized (i.e., recorded in the journal). The most common point of revenue recognition is Step 3, when the good or service is transferred to the buyer. At this point a company has normally completed the earning process and is entitled to record the revenue. Yet, there are times when each of the other steps may be the point at which revenue should be recognized. The principle of revenue recognition states that four criteria must be met before revenue can be recorded in the books:

1. The company must have completed a significant portion of the production and sales effort.
2. The amount of revenue can be objectively measured.
3. The major portion of the costs has been incurred, and the remaining costs can be reasonably estimated.
4. The eventual collection of the cash is reasonably assured.

While these guidelines are helpful, defining the point in time when all four criteria are met still requires much judgment, and can be very important because it often dramatically affects the dollar amounts on the financial statements. In a story reported recently in *The Wall Street Journal*, for example, the SEC charged three former officers of Matrix Science Corporation with significantly inflating the company's earnings. The charges alleged that the officers were able to grossly overstate net income by recording revenues on products "that haven't been shipped, or in some cases, haven't even been assembled."[7]

In another case, Stauffer Chemical, a major chemical company, was charged by the SEC with exaggerating profits by 25 percent, or $31.1 million, partially by prematurely recognizing sales.[8] *Forbes* recently reported that many struggling young companies maximize income by *front-ending* revenues. For example, Con-

---

7. Thomas R. Ricks, "Former Officers of Electronics Company Charged by SEC with Inflating Profit," *The Wall Street Journal*, 2 November 1988.

8. Geoffrey Smith, "Puddle Muddle," *Forbes*, 8 October 1984, p. 92.

tinuum, a recently organized computer software company, was estimated to have "fronted-ended some $15 million in revenues" from 1985 to 1988, by recording revenue on products that were only 60 percent to 70 percent complete.[9]

Intermediate and advanced accounting textbooks devote complete chapters to the complex and important problem of how revenues should be recognized in the wide variety of business transactions that occur. This text covers a limited number of such cases as they arise. For the time being, simply recognize that revenue recognition (1) is an important component of the matching process, (2) can be subjective, (3) can influence the financial statements significantly, and (4), in general, should be recorded at the point in the production/sales cycle (order, production, transfer, and payment) when all of the four criteria previously listed have been met.

The Principle of Consistency

The measurement principles of objectivity, matching, and revenue recognition are very general and, as such, can be applied to a variety of companies in a variety of business environments. These general principles, however, must be implemented through accounting methods, which are considerably more specific. These relatively specific methods are applicable to a much smaller set of situations.

To illustrate, the matching principle states that costs should be matched against the revenues they generate. While this principle designates that the cost of acquiring a fixed asset should be capitalized and depreciated, it provides little guidance on how the amount of depreciation should be calculated each period. An accounting method, such as straight-line depreciation, must be chosen to apply the matching principle. Straight-line depreciation, which recognizes a constant amount of depreciation each period, however, is not an appropriate application of the matching principle for all fixed assets in all situations. In certain cases a method of depreciation that recognizes large amounts of depreciation in early periods and smaller amounts later may be a better way to match revenues and expenses.

Generally accepted accounting principles, therefore, allow for a number of different, acceptable methods that can be used to account for the assets, liabilities, revenues, expenses, and dividends on the financial statements. For example, several acceptable methods may be used to account for each of the following assets: accounts receivable, inventories, long-term investments, and fixed assets. Such variety exists for two related reasons: (1) no method is general enough to apply to all companies in all situations and (2) generally accepted accounting principles are the result of a political process in which interested parties who face widely different situations are allowed and encouraged to provide input.

The principle of **consistency** states that, although there is considerable choice among methods, companies should choose a set of methods and use them from one period to the next. Its primary economic rationale is that consistency helps investors, creditors, and other interested parties to compare measures of performance and financial position from one period to the next. Presumably, if a company does not change its accounting methods, outside parties can more easily

9. Gretchen Morgenson, "They won't wait forever," *Forbes*, 16 May 1988, pp. 66, 68.

identify trends across time. In addition, management rarely wishes to change accounting methods; it had reasons for choosing the existing methods in the first place, and changing from one method to another could be viewed by outsiders as an attempt to manipulate the financial statements, reducing their credibility.

While consistency is important, it does not mean that companies never change accounting methods. If management can convince the independent auditor that the environment facing the company has changed to the point that an alternative accounting method is appropriate, the company is allowed to switch. However, such changes are not easily granted, and, when approved, the effects of the change on the financial statements are clearly disclosed. The change is usually described in the footnotes and mentioned in the auditor's report, and its effect on income is disclosed in a separate category on the income statement.

In 1987, for example, General Electric changed its method of accounting for inventory. The change was mentioned in the audit report, and the increase in net income of $281 million was disclosed as a separate item on the income statement. The following excerpt describing the change was taken from the footnotes of General Electric's 1987 financial report:

Effective January 1, 1987, GE changed its accounting procedures to include in the cost of inventories certain [costs] previously charged directly to expense. . . . The Company believes this change is preferable because it provides a better matching of production costs with related revenues in reporting operating results. In accordance with generally accepted accounting principles, the . . . effect of this change . . . is shown separately in the 1987 Statement of Earnings.

Some accountants believe that all companies should be required to use the same accounting methods. Such **uniformity,** they argue, would enable financial statement users to compare measures of performance and financial position more easily across different companies. As noted before, however, the situations faced by the variety of companies operating in the economy are so different that accounting methods that are meaningful in some circumstances are not relevant in others. Entire industries are sometimes so unique that completely new accounting methods need to be devised to capture the economics of the situations they face. Financial Accounting Standard No. 73, for example, covers specifically how railroad companies should report a change in accounting for railroad track structures. Consequently, uniformity is not a principle of accounting. It is, therefore, particularly important that financial statement users be aware of the available accounting alternatives and be able to make the adjustments required to meaningfully compare companies that use different accounting methods.

TWO EXCEPTIONS TO THE BASIC PRINCIPLES: MATERIALITY AND CONSERVATISM

Under certain circumstances the costs of applying the principles of accounting exceed the benefits. In these situations management is allowed (and, in some cases, required) to depart from the principles. All rules have exceptions, even the measurement principles of financial accounting. Two common and important exceptions are materiality and conservatism.

Materiality

Materiality states that only those transactions dealing with dollar amounts large enough to make a difference to financial statement users need be accounted for in a manner consistent with the principles of financial accounting. The dollar amounts of some transactions are so small that the method of accounting has virtually no impact on the financial statements and, thus, no effect on the related evaluation and control decisions. In such cases the least costly method of reporting is chosen, regardless of the method suggested by the principles of accounting measurement. The dollar amounts of these transactions are referred to as immaterial, and management is allowed to account for them as expediently as possible.

For example, the matching principle indicates that the cost of a wastebasket should be capitalized and depreciated over future periods because its usefulness is expected to extend beyond the current period. However, the cost of an individual wastebasket is probably immaterial, and it is costly in terms of management's time and effort to carry such items on the books. For practical reasons, therefore, the purchase price is immediately expensed. Granted, such treatment misstates income for both the current period and the future periods of the wastebasket's useful life. This misstatement, however, is extremely small (i.e., immaterial) and would have no bearing on the decisions of those who use the financial statements. In this case the costs of capitalizing and depreciating the purchase price of the wastebasket simply exceeds the benefits it would provide.

While materiality is practical, it represents a major problem area in accounting because it requires judgments that can differ considerably among investors, creditors, managers, auditors, and others. The U.S. Supreme Court has provided one of the few guidelines, defining a material item as one to which "there is substantial likelihood that a reasonable investor would attach importance in determining whether to purchase a security."[10]

In determining materiality, the size of an item is always considered, but whether it would affect the decisions of an investor or creditor is often unclear. A dollar amount that is too small to make a difference in a large company may be very significant in a small company, and not only must the size of an item be considered, but its nature can also be important. A small adjustment to the inventory account, for example, may be far more significant to financial statement users than a large adjustment to an account in the stockholders' equity section of the balance sheet. Finally, the user must be considered. A creditor's definition of materiality, for example, may be very different from that of an investor.

In summary, materiality is an important and practical exception to the principles of financial accounting measurement. Indeed, the unqualified auditor's report states that "the financial statements are free of material misstatement". Materiality is, nonetheless, very ambiguous. As stated in *Forbes*, "Too often, investors miss important information because companies deem it 'immaterial'. What does this mean? Nobody knows—and that's a big problem". The article goes on to report that Rockwell International, a multibillion-dollar conglomerate, chose not to disclose a loss that could have been as large as $220 million because it was considered immaterial.[11]

---

10. Laura Sanders, "Too Little Is Not Enough," *Forbes*, 7 November 1983, p. 106.
11. Ibid.

Conservatism

Another important exception to the principles of financial accounting measurement is conservatism. Like materiality, conservatism is practical and has evolved over time in response to cost/benefit considerations. In its simplest form, **conservatism** states that, *when in doubt*, financial statements should understate assets, overstate liabilities, speed up the recognition of losses, and delay the recognition of gains.

Conservatism does not suggest, however, that the financial statements should be intentionally understated. When given objective and verifiable evidence about a material transaction, the principles of accounting measurement should be followed, and no attempt should be made to intentionally understate assets or overstate liabilities. Only when there is significant uncertainty about the value of a transaction should the most conservative alternative be chosen.

You may wonder why financial statements are prepared on a conservative basis. Stated another way, in the face of uncertainty why not overstate, instead of understate, assets? One could argue, for example, that such overstatement would be in the best interest of a manager who is being evaluated and controlled by financial accounting information. However, as illustrated below, when the interests of all parties (managers, investors, creditors, and auditors) are considered, conservatism represents a far more practical solution.

The Nature and Cost of Legal Liability

As mentioned before, managers hire auditors to lend credibility to the financial statements. Auditors gather evidence and state opinions on whether the financial statements fairly present the financial condition of a company, and whether generally accepted accounting principles have been followed in the preparation of the financial statements. Auditors are responsible for the opinions they render, and if the financial statements are later found to be in error, company management and its auditors can be held legally liable for any damages these errors may have caused. In present-day society, where professionals (e.g., doctors, lawyers, accountants) are increasingly being held responsible for their work, such liability can result in very costly lawsuits. Recall from Chapter 1, for example, that approximately 2000 liability suits, asking for $10 billion in damages, faced public accounting firms during 1985. Such costs give rise to lower profits for auditors and managers, higher audit fees, higher prices for the goods and services provided by managers, and lower dividends for investors. In other words, the costs of legal liability are shared by all interested parties.

A Situation Involving Conservatism

Keeping the significant costs of legal liability in mind, consider the following situation. Suppose that an auditor, Ginny Hall, has been hired to audit Technic Incorporated, a company in strong financial condition except for one potential problem: Technic is presently being sued for a very large amount of money. At the time of the audit the outcome of the suit is uncertain. As far as Ginny can ascertain, there is an 80 percent chance that Technic will successfully defend itself. Technic's chief financial officer, Lew Hudson, arguing that the probability of losing the suit is low, has chosen not to disclose the lawsuit in the financial report. Technic is planning to raise capital by selling common stock in the near future and Lew feels that such a disclosure would reduce the market price of the shares. What should Ginny do, act conservatively and mention the suit in the audit report, or act as Lew wishes and provide a clean opinion?

An Error of Overstatement. Assume for the moment that Ginny does not act conservatively and makes no mention of the suit, providing a clean, unqualified audit report. A number of investors buy the shares issued by Technic at a fairly high price because, as far as they can determine, Technic is in strong financial condition. Several months later, however, Technic loses the suit and ultimately must declare bankruptcy. The investors lose their entire investments, and it is revealed at that time that both Ginny and Lew chose not to disclose the suit, even though they were aware of it when the financial statements were made public.

In this case Ginny and Lew have each made an **error of overstatement** because the investors were led to believe that Technic was in better financial condition that it actually was. The investors, who have incurred great losses, have a substantial claim against both Ginny and Lew and the company. With the help of a lawyer, the injured investors could join together and file a **class-action lawsuit,** naming Ginny and Lew as defendants. Such lawsuits are often settled for millions of dollars. For example, a recent class-action lawsuit filed against a major accounting firm, which was settled for $15 million, involved 2850 investors who together lost more than $20 million.[12] Clearly, the cost of an error of overstatement to auditors and managers, in terms of both the dollar amount of the settlement and damage to professional reputations, can be very high.

An Error of Understatement. Now assume that Ginny acts conservatively and chooses to disclose the suit in the audit report that accompanies the financial statements. This decision is difficult for her because it is against Lew's wishes and can jeopardize Ginny's future as Technic's auditor. Further, mentioning the suit will probably lower the selling price of the shares about to be issued by Technic.

Now suppose that the company successfully defends itself in the litigation that was pending at the time the financial statements were released. In this case, Ginny has made an **error of understatement.** Because she mentioned the suit, the investors were led to believe that Technic was in worse financial condition than it actually was. However, even though Ginny made an error, there are no injured stockholders and, thus, no class-action suits are filed against her or Lew.

The Relative Costs of Errors: Overstatement and Understatement

Refer now to Figure 5–6, which depicts the decision faced by Ginny and Lew in the preceding story. They could have chosen either to disclose or not disclose the suit, and later the suit would either have been won or lost, giving rise to four possible combinations: (1) disclose/win, (2) disclose/lose, (3) do not disclose/win, and (4) do not disclose/lose.

In terms of Figure 5–6, the main point of the story is that, on average, errors of overstatement (Cell 4) are much more costly than errors of understatement (Cell 1). Since these costs are shared by auditors, managers, stockholders, and others, it makes economic sense to structure the financial accounting system so that errors of overstatement are minimized. One way to achieve such an objective is to encourage conservative financial reporting.

---

12. Lee Berton, "Laventhol Settles Racketeering Suit, Paying $15 Million," *The Wall Street Journal,* 9 May 1988, p. 43.

Figure 5–6   Errors of understatement and overstatement

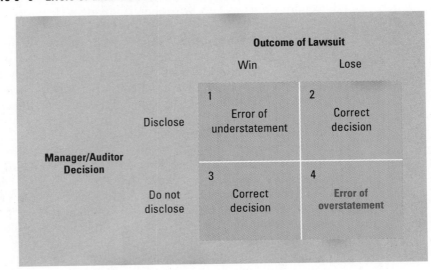

There are many examples of conservatism in the financial statements. The lower-of-cost-or-market rule, which is used to value marketable securities and inventories, has already been mentioned in this chapter and is perhaps the most evident example. Others are discussed as they arise later in the text. The following quote illustrates the economic rationale behind conservative reporting. It appeared in an article written by two accounting professors, who discuss the question of capitalizing or expensing costs incurred for research and development.

> *Virtually every time an accountant records expenditures, he or she runs the risk that a later development might, with the aid of hindsight, show that the recording was "wrong." . . . The obvious solution for avoiding this sort of situation and resulting criticisms is to expense all costs associated with the acquisition of assets where there is some significant probability that the asset will turn out to be worth less than its cost. . . . Lawsuits may force the adoption of such conservative practices [and the way to avoid them] is to expense all factors associated with assets whose value is uncertain.*[13]

THE ANNUAL REPORT OF K MART CORPORATION

Turn now to K mart's annual report located in Appendix D. There are a number of the areas in this report where the assumptions, principles, and exceptions of financial accounting are illustrated. Several are briefly described in Figure 5–7.

---

13. Harold Bierman and Roland Dukes, "Accounting for Research and Development Costs," *The Journal of Accountancy* (April 1975), pp. 48-55.

Figure 5–7   Examples of assumptions, principles, and exceptions, K mart Corporation

Assumption/Principle/ Exception	Page	Description
Economic entity	52	Consolidated financial statements include accounts of wholly-owned subsidiaries, including Builders Square, Makro, Pay Less Drug Stores, and Walden Book Company.
Fiscal period	35	Financial statements dated January 25 (fiscal year)
Fiscal period	49	Quarterly Financial Information (unaudited)
Going concern	35	Property and Equipment, major replacements and refurbishings, and certain interest charges are capitalized because they are expected to produce *future* benefits.
Stable dollar	24	While K mart uses a method to account for inventory so that cost of merchandise sold approximates current cost, the statements are prepared on a historical cost basis, and no adjustments are made for inflation in the entire financial report.
Objectivity	24	Property and Equipment are recorded at cost, not fair market value. However, K mart continually refurbishes existing stores and opens new stores, which ensures that historical cost is not too far from replacement cost.
Objectivity	30	"An audit includes examining . . . evidence supporting . . . the significant estimates made by management."
Matching	35	Property and Equipment are capitalized and depreciated principally on a straight-line basis over the estimated useful lives of the assets.
Matching	22	"Substantially all of the company's domestic inventories are measured using the last-in, first-out (LIFO) method of inventory valuation. LIFO provides a more accurate matching of current costs with current revenues."
Revenue recognition	16	The three-year summary of the general merchandise group's sales shows that sales increased 4.5% over last year.
Consistency	30	The management letter states that "the financial statements conform with generally accepted accounting principles and have been prepared on a *consistent* basis."
Materiality	36	Contingencies: "It is not expected that [the Fashion House, Inc. lawsuit] will have a material adverse effect on the company."
Materiality	46	Pension Plans: "In 1987, the company adopted Financial Accounting Standard No. 87 'Employers' Accounting for Pension Plans', which did not have a material effect on the company's pension expense."
Conservatism	35	"The company follows the practice of treating store operating costs incurred prior to opening a new retail unit as current period expenses."
Conservatism	35	"Merchandise inventories are valued at the lower of cost or market."

SUMMARY OF LEARNING OBJECTIVES

1 Identify, define, and relate the four basic assumptions of financial accounting.

The four basic assumptions of financial accounting are (1) the economic entity assumption, (2) the fiscal period assumption, (3) the going concern assumption, and (4) the stable dollar assumption. The economic entity assumption states that a company is a separate economic entity that can be identified and measured. The fiscal period assumption states that the life of an economic entity can be broken down into fiscal periods. The going concern assumption states that the life of an economic entity is indefinite. The stable dollar assumption states that the value of the monetary unit used to measure an economic entity's financial performance and position is stable across time. (Review Figure 5–1.)

These four assumptions establish the foundation upon which the system of measuring performance and financial position is built. Some of these assumptions are reasonable representations of the real world, while others are not. Those that are not, such as the stable dollar assumption, represent important limitations of financial accounting information.

2 Identify the two markets in which business entities operate, express the four alternative valuation bases in terms of these two markets, and briefly describe the valuation bases used on the financial statements.

A business entity operates in two general markets: an input market, where it purchases inputs for its operations, and an output market, where it sells the outputs that result from its operations. The four valuation bases (present value, fair market value, replacement cost, and historical cost) can be defined in terms of these two markets.

The present value of an asset or liability represents the discounted future cash flows associated with the asset of liability. Fair market value represents the sales price in the output market. Replacement costs (or current costs) are the current prices paid in the input market. Historical costs are the input prices paid when the input was originally purchased. (Review Figure 5–2.)

The financial statements contain a wide variety of valuation bases. Face value is used to value cash and short-term liabilities. Marketable securities and inventories are valued at the lower of cost or market. Accounts receivable are valued at net realizable value, a form of market value. Notes receivable, notes payable, and most long-term liabilities are valued at present value. Prepaid expenses, fixed assets, and intangible assets are valued at historical cost.

3 Identify and define the principles of financial accounting measurement.

There are four basic principles of financial accounting measurement: (1) objectivity, (2) matching, (3) revenue recognition, and (4) consistency. These principles help to determine how an entity is to be valued and thus how its performance is to be measured.

The principle of objectivity requires that the values of transactions and the assets and liabilities created by them be verifiable and backed by documentation. The matching principle states that the revenues of a given time period should be matched against the expenses required to produce them in the determination of net income. The principle of revenue recognition states that before an entity can record revenue (1) it must have completed a significant portion of the production and sales effort, (2) the revenue must be objectively measurable, (3) the major portion of the entity's production and sales costs must have been incurred or reasonably estimated, and (4) the eventual collection of cash must be assured. The principle of consistency states that the accounting methods chosen by a business entity should be the same from one period to the next.

4 Explain how the principle of objectivity determines the dollar values that appear on the financial statements.

The principle of objectivity ensures that present value is reported on the financial statements only in cases, such as contracts, where future cash flows can be objectively determined. It also ensures that market values such as fair market value and replacement costs, which are often difficult to objectively determine, are rarely reported on the financial statements (e.g., the lower-of-cost-or-market rule applied to marketable securities and inventories). Objectivity also ensures that many accounts on the financial statements are valued at historical costs and that goodwill is only recognized in situations where it is purchased in an arm's-length transaction.

5 Explain how the principles of matching and revenue recognition relate to the measure of performance.

The matching principle states that the efforts of a given period should be matched against the benefits they generate. In determining net income, benefits are usually represented as revenues, and efforts are represented by expenses, which cannot be matched against revenues until the revenues have been recognized. The principle of revenue recognition determines when revenues can be recognized. In short, the principle of revenue recognition triggers the matching principle, which in turn is necessary for determining the measure of performance.

6 Identify and describe two exceptions to the principles of financial accounting measurement, and explain the economic rationale behind them.

Two important exceptions to the principles of financial accounting measurement are materiality and conservatism. Materiality suggests that the principles of financial accounting measurement can be violated, if the dollar amount involved in a particular transaction is so small that it would not affect the decisions of financial statement users. Conservatism guides accountants, when in doubt, to understate assets, overstate liabilities, speed up the recognition of losses, and delay the recognition of gains. These two exceptions guide departures from the principles of financial accounting measurement when the costs of following them exceed the benefits. Conservatism, in particular, makes economic sense because the legal liability facing auditors and managers imposes a high potential cost on errors due to overstating assets or understating liabilities.

KEY TERMS

Class-action lawsuit (p. 229)
Conservatism (p. 228)
Consistency (p. 225)

Economic entity assumption (p. 211)
Error of overstatement (p. 229)
Error of understatement (p. 229)

Face value (p. 216)   Net realizable value (p. 216)
Fair market value (p. 216)   Objectivity (p. 220)
Fiscal period assumption (p. 211)   Output market (p. 215)
Fiscal year (p. 212)   Present value (p. 216)
Going concern assumption (p. 213)   Purchasing power (p. 214)
Historical cost (p. 216)   Replacement cost (p. 216)
Input market (p. 215)   Revenue recognition (p. 224)
Lower-of-cost-or-market rule (p. 216) Stable dollar assumption (p. 214)
Matching (p. 222)   Uniformity (p. 226)
Materiality (p. 227)   Valuation base (p. 216)

QUESTIONS FOR DISCUSSION AND REVIEW

1. List the basic assumptions, principles, and exceptions underlying the preparation of financial accounting statements. What is the difference between an assumption and a principle, an assumption and an exception, and a principle and an exception?

2. If the financial statements of two legally separate companies are combined to produce a set of consolidated financial statements, the entity for accounting purposes is different from the entity for legal purposes. In such a case, what basic accounting assumption is being invoked? State this assumption clearly.

3. A given balance sheet contains dollar amounts resulting from transactions that occurred in several different time periods. Accountants add these dollar amounts in the computation of such numbers as current assets and total assets, even though the amount of goods and services a dollar could purchase has varied widely across these time periods. What basic assumption allows accountants to make these additions? Is this assumption realistic? How are accounting reports misstated because they are based on this assumption?

4. What basic assumption allows the preparation of financial reports on a timely basis? What important trade-off is introduced because this assumption is necessary? In general, which dollar amount is more reliable: net income for a month or net income for a five-year period? Which of the two net income amounts is more timely?

5. What is a fiscal year? Why do some companies prepare financial statements on a fiscal year basis?

6. What basic assumption underlies the definition of an asset and the process of capitalizing and amortizing? Is this assumption realistic?

7. The principles of accounting measurement determine the valuation bases used on the balance sheet. The chapter describes four valuation bases. Name them.

8. Differentiate an individual company's input market from its output market. Why are these two markets relevant to financial accounting measurements? Describe each of the four valuation bases in terms of the input and output markets.

9. Name the accounts on the balance sheet, and indicate the valuation base used for each.

10. Which principle of accounting measurement is the most pervasive? Define it and describe how it determines which valuation bases are used for which balance sheet accounts.

11. Which valuation base is considered to reflect economic value? Why is this base not used to value all assets and liabilities? Under what circumstances is it used?

12. In what two ways are market values limited as valuation bases for assets and liabilities?

13. What basic principle underlies the measure of performance? State this principle and explain how it is applied to the methods used to account for inventories and fixed assets.

14. What principle triggers the matching process? That is, what principle must be applied before the matching principle can be implemented?

15. What criteria must be met before revenue can be recognized, and how does revenue recognition, in general, relate to the matching principle? As an example, explain how inventories are accounted for in terms of revenue recognition and the matching principle.

16. What basic principle of financial accounting measurement favors the use of historical costs on the balance sheet?

17. Consider a piece of machinery that was purchased two years ago for $3000, can be replaced for $4500, and can be sold for $5000. If the machinery is kept in operation, it will produce 500 widgets per year for five years. The widgets can be sold at the end of each year at a profit of $4 each. Given a 10 percent interest rate, should the machinery be kept in operation, sold, or sold and replaced? Which of the values above (historical costs, replacement costs, fair market value, or present value) was important in arriving at your decision? Which of these values would appear on the balance sheet?

18. Critique the following statement: "The financial statements are prepared on the basis of historical costs."

19. Differentiate uniformity from consistency. Which is a principle of financial accounting measurement? Why?

20. What is materiality? Why is it considered a departure from the principles of financial accounting measurement? Is there an economic reason that explains why it is followed? What factors are important in determining that which is material and that which is not?

21. What is conservatism? Why is it considered a departure from the principles of financial accounting measurement? Explain how the legal liability faced by managers and auditors might encourage conservatism in the financial statements. In general, would it be more costly to overstate or understate the value of an asset?

22. From the valuation bases used on the balance sheet, provide an example of conservatism.

EXERCISES

NOTE TO STUDENTS:
Chapter 5 describes the basic assumptions, principles, and exceptions of financial accounting. The following exercises, problems, and cases present numerical examples of the concepts we covered.

E5–1   *(The effects of inflation on holding cash)*   Assume that a corporation holds cash of $10,000 throughout a period of time in which the general price level increases by 5 percent. Does the corporation have more or less than $10,000 of purchasing power at the end of the period? By how much? Would such a gain or loss be reflected in the corporation's financial accounting statements? Why or why not?

E5–2   *(The effects of inflation on holding land)*   Palomar Paper Products purchased land in 1975 for $6000 cash. The company has held the land since that time. In 1990 Palomar purchased another tract of land for $6000 cash. Assume that prices in general increased by 50 percent from 1975 to 1990.

Required:

a. Assuming that Palomar made only these two land purchases, what dollar amount would appear in the Land account on Palomar's balance sheet as of December 31, 1990?

b. Palomar used $6000 cash to make each land purchase. Would $6000 in 1975 buy the same amount of goods and services as $6000 in 1990? If not, how much more or less, and why?

c. Explain how one would adjust the dollar amount reported in the land account as of December 31, 1990 if the stable dollar assumption were dropped.

E5–3   *(Valuation bases on the balance sheet)*   Name the valuation base(s) that are used for each of the asset and liability accounts shown here. Some assets and liabilities can use more than one valuation base.

	Historical Cost	Fair Market Value	Present Value	Replacement Cost
Cash				
Marketable Securities				
Inventories				
Prepaid Expenses				
Long-Term Investments				
Notes Receivable				
Machinery				
Equipment				
Land				
Intangible Assets				
Short-Term Payables				
Long-Term Payables				

E5–4   *(Revenue recognition)*   Cascades Enterprises ordered 2000 brackets from McKey and Company on December 1, 1990 for a contracted price of $2000. McKey completed manufacturing the brackets on January 17 of the next year and delivered them to Cascade on February 9. McKey received a check for $2000 from Cascade on March 14.

Required:

a. Assume that McKey and Company prepares monthly income statements. In which month should McKey recognize the $2000 revenue from the sale? Provide the journal entries that would be made in each of the four months.

b. Justify your answer in *(a)* in terms of the four criteria of revenue recognition.

c. Are there conditions under which the revenue could be recognized in a different month than the month you chose in *(a)?*

d. Provide several reasons why McKey's management might be interested in the timing of the recognition of revenue.

E5–5   *(The effects on income of different methods of revenue recognition)*   Gigantic Bridge Builders built a bridge for the state of Maryland over a two-year period. The contracted price for the bridge was $500,000. The costs incurred by Gigantic and the payments from the State of Maryland over the two-year period follow.

	Period 1	Period 2	Total
Costs incurred by Gigantic	$250,000	$100,000	$350,000
Payments from Maryland	$300,000	$200,000	$500,000

Required:

a. Prepare income statements for Gigantic for the two periods under the following assumptions:

(1) Revenue is recognized at the end of the project.

(2) Revenue is recognized in proportion to the costs incurred by Gigantic.

(3) Revenue is recognized when the payments are received.

b. Compute the total net income over the two-year period under each assumption.

E5–6

(Capitalize and depreciate—which assumption and principle?) JHP and Brothers purchased a panel truck for $15,000 on January 1, 1990. They estimated the life of the truck to be five years, and they planned to depreciate the entire cost using the straight-line method.

Required:

a. In line with generally accepted accounting principles, determine the amounts required here.

	1990	1991	1992	1993	1994
Original cost					
Depreciation expense					
Accumulated depreciation					
Net book value					

b. Why did you decide to capitalize rather than expense the cost of the truck? What basic assumption of financial accounting are you relying upon in this decision?

c. Why did you allocate a portion of the cost to each of the five years? What basic principle of financial accounting measurement are you relying upon in this decision.

E5–7

(The concept of materiality) Megabucks, Inc. is a multimillion dollar operation that expenses all costs under $5000. After reviewing the company's financial records, you note that many of these expenditures are for capital assets, items that are useful to the company beyond the period in which they were purchased.

Required:

a. Explain the proper accounting treatment for expenditures for items that are expected to generate benefits in the future.

b. Explain why it might make economic sense to expense some of these items. Upon what exception to the principles of financial accounting would such a decision be based?

E5–8

(Changing accounting methods and net income) The net income amounts for Jones and Bradley over the four-year period beginning in 1988 follow.

1988	1989	1990	1991
$20,000	$23,000	$22,000	$28,000

After further examination of the financial report, you note that Jones and Bradley made accounting method changes in 1989 and 1991, which affected net income in those periods. In 1989 the company changed depreciation methods. This change increased the book value of its fixed assets in each subsequent year by $5000. In 1991 the company adopted a new inventory method that increased the book value of the inventory by $13,000.

Required:

a. Consider the accounting equation, and compute the effect of each of these changes on net income in the year of the change.

b. Prepare a chart that compares net income across the four-year period, assuming no accounting changes were made by Jones and Bradley. How would your assessment of the
company's performance change after you learned of the accounting method changes?

c. What principle of financial accounting makes it difficult to make such changes? Describe the conditions under which Jones and Bradley would be allowed to make
changes in their accounting methods.

PROBLEMS

P5–1

(The effects of inflation on reported profits)   On January 1, 1990, you purchased a piece of
property for $1000. On December 31 of that year you sold the property for $2000. Assume
that the general rate of inflation for 1990 was 12 percent.

Required:

a. According to generally accepted accounting principles, prepare the journal entries for
the purchase and sale of the piece of property.

b. How much gain would be recorded in the income statement due to the sale of the property?

c. The $1000 you used to purchase the property on January 1 could have been used to
purchase any number of goods and services on January 1. Would the $2000 you re-
ceived at the end of the period enable you to purchase twice as many goods and services? Why or why not?

d. How much of this accounting gain could be attributed to inflation and how much could
be attributed to the fact that the property rose in value? Do generally accepted accounting principles make such a distinction? Why or why not?

P5–2

(Inflation and bank loans)   Assume that on January 1, Treetops Enterprises borrowed
$4760 from Banking Corporation, promising to pay $5000 at the end of one year. The effective rate of interest on the loan is approximately 5 percent ([$5000 − $4760]/$4760).
Suppose that the general rate of inflation for that year was 10 percent.

Required:

a. Record the journal entries prepared by Banking Corporation at both the payment of the
$4760 and the receipt of the $5000 one year later. How much interest revenue did
Banking Corporation recognize for the year? (*Hint:* The difference between the cash
payment and the face value of the note receivable is recorded as a discount that is converted to interest revenue over the life of the note.)

b. Do you think that Banking Corporation is better off at the end of the year by the
amount of the interest revenue? Did Banking Corporation have more or less purchasing
power at the end of the year? How much?

c. Which of the two parties, Treetops Enterprises or Banking Corporation, seems to have
ended up with the better deal? Could one determine this from a careful examination of
the financial statements prepared on the basis of generally accepted accounting principles? Why or why not?

P5–3

(The irrelevance of historical cost)   Three years ago Mallory and Sons purchased the three
assets listed in the following table. The chief financial officer, Kathy Hauser, is presently
trying to decide what to do with each asset. She has three choices for each of the assets: (1)
she can sell it, (2) she can sell it and replace it with an equivalent asset or (3) she can
simply retain it. The following information is provided to aid her decision.

Asset	Historical Cost	Replacement Cost	Fair Market Value	Present Value of Future Cash Flows Produced by Old Asset	Present Value of Future Cash Flows of Equivalent Asset
A	$8,000	$2,000	$3,000	$5,000	$10,000
B	$3,000	$4,000	$1,000	$5,000	$ 7,000
C	$4,000	$7,000	$6,000	$5,000	$10,000

Required:

a. Assuming that Kathy chooses to retain Asset A and Asset B and sell and replace Asset C, evaluate her decisions. What decisions should she have made? Support your choices.

b. How useful was the historical cost of each asset in the evaluation of the officer's decisions?

c. Assume that Kathy proceeds with her decision. According to generally accepted accounting principles, at what dollar amount would each asset be carried on Mallory's balance sheet? What principles of financial accounting would be involved?

P5-4 *(The stable dollar assumption and sales growth)* Sales data for 1989, 1990, and 1991 for Fast Growth, Inc. follow.

	1989	1990	1991
Sales	$20,000	$30,000	$40,000

After reviewing the growth in sales, Milton Smarts, the company president, commented that, according to the financial statements, sales doubled from 1989 to 1991. Assume that the general inflation rate as well as the price increase of Fast Growth's products for the period of 1989 to 1991 was 10 percent.

Required:

a. Considering price increases, did sales actually double from 1989 to 1991? By how much did the company's sales actually grow from 1989 to 1991? By what percentage did sales increase?

b. If prices had increased 25 percent from 1989 to 1991, by what percentage would sales have grown?

c. Describe how the stable dollar assumption could have misled Milton Smarts.

P5-5 *(The economic value of a company vs. its book value)* The December 31 balance sheet and the income statement for the period ending December 31 for Buyable Goods follow. (This problem requires a knowledge of present value calculations. Refer to Appendix A at the end of the text for help if necessary.)

Balance Sheet				Income Statement	
Current assets	$ 5,000	Liabilities	$ 6,000	Sales	$ 15,000
Long-lived assets	10,000	Common stock	4,000	Expenses	(12,000)
		Retained earnings	5,000	Net income	$ 3,000
		Total liabilities and			
Total assets	$15,000	stockholders's equity	$15,000		

Mr. Black is interested in purchasing Buyable Goods. He has analyzed the future prospects of the company and estimates that it should be able to maintain at least its current earnings amount for the next ten years, at which time the assets would be worthless. He also estimates that the discount rate over that time period will be 10 percent.

Required:

a. Assuming that net income is equal to cash inflows, how much should Mr. Black be willing to pay for Buyable Goods?

b. What is the book value of Buyable Goods?

c. Explain why there is a difference between the book value of Buyable Goods and the amount Mr. Black is willing to pay for it. What assumptions and/or principles of financial accounting are important here?

P5-6 *(Economic value and income vs. book value and income)*   On January 1, 1990 Barry Smith established a company by donating $50,000 and used the cash to purchase an apartment house. At the time he estimated that cash inflows due to rentals would be $30,000 per year, while annual cash outflows to manage and maintain it would be $20,000. He felt that the apartment house had a ten-year life and could be sold at the end of that time for $20,000. He also estimated that the effective interest rate during the ten-year period would be 8 percent. (This problem requires a knowledge of present value calculations. Refer to Appendix A at the end of the text for help if necessary.)

Required:

a. Prepare the journal entry that would be recorded by Barry at the purchase of the apartment. What is the book value of the building as of January 1, 1990? Assuming that Barry's estimates are correct, what is the economic value of the building? In your opinion, did Barry make a wise investment?

b. On December 31, 1990 Barry prepares financial statements and observes that his estimates were exactly correct. Assuming that cash inflows equal revenues, cash outflows equal expenses, and the cost of the apartment ($50,000) is depreciated evenly over the ten-year period, prepare the income statement and balance sheet for Barry's apartment.

c. Compute the economic income of the apartment building for 1990. Economic income equals the difference between the present value at the beginning of the year and the present value at the end of the year. Why is there a difference between accounting income and economic income?

d. What is the value on Barry's books of the apartment building at the end of 1990? What is the present value of the apartment building at that time?

P5-7 *(The differences between present value, book value, and liquidation value)*   The December 31, 1990 balance sheet of Hauser and Hall, prepared under generally accepted accounting principles, follows. (This problem requires a knowledge of present value calculations. Refer to Appendix A at the end of the text for help if necessary.)

Assets		Liabilities and Stockholders' Equity	
Cash	$ 5,000	Current liabilities	$ 4,000
Marketable securities	7,000	Long-term liabilities	10,000
Land	10,000	Common stock	40,000
Buildings and machinery	40,000	Retained earnings	8,000
		Total liabilities and	
Total assets	$62,000	stockholders' equity	$62,000

An investor believes that Hauser and Hall can generate $10,000 cash per year for ten years, at which time it could be sold for $40,000. The fair market values of each asset as of December 31, 1990 follow.

Cash	$ 5,000
Marketable securities	10,000
Land	30,000
Buildings and machinery	20,000
Total fair market value	$65,000

Required:

a. What is the book value of Hauser and Hall as of December 31, 1990?

b. What is the value of Hauser and Hall as a going concern (i.e., present value of the net future cash inflows) as of December 31, 1990? Assume a discount rate of 10 percent.

c. What is the liquidation value of Hauser and Hall (i.e, how much cash would Hauser and Hall be able to generate if each asset were sold separately and each liability were paid off on December 31, 1990)?

d. Discuss the differences among the book value of the company, the present value, and the liquidation value. Compute goodwill and explain it in terms of these three valuation bases.

P5-8

(Three different measures of income) This problem is designed to follow *(P5-7)*. Suppose that Hauser and Hall paid no dividends during 1991, and the December 31, 1991 balance sheet is listed below. (This problem requires a knowledge of present value calculations. Refer to Appendix A at the end of the text for help if necessary.)

Assets		Liabilities and Stockholders' Equity	
Cash	$15,000	Current liabilities	$ 3,000
Marketable securities	10,000	Long-term liabilities	10,000
Land	10,000	Common stock	40,000
Buildings and machinery	38,000	Retained earnings	20,000
		Total liabilities and	
Total assets	$73,000	stockholders' equity	$73,000

Assume that the investor in P5-7 was correct (i.e., the company produced $10,000 cash during 1991) and that the investor's expectations at the end of 1991 are unchanged. Assume further that an objective appraisal of the company's assets revealed the following fair market value as of December 31, 1991.

Cash	$15,000
Marketable securities	20,000
Land	33,000
Buildings and machinery	16,000
Total fair market value	$84,000

Required:

a. Compute net income for 1991 under generally accepted accounting principles.

b. Compute net income during 1991 using fair market values as the asset and liability valuation bases (i.e., $\$FMV_{1991} - \$FMV_{1990}$).

c. Compute economic income for 1991 (i.e., $\$PV_{1991} - \$PV_{1990}$). The discount rate is still 10 percent.

d. Discuss the differences among these three measures of income. Discuss some of the strengths and weaknesses of each measure.

P5-9

(Different methods of recognizing revenue) The Hillman Construction Company agreed to construct twelve monuments for the city of Elderton. The total contract price was $2.4 million, and total estimated costs were $1,140,000. The construction took place over a four-year period, and the following schedule indicates the monuments completed, costs incurred, and cash collected for each period.

Year	1	2	3	4	Total
Monuments completed	2	6	3	1	12
Costs incurred	$380,000	380,000	285,000	95,000	$1,140,000
Cash collected	$600,000	900,000	300,000	600,000	$2,400,000

Required:

a. How much revenue should Hillman recognize in each of the four periods under the three following assumptions.

(1) Revenues are recognized each year in proportion to the monuments completed.

(2) Revenues are recognized each year in proportion to the percentage of costs incurred.

(3) Revenues are recognized each year in proportion to the cash collected each year.

b. For each of the three assumptions, match the appropriate amount of cost against the recognized revenue. Determine net income for each period under the three assumptions.

c. Compare the total revenue, total cost, and total net income that result from each of the three assumptions. Note that although the timing of the recognition differs across the three assumptions, the total amount of income recognized is the same.

P5-10   *(Revenue recognition and net income)*   Hydra Aire, Inc. sells appliances to Seasons Department Store. A recent order requires Hydra Aire to manufacture and deliver 500 toasters at a price of $100 per unit. Hydra Aire's manufacturing costs are approximately $40 per unit. The following schedule summarizes the production and delivery record of Hydra.

Year	1	2	3	Total
Toasters produced	200	200	100	500
Costs incurred	$ 8,000	$ 8,000	$ 4,000	$20,000
Toasters delivered	150	200	150	500
Cash received	$10,000	$15,000	$20,000	$45,000

Required:

a. Assuming that Hydra recognizes revenue when the toasters are produced, prepare the journal entries that should be recorded to recognize revenue for each of the three years.

b. Assuming that Hydra Aire recognizes revenue at delivery, make the journal entries to recognize revenue for each of the three years.

c. Compute net income for the three periods under each of the two assumptions above.

P5-11   *(Comparing companies using different accounting methods)*   The net income and working capital accounts for two companies in the same industry, ABC Company and XYZ Company, follow.

	ABC	XYZ
1/1-12/31 Net income	$5,000	$12,000
12/31 Working capital	$8,000	$15,000

After reviewing the complete financial statements of the two companies, you note that ABC and XYZ use different inventory valuation and depreciation methods. ABC uses a method called *LIFO* to value its inventory while XYZ uses a method called *FIFO*. Had ABC used FIFO and XYZ used LIFO, their inventory accounts would have been $5000 greater and $5000 smaller, respectively. Similarly, ABC uses accelerated depreciation while XYZ uses straight-line. Had XYZ used accelerated depreciation and ABC used straight-line, their depreciation expenses for the year would have been $4,000 higher and $4,000 lower, respectively.

Required:

a. Compute net income and working capital for the two companies under the following assumptions.

Inventory Method	Depreciation Method	ABC Income/ Working Capital	XYZ Income/ Working Capital
FIFO	Straight-line		
FIFO	Accelerated		
LIFO	Straight-line		
LIFO	Accelerated		

b. Given this information, which combination of inventory and depreciation methods gives rise to the highest income and working capital numbers? Can you think of reasons why a manager would choose one method over another. Would managers always choose the method which results in the highest income? Why or why not?

c. If you were an investor, attempting to decide in which company to invest, how would you treat the fact that the two companies used different methods to account for inventory and fixed assets? Is there a principle of accounting that covers this situation? Why or why not?

P5–12   *(The economics of conservatism)*   Ted Jarvis is a CPA who has recently completed the audit of Jensen Repairs, Inc. The audited balance sheet and income statement follow.

Balance Sheet				Income Statement	
Current assets	$ 30,000	Liabilities	$ 40,000	Sales	$80,000
Long-term assets	70,000	Stockholders' equity	60,000	Expenses	(65,000)
		Total liabilities and			
Total assets	$100,000	stockholders' equity	$100,000	Net income	$15,000

During his examination Ted learned that a lawsuit is soon to be filed against Jensen. The lawsuit accuses Jensen of negligence and asks for damages over and above insurance of $30,000. If Jensen were to lose the lawsuit, the future of the business would be in jeopardy. However, as the lawyers described it to Ted, the probability that Jensen will lose the lawsuit is very low, approximately 10 percent.

Ted is unsure about whether he should require Jensen to disclose the lawsuit on the financial statements. The president of Jensen does not want it disclosed because he believes that the disclosure would cause undue concern among the company's shareholders. Ted does not want to ignore the president's request because Jensen is his most important client. On the other hand, Ted knows that if he does not require disclosure, and Jensen loses the lawsuit, he may be legally liable for the losses of the stockholders. Ted constructed the following framework to help him make his decision.

	Lawsuit Outcome	
Decision	**Win (90%)**	**Lose (10%)**
Require disclosure	Error 1	Correct decision
Do not require disclosure	Correct decision	Error 2

Required:

a. Study Ted's framework and note that he can choose to require or not require disclosure. Requiring disclosure and winning the lawsuit gives rise to Error 1. Not requiring disclosure and losing the lawsuit gives rise to Error 2. Comment on the costs that Ted would incur from each of these two errors. Which of the two errors would be more costly? Which of the two outcomes (winning or losing the suit) is more likely to occur?

b. Suppose that Ted estimates that the cost of Error 1 is $4000, and the cost of Error 2 is $60,000. Ignoring the costs and benefits of correct decisions, should Ted choose to require disclosure?

c. Explain the concept of conservatism in terms of Ted's framework.

CASES

C5-1

(Revenue recognition and matching) In April 1988, Korean Air Lines ordered nine Boeing 747 jumbo aircraft in a transaction with a potential value of over $2 billion. Six aircraft are Boeing's new 747–400 model, which sells for $135 million each. The three other aircraft and the required spare parts inventory have a contract value of $1.5 billion. The delivery schedule calls for three planes to be delivered in 1988, three in 1989, and three in 1990. The 747–400s are delivered in 1989 and 1990.

Required:

a. What amount of revenue would be reported by Boeing in 1988, 1989, and 1990 if it recognizes revenue when products are delivered? (Assume the required spare parts inventory is delivered in 1988).

b. How much revenue will be recognized in each year if Boeing waits to recognize revenue until the entire order is delivered?

c. If Boeing waits to recognize revenue until the entire order is filled, according to the matching principle, how should it account for the costs incurred to manufacture the aircraft?

C5-2

(Accounting standards and economic policy) An article published in *The Wall Street Journal* suggested that the FASB consider requiring U.S. companies to expense, instead of capitalize and amortize, goodwill. It argued that U.S. companies look more attractive than many foreign companies that are required to expense goodwill, which in turn encourages too much foreign ownership of U.S. companies. The article implied that requiring U.S. companies to write off goodwill would discourage foreign investment in the United States.

Taking issue with the article, Daniel Beresford, Chairman of the FASB, wrote a letter to the editor of *The Wall Street Journal* stating that "accounting rules are intended not to influence behavior, but to provide relevant, reliable information on which economic decisions can be based with a reasonable degree of confidence."

Required:

a. Goodwill appears as an asset on the balance sheet and results when one company purchases another for a price greater than the net fair market value of the other company's assets and liabilities. The difference is then amortized (charged as an expense) over a maximum of 40 years. Would requiring companies to expense goodwill immediately result in an increase or decrease in net income in the period when the purchase is made? Would such a requirement increase or decrease income in subsequent periods?

b. Do you think that requiring companies to expense goodwill would influence them to purchase more or fewer other companies? Why?

c. Do you think that the FASB should set accounting standards to induce desired behavior and achieve national goals?

d. By capitalizing and amortizing goodwill, what basic assumption and what principle of accounting measurement are being followed?

C5-3

(Errors of overstatement) Air Canada reported in April 1988 that "irregularities" had been discovered in the books of a subsidiary company after it was purchased in 1987. The irregularities were discovered by Air Canada's independent auditors. They suggested that some of the subsidiary's assets were overvalued, and that Air Canada paid too high a price for the subsidiary. An audit prior to the completion of the purchase did not disclose any irregularities. In its annual report, Air Canada stated: "Events have disclosed discrepancies in the value of (the purchased company's) assets at acquisition. The corporation is taking action."

Required:

a. What kind of action might Air Canada take? Against whom?

b. Does it appear that the subsidiary's management or the subsidiary's auditors acted conservatively?

c. Describe some of the costs that may be imposed on the subsidiary's management and auditors because they did not act conservatively.

C5–4

(Revenue recognition and matching) Most airlines offer promotional programs in which passengers accumulate miles over time; when they have earned enough miles, they receive free tickets. Currently, airlines do not make any accounting entries for these free tickets. The free rider merely uses available seats or, on occasion, displaces a ticketed passenger.

A panel of the American Institute of CPAs has recommended that the FASB adopt a new method of accounting for tickets issued under these programs. They propose that a portion of the fare paid when a passenger in such a program pays for a ticket be deferred until the free ride is used. For example, if a passenger purchases a $200 ticket, a portion, say $20, would not appear as revenue to the airline until the free trip is taken. It would be considered unearned revenue until then.

Required: Evaluate the proposed accounting standard in terms of the principles of revenue recognition and matching. List the criteria of revenue recognition and suggest when it would be appropriate to recognize the revenue from a ticket sale. Given your suggestion, how should the related costs be accounted for?

C5–5

(Consistency and uniformity) In 1987 General Electric (GE) made a series of accounting method changes that increased net income by a total of $858 million. The net income dollar amounts reported by GE for 1985, 1986, and 1987 follow (dollars in millions).

1985	$2,277
1986	$2,492
1987	$2,915

Required:

a. Note the constant increase in GE's net income over the three-year period. Recompute net income for 1987 assuming that the accounting changes had not been made. Which is the more appropriate comparison, the reported amounts or the recomputed amounts? Why?

b. In what three places in GE's 1987 financial report would an investor be able to find a reference to these accounting changes?

c. GE depreciates its fixed assets using a method that recognizes a relatively large portion of depreciation in the early years of an asset's useful life. IBM, on the other hand, uses the straight-line method. Briefly describe the adjustments an investor would have to make when comparing GE's performance and financial position to that of IBM.

d. Explain the difference between consistency and uniformity in terms of the accounting changes made by GE and the methods of accounting for fixed assets used by GE and IBM.

PART 2

A Closer Look at the Financial Statements

The Current Asset Classification, Cash, and Marketable Securities

Learning Objectives

1   Define current assets, working capital, current ratio, and quick ratio, and explain how these measures can be used to assess the solvency position of a company.

2   Recognize how and why managers use "window dressing" techniques to affect the reporting of current assets, working capital, and the current ratio.

3   Identify the issues considered and the techniques used when accounting for cash.

4   Define marketable securities, and identify the criteria that must be met before a security can be listed in the current asset section of the balance sheet.

5   Explain how the lower-of-cost-or-market rule is applied when accounting for marketable securities.

6   Describe why it may make economic sense to use the lower-of-cost-or-market rule, even though it gives rise to reporting problems.

≡ Part 1 of this textbook (Chapters 1 – 5) provides an overview of the entire accounting process. The discussions of the economics of financial accounting, the basic financial statements, bookkeeping procedures, the differences between cash flows and accruals, and the theory underlying accounting measurements cover the general issues important to an understanding of financial accounting. Part 2 provides more specific and detailed discussions of the accounts that compose the balance sheet, income statement, and statement of retained earnings. This chapter covers the current asset classification, cash, and marketable securities. Chapters 7, 8, 9, 10, 11, and 12, are devoted to short-term receivables, inventories, property, plant, equipment, and intangibles, current liabilities, long-term liabilities, and stockholders' equity, respectively. Long-term investments are covered in Chapter 13. Figure 6–1 is in the form of a balance sheet that is used to organize the topics covered in Part 2.

As the figure shows, the coverage of the accounts follows the order in which they appear on the balance sheet, moving from cash to intangible assets and current liabilities and the stockholders' equity accounts. All of these accounts appear on the balance sheet, but do not conclude that the income statement is ignored. Each account on the balance sheet is directly related to one or more accounts on the income statement. The Cash and Accounts Receivable accounts, for example, are the debit side of the journal entry that records a sale. Cost of Goods Sold, which appears on the income statement, is the debit side of the entry that records the outflow (at cost) of sold inventory. The costs in the Plant and Equipment accounts are systematically allocated to the income statement through depreciation expense. Indeed, for almost every permanent account on the balance sheet, there is at least one temporary account on the income statement. Consequently, a thorough discussion of the balance sheet accounts naturally implies coverage of the related income statement accounts.

The chapters in Part 2 rely heavily on the material covered in Part 1, introducing little that is entirely new. We simply discuss each account in more detail, explaining exactly how the concepts learned in Part 1 relate to the specific accounts under consideration. As this occurs, we point out where to find related discussions in the text. If you understand the material in Chapters 1 through 5, you are well on your way to understanding the material in the remainder of the text.

This chapter is divided into three sections. Section 1 covers the current asset classification and the measures of solvency and liquidity that use current assets. We first define these measures and then describe how they are used. The dollar amounts in the Cash and Marketable Securities accounts make up an important part of current assets and are therefore important components of these measures. Sections 2 and 3 consider the definitions, disclosure rules, and methods of accounting for cash and marketable equity and debt securities, respectively.

THE CURRENT ASSET CLASSIFICATION

This section first defines current assets and then describes the measures of solvency and liquidity that use them. The economic consequences and limitations of these measures are then discussed. It is important that you understand these issues because the methods used to account for cash, marketable securities, short-term receivables (Chapter 7), and inventory (Chapter 8) have a direct bearing on these measures of solvency and liquidity.

Figure 6–1   Topics covered in Part 2 (Chapters 6–13)

Assets		Liabilities and Stockholders' Equity	
Cash	Chapter 6		
Marketable securities	Chapter 6	Current liabilities	Chapter 10
Short-term receivables	Chapter 7		
Inventory	Chapter 8		
Long-term investments	Chapter 13	Long-term liabilities	Chapter 11
Property, plant, and equipment	Chapter 9		
Intangible assets	Chapter 9	Stockholders' equity	Chapter 12

Current Assets: A Definition and Relative Size for Various Industries

Current assets are so named because they are intended to be converted to cash *(liquidated)* in the near future. The exact definition of the near future is subjective, so the accounting profession has provided guidelines. According to professional standards, a **current asset** is defined as any asset that is intended to be converted into cash within one year or the company's **operating cycle,** whichever is longer.[1] As illustrated in Figure 6–2, a company's operating cycle is the time it takes the company to convert its cash to inventory (purchase or manufacture inventory), sell the inventory, and collect cash from the sale. In other words, the operating cycle is the time required for a company to go through all the required phases of the production and sales process.

As the definition of current assets states, if the operating cycle is longer than one year, it serves as the time period for current assets. Companies with different operating cycles, therefore, use different time periods to define current assets. Compare, for example, the relatively short operating cycles of grocery chains like Safeway, Albertsons, and Lucky Stores, to the operating cycles of companies in the aerospace industry like The Boeing Company and McDonnell Douglas, which require several years to manufacture aircraft. Indeed, the time periods of current assets differ widely from company to company. However, the accounts included in the current asset section on the balance sheets of virtually all companies are the

Figure 6–2   The Operating Cycle

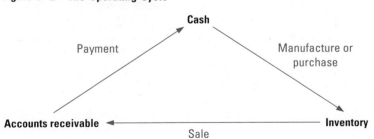

---

1. "Current Assets and Current Liabilities," *Accounting Research Bulletin no. 43, Restatement and Revision of Accounting Research Bulletin* (New York: American Institute of Accountants, 1953), Chapter 3A.

Table 6–1   Current assets as a percentage of total assets (industry averages)

Industry (no. of companies)	Average Current Assets/Total Assets
Hotel (1912)	19%
Motion picture theatres (57)	26
TV broadcasting (112)	29
Restaurants (2061)	34
Grocery stores (2295)	58
Life insurance (937)	73
Department stores (1032)	77
Wholesale sporting goods (738)	81
New and used car dealers (2120)	86

Source: Compiled from data published in *Industry Norms and Key Business Ratios* (Dun & Bradstreet, Inc., 1987).

same. They are Cash, Marketable Securities, Short-Term Accounts and Notes Receivable, Inventories, and Prepaid Expenses. The individual accounts that compose the current asset classification were briefly discussed and illustrated in Chapter 2.

The relative size of current assets differs significantly across companies in different industries. Note in Table 6–1, for example, that current assets as a percentage of total assets varies from an average of 19 percent in the hotel industry to an average of 86 percent for new and used car dealers.

The percentages in Table 6–1 vary primarily because companies in some industries carry different proportions of securities, receivables, or inventories than companies in other industries. Life insurance companies and other financial institutions, for example, carry a large proportion of short-term investments. Department stores rely heavily on credit sales and therefore carry large amounts of receivables. The most important asset for a new and used car dealer is, of course, its inventory of automobiles. Hotels, on the other hand, have a relatively small percentage of current assets; most of their investment is in property, hotel structures, and furnishings.

Measures Using Current Assets: Working Capital, Current Ratio, and Quick Ratio

The distinction between current and noncurrent assets is useful because it provides an easy-to-determine, low-cost measure of a company's ability to produce cash in the short run. Current assets are often compared to current liabilities (the liabilities expected to require cash payments within the same time period as current assets) as an indicator of a company's solvency position.[2] Reasoning that current liabilities are a measure of short-run cash outflows, these comparisons appear to be logical. Three such comparisons are working capital and two solvency ratios, the current ratio and the quick ratio. **Working capital** is defined as current assets less current liabilities; the **current ratio** is equal to current assets divided by current liabilities; and the **quick ratio** divides cash plus marketable securities plus

---

2. Current liabilities are introduced and listed in Chapter 2 and discussed extensively in Chapter 10.

Figure 6–3   Working capital, the current ratio and the quick ratio

Measure	Definition
Working capital	Current assets − current liabilities
Current ratio	Current assets ÷ current liabilities
Quick ratio	(Cash + marketable securities + short-term receivables) ÷ current liabilities

short-term receivables by current liabilities.[3] Figure 6–3 summarizes the definitions of these three measures.

The magnitude of a typical current ratio can be assessed by referring to Table 6–2. The average current ratios listed vary from .9 in the motion picture theatre industry to 3.2 for retail department stores. However, the current ratios of individual companies can vary even more. At the end of 1987, for example, Commonwealth Edison, a major electric utility, and Wendy's International, a successful fast-food operation, disclosed current ratios of .65 and .75, respectively, both of which are far below those indicated in Table 6–2.

Average current ratios vary across industries because the relative importance of current assets and the methods used to finance them vary across companies in different industries. A large dollar value of current assets, financed by long-term debt or profitable operations (retained earnings), for example, will give rise to a large current ratio.

For example, a company such as J. C. Penney, a giant in the retail industry, has current assets representing almost 70 percent of total assets. As a retail operation, J. C. Penney must carry large amounts of short-term receivables and inventories, which are financed through long-term borrowings and profitable operations. The company's current ratio is consequently relatively large, ranging between 2.5 and 3.0. The current assets of companies such as Wendy's International and McDonald's Corporation, on the other hand, represent a significantly smaller portion of total assets: 13 percent for Wendy's and 7 percent for McDonald's. The largest assets on these companies' balance sheets are land, buildings, and restaurant equipment. Both companies also rely heavily on long-term debt and profitable operations to finance asset acquisitions, but their relatively small current asset accounts cause their current ratios to be well below 1.0.

Table 6–2   Current ratios: current assets/current liabilities (industry averages)

Industry (no. of companies)	Average Current Ratio
Motion picture theatres (57)	.9
Crude oil and natural gas mining (1226)	1.3
Life insurance (937)	1.5
Book publishing (393)	2.3
Retail sporting goods (2236)	2.7
Retail department stores (1032)	3.2

Source: Compiled from data published in *Industry Norms and Key Business Ratios* (Dun & Bradstreet, Inc., 1987).

---

3. The quick ratio is sometimes calculated with only cash and marketable securities in the numerator.

The Economic Consequences of Working Capital, the Current Ratio, and the Quick Ratio

Working capital, the current ratio, and the quick ratio are often used by investors, bankers, and other lenders (e.g., bondholders) to help assess a company's ability to meet current obligations as they come due. For example, Dun & Bradstreet, a widely used service that rates the creditworthiness of a large number of U.S. businesses, includes both the current ratio and the quick ratio as solvency measures in its list of fourteen key business ratios. Another of these key ratios, sales/working capital, is described as indicating whether a company has enough (or too many) current assets to support its sales volume. The formula used by Dun & Bradstreet to determine a company's credit rating, which in turn relates to the company's ability to borrow funds and the terms of its outstanding loans, includes these fourteen ratios.[4]

The measures of working capital and the current ratio also appear in loan contracts and debt covenants, where they specify certain minimum dollar amounts or ratios that a debtor company must maintain. For example, the 1987 financial report of Cummins Engine Company, a manufacturer of heavy-duty truck engines, indicates that loan agreements entered into by the company require maintenance of a 1.25 current ratio. This means that Cummins must maintain a current ratio of 1.25, or the creditor has the right to call for the immediate payment of the entire loan principal. Similarly, McDonnell Douglas, a giant in the aerospace industry, has revolving credit agreements with a number of banks specifying that the company must maintain a certain level of working capital.

Working capital, the current ratio, and the quick ratio are also used by auditors. For example, the 1979 AICPA list of "red flags" alerting auditors to possible management fraud, includes "inadequate working capital". The AICPA reasons that low amounts of working capital may put pressure on management to fraudulently manipulate the financial records in an effort to deceive stockholders, creditors, investors, and others. In addition, examining a company's working capital and current ratio can help an auditor assess whether there is substantial doubt about a company's ability to continue operations in the future. Information that helps to predict business failures is valuable to auditors because such failures lead to investor and creditor losses, which in turn can lead to costly lawsuits against auditors.

Limitations of the Current Asset Classification

While working capital, the current ratio, and the quick ratio are used extensively in business to assess solvency, they have a number of inherent and significant weaknesses. These limitations are related to the fundamental fact that current assets and current liabilities fail to accurately reflect future cash inflows and outflows, the essence of a company's ability to meet its debts as they come due. As noted by Leopold A. Bernstein,

---

4. Many of these ratios and some others are discussed in Chapter 17, which covers how financial information is used.

> *The current ratio is not fully up to the task [of assessing short-term liquidity] because it is a static or "stock" concept of what resources are available at a given moment to meet the obligations at that moment. Moreover, working capital . . . does not have a logical or causative relationship to the future funds which flow through it. The future flows are, of course, the focus of our greatest interest in the assessment of short-term liquidity. And yet, these flows depend importantly on elements not included in the current ratio, such as sales, profits, and changes in business conditions.*[5]

Static Analysis

Working capital, the current ratio, and the quick ratio all use numbers exclusively from the balance sheet and are, therefore, static measures. They refer to a company's solvency position at only one point in time. While these measures can be compared across time to uncover trends, such analysis still fails to reflect directly the importance of operating activities on the cash position of the company. For example, W. T. Grant, once a major department store, showed a stable pattern of working capital almost up to the actual time of its bankruptcy.

Current Assets Are Poor Indicators of Cash Inflows

Working capital, the current ratio, and the quick ratio are also limited because the dollar values in a number of the current asset accounts are simply poor indicators of short-term cash inflows. Marketable securities and inventory, for example, are normally carried on the balance sheet at historical cost, which is typically a poor indicator of future cash inflows. The inventories of Nordstrom, a well-known specialty retail operation, for example, on average sell for 167 percent of their costs. Prepaid expenses represent past cash outflows, not future cash inflows.

Arbitrary Definition of Current

The definition of the time period of current assets (one year or the current operating cycle, whichever is longer) also presents problems. The choice of one year is largely arbitrary, and a company's operating cycle is often very difficult to determine. Neither time period may be relevant to a creditor trying to assess a company's ability to meet the interest and principal payments associated with a particular outstanding loan.

Consider, for example, a bank that expects full payment on an outstanding ninety-day loan. The debtor company may have a large amount of current assets on its balance sheet, but if they consist primarily of inventories, the company may be unable to meet the debt payment until the inventories are sold, which may or may not be within ninety days.

Incentives to "Window Dress"

As indicated earlier, the current asset classification is used both by financial statement readers to assess solvency and in debt contracts and covenants to control and direct management behavior. Consequently, management has incentives to choose accounting methods and make operating decisions for no reason other than to "cosmetically" inflate the balances in the current asset accounts.

For example, in 1984, Datapoint, a computer manufacturer, was charged by the SEC with materially overstating its receivables and revenues. The company

---

5. Leopold A. Bernstein, "Working Capital as a Tool," *Journal of Accountancy* (December 1981), pp. 82, 84, 86.

was apparently shipping computers without customer authorization and thereby recording sales and receivables prematurely. In 1987, General Electric changed its method of accounting for inventory and by doing so increased the dollar amount reported in its inventory account, and therefore its current assets, by $281 million. Such actions can have a significant impact on working capital or the current ratio, which in turn may affect the company's credit rating as well as determine whether a company is in violation of a loan contract or debt covenant. Later in this chapter we show how managers can manipulate the current ratio by selling and repurchasing marketable equity securities.

From these examples, it is clear that managers have discretion over the accounts in the current asset section of the balance sheet and thus have some control over measures like working capital, the current ratio, and the quick ratio. Exercising such discretion to inflate these measures is called **window dressing** and includes choosing accounting methods or making operating decisions that are designed solely to make the financial statements appear more attractive. Keep in mind, however, that while the practice of window dressing is widespread, it may not serve management's long-run interest. Managers who attempt to deceive by manipulating the dollar amounts on the financial statements risk reducing the credibility of the statements, which may actually hinder their abilities to raise debt and equity capital.

A Movement Toward Cash Flow Accounting

In view of these limitations, measures like working capital, the current ratio, and the quick ratio are rarely viewed as the only ways to assess solvency. Cash flow numbers are quickly gaining popularity as indicators of a company's ability to meet its debts as they come due. The statement of cash flows, for example, which discloses the net cash flows from operating, investing, and financing activities, is increasingly being used by investors and creditors to assess solvency. For example, Loyd C. Heath, an accounting professor at the University of Washington, states that "the emphasis in credit analysis has shifted from analysis of working capital position to dynamic analysis of future cash receipts and payments."[6]

Nonetheless, solvency and liquidity measures based on the current asset classification are still important and widely used. Working capital, the current ratio, and the quick ratio are low-cost surrogates for cash flow measures and are still used extensively by investors and creditors and in loan contracts and debt covenants. It is important, therefore, that you understand how the current asset classification is used, what its limitations are, and how it can be modified to be more useful in the future. As we move now into the discussions of each individual current asset, keep in mind that the accounting methods and operating decisions that affect these assets also affect working capital, the current ratio, and the quick ratio.

CASH

The Cash account appears in the top left-hand corner of the balance sheet and is the first asset listed in the current asset section. It consists of coin, currency, and checking accounts, as well as money orders, certified checks, cashiers' checks,

---

6. Loyd C. Heath, "Is Working Capital Really Working?" *Journal of Accountancy* (August 1980), pp. 55-62.

Table 6-3   Cash: balance sheet captions

	1986	1985	1984	1983
Cash	235	233	266	293
Cash and equivalents	117	106	89	86
Cash, including certificates of deposit or time deposits	47	55	60	59
Cash and marketable securities	201	206	185	162
Total companies	600	600	600	600

Source: *Accounting Trends and Techniques* (1987).

personal checks, and bank drafts received by a company. Remember also that cash is the standard medium of exchange and thus provides the basis for measuring all financial statement accounts.

Companies use a number of different titles to describe the Cash account on their balance sheets. *Accounting Trends and Techniques* (1987) provided the summary contained in Table 6-3 of the balance sheet captions of 600 of the largest companies in the United States. Note that the title *Cash,* while still the most common, seems to be decreasing in popularity, while *Cash and Equivalents* and *Cash and Marketable Securities* are both becoming more common on the balance sheets of U.S. companies.

The relative size of the Cash account on the balance sheet varies across companies in different industries. Table 6-4 shows that cash is a relatively small asset for household appliance manufacturers, constituting only 3 percent of total assets and 4 percent of current assets. Insurance and finance companies, on the other hand, keep relatively larger amounts of cash on hand. Fifty percent of the current assets of motion picture theaters is in the form of cash. Companies that transact in cash, such as financial institutions, motion picture theaters, and restaurants, tend to keep larger cash balances on hand than companies that sell large-ticket items (e.g., household appliances) on credit.

Three issues are particularly relevant to the study of cash in the context of financial accounting. They are: (1) restrictions on the use of cash, (2) proper management of cash, and (3) control of cash.

Table 6-4   Cash as a percentage of total assets and current assets (industry averages)

Industry (no. of companies)	Cash/Total Assets	Cash/Current Assets
Household appliance manufacturers (14)	3%	4%
General farm crops (354)	7	23
Motion picture theaters (57)	13	50
Restaurants (2061)	16	47
Single-family home construction (2342)	17	27
Accident and health insurance (199)	23	30
Mortgage banks (755)	24	36
Medical doctors' offices (301)	25	44

Source: Compiled from data published in *Industry Norms and Key Business Ratios* (Dun & Bradstreet, Inc., 1987).

Restrictions on the Use of Cash

In general, cash presents few problems from a reporting standpoint. There are no valuation problems because cash always appears on the balance sheet at face value. The only reporting issue is whether there are restrictions on its use.

Restrictions placed on a company's access to its cash are typically imposed by creditors to help insure future interest and principal payments. As part of a loan agreement, for example, a creditor may require that a certain amount of cash be held in **escrow**; that is, controlled by a trustee until the debtor's existing liability is discharged. In addition, banks often require that minimum cash balances be maintained on deposit in the accounts of customers to whom they lend money or extend credit. These amounts are called **compensating balances.**

Cash held in escrow and compensating balances are examples of cash amounts that a company may own but cannot immediately use. Such restricted cash should be separated from the general Cash account on the balance sheet, and the restrictions should be clearly described either on the balance sheet itself or in the footnotes to the financial statements. If the restricted cash is to be used for payment of obligations maturing within the time period of current assets, the separate cash account is appropriately classified as a current asset. If it is to be held for a longer period of time, it should be classified as noncurrent.

Owens-Corning Fiberglass Corporation, for example, noted in its 1986 financial report that $85 million, almost 96 percent of its $89 million cash balance, was restricted. Approximately $70 million was held in escrow to be used in the following year for the payment of a long-term debt, and $15 million was temporarily "locked" in a Brazilian bank. That same year, Atlantic Richfield Company's financial report noted that "the company maintains compensating balances for some of its various banking services and products". Both Owens-Corning and Atlantic Richfield included the restricted funds among their current assets. Manville Corporation, in its 1986 financial report, indicated that $278 million was placed in escrow in connection with bankruptcy proceedings. These funds were not included as current assets.

Proper Management of Cash

Proper cash management requires that enough cash be available to meet the needs of a company's operations, yet too much is undesirable because idle cash provides no return and loses purchasing power during periods of inflation. Maintaining a proper balance is one of management's greatest challenges. On one hand, enough cash must be available so that a company can meet its cash obligations as they come due. Purchases are often made in cash, and payments on accounts payable require cash. Wages, salaries, and currently maturing long-term debts must be honored in cash. Normally the cash needed for such operating activities is kept on the premises in the form of **petty cash** (small amounts of cash to cover day-to-day needs) or deposited in an interest-bearing checking account, where it earns a moderate rate of interest and can be withdrawn immediately as cash needs arise.

Cash in and of itself, however, is not a productive asset. Consider, for example, the popular TV game show that leaves $1 million under a plastic dome sitting out on the stage. The amount of annual interest income that is forgone by leaving that amount of cash idle, assuming a 10 percent interest rate, is $100,000 ($1,000,000 × 10%). Furthermore, during inflationary times, cash continually loses purchasing power. Assuming a 5 percent annual rate of inflation, it would require $1.05 million at the end of a year to buy the same goods and services that could have been purchased with $1 million at the beginning of the year. Consequently, cash over and above the amount needed for operations should be invested in income-producing assets like marketable securities, inventories, long-term investments, property, plant, and equipment, and intangible assets.

A company that maintains a cash balance of more than is necessary for its day-to-day needs is not operating at its full potential. It is, of course, a desirable practice to keep a little extra in the checking account to meet unforeseen cash requirements, but in general, cash in excess of the amount necessary to cover day-to-day cash obligations should be invested in assets that produce a higher return. Determining this amount and where to invest the excess is a very important concern of a company's managers.

Accountants typically do not make the decisions involved in managing cash, but many of these decisions depend on the information provided by the accounting system. One useful tool for cash management, which is an output of the accounting system, is a **cash budget,** a report that projects future cash inflows and outflows and thereby helps to assess future cash operating needs. This report, however, is generated and used internally and is not available to stockholders, investors, creditors, and other parties outside a company. It contains classified information and future projections that cannot be objectively verified and audited. Consequently, this text does not cover cash budgets; they are normally covered in managerial accounting courses.

Cash and Internal Control

Appendix 3B discusses the importance and general principles of effective internal control. Such control is the responsibility of a company's accountants and is particularly important in the area of cash. Cash control is a special concern for businesses such as grocery stores, movie theaters, restaurants, financial institutions, retail stores, department stores, and bars, which process frequent cash transactions. There are two aspects to the internal control of cash: record control and physical control.

Record Control of Cash

Record control refers to the procedures designed by a company's accountants to ensure that the cash account on the balance sheet reflects the actual amount of cash in the company's possession. Problems of record control arise when many different kinds of transactions involve cash and it is difficult to record them all accurately. Proper control of cash records requires that all cash receipts and disbursements be faithfully recorded in the cash journal and posted to the cash account in the ledger. Periodically, the dollar amount of cash indicated in the cash account in the ledger should be checked against and reconciled with the cash balance indicated on the statement provided by a company's bank. The procedures used to reconcile these two balances are discussed later in this chapter.

Physical Control of Cash

Physical control of cash refers to the procedures designed to safeguard cash from loss or theft. Problems of physical control arise because cash is the standard medium of exchange; it is universally desired and easily concealed and transported. Cash embezzlement by a company's employees is always a threat. Indeed, *U.S. News and World Report* reported that there were 12,600 arrests for embezzlement during 1986 in the United States.[7]

Proper physical control of cash requires that a minimum amount of cash be kept on a company's premises at any one time. Petty cash amounts used to cover day-to-day office expenses and cash receipts from sales or receivable payments should be handled by as few employees as possible, and stored in a safe or locked cash drawer. Cash amounts in excess of petty cash requirements should be taken to the bank at frequent intervals.

We turn now to two specific examples of basic cash control techniques: (1) the imprest petty cash system and (2) the bank reconciliation. These techniques help to achieve record control by providing mechanisms for recording certain cash inflows and outflows in the cash journal. They help to achieve physical control by identifying descrepancies between reported and actual cash as soon as they arise, so that management can investigate and attend to control problems in a more timely manner. Both the imprest petty cash system and bank reconciliations are used extensively by business organizations.

The Imprest Petty Cash System

Most companies require that a small amount of cash be kept on the premises to cover the day-to-day cash needs of their operations. Small expense payments, such as the purchase of office supplies and reimbursements for business expenses incurred by employees, require that a certain amount of cash be available at all times. Periodically, as these expenses reduce the petty cash fund, cash must be transferred from the bank to replenish it.

It is important to have a system that provides adequate record control over the petty cash disbursements. This same system must also discourage pilfering and misuse of the petty cash funds. One reasonably simple and very common method to obtain such control is the **imprest system** for petty cash disbursements. It consists of three separate steps.

1. *Establishing the petty cash fund.* An individual, often the office manager, assumes the role of the petty cash custodian. An amount of cash adequate to cover office expenses for a reasonable period of time, assume $100, is placed in the custody of this individual by a designated company official (e.g., the treasurer). The custodian is then personally responsible for the $100 cash.

2. *Operating the imprest system.* As employees receive cash from the fund to cover or reimburse themselves for office expenses, the custodian replaces the disbursed cash with a receipt, signed by the employee, indicating the nature of the expenditure. Sometimes the custodian pays the expenses directly and replaces the funds with a signed receipt. At any time, the actual cash in the fund plus the total amount of the receipts should equal the original amount used to

---

7. Harold R. Kennedy et al. "Resolving Mysterious Credit Charges," *U.S. News and World Report*, 14 March 1988, p. 108.

establish the fund ($100). As the cash is reduced, the portion of the $100 represented by the receipts becomes greater.

3. *Replenishing the petty cash fund.* When the supply of cash runs low, assume $10, the custodian must replenish it. This is done by presenting the signed receipts to the designated company official, who reimburses the custodian with enough cash to bring the fund back to the desired level. If there are no errors, the amount of cash reimbursed to the custodian equals the total dollar value of the signed receipts ($90). Any differences between these two amounts must be explained by the custodian.

Note that the imprest system exhibits several of the characteristics of an effective internal control system. First, the custodian is responsible for the fund but does not have the power to establish or replenish it. Second, the employees must sign the receipts, documenting the cash disbursements from the fund. Third, the custodian must present the signed receipts to the designated company official to replenish the fund, and differences between the cash reimbursed to the custodian and the total dollar value of the signed receipts are the clear responsibility of the custodian. These procedures involve the elements of clearly defined authority and responsibility as well as segregation of duties.

The imprest system is certainly not foolproof, but it does represent an example of how accounting systems underlie the record and physical control of a company's assets and liabilities. It helps to ensure that all petty cash receipts and disbursements are properly recorded because cash amounts paid to replenish the fund are accompanied by entries in the cash journal. The imprest system helps to ensure the physical control of cash because it provides a system of checks and balances that discourages embezzlement. Similar imprest systems are used to control cash disbursements for such items as payroll, dividends, interest, office salaries, and sales commissions.

Bank Reconciliations

Another control mechanism applied to the Cash account is the bank reconciliation. Those of you with checking accounts should already be familiar with this concept. You have probably noticed that the final cash balance on the statement the bank sends you every month rarely matches the cash balance indicated in your checkbook. A bank reconciliation explains why these two balances differ.

The balance on the bank statement may not match the balance in your checkbook for many reasons. You may have written checks, for example, that have not yet been processed by the bank. These **outstanding checks** would have been subtracted from the balance in your checkbook, but not yet subtracted from the balance on the bank statement. Similarly, **deposits** you may have made and entered on your checkbook may still be **in transit** and not yet received and recorded by the bank. The bank may also have adjusted your account for earned interest or for certain fees (e.g., **service charges** on checking accounts and **nonsufficient fund (NSF) penalties,** charges for processed checks not backed by sufficient funds) that would appear on the bank statement but not in your checkbook. A bank reconciliation is simply a systematic way of explaining the difference between the balance in your checkbook and the bank balance in terms of such items as outstanding checks, deposits in transit, bank charges, and accrued interest. Not only does it bring your checkbook up-to-date but it should catch errors made either by you or the bank.

Figure 6–4 Bank reconciliation

Cash balance per bank statement (12/31/89)		$8,200
Plus		
Deposits in transit (deposits not yet recorded by the bank)		2,350
Less		
Outstanding checks (checks recorded in company books but not yet cleared through the bank)		
#834	$250	
#836	150	
#837	350	750
Correct cash balance		$9,800
Cash balance per books (12/31/89)		$9,200
Plus		
Collections (payments on accounts receivable made directly to the bank but not yet recorded in the company books)*	$770	
Earned interest (interest earned on cash balance in bank)	50	820
Less		
Dishonored checks (recorded in books but not honored by bank due to insufficient funds)	70	
Bank charges		
Collection fee	100	
Service charge	50	220
Correct cash balance		$9,800

*Note: Banks often collect accounts receivable payments directly from the company's customers. They usually charge a fee (collection fee) for this service.

Businesses share these same concerns. They use checking accounts and at the same time keep records of cash balances in their cash ledger accounts. They receive monthly statements from banks, and invariably the cash balances on their statements do not match the balances indicated in their cash ledger accounts. Proper record control of the Cash account requires that this difference be reconciled frequently to bring a company's Cash account up-to-date and highlight errors in the records of either the bank or the company.

In practice, bank reconciliations can take a number of different forms. The most logical and useful method adjusts both the bank balance and the book balance to the correct balance, as illustrated in Figure 6–4.

Note that both the balance on the bank statement ($8200) and the balance in the books ($9200) are adjusted to the correct balance ($9800). The bank balance is adjusted for deposits in transit and outstanding checks, because these items are not reflected in the bank balance as of the statement date. The book balance is adjusted for receivables collected, earned interest, checks received but not honored by the bank, and bank charges, because these items have not yet been recorded in the company's books.

A bank reconciliation of this form is useful for three reasons: actual cash balance, adjusting journal entries, and independent verification.

1. *Actual cash balance.* It identifies the actual cash balance. It recognizes that neither the bank balance nor the book balance is up-to-date and proceeds to adjust each balance for what it fails to reflect.

2. *Adjusting journal entries.* It indicates the items that require adjusting journal entries. Any adjustment to the book balance on the bank reconciliation should be

accompanied by an entry in the company's cash journal. These entries bring the company's books (and eventually the balance sheet) to the correct cash balance. Recall the discussion of adjusting journal entries in Chapter 4, and note that these entries fall into the category of asset revaluations. The following journal entries should be made to accompany the bank reconciliation illustrated in Figure 6–4.

Cash	770		Collection Fee Expense	100	
Accounts Receivable		770	Cash		100
To record a receivable collected by the bank.			To record a collection fee.		
Cash	50		Service Charge Expense	50	
Interest Revenue		50	Cash		50
To record the earning of interest revenue.			To record a service charge.		
Accounts Receivable	70				
Cash		70			
To reverse the recording of a previously-received bad check.					

3. *Independent verification.* The bank reconciliation provides an independent verification of the company's cash balance, which is particularly useful to an auditor, who must attest that the balance sheet Cash account reflects the actual cash balance.

Bank reconciliations help to provide both record and physical control. The journal entries recorded from the bank reconciliation help to ensure that the company's records reflect its actual cash balance. The independent verification of the balance helps to identify discrepancies between the actual cash balance and the cash balance recorded in a company's records. Such discrepancies may indicate control problems that should be investigated by management. An example of a complete bank reconciliation follows.

Figure 6–5　Bank statement for Wellmar Company

First Choice Bank
1234 8th Street
Mapleton, N.Y.

Bank Statement for Wellmar Company
Statement period: November 30–December 31

Summary of Checking Account		Description of Deposits		Description of Withdrawals		
		Date	Amount	Ck. No.	Date	Amount
Beginning balance	$4,340	12/14	$2,800	4362	12/2	$ 840
Deposits	6,400	12/16	1,500	4363	12/7	750
Interest earned this period	30	12/20	2,100	4364	12/10	2,300
Withdrawals	5,350	Total	$6,400	4366	12/20	560
Service charges	60			4367	12/23	700
Collection fees	100			4369	12/24	200
Ending balance	$5,260			Total		$5,350

Assume that Wellmar Company received the bank statement in Figure 6–5 from First Choice Bank at the end of December. The accountant for Wellmar reviewed the cash journal and ledger accounts and noted that the ledger account had an ending cash balance of $5635, which differed from the $5260 balance indicated on the bank statement. It was also noted that the following checks written by Wellmar were not reflected on the bank statement.

Check Number	Amount
4365	$ 430
4368	1200
4370	285

Similarly, the accountant observed that the two deposits listed below had been entered in the company's records but were not reflected on the bank statement.

Date	Amount
12/22	$ 860
12/24	1300

Given the information above, Wellmar's accountant prepared the bank reconciliation shown in Figure 6–6. The cash journal entries resulting from the reconciliation follow.

Cash	30	
Interest Revenue		30
To record interest earned.		
Service Charge Expense	60	
Cash		60
To record service charge.		
Collection Fee Expense	100	
Cash		100
To record collection fee.		

Figure 6–6 Bank reconciliation for Wellmar Company

Cash balance per bank statement (December 31)		$5,260
Plus: Deposits in transit		
12/22	$ 860	
12/24	1,300	2,160
Less: Outstanding checks		
#4365	430	
#4368	1,200	
#4370	285	1,915
Correct cash balance (December 31)		$5,505
Cash balance per books (December 31)		$5,635
Plus: Earned interest		30
Less		
Service charge	$ 60	
Collection fees	100	160
Correct cash balance (December 31)		$5,505

MARKETABLE SECURITIES

This discussion of marketable securities is divided into three sections. The first defines marketable securities, differentiates them from long-term investments, and discusses issues considered by managers, investors, creditors, and auditors regarding the disclosure of marketable securities on the balance sheet. The second section summarizes and illustrates the financial accounting standard that prescribes the methods used to account for marketable securities.[8] Section three presents the theory and economics that underlie accounting for marketable securities, giving special emphasis to reporting problems related to the lower-of-cost-or-market rule and the concept of conservatism.

Definition of Marketable Securities

Remember that idle cash not only earns no return but during inflation actually declines in purchasing power. Nevertheless, proper cash management must ensure that enough cash is available to meet a company's day-to-day cash needs. Such cash needs tend to fluctuate, sometimes unexpectedly, making it difficult for management to consistently strike an appropriate balance between available cash and return-producing investments. In an effort to both earn a return and be able to produce cash on short-term notice, companies often purchase marketable securities. The 1986 financial report of Brown and Company, Inc., for example, indicates that it is "company policy to invest cash in excess of operating requirements in income-producing investments". Such investments, which include stocks and bonds traded on public security exchanges, provide income through dividends, interest, or price appreciation, and can be readily converted to cash when needed to meet current cash requirements.[9]

The relative size of the marketable security dollar amount on the balance sheet varies significantly across companies in different industries. Retailers such as hardware, department, clothing, and sporting good stores typically maintain marketable security amounts of less than 3 percent of total assets. Financial institutions and insurance companies, on the other hand, which have greater needs for ready cash, often carry marketable security portfolios that approximate 30–40 percent of total assets.

Marketable securities are listed in the current asset section of the balance sheet. It is important to realize that they are distinct from long-term investments in equity and debt securities, which are included in the long-term investment section. Two criteria must be met for an investment in a security to be considered current and thus warrant inclusion as a current asset:

1. The investment must be *readily marketable*.

---

8. "Accounting for Certain Marketable Securities," Statement of Financial Accounting Standards No. 12 (Stamford, Conn.: FASB, 1975).

9. Short-term investments can also consist of certificates of deposit, money market accounts, and commercial paper. Certificates of deposit are usually purchased from banks in denominations of at least $5000. They provide a fixed rate of return over a specified period of time. Money market accounts are similar to savings or checking accounts, but provide a slightly higher rate of interest and there are usually restrictions on the withdrawal of funds. Commercial paper is a short-term note issued by corporations with good credit ratings. They are usually issued in denominations of $5,000 and $10,000 and provide returns which exceed those of money market accounts.

2. Management must *intend to convert* the investment into cash within the time period of current assets (one year or the operating cycle, whichever is longer).

If either criterion is not met, the investment must be included in the long-term investment section.

The Existence of a Ready Market

Readily marketable means that the security can be sold and converted into cash on demand. Stocks and bonds that are traded actively on the public stock exchanges (e.g., New York Stock Exchange, American Stock Exchange) usually meet this criterion because a ready market exists for them. Objective market prices exist for such securities, which insure that they can be sold on very short notice. In most cases all a company must do is request that its stockbroker sell the security.

Some securities, on the other hand, are not publicly traded, often because there are restrictions on their sale. Common stocks of closely held corporations, for example, may have very limited markets because restrictions exist on who can own them (e.g., ownership is sometimes limited to family members). Objective market prices do not exist for such securities, and they cannot be readily converted into cash. Accordingly, they fail to meet the readily marketable criterion and should be listed in the long-term investment section of the balance sheet.

The Intention to Convert: Another Area of Subjectivity

The second criterion, **intention to convert** the investment to cash, is much more difficult to determine objectively. Consequently, it can be a very difficult area for the auditor, who must determine whether a company's financial statements are in conformance with generally accepted accounting principles. Simply asking managers whether they intend to sell securities within the time period of current assets does not provide sufficiently objective evidence. Recall that managers have incentives to window dress, which in this case might consist of including what would appropriately be a long-term investment in the current asset section. Such a decision might be made to increase a company's quick ratio, current ratio, or working capital number.

For example, in 1986 PepsiCo acquired two Canadian soft drink bottling operations of the Seven-Up Company from Philip Morris Companies for approximately $246 million dollars in cash. PepsiCo's financial report for that year indicated that "as it is management's intention to resell the Canadian bottling operations . . . [this investment] has been accounted for as a temporary investment and included . . . under the caption current assets". The decision to include this investment as current instead of long-term may certainly have been legitimate and, in fact, was allowed by PepsiCo's auditors, but it did serve to increase PepsiCo's current ratio by approximately 12 percent, from 1.01 to 1.13.[10]

Auditors often must infer management's intention to convert by examining the company's past practices and the nature and size of the investment in question. Has the company in the past been in the habit of selling and buying marketable securities as its cash needs rise and fall? Securities are often purchased in large

---

10. In July of 1987, consistent with management's intention, PepsiCo sold one of the bottling operations for approximately $45 million. However, the remaining investments were still disclosed as current assets on PepsiCo's 1987 balance sheet.

enough quantities to exert influence or control over another company. If so, conversion to cash in the near future would seem to be unlikely. Is the investee company a supplier or client of the investor company? Does the investor company have members on the board of directors of the investee company? Some securities are purchased as part of a fund to plan for plant expansion or the retirement of long-term debt. Is this management's intention? These and similar kinds of questions must frequently be considered by auditors in their efforts to deduce what motivates management's behavior and, accordingly, how security investments should be classified on the balance sheet.

While auditors must always be aware that management may use its discretion to manipulate the reported dollar amounts on the financial statements, it is worth noting once again that from management's perspective, upright, credible, and consistent reporting behavior is in the company's long-run best interest. Stockholders, investors, creditors, and other interested parties will place greater value on financial reports they can trust.

Accounting for Marketable Securities

Investments in securities that meet the two criteria just discussed should be classified as current and reported on the balance sheet at the **lower-of-their (aggregate)-cost-or-market** value. In applying this rule, four separate events must be considered: (1) the purchase of the securities, (2) the declaration and receipt of cash dividends, (3) the sale of the securities (at either a gain or a loss), and (4) changes in the prices of the securities on hand at the end of the accounting period.[11]

Purchase of Marketable Securities

When marketable securities are purchased, they are capitalized and recorded on the balance sheet at cost. As with other capitalized assets (inventory, long-term investments, fixed assets, and intangible assets), cost includes the purchase price as well as any *incidental acquisition costs*, such as brokerage commissions and taxes.[12] For example, assume that Goodyear Tire and Rubber Company purchased three different kinds of marketable equity securities on December 1 at the following prices:[13]

10 shares of Dow Chemical at $10/share	=	$100
20 shares of Abbott Laboratories at $12/share	=	$240
15 shares of Eli Lilly at $20/share	=	$300
	Total cost	$640

Assuming that all prices *include* brokerage commissions, the following journal entry would be made to reflect the purchase of the three securities.

---

11. This section covers the methods used to account for marketable equity securities which are described in Statement of Financial Accounting Standard No. 12, "Accounting for Certain Marketable Securities." While this standard does not explicitly cover marketable debt securities, most major U.S. companies use the same procedures to account for both marketable equity and debt securities. In line with these practices, we recommend treatment of all marketable securities in accordance with SFAS no. 12.

12. Actual brokerage commissions range from 1 percent to 5 percent.

13. For computational ease, the dollar amounts used in this example are unrealistically small. Multiplying the totals by 100 would produce numbers of a more realistic magnitude.

Marketable Securities	640	
Cash		640
To record the purchase of marketable securities.		

Declaration and Receipt of Cash Dividends

Cash dividends declared on marketable securities, to which Goodyear has a legal right, are initially recognized as a receivable and a revenue. When the cash dividend is received, the receivable is exchanged for cash. Continuing the example, suppose that on December 15 the board of directors of Abbott declared dividends of $1 per share, to be paid to the holders of its common stock on January 15. The following journal entries would be recorded in the books of Goodyear:

December 15-at declaration of dividend,			January 15-at receipt of dividend,		
Dec. 15 Dividend Receivable	20*		Jan. 15 Cash	20	
Dividend Revenue		20	Dividend Receivable		20
To record declaration of dividend.			To record receipt of dividend.		

*($1/share × 20 shares)

Sale of Marketable Securities

When marketable securities are sold, their original cost is removed from the books, and the difference between the original cost and the proceeds from the sale are recognized on the books. If the proceeds exceed the original cost, a gain is recognized; if they are less than the original cost, a loss is recognized.

Continuing the previous example, assume that on December 4, Goodyear sold five shares of Dow Chemical stock for $13/share and ten shares of Eli Lilly stock for $10/share. Assuming that brokerage commissions have already been deducted from the proceeds, these sales would give rise to the following journal entries:

Cash	65		Cash	100	
Marketable Securities (Dow)		50*	Realized Loss on Sale of Marketable Sec.	100	
Realized Gain on Sale of Marketable Sec.		15	Marketable Securities (Lilly)		200**
To record the sale of Dow.			To record the sale of Lilly stock.		
*(5 shares at $10/share)			**(10 shares at $20/share)		

or combining the two journal entries,

Cash	165	
Realized loss on sale of marketable securities	85	
Marketable securities (Dow and Lilly)		250
To record the sale of Dow and Lilly stock.		

The accounts, Realized Gain on Sale of Marketable Securities and Realized Loss on Sale of Marketable Securities represent the difference between the sale proceeds and the cost of the sold securities and therefore provide a measure of management's performance with respect to the buying and selling of marketable securities. They are temporary accounts, which are closed at the end of the accounting period, appear on the income statement and thus figure in the determination of net income. Chapter 14 points out that these book gains and losses, and others like them, appear in a special section of the income statement, entitled "Other Revenues and Expenses".

Price Changes of Marketable Securities on Hand at the End of the Accounting Period

Before discussing the methods used to account for price changes of securities on hand at the end of the accounting period, we should define three important terms with respect to marketable securities. They are *realize, recognize,* and *portfolio.*

Realized and Unrealized Gains and Losses. The term *realize* roughly means to *cash in.* It relates to securities that have been sold. The investing company no longer holds the securities that produced the gain or loss. Selling a security for $10, which originally cost $8, produces a **realized gain** of $2.

Unrealized gains or **losses** relate to price changes of securities which are still held by the investing company. For example, holding a security which decreases in price from $15 to $11 gives rise to an *unrealized* loss of $4.

Recognized and Unrecognized Gains and Losses. The term *recognize* refers to whether an economic event is recorded in the books of a company and affects the financial statements. **Recognized gains** and losses are recorded in the journal and ledger; unrecognized gains and losses are not.

Portfolio of Securities. The group of marketable securities held by a company is referred to as its **portfolio** of marketable securities. The value of the portfolio is equal to the sum of the market prices of the individual securities it contains. For example, holding three different securities with market prices of $10, $15, and $25 gives rise to a portfolio of securities with an aggregate market value of $50 ($10 + $15 + $25).

The Lower-of-Cost-or-Market Rule. The lower-of-cost-or-market rule, as applied to marketable securities, states that marketable securities on the balance sheet are to be valued at their aggregate cost or market value, whichever is lower, determined as of the balance sheet date.[14] This rule essentially means that if the aggregate market value of a company's portfolio of marketable securities at the end of the accounting period is greater than its original cost, the portfolio is carried on the balance sheet at its original cost. If, on the other hand, the aggregate market value of the portfolio of marketable securities is less than its original cost, the portfolio is carried on the balance sheet at its aggregate market value.

Continue with the previous example and assume that Goodyear prepares financial statements at the end of December. Assuming further that no other purchases or sales occurred during the month and that the market price of each security as of December 31 is different from that of December 1, the condition of Goodyear's portfolio of marketable securities is summarized as follows:

	Original Cost	12/31 Market Price
5 (10 − 5*) shares of Dow	× $10 = $ 50	× $15 = $ 75
20 shares of Abbott	× $12 = $240	× $13 = $260
5 (15 − 10*) shares of Lilly	× $20 = $100	× $ 9 = $ 45
Total original cost	$390	
Aggregate market value		$380

*Sale on December 4

---

14. "Accounting for Certain Marketable Securities," Statement of Financial Accounting Standards No. 12 (Stamford, Conn.: FASB, 1975).

Note that the price of Dow shares rose $5 during the month of December. Similarly, Abbott securities appreciated from $12/share to $13/share. However, the aggregate market value of the entire portfolio decreased $10, from $390 to $380, because the loss in value of Lilly shares ($100 − $45 = $55) more than negated the gains experienced by Dow and Abbott stocks. As of December 31, therefore, the aggregate market value of the entire portfolio ($380) is below the original cost of the securities on hand ($390). Applying the aggregate lower-of-cost-or-market rule to this set of circumstances gives rise to the following journal entry. Keep in mind that this is an adjusting journal entry made at the end of the accounting period, immediately before closing entries and the preparation of the financial statements. In terms of the classifications discussed in Chapter 4, this represents a revaluation adjusting journal entry.

Unrealized Loss on Marketable Securities	10	
Allowance for Unrealized Losses on Marketable Securities		10
To record an unrealized loss on marketable securities.		

The Unrealized Loss on Marketable Securities account is a temporary account that is closed at the end of the period and appears on the income statement. Like Gains and Losses on Sales of Marketable Securities, this account is listed in the section of the income statement designated as "Other Revenues and Expenses". The account Allowance for Unrealized Losses on Marketable Securities is a permanent account that is placed on the balance sheet immediately below the Marketable Securities account. Its credit balance serves as a contra to the debit balance in the Marketable Securities account and thereby reduces the balance sheet carrying value of marketable securities. Contra accounts like this (e.g., Allowance for Uncollectibles and Accumulated Depreciation) are found frequently on the balance sheet. The balance sheet disclosure follows.

Marketable equity securities	390	
Less: Allowance for unrealized losses on marketable securities	10	380

You may wonder why an allowance account is credited instead of the Marketable Securities account in the preceding adjusting entry. The use of an allowance account is preferred because it preserves the original cost ($390) of the securities on the balance sheet while allowing a statement of the current market value of the portfolio ($380). As the next example shows, preserving the original cost can be important when applying the lower-of-cost-or-market rule to marketable securities.

Suppose that on July 15 of the following year, Goodyear decides to sell the Lilly shares for $9 each. This transaction would give rise to the following journal entry:

Cash (5 shares × $9/share)	45	
Realized Loss on the Sale of Marketable Securities	55	
Marketable Securities (Lilly) (5 shares × $20/share)		100
To record the sale of five Lilly shares.		

This journal entry eliminates the Lilly securities from Goodyear's marketable securities portfolio and records the fact that the company realized (cashed in) a loss. Note also that the Allowance for Unrealized Losses on Marketable Securities account is not adjusted when individual securities are sold. It is adjusted only at the end of the accounting period, so that the entire portfolio can be valued on the balance sheet at the lower of its aggregate cost or market value. The value in the allowance account does not correspond to any of the individual securities that make up that portfolio.

Assuming that the share prices of Dow and Abbott remain stable throughout the following year, the state of the marketable equity securities portfolio when the financial statements are prepared at the end of December, is as follows.

	Original Cost	**Current Market Price**
5 shares of Dow	× $10 = $ 50	× $15 = $ 75
20 shares of Abbott	× $12 = $240	× $13 = $260
	Total cost $290	Aggregate market value $335

Now that the Lilly shares have been eliminated from the portfolio, the current market value of the securities on hand ($335) exceeds the original cost ($290). According to the lower-of-cost-or-market rule, Goodyear must now value marketable securities on the balance sheet at cost ($290). Such a valuation is achieved by removing the credit balance in the Allowance for Unrealized Losses on Marketable Securities account with the following adjusting journal entry:

Allowance for Unrealized Losses on Marketable Securities	10	
Recovery of Unrealized Losses on Marketable Securities		10
To record an unrealized recovery.		

The debit to the allowance account eliminates the previous $10 credit, bringing the final balance in the account to zero. As a result, the balance sheet includes only the cost of Goodyear's portfolio of marketable securities. The account Recovery of Unrealized Losses on Marketable Securities is a temporary account that is treated as a revenue and appears in the "Other Revenues and Expenses" section of the income statement. It is called a *recovery* because it represents the recapture of a loss that was recognized on the marketable securities portfolio in a previous period. It is not a gain because it does not represent an increase in the portfolio's market value over and above its original cost.

Our description of the methods used to apply the lower-of-cost-or-market rule to marketable securities might leave you feeling that these procedures are somewhat complicated and a bit confusing. Actually, however, they are the result of applying three relatively straightforward rules:

1. *Purchases are recorded at cost.* All purchases of marketable securities are recorded at cost, which includes the incidental costs of acquiring them (e.g., brokerage commissions).

2. *All realized gains and losses are recognized.* All sales of marketable securities result in realized gains or losses, computed by comparing the proceeds of the sale to the original costs of the sold securities.

At the end of the accounting period, before preparing financial statements, compute the original cost of the portfolio of marketable securities on hand and compare it to the aggregate market value of the portfolio.

3. *Unrealized losses and recoveries are recognized.* The balance in the Allowance for Unrealized Losses on Marketable Securities account should be adjusted with a journal entry so that it reflects the dollar amount of the difference between the aggregate market value of the portfolio and the original cost. The balance should be zero if the aggregate market value exceeds or is equal to the original

cost. Unrealized losses are recognized when the allowance account is increased. Recoveries of unrealized losses are recognized when the allowance account is decreased.

Some Economic and Theoretical Issues

Now that we have covered the procedures for applying the lower-of-cost or market rule to marketable securities, we present some of the economics and theory underlying these procedures. The discussion explains how the lower-of-cost-or-market rule creates some reporting problems, and examines marketable securities and objective market prices, the concept of conservatism, and the stock market crash of 1987.

The Lower-of-Cost-or-Market Rule Creates Reporting Problems

Unrealized losses on a portfolio of marketable securities are recognized, but unrealized gains are not. This inconsistent accounting treatment can produce some strange and undesirable results on the financial statements.

Suppose that both Mr. Hold and Mr. Sell begin business on December 1, 1990 by contributing $200 in cash to their solely-owned companies. On that day they both purchase ten shares of PDQ stock, each paying a total of $100 ($9 per each share and $10 in brokerage fees). Neither company enters into any transactions during the month of December, and on December 31 the market price of PDQ stock has increased to $15 per share. At this time Mr. Sell decides to sell his shares. He receives $140 ($150 less a $10 brokerage fee) and recognizes a $40 ($140 − $100) gain on the sale. He immediately uses the $140 cash and $20 additional dollars to repurchase ten PDQ shares for a total of $160 ([10 shares × $15] plus a $10 brokerage fee). Meanwhile, Mr. Hold simply holds his securities in PDQ. Given these circumstances and applying the lower-of-cost-or-market rule, the December 31 balance sheets of Mr. Hold and Mr. Sell would appear as in Figure 6−7.

It appears that Mr. Sell is financially better off than Mr. Hold. His balance sheet contains assets of greater value, and his income statement for the period, which is reflected in the retained earnings balance, shows higher income. In reality, however, Mr. Hold is in better financial condition than Mr. Sell. As of December 31, 1990 they both have ten shares of PDQ stock, but Mr. Hold has more cash because Mr. Sell had to pay $20 extra in brokerage fees. Further, Mr. Sell took time away from his business to execute additional transactions.

The reporting problem illustrated above stems from the treatment of unrealized gains by the lower-of-cost-or-market rule. Gains must be realized before they can be recognized. Mr. Sell's financial statements look better because he sold the securities and thereby cashed in a $40 gain. He was allowed to recognize it because he cashed it in. He then used the $140 he received from the sale, plus $20 additional dollars, to repurchase the PDQ securities. These transactions increased the balance sheet value of the securities to $160. Mr. Hold also enjoyed an economic gain, but because he did not cash it in, neither the balance sheet nor the income statement reflect it.

The problem illustrated above is not as critical as it could be because generally accepted accounting principles require companies to disclose the market values of their marketable securities portfolios in the footnotes to their financial statements.

Figure 6–7   Comparative balance sheets: Mr. Hold and Mr. Sell

	Mr. Hold Balance Sheet December 31, 1990		Mr. Sell Balance Sheet December 31, 1990	
Assets				
Cash	($200 − $100)	$100	($200 − 100 + 140 − 160)	$ 80
Marketable securities	(10 shares × $10)	100	[(10 shares × $15) + 10 fees]	160
Total assets		$200		$240
Liabilities and stockholders' equity				
Contributed Capital		$200		$200
Retained earnings (net income)		0	($140 − $100)	40
Total liabilities and stockholders' equity		$200		$240

Financial statement users, therefore, could ascertain that Mr. Hold, for example, had actually enjoyed an unrealized gain during the period. Nonetheless, the illustration does demonstrate that there are some real reporting problems with the lower-of-cost-or-market rule. Financial statements prepared on the basis of this rule often do not reflect the economic substance of certain transactions and therefore fail to measure management's performance accurately. Moreover, the lower-of-cost-or-market rule provides incentives for managers to act just as Mr. Sell did, cashing in securities in order to window dress the balance sheet and the income statement. As mentioned before, such actions may not be in the best interests of the company's stockholders.

Marketable Securities and Objective Market Prices

For economic reasons the financial accounting system recognizes relevant events only if they can be objectively measured. The relevant event associated with a marketable security is, of course, a change in its market price, or value. When marketable securities held by a company increase in price, the company increases in value. Conversely, a reduction in the price of a marketable security decreases the value of the investing company. It is reasonable to expect, therefore, that if changes in security prices could be objectively measured, they would be reflected in the financial statements, whether they were increases or decreases.

The prices of marketable securities, by definition, are objectively measurable. Indeed, one of the criteria for including a security in the current asset section is that a ready market exists, which in turn implies that an objective market price exists. Many marketable securities, for example, are listed on the New York or American Stock Exchanges, where official prices are published throughout all business days. Consequently, many marketable securities could be carried on the financial statements at their fair market values without violating the principle of objectivity.

Lower-of-Cost-or-Market and Conservatism

In light of the reporting problems described and the fact that the market prices of marketable securities are objectively determinable, you might wonder why generally accepted accounting principles continue to require that marketable securities be accounted for under the lower-of-cost-or-market rule. Why, for example, are marketable securities not carried on the balance sheet at market value?

The answer resides in the concept of conservatism: the lower-of-cost-or-market rule is conservative. Unrealized losses are recognized, but unrealized gains are not. Recall the discussion on conservatism in Chapter 5, which explains the economic reasoning behind conservative financial statements. From the perspective of auditors and managers, errors of understatement (conservative errors) are considerably less costly than errors of overstatement. When in doubt, understate assets, overstate liabilities, speed up the recognition of losses, and defer the recognition of gains. The liability costs associated with errors of overstatement are potentially very high. Conservative accounting rules, therefore, make economic sense, and it is not surprising that the lower-of-cost-or-market rule prevails, even though it creates reporting problems.

Lower-of-Cost-or-Market and the Stock Market Crash of 1987

On October 19, 1987 (often referred to as *Black Monday*) prices in the U.S. stock markets dropped by a larger amount than at any other time in history. This collapse had a devastating effect on the marketable security portfolios of a number of major U.S. businesses. Many companies showed multimillion-dollar unrealized losses on their 1987 financial statements. Table 6–5 lists several of these companies and the dollar amounts of the unrealized losses reported on their 1987 financial statements.

A senior vice-president for Standard & Poor's Corporation, a highly regarded credit-rating concern, pointed out in *The Wall Street Journal* that "these unrealized losses may drop [important ratios] of some corporations below the amounts required to comply with bank loan agreements. When that happens, it's a serious issue."[15] The same article also noted that these losses could seriously threaten the credit ratings of these companies.

It is particularly interesting that these companies were required to report such huge losses even though they had not sold the securities in their portfolios. Furthermore, by the end of 1988 stock market prices had substantially recovered and many of the companies were able to recognize significant unrealized recoveries on their 1988 financial statements.

Table 6–5   1987 unrealized losses on marketable securities (in millions of dollars)

Company	Reported Loss
E-II Holdings, Inc.	$114
Masco Corporation	40
Nortek Inc.	24
Sequa Corporation	24
Triangle Industries Inc.	24
Lin Broadcasting Corporation	2

Source: *The Wall Street Journal*, 26 January 1988.

---

15. Sanford Jacobs, "Black Monday Casts Dark Shadow on Corporate Profits," *The Wall Street Journal*, 26 January 1988, p. 6.

THE ANNUAL REPORT OF K MART CORPORATION

Now turn to K mart's annual report in Appendix D. Focus first on the current asset and current liability sections of the balance sheet (page 32). Current assets, which represented 57 percent and 59 percent of total assets in 1988 and 1989, consist of Cash (including temporary investments), Merchandise Inventories, Accounts Receivable, and Other Current Assets and total $7.146 billion and $6.373 for 1989 and 1988, respectively. Current liabilities consist of short-term payables, totaling $3.492 billion and $3.370 billion in 1989 and 1988. Working capital (current assets-current liabilities), the current ratio (current assets / current liabilities) and the quick ratio ([cash + short-term investments + accounts receivable] / current liabilities) for 1989 and 1988 follow.

	1989	1988
Working capital (billions)	$3.654	$3.003
Current ratio	2.046	1.891
Quick ratio	.422	.238

While both current assets and current liabilities increased during the year, the increase in current assets was greater. As a result, working capital increased by $651 million ($3.654 − $3.003) and the current ratio increased by .155 (2.046 − 1.891). A substantial increase in cash and temporary investments ($499 million) was largely responsibile, which also caused the quick ratio to almost double. Cash and temporary investments made up 7 percent of total current assets in 1988 and 13 percent in 1989. Note, however, that K mart's quick ratio is relatively low compared to its current ratio, primarily because a large percentage of its current assets are in the form of inventories.

Turn to Tables 6-1 and 6-2 in this chapter and note that K mart's current assets (as a percentage of total assets) and current ratio are somewhat lower than department stores in general. Unlike many department stores, K mart does not rely heavily on credit sales which keeps its outstanding receivables at any given time relatively low. Lower receivables indicate lower current assets and a lower current ratio.

The notes to the financial statements (page 42) indicate that K mart has bank lines of credit aggregating $599 million which require the support of compensating cash balances. Such balances are expected to average 10 percent of the credit line not in use and an additional 10 percent of any outstanding balance. Since K mart is free to withdraw the entire cash balance at any time, the compensating balances are reported as current assets on the balance sheet. The notes also indicate (page 42) that "revolving credit agreements contain certain restrictive provisions regarding the maintenance of . . . working capital."

As indicated on page 37 of the notes, "the company considers cash on hand in stores, deposits in banks, certificates of deposit and short-term marketable securities as cash and cash equivalents for the purposes of the statement of cash flows." This definition of cash is also used for the balance sheet, which shows that K mart increased its investment in temporary investments substantially during the year, from $134 million to $594 million. Consequently, most of the increase in the cash balance was actually invested in marketable securities.

The balance sheet also indicates that K mart holds significant equity investments in affiliate retail companies: $379 million in 1988 and $506 million in 1989. As described on pages 38 and 39, these investments represent significant interests in Meldisco (49%) and Coles, Myers Ltd. (22%). Such large ownership percentages suggest that these investments are not intended to be sold within the time period of current assets. These equity investments, therefore, are listed on the balance sheet as long-term.

REVIEW PROBLEM

The following information relates to the marketable security investments of Macon Construction.

a. Securities held on December 31, 1989 are described below. Prepare the appropriate journal entry that would be required under the lower-of-cost-or-market rule.

Securities	No. of Shares	Cost/Share	Total Cost	Value/Share	Total Market Value
AAA	10	$14	$140	$17	$170
BBB	25	15	375	14	350
CCC	15	8	120	10	150
			$635		$670

Solution:

The lower-of-cost-or-market rule specifies that marketable securities be carried on the balance sheet at the $635 cost of the entire portfolio because $635 is less than $670, the market value of the entire portfolio. Since the securities were recorded at cost when they were purchased originally, no adjusting journal entry is required before financial statements are prepared on December 31, 1989.

b. Early in 1990 Macon sold all of its investment in AAA securities for $18 per share. The company also sold five shares of BBB for $13 per share. During 1990 Macon received dividends of $3 per share on the remaining twenty shares of BBB and dividends of $2 per share were declared, but not yet received, on the fifteen shares of CCC stock. The per-share market values of BBB and CCC on December 31, 1990 were $12 and $10, respectively. Prepare all appropriate journal entries to reflect these facts.

Solution:

1. Cash (10 sh. × $18 per sh.)   180
     Marketable Securities (10 sh. × $14 per sh.)   140
     Realized Gain on Sale of Securities   40
     Sale of ten shares of AAA stock for $18 per share.

2. Cash (5 sh. × $13 per sh.)   65
     Realized Loss on Sale of Securities   10
       Marketable Securities (5 sh. × $15 per sh.)   75
     Sale of five shares of BBB stock for $13 per share.

3. Cash ($3 per sh. × 20 sh.)   60
     Dividend Receivable ($2 per sh. × 15 sh.)   30
       Dividend Revenue   90
     Receipt of BBB dividends and declaration of dividends on CCC stock.

4. Securities held on December 31, 1990 follow.

Securities	No. of Shares	Cost/Share	Total Cost	Value/Share	Total Market Value
BBB	20	15	$300	12	$240
CCC	15	8	120	10	150
			$420		$390

The lower-of-cost-or-market rule specifies that marketable securities on the balance sheet be carried at the $390 market value of the portfolio because $390 is less than $420, the total cost of the portfolio. Since marketable securities are recorded at cost when originally purchased, the following journal entry is required before financial statements are prepared.

Unrealized loss on marketable securities	30	
Allowance for unrealized losses ($420 − $390)		30
To record an unrealized loss on marketable equity securities.		

c. At the beginning of 1991 the remaining twenty shares of BBB stock are sold for $13 per share. During 1991 dividends declared the previous year on CCC stock are received, and a $1 per share dividend is declared, but not paid, by the board of directors of CCC. The market value of CCC stock as of the end of 1991 is $11 per share. Prepare all appropriate journal entries to reflect these facts.

Solution:

1. Cash (20 sh. × $13 per sh.)	260	
Unrealized Loss on Sales of Securities	40	
Marketable Securities (20 sh. × $15 per sh.)		300
Sale of twenty shares of BBB stock for $13 per share.		
2. Cash (15 sh. × $2 per share)	30	
Dividend receivable		30
Dividend receivable (15 sh. × $1 per sh.)	15	
Dividend revenue		15
Receipt and declaration of dividends on 15 shares of CCC stock.		

3. Securities held on December 31, 1991 follow.

Securities	No. of Shares	Cost/Share	Total Cost	Value/Share	Total Market Value
CCC	15	$8	$120	11	$165

The lower-of-cost-or-market rule specifies that marketable securities on the balance sheet be carried at the $120 total cost because $120 is less than $165, the market value of the portfolio. Since the marketable security account reflects the $120 total cost already, the allowance account should be set equal to zero. The balance in the allowance account from the previous period is $30. Thus, the following adjusting journal entry is required before financial statements are prepared.

Allowance for unrealized losses	30	
Recoveries of unrealized losses on marketable securities		30
To record a recovery on marketable equity securities.		

SUMMARY OF LEARNING OBJECTIVES

1 Define current assets, working capital, current ratio, and quick ratio, and explain how these measures can be used to assess the solvency position of a company.

Current assets are those that can be converted into cash within one year or the company's operating cycle, whichever is longer. Working capital is equal to current assets less current liabilities, those liabilities that are expected to be required for payment of the assets listed as current. The current ratio is equal to current assets divided by current liabilities. The quick ratio is equal to cash plus marketable securities plus accounts receivable, divided by current liabilities.

These low-cost measures are useful in assessing a company's solvency position because they compare a measure of short-run cash inflows to a measure of short-run cash outflows. They are often used by banks and other lenders, and they appear in many loan agreements and debt covenants, enabling lenders to protect their investments by requiring that management maintain certain levels of liquidity.

These measures are limited in their ability to indicate solvency because (1) they deal only with static balance sheet numbers, (2) many current assets (e.g., prepaid expenses) do not indicate short-term cash inflows, (3) the time period of current assets is often arbitrary or difficult to determine, and (4) managers can manipulate the accounts that compose current assets and current liabilities.

2 Recognize how and why managers use window dressing techniques to affect the reporting of current assets, working capital, and the current ratio.

Window dressing refers to management's use of discretion in reporting accounting numbers to make the financial statements appear more attractive. Such discretion is used, for example, to make it easier to attract capital, to increase bonus compensation, or to avoid violating the terms of debt contracts. There are three basic ways in which management can window dress: (1) management can choose to use accounting methods that improve the reported numbers (e.g., choice of inventory method), (2) it can bias the estimates required to apply a given accounting method (e.g., the estimate of uncollectible receivables), and (3) it can make operating decisions that directly affect the reported numbers (e.g., sell and repurchase marketable securities). The practice of window dressing is not unusual, but over a period of time it can reduce the credibility of the financial statements and actually reduce the value of management and the company in the eyes of the stockholders, investors, creditors, and others.

3 Identify the issues considered and the techniques used when accounting for cash.

Three issues are particularly important when accounting for cash:
1. *Restricted Cash.* Cash held in escrow or compensating balances are examples of restrictions on a company's use of its cash. Such restrictions should be clearly disclosed on the balance sheet or in the footnotes, and restricted cash should be included in separate accounts.
2. *Cash Management.* A company must keep enough cash on hand to meet the needs of operations, yet too much cash is undesirable because idle cash de-

clines in purchasing power during periods of inflation and provides no return. Management uses accounting information to determine the appropriate level of cash.

3. *Cash Control.* There are two aspects to the control of cash that are largely the responsibility of the company's accountants: record control and physical control. Problems of record control arise because there are many transactions that involve the Cash account, and it is often difficult to ensure that the Cash account on the balance sheet reflects the actual amount of cash in a company's possession. Problems of physical control arise because cash is universally desired and easily concealed and transported. Two methods of maintaining cash control are the imprest petty cash system and the bank reconciliation.

4   Define marketable securities and identify the criteria that must be met before a security can be listed in the current asset section of the balance sheet.

Marketable securities consist of marketable equity securities (e.g., preferred and common stocks) and marketable debt securities (e.g., corporate and government bonds). They provide income through dividends, interest, or price appreciation, and can readily be converted into cash as needed to meet current cash requirements. Two criteria must be met before an investment in a security can be listed in the current asset section of the balance sheet: (1) the security must be able to be converted into cash within the time period that defines current assets (i.e., the current operating cycle or one year, whichever is longer), and (2) management must intend to convert the security into cash within the time period that defines current assets.

5   Explain how the lower-of-cost-or-market rule is applied when accounting for marketable securities.

Marketable securities are carried on the balance sheet at the lower of their aggregate cost or market value. In applying this rule, four separate events must be considered.

1. *Purchase of marketable securities.* When marketable securities are purchased, they are capitalized and recorded on the balance sheet at cost. The cost includes the purchase price as well as any incidental acquisition costs, such as brokerage commissions and taxes.

2. *Declaration and payment of dividends.* Cash dividends declared on marketable securities are initially recognized as receivables and revenues. When a cash dividend is received, the receivable is exchanged for cash.

3. *Sale of marketable equity securities.* When marketable equity securities are sold, their original cost is removed from the books and the difference between this cost and the proceeds of the sale is recognized on the books as either a realized gain or a realized loss.

4. *End of Accounting Period Adjustment.* At the end of the accounting period, the aggregate market price of the portfolio of marketable equity securities is compared to the original cost of the entire portfolio. The balance in the Allowance for Unrealized Losses on Marketable Securities account should be adjusted with a journal entry so that it reflects the amount of the difference between the aggregate market value of the portfolio and its original cost. The balance should be zero if the aggregate market value exceeds or is equal to the original

cost. Unrealized losses are recognized when the allowance account is increased. Recoveries of unrealized losses are recognized when the allowance account is decreased.

6 Describe why it may make economic sense to use the lower-of-cost-or-market rule, even though it gives rise to reporting problems.

The lower-of-cost-or-market rule requires that unrealized losses be recognized, although unrealized gains are not. This inconsistency can lead to reporting problems. For example, companies that cash in gains on their marketable equity securities and immediately repurchase them appear to be in better financial condition than those that simply hold them, even though they have incurred transaction costs and hold assets of no greater value. Consequently, the lower-of-cost-or-market rule encourages managers to window dress by cashing in gains on marketable securities.

In spite of these reporting problems, the lower-of-cost-or-market rule may be economically justifiable on the basis of conservatism. High potential costs, primarily in the form of legal liability, face auditors and managers if they overstate assets or understate liabilities on the financial statements. The potential costs of understating assets or overstating liabilities, on the other hand, are somewhat less. Consequently, it may make economic sense to bias the reporting of uncertain events toward conservative presentation as is done with the lower-of-cost-or-market rule.

KEY TERMS

Cash budget (p. 258)
Compensating balance (p. 257)
Current asset (p. 250)
Current ratio (p. 251)
Deposits in transit (p. 260)
Escrow (p. 257)
Imprest system (p. 259)
Intention to convert (p. 265)
Lower-of-cost-or-market (p. 266)
Nonsufficient fund (NSF) penalty (p. 260)
Operating cycle (p. 250)
Outstanding checks (p. 260)

Petty cash (p. 257)
Physical control (p. 259)
Portfolio (p. 268)
Quick ratio (p. 251)
Readily marketable (p. 265)
Realized gains (losses) (p. 268)
Recognized gains (losses) (p. 268)
Record control (p. 258)
Service charge (p. 260)
Unrealized gains (losses) (p. 268)
Window dressing (p. 255)
Working capital (p. 251)

QUESTIONS FOR DISCUSSION AND REVIEW

1. What is the definition of current assets? How is it used? What weaknesses are inherent in the measure of current assets?

2. Would the current assets classification on the balance sheet of a bridge-building company mean the same as the current asset classification on the balance sheet of a small retailer? Why?

3. What is window dressing? How and why might managers manipulate the current ratio by choosing certain accounting methods or biasing estimates used in applying these methods? How might managers manipulate the current ratio by making certain operating decisions?

4. Explain why window dressing may not be in the best interest of a company, its stockholders, or its management.

5. Provide two examples of restrictions on a company's use of the cash it owns. How are these restrictions reported on the financial statements? Why should restricted cash be separated from cash that is free and clear?

6. What two issues must managers consider in their efforts to maintain the proper cash balance?

7. What is an internal control system? Why is the internal control system important to both the company and its auditors? What two methods for providing both physical and record control of the cash balance are discussed in the chapter?

8. Elmer is the custodian for the petty cash account for Enterprises International. He authorizes cash disbursements, writes up vouchers for each disbursement, and records each disbursement in the cash journal. Critically evaluate this control system for petty cash.

9. Name three characteristics of good physical cash control.

10. Describe the basic features of an imprest petty cash system. Why is it considered a good example of cash control?

11. Why are bank reconciliations useful to a company?

12. What is the basic form of a bank reconciliation? Explain how it indicates necessary adjustments to the cash account.

13. What role do marketable securities play in the management of the cash balance?

14. What two criteria must be met before an investment in a marketable security can be listed as current? Why is the second criterion so difficult to apply? How can managers window dress by structuring their investments in securities?

15. What is the difference between a realized gain and a recognized gain? Are all realized and unrealized gains of marketable securities recognized? Are all realized and unrealized losses of marketable securities recognized?

16. What are the three basic rules for accounting for marketable securities stated in generally accepted accounting principles?

17. The lower-of-cost-or-market approach for valuing marketable securities on the balance sheet is applied at the aggregate level. What does this mean, and how does it differ from applying the lower-of-cost-or-market rule to individual securities? Would applying the lower-of-cost-or-market rule at the aggregate level give rise to different balance sheet and income statement numbers than applying it to individual securities?

18. Marketable securities are carried on the balance sheet at lower of costs or market values. How is this different from carrying them at their fair market values?

19. Are any unrealized gains on marketable securities ever recognized? Before you answer, consider the fact that the lower-of-cost-or-market rule is applied on an aggregate basis.

20. What reporting problems are brought about by using the lower-of-cost-or-market rule to value marketable securities? What role does the concept of conservatism play in this valuation process? Why does conservatism make economic sense?

EXERCISES

E6-1

(*Classifying cash on the balance sheet*)   Boyer International is currently preparing its financial statements for 1990. The company has several different sources of cash and is trying to decide how to classify them. The sources of cash follow.

a. $25,000 in a checking account with The First National Bank.

b. $2000 in checks dated February 4, 1990, received from customers.

c. $250,000 in certificates of deposit through The First National Bank that are to mature on November 15, 1993.

d. $45,000 in a savings account with The First National Bank.

e. $1000 in the petty cash fund. As of December 31, 1990, there are receipts totaling $600 in the petty cash drawer.

f. $50,000 held as a compensating balance for a loan with The First National Bank. The loan agreement requires Boyer International to maintain a compensating balance equal to 10 percent of the loan balance. During 1991 the outstanding principal balance will be reduced to $350,000.

g. $10,000 in a checking account with Interstate Federal Savings.

Required: Indicate how each source listed should be classified on the December 31, 1990 balance sheet. Explain each answer.

E6-2

(*Classifying cash on the balance sheet*)   The following items relate to the financial statements of Hayes Construction Company.

a. $1000 in a checking account.

b. $5000 invested in a treasury note due to mature in ninety days.

c. $3000 in a savings account that cannot be withdrawn until a $10,000 outstanding debt is paid off.

d. $20,000 invested in securities that will be sold in two years to finance an expansion of the plant.

e. $2000 invested in IBM common shares. Management intends to liquidate this investment in less than six months.

f. $15,000 held in escrow by a bank, serving as earnest money that binds management to a real estate contract.

g. A $2000 money order received in payment from a customer.

Required: Classify each item as either: (a) unrestricted cash, (b) restricted cash, or (c) investment.

E6-3

(*Reconciling cash to the correct balance*)   The following information refers to the financial records of Space City Enterprises as of December 31.

Cash balance per books	$3480
Cash balance on bank statement	3280
Deposits in transit	1200
Outstanding checks	810
Cash collections of notes receivable for depositors	730
Dishonored checks due to nonsufficient funds (NSF)	480
Bank service charges	60

Required:

a. Prepare a bank reconciliation.

b. Prepare journal entries to bring the cash balance on the books to the correct amount.

c. What is the correct cash balance?

E6-4   *(Reconciling cash to the correct balance)*   Lowen Incorporated began operations on December 1, 1990. The December 31, 1990 bank statement and December cash ledger account for Lowen are given below.

Bank Statement

	Decreases	Increases	Balance
Balance, Dec. 1, 1990			$ 8,100
Deposits during Dec.		$12,300	20,400
Checks cleared during Dec.	$14,200		6,200
Bank service charge	25		6,175
Balance, Dec. 31, 1990			6,175

Cash Ledger Account

Dec. 1, balance	8,100	Dec. checks written	15,200
Dec. deposits	13,200		

Required:

a. Prepare a bank reconciliation.

b. Prepare journal entries to bring the balance in the Cash ledger account to the correct amount.

c. What is the correct cash balance?

E6-5   *(Reconciling cash to the correct balance)*   On December 31, 1991, the balance in Morgan Company's cash account was $78,450. The company's bank statement for the month of December indicated an ending balance of $85,270. The following information was gathered to explain the different balances.

1. Morgan Company made two deposits—one on December 30 and one on December 31—in the amounts of $19,250 and $22,765, respectively, that were not recorded by the bank until January 2, 1992.

2. The company had written checks totaling $56,335 that had not been paid by the bank by the close of business on December 31.

3. The company had made a deposit on December 9 in the amount of $19,410. The bank incorrectly recorded the deposit as $14,910.

4. The bank's service charge for the month of December was $500. Morgan Company had not recorded this charge as of December 31.

5. The company had deposited a customer's check in the amount of $2500 on December 22. The check was returned by the bank on January 2, 1992, due to insufficient funds in the customer's account.

Required:

a. Prepare a bank reconciliation.

b. Prepare journal entries to bring the balance in Morgan's Cash account to the correct amount.

c. What is the correct cash balance?

E6-6   *(Inferring deposits in transit and outstanding checks)*   The August 31 bank statement and August Cash ledger accounts for McDaniel and Sons are summarized as follows.

Bank Statement

	Decreases	Increases	Balance
Balance, August, 1, 1990			$12,800
Deposits during August		$34,200[a]	47,000
Checks cleared during August	$32,800[b]		14,200
Checks not accepted due to nonsufficient funds	2,500		11,700
Notes collected for depositors		800	12,500
Bank service charge	50		12,450
Balance, August 31, 1990			12,450

[a]Includes $2500 in transit as of July 31.
[b]Includes $3100 outstanding as of July 31.

Cash Ledger Account

Aug. 1, balance	12,200*	August checks written	32,000
Aug. deposits	33,700		

*Correct balance after July 31 adjustments

Required:

a. Compute deposits in transit and outstanding checks during August.

b. Prepare a bank reconciliation.

c. Prepare journal entries to bring the balance in the Cash ledger account to the correct amount.

d. What is the correct cash balance?

E6–7   *(Bank reconciliation and adjusting entries to the cash account)*   The June 30 bank statement for Wordinger Manufacturing is summarized below.

	Per Bank	Per Books
Balance (June 1)	$17,923	$ 21,498*
Deposits during June	79,565	91,778
Withdrawals by check during June	74,968	105,182
Bank service charge for June	25	
Balance (June 30)	$22,495	$ 8,094

*Correct balance after May 31 adjustments.

The supporting schedule for withdrawals and deposits indicates the following:

	Withdrawals		Deposits	
Check Number	Amount Per Bank	Amount Per Books	Amount Per Bank	Amount Per Books
101	$12,989	$ 12,989	$24,759	$24,759
102	10,675	a	14,250	a
104		13,190	18,781	18,781
105[b]	11,250	12,150		15,573
106	23,955	23,955	21,775	21,775
107		15,925		10,890
108	8,007	8,007		
109	8,092	8,092		
110		10,874		
	$74,968	$105,182	$79,565	$91,778

[a]These two items were recorded on the books during the month of May.
[b]The correct amount of the check was $12,150.

Required:

a. Prepare a bank reconciliation as of June 30.

b. Prepare any entries necessary on June 30 to bring the cash balance to the correct amount.

E6-8   *(Accounting for marketable securities)*   Monroe Auto Supplies engaged in several transactions involving short-term marketable securities during 1991, shown in the following list. The company had never invested in marketable securities prior to 1991.

1. Purchased 1000 shares of IBM for $50 per share.
2. Purchased 500 shares of General Motors for $60 per share.
3. Sold 750 shares of IBM for $60 per share.
4. Received a dividend of $2.00 per share from General Motors.
5. Purchased 200 shares of Xerox for $40 per share.
6. Sold the remaining 250 shares of IBM for $40 per share.
7. Sold the 200 shares of Xerox for $55 per share.
8. Sold the 500 shares of General Motors for $60 per share.

Required:

a. Prepare journal entries for each transaction.

b. What effect did these transactions have on the company's 1991 net income?

E6-9   *(Inferring marketable security adjustments from the balance sheet)*   Duke Home Security Services reported the following information regarding its short-term marketable investments in its 1990 financial report.

	1990	1989
Marketable securities	$750,000	$500,000
Less: Allowance for unrealized losses on marketable securities	50,000	35,000
	$700,000	$465,000

Required:

a. Was the difference between the portfolio market value of the marketable securities and the portfolio cost of the marketable securities greater in 1989 or 1990? Explain your answer.

b. Prepare the adjusting journal entry that is necessary on December 31, 1990, for the marketable securities under the lower-of-cost-or-market rule.

c. What is the effect of the lower-of-cost-or-market rule on net income during 1990?

E6-10   *(Inferring marketable security adjustments from the balance sheet)*   Luke Toy Enterprises began operations in 1988. The following information was extracted from the company's financial records.

	1990	1989	1988
Marketable securities	$200,000	$300,000	$250,000
Less: Allowance for unrealized losses on marketable securities	0	35,000	25,000
	$200,000	$265,000	$225,000

Required:

a. Prepare the adjusting journal entry that Luke Toy Enterprises made to adjust the carrying value of its marketable securities portfolio to lower-of-cost-or-market value at the end of 1988, 1989, and 1990.

b. Was the aggregate market value of the company's marketable securities greater than, less than, or equal to the aggregate cost of the company's marketable securities as of December 31, 1990? Explain your answer.

E6–11

(Marketable securities adjustments when there is a beginning balance in the allowance account) The following information was extracted from the December 31, 1990 balance sheets of four different companies.

	Wearever Fabrics	Frames Corp	Pacific Transport	Video Magic
Short-term marketable securities	$875,000	$500,000	$645,000	$250,000
Less: Allowance for unrealized loss on marketable securities	75,000	10,000	0	40,000
	$800,000	$490,000	$645,000	$210,000

As of December 31, 1991, the controllers of each company collected the following information concerning their short-term marketable securities.

	Wearever Fabrics	Frames Corp	Pacific Transport	Video Magic
Portfolio cost	$800,000	$600,000	$640,000	$310,000
Portfolio market value	750,000	625,000	610,000	270,000

Required:

a. What amount should each company report in the Short-Term Marketable Securities account as of December 31, 1991?

b. What amount should each company report in the Allowance for Unrealized Losses on Marketable Securities account as of December 31, 1991?

c. Prepare the necessary entry to adjust the Allowance for Unrealized Losses on Marketable Securities account for each company.

E6–12

(Lower-of-cost-or-market and a portfolio of short-term investments) Speedo Printing used some of its idle cash to invest in marketable securities. The following information is available concerning the company's investments. All of these securities were purchased during 1990, Speedo's first year of operations, and classified as short-term.

Security	Cost	12/31/90 Market Value	12/31/91 Market Value
Waste Systems, Inc.	$100,000	$98,000	$90,000
Stowe Ski Supplies	50,000	55,000	40,000
Edmunson Swimwear	80,000	60,000	65,000
Mandel Entertainment	75,000	70,000	60,000

Speedo Printing neither bought nor sold any securities during 1991.

Required:

a. Prepare the entries that were necessary during 1990 to record the acquisition of each of these securities.

b. Prepare any adjusting journal entry necessary as of December 31, 1990 associated with these securities.

c. Assume that these securities should still be classified as short-term. Prepare any adjusting journal entry necessary as of December 31, 1991 associated with these securities.

E6–13

(Realization and the lower-of-cost-or-market rule) On December 4, Emery Enterprises made its first purchase of marketable securities: 30 shares of Distinct, Inc. stock for $22 per share. On December 31, when Emery closed its books, the market value of Distinct common stock was $24 per share.

Required:

a. How much income on this investment would Emery recognize on its income statement for the period ending December 31? Why?

b. Assume that Emery sold the Distinct common stock on December 31. Prepare the journal entry to record the sale. How much income would Emery recognize on its income statement in this case?

c. Assume that the Distinct common stock is one of two kinds of securities in Emery's portfolio of marketable securities as of December 31. The portfolio is described as follows.

Securities	Cost	Market Value
Distinct	$660	$720
Zephyr	$200	$220
Total	$860	$940

Would it make any difference on Emery's income statement if it sold the Distinct common stock? Why or why not?

d. Assume that Emery's portfolio of marketable securities appeared as follows.

Securities	Cost	Market Value
Distinct	$660	$720
Zephyr	$200	$130
Total	$860	$850

Would it make any difference on Emery's income statement if it sold the Distinct common stock? Why or why not?

E6–14   *(Marketable securities and lower-of-cost-or-market)*   The following information relates to the activity in the marketable securities account of Lido International.

(1) January 28   Purchased ten shares of Able Co. stock at $12 per share.
(2) February 18   Purchased twenty shares of Baker Co. stock at $25 per share.
(3) March 15   Received dividends from Able Co. of $1 per share.
(4) April 29   Sold five shares of Able Co. for $13 per share.
(5) May 18   Received dividends from Baker Co. of $2 per share.
(6) June 1   Sold five shares of Baker Co. for $22 per share.
(7) June 30   Market value of Able shares = $14 per share
                  Market value of Baker shares = $20 per share

Required:

a. Prepare journal entries for each transaction.

b. Prepare the adjusting journal entry required if financial statements are prepared on June 30.

c. Compute the net effect of these entries on the June 30 income statement.

d. Assume that the remaining Able shares were sold on June 30. Prepare the journal entry to record the sale, the end-of-period adjusting entry, and the net effect of all transactions on the June 30 income statement.

e. Did the sale of the remaining Able shares have any effect on the June 30 income statement? Why or why not?

E6–15   *(Marketable security transactions and debt covenants)*   Near the end of 1990 Susan Johnson, chief financial officer of Microplan, Inc., prepared an estimate of the company's year-end financial statements. Excerpts from her estimate follow.

Current Assets	
Cash	$12,000
Marketable securities	35,000*
Accounts receivable	22,000
Prepaid expenses	8,000
Current liabilities	40,000

*Market value of portfolio is $48,000.

Microplan also has over $120,000 of long-term debt on which a covenant states that the company must maintain a current ratio of 2:1. After reviewing her estimate, Susan is concerned that, if nothing is done, the company will violate the debt covenant. Such a situation would give the creditor bank the right to call for payment of the entire $120,000 principal. As the financial information shows, if that occurs, Microplan will not be able to pay off the loan.

Required:

a. Compute working capital, the current ratio, and the quick ratio from the information provided by Susan. Is she correct that if nothing is done, Microplan will violate the debt covenant?

b. Assume that Microplan sells the marketable securities. Provide the journal entry to record the sale, and recompute working capital, the current ratio, and the quick ratio. Assume that brokerage fees are 2 percent of the selling price.

c. Assume that Microplan sells and immediately repurchases the securities in its portfolio of marketable securities. Provide the journal entry to record the sale, and recompute working capital, the current ratio, and the quick ratio. Assume that brokerage fees are 2 percent of the selling price and 2 percent of the purchase price.

d. What advice would you give Susan?

E6–16 *(Reporting problems with not carrying marketable securities at market value)* Tom Miller and Larry Rogers each started a business on December 1, 1989 by contributing $5000 of their own funds. Early in December both men purchased 100 shares of Diskette common stock, which was selling at the time for $24 per share. During December they both also purchased $1500 of inventory on account.

As of December 30, the market price of Diskette common stock had risen to $32 per share. Tom was delighted by the price increase but chose simply to hold the stock, expecting that the price would continue to appreciate for at least another month. Larry, on the other hand, sold his shares, but immediately repurchased them because he too believed that they would continue to appreciate. Brokerage fees on all purchases and sales of stock are 2 percent of the purchase or sales price.

Required:

a. Prepare year-end balance sheets for both Tom and Larry.

b. Compute net income, working capital, and the current ratio for both Tom and Larry.

c. From the financial statements alone, which of the two appears to be in the better financial position? Why?

d. Which of the two is in the better financial position? Why?

PROBLEMS

P6–1 *(Classifying cash on the balance sheet)*   On September 30, 1991, Print-O-Matic, Inc. entered into an arrangement with its bank to borrow $250,000. The principal is due on October 1, 1996, and the note has a stated annual interest rate of 10 percent. Under the borrowing agreement, Print-O-Matic agreed to maintain a compensating balance of $50,000 in a non-interest-bearing account. As of December 31, 1991, Print-O-Matic has an additional $225,000 in various savings and checking accounts that earn an annual rate of 5 percent. The controller intends to classify the entire $275,000 in cash as a current asset.

Required:

a. Do you agree with the classification of the $275,000 of cash as a current asset? Explain your answer.

b. Print-O-Matic reported interest expense associated with this note for the year ended December 31, 1991, in the amount of $6250 ([$250,000 × 10%] × 1/4). Do you agree with this classification? Should any other factors be considered in the interest cost? Explain.

P6–2 *(Preparing a bank reconciliation)*   Habitat Realty Company began operations on June 2, 1990. The company opened a savings and checking account with Western States Bank. On June 30 the balances in the general ledger accounts for the savings and checking accounts were $15,525 and $5163, respectively. The balances in the respective accounts on June 30 per the bank statements were $14,375 and $998. A review of the June bank statement indicated the following.

1. Habitat Realty Company was charged a $10 printing fee for its checks.
2. The company had made a transfer of $1200 from its savings account to its checking account. In error the bank recorded the transfer from the checking account to the savings account.
3. Habitat Realty earned interest of $95 on its savings account and $20 on its checking account.
4. Habitat Realty wrote checks during the month totaling $9,571. The bank paid checks totaling $8,483.
5. Habitat Realty made deposits of $19,535 and of $5809 to its savings and checking accounts, respectively. The bank recorded deposits of $15,890 and $4000 to these accounts.
6. The bank charged Habitat Realty a monthly service charge on its checking account of $25.
7. The bank returned two postdated checks totaling $1029 that Habitat Realty had deposited into its checking account. (These two checks are not included in the checking deposit total [$5809] listed in [5]).

Required:

a. Prepare separate bank reconciliations for the company's savings and checking accounts.

b. Prepare any necessary adjusting entries associated with the bank reconciliations.

c. Assume that Habitat Realty prepared a balance sheet as of June 30, 1990. What amount should the company report in the Cash account?

P6–3 *(Finding the correct cash balance)*   Kirkwood Appliances prepared the following bank reconciliation for the month of October.

Balance per bank statement (10/31/91)		$ 9,255
Add		
Deposits in transit	$ 4350	
Bank service charges	50	
Checks not honored due to insufficient funds	670	5,070
Deduct		
Outstanding checks	$1,795	
Bank error	90	
Note collected by bank	2,000	
Interest earned	125	4010
Balance per books (10/31/91)		$10,315

Required:

a. Note in the reconciliation above that Kirkwood adjusted the cash balance in the bank statement to the book balance. Convert this reconciliation to the form shown in the text, in which both the bank and the book balance are adjusted to the correct cash amount.

b. Prepare any necessary adjusting entries associated with the reconciliation.

c. Assume that Kirkwood closes its bank account on October 31, 1991. What amount of cash could the company withdraw?

P6–4 *(Applying the lower-of-cost-or-market rule to marketable securities)* O'Keefe Enterprises began investing in short-term marketable securities in 1991. The following information was extracted from its 1991 internal financial records.

Security	Purchases	Sales	Total Dividends received	12/31/91 Market Value*
Houser Company	100 shares @ $20 *2000*	60 shares @ $25 *1500*	$40	$25 *800*
Miller, Inc.	200 shares @ $45 *9000*	90 shares @ $30 *2700*	$85	35 *3850 left*
Letter Books	75 shares @ $50 *3750*	10 shares @ $55 *550*	$30	50 *3250*
Nordic Equipment	150 shares @ $75 *11250*	145 shares @ $95 *13775*	$50	90 *375*

*Per share

Required:

a. Prepare the entries to record the security purchases during 1991. For simplicity, combine all purchases into one journal entry.

b. Prepare entries to record the security sales during 1991.

c. Prepare entries to record the receipt of dividends during 1991. For simplicity, combine all dividends into one journal entry.

d. Compute the cost and market value of O'Keefe Enterprises' investment portfolio as of December 31, 1991. Prepare any necessary adjusting entries.

P6–5 *(Marketable security balance sheet disclosure and adjusting entries)* Easton Records attempts to minimize the amount of cash invested in low-interest bank accounts. The company usually invests its idle cash in short-term marketable securities. The following information was obtained from Sarah Wills, the company controller, concerning the company's investments.

Security	Purchase Date	Cost	12/31/90 Market Value	12/31/91 Market Value
Rudnicki Corp.	1/13/90	$50,000	$45,000	$50,000
Ultraplex Theaters	4/23/90	70,000	80,000	75,000
T. J. Investors	7/10/90	25,000	10,000	20,000
Cards & Gifts	10/2/90	60,000	55,000	65,000
Giant Foods	6/19/91	75,000	50,000	60,000

Based upon discussions at the end of 1990 with Ms. Wills, the company planned to hold all the investments until some time in 1991. As it turned out, no securities were sold during 1991. Based upon discussions with Ms. Wills at the end of 1991, the company plans to hold all the investments, except the investment in T. J. Investors, until some time in 1992. Easton Records plans to hold the investment in T. J. Investors for several years.

Required:

a. Present these investments as they should have been presented on the December 31, 1990 balance sheet.

b. Prepare the entry to record the purchase of Giant Foods stock.

c. What amount should be shown on the December 31, 1991 balance sheet under the account Short-Term Marketable Securities?

d. Prepare the adjusting journal entry necessary on December 31, 1991 to record the short-term marketable securities at the lower-of-cost-or-market.

P6–6   *(Marketable security purchases, sales, dividends, and end-of-period adjustments)*   Anderson Cabinets began operations during 1984. During the initial years of operations, the company invested primarily in fixed assets to promote growth. During 1990 H. Hurst, the company president, decided that the company was sufficiently stable that it could now invest in short-term marketable securities. During 1990 the company entered into the following transactions concerning marketable securities.

(1)	March 10	Purchased 1000 shares of Arctic Oil & Gas for $30 per share.
(2)	March 31	Purchased 800 shares of Humphries Manufacturing for $12 per share.
(3)	May 26	Received a cash dividend of $1.25 per share from Arctic Oil & Gas.
(4)	July 10	Purchased 1000 shares of Kingsman Game Co. for $18 per share.
(5)	September 11	Sold 800 shares of Arctic Oil & Gas for $35 per share.
(6)	September 27	Sold 500 shares of Humphries Manufacturing for $10 per share.
(7)	October 19	Purchased 1000 shares of Quimby, Inc. for $25 per share.
(8)	November 6	Received a cash dividend of $1.25 per share from Arctic Oil & Gas.
(9)	December 8	Sold the remaining shares of Arctic Oil & Gas and Humphries Manufacturing for $30 and $15, respectively.
(10)	December 31	According to *The Wall Street Journal*, the market values of these securities as of the close of business on December 31 were as follows.

Arctic Oil & Gas	$32
Humphries Manufacturing	14
Kingsman Game Company	15
Quimby, Inc.	26

Required:

a. Prepare the necessary journal entries for each of these transactions.

b. Prepare the marketable securities section of the balance sheet as of December 31, 1990.

c. Compute the impact of these transactions on the income statement for the year ended December 31, 1990.

P6–7   *(Reconstructing transactions during the period)*   Howell Shipping, Inc. reported the following items in the comparative balance sheets included in its 1991 financial report.

	1991	1990	1989
Marketable securities	$350,000	$275,000	$320,000
Less: Allowance for unrealized losses on			
marketable securities	10,000	22,000	15,000
	$340,000	$253,000	$305,000

Additional Information

(1) Howell Shipping, Inc. began operations during 1989. The company sold no marketable securities during its first year of operations.

(2) During 1990 Howell Shipping, Inc. sold marketable securities for $80,000. The company realized a loss of $20,000 on this transaction.

(3) During 1991 Howell Shipping, Inc. sold marketable securities for $15,000. The company realized a gain of $5000 on this transaction.

Required:

a. Based upon this information reconstruct all the necessary journal entries (including adjusting journal entries) associated with marketable securities for 1989, 1990, and 1991.

b. Compute the impact on the income statement for 1989, 1990, and 1991 related to the company's investments in short-term marketable securities.

P6-8

(Window dressing and the lower-of-cost-or-market rule) Levy Company and Guyer Books both invested in the same marketable securities (in the same amounts and at the same time) during 1991. The following table lists the number of shares purchased, the purchase price per share, and the market price on December 31, 1991.

Security	Number of Shares	Price per Share	Market Value Per Share
Crozier Can Company	250	$10	$12
Hamilton Housewares	100	25	20
Watson Manufacturing	200	15	45
St. Clair Computers	300	48	10
Cummings Moving Company	50	20	21

On December 31, 1991, the Levy Company sold its investment in Watson Manufacturing and immediately repurchased it. Guyer Books did not sell any of its investments during 1991.

Required:

a. Prepare the entry to record the acquisition of all securities during 1991 on the books of the Levy Company. (For simplicity, combine all the purchases into one journal entry). Also prepare the entries to record the sale and repurchase of the investment in Watson Manufacturing.

b. Prepare the entry to record the acquisition of these securities on the books of Guyer Books. (For simplicity, combine all the purchases into one journal entry).

c. Prepare any necessary adjusting entries for 1991, and compute the overall effect on net income for both companies.

d. Which company appears to be in better economic condition at the end of 1991? If we considered transaction costs, which company would be in better economic condition? Explain your answer.

e. Why do accountants adhere to the lower-of-cost-or-market rule?

P6-9

(Accounting for marketable securities over two periods) Hathaway International began operations on March 10, 1990. The company acquired the following securities during 1990.

Company	Transaction	Number of Shares	Price per Share
Desk Publishing	Purchase	1000	$10
T. Brown, Inc.	Purchase	750	12
Cityscapes	Purchase	1500	20
Wilson Cribs	Purchase	100	80

As of December 31, 1990, the market values per share of these securities were $13, $11, $17, and $60, respectively. During 1991 Hathaway International entered into the following transactions involving marketable securities.

Date	Company	Transaction	Number of Shares	Price per Share
1/10/91	Chicago Bakery	Purchase	1250	$15
3/6/91	Desk Publishing	Sale	900	14
5/23/91	Cityscapes	Sale	1500	19
6/15/91	Eagle Air Freight	Purchase	1000	50
9/20/91	Wilson Cribs	Sale	100	80
12/1/91	Rix Scooters	Purchase	500	20

As of December 31, 1991 the market values per share of the various securities were:

Desk Publishing	$16	T. Brown, Inc.	$10
Cityscapes	20	Wilson Cribs	89
Chicago Bakery	20	Eagle Air Freight	45
Rix Scooters	22		

Assume that all securities are to be classified as short-term as of December 31, 1991, and 1992.

Required:

a. As of December 31, 1990,
   (1) Compute the portfolio cost and portfolio market value of Hathaway International's investment in securities of other companies.
   (2) Compute the required balance in the Allowance for Unrealized Losses on Marketable Securities account.
   (3) Compute the change in the balance of the Allowance for Unrealized Losses on Marketable Securities account during 1990.
   (4) Prepare any necessary adjusting journal entry relating to the short-term marketable securities.

b. Prepare all the entries necessary during 1991 to record the purchase and sale of securities.

c. As of December 31, 1991,
   (1) Compute the portfolio cost and portfolio market value of Hathaway International's investment in securities of other companies.
   (2) Compute the required balance in the Allowance for Unrealized Losses on Marketable Securities account.
   (3) Compute the change in the balance of the Allowance for Unrealized Losses on Marketable Securities account during 1991.
   (4) Prepare any necessary adjusting journal entry relating to the short-term marketable securities.

CASES

C6-1

(Solvency ratios and debt covenants) Fieldcrest Cannon, Inc. manufactures and markets a broad range of home furnishing textile products. Comprising two divisions; the Bed and Bath Division and the Carpet and Rug Division, the company sells its products under several popular labels, which include: St. Mary's, Cannon, Fieldcrest, and Karastan.

In its December 31, 1987 Consolidated Statement of Financial Position, the company reported the following (dollars in thousands).

Current Assets	
Cash	$ 11,182
Accounts receivable	238,930
Inventories	262,943
Prepaid income taxes	11,821
Other current assets	4,074
Total current assets	$528,950
Current Liabilities	
Accounts payable	$ 64,142
Accrued liabilities	91,143
Current portion of debt	2,341
Total current liabilities	$157,626

Required:

a. Compute the following items as of December 31, 1987: working capital, the current ratio, and the quick ratio.

b. The company's long-term debt is almost 47 percent of total assets. Included in the long-term debt agreements are certain covenants "including requirements on the maintenance of working capital." Why might such a covenant be incorporated into a debt agreement? What could happen if Fieldcrest Cannon violated one of these covenants?

C6-2

(Working capital, debt covenants, and restrictions on management decisions) Excerpts from the June 30, 1988 balance sheet of the Quaker Oats Company are provided below (dollars in millions).

	1988	1987	1986
Current assets			
Cash and short-term investments	$ 91.2	$ 359.9	$109.5
Receivables	826.0	752.9	536.9
Inventories	539.8	486.4	413.5
Other current assets	33.3	197.4	23.0
Current liabilities	1,072.8	1,288.7	786.1

Required:

a. The notes to the company's financial statements state that "under the most restrictive terms of the various loan agreements . . . minimum working capital of $200 million must be maintained." Compute how close The Quaker Oats Company came to this restriction at the end of 1986, 1987, and 1988.

b. Assume that on July 1, 1988, The Quaker Oats Company purchased land and buildings for $600 million. Comment on how they could have financed the purchase of these assets, keeping in mind the restrictive terms of the loan agreements mentioned in (a) above.

C6–3

(Restricted cash and solvency ratios)   In its December 31, 1985 financial statement, AMAX, Inc., a coal-mining company, reported the following:

> Assets (in thousands)
> Cash and cash equivalents (Note 9) $46,700

> Note 9:
> At December 31, 1985, AMAX had on deposit with commercial banks a total of $42 million of cash and equivalents that is restricted as to use. Of that amount, $15 million was held for the January 3, 1986 repurchase of common shares from an affiliated company. The remainder represents a time deposit that is restricted to repayment of a short-term loan.

Required:

a. Why would a potential investor or creditor reading AMAX's financial statements want to know about restrictions on cash?

b. Assume the January 3 purchase of common shares will result in a long-term investment. Should the restricted cash be disclosed as current or noncurrent? Why?

c. How might disclosure of such a restriction affect the calculation of working capital, the current ratio, and the quick ratio?

d. A time deposit is like a savings account that matures and becomes available on a particular day. When the cash becomes available and the short-term loan is paid off, will working capital be increased, decreased, or unaffected? Why?

C6–4

(Marketable securities and "window dressing")   An article in *Forbes* stated that

> *The Securities and Exchange Commission is launching an earnest attack on what the Commissioner calls "cute accounting." When you have a period of economic recession, there is a tendancy for liberties to be taken. . . Some people become overly aggressive, others can be downright dishonest.*
>   *The SEC, for example, began proceedings against Clabir Corp. for substantially overstating [the value of its marketable security portfolio]. The diversified manufacturer held a 10 percent equity position in U.S. Industries. But Clabir didn't rely on the New York Stock Exchange's (NYSE) current price to value its U.S. Industries shares. Instead, Clabir relied on an oral offer from U.S. Industries to buy back its stock at a price 58 percent higher than the then current NYSE trading price, thus avoiding a writedown. The SEC thought that wasn't proper."*

> *Jill Andresley, "Indecent disclosure," *Forbes*, (13 August 1984) p. 92.

Required:

a. Briefly describe the lower-of-cost-or-market rule and explain how Clabir was able to avoid a writedown by relying on the oral buy-back offer from U.S. Industries.

b. Why did the SEC think that Clabir's method of accounting for marketable securities was improper?

c. Provide several reasons why Clabir's management might have chosen such a method, and how might the SEC's action have affected the market value of Clabir's outstanding stock? Does it appear that Clabir was window dressing in this case, and if so, does it appear to have been in the stockholders' and management's best interest? Why or why not?

C6–5

(Legal liability and conservatism) In April, 1982, Saxon Industries filed for bankruptcy. Fox & Co., Saxon's auditors, seemed to be in even deeper trouble because International Paper and Borden brought suit against Fox for a total of $6.3 million, charging that Saxon's financial statements led them to believe that the company was in better financial condition than it actually was. This assessment, in turn, caused International Paper and Borden to extend credit to Saxon in the months just prior to its collapse. In addition, Fox & Co. faced a multimillion-dollar class action suit filed on behalf of Saxon's stockholders.

Required:

a. Explain why International Paper, Borden, and Saxon's stockholders would bring suit against Fox & Co.

b. Would International Paper and Borden have the same claim if Saxon's financial statements, which were audited by Fox, had depicted the company in worse financial condition than it actually was? Why or why not?

c. Provide an economic justification for the lower-of-cost-or-market rule.

CHAPTER 7

Short-Term Receivables

Learning Objectives

1 Define and distinguish between accounts receivable and short-term notes receivable.

2 Describe the alternative methods used to account for cash discounts.

3 Differentiate between the allowance method and the direct write-off method, both of which are used to account for bad debts.

4 Explain the two basic techniques of estimating bad debts, and describe how they are used to implement the allowance method.

5 Describe the two methods used to account for short-term notes receivable.

6 Describe the economic consequences resulting from the methods used to account for short-term receivables.

≣ This chapter is devoted to accounts receivable and short-term notes receivable. These short-term receivables are included in the current asset section of the balance sheet. Recall the discussion at the beginning of Chapter 6 on current assets, working capital, the current ratio, and the quick ratio, and keep in mind that short-term receivables, like cash and marketable securities, are current assets. Consequently, the comments made in that discussion concerning window dressing and the pros and cons of using measures such as current assets, working capital, the current ratio, and the quick ratio in the assessment of solvency are also relevant here. That is, the methods used to account for short-term receivables and the dollar values attached to these accounts have a direct effect on the solvency measures used by stockholders, investors, creditors, credit-rating services, auditors, and other interested parties.

In our heavily credit-oriented economy, transactions that give rise to accounts receivable and short-term notes receivable make up a significant portion of total business transactions. Indeed, *Business Week* notes that "trade credit is a significant part of most companies' balance sheets. The Federal Reserve Board reports trade credit held by U.S. nonfinancial corporations grew by 6.4 percent during 1987, to $691 billion, and accounted for about 41 percent of their financial assets."[1] Table 7–1 contains a selected list of industries and indicates the importance of short-term receivables relative to total assets and current assets.

Restaurants and grocery stores carry relatively small levels of receivables because their customers normally pay with cash, personal checks, or bank cards such as MasterCard, VISA, and American Express.[2] Department stores, such as J. C. Penney and Sears, carry larger portions of short-term receivables because they issue their own charge cards, which their customers use extensively. Professional services, such as major public accounting firms, bill their clients and normally receive final payment several months after the billed service is complete. In addition, receivables constitute a large portion of the total assets of such firms because they carry virtually no inventory and relatively few fixed assets. Their professionals are their most important assets.[3]

ACCOUNTS RECEIVABLE: A DEFINITION

Accounts receivable arise from selling goods or services to customers who do not immediately pay cash. Often backed by oral rather than written commitments, accounts receivable represent short-term extensions of credit that are normally collectible within thirty to sixty days. These credit trade agreements are often referred to as **open accounts.** Often many such transactions are enacted between a company and its customers, and it is impractical to create a formal contract for each one. Open accounts typically reflect running balances because at the same time customers are paying off previous purchases, new purchases are being made. If an

---

1. Kathleen Madigan, "Economic Trends," *Business Week,* 11 April 1988, p. 27.

2. When a customer uses a bank card to pay for an item or service, the selling company does not carry the receivable on its balance sheet. It is "sold" to the finance company that issued the card. Such an arrangement is called *factoring.*

3. The most important assets of companies such as public accounting firms, law firms, professional sports teams, and medical offices are their employees. Yet, there is no asset account on the balance sheets of such organizations that represents these valuable human resources. Ignoring the value of human capital is an important limitation of the financial statements. This limitation is addressed again in Chapter 17, which examines the uses of financial accounting information.

Table 7–1   Short-term receivables as a percentage of total assets and current assets (1986 industry averages)

Industry	Short-Term Receivables/ Total Assets	Short-Term Receivables/ Current Assets
Restaurants	4%	12%
Grocery stores	4	7
Aircraft manufacturing	11	18
Department stores	18	23
Medical doctor offices	21	37
Accounting and auditing services	30	56
Household appliance manufacturing	31	40

Source: Compiled from data published in *Industry Norms and Key Business Ratios* (Dun & Bradstreet, Inc. 1987).

account receivable is paid in full within the specified thirty- or sixty-day period, no interest is charged. Payment after this period, however, is usually subject to a significant financial charge. Credit card arrangements with department stores, like Sears and J. C. Penney, and oil companies, like Exxon and Chevron, are common examples of open accounts.

The following journal entries illustrate the recognition of accounts receivable from (1) the sale of merchandise[4] and (2) the sale of a service.

Different entries for sale of goods vs. services

Accounts Receivable	500	
Sales		500
To record the sale on account of two items of inventory for $250 each.		

Accounts Receivable	150	
Fees Earned (or Service Revenue)		150
To record the sale on account of consulting services for $150.		

Note that the recognition of the account receivable in each case is accompanied by the recognition of a revenue: sales or fees earned (service revenue). Both the balance sheet and the income statement are therefore affected when accounts receivable are established.

Note also that the recognition of an account receivable is an application of the accrual system of accounting. Recall from Chapter 5 that revenues are recognized when the four criteria of revenue recognition are met.[5] Accounts receivable, therefore, are established in those cases where these four criteria are met prior to cash collection.

As the following journal entry below illustrates, when cash is ultimately received the accounts receivable balance is removed from the balance sheet and no revenue is recognized.

Cash	500	
Accounts Receivable		500
To record the collection of cash from an outstanding account receivable.		

The Accounts Receivable account, therefore, appears on the balance sheet during the time period between the recognition of a revenue and the receipt of the related cash payment.

---

4. The sale of merchandise also involves the outflow of inventory, which must be recognized before financial statements are prepared.

5. The four criteria of revenue recognition are: (1) the earning process is substantially complete, (2) revenue is objectively measurable, (3) post-sale costs can be estimated, and (4) cash collection is reasonably assured.

ACCOUNTING FOR AND MANAGING ACCOUNTS RECEIVABLE

The key factor in valuing accounts receivable on the financial statements is the amount of cash that the receivables are expected to generate. The cash is expected to be received in the future; in theory, therefore, present value should be used as the valuation base. The expected future cash receipt should theoretically be discounted.[6] However, as indicated earlier, the period of time from the initial recognition of an account receivable to cash collection is normally quite short (thirty to sixty days). Consequently, the difference between the amount of cash to be received and the present value of the expected cash flows from the receivable is considered immaterial. For example, the difference between $100 and the present value of $100 to be received in one month, given a 10 percent annual interest rate, is approximately $.76. Therefore, the face value of the receivable, the amount of cash to be collected, is judged to be a reasonable approximation of present value and, accordingly, provides the starting point for balance sheet valuation.

Net Realizable Value: the Valuation Base for Receivables

While the face value of the receivable represents a starting point, there are a number of reasons why it may not represent the actual amount of cash ultimately collected. Many companies, for example, offer cash discounts, allowing customers to pay lesser amounts if they pay within specified time periods. Other accounts receivable may produce no cash at all because customers simply refuse to pay (bad debts) or choose to return previously sold merchandise (sales returns). Each of these issues must be considered when placing a value on the Accounts Receivable account on the balance sheet.

Accordingly, the valuation base for the Accounts Receivable account is not the face amount of the receivables but rather the **net realizable value,** an estimate of the cash that is expected to be produced by the receivables.

Net Realizable Value of Accounts Receivable = Face Value − Adjustments for
(1) Cash Discounts, (2) Bad Debts, and (3) Sales Returns

Cash Discounts

When a good or service is sold on credit, creating a receivable, the company making the sale naturally wants to collect the cash as soon as possible. To encourage prompt payment, many companies offer discounts (called **cash discounts**) on the gross sales price. There are benefits associated with offering these discounts because collected cash can be used to earn a return, and eliminating receivables quickly reduces the costs of maintaining records for and collecting outstanding receivables. Presumably, companies that offer cash discounts believe that these benefits exceed the reduction in future cash proceeds that results from the discount.

Cash discounts simply specify that an amount of cash less than the gross sales price is sufficient to satisfy an outstanding receivable, if the cash is received within

---

6. The present value calculation is discussed and illustrated in the Appendix A at the end of the text.

a certain time period. Certain sales on account, for example, may be subject to a 2 percent (of the gross sales price) cash discount if paid within ten days. Such terms are expressed in the following way: *2/10, n/30*, which reads "two-ten, net thirty." This expression means "a discount in the amount of 2 percent of the gross sales price is available, if payment is received within ten days. To avoid finance charges over and above the gross price, payment must be received within thirty days." Other terms on cash discounts are also common: *3/20, n/30*, for example, means "a discount in the amount of 3 percent of the gross sales price is available, if payment is received within twenty days, and finance charges over and above the gross price can be avoided if payment is received within thirty days." *n/10, EOM* means that the net amount of the sale (gross price less cash discount) is due no later than ten days after the end of the month.

Cash Discounts vs. Quantity Discounts and Markdowns

Cash discounts, which can be viewed as incentives for prompt payment of open accounts, should be distinguished from quantity discounts and markdowns, which are simply reductions in sales prices. A **quantity discount** is a reduction in the per-unit price of an item if a certain quantity is purchased. "Cheaper by the dozen" is an example. **Markdowns,** which are quite common in the retail clothing industry, are reductions in sales prices normally due to decreased demand.

This distinction is important because cash discounts are reflected in the financial statements, but quantity discounts and markdowns are not. To illustrate, in conjunction with an end-of-season sale, suppose that Macy's Department Store reduces the price of a certain line of shoes from $40 to $25. This $15 markdown is simply a reduction in the sales price of the shoes and would not be reflected in Macy's books when the shoes are sold. The journal entry to record the sale of a pair of shoes would simply be:

Cash (or Accounts Receivable)	25	
Sales		25
To record the sale of merchandise.		

Note that the books give no recognition to the fact that the original sales price was $40. The asset (Cash or Accounts Receivable) and the revenue (Sales) are valued at the exchange price at the time of the transaction. The fact that the shoes were originally priced at $40 is ignored.

Accounting for Cash Discounts: Gross vs. Net Method

There are two ways to account for cash discounts: the **gross method** and the **net method.** In general, the gross method is more straightforward, requires no adjusting entries, and is more widely used in practice. It recognizes the initial sale and receivable at the gross sales price and recognizes a cash discount only if the customer pays within the designated discount period. The net method, which is theoretically preferable because it more accurately captures the economic substance of the transaction, recognizes the initial sale and receivable at the net amount (gross price less cash discount). No special recognition is made of the cash discount unless the customer pays at some time beyond the designated discount period. In this case a revenue account, called *Cash Discounts Not Taken,* is recognized on the books of the seller. The example in Figure 7–1, compares the two methods in three independent cases.

Figure 7–1 Accounting for cash discounts: gross and net methods

Given Information:

Assume that Seller Company sells goods on account with a gross sales price of $1,000 to Buyer Company on December 15, 1990 (terms 2/10, n/30). The following journal entries would be recorded on the books of Seller Company using either the gross or the net methods for three different cases.

	Gross Method			**Net Method**		
Initial sale on December 15.	Accounts Receivable	1000		Accounts Receivable	980	
	Sales		1000	Sales		980*
	Sale of goods on			Sale of goods on		
	account.			account.		
				*($1000 × [1.00 − .02])		
Case 1:						
Assume that Seller Company	Cash	980		Cash	980	
receives full payment on	Cash Discount	20		Accounts Receivable		980
December 20 (within the	Accounts Receivable		1000	Payment on account.		
10-day discount period).	Payment on account.					
Case 2:						
Assume no payments are	(No adjusting journal			Accounts Receivable	20	
received by Seller Company	entry required.)			Cash Discount Not Taken		20
prior to December 31, and				Year-end adjusting journal		
the books are closed at that				entry.		
time.						
Case 3:						
Assume full payment is	Cash	1000		Cash	1000	
received by Seller Company	Accounts Receivable		1000	Accounts Receivable		1000
on January 3 (beyond	Payment on account.			Payment on account.		
10-day discount period).						

The Gross Method. Note first that the gross method is very straightforward. It initially recognizes the transaction at $1000, the gross sales price, and thereby is based on the assumption that Buyer Company, the customer, will not receive the cash discount. If Buyer Company pays within the ten-day discount period (Case 1), a Cash Discount account is used to balance the difference between the gross receivable ($1000) and the cash proceeds ($980). Cash Discount is a temporary account that appears on the income statement of Seller Company. Its debit balance serves as a contra account to the credit balance in the Sales account, giving rise to an income statement number called *net sales*. An example of the form of this disclosure follows.

Sales	$50,000	
Less: Cash discounts	1,000	
Net sales		$49,000

Note further that if Buyer Company misses the ten-day discount (Case 2), Seller Company need not prepare an adjusting journal entry, and the $1000 cash receipt after the expiration of the discount period (Cash 3) exactly matches the gross amount in Seller Company's Accounts Receivable account.

The Net Method. The net method, on the other hand, recognizes the initial sale at $980, the net amount, thereby assuming that Buyer Company will receive the discount. If cash payment is made within the ten-day discount period (Case 1), the amount of the payment exactly matches the net amount of the receivable. If Buyer Company misses the discount period (Case 2), it owes Seller Company $1000, $20 more than was originally recorded on Seller Company's books ($980). Seller Company must, therefore, record an adjusting journal entry on December 31 that increases the receivable and recognizes (accrues) a revenue.

The revenue account, Cash Discount Not Taken, is a temporary account that is included in the Other Revenues and Expenses section of Seller Company's income statement. It is actually a finance charge, assessed against Buyer Company, for missing the discount period and is equivalent to interest revenue. In essence, Buyer Company is being charged an additional $20 for the priviledge of paying after the ten-day discount period.

The cash receipt after the expiration of the discount period of $1000 (Case 3) serves to eliminate the balance in Accounts Receivable, which is now $1000 ($980 + $20). If a cash payment was received by Seller Company after the expiration of the discount period (December 25) but before the end of the accounting period (December 31), which is not illustrated in Figure 7-1, no adjusting journal entry would have been necessary on December 31. Instead, Seller Company would have recorded the following journal entry when it received the payment and the receivable would have been removed from the books.

Cash	1000	
Accounts Receivable		980
Cash Discount Not Taken		20
To record the payment of an outstanding receivable.		

An Evaluation of The Gross and Net Methods. In comparing and evaluating these two methods, it is important that you appreciate the trade-off between good measurement theory and what is practical. In your opinion, for example, what is the economic value of the transaction in the illustration above? When the sale is made, should the receivable and the revenue be valued at $1000 or $980?

It should be clear that the economic value of the transaction is $980 because if the goods were sold for cash, the selling price would be $980. The sale and the receivable, therefore, should be valued on the books at $980, and any additional cash receipt should be considered a finance charge for late payment. Review the journal entries for the net method, and note that the transaction is treated in this way: that is, the sale and receivable are initially valued at $980 and the additional $20 is considered a finance charge revenue.

In fact, the finance charge recognized by the net method is actually quite high and it is inadvisable for buying companies to miss cash discounts. In Figure 7-1, for example, if Buyer Company missed the ten-day discount period and paid $1000 to Seller Company on January 15, 30 days after the sale, Buyer Company would have been able to use the $1000 for twenty (30 − 10) days at a cost of $20. Such a situation is equivalent to borrowing cash at a 36.5 percent ([$20/$1000] × [365 days/20 days]) annual rate of interest. Missing cash discounts, therefore, can be very expensive. Indeed, companies that miss discounts because they are short of cash would be better off to borrow from a bank at a 12 percent or 15 percent annual interest rate and use the proceeds to pay those suppliers offering cash discounts. Consequently, most buying companies attempt to make payment within the discount period. From an economic perspective, therefore, the assumption underlying the net method (i.e., the discount will be granted) is quite reasonable.

While the net method is clearly preferred to the gross method in theory, the bookkeeping procedures required to implement it are somewhat more difficult and time-consuming. For example, the adjusting journal entry required by the net method at the end of the accounting period (see Case 2 in Figure 7–1) requires the selling company to determine the dollar value of outstanding receivables that are beyond the discount period. Compiling such information can be difficult. The gross method requires no such adjusting entry.

Moreover, the gross method can be attractive to management because it allows receivables and revenues to be *front-ended*. That is, revenue from cash discounts not taken, which under the gross method is included in sales revenue, is recognized before the cash discounts are actually missed. Using the gross method, consequently, can improve the reported net income number as well as working capital, the current ratio, and the quick ratio.

Generally accepted accounting principles formally require that companies use the net method, primarily because it better captures the economic essence of cash discounts. However, the financial statement effects of the two methods are often immaterially different, and auditors usually allow the gross method. Because it is easier to implement, the gross method is normally preferred in practice. This situation provides another example of the role and importance of the materiality exception in financial accounting. That is, the more expedient gross method is allowed when it produces financial statements that are immaterially different from those produced by the theoretically superior net method. As Chapter 5 points out, however, it is often difficult to determine how much of a difference constitutes a material difference.

Accounting for Uncollectibles (Bad Debts)

In an ideal world all receivables would be satisfied and there would be no need to consider bad debts. However, accounts that are ultimately uncollectible are an unfortunate fact of life, and companies must act both to control them and to estimate their effects on the financial statements. To give you some idea of the magnitude of bad debts, Table 7–2 shows 1986 bad debts as a percentage of credit sales for several major U.S. corporations.

Controlling bad debts is a costly undertaking for many companies. The creditworthiness of potential customers can be checked by subscribing to credit-rating services such as Dun & Bradstreet, Moody's, or Standard & Poor's. Companies can create and maintain collection departments, hire collection agencies, and pursue legal proceedings. Certainly, each of these alternatives can improve cash collections, but each does so at a significant cost. In the extreme, management can institute a policy requiring that all sales be paid in cash. Such a policy would certainly eliminate collection costs and drive bad debts to zero, but it could also be extremely costly because it could dramatically reduce sales revenue. For most companies, then, bad debts are an inevitable cost of everyday operations that must be considered in the management of accounts receivable.

From an accounting standpoint, the inevitability of bad debts reduces the cash expected to be collected from accounts receivable. It thereby reduces the value of

Table 7–2   Bad debts as a percentage of credit sales

Company	Bad Debts/Credit Sales
Handy and Hardman	1%
The Wurlitzer Company	1
Whirlpool Corporation	1
J.C. Penney	1
Commonwealth Edison Company	2
Sherwin Williams Company	4
Scott Paper Company	5
Cummins Engine	5
American Telephone and Telegraph	6

Source: 1986 Annual Reports

Accounts Receivable on the balance sheet. Bad debt losses also represent after-the-fact evidence that certain sales should not have been recorded, since the fourth criteria of revenue recognition (i.e., cash collection is assured) was not met for those sales. As a result, both Accounts Receivable and net income are over-stated if bad debts are ignored. Proper accounting for bad debts, therefore, in-volves two basic adjustments: (1) a downward adjustment to Accounts Receiv-able on the balance sheet and (2) an adjustment that reduces net income.

The Allowance Method

The **allowance method** is used to account for bad debts. This method involves three basic steps: (1) the dollar amount of bad debts is estimated at the end of the accounting period, (2) an adjusting journal entry, which recognizes a bad debt ex-pense on the income statement and reduces the net balance in Accounts Receiv-able, is recorded in the books, and (3) a write-off journal entry is recorded when a bad debt actually occurs. The following example illustrates the basic steps of the allowance method.

Suppose that during 1990, its first year of operations, Q-Mart had credit sales of $20,000 and a balance in Accounts Receivable of $6000 as of December 31.

1. **Estimating bad debts.** After reviewing the relevant information Q-Mart's ac-countants estimate that 2.5 percent ($500) of its credit sales will not be col-lected.

2. **Adjusting journal entry.** The following journal entry would be recorded on December 31.

Bad Debt Expense	500	
Allowance for Doubtful Accounts		500
To record the provision for doubtful accounts.		

3. **Write-off journal entry.** On January 18, 1991, Q-Mart is notified that ABM Enterprises has declared bankruptcy and will not be able to pay the $200 it owes to Q-Mart. The following journal entry would then be recorded in the books of Q-Mart.

Allowance for Doubtful Accounts	200	
Account Receivable (ABM)		200
To write off an uncollectible account receivable (ABM).		

Step 1: Estimating Bad Debts. The allowance method requires that the dollar value of bad debts be estimated at the end of each accounting period. The most common method of estimating bad debts for financial reporting purposes is the **percentage-of-credit-sales approach.**[7] This approach simply multiplies a percentage times the credit sales of the period. In the example given, 2.5 percent ($500 ÷ $20,000) of the credit sales of 1990 were estimated to be uncollectible.

The percentage of credit sales used in the calculation of bad debt expense is based primarily on a company's past experience. For a company such as Q-Mart, which is in its first year of operations, the typical bad debt rate of the other companies in its industry may provide a useful benchmark. Nonetheless, the percentage is an estimate, which by definition is inexact and uncertain. These estimates represent an area of potential disagreement between managers, who often want the financial statements to be as attractive as possible, and auditors whose professional ethics and exposure to legal liability encourage them to prefer conservative reporting.

The problem of estimating bad debts is significant for financial institutions, which have a large portion of their assets in outstanding loans. Such problems are discussed later in the chapter in the section on notes receivable. However, most service, retail, and manufacturing companies, especially those that have been in business for many years, can estimate uncollectibles with reasonable accuracy. The major retail companies, in particular, experience bad debts at a fairly constant percentage of credit sales across time. Bad debt expense for J. C. Penney, for example, was equal to 1 percent of sales in 1985, 1986, and 1987. Thus, while it may be difficult to predict whether an individual account will be uncollectible, it is relatively easy to predict the percentage of bad debt losses from a large group of credit sales.

Step 2: Adjusting Journal Entry. The proper method of accounting for bad debts requires an end-of-period adjusting journal entry that reduces both net income and the balance sheet carrying value of Accounts Receivable. The entry recorded by Q-Mart follows.

Bad Debt Expense	500	
Allowance for Doubtful Accounts		500
To record the provision for doubtful accounts.		

Allowance for doubtful accounts. The credit side of the adjusting journal entry, Allowance for Doubtful Accounts, serves to reduce the balance sheet value of accounts receivable by $500, the expected dollar amount of bad debts.[8] Allowance for Doubtful Accounts is a permanent contra-asset account with a credit balance. It is listed immediately below, and subtracted from, Accounts Receivable on the balance sheet. The form of this disclosure in the current asset section of the balance sheet follows.

Accounts receivable	6000	
Less: Allowance for doubtful accounts	500	5500

---

7. Later in the chapter we discuss another method of estimating bad debts, called the *aging method.*

8. The account title, Allowance for Doubtful Accounts is used in this text. However, in a survey of 600 major U.S. companies, *Accounting Trends and Techniques* (1987) reports that slightly less than half of these companies use this title. The remaining companies use any of eight different descriptions, including Allowance, Allowance for Losses, and Reserve for Doubtful Accounts.

Disclosing the Allowance for Doubtful Accounts account in this way reflects the fact that less cash than is indicated by the face value of the receivables will ultimately be collected. In the case above $5500 of the outstanding receivables are expected to be received. Such disclosure helps to report Accounts Receivable at net realizable value.[9]

Bad debt expense. The debit side of the adjusting journal entry records an expense on the income statement (Bad Debt Expense). Recognizing the $500 bad debt expense in 1990 indicates that certain (unidentifiable as of December 31) credit sales should not have been recorded in 1990. It thereby serves to match the bad debt losses against the revenue recognized from these sales. This method is an application of the matching principle, which states that expenses should be matched against revenues in the proper time period.[10]

Step 3: The Write-off Journal Entry. The write-off journal entry recorded by Q-Mart reduces both the allowance account and the Accounts Receivable balance. It is particularly important to note that this entry has no effect on the income statement and only serves to remove from the books the specific account receivable of ABM. Recall from Chapter 3 and its Appendix A that the ABM account would be found in the subsidiary accounts receivable ledger, which in turn ties directly into Accounts Receivable in the general ledger. Q-Mart's journal entry follows.

Allowance for Doubtful Accounts	200	
Accounts Receivable (ABM)		200
To write off an uncollectible account receivable (ABM).		

The write-off entry has virtually no effect on the financial statements because it simply identifies a specific bad debt that (on average) was known to be uncollectible and was recognized as such at the end of the previous accounting period. Indeed, the entry does not affect the net Accounts Receivable balance, current assets, working capital, the current ratio, quick assets, or net income.

To illustrate, assume that as of December 31 net Accounts Receivable of L. S. Ayres and Company appeared as follows:

Accounts Receivable	79,000	
Less: Allowance for doubtful accounts	3,000	76,000

On January 12 of the following year, the company receives notice that Intermec Corporation will not be able to pay the $800 it owes to Ayres, and the following journal entry is recorded in the books of Ayres.

Allowance for Doubtful Accounts	800	
Accounts Receivable (Intermec)		800
To write off an uncollectible account receivable (Intermec).		

This write-off entry serves to reduce the balance of both Accounts Receivable and Allowance for Doubtful Accounts by $800. Consequently, the net Accounts Receivable balance after the write-off entry appears as follows:

---

9. Most major U.S. companies do not disclose the dollar amount in the allowance account explicitly on the balance sheet. Instead, they simply report the net amount of receivables, after the dollar amount in the allowance account has been subtracted.

10. Theoretically, the bad debt estimate represents revenues that should never have been recorded because the fourth criteria of revenue recognition (cash collection is reasonably assured) was not met. It would be more consistent, therefore, to record the adjustment as a reduction of revenue instead of an expense. Nonetheless, generally accepted accounting principles do not specifically address the issue, and most companies record the adjustment as an expense.

Accounts receivable	78,200	
Less: Allowance for doubtful accounts	2,200	76,000

Note that the write-off entry had no effect on the net realizable value of Accounts Receivable. The net balance of $76,000 is unchanged by the write-off entry because both Accounts Receivable and Allowance for Doubtful Accounts were reduced by the same dollar amount. As a result, current assets, the current ratio, working capital, the quick, ratio, and net income are all unaffected by the write-off entry. The financial statement effect occurred at the end of the previous period (Step 2) when the adjusting journal entry was recorded.

Bad debt recoveries. Specific accounts that have been written off the books are occasionally recovered later. When such a receivable is reinstated, the write-off entry is simply reversed. This procedure simply corrects what was (in retrospect) recorded in error at a previous time. For example, the recovery of a previously written-off $500 account receivable would be recorded as follows:

Accounts Receivable	500	
Allowance for Doubtful Accounts		500
To record the recovery of a $500 accounts receivable.		

If cash was received instead, the entry to record the recovery would appear as follows:

Cash	500	
Allowance for Doubtful Accounts		500
To record the recovery of $500 cash.		

So far we have implied that bad debts are discovered when a specific event occurs. For example, in the preceding illustrations the bad debt write-offs were recorded when a company received notice that a given customer was bankrupt or could not pay for some other reason. While bad debt write-offs can be recorded in this manner, it is probably more common for companies to write off bad debts when they decide that given receivables have been outstanding too long and are too costly to pursue. The following excerpt, which summarizes a typical write-off policy, was taken from the 1987 financial report of J.C. Penney Company, Inc.

> *The Company's policy is to write off accounts when the scheduled minimum payment has not been received for six consecutive months, or if any portion of the balance is more than twelve months past due, or if it is otherwise determined that the customer is unable to pay.*

Inaccurate Bad Debt Estimates. Inaccurate bad debt estimates give rise to preadjustment balances in the Allowance for Uncollectibles Account. For example, if a company estimates $4000 of bad debts on December 31, 1990, and only $3400 actually occur during 1991, as shown in Figure 7–2, the Allowance for Doubtful Accounts contains a $600 credit balance *before adjusting entries are recorded* at the end of 1991.

If instead of $3400, $4400 of bad debts actually occur during 1991, as shown in Figure 7–3, the *preadjustment December 31, 1991 balance* in Allowance for Doubtful Accounts is a $400 debit.

Because estimates are rarely correct, preadjustment balances in Allowance for Doubtful Accounts are common, but they are usually ignored because across time under- and overestimates in individual years tend to neutralize each other. However, a significant debit or credit accumulation in the preadjustment balance over

Figure 7–2   Overestimated bad debts

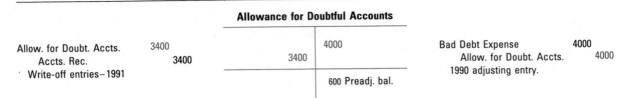

Allowance for Doubtful Accounts

Allow. for Doubt. Accts.	3400		4000		Bad Debt Expense	4000
Accts. Rec.	3400	3400			Allow. for Doubt. Accts.	4000
Write-off entries–1991					1990 adjusting entry.	
			600 Preadj. bal.			

several periods may indicate that estimates are not only inaccurate, but also biased. Consistent overestimates give rise to preadjustment credit accumulations (Figure 7–2), while consistent underestimates create preadjustment accumulations on the debit side of Allowance for Doubtful Accounts (Figure 7–3). Such accumulations often indicate that a company's estimating formula should be revised.

An Aging Schedule: Another Method of Estimating Bad Debts. As indicated earlier, Step 1 of the allowance method requires an end-of-period estimate of the dollar value of Accounts Receivable expected to be uncollectible. Many companies make such estimates by multiplying the credit sales for a period times a percentage determined from their past experiences or those of similar companies in the industry. Another common method of estimating bad debt losses is to establish an **aging schedule** of outstanding accounts receivable. This method categorizes individual accounts in terms of the length of time each has been outstanding and applies a different bad debt rate to each category. The bad debt rate applied to categories comprising older accounts is greater than that applied to categories comprising younger accounts, on the assumption that the longer an account has been outstanding, the more likely it is to be uncollectible.

Using an aging schedule to estimate bad debts. To illustrate how an aging schedule can be used to estimate bad debts, assume that each of the accounts that make up a $4000 end-of-year balance in the Accounts Receivable control account is placed into one of three categories that represent the lengths of time the accounts have been outstanding: (1) six to twelve months, (2) three to six months, and (3) less than three months. It is the company's policy to write off accounts when they become one year old. Assume also that the percentage of uncollectibles expected for each of the three categories is 30 percent for Category 1, 10 percent for Category 2, and 2 percent for Category 3. The bad debt estimate for the entire Accounts Receivable balance is computed in Figure 7–4. The $324 estimate is computed by totaling the dollar amount of the bad debts expected from each of the three categories.

Figure 7–3   Underestimated bad debts

Allowance for Doubtful Accounts

Allow. for Doubt. Accts.	4400		4000		Bad Debt Expense	4000
Accounts Rec.	4400	4400			Allow. for Doubt. Accts.	4000
Write-off entries–1991					1990 adjusting entry.	
		Preadj. bal. 400				

Figure 7–4   An aging schedule

Age of Accounts	Amount	Percent Uncollectible	Estimate
6–12 months	$ 500	30%	$150 (500 × 30%)
3–6 months	1300	10%	130 (1300 × 10%)
Less than 3 months	2200	2%	44 (2200 × 2%)
Total	$4000		$324

The end-of period adjusting entry under aging. Once the bad debt estimate is determined, the end-of-period adjusting journal entry and, accordingly, the bad debt expense can be recorded. However, it is important to note that, in contrast to the percentage-of-credit-sales approach, the dollar amount of the bad debt expense under aging is not the same as the dollar amount of the estimate. The estimate computed under aging determines the desired ending balance in the Allowance for Doubtful Accounts account, and the dollar amount of the journal entry that recognizes bad debt expense is equal to the difference between the preadjustment balance in the allowance account and the aging estimate.

To illustrate, suppose that Rogers Department Store began 1989 with a $2400 credit balance in Allowance for Doubtful Accounts. During 1989 the company wrote off $2300 in bad debts, and at year-end it used an aging schedule to estimate that $2700 in outstanding receivables would be uncollectible. The company's Allowance for Doubtful Accounts T-account, the write-off entry, and the end-of-period adjusting journal entry are shown in Figure 7–5.

The dollar amount of the bad debt expense ($2600) is computed by taking the difference between the preadjustment balance in the allowance account ($100) and the estimated bad debts determined under aging ($2700). This formula also applies when the preadjustment balance in the allowance account is a debit. In Figure 7–5, for example, if Rogers Department Store had written off $2600 of bad debts during 1989, the preadjustment balance would have been a $200 debit, and the dollar amount of the adjusting journal entry recognizing bad debt expense would have been $2900 ($200 − [−$2700]). In summary, the aging estimate specifies the dollar amount of the ending balance in the allowance account and the end-of-period adjusting journal entry, which recognizes the bad debt expense for the period, brings the preadjustment balance to that dollar amount.

Figure 7–5   Computing the end-of period adjusting journal entry with an aging estimate

Allowance for Doubtful Accounts

		2400 Beginning balance
Allowance for Doubt. Accts. 2300	2300	
Accounts Rec. 2300		
Write-off entry during 1989.		100 Preadjustment balance
		2600
		Bad Debt Expense 2600
		Allow. for Doubt. Accts. 2600
	2700 Aging estimate	Adjusting entry at end of 1989.

Note that the procedure for determining the bad debt expense when an aging estimate is used differs from the procedure used when a percentage-of-credit-sales estimate is used. The bad debt estimate, when expressed as a percentage of credit sales, directly determines the bad debt expense recognized on the income statement. This procedure achieves a direct matching between the credit sales of the period and the bad debts related to those sales. An aging estimate, on the other hand, focuses on the receivables disclosed on the balance sheet and determines the dollar amount of those accounts that are expected to be uncollectible. This balance-sheet-oriented procedure attempts to determine directly the net realizable value of the receivables, providing an indirect computation of bad debt expense. Consequently, using a percentage of credit sales is considered a better application of the matching principle, although using an aging estimate generally leads to a more accurate Accounts Receivable valuation.

Aging as a management tool. Maintaining control over outstanding accounts receivable is an important part of effective management for many companies. Because of the time value of money, receivables should be collected as quickly as possible. Bad debts should also be held to a minimum. Aging schedules help companies control bad debts in a number of significant ways.

An aging schedule, for example, can identify slow-moving accounts, thus directing collection efforts and defining the maximum costs that should be incurred by those efforts. Collection efforts should be directed toward the accounts in the older categories, but the costs associated with these efforts should not exceed the expected loss from the accounts. For example, a company may have $10,000 of accounts receivable that have been outstanding for over six months. Past experience indicates that 20 percent of such accounts are uncollectible. The $2000 ($10,000 × 20%) expected loss from these accounts determines a maximum dollar amount for the costs incurred to collect them.

An aging schedule can also be helpful in estimating how much money a company is losing in potential interest charges. Such information can be useful in deciding whether to offer cash discounts and in determining the appropriate terms for such discounts.

Although aging schedules can provide useful information, keep in mind that they can be costly to establish and maintain. For companies that rely on credit sales to a wide variety of customers, maintaining the age and balance of each account can be quite time-consuming. Computerized accounting systems are almost a necessity for efficient aging analyses and receivables control. Most large companies, of course, have computerized their receivables accounting, and when small companies change from manual to computerized accounting systems, receivables applications are often used first to improve control over accounts receivable.

The Direct Write-off Method

According to generally accepted accounting principles, the allowance method should normally be used to account for bad debts. This method is not completely objective, however, because it requires an end-of-period adjusting journal entry that is based on an estimate (percent of credit sales or aging). In those unusual cases where an estimate cannot be reasonably objective, the **direct write-off method** is used. Such cases can occur, for example, when there are no historical precedents nor experiences of similar companies upon which to base the estimate of bad debts. The direct write-off method does not require an end-of-period adjusting journal entry, which must be based on an estimate. Instead, it recognizes bad debt expense and removes outstanding receivables from the books as specific accounts are deemed to be uncollectible.

To illustrate, assume that late in 1989 an $800 sale on account is made to Morley Enterprises. During 1990 the receivable is declared to be uncollectible. Under the direct write-off method such a declaration would be accompanied by the following journal entry.

Bad Debt Expense	800	
Accounts Receivable (Morley)		800
To write off the $800 account of Morley Enterprises.		

While the direct write-off method is simple and objective, it is deficient in two fundamental ways. First, it is a poor application of the matching principle and the principle of revenue recognition. Under this method, bad debt expense is recognized when the bad debt is discovered (1990) instead of when the original revenue associated with the account was recorded (1989). Thus, the bad debt expense is not matched with the related revenue in the same time period. Stated in terms of the principle of revenue recognition, the $800 revenue in 1989 should never have been recognized because the four principles of revenue recognition were not met when the sale was made.

The direct write-off method also fails to recognize that accounts receivable will produce a lesser amount of cash than is indicated by its dollar value on the balance sheet. No allowance account is used to adjust the receivables balance to net realizable value. Consequently, accounts receivables on the balance sheet can be overstated under the direct write-off method.

Accounting for Sales Returns

For many companies it is common that merchandise that has been sold on account is returned by customers. These returns are important in the retail industry, and book publishers, like Scott, Foresman, Prentice-Hall, and Harper & Row, are especially affected because customers can often return their products sixty days or more after the initial sale. When returned items were initially sold, the sale and the associated account receivable were recognized on the books. Because sales returns are usually accompanied by either the removal of the receivable or the granting of future credit, companies with significant returns must adjust both the income statement and Accounts Receivable on the balance sheet. The methods used to account for sales returns are similar to those used to account for bad debts.

SHORT-TERM NOTES RECEIVABLE: A DEFINITION

Short-term notes receivable differ from accounts receivable primarily because they involve formal promissory notes, rather than informal promises to pay. Promissory notes usually identify the parties of the transaction and state the principal amount to be paid (the **face value,** or maturity value, of the note), the date of principal payment (maturity date), and a provision for interest (the stated interest rate). The maturity date of a short-term note receivable is usually more than sixty days from the date it is established, but less than the length of time that defines current assets. Ninety-day notes are quite common. Companies often accept notes instead of transacting on open accounts because formal notes are usually easier to enforce, can include security provisions and other management restrictions, and normally enjoy a higher priority for claims on the debtor's assets in case of bankruptcy.

Like accounts receivable, short-term notes receivable can arise from the sale of goods or services to customers. It also happens, as illustrated in the following journal entry, that a short-term note receivable is established in exchange for an account receivable. Such an exchange might occur when a company wishes to contractually obligate a slow-paying customer.

Short-Term Notes Receivable	300	
Accounts Receivable		300

To record the conversion of an account receivable to a note receivable.

However, short-term notes receivable usually result from cash loans, which are naturally common for banks and other financial institutions. The following journal entry records such a loan, a short-term note receivable in exchange for $1000 cash.

Short-Term Notes Receivable	1000	
Cash		1000

To record a short-term loan.

ACCOUNTING FOR SHORT-TERM NOTES RECEIVABLE

There are two basic methods of accounting for short-term notes receivable that are fundamentally the same. They value the assets related to the note at the same dollar amount, and they recognize the same amount of interest revenue in the same time periods. However, they involve different sets of journal entries, and the resulting disclosures are somewhat different. Method 1 recognizes the note receivable in an amount equal to the principal and accrues interest receivable over the life of the note. Method 2, on the other hand, recognizes the note receivable in the amount of the principal and the interest to be received. This method requires the recognition of a *discount*, which is converted to interest revenue over the life of the note. The following example compares the two methods.

Example: Housing Finance Company

Assume that on December 1, 1990, Housing Finance Company loans Johnson Construction $5000 in exchange for a ninety-day note with a stated annual interest rate of 12 percent. Housing Finance pays $5000 to Johnson on December 1 and receives $5150 ($5000 principal plus $150 [5000 × 12% × 3/12] interest) from Johnson on March 1, 1991. The accounting procedures under Methods 1 and 2 are compared in Figure 7–6.

Under Method 1 the face amount of the note receivable is established at $5000, the amount of the principal. One-third of the interest ($50) is accrued in 1990, and the remaining amount of the interest revenue ($100) is recognized in 1991.

Figure 7–6 Accounting for short-term notes receivable

Method 1			Method 2		
December 1, 1990			**December 1, 1990**		
Note Receivable	5,000		Note Receivable	5,150	
Cash		5,000	Cash		5,000
To record issuance of the note.			Discount on Note		150
			To record issuance of the note.		

Method 1			Method 2		
December 31, 1990 (end of period adjusting entry)			**December 31, 1990 (end of period adjusting entry)**		
Interest Receivable	50*		Discount on Note	50*	
Interest Revenue		50	Interest Revenue		50
To accrue one month of interest.			To accrue one month of interest.		

*(5,000 × 12%) ÷ 12

December 31, 1990 (balance sheet assets related to note)

December 31, 1990 (balance sheet assets related to note)

Balance Sheet December 31, 1990			Balance Sheet December 31, 1990		
Note receivable	$5,000		Note receivable	$5,150	
Interest receivable	50		Less: Discount on note	100	$5,050
Total		$5,050			

Method 1			Method 2		
March 1, 1991			**March 1, 1991**		
Cash	5,150*		Cash	5,150*	
Note Receivable		5,000	Discount on Note	100	
Interest Receivable		50	Interest Revenue		100
Interest Revenue		100	Note Receivable		5,150
To record receipt of principal and interest payment.			To record receipt of principal and interest payment.		

*5,000 + (5000 × 12% × 3/12)

Under Method 2 the face value of the note is equal to the total principal and interest ($5000 + $150), the original cash payment by Housing Finance is equal to the principal ($5000), and a discount is established in the amount of the difference: $150, the total interest to be received. The Discount on Note account is a contra-asset account that is disclosed on the balance sheet immediately below, and subtracted from, the Note Receivable account. In a sense, the discount can be viewed as unearned interest, which is amortized (converted) into interest revenue over the life of the note. The December 31 end-of-period adjusting entry amortizes one-third ($50) of the discount into Interest Revenue.

Note the disclosure under Method 2 on the December 31, 1990 balance sheet. The net balance sheet value of the note receivable is $5050, the face value ($5150) less the unamortized discount ($100 = $150 − $50). The journal entry to record the final principal and interest receipt ($5150) (1) amortizes the remaining discount into Interest Revenue ($100) and (2) writes off the Note Receivable account ($5150).

Methods 1 and 2 Compared

Although the journal entries used by Methods 1 and 2 are not the same, there is actually no difference between the resulting balance sheet and income statement values. Both methods value the assets related to the note at the same dollar amount (as of December 31, $5050), and both methods recognize equivalent dollar amounts of interest revenue in 1990 ($50) and 1991 ($100). The difference between the two methods is only a matter of disclosure. Method 1 treats the Note Receivable and the Interest Receivable related to the note independently, establishing separate accounts for each. Method 2, on the other hand, establishes a Discount on Notes Receivable account and discloses it as a contra-asset against Note Receivable on the balance sheet. The discount is treated like unearned interest revenue, in that it is converted to interest revenue as the interest on the note is earned. Under Method 2 a separate Interest Receivable account is not used.

Financial Institutions and Uncollectible Loans

The methods used to account for uncollectible notes receivable are equivalent to those used to account for bad debts. That is, generally accepted accounting principles require that the allowance method be used if uncollectibles can be estimated in a reasonably objective manner. As mentioned earlier in the chapter, estimating the dollar value of uncollectible loans is particularly important for financial institutions, because such institutions carry such large amounts of outstanding notes receivable. The 1987 balance sheet of BankAmerica Corporation, for example, indicated that $64.5 billion in loans (short- and long-term) were outstanding as of the end of the year. This amount represented 70 percent of the company's total assets. Of the $64.5 billion in loans, the company estimated that $3.3 billion (5 percent) would not be collected.

The banking and savings and loan industry has been plagued with a number of outstanding notes on which no interest or principal payments have been received. These nonperforming loans are due primarily to risky foreign investments, decreasing farm and oil prices, and a real estate slump in the Southwest. In 1988, for example, *The Wall Street Journal* reported that First Republic Bank Corporation, Texas's largest banking concern, "plans to add still more real estate and foreign loans to its $4 billion mountain of nonperforming loans . . . and will make additional provisions (on their financial statements) for loan losses and write-offs." The article went on to state that "some crucial financial ratios are slipping, and First Bank may default on about $33 million of long-term debt. Such a default could accelerate the calling of that debt and trigger calling of fully half of the corporation's $539.9 million of long-term debt. 'These factors, among others,' said Arthur Andersen & Co., independent auditors of First Bank, 'indicate that the corporation may be unable to continue in its present form.'"[11]

In another example, Seafirst Bank, the largest bank holding company in the state of Washington, found itself on the brink of bankruptcy in 1983, largely because of loans in the Southwest that were never paid. When Seafirst stock plummeted in value, irate stockholders brought a multimillion-dollar suit against the managers of Seafirst for entering into such loans and also sued the bank's audi-

---

11. Leonard M. Apcar, "String of Losses Seen by First Republic Bank," *The Wall Street Journal*, 31 March 1988, p. 3.

tors, Arthur Andersen & Co., for failing to ensure that an adequate loan-loss provision was established on the financial statements. In 1983 BankAmerica Corporation rescued the troubled Washington bank by acquiring it and pumping in needed funds, enabling it to continue operations.

These examples emphasize the point that accounting for notes receivable can be very subjective and difficult, and can lead to significant economic consequences. The next section explains how accounting for short-term receivables in general can produce economic consequences.

THE ECONOMIC CONSEQUENCES OF ACCOUNTING FOR SHORT-TERM RECEIVABLES

When accounting for short-term receivables, two general questions are of significant economic importance: (1) When should a receivable be recorded in the books? and (2) At what dollar amount should a receivable be valued on the balance sheet?

When Should a Receivable be Recorded?

Revenues and related receivables are recognized when the four criteria of revenue recognition have been met. Establishing exactly when this occurs, however, is difficult and subjective. A recent article in *Forbes* indicates that "managers have a good bit of freedom to determine when and how a sale [and the associated receivable] gets put on the books".[12] This freedom gives rise to widely different practices. For example, General Electric recognizes revenues when goods are shipped, while Harper & Row, a large book publisher, recognizes revenues when it invoices customers, sometimes a month before orders are shipped. Revenue-recognition practices even differ among companies in the same industry. A survey of 200 software companies, for example, revealed that 26 (13 percent) companies waited until cash was received before recognizing a sale, while 30 (15 percent) companies recognized a sale as soon as an order was received.[13]

Users of financial statements must realize that, even within the guidelines of generally accepted accounting principles, managers can use discretion to speed up or slow down the recognition of revenue. This concern is particularly important for transactions that occur near the end of an accounting period. Recognizing a receivable and a revenue on December 30 instead of January 2, for example, can significantly affect current assets, working capital, and net income on the December 31 financial statements.

To illustrate, suppose that current assets, current liabilities, and net income for Johnson and Sons as of December 29 are $45,000, $34,000, and $14,000, respectively. Johnson and Sons provides a service to Ace Manufacturing that is billed at $20,000. The service is ordered by Ace on December 30 and completed by Johnson and Sons on January 5. Payment is made by Ace after January 5. The current ratio, working capital position, and net income as of December 31 for Johnson and Sons are computed in Figure 7–7, assuming that (1) the revenue is

---

12. Jill Andresky, "Setting the Date," *Forbes* 16 July 1984, p. 90.
13. Ibid.

Figure 7–7 The timing of revenue and receivable recognition

	(1) Revenue is recognized on January 5.	(2) Revenue is recognized on December 30.
December 31 current ratio (current assets ÷ current liabilities)	1.32	1.91
December 31 working capital (current assets − current liabilities)	$11,000	$31,000
Net income, year ended December 31	$14,000	$34,000

recognized when the service is completed on January 5, and (2) the revenue is recognized when the service is ordered on December 30.

Note that the timing of revenue recognition can have a significant effect on important financial statement numbers. Recognizing the sale in the earlier period increased the current ratio by 45 percent, and increased working capital and net income each by $20,000. Such effects have economic significance because they may influence a company's credit rating or determine if it violates the terms of debt agreements. Since the timing of revenue and receivable recognition has a direct effect on net income and current assets, financial statement users should pay special attention to it.

Extreme cases of premature revenue and receivable recognition, or the complete fabrication of sales, is often interpreted as management fraud. The SEC, for example, recently charged three former officers of a California electronic parts manufacturer, called Matrix Science Corp., for "prematurely recognizing revenue by engaging in pre-invoicing and other accounting tricks. The SEC described pre-invoicing as recording revenue from orders for products that haven't been shipped, or in some cases haven't even been assembled. . . The officers prevented [the] outside auditors from discovering the practice by reprinting invoices and moving inventory off the premises."[14]

At What Dollar Amount Should a Receivable be Valued on the Balance Sheet?

The appropriate dollar amount at which to value receivables on the balance sheet is primarily a question of whether the outstanding receivables will, in fact, be paid. As indicated earlier, banks such as BankAmerica have billions of dollars in outstanding loans that will never produce any cash. Estimating such uncollectibles, which can significantly affect both the income statement and the balance sheet, can be a very subjective process and can lead to substantial disagreements between management and its auditors.

In 1988, for example, the auditing firm of Deloitte, Haskins & Sells postponed rendering an opinion on Federal Home Loan Bank of Dallas because the bank carried $500 million of questionable loans on its balance sheet. As stated in

---

14. Thomas E. Ricks, "Former Officers of Electronics Company Charged by SEC with Inflating Profit," *The Wall Street Journal,* 2 November 1988, p. A14.

Forbes, "since [estimating bad debts] involves judgment, there is a real temptation [for managers] to ignore potential problems and keep net income up".[15]

Another interesting example occured in 1984, when the SEC ordered two bank holding companies, IntraWest Financial Corporation and Utica Bank Shares, to increase the dollar amounts in their Allowance for Bad Loans (Debts) accounts. Waiting until the last moment, Utica increased its loan-loss provision from $2.4 million to $25 million. Other banks, apparently fearing SEC action, quickly followed suit. At Dallas's InterFirst Corporation, bad debt estimates swelled from $40 million to $430 million. Crocker National Corporation increased its bad debt estimate from $19.4 million to $119 million. Continental Illinois increased its estimate from $35 million to $262 million.[16]

These examples indicate that (1) managers are often unwilling to establish large bad debt provisions on the financial statements and (2) estimating bad debts can be a very subjective process. In conjunction with the previous discussions on the timing of revenue recognition and bad debt concerns of U.S. banks, they also suggest that the methods used to account for short-term receivables can lead to significant economic consequences. These methods can affect a company's credit rating, determine whether the terms of debt covenants are violated, accelerate bankruptcy proceedings, and bring about sizable lawsuits against managers and auditors. Indeed, the methods used to account for short-term receivables do make an economic difference.

THE COLLECTION PERIOD FOR SHORT-TERM RECEIVABLES

We have already explained how the methods used to account for short-term receivables can affect net income, the current ratio, working capital, the quick ratio, and other important financial statement numbers. Another ratio that uses the short-term receivables balance is called the **collection period.** This ratio, which is one of Dun & Bradstreet's fourteen key business ratios, is calculated as follows:

Receivable collection period = (Accounts Receivable/Sales) × 365 days

This calculation indicates how many days, in general, the short-term receivables of a given company are outstanding. Investors and creditors use it to determine how quickly a company's receivables are normally converted into cash; thus it can be helpful in determining whether a company can meet its debts as they come due. To illustrate how this ratio is calculated, consider the financial information in Figure 7–8, which was taken from the 1987 financial report of the Procter & Gamble Company.

The accounts receivable held by Procter & Gamble were outstanding, on average, for thirty-eight days in 1986 and thirty-three days in 1987. These calculations indicate that the time period between the company's sales and the collection of cash decreased from 1986 to 1987. As a basis for comparison, the average collection periods in selected industries are contained in Table 7–3.

---

15. Laura Sanders, "The SEC Takes on Loan Losses," *Forbes* 4 June 1984, p. 94.
16. Ibid.

Figure 7-8   **The calculation of collection period**

	1987	1986
Sales	$17,000*	$15,439*
Net accounts receivable	1,557	1,600
Collection period		
1986 (1,600 ÷ 15,439) × 365		38 days
1987 (1,557 ÷ 17,000) × 365	33 days	

*Dollars in millions

Note that the average collection period varies from just several days for grocery stores and new and used car dealers to over two months for accounting and medical services. The differences are largely due to the importance of accounts receivable on the balance sheet. Grocery stores and new and used car dealers carry limited receivables, while most of the sales for department stores are based on credit. Professional services normally bill their clients after completing the service and, as illustrated, receive the cash payment several months later.

THE ANNUAL REPORT OF K MART CORPORATION

Turn now to K mart's annual report located in Appendix D. As indicated on the balance sheet (page 32), short-term receivables are not particularly significant. They are included with "other current assets" in a single account which totaled $527 million in 1989 and $353 million in 1988. These dollar amounts represented 7 percent and 6 percent of current assets, and 4 percent and 3 percent of total assets, in 1989 and 1988, respectively.

Assuming that the dollar amounts in this account are all in the form of receivables, the collection periods for 1989 and 1988 can be computed as below.

Receivable collection period	=	(Accounts receivable ÷ sales) × 365 days
1989	7 days	=	($527 million ÷ $27.3 billion) × 365 days
1988	5 days	=	($353 million ÷ $25.6 billion) × 365 days

Table 7-3   **Average short-term receivable collection periods (1986 industry averages)**

Industry	Collection Period (days)
Grocery stores	3
New and used car dealers	6
Family clothing stores	14
Department stores	30
Life insurance	42
TV broadcasting	50
Crude oil and natural gas mining	68
Accounting and auditing services	69
Medical doctor offices	77

Source: Compiled from data published in *Industry Norms and Key Business Ratios* (Dun & Bradstreet, Inc., 1987).

Note that these calculations overstate actual collection periods because the dollar amount of short-term receivables is overstated. It is clear, therefore, that K mart does not rely heavily on credit sales. For example, Table 7-3, which provides collection periods for selected industries, shows that with respect to receivables K mart's operations resemble those of the average grocery store. As a discount retailer, K mart makes most of its sales in cash, personal checks, or major credit cards such as VISA or Mastercard.

Due to the immaterial nature of K mart's short-term receivables, the annual report provides no information about the methods of accounting for cash discounts, uncollectibles, or sales returns. Moreover, issues of revenue recognition are rarely a major concern of retailers, like K mart, that receive payment at the point of purchase.

REVIEW PROBLEM

This section provides a review problem that covers the methods used to account for bad debts. The facts given are accounted for using (1) the direct write-off method, (2) the allowance method with a percentage-of-credit-sales estimate, and (3) the allowance method with an aging estimate. A brief discussion of the methods follows the solution.

Assume that Credit Inc. began operations on January 1, 1989. The relevant transactions for 1989 and 1990 are summarized in the accounts receivable T-account provided in Figure 7-9. Sales on account during 1989 totaled $10,000, and cash receipts for those sales equaled $6000. The Accounts Receivable balance at the end of 1989 was $4000 ($10,000 − $6000). Sales on account during 1990 totaled $12,000, and cash receipts during the same period, from sales made in both 1989 and 1990, were $11,000. On June 5, 1990, Credit Inc. received notice that a $500 account established in 1989 would not be collectible. This account was written off, and the December 31, 1990 balance in accounts receivable is $4500 ($4000 + $12,000 − $11,000 − $500). Assume that companies in Credit's industry typically experience bad debt losses of approximately 7 percent of credit sales. Assume also that aging schedules prepared by Credit's accountants at the end of 1989 and 1990 indicated that $750 and $1100 of the outstanding accounts at those times would be uncollectible, respectively. The three methods of accounting for bad debts are also shown in Figure 7-9.

The direct write-off method makes no adjusting journal entries at the end of 1989 and 1990. It recognizes a bad debt expense and writes off the receivable on June 5, 1990, when the bad debt is discovered. Thus, the expense from the bad debt, which was related to a sale made in 1989, is inappropriately matched against revenues recognized in 1990. Furthermore, Accounts Receivable on the balance sheet at the end of both 1989 and 1990 are overstated because no adjustment is made for future bad debts.

The allowance method, using a 7 percent of credit sales estimate, gives rise to end-of-period adjusting journal entries that match bad debt expense against the revenues of the appropriate period and reduce the value of Accounts Receivable on the balance sheet to net realizable value, the amount of cash expected to be collected from the receivables. The write-off entry on June 5, 1989, has virtually no effect on the financial statements of Credit Inc.

Figure 7–9 Bad debt review problem

General Ledger

Accounts Receivable

Beginning balance	0		
1989 credit sales	10,000		
		6,000	1989 cash receipts
12/31/89 balance	4,000		
1990 credit sales	12,000		
		11,000	1990 cash receipts
		500	1990 bad debt
12/31/90 balance	4,500		

Comparison of Methods

	Direct Write-off Method	Allowance Method (percentage of credit sales estimate)		Allowance Method (aging estimate)	
	December 31, 1989	December 31, 1989		December 31, 1989	
Estimate	None	$700 (7% × $10,000)		$750	
Entry	None	Bad Debt Expense 700		Bad Debt Expense 750	
		Allow. for Doubt. Accts.	700	Allow. for Doubt. Accts.	750
	June 5, 1990	June 5, 1990		June 5, 1990	
Write-off entry	Bad Debt Expense 500	Allow. for Doubt. Accts. 500		Allow. for Doubt. Accts. 500	
	Accounts Rec. 500	Accounts Rec.	500	Accounts Rec.	500
	December 31, 1990	December 31, 1990		December 31, 1990	
Estimate	None	$840 (7% × $12,000)		$1100	
Entry	None	Bad Debt Expense 840		Bad Debt Expense 850	
		Allow. for Doubt. Accts.	840	Allow. for Doubt. Accts.	850

Allowance for Doubtful Accounts

		0	Beg. bal.
		700	12/31/89
		700	12/31/89 bal.
6/5/90	500		
		200	Preadj. bal.
		840	12/31/90
		1040	12/31/90 bal.

Allowance for Doubtful Accounts

		0	Beg. bal.
		750	12/31/89
		750	12/31/89 bal.
6/5/90	500		
		250	Preadj. bal.
		850	12/31/90
		1100	12/31/90 bal.

Note that the preadjustment balance in the Allowance for Doubtful Accounts account as of December 31, 1989 is a $200 credit ($700 estimate − $500 write-off). Either Credit overestimated its bad debt losses for 1989, or certain outstanding accounts created from 1989's credit sales may still be written off. If this preadjustment balance accumulates over a period of several years, Credit should review and possibly revise its estimating formula. Otherwise, it is ignored.

The accounts involved in the three journal entries recorded under the allowance method with an aging estimate are the same as those recorded under the allowance method with a percentage-of-credit-sales estimate. The aging estimate, however, gives rise to different dollar amounts. More importantly, note that the dollar amount of the journal entry recorded on December 31, 1990, ($850) is not the same as the bad debt estimate made on that date ($1100). It represents the dollar amount necessary to bring the final balance in the allowance account to $1100. Since the December 31, 1990 preadjustment balance in the allowance account was a credit of $250 ($750 estimate − $500 write-off), an additional credit of $850 was required to bring the final balance to $1100.

SUMMARY OF LEARNING OBJECTIVES

1 Define and distinguish between accounts receivable and short-term notes receivable.

Accounts receivable arise from transactions with customers who have purchased goods or services but have not yet paid for them. They are amounts owed by customers for goods and services sold as part of the normal operations of the business. Often backed up by oral rather than written commitments, accounts receivable represent short-term extensions of credit that are normally collectible within thirty to sixty days.

Short-term notes receivable arise from either lending arrangements or customer transactions. Unlike accounts receivable, they involve formal promissory notes that state a maturity value, a maturity date, and an annual interest rate. The time period of these notes usually extends beyond the normal thirty- to sixty-day payment period of accounts receivable, but it is usually less than one year.

2 Describe the alternative methods used to account for cash discounts.

Cash discounts are offered by companies to encourage customers to pay promptly on open accounts. Two methods are used to account for cash discounts: the gross method and the net method. Under the gross method, the original sale is recognized at the gross price, and a cash discount is not recognized unless payment is made within the discount period. Under the net method, the original sale is recognized at the discount price, and cash discount revenue is recognized if payment is made after the expiration of the discount period. While the net method better represents the economics of the transaction, the gross method is used more because it is easier to apply and there is little difference between methods.

3 Differentiate between the allowance method and the direct write-off method, both of which are used to account for bad debts.

Bad debts arise because some customers simply do not pay their open accounts. Two methods are used to account for bad debts. Under the allowance method, at the end of each accounting period the amount of uncollectibles is estimated. Then an adjusting journal entry is made to recognize bad debt expense, and a contra account to Accounts Receivable, Allowance for Doubtful Accounts, is credited. Later, when the uncollectible is actually realized, both the value of accounts receivable and the contra account are reduced. The allowance method is required under generally accepted accounting principles when the amount of bad debts can be estimated in a reasonably objective manner.

Under the direct write-off method, which is used if bad debts cannot be estimated objectively, the bad debt estimate and adjusting entry are not prepared at the end of the period. Instead, a bad debt expense is recognized when the uncollectible is realized.

4 Explain the two basic techniques of estimating bad debts and describe how they are used to implement the allowance method.

The two methods used to estimate bad debts are the percentage-of-credit-sales method and the aging method. Under the percentage-of-credit-sales method, the bad debt estimate at the end of the period is determined by multiplying a percentage, which is determined from past experience or the experience of other similar companies, by the credit sales of the period. When implementing the allowance method with a percentage-of-credit-sales estimate, the estimate determines the bad debt expense recognized for the period.

An aging estimate at the end of the period is determined by categorizing all outstanding accounts into groups based on their ages and then multiplying a different bad debt percentage times the total dollar amount in each category. The older accounts are assumed to be uncollectible with greater likelihood than the newer accounts. When implementing the allowance method with an aging estimate, the estimate is used to determine the ending balance in the Allowance for Doubtful Accounts account. In addition, an aging analysis can provide information that is helpful in determining appropriate collection and cash discount policies.

5 Describe the two methods used to account for short-term notes receivable.

Two methods are used to account for short-term notes receivable. Under the first method, a Note Receivable account is established at an amount equal to the principal. The accrual of interest involves a debit to Interest Receivable and a credit to Interest Revenue. When the combined principal and interest are received at the end of the note's life, the Note Receivable account and the Interest Receivable account are removed from the books.

The second method establishes the Note Receivable account at an amount equal to the total cash to be received, which includes both the principal amount of the note and the entire amount of interest to be received. At the same time, a Discount on Note Receivable account is credited in an amount equal to the interest to be paid on the note. This account is converted (amortized) into interest revenue over the life of the note. When the combined principal and interest payments are received at the end of the note's life, the Note Receivable account is removed from the books.

6 Describe the economic consequences resulting from the methods used to account for short-term receivables.

For many companies, short-term receivables are a significant percentage of total and current assets; accordingly, the methods used to account for them can have direct and often significant effects on such measures as current assets, working capital, the current ratio, the quick ratio, and net income. Financial statement users must realize that managers can influence these measures by speeding up or slowing down the recognition of revenue and related receivables and that the estimate of uncollectibles is very subjective. Such practices can affect a company's credit rating, determine whether debt terms are violated, accelerate bankruptcy proceedings, and bring about sizable lawsuits against managers and auditors.

KEY TERMS

Accounts receivable (p. 297)
Aging schedule (p. 308)
Allowance method (p. 304)
Cash discount (p. 299)
Collection period (p. 317)
Direct write-off method (p. 310)
Face value (p. 311)
Gross method (p. 300)

Markdown (p. 300)
Net method (p. 300)
Net realizable value (p. 299)
Open account (p. 297)
Percentage-of-credit-sales approach (p. 305)
Quantity discount (p. 300)
Short-term notes receivable (p. 311)

QUESTIONS FOR DISCUSSION AND REVIEW

1. What is the difference between an account receivable and a short-term note receivable?

2. Explain the link between accounts receivable and the income statement. How is the recognition of an account receivable related to the four criteria of revenue recognition?

3. The Sales account, which appears on the income statement, usually differs from Cash Inflows due to Operating Activities, which is found on the statement of cash flows. Why? How can accounts receivable be used to reconcile these two numbers?

4. Define window dressing, and provide three examples of how a manager may practice window dressing with respect to accounts receivable.

5. Discuss why auditors are concerned that sales on account be recognized in the proper time period and that bad debts be estimated accurately.

6. The valuation base for accounts receivable is called *net realizable value*. What is the definition of net realizable value with respect to accounts receivable?

7. Distinguish cash discounts from quantity discounts and sales discounts (markdowns). Why are quantity discounts and sales discounts not explicitly recognized in financial accounting statements?

8. Why do companies offer cash discounts? State your answer in terms of the trade-offs between the time value of money, collection costs, and the terms of the cash discount.

9. What two methods are used to account for cash discounts? Which of these methods values the sales transaction at the cash exchange value?

10. Which of the two methods of accounting for cash discounts tends to overstate the sales figure and the Accounts Receivable balance? Which of the two methods recognizes a special revenue account for financial charges associated with payments received after the end of the discount period?

11. The gross method of accounting for cash discounts is used by more companies than the net method. Yet, the net method better represents the economic value of the related transactions. Explain why in terms of costs and benefits and the concept of materiality.

12. What can companies do to reduce uncollectible accounts receivable? How could they reduce them to zero? Why don't they do it?

13. The chapter presents two methods of accounting for uncollectible accounts receivable: the allowance method and the direct write-off method. What two principles of accounting measurement are traded off when using one of these methods instead of the other? Explain why the allowance method is preferred.

14. Explain how bad debts are estimated using a percentage of credit sales. What kind of information is used by management when preparing such an estimate?

15. What is an aging of accounts receivable? Describe the computation, and explain how it provides information that is useful to managers. How can aging accounts receivable help managers set the terms of their cash discounts? What effect has the computerization of accounts receivable had on management's inclination to perform aging analyses? Why?

16. When implementing the allowance method with a percentage-of-credit-sales estimate, what role does the dollar amount of the estimate play? When implementing the allowance method with an aging estimate, what role does the dollar amount of the estimate play?

17. Discuss the role of the Allowance for Doubtful Accounts account. What financial statement numbers are affected when a bad debt is written off the books? How are current assets, working capital, the current ratio, and net income affected?

18. Suppose you are an investor attempting to decide whether to invest a substantial sum of money in a small manufacturing company. While examining the financial statements, you note that the company has shown large profits over the past several years and that the balance in Accounts Receivable is quite large. After further study, you learn that the outstanding receivables consist primarily of a few, large accounts and that the company uses the direct write-off method to account for bad debts. How and why might this information affect your investment decision?

19. If a company that uses the allowance method to account for bad debts consistently overestimates bad debts, how does this show up in the books? If the same company consistently understates the bad debt estimate, how does this show up in the books?

20. Two basic methods are used to account for notes receivable. Compare the two methods in terms of the net values of the assets related to the note (i.e., Note Receivable and Interest Receivable) and the amount and timing of interest revenue recognition. One of the methods uses a Discount on Notes Receivable account. Explain the role of this account, where it is disclosed on the balance sheet, and why it is very similar to an Unearned Revenue account, which would appear as a current liability.

EXERCISES

E7–1

(Accounting for cash discounts: gross and net methods) On May 1, 1991, Crab Cove Fishing Company sold some Maine lobster on account for a gross price of $50,000. On May 5 the company also sold some cod on account for a gross price of $20,000. The terms of both sales were 3/10, n/30. Crab Cove received payment for the first sale on May 6, 1991, and payment for the second sale on May 31, 1991.

Required:

a. Assume that Crab Cove Fishing Company uses the gross method to account for cash discounts. Prepare journal entries for each transaction.

b. Assume Crab Cove Fishing Company uses the net method to account for cash discounts. Prepare journal entries for each transaction.

E7–2

(Accounting for cash discounts: gross and net methods) On December 12, Mayliner sold goods on account for a gross price of $30,000. The terms of the sale were 2/10, n/30. As of December 31, when financial statements were prepared, no payment had been received by Mayliner. Full payment was received on January 5 of the following year.

Required:

a. Prepare journal entries for these transactions, including any necessary adjusting journal entries, under the gross method.

b. Prepare journal entries for these transactions, including any necessary adjusting journal entries, under the net method.

c. Compute the difference in net income as of December 31 between the gross and the net methods.

d. Explain why the net method is preferred to the gross method in terms of disclosure differences between the two methods. For example, would the gross profit amount reported on the income statement be different under the two methods?

e. Why is the gross method more common in practice? Assume that annual sales for Mayliner are normally about $1 million.

E7–3

(Bad debt expense under the allowance method) Olympic Medal Company began operations on January 1, 1990. The company reported the following selected items in the 1991 financial report.

	1991	1990
Gross sales	$2,750,000	$3,000,000
Accounts receivable	1,275,000	1,300,000
Actual bad debt write-offs	55,000	30,000
	80,000	57,000

A consulting company estimated that the company should not expect to collect 2 percent of gross sales.

Required:

a. Prepare the entry (and show computations) to record the estimated bad debt expense for 1990.

b. Prepare the entry (and show computations) to record the estimated bad debt expense for 1991.

c. Assume that Olympic uses an aging schedule to estimate bad debts and that at the end of 1990 and 1991, accounts with total balances of $57,000 and $80,000, respectively, were expected to be uncollectible. Prepare the entries to record the bad debt expense at the end of 1990 and 1991.

E7–4

(Accounting for uncollectibles) In its 1990 financial report Sound Unlimited reported the following items:

1. A credit balance in Allowance for Doubtful Accounts of $350,000.

2. A debit balance in accounts receivable of $6,275,000.

3. Sales of $2,500,000.

During 1990 the company was involved in the following transactions that affected Allowance for Doubtful Accounts.

(1) Wrote off accounts considered uncollectible totaling $205,000.

(2) Recovered $50,000 that had previously been written off.

Required:

a. Assume that, historically, 5 percent of sales have proven to be uncollectible. Prepare all the entries affecting Allowance for Doubtful Accounts during 1990.

b. Compute the December 31, 1989 balance in Allowance for Doubtful Accounts.

E7–5   *(Accounting for doubtful accounts: the allowance method)*   The following items were extracted from the *unadjusted* trial balance of Stein Glass Company.

Sales	$ 956,000
Accounts receivable	1,025,000
Allowance for doubtful accounts	45,000 (cr.)

The company controller has estimated, from historical data, that 4 percent of sales will be uncollectible. After analyzing individual accounts, the company's accountant wrote off $20,000 of accounts receivable as uncollectible.

Required:

a. Prepare the entry to record bad debt expense.

b. Compute the final balance in the Allowance for Doubtful Accounts account.

c. Assume that Stein Glass prepared an aging schedule of outstanding accounts receivable and estimated that accounts with a dollar value of $60,000 will be uncollectible. Prepare the entry to record the bad debt expense.

E7–6   *(Inferring bad debt write-offs and reconstructing related journal entries)*   The financial records of Jonas Services reveal the following information. The dollar amounts are end-of-year balances.

	1990	1989
Credit sales	$75,300	$59,400
Accounts receivable	9,400	8,000
Allowance for doubtful accounts	830	750
Bad debt recoveries	55	40

Jonas estimates bad debts each year at 3 percent of credit sales.

Required:

a. Compute the actual amount of write-offs during 1990.

b. Prepare journal entries to summarize the activity in Accounts Receivable and the related allowance account during 1990.

c. Assume that Jonas Services prepared an aging schedule to estimate bad debts. If write-offs during 1990 were $2000, compute the bad debt expense recognized on the 1990 income statement.

E7–7   *(Two methods to account for short-term notes receivable)*   Frederickson Financial loaned $7000 to Slayden Brothers on December 1, 1989. The ninety-day note (both principal and interest) was due March 1 of the following year and had a stated annual interest rate of 12 percent.

Required:

a. Prepare the journal entries on Frederickson Financial's books related to this note that were recorded on December 1, when the note was issued, on December 31, when financial statements were prepared, and March 1, when the note was paid in full assuming the following:

(1) The note receivable is recorded at face value, and no discount is recognized.

(2) The note receivable is recorded at face value plus interest, and a discount is recognized.

b. Does Method 1 affect the December 31 financial statements differently from Method 2? Explain your answer in terms of the effects on net income and current assets as well as in terms of general balance sheet and income statement disclosure.

E7–8

(Preadjustment balances in the allowance account and estimates based on the accounts receivable balance)   On December 31, 1990, The Avery Company had a debit balance in Accounts Receivable of $5,545,000 and a preadjustment credit balance in Allowance for Doubtful Accounts of $100,000. The controller of the company analyzed all of the outstanding accounts and decided that the company would probably be unable to collect accounts totaling $195,000. However, the controller was unable to determine exactly which accounts would prove to be uncollectible.

Required:

a. Explain why a company would have a preadjustment balance in Allowance for Doubtful Accounts.

b. What balance should be reported in Allowance for Doubtful Accounts as of December 31, 1990?

c. Prepare any adjusting journal entries necessary as of December 31, 1990.

E7–9

(Preparing the end-of-period entry using an aging estimate)   Champion Sporting Equipment reported a balance in Accounts Receivable of $1 million on December 31, 1990. Using an aging schedule, the company estimated that $50,000 of the total Accounts Receivable balance would prove to be uncollectible.

Required:

a. Assume that prior to adjusting journal entries on December 31, 1990, Allowance for Doubtful Accounts had a credit balance of $10,000. Prepare the adjusting journal entry to record bad debt expense.

b. Assume that prior to adjusting journal entries on December 31, 1990, Allowance for Doubtful Accounts had a debit balance of $5000. Prepare the adjusting journal entry to record bad debt expense.

E7–10

(Preparing an aging schedule and recording bad debt expense)   Potter Stables uses the aging method to estimate its bad debts. Sherman Potter, the company president, has given you the following aging of accounts receivable as of December 31, 1991, along with the historical probabilities that the account balances will not be collected.

Account Age	Balance	Noncollection Probability
Current	$200,000	2%
1-45 days overdue	110,000	5
46-90 days overdue	68,000	8
90 or more days overdue	25,000	15

Required:

a. Assume that Potter Stables has a preadjustment credit balance of $15,000 in Allowance for Doubtful Accounts as of December 31, 1991. Prepare the entry to record bad debt expense for 1991.

b. Assume that Potter Stables has a credit balance of $10,000 in Allowance for Doubtful Accounts as of January 1, 1991. During 1991, the company wrote off $14,000 of open accounts receivable considered to be uncollectible. The company also recovered $3000 of accounts previously written off. Prepare the entry to record bad debt expense for 1991.

PROBLEMS

P7–1 (*Accounting for cash discounts*)   Klinger Dress Company made a sale on account on July 5, 1991, for a gross price of $150,000. The company made another sale on account on July 21, 1991, for a gross price of $80,000. The terms of both sales were 2/15, n/30. The company received payment for the first sale on August 30, 1991, and for the second sale on July 31, 1991. Klinger Dress Company makes monthly adjusting journal entries.

Required:

a. Assume Klinger Dress Company uses the net method to account for cash discounts. Prepare journal entries for each transaction.
b. Assume Klinger Dress Company uses the gross method to account for cash discounts. Prepare journal entries for each transaction.

P7–2 (*Cash discounts: gross and net methods*)   Barlow Corporation made two sales on account during the month of May. The first sale was made on May 2 for $10,000, and the second was made on May 10 for $20,000. The terms of each sale were 3/15, n/30. The first sale was settled on May 13, and the second was settled on June 18. The company prepares monthly adjusting entries.

Required:

a. Assume that Barlow Corporation uses the net method to account for sales discounts. Prepare all the necessary journal entries associated with these transactions.
b. Assume that Barlow Corporation uses the gross method to account for sales discounts. Prepare all the necessary journal entries associated with these transactions.
c. Assume that Barlow Corporation uses the net method to account for sales discounts, and assume that the company received $14,550 on May 20 and the remainder on June 27 in settlement of the second sale on account. Prepare all the necessary journal entries associated with the second sale.
d. Assume that Barlow Corporation uses the gross method to account for sales discounts, and assume that the company received $14,550 on May 20 and the remainder on June 27 in settlement of the second sale on account. Prepare all the necessary journal entries associated with the second sale.

P7–3 (*Cash discounts: gross method, net method, and missing discounts*)   During the month of March, QNI Corporation made the following credit sales and had the following related collections. QNI prepares financial statements for the first quarter of operations at the end of March.

(1) March 3   Sold goods to AAA company for a gross price of $1200. The terms of the sale were 2/10, n/30.
(2) March 8   Sold goods to BBB company for a gross price of $800. The terms of the sale were 2/10, n/30.
(3) March 11   Received full payment from AAA.
(4) March 28   Received full payment from BBB.

(5) March 29   Sold goods to CCC Company for a gross price of $1600. The terms of sale were 2/10, n/30.

Required:

a. Prepare the journal entries to record these transactions under the gross method.

b. Prepare the journal entries to record these transactions under the net method.

c. Describe the differential effects of the two methods on the income statement prepared at the end of the first quarter.

d. Note that BBB missed the discount period by ten days. Compute the annual interest rate BBB paid for the use of the $800 for that ten-day period. Assuming that BBB can borrow money from the bank at 14 percent, what should BBB have done differently?

P7-4   *(Underestimating bad debts over time)*   Financial information for Stable Toddlers, Inc. follows.

	1990	1989	1988
Credit sales	$205,000	$200,000	$180,000
Actual bad debt write-offs	10,000	9,000	7,000

The company estimates bad debts for financial reporting purposes at 3 percent of credit sales. The balance in Allowance for Doubtful Accounts as of January 1, 1988, was $10,000.

Required:

a. Provide the journal entries related to Allowance for Doubtful Accounts for 1988, 1989, and 1990.

b. Compute the balance in Allowance for Doubtful Accounts as of December 31, 1990.

c. If you were auditing Stable Toddlers, what advice would you give them with respect to their bad debt estimate? How did you come to your conclusion?

d. Compute the bad debt expenses that would have been recognized for 1988, 1989, and 1990 if the company used the direct write-off method. Compare these amounts to those determined under the allowance method.

P7-5   *(Accounting for uncollectibles over two periods)*   Glacier Ice Company uses a percentage-of-net-sales method to account for estimated bad debts. Historically, 3 percent of net sales have proven to be uncollectible. During 1990 and 1991 the company reported the following:

	1990	1991
Gross sales	$1,500,000	$2,000,000
Sales discounts	100,000	125,000
Sales returns	50,000	25,000

Required:

a. Prepare the necessary adjusting entry on December 31, 1990 to record the estimated bad debt expense for 1990.

b. Assume that the January 1, 1990 balance in Allowance for Doubtful Accounts was $65,000 (credit) and that $70,000 in bad debts were written off the books during 1990. What is the December 31, 1990 balance in this account *after adjustments?*

c. Prepare the necessary adjusting entry on December 31, 1991 to record the estimated bad debt expense for 1991.

d. What is the December 31, 1991 balance in Allowance for Doubtful Accounts? Assume that $85,000 in bad debts were written off the books during 1991.

P7-6   *(Ignoring potential bad debts can lead to serious overstatements)*   The following financial information represents Johnson Company's first year of operations, 1990.

Income Statement		Balance Sheet	
Sales	$200,000	Cash	$ 5,000
Cost of goods sold	102,000	Accounts receivable	85,000
Gross profit	98,000	Other assets	40,000
Expenses	65,000	Total assets	$130,000
Net income	$ 33,000		
		Current liabilities	$ 13,000
		Long-term note payable	80,000
		Stockholders' equity	37,000
		Total liabilities and	
		stockholders' equity	$130,000

After reading Johnson's financial statements, you conclude that the company had a very successful first year of operations. However, after further examination you note that the expense figure on the income statement contains no bad debt expense. You also realize that a large percentage of Johnson's sales were to three customers, one of which, Litzenberger Supply, is in very questionable financial health although still in business. Litzenberger owes Johnson $50,000 as of the end of 1990.

Required:

a. Adjust the financial statements of Johnson Company to reflect a more conservative reporting with respect to bad debts. That is, establish a provision for the uncollectibility of Litzenberger's account. Recompute net income. How does this adjustment affect your assessment of Johnson's first year of operations?

b. Why would auditors probably require that Johnson choose the more conservative reporting?

c. Johnson's chief financial officer claims that no bad debt charge should be recorded because Litzenberger is still conducting operations as of the end of 1990. How would you respond to this claim?

P7–7   *(Estimating uncollectibles, financial ratios, and loan agreements)*   Excerpts from the 1990 financial statements of Finley, Ltd., a service company, follow.

Fees earned	$240,000
Accounts receivable	68,000
Allowance for doubtful accounts	3,400
Total current assets	105,000
Total current liabilities	65,000
Net income	15,000
Dividends declared	5,000
Bad debt expense	3,400

Auditors from Price and Company reviewed the financial records of Finley and found that a credit sale (for services rendered) of $10,000, which was included in the Fees earned amount above, should not have been recognized until January 20, 1991. The auditors also noted that a more reasonable estimate of future bad debts would be 10 percent of the Accounts Receivable balance. The auditors have informed Finley's management that the audit opinion will be qualified if Finley does not adjust the financial statements accordingly.

Required:

a. Compute the effect of the auditor's recommended adjustments on the 1990 Fees earned, Accounts Receivable, Allowance for Doubtful Accounts, current ratio, working capital, and net income reported by Finley.

b. Assume that Finley has a loan agreement with a bank requiring it to maintain a current ratio of 1.5 and limiting its annual dividend payment to 50 percent of net income. How might these restrictions have influenced the reporting decisions of Finley's managers?

P7-8   *(Uncollectibles: direct write-off and the allowance method)*   Grace Linen Service began operations on January 28, 1988. The company uses the direct write-off method to account for uncollectible accounts. Over the past five years the company has written off the following items.

(1) July 6, 1988   Wrote off $10,000 as uncollectible from a sale made on March 1, 1988.

(2) Feb. 3, 1989   Wrote off $50,000 as uncollectible from a sale made on October 28, 1988.

(3) Sept. 11, 1989   Wrote off $25,000 as uncollectible from a sale made on December 20, 1988 ($12,000) and a sale made on May 10, 1989 ($13,000).

(4) Mar. 24, 1990   Recovered $5000 that had been written off on February 3, 1989. It is company policy to credit Bad Debt Expense when an account is recovered.

(5) Aug. 8, 1991   Wrote off $75,000 as uncollectible from sales made in 1988 ($20,000), in 1989 ($25,000), and in 1990 ($30,000).

(6) Dec. 2, 1991   Wrote off $5000 as uncollectible from a sale made on April 26, 1991.

(7) Sept. 19, 1992 Wrote off $90,000 as uncollectible from sales in 1988 ($5000), in 1989 ($30,000), in 1990 ($25,000), in 1991 ($20,000), and in 1992 ($10,000).

Additional Information

a. Over the period 1988 to 1992, Grace Linen Service realized the following sales and reported the following ending balances in accounts receivable.

	Sales	Accounts Receivable
1988	$1,000,000	$ 950,000
1989	975,000	900,000
1990	1,025,000	1,200,000
1991	1,032,000	1,175,000
1992	990,000	1,095,000

b. At the beginning of operations, a consultant had informed Grace Linen Service that the company should expect not to collect 8 percent of total sales.

Required:

a. Prepare the entries for these transactions as Grace Linen Service prepared them.

b. Prepare the entries for these transactions, including an estimate of bad debts, that would be required under the allowance method, and compute the ending annual balance in Allowance for Doubtful Accounts.

c. List the bad debt expense and the balance sheet value of Accounts Receivable for each year over the five-year period for both the direct write-off method and the allowance method. Use the following format.

	1988	1989	1990	1991	1992
Direct write-off					
Bad debt expense					
Accounts receivable value					
Allowance					
Bad debt expense					
Accounts receivable value					

Compute the total bad debt expense over the five-year period under the two methods. Why is the allowance method preferred to the direct write-off method?

P7-9   *(Cash discounts, uncollectibles, and notes receivable)* Hamilton Enterprises entered into the following transactions during 1990.

(1)	Jan. 4	Sold merchandise valued at $525,000 in exchange for a six-month note with a stated annual interest rate of 8 percent. No discount was recognized on the note.
(2)	Feb. 15	Sold merchandise on account for $665,000.
(3)	March 5	Collected $235,000 on an open receivable. The sale had been made on December 29, 1989.
(4)	March 29	Bill Hinkley informed the company that he was moving to Brazil and would not be paying $98,000 owed to the company.
(5)	April 15	Sold merchandise on account for $500,000.
(6)	April 23	Collected $485,000 from the sale made on April 15, 1990.
(7)	May 30	One of the company's customers, The Hardware Hutch, had declared bankruptcy on October 22, 1989, at which time Hamilton Enterprises wrote off the entire balance of $43,000 as uncollectible. The company has now received a check from the customer for $15,000. Hamilton is doubtful that the remaining $28,000 will ever be collected.
(8)	June 4	Collected the principal and interest on the note received on January 4, 1990.
(9)	June 27	Sold merchandise on account for $750,000.
(10)	July 1	Collected $788,000 on open accounts. $400,000 was from the sales made on February 15, and the remaining amount was from the sale made on June 27.
(11)	August 31	Wrote off accounts totaling $146,000 deemed as uncollectable.
(12)	Sept. 18	Collected $200,000 on an open account. The sale had been made on February 15.
(13)	Oct. 30	Sold merchandise on account for $200,000.
(14)	Nov. 12	Collected $20,000 from The Hardware Hutch. Hamilton now believes that the remaining balance will be collected sometime in the future (see transaction (7) on May 30).
(15)	Dec. 20	Sold merchandise on account for $150,000.

Additional Information

a. The company offers a cash discount on all credit sales. The terms are 3/15, n/45. The company uses the gross method to account for cash discounts.

b. The January 1, 1990 balance in Allowance for Doubtful Accounts was a credit of $500,000, and the Accounts Receivable balance was a debit of $3,750,000.

c. Historically, 3 percent of credit sales have proven to be uncollectible. (*Hint:* Credit sales only include sales on account, not sales made in exchange for notes.)

d. Cash sales for the year totaled $5,794,000

e. Hamilton Hardware does not make monthly adjusting entries.

Required:

a. Prepare journal entries for each transaction.

b. Prepare the entry to record bad debt expense for 1990.

c. Compute the ending balance in both Accounts Receivable and Allowance for Doubtful Accounts.

P7–10

(Accounting for short-term notes receivable)   Northwest Plumbing Supply entered into the following transactions involving short-term notes receivable during 1990.

(1) Jan. 29   Sold merchandise with a sales value of $45,000 in exchange for a three-month note with a stated annual rate of 10 percent.

(2) Mar. 1   Loaned $10,000 to one of the company's employees. The note called for a 12 percent annual interest rate and was to be paid in full at the end of the year.

(3) April 29   Note issued on Jan. 29 is repaid.

(4) May 31   Accepted a five-month note with a stated annual rate of 9 percent in payment of a $15,000 open account receivable.

(5) July 14   Sold merchandise for $25,000. Five thousand dollars was collected in cash, and the remainder was accepted in the form of a six-month note with a stated annual rate of 12 percent.

(6) Oct. 31   Note issued on May 31 is repaid.

(7) Dec. 1   Sold merchandise for $30,000 in exchange for a forty-five-day note with a stated annual rate of 8 percent.

Required:

a. Assuming that the notes are recorded at face value and no discount is recognized, prepare journal entries that would cover the following:
   (1) The issuance of the notes
   (2) The principal and interest payments
   (3) The adjusting entries on December 31

b. Assume that the notes are recorded at face value plus interest and a discount is recognized. Prepare journal entries to cover the same items as in (a).

P7–11

(Preparing an aging schedule and implementing the allowance method)   Burns Medical Supplies uses the aging method to estimate bad debts. The breakdown of accounts receivable as of December 31, 1990 with related estimates of collection probability follow.

Account Age	Balance	Collection Probability
Current	$3,050,000	99%
1–30 days past due	1,500,000	97
31–100 days past due	650,000	90
101–200 days past due	250,000	85
Over 200 days past due	100,000	55

Required:

a. Assume that Burns Medical Supplies has a credit balance of $200,000 in Allowance for Doubtful Accounts prior to adjusting as of December 31, 1990. Prepare the entry to record bad debt expense for 1990.

b. Assume that Burns Medical Supplies has a credit balance of $200,000 in Allowance for Doubtful Accounts as of January 1, 1990. During 1990, the company deemed $450,000 of open accounts receivable to be uncollectible and wrote them off. The company also recovered $300,000 of accounts previously written off. Prepare the entry to record bad debt expense for 1990.

P7–12

(Bad debt estimates based on the Accounts Receivable balance)   Bremen Brewery estimates bad debts as a percentage of credit sales. Historically, 4 percent of credit sales have proven to be uncollectible. At the beginning of 1990 the company reported a credit balance in Allowance for Doubtful Accounts of $514,000. Credit sales during 1990 totaled $12,875,000. Actual bad debt write-offs during the year totaled $650,000.

To check the adequacy of the allowance balance, on December 31 (1990) Don Harris, the company controller, prepared an aging of the accounts receivable subsidiary ledger. The breakdown of the accounts with related estimates of collection probability follows.

Age Category	Account Balance	Collection Probability
Current	$3,870,000	98.75%
1–30 days past due	2,578,000	97.25
31–90 days past due	1,364,000	91.50
91–150 days past due	743,000	86.00
Over 150 days past due	549,000	50.00

Required:

a. Assume that Bremen Brewery uses a percentage of credit sales to estimate bad debts for external reporting purposes. Prepare the entry to record bad debt expense for 1990.

b. Based on the aging analysis, what amount of bad debts should Bremen expect? If Bremen uses the aging analysis to estimate bad debts for financial reporting purposes, prepare the entry to record bad debt expense for 1990.

c. Assume that each of the collection probabilities listed in the chart above was 1 percent less (for example, the accounts classified as current would now have a collection probability of 97.75). What amount of bad debts should Bremen expect?

d. Why should companies that use a percentage of credit sales to estimate bad debts periodically examine the accuracy of their estimates with an aging of accounts receivable?

e. Assume that the aging analysis used in (b) was conducted with the expectation that no additional efforts would be made to collect past-due accounts. Assume also that costly additional collection efforts could decrease the bad debt losses. How could the aging analysis help to determine how much cost to incur in an effort to collect past-due accounts?

P7–13   *(Accounting for uncollectibles and the aging estimate)*   In an attempt to include all relevant information for decision-making purposes, Hollow Tubing Company estimates bad debts using the aging method. However, for external reporting purposes, the company estimates bad debts as a percentage of credit sales. Hollow Tubing prepares monthly adjusting journal entries. From trends over the past five years, the company controller has estimated that 2 percent of monthly credit sales will prove to be uncollectible. Following are the monthly credit sales and bad debt write-offs for Hollow Tubing Company for 1990.

Month	Cash Collections	Credit Sales	Write-offs
January	$ 1,200,000	$ 1,000,000	
February	1,050,000	925,000	
March	910,000	1,010,000	
April	1,000,000	975,000	87,000
May	875,000	950,000	
June	1,080,000	1,200,000	
July	950,000	1,150,000	52,000
August	1,011,000	1,075,000	
September	1,105,000	1,025,000	
October	980,000	980,000	
November	1,100,000	900,000	
December	865,000	750,000	100,000
Total	$12,126,000	$11,940,000	$239,000

On December 31, 1990, the controller prepared the following aging of accounts receivable.

Account Classification	Balance	Percent Uncollectible
Current	$ 700,000	2.0%
1–30 days past due	1,200,000	5.5
31–75 days past due	550,000	10.0
Over 75 days past due	800,000	25.0

The Allowance for Doubtful Accounts balance on Jan. 1, 1990, was a credit of $70,000.

Required:

a. Prepare the adjusting journal entry necessary on December 31, 1990, so that the statements will be in accordance with the company's external reporting policies. Remember that the company prepares monthly adjusting journal entries.

b. Compute the balance in Allowance for Doubtful Accounts after the entry in a. has been recorded.

c. Compute the balance in Accounts Receivable as of January 1, 1990.

d. Compute the estimated bad debts using the aging method. Prepare the necessary entry. Remember that the company prepares monthly adjusting journal entries.

e. Why would a company want to estimate bad debts using two different methods? Which of the two methods is more costly and time-consuming to implement? Which provides more useful information?

CASES

C7–1

(Outstanding accounts receivable: ages, collection rates, and adjusting journal entries) In *Business Week*, TRW Inc.'s Information Services Division reported the results of a survey of 8000 companies.* It found that 78.5 percent of their fourth-quarter 1987 accounts receivable were current (i.e., within a thirty-day grace period). Of all outstanding receivables, 16.5 percent were between thirty and sixty days old, and 5 percent were over sixty days old.

*Kathleen Madigan, "Economic Trends," *Business Week,* 11 April 1988, p. 27.

Required:

a. In order to provide responses to this survey, what schedule must the participating companies have prepared? Describe this schedule.

b. As of January 31, 1988, Toys "Я" Us reported $63,534,000 of outstanding accounts receivable. Assume that the ages of the outstanding accounts of Toys "Я" Us are typical of the percentages found by TRW and that the probability of collection for these accounts is as follows.

Ages of Account	Probability
Current	99%
30–60 days	96
Over 60 days	80

Compute the bad debt estimate for Toys "Я" Us.

c. Provide the adjusting journal entry recorded in the books of Toys "Я" Us, assuming that the preadjustment balance in Allowance for Doubtful Accounts was a debit of $840,000.

C7-2   *(Cash discounts, from the company's and the customer's standpoint)*   During the month of July, 1988, major U.S. retailers, such as Sears and J. C. Penney, reported only slight gains in sales. An analyst for this industry said that "consumers are stretched with debt," indicating that they were unwilling to increase their current levels of debt. In an effort to increase sales, some of the retailers are considering offering cash discounts for customers who pay cash immediately or within a very short period of time (e.g., ten days).

Required:

a. Most large retail companies currently assess no finance charge for outstanding accounts of less than thirty days. Suppose that a company, such as Sears, changed its credit policy and began granting cash discounts with terms of 2/10, n/30. Would such a policy necessarily increase sales volume? Why or why not? What would happen, for example, if the cash discount rate were set too high?

b. Assume that you purchased merchandise from Sears on account with a gross price of $500 under terms of 2/10, n/30. If you paid your account in ten days, how much would you have to pay? If you paid your account in twenty days, how much would you pay, and at what annual rate of interest would you be paying? If you paid your account in thirty days, how much would you pay, and at what annual rate of interest would you be paying?

C7-3   *(Bad debt rates over time)*   The following information was computed from the 1987 financial report of the merchandising division of Sears, Roebuck and Co. (dollars in millions).

	1987	1986	1985
Merchandise sales	$25,875	$24,811	$24,274
Credit sales as a percentage of total	59%	61%	62%
Bad debt expense	$ 291	$ 350	$ 224
Bad debt write-offs	$ 256	$ 243	$ 186

Required:

a. Assume that Sears uses a percentage of credit sales to estimate bad debts. Compute the percentages experienced by Sears in 1985, 1986, and 1987.

b. Assume that the merchandise division of Sears began 1985 with a $200 credit balance in Allowance for Doubtful Accounts. Prepare the journal entries that affected the allowance account for 1985, 1986, and 1987, and compute the balance as of December 31, 1987.

c. Have the rates used by Sears to estimate bad debts been consistently over or under its bad debt experience? How can you tell? Would you expect Sears's auditor to encourage the company to lower its bad debt estimate? Why or why not?

C7-4   *(Uncertain loans, accounting procedures, and audit qualifications)*   The Farm Credit System is the nation's largest lender to farmers. In the fourth quarter of 1987 it posted a profit of $179 million, avoiding a loss by using an unusual accounting technique. As reported in *The Wall Street Journal*, "the System would have posted a fourth-quarter loss of about $43 million had it not taken $222 million out of its reserve for loan losses [Allowance for Doubtful Accounts] . . . . The System began that practice in the 1987 second quarter, as federal subsidy payments buoyed the farm economy and problem loans declined. The practice is highly unusual, though not a violation of generally accepted accounting principles."[*]

---

[*]Jeff Bailey, "Farm credit posts 4th-Quarter profit, reflecting unusual accounting method," *The Wall Street Journal*, 19 February 1988, p. 40.

Required:

a. Prepare the journal entry recorded by the Farm Credit System described above. Explain why such an entry was described as "highly unusual".

b. Explain how subsidy payments from the U.S. government to farmers would allow the Farm Credit System to justify such as accounting practice.

c. The article goes on to report that "The System's auditor, Price Waterhouse, . . . qualified its opinion of the System's financial statements. . . .The qualification for the 1987 books is based on uncertainties of parts of the 1987 federal bailout being implemented." Why would Price Waterhouse qualify the System's financial statements due to uncertainties over the federal subsidy payments?

C7-5

(Nonperforming loans, write-offs, and outstanding debt)   This chapter notes that First Republic Bank, the largest banking concern in Texas, experienced serious financial problems in 1988 because many of its outstanding loans were not performing. It also points out that writing off these loans had caused certain financial ratios to drop, which could trigger the calling of approximately $270 million of the company's long-term debt. These problems influenced the bank's auditor to question whether the bank could continue in its present form.

Required:

a. What does it mean to *call a debt,* and why would this present a problem for First Republic Bank?

b. Explain how loan write-offs could cause financial ratios to drop and trigger the calling of debt.

c. Would the bank's auditors be likely to issue an unqualified opinion on First Republic Bank? Why or why not?

Merchandise Inventory

Learning Objectives

1 Define inventory, and describe how the methods used to account for it affect the financial statements.

2 Identify the four main issues that must be addressed when accounting for inventory.

3 Describe the general rules for including items in inventory and attaching costs to these items.

4 Explain the differences between the perpetual and periodic methods and the tradeoffs involved in choosing between them.

5 Identify the three cost flow assumptions and the measurement and economic trade-offs that must be considered when choosing from among them.

6 Explain how to apply the lower-of-cost-or-market rule to ending inventories.

≣ Inventory refers to items held for sale in the ordinary course of business. It is very important to retail and manufacturing enterprises, whose performance depends significantly on their sales. The demand for a company's products is often the most important determinant of its success. Indeed, the 1987 financial report of Eastman Kodak Company opened with the following comments from the company's chief executive officer. "Worldwide sales rose 15 percent to $13.3 billion, an all-time high. While the company's flagship products, Kodacolor films and Ektacolor papers led the advance, all five business groups contributed. Unit volume was the driving force."

Stockholders, creditors, managers, and auditors are all justifiably interested in the amount, condition, and marketability of a company's inventory. Stockholders are interested in future sales, profits, and dividends, all of which are related to the demand for inventory, and in the efficiency with which managers acquire, carry, and sell inventory. Creditors are interested in the ability of inventory sales to produce cash that can be used to meet interest and principal payments. Creditors may also view inventory as potential collateral or security for loans. Management must ensure that inventories are acquired (or manufactured) and carried at reasonable costs. Enough inventory must be carried and available to meet constantly-changing consumer demands, yet carrying too much inventory can be very costly.[1] Auditors must ensure that the inventory dollar amount disclosed in the financial statements is determined using generally accepted accounting principles and reflects the value of the inventories actually owned. The value and marketability of a company's inventory can also provide an indication of its ability to continue as a going concern.

INVENTORY ACCOUNTING AND THE FINANCIAL STATEMENTS

The methods used to account for inventories can have a significant effect on the financial statements for two basic reasons. First, inventory is often quite large compared to the other assets on the balance sheet, especially for retail and manufacturing operations. Second, the methods used to account for inventory directly affect (1) cost of goods sold, which in turn affects net income, and (2) the dollar amount at which inventory is carried on the balance sheet, which in turn affects current assets, working capital, the current ratio, and other important financial ratios.

The Relative Size of Inventories

While the relative size of inventories varies across companies in different industries, for many companies inventory is both the largest current asset and the largest of all assets on the balance sheet. Table 8−1 shows reported inventory amounts as a percentage of total assets and current assets for a selected group of

---

1. In recent years U.S. manufacturers have become especially concerned with the levels of inventory they maintain. This concern is particularly important in the automobile industry, where U.S. automakers, like General Motors, Ford, and Chrysler compete with Japanese companies, like Honda, Toyota, and Mitsubishi, who are able to save substantial costs by carrying lower levels of inventory.

Table 8–1   Inventory as a percentage of total assets and current assets (industry averages)

Industry (number of firms)	Inventory/Total Assets	Inventory/Current Assets
Financial Institutions		
Accident and health insurance (199)	0%	0%
Life insurance (937)	1	1
Services		
Accounting and auditing services (1335)	2	3
Hotels (1912)	2	14
Manufacturing		
Aircraft manufacturing (35)	28	45
Household appliance manufacturing (14)	38	49
Retailers		
Grocery stores (2295)	35	60
Department stores (1032)	45	58
Hardware (2239)	52	68
Sporting goods (2236)	58	74
New and used cars (2120)	64	74

Source: Compiled from data published in *Industry Norms and Key Business Ratios* (Dun & Bradstreet, Inc., 1987).

industry classifications. The same information for a selected group of major U.S. companies is provided in Table 8–2. Note that financial institutions and services rely very little on inventories, but they are very important to manufacturers and retailers.

The Effects of Inventory Accounting on Cost of Goods Sold and the Inventory Account

When inventory is acquired, either through purchase or manufacture, the costs of acquiring it are placed in the Inventory account. Consistent with the matching principle, in the period when the inventories are sold these costs are transferred to

Table 8–2   Inventory as a percentage of total assets and current assets (selected companies)

Company (description)	Inventory/Total Assets	Inventory/Current Assets
H & R Block (tax preparation service)	0%	0%
Wendy's International (restaurant)	3	20
Marriott Corporation (hotels)	3	20
Scott Paper Company (forest products)	10	37
Merck (pharmaceuticals)	12	22
Sherwin Williams Company (paint products)	25	37
Sundstrand (electronic systems)	30	60
Toys "R" Us (specialty retail chain)	38	87
McDonnell Douglas Corporation (aerospace)	44	70

Source: 1987 annual reports.

Figure 8-1   Allocating the cost of inventory to cost of goods sold and ending inventory

General Journal

Inventory	2,000	
Accounts Payable		2,000
To record the purchase of inventory		
on account.		
Cost of Goods Sold	1,200	
Inventory		1,200
To record the sale of inventory.		

Allocation of Inventory Cost

Ending inventory ($2,000 − $1,200)	$ 800	
Cost of goods sold	1,200	
Total inventory acquisition cost		$2,000

the Cost of Goods Sold account, which appears on the income statement. Inventory costs that have not been transferred to cost of goods sold, remain in the Inventory account and appear on the balance sheet.

To illustrate, assume that in its first year of operations Lawrence Enterprises purchased inventory on account for $2000. During the year a portion of this inventory, with a cost of $1200, was sold. As shown in Figure 8-1, $800 of the inventory cost would appear in the Inventory account on the year-end balance sheet, and $1200 would appear in Cost of Goods Sold.

The entries and calculation in Figure 8-1 show that the costs of acquiring inventory are either allocated to Cost of Goods Sold or the Inventory account. The portion of the costs allocated to Cost of Goods Sold ($1200) appears on the income statement and reduces net income, and the portion allocated to inventory ($800) appears on the balance sheet and increases current assets, working capital, and the current ratio.

In this example it is very clear how the inventory cost should be allocated between Cost of Goods Sold and the Inventory account. In practice, however, this allocation is often difficult to determine. As demonstrated later in the chapter, there are a number of acceptable methods of making such an allocation and the choice of method can have significant effects on the financial statements.

To illustrate, consider the partial income statement and balance sheet of Lauren, Inc. which appear under "Given Information" in Figure 8-2. Assume that during the year Lauren purchased inventories at a cost of $20,000 and can choose between two methods of allocating this cost between the Cost of Goods Sold and Inventory accounts. Method 1 allocates $15,000 to Cost of Goods Sold and $5000 to Inventory; Method 2 allocates $5000 to Cost of Goods Sold and $15,000 to Inventory.

The financial statements that result from the two methods are shown in Figure 8-2. Note that Method 2 shows higher net income and higher current assets by $10,000, the difference between the dollar amounts allocated to Cost of Goods Sold and Inventory by the two methods. By allocating less of the $20,000 inventory cost to Cost of Goods sold and more to inventory, Method 2 enables Lauren to report

Figure 8–2 The financial statement effects of alternative inventory methods: Lauren, Inc.

Given Information

Excerpt from Income Statement		Excerpt from Balance Sheet	
Sales	$50,000	Current assets[b]	$20,000
Expenses[a]	40,000	Current liabilities	25,000

[a]Excluding cost of goods sold
[b]Excluding inventory

Inventory Allocation Method 1

Inventory acquisition costs

Cost of Goods Sold $15,000 ← 20,000 → $5,000 Inventory

Excerpt from Income Statement		Excerpt from Balance Sheet	
Sales	$50,000	Current assets	$25,000
Cost of goods sold and expenses	55,000	Current liabilities	25,000
Net loss income (loss)	$ (5,000)	Working capital	0
		Current ratio	1.0

Inventory Allocation Method 2

Inventory acquisition costs

Cost of Goods Sold $5,000 ← $20,000 → $15,000 Inventory

Excerpt from Income Statement		Excerpt from Balance Sheet	
Sales	50,000	Current assets	$35,000
Cost of goods sold and expenses	45,000	Current liabilities	25,000
Net income	$ 5,000	Working capital	$10,000
		Current ratio	1.4

higher levels of net income, current assets, working capital, and the current ratio. It is important to realize that the method of choice has no bearing on the actual amount of inventory held or sold by the company. It only affects the dollar values of inventory and cost of goods sold reported on the financial statements.

In practice, the method used to account for inventory can have significant effects on the financial statements. In 1987, for example, General Electric Company (GE) changed its method of accounting for inventory, choosing to allocate a greater portion of costs to the Inventory account. This change, which was approved by the company's auditors, increased GE's net income and working capital position by $281 million. In terms of the preceding examples, by allocating $281 million additional costs to inventory on the balance sheet, GE matched $281 million fewer costs against revenues on the income statement.

Fabricating inventories and manipulating the allocation of inventory costs between the Inventory and Cost of Goods Sold accounts is a technique used by some unethical managers to fraudulently inflate the value of a company's inventory and net income. In a case reported recently in *The Wall Street Journal*, Eddie Antar, the founder of Crazy Eddie, Inc., a consumer-electronics retailer, was accused of "falsifying inventory and profit reports [by] inflating the March 1987 inventory balance by $10 million . . . and, among other things, improperly includ-

Figure 8–3   Accounting for inventory: Four important issues

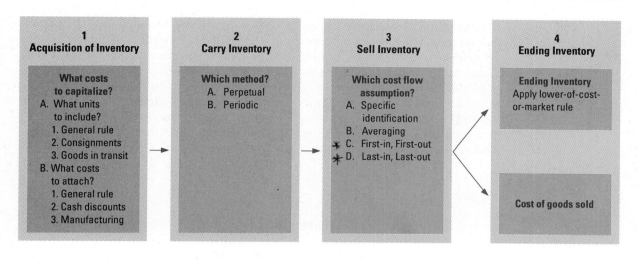

ing $4 million in merchandise that was being returned to suppliers."[2] In effect, this scheme boosted profits and inventory values by allocating too much cost to the Inventory account and too little to Cost of Goods Sold. The shareholders of Crazy Eddie, Inc., whose shares dropped in value from $21.63 per share in 1986 to $1.31 in mid-1988, brought a multimillion-dollar class-action suit against both Mr. Antar and the company's original auditor, who has since been fired by the company's new management.

ACCOUNTING FOR INVENTORY: FOUR IMPORTANT ISSUES

Figure 8–3 summarizes four important issues that must be addressed when accounting for inventory. At the top of the figure, the life cycle of inventory is divided into four segments. Inventory is (1) acquired, through purchase or manufacture, and then (2) carried on the company's balance sheet. It is then either (3) sold, or it remains on the balance sheet as (4) ending inventory. At each of these four points an important issue in financial accounting must be addressed.

Acquiring Inventory: What Costs to Capitalize?

When inventory is acquired, its cost is capitalized and placed in the Inventory account on the balance sheet. Determining this capitalized cost consists of two separate decisions: (1) what units to include in inventory and (2) what costs to attach to each unit. A general rule guides each decision, but neither is always straightforward. Each depends upon a number of considerations, including legal statutes, the method of accounting for inventory purchases, and the nature of the company.

---

2. Jeffrey A. Tannenbaum, *Filings by Crazy Eddie Suggest Founder Led Scheme to Inflate Company's Value, The Wall Street Journal,* 31 May 1988, p. 32.

Carrying Inventory: Which Method?

Once the capitalized inventory cost has been determined, a method of carrying the inventory on the books must be chosen. There are two methods: the perpetual method and the periodic method. The **perpetual method** maintains an up-to-date (perpetual) record of inventory, recording inventory inflows at each purchase and inventory outflows at each sale. The **periodic method** records each purchase as it occurs but does not record an inventory outflow when goods are sold. Instead, at the end of the accounting period (periodically) an inventory count is made and a journal entry is recorded to bring the inventory to the appropriate balance. In general, the perpetual method requires more bookkeeping procedures but provides more timely and useful information.

Selling Inventory: Which Cost Flow Assumption?

As indicated earlier in the chapter, the most important and difficult question of inventory accounting often involves how to allocate the capitalized inventory cost between cost of goods sold and ending inventory. In those relatively unusual cases when the exact cost of sold inventory is known, this amount can be allocated to cost of goods sold. Such a method is called the **specific identification** procedure. In most cases, however, inventory sales are so frequent, and the inventory items are so extensive and diverse that the exact cost of sold inventory is not known. When this occurs, an assumption about how inventory costs flow through the company must be made.

There are three basic assumptions: (1) the averaging assumption, the (2) first-in, first-out (FIFO) assumption, and the (3) last-in, first-out (LIFO) assumption. The **averaging assumption** simply computes an average cost for each inventory item and multiplies the number of items sold times this average to arrive at cost of goods sold. **First-in, first-out (FIFO)** assumes that items are sold in the order in which they are acquired. Relatively old inventory costs, therefore, are allocated to cost of goods sold, leaving the costs of the most recent inventory acquisitions in inventory. **Last in, first out (LIFO)** invokes the opposite assumption: the costs of the most current inventory acquisitions are allocated to cost of goods sold, while the costs of the first items acquired remain in inventory. The assumption chosen can have significant effects on the financial statements.

Once again, keep in mind that the assumption chosen has no bearing on the actual inventory sold and held by a company. It only determines the costs allocated to the Cost of Goods Sold and Inventory accounts.

Ending Inventory: Applying the Lower-of-Cost-or-Market Rule

After the capitalized inventory cost has been allocated between the Cost of Goods Sold and Inventory accounts, the dollar amount in the inventory account is at cost. In applying the lower-of-cost-or-market rule, this amount must be compared to the market value of the inventory. If the cost is less than the market value, the Inventory account remains at cost. If the cost is greater than the market value, the inventory must be *written down* to market value with an adjusting journal entry. This procedure can be troublesome because the market value of inventory is often difficult to determine.

ACQUIRING INVENTORY: WHAT COSTS TO CAPITALIZE?

Inventory costs are capitalized because inventories are assets that provide future economic benefits. When inventories are sold, these benefits are realized, and according to the matching principle, the capitalized cost should at this time be matched against the revenue recognized from the sale. Determining the amount of capitalized cost involves two steps: the number of items or units that belong in inventory must first be determined, and then costs must be attached to each item.

What Items or Units to Include?

Decisions as to what items or units to include in inventory are governed by a general rule. However, the general rule is not always simple to apply.

General Rule

Items should be included in a company's inventory if they are being held for sale and the company has complete and unrestricted ownership of them. Such ownership indicates that (1) the company bears the complete loss if the inventory is lost, stolen, or destroyed and (2) the company owns all rights to the benefits produced by the items.

In most cases ownership is accompanied by possession: companies that own inventory are usually in possession of it. Under these circumstances, determining the number of units that belong in inventory is straightforward: the number of inventory units on the company's premises can simply be counted. In some cases, however, ownership is not accompanied by possession and it becomes somewhat more difficult to find and determine the appropriate number of inventory units. Consignments and goods in transit are two common examples.

Consignments

In a **consignment,** a *consignor* (the owner) transfers inventory to a *consignee* (receiver), who takes physical possesssion and places the inventory up for sale. When it is sold, the consignee collects the sales proceeds, keeps a percentage of the proceeds for the service, and transfers the remainder to the consignor.

When accounting for consignments, it is important to realize that ownership, not physical possession, determines the balance sheet upon which consigned inventory is disclosed. Since consigned inventory is owned by the consignor, it belongs on the consignor's balance sheet, even though it is physically located on the consignee's premises. When preparing and auditing financial statements, managers and auditors must be careful to treat consigned inventory in the appropriate manner: including it on the wrong balance sheet, would misstate the inventory balance, current assets, cost of goods sold, gross profit, and net income.

Goods in Transit

When inventory is sold, the seller records a sale, and the buyer records a purchase. Theoretically, both parties should record the transaction at exactly the same moment: the point in time when the ownership of the inventory transfers from the seller to the buyer. For practical purposes, however, most sales are recorded when goods are shipped, and most purchases are recorded when goods are received. Since goods are often in transit between the seller and the buyer for as long as several days, sellers and buyers often record the same transaction at

Figure 8–4 Accounting for goods in transit

Shipping Terms	Owner in Transit	Journal Entries
FOB shipping point	Buyer	Buyer (debit Inventory, credit Accounts Payable or Cash)* Seller (debit Accounts Receivable or Cash, credit Sales) (debit Cost of Goods Sold, credit Inventory)*
FOB destination	Seller	Buyer (no entries) Seller (no entries)

*Assumes that buyer and seller both use the perpetual inventory method.

two different points in time. This practice is acceptable except in cases where there are **goods in transit** at the end of an accounting period. For example, suppose that Buyer & Co. (located in Seattle, WA) purchased goods on account from Seller Inc. (located in New York, NY) on December 29, 1989. Seller delivered the goods immediately to XYZ Trucking Co., and on December 31, the balance sheet date for both Buyer and Seller, the goods are in transit.

Accounting for this transaction in an appropriate manner involves determining who owns the goods while they are in transit. The most common way of determining ownership is to examine the freight terms associated with the shipment. These terms normally indicate which party bears the responsibility for shipping the goods and thereby owns them while they are in transit. Freight terms are usually expressed in one of two ways: FOB shipping point or FOB destination.

FOB (free on board) shipping point indicates that the seller is responsible for the goods only to the point from which they are shipped. In the example, if the goods were shipped FOB shipping point, Seller, Inc. would be responsible to deliver the goods to XYZ Trucking. From that point to Seattle, Buyer would be considered the owner of the goods, and their value would belong on Buyer's December 31 balance sheet. Both an inventory purchase on Buyer's books and a sale on Seller's books should be recorded.

FOB (free on board) destination indicates that the seller is responsible for the goods all the way to their destination. If the goods in the example were shipped FOB destination, Seller, Inc. would be considered the owner of the goods until they reached Seattle. In this case the goods would belong in Seller's inventory, and neither a purchase nor a sale would be recognized as of December 31. Figure 8–4 summarizes the rules of accounting for goods in transit as of the end of an accounting period.

Transactions near the end of an accounting period are often difficult both to account for correctly and to audit. Managers and auditors must examine freight invoices and other related documents to ensure that sales and purchases are placed in the proper accounting periods and that, as of the balance sheet date, the number of inventory units on a company's balance sheet accurately reflects the inventory units actually owned.

What Costs to Attach?

Once the number of items to be included in inventory has been determined, costs must be attached to these items to produce the total capitalized inventory cost. The general rule that guides this process, and how it applies to inventory purchases and manufacturing operations are discussed in the following sections.

General Rule

All costs associated with the manufacture, acquisition, storage or preparation of inventory items should be capitalized and included in the Inventory account. Included are the costs required to bring inventory items to saleable condition, such as the costs of purchasing, shipping in (called **freight in** or **transportation-in**), manufacturing, and packaging. This rule is not difficult to apply in most cases, but two relatively common areas require further discussion. They are (1) accounting for cash discounts on inventory purchases and (2) determining the costs of manufacturing inventories.

Accounting for Cash Discounts: Gross Method and Net Method

Chapter 7 discusses accounting for cash discounts from the seller's point of view. There we commented that two methods are used to account for cash discounts: the gross method and the net method. The *gross method* establishes a credit sale and the corresponding account receivable at the gross price and recognizes a discount if payment is received within the discount period. The *net method* establishes credit sales and receivables at the net price (gross price − cash discount) and recognizes interest revenue if payment is received after the discount period. The net method reflects the economics of the transaction more accurately than the gross method, but it is more difficult to implement because it requires an adjusting journal entry at the end of the accounting period. Because the difference in the effects on the financial statements of the two methods is often immaterial, the gross method is normally acceptable and is more common in practice.

The issues involved in accounting for cash discounts in this chapter are exactly the same, except that now we discuss them from the buyer's point of view. Figure 8−5 illustrates the journal entries involved in accounting for cash discounts on inventory purchases.[3]

Because we have already discussed cash discounts in the context of credit sales and accounts receivable, we provide only a few comments here. Note first that if the $20 discount is received under the gross method (Case 1), the carrying value of the inventory is reduced by $20. Perhaps more important, however, is the Purchase Discounts Lost account, which is recognized under the net method if payment is made after the discount period. If material, the dollar amount in this account is treated as a separate expense on the income statement, much like interest expense. Recall from Chapter 7 that missing cash discounts can be very costly, and failing to take advantage of these discounts can indicate problems in a company's cash position or cash management policies. The dollar amount in the "Purchase Discounts Lost" account can indicate the extent of such a problem.

Determining the Costs of Manufacturing Inventories

Retail companies, like Sears, Wall-Mart Stores, K mart, May Department Stores, J. C. Penney, and others simply purchase inventories (usually from manufacturers) and sell them for prices that exceed their costs. Retailers primarily provide a distribution service, rarely changing or improving the inventories they sell. As a result, the capitalized inventory cost for a retail operation consists primarily of only two components: (1) the purchase cost and (2) freight-in. If K mart, for ex-

---

3. This example assumes that the purchasing company uses the perpetual method of inventory accounting.

Figure 8–5   Accounting for inventory purchases: gross and net methods

Given Information
Assume that goods with a gross sales price of $1,000 are purchased on December 15, 1990 (terms 2/10, n/30).

	Gross Method			Net Method		
Initial purchase on December 15	Inventory	1000		Inventory	980	
	Accounts Payable		1000	Accounts Payable		980*
	Purchase of inventory.			Purchase of inventory.		
				*($1000 × [1.00 − .02])		
Case 1:						
Assume full payment on December 20 (within 10-day discount period).	Accounts Payable	1000		Accounts Payable	980	
	Inventory		20	Cash		980
	Cash		980	Payment on account.		
	Payment on account.					
Case 2:						
Assume no payments received on December 25 and books are closed on December 31.	(No adjusting journal entry required.)			Purchase Discount Loss	20	
				Accounts Payable		20
				Year-end adjusting journal entry.		
Case 3:						
Assume full payment on January 3 (beyond 10-day discount period).	Accounts Payable	1000		Accounts Payable	1000	
	Cash		1000	Cash		1000
	Payment on account.			Payment on account.		

ample, purchases merchandise for $5000 cash and pays $500 to have the goods shipped to one of its stores, the following journal entry would be recorded.[4]

Inventory	5500	
Cash		5500
To record the purchase of inventory and the freight-in charges.		

The operations of **manufacturing companies,** like IBM, General Electric, General Motors, Procter & Gamble, RJR Nabisco, and Johnson & Johnson, on the other hand, are much more complex. These companies purchase raw materials, and use processes involving labor and other costs to manufacture their inventories. The capitalized inventory cost therefore includes the cost of acquiring the raw materials, the cost of the labor used to convert the raw materials to finished goods, and other costs that support the production process. These other costs are called **overhead** and include such items as indirect materials (e.g., paint, screws, nails, etc.), indirect labor (e.g., salaries of line managers), depreciation of fixed assets, and utility and insurance costs.

The capitalized inventory costs of manufacturing operations include all costs required to bring the inventory to saleable condition. In this general respect ac-

---

4. The journal entry assumes that K mart uses the perpetual method of inventory accounting.

counting for manufacturing operations is no different than accounting for retail operations. However, in manufacturing, virtually any cost that can be linked to the production process should be allocated to the Inventory account. Costs like depreciation, wages and salaries, rent and insurance, therefore, are often capitalized as part of the inventory cost and, accordingly, are matched against revenues when the finished inventory is sold.

This textbook is primarily devoted to the methods of accounting for retail and service companies. The methods used to account for manufacturing operations are covered in managerial and cost accounting courses.

CARRYING INVENTORY: THE PERPETUAL OR PERIODIC METHOD?

Two methods are used to record and carry inventory on the books: the perpetual method, which we have used so far in this chapter, and the periodic method. These methods differ in two ways. First, they use different accounts to record inventory purchases. The perpetual method records purchases directly in the Inventory account, and the periodic method records purchases in a separate Purchases account.[5] Second, the two methods determine Cost of Goods Sold and Inventory in different ways. The perpetual method keeps an up-to-date record in the Inventory account, allocating inventory costs to the Cost of Goods Sold account each time an item is sold. Under the periodic method, inventory purchases are recorded as they occur, but Inventory and Cost of Goods Sold are not determined until the end of the period after an inventory count is taken. The dollar amounts of these accounts are then recorded in the books during the closing process. An example that compares the two methods appears in Figure 8–6.

Under the perpetual method the inventory account is increased (debited) when inventory is purchased and decreased (credited) when inventory is sold. As a result, a *perpetual* balance, which should equal the inventory on hand at all times, is maintained in the Inventory account. As Figure 8–7 shows, the balance of the Inventory account on the balance sheet can simply be taken from the ending balance in the Inventory T-account. Cost of Goods Sold is also kept up-to-date because the cost of sold inventory is transferred from the Inventory account to Cost of Goods Sold at each sale.

Under the periodic method, inventory purchases are recorded in a separate Purchases account and no record is made of inventory outflows when inventory is sold. No inventory costs, therefore, are transferred to Cost of Goods Sold during the period. As a result, the balance in the Inventory T-account at the end of the period is still the dollar amount of the beginning balance, and the balance in Cost of Goods Sold is zero. These amounts must be adjusted to reflect the end-of-period dollar amounts in the two accounts, which is achieved in three steps:

1. An inventory count is taken.
2. Costs are attached to the number of items determined by the count.
3. A journal entry is recorded.

---

5. The periodic method also records freight-in, cash discounts on purchases, and purchase returns in separate accounts, the perpetual method records these items directly in the Inventory account. Exploring such differences, however, introduces complications that are beyond the scope of this textbook.

Figure 8−6   Perpetual and periodic methods

Given Information

Assume that inventory at the beginning of December is $2,500 (125 units at $20 per unit). The following transactions occurred during December.

December 10: Purchased 100 units of inventory on account for $20 per unit.

Perpetual Method			Periodic Method		
Inventory	2,000[a]		Purchases	2,000[a]	
Accounts Payable		2,000	Accounts Payable		2,000
Purchase of inventory.			Purchase of inventory.		

   [a](100 units × $20)

December 20: Sold 50 units of inventory for cash @ $30 per unit.

Perpetual Method			Periodic Method		
Cash	1,500[a]		Cash	1,500[a]	
Sales		1,500	Sales		1,500
Sale of inventory.			Sale of inventory.		
Cost of Goods Sold	1,000[b]		(No entry recorded to reflect		
Inventory		1,000	outflow of inventory.)		
To record outflow of					
inventory.					

   [a](50 units × $30)
   [b](50 units × $20)

December 31: Books are closed and financial statements are prepared.

Perpetual Method	Periodic Method		
(No journal entry required.)	Cost of Goods Sold	1,000[a]	
	Inventory (ending)	3,500[b]	
	Purchases		2,000
	Inventory (beginning)		2,500
	To record cost of goods		
	sold and ending inventory.		

[a]$2,500 + $2,000 − $3,500
[b]An inventory count is required to determine the number of remaining units (175 units × $20)

In the preceding example we assumed that the inventory count determined the following:

- There were 175 units on hand at the end of the period.
- A $20 cost was attached to each of the 175 units (175 units × $20 = $3500).
- The following journal entry was recorded.

Cost of Goods Sold	1000	
Inventory (ending)	3500	
Purchases		2000
Inventory (beginning)		2500
To record cost of goods sold and ending inventory.		

Figure 8–7   Inventory T-account: The perpetual method

	Inventory		
Beginning balance	2,500		
12/10 purchase	2,000		
		1,000	12/20 sale
Ending balance	3,500		

The entry, which is recorded during the closing process, performs four functions: (1) it closes the Purchases account (credit to Purchases, $2000), (2) it removes the beginning inventory amount from the Inventory T-account (credit to Inventory, $2500), (3) it records the ending inventory amount (debit to Inventory, $3500), and (4) it recognizes the cost of goods sold for the period ($1000). Note that the dollar amount recorded in the Cost of Goods Sold account is the amount necessary to bring the debits and credits of the journal entry into balance. Once the balance in the Inventory account has been determined, the cost of goods sold can also be calculated using the following formula:[6]

$$\text{Cost of Goods Sold} = \text{Beginning Inventory} + \text{Purchases} - \text{Ending Inventory}$$
$$\$1000 \quad = \quad \$2500 \quad + \quad \$2000 \quad - \quad \$3500$$

Perpetual and Periodic Methods: Costs and Benefits

The perpetual method requires more bookkeeping procedures than the periodic method because it recognizes the cost of goods sold and the outflow of inventory at each sale. Further, both methods require that an end-of-period inventory count be taken: the perpetual method to check the accuracy of the ending balance in the Inventory ledger account, and the periodic method to determine an ending inventory amount. As a result, many companies, especially those that sell large volumes of widely different inventory items (e.g., a department store), use the periodic method because it is less costly for them to implement. Bear in mind, however, that the periodic method provides less useful information for both a company's management and those who use its financial statements. To illustrate, consider the following example.

Suppose that Retail International is a medium-sized retail store that began in 1989 with 45,000 units of inventory. During 1989 the company purchased 42,000 units, sold 27,000 units, and lost (either broken, misplaced, or stolen) 8000 units. Assuming that the cost of each unit is $1, the actual ending inventory balance for Retail International would be as follows:

$$\text{End. Inv.} = \$52,000 = \text{Beg. Inv.} + \text{Purchases} - \text{Sales (at cost)} - \text{Lost Inv.}$$
$$\$45,000 + \$42,000 - \$27,000 - \$8000$$

---

6. A more complete formula for cost of goods sold, which includes freight-in, purchase discounts, and purchase returns is provided below.

Cost of Goods Sold = beginning inventory + Net purchases* + freight-in − Ending inventory
*Net purchases = Purchases − Purchase discounts − Purchase returns

The Periodic Method

Assume that Retail International uses the periodic inventory method. The company would record the purchases as they were made, but would not recognize the cost of goods sold as the units were sold. At the end of 1989, an inventory count would indicate that there were 52,000 units of inventory on hand. Each unit has a cost of $1, so the following entry would be recorded during the closing process.

Cost of Goods Sold	35,000	
Inventory (ending, $1 × 52,000 units)	52,000	
Purchases		42,000
Inventory (beginning)		45,000
To record ending inventory and the cost of goods sold.		

This entry serves to remove from the books the $42,000 in the Purchases account and the $45,000 of beginning Inventory. The ending inventory balance ($52,000) would be determined by the inventory count. Note that Cost of Goods Sold ($35,000) is not determined independently. Instead, it represents the dollar amount required to bring the journal entry into balance. Consequently, under the periodic method Retail International and those who read the financial statements can only ascertain that $35,000 of inventory is gone. There is no indication on the financial statements that inventory with a cost of $8000 was lost: the loss is "buried" in the Cost of Goods Sold account.

The Perpetual Method

Assume instead that Retail International uses the perpetual method. Figure 8–8 includes the journal entries to record the inventory purchases and sales as well as the Inventory T-account.

Inventory purchases and sales are recorded directly in the Inventory T-account, and the year-end balances in Inventory and Cost of Goods Sold are $60,000 and $27,000, respectively. At year-end, an inventory count reveals that units with a cost of $52,000 are on hand. By comparing the Inventory T-account balance ($60,000) with the actual goods on hand ($52,000), Retail International is now aware that $8000 of inventory is unaccounted for, and management is alerted to a control problem (e.g., shoplifting, inaccurate record keeping, breakage) that should be addressed and corrected. The following journal entry would be recorded at the end of 1989:

Figure 8–8   Perpetual inventory method: Retail International

---

General Journal

Inventory	42,000	
Accounts Payable		42,000
To record the inventory purchases.		
Cost of Goods Sold	27,000	
Inventory		27,000
To record the cost of goods sold inventories.		

General Ledger

Inventory

Beginning inventory	45,000		
Purchases	42,000		
		27,000	Sold inventories
Ending inventory	60,000		

Inventory Shortage	8000	
Inventory		8000
To record inventory shortage for the period.		

The Inventory Shortage account would be treated as a separate expense on the income statement and, if material, would indicate to financial statement users and management that Retail International should review its inventory control procedures.

This illustration represents only one of many ways in which the perpetual method provides more useful information than the periodic method. Although the perpetual method requires additional bookkeeping procedures, computer systems have recently reduced the costs of such procedures significantly. As a result, more and more companies, even those that handle high volumes of widely diversified inventories, are moving toward the perpetual method. The major supermarket chains like Safeway, Giant Foods, and Lucky Stores, Inc. represent a case in point. Many have recently moved to automated bar code sensors, devices that reduce the cost of using the perpetual method for merchandisers who sell a wide variety of relatively low-cost items. Similarly, many of the major retailers, like K mart, Sears, and J. C. Penney are moving toward perpetual systems.

Errors in the Inventory Count: The Perpetual and Periodic Methods

Inventory counts are made at the end of each period under both the perpetual and periodic methods. It is often difficult to ensure that such counts are accurate because many companies carry so many different kinds of inventory that each group of items cannot be counted at a reasonable cost. In such cases auditors and managers rely on estimates, and sometimes errors are committed.

An error in an inventory count will misstate both inventory on the balance sheet and net income on the income statement of that period. Such errors also misstate net income in the subsequent period by an equal dollar amount in the opposite direction. For example, an error in the inventory count taken at the end of 1989 that understates inventory by $2000 will also understate 1989's net income by $2000. In addition, this error will cause net income of 1990 to be overstated by $2000. Such effects occur whether a company uses the perpetual method or the periodic method.

To illustrate, assume that Rainier Corporation began operations on January 1, 1989. Figure 8–9 summarizes the transactions entered into by the company during 1989 and 1990 and contains accurate inventory balances and income statements for the two years. Assume that the only expenses incurred by the company were the costs of sold inventories.

Suppose that Rainier Corporation made no accounting errors during 1989 or 1990, except that it failed to include 20 items of inventory, each with a cost of $1, in its inventory count at the end of 1989. Inventory was thus determined incorrectly to be $280 instead of $300. Inventory was correctly counted at the end of 1990. The Inventory T-account, the cost of goods sold, and the inventory calculations for 1989 and 1990 under both the perpetual and periodic methods appear in Figure 8–10. Income statements prepared with the accurate information and under the perpetual and periodic methods are shown in Figure 8–11.

Figure 8–9   Rainier Corporation: transactions for 1989–1990

1989	Inventory	Sales
(1) Purchased 500 units of inventory for $1 per unit.	$500	
(2) Sold 200 units of inventory for $3 per unit.	200	$ 600
Ending inventory	$300	

Sales ($600) − Cost of goods sold ($200) = Net income ($400)

1990	Inventory	Sales
Beginning inventory	$300	
(1) Purchased 600 units of inventory for $1.	600	
(2) Sold 700 units of inventory for $3 per unit.	700	$2100
Ending inventory	$200	

Sales ($2100) − Cost of goods sold ($700) = Net income ($1400)

The error in the 1989 inventory count caused both methods to value ending inventory at $280, $20 below the correct amount. Under the perpetual method, the dollar amount in the Inventory T-account before the year-end count was taken ($300) was incorrectly reduced by what was believed to be a $20 shortage. Under the periodic method, the inventory count directly determined the ending inventory balance. Note in Figure 8–11 that the error caused both the perpetual and the periodic methods to understate net income by $20: the perpetual method, because an erroneous shortage expense was recorded, and the periodic method, because the cost of goods sold was overstated by $20.

In 1990, after taking a correct inventory count at year-end ($200), a recovery is recognized under the perpetual method because the Inventory balance prior to the count was only $180. This recovery caused 1990 net income to be overstated by $20. Under the periodic method, the ending inventory of 1989, which is understated by $20, becomes the beginning inventory of 1990. As a result, the cost of goods sold in 1990 is understated by $20, and net income is $20 overstated.

Figure 8–10   Inventory errors: perpetual and periodic methods

Perpetual Method

Inventory

Purchase	500		
		200	Sale
		20	Shortage
12/31/89	280		
Purchase	600		
		700	Sale
Recovery	20		
12/31/90	200		

Periodic Method

Cost of Goods Sold calulation

Cost of goods sold	=	Beginning inventory	+	Purchases	−	Ending Inventory
1989						
$220	=	$0	+	$500	−	$280
1990						
$680	=	$280	+	$600	−	$200

Figure 8–11   Comparative income statements: Rainer Corporation

	Accurate	Perpetual	Periodic
1989			
Sales	$ 600	$ 600	$ 600
Cost of goods sold	200	200	220
Shortage	—	20	—
Net income	$ 400	$ 380	$ 380
1990			
Sales	$2,100	$2,100	$2,100
Cost of goods sold	700	700	680
Recovery	—	20	—
Net income	$1,400	$1,420	$1,420

In summary, a single error in the counting of inventory caused net income of 1989 and net income of 1990 to be misstated by equal dollar amounts ($20) in opposite directions. Although both income statements are incorrect, the balance sheet as of the end of 1990 is properly stated. The accurate inventory count at year-end corrected the Inventory balance, and the $20 understatement of retained earnings due to understated net income in 1989 was counterbalanced by a $20 overstatement to net income in 1990.

Inventory errors are not unusual and at times can be quite significant. *The Washington Post* (23 June 1988), for example, reported that Comnet Corp., a computer software and health-care products company, discovered that management had unintentionally overvalued inventories by $1.6 million on the company's 1988 financial statements. Consequently, Comnet's 1988 reported net income of $2.6 million should have been reduced to $1.0 million.

SELLING INVENTORY: WHICH COST FLOW ASSUMPTION?

We have already indicated that the most important and difficult question of inventory accounting often involves how to allocate the capitalized inventory cost between the cost of goods sold and ending inventory. The examples so far have assumed that the cost of the sold inventory is known, but such situations are relatively unusual. In most cases companies are unable to determine exactly which items are sold and which items remain in ending inventory. When this occurs an assumption must be made about the cost flow of the inventory items. The assumption chosen can significantly affect net income, current assets, working capital, and the current ratio because it determines the relative costs allocated to the cost of goods sold and ending inventory.

This section first discusses the specific identification method, which is used when the cost of the sold inventory items can be determined. We then cover three cost flow assumptions that are used extensively in practice: averaging, First-in, First-out (FIFO), and Last-in, First-out (LIFO). Each assumption is illustrated under both the perpetual and the periodic methods.

Specific Identification

In some cases, especially with relatively infrequent sales of large-ticket items (e.g., jewelry, furniture, automobiles, land), it is possible to specifically identify which inventory items have been sold and which remain. In such situations the allocation of inventory cost between the cost of goods sold and ending inventory is relatively straightforward. Suppose, for example, that on March 1, Used Cars & Co. had three 1989 Honda Accords for sale. Cars 1 and 2 were purchased from the same dealer at a cost of $10,000 each. Car 3 was purchased recently at an auction for $12,000. The three cars are in equivalent condition, and the selling price for each is $18,000. The March 1 inventory for Used Cars & Co. follows.

Car	Cost
1	$10,000
2	$10,000
3	$12,000
Total	$32,000

Assume that on March 15, Sammy Sportsman agrees to purchase any one of the three cars for $18,000. Used Cars gives Sammy Car 3 (cost = $12,000) and the following journal entries (perpetual method) are recorded:

Cash	18,000	
Sales		18,000
Cost of Goods Sold	12,000	
Inventory		12,000
To record the sale of a Honda		
with a cost of $12,000 for $18,000.		

It is fairly clear in this situation that $12,000 should have been allocated to Cost of Goods Sold, and $20,000 should remain in ending inventory. An inventory item (Car 3) with a cost of $12,000 was sold. Thus, the specific identification procedure is a relatively straightforward way to determine the cost of goods sold and ending inventory. Nonetheless, it does have limitations.

First, the specific identification procedure is impractical for most companies, which cannot specifically identify which inventory is sold and which inventory remains on hand. Its use is limited primarily to operations that experience infrequent sales of large-ticket items.

A second limitation is that in many cases specific identification allows a manager to manipulate net income and the ending inventory value. Suppose in the example that the manager of Used Cars & Co. chose to give Sammy Sportsman either Car 1 or Car 2, instead of Car 3. Recall that Sammy was indifferent among the three automobiles. In this situation the following journal entries would have been recorded.

Cash	18,000	
Sales		18,000
Cost of Goods Sold	10,000	
Inventory		10,000
To record the sale of a Honda		
with a cost of $10,000 for $18,000.		

The decision to give Sammy Car 1 or Car 2 would have produced net income and ending inventory values that were $2000 ($12,000 − $10,000) greater than the decision to give Sammy Car 3. The specific identification procedure allowed the manager to manipulate income and inventory by choosing which inventory item to deliver to the customer. While manipulating the financial statements in this way is not a misrepresentation, it does allow management to influence the timing of income recognition.

Three Inventory Cost Flow Assumptions: Averaging, FIFO, and LIFO.

The inventories of many companies are acquired at so many different prices that it is impossible to specifically identify the costs of the items sold and the costs of the items in ending inventory. In such cases an assumption must be invoked. To illustrate and compare the three different cost flow assumptions, consider the following example. The chart in Figure 8–12 describes the inventory purchase and sales data for Discount Sales Company during its first year of operations.

Beginning inventory consisted of 20 units, a total of 60 units were purchased, and 35 units were sold during the year, producing an ending inventory of 45 units. Note that each unit of beginning inventory had a cost of $4, Purchase 1 was at a $5 unit cost, and Purchase 2 was at a $6 unit cost. Inventory costs increased during the period. Total capitalized inventory costs were $410, and $330 ($150 + $180) of those costs represented new purchases. Sold units were priced at $15 each. The following assumptions each allocate the $410 of capitalized inventory cost to Cost of Goods Sold and Inventory in a different way.

Averaging Assumption/Perpetual Method: A Moving Average
Under the perpetual method, the cost of sold inventory must be transferred to the Cost of Goods Sold account at each sale. A per-unit average cost, therefore, can be computed at the time of each sale by dividing the total cost of the available units by the number of available units. Since purchases are being made throughout the period at different costs, the per-unit average varies throughout the period. For this reason the per-unit average computed under the perpetual method is called a *moving average*. Figure 8–13 shows the relevant journal entries and the moving-average ending inventory and cost of goods sold computations for Discount Sales Company.

Figure 8–12   Inventory purchase and sales schedule: Discount Sales Company

Description	No. Units	×	Cost	or	Sales Price	Total Sales Proceeds	Total Costs
Beginning inventory	20	×	$4				$ 80
Purchase 1	30	×	5				150
Sale 1	10	×			$15	$150	
Purchase 2	30	×	6				180
Sale 2	25	×			15	375	
Ending Inventory	45						——
Capitalized inventory costs							$410
Units sold	35						
Total sales proceeds						$525	

Figure 8–13   Averaging assumption: perpetual method

Sale 1			Sale 2		
Cost of Goods Sold ($4.60[a] × 10 u)	46		Cost of Goods Sold ($5.20[b] × 25 u)	130	
Inventory		46	Inventory		130
Sale of inventory at $4.60 per			Sale of inventory at $5.20 per		
unit.			unit.		

[a][(20 u × $4) + (30 u × $5)] ÷ (20 u + 30 u)

[b][(40 u × $4.60) + (30 u × $6.00)] ÷ (40 u + 30 u)

Cost of goods sold = $46 + $130 = $176
Ending inventory = $80 + $150 − $46 + $180 − $130 =   234
Total capitalized inventory cost $410

At Sale 1, the per-unit cost is computed by dividing the total costs of the available units (beginning inventory [$80] and Purchase 1 [$150]) by the number of available units (beginning inventory [20] and Purchase 1 [30]). At Sale 2, note that the 40 remaining units from beginning inventory and the first purchase are valued at the per-unit average computed at Sale 1 ($4.60). Note also that the per-unit average cost at Sale 2 ($5.20) is greater than the per-unit average cost at Sale 1 ($4.60). The increase occurred because goods with a $6 unit cost that were purchased between Sale 1 and Sale 2 were included in the per-unit average cost calculation at Sale 2.

Averaging Assumption/Periodic Method: A Weighted Average

The averaging assumption applied to the periodic method involves the same per-unit calculation as under the perpetual method, except that it is only applied once, at the end of the period after the inventory count is taken. The total capitalized inventory cost ($410) is divided by the number of available units (80 = 20 + 30 + 30) to compute the per-unit average cost ($5.125 = $410 ÷ 80 units). Ending inventory is calculated by multiplying the per-unit average cost times the number of units on hand ($231 = $5.125 × 45 units). Once ending inventory is determined, the cost of goods sold can be calculated in the following manner. Note once again that the total capitalized inventory cost is allocated between Cost of Goods Sold and ending inventory.

Cost of Goods Sold	=	Beginning Inventory	+	Purchases	+	Ending Inventory
$179	=	$80	+	$330	−	$231
						(45 units × $5.125)

Cost of goods sold   = $179
Ending inventory   =   231
Total capitalized inventory cost = $410

First-in, First-out (FIFO) Assumption/Perpetual Method

Under the FIFO assumption, the costs of the units sold are assumed to be equal to the costs of the oldest available units in the financial records. Consequently, the 10 units sold at Sale 1 are assumed to come from the 20 units available in beginning inventory. The 25 units sold at Sale 2 are assumed to come first from the 10

Figure 8–14 FIFO assumption: perpetual method

Sale 1			Sale 2		
Cost of Goods Sold (10 u × $4[a])	40		Cost of Goods Sold	115[b]	
Inventory		40	Inventory		115
Sale of 10 units of inventory.			Sale of 25 units of inventory.		
[a]Cost of units in beginning inventory			[b](10 units × $4) + (15 units × $5)		

Cost of goods sold = $40 + $115 = $155
Ending inventory   = $80 + $150 − $40 + $180 − $115 =   255
Total capitalized inventory cost $410

remaining units in beginning inventory and then 15 of the units acquired at Purchase 1. Under the FIFO assumption, the cost of the ending inventory always consists of the costs of the most recently purchased units. Figure 8–14 shows the relevant journal entries and the ending inventory and Cost of Goods Sold computations for Discount Sales Company.

FIFO Assumption/Periodic Method

Under the periodic method, the FIFO assumption is only applied once, at the end of the period after the inventory count is taken. The 45 units in ending inventory are assumed to consist of those most recently purchased: that is, the 30 units from Purchase 2 and the 15 units from Purchase 1. Ending inventory and Cost of Goods Sold are computed as follows:

$$\text{FIFO ending inventory} = (30 \text{ units from Purchase 2} \times \$6/\text{unit}) \ \$180$$
$$+ (15 \text{ units from Purchase 1} \times \$5/\text{unit}) \ \underline{75}$$
$$\$255$$

Cost of Goods Sold = Beginning Inventory + Purchases − Ending Inventory
     $155   = $80   + $330   − $255

Cost of goods sold   = $155
Ending inventory   = 255
Total capitalized inventory cost = $410

Note that under the FIFO assumption, ending inventory ($255) and Cost of Goods Sold ($155) are the same whether the perpetual or the periodic method is used. The computations are equivalent because FIFO assumes that the units are sold in the same order in which they are purchased. That is, under both the perpetual and the periodic methods, the same units are assumed to be sold. As the next section shows, this equivalence does not hold for the LIFO assumption.

Last-in, First-out (LIFO) Assumption/Perpetual Method

Under the LIFO assumption, the costs of the units sold are assumed to be equal to the costs of those most recently purchased. Consequently, the 10 units sold at Sale 1 are assumed to come from the 30 units purchased at Purchase 1. The 25 units sold at Sale 2 are assumed to come from Purchase 2. If more than 30 units had been sold at Sale 2, the additional units would have been assumed to come from the remaining units acquired at Purchase 1. Under the LIFO assumption, the

Figure 8–15   LIFO assumption: perpetual method

Sale 1

Cost of Goods Sold (10 u × $5ª)	50	
Inventory		50

Sale of 10 units of inventory.

ªCost of units from Purchase 1.

Sale 2

Cost of Goods Sold (25 u × $6ᵇ)	150	
Inventory		150

Sale of 25 units of inventory

ᵇCost of units from Purchase 2.

Cost of goods sold = $50 + $150 = $200
Ending inventory = $80 + $150 − $50 + $180 − $150 =   210
Total capitalized inventory cost $410

---

cost of the ending inventory always consists of the costs of the oldest available units in the financial records. The relevant journal entries and the ending inventory and cost of goods sold computations for Discount Sales Company appear in Figure 8–15.

LIFO Assumption/Periodic Method

Under the periodic method, the LIFO assumption is only applied once, at the end of the period after the inventory count is taken. The 45 units in ending inventory are assumed to consist of the oldest available in the financial records: that is, the 20 units from beginning inventory and 25 units from Purchase 1. Ending inventory and Cost of Goods Sold are computed as below:

LIFO ending inventory   = (25 units from Purchase 1 × $5/unit) $125
                        + (20 units from beginning inventory × $4/unit)   80
                                                                         $205

Cost of Goods Sold = Beginning Inventory + Purchases − Ending Inventory
       $205   = $80   + $330   − $205

Cost of goods sold   = $205
Ending inventory   = $205
Total capitalized inventory cost = $410

Under the LIFO assumption, the dollar amounts of ending inventory ($205) and Cost of Goods Sold ($205) with the periodic method are different from ending inventory ($210) and Cost of Goods Sold ($200) with the perpetual method. The difference occurs because LIFO assumes that goods are sold in a different order from the one in which they are purchased. When the periodic method is used, this assumption can give rise to illogical results.

In the preceding illustration, for example, under the LIFO/periodic method the 45 units in ending inventory are assumed to consist of the 20 units in beginning inventory and 25 of the 30 units acquired at Purchase 1. This assumption implies that 5 of the 10 units sold at Sale 1 came from units acquired at Purchase 2. Such a sequence of events, however, could not have actually happened: Purchase 2 occurred *after* Sale 1. This illogical result does not occur under the LIFO/perpetual method.

Table 8–3   Financial statement effects of the three inventory cost flow assumptions

	FIFO	Averaging	LIFO
Sales (35 units × $15)	$525	$525	$525
Cost of goods sold	155	176	200
Gross profit	370	349	325
Expenses	150	150	150
Net income before taxes	$220	$199	$175
Ending inventory	$255	$234	$210
Cost of goods sold	155	176	200
Total capitalized inventory cost	$410	$410	$410

Inventory Cost Flow Assumptions: Effects on the financial Statements

Table 8–3 compares the averaging, FIFO, and LIFO cost flow assumptions with respect to the cost of goods sold, gross profit, net income and ending inventory. These comparisons are based on the information from the previous example using the perpetual method.[7] Assume further that Discount Sales Company incurred $150 of expenses (excluding the cost of goods sold) during the period.

Several features about the comparisons in Table 8–3 are noteworthy. First, under all three cost flow assumptions the entire $410 of capitalized inventory cost is allocated either to ending inventory or Cost of Goods Sold. The three assumptions differ in that they give rise to different allocations.

Second, the relative dollar amounts on the financial statements produced by the three assumptions are driven by the changes in the inventory purchase costs that occurred during the period. In this illustration, for example, per-unit inventory purchase costs increased during the period from $4 for beginning inventory, to $5 for Purchase 1, to $6 for Purchase 2. This cost increase caused ending inventory under FIFO ($255) to be greater than ending inventory under averaging ($234), which in turn was greater than ending inventory under LIFO ($210). Inventory cost increases also caused Cost of Goods Sold under FIFO ($155) to be less than Cost of Goods Sold under averaging ($176), which in turn was less than Cost of Goods Sold under LIFO ($200). We chose to illustrate an inflationary trend because in reality prices tend to increase over time. However, it is important to realize that if inventory costs had decreased during the period, the orders shown above would have been reversed: the LIFO assumption would have resulted in the greatest ending inventory and the least Cost of Goods Sold dollar amounts. In fact, had inventory costs remained stable throughout the period, no differences would have resulted: all three assumptions would have reported the same ending inventory and Cost of Goods Sold amounts.

Finally, in the example, the FIFO assumption gave rise to the highest, and the LIFO assumption gave rise to the lowest, net income and ending inventory dollar amounts. In times of increasing inventory costs, therefore, using the FIFO as-

---

7. Although the actual dollar amounts of ending inventory and Cost of Goods Sold are usually different under the periodic method, the general relationships among the cost flow assumptions are the same.

sumption can boost important financial ratios, such as earnings per share, working capital, and the current ratio. Choosing LIFO, on the other hand, may value inventories at unrealistically low levels. *Forbes* warns that financial statement users should pay close attention to a company's inventory cost flow assumption because it can "significantly distort" important financial ratios.[8]

Inventory Cost Flow Assumptions: Effects on Federal Income Taxes

As the previous example shows, if inventory costs are increasing, using the LIFO assumption gives rise to the lowest net income amount. During inflationary times, therefore, the LIFO assumption is an attractive alternative for determining a company's federal income tax liability, which is computed as a percentage of taxable income: less taxable income means less federal income tax liability.

Federal income tax law states that if a company uses the LIFO assumption for computing its tax liability, it must also use the LIFO assumption for preparing its financial statements. If a company uses a cost flow assumption other than LIFO for tax purposes, it can use the LIFO, averaging, or FIFO assumption for financial reporting. This regulation is called the **LIFO conformity rule,** and it causes most companies to use the same cost flow assumption for both income tax and financial reporting purposes. Companies that choose LIFO for tax purposes must use it for reporting purposes. Companies that want to use FIFO for reporting purposes may not use LIFO for tax purposes.

Table 8–4 shows the effects of the different cost flow assumptions on federal income taxes. The comparison uses the numbers from Table 8–3, except that federal income taxes have been assessed as a percentage (34 percent) of net income before taxes and are listed as an expense on the income statement.

Note in Table 8–4 that, in times of rising inventory costs, if a company chooses to minimize its federal income taxes by using the LIFO assumption, it must report lower net income and inventory on its financial statements. The effects on the financial statements of using LIFO can be significant. For example, the inventories of Bethlehem Steel, a LIFO user, are valued at about a billion dollars less than they would be under FIFO, approximately $24.15 per share.[9] In another example,

Table 8–4 Income tax effects of the three inventory cost flow assumptions

	FIFO	Averaging	LIFO
Sales (35 units × $15)	$525	$525	$525
Cost of goods sold	155	176	200
Gross profit	370	349	325
Expenses	150	150	150
Net income before taxes	220	199	175
Federal income taxes (34%)	75	68	60
Net income after taxes	$145	$131	$115

8. Karen Cook, "Sacking the Mattress," *Forbes,* 6 July 1981, p. 114.

9. Ibid.

DuPont reduced its current assets and reported net income by $612 million when it changed from FIFO to LIFO.

On the other hand, companies using the FIFO assumption to boost reported net income and ending inventory must pay additional federal income taxes. These additional tax payments can be very significant. For example, in an article in *The Wall Street Journal*, Gary Biddle, an accounting professor, reported that Eastman Kodak saved $204 million in taxes between 1974 and 1978 by choosing LIFO instead of FIFO. In a single year Amoco, General Electric, and U.S. Steel together would have paid $3 billion in additional taxes if they had used FIFO.[10]

Choosing an Inventory Cost Flow Assumption: Trade-offs

For most companies it is impractical to specifically identify the inventory items sold during a given period. Management must, therefore, choose from among the three assumptions discussed above. *Accounting Trends and Techniques* (1987) reports that of 600 major U.S. companies surveyed, 393 (66 percent) used LIFO, 383 (64 percent) used FIFO, and 223 (37 percent) used averaging for at least some of their inventories. Most of these companies used different methods for different kinds of inventory. Of those using LIFO, 229 (58 percent) used it for 50 percent or more of their inventories. The choice of a cost flow assumption is a difficult problem that depends on the situation faced by a given company.

Before considering the trade-offs involved in choosing an inventory cost flow assumption, remember that the assumption does not necessarily reflect the actual movement of the inventory. In fact, there is often no relationship between the assumption used to value the inventory for reporting purposes and the actual cost of the inventory on hand. Choosing a cost flow assumption is largely independent of the nature of the inventory itself.

It is also difficult to change a cost flow assumption once it has been chosen. As discussed in Chapter 5, the principle of consistency requires that accounting methods be consistent from year to year, and such changes, even when approved by an auditor, must be fully described in the footnotes, mentioned in the audit report, and their effect on income must be separately disclosed on the income statement. Recently, only a few major U.S. companies have changed their inventory cost flow assumptions. In 1986, for example, *Accounting Trends and Techniques* reports that only 4 of the 600 major U.S. companies surveyed chose to make such a change.

The trade-offs involved in choosing an inventory cost flow assumption are divided into two categories: (1) income and asset measurement and (2) economic consequences. *Income and asset measurement* refers to how well each assumption produces measures that reflect the actual financial condition of a company. *Economic consequences* refer to the costs and benefits associated with using a particular assumption.

Income and Asset Measurement

In terms of income and asset measurement, neither LIFO nor FIFO is clearly preferred. The LIFO assumption is a better application of the matching principle than the FIFO assumption. LIFO allocates the most current purchase costs to Cost of

---

10. Gary Biddle, "Paying FIFO Taxes: Your Favorite Charity," *The Wall Street Journal,* 19 January 1981, p. 18.

Goods Sold, where they are matched against current sales in the determination of net income. FIFO matches relatively old costs against current revenues.

FIFO, on the other hand, is generally viewed as producing a more current measure of inventory on the balance sheet. Ending inventory under FIFO reflects the costs of the most recent purchases, LIFO reports ending inventory in terms of older, less relevant, costs. Using LIFO over a period of time, therefore, can give rise to ending inventory costs that are grossly out-of-date. An article in *Forbes* stated that using LIFO leads to a "less realistic balance sheet." Union Carbide's net worth (assets − liabilities), for example, was understated by about 18 percent simply because it used LIFO, and the *inventory turnover* (Cost of Goods Sold / Inventory) of Monsanto, another LIFO user, was overstated by approximately 50 percent.[11]

Economic Consequences

Economic consequences refer to the costs and benefits associated with income taxes and liquidity problems, bookkeeping costs, LIFO liquidations and purchasing practices, debt and compensation contracts, and the capital market.

Income Taxes and Liquidity. Often the most important economic consideration when choosing an inventory cost flow assumption is the tax consequence. When inventory costs are rising, LIFO yields a lower net income number than FIFO, resulting in a lower tax liability. Consequently, choosing LIFO can improve a company's liquidity position by minimizing cash payments for income taxes. As mentioned earlier, the magnitudes of such savings can be significant.

Using FIFO can create liquidity problems. In times of rising prices, FIFO produces higher income than LIFO because it matches relatively old costs against current revenues. Because old costs are lower than current costs, FIFO creates **paper profits,** profits that are due to rising inventory costs instead of efficient operations. Paper profits appear on the income statement, but they are not backed by cash inflows. Unfortunately, these inflated profits are also used to determine a company's tax liability, which must be paid in cash. As a result, operating cash inflows may not be sufficient to cover the required cash outflows, and the company's liquidity position suffers.

In 1974 and 1975, for example, while the U.S. experienced economic recession and double-digit inflation, many U.S. companies suffered serious liquidity problems. In response over 400 FIFO users adopted LIFO. It has been estimated that the income tax savings enjoyed by these companies averaged approximately $26 million each.[12] Unquestionably, this tax savings did much to ease their cash flow problems.

Bookkeeping Costs. While LIFO usually brings about a lower tax liability than FIFO, it requires more bookkeeping procedures and is generally more costly to implement. For example, accounting professors Michael Granof and Daniel Short conducted a survey of FIFO users and found that many companies did not adopt LIFO because "the record keeping requirements of LIFO are burdensome and costly."[13] Indeed, short-cut methods for estimating LIFO have been devised to reduce the costs of maintaining LIFO records.

---

11. Richard Greene, "No Free LIFO," *Forbes*, 6 December 1982, p. 168, 171.

12. Gary Biddle, "Paying FIFO Taxes: Your Favorite Charity," *The Wall Street Journal*, 19 January 1981, p. 18.

13. Michael Granof and Daniel Short, "For Some Companies FIFO Accounting Makes Sense," *The Wall Street Journal*, 30 August 1982, p. 12.

LIFO Liquidation and Inventory Purchasing Practices. The use of LIFO can give rise to grossly overstated net income amounts when inventory levels are cut back. Consider, for example, Atlantic Richfield, a giant in the oil industry and a long-time LIFO user. In the early 1980s the dollar amount in the company's inventory balance consisted of very old, very low, and very outdated costs. Then an oil glut occurred, and the market price of oil decreased sharply. In response, Atlantic Richfield and a number of other oil companies cut inventory levels significantly. This action caused the low and outdated costs in inventory to be matched against Atlantic Richfield's current revenues. The result was a $105 million increase in the company's profits. That same year the profits of Gulf Oil, Standard Oil of California, and Texaco, other LIFO users, were inflated for the same reason by $200 million, $165 million, and $315 million, respectively.[14] Unfortunately, these high profits were due to the liquidation of LIFO inventories, not the effective and efficient operations of the oil companies or the condition of the oil industry, which at the time was suffering. Moreover, additional income taxes had to be paid on these profits.

Many LIFO users allow such inventory liquidations to occur, but other companies intentionally avoid them by maintaining their inventory purchases to prevent their inventory levels from diminishing. Such a practice avoids increased taxes, but, at the same time, can give rise to other problems. It may not be the appropriate time to purchase inventory. Inventory costs may be at a seasonal high, for example, or significant discounts may not be available. Further, such action does nothing to solve the problem associated with LIFO's understated inventory valuation; it merely postpones a problem that grows worse with each passing year.

Debt and Compensation Contracts. FIFO may be attractive to management because, when inventory costs are rising, FIFO produces higher reported net income and higher inventory values than LIFO. Compensation paid to management expressed as a percentage of FIFO income tends to be higher than compensation based on LIFO income. In addition, debt covenants using ratios based on FIFO will impose less restrictive constraints on managers than those based on LIFO.

The Capital Market. Management may also choose FIFO over LIFO because it believes that FIFO's higher net income and inventory amounts are valued more highly by investors and creditors in the capital market. They reason that using FIFO could improve the company's credit rating, which may lead to better terms on its borrowings and higher prices for its outstanding debt securities. Some believe that FIFO may also bring about higher prices for the company's outstanding equity securities. For example, one manager, when asked by Granof and Short in the survey mentioned earlier, "why [the company] did not use LIFO," responded that using LIFO "would depress the market price of its stock."[15] If such assertions are correct, using FIFO would make it easier to raise capital as well as increase management's value in the managerial labor market.

The validity of this reasoning is still open to question. A number of research studies in accounting suggest that the stock market "looks through" a company's accounting methods and values the company on the basis of the underlying cash flows. Since using LIFO usually saves taxes, these studies suggest, and some support the conclusion, that companies using LIFO are more highly valued by the

---

14. Laura Sanders and Laura Rohman, "A LIFO Boomerang," *Forbes,* 17 January 1983, p. 101, 104.
15. Granof and Short, "For Some Companies FIFO Accounting Makes Sense," p. 12.

stock market than companies using FIFO. However, the evidence is mixed, and all such conclusions are still tentative.[16]

Under generally accepted accounting principles, companies using LIFO are allowed to report in the footnotes to the financial statements what the value of their inventories would be if they used FIFO. The quote below was taken from the 1986 financial report of Adolph Coors Company.

> *Inventories: Inventories are stated at the lower-of-cost-or-market. Cost is determined by the last-in, first-out (LIFO) method for substantially all inventories. Current costs, as determined principally on the first-in, first-out method, exceeded LIFO cost by $57,432,000.*

Such a disclosure enables capital market investors and creditors to compute the amount of net income and other relevant financial ratios that would result if a company used FIFO instead of LIFO. It should, therefore, help to reduce any of the negative impact on stock prices that might result from using LIFO.

ENDING INVENTORY: APPLYING THE LOWER-OF-COST-OR-MARKET RULE

The inventory cost flow assumption determines the capitalized cost allocated to ending inventory. However, inventories on the balance sheet are not necessarily carried at this dollar amount. Based on conservatism, ending inventory, similar to marketable securities, is valued at cost or market value, whichever is lower.

Applying the lower-of-cost-or-market rule to ending inventory is accomplished by comparing the cost allocated to ending inventory to the market value of the inventory. If the market value exceeds the cost, no adjustment is made and the inventory remains at cost. If the market value is less than the cost, the inventories are written down to market value with an adjusting journal entry.

Suppose, for example, that ABC enterprises uses the FIFO assumption, which gives rise to an ending inventory of $100. If the market value of the inventory is $150, no adjusting journal entry need be recorded. The ending inventory remains at cost because cost ($100) is lower than market value ($150). If the market value of the inventory is $80, however, the inventory would have to be written down (reduced) from $100 to $80. The following journal entry represents one way of recording such a writedown.

Loss on Inventory Write-down ($100 − $80)   20
    Inventory   20
To write-down the inventory to market value.

Inventory writedowns are fairly common and sometimes quite large. In its 1987 financial report, for example, American Telephone & Telegraph Company reported an inventory loss of approximately $761 million, attributed primarily to obsolete communications equipment and office automation products. In 1988 TII

16. See, for example, the section on "Accounting Alternatives and the Capital Market" in *Financial Accounting Theory*, 3d ed., ed. Stephen Zeff and Thomas Keller (New York: McGraw-Hill, 1985, p. 569).

Industries, Inc., a manufacturer of high voltage power systems and electronic products, booked an inventory writedown in the amount of $13 million, stemming from customer changes in product specifications.[17]

In the preceding illustration, applying the lower-of-cost-or-market rule was relatively straightforward. In reality, however, the process is somewhat more complex because inventory market values are rarely easy to determine.

Determining Market Values for Inventories and Applying the LCM Rule

The accounting profession has concluded that there are three possible market values which can be used to compare with historical cost when applying the lower-of-cost or market rule: (1) **replacement cost,** the price a company would have to pay to replace its inventories, (2) **net realizable value,** the amount a company can expect to receive for its inventories less the costs of completing and selling them, and (3) **net realizable value less a normal profit margin,** which is equal to (2) less a company's normal markup.

Given these three market values applying the lower-of-cost-or-market rule to inventories involves four steps.

1. Determine *historical cost*. This is the dollar amount allocated to ending inventory after the cost flow assumption is applied.
2. Choose the *appropriate market value* from replacement cost, net realizable value, and net realizable value less a normal profit margin. Replacement cost is chosen if it is between net realizable value and net realizable value less a normal profit margin. If replacement cost exceeds net realizable value (referred to as the "ceiling"), net realizable value is chosen. If replacement cost is less than net realizable value less a normal profit margin (referred to as the "floor"), net realizable value less a normal profit margin is chosen. It always turns out that the *middle of the three market values* is the appropriate one.
3. *Compare* historical cost (Step 1) to the appropriate market value (Step 2) and choose the lower of the two.
4. If historical cost is less than the appropriate market value, no adjusting journal entry need be made. If historical cost is greater than the appropriate market value, an *adjusting journal entry* of the following form should be recorded in the books.

Loss on Inventory Write-down	XX	
Inventory		XX

Assume, for example, that the information contained in Figure 8–16 was compiled from the inventory records of four different companies. In the case of company A, replacement cost ($180) is between net realizable value ($210) and net realizable value less a normal profit margin ($150). Replacement cost is the appropriate market value and is, therefore, compared to historical cost. Replacement

---

17. "Who's News?," *The Wall Street Journal,* 22 April 1988, p. 36.

Figure 8–16   The lower-of-cost-or-market

	Historical Cost	Replacement Cost	Net Realizable Value	Net Realizable Value Less Normal Profit	Lower-of-cost or Market
Company A	$200	$180	$210	$150	$180
Company B	$350	$375	$360	$310	$350
Company C	$125	$100	$150	$120	$120
Company D	$480	$500	$530	$490	$480

cost ($180) is less than historical cost ($200) and serves as the basis for inventory valuation. Since inventories are presently at historical cost, the following journal entry would be recorded in the books.

```
Loss on Inventory Write-down               20
     Inventory                                      20
     To write-down inventory to market value.
```

For company B, net realizable value ($360) is the middle market value and is compared to historical cost ($350). Historical cost is lower, so no journal entry need be prepared. For company C, replacement cost is below net realizable value less a normal profit margin and thus net realizable value less a normal profit margin ($120) represents the appropriate market value. It is below historical cost ($125), so the inventory must be written down with the journal entry that appears below.

```
Loss on Inventory Write-down                5
     Inventory                                       5
     To write-down inventory to market value.
```

In case D replacement cost ($500) is the middle market value and above historical cost ($480). Consequently, no adjusting entry is recorded and the ending inventory remains at historical cost.

The Lower-of-Cost-or-Market Rule: A Critique

The lower-of-cost or market rule, whether applied to inventories or marketable securities, is often criticized because it treats price increases differently than price decreases. The rule gives prompt recognition in the books to decreases in market value but fails to do the same for increases.

The rule also requires that losses be recognized before being realized. For example, consider an inventory item with an original cost of $10 that is written down to $8, its market value. A $2 loss is immediately recognized on the income statement. Suppose that during the next accounting period the item's market value increases to $12, and it is sold. A $4 gain ($12 − $8) would be recognized on this transaction. As a result, the first period would show a $2 loss and the second period would show a $4 gain. Some accountants argue that a $2 gain ($12 − $10) should be recognized in Period 2, and that no loss should be recognized in Period 1.

There is little doubt that the lower-of-cost-or-market rule produces inconsistent measures of net income and other important financial numbers. Problems due to these inconsistencies are discussed in Chapter 6 (marketable securities). However, it is important to keep in mind that conservative accounting is a response to the liability faced by those who must provide and audit financial statements. The potential costs to these parties associated with understating inventories and profits are typically less than those associated with overstating them. From an economic standpoint, therefore, the lower-of-cost-or-market rule may be justifiable, even though it produces inconsistent and somewhat distorted measures on the financial statements. In any event, investors, creditors, managers, auditors, and other interested parties must be aware of these inconsistencies.

INVENTORY TURNOVER

The methods used to account for inventories have economic importance because the measures they affect, such as net income, earnings per share, the current ratio, and working capital, are important to financial statement users in assessing earning power and solvency. These measures help to determine credit ratings and are also used in contracts designed to control the business decisions of management.

Another commonly used measure, which involves the reported inventory dollar amount, is the inventory turnover ratio. This measure, which is one of Dun & Bradstreet's 14 key business ratios, is calculated in the following way:

Inventory Turnover Rate = Cost of Goods Sold ÷ Average Inventory*

*Average Inventory = (Beginning Inventory + Ending Inventory) ÷ 2

Inventory turnover indicates the speed with which inventories move through a company. It compares the amount of inventory carried by the company to the volume of goods sold during a particular accounting period, reflecting the number of times the inventory *turned over* during the period. For example, if Cost of Goods Sold is $30,000, and average inventory is $10,000, then inventory turned over three ($30,000 ÷ $10,000) times during the period. In other words, the company sold three times as much inventory as it carried, on average, during the period. Table 8–5 contains the average inventory turnovers for a selected group of industries.

Family clothing, sporting goods, and department stores turn over their inventories approximately once every season, or four times per year. Grocery stores, because they deal in produce, turn over their goods much more often. Restaurants, who deal predominantly in fresh foods, turn over their inventories every five or six days. For a more complete discussion of this ratio, see Chapter 17.

THE ANNUAL REPORT OF K MART CORPORATION

Turn now to K mart's annual report located in Appendix D. K mart is the world's largest discount retailer and a major operator of drug stores, warehouse home improvement centers, and book stores. Consequently, the marketability, control, and management of its inventory are critical to its success. The balance sheet

Table 8-5   Annual inventory turnovers: Cost of Goods sold/average inventory (industry averages)

Industry (No. of firms)	Annual Inventory Turnover
Family clothing (1373)	3
Sporting goods (2236)	4
Hardware (2239)	4
Department stores (1032)	5
Aircraft manufacturing (35)	6
Grocery stores (2295)	17
Single family home construction (2342)	29
Restaurants (2061)	60

Source: Compiled from data published in *Industry Norms and Key Business Ratios* (Dun & Bradstreet, Inc., 1987).

(page 32) reports that merchandise inventories represented 79 percent ($5.67 billion/$7.1 billion) of current assets and 47 percent ($5.67 billion/$12.1 billion) of total assets as of January 25, 1989. One year earlier inventories comprised 87 percent ($5.57 billion/$6.373 billion) of current assets and 50 percent ($5.57 billion/ $11.1 billion) of total assets.

Page 35 of the footnotes indicates that "merchandise inventories are valued at the lower of cost or market, using the retail method,[18] on the last-in, first-out basis for substantially all domestic inventories and the first-in, first-out basis for the remainder." The section entitled Merchandise Inventories (page 37) discloses that the inventory balance sheet value would be $898 million (1989) and $738 (1988) higher if K mart used the first-in, first-out assumption.

While inventory represents the largest item on K mart's balance sheet, note that it decreased as a percentage of both current assets and total assets during the past year. Some of the decrease may be attributable to the point-of-sale (POS) automated systems which have been installed in an increasing number of K mart stores (page 17). As noted on page 18, using this online perpetual inventory system and information from "the satellite network, centralized buying will result in better in-stock positions in K mart stores, improved inventory control and turnover, and increased sales volume."

The income statement (page 31) shows that Cost of Merchandise Sold is the largest expense item. In 1989, 1988, and 1987 it represented 73 percent, 72 percent, and 72 percent of Sales, respectively. The section on Effects of Inflation (page 24) reports again that "K mart, like most nonfood retailers, uses the LIFO method [and as a result] cost of merchandise sold approximates current cost." Page 22, under the caption Cost of Merchandise Sold, indicates further that "LIFO provides a more accurate matching of current costs with current revenues."

The discussion on page 22 also notes that Cost of Merchandise Sold (as a percentage of Sales) increased during 1988, stating that the higher percentage "was attributable to an increased emphasis by the general-merchandising group on competitive pricing and price leadership, the inclusion of lower-margined Makro

---

18. The retail inventory method is used by many retailers to estimate the year end inventory balance and cost of goods sold amount. We do not cover it in this text as it is normally discussed in intermediate accounting.

stores . . . and an increased LIFO charge." In other words, K mart reduced its sales prices at the same time the LIFO assumption matched current inflated inventory costs against revenues, giving rise to higher Cost of Goods Sold charges.

Assuming that the inventory balance as of January 27, 1988 ($5.571 billion) is equal to the average balance during the preceding year, K mart's inventory turnover ratios for 1989 and 1988 can be calculated as follows.

	Inventory Turnover	=	Cost of Goods Sold	÷	Average Inventory
1989	3.54	=	$19.914	÷ [($5.671 + $5.571) ÷ 2]
1988	3.33	=	$18.564	÷ $5.571

On average, K mart turns over its inventory between 3 and 4 times per year, or roughly once every 100 days. Such turnover approximates the averages for family clothing, sporting goods, hardware, and department stores reported in Table 8−4. Note that the ratio increased in 1989 because the increase in Cost of Goods Sold exceeded the increase in the inventory balance. This result supports the statement made on page 18 that the POS systems are improving inventory turnover. However, on page 26 the inventory turnover ratio is calculated using replacement cost as measured by the first-in, first-out (FIFO) method of inventory. These calculations show a decrease of 3.1 to 3.0 from 1988 to 1989.

REVIEW PROBLEM

On December 1, Jane Lee contributed $1000 of her own funds to begin an Oriental grocery store that sells white rice. The rice is kept in a large bin, and customers help themselves by filling plastic bags with a large scoop. During December the transactions described in Figure 8−17 took place. Assume that Jane incurred cash expenses (excluding the cost of goods sold and inventory shortages) of $400 during December, and she pays income taxes at a rate of 30 percent of net income before taxes on December 31.

Jane purchased rice on two occasions at two different prices. By multiplying the number of pounds purchased times the cost per pound, the total capitalized inventory cost for January can be computed ($510). Three hundred pounds of rice were sold for a price of $5/lb., creating total sales of $1500 (300 lb × $5).

Figure 8−17   December transactions for JL Oriental Foods

Date	Description	Total Inventory Cost
December 1	Contribution of $1,000 by owner, Jane Lee	
December 7	Purchased 300 pounds of rice for $1.00 per pound	$300
December 25	Sold 250 pounds of rice for $5.00 per pound	
December 27	Purchased 150 pounds of rice for $1.40 per pound	210
December 28	Sold 50 pounds of rice for $5.00 per pound	
December 29	Paid cash expenses of $400	
December 31	Paid income tax liability	
Total capitalized inventory cost		510

Figure 8–18   Perpetual method: FIFO assumption

JL Oriental Foods Income Statement For the Month Ended December 31, 1990	
Sales (300 lb. × $5)	$1,500
Cost of goods sold	300[a]
Gross profit	1,200
Inventory shortage	14[b]
Expenses	400
Net income before taxes	786
Income tax expense ($786 × .30)	236
Net income after taxes	$ 550

[a]300 lb. sold × $1.00 per lb.
[b]10 lb. lost × $1.40 per lb.

JL Oriental Foods Balance Sheet December 31, 1990	
Cash	$1,354[c]
Inventory	196[d]
Total assets	$1,550
Common stock	1,000
Retained earnings	550
Total liabilities and stockholders' equity	$1,550

[c]**Capital contribution − Purchases + Sales − Expenses − Taxes**
$1,000   − ($300 + $210) + $1,500 − $400   − $236
[d]140 lb. × $1.40

On December 31, when financial statements are prepared, Jane is able to determine beginning inventory ($0) and total purchase costs ($510) because she recorded the purchases as they were made. Assume that Jane took an inventory at this time (i.e., weighed the rice) and noted that there were 140 pounds of rice on hand (i.e., 10 lbs. were lost). The following figures (8–18 through 8–21) contain the income statements and balance sheets prepared by JL Oriental Foods under the perpetual and periodic methods and the FIFO and LIFO cost flow assumptions.

In Figure 8–22 the net income, ending inventory, and cash balance produced under the four combinations of inventory methods and cost flow assumptions are compared. Note that FIFO produces the same results whether the perpetual or periodic method is used. LIFO does not. The dollar amounts under LIFO/perpetual are closer to FIFO than are the amounts produced by LIFO/periodic. FIFO net income and ending inventory (perpetual and periodic) are greater than LIFO net income and ending inventory. The cash balances under LIFO (perpetual and periodic) are greater than the cash balances under FIFO because LIFO's lower net income gives rise to a lower tax liability. The relationships among these four combinations generally hold when inventory costs are rising.

Figure 8–19   Periodic method: FIFO assumption

JL Oriental Foods
Income Statement
For the Month Ended December 31, 1990

Sales (300 lb. × $5)	$1,500
Cost of goods sold	314[a]
Gross profit	1,186
Expenses	400
Net income before taxes	786
Income tax expense ($786 × .30)	236
Net income after taxes	$ 550

[a]Beginning inventory +   Purchases   − Ending inventory
   $0   + ($300 + $210) − (140 lb. × $1.40)

JL Oriental Foods
Balance Sheet
December 31, 1990

Cash	$1,354[b]
Inventory	196[c]
Total assets	$1,550
Common stock	1,000
Retained earnings	550
Total liabilities and stockholders' equity	$1,550

[b]Capital contribution −   Purchases   + Sales − Expenses − Taxes
   $1,000   − ($300 + $210) + $1,500 − $400   − $236
[c]140 lb. × $1.40

Assume that on December 31 the replacement cost of rice drops suddenly to $1.20 per pound.[19] The total replacement cost of Jane's 140 pounds of rice, therefore, is $168 (140 lb × $1.20). If Jane used the FIFO assumption, she would record the following journal entry to apply the lower-of-cost or market rule.

Loss on Inventory Write-down	28*	
Inventory		28
To record the write-down of inventory to market value.		
*$196 − $168		

If Jane used the LIFO assumption with the perpetual method, she would record the following journal entry to apply the lower-of-cost or market rule.

Loss on Inventory Write-down	8*	
Inventory		8
To record the write-down of inventory to market value.		
*$176 − $168		

---

19. Assume that replacement cost is below net realizable value and above net realizable value less a normal profit margin.

If Jane used the LIFO assumption with the periodic method, she would record no journal entry, because the cost of the ending inventory ($140) is already below the replacement cost ($168).

Figure 8-20   Perpetual method: LIFO assumption

JL Oriental Foods
Income Statement
For the Month Ended December 31, 1990

Sales (300 lb. × $5)	$1,500
Cost of goods sold	320[a]
Gross profit	1,180
Inventory shortage	14[b]
Expenses	400
Net income before taxes	766
Income tax expense ($766 × .30)	230
Net income after taxes	$ 536

[a](250 lb. sold × $1.00) + (50 lb. sold × $1.40)
[b](10 lb. lost × $1.40)

JL Oriental Foods
Balance Sheet
December 31, 1990

Cash	$1,360[c]
Inventory	176[d]
Total assets	$1,536
Common stock	1,000
Retained earnings	536
Total liabilities and stockholders' equity	$1,536

[c]Capital contribution − Purchases + Sales − Expenses − Taxes
  $1,000   − ($300 + $210) + $1,500 − $400   − $230
[d](50 lb. × $1.00) + (90 lb. × $1.40)

Figure 8-21   Periodic method: LIFO assumption

JL Oriental Foods
Income Statement
For the Month Ended December 31, 1990

Sales (300 lb. × $5)	$1,500
Cost of goods sold	370[a]
Gross profit	1,130
Expenses	400
Net income before taxes	730
Income tax expense ($730 × .30)	219
Net income after taxes	$ 511

[a]Beginning inventory +   Purchases   − Ending inventory
      $0   + ($300 + $210) − (140 lb. × $1.00)

JL Oriental Foods
Balance Sheet
December 31, 1990

Cash	$1,371[b]
Inventory (140 lb. × $1.00)	140
Total assets	$1,511
Common stock	1,000
Retained earnings	511
Total liabilities and stockholders' equity	$1,511

[b]Capital contribution −   Purchases   + Sales − Expenses − Taxes
      $1,000   − ($300 + $210) + $1,500 − $400   − $219

Figure 8-22   Inventory assumption: method comparisons

	FIFO/Perpetual	FIFO/Periodic	LIFO/Perpetual	LIFO/Periodic
Net income	$ 550	$ 550	$ 536	$ 511
Ending inventory	196	196	176	140
Cash balance	$1,354	$1,354	$1,360	$1,371

SUMMARY OF LEARNING OBJECTIVES

1 Define inventory, and describe how the methods used to account for it affect the financial statements.

Inventory includes asset items held for sale in the ordinary course of business. The ending inventory balance appears on the balance sheet and, for manufacturing and retail companies, is often the largest current asset. The methods used to account for inventory affect the allocation of the capitalized inventory cost between ending inventory and the Cost of Goods Sold. This allocation, in turn, affects net income and the ending inventory amount reported on the balance sheet. The effects of inventory accounting methods in the current and subsequent periods can be assessed by examining the following formula:

Cost of Goods Sold = Beginning Inventory + Purchases − Ending Inventory

The ending inventory valuation of the current period decreases cost of goods sold and, thereby, increases gross profit and net income. Ending inventory of the current period becomes beginning inventory of the subsequent period. Beginning inventory increases cost of goods sold and decreases gross profit and net income.

2 Identify the four main issues that must be addressed when accounting for inventory.

The four main issues that must be addressed when accounting for inventories are (1) what costs to include in the capitalized inventory cost (what items to include and what costs to attach to these items), (2) which method to use to carry the inventory (perpetual or periodic), (3) which cost flow assumption to use (specific identification, averaging, FIFO, or LIFO), and (4) how to apply the lower-of cost-or-market value rule.

3 Describe the general rules for including items in inventory and attaching costs to these items.

Items held for sale should be included in a company's inventory if the company has complete and unrestricted ownership of them. In a consignment, even though the inventory is in the possession of the consignee, it should be reported on the consignor's balance sheet. Goods in transit as of the balance sheet data that were sent FOB shipping point should be included in the buyer's inventory. Goods in transit as of the balance sheet date that were sent FOB destination should be included in the seller's inventory.

Any cost required to bring an inventory item to saleable condition should be capitalized and treated as an inventory cost. This includes all costs that can reasonably be associated with the manufacture, acquisition, storage, or preparation of inventory items.

4 Explain the differences between the perpetual and periodic methods and the tradeoffs involved in choosing between them.

The perpetual method keeps an up-to-date record of all inventory flows. Inventory purchases are recorded in the inventory account at cost, and Cost of Goods Sold is debited for the cost of items when they are sold.

The periodic method updates the Inventory account at the end of each accounting period. Inventory purchases are recorded in the Purchases account at cost, but cost of goods sold is not recognized when the inventory is sold. Instead, at the end of each accounting period, an inventory count is taken and the Inventory and cost of goods sold balances are updated during the closing process.

The perpetual method requires more bookkeeping procedures than the periodic method and is therefore usually more costly to implement. However, the perpetual method provides more up-to-date information. As computer systems have reduced the processing costs of maintaining inventory records, the perpetual method has become more popular.

5 Identify the three cost flow assumptions and the measurement and economic trade-offs that must be considered when choosing from among them.

The three cost flow assumptions are averaging, first-in, first-out (FIFO), and last-in, first-out (LIFO). Under averaging, average costs are allocated to the goods sold and the goods that remain in ending inventory. When the averaging assumption is combined with the perpetual method, it is known as a *moving average*. When the averaging assumption is combined with the periodic method, it is known as a *weighted average*.

Under FIFO, the first items purchased are assumed to be the first items sold. This assumption matches old inventory costs with sales but places relatively up-to-date inventory costs on the balance sheet. In times of rising inventory costs, this assumption tends to inflate net income and increase a company's tax liability.

Under LIFO, the most recent items purchased are assumed to be the first items sold. This assumption matches current inventory costs with sales but tends to place old and outdated inventory costs on the balance sheet. LIFO can also be costly to implement and can encourage managers to purchase inventory items at inappropriate times. However, this assumption provides a reasonable measure of net income and in times of rising inventory costs, it helps to minimize a company's tax liability.

Numbers like net income, earnings per share, the current ratio, and working capital, which are partially determined by the inventory cost flow assumption, are used by investors, creditors, and other interested parties to assess earning power and solvency. These and other measures that use the reported inventory number, are also used in contracts (e.g., debt covenants and management compensation) designed to control the business decisions of managers. Another common measure used by investors and creditors is the inventory turnover ratio. It compares the amount of inventory carried by the company to the volume of goods sold during a particular accounting period, reflecting the number of times the inventory turned over during the period.

6 Explain how to apply the lower-of-cost-or-market rule to ending inventories.

There are four steps involved in applying the lower-of-cost-or-market rule to inventory: (1) determine historical cost (the dollar amount allocated to ending inventory after the cost flow assumption is applied), (2) choose the appropriate market value (the middle value of replacement cost, net realizable value, or net realizable value less a normal profit margin), (3) compare historical cost to the appropriate market value and choose the lower dollar amount. If historical cost is greater than the market value, (4) make an adjusting journal entry that reduces the book value of the inventory to the chosen market value.

KEY TERMS

Averaging assumption (p. 344)
Consignment (p. 345)
First-in, First-out (FIFO) (p. 344)
FOB destination (p. 346)
FOB shipping point (p. 346)
Freight-in (p. 347)
Goods in transit (p. 346)
Inventory turnover (p. 369)
Last-in, first-out (LIFO) (p. 344)
LIFO conformity rule (p. 362)
Manufacturing companies (p. 348)

Net realizable value (p. 367)
Net realizable value less normal profit
  margin (p. 367)
Overhead (p. 348)
Paper profits (p. 364)
Periodic method (p. 344)
Perpetual method (p. 344)
Replacement cost (p. 367)
Retail companies (p. 347)
Specific identification (p. 344)
Transportation-in (p. 347)

QUESTIONS FOR DISCUSSION AND REVIEW

1. What is inventory? Why are managers, investors, creditors, and auditors interested in the methods used to account for it?

2. How is the Inventory account on the balance sheet linked to the income statement? How does the allocation of the capitalized inventory cost affect the financial statements?

3. Name the four major issues that must be addressed when accounting for inventory. Briefly describe each issue and explain how it is related to the others.

4. What is the general rule for deciding what items to include in inventory? What is a consignment, and how does it relate to inventory accounting? How might consignments be difficult for auditors?

5. Assume that Rawlers Corporation acts as a consignee for Matton Manufacturing. If Matton's inventory is mistakenly included on the balance sheet of Rawlers, how will the financial statements of Rawlers be misstated?

6. What factors must be considered when attempting to determine who owns goods that are in transit at the end of an accounting period? What is the meaning of *FOB shipping point* and *FOB destination?* How might these shipping terms be helpful in determining whether or not a sale or purchase has been completed as of the end of an accounting period?

7. What is the general rule for deciding what costs to attach to inventory items? Discuss the basic differences between a retailer and a manufacturer and how these differences affect inventory accounting.

8. On which financial statement would you find a Purchase Discount Lost account? Of what significance is it, and what does it tell you about the method of accounting used by a company for its inventory purchases?

9. What is the basic difference between the perpetual and the periodic inventory methods? Which method is easier to implement? Why?

10. The advent of computer systems has caused a number of companies to switch from the periodic method of carrying inventory to the perpetual method. Why would companies do this? What advantages does the perpetual method have over the periodic method? Provide an example.

11. The specific identification method is a procedure for determining which inventory costs are allocated to Cost of Goods Sold and which inventory costs are allocated to ending inventory. What are the advantages and disadvantages of this procedure? How

can this procedure be used by a manager to manipulate net income and other financial ratios?

12. What is the basic difference between the FIFO and the LIFO cost flow assumptions? If inventory costs are stable across time, is there any difference between the cost of goods sold and ending inventory produced under FIFO and LIFO? Why or why not?

13. What is the moving-average flow assumption? Why is it called a moving average?

14. Under the FIFO assumption, do the ending inventory and Cost of Goods Sold figures differ under the periodic method and the perpetual method? Why or why not?

15. Under the LIFO assumption, do ending inventory and Cost of Goods Sold differ under the periodic method and the perpetual method? Why or why not?

16. From a measurement standpoint, which assumption (FIFO or LIFO) is preferred? State your answer in terms of the matching principle and the balance sheet valuation of inventory.

17. State the LIFO conformity rule. How might this rule affect a manager's decision to choose an inventory flow assumption?

18. List the economic advantages and disadvantages of LIFO and FIFO and explain why companies choose one or the other.

19. Is it advisable simply to choose FIFO because in times of rising inventory costs it provides higher inventory and net income numbers? Might a higher income number increase the value of a company's capital stock? Discuss.

20. What is a *LIFO liquidation*, and how might one inflate net income?

21. In periods of rising inventory costs, why would a manager who uses LIFO want to avoid a year in which sales significantly exceed purchases? How might it be done? What problems may be associated with this strategy?

22. Describe the lower-of-cost-or-market rule as applied to inventories. Why is it viewed as inconsistent by a number of its critics? From a measurement standpoint, do these arguments have merit? If so, how would the lower-of-cost-or-market rule have to be justified?

23. Why is applying the lower-of-cost or market rule to inventories often difficult? Are inventory market values objectively determined? What three market values are considered in the rule? Which market value is preferred if it does not exceed the "ceiling" or dip below the "floor"? Which market value serves as the "ceiling"? Which market value serves as the "floor"?

24. What is inventory turnover? What problems could be indicated by low inventory turnover? What problems could be indicated by high inventory turnover?

EXERCISES

E8-1

(Accounting for inventory purchases: gross and net methods) Nick's Fish Market purchased Maine lobster on account on October 10, 1991, for a gross price of $35,000. Nick also purchased Alaskan king crab on account on October 11, 1991, for a gross price of $20,000. The terms of both sales were 3/15, n30. Nick paid for the first purchase on October 20, 1991, and for the second purchase on October 30, 1991. He uses the perpetual inventory method.

Required:

a. Assume Nick's Fish Market uses the gross method to account for cash discounts. Prepare journal entries for each transaction.

b. Assume Nick's Fish Market uses the net method to account for cash discounts. Prepare journal entries for each transaction.

E8–2   *(Accounting for inventory purchases: gross and net methods)*   Bertanelli Corporation purchased inventory on account on March 3, 1991, for a gross price of $200,000. The company purchased additional inventory on account on March 10, 1991, for a gross price of $180,000. The terms of both sales were 2/12, n30. Bertanelli Corporation paid for the first purchase on April 25, 1991, and for the second purchase on March 20, 1991. The company prepares monthly adjusting journal entries and uses the perpetual inventory method.

Required:

a. Assume Bertanelli Corporation uses the net method to account for cash discounts. Prepare journal entries for each transaction.
b. Assume Bertanelli Corporation uses the gross method to account for cash discounts. Prepare journal entries for each transaction.

E8–3   *(Compute the missing values and prepare the closing journal entry under the periodic method)* The following information was extracted from the financial records of House Designs.

	12/31/93	12/31/92	12/31/91	12/31/90
Beginning inventory	$110,000	?	$125,000	$100,000
Purchases	?	75,000	60,000	50,000
Purchase discounts	(10,000)	?	(5,000)	?
Cost of goods available for sale	155,000	190,000	?	135,000
Ending inventory	75,000	?	135,000	?
Cost of goods sold	?	80,000	45,000	10,000

Required:

a. Compute the missing information for each year.
b. Assume that the House Designs uses the periodic method to account for inventory. Prepare the closing entry to recognize ending inventory and Cost of Goods Sold at the end of each year.

E8–4   *(The financial statement effects of inventory errors)*   Cummings Novelty Corporation reported the following items in its 1990 financial report.

	1990		1989	
Sales		$400,000		$250,000
Cost of goods sold				
Beginning inventory	190,000		175,000	
Purchases	240,000		125,000	
Goods available for sale	430,000		300,000	
Less: Ending inventory	235,000		190,000	
Cost of goods sold		195,000		110,000
Gross profit		$205,000		$140,000

Additional Information

The ending inventory amount was obtained by a physical count of the inventory on hand at the end of the year. Counting errors caused the ending inventory in 1989 to be understated by $10,000 and the ending inventory in 1990 to be overstated by $5000.

Required:

a. Compute the impact of these errors on Cost of Goods Sold for the year ended December 31, 1989, and on the Inventory balance as of December 31, 1989.

b. Compute the impact of these errors on Cost of Goods Sold for the year ended December 31, 1990, and on the inventory balance as of December 31, 1990.

c. What is the impact of these errors on Cost of Goods Sold over the two-year period ended December 31, 1990?

E8–5   *(Goods in transit as of the end of the accounting period)*   Austin Manufacturing engaged in five transactions involving inventory at the end of 1990:

(1) Ordered $50,000 of inventory on December 29, 1990. The goods were shipped on December 30, 1990, with the terms FOB shipping point. Austin received the inventory on January 4, 1991.

(2) Received an order to sell inventory with a cost of $25,000. The goods were shipped to the customer on December 29, 1990, and received on January 2, 1991. The terms of the sale were FOB destination.

(3) Received an order to sell inventory with a cost of $40,000. The goods were shipped to the customer on December 31, 1990, and received on January 3, 1991. The terms of the sale were FOB shipping point.

(4) Ordered $75,000 of inventory on December 30, 1990. The inventory was shipped on December 31, 1990, with the terms FOB destination. Austin received the inventory on January 3, 1991.

(5) Ordered $10,000 of inventory on December 27, 1990. The inventory was shipped on December 27, 1990, with the terms FOB destination. Austin received the inventory on December 31, 1990.

Required:

a. For each transaction, indicate whether Austin Manufacturing has legal title to the inventory as of December 31, 1990.

b. Assume that Austin Manufacturing took a physical count of its inventory at the close of business on December 31, 1990. For each transaction, indicate whether the inventory would have been on hand for Austin Manufacturing to include in its physical count.

c. For each transaction, indicate in what direction and by what amount the Inventory account as of December 31 would have to be adjusted.

E8–6   *(Carrying inventories: perpetual and periodic methods)*   The following information comes from the records of Parson's Discount House.

Beginning inventory	$32,000
Inventory purchases	84,000
Transportation-in	3,500

An inventory count taken at year-end indicates that inventory with a cost of $50,000 is on hand as of December 31, 1990.

Required:

a. Assume that Parsons uses the periodic inventory method. Compute Cost of Goods Sold and prepare the year-end closing journal entry.

b. Assume that Parsons uses the perpetual method and that inventory purchases and transportation-in are both reflected in the Inventory account, which shows an ending balance of $52,000. Compute Cost of Goods Sold under the perpetual method along with any adjusting entries required at the end of the period.

c. Explain why the periodic method produces a value for Cost of Goods Sold that is different from that produced by the perpetual method. What information does the perpetual method provide that is not provided by the periodic method?

E8–7   *(Income manipulation under specific identification)* Marian's Furs specializes in full-length mink coats. As of January 1, Marian had four top-of-the-line coats. Although the four coats are equivalent, they were purchased the previous year at different costs:

	Cost
Coat 1	$7200
Coat 2	$7600
Coat 3	$8000
Coat 4	$7000

·During January a customer decided to buy any one of the mink coats for $10,000. This was the only sale in January.

Required:

a. If Marian wished to maximize January's profits and ending inventory, which of the minks would she have given to the customer? Compute the gross profit on the sale and January's ending inventory. Discuss why Marian might wish to maximize profits and ending inventory.

b. If Marian wished to minimize January's profits and ending inventory, which of the minks would she have given to the customer? Compute the gross profit on the sale and January's ending inventory. Discuss why Marian might wish to minimize profits and ending inventory.

E8–8   *(Computing Cost of Goods Sold and ending inventory under the LIFO, FIFO, and averaging assumptions)* Mayflower Wood Wholesalers entered into the following transactions during 1990 involving inventory.

Date	Purchases	Sales (Units)
Beginning Inventory	12 @ $5.50	
1/12/90	8 @ $5.75	
3/10/90		15
5/30/90	25 @ $5.80	
8/14/90	10 @ $6.00	
10/29/90		23
11/18/90	20 @ $6.05	
12/8/90		26
12/11/90		10
12/27/90	30 @ $6.20	

Required: Assume that Mayflower Wood Wholesalers uses the perpetual inventory method and conducted a year-end inventory count that revealed 28 units on hand. Compute the cost of goods sold, shortage expense, and ending inventory reported on the December 31, 1990 financial statements if the company follows the

a. LIFO cost flow assumption

b. FIFO cost flow assumption

c. Averaging cost flow assumption

(Hint: Assume that inventory shortages are valued as if the units had been sold on December 31.)

E8–9   *(Inventory assumptions and manipulating income under specific identification)* Vinnie's House of Televisions has 75 identical 27-inch color monitors in stock on January 1, 1990. Vinnie maintains records of the serial numbers of each monitor to track their costs. Vinnie purchased 75 of the monitors on December 5, 1989 for $450 each, 60 on January 2, 1990 for $500 each, and an additional 65 on January 15, 1990 for $600 each. Each monitor is priced to sell at $1000. Vinnie sold 150 monitors during the month of January.

Required:

a. Compute gross profit and ending inventory for the month if the company uses the periodic method and adheres to each of the following:

   (1) FIFO cost flow assumption

   (2) Averaging cost flow assumption

   (3) LIFO cost flow assumption

b. Assume that Vinnie uses the specific identification method to compute the cost of goods sold. Explain how Vinnie could manipulate the gross profit number. What are the highest and the lowest gross profit amounts Vinnie could report? What are some possible factors that could motivate Vinnie to report either the highest or the lowest net income amount?

E8–10   *(Inventory flow assumptions over several periods and income taxes)*   Hanberry Bottling Company began business in 1986. Inventory units purchased and sold for the first year of operations and each of the following four years follow.

	Units Purchased	Cost Per Unit	Units Sold
1986	10,000	$10	6,000
1987	12,000	15	15,000
1988	5,000	16	3,000
1989	10,000	20	9,000
1990	2,000	22	6,000

Inadequate cash flows forced the Hanberry Bottling Company to cease operations at the end of 1990.

Required:

a. Compute Cost of Goods Sold for each of the five years if the company uses the following:

   (1) LIFO cost flow assumption

   (2) FIFO cost flow assumption, and

   (3) averaging cost flow assumption.

b. Does the choice of a cost flow assumption affect total net income over the life of a business? Explain your answer.

c. If the choice of a cost flow assumption does not affect net income over the life of a business, how does the choice of a cost flow assumption give rise to a tax benefit?

E8–11   *(Different inventory methods and cost flow assumptions)*   Benston Enterprises had 15,000 units of inventory on hand as of January 1, 1991, and each unit had a cost of $5. The following information was extracted from the inventory records of Benston Enterprises for 1991.

Inventory Purchases

2/15/91	10,000 units @ $10 per unit
4/25/91	15,000 units @ $15 per unit
9/18/91	10,000 units @ $20 per unit
11/1/91	30,000 units @ $25 per unit
12/7/91	15,000 units @ $30 per unit

Inventory Sales

3/15/91	15,000 units
5/10/91	10,000 units
10/9/91	25,000 units
12/2/91	25,000 units

Required: Compute the cost of goods sold and ending inventory under the following four method/assumption combinations.

a. Perpetual/FIFO

b. Periodic/FIFO

c. Perpetual/LIFO

d. Periodic/LIFO

E8–12

(Inventory turnover) The following information was taken from the financial records of Sharp Machines.

	1990	1989	1988	1987
Sales	$55,000	$53,000	$42,000	$35,000
Inventory	12,000	10,000	9,000	5,000

Sharp maintains a gross profit of 60% of sales.

Required

a. How many times did Sharp turn over its inventory in 1988, 1989, and 1990?

b. On average, how many days did it take the company to turn over its inventory in 1988, 1989, and 1990?

c. What trend seems to be developing and what factors might cause such a trend?

E8–13

(Combining inventory methods and flow assumptions) The following information concerning inventory was extracted from the financial records of West Coast Grocers, Inc.

Date	Purchases	Sales (units)
Beginning inventory	10,000 @ $10	
2/10/90	12,000 @ $15	
5/20/90		10,000
6/30/90	15,000 @ $20	
9/10/90	18,000 @ $25	
10/9/90		20,000
11/1/90	14,000 @ $30	
12/8/90		16,000
12/9/90	20,000 @ $40	

Additional Information

1. The company had sales volume during 1990 of $2,000,000.

2. The company incurred expenses during 1990, excluding cost of goods sold, of $250,000.

Required:

a. Compute the total number of units available, the number of units sold, and the number of units in ending inventory as of December 31, 1990.

b. Prepare income statements for each of the following combinations.

	Method	Assumption		Method	Assumption
(1)	Periodic	FIFO	(4)	Perpetual	FIFO
(2)	Periodic	Averaging	(5)	Perpetual	Averaging
(3)	Periodic	LIFO	(6)	Perpetual	LIFO

E8-14

(Applying the lower-of-cost or market rule) The following information concerns the ending inventory of five different companies.

Company	Historical Cost	Net Realizable Value	Replacement Cost	Net Realizable Value Less a Normal Profit Margin
Wheaton	$32,300	$40,000	$35,600	$34,300
Loners	64,200	63,100	65,800	59,200
Flowe	17,400	18,300	16,000	13,100
Roberts	6,500	8,200	4,300	7,100
Strayling	26,300	26,800	18,900	22,900

Required:

a. In each case choose the market value which is to be compared to historical cost when applying the lower-of-cost or market rule.

b. In each case choose the value at which ending inventory should be carried on the balance sheet.

c. In each case prepare the journal entries that would be required under the lower-of-cost or market rule.

PROBLEMS

P8-1

(Misstated income under the gross method) On December 15 and 26, Brown and Swazey purchased merchandise on account for gross prices of $4000 and $6000 respectively. Terms of both purchases were 2/10, n30. As of December 31, both accounts were outstanding. The company uses the perpetual inventory method, and none of these items have been sold.

Required:

a. Provide all the journal entries that would be recorded in December under both the gross and the net methods.

b. By how much and in what direction is net income misstated for these two transactions under the gross method?

c. By how much and what direction is gross profit misstated for these two transactions under the gross method?

d. Assume that both accounts are paid in full on January 2. Provide the journal entries that would be recorded under both the gross and the net methods.

P8-2

(The gross and net methods and partial payments) Phelps Corporation made two purchases of inventory on account during the month of March. The first purchase was made on March 5 for $15,000, and the second purchase was made on March 10 for $30,000. The terms of each purchase were 2/10, n30. The first purchase was settled on March 13, and the second was settled on July 18. The company prepares monthly adjusting entries and uses the perpetual inventory method.

Required:

a. Assume that Phelps Corporation uses the net method to account for cash discounts. Prepare all the necessary journal entries associated with these transactions.

b. Assume that Phelps Corporation uses the gross method to account for cash discounts. Prepare all the necessary journal entries associated with these transactions.

c. Assume that Phelps Corporation uses the net method to account for cash discounts and that, with respect to the second purchase, the company settled 2/3 of the account payable balance on March 19 and settled the remaining balance on August 7. The first purchase was settled on March 13. Prepare all the necessary journal entries associated with the second purchase.

d. Assume that Phelps Corporation uses the gross method to account for cash discounts and that, with respect to the second purchase, the company settled 2/3 of the accounts payable balance on March 19 and settled the remaining balance on August 7. The first purchase was settled on March 13. Prepare all the necessary journal entries associated with the second purchase.

P8–3   *(The financial effects of inventory errors)*   The information below was taken from the records of Schmitt Brothers.

	1991	1990	1989
Sales	$100,000	$90,000	$85,000
Cost of goods sold	50,000	42,000	40,000
Gross profit	50,000	48,000	45,000
Expenses	37,000	32,000	20,000
Net income	$ 13,000	$16,000	$25,000

You are auditing the Schmitt Brothers' books in early 1992 and discover that their inventory counting procedures are flawed. Accordingly, ending inventory was overstated by $2000 in 1989, understated by $3000 in 1990, and overstated by $1000 in 1991. Schmitt uses the periodic inventory method.

Required: Compute the corrected cost of goods sold and net income for 1989, 1990, and 1991.

P8–4   *(The financial statement effects of inventory in transit and consignments)*   The income statement and balance sheet as of December 31, 1990, for Rodman and Sons are provided below. The company uses the FIFO cost flow assumption.

Income Statement

Sales	$200,000
Cost of goods sold	130,000
Gross profit	70,000
Selling and administrative expenses	40,000
Net income	$ 30,000

Balance Sheet

Cash	$ 35,000	Current liabilities	$ 20,000
Inventory	40,000	Long-term liabilities	50,000
Noncurrent assets	120,000	Stockholders' equity	125,000
		Total liabilities and	
Total assets	$195,000	stockholders' equity	$195,000

While examining the company's financial statements, the auditor noted that the following items were ignored when the financial statements were prepared.

Purchases in transit on December 31, 1990

Amount	Shipping terms
$10,000	FOB shipping point
6,000	FOB destination

Cost of inventory out on consignment (recorded as a purchase
but ignored in the physical ending inventory count $12,000

Required:

a. Prepare the income statement and balance sheet for Rodman and Sons in light of the additional information discovered by the auditor.

b. Does it make any difference whether Rodman uses the perpetual or the periodic inventory method? Why or why not?

P8–5 *(Including goods in transit and consignments in ending inventory)*   Yakima Sporting Goods reported the following information as of December 31, 1990:

Inventory (based upon a physical count on 12/31/90)	$2,345,000
Accounts payable	778,000

Additional Information

(1) Yakima Sporting Goods had ordered $125,000 of merchandise from its suppliers on December 27, 1990, with the terms FOB destination. The goods were shipped on December 31, 1990, and received on January 2, 1991.

(2) Included in the physical inventory count was $55,000 in merchandise held on consignment for Power Sunblock Company.

(3) Yakima Sporting Goods received a freight bill for items purchased during December 1990 in the amount of $18,000 on January 6, 1994. These freight charges had not been included in either Inventory or Accounts Payable as of December 31, 1990. Two-thirds of the merchandise purchased during December 1990 was still in the inventory as of December 31, 1990.

(4) Yakima Sporting Goods shipped a large order to an out-of-city customer in the amount of $75,000 (at retail) on December 30, with the terms FOB destination. The customer received the goods on January 2, 1991. Cost of goods sold is 80 percent of the retail price.

(5) Yakima Sporting Goods received a shipment from a vendor on December 30, 1990, which was included in the physical inventory count. The vendor invoice of $30,000 was not included in Accounts Payable as of December 31, 1990, due to a temporary breakdown in the company's internal controls.

(6) Yakima Sporting Goods had $50,000 of weightlifting equipment on consignment at a local health club as of December 31, 1990. The equipment was not included in the company's physical inventory count.

Required:

a. Prepare a schedule in the following format.

	Inventory	Accounts Payable
Reported amounts	$2,345,000	$778,000
Adjustments		
(1)		
(2)		
(3)		
(4)		
(5)		
(6)	_____	_____
Total Adjustments	_____	_____
Adjusted amounts		

b. Complete the schedule for each item listed above. If the item requires no adjustment, state "No effect."

P8-6

(Examining goods in transit at the end of the period) Chung Graphics Software Company took a physical count of all inventory in its possession at the close of business on December 31, 1990. The count indicated $500,000 of inventory on hand, and the company adjusted its books to this amount. No further entries were made to the inventory account during 1990. The company's year end is December 31. While performing the audit of the company's financial statements, the auditors discovered the following transactions involving inventory near December 31.

Type of Transaction	Date Shipped	Date Received	Inventory Amount	Terms
Purchase	12/30/90	1/4/91	$35,000	FOB Shipping point
Purchase	12/29/90	12/31/90	25,000	FOB Shipping point
Purchase	12/27/90	1/2/91	10,000	FOB Destination
Sale	12/29/90	1/4/91	30,000	FOB Shipping point
Sale	12/30/90	12/31/90	20,000	FOB Destination
Sale	12/30/90	1/3/91	15,000	FOB Destination

The following items were extracted from the company's unadjusted trial balance.

Purchases	$980,000 (debit)
Inventory (beginning)	675,000 (debit)

Required:

a. Prepare the closing entry that Chung Graphics made based on its physical count to record Cost of Goods Sold for the year ended December 31, 1990.

b. For each transaction, explain whether ending inventory and/or Cost of Goods Sold would have to be adjusted.

c. Prepare the entry necessary to record the impact of the inventory transactions examined by the auditors. What should be the balance in ending inventory as of December 31, 1990?

P8-7

(The financial statement and income tax effects of averaging, FIFO, and LIFO) The purchase schedule for Lumbermans and Associates is provided below.

Date	Items Purchased	Cost per Item
March 15	5,000	$1.20
July 30	8,000	$1.40
December 17	9,000	$1.50
Total	22,000	

The inventory balance as of the beginning of the year was $15,000 (15,000 units @ $1), and an inventory count at year-end indicated that 11,000 items were on hand. The company uses the periodic inventory method. Sales and expenses (excluding Cost of Goods Sold) totaled $55,000 and $15,000, respectively. The federal income tax rate is 30 percent of taxable income.

Required:

a. Prepare three income statements, one under each of the assumptions: FIFO, averaging, and LIFO.

b. How many tax dollars would be saved by using LIFO instead of FIFO?

c. Assume that the market value of an inventory item dropped to $1.35 as of year-end. Apply the lower-of-cost-or-market rule and provide the appropriate journal entry (if necessary) under the FIFO, averaging, and LIFO assumptions.

d. Repeat (a) above assuming that the costs per item were as follows.

Beginning inventory	$1.60
March 15	$1.50
July 30	$1.40
December 17	$1.20

Which of the three assumptions gives rise to the highest net income and ending inventory amounts now? Why?

P8-8

(Avoiding LIFO liquidations) IBT has used the LIFO inventory cost flow assumption for five years. As of December 31, 1989, IBT had 700 items in its inventory and the $9000 inventory dollar amount reported on the balance sheet consisted of the following costs.

When Purchased	Number of Items	Cost per Item	Total
1985	500	$12	$6000
1987	200	$15	$3000
Total	700		$9000

During 1990, IBT sold 800 items for $50 each and purchased 400 items at $30 each. Expenses other than the cost of goods sold totaled $20,000, and the federal income tax rate is 30 percent of taxable income.

Required:

a. Prepare IBT's income statement for the year ending December 31, 1990.

b. Assume that IBT purchased an additional 400 items on December 20, 1990, for $30 each. Prepare IBT's income statement for the year ending December 31, 1990.

c. Compare the two income statements and discuss why it might have been wise for IBT to purchase the additional items on December 20. Discuss some of the disadvantages of such a strategy.

P8-9

(Using LIFO and saving tax dollars) Financial statements as of December 31, 1990, for Rechoff Company are provided below. Rechoff uses the FIFO inventory cost flow assumption.

Income Statement

Sales		$80,000
Cost of goods sold		
Beginning inventory	$20,000	
Purchases	40,000	
Goods available for sale	60,000	
Less: Ending inventory	25,000	
Cost of goods sold		35,000
Gross profit		45,000
Selling & administrative expenses		20,000
Net income before taxes		25,000
Federal income tax (30%)		7,500
Net income		$17,500

Balance Sheet

Cash	$15,000	Current liabilities	$18,000
Inventory	25,000	Long-term liabilities	20,000
Other noncurrent assets	40,000	Stockholders' equity	42,000
		Total liabilities and	
Total assets	$80,000	stockholders' equity	$80,000

On December 31, 1990, Rechoff decided to change from the FIFO to the LIFO inventory cost flow assumption. The ending inventory value under the LIFO assumption is $15,000.

Required:

a. Compute the change in Rechoff's current ratio associated with the change from FIFO to LIFO. Round to two decimal places.

b. Compute the change in Rechoff's gross profit and net income associated with the change from FIFO to LIFO. Assume that the dollar amount of the change is reflected in Cost of Goods Sold.

c. How many tax dollars would be saved by the change from FIFO to LIFO?

d. Discuss some of the disadvantages associated with the change to LIFO.

P8–10   *(LIFO liquidations, income tax implications, and year-end purchases)*   Ruhe Auto Supplies began operations in 1979. The following represents the company's inventory purchases and sales in the first and subsequent years of operations.

Year	Units Purchased	Cost per Unit	Units Sold
1980	20,000	$ 5	5,000
1981	8,000	10	9,000
1982	7,000	15	7,000
1983	8,500	20	7,000
1984	6,000	25	7,500
1985	7,500	30	7,000
1986	9,000	50	8,000
1987	8,000	65	9,000
1988	9,500	70	9,000
1989	7,000	75	8,000
1990	8,500	80	8,500
1991	9,000	85	7,500
1992	8,500	90	9,500
1993	9,500	95	20,000

Additional Information

1. The company's federal income tax rate is 30 percent.

2. For the year ended December 31, 1993 Ruhe Auto Supply generated $3,000,000 in revenues and incurred $800,000 in expenses (exclusive of Cost of Goods Sold).

3. Ruhe Auto Supply uses the periodic method and the LIFO cost flow assumption to account for inventory.

Required:

a. Compute ending inventory as of December 31, 1992. Identify the number of units in ending inventory and the costs attached to each unit.

b. Compute the company's 1993 income tax liability and net income after taxes for the year ended December 31, 1993.

c. Assume that Ruhe Auto Supply was able to purchase an additional 10,500 units of inventory on December 31, 1993 for $95 per unit. Would you advise the company to purchase these additional units? Explain your answer.

P8–11   *(The gross method, the periodic method, and the LIFO and FIFO cost flow assumptions)*   The Magic Teddy Bear Toy Company entered into the following transactions during January 1990.

(1) January 3: Purchased 8000 teddy bears @ $20 each with the terms 2/10, n 30.

(2) January 3: Sold 2000 teddy bears @ $50 each for cash.

(3) January 9: Sold 4000 teddy bears @ $50 each on account.

(4) January 10: Settled the purchase made on January 3.

(5) January 15: Purchased 10,000 teddy bears. Three thousand of the bears were purchased for cash at $24.50 each, and the remaining bears were purchased on account for a gross price of $25.00 each (terms 2/10, n 30).

(6) January 19: Purchased 7000 teddy bears @ $26 each with the terms 2/10, n 30.

(7) January 23: Paid for one-half of the teddy bears purchased on account on January 15.

(8) January 27: Purchased 2000 teddy bears @ $28 each for cash.

(9) January 28: Settled the remaining open account from the purchase made on January 15.

(10) January 28: Settled the open account from the purchase made on January 19.

(11) January 29: Sold 6000 teddy bears @ $60 each for cash.

(12) January 30: Sold 5000 teddy bears @ $60 each on account.

(13) January 31: Purchased 1000 teddy bears @ $30 each for cash.

(14) January 31: Received a freight bill covering all purchases made during January 1990 in the amount of $28,000.

The Magic Teddy Bear Company has 5000 teddy bears @ $19 each on hand as of January 1, 1990.

Required: Assume that The Magic Teddy Bear Toy Company accounts for purchase cash discounts under the gross method and uses the periodic inventory method. Prepare all necessary entries, including adjusting journal entries, during January 1990 if the company uses the following:

a. LIFO cost flow assumption

b. FIFO cost flow assumption

(*Hint:* Compute the total cost per unit in order to calculate ending inventory and Cost of Goods Sold.)

P8–12   *(Different inventory methods, cost flow assumptions, and shortages)*   The following information was extracted from the 1990 financial records of F. S. Larson, Inc.

Date	Purchases	Total Cost
Beginning Inventory	12,000 @ $10	$ 120,000
2/10/90	10,000 @ $15	150,000
6/30/90	15,000 @ $20	300,000
9/10/90	17,000 @ $25	425,000
11/1/90	14,000 @ $30	420,000
12/9/90	5,000 @ $40	200,000
		$1,615,000

Assume that F. S. Larson, Inc. made the following sales of inventory during 1990 and that a year-end count indicated 26,000 units of inventory on hand.

5/20/90	10,000 units
10/9/90	20,000 units
12/8/90	16,000 units

Required:

a. Assume that F. S. Larson, Inc. accounts for inventory using the perpetual method and the LIFO cost flow assumption. What amount should the company report for Inventory, Cost of Goods Sold, and shortage expense as of December 31, 1990?

b. Assume that F. S. Larson, Inc. accounts for inventory using the perpetual method and the FIFO cost flow assumption. What amount should the company report for Inventory, Cost of Goods Sold, and shortage expense as of December 31, 1990?

c. Assume that F. S. Larson, Inc. accounts for inventory using the periodic method and the FIFO cost flow assumption. Prepare the necessary closing entry for inventory as of December 31, 1990. What amount of shortage expense would be disclosed on the income statement?

P8–13   *(Comparing the financial statement effects of FIFO and LIFO when combined with the perpetual and periodic methods)*   Lewis Medal Shop had 1000 units of inventory on hand as of January 1, 1990. Each unit was recorded on the balance sheet at $5. On June 10 the company received a shipment of 2000 medals at a total cost of $20,000. During 1990, Lewis Medal Shop made three sales: 900 units on March 6, 1200 units on July 19, and 200 units on December 1. All purchases were made on account. A count of inventory on December 31 reveals 700 medals on hand.

Required:

a. Prepare all the journal entries necessary during 1990 associated with inventory if the company uses the following:

   (1) Periodic method/FIFO assumption.

   (2) Periodic method/LIFO assumption.

   (3) Perpetual method/FIFO assumption.

   (4) Perpetual method/LIFO assumption.

b. Which method/assumption combination results in the lowest Cost of Goods Sold amount and the highest ending inventory balance? Which method/assumption combination results in the highest Cost of Goods Sold amount and lowest ending inventory balance?

c. Under LIFO, why does the periodic method give rise to a Cost of Goods Sold number that is different from that produced by the perpetual method?

P8–14   *(Inventory methods, flow assumptions, and income taxes)*   Starfire Video entered into the following transactions involving inventory during 1990.

   (1) Purchased 600 movie videos for $15 each.

   (2) Sold 100 movie videos for $40 each.

   (3) Purchased 200 music videos for $12 each.

   (4) Purchased 300 movie videos for $18 each.

   (5) Purchased 100 movie videos for $20 each.

   (6) Sold 250 movie videos for $40 each.

   (7) Sold 200 movie videos for $45 each.

   (8) Purchased 400 movie videos for $22 each.

   (9) Sold 100 music videos for $35 each.

   (10) Sold 400 movie videos for $45 each.

   (11) Purchased 200 movie videos for $25 each.

Additional Information

1. At the beginning of the year Starfire Video reported the following inventory:

   200 movie videos @ $13 each

   50 music videos @ $10 each.

2. The purchase prices listed above do not include any freight. Starfire Videos is charged 50¢ freight for each video purchased. Freight costs, however, are already reflected in the costs of beginning inventory.

3. The movie videos and the music videos are accounted for separately.

4. Based upon a physical count of inventory at the end of the year, Starfire Video had the following inventory: 850 movie videos and 150 music videos.

5. All inventory was purchased on account and all sales were for cash.

Required:

a. Assume that Starfire Videos uses the LIFO cost flow assumption. Prepare all journal entries, including closing entries, necessary during 1990 for inventory if the company uses the following:

   (1) periodic method
   (2) perpetual method.

b. Assume that Starfire Videos uses the FIFO cost flow assumption. Prepare all journal entries, including closing entries, necessary during 1990 for inventory if the company uses the following:

   (1) periodic method
   (2) perpetual method.

c. Assume that Starfire's goal is to minimize tax payments. Which cost flow assumption should the company select?

P8-15   *(Applying the lower-of-cost or market rule)*   J. Hartney, controller of Babbit Plumbing, has compiled the following information to aid him in applying the lower-of-cost or market rule to the company's inventory.

	Replacement Cost	Net Realizable Value	Normal Profit	Historical Cost
Item A	$50	$55	$ 7	$60
Item B	61	60	10	55
Item C	72	75	1	77
Item D	33	50	5	44
Item E	40	47	9	50
Item F	38	40	1	40
Item G	12	15	5	8
Item H	10	8	1	5

Required:

a. Compute the amount that Babbit Plumbing should report in the account "Inventory" under the lower-of-cost or market rule assuming that the company applies this rule to each item individually.

b. Prepare any journal entries necessary to adjust inventory to the lower-of-cost or market.

CASES

C8-1   *(The lower-of-cost-or-market rule and the recognition of loss/income)*   TII industries makes overvoltage protectors, power systems, and electronic products primarily for use in the communications industry. In April, 1988, the company reported that it will take "a substantial inventory write-down" that will result in a loss for its third quarter, ending June 24. The write-down was estimated to be $12 million and stems from customers's changes in product specifications.

Required:

a. Provide the journal entry to record the writedown. Is the loss realized or unrealized? Why?

b. Assume that the original cost of the inventory was $52 million and that it was written down to its replacement (market) value of $40 million. If TII Industries sells it for $48 million cash in the following period, what journal entries would be recorded? Assume that TII uses the perpetual inventory method.

c. Applying the lower-of-cost-or-market rule in this case would cause TII to recognize a loss in the period of the write-down and income in the subsequent period. Does such recognition seem appropriate? Why or why not?

C8-2   *(LIFO and FIFO inventory values)*   In its December 31, 1984 financial statement, Armstrong World Industries, a maker of furniture, showed inventories of $202,215,000. Included in the notes to the financial statements was the following excerpt:

> *Inventories are valued at the lower of cost or market. The materials portion of substantially all domestic inventories is valued using the last-in, first-out method. . . . Other inventories are generally determined on a first-in, first-out method.*
>
> *Approximately 60 percent of the company's total inventory is valued on a LIFO basis. Such values were lower than would have been reported on a total FIFO basis by $96.3 million.*

Required:

a. Why would a potential investor or creditor who is considering investing in Armstrong securities be interested in the difference between LIFO and FIFO inventory values?

b. If the company had used FIFO for all its inventory, would it have reported a different net income? By how much and in what direction would net income have changed?

c. Assuming an income tax rate of 30 percent, approximately how much more income tax would Armstrong have paid if it switched to FIFO?

d. The notes indicate that inventory valued on a LIFO basis has a lower value than on a FIFO basis. What would cause this to be true?

C8-3   *(LIFO liquidation)*   In its 1987 annual report, General Motors Corporation reported the following:

	1987	1986
Sales	$100,118,500	$101,506,000
Inventories	7,939,700	7,235,100

Note 1 (in part)

> *Inventories are stated generally at cost, which is not in excess of market. The cost of all domestic inventories . . . is determined by the last-in, first-out method . . . As a result of decreases in U.S. inventories, certain LIFO inventory quantities were liquidated. These inventory adjustments favorably affected income before taxes.*

Required:

a. Explain how liquidating LIFO inventories can "favorably affect income before taxes."

b. What affect did this LIFO liquidation have on GM's 1987 income tax liability?

c. How could GM have avoided the LIFO liquidation?

C8-4

(Choosing FIFO or LIFO)   In 1983 a partner from a major accounting firm made the following comment when asked about the accounting methods used by companies in the software industry: "Accounting policies that have adverse short-term effects on financial statements cannot help the industry raise capital."*

*Eamonn Fingleton, "Capital Offense," Forbes, 17 January 1983, pp. 100–101.

After reading such a comment, one might conclude that managers who wish to raise capital by borrowing from banks or issuing equity or debt securities, should choose the FIFO cost flow assumption instead of LIFO. Yet, others have written that they are "puzzled" about why thousands of U.S. companies use FIFO instead of LIFO.*

*Gary Biddle, "Paying FIFO Taxes: Your Favorite Charity," The Wall Street Journal, 19 January 1981, p. 18.

Required: List and briefly explain some of the major trade-offs that must be faced by management when choosing between LIFO and FIFO.

C8-5

(Fraudulent inventory manipulation)   In 1982 Saxon Industries went into bankruptcy amid a storm of complaints charging inflated inventories and unsubstantiated bookkeeping entries. Saxon's shareholders brought a multimillion-dollar suit against the company's auditors, who were unaware of what was later found to be a massive management fraud.

Required:

a. Explain how the management of Saxon could have used bookkeeping entries to "inflate" inventories and profits.

b. If a company inflates profit in a given year by fraudulently writing up inventory values, what happens to profit in the following year if the books are kept correctly in that year? To prevent this, what must management do in that second year?

c. Why would Saxon's stockholders sue the auditors instead of the company's management?

Long-Lived Assets

Learning Objectives

1 Define long-lived assets and describe how the matching principle underlies the methods used to account for them.

2 Identify the three major questions that must be addressed when accounting for long-lived assets and how the answers to these questions can affect the financial statements.

3 Identify the costs that should be included in the capitalized cost of a long-lived asset.

4 Describe the accounting treatment of postacquisition expenditures.

5 Explain how the cost of a long-lived asset is allocated over its useful life, and describe the alternative allocation methods.

6 Specify how to account for the disposition of long-lived assets.

7 Identify the major economic consequences associated with the methods used to account for long-lived assets.

8 (Appendix 9A) List and describe intangible assets and the methods used to account for them.

≣ This chapter concerns long-lived assets, assets that are used in the operations of a business, providing benefits that extend beyond the current operating period. Included in this category of assets are land, buildings, machinery, equipment, natural resource costs, intangible assets, and deferred costs.

Land includes the cost of real estate that is used in the operations of the company. **Fixed assets,** such as buildings, machinery, and equipment, are often located on this real estate. **Natural resource costs** include the costs of acquiring the rights to extract natural resources. Such costs are very important in the operations of the extractive industries (e.g., mining, petroleum, and natural gas). **Intangible assets** are characterized by rights, privileges, and benefits of possession rather than physical existence. Examples include the costs of acquiring patents, copyrights, trademarks, and goodwill. **Deferred costs** represent a miscellaneous category of intangible assets, often including prepaid expenses that provide benefits for a length of time that extends beyond the current period, organizational costs, and other start-up costs associated with beginning operations (e.g., legal and licensing fees). The methods used to account for land, fixed assets, and natural resource costs (often using an account called *Property, Plant, and Equipment)* are covered in the main text of this chapter. Intangible assets and deferred costs are discussed in the appendix.

Stockholders, investors, creditors, managers, and auditors are interested in the nature and condition of a company's long-lived assets because such assets represent the company's capacity to produce and sell goods and/or services in the future. Planning and executing major capital expenditures in such items as land, buildings, and machinery are some of management's most important concerns. For many companies, long-lived assets are the largest asset category on the balance sheet. The long-lived assets of The Procter & Gamble Company, for example, a major manufacturer of consumer products, are valued on the balance sheet at over $8 billion, more than 60 percent of total assets.

THE RELATIVE SIZE OF LONG-LIVED ASSETS

The relative size of long-lived assets on the balance sheets of major U.S. companies varies across industries. Table 9–1 contains the ratio of noncurrent assets to total assets for a selected group of industries.

Table 9–1   Noncurrent assets/total assets (selected industries)

Industry (No. of Companies)	Noncurrent Assets/Total Assets
New and used car dealers (2120)	14%
Family clothing (1373)	22
Department stores (1032)	23
Hardware (2239)	23
Grocery stores (2295)	42
Crude oil and natural gas (1226)	62
Restaurants (2061)	65
Hotels (1912)	80
Motion picture theatres (57)	84

Source: Compiled from data published in *Industry Norms and Key Business Ratios* (Dun & Bradstreet, Inc., 1987)

Note that the ratio varies from 14 percent for new and used car dealers to 84 percent for motion picture theatres.[1] The industries with the lower percentages are generally retailers (i.e., new and used cars and family clothing, department, hardware, and grocery stores) who invest heavily in inventories. The extractive industries, manufacturers, and some services (e.g., restaurants and hotels) require large amounts of property, plant, and equipment to support their operations. For example, Amoco Corporation (petroleum and natural gas), IBM (computer manufacturer), and Wendy's International (fast food restaurants) carry 72 percent, 51 percent, and 78 percent, respectively, of their total assets in the form of long-lived assets.

LONG-LIVED ASSET ACCOUNTING: GENERAL ISSUES AND FINANCIAL STATEMENT EFFECTS

The matching principle states that efforts (expenses) should be matched against benefits (revenues) in the period when the benefits are recognized. The cost of acquiring a long-lived asset, which is expected to generate revenues in future periods, is therefore capitalized in the period of acquisition. As the revenues associated with the long-lived asset are recognized, these costs are amortized (i.e., converted to expenses) with a periodic adjusting journal entry. Stated another way, since expenses represent the costs of assets consumed in conducting business, at the end of each accounting period an entry is recorded to reflect the expense associated with the portion of the long-lived asset consumed during that period.

The form of the journal entries to capitalize and amortize a piece of equipment follows. Assume that the equipment is purchased on January 1 for $10,000, and its cost is amortized evenly over its four-year useful life. Recall that amortization of a fixed asset is called *depreciation* and that the dollar amount of the depreciation expense recognized each year is accumulated in an Accumulated Depreciation account.

Jan. 1	Equipment	10,000	
	Cash		10,000
	To record the acquisition of equipment for $10,000.		
Dec. 31	Depreciation Expense	2,500	
	Accumulated Depreciation		2,500
	To recognize depreciation during the first year of the asset's useful life.		

The preceding description and journal entries indicate that three basic questions must be answered in the process of accounting for long-lived assets:

1. What dollar amount should be included in the capitalized cost of the long-lived asset?

2. Over what time period should this cost be amortized?

3. At what rate should this cost be amortized?

As the following illustration shows, the answers to these questions can have significant effects on the financial statements.

---

1. These ratios overstate the percentage of long-lived assets to total assets because the numerator contains long-term investments. However, the companies in the industries selected generally do not have a large amount of long-term investments.

Figure 9-1   The effects of depreciation period on the financial statements: Rudman Mfg.

Case 1: $12,000 cost is capitalized and depreciated evenly over a three-year period.

	Year 1		Year 2		Year 3	
Equipment	12,000					
Cash		12,000				
Depreciation Expense	4,000		Depreciation Expense	4,000	Depreciation Expense	4,000
Accumulated Depreciation		4,000	Accumulated Depreciation	4,000	Accumulated Depreciation	4,000
Balance sheet value:*	$8,000		$4,000		$0	

Case 2: $9,000 cost is capitalized and depreciated evenly over a three-year period.

	Year 1		Year 2		Year 3	
Equipment	9,000					
Cash		9,000				
Installation Expense	3,000					
Cash		3,000				
Depreciation Expense	3,000		Depreciation Expense	3,000	Depreciation Expense	3,000
Accumulated Depreciation		3,000	Accumulated Depreciation	3,000	Accumulated Depreciation	3,000
Balance sheet value:*	$6,000		$3,000		$0	

Case 3: $12,000 cost is capitalized and depreciated evenly over a two-year period.

	Year 1		Year 2		Year 3	
Equipment	12,000					
Cash		12,000				
Depreciation Expense	6,000		Depreciation Expense	6,000		
Accumulated Depreciation		6,000	Accumulated Depreciation	6,000		
Balance sheet value:*	$6,000		$0		$0	

Case 4: $12,000 cost is capitalized and depreciated over a three-year period at an accelerated rate.

	Year 1		Year 2		Year 3	
Equipment	12,000					
Cash		12,000				
Depreciation Expense	6,000		Depreciation Expense	4,000	Depreciation Expense	2,000
Accumulated Depreciation		6,000	Accumulated Depreciation	4,000	Accumulated Depreciation	2,000
Balance sheet value:*	$6,000		$2,000		$0	

*Balance sheet value, also known as *book value,* equals capitalized cost less accumulated depreciation.

Assume that Rudman Manufacturing acquired equipment for a purchase price of $9000 and paid $3000 to have it installed on January 1. Figure 9–1 compares the journal entries to record the acquisition and the depreciation charge, and the resulting balance sheet value of the equipment in four different cases. In Case 1 Rudman capitalizes the entire $12,000 cost and depreciates it evenly ($4000 per year) over a three-year period. In Case 2 Rudman capitalizes the $9000 purchase cost, expenses the $3000 installation charge, and depreciates the purchase cost

Table 9-2   Comparative expense amounts and balance sheet values

	Year 1	Year 2	Year 3	Total Expenses
Case 1				
Expense	$4000	$4000	$4000	$12,000
Balance sheet value	8000	4000	0	
Case 2				
Expense	6000	3000	3000	12,000
Balance sheet value	6000	3000	0	
Case 3				
Expense	6000	6000	0	12,000
Balance sheet value	6000	0	0	
Case 4				
Expense	6000	4000	2000	12,000
Balance sheet value	6000	2000	0	

evenly ($3000 per year) over a three-year period. In Case 3 Rudman capitalizes the entire $12,000 cost and depreciates it evenly ($6000 per year) over a two-year period. In Case 4 Rudman capitalizes the entire $12,000 cost and depreciates it over a three-year period using an *accelerated rate:* that is, greater depreciation charges are recognized in the early years of the asset's life.

Comparing Case 1 to Case 2 illustrates the financial statement effects of varying the amount of capitalized cost. Note that increasing the amount of capitalized cost reduces the total expense recognized in Year 1, but increases the depreciation expense recognized during each year of the asset's useful life.

Comparing Case 1 to Case 3 illustrates the financial statement effects of varying the estimated useful life. As the life estimate gets shorter (longer), the amount of depreciation expense recognized in each year increases (decreases). In the extreme case, estimating the useful life of an asset at one year is equivalent to expensing its cost.

Comparing Case 1 to Case 4 illustrates the financial statement effects of varying the depreciation rate. Using an accelerated rate increases the amount of depreciation expense recognized in the early years, but gives rise to smaller amounts of depreciation expense in later years.

The differences among the four cases with respect to the amount of expense recognized and the balance sheet value of the equipment are summarized in Table 9-2. It is important to note that the total amount of expense recognized under the four cases is the same ($12,000). Varying the capitalized cost, estimated life, and depreciation rate only affects the timing of the expense recognition throughout the three-year period.

Choosing to capitalize and amortize or expense the costs associated with acquiring long-lived assets can have significant effects on the financial statements. For example, Rodeway Express, a large trucking company, reduced its net income by $27 million when it was forced to expense, instead of capitalize, the cost of acquiring restricted operating routes.[2] The major railroads, including Burlington Northern, CSX, Sante Fe, Norfolk & Western, and Union Pacific, increased profits

---

2. Thomas Baker, "Reality Takes the Wheel," *Forbes*, 27 October 1980, pp. 133–34.

Figure 9–2 Accounting for long-lived assets

Acquisition	Use	Disposal

1. What cost to capitalize?
  a. General rule
  b. Specific issues
    (1) Land
    (2) Lump-sum purchases
  c. Construction
	1. Postacquisition expenditures
	  a. Betterments
	  b. Maintenance
	2. Cost Allocation
	  a. Estimate useful life
	  b. Estimate salvage value
	  c. Choose allocation method
	    (1) Straight-line
	    (2) Accelerated
	    (3) Activity
	  d. Allocation for tax purposes
		1. Retirement—discontinue asset
		2. Sale—exchange asset for cash
		  or receivable
		3. Trade-in—exchange of
		  long-lived assets

by an average of 25 percent when they were allowed to capitalize and amortize, instead of expense, the costs of laying track. The net income of Comserv, a Minneapolis-based maker of software systems, was boosted by $6.5 million in 1982 because the company chose to capitalize and amortize, instead of expense, software development costs.[3]

Changing the useful-life estimate or adjusting the rate at which a long-lived asset is amortized can also significantly affect the financial statements and important financial ratios. American Airlines decreased expenses by $14.6 million and increased earnings per share from $.72 to $1.11 when it decided to depreciate the cost of its aircraft over a longer period of time.[4] Burlington Northern's 1986 financial report disclosed that the company's net income was reduced by $336 million when it changed the rate at which it depreciated its railroad assets.

AN OVERVIEW OF LONG-LIVED ASSET ACCOUNTING

Figure 9-2 summarizes and organizes the topics covered in the remainder of the chapter. As shown at the top of the figure, there are three points in time during the life of a long-lived asset when important accounting issues must be addressed: (1) when the long-lived asset is acquired (purchased or manufactured), (2) while the long-lived asset is in use, and (3) when the long-lived asset is disposed of.

Acquisition: What Costs to Capitalize?

A general rule guides the choice of what costs to capitalize when a long-lived asset is acquired. It states that all costs required to get a long-lived asset into serviceable condition and location should be capitalized. However, applying this rule is not always straightforward. We discuss several such examples in the sections on land, lump-sum purchases, and construction of long-lived assets.

---

3. Gerald Odening, "They've Been Working on the Railroad," *Forbes,* 20 July 1981, p. 83.
4. Jane Carmichael, "The Wild Blue Yonder," *Forbes,* 9 November 1981, pp. 94, 96.

Use of Long-Lived Assets: Postacquisition Expenditures and Cost Allocation

Postacquisition expenditures represent costs incurred to improve or maintain long-lived assets after they have been acquired. Such costs are classified into either of two categories: betterments or maintenance. A **betterment** improves a long-lived asset and is therefore capitalized. A **maintenance expenditure,** which simply maintains a long-lived asset, is treated as an expense.

The process of amortizing the cost of a long-lived asset over its useful life involves estimating the useful life and salvage value and choosing an allocation method or rate. The straight-line, accelerated, and activity methods are three alternative allocation rates that are allowed under generally accepted accounting principles. The process of amortizing a fixed asset is called **depreciation.** The process of amortizing a natural resource cost is called **depletion.** The process of amortizing an intangible asset is called **amortization.**

An issue separate from financial accounting but important to management is the choice of a depreciation method for tax purposes. The section following the discussion of the straight-line and accelerated methods addresses this issue.

Disposal: Retirement, Sale, or Trade-in?

Long-lived assets are disposed of in one of three ways: (1) retirement, (2) sale, or (3) trade-in. **Retirement** simply means to discontinue using the long-lived asset. A **sale** involves exchanging the long-lived asset for cash or a receivable. **Trade-ins** involve exchanging long-lived assets and often cash for other long-lived assets.

We note throughout this chapter that generally accepted accounting principles address each of the issues briefly described above. Yet, in almost every case, the guidelines provided are not very precise, and management is allowed much discretion. We emphasize the point that such discretion can significantly affect the financial statements.

WHAT COSTS TO CAPITALIZE?

The capitalized cost of a long-lived asset includes all costs required to bring it into serviceable or usable condition and location. Such costs include not only the actual purchase cost of the asset but also costs like freight, installation, taxes, and title fees. For example, suppose that the purchase cost of a piece of equipment is $25,000, and it costs $2000 to have it shipped in, $1500 to have it installed, and taxes and title fees total $500 and $300, respectively. The total capitalized cost of the equipment would then be $29,300 ($25,000 + $2,000 + $1,500 + $500 + $300), and the following journal entry would be entered to record the acquisition, assuming that cash is paid for the equipment.

Equipment	29,300	
Cash		29,300
To record the acquisition of equipment.		

Purchasing a long-lived asset often involves a substantial investment, which is frequently financed by the purchasing company. That is, a note payable (instead

Figure 9-3   Determining the capitalized cost of machinery purchased in exchange for a note payable

Calculate Capitalized Cost	
Purchase price (200,000 × 1.7355*)	$347,100
Freight	1,000
Installment costs	2,500
Idle time	5,000
Capitalized cost	$355,600

General Journal

Machinery	355,600	
Discount on Note Payable (plug)	52,900	
Note Payable (200,000 + 200,000)		400,000
Cash (1,000 + 2,500 + 5,000)		8,500
To record the acquisition of machinery.		

*Table factor (present value of an ordinary annuity: $n = 2$, $i = 10\%$).

of cash) is exchanged for the long-lived asset. In such cases the purchase price of the long-lived asset is equal to the present value of the future cash payments specified by the note payable. The discount rate used in the present value calculation is equal to the prevailing rate of interest for similar transactions.

To illustrate, suppose that a company purchases a machine and signs a long-term note stating that the company must pay $200,000 at the end of Year 1 and again at the end of Year 2. No interest is stated on the note. Freight costs are $1000 and the wages of two workers who install the machine are $2500. A portion of the plant was idle while the machine was being installed, and wages paid to the employees during this idle time were $5000. Assume that the prevailing rate of interest for similar transactions is 10 percent. Figure 9-3 shows the computation of the capitalized cost and the journal entry to record the purchase.

Note first that the purchase price of the machine is equal to the present value of the two-year $200,000 annuity payment ($347,100), and the total capitalized cost of the machinery ($355,600) includes freight, installation, and idle time. The note payable in the journal entry is equal to the total cash payments ($200,000 + $200,000) specified by the note, the freight, installation, and idle-time charges were paid in cash.

For the time being, view the Discount on Note Payable account as a plug to make the journal entry balance. Actually, this account represents the difference between the $347,100 purchase price of the machine and the $400,000 note payable. The nature of this account and how it is treated on the financial statements is discussed more fully in Chapter 11, which covers long-term liabilities.

The Acquisition of Land

All costs incurred to acquire land and make it ready for use should be included in the Land account. They include (1) the purchase price of the land; (2) closing costs, such as title, legal, and recording fees; (3) costs incurred to get the land in condition for its intended use, such as razing old buildings, grading, filling, draining and clearing; (4) assumptions of any back taxes, liens, or mortgages; and (5) additional land improvements assumed to be permanent, such as landscaping, street lights, sewers, and drainage systems.

While the costs incurred to acquire land and prepare it for use are capitalized, *they are not amortized* over future periods. The process of amortization requires the estimate of a useful life. Because land is considered to have an indefinite life, its cost cannot be amortized.

Figure 9-4   Land and land improvements: King Enterprises

Land Account (not subject to amortization)			Land Improvements Account (subject to amortization)		
Purchase price		$30,000	Fence	$5,500	
Title and closing		1,000	Roadway	4,200	
Land preparation costs	$10,000		Total costs	$9,700	
Less: Sale of timber	8,000	2,000			
Sewer and power		3,000			
Street light assessment		2,500			
Total costs		$38,500			

General Journal

Land	38,500	
Cash		38,500
To record the purchase and preparation of land.		

General Journal

Land Improvements	9,700	
Cash		9,700
To record land improvements.		

Land Improvements: Indefinite or Limited Life?

A distinction should be made between land improvements with indefinite lives and those with limited lives. Land improvements with indefinite lives are included in the Land account and are not subject to amortization. Land improvements with limited lives are recorded in a separate account and amortized over their limited lives.

A common case occurs when land is purchased as a site for the construction of a new building. In such cases all costs incurred up to the excavation for the building are considered necessary to get the land in condition for its intended purpose. They are viewed as having an indefinite life and appear in the Land account. Removal of old buildings, clearing, grading, and filling are considered land costs, and any proceeds obtained during this process, such as the salvage value of building materials or the sale of cleared timber, serve to reduce the cost of the land. Special assessments for local improvements, such as sidewalks and street lights, are also charged to the Land account because they are relatively permanent and are maintained by local government. However, land improvements with limited lives, such as driveways, walkways, fences and parking lots, are recorded in a special Land Improvement account. These costs are amortized over their useful lives.[5]

An Example: Land or Land Improvement?

Assume that King Enterprises paid $30,000 cash for a wooded tract of land where it intends to build a new facility. Additional title and closing costs totaled $1000. It cost $10,000 to harvest the timber and grade the site. The timber was subsequently sold for $8000. The installation of sewer and power systems cost $3000, and street lights were installed by the county for a $2500 assessment fee. King Enterprises erected a fence around the site for $5500 and a small roadway was prepared for $4200. Figure 9-4 shows the computation of the dollar amounts in the Land and the Land Improvement accounts and the related journal entries.

---

5. *Accounting Trends and Techniques* (New York: American Institute of Certified Public Accountants (AICPA), 1987) reports that, of the 600 major U.S. companies surveyed, 393 used a Land account only, and 111 used a Land and Improvements account, p. 143.

Figure 9–5   Cost allocation on the basis of relative fair market values

Asset	Fair Market Value	Relative Cost Allocation
Inventory	$20,000	$16,000 ([$20,000 ÷ $50,000] × $40,000)
Land	10,000	8,000 ([$10,000 ÷ $50,000] × $40,000)
Equipment	20,000	16,000 ([$20,000 ÷ $50,000] × $40,000)
Total	$50,000	$40,000

Lump-Sum Purchases

A special problem arises when more than one long-lived asset is purchased at a single (lump-sum) price. In such situations the total purchase cost must be broken down and allocated to the individual assets.

Relative Fair Market Value

If the fair market values of the purchased assets can be objectively determined, the total purchase cost can be allocated to each asset on the basis of its relative fair market value. This cost allocation scheme is based on the assumption that costs vary in direct proportion to sales value.

To illustrate, assume that ABC Incorporated purchases three assets (inventory, land, and equipment) from Liquidated Limited, a company that is in the process of liquidation. The total price for the assets is $40,000. The individual fair market values of the three assets and the allocation of the $40,000 purchase cost to each asset appear in Figure 9–5.

Note that the cost allocated to each asset is in direct proportion to the asset's portion of the total fair market value. The inventory, for example, accounts for 40 percent ($20,000/$50,000) of the total fair market value and thereby receives 40 percent ($16,000/$40,000) of the total cost. The equipment is treated similarly. Land accounts for 20 percent ($10,000/$50,000) of the total fair market value and receives 20 percent ($8,000/$40,000) of the total cost.

Remember also that while all three costs are capitalized, each is treated differently in the future. The $16,000 inventory cost will be converted to Cost of Goods Sold when the inventory is sold, the $8000 land cost is not subject to amortization, and the $16,000 equipment cost will be depreciated over the equipment's useful life.

Land and Building Purchased Together

In the preceding example each asset's fair market value could be objectively determined. In some situations, however, such a determination is difficult because the assets cannot be separated. A common case occurs when land and a building are purchased together for a single price.

If the individual fair market values of the land and the building cannot be determined objectively, the total purchase cost could be allocated by assessing the fair market value of the land without the building, and allocating this amount to the Land account. The remaining cost (the difference between the value of the land and the lump-sum purchase price) is allocated to the building. Real estate tax appraisals are often relied upon in such cases.

For example, assume that a tract of land with a building is purchased for $150,000. An objective appraisal estimates the value of the land without the building to be $100,000. The cost of the land, therefore, is determined to be $100,000, and the cost of the building is set at $50,000 (150,000 − 100,000). The cost of the building is depreciated over its useful life, but the cost of the land is not.

Construction of Long-Lived Assets

When companies construct their own long-lived assets, all costs required to get the assets into operating condition must be included in the long-lived asset account, including the costs of materials, labor, and overhead used in the construction process. The costs may also include interest on funds borrowed to finance the construction. For example, note the following excerpts from the 1986 financial reports of Adolph Coors Company and Standard Oil Company.

• Adolph Coors Company: "Properties: The Company has engineering and construction staffs responsible for the majority of plant expansion projects and installation of machinery and equipment. Capitalized costs of projects undertaken internally consist of direct materials, labor, and allocated overhead."

• Standard Oil Company: "Capitalized Interest: Interest costs incurred in connection with significant expenditures for the construction or acquisition of property, plant, and equipment are capitalized."

Although determining the costs of materials and labor is relatively straightforward, allocating overhead and interest to the cost of long-lived assets can be difficult and is often arbitrary. Such issues are normally covered in management accounting courses.

POSTACQUISITION EXPENDITURES: BETTERMENTS OR MAINTENANCE?

Costs are often incurred subsequent to the acquisition or manufacture of a long-lived asset. Such expenditures serve either to improve the existing asset or merely to maintain it. Costs incurred to improve the asset are called *betterments*, and costs incurred merely to repair it or maintain its current level of productivity are classified as *maintenance*.

The following guidelines are often used to distinguish betterments from maintenance expenditures. In order to be considered as a betterment, a postacquisition expenditure must improve the long-lived asset in one of four ways:

1. Increase the asset's useful life

2. Improve the quality of the asset's output

3. Increase the quantity of the asset's output

4. Reduce the costs associated with operating the asset

Betterments are usually infrequent and tend to involve large dollar amounts. Maintenance expenditures, on the other hand, fail to meet any of the criteria mentioned above, and tend to be periodic and involve relatively smaller dollar amounts.

Postacquisition expenditures classified as betterments should be capitalized, added to the cost of the long-lived asset, and then amortized over its remaining life. Expenditures classified as maintenance should be treated as current expenses. For example, note the following excerpts from the 1986 financial reports of American Standard Inc. and Adolph Coors Company.

• American Standard, Inc.: "Facilities: The company capitalizes in the Facilities accounts costs, including interest during construction, of fixed-asset additions, improvements, and betterments that add to productive capacity or extend the asset life. Maintenance and repair expenditures are charged against income."
• Adolph Coors Company: "Properties: Expenditures for new facilities and significant betterments of existing properties are capitalized at cost. Maintenance and repairs are expensed as incurred."

Distinguishing between a betterment and a maintenance expenditure, even with the criteria mentioned above, is often difficult in practice. Consequently, since most postacquisition expenditures are relatively small, they are usually considered immaterial and are expensed accordingly.

To illustrate the accounting treatment for betterments and maintenance expenditures, assume that Jerry's Delivery Service purchased an automobile on January 1, 1989, for $10,000. The purchase cost was capitalized, and the useful life of the automobile was estimated to be four years from the date of purchase. Each year Jerry had the car tuned up and serviced at a cost of $300. During the second year the muffler was replaced for $80, and during the third year the car was painted at a cost of $450. At the beginning of the fourth year Jerry paid $1000 to have the engine completely overhauled. The overhaul increased the automobile's expected life beyond the original estimate by an additional year. Figure 9–6 traces the book value, depreciation, and maintenance expenses associated with the automobile over its five-year life.

Note that all postacquisition costs were treated as expenses except for the overhaul, which increased the automobile's life. The $1000 cost of the overhaul was capitalized at the beginning of the fourth year and, with the book value ($2,500) at that time, was depreciated evenly over the remaining two years of the car's useful life.

Figure 9–6   Betterments and maintenance expenditures: Jerry's Delivery Service

	1989	1990	1991	1992	1993
Book value (1/1)	$10,000	$7,500	$5,000	$2,500	$1,750
Overhaul				1,000	
Less: Depreciation	2,500[b]	2,500	2,500	1,750[c]	1,750
Book value[a] (12/31)	$ 7,500	$5,000	$2,500	$1,750	$ 0
Maintenance expenses					
Tune-up and service	300	300	300	300	300
Muffler replacement		80			
Paint job			450		

[a]Book value equals cost less accumulated depreciation.
[b]2,500 = ($10,000 ÷ 4 years)
[c]1,750 = ($2,500 + $1,000) ÷ 2 years

COST ALLOCATION: AMORTIZING CAPITALIZED COSTS

Once the cost of a long-lived asset has been determined, it must be allocated over the asset's useful life. Such allocation is necessary if the costs are to be matched against the benefits produced by the asset. The allocation process requires three steps: (1) the useful life and (2) salvage value of the long-lived asset must be estimated, and (3) an allocation method must be chosen.

Estimating the Useful Life and Salvage Value

Accurately estimating the useful life and salvage value of a long-lived asset is extremely difficult. An important consideration is the **physical obsolescence** of the asset. At what time in the future will the asset deteriorate to the point when repairs are not economically feasible, and what will be the asset's salvage value at that time? It is virtually impossible to predict accurately the condition of an asset very far into the future, let alone predict the **salvage value,** the dollar amount that can be recovered when the asset is sold, traded in, or scrapped.

The problem of predicting useful lives and salvage values is complicated further by technological developments. The usefulness of a long-lived asset is largely determined by technological advancements, which could at any time render certain long-lived assets obsolete. **Technical obsolescence,** in turn, could force the early replacement of a long-lived asset that is still in reasonably good working order.

As a result, generally accepted accounting principles provide no clear guidelines for determining the useful lives and future salvage values of long-lived assets. In practice, many companies assume salvage value to be zero and estimate useful lives by referring to guidelines developed by the Internal Revenue Service. These guidelines, however, were established for use in determining taxable income and need not be followed in the preparation of the financial statements. Consequently, management can use its own discretion when estimating salvage values and useful lives. As long as the estimates seem reasonable and are applied in a systematic and consistent manner, auditors generally allow managers to do what they wish in this area. Table 9–3 shows the range of estimated useful lives for different kinds of fixed assets reported by 600 major U.S. companies.

Financial Statement Effect of the Useful-Life Estimate
The relatively wide ranges reported for some of the categories in Table 9–3 can complicate the decisions of financial report users because these estimates can have a significant effect on net income and the balance sheet carrying amounts of long-lived assets. Consider the following example.

Table 9–3   Estimated useful lives of fixed assets

Fixed Asset Category	Estimated Useful Lives
Buildings and additions	10–50 years
Machinery and equipment	5–20 years
Office equipment	10 years
Automotive equipment	3–5 years

Source: Accounting Trends and Techniques (New York: American Institute of Certified Public Accountants, 1987).

Figure 9–7   Financial statement effect of the useful life estimate: a comparison

Excerpt from Income Statement

	Transcontinental		Seaways	
Revenues	$1,000,000		$1,000,000	
Other expenses	500,000		500,000	
Depreciation	300,000[a]		200,000[b]	
Net income	$ 200,000		$ 300,000	

[a]($3,000,000 ÷ 10 yrs)
[b]($3,000,000 ÷ 15 yrs)

Excerpt from Balance Sheet

Aircraft (historical cost)	$3,000,000		$3,000,000	
Less: Accumulated depreciation ·	1,500,000[c]	1,500,000	1,000,000[d]	2,000,000

[c]($300,000 × 5 years)
[d]($200,000 × 5 years)

Assume that Transcontinental Airways depreciates its aircraft over a ten-year period, while Seaways International, its main competitor, depreciates its planes over fifteen years. Assume further that these two airlines are of equal value, and in the current year both show $1 million of revenue and $500,000 in expenses other than depreciation. Each airline purchased its aircraft five years ago for $3 million, and both take equal amounts of depreciation from one year to the next. Both companies estimate the salvage values of the planes to be zero. Figure 9–7 shows the current year's income statements and the balance sheet carrying amounts (book value) of each company's aircraft.

It is relatively clear from this example that the useful-life estimate had a significant impact on the reported incomes of the two companies. Net income for Seaways, which estimated a fifteen-year useful life, is $100,000 greater than that of Transcontinental, which estimated a useful life of ten years. The balance sheet at the end of the fifth year also shows a substantial difference, with Seaways reporting a book value of its aircraft that is $500,000 greater than that reported by Transcontinental.

Such differences could complicate the decisions of individuals who use financial statements to compare the performance of the two companies. Both airlines are in economically equivalent positions, yet their financial statements suggest otherwise. This problem is particularly evident in the airline industry, in which many companies use different estimated lives for depreciation. Prior to 1986, Delta Air Lines, for example, took only ten years to depreciate its aircraft, while American used fourteen to sixteen years for most of its aircraft.[6]

Revising the Useful-Life Estimate
Estimating the useful life of a long-lived asset when it is acquired is a very subjective process. After using a long-lived asset for several years, companies often find that their original estimates were inaccurate. Footnote 6 noted that in 1986 Delta Airlines increased the estimated useful life of its aircraft from ten to fifteen years.

---

6. Carmichael, "The Wild Blue Yonder." Note also that in 1986 Delta increased the estimated life of most of its aircraft to 15 years, pp. 94, 96.

In such situations the portion of the long-lived asset's depreciation base (cost-salvage value) that has not yet been depreciated is simply depreciated over the remainder of the revised useful life.

To illustrate, suppose that Delta Airlines purchased aircraft for $110,000 on January 1, 1980, and at the time estimated the useful life of the aircraft and the salvage value to be ten years and $10,000, respectively. If the company depreciated equal portions ($10,000) of the amount subject to depreciation ($100,000) each year, it would have recognized $50,000 dollars of accumulated depreciation by the end of 1984, and the aircraft would be reported on the 1984 balance sheet in the following manner:

Aircraft	$110,000	
Less: Accumulated depreciation	50,000	60,000

Assume that as of January 1, 1985, the company's accountants believed that the aircraft would actually be in service through 1994, ten years beyond the present time, and fifteen years from the date of acquisition (1980). In other words, the company changed its original useful-life estimate from ten to fifteen years. At that point Delta would not make a correcting journal entry to restate the financial statements of the previous periods. Instead, it would simply depreciate the remaining depreciation base ($60,000 − $10,000) over the remaining life of the aircraft (ten years). The following journal entry would be recorded in the company's books at the end of 1985, and at the end of each year until and including December 31, 1994.

Dec. 31	Depreciation Expense ($50,000/10 yr)	5000	
	Accumulated Depreciation		5000
	To record depreciation on aircraft.		

Cost-Allocation Methods

The useful-life estimate determines the period of time over which a long-lived asset is to be amortized. The salvage-value estimate in conjunction with the capitalized cost determines the **depreciation base**[7] (capitalized cost − salvage value): the dollar amount of cost that is amortized over the asset's useful life. The cost-allocation methods discussed in this section determine the rate of amortization or, in other words, the amount of cost that is to be converted to an expense during each period of a long-lived asset's useful life. Three basic allocation methods are allowed under generally accepted accounting principles: (1) straight-line, (2) accelerated, and (3) activity.

The Straight-Line Method of Amortization (Depreciation)
The discussions and most of the examples so far have assumed that equal dollar amounts of a long-lived asset's cost are amortized during each period of its useful life. This assumption, which is referred to as the **straight-line method,** is used by most companies to depreciate their fixed assets and by almost all companies to amortize their intangible assets.[8] Management probably chooses the straight-line

---

7. *Depletion base* and *amortization base* are the terms used for natural resource costs and intangibles, respectively.

8. *Accounting Trends and Techniques* (New York: AICPA, 1987) reports that, of the 600 major U.S. companies surveyed, 561 (94 percent) used the straight-line method to depreciate at least some of their fixed assets. The straight-line method is used predominantly to depreciate buildings, p. 296.

Figure 9–8   The straight-line method: Midland Plastics

Formula

Straight-line depreciation	=	(Cost − Salvage Value)*	÷	Estimated Life
$2,400 per year	=	($15,000 − $3,000)	÷	5 years

*Depreciation base

General Journal

Depreciation Expense	2,400	
Accumulated Depreciation		2,400
To record annual depreciation		

method because, in comparison to the other methods, it is simple to apply and tends to produce higher net income numbers and higher long-lived asset book values in the early years of a long-lived asset's life. Consider the following example.[9]

Assume that Midland Plastics purchased a Van Wagon for $15,000 on January 1, 1987. The life and salvage value of the wagon are estimated to be five years and $3000, respectively. Under the straight-line method, the annual depreciation expense would be calculated as shown in Figure 9–8, which also includes the related adjusting journal entry.

Under the straight-line method, the same dollar amount of depreciation is recognized in each year of the asset's useful life. At $2400 per year for five years, the total amount of depreciation taken would be $12,000, the depreciation base. At the end of the wagon's estimated life, its book value ($15,000 − $12,000) is equal to its estimated salvage value ($3000).

The other two methods, sum-of-the years'-digits and the double-declining-balance are *accelerated* methods of amortization. They are called **accelerated methods** because greater amounts of the capitalized cost are allocated to the earlier periods of the asset's life than to the later periods. Accelerated methods are used by some companies to depreciate fixed assets when preparing financial reports. Apple Computer, Inc. and Liz Claiborne, Inc., for example, use double-declining-balance as their primary depreciation method, while General Electric Company uses the sum-of-the-years'-digits method. *Accounting Trends and Techniques* (1987) reports that sum-of-the-years'-digits is the predominant method used to depreciate machinery and office equipment, while the double declining-balance method is commonly used to depreciate automotive equipment.

Sum-of-the- Years'-Digits Method

To illustrate the **sum-of-the-years'-digits method,** assume the same facts as in the previous example: a wagon with an estimated useful life of five years and an estimated salvage value of $3000, is purchased for $15,000 on January 1, 1987. The general formula and calculations for each year for Midland Plastics Company appear in Figure 9–9.

Under the sum-of-the years'-digits method, the depreciation amount in a given year is computed by multiplying the depreciation base times the ratio of the remaining years in the asset's life *(R)* to (N [N + 1] ÷ 2), where N equals the esti-

---

9. The information from this example is also used in the illustrations of the accelerated methods that follow.

Figure 9–9 Sum-of-the-years'-digits method: Midland Plastics

Formula

Sum-of-the-Years'-Digits Depreciation = (Cost − Salvage Value)* × $\dfrac{R}{N(N+1) \div 2}$

where R = the remaining useful life of the asset as
of the beginning of the current year
N = the entire estimated useful life

*Depreciation base

Calculations

1987: ($15,000 − $3,000) × $\dfrac{5}{5(5+1) \div 2}$ = $ 4,000

1988: ($15,000 − $3,000) × $\dfrac{4}{5(5+1) \div 2}$ = $ 3,200

1989: ($15,000 − $3,000) × $\dfrac{3}{5(5+1) \div 2}$ = $ 2,400

1990: ($15,000 − $3,000) × $\dfrac{2}{5(5+1) \div 2}$ = $ 1,600

1991: ($15,000 − $3,000) × $\dfrac{1}{5(5+1) \div 2}$ = $\underline{\$\ \ \ 800}$

Total depreciation expense recognized $\underline{\underline{\$12,000}}$

---

mated useful life. Note that R decreases by 1 as each year passes and (N [N + 1] ÷ 2) is equal to (5 + 4 + 3 + 2 + 1), the sum of the digits in the estimated useful life. This computation differs from the straight-line method in that it produces a decreasing amount of depreciation in each subsequent year. Yet, similar to the straight-line method, at the end of the asset's estimated useful life the book value ($15,000 − $12,000) is equal to the estimated salvage value ($3000).

Double-Declining-Balance Method

To illustrate the **double-declining-balance method,** assume once again the facts of the preceding example. Figure 9–10 shows the general formula and calculations for each year.

Under the double-declining-balance method, each year's depreciation is computed by multiplying 2 times the book value of the asset (cost − accumulated depreciation) and dividing the result by N, the estimated useful life.[10] Note that salvage value is not part of the general formula. However, the book value of the asset cannot be reduced below the asset's estimated salvage value. In 1990, for example, only the amount of depreciation ($240) necessary to bring the asset's book value ($15,000 − $11,760) to its estimated salvage value ($3000) was recognized. In 1991 no depreciation expense was recognized.

---

10. The formula for the double-declining-balance method can also be expressed as: (Cost − accumulated depreciation) × (2 × the straight-line rate). The straight-line rate is equal to the percentage of the depreciation base charged each year under the straight-line method (1/N). Using the numbers in the example above, this formula appears as follows: ($15,000 − accumulated depreciation) × 40 percent.

Figure 9-10 The double-declining-balance method: Midland Plastics

Formula

Double-Declining-Balance Depreciation = (2 × Book Value) ÷ N
where   Book value* = cost − accumulated depreciation
        N = the estimated useful life
*The book value cannot be reduced below the salvage value.

Calculations

1987:	(2 × $15,000) ÷ 5 = Accumulated depreciation = $6,000	$ 6,000
1988:	(2 × [$15,000 − $6,000]) ÷ 5 = Accumulated depreciation = $9,600 ($6,000 + $3,600)	$ 3,600
1989:	(2 × [$15,000 − $9,600]) ÷ 5 = Accumulated depreciation = $11,760 ($9,600 + $2,160)	$ 2,160
1990:	Reduce book value ($15,000 − $11,760) to salvage value ($3,000) Accumulated depreciation = $12,000 ($11,760 + $240)	$ 240
1991:	No depreciation recognized because book value cannot be reduced below salvage value	$ 0
	Total depreciation expense recognized	$12,000

Straight-Line, Sum-of-the-Years'-Digits, and Double-Declining-Balance: A Comparison

This section compares the financial statement effects of the three cost-allocation methods discussed above. The general formulas, the depreciation expenses, and the related book values for each year of the estimated useful life under each of the three methods appear in Figure 9–11. This comparison uses the same information given in the previous examples.

Figure 9-11 Depreciation methods compared

	Straight-Line (SL = [C − SV] ÷ N)			Sum-of-the-Years'-Digits $\left(SYD = [C − SV] \times \frac{R}{N(N+1) \div 2}\right)$			Double-Declining-Balance $\left(\frac{2 \times BV}{N}\right)$		
	Expense	**Book Value**		**Expense**	**Book Value**		**Expense**	**Book Value**	
1987	2,400	15,000		4,000	15,000		6,000•	15,000	
		−2,400	**12,600**		−4,000	**11,000**		−6,000	**9,000**
1988	2,400	15,000		3,200	15,000		3,600	15,000	
		−4,800	**10,200**		−7,200	**7,800**		−9,600	**5,400**
1989	2,400	15,000		2,400	15,000		2,160	15,000	
		−7,200	**7,800**		−9,600	**5,400**		−11,760	**3,240**
1990	2,400	15,000		1,600	15,000		240	15,000	
		−9,600	**5,400**		−11,200	**3,800**		−12,000	**3,000**
1991	2,400	15,000		800	15,000		0	15,000	
		−12,000	**3,000**		−12,000	**3,000**		−12,000	**3,000**

Table 9-4   The comparative effects on net income of different amortization methods

Method	1987	1988	1989	1990	1991	Total
Straight-line	$4600	$4600	$4600	$4600	$4600	$23,000
Sum-of-the-years'-digits	3000	3800	4600	5400	6200	23,000
Double-declining-balance	1000	3400	4840	6760	7000	23,000

The straight-line method results in the same amount of depreciation ($2400) in each of the five years. The two accelerated methods (sum-of-the-years' digits and double-declining-balance) show greater amounts of depreciation in the early periods of the asset's life (1987 and 1988) and lesser amounts of depreciation in the later periods (1990 and 1991). All three methods recognize total depreciation of $12,000 over the five-year period and thus depreciate the long-lived asset only to its salvage value ($3000).

Choosing among the three methods can have a significant effect on the timing of reported income. Assume that Midland Plastics, which purchased the wagon in the preceding examples, has revenues of $12,000 and expenses other than depreciation of $5000 in each of the five years, 1987–91. Table 9–4 contains the income numbers for each of the three methods for each of the five years.

The net income numbers appearing in Table 9–4 were determined in the following manner:

Net income = $12,000 (revenues)   − $5000 (other expenses)   −   depreciation expense

For example, under the straight-line method for all five years:

$4600   = $12,000   − $5000   − $2400

Under the sum-of-the-years'-digits method for 1987:

$3000   = $12,000   − $5000   − $4000

Note first that the total income recognized across the five-year period is the same ($23,000) under each method because each method recognizes $12,000 ($15,000 − $3000) of depreciation expense over the life of the asset. However, the amount of depreciation recognized in each period differs across the three methods, giving rise to different income patterns over the life of the asset. The graph in Figure 9–12 compares these income patterns.

Two aspects about this graph are important and generalizable. First, compared to both accelerated methods, net income under the straight-line method is higher in the early periods and lower in the later periods of the asset's estimated useful life. Second, the change in net income from one period to the next is greater under the double-declining-balance method than it is under the sum-of-the-years'-digits method, which in turn is greater than under the straight-line method. The double-declining-balance method, therefore, is the most extreme form of accelerated depreciation. Relatively speaking, the double-declining-balance method (and to a lesser extent, the sum-of-the-years'digits method) gives the impression that net income is low in the early periods but increases rapidly over the life of the asset. The straight-line method measures net income as higher in the early periods and remaining constant over the asset's life.

Figure 9–12   Effects of depreciation methods on net income

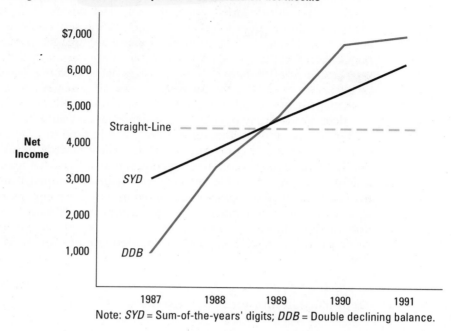

Note: *SYD* = Sum-of-the-years' digits; *DDB* = Double declining balance.

Figure 9–12 is based on the assumption that revenues and nondepreciation expenses are constant throughout the five-year period. Different assumptions about revenues and expenses would change the positions of each plot on the graph. However, the relative positions of the three plots would remain the same, and the preceding statements comparing the three methods would still be valid.

How Does Management Choose an Acceptable Depreciation Method?

Management may choose a given depreciation method for a variety of reasons. Perhaps the most obvious reason is that the method has a significant and desired effect on important financial ratios, such as earnings per share, that are used by stockholders, investors, and creditors to evaluate management performance. When RTE Corporation, an electrical equipment manufacturer, more than doubled earnings per share by changing its depreciation method, its controller justified the action by stating: "We realize that compared to our competitors, our [past] conservative [accelerated] method of depreciation may have hurt us with investors because of its negative impact on net earnings." In a similar context, Inland Steel's controller commented "Why should we put ourselves at a disadvantage by depreciating more conservatively [i.e., accelerated methods] than other steel companies do?"[11]

As stated before, however, changing accounting methods, such as the depreciation method, to inflate net income in an effort to positively influence the assess-

11. Jill Andresky, "Double Standard," *Forbes,* 22 November 1982, p. 178.

ments of investors and creditors may not be an effective strategy. Some evidence suggests that stock market prices do not react positively to such changes, and many accountants question whether credit-rating services, like Dun & Bradstreet, adjust their ratings. In fact, knowledgable stockholders, investors, and creditors may interpret a change to a less conservative depreciation method (e.g., from accelerated to straight-line) as a negative signal, indicating that management may be attempting to hide poor performance that it anticipates in the future.

Management may also consider compensation contracts based on net income and debt covenants when choosing a depreciation method. Compared to accelerated methods, straight-line, for example, would tend to produce greater amounts of net-income-based compensation in the early periods of an asset's useful life. Similarly, the depreciation method chosen may affect whether a company violates a debt covenant. The 1986 financial report of McDonnell Douglas, for example, indicated that a credit agreement entered into by the company required that a certain balance in the Retained Earnings account be maintained. Since the depreciation method affects net income, which in turn affects the balance in retained earnings, the depreciation method can determine whether the covenant is violated.

Depreciation Methods for Income-Tax Purposes

Management is not required to choose the same depreciation method for income-tax purposes that it uses for financial reporting. Indeed, many companies, such as Sundstrand Corporation (aerospace) and Merck and Company, Inc. (pharmaceuticals), use the straight-line method for reporting and an accelerated method for tax purposes. *Forbes* reports that "Like most businesses, Anheuser-Busch keeps two sets of books, one for tax purposes and one for its owners. [The company] uses accelerated depreciation for taxes but straight-line for reporting to investors." Such a strategy gives rise to significant tax savings for these companies. In 1980, for example, Anheuser-Busch saved $67.8 million in taxes by using accelerated depreciation instead of straight-line for tax purposes.[12]

We have shown that estimating useful lives and salvage values in addition to choosing among alternative depreciation methods gives management considerable flexibility in reporting the amount of depreciation on the financial statements. However, the current rules specified in the **Internal Revenue Code,** which cover depreciation for tax purposes, are much less flexible.

The **Modified Accelerated Cost-Recovery System (MACRS)** defines the maximum amount at which the cost of a fixed asset can be depreciated for the purpose of determining taxable income in a given year. To determine this amount, a fixed asset is placed into one of eight categories, based on its estimated useful life as specified in the **Asset Depreciation Range (ADR)** system. The ADR is a document published by the Internal Revenue Service that defines the minimum allowable useful lives for various kinds of fixed assets. In the MACRS each of the eight categories is then linked with an allowable depreciation method, as indicated in Table 9–5.

Automobiles, for example, are placed in Category 2, which allows them to be depreciated over a five-year life using the double-declining-balance method.

---

12. Jane Carmichael, "Rollover," *Forbes,* 18 January 1982, pp. 75, 78.

Table 9–5 Depreciation rules for income-tax purposes

Category	Estimated Life as Stated in ADR	Allowable Depreciation Method as Stated in MACRS
1	3 years	Double-declining-balance
2	5 years	Double-declining-balance
3	7 years	Double-declining-balance
4	10 years	Double-declining-balance
5	15 years	150% declining-balance*
6	20 years	150% declining-balance*
7	27.5 years	Straight-line
8	31.5 years	Straight-line

*Formula = (1.5 × [Cost − accumulated depreciation]) ÷ life

Equipment and machinery are normally included in Categories 1, 2, 3, or 4 and are therefore depreciated over lives ranging from 3–10 years, using the double-declining-balance method. Apartments, buildings, and warehouses are generally classified in Categories 7 or 8, which are subject to the straight-line method over an estimated life of either 27.5 or 31.5 years.

For purposes of determining taxable income, management should use the depreciation strategy that provides the greatest benefit for the company. The appropriate strategy, however, is not entirely obvious because income-tax payments are based on income and, as Table 9–4 shows all depreciation strategies give rise to the same total income over the life of an asset. Consequently, all depreciation strategies produce the same total dollar amount of income-tax payment over the life of the asset.

The key consideration in management's choice of a depreciation strategy for tax purposes, therefore, is the *timing* of the income tax payments produced by the strategy. Accelerated methods and shorter estimated lives are preferred for tax purposes because they save tax dollars in the early years of the asset's life and, thereby, minimize the present value of the stream of income tax payments.

To illustrate, consider the net income numbers resulting from the previous illustration that compared the alternative depreciation methods. These numbers are summarized in Table 9-6.

The total income recognized under the three methods is the same ($23,000). Now assume a corporate income-tax rate of 30 percent. The income-tax payments reported in Table 9–7 would then be due under each of the three methods for each of the five years. The table also provides the present value of each stream of tax payments, assuming a 10 percent discount rate.

The tax payments included in Table 9–7 are simply the income numbers in Table 9–6 multiplied by the 30 percent tax rate. The total tax payments are equal

Table 9–6 The comparative effects on net income of different depreciation methods

Method	1987	1988	1989	1990	1991	Total
Straight line	$4600	$4600	$4600	$4600	$4600	$23,000
Sum-of-the-Years'-Digits	3000	3800	4600	5400	6200	23,000
Double Declining Balance	1000	3400	4840	6760	7000	23,000

Table 9–7   Income-tax payments (30 percent of income)

Method	1987	1988	1989	1990	1991	Total	Present Value*
Straight Line	$1380	$1380	$1380	$1380	$1380	$6900	$5231
Sum-of-the-Years'-Digits	900	1140	1380	1620	1860	6900	5058
Double Declining Balance	300	1020	1452	2028	2100	6900	4896

*The sums of all payments discounted separately using the table for the present value of a single sum.

across all three methods ($6900), but the present values of the tax payments are not. The double-declining-balance method has the lowest present value ($4896), followed by sum-of-the-years' digits ($5058), and straight line ($5231). Thus, the more accelerated the depreciation method, the lower the present value of the tax payments. In general, the depreciation method chosen for tax purposes should be the one that recognizes the greatest amount of depreciation in the early years of an asset's life.

The Activity (Units-of-Production) Method and Natural Resource Depletion

The **activity method**[13] allocates the cost of a long-lived asset to future periods on the basis of its activity. This method is used primarily in the mining, oil, and gas industries to deplete the costs associated with acquiring the rights to and extracting natural resources, as noted, for example, in the following excerpt from the 1986 financial report of Diamond Shamrock Corporation, a large mining operation: "Coal, oil, gas, and other raw material resources are depleted on a units-of-production basis generally over estimated aggregate recoverable reserves.

The estimated life under this method is expressed in terms of units of activity (e.g., miles driven, units produced, barrels extracted) instead of years, as is done under the previous methods. In periods when an asset is very active (e.g., production is high), a relatively large amount of the cost is amortized. In periods when the asset is less active, relatively fewer costs are amortized.

For example, assume that a company purchases mining properties for $1 million in cash. It estimates that the properties will yield 500,000 saleable tons of ore, and during the first year of production the company mines 10,000 tons. The computation of the depletion rate and the journal entries which would be made to record this series of events appear in Figure 9–13.

Depletion: A Cost of Inventory
Ordinarily, depletion is not immediately expensed. Instead, it is carried on the books until the output is sold. Since the depletion cost can be associated directly with the output, it should be matched against the revenue generated from the output. In other words, depletion is a cost of production, which should be capitalized as part of the cost of the minerals inventory. Minerals Inventory is then converted to Cost of Goods Sold in the accounting period when the minerals are sold and the revenue from the sale is recognized.

---

13. Referred to as the *units-of-production* method in *Accounting Trends and Techniques* (New York: AICPA, 1987), p. 146.

Figure 9-13 Depletion rate and related journal entries

Depletion rate: $1,000,000 ÷ 500,000 estimated tons = $2 per ton

General Journal

Mineral Deposits	1,000,000	
Cash		1,000,000
To record the acquisition of the right to extract the ore.		
Depletion (10,000 tons × $2 per ton)	20,000	
Mineral Deposits (or Accumulated Depletion)		20,000
To record the depletion for the first year.		

Assume, for example, that Econ Oil Company paid $500,000 for the rights to drill oil at a certain site. Company engineers estimate that the site will produce 100,000 barrels. Suppose further that during the first year Econ extracts 20,000 barrels and sells 15,000 for $15 each. The journal entries shown in Figure 9-14 would be entered to record these events.

In the figure, the amount of depletion ($100,000) is based on a production of 20,000 barrels and is capitalized as part of Mineral Inventory.[14] Mineral Inventory is then converted to Cost of Goods Sold ($75,000) when the 15,000 barrels are sold. At year-end, therefore, $25,000 ($100,000 − $75,000) remains in the Mineral Inventory account, awaiting the sale of the 5000 (20,000 − 15,000) barrels still on hand.

Figure 9-14 Depletion as a cost of inventory: Econ Oil

Depletion rate: $500,000 ÷ 100,000 barrels = $5 per barrel.

General Journal

Mineral Deposits	500,000	
Cash		500,000
To record the acquisition of the drilling rights.		
Mineral Inventory (Depletion)	100,000	
Mineral Deposits (or Accumulated Depletion)		100,000
To record depletion (20,000 barrels extracted × $5 per barrel).		
Accounts Receivable (15,000 × $15)	225,000	
Sales		225,000
Cost of Goods Sold (15,000 × $5)	75,000	
Minerals Inventory		75,000
To record the sale of 15,000 barrels @ $15 each.		

14. Other costs, such as materials, labor, and overhead, would also be capitalized as part of inventory cost and allocated to Cost of Goods Sold when the oil is sold.

Long-Lived Assets Used in the Extraction Process

In addition to the costs of acquiring the rights to extract natural resources, a mining or drilling company also purchases or builds equipment and structures that are used in the actual extraction process. If such long-lived assets are associated solely with a specific mineral deposit, the purchase or construction costs should be capitalized and depleted, using the activity method, along with the costs of acquiring the rights to the deposit. If, on the other hand, the assets are used to extract minerals at many locations, they are considered fixed assets, and their costs are capitalized and depreciated using one of the alternative depreciation methods. The excerpt below is from the 1986 financial report of Standard Oil Company and describes how it treats such costs.

Depreciation, Depletion, and Amortization Costs: Depreciation of the trans-Alaska pipeline is computed by the units-of production method based on estimated applicable proven oil reserves. Depletion and depreciation of proved oil and gas properties and depletion of mine development costs, mineral lands and leaseholds are computed for each oil and/or gas reservoir or mine using the units-of-production method based on applicable reserves. Other property, plant, and equipment is depreciated principally by the straight-line method over estimated lives which are revised periodically based on experience.

Figure 9-15   Depletion and depreciation: Econ Oil

General Journal		
Mineral Rights	1,000,000	
Assembly Costs	250,000	
Machinery	100,000	
Cash or Payables		1,350,000
To record the acquisition of the drilling rights, the costs of assembling the oil rig, and the costs of additional machinery.		

Depletion rate: ($1,000,000 + $250,000) ÷ 625,000 barrels = $2 per barrel

Mineral Inventory (Depletion)	200,000	
Mineral Rights [100,000 × ($1,000,000 ÷ 625,000)]		160,000
Assembly Costs [100,000 × ($250,000 ÷ 625,000)]		40,000
To record depletion of rights and temporary assets (100,000 barrels × $2 per barrel).		
Accounts Receivable (60,000 × $15)	900,000	
Sales		900,000
Cost of Goods Sold (60,000 × $2 per barrel)	120,000	
Minerals Inventory		120,000
To record the sale of 60,000 barrels @ $15 per barrel.		

Depreciation rate: $100,000 ÷ 10 years = $10,000 per year

Depreciation Expense	10,000	
Accumulated Depreciation		10,000
To record depreciation of machinery.		

To illustrate, assume that Econ Oil paid $1 million for the drilling rights to a tract of land in west Texas. The company also assembled an oil rig at a cost (labor) of $250,000, which will be dismantled after the drilling is complete. Other machinery used in the drilling operation cost $100,000 and is expected to be used later at other sites. Engineers estimate that this site will produce 625,000 barrels of oil, and the machinery is depreciated over a ten-year period using the straight-line rate. Salvage value is estimated to be zero.

During the first year Econ Oil extracts 100,000 barrels of oil and sells 60,000 at a price of $15 per barrel. The journal entries for the first year appear in Figure 9–15.

In the example, the costs of acquiring the drilling rights, assembling the temporary oil rig, and purchasing the machinery are all capitalized. The costs of assembly are depleted as the oil is extracted because such costs are associated only with the present site. Accordingly, these costs are converted to inventory and matched against revenues as the oil is sold. The cost of the machinery, which will be used at a number of drilling sites, is subject to depreciation and is therefore expensed over its useful life.

DISPOSAL: RETIREMENTS, SALES, AND TRADE-INS

Long-lived assets are acquired at cost, amortized as they are used in the operations of a business, and eventually disposed of. The disposal can take one of three forms: retirement, sale, or trade-in. The accounting procedures followed in all three cases have much in common. The cost and accumulated depreciation (or *net cost*, as in the case of intangibles and natural resources) of the long-lived asset are removed from the books when the asset is disposed of, and any receipt or payment of cash or other assets is recorded. A gain or loss on the exchange is recognized in the amount of the difference between the book value of the asset and the net value of the receipt. Such gains and losses are usually found in the "other revenues and expenses" section of the income statement. Consider, for example, the following excerpt from the 1986 financial report of Kerr Glass Manufacturing Corporation: "When properties are retired, related accumulated depreciation is removed from the accounts, and the resulting gain or loss is credited or charged to operations."

Retirements of Long-Lived Assets

Occasionally, companies retire or abandon their long-lived assets. Such action is often due to obsolescence, the lack of a market for the asset in question, or closure by a regulatory body. If cash is received (e.g., scrap value) in the retirement, as is often the case, the transaction is handled as a sale, which is covered in the next section. In the event that no cash is received, the original cost and accumulated depreciation of the long-lived asset are simply written off the books. No gain or loss is recognized if the asset is fully depreciated at the time of the retirement. A loss is recognized if the asset is not yet fully depreciated.

For example, assume that Ajax and Brothers retired two pieces of equipment that were purchased ten years ago. No cash was received for either piece. Item 1 was purchased for $10,000 and was depreciated over eight years with no ex-

422

pected salvage value. At the time of its retirement it was fully depreciated (i.e., accumulated depreciation was $10,000). Item 2 was purchased for $13,000 and was expected to have a $1000 salvage value after its useful life of twelve years. At the time of its retirement the Accumulated Depreciation account was equal to $10,000. The journal entries accompanying the retirement of the two pieces of equipment are given below.

Accumulated Depreciation	10,000	
Equipment		10,000
To record the retirement of Item 1.		
Loss on Retirement	3,000	
Accumulated Depreciation	10,000	
Equipment		13,000
To record the retirement of Item 2.		

No gain or loss is recognized on the retirement of Item 1 because an asset with a book value of zero was simply abandoned. The $3000 loss on the retirement of Item 2 is recognized because the disposal of an asset with a book value of $3000 generated no benefit.

Utility companies have recently faced the possible closure of a number of power plants due to cost overruns and inefficient management. Such an action can give rise to a substantial loss on the financial statements. For example, the 1987 financial report of Commonwealth Edison, a giant electric utility, indicates that the company may be required by the Illinois Commerce Commission to retire several newly completed plants. The potential write-off was so significant that Arthur Andersen, Commonwealth's auditors, rendered a qualified opinion on the utility's financial statements.

Sales of Long-Lived Assets

Accounting for sales of long-lived assets is essentially the same as accounting for retirements, except that cash is received in the exchange. The capitalized cost and accumulated depreciation associated with the asset are written off the books and the receipt of cash is debited. Gains and losses are usually recognized because the cash received is rarely equal to the book value of the sold asset. In all long-lived asset disposals, accumulated depreciation should be updated to the point of the disposal. That is, depreciation expense and accumulated depreciation must be recognized from the most recent financial statement date to the date of sale. Such an entry properly matches expenses to revenues in the period of the sale and updates the book value of the asset to the date of sale.[15]

For example, Computer Services purchased office furniture on April 1, 1987, for $24,000. At the time of the purchase the company estimated the useful life of

---

15. Long-lived assets are rarely acquired or disposed of on the first or last day of the accounting period. In practice, therefore, companies must consider whether they wish to compute depreciation for partial periods. This text does not cover such computations for two reasons. First, many companies follow either of two policies: (1) recognize a full year of depreciation in the year of acquisition and zero depreciation in the year of disposition, or (2) recognize zero depreciation in the year of acquisition and a full year of depreciation in the year of disposition. Such policies eliminate the need to compute depreciation for partial periods. Second, computing depreciation for a partial period can get somewhat involved, especially under the accelerated methods, and we leave such discussion to intermediate accounting textbooks.

Figure 9–16 The sale of a long-lived asset: Computer Services

	Depreciation Computations		Accumulated Depreciation
1987	(Year of acquisition)	$ 0	$ 0
1988	($24,000 − $4,000) ÷ 10 years	2,000	2,000
1989	($24,000 − $4,000) ÷ 10 years	2,000	4,000
1990	(Year of disposition)	2,000	6,000

General Journal

1990			
July 1	Depreciation Expense	2,000	
	Accumulated Depreciation		2,000
	To update depreciation in the year of disposition.		
July 1	Cash	13,000	
	Accumulated Depreciation	6,000	
	Loss on Sale	5,000	
	Furniture		24,000
	To record the sale of a long-lived asset.		

the furniture to be ten years and the salvage value to be $4000, and it used the straight-line method of depreciation. On July 1, 1990 (three years and four months later), Computer Services remodeled its office and sold all the original furniture for $13,000. The company policy on recognizing depreciation for partial periods is to recognize no depreciation in the year of acquisition and a full year's depreciation in the year of disposition. The relevant calculations and the related journal entries appear in Figure 9–16.

On the date of sale, the depreciation is updated, and the sale is recorded. The loss on the sale ($5000) represents the difference between the updated book value ($24,000 − $6000) and the cash proceeds ($13,000).

Trade-ins of Long-Lived Assets

In a trade-in, two or more assets are exchanged, and cash is often received or paid. The methods used to account for such transactions depend on whether the exchanged assets are similar or dissimilar. This text limits its coverage to exchanges of **dissimilar assets,** those that are of a different general type, perform different functions, and are employed in different lines of business. The methods used to account for exchanges of similar assets are normally covered in intermediate accounting textbooks.

In general, the accounting procedures described in the sections on retirements and sales of long-lived assets also apply when dissimilar assets are exchanged. That is, the depreciation of the asset given up is updated, its capitalized cost and accumulated depreciation are written off the books, and the receipt or payment of cash is recorded. However, a problem arises when accounting for exchanges of dissimilar assets because the dollar amount at which the asset received should be valued on the balance sheet is difficult to determine. This problem, in turn, makes it equally difficult to measure the gain or loss that is recognized on the exchange.

In general, the asset received in a trade-in should be valued on the balance sheet at either: (1) the fair market value of the assets given up or (2) the fair market value of the assets received, whichever is clearly more evident and objectively determinable. Applying this rule is often difficult because the list price of an asset does not necessarily reflect its fair market value, and determining the fair market value of the asset given up is normally very subjective. Often the accountant must consult industry publications or obtain data on recent transactions involving similar assets to determine fair market values.

For example, Mastoon Industries exchanged a delivery truck, which originally cost $17,000 (Accumulated Depreciation = $9000) for a new printing press. The dealer agreed to accept the truck plus $12,000. Based on a list price of $18,000 for the printing press, the dealer claims to be granting a $6000 ($18,000 − $12,000) trade-in allowance on the truck. However, the accountant for Mastoon finds that recent sales of comparable printing presses have realized, on average, $16,000 and a publication of used truck prices indicates that the value of the truck is approximately $5000.

Given these facts, there are two acceptable ways to value the printing press on the balance sheet of Mastoon: (1) the fair market value of the assets given up ($17,000 = $12,000 cash + $5000 value of truck) or (2) the fair market value of the asset received ($16,000 determined from recent sales). The journal entries for each method follow.

Printing Press	17,000	
Accumulated Depreciation	9,000	
Loss on Trade-in	3,000	
Truck		17,000
Cash		12,000
To record the trade-in by valuing the printing press at the fair market value of the assets given up.		

Printing Press	16,000	
Accumulated Depreciation	9,000	
Loss on Trade-in	4,000	
Truck		17,000
Cash		12,000
To record the trade-in by valuing the printing press at the fair market value of the asset received.		

The two journal entries are exactly the same except for the value of the printing press and the amount of loss recognized on the transaction. In Case 1 the printing press is valued at $17,000, and the loss is $3000; in Case 2 the printing press is valued at $16,000 and the loss is $4000. From the given information, it is not completely clear which of the two journal entries represents the preferred accounting treatment. The answer depends on the relative objectivity and accuracy of the two fair market value estimates. As the general rule states, the most objective and accurate estimate should be used.

Note also that the list price ($18,000) was not used as the fair market value of the printing press. List prices are nothing more than invitations to negotiate, and astute buyers can often bargain for lower prices. Moreover, since the actual fair market value of the printing press seems to be $16,000 instead of $18,000, a better estimate of the trade-in allowance on the truck is $4000 ($16,000 − $12,000) rather than $6000 ($18,000 − $12,000). It is not uncommon for dealers, especially in the automobile industry, to lead customers to believe that they are receiving more for their trade-ins than they actually are.

As indicated earlier, this discussion covers only exchanges of dissimilar assets because the methods used to account for exchanges of similar assets are quite complex. For example, although book losses are recognized when similar assets are exchanged, book gains are only recognized in proportion to the amount of cash received. Nonetheless, even though the coverage has been limited, it is relatively clear that accounting for trade-ins represents another point at which subjectivity and judgment have a substantial influence on the appearance of the financial statements.

ACCOUNTING FOR LONG-LIVED ASSETS: A REVIEW AND CRITIQUE

The introduction to this chapter noted that accounting for long-lived assets basically involves addressing three questions: (1) What dollar amount should be included in the capitalized cost of the long-lived asset? (2) Over what time period should this cost be amortized? (3) At what rate should this cost be amortized? The answers to these questions, though guided by the matching principle, can lead to reporting problems and misunderstandings.

Problems with Historical Cost

Long-lived assets are capitalized at historical cost when they are acquired. This procedure gives rise to problems for two fundamental reasons. First, there is some question about the usefulness of historical cost for decision-making purposes. Investors and creditors, for whom the financial statements are primarily intended, may find that the historical cost of a long-lived asset is not particularly relevant to the decisions they face. The asset's present value, fair market value, or replacement cost may represent more relevant and useful information. However, these valuation bases do not underlie the dollar amount at which long-lived assets are carried on the balance sheet. The general limitations of historical cost and the procedures that can be used to carry long-lived assets on the balance sheet at replacement cost and fair market value are discussed in Chapter 17 and Appendix C at the end of the text.

The second problem with historical cost is that, although it is generally more objective than the other valuation bases, often it must be determined in a relatively subjective manner. Examples discussed in the text include land improvements, lump-sum purchases, constructing long-lived assets, and determining the costs of long-lived assets received from trade-ins. In such cases managers can subjectively influence important financial statement numbers.

Problems with Cost Allocation

Accurately predicting the useful life and the salvage value of a long-lived asset is virtually impossible. It is also extremely difficult to choose a method of depreciation that allocates the cost of a fixed asset on the basis of revenues it generates. Most fixed assets have very little to do with the direct generation of revenues. Instead, they help to support a general process that eventually leads to revenues.

Consequently, there is no way to apply the matching principle in this case with any degree of confidence. Managers are left to choose from several alternatives and are generally allowed to do what they wish as long as the method chosen is reasonable and systematic. In several areas of the chapter we demonstrated how financial statement numbers are sensitive to the different cost-allocation methods.

Misconceptions About Cost Allocation

Two aspects about the cost-allocation process are often misunderstood. First, the goal of the cost-allocation process is to achieve a reasonable matching of revenues and expenses. It is not an attempt to carry the long-lived asset on the balance sheet at present value, fair market value, or replacement cost. The book value of a long-lived asset cannot be viewed as an approximation of any of these valuation bases. Book value is simply historical cost less accumulated amortization: nothing more, nothing less.

It is often claimed that an objective of cost allocation is to provide funds for the future replacement of long-lived assets as they are sold or retired. In a direct sense this claim is clearly untrue. The basic depreciation entry, for example, which is illustrated below, does not involve cash. Cash is neither received nor transferred to some replacement fund. Cost allocation does not in and of itself provide funds for replacement.

Depreciation Expense	100	
Accumulated Depreciation		100
To record the depreciation of a fixed asset.		

However, in an indirect way, depreciation can provide funds for future replacement of long-lived assets. Depreciation expense, like all other expenses, is deducted from revenues and thus reduces net income. To the extent that taxable income is also reduced, depreciation saves tax dollars. These dollars could be set aside for the replacement of long-lived assets. In addition, dividends paid by a corporation are usually based on net income. Accordingly, depreciation may reduce dividend payments. This savings could also be set aside for the purpose of replacing long-lived assets.

Thus, the depreciation journal entry, which does not reflect a cash inflow in and of itself, can reduce cash outflows due to taxes and dividends. In this way it might indirectly be viewed as providing funds for the replacement of long-lived assets. Nevertheless, the cash saving is usually considerably less than the dollar amount of the depreciation entry and there is certainly no guarantee that either the cash saving will equal the cost of replacing the long-lived asset or that management will choose to use it in that way.

THE ANNUAL REPORT OF K MART CORPORATION

Turn now to K mart's annual report located in Appendix D. As of January 25, 1989 the Property and Equipment (net) account on the Balance Sheet (page 32) equalled $3.896 billion, over 32 percent of K mart's total assets. The chart on page 18 indicates that during 1988 K mart opened 64 new K mart stores in the United States and Canada. The discussion also states that "in addition to the store expansion program, K mart Corporation continues to modernize and refurbish stores, creating a more appealing and convenient shopping atmosphere. The company is concentrating efforts on allocating more space to apparel departments and updating home care centers, Kitchen Korners, electronics and domestic centers. During 1988, 163 K mart stores were completely refurbished, including an updated floor plan emphasizing apparel, a better merchandising mix and new fixturing." The Statement of Cash Flows (page 33) indicates that K mart invested $570 million in additions to owned property during the year.

The section entitled Property Owned (page 35) describes the methods used to account for long-lived asset additions and disposals. It indicates that "land, buildings, leasehold improvements and equipment are recorded at cost. Major replacements and refurbishings are charged to the property accounts while replacements, maintenance and repairs that do not improve or extend the life of their respective assets are expensed currently. The company capitalizes interest cost as part of the cost of constructing capital assets. The costs of all properties retired and the accumulated depreciation thereon are eliminated from the accounts and the resulting gain or loss is taken into income." In addition, as indicated in the section entitled Pre-Opening and Closing Costs, "the company follows the practice of treating store operating costs incurred prior to opening a new retail unit as current period expenses."

The Property and Equipment chart on page 37 provides more complete information about the Property and Equipment account, which is only disclosed at its net amount on the Balance Sheet. As indicated, the property owned is composed primarily of furniture and fixtures ($3.353 billion) and property held under capital leases ($2.416 billion).[16] The accumulated depreciation and amortization total is $3.896 billion, representing 55 percent of the total cost.

The Statement of Cash Flows, which is prepared under the indirect method (see Chapter 4 appendix or Chapter 15), reports that depreciation and amortization during the year was $437 million, a $36 million increase over the previous year. On the Income Statement depreciation expense is included with Selling, General and Administrative Expenses, where it represents only 1.6 percent ($437 million ÷ $27.301 billion) of Sales. Note on page 35, under the section entitled Depreciation, that "the company computes depreciation on owned property principally on the straight-line method for financial reporting purposes and on accelerated methods for income tax purposes. Most store properties are leased and improvements are amortized over the term of the lease but not more than 25 years. Other annual rates used in computing depreciation for financial statement purposes are 2 percent to 4 percent for buildings, 10 percent to 14 percent for store fixtures and 5 percent to 33 percent for other fixtures and equipment." Also, at the bottom of page 24 it states that "because the company is continually refurbishing existing stores and opening new stores, depreciation and amortization expense more closely approximates current cost."

Other Assets and Deferred Charges on the Balance Sheet totaled $578 million as of January 25, 1989. Very little information is provided in the annual report about this account, which probably includes various intangible assets, prepaid expenses, and goodwill. The section entitled New Ventures on page 36, however, discloses that in March 1988 K mart purchased a 51 percent interest in Makro

---

16. The methods used to account for property held under capital leases are discussed in Chapter 11.

Inc., from SHV North America Corporation. It indicates further that "the excess of cost over the fair market value of the assets acquired [Goodwill], which is not significant, is being amortized over 40 years on a straight-line basis." Intangible assets, including goodwill, are discussed in the Appendix of this chapter.

REVIEW PROBLEM

Norby Enterprises purchased equipment on January 1, 1988, for $8000. It cost $1500 to have the equipment shipped to the plant and $500 to have it installed. The equipment was estimated to have a five-year useful life and a salvage value of $1000. On January 1, 1991, the equipment was overhauled at a cost of $1000, and the overhaul extended its estimated useful life by an additional year (from five to six years). On January 1, 1992, the equipment and $13,000 cash were traded in for a dissimilar piece of equipment with a fair market value of $15,000. Norby uses the straight-line method of depreciation. The computations and journal entries related to the acquisition, depreciation, overhaul, and disposal of the equipment appear in Figure 9–17.

Figure 9–17 Solution to review problem: Norby Enterprises

Description/Date	Journal Entry			Accumulated Depreciation	Book Value[a]
Acquisition of equipment (1/1/88)	Equipment Cash	10,000[b]	10,000	0	10,000
Depreciation[c] (12/31/88)	Depreciation Expense Accumulated Depreciation	1,800	1,800	1,800	8,200
Depreciation[c] (12/31/89)	Depreciation Expense Accumulated Depreciation	1,800	1,800	3,600	6,400
Depreciation[c] (12/31/90)	Depreciation Expense Accumulated Depreciation	1,800	1,800	5,400	4,600
Overhaul (1/1/91)	Equipment Cash	1,000	1,000	5,400	5,600
Depreciation[d] (12/31/91)	Depreciation Expense Accumulated Depreciation	1,533	1,533	6,933	4,067

Trade-in (1/1/92)	Equipment (new)
	Accumulated Depreciation
	Loss on Trade-in
	    Equipment (old)
	    Cash
		15,000
		6,933
		2,067
			11,000
			13,000		

Computations

[a]Book value = Equipment cost − accumulated depreciation

[b]Equipment cost: $8,000 purchase + $1,500 shipping + $500 installation = $10,000

[c]Depreciation expense before overhaul: ($10,000 cost − $1,000 salvage) ÷ 5-year life = $1,800

[d]Depreciation expense after overhaul: ($4,600 book value + $1,000 overhaul − $1,000 salvage) ÷ 3-year remaining life = $1,533

SUMMARY ANSWERS TO LEARNING OBJECTIVES

1 Define long-lived assets and describe how the matching principle underlies the methods used to account for them.

Long-lived assets are assets that are used in the operations of the business, providing benefits that extend beyond the current accounting period. Included are land (not held for resale), buildings, machinery, equipment, costs incurred to acquire the right to extract natural resources, intangible assets, and deferred costs.

According to the matching principle, efforts (expenses) should be matched against benefits (revenues) in the period when the benefits are recognized. Since the benefits provided by long-lived assets extend beyond the current period, the costs of acquiring long-lived assets are capitalized in the period of acquisition and then amortized as their useful lives expire.

2 Identify the three major questions that must be addressed when accounting for long-lived assets and how the answers to these questions can affect the financial statements.

Accounting for most long-lived assets consists primarily of answering three questions: (1) What dollar amount should be included in the capitalized cost of the long-lived asset? (2) Over what time period should this cost be amortized? (3) At what rate should this cost be amortized? These questions are addressed for all long-lived assets except land, which is not subject to amortization.

Answering these questions in various ways can have significant effects on the timing of asset and income recognition. Capitalizing instead of expensing a cost defers expense recognition, giving rise to higher asset values and net income in the period of acquisition. Similarly, allocating the cost of a long-lived asset over a long, instead of a short, period of time defers expense recognition and creates higher asset and income values in the early years of the asset's life. However, these financial statement effects are a matter of timing, not magnitude. That is, a method giving rise to higher asset and income values in the early years of an asset's life will create lower asset and income values in the later years.

3 Identify the costs that should be included in the capitalized cost of a long-lived asset.

The general rule states that all costs required to get a long-lived asset into serviceable condition should be capitalized. This includes not only the cost of purchasing a long-lived asset, but also costs such as freight, installation, taxes, title fees, idle time while the asset is being installed, the costs of preparing land for use in the business, indirect overhead costs incurred while manufacturing a long-lived asset, and interest costs on borrowed funds used to construct long-lived assets. When long-lived assets are purchased as part of a group of assets for a single, lump-sum price, the overall price is allocated to each asset on the basis of its relative fair market value.

4 Describe the accounting treatment of postacquisition expenditures.

Postacquisition expenditures are costs incurred subsequent to the acquisition or manufacture of a long-lived asset. Costs incurred to improve the asset (as defined by a set of criteria) are called *betterments*, and should be capitalized as part of the cost of the asset and amortized over its remaining life. Betterments are usually infrequent and tend to involve relatively large dollar amounts.

Costs incurred to repair an asset or maintain its current level of productivity are classified as maintenance, and are immediately expensed. Maintenance expenditures tend to be periodic and relatively small. Most postacquisition expenditures are small, and it is often difficult to distinguish between a betterment and a maintenance expenditure. On the basis of materiality, therefore, most postacquisition expenditures are expensed.

5 Explain how the cost of a long-lived asset is allocated over its useful life, and describe the alternative allocation methods.

To allocate the cost of a long-lived asset over its useful life, three issues must be addressed: (1) the useful life must be estimated, (2) the salvage value must be estimated, and (3) a cost-allocation method must be chosen. The useful-life estimate defines the period of time over which the asset's cost is to be amortized. The capitalized cost less the salvage value defines the amortization base, the total amount of cost to be amortized. The cost-allocation method determines the amount of cost to be amortized each period.

Accurately estimating the useful life and salvage value of a long-lived asset is difficult. The asset's physical obsolescence should be considered, and issues like changing demands and technological developments complicate the process. At a minimum, the estimates must be reasonable and applied in a systematic and consistent manner. Nonetheless, these estimates are very subjective and leave much to the discretion of managers. Further, they can have significant effects on the financial statements.

Three basic cost-allocation methods are considered systematic and reasonable: (1) straight-line, (2) accelerated, and (3) activity. The straight-line method recognizes equal amounts of depreciation each period throughout the life of the asset. This method is used by most companies to depreciate buildings for financial reporting purposes and to amortize intangible assets for both financial reporting and tax purposes.

Accelerated methods, including sum-of-the-years'-digits and double-declining-balance, recognize larger amounts of depreciation in the early periods of an asset's life and smaller amounts in the later periods. These methods are used predominantly to depreciate machinery and office and automotive equipment. For long-lived assets like machinery and equipment, these methods are allowed for tax purposes, and are attractive because they reduce tax payments in the early periods of the asset's life.

The activity method bases the amount of amortization each period on the activity of the asset during that period. The life of the asset is expressed in terms of a unit of activity, and as each unit is produced, a portion of the asset's cost is amortized. This method is primarily used to record the depletion of natural resources.

6 Specify how to account for the disposition of long-lived assets.

Long-lived assets are disposed of through retirement, sale, or trade-in. When a long-lived asset is retired for no cash, the original cost and accumulated depreciation of the asset is written off the books, and a loss is recognized if the asset is not fully amortized as of the time of the retirement.

When long-lived assets are sold for cash, Cash is debited, the original cost and accumulated depreciation are written off the books and a gain or loss, which represents the difference between the book value of the asset and the proceeds, is recognized on the transaction.

When two dissimilar assets and cash are exchanged, the cash receipt or payment is recorded, the original cost and accumulated depreciation of the asset given up are written off the books, the asset received is given a dollar value, and a gain or loss is recognized on the transaction. The general rule for valuing the asset received is to use the fair market value of the assets given up (cash and the asset given up) or the fair market value of the asset received, whichever is clearly more objectively determinable. After the asset received is assigned a dollar value, a gain or loss is recognized. Exchanges involving similar assets are accounted for in a different manner: losses are recognized in the same way, but gains are only recognized in proportion to the cash received.

7 Identify the major economic consequences associated with the methods used to account for long-lived assets.

The methods used to account for long-lived assets can have significant economic effects. The amount of cost to capitalize, the chosen amortization method, and the dollar values assigned to assets received in exchanges can have significant effects on the timing of net income and important financial ratios. These numbers are used by interested parties to evaluate management and assess earning power, solvency, and determine credit ratings. They are also used in compensation contracts and debt covenants to control and direct management behavior.

A P P E N D I X   9 A

Intangible Assets and Deferred Costs

Intangible assets are characterized by the rights, privileges, and benefits of possession rather than by physical existence. Some accountants also suggest that intangible assets have a higher degree of uncertainty than tangible assets. Among other items, they include the costs of acquiring copyrights, patents, trademarks, trade names, licenses, and goodwill. Deferred costs include prepaids, which extend beyond the current accounting period, and the costs incurred prior to the point when a company is fully operational (start-up or organizational costs). Such assets are often reported on the balance sheet as "Other assets." In general, the costs of acquiring intangible assets and deferred costs should be capitalized, and professional standards require that they be amortized over their useful lives, but not to exceed 40 years. Most companies use the straight-line method to amortize intangibles for both reporting and tax purposes.

The useful life of an intangible asset is often difficult to estimate, and the decline in service potential is often almost impossible to measure. As a result, the allocation of the capitalized cost to future periods is very subjective, and different intangible assets are treated in different ways. Table 9A–1 shows the amortization periods of the more common intangible assets and deferred costs used by a selected group of 600 major U.S. companies during 1986.

Table 9A–1   Amortization periods, 1986 (number of companies)

Period	Goodwill	Patent	Trademark	License	Software
40 years	151	—	5	1	—
"Not exceeding 40 years"	73	5	4	2	—
25–30 years	16	—	—	—	—
20 years	18	—	1	1	—
10–15 years	18	3	1	1	—
Legal/estimated life	15	44	22	10	9
Other	31	11	6	8	9
Total	322	63	39	23	18

Source: *Accounting Trends and Techniques* (New York: American Institute of Certified Public Accountants, 1987).

COPYRIGHTS, PATENTS, AND TRADEMARKS

Copyrights are exclusive rights granted by law to control literary, musical, or artistic works. They are granted for fifty years beyond the life of the creator. Patents are granted by the U.S. Patent Office, and they give the holders exclusive rights to use, manufacture, or sell a product or process for a period of ten years. A trademark or trade name is a word, phrase, or symbol that distinguishes or identifies a particular enterprise or product. The right to use a trademark is also granted by the U.S. Patent Office exclusively to the holder. The trademark lasts for a period of twenty years but can be renewed indefinitely. Kleenex, Pepsi-Cola, Excedrin, and Wheaties are just a few examples of trade names that are so familiar that they are now a part of our culture.

THE COSTS OF DEVELOPING COMPUTER SOFTWARE

Effective for financial statements with fiscal years beginning after December 15, 1985, SFAS No. 86 specifies that costs of developing and producing computer software products to be sold or leased be capitalized and amortized over their economic lives. Prior to this standard such costs were expensed, and many small software development companies claimed that this practice understated net income, making it very difficult to attract outside capital. This standard had a significant impact on the financial statements of many companies involved in the development of computer software. For example, consider the excerpt below from the 1986 financial report of Wang Laboratories, Inc. Note that the net effect of the change increased 1986 net income by $19.3 million.

Effective July 1, 1985, the Company adopted a change of accounting for costs of computer software. The change was made in accordance with provisions of Statement of Financial Accounting Standards No. 86, which specifies that certain costs incurred in the development of computer software to be sold or leased to customers, are to be capitalized and amortized over the economic useful life of the software product. Total costs capitalized during the year ended June 30, 1986 approximated $21.1 million, of which $1.8 million has been amortized and charged to expense.

GOODWILL

When one company purchases another for a dollar amount that is greater than the net fair market value of the purchased company's assets and liabilities, goodwill is recognized on the purchasing company's balance sheet. Goodwill is a common asset on the balance sheets of the major U.S. companies. Table 9A–1 shows that 322 of the 600 companies surveyed disclosed goodwill on their balance sheet. For many companies, such as Chrysler Corporation, Marriott Corporation, and General Electric, goodwill is quite significant. It accounts for 10 percent or more of their total assets.

To illustrate how goodwill is acquired, consider PepsiCo's acquisition of several major bottling operations from Philip Morris Companies and Kentucky Fried Chicken from RJR Nabisco, Inc. in 1986 for a total of $1,678.3 million dollars. The fair market values of the assets and liabilities purchased by PepsiCo in these transactions were $1,191.4 million and $458.5 million, respectively. Accordingly, the following journal entry was recorded on PepsiCo's books. Assets in the journal entry include cash, receivables, inventories, investments, and long-lived assets; liabilities include short-term payables and long-term debts.

Assets	1,191,400,000	
Goodwill	945,400,000	
Liabilities		458,500,000
Cash		1,678,300,000
To record the purchase of the bottling operations and Kentucky Fried Chicken.		

Similarly, in 1986 Brunswick Corporation purchased Bayliner Marine Corporation and Sea Ray Industries, Inc. for a total cost of $779 million. Brunswick received assets of $707.9 million and liabilities of $140.2 million. Consequently, Brunswick recorded the following journal entry on its books. As in the preceding entry assets include cash, receivables, inventories, investments, and long-lived assets; liabilities include short-term payables and long-term debts.

Assets	707,900,000	
Goodwill	211,300,000	
Liabilities		140,200,000
Cash		779,000,000
To record the purchase of Bayliner and Sea Ray.		

Note in both transactions that the amount of goodwill is simply the difference between the purchase price and the net value of the purchased companies' assets and liabilities. It represents PepsiCo's and Brunswick's assessments that the purchased companies are worth more as working units than is indicated by the values of their individual assets and liabilities.

Goodwill is a long-lived asset, and for financial reporting purposes, it is amortized over a period of time not to exceed forty years, normally using the straight-line method. Note in Table 9A–1 that major U.S. companies use a variety of periods over which to amortize goodwill. In fact, goodwill acquired before October 31, 1970 need not be amortized at all, and many companies leave it on the balance sheet indefinitely.[17]

---

17. *Accounting Trends and Techniques* (New York: AICPA, 1987) reports that 84 of the 600 major U.S. companies surveyed did not amortize goodwill acquired prior to October 31, 1970, p. 163.

It is also important to realize that goodwill is not subject to amortization for income-tax purposes. The Internal Revenue Service has taken the controversial position that goodwill is fundamentally an investment with an indefinite useful life, similar to land, and as such should not be amortized for purposes of determining taxable income. Consequently, goodwill acquired since late 1970 must be amortized for financial reporting purposes, but cannot be amortized for income tax purposes. If income tax law were to allow the amortization of goodwill, corporate acquisitions would become much more attractive from an economic standpoint.

ORGANIZATIONAL COSTS

Organizational costs represent another controversial area in accounting for intangible assets. These are costs incurred prior to the start of a company's operations, typically including fees for underwriting, legal and accounting services, licenses, titles, and promotional expenditures. It is relatively clear that such costs are incurred to generate future revenues, and therefore it seems that organizational costs should be capitalized. However, the service potential of such an asset cannot be associated with any future revenue in particular and thus it is difficult to determine how it should be amortized. In a sense, organizational costs are of value to the company throughout its entire life. Does that mean that they should be left on the balance sheet indefinitely? Conceptually they may, but as stated earlier, professional pronouncements require that intangible assets be amortized over a period of time not to exceed forty years.

Unlike goodwill, organizational costs can be amortized in the determination of taxable income. For such purposes, most companies choose to amortize organizational costs over a useful life that is much shorter than that chosen for financial reporting purposes.

RESEARCH AND DEVELOPMENT COSTS

Research and development (R&D) costs are incurred to generate revenue in future periods through the creation of new products or processes. Such costs are significant for many major U.S. manufacturers. In 1987, for example, Eli Lilly and Company, Dow Chemical, and Abbott Laboratories invested $466 million, $670 million, and $361 million, respectively, in research and development. That same year, IBM and the Boeing Company invested $5.4 billion and $824 million, respectively, in R&D.

The matching principle clearly suggests that R&D costs should be capitalized and amortized over future periods. However, it is difficult to match specific research and development expenditures with the creation of specific products or processes. Some R&D expenditures are for basic research, others lead to failures, and still others provide only indirect benefits, or benefits that could not have been foreseen when the expenditure was incurred.

Concerned with the wide variety of practices used by companies to capitalize and amortize R&D expenditures, in 1974 the FASB published SFAS No. 2. This pronouncement required that expenditures for most types of R&D costs be expensed in the year incurred, rather than capitalized as intangible assets and then amortized. While this pronouncement promoted uniformity of accounting practices in the area of R&D, relieved pressures on auditors and managers to subjectively determine which R&D costs should be capitalized, and reduced some of management's ability to manipulate the financial statements, it is definitely inconsistent with the matching principle. In line with this standard, many R&D costs that will clearly benefit future periods are being immediately expensed. As with organizational costs, accounting for R&D costs represents an example of theoretical measurement principles being compromised in the interest of practical considerations.

The requirement to expense all R&D costs can have a significant effect on the financial statements. Had IBM, for example, been allowed to capitalize half of its R&D expenditures in 1987, its net income would have increased from $5.3 billion to approximately $8 billion. There is also some evidence to suggest that the negative effects on net income and other important financial ratios of SFAS No. 2 serve to discourage companies, especially small research-oriented firms, from making R&D expenditures.

SUMMARY OF LEARNING OBJECTIVE

8   List and describe intangible assets and the methods used to account for them.

Intangible assets are characterized by the rights, privileges, and benefits of possession rather than by physical existence. They include the costs of acquiring copyrights, trademarks, and patents as well as the costs incurred before a company is fully operational and goodwill, the difference between the price paid when a company is purchased and the total fair market value of the company's individual assets and liabilities. The costs of intangible assets are capitalized, and professional standards require that they be amortized over their useful lives but not to exceed forty years. Most companies use the straight-line method to amortize intangibles for both reporting and tax purposes. Goodwill is not amortized for tax purposes. Although the matching principle suggests that research and development costs be capitalized and amortized, such costs are expensed when incurred.

KEY TERMS

Accelerated method (p. 411)
Activity method (p. 418)
Amortization (p. 402)
Asset Depreciation Range (ADR) (p. 416)
Betterment (p. 402)
Deferred cost (p. 397)
Depletion (p. 402)
Depreciation (p. 402)
Depreciation base (p. 410)
Dissimilar assets (p. 423)
Double-declining-balance method (p. 412)
Fixed assets (p. 397)
Intangible assets (p. 397)
Internal Revenue Code (p. 416)

Land (p. 397)
Maintenance expenditure (p. 402)
Modified Accelerated Cost-Recovery System (MACRS) (p. 416)
Natural resource cost (p. 397)
Physical obsolescence (p. 408)
Postacquisition expenditure (p. 402)
Retirement (p. 402)
Sale (p. 402)
Salvage value (p. 408)
Straight-line method (p. 410)
Sum-of-the-years'-digits method (p. 411)
Technical obsolescence (p. 408)
Trade-in (p. 402)

QUESTIONS FOR DISCUSSION AND REVIEW

1. List and define the different kinds of long-lived assets. Why are long-lived assets of interest to stockholders, investors, creditors, managers, and auditors?

2. The chapter mentions three basic issues that must be addressed when accounting for long-lived assets. What are these issues and how are they related to the matching principle?

3. Differentiate among land, fixed assets, natural resource costs, and intangible assets. In each case how is the capitalized cost allocated to future periods? What accounts are involved?

4. The different methods of accounting for long-lived assets give rise to timing differences in asset and income recognition. Explain what this means and provide an illustration.

5. Long-lived assets are (1) acquired, (2) used, and then (3) disposed of. Briefly describe the accounting issues that are addressed at each of these three stages.

6. What is the general rule for determining the amount of cost that should be capitalized for a long-lived asset? What kind of costs are typically included?

7. How is the cost of a long-lived asset determined when the asset is purchased in exchange for a long-term note payable?

8. Distinguish between the costs included in the Land account and the costs included in the Land Improvements account. How are they accounted for differently?

9. How is the cost of a lump-sum purchase allocated to the component items purchased? If inventory, land, and equipment were all purchased for one lump sum, why would it make a difference on the financial statements how the total cost was allocated to each item?

10. What are postacquisition expenditures? Differentiate a betterment from a maintenance expenditure, and describe the methods used to account for each. What criteria are used to define a betterment? Describe the role of materiality with respect to accounting for betterments and maintenance expenditures.

11. What three steps are required to allocate the cost of a long-lived asset over its useful life? How do these three steps affect the measurement of assets and net income?

12. The chapter describes and illustrates four cost-allocation methods. Describe each method and compare their effects on the income statement and the balance sheet. Which methods tend to make a company look as if its performance is improving? In those cases where there is a close association between the activity of a long-lived asset and its decline in service potential, which method represents the best application of the matching principle? Why?

13. Provide an example of how the terms of an outstanding loan liability (i.e., debt covenant) might influence a manager to choose a particular depreciation method.

14. Explain why a large, well-established company might not choose to change from an accelerated method of depreciation to straight-line? How might investors and creditors interpret such a move?

15. Briefly describe the tax law with respect to the depreciation of fixed assets. Why do most companies choose one depreciation method for reporting purposes and another for tax purposes? When managers have a choice, why do they generally depreciate fixed assets for tax purposes using as short a life as possible and the double-declining-balance method? Are fewer tax dollars paid over the life of the asset?

16. Describe the activity method and how it is used to deplete the costs of acquiring rights to extract natural resources. When should the depletion cost be matched against revenue? How is this accomplished? When long-lived assets are used in the extraction process, how is it determined that some are subject to depletion, while others are subject to depreciation?

17. List the three ways described in the chapter to dispose of long-lived assets. What do the methods used to account for these three events have in common?

18. What is the general rule for valuing an asset received in exchange for a dissimilar asset and cash? Prepare the form of a journal entry (i.e., debited and credited accounts but no dollar amounts) used to record such a transaction. Assume that a loss is recognized on the exchange.

19. What are the two fundamental problems with valuing long-lived assets at historical cost? What problems are there with the cost-allocation process?

20. Some claim that an objective of allocating the costs of long-lived assets to future periods is to provide funds for the future replacement of those assets. Evaluate this statement, pointing out both how it is inaccurate as well as how, in an indirect way, it might be viewed as correct.

21. *Appendix 9A.* List and define five different intangible assets. What methods are used to allocate the cost of intangible assets to future periods?

22. *Appendix 9A.* What is goodwill, and how is it recognized on the financial statements?

23. *Appendix 9A.* How are the methods used to account for research and development costs inconsistent with the matching principle? Why have they not been changed?

EXERCISES

E9-1

(Different amortization methods achieve different objectives)   The controller of Bedrock Furniture Store is currently trying to decide what depreciation method to use for a particular fixed asset. The controller has prepared the following list of possible objectives that might be accomplished through a depreciation method. Which method (s)

a. Most closely matches the asset's cost with the benefits resulting from the asset's use?

b. Allocates the cost of the asset over the asset's useful life?

c. Generates the largest net income in the last year of the asset's useful life?

d. Does not use the asset's salvage value in computing the depreciation expense?

e. Is best for tax purposes, (i.e., minimizes the present value of future tax payments)?

f. Recognizes an equal charge to expense every period?

g. Generates the largest depreciation expense in the asset's last year?

h. Does not allow the asset's book value to drop below the asset's salvage value?

Required: Consider each objective independently and indicate the depreciation method or methods that achieve each objective.

E9-2

(Determining the capitalized cost and depreciation base)   Lowery, Inc. purchased new plant equipment on January 1, 1991. The company paid $850,000 for the equipment, $50,000 for transportation of the equipment, and $10,000 for insurance on the equipment while it was being transported. The company also estimates that over the equipment's useful life, it will require additional power, which will cause utility costs to increase $90,000. The equipment has an estimated salvage value of $75,000.

Required:

a. What amount should the company capitalize for this equipment on January 1, 1991?

b. What is the depreciation base of this equipment?

c. What amount will be depreciated over the life of this equipment?

E9–3   *(Allocating cost on the basis of relative market value)*   AJB Real Estate purchased a ten-acre tract of land for $80,000. The company divided the land into four lots of two and one-half acres each. Lot 1 had a beautiful view of the mountains and was valued at $40,000. Lot 2 had a stream running through it and was valued at $30,000. Lots 3 and 4 were each valued at $15,000. Assume that each lot is sold for the values indicated. Compute the profit on each of the four sales.

E9–4   *(Betterments or maintenance?)*   The following items represent common postacquisition expenditures incurred on machinery. Identify each as a betterment or a maintenance item.

a. Lubrication service
b. Painting costs
c. Cleaning expenditures
d. Rewiring costs to increase operating speed
e. Repairs
f. Replacement of defective parts
g. An overhaul to increase useful life
h. Cost of a muffler to reduce machine noise
i. Costs of redesign to increase output

E9–5   *(Depreciation calculations and journal entries)*   Conlon Corporation purchased a new computer system on January 1, 1989, for $350,000 cash. The company also incurred $25,000 in installation costs and $10,000 to train its employees on the new system. The computer system has an estimated useful life of five years and an estimated salvage value of $85,000.

Required:

a. Prepare the entry to record the acquisition of the computer system.
b. Calculate the depreciation expense recognized each year over the life of the system for each of the following assumptions:
   1. Conlon uses straight-line depreciation.
   2. Conlon uses sum-of-the-years'-digits depreciation.
   3. Conlon uses double-declining-balance depreciation.
c. Provide the journal entry recorded by Conlon at the end of 1989 under the double-declining-balance method.

E9–6   *(Computing depreciation and choosing a depreciation method)*   Benick Industries purchased a new lathe on January 1, 1989, for $145,000. Benick estimates that the lathe will have a useful life of four years and that the company will be able to sell it at the end of the fourth year for $20,000.

Required:

a. Compute the depreciation expense that Benick Industries would record for 1989, 1990, 1991, and 1992 under each of the following methods:
   1. Straight-line depreciation
   2. Sum-of-the-years'-digits depreciation
   3. Double-declining-balance depreciation
b. If you were the president of Benick Industries, what might you consider when choosing a depreciation method for financial reporting purposes? Why?

E9–7   *(How the matching principle is applied affects the timing of income recognition)*   The condensed balance sheet as of December 31, 1990 for Van Den Boom Enterprises follows.

Assets		Liabilities and Stockholders' Equity	
Current assets	$40,000	Liabilities	$35,000
Land	50,000	Stockholders' equity	55,000
		Total liabilities and	
Total assets	$90,000	stockholders' equity	$90,000

Revenues and expenses (other than amortization) are predicted to be $50,000 and $20,000, respectively for 1991, 1992, and 1993. All revenues and expenses are received or paid in cash. On January 1, 1991, Van Den Boom pays $30,000 cash for an item.

Required:

a. Assume that Van Den Boom Enterprises only engaged in operating activities during 1991, 1992, and 1993. Prepare income statements for 1991, 1992, and 1993 and the balance sheet as of December 31, 1993 assuming the $30,000 cash payment is treated in each of the following ways:

1. Immediately expensed
2. Capitalized and amortized evenly over two years
3. Capitalized and amortized evenly over three years

b. Compute the total income recognized over the three-year period under each assumption above.

c. What is interesting about the 12/31/93 balance sheet prepared under all three assumptions?

E9-8   *(Revising the estimated life)*   Moiston Products purchased a machine on January 1, 1987, for $15,000 and estimated its useful life and salvage value at five years and $3000, respectively. On January 1, 1990, the company added three years to the original useful-life estimate.

Required:

a. Compute the book value of the machine as of January 1, 1990, assuming that Moiston uses the straight-line method of depreciation.

b. Prepare the journal entry entered by the company to record depreciation on December 31, 1990.

E9-9   *(The activity method of depreciation)*   Acme Trucking purchased a truck for $25,000 on January 1, 1989. The useful life of the truck was estimated to be either five years or 200,000 miles. Salvage value was estimated at $5000. Over the actual life of the truck it logged the following miles:

Year 1	48,000 miles
Year 2	35,000 miles
Year 3	40,000 miles
Year 4	25,000 miles
Year 5	35,000 miles
Year 6	10,000 miles

At the end of the sixth year, the truck was sold for $3000.

Required: Prepare the journal entries to record depreciation over the life of the truck, and its sale, assuming these methods:

1. Activity method
2. Straight-line method

E9-10   *(Which costs are subject to depreciation?)*   Firton Brothers purchased a tract of land that included an abandoned warehouse for $80,000. The warehouse was razed and the site was
prepared for a new building at a cost of $15,000. Scrap materials from the warehouse were
sold for $5000. A building was then constructed for $140,000, a driveway and parking lot
were laid for $22,000, and permanent landscaping was completed for $4000. Firton Brothers depreciates fixed assets over a twenty-year period using the straight-line method.

Required:

a. Compute the amount of cost to be placed in the Land, Land Improvements, and Building accounts.
b. Assuming a salvage value of zero, compute the depreciation expense associated with the
   items above for the first year.

E9-11   *(The effect of estimated useful life on income and dividends)*   Stork Freight Company owns and
operates fifteen planes that deliver packages worldwide. The planes were purchased on
January 1, 1985, for $1 million each. The company estimates that the planes will be
scrapped after twelve years. Stork Freight uses straight-line depreciation.

Required:

a. Assume that in a typical year the company generates revenues of $47 million and oper-
   ating expenses (excluding depreciation expense) of $25 million. Prepare an income
   statement for a typical year.
b. Assume that the company had originally estimated the useful life at six, instead of
   twelve, years. Prepare an income statement for a typical year. What is the percent
   change in net income?
c. Assume that the company policy is to pay dividends in the amount of 70 percent of net
   income. Compute the difference in the dividend payment between the two cases above.

E9-12   *(Fixed asset sales)*   Savory Enterprises reported the following information regarding the
company's fixed assets in the footnotes to the company's 1990 financial statement.

Office furniture	$500,000	
Less: Accumulated depreciation, office equipment	300,000	200,000

Required:

a. Assume that Savory Enterprises sells all of its office furniture for $275,000 in cash on
   January 1, 1991. Prepare the entry to record the sale.
b. Assume that Savory Enterprises sells all of its office furniture for $105,000 in cash on
   January 1, 1991. Prepare the entry to record the sale.

E9-13   *(Retiring, selling, and trading in a fixed asset)*   Edam Company purchased equipment on January 1, 1988, for $25,000. The estimated useful life of the equipment is five years, the sal-
vage value is $5000 and the company uses the double-declining-balance method to depre-
ciate fixed assets.

Required:

a. Provide the journal entry if the equipment is scrapped after three years.
b. Provide the journal entry if the equipment is scrapped after five years.
c. Provide the journal entry if the equipment is sold for $8000 after three years.
d. Provide the journal entry if, at the end of the fifth year, the equipment and $28,000
   cash are traded in for a dissimilar asset with an objectively determined fair market value
   of $30,000.

E9-14

(An error in recording the acquisition of a fixed asset) Lewis Real Estate purchased a new photocopy machine on January 1, 1990, for $200,000. The company's bookkeeper made the following entry to record the acquisition.

| Depreciation Expense | 200,000 | |
| Cash | | 200,000 |

The photocopy machine has an estimated useful life of four years and an estimated salvage value of $40,000. Lewis Real Estate did not make any adjusting entry on December 31, 1990. Furthermore, the company never discovered the error.

Required:

a. Assume that Lewis Real Estate uses the straight-line method to depreciate its fixed assets. Compute the values for the following chart.

	Depreciation Expense per Company's Books	Correct Depreciation Expense	Annual Difference	Cumulative Difference
1990				
1991				
1992				
1993				
Total				

b. In what direction and by how much will the account Accumulated Depreciation be misstated as of December 31, 1992?

c. In what direction and by how much will the account Retained Earnings be misstated *prior* to closing entries on December 31, 1992?

d. In what direction and by how much will the account Retained Earnings be misstated *after* closing entries on December 31, 1992?

E9-15

(Depletion and matching) Natural Extraction Industries paid $2 million for the right to drill for oil on a tract of land in west Texas. Engineers estimated that this oil deposit would produce 100,000 barrels of crude oil.

Required:

a. During the first year of operations Natural Extraction extracted 30,000 barrels of oil and sold 10,000 barrels. Prepare the entries to record Depletion and Cost of Goods Sold for the first year.

b. During the second year the company extracted 50,000 barrels and sold 65,000. Prepare the entries to record Depletion and Cost of Goods Sold for the second year.

c. Provide the balance sheet disclosure for the Oil Inventory account and the Oil Deposits account as of the end of the second year.

E9-16

(Appendix 9A: Intangible assets: expense or capitalize and amortize?) Mandel Corporation incorporated on January 1, 1989, and incurred $45,000 in organization costs.

Required:

a. Should Mandel Corporation capitalize or expense these costs? Defend your answer.

b. If these costs are capitalized, over what period of time should they be amortized? Provide the amortization journal entry for a single year if the maximum period of time is chosen.

c. What arguments could be used to justify capitalizing organization costs but not allocating them to future periods?

d. Assume that during 1989, Mandel acquired a patent for $65,000. Should this cost be expensed or capitalized? Why one and not the other?

e. Assume that during 1989, Mandel invested $220,000 to research and develop new products. Should these costs be expensed or capitalized?

f. What arguments could be used to justify capitalizing research and development costs and, if capitalized, how should these costs be amortized to future periods?

E9–17   *(Appendix 9A: The capitalized cost of a patent)*   The following information was extracted from the internal financial records of North Robotics regarding a patent filed in 1990 for a new robotics arm used for manufacturing.

(1) Legal and filing fees of $50,000 were paid during 1990 for filing the patent.

(2) Legal fees of $200,000 were incurred and paid during 1991 to defend the patent against infringement by another company.

The patent was granted on December 31, 1990. The company estimated that the patent would provide an economic benefit to the company for five years. It is company policy not to amortize intangible assets in the year of acquisition.

Required:

a. Assume that North Robotics successfully defended its patent against the infringement.

    (1) What amount should North Robotics report for this patent on the company's December 31, 1990 balance sheet?

    (2) What amount should North Robotics report for this patent on the company's December 31, 1991 balance sheet?

    (3) Prepare the entry to amortize the patent on December 31, 1991.

b. Assume that North Robotics was unsuccessful in defending its patent against the infringement.

    (1) What amount should North Robotics report for this patent on the company's December 31, 1990 balance sheet?

    (2) What amount should North Robotics report for this patent on the company's December 31, 1991 balance sheet?

    (3) Prepare the entry to write off the patent.

PROBLEMS

P9–1   *(Determining capitalized cost and the depreciation base)*   Stonebrecker International recently purchased new manufacturing equipment. The equipment cost $1 million. The company also incurred additional costs related to the acquisition of the equipment. The total cost to transport the equipment to Stonebrecker's plant was $50,000, half of which was paid by Stonebrecker. The company also paid $5000 to insure the equipment while it was being transported to its plant. The initial installation costs totaled $40,000. After installing the equipment, however, it was discovered that the floor under the equipment would have to be reinforced. Materials and direct labor to reinforce the floor totaled $20,000. While the equipment was being installed and the floor was being reinforced, the plant workers could not perform their normal functions. The cost to Stonebrecker of the employee downtime was $10,000. Stonebrecker estimates that the equipment will have a salvage value in ten years of $100,000.

Required:

a. What dollar amount should Stonebrecker capitalize on its books for this equipment.

b. Prepare the journal entry to capitalize the equipment.

c. What is the depreciation base of this equipment?

d. Over the life of this equipment, what dollar amount will be depreciated under the straight-line method? Under the sum-of-the-years'-digits method? Under the double-declining-balance method?

P9–2 *(Lump-sum purchases and cost allocation)*   The JRF Company purchased a building, some office equipment, two cranes, and some land on January 1, 1989, for a total of $1 million cash. JRF Company has obtained the following appraisals of these assets.

Asset	Fair Market Value on 1/1/89	Estimated Life	Estimated Salvage Value
Building	$300,000	20 years	$75,000
Office equipment	150,000	3 years	35,000
Crane 1	75,000	5 years	15,000
Crane 2	75,000	5 years	15,000
Land	600,000	Indefinite	

JFR company uses the straight-line method to depreciate fixed assets.

Required:

a. Prepare the journal entry to record the purchase.

b. Prepare the journal entry to record depreciation expense for each type of asset for the year ended December 31, 1989.

c. Assuming that all of these assets are still held as of December 31, 1992, present these fixed assets as they would be shown on the December 31, 1992 balance sheet.

P9–3 *(Determining capitalized cost and depreciating)*   Gidley, Inc. purchased a piece of equipment on January 1, 1989. The following information is available for this purchase.

Purchase Price	$900,000	Salvage Value	$50,000
Transportation	$100,000[a]	Useful Life	4 Years
Installation	$130,000[b]		

[a]Included in the transportation cost is $1000 for insurance covering the shipment of the equipment to Gidley.
[b]Included in the cost of installation is $80,000 in wages paid to employees who helped install the equipment.

Required:

a. Compute the cost of the fixed asset that should be capitalized.

b. Prepare the entry to record depreciation expense for the year ended December 31, 1989, assuming the company uses each of the following:

(1) Sum-of-the-years'-digits depreciation method

(2) Double-declining-balance depreciation method

(3) Straight-line depreciation method

c. Assuming that the equipment was sold on January 1, 1991 for $250,000, prepare the entry to record the sale of the equipment assuming the company uses each of the following methods:

(1) Sum-of-the-years'-digits depreciation method

(2) Double-declining-balance depreciation method

(3) Straight-line depreciation method

P9–4 *(Determining cost when an asset is purchased in exchange for a note payable)*   Hathaway Enterprises purchased equipment on January 1, 1989, in exchange for a three-year non-interest-bearing note. The note called for a down payment of $100,000 and payments of $100,000 at the end of each year for three years. The estimated useful life of the equipment is five years, and the salvage value is estimated to be $50,000. Hathaway uses the straight-line method to depreciate fixed assets. The company's discount rate is 10 percent. (This problem requires knowledge of present value techniques that are discussed in Appendix A at the end of the text.)

Required:

a. Compute the capitalized cost of the equipment.

b. Provide the journal entry to record depreciation on the machinery at the end of 1989.

c. Assume that the machinery is sold for $90,000 on January 1, 1993. Provide the entry to record the sale.

P9–5

(Accounting for betterments and maintenance costs) Magneto Manufacturing purchased a dryer for $45,000 on January 1, 1989. The estimated life of the dryer is five years, and the salvage value is estimated to be $5000. Magneto uses the straight-line method of depreciation.

On January 1, 1993, Magneto paid $10,000 to have the dryer overhauled, which increased the speed of the dryer and extended its useful life to December 31, 1996. Each year Magneto pays $500 to have the dryer serviced. On November 12, 1992, a major repair was required at a cost of $2500.

Required:

a. Provide the journal entry on January 1, 1989 to record the purchase of the dryer.

b. How should the service and repair costs be treated on the books of Magneto?

c. Compute the depreciation expense that would be recognized during each year of the dryer's eight-year useful life.

P9–6

(Accounting for betterments) Hulteen Hardware purchased a new building on January 1, 1989, for $1,500,000. The company expects the building to last twenty-five years and expects to be able to sell it then for $150,000. During 1994 the building was painted at a cost of $5000. Almost ten years after acquiring the building, the roof was destroyed by a storm. The company had a new roof constructed at a cost of $200,000. The new roof was completed on January 1, 1999, and it is expected to extend the life of the building by five years, to a total of thirty years. All other estimates are still accurate. Hulteen Hardware uses the straight-line method to depreciate the cost of all fixed assets.

Required:

a. Prepare the entry to record the purchase of the building, assuming that the company paid cash.

b. Prepare the entry to record the purchase of the new roof on January 1, 1999.

c. Prepare the entry to record depreciation expense for the year ended December 31, 1999.

d. Prepare the journal entry that would be recorded if the building was sold for $1,200,000 on December 31, 2004.

P9–7

(Revising the estimated life with different methods of depreciation) Balmer Copy Center purchased a machine on January 1, 1985, for $150,000 and estimated its useful life and salvage value at ten years and $30,000, respectively. On January 1, 1990, the company added three years to the original useful-life estimate.

Required:

a. Compute the book value of the machine as of January 1, 1990, assuming that Balmer recognizes depreciation using straight-line.

b. Prepare the journal entry to record depreciation entered by the company on December 31, 1990, assuming that Balmer uses straight-line.

P9-8

(Why is double-declining-balance preferred for tax purposes?) Note: Knowledge of the time value of money is necessary for this problem (see Appendix A). Ellery and Son purchased equipment for $20,000 on January 1, 1989. Ellery can use the double-declining-balance method for tax purposes but does not understand why he should prefer it over straight-line. Given the following information, what is your advice?

Estimated useful life	4 years
Estimated salvage value	$ 5,000
Expected revenues over each of the next four years	$100,000
Expected expenses (excluding depreciation) over each of the next four years	$ 60,000
Tax rate (percent of net income)	30 percent

Required:

a. Which of the two methods will give rise to the greater amount of depreciation over the life of the equipment? Support your answer with computations.

b. Which of the two methods will result in the payment of less taxes over the life of the equipment? Support your answer with computations.

c. Why is the double-declining-balance method preferred for tax purposes?

d. Assume a discount rate of 10 percent. How much money would be saved by using double-declining-balance instead of straight-line?

P9-9

(The effect of depreciation on taxes, bonuses, and dividends) Bentley Poster Company pays income taxes on net income at the rate of 32 percent. The company pays a bonus to its officers of 8 percent of net income after taxes and pays dividends to its stockholders in the amount of 75 percent of net income after taxes. On January 1, 1990 the company purchased a fixed asset for $100,000. Such assets are usually depreciated over a ten-year period. Salvage value is expected to be zero. Assume that the bonus payment is not included as an expense in the calculation of taxable income and reported income.

Required: Assume that revenues and expenses (excluding depreciation) for 1990 are $250,000 and $140,000, respectively. Compute the tax, bonus and dividend payment for 1990 if the company uses the following:

a. The straight-line method of depreciation

b. The double-declining-balance method of depreciation

c. The straight-line method of depreciation, assuming a five-year useful life

P9-10

(The effect of the estimated useful life on net income, bonuses, and dividends) Jonas Morley manages Weatherly Enterprises and is paid a salary plus a bonus of 10 percent of the company's net income for the year. The company is in the process of purchasing a piece of machinery in exchange for a five-year non-interest-bearing note that specifies a payment of $25,000 at the end of each year for five years. The present value of the note is $105,340. The note also stipulates that company dividends cannot exceed 50 percent of net income (computed before the bonus) in any one year. Weatherly uses the straight-line method to depreciate fixed assets and assumes zero salvage value. Assume that the bonus payment is not included as an expense in calculating net income.

Required:

a. At what dollar amount should the machine be capitalized?

b. Compute Morley's bonus and the maximum dividend payment that can be made by the company if revenues are $100,000, expenses other than depreciation are $40,000, and the useful life of the equipment is assumed to be ten years.

c. Compute Morley's bonus and the maximum dividend payment that can be made by the company if revenues are $100,000, expenses other than depreciation are $40,000, and the useful life of the equipment is assumed to be five years.

d. In general, would Morley prefer a short or a long estimated useful life? Why?

e. Why would the holder of the note want to restrict Weatherly's ability to pay dividends?

P9–11   *(Expensing what should be capitalized can misstate net income)*   Westmiller Construction Company purchased a new truck on December 31, 1988, for $18,000. The truck has an estimated useful life of three years and an estimated salvage value of $6000. When the truck was purchased, the company's accountant made the following entry:

| Truck Expense | 18,000 | |
| Cash | | 18,000 |

Over the life of the truck, the company made no other entries associated with it.

Required:

a. What entry should Westmiller Construction Company have made on December 31, 1988?

b. Assuming that the straight-line method of depreciation should have been used, and the error was not discovered, in what direction and by how much was net income misstated in 1988 and 1989?

c. Assuming that the double-declining-balance method of depreciation should have been used, and the error was not discovered, in what direction and by how much was net income misstated in 1988 and 1989?

P9–12   *(Inferring a depreciation method and related journal entries)*   JoyDon Enterprises reports the following information in its 1988 financial report:

	12/31/88		12/31/87	
Plant equipment	$1,000,000		$750,000	
Less: Accumulated depreciation—plant equipment	590,000	410,000	490,000	260,000

Additional Information

(1) JoyDon Enterprises began operations on January 1, 1986, and the entire Plant Equipment balance reported on December 31, 1987 was purchased for cash on the first day of operations. This equipment had an estimated salvage value of $50,000 and an estimated useful life of four years. The company neither bought nor sold any plant equipment during 1986 and 1987.

(2) On January 1, 1988, JoyDon Enterprises sold for cash some plant equipment that originally cost $200,000, at a book gain of $25,000. When the equipment was acquired on January 1, 1986, it had no estimated salvage value. The original estimates for the salvage value and the useful life are still accurate for the remaining equipment.

(3) The company purchased additional plant equipment on January 1, 1988, for cash. This equipment is expected to be scrapped after five years and has an estimated salvage value of $30,000.

Required:

a. Prepare the entry to record the plant equipment acquired on January 1, 1986.

b. What method does the company use to depreciate plant equipment?

c. Prepare the entry to record the depreciation expense for the year ended December 31, 1986.

d. Prepare the entry to record the depreciation expense for the year ended December 31, 1987.

e. Prepare the entry to record the sale of the plant equipment on January 1, 1988.

f. Prepare the entry to record the plant equipment acquired on January 1, 1988.

g. Prepare the entry to record the depreciation expense for the year ended December 31, 1988.

P9–13   *(Selling and trading in fixed assets)*   Webb Net Manufacturing purchased a new net weaving machine on January 1, 1989, for $500,000. The new machine has an estimated life of five years and an estimated salvage value of $100,000. It is company policy to use straight-line depreciation for all of its machines.

Required:

a. Assume that Webb Net Manufacturing sells this machine on January 1, 1992 for $325,000. Prepare the entry to record this transaction.

b. Assume that Webb Net Manufacturing sells this machine on June 30, 1992 for $320,000. Prepare the entry or entries to record this transaction.

c. Assume that Webb Net Manufacturing trades in this machine for a tract of land on January 1, 1992. The list price of the land is $250,000 and it has an appraised value of $210,000. The company is granted a trade-in allowance on the machine of $75,000 and pays an additional $175,000 in cash for the land. The net weaving machine is appraised at $75,000. Prepare the entry to record the trade-in assuming the land is valued as follows:

  (1) The fair market value of the asset received.

  (2) The fair market value of the assets given up.

P9–14   *(Natural resources: different methods of cost allocation depending on the nature of the asset)*   Garmen Oil Company recently discovered an oil field on one of its properties in Texas. In order to extract the oil, the company purchased drilling equipment on January 1, 1989, for $625,000 cash and also purchased a mobile home on the same date for $24,000 cash, to serve as on-site headquarters. The drilling equipment has an estimated useful life of twelve years but will be abandoned when the company shuts down this well. The mobile home has an estimated useful life of seven years and an estimated salvage value of $3000. The company expects to use the mobile home on other drilling sites after work on this site is completed.

Company geologists estimated correctly that the well would produce two million barrels of oil. Actual production from the well for 1989, 1990, and 1991 was 600,000 barrels, 750,000 barrels and 650,000 barrels, respectively. All extracted barrels were immediately sold. This well is now dry and Garner Oil has shut it down.

Required:

a. Prepare the entry to record the purchase of the drilling equipment and the mobile home.

b. Prepare the entries to allocate the cost of the drilling equipment to Minerals Inventory and Cost of Goods Sold for 1989, 1990, and 1991.

c. Prepare the entries to record depreciation expenses for 1989, 1990, and 1991 for the mobile home using the straight-line method. Why are different methods used to allocate the costs of the drilling equipment and the mobile home?

d. Assume that Garmen Oil discovered that the well was dry at the end of 1990 (i.e., the well only produced 1,350,000 barrels of oil). Repeat Parts (b) and (c).

P9–15   *(Appendix 9A: Recognizing and amortizing goodwill)*   On January 1, 1990, Diversified Industries purchased Specialists, Inc. for $1,500,000. The balance sheet of Specialists, Inc. at the time of the purchase follows.

Assets		Liabilities and Stockholders' Equity	
Current assets	$650,000	Liabilities	$250,000
Long-lived assets	330,000	Stockholders' equity	730,000
		Total liabilities and	
Total assets	$980,000	stockholders' equity	$980,000

The total fair market value of the individual assets of Specialists is $1,200,000 and the liabilities are valued on the balance sheet at fair market value.

Required:

a. How can the fair market value of Specialists' assets exceed the value of the assets on the balance sheet?

b. Why would Diversified pay more for Specialists than the fair market value of the assets less the liabilities?

c. Provide the journal entry to record the purchase.

d. Assume that Diversified chooses accounting methods to maximize reported net income each year. What journal entry would Diversified record on December 31, 1990, with respect to this purchase?

e. The Internal Revenue Code states that goodwill cannot be amortized for tax purposes. Provide an argument in support of this position.

CASES

C9–1   *(Lump-sum sales and purchases)*   MGM Grand, Inc., purchased two Las Vegas casinos and the adjoining land for a total of $167 million in late February 1988. In April, the company agreed to sell one of the casinos and 58.7 acres of adjacent land for $110 million.

Required:

a. What issues need to be addressed in order to determine the gain or loss resulting from the sale of one of the hotels? How should the cost of the sold hotel be established?

b. Assume that each hotel had a cost of $75 million and the adjacent land originally cost $17 million. Provide the journal entry prepared by MGM Grand to record the sale.

c. Explain how the hotel and the land would each be valued on the balance sheet of the purchasing company.

d. Assume that an appraiser assesses the value of the land without the hotel to be $43 million. Compute the annual depreciation charge recognized by the purchasing company if it depreciates buildings using the straight-line rate over a period of twenty-five years. Assume no salvage value.

C9–2   *(The effect of the depreciation method on book gains recognized on a sale)*   Allegis Corporation is the parent of United Air Lines, Inc. In May 1988, Allegis agreed to sell half of its interest in its Apollo computer reservation system to four European airlines and U.S. Air Group, Inc., for $500 million. Assume the entire system cost Allegis $850 million to develop, and that it has been in place five of its estimated fifteen-year useful life and was depreciated using the double-declining-balance method with no salvage value.

Required:

a. Compute the depreciation charge recognized by Allegis for each of the five years.

b. Provide the journal entry to record the sale.

c. Assume that Allegis uses the straight-line method of depreciation and repeat a. and b. above.

d. Which of the two depreciation methods gave rise to the largest book gain on the sale? Why?

e. For both methods, subtract the total depreciation expense recognized over the five years from the book gain recognized on the sale.

C9–3

(Depreciation methods: income recognition and income taxes) International Lease Finance Corporation (ILFC) purchases aircraft which it then leases to airlines. In May 1988 the company sold three of its leased aircraft to two airlines for a total of $29 million. Assume the planes were acquired three years ago for cash at a cost of $25 million each, at which time they were estimated to have a ten-year useful life and no salvage value. Assume also that ILFC generated revenues of $100 million during each of the three years and incurred annual expenses (excluding depreciation and gains or losses from aircraft sales) of $60 million. Note: Knowledge of the time value of money is necessary to answer point d. in the required section below. Refer to Appendix A at the end of the text.

Required:

a. Compute net income for each of the three years, assuming that ILFC uses the straight-line method of depreciation. Include the sales of the aircraft in the net income calculation of the third year.

b. Compute net income for each of the three years, assuming that ILFC uses the sum-of-the-years'-digits method. Include the sale of the aircraft in the net income calculation of the third year.

c. Assuming an income tax rate of 30 percent, compute the total dollar amount of income taxes paid by ILFC over the three-year period under each of the two methods.

d. Assume a discount rate of 10 percent and compute the benefit associated with using the sum-of-the-years' digits method instead of straight-line for income-tax purposes.

C9–4

(Recognizing depreciation and economic consequences) In the past, private colleges, which are subject to the accounting and reporting standards for nonprofit entities, have not been required to recognize depreciation on their financial statements. However, *The Wall Street Journal* recently reported that "many of the nations 1500 private colleges are considering ignoring a new accounting rule that would require them to depreciate buildings and equipment. . . . Several colleges received assurances from Standard & Poor's Corp. and Moody's Investors Services, Inc. that the bond-rating agencies wouldn't lower the colleges' bond ratings based on noncompliance with the FASB Statement. . . . The FASB's rules have the informal blessing of the Securities and Exchange Commission and, if not followed, would result in a qualified [audit] opinion. Such qualifications could cloud the status of some college bonds by triggering spending limits in bond covenants."

Lee Berton, "Several private colleges may ignore new accounting rule on depreciation," *The Wall Street Journal*, 4 February 1988, p. 28.

Required:

a. Explain why colleges might not want to recognize depreciation on their financial statements.

b. Why would such institutions be interested in the assurances described above from companies such as Standard & Poor's and Moody's?

c. Why might an auditor qualify the audit opinion on a college that did not conform to this accounting rule?

d. Why would a spending limit be part of a bond covenant, and how could a qualified audit opinion trigger such a limit?

C9-5   *(Betterments or maintenance and subsequent depreciation)*   Ford Motor Company said it would spend $200 million to refurbish its Mustang assembly plant in Dearborn, Michigan. The aging factory had been discussed as a candidate for closing, but Ford's current capacity of Mustang production is barely able to keep pace with demand.

Required:

a. What issues must be considered when deciding whether to capitalize or expense the $200 million expenditure?

b. Under what conditions could the $200 million cost be expensed even if it improved instead of maintained the plant?

c. Assume that the $200 million cost is capitalized and that the refurbishment extends the useful life of the factory. Explain how Ford will compute depreciation on its factory over its remaining useful life.

Current Liabilities, Contingencies, Retirement Costs, and Deferred Income Taxes

Learning Objectives

1   Define liabilities and current liabilities.

2   Distinguish between determinable current liabilities and contingent liabilities.

3   List the determinable current liabilities, and briefly explain the nature of each.

4   Explain why bonus systems and profit sharing arrangements are used to compensate management, and describe the incentives they create.

5   Describe the methods used to account for contingencies and how they apply to warranties.

6   Explain the fundamentals involved in accounting for pensions and post-retirement health care and insurance costs.

7   Explain the fundamentals involved in accounting for deferred income taxes.

8   Describe the economic consequences associated with reporting liabilities on the financial statements.

9   (Appendix 10A) Describe the two basic kinds of pension plans, and discuss the fundamentals involved in accounting for each.

≣ This chapter and the next (Chapter 11) are devoted to liabilities: obligations of a company to disburse assets or provide services in the future. Liabilities are divided on the balance sheet into two categories: current liabilities and long-term liabilities. Current liabilities primarily include short-term payables; long-term liabilities relate to long-term notes, bonds, leases, pensions, and deferred income taxes. This chapter introduces liabilities in general and covers the methods used to account for current liabilities. Accounting for pensions, post-retirement health care and insurance costs, and deferred income taxes is also briefly reviewed and the liabilities related to pensions are discussed more completely in the appendix. Chapter 11 is devoted to long-term notes, bonds, and leases. These three liabilities are covered in a single chapter because the same basic method, called the *effective interest method,* is used to account for them.

WHAT IS A LIABILITY?

The definition of a liability in the context of financial accounting is somewhat ambiguous and difficult to state precisely. While generally defined as obligations to give up assets or provide services in the future, the liabilities listed on the balance sheet entail a wide variety of items, including credit balances with suppliers, debts from borrowings, services yet to be performed, withholdings from employees' wages and salaries, dividend declarations, product warranties, deferred income taxes, and a number of complex financing instruments. There is some question whether all these items are liabilities in an economic sense as well as whether all the economic liabilities of a company are included on its balance sheet. For example, we discuss later that deferred income taxes, although often the largest liability on the balance sheet, may never result in a future cash outflow. Significant future cash outflows due to obligations to employees under existing pension and health care plans, on the other hand, may not be reported on the balance sheet at all.

The FASB recently defined liabilities as "probable future sacrifices of economic benefits arising from present obligations of a particular entity to transfer assets or provide services to other entities in the future as a result of past transactions or events." The Board commented further that all liabilities appearing on the balance sheet should have three characteristics in common: (1) they should be present obligations that entail settlements by probable future transfers or uses of cash, goods, or services; (2) they should be unavoidable obligations; and (3) the transaction or event obligating the enterprise must have already happened.[1]

THE RELATIVE SIZE OF LIABILITIES ON THE BALANCE SHEET

The importance of liabilities on the balance sheet varies across companies in different industries. Table 10–1 contains liabilities as a percentage of total assets, often referred to as the **debt ratio,** for selected industries.

Note that this percentage varies from 36 percent for family clothing stores to 68 percent for new and used car dealers. Companies in the industries with relatively

---

1. Financial Accounting Standards Board (FASB) "Elements of Financial Statements of Business Enterprises," *Statement of Financial Accounting Concepts No. 3* (Stamford, Conn.: FASB, 1980), pars. 28 and 29.

Table 10–1   Average liabilities/total assets (selected industries)

Industry (No. of Companies)	Liabilities/Total Assets
Family clothing stores (1373)	36%
Accounting and auditing services (1335)	40
Department stores (1032)	40
Hardware stores (2239)	43
Aircraft manufacturing (35)	48
Grocery stores (2295)	51
Mortgage bankers (755)	53
Accident and health insurance (199)	60
New and used cars (2120)	68

Source: Compiled from data published in *Industry Norms and Key Business Ratios* (Dun & Bradstreet, Inc., 1987)

less total liabilities rely heavily on equity issuances and profitable operations for their financing needs. Financial institutions, on the other hand, borrow extensively because such debts can be secured with available financial assets. Companies in the new and used car industry rely heavily on liabilities because they borrow heavily to finance their extensive automobile inventories.

CURRENT LIABILITIES

Current liabilities are normally debts that must be paid within one year. A more precise definition, however, includes obligations that are expected to require the use of current assets or the creation of other current liabilities. Current liabilities include obligations to suppliers (accounts payable), short-term debts, current maturities on long-term debts, dividends payable to stockholders, deferred revenues (services yet to be performed that are expected to require the use of current assets), third-party collections (e.g., sales tax and payroll deductions), periodic accruals (e.g., wages and interest), and potential obligations related to pending or threatened litigation, product warranties, and guarantees.

Table 10–2 shows excerpts from the 1986 balance sheets of Union Carbide Corporation and Philip Morris Companies, Inc. It illustrates typical balance sheet current liability sections.

The Relative Size of Current Liabilities on the Balance Sheet

The relative size of current liabilities on the balance sheet varies across companies from different industries. Table 10–3 contains the average current liability/total liability ratio of companies in selected industries.

Note that the ratio varies from 27 percent in the hotel industry to 80 percent for accident and health insurance companies, and that in eight of the ten industries listed in Table 10–3, current liabilities represent over 50 percent of total liabilities. In general, companies in the service industry (e.g., hotels and restaurants) invest primarily in long-term assets, such as property, plant, and equipment, which are financed through long-term borrowings. As a result, they tend to rely less heavily on current liabilities. The current liabilities of Marriott Corporation

Table 10–2 Typical balance sheet current liability sections

Union Carbide Corporation	1986*	1985*
Accounts payable	$ 414	$ 327
Short-term debt	388	821
Payments due within one year on long-term debt	71	201
Accrued income and other taxes	280	147
Other accrued liabilities	728	886
Total current liabilities	$1,881	$2,382

Philip Morris Companies, Inc.	1986	1985
Notes payable	$ 864	$ 595
Current portion of long-term debt	103	83
Accounts payable	813	946
Accrued liabilities		
Taxes, except income taxes	531	484
Employment costs	405	426
Other	1,031	952
Income taxes payable	557	362
Dividends payable	178	119
Total current liabilities	$4,482	$3,967

*Dollars in millions.

Table 10–3 Average current liabilities/total liabilities (selected industries)

Industry (No. of Companies)	Liabilities/Total Liabilities
Hotels (1912)	27%
TV broadcasting (112)	48
General farm crops (354)	51
Grocery stores (2295)	57
Hardware stores (2239)	63
Department stores (1032)	65
Family clothing stores (1373)	69
Mortgage bankers (755)	77
Household appliance manufacturing (14)	78
Accident health insurance (199)	80

Source: Compiled from information published in *Industry Norms and Key Business Ratios* (Dun & Bradstreet, Inc., 1987).

and McDonald's Corporation, for example, represent only 24 percent and 21 percent, respectively, of total liabilities.

Retail companies, on the other hand, finance their relatively heavy investment in receivables and inventories with a greater percentage of current liabilities. The current liabilities of J. C. Penney and the merchandise group of Sears, Roebuck and Co. represent 40 percent and 51 percent, respectively, of total liabilities. Financial institutions, such as banks, rely almost exclusively on customer deposits and other short-term borrowings. The current liabilities of BankAmerica Corporation and the Bank of New York represent 95 percent and 97 percent, respectively, of total liabilities.

Valuing Current Liabilities on the Balance Sheet

Most liabilities involve future cash outflows that are specified by formal contract or informal agreement. They can therefore be predicted objectively, and present value methods can be used to value liabilities on the balance sheet. In the case of current liabilities, however, the time period until payment is relatively short and the difference between the **face value** (actual cash payment when the liability is due) of the liability and its present value (discounted future cash payment) is considered to be immaterial. Thus, in the interest of materiality and expediency current liabilities are usually recorded on the balance sheet at face value.

Reporting Current Liabilities: An Economic Consequence

In most cases the face value of a current liability is easy to determine, and balance sheet valuation is straightforward. The primary problem is one of discovery, ensuring that all existing current liabilities are reported on the balance sheet. Failure to discover and report an existing current liability misstates the financial statements and any of the financial measures that include current liabilities. Two particularly important financial measures are the current ratio (current assets/current liabilities) and working capital (current assets − current liabilities). These two measures are used by stockholders, investors, creditors, and others primarily to assess solvency and are frequently found in loan contracts. For example, a recent financial statement of Cummins Engine Co., a manufacturer of heavy-duty truck engines, describes a loan agreement that requires Cummins to maintain a current ratio of 1.25 : 1.

Debt restrictions like the one imposed on Cummins Engine can discourage management from reporting current liabilities on the balance sheet. Consider, for example, JFP Company, which borrows $1 million from Thrifty Bank. The loan contract states that the loan is in default if JFP's current ratio, as reported on the balance sheet, dips below 2 : 1. Defaulting on this loan could mean that JFP must immediately pay the outstanding balance; in most cases, however, the company would be forced to renegotiate the terms of the loan with Thrifty Bank. Such renegotiations would probably require that JFP make costly concessions, normally in the form of less desirable loan terms (e.g., higher interest rates, additional collateral).

At year end JFP's accountants determine that current assets equal $100,000. If current liabilities are determined to be $50,000 or less, the current ratio will be at least 2 : 1, and the loan will not be in default. On the other hand, if current liabilities are determined to be greater than $50,000, the current ratio would dip below 2 : 1 and JFP would be in violation of the loan contract, which could lead to serious financial problems.

If JFP's management fails, either intentionally or unintentionally, to report a given current liability on the balance sheet, it can avoid violating the terms of the loan contract and the related financial consequences. Management, therefore, has an incentive either to ignore existing current liabilities or to structure transactions so that current liabilities do not have to be recorded. In such cases auditors must make special efforts to ensure that all existing current liabilities are properly reported on the balance sheet.

Figure 10–1   Outline of current liabilities

Determinable Current Liabilities	Contingent Liabilities

Determinable Current Liabilities

A. Accounts payable
B. Short-term debts
   1. Short-term notes
   2. Current maturities of long-term debts
C. Dividend payable
D. Deferred revenues
   1. Returnable deposits
   2. Advance sales
E. Third-party collections
F. Accrued liabilities
   1. Determinable
   2. Conditional
      a. Income taxes
      b. Incentive compensation

Contingent Liabilities

A. Lawsuits
B. Warranties

ACCOUNTING FOR CURRENT LIABILITIES

All current liabilities, because they represent probable future outlays, involve an element of uncertainty. The relative degree of uncertainty associated with a given current liability gives rise to the following two categories: (1) determinable current liabilities (reasonably certain) and (2) contingent current liabilities (dependent upon a future event). Figure 10–1 provides an outline of the current liabilities covered in this section.

Determinable Current Liabilities

In general, **determinable current liabilities** can be precisely measured, and the amount of cash needed to satisfy the obligation and the date of payment are reasonably certain. However, because they are often small and frequently result from unwritten extensions of credit or unrecorded accruals, they can present problems of discovery. Determinable current liabilities include accounts payable, short-term debts, dividends payable, deferred revenues, third-party collections, and accrued liabilities.

Accounts Payable

Accounts payable are dollar amounts owed to others for goods, supplies, and services purchased on **open account.**[2] They arise from frequent transactions between a company and its suppliers that are normally not subject to specific, formal con-

---

2. Accounts payable are often referred to as *trade accounts payable*. *Accounting Trends and Techniques* (New York: AICPA, 1987, p. 177) reports that 125 of the 600 major U.S. companies surveyed used that phrase.

tracts. These extensions of credit are the practical result of a time lag between the receipt of a good, supply, or service and the corresponding payment. The time period is usually short (e.g., thirty to sixty days) and is indicated by the terms of the exchange (e.g., 2/10, n/30).

Measuring the amount of accounts payable is not particularly difficult, because invoices received from creditors (suppliers) normally specify the due dates, terms of sale, and the exact amounts of cash that are required to discharge the obligations. However, particular attention must be paid to transactions occurring near the end of an accounting period (e.g., goods in transit) to ensure that the good received and the related account payable are both recorded in the proper period. Recall from Chapter 8, where inventory purchases were discussed, that the shipping terms (i.e., FOB shipping point or FOB destination) usually indicate when the ownership of the goods transfers from the seller to the buyer.

Accounts payable are usually associated with inventory purchases, and the form of a typical journal entry is indicated below.

Inventory	500	
Accounts Payable		500
To record a purchase of inventory priced at $500.		

The money value assigned to this journal entry can be at either the gross amount (without cash discount) or the net amount (with cash discount) of the exchange. Journal entries under the gross and net methods are discussed in both Chapter 7 (short-term receivables) and Chapter 8 (inventories).

The relative importance of accounts payable on the balance sheet varies across major U.S. companies. Table 10–4 below lists accounts payable as a percentage of current liabilities for a selected group of companies in the United States as of the end of 1987.

Note that while there are considerable differences in the percentages, companies do not seem to form groups on the basis of industry membership. McDonnell Douglas, ARCO, DuPont, Chevron, Chrysler and Boeing, for example, all represent various forms of manufacturing, yet their percentages vary considerably. Indeed, McDonnell Douglas and Boeing, which are competitors in the same industry, have very different percentages. Similarly, the percentages of ARCO and Chevron are very different.

Table 10–4   Accounts payable/current liabilities (selected companies)

Company	Accounts Payable/Current Liabilities
McDonnell Douglas (aerospace manufacturing)	22%
ARCO (oil company)	26
DuPont (research and manufacturing)	39
Wendy's International (fast-food restaurants)	42
Marriott Corporation (hotels)	45
Chevron (oil company)	51
Chrysler Corporation (automobile manufacturing)	56
J. C. Penney (retail goods)	59
The Boeing Company (aerospace manufacturing)	63

Source: 1987 financial reports.

Short-Term Debts

Short-term debts (or short-term borrowings) typically include short-term bank loans, commercial paper, lines of credit, and current maturities of long-term debt.[3] **Commercial paper** represents short-term notes (30 to 270 days) issued for cash by companies with good credit ratings to other companies. A **line of credit** is usually granted to a company by a bank or group of banks, allowing it to borrow up to a certain maximum dollar amount, interest being charged only on the outstanding balance. Issued commercial paper and existing lines of credit are an indication of a company's ability to borrow funds on a short-term basis; thus, they are very important to investors and creditors who are interested in assessing solvency. Consequently, such financing arrangements are extensively described in the footnotes. The excerpt below, for example, is from the 1986 financial report of Black and Decker Corporation and describes the company's short-term debt.

Short-Term Borrowings	1986*	1985*
Commercial paper	$67,000	—
Bank loans	61,250	34,534
Unsecured notes	73,000	—
Current maturity of long-term debt	10,632	2,948

*Dollars in thousands.

In September 1986 the Corporation entered into a $90,000 revolving credit facility extending to December 31, 1988 with several commercial banks. The agreement provides for credit availability each July 1 and December 31 to support the issue of commercial paper during the peak seasonal period. Interest rates under the agreement can vary. In 1986 the Corporation also initiated a commercial paper program that makes available to the Corporation up to $100,000 of short-term financing at prevailing interest rates for periods ranging from 7 to 183 days. Under the terms of informal line-of-credit arrangements, the Corporation may borrow up to an additional $196,000 on such terms as may be mutually agreed upon. These arrangements do not have termination dates and are reviewed periodically.

The methods used to account for short-term notes and current maturities on long-term debts are discussed below.

Short-Term Notes. Short-term notes usually arise from cash loans and are generally payable to banks or loan companies. In most cases the life of a note is somewhere between thirty days and one year, and the bank or loan company lends the borrowing company less cash than is indicated on the face of the note. At the **maturity date** (when the loan is due), the borrowing company pays the lending institution the face amount of the note and the difference between the face amount and the amount of the loan is treated as interest.

For example, suppose that on January 1, Freight Line Industries borrows $9400 from Commercial Loan Company and signs a six-month note with a face amount of $10,000. The journal entry to record this transaction is provided below.

---

3. *Accounting Trends and Techniques* (New York: AICPA, 1987, p. 175) reports that 405 of the 600 major U.S. companies surveyed indicated short-term debt on their balance sheets. Of these 405 companies, 46 disclosed commercial paper arrangements.

Cash	9400	
Discount on Note Payable	600	
Note Payable		10,000
To record the issuance of a short-term note payable.		

The Discount on Notes Payable account serves as a contra account to notes payable on the balance sheet and represents interest that is not yet owed but will be recognized in the future. Assuming that financial statements are prepared monthly, one sixth of the discount would be converted to interest expense each month by an adjusting journal entry of the following form:

Interest Expense ($600/6)	100	
Discount on Notes Payable		100
To record the accrual of interest on a short-term note.		

After this entry is recorded at the end of the first month, the balance of the discount would have been reduced to $500, and the balance sheet carrying amount of the note would be as follows. The net balance ($9500) represents the amount of cash that would be required to pay off the note as of the balance sheet date.

| Note Payable | $10,000 | |
| Less: Discount on Note Payable | 500 | $9,500 |

Note in this example that the discount is amortized using the straight-line method (i.e., equal amounts of interest expense are recognized each month). Generally accepted accounting principles specify that discounts on notes payable should be amortized using a procedure called the effective interest method (see Chapter 11). However, the time period of a short-term note is so short that the difference between the straight-line method and the effective interest method is immaterial. Thus, in the interest of materiality and expediency, the straight-line method is acceptable.

Current Maturities of Long-Term Debts. Long-term debts are often retired through a series of periodic installments. The installments that are to be paid within the time period that defines current assets (one year or the current operating cycle, whichever is longer) should be included on the balance sheet as current liabilities; the remaining installments should be disclosed as long-term liabilities.

For example, assume that on December 31, 1989, Wright and Sons borrows $50,000, which is to be paid back in annual installments of $7000 each. The first payment, which is due on December 31, 1990, will consist of $5000 in interest and $2000 in principal. On the December 31, 1989 balance sheet the associated payable would be disclosed in the following way. Note that the $50,000 principal amount is divided into $2000, which is due in the current period, and $48,000, which is long-term. The $5000 in interest will be accrued at the end of 1990 after the company has had use of the funds.

Current liabilities	
Current maturity of long-term debt	2000
Long-term liabilities	
Long-term note payable	48,000

Current maturities on long-term debts can be quite large, but they rarely represent a major portion of current liabilities. In the 1987 financial report of Goodyear Tire & Rubber Company, for example, current maturities in the amount of $90 million were disclosed. Although significant, this amount represented only 4 percent of the company's current liabilities.

Dividends Payable

A liability is created when the board of directors of a corporation declares a dividend to be paid to the stockholders. It is listed as current because dividends are usually paid within several months of declaration. When a cash dividend of $5000 is declared, for example, the following journal entry is recorded.

Dividend	5000	
Dividend Payable		5000
To record the declaration of a cash dividend.		

The Dividend account is a temporary account that is closed directly to Retained Earnings at the end of the accounting period. Dividend Payable is a current liability that is removed from the books when the dividend is paid.

Dividend Payable	5000	
Cash		5000
To record the payment of a cash dividend.		

Dividends are declared for many different reasons and can be paid in several different forms. These issues are discussed in Chapter 12, where stockholders' equity is covered.

Deferred (Unearned) Revenues

Payments are often received before contracted services are performed. In such cases liabilities are created, because the companies receiving the payments have obligations that must be fulfilled. These obligations may consist of delivering goods, executing services, or simply returning cash. If satisfying the obligation is expected to require the use of current assets, these receipts should be recorded as current liabilities. The basic journal entry used to account for such receipts appears as follows.

Cash	800	
Deferred Revenue		800
To record the receipt of $800 cash for a service yet to be rendered.		

Deferred revenues, also called *unearned revenues* or *receipts in advance*, take a number of different forms. Two examples are common in the airline industry. Passenger tickets are frequently paid several months before they are used, often because special discount fares are available with prepayment. These receipts are not immediately treated as revenues by the airlines but are recorded as Air Traffic Liability and listed in the current liability section of the balance sheet. These liabilities are converted to revenue as the tickets are used. Similarly, the frequent-flyer programs offered by a number of the major airlines create obligations, as customers build up mileage credits, that must be paid in the form of free airline tickets. These liabilities should be recognized as the mileage credits are earned.

The following two sections discuss the methods used to account for deferred revenue more completely.

Advance Sales. Businesses often sell rights to future services or goods. Examples include gift certificates sold by retail stores that are redeemable in merchandise, coupons sold by restaurants that can be exchanged for meals, and tickets and tokens sold by transportation companies that are good for future fares. In such cases these businesses have received cash before they have performed a service or provided a good.

One of the primary criteria of revenue recognition is that the earning process must be substantially complete. In the case of advanced sales, therefore, revenue should not be recognized at the time the cash is received. The earning process is not yet complete. Instead, a liability (i.e., deferred revenue) should initially be recorded. This liability is then converted to revenue as the related services are performed or the relevant goods are delivered. If providing the related services or relevant goods is expected to require the use of current assets, deferred revenue should be classified as a current liability.

To illustrate, assume that Seattle Metro Transit sells bus passes that are good for one month for $20.00 each. On December 15 the transit company sells 50 passes for a total of $1000. The following journal entries would be recorded on December 15 and December 31, after one-half month had expired.

Dec. 15	Cash	1,000	
	Deferred Revenue		1,000
	To record the sale of 50 bus passes.		
Dec. 31	Deferred Revenue	500	
	Fees Earned		500
	To record the completion of one-half the service.		

Returnable Deposits. Deposits are often paid by customers to guarantee performance or to cover expected future obligations. It is quite common, for example, for the owner (lessor) of an apartment complex to require that lessees pay a damage deposit upon entry. Such deposits provide cash that can be used to pay possible future obligations in the event of damages to the rental property, which are the responsibility of the lessee. When the cash deposit is received, the lessor should not recognize revenue. Rather, a liability, Returnable Deposits, should be credited. This liability is removed from the books when the cash is returned to the lessee, or as expenses associated with repairing damaged property are incurred.

For example, assume that on January 14, Judy Nirodi signs a one-year lease with Pigskin Apartments for a two-bedroom apartment. The lease requires a $300 damage deposit. At the end of the year Judy leaves the apartment and Pigskin incurs $120 to repair damages for which Judy is responsible. On December 31 Pigskin returns $180 ($300 − $120) to Judy. The following journal entries would be entered by Pigskin to record these events.

Jan. 14	Cash	300	
	Returnable Deposit		300
	To record the receipt of a $300 damage deposit.		
Dec. 31	Returnable Deposit	120	
	Cash		120
	To record the damage repairs.		
Dec. 31	Returnable Deposit	180	
	Cash		180
	To record the cash payment to Judy.		

Third-Party Collections

Companies often act as collecting agencies for government or other entities. The price paid for an item at K mart, for example, includes sales tax, which K mart must periodically remit to the proper government authority. Companies are also required by law to withhold from employee wages social security taxes as well as an amount approximating the employee's income tax.[4] These withholdings are periodically sent to the federal government. In addition to payroll tax deductions, companies often withhold insurance premiums or union dues, which in turn must be passed on to the appropriate third party. In each of these cases a liability is created; the company receives or holds cash that legally must be paid to a third party. The liability is discharged when the cash payment is made. These liabilities are usually considered current because payment is expected within the time period of current assets.

To illustrate, assume that Sears, Roebuck sells a small tractor for $1000, which includes $50 in sales tax. The proper journal entry to record the sale follows.

Cash (or Accounts Receivable)	1000	
Sales Tax Payable		50
Sales		950
To record the sale of merchandise.		

When Sears pays the sales tax to the proper government authority, the following entry is recorded.

Sales Tax Payable	50	
Cash		50
To record the payment of sales taxes.		

To illustrate the liabilities associated with payroll deductions, assume that an assembly-line worker for General Motors earns gross wages of $3000 per month. However, $210 of that amount is withheld for social security taxes, $300 is withheld for income taxes, and $20 is withheld for union dues. These facts would give rise to the following journal entry when the monthly wage payment is made.

Wage Expense	3000	
Withholding Taxes Payable		300
Social Security Taxes Payable		210
Union Dues Payable		20
Cash		2470
To record payroll at the end of the month.		

Assuming General Motors pays all these liabilities at one time, the following journal entry would be recorded when the liabilities are discharged.

Withholding Taxes Payable	300	
Social Security Taxes Payable	210	
Union Dues Payable	20	
Cash		530
To record the payment of payroll liabilities.		

---

4. Companies must not only withhold employee social security taxes; they must also match them. That is, employers must pay to the government a dollar amount equal to that withheld from the employee's wages. Such payments can be quite large. In 1987, for example, General Motors paid well over $100 million in matched social security taxes.

Accrued Liabilities

Obligations are often created prior to the payment of cash. The recognition of such an obligation gives rise to an accrued liability. Accrued liabilities can be divided into two categories: determinable and conditional. *Determinable accrued liabilities* can be measured with reasonable precision, and the amount of cash needed to satisfy the obligation as well as the date of payment are relatively certain. *Conditional accrued liabilities* are based on net income, which cannot be determined until the end of the accounting period.

Determinable Accrued Liabilities. The matching principle states that net income in a particular period is the result of matching the revenues realized in that period with the expenses required to produce them. Revenues represent asset inflows (or discharge of liabilities) due to operations, and expenses represent the asset outflows (or the establishment of liabilities) required to generate the revenues. Determinable accrued liabilities arise when services or resources are used before payment is made, and they are recognized in the books at the end of the accounting period with an adjusting journal entry. Accrued liabilities are included in the current liability section of the balance sheet because they are usually paid early in the following accounting period.

Examples of determinable accrued liabilities include wages and salaries payable, interest payable, rent payable, insurance payable, and property taxes payable. These payables are often combined into one account on the balance sheet called Accrued Liabilities. To illustrate the method used to account for accrued liabilities, assume that Menlow Sisters borrowed $10,000 on December 1, 1989, and agreed to make semiannual interest payments at an annual rate of 12 percent. On December 31, after one month had passed, the following adjusting journal entry would be recorded when Menlow prepared the financial statements.

Dec. 31	Interest Expense [(10,000 × .12)/12]	100	
	Interest Payable		100
	To record accrued interest payable.		

When the semiannual interest payment is made on June 1, 1990, the following journal entry would be recorded. (For a more complete discussion of accrual accounting and accrued liabilities, see Chapter 4.)

June 1	Interest Payable	100	
	Interest Expense [10,000 × .12 × (5/12)]	500	
	Cash		600
	To record the payment of interest.		

Errors in Recording Accrued Liabilities. Managers and auditors must be careful that all existing liabilities are reported on the balance sheet, especially when reporting determinable accrued liabilities, which are not always evidenced by documentable exchanges and can be easily overlooked. Failure to record an accrued liability overstates net income, working capital, and the current ratio in the current period. As mentioned earlier, because such numbers are important to financial statement users and appear in debt and compensation contracts, management may have incentives to overlook or understate certain accrued liabilities.

However, it is also important to realize that failing to accrue a liability in a given period, while overstating income in that period, understates net income in the *subsequent* period. Suppose, for example, in the previous illustration, that Menlow Sisters failed to accrue the $100 interest payable at the end of 1989. Clearly, such an error would understate expenses and current liabilities in 1989. At the same time, however, this error would also have resulted in the following journal entry being recorded on June 1, 1990.

June 1	Interest Expense	600	
	Cash		600
	To record the payment of interest.		

The $600 of interest expense recognized in 1990 is $100 more than would have been recognized if interest had been accrued at the end of 1989. The $100 interest expense overstatement, in turn, causes 1990 net income to be understated by $100. Thus, errors in recording of accrued liabilities give rise to errors in the timing of income recognition, rather than the amount of income.

Conditional Accrued Liabilities. Some accrued liabilities cannot be determined until the end of the accounting period because they are based on net income, which cannot be computed until that time. These are known as **conditional accrued liabilities;** income taxes payable and payables associated with employee incentive compensation plans are two examples.

Income-tax liability. Income tax liability for a corporation is based on a percentage of taxable income in accordance with the rules stated in the Internal Revenue Code. Presently, the income rate paid by corporations is approximately 34 percent of taxable income. Most corporations are required by law at the beginning of each year to estimate their tax liabilities for the entire year and to make quarterly tax payments based on these estimates.

For example, assume that on January 1, 1991, Raleigh Trucking Company estimates 1991 taxable income and tax liability to be $58,800 and $20,000 ($58,800 × .34), respectively. The company makes payments of $5000 each quarter (April, June, September, and December) throughout the year. At year end Raleigh calculates its actual 1991 taxable income and tax to be $80,000 and $27,200 ($80,000 × .34), respectively. Raleigh has therefore underpaid its 1991 taxes by $7200 ($27,200 − $20,000), and a liability must be recorded on the balance sheet. The following journal entries would be recorded to reflect these events.

	Recorded in April, June, September, and December:		
	Income Tax Expense	5000	
	Cash		5000
	To record quarterly tax payments.		
Dec. 31	Income Tax Expense	7200	
	Income Tax Payable		7200
	To accrue income tax liability at year end.		

When the income-tax liability is paid the following year, the following journal entry is recorded.

Income Tax Payable	7200	
Cash		7200
To record the payment of income tax liability.		

Incentive compensation. Basing compensation on net income and/or stock prices is a very popular way to pay managers. Such payments comprise a significant portion of the total compensation of virtually all upper-level executives in major U.S. corporations. Profit-sharing arrangements, which are also based on a measure of net income, are frequently used to compensate employees at lower levels of the corporate hierarchy. *Accounting Trends and Techniques* (AICPA, 1987) reports that 553 incentive compensation plans were described in the financial reports of the 600 major U.S. companies selected for study.

Incentive compensation plans can take a number of different forms. AMP Incorporated, for example, has two incentive bonus plans: (1) a stock plus cash plan and (2) a cash plan. Executive compensation under the first plan is related to the market value of the company's stock; compensation under the second is a percentage of the company's net income. The formula for Chrysler's incentive compensation plan includes a provision of 8 percent of consolidated net income. Exxon's incentive program indicates that the total amount distributed cannot exceed 3 percent of net income or 6 percent of capital invested (as defined by the plan).

Incentive compensation is particularly significant in the automobile industry. In 1987, for example, General Motors distributed bonuses to its top executives totaling $157 million, which was described in *The Wall Street Journal* as "anemic" compared to the executive bonuses paid at Ford Motor Company. Ford also paid its workers an average of $3700 each in profit sharing. Lee Iacocca of the Chrysler Corporation has received the greatest amount of incentive compensation. From 1984 to 1987 he received nearly $50 million in total compensation, of which less than $4.2 million was in the form of salary.[5]

From an accounting standpoint, liabilities associated with incentive compensation plans must be accrued at year end because they are based on measures (e.g., net income or stock prices) that cannot be determined until that time. They are listed as current on the balance sheet because they are typically distributed to management early the following period, at which time the liability is discharged.

Suppose, for example, that Tom Turnstile, an executive for Maylein Stoneware, is paid a bonus each year in the amount of 3 percent of net income. If net income is determined at year end to be $300,000, Turnstile's bonus is $9000 ($300,000 × .03), and the following journal entry is recorded.

Bonus Expense	9000	
Bonus Liability		9000
To accrue the bonus liability.		

When the bonus is paid the following year, the journal entry below is recorded.

Bonus Liability	9000	
Cash		9000
To record payment of the bonus.		

Incentive compensation plans are popular because they help a company's stockholders induce managers and employees to act in a manner consistent with their objectives. By basing compensation on net income or stock prices, such plans encourage management to maximize net income or stock prices, an objective that is also in the interests of the stockholders. Keep in mind, however, that managers have incentives to influence the measure of net income through oper-

---

5. Jacob Schlesinger, "GM Officials Get Short-Term Incentives Despite Plan to Emphasize Long-Term," *The Wall Street Journal*, 18 April 1988, p. 4.

ating decisions, the choice of accounting methods, estimates, assumptions, the timing of accruals, or even intentional misstatements.[6]

To illustrate, suppose in the previous example that Tom Turnstile, who receives a bonus equal to 3 percent of net income each year, is the chief executive officer and accountant for Maylein Stoneware. At year end, rather than reporting net income at $300,000 as stated in the example, he overlooks a $20,000 accrual, chooses an accounting method that recognizes $20,000 less of expenses (e.g., FIFO), or postpones $20,000 in research and development expenditures. Any of these acts would cause expenses to be $20,000 less than otherwise and net income to be $320,000. Tom's bonus would then be $9600 ($320,000 × .03) instead of $9000 ($300,000 × .03), an increase of $600.

In summary, while executive compensation systems based on net income encourage management to act in the interests of the stockholders, they also encourage management to manipulate the measure of net income. All interested parties should be aware that management is motivated by such incentives and can exert such control. However, it may not be in management's interest to do so. As illustrated earlier, most manipulations reverse themselves in the subsequent period, and stockholders, investors, and creditors may discount the value of companies that provide financial statements of questionable credibility.

CONTINGENCIES AND CONTINGENT LIABILITIES

As defined by the FASB, "a contingency is an existing condition, situation, or set of circumstances involving uncertainty as to possible gain or loss to an enterprise that will ultimately be resolved when one or more future events occurs or fails to occur."[7] A common example is a pending lawsuit that will be settled in the future by the decision of a court. If the possible future outcome represents an increase of assets or a decrease of liabilities, the existing condition is considered a **gain contingency.** If the possible outcome represents a decrease in assets or an increase in liabilities, the condition is considered a **loss contingency.**

Before discussing the methods used to account for contingencies, study the following scenario carefully. It is designed to illustrate some of the economic issues involved in reporting contingencies.

Contingent Liabilities: A Scenario

Suppose that Harry Jones, the accountant for Chemical Enterprises, is preparing the financial statements as of December 31, 1990. Chemical Enterprises is in need of cash and plans to submit the financial statements to First National Bank with an application for a sizable loan. First National has required that the statements Harry prepares be audited by an independent CPA. To conduct the audit, Chemical has hired the firm of Arthur Mitchell & Co.

---

6. A number of research studies in accounting support the conclusion that management's choice of accounting methods (e.g., FIFO vs. LIFO, straight-line vs. accelerated depreciation) is influenced by the existence and nature of executive compensation plans.

7. FASB, "Accounting for Contingencies," *Statement of Financial Accounting Standards No. 5* (Stamford, Conn.: FASB, 1987), par. 1.

The preparation of the statements has gone smoothly for Harry, except for one rather significant problem. Several months ago a small amount of toxic liquid from one of Chemical's plants seeped into the water supply of a small midwestern town. The extent of Chemical's responsibility and the nature and extent of any physical harm to the town's residents are uncertain. Nonetheless, the town has filed suit against Chemical for $1 million, and the court case is currently in process. After reviewing the facts of the case, Chemical's lawyers estimate that there is a 70 percent chance that Chemical will successfully defend itself against the lawsuit.

Harry is uncertain how this lawsuit should affect the financial statements of Chemical as of December 31, 1990. As he sees it, the following alternatives represent the three possible ways to account for it.

1. Ignore the suit on financial statements.
2. Disclose and describe the suit in the footnotes to the financial statements.
3. Recognize a loss on the income statement and a liability on the balance sheet in the amount of $1 million, and disclose and describe the suit in the footnotes.

Alternative 1: Ignore

Under the first alternative, the lawsuit would not be mentioned anywhere in the financial statements. No loss has occurred as of December 31, 1990, and there is a 70 percent chance, according to the lawyers, that no loss will occur at all. Chemical's management might be inclined to favor this alternative over the others because they suspect that disclosing the lawsuit (Alternative 2) or adjusting the financial statements to reflect it (Alternative 3) could endanger the bank loan or at least make the terms (e.g., interest rate) of the loan less favorable. Ignoring the lawsuit would avoid a negative effect on the financial ratios in general as well as on any contracts based on them.

However, the auditor, Arthur Mitchell & Co., is also aware of the lawsuit and is likely to render a qualified opinion on the financial statements unless some recognition is made of the potential loss. If it is not disclosed, and the auditor grants a *clean opinion*, then if the bank makes the loan, the auditor may be liable for any losses the bank incurs if Chemical loses the suit. Ignoring the lawsuit would not be a conservative choice for either the auditor or management, and may expose them both to significant legal liability.

Alternative 2: Disclose

The second alternative entails disclosing the nature and amount of the lawsuit as well as the opinions of Chemical's legal council. This alternative would describe the situation to the bank as well as other financial report users, but it would have no effect on the dollar amounts in the financial statements. Consequently, financial ratios and contracts written in terms of financial statement numbers would remain unaffected. However, the bank could make any adjustments it saw fit and thereby assess for itself the magnitude of the potential problem.

Alternative 3: Accrue

The final alternative is to accrue the loss and the related liability on the financial statements. If Harry chooses this action, he would make the following adjusting journal entry on December 31, 1990:

Contingent Loss	1,000,000	
Contingent Liability		1,000,000
To accrue a contingent liability.		

The Contingent Loss account is a temporary account and would appear on the income statement. It would serve to reduce net income. The Contingent Liability account would appear on the liability side of the balance sheet and be classified as current if payment were expected in the time period that defines current assets. If Chemical loses the suit and pays the residents of the town, the contingent liability would be written off in the following manner:

Contingent Liability	1,000,000	
Cash, Payables, etc.		1,000,000
To record the payment of a contingent liability.		

Alternative 3 would probably be very unattractive to the management of Chemical. Having to recognize the contingent loss and the associated liability on the financial statements would not only endanger the bank loan but could make important financial ratios appear much less favorable. It could, therefore, put the company in technical default on existing debt covenants as well as reduce compensation from bonus and profitsharing plans. Furthermore, the court might interpret accrual of the loss as Chemical's own admission that the suit is lost, reducing Chemical's chances of a successful defense.

On the other hand, accruing the contingent loss is the most conservative choice. It would therefore substantially reduce the liability faced by both the auditor and Chemical's management, and possibly increase the credibility of both parties in the view of financial statement users.

Accounting for Contingencies

Choosing the appropriate accounting treatment for the situation depicted in the preceding scenario is not a simple matter. Each of the three alternatives is attractive in some respects and unattractive in others. The FASB has addressed this problem by preparing Standard No. 5, "Accounting for Contingencies,"[8] which provides guidelines that should be followed when accounting for contingencies. This standard first distinguishes between gain contingencies, which involve possible future gains, and loss contingencies, which involve possible future losses. As Table 10−5 shows, the methods used to account for these two contingencies are quite different.

Gain Contingencies

Accounting for gain contingencies is quite straightforward. They are never accrued on the financial statements and are rarely disclosed in the footnotes.[9] They are not recognized until they are actually realized. This treatment is consistent with both the principle of objectivity and the concept of conservatism. It avoids any subjective estimates involved in predicting the outcomes of contingent events and ensures that the financial statements do not reflect gains that may not actually occur.

---

8. Ibid.

9. *Accounting Trends and Techniques* (New York: AICPA, 1987, p. 65) reports that, of the 600 major U.S. companies examined, only 22 disclosed contingent gains due to lawsuits, and 361 reported contingent losses due to lawsuits.

Table 10-5   Accounting for contingencies

Contingency	Probability of Occurrence	Accounting Treatment
Loss contingency	Remote	Ignore
	Reasonably possible	Disclose all available information
	Probable and estimable	Accrue and disclose
Gain contingency	Remote	Ignore
	Reasonably possible	Ignore
	Probable	Sometimes disclose

Loss Contingencies

Accounting for loss contingencies is somewhat more involved. The probability of a loss occurring from a contingent situation should be classified as either remote, reasonably possible, or probable. If the probability is remote, the loss need not be disclosed. If the probability is considered reasonably possible, the potential loss and all relevant information about it should be disclosed in the footnotes. If the loss is viewed as probable and the amount can be estimated, the potential loss and associated liability should be accrued on the financial statements, and the nature of the loss should be described in the footnotes. Accrued loss contingencies are considered current liabilities if they are to be paid in the time period defining current assets.

Classifying contingent losses as remote, reasonably possible, or probable and estimating the dollar amount of probable contingent losses can be highly subjective. Managers and auditors often consult with legal council or other experts, but in areas like lawsuits it is very difficult to predict outcomes accurately. Consequently, relatively few contingent losses stemming from lawsuits are actually accrued on the financial statements.

Ignoring potential losses from litigation is also relatively rare. Such a practice is not conservative and can expose management and the auditor to significant levels of legal liability. Therefore, as a practical matter, most contingent losses related to pending litigation are simply disclosed. Opinions of legal council, estimates of the dollar amounts of the settlements, and other available information concerning potential losses from litigation are usually described in the footnotes to the financial statements. The following excerpt, for example, is from the 1986 financial report of Amoco Corporation.

> *Litigation: Suits are pending in various states and federal courts in Illinois against Amoco . . . seeking damages for pollution. . . . Amounts originally claimed for pollution damage aggregated about $1.9 billion, but the amount of claims being asserted currently is estimated at approximately $300 million. The suits are not expected to have a material adverse effect on the corporation's consolidated financial position.*

While the loss contingencies described in the excerpt above "are not expected to have a material adverse effect" on Amoco's financial position, some loss contingencies can be very significant. In 1988, for example, Rockwood Holding Co. was issued a qualified opinion by its independent auditors "in connection with litigation related to credit insurance."[10] As reported in *Forbes*, such qualifications

---

10. "Qualified Opinion on Rockwood Holding Year-End Results Set," *The Wall Street Journal,* 11 April 1988.

are issued by auditors to "protect themselves from future litigation" by alerting investors and "bank credit officers to important footnotes" and material uncertainties about the future of the company.[11]

Warranties: Accrued Loss Contingencies

Although most contingent losses related to pending litigation are usually only disclosed, certain loss contingencies are normally accrued. In these cases the losses are highly probable and can be estimated with reasonable accuracy. Maintenance and repair warranties on previously sold products are common examples.

In a **warranty,** a seller promises to remove deficiencies in the quantity, quality, or performance of a product sold to a buyer. Warranties are usually granted for a specific period, during which time the seller promises to bear all or part of the costs of replacing defective parts, performing necessary repairs, or providing additional services. From the seller's standpoint, warranties entail uncertain future costs. It is unlikely that all buyers will take advantage of the warranties granted to them, but enough of them do so to consider the future costs probable and reasonably estimable. Thus, warranties are normally accounted for as accrued contingent losses.

For example, suppose that Hauser and Sons sold ten word processors on July 1 for $1000 each. Each word processor is under warranty for parts and labor for one year and, based on past experience, the company estimates that, on average, warranty costs will be $100 per unit. During the remainder of the year several machines require servicing and as of December 31, $350 of warranty costs had been incurred. The following journal entries would be recorded to reflect these events.

Cash or Accounts Receivable	10,000	
Sales (10 × $1,000)		10,000
To record the sale of ten word processors.		
Warranty Expense (10 × $100)	1000	
Contingent Warranty Liability		1000
To recognize the contingent liability associated with the warranty.		
Contingent Warranty Liability	350	
Cash, Wages Payable, or Parts		350
To record warranty costs incurred during the year.		

Several features about this accounting treatment are noteworthy. First, the contingent liability is created when the word processors are sold because at that time Hauser and Sons are responsible for future services. Accordingly, the entire expected warranty expense related to the sale of the ten word processors is recognized in the period of sale, even though only a $350 cost is actually incurred. The total warranty expense is thereby matched against sales revenue in the period of sale. Note also that the balance in the Contingent Warranty Liability account at the end of the period is $650 ($1,000 − $350), indicating that costs of $650 are still expected during the following six-month period due to warranties. This amount would be listed as a current liability on the December 31 balance sheet. As the following entry illustrates, the $650 contingent liability is removed from the books when costs are incurred to service the warranties as they are exercised in the second period.

---

11. Jane Carmichael, "The End of the Red Flag," *Forbes*, 23 November 1981, pp. 115–16.

Contingent Liability	650	
Cash, Wages Payable, etc.		650
To record the payment of previously recognized warranty liabilities.		

The excerpt below is from the 1986 financial statements of Winnebago Industries, Inc., a manufacturer of recreational vehicles. It contains the current liability section of the balance sheet and a footnote describing the company's liability on product warranties.

	1986*	1985*
Current maturities of long-term debts	$ 1,050	$ 1,171
Bank acceptances	—	3,363
Notes payable	15,000	—
Accounts payable	23,639	19,905
Accrued expenses	12,410	11,636
Income taxes payable	5,823	4,265
Liabilities on product warranties	5,476	4,825
Total current liabilities	$63,398	$45,165

Note 1: Provision for warranty claims: Estimated warranty costs are provided at the time of sale of the warranty products.

*Dollars in thousands.

Similarly, the Polaroid Corporation, a manufacturer of camera equipment, also experiences material warranty costs that are accrued before they are actually incurred. The following excerpt is from its 1986 financial report: "Product Warranty: Estimated product warranty costs are accrued at the time the products are sold."

RETIREMENT COSTS: PENSIONS AND POST-RETIREMENT HEALTH CARE AND INSURANCE

This section introduces and briefly describes pension and post-retirement health care and insurance liabilities. A more complete discussion of pensions appears in the appendix.

A **pension** is a sum of money paid to a retired or disabled employee, the amount of which is usually determined by the employee's years of service. For most large companies, pension plans are an important part of the employees' compensation packages, and they are part of almost all negotiated wage settlements.[12] Pension plans are backed by contractual agreements with the employees and are subject to federal regulation.

Most pension plans are structured so that an employer periodically makes cash payments to a pension fund, which is a legal entity distinct from the sponsoring company. The cash, securities, and other income-earning investments that make up the fund are usually managed by someone outside the company, and the assets in the pension fund do not appear on the company's balance sheet. The employer's cash contributions plus the income generated through the fund's management (i.e., dividends, interest, capital appreciation) provide the cash that is distributed to employees upon retirement. The terms of the pension plan determine the amounts to which individual employees are entitled (benefits).

---

12. *Accounting Trends and Techniques* (New York: AICPA, 1987, p. 274) reports that, of the 600 major U.S. companies surveyed, 560 disclosed the existence of a pension plan.

Pension liability, which appears in the long-term liability section on the balance sheet of some companies, is an estimate of the difference between the dollar amount contributed by the company to the pension fund and the total contributions necessary to maintain a fund large enough to meet the employee benefits guaranteed by the company.

For example, assume that Jonas Company has contributed $50,000 to its pension fund since it was established. It has been estimated that contributions of $75,000 would have been necessary to maintain a fund large enough to pay the benefits promised to the present employees. Thus, Jonas should report a long-term pension liability of $25,000 ($75,000 − $50,000).

As specified in Financial Accounting Standards Nos. 87 and 88, the accounting methods and disclosure requirements for pension plans are complex and extensive.[13] The following excerpt from the 1986 financial report of Ashland Oil, Inc., represents only a small portion of the required disclosures.

Employees' Pension and Retirement Benefits: Ashland sponsors pension and retirement plans which cover substantially all employees, other than union employees covered by multiemployer pension plans under collective bargaining agreements. Benefits under these plans generally are based on the employees' years of service and compensation during the years immediately preceding retirement. Ashland's general funding policy is to contribute amounts deductible for federal income tax purposes.

Accounting for pension plans is quite subjective, relying heavily on estimates and assumptions. Further, a small change in an important estimate can have a significant effect on both the amount funded by the company and the net income figure reported on its income statement. For example, to determine what a company must contribute to the pension plan each year, company accountants must estimate the fund's future annual return. In 1981 Eastern Airlines changed this estimate and reduced its annual pension contribution by $25 million, increasing 1981 net income by that same amount. Similarly, it was reported that if Bethlehem Steel would increase its estimate of its pension fund's future return by only 1 percent, it would decrease its pension liability by as much as $200 million.[14]

Most large companies cover a portion of the health care and insurance costs incurred by employees after retirement (i.e., **post-retirement health care and insurance costs**). Similar to pensions, such coverage is part of employee compensation and is earned over an employee's years of service. Unlike pensions, however, most companies neither set up funds to pay these future costs nor accrue the related liabilities as the employees earn the coverage. Instead, the expense associated with these costs is simply recognized when the health care payments are made after the employee retires. Such a policy is referred to as a pay-as-you-go approach.

The FASB has recently proposed that companies estimate and record the liability associated with post-retirement health care and insurance costs and begin accruing them starting in 1992. In other words, the FASB has proposed that these costs be accounted for in a manner similar to pensions, stating that "such ac-

---

13. FASB, "Employers' Accounting for Pension Plans," *Statement of Financial Accounting Standards Nos. 87 and 88* (Stamford, Conn.: FASB, 1985).

14. Thomas Baker, "Reading the Tea Leaves," *Forbes*, 22 June 1981, pp. 76, 78.

counting changes are needed to improve disclosure to investors, to provide better comparisons of financial data among companies and industries, and to require companies to accrue for expenses they promise to pay."[15]

This proposal is one of the most controversial in the history of the FASB. *Barron's* (April 17, 1989) reports that "estimates of the size of this new liability [for the entire economy] range from $400 billion to $1 trillion, depending on whose . . . assumptions you accept. Even with the smaller figure, adopting the FASB approach would saddle some companies with an annual expense that could cut reported profits by as much as 130%." *The Wall Street Journal* (March 21, 1989) adds that many corporate executives maintain that "the FASB doesn't seem to care what it does to the U.S. economy, and its credibility gap with business is growing . . . General Motors Corp.'s reported annual profits after 1992 could come close to being wiped out by the latest proposal on accruing [these costs]. . . . Such discontent with the FASB has spurred such powerful lobbying groups as the Business Roundtable to ask for more voice in the FASB deliberations." *Fortune* (December 19, 1988) points out further that "many executives . . . contend that future health costs simply cannot be measured . . . [while] others argue that the rules will prompt companies to seek some way to avoid paying the benefits they have promised."

It is presently impossible to predict how this issue will be resolved. It is clear, however, that potentially a very large liability is not being reported on the balance sheets of most major U.S. companies. This issue also provides a dramatic illustration of the economic consequences of accounting standards and the political environment in which they are set.

DEFERRED INCOME TAXES

We have noted several times that the rules for computing taxable income are different from generally accepted accounting principles, which specify how financial accounting net income is to be measured. The most common case arises when a company depreciates its fixed assets using an accelerated method in computing taxable income and the straight-line method in preparing the financial statements. Such a strategy saves income taxes in the early periods of the asset's useful life, as illustrated in Chapter 9, but this benefit reverses itself in later years, leading to additional income tax payments.

To illustrate, suppose that Midland Plastics purchased a piece of equipment on January 1, 1988, for $9000. The equipment is expected to have a three-year useful life and no salvage value. Midland computes depreciation using the double-declining-balance method for income-tax purposes and straight-line for reporting purposes. By doing so, Midland is creating a tax savings in 1988 (the first year of the asset's life) but at the same time is creating an obligation to pay additional taxes in the later years, 1989 and 1990. Table 10–6 provides a schedule of the tax savings for 1988 and the additional tax payments for 1989 and 1990. Assume that Midland pays income taxes at a rate of 30 percent of taxable income.

Note that the use of the double-declining-balance method creates a tax savings of $900 in 1988, the first year of the equipment's useful life. In 1989 and 1990, however, this benefit reverses itself, giving rise to additional tax payments of $300

---

15. Lee Berton, "Accounting-Board Rulings Make Business See Red." *The Wall Street Journal*, 21 March, 1989.

Table 10-6   Income tax savings and reversals

Year	Dollar Amounts of Depreciation			Amount of Excess (Under) Depreciation		Tax Rate		Income Tax Benefit (Disbenefit)
	Double-Declining-Balance[a]		Straight-Line[b]					
1988	$ 6000	—	$ 3000	=	$ 3000	×	30%	=	$900
1989	2000	—	3000	=	(1000)	×	30%	=	(300)
1990	1000	—	3000	=	(2000)	×	30%	=	(600)
Total	$ 9000		$ 9000		$ 0				$ 0

[a]($9000 − accumulated depreciation) × 2(straight-line rate [33%])
[b]$9000/3 yr.

in 1989 and $600 in 1990. As of the end of 1988, Midland can view these additional tax payments as liabilities because they represent future obligations. Specifically, additional tax payments that total $900 ($300 + $600) are expected in 1989 and 1990. This liability is reported on the balance sheet and referred to as **deferred income taxes.** Midland Plastics, in other words, would report a deferred income tax liability of $900 in the long-term liability section of its 1988 balance sheet.

During 1989 and 1990, as the tax benefit reverses itself and Midland pays the additional taxes, the deferred income tax liability is reduced by $300 in 1989 and by $600 in 1990. Consequently, as of the end of 1990, after the useful life of the equipment has expired, the deferred income tax liability has been reduced to zero.

In summary, using double-declining-balance instead of straight-line gives rise to an immediate tax benefit and a future liability (deferred income taxes) that is discharged as additional taxes are paid over the life of the asset. Preparing the journal entry to record the recognition or discharge of deferred income taxes consists of three steps:

1. Compute the income tax benefit (or disbenefit) as illustrated in Table 10-6. The dollar amount of a tax benefit (1988) is entered as a credit to the Deferred Income Tax account. The dollar amounts of tax disbenefits (1989 and 1990) are entered as debits to the Deferred Income Tax account in future periods.

2. Compute the company's income tax liability (taxable income × corporate income tax rate). This dollar amount is entered as a credit to the Income Taxes Payable account.

3. Enter a debit to the Income Tax Expense account in an amount that brings the journal entry into balance.

To illustrate, assume in the preceding example that Midland Plastics recognized taxable income in the amount of $10,000 for each of the three years 1988, 1989, and 1990. The company's tax liability, therefore, in each year was $3000 ($10,000 × .30). Given this information, Figure 10-2 contains the journal entries and the balance sheet carrying values of the Deferred Income Tax account for the three-year period.

In 1988 a deferred tax liability of $900 is recognized because Midland, which uses the double-declining-balance method for tax purposes, expects to pay additional income taxes of $300 and $600 over the next two years. An income tax

Figure 10–2   Deferred income taxes

	1988			1989			1990		
General journal	Income Tax Expense (plug)	3,900		Income Tax Expense (plug)	2,700		Income Tax Expense (plug)	2,400	
	Deferred Income Taxes		900	Deferred Income Taxes	300		Deferred Income Taxes	600	
	Income Tax Payable		3,000	Income Tax Payable		3,000	Income Tax Payable		3,000
Balance sheet excerpt	Deferred income taxes		900	(900 − 300)	600		(600 − 600)	0	

liability of $3000 is also recognized, and Income Tax Expense is debited for an amount ($3900) that brings the journal entry into balance. In 1989 and 1990, as Midland pays the additional taxes, the Deferred Income Tax account is reduced. In both years an income tax liability is recognized for $3000, and the dollar amount of the debit to Income Tax Expense makes the journal entry balance.

Deferred income taxes represent a significant liability on the balance sheet of many major U.S. companies.[16] The excerpt below is from the 1986 financial report of Briggs and Stratton Corporation. As of December 31, 1986, the company reported a deferred tax liability of more than $38 million.

Deferred income taxes: Deferred income taxes, classified as a noncurrent liability, provide for the tax effects of timing differences . . . in different periods for tax and financial reporting purposes. These timing differences principally result from additional tax deductions available due to the use of accelerated methods of depreciation and shorter asset lives for tax purposes.

The size of the Deferred Income Tax account is usually related to the size of a company's investment in fixed assets. Large manufacturing companies, such as IBM, DuPont, ARCO, and Chrysler, as a result, often carry huge balances in their deferred tax accounts. Such companies normally depreciate their fixed assets using accelerated methods for tax purposes and straight-line for financial reporting purposes, and the resulting differences between taxable income and financial accounting income can be quite large.[17] On the other hand, financial institutions, which carry limited investments in fixed assets, rarely show balances in the Deferred Income Tax account. Indeed, Chase Manhattan Bank, the American Express Company, and Safeco Insurance report no deferred income taxes on their balance sheets.

As explained earlier, the Deferred Income Tax account can be viewed as a liability for additional income taxes that must be paid in the future as certain tax benefits reverse themselves. However, if a company consistently purchases more fixed assets than it retires, it can indefinitely postpone the reversal period and the payment of the additional income taxes. At the same time, the credit balance in

16. The Deferred Income Tax account can have a debit balance. However, such cases are relatively uncommon, and the methods used to account for them are beyond the scope of this text.

17. *Accounting Trends and Techniques* (New York: AICPA, 1987, p. 301) reports that, of the 600 major U.S. companies surveyed, 488 disclosed timing differences due to the use of a different depreciation method for reporting purposes than the method used for tax purposes.

Table 10–7   Deferred income tax liability (selected U.S. companies)

Company	Deferred Tax Liability (millions)	Percent of Total Assets
ARCO	$3,641	16%
J. C. Penney	1,375	12
DuPont	2,801	10
IBM	5,150	8
Chrysler	1,196	6
McDonald's	440	6

Source: 1987 financial reports.

the Deferred Income Tax account continues to accumulate. Many of the largest companies in the U.S. have accumulated significant dollar amounts in deferred income taxes simply because they have continued to grow over a long period of time, consistently purchasing more fixed assets than they retire.[18]

To illustrate the size of the Deferred Income Tax account, Table 10–7 contains the dollar amounts of deferred income taxes disclosed on the 1987 balance sheets of selected major U.S. companies. The table also shows this amount as a percentage of each company's total assets.

In spite of such large balances, many accountants argue that deferred income taxes do not represent economic liabilities. Because they can be postponed indefinitely, they do not lead to future cash outflows. An article in *Forbes* magazine noted: "These numbers are not valid because most deferred taxes never actually get paid. In the real world . . . companies continually make plant and equipment purchases that create new deductions. The result: treating deferred taxes as a liability presents an inaccurate picture of liquidity and cash flow."[19] The national director for accounting and auditing for Seidman & Seidman commented further: "The deferred taxes on the balance sheet bear no relationship to what is actually going to be owed. So the current method of income tax accounting makes it impossible for the investors to evaluate a company's liquidity, solvency, or cash flow."[20]

Another interesting aspect about deferred income taxes is that income statement gains and losses can be recognized when income tax rates change. Consider, for example, the General Electric (GE) Company, which had accumulated excess depreciation (i.e., accelerated in excess of straight-line) of approximately $4 billion as of the end of 1986. At the 1986 income tax rate of 48 percent, these benefits translated to a deferred income tax liability of $1.92 billion ($4 billion × 48%), which GE reported on its 1986 balance sheet. However, in 1987 the corporate income tax rate was reduced to 34 percent, and using the new tax rate, GE recalculated its deferred income tax liability to be $1.36 billion ($4 billion × 34%). Reducing the liability gave rise to an approximate gain of $560 million ($1.92 billion − $1.36 billion) that was recognized in 1987 and recorded with the following journal entry.

---

18. Jane Carmichael, "Rollover," *Forbes*, 18 January 1982, pp. 75, 78.

19. Jill Andresky, "Leaving Well Enough Alone," *Forbes*, 7 May 1984, p. 206.

20. Carmichael, "Rollover." pp. 75, 78.

Deferred Income Taxes	560	
Gain on Change in Income Tax Rate		560
To record a gain due to reductions in future income tax rates.		

The methods used to account for deferred income taxes are controversial and actually much more complicated than indicated in this discussion. More in-depth coverage can be found in intermediate accounting texts. Nonetheless, this issue is important to all interested parties because calculating the amount of deferred tax and considering it a liability or otherwise can have significant economic consequences.

REPORTING LIABILITIES ON THE BALANCE SHEET: ECONOMIC CONSEQUENCES

The reported values of current liabilities, pension and post-retirement health care and insurance liabilities, and deferred income taxes affect important financial ratios that stockholders, investors, creditors, and others use to assess management's performance and a company's financial condition. Seven of Dun & Bradstreet's fourteen key business ratios, for example, directly include a measure of liabilities: (1) quick ratio ([cash + receivables]/current liabilities), (2) current ratio (current assets/ current liabilities), (3) current liabilities/net worth, (4) current liabilities/inventory, (5) total liabilities/net worth, (6) sales/net working capital, and (7) accounts payable to sales. Such ratios are also found in debt contracts designed to direct and control the business decisions of management. Consequently, the balance sheet values of liabilities and underlying debt contracts are very important to all financial statement users.

Stockholders and Investors

Stockholders and investors are concerned with liabilities and the contracts that underlie them because interest payments must be met before dividends can be distributed. Also, in the event of liquidation, outstanding payables must be satisfied before stockholders are paid. Many loan contracts, for example, restrict the amount of dividends that can be paid in any one year to the common stockholders. The 1987 financial report of Sherwin Williams and Company, a manufacturer of paint products, states that certain debt covenants restrict the payment of dividends and other distributions on the company's stock. As of December 31, 1987, $179 million was available for cash dividends on common stock.

Creditors

The creditors of a company have a special interest in the liabilities held by others. These liabilities compete for the resources that must be used to satisfy the obligations owed to them. Creditors often protect their interests by writing terms in loan contracts that require collateral in the case of default or restrict a company's future borrowings. Referring again to the 1987 financial report of Sherwin Williams, these same debt covenants disallowed certain investments and limited the incurrence of future debts.

Management

Management views short- and long-term borrowings and the related liabilities as important sources of capital for operating, investing, and financing activities. A recent article in *Forbes* states that "most companies spend lots of time figuring out when and how to borrow money. That makes sense. Proper timing of debt can save millions in interest payments."[21] On its 1988 balance sheet the Quaker Oats Company, for example, disclosed $1.7 billion of outstanding liabilities, representing 58 percent of its financing sources. That amount is certainly a significant sum that requires astute and careful management to ensure that sufficient cash is on hand to meet the required payments as they come due. In 1988 alone, Quaker Oats paid approximately $323 million in interest and principal to service its outstanding debt.

While management must rely on borrowings for its financing needs, it has incentives to understate liabilities on the balance sheet. Indeed, a well-known article in *Forbes* began: "The basic drives of man are few: to get enough food, to find shelter, and to keep debt off the balance sheet."[22] Additional debt on the balance sheet, for example, can reduce a company's credit rating, making it increasingly difficult to attract capital in the future. In 1988 Standard & Poor's Corp., an established credit-rating service, lowered the credit rating of Fleming Company because the company financed an acquisition with borrowings that increased its total debt by $375 million. In reaction to Standard & Poor's announcement, the market price of the company's outstanding debt immediately dropped.

Additional debt on the balance sheet can also decrease the current ratio, increase the debt/asset ratio, and increase the debt/equity ratio. Such changes could cause a company to violate its debt covenants and in general cause it to be viewed as more risky by outside investors and creditors. The national director of accounting and auditing at Seidman & Seidman, for example, points out that "removing large amounts of debt can present a more favorable impression of debt-to-equity ratios, working capital ratios, and the returns on assets invested in the business."[23]

There are also situations, however, when management may wish to report additional liabilities on the balance sheet. For example, by reporting additional accrued liabilities in the current period, management may be able to report higher net income amounts in future periods. Such a strategy is not unusual for companies that are experiencing exceptionally poor years as well as for those experiencing exceptionally good years.

In 1988, for example, while in the midst of bankruptcy proceedings, LTV Corporation accrued a number of significant liabilities, including post-retirement health care and insurance costs, none of which were required at the time by generally accepted accounting principles. A spokesman for LTV was quoted in *The Wall Street Journal* (22 November 1988) as saying, "[the company] took the special charges because it believes it should record all its liabilities while in [bankruptcy] proceedings. It's a unique opportunity for us to take it at a time when it does the least harm." As noted later in the article, "LTV likely wants a fresh start when it emerges from bankruptcy-law proceedings." Such a strategy is known as

---

21. Richard Morris, "None for Me, Thanks," *Forbes*, 22 October 1984, p. 134.
22. Richard Greene, "The Joys of Leasing," *Forbes*, 24 November 1980, p. 59.
23. Anne McGrath, "The Best of Both Worlds," *Forbes*, 26 September 1983, pp. 106, 108.

taking a bath. By accumulating a number of losses in a single, exceptionally poor year, a company can avoid having to recognize these losses in future years.

Alternatively, companies experiencing exceptionally good years may also choose to accrue additional liabilities. The article just cited also pointed out that a number of companies "with strong equity positions" may wish to take early recognition of certain liabilities and, in effect, "bite the bullet early." This strategy recognizes losses in a year where they will be overwhelmed by other items of income. It also avoids having to recognize the losses in later years, which may not be so exceptional.

Auditors

Auditors must attest that all liabilities are identified and properly reported on the balance sheet. Auditors are particularly careful in this area because significant unreported liabilities may lead to losses incurred in the future by investors and creditors for which auditors may be held liable. For example, Peat, Marwick, and Main, a major accounting firm, recently withdrew its opinions on Bombay Palace Restaurants, Inc., accusing the company of supplying false information and invoice documents with respect to certain material liabilities.[24]

THE ANNUAL REPORT OF K MART CORPORATION

Turn now to K mart's annual report located in Appendix D. It provides information about the company's current liabilities, employee incentive plan, contingent liabilities, pension plans, and deferred income taxes.

The Balance Sheet (page 32) shows that total current liabilities for 1988 and 1989 were $3.37 billion and $3.492 billion, respectively. Current liabilities consisted primarily of accounts payable, accrued payrolls and other liabilities, taxes other than income taxes, and income taxes. K mart's current ratios (called working capital ratios on page 14) for 1987, 1988, and 1989 were 1.7, 1.9, and 2.0. As indicated on page 26, "the working capital ratio demonstrates the company's ability to meet short-term obligations . . . the improvement in 1988 is primarily due to increased cash and investments partially offset by a slight increase in accounts payable. The improvement in 1987 was due to an increase in inventory and a decrease in short-term borrowings."

Current maturities on long-term debts are reported on the charts appearing on pages 41 and 43, which describe Long-Term Debt and Leases, respectively. As of January 25, 1989 the portion of long-term debt due within one year was only $1 million while lease payments due within one year totaled $89 million. These two amounts are included on the Balance Sheet in the account Accrued Payrolls and Other Liabilities.

Note on the Income Statement (page 31) that K mart recognized Income Tax Expense of $441 million, which represented approximately 35 percent of Income Before Taxes ($1.244 billion). The components of the expense calculation are disclosed on page 40. The outstanding income tax liabilities as of January 25, 1989 and January 27, 1988 were $226 and $211 million, respectively, and the actual

---

24. "Auditor Resigns, Withdraws Opinions on Some Reports," *The Wall Street Journal,* 14 May 1988.

income tax payment during the current year was $423 million (page 37). Note that this payment was applied to both the 1988 and the 1989 income tax liability.

The employee incentive plan, referred to as the Stock Option Plan, is described on page 48. While the description is somewhat beyond the scope of this text, the Plan basically provides officers and key employees with the right to purchase K mart stock at specified prices. Most plans of this nature base the granting of such rights on the achievement of certain company goals, normally expressed in terms of various measures of income.

A contingency is described on page 36. Legal judgment in the amount of $79 million, as of January 25, 1989, was recently rendered against K mart. The company is planning an appeal and has chosen not to accrue a contingent liability because "while management and legal counsel are presently unable to predict the outcome or to estimate the amount of any liability the company may have with respect to this lawsuit, it is not expected that this matter will have a material adverse effect on the company."

K mart's pension plans are described on pages 46 and 47.[25] Note first that the U. S. employees are covered by a defined benefit plan while employees in Canada are covered by a defined contribution plan. The discussion also indicates that "the company's policy is to fund at least the minimum amounts required by the Employee Retirement Income Security Act of 1974 . . . the company made no contribution to its principal pension plan in fiscal 1988, 1987 or 1986 . . . [and] pension expense was $35 million in both 1988 and 1987, and $9 million in 1986." K mart discloses no pension liability on its balance sheet because, as indicated in the chart on page 47, the estimated market value of the pension fund's assets ($986 million) exceeds the projected benefit obligation ($871 million). Note also that no mention is made of post-retirement health care and insurance costs in the entire annual report.

The section entitled Income Taxes on page 35 indicates that "deferred income taxes are provided on nonpermanent differences between financial statement and taxable income." The section entitled Depreciation discloses further that "the company computes depreciation on owned property principally on the straight-line method for financial statement purposes and on accelerated methods for income tax purposes." As a result, a Deferred Income Tax account appears on the Balance Sheet and contains balances of $220 million (1989) and 200 million (1988). These amounts represent approximately 3 percent of total liabilities (current and long-term).

The dollar amount of the Deferred Income Tax account is relatively small because K mart does not invest heavily in fixed assets. Note on page 40 that the excess of tax over book depreciation is only $43 million, which represents less than .2 percent of total expenses. Note also on pages 22 and 41 that K mart chose not to elect Financial Accounting Standard No. 95, which recently changed the method of accounting for deferred income taxes to reflect the method described earlier in the chapter. Had K mart adopted the new standard, it would have used a lower income rate in the deferred tax calculation, thereby reducing its Deferred Income Tax amount and increasing reported net income. However, because deferred income taxes are relatively small, the additional income recognized by the company "was not considered material."

---

25. The discussion on pension plans assumes that you have read the Appendix at the end of the chapter.

REVIEW PROBLEM

Before adjustments and closing on December 31, 1990 the financial records of Martin Brothers indicated the following balances.

Cash	$23,000	Accounts Payable		$13,000
Accounts receivable	14,000	Short-term notes	$10,000	
Inventory	32,000	Less: Discount on notes	(1,000)	9,000
		Deferred revenues		3,000
		Other current liabilities		13,000
Total current assets	$69,000	Total current liabilities		$38,000

The terms of an outstanding long-term note payable state that Martin must maintain a current ratio of 1.5, or the note will be in default. The current ratio computed from the information above is 1.82 ($69,000 ÷ $38,000). However, the following transactions are not reflected in the preceding preadjustment and preclosing balances.

(1) Merchandise purchased on account for $5000 was in-transit as of December 31, 1990. The terms of the purchase were FOB shipping point.

(2) One-half of the interest on the $10,000 short-term note payable should be accrued as of December 31.

(3) A $4000 installment on a long-term debt will be due on March 31, 1991. Martin Brothers intended to withdraw $4000 from a fund, listed on the balance sheet as a long-term investment, to meet the payment.

(4) One-third of the deferred revenue has been earned as of December 31.

(5) Wages in the amount of $4000 are owed as of December 31. Federal income and social security taxes withheld on these wages equal $800 and $400, respectively.

(6) The total income tax liability for 1990 was estimated at year end to be $34,000. Income tax payments during the year totaled $32,000.

(7) Albinus, Inc. brought suit against Martin Brothers early in 1990. As of December 31, Martin's legal counsel estimates that there is a 50 percent probability that Martin will lose the suit in the amount of $8000. If Martin loses the suit, payment will be due within the next year.

Required. Provide the journal entry, if necessary, for each additional transaction, and compute the current ratio after all adjustments have been recorded. Is Martin in violation of the debt covenant? (Figure 10-3 presents the solution to this problem.)

Martin Brothers will be in default on the long-term liability if the contingent loss is accrued. The current ratio (1.31) will be below the ratio required in the debt covenant (1.5). If the contingent loss is only disclosed, the 1.53 current ratio will meet the requirements of the covenant.

Figure 10–3 Solution to review problem: Martin Brothers

Transaction	Current Assets	Journal Entry			Current Liabilities
	$69,000				$38,000
(1)	+5,000	Inventory	5000		+5,000
		Accounts Payable		5000	
		To record the purchase of inventory on account.			
(2)		Interest Expense	500		+500
		Discount on Note		500	
		To record the accrual of interest on an outstanding note.			
(3)		No entry—not payable from current assets.			
(4)		Deferred Revenue	1000		(1,000)
		Earned Revenue		1000	
		To record the recognition of revenue.			
(5)		Wage Expense	4000		+4,000
		Federal Income Tax Payable		800	
		Social Security Tax Payable		400	
		Wages Payable		2800	
		To record payroll and related taxes.			
(6)		Income Tax Expense	2000		+2,000
		Income Tax Payable		2000	
		To record income tax liability.			
(7)		Depends upon whether a 50 percent probability is considered "reasonably possible" or "probable."			
		If the loss is considered "reasonably possible," it is only disclosed and not included as a current liability.			
		If the loss is considered "probable," the contingent loss is accrued with the following journal entry:			
		Contingent Loss	8000		+8,000
		Contingent Liability		8000	
		To record a contingent loss.			
	$74,000 =	Total current assets			
		Total current liabilities			
		Not including contingent loss			$48,500
		Including contingent loss			$56,500

Current ratio not including contingent loss = 1.53 ($74,000 ÷ $48,500)
Current ratio including contingent loss   = 1.31 ($74,000 ÷ $56,500)

SUMMARY OF ANSWERS TO LEARNING OBJECTIVES

1 Define liabilities and current liabilities.

The FASB recently defined liabilities as "probable future sacrifices of economic benefits arising from present obligations of a particular entity to transfer assets or provide services to other entities in the future as a result of past transactions or events." (See footnote 1.) All liabilities appearing on the balance sheet should have three characteristics in common: (1) they should be present obligations that entail settlements by probable future transfers or uses of cash, goods or services; (2) they should be unavoidable obligations; and (3) the transaction or event obligating the enterprise must have already happened.

Current liabilities are obligations that are expected to require the use of current assets or the creation of other current liabilities. They include obligations to suppliers, short-term notes payable, current maturities of long-term debts, dividends payable to stockholders, deferred revenues, third-party collections, periodic accruals, and potential obligations related to pending or threatened litigation, product warranties, and guarantees.

2 Distinguish between determinable current liabilities and contingent liabilities.

Determinable current liabilities can be precisely measured, and the amounts of cash needed to satisfy the obligations and the dates of payment are reasonably certain. Examples include accounts and short-term notes payable, dividends payable, deferred revenues, third-party collections, and accrued liabilities.

A contingent liability results from an existing condition that can lead to a negative outcome in the future, depending on the occurrence of a given event. Examples include lawsuits, warranties, and guarantees.

3 List the determinable current liabilities, and briefly explain the nature of each.

Determinable current liabilities include accounts payable, short-term notes payable, current maturities of long-term debts, dividends payable, deferred revenues, third-party collections, and accrued liabilities. Accounts payable are dollar amounts owed to others for goods, supplies, and services purchased on open account. Short-term notes arise from loans or purchases and specify an interest rate and a maturity date. In most cases the life of the note is between thirty days and one year. Current maturities on long-term debts represent installments on long-term notes that are due within the time period of current assets.

Dividends payable represent dividend payments that have been declared by the board of directors but not yet distributed to stockholders. Deferred revenues represent payments that have been received before contracted services have been performed, for example, returnable deposits and advance sales.

Third-party collections represent situations where a company acts as a collection agency for government or other entities. Examples include sales taxes and withholdings from employee wages for federal income taxes and social security. Accrued current liabilities can include items like interest, wages, insurance, and rent as well as accruals like income tax liability and employee bonuses, which are conditional on net income.

4   Explain why bonus systems and profit sharing arrangements are used to compensate management, and describe the incentives they create.

Bonus systems are popular because they provide a means for stockholders to induce management and other employees to act in a manner consistent with the objectives of the stockholders. Such incentives are created by basing compensation on profits. Management has some control, however, over the measure of profits, through operating decisions, the choice of accounting methods, estimates, assumptions, and the timing of accruals. Managers can use this control to increase their bonus compensation.

5   Describe the methods used to account for contingencies and how they apply to warranties.

Contingencies are divided into two categories: gain contingencies and loss contingencies. Gain contingencies are almost never accrued and are very rarely disclosed in the footnotes.

The probability of a loss contingency should be classified as either remote, reasonably possible, or probable. If the probability is remote, the loss need not be disclosed. If the event is reasonably possible, the potential loss and all relevant information about it should be disclosed in the footnotes. If the event is viewed as probable and the amount of the loss can be estimated, the potential loss and associated liabilities should be accrued on the financial statements and described in the footnotes.

In a warranty, a seller promises to remove deficiencies in the quantity, quality, or performance of a product sold to a buyer. Warranties are usually granted for specific periods of time, during which the seller promises to bear all or part of the costs of replacing defective parts, performing necessary repairs, or providing additional services. From the seller's standpoint, warranties entail uncertain future costs. Not all buyers will take advantage of the warranties granted to them, but enough of them do so to consider the future costs probable and reasonably estimable. Thus, warranties are normally accounted for as accrued contingent losses.

When a sale is made that includes a warranty, the sale is recorded and warranty expense and contingent warranty liability are recognized in the amount of the estimated future warranty costs. As the warranty costs are incurred, the contingent warranty liability is reduced.

6   Explain the fundamentals involved in accounting for pensions and post-retirement health care and insurance costs.

A pension is a sum of money paid to a retired or disabled employee, the amount of which is usually determined by the employee's years of service. Most pension plans are structured so that a company, the employer, periodically makes cash payments to a pension fund, which is managed by a separate entity and does not appear on the company's balance sheet. The fund then provides the cash distributed to employees upon retirement. Pension liabilities should be accrued as employees earn the rights to future pension payments and the Pension Liability account, which appears in the long-term liability section of the balance sheet, is an estimate of the difference between the dollar amount contributed to the fund and the total contributions necessary to maintain a fund large enough to meet the employee benefits guaranteed by the company.

Most large companies also cover a portion of the health care and insurance costs incurred by employees after retirement. Presently, these companies neither set up funds to pay these future costs nor accrue them as they are earned by the employees. The FASB has recently proposed that companies estimate and record the liability associated with these costs and begin accruing them in 1992. Industry has been very critical of this proposal, claiming that the potential huge liability (1) cannot be estimated objectively, (2) will hurt important financial ratios and numbers, and (3) may cause companies to discontinue providing post-retirement health care and insurance benefits to employees.

7 Explain the fundamentals involved in accounting for deferred income taxes.

Using accelerated methods to depreciate fixed assets instead of straight-line methods, gives rise to an immediate tax benefit that reverses itself in later periods. The future tax payments associated with such reversals represent a liability (deferred income taxes) that is discharged as the additional taxes are paid over the life of the asset. Preparing the journal entry to record the recognition or discharge of deferred income taxes consists of three steps:

1. Compute the income tax benefit (or disbenefit) due to using accelerated depreciation instead of straight-line. The dollar amount of a tax benefit is entered as a credit to the Deferred Income Tax account. The dollar amounts of tax disbenefits are entered as debits to the Deferred Income Tax account in future years.

2. Compute the company's income tax liability (taxable income × corporate income tax rate). This dollar amount is entered as a credit to the income taxes payable account.

3. Enter a debit to the Income Tax Expense account in an amount that brings the journal entry into balance.

Deferred income taxes represent a significant item listed in the liability section of the balance sheets of many major U.S. companies. Large balances accumulate in the deferred income tax account because growing companies purchase fixed assets more quickly than they dispose of them. The tax benefits associated with using accelerated depreciation, therefore, do not reverse. Many accountants claim that deferred income taxes do not represent a liability in an economic sense because the additional taxes will never be paid.

8 Describe the economic consequences associated with reporting liabilities on the financial statements.

Disclosing a liability on the balance sheet affects important financial ratios (e.g., current ratio, debt/equity, debt/assets) that are used by stockholders, investors, creditors, and others (1) to assess the financial performance and condition of a company and (2) to direct and control the actions of managers through contracts. Each of these parties has an economic interest in the amount of debt that must be paid by a company. Financial ratios, which use balance sheet liabilities, are often found in debt contracts to protect creditors by limiting future borrowings, dividend payments, and other management actions. Such economic consequences create incentives that encourage managers in certain situations to understate, and in other situations to overstate, liabilities.

APPENDIX 10A

Accounting for Pensions

There are two primary types of pension plans: a defined-contribution plan and a defined-benefit plan. The definitions of these plans and the methods used to account for them are discussed and illustrated in this appendix.

DEFINED-CONTRIBUTION PLAN

Under a **defined-contribution plan,** an employer agrees only to make a series of contributions of a specified amount to the pension fund. These periodic cash payments are often based on employee wages or salaries, and each employee's percentage interest in the total fund is determined by the proportionate share contributed by the employer on the employee's behalf. Under this type of plan, the employer makes no promises regarding how much the employees will receive upon retirement. The actual benefits depend upon the investment performance of the fund. The employer guarantees only the inputs (contributions), not the outputs (benefits). Most university business school professors are covered by such a plan.

Accounting for a defined-contribution plan is relatively simple because once the employer makes the contribution, the sponsoring company faces no further liability. The cash payment is simply expensed, as in the following journal entry.

Pension Expense	1000	
Cash		1000
To record a contribution of $1000 to a defined-contribution plan.		

DEFINED-BENEFIT PLAN

Under a **defined-benefit plan** the employer promises to provide each employee with a specified amount of benefit upon retirement. Such a guarantee is somewhat more difficult than promising to make specified contributions because the benefits are received by the employees in the future and are therefore uncertain. The benefits must be predicted, and the employer must contribute enough cash so that the contributions plus the earnings on the assets in the fund will be sufficient to provide the promised benefits as they come due. The employees of most major U.S. companies are covered by defined benefit plans.[26]

In the past many employers under defined-benefit plans either set aside no funds or failed to set aside enough to cover their future pension obligations. They simply paid the obligations as they came due, often out of the company's current

---

26. The social security system currently operating in the United States is a type of defined-benefit pension plan; the Federal government promises U.S. citizens a specified amount of benefit at age 65. Presumably, these benefits are paid out of a fund that contains income-earning securities.

operating capital. This practice not only represented poor financial management but, on occasion, left retired employees short of their rightful pension benefits. To help assure that retired employees received what was promised to them, Congress passed the **Employment Retirement Income Security Act** (ERISA) in 1974, which requires employers to fund their plans at specified minimum levels and provides other safeguards designed to protect employees.

The basic accounting procedures and the theories underlying accounting for defined-benefit pension plans are really quite simple. In accordance with the matching principle, pension expense and the associated liability are accrued each period as employees earn their rights to future benefits (i.e., during the years when the employees provide services and help the company to generate revenues). The periodic adjusting journal entry to record this accrual takes the following form:

Pension Expense	800	
Pension Liability		800
To accrue an $800 pension liability.		

The periodic cash payments made by the employer to the pension fund simply reduce the pension liability as in the following journal entry, and the pension liability that appears on the balance sheet is simply the difference between the accrued liability and the cash payments. A large pension liability indicates that a significant amount of the expected pension costs has yet to be funded.

Pension Liability	1500	
Cash		1500
To record a $1500 cash payment to the pension fund.		

The primary difficulties in accounting for and managing a defined-benefit plan are in (1) determining the appropriate dollar amount of the periodic accrual entry (i.e., Pension Expense debit and Pension Liability credit) and (2) deciding how much cash needs to be contributed to the pension fund to cover the eventual liability. The ultimate pension cost cannot be known for certain until the employees have received all the benefits to which they are entitled. This will not be known until the employees' deaths as well as the deaths of their survivors, who may also be entitled to certain benefits. Unpredictable factors like employee life expectancies, employee turnover rates, future salary and wage rates, and pension-fund growth rates all have a bearing on this determination.

Most companies hire **actuaries,** statisticians who specialize in such areas as assessing insurance risks and setting premiums, to establish estimates of the future pension costs and to provide methods for allocating those future costs to current periods (called *actuarial cost methods*). Generally accepted accounting principles require that an employer periodically recognize an expense and an associated liability in an amount that is established by one of many acceptable actuarial methods. The amount of this accrual is usually equal to an estimate of the present value of the pension benefits earned by employees during a given period. These amounts are very inexact, depending largely on subjective estimates and assumptions. As a matter of policy, contractual obligation or law (ERISA), most companies make periodic cash payments to their pension plans in amounts that approximate the accruals they have chosen to record. Thus, the pension liability appearing on most balance sheets is either zero or relatively small.

Assume, for example, that an acceptable actuarial method indicates that Schmitt Associates should accrue $25,000 each year for their defined-benefit pension plan. This estimate would give rise to the following journal entry.

Pension Expense	25,000	
Pension Liability		25,000
To accrue the estimated pension liability.		

If Schmitt decides to fund 80 percent of the liability in the current year, the following cash payment and journal entry would be recorded. The unfunded pension liability, therefore, would be $5000 ($25,000 − $20,000).

Pension Liability	20,000	
Cash ($25,000 × .80)		20,000
To fund 80 percent of the estimated pension liability.		

SUMMARY OF LEARNING OBJECTIVE

9   Describe the two basic kinds of pension plans, and discuss the fundamentals involved in accounting for each.

There are two primary types of pension plans: defined-contribution plans and defined-benefit plans. Under a defined-contribution plan, the employer agrees only to make a series of contributions of a specified amount to the pension fund. Cash payments are expensed as they are made.

Under a defined-benefit plan, the employer promises to provide each employee with a specified amount of benefit upon retirement. In accordance with the matching principle, pension expense and the associated liability are accrued each period as the employees earn their rights to future benefits. The periodic cash payments made by the employer to the pension fund simply reduce the pension liability. The pension liability that appears on the balance sheet is the difference between the accrued liability and the cash payments.

KEY TERMS

Actuaries (p. 487)
Commercial paper (p. 458)
Conditional accrued liability (p. 464)
Debt ratio (p. 452)
Deferred income taxes (p. 474)
Defined-benefit plan (p. 486)
Defined-contribution plan (p. 486)
Determinable current liability (p. 456)
Employment Retirement Income Security Act (p. 487)

Face value (p. 455)
Gain contingency (p. 466)
Line of credit (p. 458)
Loss contingency (p. 466)
Maturity date (p. 458)
Open account (p. 456)
Pension (p. 471)
Post-retirement health care and insurance costs (p. 472)
Warranty (p. 470)

QUESTIONS FOR DISCUSSION AND REVIEW

1. Define a liability, and identify the three characteristics all balance-sheet liabilities have in common.

2. What is the definition of a current liability? Why are current liabilities defined in terms of current assets?

3. Define and differentiate determinable, conditional, and contingent liabilities. Provide several examples of each.

4. Define accounts payable. Why does the auditor pay special attention to the inventory purchases occurring near the end of an accounting period?

5. Under what conditions should the current installment payment on a long-term debt be disclosed as a current liability on the balance sheet?

6. Are short-term deferred revenues, such as returnable deposits and advance sales, expected to be discharged with current assets in the near future? Discuss.

7. Provide two examples of third-party collections. Do they require cash payments from the company's standpoint? Discuss.

8. Certain liabilities cannot be determined until the end of the accounting period. Two examples are the liabilities associated with income taxes and bonus agreements. What term is used to describe these liabilities, and why can they not be determined until the end of the accounting period?

9. Why do companies compensate their employees through bonus agreements and profit-sharing plans? What role do financial statement numbers play in these compensation schemes, and how might this method of compensation influence the reporting and operating decisions of management?

10. What is a contingent loss, and under what conditions must it be accrued? Under what conditions are contingent losses ignored or simply disclosed? The guidelines that specify the methods of accounting for contingent liabilities are very subjective. Discuss some of the factors that might influence managers and auditors to want to account for the same contingent liability in different ways.

11. How are gain contingencies accounted for? Why are gain contingencies accounted for in a different manner than loss contingencies?

12. Explain why product warranties are classified as contingent liabilities. Under what conditions are the costs associated with product warranties accrued? Briefly explain the procedures involved when accounting for product warranties.

13. Briefly explain what a pension plan is, and why the assets in the pension fund do not appear on a company's balance sheet. Why does a pension liability sometimes appear on the balance sheet?

14. Define post-retirement health care and insurance costs and explain how the FASB proposes that they be accounted for. Why has the proposal been so controversial?

15. Why do companies use accelerated methods to depreciate their fixed assets for tax purposes? How does this practice lead to the recognition of a liability?

16. Do deferred income taxes actually represent liabilities? Will they require the future payment of assets? Why are deferred liabilities so large for many major U.S. corporations? Discuss.

17. Recently the income tax rate for U.S. corporations was reduced. How did the new rate allow some U.S. corporations to recognize significant gains on their income statements?

18. Why is it important to disclose and value all liabilities appropriately on the balance sheet? Why is it important to stockholders, investors, creditors, management, and auditors?

19. Explain why financial statement ratios like the current ratio are found in debt covenants. How might such covenants affect the reporting and operating decisions of management?

20. How can management benefit from understating liabilities? Why is such a practice often not effective?

21. In what situations might a manager wish to overstate liabilities?

22. When a manager manipulates liabilities, what important financial statement numbers are affected? Is it necessarily in management's best interest to perform such manipulations? Why?

23. (*Appendix* 10A) What is the difference between a defined-contribution pension plan and a defined-benefit pension plan? What are the major difficulties involved with accounting for a defined-benefit pension plan?

24. (*Appendix* 10A) What is ERISA, and why was it instituted? What role do actuarial estimates play in accounting for defined-benefit pension plans?

EXERCISES

E10–1

(Reporting current liabilities and the current ratio)   Gemini Incorporated reported current assets of $15,000 and current liabilities of $12,000 on its December 31, 1990 balance sheet. After examining the financial records, the auditor discovered that the following items had either been ignored or were mistakenly recorded in the books.

(1) An inventory purchase of $2000, which was in transit as of December 31 and shipped FOB shipping point, was not recorded. The purchase was made on account.

(2) An inventory purchase of $1200, which was in transit as of December 31 and shipped FOB destination, was recorded. The purchase was made on account.

(3) An $1800 installment payment on a long-term note payable, due on March 15, 1991, was not included as current. The entire liability was included as long-term.

(4) Short-term payables in the amount of $2200 were listed as current even though they were part of a line of credit that will allow them to be immediately refinanced when they become due.

Required: Compute the amounts needed in the following chart by indicating the effect of each listed item on current assets and current liabilities. Compute Gemini's current ratio after the adjustments.

	Current Assets	Current Liabilities
	$15,000	$12,000
1.		
2.		
3.		
4.	_____	_____
Total		

E10–2

(Why are current liabilities carried at face value instead of present value?)   Twin Rivers Enterprises reports $25,000 in Accounts Payable on the balance sheet as of December 31, 1990. These payables, on average, will be paid in ten days. Note: Knowledge of present value is required to do this exercise (see Appendix A at the end of the text).

Required:

a. Assuming a 12 percent discount rate, approximate the present value of the cash outflows associated with the accounts payable.

b. Why are accounts payable carried on the balance sheet at face value instead of present value?

E10–3   *(Financing with long-term debt, contract terms, and the current ratio)*   Darrington and Darling borrowed $100,000 from Commercial Financing to finance the purchase of fixed assets. The loan contract provides for a 12 percent annual interest rate and states that the principal must be paid in full in ten years. The contract also requires that Darrington and Darling maintain a current ratio of 1.5:1. Before Darrington and Darling borrowed the $100,000, the company's current assets and current liabilities were $130,000 and $80,000, respectively.

Required:

a. Compute the company's current ratio if it invests $50,000 of the borrowed funds in fixed assets and keeps the rest as cash or short-term investments. To what dollar amount can current liabilities grow before the company violates the debt contract?

b. Compute the company's current ratio if it invests $80,000 of the borrowed funds in fixed assets and keeps the rest as cash or short-term investments. To what dollar amount can current liabilities grow before the company violates the debt contract?

c. Compute the company's current ratio if it invests the entire $100,000 of the borrowed funds in fixed assets. To what dollar amount can current liabilities grow before the company violates the debt contract?

E10–4   *(Accruals, the current ratio, and net income)*   Martha Lane Electronics recognizes expenses for wages, interest, and rent when cash payments are made. The following related cash payments were made during December 1990.

(1) December 1	Paid $2400 for rent to cover the subsequent twelve months.
(2) December 5 and 20	Paid wages in the amount of $6000. Wages in the amount of $6000 are paid on the fifth and the twentieth of each month for the fifteen days just ended. The next payment will be on January 5, 1991.
(3) December 15	Paid $600 interest on an outstanding note payable. The note has a face value of $10,000 and a twelve percent annual interest rate. Interest payments in the amount of $600 are made every six months.

As of December 31 the current assets and current liabilities reported on Martha Lane's balance sheet were $24,000 and $15,000, respectively. Martha Lane's income statement reported net income of $7500.

Required: Compute Martha Lane's current ratio and net income if the company were to account for wages, interest, and rent on an accrual basis.

E10–5   *(Short-term notes payable and the actual rate of interest)*   On December 1 Alton's Department Store borrowed $19,250 from First Bank and Trust. Alton signed a ninety-day note with a face amount of $20,000. The interest rate stated on the face of the note is 15 percent per year.

Required:

a. Provide the journal entry recorded by Alton on December 1.

b. Provide the adjusting entry recorded by Alton on December 31 before financial statements are prepared. Show how the note payable would be disclosed on the December 31 balance sheet.

c. Compute the actual annual interest rate on the note. (*Hint:* Note that Alton only had the use of $19,250 over the period of the loan.)

d. Why is the actual interest rate different from the rate stated on the face of the note?

E10–6　　*(Current maturities and debt covenants)*　On January 1, 1986, Lacey Treetoppers borrowed $150,000, which is to be paid back in annual installments of $10,000 on December 30 of each year.

Required:

a. Assuming that Lacey has met all payments on a timely basis, how should this liability be reported on the December 31, 1990 balance sheet?

b. Assume that during December of 1990 the management of Lacey realizes that including the upcoming $10,000 installment as a current liability reduces the company's current ratio below 2:1, the ratio required in a long-term note payable signed by the company. Discuss how management might be able to avoid classifying the current maturity as a current liability.

E10–7　　*(Returnable deposits)*　Dunhill Terrace rented a two-bedroom apartment to Kathie Cudney on July 1, 1990. Kathie signed a one-year lease and paid a damage deposit upon entry of $200. On June 30, 1991, at the end of the lease period, Kathie vacated the apartment. At that time the apartment was inspected, and damages caused by Kathie were repaired at a cost of $48. The remainder of the deposit was returned to Kathie.

Required:

a. Prepare the journal entries recorded by Dunhill Terrace for the following:
   1. The receipt of the $200 damage deposit
   2. Payment for the repairs
   3. Payment to Kathie

b. Why is the damage deposit not recorded as a revenue when it is received?

E10–8　　*(Gift certificates and deferred revenue)*　Norsums Department Store sells gift certificates that are redeemable in merchandise. During 1990 Norsums sold gift certificates for $22,000. Merchandise with a total price of $13,000 was redeemed during the year. The cost of the sold merchandise to Norsums was $8000. Norsums sold gift certificates for the first time in 1990.

Required:

a. Record the sale of the gift certificates.

b. Record the redemptions during 1990. Assume that Norsums uses the perpetual inventory method.

c. Compute the balance in the Deferred Revenue account as of December 31, 1991, assuming that gift certificates were sold for $15,000 in 1991 and merchandise with a total price of $20,000 was redeemed.

E10–9　　*(Third-party collections and payroll accounting)*　On November 25 Ed Soper received his monthly paycheck from Linson Motor Services. The employee earnings statement that accompanied the check indicated the following:

Gross monthly earnings	$3063
Social security taxes withheld	230
Federal taxes withheld	523
Contribution to United Way	25
Contribution to savings account	50
Net pay	$2235

Required:

a. Briefly describe why Ed earned $3063 but was only paid $2235.

b. Prepare the journal entry recorded by Linson Motor Services when Ed is paid.

c. Prepare the journal entries recorded by Linson when the social security taxes, federal income taxes, United Way contribution, and savings plan payments are made.

E10–10   *(Quarterly tax payments and federal tax liability)*   Graves Landscaping pays federal income taxes at a rate of 34 percent of taxable income. On January 1, 1990, Graves estimated that taxable income would be $200,000 for 1990 and based their quarterly tax payments on that amount. Quarterly tax payments of $17,000 were made on April 15, June 15, September 15, and December 15. As of December 31, 1990, actual taxable income was determined to be $215,000.

Required:

a. Provide the journal entries that Graves recorded when the quarterly tax payments were made on April 15, June 15, September 15, and December 15.

b. Provide the journal entry to accrue the federal tax liability as of December 31, 1990.

E10–11   *(Gain and loss contingencies)* . Thor Power has brought suit against Regional Supply in the amount of $150,000 for patent infringement. As of December 31 the suit is in process, and the attorneys have determined that there is a greater than 50 percent chance that Thor Power will win the entire $150,000.

Required:

a. How should Thor Power account for the situation described above?

b. How should Regional Supply account for the situation described above? Briefly describe some of the factors that might affect how Regional Supply chooses to account for this situation.

c. Why would the two companies account for the same facts in different ways?

E10–12   *(Bonus plans and contingent losses)*   Stice Brothers recently instituted a bonus plan to pay its executives. The plan specifies that net income must exceed $100,000 before any bonus payments are made. Cash in the amount of 10 percent of net income in excess of $100,000 is placed in a bonus pool, which is to be shared evenly by each of the executives. Ignore income taxes and assume that the bonus payment is not included as an expense in the calculation of net income.

Required:

a. Briefly describe why a company would institute a bonus plan, and compute the amount in the bonus pool if Stice Brothers shows net income of $130,000. Prepare the journal entry that would be recorded to reflect the bonus liability at the end of the year.

b. How much is in the bonus pool if Stice Brothers shows net income of $90,000? Assume that as of the end of the year Stice Brothers is being sued for $40,000. The company's legal counsel believes that there is an 80 percent chance that Stice will lose the suit, and the entire $40,000 will have to be paid. Assume also that the suit was ignored when the $90,000 net income was computed. Why might Stice's management wish to accrue the loss from the suit in 1990 instead of simply disclosing it?

E10–13   *(Warranty costs: contingent losses or expense as incurred?)*   During 1990 Seahawk Outboards sold 200 outboard engines for $250 each. The engines are under a one-year warranty for parts and labor, and from past experience, the company estimates that, on average, warranty costs will equal $20 per engine. As of December 31, 1990, 50 engines had been serviced at a total cost of $1200. During 1991 engines were serviced at a total cost of $2800.

Required:

a. Prepare the journal entries that would be recorded at the following times:
   1. During 1990 to record the sale of the engines
   2. During 1990 to accrue the contingent loss on warranties
   3. During 1990 and 1991 to record the actual warranty costs incurred.

b. Compute the effect on 1990 and 1991 net income if Seahawk chose not to treat the warranty costs as contingent losses. Instead, they chose to expense warranty costs as they were incurred. Compute the total net income for 1990 and 1991 for each of the two accounting treatments.

E10–14   *(Pension contributions and unfunded pension liability)*   Seasaw Seasons instituted a pension plan for its employees three years ago. Each year since the adoption of the plan, Seasaw has contributed $10,000 to the pension fund, which is managed by Fiduciary Trust Associates. As of the end of the current year, it was estimated that contributions of $45,000 would have been necessary to maintain a fund large enough to provide the benefits promised to the employees when they retire.

Required:

a. Prepare the journal entries that were recorded by Seasaw as it contributed cash to the pension fund.

b. How much pension liability should be recorded on Seasaw's balance sheet as of the end of the current year?

E10–15   *(Deferred taxes and the tax rate)*   Swingley Company uses an accelerated method to depreciate its fixed assets for tax purposes and the straight-line method for reporting purposes. In 1990 the accelerated method recognized depreciation of $35,000, while the straight-line method recognized depreciation of $20,000. Taxable income and net income before taxes for that year were $65,000 and $80,000, respectively.

Required:

a. If the federal income tax rate is 40 percent, prepare the journal entry recorded by Swingley to accrue its 1990 tax liability.

b. If the federal income tax rate is 30 percent, prepare the journal entry recorded by Swingley to accrue its 1990 tax liability.

c. Briefly explain why the Deferred Tax account is considered a liability on the balance sheet and why it is less when the tax rate is 30 percent than when the rate is 40 percent.

PROBLEMS

P10-1   *(Distinguishing current from long-term liabilities)*   Judy Morgan, controller of Boulder Corporation, is currently preparing the 1990 financial report. She is trying to decide how to classify the following items.

(1) Account payable of $250,000 owed to suppliers for inventory.

(2) A $50,000 note payable that matures in three months. The company is planning to acquire a five-year loan from its bank to pay off the note. The bank has agreed to finance the note.

(3) A $500,000 mortgage; $75,000 payable within twelve months, and the remaining $425,000 to be paid over the next six years.

(4) The sum of $10,000 owed to the phone company for service during December.

(5) Advances of $25,000 received from a customer. The contract between the customer and Boulder Corporation states that if the company does not deliver the goods within six months, the $25,000 is to be returned to the customer.

(6) The sum of $15,000 due to the federal government for income tax withheld from employees during the last quarter of 1990. The government requires that withholdings be submitted by the end of the next quarter to the Internal Revenue Service.

(7) A $125,000 note payable; $30,000 is payable within twelve months, and the remaining $95,000 is to be paid over the next two years. Boulder Corporation plans to issue common stock to the creditor for the portion due during the next twelve months.

(8) The company declared a cash dividend of $80,000 on December 29, 1990. The dividend is to be paid on January 21, 1991.

Required:

a. Classify each of the items as a current liability or as a long-term liability. (*Note:* some items may be partially classified as current and as long-term.)

b. Compute the total amount that should be classified as current liabilities.

c. Compute the total amount that should be classified as long-term liabilities.

P10-2   *(Recognizing current liabilities can restrict dividend payments)*   Sealby and Sons borrowed $500,000 from Guarantee Bankers to finance the purchase of equipment costing $360,000 and to provide $140,000 in cash. The note states that the loan matures in twenty years, and the principal is to be paid in annual installments of $25,000. The terms of the loan also indicate that Sealby must maintain a current ratio of 2:1 and cannot pay dividends that will reduce retained earnings below $200,000. The balance sheet of Sealby, immediately prior to the bank loan and the purchase of the equipment, follows.

Current assets	$ 120,000	Current liabilities	$ 100,000
Noncurrent assets	1,500,000	Long-term liabilities	300,000
		Capital stock	1,000,000
		Retained earnings	220,000
		Total liabilities and	
Total assets	$1,620,000	stockholders' equity	$1,620,000

Required: The board of directors of Sealby is about to declare a dividend to be paid to the shareholders early in 1991. After accepting the loan and purchasing the equipment, how large a dividend can the board pay and not violate the terms of the debt covenant?

P10-3   *(Recognizing current liabilities and violating debt covenants)*   Before adjustments and closing on December 31, 1990, the current accounts of Barnaby Jones and Associates indicated the following balances.

	Debit	Credit
Cash	$40,000	
Accounts receivable	50,000	
Allowance for doubtful accounts		$ 2,000
Inventory	52,000	
Accounts payable		30,000
Deferred revenues		25,000
Warranty liabilities		5,000
Other current liabilities		10,000

The terms of an outstanding long-term note payable state that Barnaby Jones must maintain a current ratio of 2:1 or the note will become due immediately. The following items are not reflected in the balances above.

(1) Bad-debt losses in the amount of 6 percent of the outstanding accounts receivable balance are expected.

(2) The warranty liability on outstanding warranties is estimated to be $12,000.

(3) Forty percent of the deferred revenue had been earned as of December 31.

(4) Five thousand dollars, listed above under "Other current liabilities," is part of a line of credit and is expected to be immediately refinanced on a long-term basis when due.

(5) The total income tax liability for 1990 was estimated at year end to be $23,000. Estimated tax payments during the year totaled $20,000.

(6) Trademans, Inc. brought suit against Barnaby Jones early in 1990. As of December 31, Barnaby Jones's legal counsel estimates that there is a 60 percent probability that the suit will be lost in the amount of $10,000. If the suit is lost, payment will most likely be due in the next year.

Required:

a. Prepare the journal entries that would be recorded (if necessary) for each of the six items listed.

b. After preparing the journal entries, compute the company's current ratio assuming that the contingent liability described in (6) is not accrued.

c. After preparing the journal entries, compute the company's current ratio assuming that the contingent liability described in (6) is accrued.

d. If you were Barnaby Jones's auditor, would you require that the contingent liability be accrued? Discuss.

P10-4   *(Advance deposits and deferred revenues)* Trudy Rental Properties owns and manages twenty-five rental units. Each unit rents for $400 per month, and Trudy requires a $300 damage deposit and the first month's rent from each new tenant before entry. When a tenant leaves, the apartment is inspected for damages, and the $300 damage deposit is used to cover repairs. Any of the $300 that remains after the repairs are completed is returned to the tenant.

On December 15 Trudy rented three apartments, receiving the $300 damage deposit and the first month's rent in each case. On December 31 a tenant moved out. Damages caused by the tenant were repaired at a cost of $220, and the remaining $80 was returned to the tenant on January 10.

Required: Prepare journal entries to record the following:

a. The cash receipts from the new tenants on December 15

b. The payment for repairs on December 30

c. Any related adjusting journal entries required on December 31

d. The $80 cash payment to the tenant on January 10.

P10–5

(Computing sales tax liability when sales tax is included in the price of the item sold)   On April 12 General Home Appliance sold a toaster for $48.15 cash. The total sales price included a 7 percent sales tax, which must be remitted to the state government at the end of the month.

Required:

a. Prepare the journal entry to record the sale. General Home Appliances uses the periodic inventory method. (*Hint:* The sales tax is computed as a percentage of the price of the item sold.)

b. Provide the journal entry to record the payment of the sales tax to the government at the end of April.

P10–6

(Payroll tax withholdings)   Makert Marketing Services pays its employees on the 25th of every month for the first fifteen days of that month. The following information is available for the pay period June 1–June 15.

Gross wages	$1,000,000
Health and life insurance withholding	21,000
FICA (social security) withholding percentage	7.5%
Federal income tax withholding percentage	9.0%

Required:

a. Compute the amount of money withheld from the employees for the following:
   (1) FICA (social security)
   (2) Federal income taxes.

b. Compute the employees' total take-home pay.

c. Prepare the entries necessary on June 15 associated with these wages.

d. Prepare the entries necessary on June 25 associated with these wages.

P10–7

(Estimated income tax payments and accrued tax liability)   Trailor Homes showed a federal income tax liability of $15,000 on its 1990 balance sheet. At the beginning of 1991, for purposes of estimated tax payments, the company estimated its taxable income to be $250,000 during 1991. Trailor pays a federal income tax rate of 30 percent of taxable income. The company made the following tax payments during 1991.

April	$33,750
June	18,750
September	18,750
December	18,750

Actual taxable income for the year, determined at the end of 1991, was $300,000.

Required:

a. Prepare the journal entries to record the tax payments during 1991.

b. Provide the journal entry to accrue Trailor's income tax liability as of December 31, 1991.

P10–8

(Issues surrounding the recognition of a contingent liability)   While shopping on October 13, 1990 at the Floor Wax Shop, Tom Jacobs slipped and seriously injured his back. Mr. Jacobs believed that the Floor Wax Shop should have warned him that the floors were slick; hence, he sued the company for damages. As of December 31, 1990, the lawsuit was still in progress. According to the company's lawyers, it was probable that the company would lose the lawsuit. The lawyers also believed that the company could lose somewhere between $250,000 and $1,500,000, with a best guess of the loss of $896,000. The lawsuit was eventually settled in favor of Mr. Jacobs on August 12, 1991 for $675,000.

Required:

a. Discuss the issues that the Floor Wax Shop must address in deciding how to report this lawsuit in the 1990 financial report.

b. If you were auditing the Floor Wax Shop, how would you recommend that this lawsuit be reported in the 1990 financial report? Why?

c. Assume that a contingent liability of $896,000 is accrued on December 31, 1990. What journal entry would the company record on August 12, 1991, the date of the settlement?

P10–9   *(Accruing warranty costs before they are incurred)*   Arden's Used Cars offers a one-year warranty from date of sale on all cars. From historical data, Mr. Arden estimates that, on average, each car will require the company to incur warranty costs of $750. The following is the activity related to the cars during 1990.

(1)	February 2	Sold five cars
(2)	March 23	Sold ten cars
(3)	May 30	Incurred warranty costs of $3000 on four cars sold in 1989
(4)	July 5	Sold 8 cars
(5)	September 2	Incurred warranty costs of $5000 on five cars sold in 1990
(6)	November 15	Incurred warranty costs of $6000 on one car sold in 1990
(7)	December 20	Sold twelve cars

Required:

a. Assume that the cars were sold for an average of $8000. Prepare the entry to record the car sales during 1990 (combine all the sales and make one entry).

b. Prepare the individual entries to record the warranty costs incurred. Assume that the breakdown of warranty costs is 45 percent wages (paid in cash) and 55 percent parts.

c. Arden accrues its warranty liability with a single adjusting journal entry at year end. Prepare that entry.

d. Compute the year-end warranty liability. The beginning balance in the warranty liability account was $3000.

e. Explain why accountants estimate the warranty expense in the year of sale instead of recording the expenses as the costs are incurred.

P10–10   *(Advertising campaigns can give rise to contingent liabilities)*   To kick off its 1990 advertising campaign, Kelly's Breakfast Cereal is offering a $1 refund in exchange for five cereal box tops. The company estimates that the tops of 10 percent of the cereal boxes sold will be returned for the refund. The cereal boxes are sold for $2.00 each. During 1990 and 1991, 20,000 and 28,000 cereal boxes are sold, respectively, and 1500 and 2000 box tops are received for refunds during 1990 and 1991, respectively.

Required:

a. Prepare the journal entries to record the sale of the cereal boxes, the recognition of the contingent liability associated with the potential refunds, and the actual refund payments for 1990 and 1991.

b. Compute the liabilities associated with the potential refunds as of the end of 1990 and 1991.

P10–11   *(Deferred income taxes, changes in tax rates, and investment in long-lived assets)*   Acme, Inc. purchased machinery at the beginning of 1986 for $10,000. Management used the straight-line method to depreciate the cost for financial reporting purposes and the double-declining-balance method to depreciate the cost for tax purposes. The life of the machinery was estimated to be four years, and the salvage value was estimated at zero. Revenues less expenses other than depreciation (for financial reporting and tax purposes) equaled $50,000 in 1986, 1987, 1988, and 1989. Acme pays income taxes at the rate of 30 percent of taxable income.

Required:

a. Prepare the journal entries to accrue income tax expense and income tax liability for 1986, 1987, 1988, and 1989. Indicate the balance in the Deferred Income Tax account as of the end of each of the four years.

b. Assume that the tax rate was changed by the federal government to 20 percent at the beginning of 1988. Repeat the exercise in (a). Would it be appropriate to recognize a gain at the end of 1988 to reflect the tax rate decrease? Why or why not, and, if so, how much of a gain?

c. Assume that Acme purchased additional machinery at the beginning of 1987 and 1989. Each purchase was for $10,000 and each machine had a four-year estimated life and no salvage value. Once again, straight-line depreciation method was used for reporting purposes, and double-declining-balance for tax purposes. Repeat the exercise in (a). Why is the Deferred Income Tax account one of the largest liabilities on the balance sheets of many major U.S. companies?

P10–12   *(Appendix 10A: Accruing and funding pension liabilities)*   Silverton Company instituted a defined-benefit pension plan for its employees at the beginning of 1986. An actuarial method that is acceptable under generally accepted accounting principles indicates that the company should contribute $20,000 each year to the pension fund to cover the benefits that will be paid to the employees. Silverton funded 80 percent of the liability in 1986 and 1987, 90 percent in 1988 and 1989, and 100 percent in 1990.

Required:

a. Prepare the journal entries to accrue the pension liability and fund it for 1986, 1987, 1988, 1989, and 1990.

b. Compute the balance in the Pension Liability account as of December 31, 1990.

CASES

C10–1   *(Debt covenants and inventory purchases)*   Morton Thiokol, a maker of chemicals, aerospace components, and salt, reported the following in its 1987 financial statements.

	1987*	1986*
Current assets	$728.6	$596.6
Current liabilities	473.2	353.0

*Dollars in millions

Required:

a. Assume that Morton Thiokol issued long-term notes in 1985 that contained a restrictive covenant requiring the company to maintain a current ratio of 1.5 and $200 million in working capital. Is the company in danger of violating this covenant?

b. Explain what would happen if the company violated the debt covenant.

c. Assume that at the end of 1987, Morton Thiokol considered a $40 million inventory purchase. If the company had the necessary cash, why should management have paid cash for the inventory instead of purchasing it on account? Support your answer with calculations.

C10–2   *(Receipts in advance: measurement theory and financial statement effects)*   Ingersoll-Rand manufactures specialized heavy-duty construction equipment. Included in the current liabilities
section of its 1987 financial statements are "Customers' Advance Payments" of
$12,918,000. The notes to the financial statements indicate that, although payments are
collected in advance from customers, revenues are recognized when products are shipped.

Required:

a. Are the payments collected in advance considered deferred revenues? How do you
know?

b. What journal entry does the company record when it receives cash for the advance payments? What journal entry is recorded when the products are shipped? Explain this accounting treatment in terms of the principles of revenue recognition and matching.

c. How does this accounting treatment affect important financial ratios, such as earnings
per share, the current ratio, and the debt/equity ratio, in the current as well as future
periods?

C10–3   *(Accounting for warranties as a contingency)*   General Motors Corporation reported the following in its 1987 financial statements.

Current liabilities	
Taxes, other than income	$1,155.2*
Payrolls	2,206.6
Employee benefits	487.2
Warranties	3,907.9
Other	7,428.8

*Dollars in millions.

Required:

a. What journal entry was made to record Warranties, assuming that all $3,907.9 million
related to sales in 1987? Explain in general how this dollar amount was determined.

b. Suppose that General Motors satisfied warranty claims of $7,500,000 during 1988.
What journal entry would be made to reflect this event?

c. Describe the methods used to account for loss contingencies, and explain how accounting for warranties represents an example.

d. When accounting for contingencies, how can management manipulate financial ratios
and still be within the guidelines set by generally accepted accounting principles?

C10–4   *(Recognizing a contingent liability from a lawsuit)*   Chrysler Corporation agreed to pay $11.5
million to settle a suit brought by a woman who was paralyzed during an automobile accident in 1984. The payment, made in 1988, was the result of a 1986 judgment that in-
structed Chrysler to pay $9.5 million. The difference between the amount of the judgment
and the amount Chrysler agreed to pay represents interest from the time of the original
verdict.

Required:

a. Provide the journal entries (if any) and indicate what footnote disclosure would have
been made in 1984, 1986, 1987 (accrued interest), and 1988. Assume an interest rate of
11 percent and that the loss was reasonably possible as of 1984, but its amount was not
estimable until the 1986 judgment.

b. Where would the contingent liability appear in the 1986 and 1987 financial statements?

C10–5   *(Deferred income taxes: liabilities?)*   In its 1987 financial report, PepsiCo, Inc. reported the
following.

Current liabilities	$2,722.8*
Long-term debt	2,986.7
Deferred income taxes	804.6
Stockholders' equity	2,508.6
Total liabilities and stockholders' equity	$9,022.7

*Dollars in millions.

Required:

a. What are deferred income taxes, how do they arise, and why are they considered long-term liabilities?

b. How do deferred income taxes accumulate to such large amounts on the balance sheets of many major U.S. Companies?

c. Assume that PepsiCo is subject to a debt covenant requiring that the company maintain a debt/total assets ratio of no greater than .70. Compute the debt/total assets ratio for the company and discuss how management might be able to argue that it had not actually violated the covenant.

C10–6

(*"Taking a bath" during bankruptcy proceedings*) A major defense contractor, LTV, faced with huge liabilities, sought Chapter 11 protection in 1988. Under Chapter 11, a company continues to operate but is protected from creditors while it tries to work out a reorganization plan. At that time the company's management chose to accrue a $2.26 billion liability to reflect the potential cost of medical and life insurance benefits for its 118,000 current and retired employees. At the time this charge was not required by generally accepted accounting principles. *The Wall Street Journal* reported that the company chose to recognize the charge at this time because "if the company waited until after it negotiated new credit agreements and emerged from bankruptcy-law proceedings before taking the $2 billion charge, the additional liability could trigger violations of its debt covenants."*

*Karen Blumenthal, "LTV to reserve $2.26 billion for retirees, *The Wall Street Journal*, 22 November 1988, pp. A3, A4.

Required:

a. Provide the journal entry to record the $2.26 billion charge recognized by LTV.

b. Explain how taking the charge before negotiating new credit agreements could avoid violating debt covenants.

c. It was also reported that LTV took several other significant charges while it was under bankruptcy proceedings. In addition to its concern about debt covenants, in general, why might management have chosen to take these charges at this time?

C10–7

(*Executive compensation: form and incentives*) *The Wall Street Journal* (20 April 1988) reported that from 1985 to 1987 Lee Iacocca, chief executive officer of Chrysler Corporation, earned $50 million in compensation, of which less than $4 million was in the form of salary. The remaining $46 million was in the form of bonuses paid in Chrysler common stock and cash.

Required:

a. Explain why a company's board of directors would use incentive compensation schemes, such as bonuses, to pay top management.

b. Bonuses are often in the form of common stocks. How could compensating management with common stock benefit a company's stockholders?

c. In general, how are the amounts of most bonuses determined, and what incentives does such a determination provide for management?

C10–8

(Replacing currently maturing debt with a short-term note)   General Cinema Corporation operates the leading movie theater circuits in the United States, is an independent bottler of Pepsi-Cola and related products, and also owns several "high-end" retail stores, including Neiman-Marcus. In its 1987 financial statements, the company reported the following in the current liabilities section.

Long-term liabilities—due within one year	$ 7,014,000
Total current liabilities	$339,304,000

In the notes to the financial statements, the company profiles all the components of its long-term debt.

Required:

a. What kind of assets must General Cinema use to repay the long-term liabilities in order for the portion due within one year to be classified as a current liability?

b. If General Cinema plans in the foreseeable future to refinance the amount of currently maturing long-term debt by issuing long-term notes, how should the debt be classified, as current or long-term? Why?

c. Why might management consider such a refinancing strategy? State your answer in terms of important financial ratios and debt covenants.

Long-Term Liabilities: Notes, Bonds, and Leases

Learning Objectives

---

1 Define long-term notes payable, bonds payable, and leasehold obligations, and explain how companies use these instruments as important sources of financing.

2 Identify the important economic consequences associated with reporting long-term liabilities on the balance sheet.

3 Differentiate the stated interest rate from the effective interest rate, and explain how differences between these rates can lead to recognizing discounts and premiums on notes and bonds payable.

4 Describe the basic rules of the effective-interest method.

5 Explain the methods used to account for long-term notes payable, especially in cases where the effective interest rate is greater than the stated interest rate.

6 Identify and define the essential terms associated with bonds, and explain the methods used to account for bond issuances, recognizing interest expense over the life of the bond, and bond redemptions.

7 Differentiate operating leases from capital leases, and explain the methods used to account for capital leases.

8 (Appendix 11A) Identify the important factors that affect bond prices.

≣ This chapter is devoted to long-term notes payable, bonds payable, and lease-hold obligations. **Notes payable** are obligations evidenced by formal notes. They normally involve direct borrowings from financial institutions or arrangements to finance the purchase of assets. **Bonds payable** are notes that have been issued for cash to a large number of creditors, called *bondholders*. **Leasehold obligations** refer to future cash payments (e.g., rent) that are required for the use or occupation of property during a specified period of time. Each of these liabilities represents an obligation to disburse assets (usually cash) at a time beyond the period that defines current assets. The formal contracts underlying such arrangements specify the principal amount of the debt, the periodic interest payments, the time over which the interest and principal are to be paid, security provisions (e.g., collateral), and a number of other provisions, many of them designed to protect the interests of the lenders.

Long-term borrowing arrangements, such as notes, bonds and leases, are a common and major source of capital and financing for companies throughout the world. Funds used to acquire other companies, purchase machinery and equipment, finance plant expansion, pay off debts, repurchase outstanding stock, and support operations are often generated by issuing long-term notes and bonds, or entering into lease agreements. Ralston Purina Company, for example, increased long-term borrowings by $646.9 million during 1986, primarily to finance the acquisitions of Eveready Batteries and the Continental Baking Company.

Accounting Trends and Techniques (New York: AICPA, 1987) reports that, of the 600 major U.S. companies surveyed, 508 (85 percent) disclosed long-term notes payable, 265 (44 percent) disclosed bonds payable, and 448 (75 percent) disclosed leasehold liabilities. In 1966 Exxon Corporation reported long-term liabilities of $4.3 billion, consisting of approximately $2.9 billion in long-term notes, $866 million in outstanding bonds payable, and $505 million in leasehold obligations.

THE RELATIVE SIZE OF LONG-TERM LIABILITIES

Table 11–1 indicates the relative size of long-term liabilities on the balance sheets of U.S. companies for a selected group of industries. For each industry the table indicates: (1) long-term liabilities as a percentage of total assets, (2) long-term liabilities as a percentage of total liabilities, and (3) long-term liabilities as a percentage of stockholders' equity.[1] Companies generate assets in three different ways: borrowings, equity issuances, and profitable operations. Long-term liabilities/total assets indicates the relative importance of long-term liabilities in generating a company's assets. Long-term liabilities/total liabilities indicates the importance of long-term liabilities relative to current liabilities. Long-term liabilities/ stockholders' equity indicates the importance of long-term liabilities relative to equity issuances and profitable operations as sources of financing.

The importance of long-term liabilities as a source of financing (column 1) ranges from 8 percent for new and used cars to 44 percent for hotels. The magni-

---

1. Long-term liabilities on Table 11-1 include deferred income taxes, but many accountants believe that deferred income taxes do not represent a liability in an economic sense. As companies grow, they continually increase their investments in long-lived assets. The benefits associated with using accelerated depreciation instead of the straight-line method for tax purposes, therefore, are continually greater than the additional taxes paid in the reversal years, which in turn causes the balance in the Deferred Income Tax account to accumulate. In a sense, the future cash payments reflected by the balance in the Deferred Income Tax account are never paid. See Chapter 10 for further discussion on deferred income taxes.

Table 11-1   The relative size of long-term liabilities (LTL) (industry averages)

Industry (no. of companies)	LTL/ Assets	LTL/ Total Liabilities	LTL/ Stockholders' Equity
New and used car dealers (2120)	8%	12%	25%
Mortgage banks (755)	12	23	26
Department stores (1032)	14	35	23
Crude oil and natural gas (1226)	15	37	25
Hardware stores (2239)	16	37	28
Accounting and auditing services (1335)	16	40	27
Life insurance (937)	17	35	33
Aircraft manufacturing (35)	18	38	35
Grocery stores (2295)	22	43	45
Motion picture theaters (57)	32	54	78
Hotels (1912)	44	73	110

Source: Compiled from data published in *Industry Norms and Key Business Ratios* (Dun & Bradstreet, Inc., 1987)

tude of this percentage depends, in general, on the importance of long-term assets (investments and long-lived assets) held by a company because such assets are often financed with long-term liabilities. Financial institutions and professional services, for example, do not invest heavily in long-term assets. Consequently, such companies do not rely on long-term financing arrangements. To illustrate, the long-term liability/total asset ratio for Chase Manhattan Bank and H&R Block are only 4 percent and 1 percent, respectively. On the other hand, companies in the hotel industry invest heavily in long-lived assets, which are commonly financed with long-term liabilities. The long-term liability/total asset ratio for Marriott Corporation, for example, is approximately 50 percent.

The amount of long-term liabilities as a percentage of total liabilities (column 2) is less than 50 percent for most industries. Thus, current liabilities generally represent a more important source of financing than long-term liabilities. As of December 31, 1987 the dollar value of IBM's current liabilities, for example, was almost twice as great as the dollar value of its long-term liabilities. Indeed, some major U.S. companies, such as Polaroid Corporation, carry no long-term debt on their balance sheets.

Similarly, the long-term liability/stockholders' equity ratios indicate that equity issuances and profitable operations are generally more important sources of financing than long-term liabilities. As of December 31, 1987, the balance in the stockholders' equity accounts for DuPont, for example, was 2.9 times greater than the balance sheet value of its long-term liabilities. However, for certain companies the value of long-term liabilities exceeds stockholders' equity. On its December 31, 1987 balance sheet, the Marriott Corporation reported long-term liabilities of over $3 billion and stockholders' equity of only $811 million.

THE ECONOMIC CONSEQUENCES OF REPORTING LONG-TERM LIABILITIES

Chapter 10 describes the economic consequences of disclosing liabilities on the balance sheet. We pointed out that investors and creditors commonly use financial ratios involving liabilities to assess earning power and solvency. Such ratios are used, for example, to determine credit ratings, which directly affect a company's ability to borrow funds as well as the interest rate it pays. Indeed, seven of Dun & Bradstreet's fourteen key business ratios directly involve a measure of liabilities.

To illustrate the importance of credit ratings to major U.S. companies, consider the following quote from the 1987 financial report of Monsanto, a major manufacturer of chemical and agricultural products, pharmaceuticals, low-calorie sweeteners, and industrial equipment.

> *Management desires to maintain Monsanto's "A" or equivalent debt rating, which management believes assures adequate financial flexibility and access to the full range of worldwide debt markets. . . . Management intends to manage [certain ratios] at levels consistent with Monsanto's bond rating objective.*

Another important economic consequence associated with long-term liabilities results from their underlying contracts (or covenants). To ensure that companies meet their interest and principal payments, creditors often impose restrictions, which are written directly in the debt contracts, on the activities of management. As a condition of a loan, for example, a bank may require that the debtor company maintain a debt/equity ratio of less than .75. Such restrictions limit management's ability to borrow, which in turn reduces the number of other creditors who have legal rights to the company's assets.

Published financial reports often describe such limitations. As of December 31, 1987, the credit agreements entered into by Anchor Hocking Corporation, for example, "require the Company to maintain stated minimum working capital and net worth [stockholders' equity] amounts plus specific liquidity and long-term solvency ratios." Cabot Corporation's long-term loan agreements "contain provisions specifying certain limitations on the Company's operations including the amount of future indebtedness, investments, and dividends." Coleco Industries, Inc. must honor a credit agreement that "contains various covenants including maintenance of working capital, net worth and pretax income, ratio of debt to net worth, restrictions on unsecured indebtedness, and prohibition of the payment of cash dividends."

The terms of these covenants are important to stockholders, investors, creditors, management, and auditors because they can significantly limit management's operating activities, including the payment of dividends. Further, violating such covenants may require the immediate payment of the principal on a debt, which in some cases can be financially disastrous. For example, as its financial condition continued to worsen in 1988, a spokesman for First RepublicBank commented in *The Wall Street Journal* (31 March 1988):

> *Some crucial financial ratios are slipping, and the company may default [violate debt covenants] . . . on about $33 million of long-term debt. Such a default could accelerate the calling of that debt and may trigger calling fully half of the corporation's $539.9 million of long-term debt. [The problems are so severe that] the corporation may be unable to continue in its present form [and the company's auditors] will be unable to express an opinion on First RepublicBank's year-end financial statements.*

Indeed, financial ratios involving measures of liabilities have a direct bearing on management's ability to attract outside capital and are used in contracts to control and direct management's behavior. As such, management has economic incentives to "manage" the amount of debt reported on the balance sheet. Such manipulation can occur when accounting methods are chosen, when estimates and judgments are relied upon in applying the chosen accounting methods, or in structuring transactions and making operating decisions that affect reported liabilities.

In most cases, management has incentives not to report debt on the balance sheet. Reporting additional debt can lower credit ratings, violate debt covenants, and in general characterizes the company to investors and creditors as more risky. However, as discussed in Chapter 10, there are cases where management chooses to accelerate the recognition of liabilities and losses that would not have to be recognized under generally accepted accounting principles. This phenomenon is not unusual for companies experiencing either exceptionally poor or exceptionally good years. A company experiencing an exceptionally poor year may accelerate the recognition of liabilities and losses to **take a bath** in the current year, and avoid having to recognize those losses in later years as it attempts to reverse its poor performance. A company experiencing an exceptionally good year may accelerate the recognition of liabilities and losses in an effort to **smooth income** from one year to the next. Accelerating the recognition of a loss in an exceptionally good year reduces net income in that year and thus increases income in future years when the company's profits may not be so high.

It is important that stockholders, investors, creditors, and auditors be aware that management has incentives to manage liabilities. While most managers are ethical, some are not. Further, the liabilities reported on the balance sheet can be managed without violating generally accepted accounting principles. As we proceed through this chapter, we point out areas of accounting for long-term liabilities where management must rely on judgment and thus may affect the dollar value reported for long-term liabilities.

ACCOUNTING FOR LONG-TERM LIABILITIES: PRESENT VALUE, THE EFFECTIVE INTEREST RATE, AND THE EFFECTIVE-INTEREST METHOD

Chapter 5 points out that present value is the goal of financial accounting measurement, but that accountants often report other measures (e.g., historical cost) on the financial statements. Present value normally cannot be measured with sufficient objectivity because its calculation requires two extremely subjective estimates: (1) future cash flows must be predicted and (2) the predicted cash flows must be discounted at an uncertain interest rate.

In the case of long-term liabilities, however, these two estimates are much less subjective. The timing and the amount of the future cash outflows associated with these obligations are specified by contract and are therefore predictable. Further, a discount rate can be determined by inferring the effective (actual) rate of interest on the obligation, which normally differs from the rate of interest stated on the debt contract. As a result, much of the subjectivity associated with calculating present value is absent when accounting for long-term liabilities, and such obligations can be valued on the balance sheet at an estimate of present value without violating the principle of objectivity or exposing the manager and auditor to excessive levels of legal liability.

The Effective Interest Rate

The following section covers the method used to account for long-term liabilities. Before moving to that discussion, however, it is important to define the effective interest rate, distinguish it from the interest rate stated on the debt contract, and show how it can be determined.

The **stated interest rate** is the annual interest rate stated directly on the contract. The stated interest rate times the maturity value, the amount paid when the obligation matures, determines the periodic interest payments. The **effective interest rate** is the actual interest rate paid by the borrower. It may or may not equal the stated interest rate. The effective rate is determined by finding the discount rate that sets the present value of the obligation's cash outflows equal to the amount originally borrowed. The following examples show how the effective rate is determined for three different debt contracts.

Case 1: Non-interest-bearing Obligation

Assume that IBM borrowed $8573, promising to pay the lender $10,000 at the end of two years. The cash flows associated with this obligation follow.

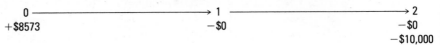

This debt has a maturity of two years, a principal of $10,000, and a stated interest rate of 0 percent ($0/$10,000). Such obligations are known as **non-interest-bearing debts.** It is important to realize that, even though the interest rate stated on the obligation is zero, IBM is actually paying interest. The company is paying $1427 over a two-year period, because $10,000 is being paid back although only $8573 was borrowed. The effective (actual) rate of interest on the loan is calculated by finding that interest rate which, when used to discount the $10,000 in two years, results in a present value of $8573. This calculation can be set up in the following way.

$$PV = \text{Future cash payment} \times (PV \text{ table factor:single sum})$$
$$\$8573 = \qquad \$10,000 \qquad \times (PV \text{ table factor:single sum})$$

Rearranging,

$$PV \text{ table factor} = \$8573 \div \$10,000$$
$$= \qquad .8573$$

Since $n = 2$, therefore i (the effective interest rate) $= 8\%$

The present value of $10,000 paid in two years is set equal to $8573, the proceeds from the loan. By rearranging the terms of the equation, the PV table factor (single sum) is found to be .8573. Since n (the number of periods) is equal to 2, one can move across the second row of the Present Value of a Single Sum table (Appendix A — Table 4) to find the table factor of .8573. This factor corresponds to an 8 percent discount rate.

Case 2: Stated Rate Less Than Effective Rate

Assume that IBM borrowed $9465, promising to pay $500 in interest at the end of each year for two years and to pay back $10,000 at the end of the second year. The cash flows associated with the obligation appear below.

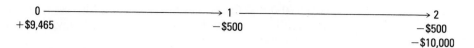

The amount borrowed on the loan is $9,465, the time to maturity is two years, the principal is $10,000, and the stated annual interest rate is 5 percent ($500 ÷ $10,000). Once again, the effective interest rate paid by IBM is different from the stated rate because the company not only paid $500 in each of two years, but also paid $10,000 at maturity when only $9465 was originally borrowed. Determining the effective interest rate in this case is done as in the previous case, but it is somewhat more difficult because it normally requires the use of the trial-and-error method. The calculations are shown in Figure 11–1.

After setting up the basic equation at the top of the figure, we simply plugged different interest rates into the formula until we found the solution. Using a 10 percent interest rate, for example, produced a present value of $9132, which was too low. A 10 percent discount rate, therefore, is too high. A 6 percent interest rate, on the other hand, produced a present value of $9817, which was too high, meaning that a 6 percent discount rate is too low. At this point it was clear that the solution was between 6 percent and 10 percent. We tried 8 percent and found that rate to be correct. That is, discounting the future cash flows of the obligation at 8 percent produced a present value equal to the proceeds of the loan ($9465).

Case 3: Stated Rate Equals Effective Rate

Assume that IBM borrowed $10,000, promising to pay $1000 in interest at the end of each year for two years and to pay back the $10,000 at the end of the second year. The associated cash flows follow.

```
0 ─────────────────────────→ 1 ─────────────────────────→ 2
+$10,000                       −$1,000                      −$1,000
                                                            −$10,000
```

The amount borrowed on the loan is $10,000, the time to maturity is two years, the principal is $10,000, and the stated annual interest rate is 10 percent

---

Figure 11–1   Inferring the effective interest rate on a note payable

PV	=	Interest	×	(*PV* Table Factor)	+	Maturity	×	(*PV* Table Factor)
$9,465	=	$ 500	×	(*PV* annuity: *n* = 2, *i* = ?)	+	$10,000	×	(*PV* single sum: *n* = 2, *i* = ?)
Try 10%								
PV	=	$ 500	×	(1.735)	+	$10,000	×	(.8264)
PV	=	$9,132						
Try 6%								
PV	=	$ 500	×	(1.833)	+	$10,000	×	(.8900)
PV	=	$9,817						
Try 8%								
PV	=	$ 500	×	(1.783)	+	$10,000	×	(.8573)
PV	=	$9,465						

($1000/$10,000). In this case the effective interest rate is also 10 percent because the present value of the interest and principal payments discounted at 10 percent equals $10,000. Specifically,

$$
\begin{aligned}
PV &= \quad\quad PV \text{ of interest payments} \quad\quad + \quad\quad PV \text{ of principal payment} \\
&= \$1000 \; (PV \text{ of annuity}: n = 2, \, i = 10\%) + \$10,000 \; (PV \text{ of lump sum}: n=2, \, i = 10\%) \\
&= \$1000 \; (1.7355) \quad\quad\quad\quad\quad\quad\quad + \$10,000 \; (.82645) \\
&= \$10,000
\end{aligned}
$$

To summarize, this section demonstrates how to determine the effective interest rate from the cash flows specified by three different debt contracts: a non-interest-bearing obligation, a debt with a stated rate less than the effective rate, and a debt with a stated rate equal to the effective rate. It is important to realize that the stated interest rate defines the periodic cash flows associated with the obligation, while the effective interest rate reflects the economic cost of the loan. If given the choice, for example, IBM would prefer the obligations described in Case 1 or Case 2 to the obligation described in Case 3 because the effective interest rate (8 percent) is lower. As the next section explains, the method used to account for long-term liabilities is based on the effective rate of interest.

The Effective-Interest Method

The method used to account for long-term liabilities is called the **effective-interest method.** It bases both the dollar amount of the long-term liability on the balance sheet and the dollar amount of the related periodic interest expense on an estimate of the present value of the obligation's future cash payments. It consists of the following two general rules.

1. The balance-sheet value of a long-term liability is determined by the present value of the liability's future cash outflows, discounted at the effective interest rate at the time of issuance. The effective interest rate remains constant over the life of the obligation.

2. The interest expense recognized during each period of the liability's life is equal to the effective interest rate multiplied times the balance-sheet value of the liability as of the beginning of that period. The balance-sheet value of the liability approaches the maturity value over the life of the obligation.

While the general rules of the effective-interest method are relatively straightforward, they must be applied to long-term debt contracts that take a wide variety of forms. Consequently, in certain cases implementing this method can seem to be somewhat complex. The remainder of the chapter is devoted to applying these rules to different kinds of long-term liabilities. The following discussion illustrates how the effective-interest method is applied to different kinds of notes payable. We then apply the method to bonds and finally demonstrate how long-term lease obligations are accounted for under the effective-interest method.

LONG-TERM NOTES PAYABLE

Long-term notes are issued by companies to banks and other lenders to acquire cash, which is used to finance operations, acquire long-term investments, acquire long-lived assets, pay other debts, pay dividends, and repurchase outstanding stock. The notes usually specify (1) the **principal** amount, which is to be paid on the **maturity date;** (2) an annual interest (stated) rate, which determines the periodic interest payments and is expressed as a percentage of the principal; and (3) any assets **(collateral)** that might be pledged as security in case the interest or principal payments are not met. As indicated earlier, such notes often include additional provisions *(restrictive covenants)* designed to protect the interests of the lenders.

Issuing long-term notes is a popular way for major U.S. companies to raise capital. Both **secured** (backed by collateral) and **unsecured notes** are widely used. *Accounting Trends and Techniques* (AICPA, 1987) reports that, of the 600 major U.S. companies surveyed, 418 (70 percent) disclosed unsecured notes and 90 (15 percent) disclosed notes that were backed by collateral. The following excerpt from the long-term liability section of the 1986 financial report of McKesson Corporation illustrates how long-term notes payable are commonly disclosed. The interest rates disclosed are the effective interest rates of the outstanding notes.

	1986*	1985*
Notes payable to banks	$71.8	$17.9
8 7/8% notes due 1991	74.6	—
10 3/4% notes due 1995	74.8	—
8.65% to 10.25% notes due 1987–90	61.7	—
6.05% to 12.75% notes due through 2012	42.3	25.1

*Dollars in millions.

Accounting for Long-Term Notes Payable

The effective-interest method is used to account for long-term notes payable. As stated earlier, this method values the note payable on the balance sheet at the present value of the future cash flows required under the terms of the note, discounted at the effective interest rate. It also determines the interest expense for each period by multiplying the effective interest rate times the balance-sheet value of the note at the beginning of that period. The following examples account for three different notes payable:

Case 1	Stated rate equal to effective rate
Case 2	Non-interest-bearing note
Case 3	Stated rate less than effective rate

Case 1: Stated Rate Equal to Effective Rate

Assume that on January 1, 1990, Apple Company borrows $5000 from First National Bank. The terms of the loan specify that Apple must pay back the $5000 on December 31, 1991, and make interest payments of $550 on December 31, 1990, and December 31, 1991. In other words, the amount borrowed is $5000 and the note has a principal of $5000, a time to maturity of two years, and a stated annual interest rate of 11 percent ($550/$5000). Discounting the future cash outflows (interest and principal payments) at 11 percent results in a present value of $5000, so the effective interest rate on this note is also 11 percent. The cash flows associated with the note and the related journal entries appear in Figure 11–2.

When Apple issues the note, the cash proceeds ($5000) are recorded and the note payable is established in the amount of the principal ($5000). When the note is paid back at maturity (December 31, 1991), the note payable is written off the books, and cash in the amount of the principal is credited.

Figure 11–2   Accounting for notes payable (stated rate equal to effective rate)

Cash Flows

```
    1/1/90 ─────────────────────────→12/31/90 ─────────────────────────→12/31/91
    +$5,000                            −$550                              −$ 550
                                                                          −$5,000
```

General Journal

Cash	5,000		Interest Expense	550^a		Interest Expense	550^a	
Note Payable		5,000	Cash		550^b	Cash		550^b
To record issuance of the note.			To record the first interest payment.			Note Payable	5,000	
						Cash		5,000
						To record the final interest payment and principal payment.		

^{a}Effective rate (11%) × balance-sheet value ($5,000)
^{b}Stated rate (11%) × principal ($5,000)

On December 31, 1990, and December 31, 1991, cash interest payments are made, and interest expense amounts are recognized, both for $550. It is important to realize that interest expense is computed by multiplying the effective interest rate (11 percent) times the balance-sheet value of the note ($5000), while the cash interest payment is computed by multiplying the stated interest rate (11 percent) times the principal ($5000). For this particular note, interest expense is equal to the cash interest payment because the effective rate is equal to the stated rate, and the balance-sheet value is equal to the principal. As illustrated in Cases 2 and 3, these equalities do not always occur.

Case 2: Non-interest-bearing Note
Assume that on January 1, 1990, Apple Company borrows $6733 from First National Bank. The terms of the loan specify that Apple must pay back $8000 on December 31, 1991, and make no interest payments over the period of the loan. In other words, the amount borrowed is $6733, and the note has a principal of $8000, a time to maturity of two years, and a stated annual interest rate of 0 percent ($0/$8000). Discounting the future cash outflows (interest and principal payments) at 9 percent results in a present value of $6733, so the effective interest rate on this note is 9 percent. Figure 11–3 illustrates the cash flows and the methods used to account for this note.

When Apple issues the note on January 1, 1990, the cash proceeds ($6733) are recorded, and the note payable is established in the amount of the principal ($8000). The cash proceeds do not equal the principal, so **"Discount on Note Payable"** in the amount of $1267 is recognized. As shown in Figure 11–3, this account, called a *contra-liability*, is disclosed on the liability side of the balance sheet and is subtracted from the Long-Term Note Payable account. Thus, the balance-sheet value of the note payable is equal to $6733, which is the principal ($8000) less the discount ($1267) or, in other words, the present value of the future cash payments discounted at 9 percent (the effective interest rate). The $1267 discount can be viewed as interest expense waiting to be recognized over the two-year life of the note.

Figure 11–3   Accounting for long-term notes payable (non-interest-bearing note)

Cash Flows

```
1/1/90 ─────────────────────────→12/31/90 ──────────────────────────→12/31/91
   +$6,733                           −$0                                 −$  0
                                                                         −$8,000
```

General Journal

Cash	6,733	
Discount on Notes	1,267	
Note Payable		8,000
To record the issuance of a note.		

Interest Expense	606[a]	
Discount on Notes		606
To record accrued interest on a note.		

Interest Expense	661[b]	
Discount on Notes		661
To record accrued interest on a note.		
Note Payable	8,000	
Cash		8,000
To record a principal payment on a note.		

[a]$6,733 × 9%
[b]$7,339 × 9%

Balance-Sheet Value

Note payable	8,000	
Less: Discount on note	1,267	6,733

Note payable	8,000	
Less: Discount on note	661	7,339

General Ledger

Discount on Notes Payable			
(1/1/90)	1,267		
		606	(12/31/90 adjustment)
(12/31/90)	661		
		661	(12/31/91 adjustment)
	0		

The adjusting entry on December 31, 1990, serves to amortize a portion of the discount ($606) and to recognize interest expense on the note. It reflects the fact that Apple is incurring interest on the note even though the stated interest rate is zero. The amount of interest expense is determined by multiplying the effective rate (9 percent)—the actual interest rate paid by Apple—times the balance-sheet value of the note payable ($6733) at the beginning of the period. This calculation is the essence of the effective-interest method. After the adjusting entry is recorded, the balance-sheet value of the note payable is increased to $7339 because the discount, which is subtracted from the note payable on the balance sheet, has been reduced to $661.

The adjusting entry on December 31, 1991, serves to amortize the remainder of the discount ($661) and to recognize the interest expense during 1991. Once again, the amount is determined by multiplying the effective rate times the balance-sheet value of the note payable at the beginning of the period. This time, however, the balance-sheet value of the note is $7339, and the amount of interest expense recognized is $661. Note also that the balance-sheet value of the note approached the maturity value over the life of the note and that on the maturity date the discount is reduced to zero, and the principal of the note is paid.

Case 3: Stated Rate Less than Effective Rate

Assume that on January 1, 1990, Apple Company borrows $7572 from First National Bank. The terms of the loan specify that Apple must pay back $8000 on December 31, 1991, and make annual interest payments of $400 over the period of the loan. Thus, the amount borrowed is $7572, and the note has a principal of $8000, a time to maturity of two years, and a stated annual interest rate of 5 percent ($400/$8000). Discounting the future cash outflows (interest and principal payments) at 8 percent results in a present value of $7572, so the effective interest rate is 8 percent. Figure 11—4 illustrates the cash flows and the methods used to account for this note.

Figure 11—4   Accounting for long-term notes payable (stated rate less than effective rate)

Cash Flows

1/1/90	12/31/90	12/31/91
+$7,572	−$400	−$ 400
		−$8,000

Journal Entries

Cash	7,572		Interest Expense	606[a]		Interest Expense	622[b]	
Discount on Notes	428		Discount on Notes		206	Discount on Notes		222
Note Payable		8,000	Cash		400	Cash		400
To record the issuance of a note.			To record the accrual and payment of interest on a note.			To record the accrual and payment of interest on a note.		
						Note Payable	8,000	
						Cash		8,000
						To record a principal payment on a note.		

[a]$7,572 × 8%
[b]$7,778 × 8%

Balance-Sheet Value

Note payable	8,000		Note payable	8,000	
Less: Discount on note	428	7,572	Less: Discount on note	222	7,778

General Ledger

	Discount on Notes Payable		
(1/1/90)	428		
		206	(12/31/90 adjustment)
(12/31/90)	222		
		222	(12/31/91 adjustment)
	0		

When Apple issues the note on January 1, 1990, the cash proceeds ($7572) are recorded, and the note payable is established in the amount of the principal ($8000). The cash proceeds do not equal the principal, so Discount on Note Payable in the amount of $428 is recognized. The balance-sheet value of the note payable is equal to $7572, which is the principal ($8000) less the discount ($428), or the present value of the future cash payments discounted at 8 percent (the effective interest rate). Once again, the $428 discount can be viewed as interest expense waiting to be recognized over the two-year life of the note.

At the end of the first period, interest expense is recognized in the amount of $606, which is determined by multiplying the effective rate (8 percent) times the balance-sheet value of the note ($7572) at the beginning of the period. The $400 cash interest payment is recorded, and the discount is credited for the difference ($206). The amortized amount of the discount represents the portion of the interest cost not reflected by the $400 cash interest payment. Recall that Apple originally received only $7572 and is required to return $8000. As of the end of the first period, the balance-sheet value of the note payable has been increased to $7778 because the discount, which is subtracted from the note payable on the balance sheet, has been reduced to $222.

On the maturity date, interest expense in the amount of $622 is recognized, the $400 cash interest payment is recorded, and the remainder of the discount ($222) is amortized. Once again, the amount of interest expense is determined by multiplying the effective rate (8 percent) times the balance-sheet value of the note payable at the beginning of the period ($7778). Note also that the $8000 principal payment is made at the maturity date.

To illustrate how companies disclose the methods used to account for long-term notes issued at a discount, consider the following excerpt from the 1987 financial report of The New York Times Company.

> In connection with the 1985 acquisition of certain newspapers, the Company issued 10-year notes with an aggregate stated value of $162,300,000, which has been discounted at an [effective] interest rate of 11.85 percent for financial reporting purposes. The original difference of $12,600,000 between the stated value of the notes and the amount that results from discounting the notes at 11.85 percent [the discount] is being amortized as interest expense over the term of the notes.

The Straight-Line Method

The effective-interest method ensures that the periodic interest expense reported on the income statement is based on the value of the outstanding note payable and the effective (actual) interest rate. It also ensures that the note payable is carried on the balance sheet at an estimate of the present value of its future cash flows. Instead of the effective-interest method, many companies amortize Discounts on Notes Payable using the straight-line method. That is, they amortize equal amounts of the discount into interest expense during each period of the note's life. For example, referring to the illustration in Figure 11−4, in both 1990 and 1991 the discount would be amortized in the amount of $214 ($428 ÷ 2 years) and interest expense would be recognized in the amount of $614 ($400 + $214).

According to generally accepted accounting principles, the straight-line method is acceptable only if it results in numbers (i.e., interest expense and book value of the note payable) that are not materially different from those produced by the effective-interest method. While the straight-line method may be simpler to apply, it misstates periodic interest expense and the balance-sheet value of the note because it fails to reflect the actual interest rate paid by the borrower.

BONDS PAYABLE

Companies issue bonds to raise large amounts of capital, usually to finance expensive, long-term projects. In 1987, for example, Coca-Cola Enterprises collected approximately $263 million from bond issuances and used it primarily to finance capital expenditures totaling $206 million and the acquisition of several bottling companies. From 1985 through 1987, McDonnell Douglas issued bonds that produced $750 million, most of which was used to expand its productive capacity. In 1987 Colgate-Palmolive issued $150 million in thirty-year bonds, which received A1 and A+ ratings from the Moody's and Standard & Poor's rating agencies. As disclosed in the company's financial report, the additional cash was used to finance "acquisitions in the United States and internationally to complement core business activity."

Bonds are normally sold to the public through a third party, such as an investment banker or a financial institution. They involve formal commitments requiring the issuing company to make cash interest payments to the bondholder and a principal payment (usually in the amount of $1000 per bond) when the bond matures, which is usually between five and thirty years from the date of issuance. After bonds are initially issued, they are generally freely negotiable: that is, they can be purchased and sold in the open market. Both the New York and the American Security Exchanges maintain active bond markets. During 1987, for example, bond transactions on the New York and American Exchanges totaled approximately $4.4 billion and $309 million, respectively.[2]

Bond Terminology

Figure 11-5 summarizes the important components of a bond. The **life** of the bond is the time period extending from the date of its issuance to its maturity date, usually somewhere between five and thirty years. At the maturity date, the end of the bond's life, an amount of cash equal to the face value (*principal, par value,* or *maturity value*) is paid to the bondholder. The *face value,* the amount written on the face of the bond, is usually $1000. The **interest payment,** which is paid to the bondholders on each semiannual interest payment date, is computed by multiplying the annual interest rate stated on the bond (the stated or coupon rate) times the face value of the issuance. This amount is then divided by 2 because the stated rate is an annual rate, and the interest payments are made every six months. The **proceeds,** the amount collected by the issuing company when the bonds are issued, are equal to the price paid by the purchasers of the bonds multiplied by the number of bonds issued. This amount is usually net of the issuance costs incurred by the issuing company.

To illustrate, on June 15, 1988, Associated Corporation of North America issued 200,000 bonds, each with a face value of $1000 and a stated interest rate of

2. *The Wall Street Journal,* 13 June 1988, p. 20

Figure 11-5 Bond terminology

Issuance Date		Time to Maturity				Maturity Date
0	6 months	1 year	6 months	2 years	(etc.) . . .	

Cash Flows

Proceeds at Issuance	Interest Payment	Interest Payment	Interest Payment	Interest Payment	. . .	Interest Payment
						Face Value Payment

Terms of Bond Contract

Life: Time period from date of issuance to the maturity date, usually from five to thirty years.

Maturity date: Date when the dollar amount written on face of bond (face value) and final interest payment are paid to the bondholder.

Face value: Dollar amount written on the bond certificate. Sometimes referred to as the *principal, par value,* or *maturity value,* the face value is usually $1000.

Interest payment: The interest rate stated on the bond multiplied by the face value. This rate is called the *stated rate,* or *coupon rate,* and it is usually fixed for the entire life of the bond.

Proceeds at issuance: Dollar amount collected when the bonds are issued, equal to the price the buyers paid for each bond multiplied by the number of bonds issued. This amount is usually net of issuance fees.

Effective interest rate: The actual interest rate paid on the bond. The rate, when used to discount the future interest and principal cash payments, results in a present value that is equal to the amount received by the issuer.

Other Provisions of the Bond Contract

Restrictions: The bond contract may restrict the issuing company in certain ways to ensure that the interest and principal payments will be made. For example, a certain current ratio or level of working capital may be required, dividends may be restricted, or additional debt may be limited.

Security: The bond contract may specify that collateral be paid in case of default (i.e., interest or principal payments are not made). Unsecured bonds are called *debentures.*

Call provision: The bond contract may specify that the issuing company can buy back (retire) the bonds at a specified price after a certain date during the life of the bond. The specified price is usually greater than the face value.

9 percent, due to mature five years later, on June 15, 1993. Associated collected $996.05 on each bond, which totaled $199,210,000 for the entire bond issuance. In terms similar to those in Figure 11-5, the cash flows associated with this bond issuance and the calculations of the proceeds, the semiannual interest payment, and entire maturity value are shown in Figure 11-6.

In addition to the face value, maturity date, and stated interest rate, the bond contract may include a number of other important provisions. Three such provisions are described in Figure 11-5: restrictive covenants, security, and call provisions.

Figure 11–6 Example of bond issuance: Associated Corporation of North America (dollars in thousands)

Issuance Date		Time to Maturity: Five Years			Maturity Date
(6/15/88)					(6/15/93)
0	6 months	1 year	6 months	2 years . . .	5 years
Proceeds	Interest	Interest	Interest	Interest . . .	Interest and face value
+$199,210[a]	−$9,000[b]	−$9,000	−$9,000	−$9,000	−$ 9,000 −$200,000

[a]200,000 bonds $\times$ $996.05 = $199,210
[b](200,000 bonds $\times$ $1,000 $\times$ 9%) ÷ 2 = $9,000

Restrictive **covenants** are imposed by bondholders to protect their interests and may restrict management in a number of significant ways. Nordstrom, a large specialty store operating primarily in the western part of the United States, states in its 1987 financial report that the company has entered into long-term debt agreements that (1) limit additional long-term debt and lease obligations; (2) require that working capital must be at least $50 million or 25 percent of current liabilities, whichever is greater; (3) limit short-term borrowings; and (4) restrict dividends to shareholders.

Security provisions also protect the interests of bondholders by ensuring that assets are pledged in case of default. As of December 31, 1987, H&R Block, for example, had outstanding bonds with a balance-sheet value of $4,944,000, which were collateralized by land, buildings, and equipment with a balance-sheet value of $5,050,000. Bonds with no assets backing them are called **unsecured bonds** or **debentures.** At December 31, 1987, General Motors Corporation had outstanding debentures valued on the balance sheet at $602 million. Debentures with a very low priority among the issuing company's assets in case of liquidation are referred to as *junk bonds.*[3]

A **call provision** grants to the issuing company the right to retire (repurchase) outstanding bonds after a designated date for a specified price. This provision serves to protect the interests of the issuing company, enabling it to remove the debt if economic conditions are appropriate. If interest rates and the economy fall, for example, a company may wish to repurchase outstanding bonds that require relatively high interest payments. The following excerpt from the 1987 financial report of Texas Instruments, a developer and manufacturer of computer and electronic equipment, refers to a call provision on certain of the company's outstanding bonds. Note that this particular provision allows either Texas Instruments (in 1990) or the bondholders (in 1994) to redeem the debt at a specified price.

In September 1987, the company issued $300 million of . . . debentures. The debentures may be redeemed, at the company's option, beginning in September 1990, at specified prices, and may be redeemed, at the holders' option, at par during a thirty-day period beginning in September 1994.

---

3. A number of companies and other entities have recently issued junk bonds, often to finance large corporate acquisitions, and there is some concern that issuing such large amounts of unsecured bonds reduces the stability of the financial markets. Junk bonds are very similar to preferred stock, which is discussed in Chapter 12.

The Price of a Bond

Bond prices are basically determined by what potential bondholders are willing to pay for the right to receive the semiannual interest payments and cash in the amount of the face value at maturity. The credit rating of the issuing company, the stated interest rate, and the restrictions, security arrangements, and many other provisions of the bond contract directly influence the price at which bonds are issued. Bonds issued by companies with high credit ratings, offering high stated interest rates, and backed by collateral tend to sell for higher prices than unsecured bonds issued by companies with low credit ratings, offering low stated interest rates. The appendix at the end of this chapter discusses more completely how bond prices are determined.

Bond prices are usually expressed as a percentage of the face value ($1000), and may be less than, equal to, or greater than the face value. Bonds issued for less than $1000 are issued at a *discount*. Bonds issued for $1000 are issued at *face (or par) value*. Bonds issued for greater than $1000 are issued at a *premium*.

On June 6, 1988, for example, Associated Corporation of North America, United Airlines, Inc., and Ford Motor Company each announced a major bond issuance in *The Wall Street Journal*. Associated offered 200,000 bonds with a time to maturity of five years and a stated interest rate of 9 percent at a discount price of 99.605 ($996.05 per bond). United Airlines offered 500,000 bonds with a maturity of ten years and a stated interest rate of 13 percent at 100.0 of face value ($1000 per bond). Ford offered 75,000 bonds with a time to maturity of three years and a stated interest rate of 13 percent at a premium price of 100.6 ($1006 per bond).

The Effective Rate and the Stated Rate

As in the case of long-term notes payable, the effective (actual) rate of interest paid on a bond is not necessarily equal to the stated rate. The effective rate is that rate which, when used to discount the future interest and face value payments, results in a present value that is equal to the issuance price. Depending on the relationship between the issuance price and the face value, the effective rate of interest on a bond may be lower than, equal to, or higher than the stated interest rate. The relationship among the price, the effective interest rate, and the stated interest rate is summarized below.

1. When the issuance price of a bond is greater than its face value *(premium)*, the effective rate is less than the stated rate.
2. When the issuance price of a bond is less than its face value *(discount)*, the effective rate is greater than the stated rate.
3. When the issuance price of a bond is equal to its face value *(par)*, the effective rate is equal to the stated rate.

Table 11−2 illustrates these three relationships. The effective interest rates of three different bonds are compared. Each bond has a $1000 face value, a five-year life, and a 6 percent stated annual interest rate (paid semiannually). They differ in that one is issued at a discount (91.9), one is issued at a premium (109.0), and one is issued at par (100.0). In each case the effective interest rate is determined

Table 11–2   Bond prices and the relationship between the effective rate and the stated rate

Effective Rate		Stated Rate	Face Value	Price (Present Value)	Type of Issued
8%	>	6%	$1000	$ 919 = 30(8.1109) + $1000(.6756)	Discount
4%	<	6%	$1000	$1090 = 30(8.9826) + $1000(.8203)	Premium
6%	=	6%	$1000	$1000 = 30(8.5302) + $1000(.7441)	Par

by finding that rate which, when used to discount the interest and face value payments, results in a present value that equals the given price.[4]

In the first case the effective rate is greater than the stated rate because the bond is issued at an $81 ($1000 − $919) discount. The issuing company is actually paying more than the stated rate because it receives only $919 for a bond on which it will pay $1000 at maturity.

In the second case the effective rate is less than the stated rate because the bond is issued at a $90 ($1090 − $1000) premium. The issuing company is actually paying less than the stated rate because it receives $1090 for a bond on which it will only pay $1000 at maturity.

In the final case the effective rate is equal to the stated rate because the bond is issued at par. The issuing company is actually paying the amount of interest indicated by the stated rate because it receives $1000 for a bond on which it will pay $1000 at maturity.

Accounting for Bonds Payable

The effective-interest method is also used to account for bonds payable. To review, applying the effective-interest method involves two basic rules: (1) the balance-sheet value of the bond liability is equal to the present value of the future cash outflows associated with the bond, discounted at the effective interest rate as of the issuance date; and (2) the interest expense recognized during each period of the bond's life is determined by multiplying the effective interest rate times the balance-sheet value of the bond liability as of the beginning of that period. The following examples use the effective-interest method to account for three different bonds: one issued at face (par) value, one issued at a discount, and one issued at a premium. The following information is used in all three cases.

Assume that Reebok International issues ten bonds, each with a face value of $1000, a stated interest rate of 10 percent, and time to maturity of two years.[5]

---

4. When using present value tables to infer an effective interest rate or to compute the price of a bond, keep in mind that interest payments are made on a semiannual basis. Accordingly, when finding the table factors for the interest payment annuity and the lump sum payment, the number of periods must be doubled and the discount rate must be halved. For example, the present value of a bond with a ten-year life, a $1000 face value, and a 10 percent stated interest rate, discounted at 8 percent, would be computed as below. Note that the table factors are based on an N of 20 (10 × 2) and an i of 4 percent (8%/2).

PV = Semiannual interest (PV of annuity: N = 20, i = 4%) + Face value (PV lump sum: N = 20, i = 4%)
  = $50   (13.59)   + $1000   (.456)
  = $679.50   + $456
  = $1135.50

5. Bonds are normally issued in much greater amounts, and their lives are usually considerably longer than two years. We have chosen a two-year life and a relatively small issuance to make the example manageable within the structure of this text. The shortened example, however, is sufficient to illustrate the important concepts.

Figure 11–7   Cash flows for bonds payable: three cases compared

Face value: 10 bonds × $1,000 per bond   = $10,000
Semiannual interest payment: ($10,000 × 10%) ÷ 2   = $ 500

Issuance Date	6 months	1 year	6 months	Maturity Date
Case 1: Issued at $10,000 (face)				
+$10,000	−$500	--$500	−$500	−$ 500
				−$10,000
Case 2: Issued at $9,654 (discount)				
+$9,654	−$500	−$500	−$500	−$ 500
				−$10,000
Case 3: Issued at $10,363 (premium)				
+$10,363	−$500	−$500	−$500	−$ 500
				−$10,000

Interest payments of $500 ([$10,000 × 10 percent]/2) are to be made semiannually. In Case 1, the bonds are issued at face (par), so that the effective rate (10 percent) equals the stated rate (10 percent). In Case 2, the bonds are issued at a discount, so that the effective rate (12 percent) is greater than the stated rate (10 percent). In Case 3, the bonds are issued at a premium, so the effective rate (8 percent) is less than the stated rate (10 percent). Figure 11–7 shows the cash flows associated with the three bond issuances. Note that the cash flows are identical for all three bond issuances except for the issuance price.

Case 1: Bonds Issued at Par
In Case 1 the bonds are issued at par ($10,000) and the effective rate (10 percent) is equal to the stated rate (10 percent). The journal entries, balance-sheet values of bonds payable, and present value of the future cash flows discounted at the effective interest rate are shown in Figure 11–8.

When bonds are issued at par, the journal entries are very straightforward because neither a discount nor a premium need be considered. The Bonds Payable account is simply carried on the balance sheet at $10,000 until maturity. Note that the present value of the remaining cash flows, discounted at 10 percent, is also equal to $10,000 throughout the life of the bond. The interest expense recognized in each six-month period ($500), which appears on the income statement, is calculated by multiplying the effective interest rate (5 percent = 10 percent/2) times the balance-sheet value of the bonds payable at the beginning of the period ($10,000). This calculation is consistent with the effective-interest method and in this case gives rise to an amount that is equal to the $500 cash payment. These two dollar amounts are equal because the effective rate, which determines the interest expense, is equal to the stated rate, which determines the interest payment.

Figure 11-8 Bonds issued at face value: Case 1

Date	Journal Entry		Balance-Sheet Value	Present Value
Issue	Cash	10,000		
	Bonds Payable	10,000	$10,000	$10,000
	To record a bond issuance.			
6 months	Interest Expense	500		
	Cash	500	10,000	10,000
	To record the payment of interest.			
1 year	Interest Expense	500		
	Cash	500	10,000	10,000
	To record the payment of interest.			
6 months	Interest Expense	500		
	Cash	500	10,000	10,000
	To record the payment of interest.			
Maturity	Interest Expense	500		
	Cash	500	10,000	10,000
	To record the payment of interest.			
	Bonds Payable	10,000		
	Cash	10,000	0	0
	To record the payment of principal.			

Interest expense = Balance-sheet value at beginning of period × [effective interest rate (10%) ÷ 2]
Cash interest payment = ($10,000 × 10%) ÷ 2
Balance-sheet value = Face value ($10,000)
Present value = Remaining cash outflows discounted at effective interest rate (10%)

Case 2: Bonds Issued at a Discount

In Case 2 the bonds are issued at a $346 discount, and the effective rate of interest (12 percent) is greater than the stated rate (10 percent). Figure 11-9 shows the journal entries, balance-sheet value of bonds payable, and present value of the future cash flows discounted at the effective interest rate.

The bond payable is initially recorded at $10,000, which is greater than the $9654 cash proceeds; consequently, a $346 **Discount on Bonds Payable** is recognized. This discount is disclosed on the balance sheet as a contra-liability and is subtracted from the Bonds Payable account. As before, it can be viewed as interest expense waiting to be recognized over the life of the bond. The balance sheet disclosure of the Bonds Payable account and the discount at issuance appears as follows:

Bonds payable	$10,000	
Less: Discount on bonds payable	346	$9654

In applying the effective-interest method, interest expense is calculated each period by multiplying the effective interest rate (6 percent = 12 percent/2) by the balance-sheet value of the bond liability at the beginning of the period. For example, at the end of the first six-month period, the $579 interest expense is computed thus: 6 percent × $9654. The cash interest payment is only $500, so $79 is credited to the Discount account. The $79 of amortized discount represents the interest cost, recognized in the first period, associated with receiving only $9654 for a bond that requires a payment of $10,000 at maturity. The remaining (unamortized) portion of the discount ($267 = $346 − $79) is subtracted from Bonds

Figure 11–9   Bonds issued at a discount: Case 2

Date	Journal Entry			Balance-Sheet Value	Present Value
Issue	Cash	9,654			
	Discount on Bonds	346			
	Bonds Payable		10,000	$ 9,654	$ 9,654
	To record a bond issuance.				
6 months	Interest Expense	579			
	Discount on Bonds		79	+79	
	Cash		500	9,733	9,733
	To record the payment of interest and amortization of the discount.				
1 Year	Interest Expense	584			
	Discount on Bonds		84	+84	
	Cash		500	9,817	9,817
	To record the payment of interest and amortization of the discount.				
6 months	Interest Expense	589			
	Discount on Bonds		89	+89	
	Cash		500	9,906	9,906
	To record the payment of interest and amortization of the discount.				
Maturity	Interest Expense	594			
	Discount on Bonds		94	+94	
	Cash		500	10,000	10,000
	To record the payment of interest and amortization of the discount.				
	Bonds Payable	10,000			
	Cash		10,000	0	0
	To record the payment of principal.				

Interest expense = Balance-sheet value at beginning of period × [effective interest rate (12%) ÷ 2]
Cash interest payment = ($10,000 × 10%) ÷ 2
Balance-sheet value = Face value ($10,000) less unamortized discount
or
Balance-sheet value at beginning of period + discount amortized during period
Present value = remaining cash outflows discounted at effective interest rate (12%)

Payable on the balance sheet to bring its balance-sheet value to present value ($9733).[6] This process is repeated every six months throughout the life of the bond, and eventually the entire discount is amortized into interest expense. Note also that the effective-interest method keeps the balance-sheet value of the bond liability equal to the present value of the remaining cash flows, discounted at 12 percent, throughout the life of the bond.

The 1987 financial report of Colgate-Palmolive Company illustrates how the company discloses bonds issued at a discount. Note in this excerpt that Colgate-Palmolive, like most major U.S. corporations, discloses bonds payable at a dollar amount that is net of the discount.

---

6. Subtracting the unamortized portion of the discount from Bonds Payable is equivalent to adding the amortized amount of the discount to the balance-sheet value, which is shown in Figure 11–9.

	1987*	1986*
$150,000 face amount debentures due 2017 (less unamortized discount of $3660) at an effective interest rate of 9.98%.	$146,340	—
$62,400 face amount bonds due 1955 (less unamortized discount of $7027) at an effective interest rate of 10.3%.	55,373	$54,190

*Dollars in thousands.

Case 3: Bonds Issued at a Premium

In Case 3 the bonds are issued at a $363 premium, and the effective rate of interest (8 percent) is less than the stated rate (10 percent). The journal entries, balance-sheet value of bonds payable, and present value of the future cash flows discounted at the effective interest rate appear in Figure 11–10.

The bond payable is initially recorded at $10,000, which is less than the $10,363 cash proceeds, so a $363 **Premium on Bonds Payable** is recognized. This premium is disclosed on the balance sheet as an addition to the Bonds Payable account. It can be viewed as a reduction in interest expense (or a deferred revenue) waiting to be recognized over the life of the bond. The balance sheet disclosure of the Bonds Payable account and the premium at issuance appear as follows:

Bonds payable	$10,000	
Plus: Premium on bonds payable	363	$10,363

In applying the effective-interest method, interest expense is calculated each period by multiplying the effective interest rate (4 percent = 8 percent ÷ 2) by the balance-sheet value of the bond liability at the beginning of the period. For example, at the end of the first six-month period, the $415 interest expense is equal to 4 percent × $10,363. The cash interest payment is $500, so $85 is debited to the Premium account. The $85 of amortized premium represents reduced interest cost, recognized in the first period, associated with receiving $10,363 for a bond that requires a payment of only $10,000 at maturity. The remaining (unamortized) portion of the premium ($278 = $363 − $85) is added to Bonds Payable on the balance sheet to bring its balance-sheet value to the present value ($10,278).[7] This process is repeated every six months throughout the life of the bond and eventually the entire premium is amortized into interest expense. Note, once again, that the effective-interest method keeps the balance-sheet value of the bond liability equal to the present value of the remaining cash flows, discounted at 8 percent, throughout the life of the bond.

Discount and Premium Amortization Schedules

A common way to illustrate the amortization of a discount or premium over the life of a bond issuance is to prepare an **amortization schedule** which has been done in Figures 11–11 and 11–12 for Cases 2 and 3, respectively. Review these two amortization schedules and note that they are simply another way to illustrate what is shown in Figures 11–9 and 11–10.

Issuing Bonds at Par, Discount, or Premium: A Comparison

The dollar amounts of interest expense and the balance-sheet values of Bonds Payable over the lives of the bonds are compared across Case 1 (par), Case 2 (discount), and Case 3 (premium) in Table 11–3.

---

7. Adding the unamortized portion of the premium to Bonds Payable is equivalent to subtracting the amortized amount of the premium from the balance-sheet value, which is shown in Figure 11–10.

Figure 11–10   Bonds issued at a premium: Case 3

Date	Journal Entry			Balance-Sheet Value	Present Value
Issue	Cash	10,363			
	Premium on Bonds Payable		363		
	Bonds Payable		10,000	$10,363	$10,363
	To record a bond issuance.				
6 months	Interest Expense	415			
	Premium on Bonds Payable	85		−85	
	Cash		500	10,278	10,278
	To record the payment of interest and amortization of the premium.				
1 Year	Interest Expense	411			
	Premium on Bonds Payable	89		−89	
	Cash		500	10,189	10,189
	To record the payment of interest and amortization of the premium.				
6 months	Interest Expense	407			
	Premium on Bonds Payable	93		−93	
	Cash		500	10,096	10,096
	To record the payment of interest and amortization of the premium.				
Maturity	Interest Expense	404			
	Premium on Bonds Payable	96		−96	
	Cash		500	10,000	10,000
	To record the payment of interest and amortization of the premium.				
	Bonds Payable	10,000			
	Cash		10,000	0	0
	To record the payment of principal.				

Interest expense = Balance-sheet value at beginning of period × [effective interest rate (8%) ÷ 2]
Cash interest payment = ($10,000 × 10%) ÷ 2
Balance-sheet value = Face value ($10,000) plus unamortized premium
or
Balance-sheet value at beginning of period − premium amortized during period
Present value = remaining cash outflows discounted at effective interest rate (8%)

Note that interest expense is constant when bonds are issued at par, increasing when bonds are issued at a discount, and decreasing when bonds are issued at a premium. Similarly, the balance-sheet value of Bonds Payable is constant when bonds are issued at par, increasing when they are issued at a discount, and decreasing when they are issued at a premium. The balance-sheet value in all cases is $10,000 when the bonds are paid off at maturity.

The Straight-Line Method

The calculations in Cases 2 and 3 amortize the discount and premium using the effective-interest method. As with long-term notes payable, many companies amortize bond discounts and premiums using the straight-line method. Under this method, equal dollar amounts are amortized in each period. In Case 2 above, for example, the $346 discount would be amortized at a rate of $86.50 ($346 ÷ 4)

Figure 11-11   Amortization schedule: bonds issued at a discount (Case 2)

$10,000 bond issuance   Life = 2 years   Stated interest rate = 10%   Effective interest rate = 12%

Date	Interest Expense (6% × book value)	Interest Payment (5% × face value)	Unamortized Discount	Balance-Sheet Value (face value − unamortized discount or book value + amortized discount)
Issue	—	—	$346	$ 9,654
6 months	$579	$500	−79	+79
			267	9,733
1 year	584	500	−84	+84
			183	9,817
6 months	589	500	−89	+89
			94	9,906
Maturity	594	500	−94	+94
			0	$10,000

Figure 11-12   Amortization schedule: bonds issued at a premium (Case 3)

$10,000 bond issuance   Life = 2 years   Stated interest rate = 10%   Effective interest rate = 8%

Date	Interest Expense (4% × book value)	Interest Payment (5% × face value)	Unamortized Premium	Balance-Sheet Value (face value + unamortized premium or book value − amortized premium)
Issue	—	—	$ 363	$10,363
6 months	$415	$500	−85	−85
			278	10,278
1 year	411	500	−89	−89
			189	10,189
6 months	407	500	−93	−93
			96	10,096
Maturity	404	500	−96	−96
			0	$10,000

per six-month period. In Case 3 the $363 premium would be amortized at a rate of $90.75 ($363 ÷ 4) per six-month period. Once again, while the straight-line method may be simpler to apply, generally accepted accounting principles allow it only if it results in financial statement numbers that are not materially different from those produced by the effective-interest method. The straight-line method is conceptually deficient because it fails to reflect the actual rate of interest paid by the issuing company.

Bonds Issued Between Interest-Payment Dates

Bonds are rarely issued exactly on an interest payment date. For example, Carolco Pictures, Inc. issued 52,500 debt securities on June 15, 1988, for $1000 each. The securities have a stated annual interest rate of 14 percent, which is to be paid

Table 11-3   Issuing bonds at par, discount, or premium: comparing Interest Expense and Bond Payable

Date	Case 1 Par		Case 2 Discount		Case 3 Premium	
	Interest Expense	Bond Payable	Interest Expense	Bond Payable	Interest Expense	Bond Payable
Issue		$10,000		$ 9,654		$10,363
6 months	$500	10,000	$579	9,733	$415	10,278
1 year	500	10,000	584	9,817	411	10,189
6 months	500	10,000	589	9,906	407	10,096
Maturity	500	10,000	594	10,000	404	10,000

semiannually on June 1 and December 1. Each June 1 and December 1 throughout the term of the securities, therefore, Carolco pays bondholders $70 ([$1000 × 14 percent] ÷ 2) in interest on each bond.

Since the bonds were issued on June 15 instead of on June 1, the interest payment date, the bondholders had held the bonds only five and one-half months when they received a full, six-month interest payment of $70 per bond on December 1.

Carolco compensated for this apparent inequality by charging the bondholders for two weeks of accrued interest ($5.44 = $70 × [14 days ÷ 180 days]) when the bonds were issued on June 15, in addition to the $1000 purchase price. Accordingly, Carolco collected $1005.44 for each bond (total: $52,785,600 = 52,500 × $1005.44) and recognized $285,600 ($5.44 × 52,500) as accrued interest payable when the securities were issued. The accrued interest payable was removed from the books when the first interest payment was made on December 1, 1988. The journal entries below were recorded by Carolco on June 15, when the securities were issued, and on December 1, when the first interest payment was made.[8]

June 15	Cash (52,500 × $1005.44)	52,785,600	
	Bond Payable (52,500 × $1000)		52,500,000
	Accrued Interest Payable (52,500 × $5.44)		285,600
	To record the issuance of debt securities for $1000 plus accrued interest.		
Dec. 1	Accrued Interest Payable	285,600	
	Interest Expense	3,389,400	
	Cash ($52,500,000 × 7%)		3,675,000
	To record the payment of interest.		

It is very common to charge accrued interest when bonds are issued on dates other than the interest payment dates. For example, on June 3, 1988, Heller Financial, Inc. advertised a $100,000,000 debt issuance in *The Wall Street Journal* for 99.78 plus accrued interest. Soon thereafter Jones Intercable advertised a $150,000,000 bond issuance for 98.50 plus accrued interest.

---

8. When issuing bonds, some companies credit Interest Expense for the amount of accrued interest. When the subsequent interest payment is made, Interest Expense is debited for the dollar amount of the entire payment.

The Effective-Interest Method and Changing Interest Rates

We have stated on several occasions that the effective-interest method values long-term liabilities on the balance sheet at the present value of the liability's future (remaining) cash flows, discounted at the effective interest rate *as of the date of issuance*. Under this method the same effective interest rate is used throughout the life of the liability, even though interest rates in the financial markets vary substantially. By ignoring changes in market interest rates, the effective-interest method fails to recognize economic gains and losses that affect the issuing company's financial condition.

   To illustrate, assume that Olsen Foods issued ten bonds of $1000 face value for $1000 each. The stated annual interest rate is 8 percent, and the bonds mature at the end of five years. Because the bonds were issued at face value, the effective interest rate is also 8 percent, and under the effective-interest method the following journal entry would be recorded at issuance.

Cash (10 × $1,000)	10,000	
Bond Payable		10,000
To record a bond issuance.		

   Throughout its five-year life the bond payable would be carried on the balance sheet at $10,000, the present value of the remaining cash flows, discounted at 8 percent, the effective interest rate as of the issue date. If market interest rates fall by 2 percent during the first year of the bond's life, however, the economic value of the bond liability becomes $10,702, the present value of the remaining cash flows discounted at 6 percent (8% − 2%).[9] As a result, Olsen would incur an economic loss of approximately $702 ($10,702 − $10,000). The intuition underlying such a loss is that Olsen is paying an effective rate of 8 percent on its outstanding bonds while market rates are somewhat lower.

   If, on the other hand, market interest rates rise by 2 percent during the first year, the economic value of the bond liability becomes $9354, the present value of the remaining cash flows discounted at 10 percent (8% + 2%).[10] Olsen therefore, would enjoy an economic gain of approximately $646 ($10,000 − $9,354). The underlying intuition is that Olsen is paying only 8 percent on its outstanding bonds while market interest rates are somewhat higher.

   Neither the economic loss nor the economic gain in the example above would be recognized under the effective-interest method. It is difficult to objectively determine the interest rate that should be used to discount the remaining cash flows, and no exchange transaction has occurred, where a verifiable gain or loss could be recognized. Consequently, the principle of objectivity ensures that the effective-interest method does not carry the bond liability on the balance sheet at present value in an economic sense. Rather, the bond liability is carried at an es-

---

9. We assume that when market interest rates decrease by 2 percent, the effective interest rate on these bonds also decreases by 2 percent. Under this assumption, the present value of the remaining cash flows are as follows (note that interest payments are semiannual):

$10,702 = $400 (*PV* annuity: $n = 8, i = 3\%$) + $10,000 (*PV* single sum: $n = 8, i = 3\%$)
   = $400   (7.01969)   + $10,000   (.78941)

10. We assume that when market interest rates increase by 2 percent, the effective interest rate on these bonds also increase by 2 percent. Under this assumption, the present value of the remaining cash flows are as follows (note that interest payments are semiannual):

$9354 = $400 (*PV* annuity: $n = 8, i = 5\%$) + $10,000 (*PV* single sum: $n = 8, i = 5\%$)
   = $400   (6.46321)   + $10,000   (.67684)

timate of present value, which relies on the assumption that the effective interest rate is constant throughout the life of the bond. Financial statement users should be aware that this assumption ensures that economic gains and losses resulting from interest rate fluctuations are not recognized on the financial statements. Moreover, as we discuss later, changing market interest rates often encourage management to repurchase or redeem outstanding bonds prior to maturity. Financial statement gains and losses are recognized on such redemptions.

Bond Redemptions

Bonds can be **redeemed** (repurchased or retired) on or before the maturity date. When this occurs, the dollar amount in the Bond Payable account and any unamortized discount or premium are written off the books, a cash payment is recorded, and a gain or loss is recognized on the redemption.

Bond Redemptions at Maturity

When bonds are redeemed at the maturity date, the issuing company simply pays cash to the bondholders in the amount of the face value and removes the bond payable from the balance sheet. At maturity, the bond payable is equal to the face value because, after the final entry to record interest expense, any discount or premium on the bonds will have been completely amortized. Journal entries to record bond redemptions at the maturity dates for bonds issued at face (Case 1), at a discount (Case 2), and at a premium (Case 3) appear in Figures 11−8, 11−9, and 11−10, respectively. Note that in all three cases the journal entry to record the redemption takes the following form.

Bond Payable	10,000	
Cash		10,000
To record the redemption of bonds with a $10,000 face value at maturity.		

Bond Redemptions Before Maturity

Many companies exercise call provisions and redeem bonds before the maturity date. As indicated earlier, as economic conditions (especially interest rates) change, companies may wish to retire long-term debts. To illustrate, consider companies that issued bonds in the late 1970s when interest rates were at all-time highs. A number of these companies issued bonds with stated rates in excess of 15 percent. By the mid-1980s, interest rates had fallen, and many of these companies redeemed their bonds and issued new bonds with considerably lower stated rates. In 1986, for example, Ralston Purina Company redeemed $300.8 million of its outstanding debentures prior to scheduled maturity. The Greyhound Corporation redeemed a substantial amount of long-term debt prior to maturity in both 1983 and 1987.

The methods used to account for a bond redemption prior to maturity involve (1) updating the amortization of any discount or premium and (2) recording an entry to reflect the redemption. This entry records a cash payment, removes from the balance sheet the bond payable and the remaining unamortized discount or premium, and recognizes a gain or loss on the transaction. For example, if bonds with a $100,000 face value and a $5000 unamortized discount are redeemed for $102,000, the following journal entry would be recorded. Assume that the discount has been amortized up to the date of the redemption.

Bond Payable	100,000	
Loss on Redemption	7,000	
Discount on Bonds Payable		5,000
Cash		102,000
To record the redemption of bonds prior to maturity.		

The $7000 loss on redemption would decrease net income and appear in a separate section of the income statement, referred to as *extraordinary items*.[11] The $300.8 million bond redemption by Ralston Purina referred to above resulted in a $23.7 million loss, which appeared on the company's 1986 income statement.

If bonds with a $100,000 face value and a $3000 unamortized premium are redeemed for $102,000, the following journal entry is recorded, and a gain on the redemption is recognized on the income statement. One of the bond redemptions by Greyhound Corporation referred to above resulted in a $14.7 million gain, which appeared on the company's 1983 income statement.

Bond Payable	100,000	
Premium	3,000	
Cash		102,000
Gain on Redemption		1,000
To record the redemption of bonds prior to maturity.		

LEASES

A **lease** is a contract granting use or occupation of property during a specified period of time in exchange for rent payments. Such contracts are a very popular way to finance business activities. Companies often lease, rather than purchase, land, buildings, machinery, equipment, and other holdings, primarily to avoid the risks and associated costs of ownership. *Accounting, Trends and Techniques* (New York: AICPA, 1987) reports that, of the 600 major U.S. companies surveyed, 555 (93 percent) disclosed some form of material lease arrangement. In 1987, Chevron Corporation, McDonnell Douglas, and Coca-Cola Enterprises reported lease expenses of $275 million, $165 million, and $25 million, respectively.

A number of commercial airlines have recently moved toward leasing as a means of financing new aircraft. *The Wall Street Journal* reported that "International carriers such as Lufthansa, British Airways, Singapore Airlines and Malaysian Airlines have viewed [leasing] as more attractive than issuing public debt or arranging bank financing to purchase planes outright. Small airlines, such as Seattle-based Alaska Air Group, have been leasing companies' principal customers. America West Airlines, based in Phoenix, Ariz., says "its launch in 1983 would not have been possible if it had had to purchase outright its $70 million of aircraft."[12]

For purposes of financial accounting, lease arrangements are divided into two categories: operating leases and capital leases.

Operating Leases

In a pure leasing arrangement an individual or entity *(lessor)*, who owns land, buildings, equipment, or other property, transfers the right to use this property to

---

11. Extraordinary items are discussed in Chapter 14.
12. Eileen White Rerd, "For Airplane Lessors Business Is Greater," *The Wall Street Journal*, 20 May 1988, p. 12.

another individual or entity *(lessee)* in exchange for periodic cash payments over a specified period of time. Normally, the terms of the lease are defined by contract, and over the period of the lease, the owner is responsible for the property's normal maintenance and upkeep. The lessee assumes none of the risks of ownership, and at the end of the lease, the right to use the property reverts to the owner.

These types of agreements are called **operating leases,** and accounting for them is straightforward. The property is reported as an asset on the owner's balance sheet, and the periodic rental payments are recorded as rent revenue on the owner's income statement. If applicable, as in the case of a fixed asset, the capitalized cost of the property is depreciated by the owner. The lessee, on the other hand, recognizes no asset or liability, but simply reports rent expense on the income statement as the periodic rent payments are accrued.

Capital Leases

Many contractual arrangements, which appear on the surface to be leases, are actually installment purchases, where the risks and benefits of ownership have been transferred to the lessee. The present value of the periodic lease payments, for example, may approximate the fair market value of the property. It is also possible that the property may revert to the lessee at the end of the lease period. Further, the period of the lease may be equivalent to the asset's useful life. In such situations the lessee has actually purchased the property from the lessor and is paying it off in installments. Such leases are referred to as **capital leases,** and they should be treated on the financial statements as purchases. That is, the leased property should be included as an asset on the balance sheet of the lessee, and the obligation associated with the future lease payments should be reported as a liability.

Suppose that on January 1, 1990, Hitzelberger Supply (lessee) signs an agreement to lease a bulldozer from Jones and Sons (lessor) for a period of two years. The contract specifies that Hitzelberger must pay $10,000 on December 31 of 1990 and 1991, and the bulldozer can be purchased by Hitzelberger at the end of the lease for a nominal sum. The market price of the bulldozer at the time of the agreement is $17,355, leading to an effective interest rate of 10 percent, which is equivalent to the interest rate that would be charged if Hitzelberger borrowed funds to purchase the bulldozer.[13]

Hitzelberger should account for this arrangement as a capital lease because the effective rate is equivalent to the market interest rate (i.e., the present value of the lease payments discounted at the market rate approximates the fair market value of the bulldozer), and the company can purchase the bulldozer at the end of the lease period for a nominal sum. Although the transaction is described as a lease, economically it is actually an installment sale. Assuming that the bulldozer is depreciated on a straight-line basis over a five-year useful life and that this agreement is considered a capital lease, the entries shown in Figure 11–13 would be recorded by Hitzelberger over the life of the lease.

As with long-term notes payable and bonds payable, the effective-interest method is used to compute the interest expense and to amortize the lease liability. Specifically, the annual interest expense associated with the installment purchase is computed by multiplying the effective interest rate (10 percent) times the bal-

---

13. The effective rate of interest is determined by finding that rate which, when used to discount the future cash flows of the lease, results in a present value that is equal to the market price of the bulldozer.

Figure 11-13   Accounting for a capital lease: Hitzelberger Supply

General Journal

1990	Jan. 1	Machinery ($10,000 × 1.7355*)	17,355	
		Lease Liability		17,355
		To record a capital lease when the lease agreement is signed.		
		*Present value of annuity table: $n = 2, i = 10\%$		
	Dec. 31	Depreciation Expense (17,355 ÷ 5)	3,471	
		Accumulated Depreciation		3,471
		Interest Expense (10% × 17,355)	1,736	
		Lease Liability (plug)	8,264	
		Cash (annual payment)		10,000
		To record depreciation and the first $10,000 lease payment.		
1991	Dec. 31	Depreciation Expense (17,355 ÷ 5)	3,471	
		Accumulated Depreciation		3,471
		Interest Expense (10% × $9,091*)	909	
		Lease Liability (plug)	9,091	
		Cash (annual payment)		10,000
		To record depreciation and the second $10,000 payment.		
		*Unamortized lease liability ($17,355 − $8,264)		

ance-sheet value of the liability, and the dollar amount of the liability amortized each period is equal to the difference between the cash payment and the interest expense. This procedure ensures that the lease liability is carried on the balance sheet at present value throughout the life of the lease, assuming that the effective interest rate remains constant over that time period. Note also that Hitzelberger depreciates the cost of the machinery, which reflects the fact that for purposes of financial accounting, Hitzelberger is considered the owner of the bulldozer.

Capital-Lease Amortization Schedules

As with bonds, amortization schedules are also used to illustrate the amortization of capital leases over their lives. Assume that a piece of equipment is purchased through a capital lease requiring the lessee to pay $5000 per year for five years. The effective interest rate on the transaction is 8 percent. The amortization schedule for this lease appears in Figure 11−14.

Once again, the lease liability is valued on the balance sheet at the present value of the future cash outflows discounted at the effective interest rate (8 percent), which is assumed to be constant throughout the life of the lease. Interest expense for a given period is computed by multiplying the effective interest rate times the balance-sheet value of the liability as of the beginning of that period.

Figure 11-14 Capital lease amortization schedule

Year	Cash Payment		Interest Expense*	Lease Liability
				$19,964
1	$5,000	—	$1,597	(3,403)
				16,561
2	5,000	—	1,325	(3,675)
				12,886
3	5,000	—	1,031	(3,969)
				8,917
4	5,000	—	713	(4,287)
				4,630
5	5,000	—	370	(4,630)
				0

*Interest expense = 8% × Balance-sheet value of lease liability at beginning of year

Accordingly, as the lease liability becomes smaller with each succeeding year, the dollar value of the interest expense also decreases. At the end of the lease, the liability has been reduced to zero. Although not illustrated in Figure 11-14, keep in mind that the cost of the machinery ($19,964) should be depreciated using one of the methods allowed under generally accepted accounting principles.

Operating Leases, Capital Leases, and Off-Balance-Sheet Financing

Both operating leases and capital leases are commonly reported on the financial statements of U.S. companies. *Accounting Trends and Techniques* (New York: AICPA, 1987) reports that, of the 600 companies surveyed, 373 (62 percent) disclosed both operating and capital leases, 107 (18 percent) disclosed operating leases only, and 75 (12 percent) disclosed capital leases only.

It is important to realize how the accounting treatment of an operating lease differs from that of a capital lease. From the lessee's standpoint, an operating lease simply gives rise to a periodic rent expense, while a capital lease involves the recognition of an asset, a leasehold liability, and an additional depreciation expense. Because accounting for capital leases increases liabilities and recognizes depreciation expense, which can affect important financial ratios negatively, companies have incentives to structure lease agreements so that they are accounted for as operating leases. Indeed, a 1981 study sponsored by the Financial Accounting Standards Board found "that a majority of the companies surveyed were structuring the terms of new lease contracts to avoid capitalization."[14] Such attempts to finance asset acquisitions without having to report liabilities on the balance sheet may be economically sound in view of the importance of financial ratios in debt covenants and investor and creditor decisions. In one particular case, *Forbes* magazine reported that Dierckx Equipment Corporation, a small privately-owned company, could "endanger its credit rating" by capitalizing its leases.[15]

14. FASB, "FASB-Sponsored Research Finds Majority of Leases Structured to Avoid Capitalization," *Status Report*, 1 September 1981 (Stamford, Conn.: FASB).
15. Jay Gissen, "The World According to GAAP," *Forbes*, 8 June 1981, pp. 148, 150.

In 1977, the Financial Accounting Standards Board issued an accounting standard that identified a set of criteria for distinguishing capital leases from operating leases. In general, these criteria attempted to identify when a leasing arrangement actually represents an installment purchase and therefore should be treated as such (i.e., a capital lease) on the financial statements. While these criteria are useful, they have not removed all the subjectivity involved in classifying leases. For example, the FASB research study reported above, which noted that many companies attempt to avoid lease capitalization, was conducted in 1981, four years after these criteria were issued. Consequently, financial statement users should closely review the lease terms disclosed in the footnotes of financial statements and ascertain for themselves whether a leasing arrangement is in fact a rental agreement or an installment purchase.

THE ANNUAL REPORT OF K MART CORPORATION

Turn now to K mart's annual report located in Appendix D. The Balance Sheet (page 32) shows that long-term liabilities (exclusive of Deferred Income Taxes) consist of Capital Lease Obligations ($1.588 billion), Long-Term Debt ($1.358 billion), and Other Long-Term Liabilities ($459 million). The 11-Year Financial Summary on page 14 also reports the dollar amounts of Long-Term Debt and Capital Lease Obligations as well as Debt and Equivalent as a percent of Total Capitalization. This ratio, which is further described on page 28, is the result of dividing Long-Term Liabilities (including current maturities) by Total Capitalization (Long-Term Liabilities + Deferred Income Taxes + Stockholders' Equity). It equalled 38 percent, 39.4 percent, and 43.2 percent at the end of 1988, 1987, and 1986, respectively.

Note that Debt and Equivalent as a percent of Total Capitalization does not correspond to any of the ratios reported in Table 11-1, which includes Long-Term Liabilities as percentages of Total Assets, Total Liabilities, and Stockholders' Equity. As of January 25, 1989, K mart's long-term liabilities represented 28 percent of total assets, 49 percent of total liabilities, and 68 percent of stockholders' equity. The magnitudes of these percentages indicate that K mart carries a relatively large amount of long-term debt when compared to general industry averages, somewhat more than grocery stores and somewhat less than motion picture theaters and hotels.

K mart's Capital Lease Obligations represent its largest long-term liability. The section describing leases on page 43 reports that "the company conducts operations primarily in leased facilities." Both capital and operating leases are substantial, indicated by the chart on page 43 which reports that minimum lease payments due in the future total $4.731 billion and $4.650 billion for capital and operating leases, respectively. The methods used to account for capital and operating leases are described on page 35 which discloses that "the company accounts for capital leases . . . as the acquisition of an asset and the incurrence of an obligation . . . the asset is amortized using the straight-line method and the obligation, including interest thereon, is liquidated [amortized] over the life of the lease. All other leases (operating leases) are accounted for by recording periodic rental expense over the life of the lease." The section on Property and Equipment (page 37) reports Property under Capital Leases of $2.416 billion and accumulated depreciation and amortization on such property of $1.105 billion. In addition, the

Income Statement (page 31) discloses interest expense on Capital Lease Obligations of $174 million.

K mart's outstanding long-term debt, which includes various debentures (unsecured bonds), notes, and commercial paper, is extensively described on pages 41 and 42 and the interest expenses recognized on such debt totaled $172 million during 1988. Debentures account for most of the total, three issuances of which were made at discounts. Stated interest rates on the debentures range from 8⅛ percent to 12½ percent and maturity dates range from 1997 to 2017. The debentures contain call provisions and "in December 1986, the company called for early redemption on all $250 million of its 12¾ percent sinking fund debentures due March 1, 2015." The Income Statement shows that a $16 million extraordinary gain was recognized on the transaction. Note also that "interest [on the debentures] is payable semiannually on June 1 and December 1 of each year."

While outstanding debentures represent K mart's primary long-term debt, a major source of financing during 1988 was a $300 million medium-term note issuance, which is described on pages 27 and 41. The cash proceeds from this issuance are included on the Statement of Cash Flows (page 33). As indicated on page 41, "the average coupon rate of these notes is 9.25 percent and the average term of the notes is 6.2 years." Note on page 41 that this issuance represents the only medium-term notes presently outstanding.

Finally, the bottom of page 42 indicates that "the company has entered into revolving credit agreements with various banks" which would allow K mart to borrow $340 million as of January 25, 1989. As of that date, "the company had no outstanding borrowings under these agreements." However, these agreements limit K mart, as they "contain certain restrictive provisions regarding the maintenance of net worth [stockholders' equity], working capital, coverage ratios and payment of cash dividends. At January 25, 1989, $2,351 million of consolidated retained earnings were free of such restrictions." Note on the Balance Sheet (page 32) that K mart reports Retained Earnings of $4,345 million as of January 25, 1989.

REVIEW PROBLEM

Assume that Union Carbide issues 500 bonds each with a $1000 face value on January 15, 1991. The five-year bonds have an annual stated interest rate of 6 percent, to be paid semiannually on December 31 and June 30. The bonds are issued at 91.89 plus accrued interest, providing an effective annual interest rate of 8 percent. A call provision in the bond contract states that the bonds can be redeemed by Union Carbide after December 31, 1991, for 96.0. Assume that Union Carbide exercises this provision on July 1, 1992.

Figure 11–15 provides the cash flows, journal entries, discount balance, and net book value of the bonds from the time of the bond issuance to the redemption. An explanation of each calculation follows.

Cash Flow Calculations

Proceeds. The proceeds of the bond issuance ($459,443) were calculated by multiplying the number of bonds issued (500), times the price per bond ($918.89).

Figure 11–15   Review problem

Terms: Number of bonds issued: 500   Interest payment dates: Dec. 31, June 30
Face value: $1,000   Issue date: January 15, 1991
Stated interest rate: 6%   Price: .9189 ($461,650) plus accrued interest ($1,250)
Time to maturity: 5 years   Effective interest rate: 8%

Call Provision: Redeemable after 12/31/91 for .9600

				6/30/92
12/31/90—————	→1/15/91—————————	→6/30/91—————————	→12/31/91—————————	→7/1/92

Cash Flows	+$459,443 (proceeds)	−$15,000 (interest)	−$15,000 (interest)	−$15,000 (interest)
	+$1,250 (accrued interest)			−$480,000 (redemption)

General Journal	Cash 460,693
	Discount 40,557
	  Bond Pay. 500,000
	  Int. Pay. 1,250
	To record a bond issuance.
		Int. Exp. 17,128
		Int. Pay. 1,250
		  Cash 15,000
		  Discount 3,378
		To record the payment of interest and amortization of the discount.
			Int. Exp. 18,513
			  Cash 15,000
			  Discount 3,513
			To record the payment of interest and amortization of the discount.
				Int. Exp. 18,653
				  Cash 15,000
				  Discount 3,653
				To record the payment of interest and amortization of the discount.
				
				Bond Payable 500,000
				Loss on Redemp. 10,013
				  Discount 30,013
				  Cash 480,000
				To record a bond redemption.

Discount Balance	$40,557	$40,557 − $3,378 = $37,179	$37,179 − $3,513 = $33,666	$33,666 − $3,653 = $30,013 (before redemption)

Net Book Value of Bond Payable	$500,000 − $40,557 = $459,443	$500,000 − $37,179 = $462,821	$500,000 − $33,666 = $466,334	$500,000 − $30,013 = $469,987 (before redemption)

Bond Pay. = Bond Payable
Int. Pay. = Interest Payable
Int. Exp. = Interest Expense

Interest Payments. The semiannual interest payment ($15,000) was calculated by multiplying the number of bonds issued (500), times the face value of each bond ($1000), times half the stated annual interest rate (3 percent).

Accrued Interest (1/15/91). The accrued interest on January 15 ($1250) was calculated by multiplying the semiannual interest payment ($15,000) times the ratio of the time since the last interest payment date (15 days) divided by 180 days (i.e., half a year).

Redemption Payment (7/1/92). The payment required to redeem the bonds on July 1, 1992 ($480,000) was calculated by multiplying the number of bonds issued (500) times the redemption price per bond ($960).

Journal Entry Calculations

At Issuance. Cash ($463,693) was calculated by adding the cash proceeds ($459,443) to the accrued interest ($1250). Bond Payable ($500,000) was calculated by multiplying the number of bonds issued (500) times the face value of each bond ($1000). Interest Payable is equal to accrued interest ($1250), and the discount ($40,557) represents an interest cost waiting to be recognized over the life of the bond. It arises because the bond issuance, which will require a $480,000 cash payment at maturity, generated only $459,443 at issuance.

Interest Payments and Discount Amortization. The calculation of the cash interest payment is described above. The effective interest rate (8 percent) was computed by finding the rate that produced a present value equal to the price ($459,443). The amount of interest expense recognized each period was calculated by multiplying half the effective interest rate (4 percent) times the net book value of the bond payable ($500,000 − unamortized discount) at the beginning of the period.[16] The credit to the discount represents the additional interest expense recognized each period because the bonds were issued at a discount.

Redemption (7/1/92). The calculation of the cash payment at redemption ($480,000) was described earlier. The balance-sheet value of the bonds at the time of the redemption (Bond Payable: $500,000, Discount: $30,013) is removed from the books. The Loss on Redemption ($10,013) represents the difference between the cash paid to redeem the bonds and the balance-sheet value of the bonds as of July 1, 1992.

Discount Balance and Balance-Sheet Value of Bonds Payable

The ending discount balance each period was calculated by subtracting the amount of the discount amortized during the period from the balance at the beginning of the period. The balance-sheet value of the bonds payable at the end of each period was calculated by subtracting the unamortized discount from the face value of the bond issuance ($500,000).

SUMMARY OF LEARNING OBJECTIVES

1 Define long-term notes payable, bonds payable, and leasehold obligations, and explain how these instruments are used by companies as important sources of financing.

Long-term liabilities include notes payable, bonds payable, and leasehold obligations. They represent obligations that require the disbursement of assets (usually cash) at a future time beyond the period that defines current assets. Notes payable refer to obligations evidenced by formal notes. They normally involve direct borrowings from financial institutions or an arrangement to finance the purchase of assets. Bonds payable are notes issued for cash to a large number of creditors,

---

16. On June 30, 1991, the amount of interest expense computed ($18,378) is reduced by the interest payable ($1250), to give $17,128. This adjustment is made because the bonds were only held for 5 1/2 months.

called *bondholders*. Leasehold obligations refer to future cash payments (i.e., rent) that are required for the use or occupation of property during a specified period of time.

Long-term notes, bonds and leases are common and major sources of capital for companies throughout the world. Funds used to acquire other companies, purchase machinery and equipment, finance plant expansion, pay off debts, repurchase outstanding stock, and support operations are often generated by issuing long-term notes, bonds, or entering into lease agreements.

2 Identify the important economic consequences associated with reporting long-term liabilities on the balance sheet.

Investors and creditors commonly use financial ratios involving liabilities to assess earning power and solvency. Such ratios are used to determine credit ratings, which directly affect a company's ability to borrow funds as well as the interest rates it pays on these funds. The methods used to account for long-term liabilities affect these ratios and thereby affect investor and creditor assessments of earning power, solvency, and credit ratings.

Another important economic consequence associated with long-term liabilities results from their underlying contracts (or covenants). To ensure that companies meet their interest and principal payments, creditors often impose restrictions, which are written directly in the debt contracts, on the activities of managers. The terms of these covenants, which are expressed in terms of financial accounting ratios, are important to managers, creditors and investors because they can significantly limit management's operating activities as well as future dividends. Violating such covenants can require the immediate payment of the principal on the debt, which in some cases can be financially disastrous.

These economic consequences give managers incentives not to disclose debt on the balance sheet. A common practice is to structure leasing arrangements so that they can be accounted for as operating leases, which avoids having to recognize a leasehold liability and additional depreciation expense. In certain cases, however, management may wish to accelerate the recognition of liabilities and related losses. Companies experiencing exceptionally poor performance may wish to "take a bath," while companies experiencing exceptionally good performance may wish to smooth net income over time.

3 Differentiate the stated interest rate from the effective interest rate, and explain how differences between these rates can lead to recognizing discounts and premiums on notes and bonds payable.

The stated interest rate is the annual interest rate stated directly in the loan contract. The stated interest rate times the *principal,* the amount paid when the obligation matures, determines the annual interest payments. The effective interest rate is the actual interest rate paid by the borrower. It may or may not equal the stated interest rate. The effective rate is determined by finding the discount rate that results in a present value equal to the amount originally borrowed.

The relationship among the proceeds generated at issuance of an obligation, the effective interest rate, and the stated interest rate is summarized as follows:

1. When the proceeds from an obligation (note or bond) are equal to its face value, the obligation is issued at par, and the effective rate is equal to the stated rate.

2. When the proceeds from an obligation exceed its face value, the obligation is issued at a premium, and the effective rate is less than the stated rate.

3. When the proceeds from an obligation are less than its face value, the obligation is issued at a discount, and the effective rate is greater than the stated rate.

4   Describe the basic rules of the effective-interest method.

The effective-interest method consists of the following two general rules.

1. The balance-sheet value of a long-term liability is determined by the present value of the liability's future cash outflows, discounted at the effective interest rate at the time of issuance. The effective interest rate is assumed to remain constant over the life of the obligation.

2. The interest expense recognized during each period of the liability's life is equal to the effective interest rate multiplied by the balance-sheet value of the liability as of the beginning of that period. The balance-sheet value of the liability approaches the maturity value over the life of the obligation.

5   Explain the methods used to account for long-term notes payable, especially in cases where the effective interest rate is greater than the stated interest rate.

The effective-interest method is used to account for long-term notes payable. At issuance, Cash is debited in the amount of the proceeds, Note Payable is credited in the amount of the principal, and if the effective rate is greater than the stated rate, a Discount account is debited in the amount of the difference. Periodic interest expense is calculated by multiplying the effective interest rate times the balance-sheet value (principal less unamortized discount) of the note at the beginning of the period. At the same time, the discount is amortized. When the principal is paid at the maturity date, Cash is credited in the amount of the principal, and the note payable is removed from the balance sheet. Any discount should be completely amortized by the maturity date.

6   Identify and define the essential terms associated with bonds, and explain the methods used to account for bond issuances, recognizing interest expense over the life of a bond, and bond redemptions.

The life of a bond is the time period extending from the date of its issuance to the maturity date. At the maturity date, the face value is paid to the bondholders. The interest payment, which is paid to the bondholders on each semiannual interest payment date, is computed by multiplying the annual interest rate stated on the bond by the face value of the issuance. This amount is then divided by 2, because the stated rate is an annual rate, and the interest payments are made every six months. The proceeds of a bond issuance equal the price paid by the purchasers times the number of bonds issued. This amount is usually net of the issuance costs incurred by the issuing company. Restrictive covenants are imposed by bondholders to protect their interests and may restrict management in a number of significant ways. Security provisions also protect the interests of bondholders by ensuring that assets are pledged in case of default. Call provisions grant to the issuing company the right to retire outstanding bonds after a designated date for a specified price.

The effective-interest method is used to account for bonds. At issuance, Cash is debited in the amount of the proceeds, Bond Payable is credited in the amount of the face value, and a Discount or Premium is recognized if the effective rate differs from the stated rate. Interest expense is recognized periodically by multiplying the effective interest rate times the net book value of the bond payable at the beginning of the period. Cash is credited in the amount of the interest payment, and the premium or discount is then amortized. At redemption prior to maturity, amortization of any discount or premium is updated, and an entry is recorded to reflect the redemption. This entry credits Cash for the redemption price, removes the bonds payable and any unamortized premium or discount from the books, and recognizes a gain or loss on the redemption. When bonds are redeemed at maturity, Cash is credited for the face value, and the bond payable is removed from the balance sheet. Any discount or premium will have been completely amortized by the maturity date.

7   Differentiate operating leases from capital leases, and explain the methods used to account for capital leases.

In an operating lease arrangement, an individual or entity (lessor), who owns land, buildings, equipment or other property, transfers the right to use this property to another individual or entity (lessee) in exchange for periodic cash payments over a specified period of time. The terms of the lease are defined by contract, and over the period of the lease the owner is responsible for the property's normal maintenance and upkeep. The lessee assumes none of the risks of ownership, and at the end of the lease, the rights to use the property revert to the owner. Capitalized leases are lease agreements that are actually installment purchases, where the risks and benefits of ownership are transferred from the lessor to the lessee.

The effective-interest method is used to account for capital lease liabilities. When the lease agreement is initiated, the leased asset is debited, and the lease obligation is credited in the amount of the present value of the future cash flows specified in the lease, discounted at the effective interest rate at that time. The asset is depreciated separately, and interest expense on the lease obligation is computed periodically by multiplying the effective interest rate by the balance-sheet value of the obligation at the beginning of the period. Cash is credited in the amount of the periodic lease payment, and the lease liability is amortized in the amount of the difference between the interest expense and the cash payment. Under this method, the lease liability is completely amortized over the life of the lease.

A P P E N D I X   1 1 A

The Determination of Bond Prices

The chapter states that bond prices are determined by the dollar amount potential bondholders are willing to pay for them. That is, what will investors pay for the right to receive the semiannual interest payments and a cash payment in the amount of the face value at maturity? This appendix identifies and discusses factors considered by debt investors when deciding whether to purchase bonds. These factors have a direct bearing on bond prices.

Suppose, for example, that on June 9, 1988, you were reading *The Wall Street Journal,* looking to purchase a bond. You note that on that day Sears, Roebuck & Company lists bonds with the following terms:

Face value	$1000
Time to maturity	18 years
Stated annual interest rate (paid every 6 months)	8%
Current price	85 1/4, or $853

The decision to buy the bond involves three steps: (1) determine the effective rate of return, (2) determine your required rate of return, and (3) compare the effective rate to the required rate.

DETERMINE THE EFFECTIVE (ACTUAL) RATE OF RETURN

The effective rate of return is that rate which, when used to discount the bond's future cash flows (interest and principal payments), results in a present value that is equal to the price. In this case the effective rate of return would be calculated in the following way.

$PV =$ PV of interest payments   +   PV of face value payment
$853 = \$40$ (*PV* annuity: $n = 36, i = ?$) + $1000 (*PV* single sum: $n = 36, i = ?$)
At $i =$ approximately 10%, $PV = \$853$

Once you have determined that the effective annual rate of return on the bond is approximately 10 percent, you must decide whether or not 10 percent is a large enough return to satisfy you. In other words, what is your required annual rate of return on Sears, Roebuck bonds? Is it greater than or less than 10 percent? If it is greater than 10 percent you will not purchase the bond. If it is less than or equal to 10 percent, you will purchase the bond.

DETERMINE THE REQUIRED RATE OF RETURN

Your required rate of return is determined by adding the return you could receive from investing your money in a risk-free security (i.e., the risk-free return) to the risk premium you would attach to Sears, Roebuck bonds. This expression follows.

Required rate of return = Risk-free return + Risk premium

Determine the Risk-Free Return

The **risk-free return** is the annual return you could receive by investing in a risk-less security. *Riskless securities* are so-called because there is virtually no doubt that the interest and principal payments will be honored. They are often backed by the federal government. The bank interest rate on savings accounts probably represents the lowest estimate of the risk-free return. The annual return on **certificates of deposit,** where a given amount of money is lent to a financial institution for a specified period of time, represents another, perhaps more relevant, example. The annual returns on **treasury notes,** which can be purchased from the federal government and mature up to six months from the date of issue, provide another approximation of the risk-free rate of return.

Keep in mind that the actual risk-free rate can only be approximated and that it fluctuates from day to day based on such factors as changes in the **prime interest rate** (the interest rate charged by banks to their preferred customers), changes in the **discount rate** (the lending rate charged to banks by the Federal Reserve Board), and the inflation rate expected in the future. On June 9, 1988, when you were deciding whether or not to purchase the Sears bonds, a reasonable approximation of the riskless rate was 7 percent.

Determine the Risk Premium

The **risk premium** is expressed as a percentage and reflects the probability that Sears will default on the periodic interest payments or the face value payment at maturity. If this probability is high, these bonds would be classified as a high-risk investment, and the risk premium would be relatively large, say 5–10 percent. If, on the other hand, the probability of default is low, the risk premium would be considerably less, say 1–3 percent.

The risk premium is associated specifically with the company issuing the bonds. It is determined by a number of factors, including the credit rating of the company and the bond issuance, the financial statements of the company, future movements in the economy and how these movements may affect the operations of the company, and the contract underlying the bond issuance. For example, restrictions on such factors as operations, the addition of future debt, and future dividend payments, as well as provisions for collateral and call privileges can affect the risk premium.

Assume that you have assessed the factors described above and have determined that the risk premium associated with the Sears bonds is 2 percent.

COMPARE THE EFFECTIVE RATE TO THE REQUIRED RATE

The effective rate of return on the Sears bond is 10 percent. You have determined that your required rate of return is 9 percent (7 percent risk-free rate + 2 percent risk premium). Since the effective rate exceeds your required rate, you will purchase the bond. The bond is selling for $853 and, in fact, you would be willing to pay $920 for the bond, which is the present value of the bond's future cash payments discounted at 9 percent, your required rate. However, had your required rate of return been greater than 10 percent, either due to a higher risk-free rate or a higher risk premium, you would not have purchased the bonds, and would not do so until the price decreased considerably.

FACTORS DETERMINING BOND PRICES

Bond prices, therefore, are determined by a market of investors, each assessing the general risk-free rate as well as the risk premium associated specifically with the issuing company. Any factor affecting either of these two items affects bond prices. Specifically, factors that decrease either the risk-free rate or the risk premium tend to increase bond prices. Conversely, factors that increase either one will tend to decrease bond prices. Several examples follow.

In Spring of 1987, *The Wall Street Journal* reported that "Federal Reserve Board chairman, Alan Greenspan, confirmed that the Fed eased its grip on credit, allowing interest rates to fall." This action reduced the risk-free rate; accordingly, bond prices should have risen. Indeed, the same article notes that Greenspan's comments spurred a rally in bond prices.

In Spring of 1986, the *New York Times* reported that Merrill Lynch and Company "lost $250 million in a given month because bonds that it owned plummeted in value when interest rates surged." The increase in general interest rates increased the risk-free rate of interest and thus decreased the prices of the bonds held by Merrill Lynch.

The inverse relationship between the risk premium and bond prices illustrates clearly why companies are so interested in their credit ratings. A decrease in a company's credit rating ordinarily leads to an increase in the market's assessment of the company's risk premium and, accordingly, a decrease in the value of the company's debt. For example, on June 10, 1988, Standard & Poor's Corporation, a credit-rating agency, downgraded $310 million of long-term debt issued by American Stores, a holding company based in Salt Lake City. Standard & Poor's justified the downgrade by claiming that "financial risk will increase sharply" as a result of American's recent $2.5 billion acquisition of Lucky Stores, Inc. The value of American's debt decreased when Standards & Poors made this announcement.[17]

SUMMARY OF LEARNING OBJECTIVE

8   Identify the important factors that affect bond prices.

Bond prices are determined by what potential bondholders are willing to pay for the cash flows associated with the bond. The decision to buy a bond involves three steps: (1) determine the effective rate of return provided by the bond, (2) determine your required rate of return, and (3) compare the effective rate to the required rate. If the effective rate is greater than the required rate, purchase the bond. If the effective rate is less than the required rate, do not purchase the bond.

The effective rate of return is the rate that yields a present value that is equal to the price when used to discount the bond's future cash flows. The required rate of return is determined by adding the return you could receive from investing your money in a risk-free security to the risk premium you would attach to the issuing company.

The risk-free return is that annual return that could be received by investing in a riskless security. It is influenced by the discount rate set by the Federal Reserve Board, the prime rate of interest, and expectations about future inflation. The risk premium reflects the probability that the issuing company will default on the periodic interest payments or the face value payment at maturity. The risk premium is determined by such factors as the credit rating and financial statements of the company, future movements in the economy and their effect on the operations of the company, and the contract underlying the bond issuance.

---

17. *The Wall Street Journal,* 10 June 1988.

KEY TERMS

Amortization schedule (p. 524)	Maturity date (p. 511)
Bonds payable (p. 504)	Non-interest-bearing debt (p. 508)
Call provision (p. 518)	Notes payable (p. 504)
Capital lease (p. 531)	Operating lease (p. 531)
Certificate of deposit (p. 541)	Premium on bonds payable (p. 524)
Collateral (p. 511)	Prime interest rate (p. 542)
Covenant (p. 518)	Principal (p. 511)
Debenture (p. 518)	Proceeds (p. 516)
Discount on note (bond) payable (pp. 512, 522)	Redeem (redemption) (p. 529)
	Risk-free return (p. 541)
Discount rate (p. 542)	Risk premium (p. 542)
Effective-interest method (p. 510)	Secured note (bond) (p. 511)
Effective interest rate (p. 508)	Smooth income (p. 507)
Interest payment (p. 516)	Stated interest rate (p. 508)
Lease (p. 530)	"Take a bath" (p. 507)
Leasehold obligation (liability) (p. 504)	Treasury notes (p. 541)
Life (p. 516)	Unsecured notes (bonds) (pp. 511, 518)

QUESTIONS FOR DISCUSSION AND REVIEW

1. Define long-term notes payable, bonds payable, and leasehold obligations, and explain to what extent companies use such instruments to finance operations. What kinds of projects are long-term liabilities usually used to finance?

2. Explain how a debt covenant can have an important economic consequence on a company's financial condition.

3. Why might management wish to avoid reporting debt on the balance sheet?

4. Identify circumstances in which management might wish to accelerate the recognition of debt and related losses on the financial statements.

5. Why are long-term liabilities carried on the balance sheet at an estimate of present value, while long-lived assets are not?

6. What is the stated interest rate, and how does it differ from the effective interest rate? If you were a manager deciding to borrow money, explain how both the stated rate and the effective rate would affect your decision.

7. Briefly explain how the effective interest rate on an obligation is computed. Why is it more difficult to compute the effective interest rate for a note with a stated interest rate greater than zero than for a non-interest-bearing note?

8. State the two basic rules of the effective-interest method. Give several examples using the effective-interest method to value balance sheet liabilities.

9. What method is used to account for long-term notes payable? If the proceeds from a long-term note are less than the principal, what is the relationship between the stated rate of interest and the effective rate?

10. Why might a company decide to borrow money by issuing a note with a stated interest rate of zero?

11. Explain the process used to amortize a discount on a long-term note payable.

12. When is the straight-line method an acceptable way to amortize discounts and premiums associated with long-term notes and bonds payable? Why is that method not recommended from a conceptual standpoint?

13. Why is issuing bonds such a popular way to raise large amounts of capital?

14. Figure 11–5 identifies nine terms that are important for an understanding of bond contracts. List and briefly explain each of them.

15. What is a debenture? Why might IBM be able to issue debentures frequently, while Jones Airlines, Inc., a less dependable business, might not?

16. Why might a company choose to have a call provision written into a bond contract? In general, how would adding such a provision tend to affect the issue price of the bonds?

17. When a bond is issued at a discount, what is the relationship between the stated interest rate and the effective interest rate? When a bond is issued at a premium, what is the relationship between the stated rate and the effective rate?

18. What method is used to account for bond liabilities? How is the interest expense associated with the bond issuance determined each period? Why does the interest expense normally differ from the cash interest payment?

19. When bonds are issued between interest payment dates, how is the cash collected from the bond issuance computed?

20. Does the effective-interest method ensure that bond liabilities are carried on the balance sheet at present value in an economic sense? Why or why not?

21. Why is a gain or loss usually recognized when a company redeems outstanding bonds prior to maturity?

22. Why is leasing such a popular form of financing for many companies? Distinguish a capital lease from an operating lease.

23. Explain the methods used to account for capital leases. How is the lease obligation amortized over the life of the lease?

24. What is off-balance-sheet financing? Why might a company structure a lease so that it is considered an operating lease instead of a capital lease?

25. (*Appendix 11A*) Describe the three steps involved when deciding whether to purchase a bond. Define the required rate of return, the risk-free return, and the risk premium, and explain how they are related.

26. (*Appendix 11A*) Explain how a reduction in a company's credit rating would affect the prices at which the company could issue bonds.

27. (*Appendix 11A*) If you were holding a portfolio of bonds, would you want future interest rates to increase or decrease? Why?

EXERCISES

E11–1

(*Disclosing debt and debt covenants*) The balance sheet as of December 31, 1990, for Roseton Enterprises follows.

Assets		Liabilities and Stockholders' Equity	
Current assets	$200,000	Current liabilities	$200,000
Noncurrent assets	700,000	Long-term liabilities	300,000
		Stockholders' equity	400,000
		Total liabilities and	
Total assets	$900,000	stockholders' equity	$900,000

During 1990 Roseton entered into a loan agreement that required the company to maintain a debt/equity ratio of less than 2:1.

Required:

a. How much additional debt can Roseton take on before it violates the terms of the loan agreement?

b. Assume that during 1991 Roseton had revenues of $950,000 and expenses of $800,000. Assume that all revenues and expenses were in cash. How much additional debt can Roseton take on before it violates the terms of the loan agreement?

c. Assume again that during 1991 Roseton has cash revenues of $950,000 and cash expenses of $800,000. If Roseton pays a cash dividend of $100,000, how much additional debt can it take on before violating the terms of the loan agreement? If Roseton declares, but does not pay, the dividend during 1991, does it make a difference in the amount of additional debt the company can take on?

E11-2   *(Annual or semiannual interest payments?)*   Hathaway Manufacturing issued long-term debt on January 1, 1990. The debt has a face value of $100,000 and an annual stated interest rate of 10 percent. The debt matures on January 1, 1995.

Required:

a. Assume that the debt agreement requires Hathaway Manufacturing to make annual interest payments every January 1. Set up a time line that indicates the timing and magnitude of the future cash outflows for this long-term debt.

b. Assume that the debt agreement requires Hathaway Manufacturing to make semiannual interest payments every July 1 and January 1. Set up a time line that indicates the timing and magnitude of the future cash outflows for this long-term debt.

c. Under the conditions of (a) and (b), compute the present value of these two debt agreements if the effective rate of interest is equal to the stated rate of interest.

E11-3   *(The relationships among the stated rate, effective rate, and issuance price of a liability)*   The stated and effective interest rates for several notes and bonds follow. Indicate whether each note/bond would be issued at a discount, par value, or a premium.

Note/Bond	Stated Interest Rate	Effective Interest Rate
1	10%	10%
2	12	8
3	9	11
4	10.5	10

E11-4   *(Computing the proceeds from various notes)*   Compute the proceeds from the following notes payable. Interest payments are made annually.

Proceeds	Stated Interest Rate	Effective Interest Rate	Face Value	Life
?	0%	10%	$ 1,000	2 years
?	0	8	5,000	5 years
?	5	12	8,000	5 years
?	8	8	3,000	8 years
?	10	6	10,000	10 years

E11-5   *(Notes issued at a discount and the movement of interest expense)*   AAA Rentals borrowed $5674 on a five-year, non-interest-bearing note with a face value of $10,000. The effective interest rate on the note was 12%.

Required:

a. Prepare the journal entry to record the initial borrowing.

b. How much interest expense should AAA recognize on the note payable during the first year?

c. What is the balance-sheet value of the note at the end of the first year?

d. Will the interest expense recognized by AAA in the second year be greater than, equal to, or less than the interest expense recognized in the first year? Why?

e. Will the interest expense recognized in the third year be greater than, equal to, or less than the interest expense recognized in the second year?

E11-6

(Accounting for notes payable with various stated interest rates)   Candleton signed a two-year note payable with a face value of $5000 and an effective interest rate of 8 percent. Interest payments on the note are made annually.

Required: Provide the journal entries that would be recorded over the life of the note assuming the following stated interest rates.

a. 8 percent

b. 0 percent

c. 6 percent

E11-7

(Determining the effective interest rate)   On January 1, 1991, Wilmes Floral Supplies borrowed $4826 from Bower Financial Services. Wilmes Floral Supplies gave Bower a $5000 note with a maturity date of December 31, 1992. The note specified an annual stated interest rate of 8 percent.

Required:

a. Compute the present value of the note's future cash flows at the following discount rates.

   (1) 8 percent

   (2) 10 percent

   (3) 12 percent

b. What is the effective interest rate of the note?

c. Determine the effective interest rate on the note if Floral Supplies originally borrowed $5000.

E11-8

(Financing asset purchases with notes payable)   MacFarland Enterprises purchased a building on January 1, 1991, in exchange for a three-year non-interest-bearing note with a face value of $693,000. Independent appraisers valued the building at $550,125.

Required:

a. At what amount should this building be capitalized?

b. Compute the present value of the note's future cash flows using the following discount rates.

   (1) 6 percent

   (2) 8 percent

   (3) 10 percent

c. What is the effective interest rate of this note?

E11-9

(Inferring an effective interest rate from the financial statements)   The following information was extracted from the financial records of Leong Cosmetics.

	1990	1989
Notes payable	$100,000	$100,000
Less: Discount on notes payable	6,000	7,280
Interest expense	$ 8,280	$ 8,100

Required:

a. What is the effective interest rate on the note payable?

b. Prepare the journal entry to record interest expense during 1990.

E11-10 *(Computing bond issuance proceeds and the movement of balance-sheet value and interest expense over the bond's life)*   Three different bond issuances are listed here with interest payments made semiannually.

Bond Issuance	Face Value	Stated Interest Rate	Effective Interest Rate	Life
A	$200,000	8%	8%	20 years
B	$500,000	10	8	20 years
C	$800,000	8	10	15 years

Required:

a. Compute the proceeds of each bond issuance.

b. For each bond issuance, indicate whether the balance-sheet value of the bond liability will increase, decrease, or remain constant over the life of the bond.

c. For each bond issuance, indicate whether the interest expense recognized each period will increase, decrease, or remain constant over the life of the bond.

E11-11 *(Accounting for bonds issued at face value)*   On January 1, 1990, Collins Copy Machine Company issued ten $1000 face-value bonds with a stated annual rate of 12 percent that mature in ten years. Interest is paid semiannually on June 30 and December 31. The bonds had an effective interest rate of 12 percent.

Required:

a. Without computing the present value of the bonds, state whether Collins Company will issue these bonds at par value, at a premium, or at a discount. Explain your answer.

b. Prepare the entry to record the issuance of these bonds on January 1, 1990.

c. Prepare all the entries associated with these bonds during 1990 (excluding the entry to record the issuance).

d. Compute the balance-sheet value of the bond liability as of December 31, 1990.

e. Compute the present value of the bond's remaining cash flows as of December 31, 1990, using the 12 percent effective interest rate.

E11-12 *(Accounting for bonds issued at a discount)*   Tingham Village issued 1500 five-year bonds on July 2, 1990. The interest payments are due semiannually (January 1 and July 1) at an annual rate of 8 percent. The effective interest rate on the bonds is 10 percent. The face value of each bond is $1,000.

Required:

a. Prepare the journal entry that would be recorded on July 1, 1990, when the bonds are issued.

b. Prepare the journal entry that would be recorded on December 31, 1990.

c. Compute the balance-sheet value of the bond liability as of December 31, 1990.

d. Compute the present value of the bond's *remaining* cash flows as of December 31, 1990, using an effective interest rate of 10 percent.

E11-13 *(Changing market interest rates and economic gains and losses)*   Treadway Company issued bonds with a face value of $10,000 on January 1, 1988. The bonds were due to mature in five years and had a stated annual interest rate of 10 percent. The bonds were issued at face value. Interest is paid semiannually.

Required:

a. As of December 31, 1988, market interest rates had decreased by 2 percent, and the market price of Treadway bonds reflected the entire change. Compute the present value of Treadway's bond liability as of that date using the new effective interest rate (8 percent), and determine the economic gain or loss experienced by the company.

b. Assume instead that as of December 31, 1988, market interest rates had increased by 2 percent, and the market price of Treadway's bonds reflected the entire change. Compute the present value of Treadway's bond liability as of that date, using the new effective interest rate (12 percent), and determine the economic gain or loss experienced by the company.

c. What is the intuition underlying such gains and losses, and why are they not reflected on the financial statements?

E11–14   *(Issuing bonds between interest-payment dates)*   Johnson and Curry issued bonds with a face value of $500,000 on January 31, 1990. The bonds were issued at par, and the interest rate stated on the bonds was 12 percent, to be paid semiannually on January 1 and July 1.

Required:

a. Prepare the journal entry to record the bond issuance on January 31, 1990.

b. Prepare the journal entry to record the first interest payment on July 1, 1990.

E11–15   *(Redeeming bonds not originally issued at par)*   On September 10, 1986, Lacey Paper Products issued bonds with a face value of $500,000 for a price of 96. During 1991 Lacey exercised a call provision and redeemed the bonds for 101. At the time of the redemption, the bonds had a balance-sheet value of $488,000.

Required:

a. Prepare the journal entry to record the redemption.

b. Assume that the bonds were issued in 1986 for 102, and at the time of redemption they had a balance-sheet value of $502,000. Prepare the journal entry to record the bond redemption.

E11–16   *(Updating amortization and retiring a bond issuance)*   Marker Musical Products issued bonds with a face value of $100,000 and an annual stated interest rate of 8 percent on January 1, 1988. The effective interest rate on the bonds was 10 percent. Interest is paid semiannually on July 1 and January 1. As of December 31, 1990, the company reported the following dollar amounts for these bonds:

Bonds payable	$100,000
Less: Discount on bonds payable	3,546
	$ 96,454

Marker Musical Products retired the bonds on July 2, 1991, by repurchasing them for $98,250 in cash.

Required:

a. Provide the journal entry recorded on July 1, 1991, when the interest payment is made.

b. Prepare the journal entry to record the retirement of the bonds.

E11–17   *(Accounting for leases and the financial statements)*   Tradeall, Inc. leases automobiles for its salesforce. On January 1, 1990, the company leased 100 automobiles and agreed to make lease payments of $3500 per automobile each year. The lease agreement expires on December 31, 1994, at which time the automobiles can be purchased by Tradeall for a nominal price. Assume an effective rate of 8 percent.

Required:

a. Compute the annual rental expense if the lease is treated as an operating lease.

b. Prepare the journal entry on January 1, 1990, if the lease is treated as a capital lease.

c. Assume that the automobiles are depreciated over a five-year life, using the straight-line method. Compute the total rental expense (interest and depreciation) associated with the lease during the first year, if the lease is treated as a capital lease.

d. Which of the two methods of treatment (operating or capital) would give rise to a higher net income in the first year? Which method would give rise to a lower debt/equity ratio?

e. Define off-balance-sheet financing, and explain how leases can be arranged to practice it.

E11–18   *(Financing asset purchases)*   Fredericksen Motors plans to acquire a building and can either borrow cash from a bank to finance the purchase or lease the building from the current owner. The sales price of the building is $74,694. If the company wishes to finance the purchase with a bank loan, it must sign a twenty-year note with a face value of $74,694 and a stated interest rate of 12 percent. If the company leases the building, it must make an annual lease payment of a constant-dollar amount for twenty years, at which time the building can be purchased for a nominal fee.

Required:

a. Compute the annual lease payment that would make the two alternatives equivalent. Ignore the nominal purchase fee at the end of year twenty.

b. Describe how the timing of the cash flows would differ between the two alternatives.

c. Provide the journal entries that would be recorded when the building is acquired if the company (1) finances the purchase with a bank loan, (2) leases the building and accounts for it as a capital lease, or (3) leases the building and accounts for it as an operating lease.

d. If the company leases the building and accounts for it as a capital lease, compute the balance-sheet value of the lease liability after the second lease payment.

e. Compute the present value of the remaining lease payments as of the end of the second year.

E11–19   *(Inferring the effective rate of interest)*   Compute the effective rate of interest on the following long-term debts. Interest payments on the notes are made annually and interest payments on the bonds are made semiannually.

Debt	Proceeds	Face Value	Life	Stated Interest Rate
Note	$10,000	$ 10,000	5 years	8%
Note*	37,594	100,000	7 years	0
Note	922	1,000	5 years	7
Bond	11,635	10,000	10 years	6
Bond	45,710	50,000	20 years	9

E11–20   *(Appendix 11A: The decision to purchase a bond)*   Acme bonds are selling on the open market at 89.16. The bonds have a stated interest rate of 8 percent and mature in 8 years. Interest payments are made semiannually.

Required:

a. Assume that your required rate of return is 12 percent. Would you buy the bonds? Why or why not?

b. At what required rate of return would you be indifferent to purchasing the bonds?

PROBLEMS

P11-1

(Computing the face value of a note payable)   On December 31, 1989, East Race Kayak Club decides it needs to borrow $20,000 for two years. The Bend Bank currently is charging a 12 percent effective annual interest rate on similar loans.

Required:

a. Assume that the club borrows $20,000 and signs a two-year note with a 12 percent stated annual interest rate. What would be the face amount of the note payable?

b. Assume that the club borrows $20,000 and signs a two-year note with a stated annual interest rate of zero. What would be the face amount of the note payable?

c. Prepare the journal entry to record the note payable, assuming that the club signs

   (1) the note in (a).

   (2) the note in (b).

d. Prepare the entries necessary on December 31, 1991 assuming that the club signs

   (1) the note in (a) (interest payable on December 31).

   (2) the note in (b).

P11-2

(Accounting for bonds with an effective rate greater than the stated rate)   Hartl Enterprises is-sued five $1000 bonds on September 30, 1989, with a stated annual interest rate of 10 percent. These bonds will mature on October 1, 1999, and have an effective rate of 12 per-cent. Interest is paid semiannually on October 1 and April 1. The first interest payment will be made on April 1, 1990.

Required:

a. Without computing the present value of the bonds, will they be issued at par value, at a discount, or at a premium? Explain your answer.

b. Prepare the entry to record the issuance of the bonds on September 30, 1989.

c. Prepare any adjusting journal entries necessary on December 31, 1989.

d. Prepare the entry to record the interest payment on April 1, 1990.

P11-3

(The balance-sheet value of debt and the long-term debt/equity ratio)   The balance sheet as of December 31, 1990, for Connerty Corporation follows.

Assets		Liabilities and Stockholders' Equity	
Current assets	$ 85,000	Current liabilities	$ 70,000
Noncurrent assets	125,000	Long-term liabilities	40,000
		Stockholders' equity	100,000
		Total liabilities and	
Total assets	$210,000	stockholders' equity	$210,000

Required:

a. Compute Connerty Corporation's long-term debt/equity ratio.

b. Assume that Connerty Corporation is considering borrowing money and signing a five-year note with the following terms.

Face value	$40,000
Stated interest rate	0%
Effective interest rate	11%

Compute the proceeds of the note, and compute the company's long-term debt/equity ratio if it decides to borrow the money.

c. Assume that Connerty Corporation is considering issuing bonds that mature on December 31, 2010. The bonds have a face value of $40,000, a stated interest rate of 10 percent, and an effective interest rate of 8 percent. Compute the proceeds from the bond issuance, and compute the company's long-term debt/equity ratio if it issues the bonds. The bonds pay interest semiannually.

P11–4   *(Accounting for notes issued at a discount and at face value)*   Patnon Plastics needed some cash to finance expansion. Patnon issued the following debt to acquire the cash.

(a) A five-year note with a stated interest rate of zero, a face value of $10,000, and an effective interest rate of 12 percent.

(b) A seven-year note with an annual stated rate of 6 percent and a face value of $35,000. Interest is paid annually on December 31. The effective interest rate is 9 percent.

(c) A ten-year note with an annual stated rate of 10 percent and a face value of $50,000. Interest is paid semiannually on June 30 and December 31. The effective interest rate is 10 percent.

All three notes were issued on January 1, 1990.

Required:

a. Compute the proceeds from each of the three notes.

b. Prepare the entries to record the issuance of each note.

c. Prepare the entry to record the interest paid on June 30, 1990, on the ten-year note.

d. Prepare the entries to record the interest paid on December 31, 1990, on the seven-year note and the ten-year note.

e. Prepare the adjusting entry required on December 31, 1990, to recognize accrued interest on the five-year note.

P11–5   *(Issuing notes to finance the purchase of an asset)*   Bauer Sporting Goods purchased a building on January 1, 1988, in exchange for two notes payable. The first note matured in six years, had a stated interest rate of zero, and a face value of $465,000. The second note had a face value of $500,000, a three-year maturity, and a stated annual interest rate of 9 percent. Interest payments on the second note are due at the end of each year. The effective annual interest rate on the notes is 8 percent.

Required:

a. At what amount did Bauer Sporting Goods capitalize this building (i.e., what was the cost of the building)?

b. Prepare the entry to record the acquisition of the building.

c. Prepare the necessary adjusting entries associated with these notes on December 31, 1988.

P11–6   *(The effects of various notes payable on the financial statements)*   The balance sheet as of December 31, 1990, for Cherrington Sons follows.

Assets		Liabilities and Stockholders' Equity	
Current assets	$ 40,000	Current liabilities	$ 30,000
Noncurrent assets	80,000	Long-term liabilities	60,000
		Stockholders' equity	30,000
		Total liabilities and	
Total assets	$120,000	stockholders' equity	$120,000

The company needs capital to finance operations and purchase new equipment. Cherrington is not certain how much money it will need and is considering one of the following three-year notes payable. Each note would mature on January 1, 1994.

(a) Face value = $50,000   Stated interest rate = 0%   Proceeds = $37,566
(b) Face value = $50,000   Stated interest rate = 10%*   Proceeds = $50,000
(c) Face value = $50,000   Stated interest rate = 6%*   Proceeds = $45,027

*Interest paid annually.

Required:

a. Determine the effective interest rate of each note.

b. Compute the amounts that would complete the following table.

	Interest Expense (a)	Interest Expense (b)	Interest Expense (c)
Year 1			
Year 2			
Year 3			

c. Cherrington can earn a 12% return on the borrowed money. Compute the annual income (return − interest expense) generated from each of the three notes.

d. Compute the amounts that would complete the following chart. (*Hint:* Consider the effect of annual income from Part c on stockholders' equity.

	Debt/Equity (a)	Debt/Equity (b)	Debt/Equity (c)
12/31/91			
12/31/92			
12/31/93			

e. Discuss some of the trade-offs involved in choosing among the three notes.

P11–7   *(The difference between cash interest payments and interest expense)*   Earl Rix, president of Rix Driving Range and Health Club, has provided you with the following information:

Balance Sheet	**1990**	**1989**
Notes payable	$800,000	$800,000
Less: Discount on notes payable	55,000	70,000
Income Statement		
Interest expense	$ 95,000	

The stated annual interest rate on the notes is 10 percent, and interest is paid annually on December 31. The $95,000 in interest expense is due solely to these notes.

While reviewing the company's 1990 financial statements, Mr. Rix is having difficulty understanding why the amount charged to interest expense does not equal the amount of cash actually disbursed during 1990 in payment of the interest on these notes.

Required:

a. Assuming that Rix Driving Range and Health Club makes all of its interest payments on time, how much cash was actually disbursed during 1990 for interest payments on these notes?

b. Explain to Mr. Rix why interest expense does not equal the amount of cash disbursed for interest. What does the difference between the cash disbursed and the amount charged as interest expense represent?

c. What was the effective interest rate at the time the notes were issued?

d. Provide the journal entry to record the payment of interest on December 31, 1990.

P11–8   *(The effective-interest method, interest expense, and present value)*   Hartney Enterprises issued ten $1000 bonds on June 30, 1990, with a stated annual interest rate of 18 percent that mature in fifteen years. Interest is paid semiannually on December 31 and June 30. The effective interest rate as of June 30, 1990, the date of issuance, was 20 percent.

Required:

a. Compute the present value of the cash flows associated with these bonds on June 30, 1990, using the following format:

Face value		XX
Present value of cash payment at maturity	XX	
Present value of cash interest payments	+XX	
Less: Total present value		XX
Discount (premium) on bonds		XX

b. Compute the present value of the remaining cash flows associated with these bonds on December 31, 1990. What does the present value on December 31, 1990, represent?

c. What does the difference between the present value of the remaining cash flows associated with these bonds on June 30, 1990 and December 31, 1990, represent? (Hint: The discount factors for the interest and principal payments are 9.36961 and .06304, respectively.)

d. Prepare the entry to record the interest payment on December 31, 1990, using the effective-interest method. Is the amount of Discount on Bonds Payable amortized in this entry the same as the amount found in (c)? Why or why not?

P11-9   *(The effective-interest method and the straight-line method: effects on the financial statements)*
Ross Running Shoes issued five $1000 bonds with a stated annual rate of 10 percent on June 30, 1990. These bonds mature on June 30, 1993. The bonds have an effective interest rate of 8 percent, and interest is paid semiannually on December 31 and June 30.

Required:

a. How much must Ross Running Shoes invest in a bank on June 30, 1990, at an annual rate of 8 percent to meet all the future cash flow requirements of these bonds and have no money left after repaying the principal on June 30, 1993?

b. Prepare the entry to record the interest payment on December 31, 1990. Assume that the company uses the effective-interest method.

c. Prepare the entry to record the interest payment on December 31, 1990. Assume that the company uses the straight-line method to amortize the premium.

d. Which method (effective-interest or straight-line) of amortizing the premium will allow Ross Running Shoes to recognize the higher amount of net income in 1990?

e. Which method (effective-interest or straight-line) of amortizing the premium will allow Ross Running Shoes to recognize the higher amount of net income in 1993?

P11-10   *(Why the effective-interest method is preferred to the straight-line method)*   Consider the three notes payable listed here. Each was issued on January 1, 1990, and matures on December 31, 1992. Interest payments are made annually on December 31.

Note	Face Value	Stated Interest Rate	Effective Interest Rate
A	$1000	8%	10%
B	1000	10	10
C	1000	10	8

Required:

a. Compute the present value of the remaining cash outflows for each note at each date.

Note	1/1/90	12/31/90	12/31/91
A			
B			
C			

b. Compute the balance-sheet value of each note payable at each of the above dates using the effective-interest method.

c. Compute the balance-sheet value of each note payable at each of the above dates using the straight-line method.

d. Why is the effective-interest method preferred to the straight-line method for financial reporting purposes?

P11–11

(Issuing bonds between interest payment dates)   The Malcomb House issued ten-year bonds with a face value of $800,000 on July 31, 1990. The bonds had a 12 percent effective interest rate and a stated rate of 12 percent. The interest payments were to be made semiannually on January 1 and July 1.

Required:

a. Prepare the journal entry to record the bond issuance on July 31, 1990.

b. Prepare the journal entry that would be recorded on December 31, 1990.

c. Prepare the journal entry to record the first interest payment on January 1, 1991.

P11–12

(Redemptions and updating amortization)   Stern & Lewis Pork Ranch reported the following account balances in the December 31, 1989, financial report.

Bonds payable	$500,000
Premium on bonds payable	12,600

The bonds have a stated annual interest rate of 8 percent and an effective interest rate of 6 percent. Interest is paid on June 30 and December 31.

Required:

a. Prepare the entry necessary on January 1, 1990, if the bonds are called at 102.

b. Prepare the entry necessary on January 1, 1990, if the bonds are called at 110.

c. Prepare the entry to record the payment of interest on June 30, 1990, if the bonds are not called on January 1, 1990.

d. Prepare the entry necessary on July 1, 1990, if the bonds are called at 107.

P11–13

(Call provisions and bond market prices)   Ficus Tree Farm issued ten $1000 bonds with a stated annual interest rate of 14 percent on January 1, 1990, that mature on January 1, 1995. Interest is paid semiannually on June 30 and December 31. The bonds were sold at a price that resulted in an effective interest rate of 16 percent. The bonds can be called for 103.5 beginning June 30, 1992.

Required:

a. Prepare the entry on January 1, 1990, to record the issuance of these bonds.

b. Prepare the entry on June 30, 1990, to record the payment of interest.

c. Assume that Ficus wishes to retire the bonds on June 30, 1992. If the bonds are selling on the open market on that date at a price that would result in a return on 12 percent, should Ficus exercise the call provision or simply attempt to buy the bonds at the market price?

d. Is it likely that Ficus would be able to buy back all outstanding bonds on the bond market at market prices?

e. Prepare the entries necessary on June 30, 1992, if Ficus chooses to exercise the call provision.

P11–14

(Tax deductible bond interest and the present value of cash outflows)   Jennings Corporation is contemplating issuing bonds in an effort to raise cash to finance an expansion. Before issuing the debt, the controller of the company wants to prepare an analysis of the cash flows and the interest expense associated with the issuance.

Jennings Corporation is considering issuing one hundred $1000 bonds on June 30, 1990, that mature on June 30, 1994. The bonds will have a stated annual interest rate of 8 percent, and interest is to be paid semiannually on December 31 and June 30. The bonds will have an effective interest rate of 12 percent.

Required:

a. Compute the amounts that would complete the following table with respect to the bond issuance being considered by Jennings.

Date	Interest Expense	Cash Payment	Unamortized Discount	Balance-Sheet Value
6/30/90				
12/31/90				
6/30/91				
12/31/91				
6/30/92				
12/31/92				
6/30/93				
12/31/93				
6/30/94				

b. Find the difference between the total cash inflow from issuing the bonds and the total cash outflows from interest and principal payments.

c. Recognizing that cash interest payments are tax deductible, and assuming a tax rate of 34 percent, recompute the difference you found in (b).

d. Repeat (c), but now consider the time value of money by using the effective rate on these bonds to compute the present value of the net future cash outflows due to interest and principal payments.

P11–15

(Accounting for a capital lease)   Taylor Company acquired some equipment on January 1, 1990, through a leasing agreement that required an annual payment of $15,000. Assume that the lease has a term of five years and that the life of the equipment is also five years. The lease is treated as a capital lease, and the fair market value of the equipment is $59,890.65. Taylor uses the straight-line method to depreciate its fixed assets. The effective annual interest rate on the lease is 8 percent.

Required:

a. Compute the amounts that would complete the table, and provide the related journal entries.

Date	Balance-Sheet Value of Equipment	Leasehold Obligation	Interest Expense	Depreciation Expense	Rent Expense	Total Expense
1/1/90						
12/31/90						
12/31/91						
12/31/92						
12/31/93						
12/31/94						

b. Compute the same amounts if the lease is treated as an operating lease.

P11–16

(Some economic effects of lease accounting)   The balance sheet as of December 31, 1990, for Thompkins Laundry follows.

Assets		Liabilities and Stockholders' Equity	
Current assets	$10,000	Current liabilities	$10,000
Noncurrent assets	60,000	Long-term liabilities	20,000
		Stockholders' equity	40,000
		Total liabilities and	
Total assets	$70,000	stockholders' equity	$70,000

The $20,000 of long-term debt on the balance sheet represents a long-term note that requires Thompkins to maintain a debt/equity ratio of less than 1:1. If the covenant is violated, the company will be required to pay the entire principal of the note immediately.

On January 1, 1991, Thompkins entered into a lease agreement. The agreement provides the company with laundry equipment for five years, for an annual rental fee of $5000.

Required:

a. Compute Thompkins' debt/equity ratio as of January 1, 1991, if the company treats the lease as an operating lease.

b. Compute Thompkins' debt/equity ratio as of January 1, 1991, if the company treats the lease as a capital lease. Assume an effective interest rate of 12 percent.

c. Compare the expenses recognized during 1991 if the lease is treated as operating to the expenses recognized during 1991 if the lease is treated as capital. Assume that the leased equipment has a five-year useful life and is depreciated using the straight-line method.

d. Discuss some of the reasons why Thompkins would want to treat the lease as an operating lease. How might the company arrange the terms of the lease so that it will be considered an operating lease?

P11–17

(Financing asset purchases with notes and inferring the effective rate of interest) Memminger Corporation purchased equipment on January 1, 1990. The terms of the purchase required that the company pay $500 in interest at the end of each year for five years and $10,000 at the end of the fifth year. The fair market value of the equipment on January 1, 1990, was $8802.

Required:

a. Prepare the journal entry that would be recorded on January 1, 1990.

b. Compute the effective interest rate on the note payable.

c. Prepare the journal entry that would be recorded when the first interest payment is made on December 31, 1990.

d. Compute the net book value of the note payable as of December 31, 1990.

P11–18

(Appendix 11A: Determinants of bond market prices) Flowers and Sons bonds are selling on the open market at par value. The bonds have a stated interest rate of 9 percent and mature in five years. You have determined that the riskless rate of return is 7 percent.

Required:

a. What is the maximum risk premium you could attach to these bonds and still be willing to purchase them?

b. Assume that Standard & Poor's, a credit-rating service, lowers the credit rating of Flowers and Sons bonds, and this action causes you to increase your risk premium from 2 percent to 5 percent. What price would you be willing to pay for the bonds?

c. (Independent of [b].) Assume that you read in *The Wall Street Journal* that the prime rate has been cut by 1 percent. All other factors being equal, would this news tend to increase or decrease the market price of Flowers and Sons bonds? Why? Assuming that reducing the prime rate by 1 percent reflects a reduction in the riskless rate of 1 percent, estimate the magnitude of such an effect.

CASES

C11-1   *(Repurchasing outstanding debt)*   Sun Company, an oil-refining concern, purchased all of its outstanding 8 1/2 percent (stated rate) debentures due November 15, 2000 as part of a re-structuring plan. The balance-sheet value of each outstanding debenture at the time of the repurchase was $875,000. The company paid $957.50 for each $1000 face value bond, plus accrued interest from May 15, the most recent interest payment date. The settlement date, when the bondholders received their cash, was August 2.

Required:

a. What is a debenture? Would such bonds tend to be issued for higher or lower prices than secured bonds? Why?
b. Briefly discuss why a company would repurchase its outstanding debt.
c. Explain how this repurchase would affect (increase, decrease, or no effect) the components of the accounting equation: assets, liabilities, stockholders' equity. Would a gain or loss be recognized on the transaction?
d. How much cash was paid for each bond on August 2? Be sure to include accrued interest.

C11-2   *(Accounting for a bond issuance)*   BP America, Inc., the U.S. subsidiary of the British Petroleum Company issued $200,000,000 bonds with a stated rate of 10 percent due in 2018. Interest payment dates are July 1 and January 1. The bonds were issued on July 1, 1988, at a price of 99.325.

Required:

a. By comparing the issue price to the par value of the bonds, determine whether the bonds were issued at a discount or at a premium.
b. Provide the journal entry to record the issuance of the bonds on July 1, 1988.
c. Determine the effective interest rate on the bonds. Round to the nearest whole number.
d. Provide the journal entry to record the first interest payment on January 1, 1989.
e. Assume that by July 1, 1989, the market rate of interest had increased by 2 percent, all of which was reflected in the price of the bond. Compute the price of the bonds, after the July 1 interest payment, and compare it to the balance-sheet value. Why are these two numbers different?
f. Provide the entry to record a redemption, assuming that BP America redeems the bonds on July 1, 1989, for the market price. Assume that the interest payment has already been made.
g. Provide an intuitive explanation of the gain or loss recognized on the redemption. Would this gain or loss have been recorded if BP America had not redeemed the bonds? Why or why not?

C11-3   *(Bonds with a stated interest rate of zero)*   In 1981, J. C. Penney Company issued bonds with a face value of $200 million and a stated interest rate of zero, which matured in 1989, for 33.24. That same year Martin Marietta, Northwest Industries, and Alcoa also issued bonds with stated interest rates of zero.

Required:

a. Why would an investor purchase a bond with a stated interest rate of zero?

b. Compute the effective interest rate on the bond issuance.

c. In terms of its cash flows, explain why a company might wish to issue bonds with a stated interest rate of zero.

d. At what price would the bonds have been issued if the stated interest rate had been 5 percent? 18 percent?

C11-4   *(Buy or lease: financial statement effects)* Assume that United Airlines is planning to purchase a jet passenger plane, with a price of $45,636,480, from The Boeing Company. United is considering structuring the transaction in one of two ways. In Alternative 1, United would borrow the necessary cash from Federal City Bank and sign a note requiring payments of $6 million at the end of each year for fifteen years. The proceeds from the loan would then be used to purchase the airplane. In Alternative 2, United would lease the airplane from Boeing and make annual lease payments of $6 million for fifteen years, at which time it could purchase the airplane from Boeing for a nominal sum. United depreciates its aircraft over a useful life of fifteen years using the straight-line method.

Required:

a. Determine the effective interest rate on the note and the lease arrangement.

b. Provide the journal entries that would be recorded under Alternative 1 to reflect the borrowing and the purchase of the airplane.

c. Provide the journal entry that would be recorded under Alternative 2 when the lease agreement is signed, if the lease is treated as a capital lease.

d. Compare the effects on the financial statements caused by (b) and (c).

e. Provide the journal entry that would be recorded under Alternative 2 when the lease agreement is signed, if the lease is treated as an operating lease.

f. Which of the two alternatives would represent an example of off-balance-sheet financing? Explain why United might want to structure the transaction in this way.

C11-5   *(Appendix 11A: Refinancing outstanding debt)* Standard & Poor's Corporation, a bond-rating service, assigned a *single-B* rating to bonds issued by MGM/UA Communications Company. This rating was higher than the ratings assigned to previous bond issuances of the company. Standard & Poor's decision to upgrade the rating was based on how MGM/UA planned to use the funds, which involved the repayment of outstanding bank loans with high rates of interest.

Required:

a. Explain the relationship between the Standard & Poor's rating and the price at which the bonds can be issued. That is, if the rating is upgraded or downgraded, what happens to the price? Answer the question in terms of the risk premium attached by investors and creditors to MGM/UA.

b. Why would a company issue bonds and use the proceeds to pay off a loan? Assuming that the bonds are at face value, which is equal to the principal amount of the outstanding bank loans, how would these two transactions affect the company's financial statements?

c. Assume that MGM/UA planned to use the funds to finance the purchase of additional plant assets. How would these two transactions (the bond issuance and the purchase of assets) affect the financial statements, and do you suppose that Standard & Poors would have upgraded its rating? Why or why not?

CHAPTER 12

Stockholders' Equity

Learning Objectives

1 Identify the three forms of financing, and describe the relative importance of each to major U.S. corporations.

2 Distinguish debt from equity, and explain why such a distinction is important to investors and creditors, managers, and accountants.

3 Explain the economic consequences associated with the methods used to account for stockholders' equity.

4 Describe the basic characteristics of the corporate form of organization.

5 Describe the rights associated with preferred and common stock and the methods used to account for stock issuances.

6 Distinguish among the market value, book value, par value, and stated value of a share of common stock.

7 Define treasury stock, explain why corporations acquire it, and summarize the methods used to account for it.

8 Define cash and property dividends, and describe some of the dividend strategies followed by corporations.

9 Distinguish among an ordinary stock dividend, a stock split in the form of a dividend, and a stock split. Summarize the methods used to account for each and briefly explain why corporations declare stock splits and stock dividends.

10 Explain how retained earnings are appropriated and why corporations follow such a practice.

11 (Appendix 12A) List the basic features of a partnership and briefly describe the methods used to account for its formation, the allocation of partnership profits, and partner withdrawals.

≣ Companies can generate assets from three different sources: (1) borrowings, (2) issuing equity securities, and (3) retaining funds generated through profitable operations. Each of these sources is represented on the right side of the basic accounting equation (balance sheet), which is depicted in Figure 12–1.

Chapters 10 and 11 are devoted to current and long-term liabilities, which represent the first of the three financing sources illustrated in Figure 12–1. This chapter is devoted to stockholders' equity, which comprises the other two financing sources: (2) contributed capital and (3) earned capital. **Contributed capital,** which reflects contributions from a company's owners, consists of three components: preferred stock, common stock, and additional paid-in capital. The major component of **earned capital** is retained earnings, a measure of the assets that have been generated through a company's profitable operations and not paid to the owners in the form of dividends. The total dollar amount of stockholders' equity is also referred to as a company's **net assets, book value,** or **net worth.**

Contributed and earned capital are important financing sources for many major U.S. companies. Funds used to acquire other companies, purchase machinery and equipment, finance plant expansion, pay off debts, and support operations are often generated by issuing preferred stock, issuing common stock, and retaining funds provided by profitable operations. In 1987, for example, Chrysler Corporation issued 14.9 million shares of common stock and 300,000 shares of preferred stock, with a combined value of $518 million, to finance the acquisition of American Motors Corporation. At the same time, 23 percent of the total assets reported on Chrysler's balance sheet ($19.9 billion) were provided by retained earnings, reinvested profits that were generated in previous periods.

THE RELATIVE IMPORTANCE OF LIABILITIES, CONTRIBUTED CAPITAL, AND EARNED CAPITAL

Table 12–1 indicates the relative importance of liabilities, contributed capital, and earned capital (retained earnings) on the balance sheets of a selected group of twelve major U.S. companies. While these companies are not representative of all U.S. companies, the group does include a wide variety of operations.

The relative size of stockholders' equity on the balance sheets of these companies can be computed by summing the percentages of assets provided by contributed capital and retained earnings. On average, stockholders' equity accounts for 43 percent (13% + 30%) of the companies' assets. Current and long-term liabilities account for 57 percent. Thus, major U.S. companies tend to rely more heavily on debt as a source of financing than on contributed and earned capital.

Figure 12–1   The basic accounting equation

		Stockholders' Equity	
Assets = (1) Liabilities +	(2) Contributed capital	+	(3) Earned capital
	Preferred stock		Retained earnings
	Common stock		
	Additional paid-in capital		

Table 12–1 The relative importance of liabilities, contributed capital, and retained earnings (percentage of total assets)

Company (Description)	Liabilities	Contributed Capital	Retained Earnings
Alcoa (aluminum manufacturing)	52%	18%	30%
Amoco (petroleum and chemical)	51	9	40
American Telephone and Telegraph (communications)	62	25	13
BankAmerica (financial services)	96	2	2
Boeing (aircraft manufacturing)	59	11	30
Columbia Broadcasting Systems (broadcasting)	66	11	23
Delta (airlines)	64	12	24
General Motors (automobile manufacturing)	62	9	29
H&R Block (tax services)	44	12	44
J. C. Penney (retail goods)	61	9	30
Microsoft (computer software development)	17	27	56
Walt Disney (children's entertainment)	51	9	40
Average	57%	13%	30%

Source: 1987 annual reports.

Within stockholders' equity, retained earnings (30 percent) appears to be a more important source of financing than contributed capital (13 percent). The relative importance of retained earnings can be partially explained by the fact that Table 12–1 consists only of successful, established companies, which have generated profits over many years. Younger, less-established companies often have not been either profitable enough or in existence long enough to rely heavily on internally generated funds as a source of financing.

Note, however, that there is some variation across the different companies. BankAmerica, for example, relies almost exclusively on debt financing. Such reliance is typical of banks and other financial institutions. Ninety-five percent of the assets of The Bank of New York Company, Inc., for example, can be attributed to various forms of borrowing. Note also that Microsoft, a member of the fast-growing computer software industry, has relied heavily on retained earnings as a source of financing, even though it is a relatively new company. Such reliance can be attributed to two factors: (1) Microsoft has been extremely profitable in its short history, and (2) the company has a policy of paying no dividends.

DEBT AND EQUITY DISTINGUISHED

Chapters 10 and 11 present the basic characteristics of the debt contracts between a company and its creditors. This section describes how the nature of this relationship differs from that between a company and its stockholders. As discussed later, such a distinction is important to investors, creditors, management, and auditors.

Characteristics of Debt

When a company borrows money, it establishes a relationship with an outside party, a *creditor* or *debtholder*, whose influence on the company's operations is defined by a formal legal contract, containing a number of specific provisions. The maturity date defines the end of the contract. The interest and principal payments are defined by the stated interest rate and the schedule of payments over the period of the loan. If these payments are not met on a timely basis, the contract is in default, and the creditor can take legal action against the company. In such cases the debtholder's rights to the assets of the company are covered in the security provisions written in the debt contract. Further, as mentioned before, creditors can protect their interests by requiring in the contract that a company restrict its dividend payments or maintain certain levels of working capital and/or various accounting ratios over the period of the loan.

Debtholders can affect a company's operations through the debt contract, but they have no direct voice in the management of the company. They cannot vote in the election of the board of directors, and therefore have no direct influence over management compensation, the decision to hire or fire management, and the general policies of the corporation. Finally, interest payments on debt are considered expenses of the company's operations by both generally accepted accounting principles and the Internal Revenue Service. Thus, interest expense appears on the income statement for external reporting purposes, and interest payments are a deductible expense in the computation of taxable income.

Characteristics of Equity

When a corporation raises capital by issuing stock, it establishes a relationship with an owner, often referred to as an *equityholder,* or *stockholder.* Unlike debt, an equity relationship is not evidenced by a precisely specified contract. There is no maturity date, because a stockholder is an owner of a company until it ceases operations, or until the equity interest is transferred to another party. Dividend payments are at the discretion of the board of directors, and stockholders have no legal right to receive dividends until they are declared. In case of bankruptcy, the rights of the stockholders to the available assets are subordinate (secondary) to the rights of the creditors, who are paid in an order which can usually be determined by examining the terms in the debt contracts. The stockholders receive the assets that remain. That is, a corporation's owners have a **residual interest** to the corporation's assets in case of bankruptcy.

Stockholders, however, can exert significant influence over corporate management. Each ownership share carries a vote that is cast in the election of the board of directors at the annual stockholder's meeting. The board, whose function is to represent the interests of the stockholders, declares dividends, determines executive compensation, has the power to hire and fire management, and sets the general policies of the corporation. In addition, certain significant transactions, such as the issuance of additional stock, often must be approved by vote of the stockholders.

Finally, distributions by a corporation to the stockholders (dividends) are not considered operating expenses by either generally accepted accounting principles or the Internal Revenue Service. They are considered a return on the owners' original investments. Consequently, dividends are neither included as expenses on the income statement, nor are they considered deductible expenses in the computation of taxable income. On the financial statements, dividends serve to reduce retained earnings without passing through the income statement and income summary. Figure 12–2 summarizes the fundamental differences between debt and equity discussed in this section.

Figure 12–2   Characteristics of debt and equity

Debt	Equity
1. Formal legal contract	1. No legal contract
2. Fixed maturity date	2. No fixed maturity date
3. Fixed periodic interest payments	3. Discretionary dividend payments
4. Security in case of default	4. Residual asset interest
5. No direct voice in management; influence through debt covenants	5. Vote for board of directors
6. Interest is an expense.	6. Dividends are not an expense, but a distribution of retained earnings.

Why Is It Important to Distinguish Debt from Equity?

It is important to distinguish debt from equity for a number of different reasons, depending primarily on the perspective of the interested party. The following sections describe the importance of such a distinction from the separate perspectives of capital providers (investors or creditors), management, and accountants and external auditors.

Debt vs. Equity: the Capital Provider's Perspective

Capital providers include individuals and entities who hold debt and equity securities. Debt securities primarily include notes receivable and bonds, and equity securities include stocks. As mentioned before, active markets exist where such securities are purchased and sold. This section discusses some of the basic trade-offs between investing in debt and equity securities.

Owning an equity security is usually riskier than owning a debt security. The interest and principal payments associated with debt investments are backed by legal contracts and, in general, are more predictable and dependable than discretionary dividend payments. Debt contracts often include security provisions, and in case of bankruptcy, debtholders have higher priority claims to the existing assets than equityholders, who are often left with nothing. As evidence of the riskier nature of equity securities, stock prices tend to be more volatile than bond prices on the major security exchanges.

A characteristic of the additional risk associated with equity investments is that they can produce higher returns than debt investments. When companies perform exceptionally well, equityholders often receive exceedingly large returns, either in the form of dividends or price appreciation of their securities. Debtholders, on the other hand, are limited only to the interest and principal payments specified by the debt contract. For example, Microsoft, described earlier as a fast-growing computer software manufacturer, had an exceptional fiscal year ending June 30, 1987. During that time the price of its stock increased from $13/share to over $64/share, an annual return for the stockholders of 492 percent. In contrast, during that same year the company paid only a 10 percent return to its debtholders (i.e., interest rate on outstanding loans).

Debt vs. Equity: Management's Perspective

The decision by management to raise capital by issuing debt or equity is complex. Factors like present and future interest rates, the company's credit rating, the relative amount of debt and equity in the company's capital structure and balance sheet, the condition of the economy, and the nature of the company's operations are usually relevant. This section mentions only a few of the basic and significant trade-offs involved in such a decision.

Issuing debt limits a company in a number of important ways. Contractual interest and principal payments must be met in the future, and assets often must be pledged as security (collateral) during the period of the debt. As of the end of 1987, for example, Chevron Corporation reported that capital lease obligations were expected to require cash payments in the future of approximately $1.3 billion. Additional debt may also lower a company's credit rating and reduce its ability to borrow in the future. During 1988, for example, Standard & Poor's lowered the credit rating of American Standard bonds, citing the extensive additional debt incurred by the company to finance a recent acquisition.[1] Finally, as shown many times in this text, the debt contract itself may restrict a company's future borrowing power, restrict dividends, or require that certain accounting ratios be maintained at or above specified levels.

On the other hand, raising capital by issuing debt is attractive because interest payments are *tax deductible*. Amoco Corporation, for example, saved approximately $180 million in federal income taxes during 1987 because it was able to deduct the interest on its outstanding debts for tax purposes. Issuing debt, therefore, is generally considered less expensive than issuing equity, as dividend payments are not tax deductible. In general, if management can use debt capital to earn revenues that exceed the after-tax cost of the debt, it is using a concept called **leverage** to provide a return for the stockholders. As indicated in Table 12–1, such a practice appears to be common, in that large U.S. corporations tend to rely more heavily on debt than on equity. The tax deductibility of interest, which significantly reduces the cost of issuing debt, is definitely one of the main reasons.

Another advantage of raising capital by issuing debt instead of equity is that issuing equity can dilute the ownership interests of the existing stockholders. Suppose, for example, that Mr. Jones owns 10 percent of XYZ Corporation, 1000 of the 10,000 outstanding shares. If XYZ issues an additional 10,000 shares, and Mr. Jones purchases none, his ownership interest decreases from 10 percent to 5 percent (1000/20,000).[2] Such **dilution,** if not accompanied by higher profits, can reduce both the future dividends paid to Mr. Jones and the market price of his shares.

Dilution also reduces the proportionate control of the existing shareholders and, accordingly, can increase the likelihood of a **takeover** by an outsider. In a takeover, another company, an investor, or group of investors (sometimes called a *raider*) purchases enough of the outstanding shares to gain a controlling interest in the purchased company. The voting power attached to the acquired shares is often used by the raider to elect a new board of directors. Such action can be followed by the replacement of existing management and substantial changes in the nature of the purchased company. Corporate takeovers have recently been very common in the United States. In early 1988, for example, the front page of *The Wall Street Journal* reported that "takeover activity reached a recent peak with the

1. *The Wall Street Journal,* 20 June 1988, p. 20.

2. Some stock certificates carry with them a preemptive right, which allows existing shareholders to share proportionately in any new issues of stock. Also, additional stock issuances sometimes require the approval of the existing stockholders.

announcement of six transactions totaling $5.4 billion. The flurry, fueled by low stock prices, isn't expected to slow soon."

Not even the largest U.S. companies have escaped such takeovers. RJR Nabisco, for example, was recently purchased by a group of investors for approximately $23 billion. Many of the company's top executives were replaced immediately after the buy-out.

Corporate managers, whose jobs are threatened by takeovers, are understandably concerned with the dilutive effects of equity issuances. Indeed, new equity issuances have been relatively less common in the past few years. In fact, many companies, like Walt Disney and Avco, have recently entered into programs of buying back their own previously issued shares.[3] Such transactions, called **treasury stock** purchases because the acquired shares are often held in the corporation's treasury for reissuance at a later date, make a company less attractive as a takeover target by reducing its cash balance and increasing the proportionate control of the remaining stockholders. In 1986, for example, Safeway Stores, Inc. purchased all of its publicly-traded outstanding stock to elude a takeover attempt by Dart Group Corporation. In other words, the company *went private:* the only shares left outstanding were those held by stockholders who withdrew them from the public markets.

Debt vs. Equity: the Accountant's and Auditor's Perspective

From a financial accounting standpoint, the distinction between debt and equity is important for two reasons: (1) debt and equity issuances are disclosed in different sections of the balance sheet, and (2) debt transactions affect the income statement, while equity transactions do not.

Debt issuances are disclosed in the liability section of the balance sheet, while equity issuances are included in the stockholders' equity section. Proper classification is important because the debt/equity distinction affects a number of financial ratios, which are used by investors and creditors and in debt covenants and executive compensation agreements.

Interest payments on outstanding debts and book gains and losses, recognized when debt is redeemed, appear on the income statement and affect the computation of net income. In contrast, transactions involving equity securities, like dividends and the reissuance of treasury stock, do not enter into the computation of net income.

Figure 12—3 summarizes why distinctions between debt and equity are important to investors and creditors, management, and accountants and auditors. These distinctions give rise to economic consequences that are discussed in the following section.

THE ECONOMIC CONSEQUENCES ASSOCIATED WITH ACCOUNTING FOR STOCKHOLDERS' EQUITY

The economic consequences associated with accounting for stockholders' equity arise from the effects of financial ratios (e.g., debt/equity) that include the dollar amount of stockholders' equity or its components. Such ratios affect a company's stock prices, credit rating, and any debt covenants that restrict additional borrow-

---

3. Jinny St. Goar, "The Footnote Follies," *Forbes* 11 March 1985.

Figure 12-3 Distinctions between debt and equity from different perspectives

Interested Party	Debt	Equity
Investors and Creditors	Lower investment risk	Higher investment risk
	Fixed cash receipts (contractual interest and principal)	Variable cash receipts (discretionary dividends and stock appreciation)
Management	Contractual future cash payments	Dividends are discretionary
	Effects on credit rating	Effects of dilution/takeover
	Interest is tax deductible	Dividends are not tax deductible
Accountants and Auditors	Liability section of balance sheet	Stockholders' equity section of balance sheet
	Income statement effects from debt transactions	No income statement effects from equity transactions

ings, the payment of dividends, or the repurchase of outstanding equity shares (i.e., treasury stock purchases). Four of Dun & Bradstreet's fourteen key business ratios explicitly use the dollar value of stockholders' equity (net worth) in their calculations: (1) current liabilities/net worth, (2) total liabilities/net worth, (3) fixed assets net worth, and (4) return on net worth. Dun & Bradstreet uses the values of these ratios to determine a company's credit rating, which in turn can affect the terms (e.g., market price, interest rate, security, restrictive covenants) of the company's debt issuances.

As discussed in Chapters 10 and 11, many companies "manage" their debt/equity ratios to maintain or improve their credit ratings. The dollar value of stockholders' equity is the denominator of the debt/equity ratio and, therefore, the methods used to account for stockholders' equity may influence a company's credit rating and ability to borrow. In general, as a company's debt/equity ratio increases, its credit ratings fall. In 1988, for example, American Stores, a supermarket and drugstore chain, agreed to acquire Lucky Stores, Inc. To finance the acquisition, American Stores raised additional capital, which it reported as debt on its balance sheet, increasing the company's debt/equity ratio. Moody's Investor Service responded by lowering the credit rating on American Stores' outstanding bonds, which was followed by a decrease in the market price of the bonds.

On the other hand, as companies reduce their reliance on debt and increase their reliance on equity issuances and especially retained earnings, as sources of financing, their credit ratings tend to rise. In its 1987 financial report, for example, General Electric commented that during the year its debts were "substantially reduced," leading the major debt-rating agencies to evaluate the company's credit rating as being of the highest standing, *AAA*. Such a rating enabled General Electric to get the best possible terms on its debt issuances as well as maintain or increase the value of the company's outstanding debt securities. That same year AT&T's annual report stated that it was able to maintain its credit rating because "strong . . . operations permitted it to reduce its utilization of external sources of financing."

Chapter 11 describes how the links among debt ratios, credit ratings, and debt covenants can encourage companies to practice *off-balance-sheet financing*. Such practices are also a concern in this chapter, because the distinction between debt and equity is not always clear-cut. Many securities issued to raise capital have characteristics of both debt and equity (see Figure 12–2). Such **hybrid securities,** as they are called, are difficult to classify on the balance sheet as either debt or equity. This ambiguity allows management to structure the terms of debt issuances so that they appear as equity and can therefore be reported in the stockholders' equity section of the balance sheet. Such a strategy might serve to reduce a company's debt/equity ratio. As you will see later in the chapter, certain preferred stocks, for example, share many of the characteristics of bonds. An article in *Forbes* cautions financial report users about hybrids, commenting that they "are clever ways to raise cash . . . simply [a form of] off-balance-sheet financing masquerading as equity."[4]

Another important economic consequence associated with the stockholder equity section of the balance sheet relates to restrictions on dividend payments and the repurchase of previously issued, outstanding stock imposed by certain debt covenants. Such restrictions can be very significant. For example, under the terms of covenants with its debtholders, as of January of 1988, Turner Broadcasting System, Inc. was prohibited from paying cash dividends.

Similar restrictions may be less binding. The 1987 financial report of The New York Times Company, for example, indicated that "certain debt agreements include provisions requiring that stockholders' equity be maintained at a level greater than $530 million," which at that time represented approximately 64 percent of the company's stockholders' equity balance. Similarly, The Pillsbury Company reported the following in its 1987 financial report:

> *Certain debt agreements contain restrictions relating to the payment of dividends and the purchase by the Company of its common stock. Under the most restrictive of these provisions, approximately $225 million of retained earnings at May 31, 1987, was available for dividends and the purchase of common stock of the Company.*

Such restrictions protect the interests of creditors by keeping a company from paying all of its available cash to the shareholders through excessive dividends or stock repurchases. As discussed in Chapter 11, violating these restrictions normally requires that the timing of the outstanding debt payments be significantly accelerated or, in the extreme case, that the entire debt be repaid immediately. Investors, creditors, managers, and auditors should be aware of these restrictions, because either of these outcomes can give rise to serious financial problems. Note also that the methods used to account for stock issuances, dividends, treasury stock purchases, and retained earnings, which are covered later in the chapter, can determine whether such restrictions have been violated.

The remainder of the chapter describes the corporate form of business organization and covers the methods used to account for the stockholders' equity section of a corporation. Appendix 12A describes proprietorships and partnerships and introduces the methods used to account for the owners' equity section of these forms of business organization.

---

4. Richard Greene, "What, and Whose, Bottom Line?" *Forbes,* 7 October 1985, p. 101.

THE CORPORATE FORM OF ORGANIZATION

A **corporation** is a legal entity, separate and distinct from its owners (stockholders). A corporation must be chartered by the state in which its corporate headquarters is located. The chartering process requires the submission of certificates of incorporation and supplementary application forms as well as the payment of the necessary fees. The certificate of incorporation specifies the corporation's purpose, the number of shares it is authorized to issue, and the individuals composing the board of directors. Formal bylaws must be adopted that cover such matters as the issuance and transfer of stock and the meetings of the directors and the stockholders. A corporation has an indefinite life, which continues regardless of changes in ownership. Stockholders of a corporation are usually free to transfer their ownership interests to anyone they wish.

Corporations are usually formed by one or more individuals, known as **promoters,** who organize the corporation, apply for a charter and establish the corporate bylaws. The promoters contribute cash, other assets or services in exchange for proportionate amounts of the equity. If additional equity financing is necessary, the promoters arrange for shares of stock to be sold either to the general public **(public placement),** which can be extremely expensive and involve extensive audits and much paperwork, or to other specific parties **(private placement).** Corporations can be new businesses, or they are often formed from existing proprietorships or partnerships.

As discussed earlier, corporations are owned by stockholders who annually elect a board of directors. The board represents the stockholders' interests in the management of the business and has the power to declare dividends, hire and fire management, determine executive compensation, and in general, set long-term corporate goals and all policy. Typically, the Board meets four times per year to review the progress and future plans of the management and to decide whether to declare dividends. Often a number of the board members and managers are also stockholders.

Limited Liability

In a corporation, the liability of the stockholder is limited to the dollar amount of their investments. In other words, the maximum loss a shareholder can sustain is equal to the shareholder's investment. Shareholders' personal assets are not at risk, which means that they cannot be legally required to use personal assets to satisfy the obligations of the corporation. Only in rare cases (e.g., shareholder fraud) can action be taken directly against shareholders, and even in these cases, shareholders are not liable for the negligent or fraudulent action of one another. As a legal entity, a corporation provides a shield that protects the personal assets of the shareholders from the corporate creditors. An individual who chooses to take legal action against a corporation must sue the corporation as an entity, not the individual stockholders.

The limited liability feature of the corporate form makes it well suited to raise large amounts of capital through large equity issuances. Many investors are willing to purchase ownership interests in corporations, knowing that their potential gains are unlimited but their losses can be no greater than their initial investments. While corporate shareholders are understandably concerned with the effectiveness of management, such concern is lessened by the fact that even the worst mismanagement at no time places their personal assets at risk. Limited liability is one important reason why most large businesses tend to be corporations.

Corporate Income Taxes

Corporations, as legal entities, are subject to both federal and state income taxes. The corporate income tax rate, which is approximately 34 percent, is assessed against a corporation's taxable income, and the corporation itself is liable for the tax payment. The amount of income tax paid by the corporation is neither determined nor affected by the amount of dividends declared by the board of directors. However, dividends received by a shareholder must be included in the shareholder's taxable income. In a sense, therefore, corporate profits are taxed twice: once at the corporate level and again when a shareholder receives dividends. Such **double taxation** is a disadvantage of the corporate form of organization.

Stockholder Returns: Capital Appreciation and Dividends

Returns to shareholders of large corporations that are listed on the public security exchanges come in either of two forms: (1) price appreciation of their shares or (2) dividends. Publicly-traded stocks are easily transferable, and objective market prices are readily available. Thus, shareholders can cash in their investments at any time they choose. Many publicly-traded corporations also pay quarterly dividends. On the other hand, shareholders of small corporations, whose stock is not traded on public security exchanges, find it more difficult to sell their shares. Their returns come primarily in the form of dividends.

ACCOUNTING FOR CORPORATE STOCKHOLDERS' EQUITY

The stockholders' equity section of the balance sheet consists of two major components: (1) contributed capital, which primarily reflects contributions of capital from shareholders and includes the Preferred Stock, Common Stock, and Additional Paid-in Capital[5] accounts, and (2) earned capital, which reflects the amount of assets earned and retained by the corporation and consists essentially of the Retained Earnings account. An example of the stockholders' equity section of a corporate balance sheet appears in Figure 12−4. Spend a moment to review it because it provides an outline of the remaining discussion in this chapter.

Preferred Stock

Preferred stock is so called because preferred stockholders have certain rights that are not shared by common stockholders. These special rights relate either to the

---

5. While the title *Additional Paid-in Capital* is the most common, there is some variation across companies. For example, The New York Times Company uses *Additional Capital*, Goodyear Tire and Rubber uses *Capital Surplus*, and Chevron Corporation uses *Capital in Excess of Par Value*.

Figure 12–4   Stockholders' equity section of balance sheet

Contributed capital		
Preferred stock (authorized, issued and outstanding shares, asset preference, dividend preference, par value, cumulative, nonparticipating)	$ 3,000	
Common stock (authorized, issued and outstanding shares, par value/ stated value/no par)	15,000	
Additional paid-in capital (preferred stock, common stock, treasury stock, stock dividends)	86,000	
Total contributed capital		$104,000
Earned capital		
Retained earnings	125,000	
Total earned capital		125,000
Less: Treasury stock (cost method)		20,000
Total stockholders' equity		$209,000

receipt of dividends or to claims on assets in case of liquidation. **Preferred stock as to dividends** confers the right, if dividends are declared by the corporation's board of directors, to receive a certain specified dividend payment before the common stockholders receive dividends. **Preferred stock as to assets** carries a claim to the corporation's assets, in case of liquidation, with a higher priority than the claim carried by common stock. The exact characteristics and terms of preferred stock vary from one issue to the next. The following sections describe some of the more important features of preferred stock.

Authorized, Issued, and Outstanding Preferred Shares

Authorized preferred shares are the number of shares a corporation is entitled to issue by its corporate charter. Additional authorizations must be approved by the board of directors and are often subject to shareholder vote. For example, the following excerpt was taken from the 1987 financial report of the American Express Company: "The Board of Directors is authorized to permit the Company to issue up to 20 million preferred shares without further shareholder approval."

Issued preferred shares have been issued previously by a corporation and may or may not be currently outstanding. Some issued shares may have been repurchased by the corporation and held as treasury stock.

Outstanding preferred shares are the shares presently held by the stockholders. Issued shares less repurchased shares equal outstanding shares. *Accounting Trends and Techniques* (New York: AICPA, 1987) reports that, of the 600 major U.S. corporations surveyed, approximately 30 percent had outstanding preferred issuances.

The number of authorized, issued, and outstanding preferred shares should be disclosed in the financial report. The New York Times Company, for example, disclosed in its 1987 financial report that the shareholders had authorized 110,000 shares of preferred stock, of which 91,659 had been issued, and 26,663 were presently outstanding.

Many major U.S. corporations have authorized preferred stock issuances but have chosen not to issue them. In such cases the number of authorized shares should still be disclosed in the financial report. As of the end of 1987, for example, Goodyear Tire and Rubber Company (50 million shares), Ralston Purina

Company (6 million shares), Johnson & Johnson (2 million shares), and Pillsbury (500,000 shares) disclosed authorized preferred shares, none of which had been issued.

Preferred Dividend Payments

The terms of preferred stocks usually include a specific annual dividend that is paid to the preferred stockholders before any payments are made to the common stockholders, assuming a dividend is declared by the Board. The remaining amount of the dividend is then paid to the common stockholders. The amount of the preferred annual dividend payment is normally expressed as either an absolute dollar amount or as a percentage of a dollar amount referred to as the **par value** of the preferred stock.[6]

For example, if dividends are declared in a given year, the holder of 1 share of $5 preferred stock would receive a $5 dividend. The holder of 1 share of 4 percent preferred stock with a par value of $100 would receive a $4 (4% × $100) dividend. As of December 31, 1987, General Motors had two kinds of preferred shares outstanding, differentiated by the per-share amount of the annual dividend payment: a $5.00 series and a $3.75 series. GTE, on the other hand, had outstanding preferred stock that paid an annual dividend of 5% of the $50 par value ($2.50).

To illustrate the allocation of a dividend between preferred and common stock, during 1987 the board of directors of DuPont declared and paid a total dividend of $802 million. During the year, approximately 1.68 million shares of $4.50 preferred stock, .7 million shares of $3.50 preferred stock, and 240 million shares of common stock were outstanding. The dividend allocation to the preferred and common stockholders is shown in Figure 12–5.

The shareholders holding the $4.50 preferred stock each received $4.50 per share. Those holding the $3.50 preferred stock each received $3.50 per share. These payments accounted for $10 million of the total dividend. The remaining $792 million were paid to the common stockholders on a per-share basis. Specifically, $3.30 was paid on each of the 240 million common shares outstanding.

The important point is that had DuPont declared and paid only a $12 million dividend, the preferred shareholders would have still received $10 million. The remaining $2 million would have been paid to the common shareholders on a per-share basis. Had DuPont declared and paid a dividend of less than $10 million, the common shareholders would have received nothing.

Cumulative-Noncumulative Preferred Stock

To continue the preceding example, how would the preferred shareholders be affected if DuPont declared and paid no dividends in 1987, or a dividend of less than $10 million? For example, if it paid a total dividend of $4 million, would the preferred shareholders forego the $6 million ($10 million − $4 million) missed dividend completely, or would they have a right to the $6 million as future dividends are declared and paid in subsequent periods?

With **cumulative preferred stock,** when a corporation misses a dividend, **dividends in arrears** are created in the amount of the missed preferred dividend. In

---

6. The concept of par value is discussed more completely later in the chapter when we cover common stock. At that time we point out that par value has little or no economic meaning. In the case of preferred stock, however, par value is meaningful in that it is sometimes used to determine the annual dividend payment to the preferred stockholders

Figure 12–5   Allocation of a dividend between preferred and common stock

Preferred dividend		
$4.50 preferred stock × 1.68 million shares	$7.55 million	
$3.50 preferred stock × .7 million shares	2.45 million	$ 10 million
Common dividend ($3.30 × 240 million shares)		792 million
Total dividend		$802 million

future periods, as dividends are declared, dividends in arrears are first paid to the preferred stockholders, who then receive their normal, annual dividend. Finally, the common stockholders are paid from what remains. If the preferred stock is *noncumulative*, no dividends in arrears are created for missed dividends, and the preferred stockholders receive only their normal, annual dividend in future periods as dividends are declared.

To illustrate, suppose that PDQ Corporation had 5000 shares of $100 par value, 10 percent, cumulative preferred stock outstanding. No dividend is paid during 1990, a $30,000 dividend is paid in 1991, and a $150,000 dividend is paid in 1992. Figure 12–6 lists the dividends paid to the preferred and common stockholders in each of the three years.

In 1990 no dividends are declared, and because the preferred stock is cumulative, dividends in arrears in the amount of the missed dividend ($50,000) are created. In 1991 the entire $30,000 dividend is paid to the preferred stockholders. This payment reduces the original amount of dividends in arrears to $20,000 ($50,000 − $30,000) but fails to cover the $50,000 to be paid to the preferred stockholders during 1991. Thus, an additional $50,000 in dividends in arrears are created, bringing the total at the end of 1991 to $70,000. The $150,000 dividend in 1992 is first applied to the $70,000 dividends in arrears, then $50,000 is paid to the preferred stockholders for the current year, and the remainder ($30,000) is distributed to the common stockholders.

Had the preferred stock in the example above been noncumulative, the preferred stockholders would have received all of the $30,000 dividend in 1991, but in 1992 they would have received only the $50,000 annual dividend. They would have received no dividends in arrears, and the common stockholders would have received $100,000.

It is important to realize that dividends in arrears are not liabilities to the corporation and therefore are not listed on the balance sheet. They do not represent legal obligations to the preferred stockholders because dividends are at the discretion of the board of directors. The liability is created at the time the dividends are

Figure 12–6   Dividend payments on cumulative preferred stock

Year	Dividends Paid	Dividends in Arrears	Preferred Stock Dividend	Common Stock Dividend
1990	0	$50,000	0	0
		[5000 sh ($100 × 10%)]		
1991	$ 30,000	$70,000	$ 30,000	0
		($50,000 − $30,000 + $50,000)		
1992	$150,000	0	$120,000	$30,000
			($70,000 + $50,000)	($150,000 − $120,000)

declared and only in the amount of the dividends. However, the corporation must keep track of dividends in arrears because they must be clearly disclosed in the financial report. Such information is particularly interesting to creditors as well as potential and existing stockholders because it may signal a shortage of cash in the corporation. The amount of dividends in arrears may also affect the dividends that common stockholders can expect to receive in the future.

Almost all preferred stock issuances are cumulative, and among major U.S. companies dividends in arrears are relatively rare. However, in 1986 and 1987, in an effort to save cash, Bethlehem Steel omitted dividends on its $5 and $2.50 cumulative preferred stocks. Accordingly, the company disclosed dividends in arrears of $22.5 million in its 1987 financial report. In 1988, as the outlook in the steel industry improved, Bethlehem Steel paid these back dividends.

Participating/Nonparticipating Preferred Stock

When a dividend is declared, the holders of cumulative preferred stock have a right to any dividends in arrears as well as the annual dividend payment specified by the terms of the preferred stock. If the total dividend exceeds this amount, the remainder is normally paid to the common stockholders on a per-share basis. If the preferred stock carries a **participating** feature, however, the preferred stockholders not only have a right to dividends in arrears and the annual dividend payment, but they also share in the remaining amount of the dividend with the common stockholders. The extent to which the preferred stockholders participate in the remaining dividend is often expressed as a percentage of the par value of the preferred stock. Nonparticipating preferred stock, which is much more common, carries no rights to share in the remaining dividend.

To illustrate a participating feature, assume that Hauser Construction declares a $20,000 dividend to be paid to the preferred and common stockholders. At the time of the dividend, 1000 shares of 5 percent preferred stock with a par value of $100 are outstanding, and dividends in arrears total $5000. The preferred stock contains a feature that allows it to participate at the rate of 2 percent of the $100 par value. Figure 12−7 shows the allocation of the $20,000 dividend between the preferred and common stockholders.

The holders of the cumulative and participating preferred stock receive $5000 in payment of the dividends in arrears, $5000 as determined by the annual dividend payment, and $2000 due to the participation feature. The remaining $8000 is distributed to the common stockholders on a per-share basis.

Preferred Stocks: Debt or Equity?

We have described how most preferred stocks (1) carry higher priority than common stocks in the event of liquidation, (2) specify annual dividend payments of a fixed amount, (3) are cumulative, and (4) do not contain a participation feature. In addition, preferred stocks normally do not carry a right to vote in the election of the board of directors, and many contain a call provision that allows the corporation to redeem the stock for a specified price after a specified date.

Recall the discussion earlier in the chapter on the characteristics of debt and equity (see Figure 12−2), and note how the features listed above closely resemble debt. In fact, in some cases the Internal Revenue Service has allowed corporations to deduct from taxable income the dividends paid on securities classified on the balance sheet as preferred stocks. Preferred stocks are definitely hybrid securities, which have characteristics of both debt and equity. They are, therefore, difficult to

Figure 12–7   Participating preferred stock

Total dividend		$20,000
Less: Payments to preferred stockholders		
Dividends in arrears	$5,000	
Annual dividend payment (1,000 × $100 × 5%)	5,000	10,000
Remaining dividend		10,000
Less: Participating feature (1,000 × $100 × 2%)		2,000
Payment to common stockholders		$ 8,000

classify on the balance sheet. In most cases the Preferred Stock account is disclosed at the top of the stockholders' equity section, where it is located immediately below long-term liabilities. In some cases, however, preferred stocks are disclosed as debt. On its 1987 balance sheet, for example, Burlington Northern, a major U.S. company in transportation and natural resource mining, reported two preferred stock issuances in the long-term liability section of the balance sheet. Financial statement users interested in computing ratios that involve distinctions between debt and equity (e.g., debt/equity), may find it more useful to treat the preferred stock account as a long-term liability.

Classifying hybrid securities, like preferred stocks, is indeed a difficult area for accountants and auditors, primarily because the distinction between debt and equity is not always clear-cut, and the guidelines specified by generally accepted accounting principles are not very specific. In a recent article in *Forbes*, the national director of accounting and auditing at a major accounting firm noted that "the distinction between debt and equity has become so muddied that the accounting rules seem more arbitrary than ever."[7] Consequently, by issuing certain kinds of preferred stock management can raise what is essentially debt capital without increasing the liabilities reported on the balance sheet. Because preferred stock carries no voting power, such a strategy also avoids the problems of dilution and possible takeover associated with issuing common stock. As noted in *Forbes*, "Companies anxious to protect their credit ratings, and unwilling to issue more [common] stock for fear of diluting earnings per share or inviting takeover bids, have turned to these ingenious instruments [preferred stocks] to lower the cost of raising money. But pity the poor accountant who must categorize these hothouse hybrids."[8]

Accounting for Preferred Stock Issuances

When preferred stocks are issued for cash, the Cash account is debited for the proceeds, and if the preferred stock has no par value, the Preferred Stock account is credited for the dollar amount of the proceeds. For example, in 1984 McDonald's Corporation issued 1,331,000 shares of no-par preferred stock for $50 per share. The company recorded the following journal entry to reflect this transaction.

Cash	66,550,000	
Preferred Stock (1,331,000 sh × $50)		66,550,000
To record the issuance of no-par value preferred stock.		

---

7. Richard Greene. "What, and Whose, Bottom Line?" *Forbes*, 7 October 1985, p. 101.

8. Jinny St. Goar, "Creative Paper," *Forbes*, 3 June 1985, pp. 178, 180.

If preferred stock is issued with a par value, the Cash account is debited for the proceeds, the Preferred Stock account is credited for the par value times the number of shares issued, and the Additional Paid-in Capital (Preferred Stock) account is credited for the remainder. The dollar amount credited to the Additional Paid-in Capital (Preferred Stock) account represents the difference between the total issuance price of the stock and the par value of the issuance. For example, during 1982 Weyerhaeuser Company issued 147,000 shares of $1.00 par value preferred stock for $11 per share. The company recorded the following journal entry.

Cash (147,000 sh × $11)	1,617,000	
Preferred Stock (147,000 sh × $1)		147,000
Additional Paid-in Capital (P/S)		1,470,000
To record the issuance of $1 par value preferred stock.		

Note that par value determines how the total proceeds from the issuance are allocated between the Preferred Stock and the Additional Paid-in Capital accounts. When preferred stock has no par value, all of the proceeds are accounted for in the Preferred Stock account. Refer back to the stockholders' equity section in Figure 12−4, and note where the Preferred Stock account and the Additional Paid-in Capital (Preferred Stock) accounts are disclosed on the balance sheet.

Common Stock

Unlike preferred stock, common stock is typically not characterized by a wide variety of features that differ from issuance to issuance. Moreover, common stock is not designed to provide a fixed return over a specified period of time. Rather, as a true equity security, common stock is characterized by three fundamental rights: (1) the right to receive dividends if they are declared by the board of directors, (2) a residual right to the corporation's assets in case of liquidation, and (3) the right to exert control over management, which includes the right to vote in the annual election of the board of directors and the right to vote for or against certain significant transactions proposed by management (e.g., the authorization of additional shares, large purchases of outstanding shares, major acquisitions). As discussed earlier, from the investor's standpoint such rights give rise to a security which is riskier than either debt or preferred stock but, at the same time, has the potential for much higher returns.

Market Value, Book Value, Par Value, and Stated Value
The value of the common stock issued by a corporation can be described in a number of different and often confusing ways. This section clarifies some of this confusion by differentiating among the market value, book value, par value, and stated value of a share of common stock.

Market Value. The **market value** of a share of stock, common or preferred, at a particular point in time is the price at which the stock can be exchanged on the open market. This amount varies from day to day, based primarily on changes in investor expectations about the financial condition of the issuing company, interest rates, and other factors. The market prices of the common stocks of publicly-traded companies are usually disclosed in their financial reports. The 1987 financial report of Walt Disney, for example, disclosed that the market price of the company's common stock fluctuated from a low of approximately $39 per share to a high of slightly over $46 during the year ending December 31, 1987.

Book Value. The **book value** of a share of common stock is determined by the following formula.

$$\text{Book value of common stock} = \frac{\text{Stockholders' equity} - \text{Preferred capital}}{\text{Number of common shares held by the shareholders}}$$

It is simply the book value of the corporation (less preferred capital), as indicated on the balance sheet, divided by the number of common shares presently held by the shareholders. This value rarely approximates the market value of a common share because the balance sheet, in general, does not represent an accurate measure of the market value of the company. As of December 31, 1987, the book value of Walt Disney common stock was $14 per share, considerably below the range of market value ($39–$46) indicated in the previous paragraph.

Par Value. The **par value** of a share of common stock has no relationship to its market value or book value and, for the most part, has no economic significance. At one time, it represented a legal concept, instituted by some states, that was intended to protect creditors by making common stockholders liable for at least the par value of the stock, even if their investments were for amounts less than par. In such cases the liability of the stockholders was no longer limited to their investments in the corporation. Over time, however, the concept of par value proved to be ineffective because corporations simply assigned par values to common shares that were far below their issuance prices. It was not uncommon for corporations to issue either no-par common stock or common stock with extremely low par values. For example, the par value of Walt Disney Company common stock as of December 31, 1987 is only $.10 per share.

Stated Value. Many states attempted to protect corporate creditors by substituting the concept of stated value for par value. This legal concept requires that dividends paid to stockholders cannot exceed the dollar amount in stockholders' equity less the **stated value** of the stock, multiplied by the number of shares held by the shareholders. For example, if the value of stockholders' equity of a corporation was $100,000 and the corporate shareholders held 5000 shares with a stated value of $5 each, the corporation could pay a maximum dividend of $75,000 ($100,000 − [5000 × $5]). Such a limitation prohibited a corporation from declaring a dividend that effectively distributed all the corporate assets to the stockholders. It served to protect corporate creditors, especially in the case of liquidation, by helping to ensure that corporate assets were available to satisfy creditor claims.

Most states, however, have subsequently required that dividends cannot be paid in excess of the dollar amount of retained earnings. Since this amount is almost always less than stockholders' equity less the stated value of the shares held by the stockholders, this new limitation effectively rendered the concept of stated value legally and economically meaningless. Furthermore, as indicated before, many debt covenants limit a company's ability to pay dividends to amounts that are far below the balance in retained earnings.

Table 12–2   Limitations on dividends

Stated value	$40,000 ($50,000 − [1,000 × $10])
Retained earnings	$20,000
Debt covenant	$ 5,000 ($20,000 − $15,000)*

*Dividends reduce retained earnings directly

To illustrate, assume that the shareholders of Washington Corporation hold 1000 shares, each with a stated value of $10. Total stockholders' equity is $50,000, and retained earnings are $20,000. A debt covenant entered into by the corporation requires that the balance in Retained Earnings be maintained at no less than $15,000. The maximum dividend allowed under the stated value limitation, the retained earnings limitation, and the debt covenant are computed in Table 12–2.

In this case Washington Corporation can pay a maximum dividend of $5000 without violating the debt covenant. Had the corporation not entered into the debt covenant, it could have legally paid a dividend of $20,000, the amount in Retained Earnings. Under no circumstances, however, could the corporation have paid a legal dividend of $40,000, the amount of the stated value limitation. As a result, in this case, and in almost all others, stated value has no legal or economic significance.

While the par and stated value of a share of common stock have no legal or economic significance, these values do have financial accounting significance. As the next section demonstrates, under generally accepted accounting principles, these values are used in the journal entries to record certain common stock transactions. In our opinion, attributing any significance, accounting or otherwise, to the par or stated value of common stock is unwarranted. In the remainder of the text the term *par value* means both par and stated value.

Accounting for Common Stock Issuances

As for preferred stock, common stock issuances must be authorized in the corporate charter and approved by the board of directors and sometimes the stockholders. Similarly, the number of shares of common stock outstanding may differ from the number of common shares originally issued. As of December 31, 1987, for example, the corporate charter and stockholders of Johnson & Johnson had authorized 270 million shares of common stock; 192 million had been issued, and 172 million were currently outstanding: 20 (192 − 172) million had been repurchased by the company and were held in the form of treasury stock.

The methods used to account for common stock issuances are essentially the same as those used for preferred stock. When no-par common stock is issued for cash, the Cash account is debited for the proceeds and the Common Stock account is credited for the entire dollar amount. For example, during the 1987 fiscal year Apple Computer, Inc. issued 4.98 million shares of no-par common stock for an average price of $17.592 per share (total cash proceeds of $87.61 million). Accordingly, the company prepared the following journal entry.

Cash	87,610,000	
Common Stock		87,610,000
To record the issuance of no-par common stock.		

When common stock with a par value is issued for cash, the Cash account is debited for the total proceeds, the Common Stock account is credited for the number of shares issued times the par value per share, and the Additional Paid-in Capital (Common Stock) account is credited for the remainder. The dollar amount credited to the Additional Paid-in Capital (Common Stock) account represents the difference between the total issuance price of the stock and the par value of the issuance. For example, when Coca-Cola Enterprises issued 71.4 million shares of $1 par value common stock for $15.62 per share in 1985, the company recorded the following journal entry.

Cash	1,115,270,000	
Common Stock (71.4 million sh × $1)		71,400,000
Additional Paid-In Capital (C/S)		1,043,870,000
To record the issuance of $1 par value common stock.		

Treasury Stock

Outstanding common stock is often repurchased and either (1) held *in treasury,* awaiting to be reissued at a later date, or (2) retired.[9] Repurchases of this nature normally must be authorized and approved by a company's stockholders and board of directors. Treasury stock carries none of the usual rights of common stock ownership. That is, when outstanding shares are repurchased, they lose their voting power and their right to receive dividends.

Why Companies Purchase Treasury Stock

There are many reasons why corporations purchase outstanding common shares and hold them in treasury. Perhaps the most common is to support employee compensation plans. General Mills, for example, purchased over two million of its own common shares in both 1984 and 1986, bringing the total number of shares in treasury to 13.8 million. During that time period approximately 1.8 million shares were issued to employees as compensation for services and over 6 million additional shares could be issued at the option of the employees.

As mentioned earlier, other companies, such as Walt Disney, Avco, Gillette, and Safeway, have recently entered into common stock buy-back programs to fend off possible takeover attempts. By purchasing its own outstanding common stock a company can discourage takeovers by reducing its cash balance and increasing the proportionate control of the remaining shareholders. Gillette, for example, entered into a plan to purchase 11 million of its outstanding common shares in 1986. In doing so, the company blocked a takeover attempt by purchasing the 13.9 percent interest held at that time by the Revlon Group, Inc. Columbia Broadcasting Systems (CBS) blocked a takeover attempt by Ted Turner (Turner Broadcasting Systems) by repurchasing a substantial portion of its outstanding common stock.

Purchasing treasury stock can also increase the market price of a company's outstanding stock. For example, when General Motors announced its plan to spend $5 billion dollars to purchase over 20 percent of its outstanding stock in 1987, the price of the company's stock rose immediately from $76 per share to $79.

---

9. Repurchased preferred shares are normally retired and are not held as treasury stock.

Finally, a treasury stock purchase can serve to increase a company's earnings per share (net income/outstanding common shares). In a recent article, *Forbes* magazine reported that treasury stock purchases "reduce shares outstanding and hype [i.e., inflate] per-share earnings."[10] For example, by repurchasing 12.2 million common shares in 1982, Gulf Oil Company significantly lessened a decrease in its earnings per share. This strategy made Gulf's financial performance appear relatively better than that of many companies in the oil industry, which at the time was experiencing a slump in the price of oil.

While most repurchased common shares are held in treasury, they are sometimes retired and disposed of. Such an action enables management to return cash to the stockholders and reduce the scale of a company's operations. Retired treasury shares have the status of authorized and unissued shares.

Accounting for Treasury Stock: The Cost Method

There are two primary methods of accounting for treasury stock: (1) the cost method and (2) the par value method. While either method is acceptable under GAAP, the cost method, which is covered below, is simpler and more widely used.[11]

Purchasing Treasury Stock. Under the cost method, when a company purchases its own outstanding common stock, a permanent account, called Treasury Stock, is debited for the cost of the purchase. This account is disclosed below retained earnings in the stockholders' equity section of the balance sheet (see Figure 12–4). For example, during 1987 Chrysler Corporation purchased 11.1 million shares of treasury stock for a total cost of $391 million. To record this transaction the company made the following journal entry.

Treasury Stock	391,000,000	
Cash		391,000,000
To record the purchase of treasury stock.		

This transaction brought the total number of treasury shares held by Chrysler to 23.4 million, and the stockholders' equity section of Chrysler's 1987 balance sheet appeared as in Figure 12–8.

Some accountants have argued that treasury stock, similar to marketable securities, represents an asset that should be disclosed on the balance sheet. This argument rests on the premise that treasury stock can be sold and will eventually produce cash. In practice, however, treasury stock is listed on the balance sheet as a reduction to stockholders' equity primarily because it is illogical to view a corporation as owning part of itself. Unlike purchasing securities issued by another company (marketable securities), purchasing treasury stock reduces the scale of the purchasing company's operations as well as the equity interests of the stockholders. Further, corporations can always produce cash by issuing authorized and unissued shares. Are such shares assets? Note in Chrysler's case that 500 million common shares have been authorized while only 244.7 million have been issued. Few would argue that the 255.3 (500 − 244.7) million authorized and unissued shares should be listed as balance sheet assets.

---

10. Christopher Power, "The Gimmicks of '82," *Forbes*, 14 March 1983, pp. 96, 98.

11. In theory, the cost method is appropriate when the repurchased shares are held in treasury, while the par value method is appropriate when the repurchased shares are retired. The par value method accounts for the purchase of outstanding common shares as a retirement, whether or not they are actually retired.

Figure 12-8 Purchase of treasury stock

Chrysler Corporation **Balance Sheet** **Stockholders' Equity Section** **December 31, 1987**	

Preferred stock (5.7 million shares of $1 par value, $2.375 cumulative convertible preferred stock authorized; .3 million shares issued)	$ 300,000
Common stock (500 million shares of $1 par value authorized, 244.7 million shares issued)	244,700,000
Additional paid-in capital	2,374,300,000
Retained earnings	4,581,300,000
Treasury stock—common stock, at cost: (23.4 million shares)	(697,700,000)
Total stockholders' equity	$6,502,900,000
.Source: 1987 annual report.	

The Treasury Stock account is disclosed immediately below retained earnings because in many states dividends cannot legally exceed retained earnings less the cost of all shares held in treasury. Such laws are designed to protect creditors by keeping a corporation from distributing all of its cash to the shareholders in the form of dividends or stock repurchases. By subtracting the dollar amount in the Treasury Stock account from retained earnings, financial statement readers can determine the maximum amount of cash that legally can be paid to the shareholders as of the balance sheet date.

Reissuing Treasury Stock for More than Acquisition Cost. Common stock held in treasury is often reissued at a later date. If it is reissued at a price greater than its accquisition cost, the Cash account is debited for the proceeds, the Treasury Stock account is credited for the cost, and the difference is credited to the Additional Paid-in Capital (Treasury Stock) account. For example, in 1987 PepsiCo, Inc. reissued 139,000 shares of treasury stock, which had an acquisition cost of $2.7 million, for a total of $5.3 million. Accordingly, the company recorded the following journal entry.

Cash	5,300,000	
Treasury Stock		2,700,000
Additional Paid-in Capital (T/S)		2,600,000
To record the reissuance of treasury stock.		

Note that the treasury shares were reissued for a dollar amount that exceeded the acquisition cost, and Additional Paid-in Capital (Treasury Stock) was credited for the difference. Additional Paid-in Capital is credited instead of a *gain*, which would appear on the income statement and be closed to Retained Earnings, because this transaction represents an exchange with the stockholders of the corporation. It is not an operating transaction, and it is illogical for a corporation to recognize a gain at the expense of its stockholders. Consequently, the amount of the proceeds from the issuance of treasury stock in excess of its acquisition cost is added to the contributed capital portion of stockholders' equity, rather than to earned capital.

Reissuing Treasury Stock for Less than Acquisition Cost. If treasury stock is reissued for less than the acquisition cost, the Cash account is debited for the proceeds, the Treasury Stock account is credited for the acquisition cost, and Additional Paid-in Capital (Treasury Stock) is debited for the difference, if there is a sufficient balance in the account to cover this difference. If the difference between the acquisition cost and the proceeds exceeds the balance in the Additional Paid-in Capital (Treasury Stock) account, Retained Earnings is debited.

For example, in 1986 Eli Lilly and Company reissued 1,271,036 treasury shares, with an acquisition cost of $68.5 million, for $44.5 million. At the time of the transaction, the balance in the Additional Paid-in Capital (Treasury Stock) account exceeded $24 million, the difference between the cost and the proceeds. The following journal entry, therefore, was recorded to reflect the transaction.

Cash	44,500,000	
Additional Paid-in Capital (T/S)	24,000,000	
Treasury Stock		68,500,000
To record the reissuance of treasury stock.		

In 1984 The Pillsbury Company reissued 300,000 shares of treasury stock, which had an acquisition cost of $12.9 million, for a total of $11.7 million. The balance in the Additional Paid-in Capital (Treasury Stock) account at the time of the reissuance was zero. Accordingly, the following journal entry was recorded.

Cash	11,700,000	
Retained Earnings	1,200,000	
Treasury Stock		12,900,000
To record the reissuance of treasury stock.		

Note that in both preceding examples, an income statement loss is not recognized when treasury stock is reissued for an amount less than the acquisition cost. Reissuing treasury stock is a capital transaction and as such should not affect the income statement. However, debiting Retained Earnings, when the dollar amount in the Additional Paid-in Capital (Treasury Stock) account is insufficient to cover the difference, is a questionable practice: it is treated as a reduction of earned capital when, in fact, it represents a return of contributed capital.

The Magnitude of the Treasury Stock Account

The dollar values of the Treasury Stock account on the balance sheets of major U.S. corporations are often quite significant. As indicated in Table 12−3, it is not unusual for it to exceed the dollar value of the corporation's total contributed capital (preferred stock, common stock, and additional paid-in capital). This phenomenon can occur because treasury stock is often acquired at a price that is considerably higher than the original issuance price of the shares.

Retained Earnings

Retained earnings is a measure of previously recognized profits that have not been paid to the shareholders in the form of dividends. As indicated in Table 12−1, major U.S. corporations rely heavily on internally generated funds as a source of capital. This section discusses two factors that affect the Retained Earnings balance: (1) dividends and (2) appropriations.

Table 12–3   The dollar value of treasury stock/total contributed capital (dollars in millions)

Company	Treasury Stock ÷ Contributed Capital		
Time, Inc.	$453/319	=	1.42
Colgate-Palmolive	477/323	=	1.48
General Mills	379/221	=	1.71
Gillette	628/292	=	2.15
Exxon	7,936/2,822	=	2.81
Ralston Purina	1,592/292	=	5.45

Source: 1987 annual reports.

Dividends

Dividends are distributions of cash, property, or stock to the stockholders of a corporation. They are declared by a formal resolution of the corporation's board of directors (usually quarterly), and the amount is usually announced on a per-share basis.

Cash dividends represent distributions of cash to the stockholders. Property dividends **(dividends in kind)** are distributions of property, usually debt or equity securities in other companies. **Stock dividends** are distributions of a corporation's own shares. Cash dividends are by far the most common. *Accounting Trends and Techniques* (New York: AICPA, 1987) reports that, of the 600 major U.S. companies surveyed, 487 (81 percent) paid cash dividends, during 1986, 17 (3 percent) paid property dividends, and 12 (2 percent) paid dividends in the form of stock.[12]

As Figure 12–9 shows, three dates are relevant when dividends are declared: (1) the **date of declaration,** when the dividends are declared by the board, (2) the **date of record,** which determines who is to receive the dividend, and (3) the **date of payment,** when the distribution is actually made. A typical dividend announcement reads as follows: "The Board of Directors of Bennet Corporation, at its regular meeting of March 10, 1990, declared a quarterly dividend of $5 per share, payable on April 20, 1990, to stockholders of record on April 2, 1990." In this announcement March 10 is the date of declaration, April 2, the date of record, and April 20, the date of payment.

Dividend Strategy. When and how much of a dividend to declare depends on a number of factors, such as the nature, financial condition, and desired image of the company, as well as legal constraints. If dividends are to be paid in cash, the board of directors must first be certain that the corporation has sufficient cash to meet the payment. Such a determination requires a projection of the operating cash flows of the company, including, for example, analyses of the company's current cash position, future sales, receivables, inventory purchases, and fixed-asset replacements. It is usually wise to make sure that the company's operating cash needs are met before cash dividends are paid.

The goals of a corporation and the nature of its activities may also have a bearing on dividend policy. Some companies, like Toys "Я" Us, Inc. and Microsoft Corporation, are relatively young, fast-growing companies that have adopted pol-

---

12. Some companies distributed more than one kind of dividend, and others distributed no dividends of any kind.

Figure 12–9   Important dividend dates

Date of Declaration	Date of Record	Date of Payment
Board of Directors declares dividend, and liability is established.	Shareholders holding stock at this date receive the dividend when paid.	Dividend is paid to shareholders of record.

icies of paying no dividends. Such companies, often called growth companies, re-invest their earnings primarily to support growth without having to rely too heavily on debt and dilutive equity issuances. The shareholders receive their investment returns in the form of stock price appreciation. The following excerpt is from the 1987 financial report of Toys "Я" Us, Inc.

> *The Company has followed the policy of reinvesting earnings in the business and, consequently, has not paid any cash dividends. At the present time, no change in this policy is under consideration by the Board of Directors. The payment of cash dividends in the future will be determined by the Board of Directors in light of conditions then existing, including the Company's earnings, financial requirements and condition, opportunities for reinvesting earnings, business conditions, and other factors.*

More established companies, such as General Electric and Johnson & Johnson, normally pay quarterly dividends in the amount of 30–40 percent of net income and also attempt to consistently increase their dividend payments from year to year. This policy, which provides a consistent dividend while retaining some funds to finance available growth opportunities, tends to refect an image of stability, strength, and permanence. The following excerpt, for example, is from the 1987 financial report of General Electric.

> *Dividends paid totaled $1.777 billion in 1987 [$1.29 per share]. At the same time, the Company retained sufficient earnings to support enhanced productive capability and to provide adequate financial resources for internal and external growth opportunities. [This increase] in dividends declared . . . marked the twelfth consecutive year of dividend growth.*

Some companies consistently increase dividends from year to year, but the distributions do not represent a consistent percentage of net income. Eastman Kodak Company, for example, has increased its dividends each year since 1977. However, as a percentage of net income, dividend payments over that time period varied from around 40 percent in 1978 to over 100 percent in 1983, 1985, and 1986. Apparently, the boards of such companies believe that dividend payments should show consistent growth regardless of how well the company does from one year to the next.

As mentioned before, state laws and debt covenants can also limit the payment of dividends. In most states the dollar amount of retained earnings less the cost of treasury stock sets a limitation on the payment of dividends. In addition, the terms of debt contracts may further limit dividend payments to an even smaller portion of retained earnings. As of December 31, 1987, for example, Sears, Roebuck & Company had a balance of retained earnings less treasury stock of over $11 billion. Yet certain indenture agreements existing at the time limited dividend payments to a maximum amount of $1.1 billion.

Accounting for Cash Dividends. When the board of directors of a corporation declares a cash dividend, a liability in the amount of the fair market value of the dividend is created on the date of declaration. At this time a Cash Dividend account is debited, and a current liability account, Dividend Payable, is credited for a dollar value equal to the per-share amount times the number of outstanding shares. Cash Dividend is a temporary account that is closed directly to Retained Earnings at the end of the accounting period. The Dividend Payable account is removed from the balance sheet when the dividend is paid on the date of payment. No entry is recorded on the date of record. The shareholders as of the date of record are simply the recipients of the dividend.

To illustrate, in December 1987 the Board of Directors of Marriott Corporation declared a fourth-quarter cash dividend of $.20 per share on 118.8 million common shares outstanding. The following journal entry was recorded on that date.

Cash Dividend	23,760,000	
Dividend Payable (118.8 million sh × $.20/sh)		23,760,000
To record the declaration of a cash dividend.		

Marriott recorded the following entry on the date of payment.

Dividend Payable	23,760,000	
Cash		23,760,000
To record the payment of a cash dividend.		

Accounting for Property Dividends. Dividends paid with a corporation's noncash assets can be in whatever form the board of directors designates, such as inventory, real estate, or securities. For practical purposes, however, most property dividends are paid in the form of securities issued by other companies (e.g., marketable securities).

When the board of directors declares a property dividend, a liability in the amount of the fair market value of the property to be distributed is created on the date of declaration. If, on the date of declaration, the fair market value of the property exceeds its balance-sheet value, the balance-sheet value must be increased, and a gain is recognized in the amount of the difference between the balance-sheet value and the fair market value. If the fair market value of the property is less than the balance-sheet value, a loss must be recognized in the amount of the difference between the balance-sheet value and the fair market value. Such gains and losses are disclosed on the income statement under the section entitled "Other gains and losses."

After the balance-sheet value of the property is adjusted to fair market value, property dividends are treated exactly as cash dividends: (1) on the date of declaration, the Dividend account is debited, and the associated liability is credited in the amount of the fair market value of the property; (2) on the date of record, no entry is recorded; and (3) on the date of payment, the property and the liability are removed from the books. As with cash dividends, the Property Dividend account is closed directly to Retained Earnings at the end of the accounting period.

To illustrate, Leighton Corporation transferred marketable securities with a cost of $550,000 to its stockholders by declaring a property dividend on December 28,

Figure 12-10   A property dividend

1986
Dec. 28
	Marketable Securities ($580,000 − $550,000)
	    Gain on Appreciation of Securities
	    To adjust the property to fair market value.
		30,000	30,000

Dec. 28	Property Dividend
	    Dividend Payable
	    To record the declaration of the property
	        dividend.
		580,000	580,000

1987 Jan. 15	(No entry.)		

Jan. 30	Dividend Payable
	    Marketable Securities
	    To record the payment of the property
	        dividend.
		580,000	580,000

1986, to be distributed on January 30, 1987, to the stockholders of record on January 15. The fair market value of the securities on December 28, the date of declaration, was $580,000. The entries contained in Figure 12–10 would be recorded at each of the three dates.

Figure 12–11 summarizes and illustrates the journal entries involved in accounting for cash and property dividends. The figure covers the methods used to account for three independent cases: (1) a cash dividend of $800, (2) a property dividend in the form of securities with a fair market value of $800 and a balance-sheet value of $760, and (3) a property dividend in the form of securities with a fair market value of $800 and a balance-sheet value of $860. In each case the entries recorded on the date of declaration, the date of record, and the date of payment are provided.

Review the journal entries associated with each case, and note the general rule for valuing dividends. It states that dividends are recorded at the fair market value, as of the date of declaration, of the assets distributed to the stockholders. Note also that by adjusting the property to be distributed to its fair market value, property dividends are accounted for as if the property were first sold (converted into cash), and then the cash proceeds from the sale were distributed to the stockholders.

Stock Splits and Stock Dividends. Corporations can distribute additional shares to existing stockholders by declaring either a stock split or a stock dividend. For practical purposes, there is very little difference between these two actions. In both cases the existing shareholders receive additional shares, and in neither case are the assets or liabilities of the corporation increased or decreased.

In a **stock split** the number of outstanding shares is simply "split" into smaller units, which requires the corporation to distribute additional shares. A 2:1 stock split, for example, serves to double the number of outstanding shares, which requires that the company distribute an additional share for each common share outstanding. A 3:1 stock split effectively triples the number of outstanding shares,

Figure 12–11 Accounting for cash and property dividends

General Rule: Dividends are recorded at the fair market value, as of the date of declaration, of the assets distributed to the stockholders.

Date of Declaration——————————→**Date of Record**——————————→**Date of Payment**

Case 1: $800 cash dividend

Cash Dividend	800		No entry	Dividend Payable	800	
Dividend Payable		800		Cash		800
To record the declaration of a cash dividend.				To record the payment of a property dividend.		

Case 2: Property dividend—securities with a fair market value of $800 and a balance-sheet value of $760

Securities	40	
Gain on Appreciation		40
To adjust the securities to market value.		

Property Dividend	800		No entry	Dividend Payable	800	
Dividend Payable		800		Securities		800
To record the declaration of a property dividend.				To record the payment of a property dividend.		

Case 3: Property dividend—securities with a fair market value of $800 and a balance-sheet value of $860

Loss on Securities	60	
Securities		60
To adjust the securities to market value.		

Property Dividend	800		No entry	Dividend Payable	800	
Dividend Payable		800		Securities		800
To record the declaration of a property dividend.				To record the payment of a property dividend.		

which the company executes by distributing two additional shares for each one outstanding. In a 3:2 stock split, one additional share is issued for every two outstanding.

In a **stock dividend** additional shares, usually expressed as a percentage of the outstanding shares, are issued to the stockholders. Large stock dividends have essentially the same effect as stock splits. Both a 100 percent stock dividend and a 2:1 stock split, for example, double the number of outstanding shares. Similarly, both a 50 percent stock dividend and a 3:2 stock split increase outstanding shares by 50 percent. Professional accounting standards recommend that relatively large stock dividends (over 25 percent) be referred to as **stock splits in the form of dividends.** Stock splits and stock splits in the form of dividends are relatively common. *Accounting Trends and Techniques* (New York: AICPA, 1987) reports that, of the 600 major U.S. companies surveyed, 105 (18 percent) reported a stock split or a large stock dividend during 1986. Of those 105 issuances, 9 percent were less than 3:2, 35 percent were 3:2, 50 percent were 2:1, and 6 percent were greater than 2:1. Relatively small stock dividends (less than 25 percent), which are somewhat less common than either stock splits or stock splits in the form of dividends, are referred to as **ordinary stock dividends.**

Accounting for Stock Dividends and Stock Splits. Stock dividends and splits can be divided into three categories: (1) ordinary stock dividends (<25 percent), (2) stock splits in the form of dividends (>25 percent) and (3) stock splits. While each category is accounted for in a slightly different manner, it is important to realize that such actions affect neither the corporation's assets nor its liabilities. Only accounts within the stockholders' equity section (i.e., Common Stock, Additional Paid-in Capital, or Retained Earnings) are adjusted.

Ordinary Stock Dividends. When the board of directors of a corporation declares an ordinary stock dividend, a Dividend account is debited for the number of shares to be issued times the fair market value of the shares, the Common Stock account is credited for the number of shares issued times the par value, and Additional Paid-in Capital is credited for the remainder.[13]

To illustrate, assume that ATP International has 100,000 shares of $1 par value common stock outstanding, each with a fair market value of $25. The company would record the following journal entry if the board of directors decided to distribute 5000 additional shares by declaring a 5 percent stock dividend.

```
Stock Dividend ([100,000 × .05] × $25/sh)        125,000
    Common Stock (5,000 sh × $1/sh)                          5,000
    Additional Paid-in Capital (Stock Dividend)            120,000
    To record a 5 percent stock dividend.
```

Note that no assets or liabilities are involved in the transaction. Retained Earnings is reduced after the Stock Dividend account is closed at the end of the accounting period, and the Common Stock and Additional Paid-in Capital (Stock Dividend) accounts are both increased. In other words, Retained Earnings have been *capitalized*. Earned capital has been transferred to contributed capital. Note also that if the issued stock has a par value of zero, the entire amount of the stock dividend is credited to the Common Stock account.

Stock Splits in the Form of Dividends. Under generally accepted accounting principles, stock dividends in excess of 25 percent should be valued at the par value of the issued stock. That is, a dollar amount equal to the par value of the stock times the number of issued shares should be transferred from Retained Earnings to the Common Stock account.

To illustrate, in 1986 the Board of Directors of Toys "Я" Us, Inc. declared a 3:2 stock split in the form of a 50 percent stock dividend. Prior to the declaration the company had 8.4 million shares of common stock outstanding, each with a par value of $.10. To execute the stock split, the company distributed 4.2 million additional shares and recorded the following journal entry.

```
Stock Dividend                                        420,000
    Common Stock (4.2 million sh × $.10 par)                   420,000
    To record a 3:2 stock split in the form of a 50 percent stock dividend.
```

As in the case of an ordinary stock dividend, no assets or liabilities are involved in the transaction. Retained Earnings is reduced after the Stock Dividend account is closed at the end of the accounting period, and the Common Stock account is increased. Again, earned capital is transferred to contributed capital. However, unlike ordinary stock dividends, the amount transferred from Retained Earnings to the Common Stock account in this case is determined by the par value of the stock. If the issued stock has a par value of zero, there is no dollar amount to transfer from Retained Earnings to the Common Stock account, and no entry is made to record the transaction.

---

13. We assume here that the stock dividend is declared and issued on the same day.

Figure 12-12 Accounting for ordinary stock dividends, stock splits in the form of dividends, and stock splits

Form of Distribution	Accounts Affected			Basis for Valuation
Ordinary stock dividend (less than 25%)	Stock Dividend (R/E)	XX		Fair market value of issued stock
	Common Stock		XX	
	Additional Paid-in Capital (S/D)		XX	
Stock split in the form of a dividend (greater than 25%)	Stock Dividend (R/E)	XX		Par value of issued stock
	Common Stock		XX	
Stock split	No entry			No entry

Stock Splits. Under generally accepted accounting principles, no entry is recorded in the books when stock splits are declared. The corporation should simply record the fact that the par value of the issued stock has been reduced in proportion to the size of the split. A 3:1 split, for example, triples the number of outstanding shares and reduces the par value of each share to one-third of its original value. If the stock has no par value, the par value need not be adjusted.

To illustrate, in 1987 the Board of Directors of General Electric approved a 2:1 stock split and recorded no journal entry to reflect the action. The 463 million outstanding shares, each with a par value of $1.25, were simply replaced by 926 (463 × 2) million outstanding shares, each with a par value of $.625 ($1.25÷2). In other words, an additional share with a par value of $.625 was distributed for each share outstanding.

Figure 12-12 summarizes the methods, recommended under generally accepted accounting principles, to account for ordinary stock dividends, stock splits in the form of dividends, and stock splits. While these represent the recommended methods, there is controversy in the area, and actual practices do vary. *Accounting Trends and Techniques* (New York: AICPA, 1987), for example, reported that of the 105 stock splits and large stock dividends reported, 33 companies debited Retained Earnings and credited Common Stock, 60 debited Additional Paid-in Capital and credited Common Stock, and 12 recorded no journal entry. Such controversy exists because there is considerable doubt about whether stock dividends and stock splits actually represent economic exchanges between a corporation and its shareholders and, accordingly, whether any journal entry should be recorded at all. Certainly no assets or liabilities are exchanged, and there is little theoretical justification for using either the market value of the stock or its par value, which has limited economic significance, to value the distribution.

Why Do Companies Declare Stock Dividends and Stock Splits? To understand the reasons behind stock dividends and stock splits, it is important to realize that such actions do not distribute additional assets to the shareholders. Their proportionate ownership of the company after the dividend or split is the same as it was before the dividend or split. For example, a shareholder who owns 10 of a company's 100 outstanding shares, owns 10 percent of the company. After a 2:1 stock split, the shareholder will own 20 of the company's 200 outstanding shares, which still represents a 10 percent interest. Consequently, unlike cash or property dividends, corporations do not declare stock dividends or stock splits to distribute assets to the shareholders.

Perhaps the most popular reason for declaring a stock split or a large stock dividend is to reduce the per share price of the outstanding shares so that investors can more easily purchase them. When IBM, for example, declared a 4:1 stock split, which quadrupled the number of outstanding shares, the per-share price of IBM stock immediately decreased from $300 to $75 ($300÷4). The managements of many corporations believe that such an action encourages better public relations and wider stock ownership.

The reasons for ordinary stock dividends (<25 percent) are less clear. Such distributions have a relatively small effect on the number of outstanding shares and thus do little to reduce per-share prices and broaden stock ownership. Alternatively, corporations that are short of cash may distribute stock dividends instead of cash dividends, so that the shareholders are at least receiving something. Such a publicity gesture may satisfy stockholders, especially if they believe that they are the recipients of additional assets. Finally, corporations may issue stock dividends to capitalize a portion of Retained Earnings. By reducing Retained Earnings, a stock dividend places a more restrictive limitation on future dividend payments.

Appropriations of Retained Earnings

An **appropriation of retained earnings** is a book entry, involving only the Retained Earnings account, that serves to restrict a portion of retained earnings from the payment of future dividends. It involves no asset or liability accounts. Such entries are executed either at the discretion of the board of directors or in conformance with the terms of contracts (e.g., debt covenants).

Suppose, for example, that the board of directors of Rosebud Corporation plans to expand the company's main manufacturing plant. To save cash so that the expansion can be funded internally, the board has decided to place a restriction on the payment of future dividends. Accordingly, a resolution is passed stating that the company cannot pay dividends that reduce Retained Earnings below $300,000. The following journal entry could accompany this resolution.

Retained Earnings	300,000	
Restricted Retained Earnings		300,000
To record an appropriation of retained earnings.		

Assuming that the balance in the company's Retained Earnings account before the appropriation was $500,000, the stockholders' equity section of Rosebud's balance sheet after the resolution would appear as in Figure 12–13.

Figure 12–13 Appropriation of retained earnings

Rosebud Corporation Balance Sheet Stockholders' Equity December 31, 1990		
Common stock		$1,200,000
Additional paid-in capital		2,500,000
Retained earnings		
Restricted	300,000	
Unrestricted	200,000	500,000
Total stockholders' equity		$4,200,000

Appropriations of retained earnings that result from contractual restrictions are accounted for in a similar manner. If a long-term debt covenant requires that a company maintain a Retained Earnings balance of at least $650,000, that dollar amount is transferred from Retained Earnings to Restricted Retained Earnings.

Retained Earnings	650,000	
Restricted Retained Earnings		650,000
To record an appropriation of retained earnings.		

In practice, most companies simply disclose the existence, nature, and dollar amount of restricted retained earnings instead of recording the journal entries illustrated. Nordstrom, for example, disclosed the following information about restricted retained earnings in its 1987 financial report and chose not to adjust the balance of Retained Earnings: "Senior Note Agreements contain restrictive covenants which . . . restrict dividends to shareholders to a formula amount (under the most restrictive formula, approximately $247,342 of retained earnings was not restricted)."

THE STATEMENT OF STOCKHOLDERS' EQUITY

Generally accepted accounting principles require that the changes during the period in the dollar balances of the separate accounts composing the stockholders' equity section be disclosed in the financial report. A company can either disclose such changes in the footnotes or in a separate financial statement called the **statement of stockholders' equity.** An example of such a statement, summarized, appears in Figure 12–14.

Figure 12–14   Statement of stockholders' equity

DuPont
Statement of Stockholders' Equity
For the Years Ended Dec. 31, 1985, 1986, and 1987
(dollars in millions)

	1987	1986	1985
Preferred stock	$ 237	$ 237	$ 237
Common stock	398	400	401
Additional paid-in capital			
Balance at beginning of year	4,535	4,492	4,455
Common stock			
Issued	57	80	37
Treasury stock	(37)	(37)	—
Balance at end of year	4,555	4,535	4,492
Retained earnings			
Balance at beginning of year	8,202	7,529	7,142
Net income	1,786	1,538	1,118
Dividends	(802)	(744)	(731)
Treasury stock	(132)	(121)	—
Balance at end of year	9,054	8,202	7,529
Total stockholders' equity	$14,244	$13,374	$12,659

Source: 1987 annual report.

THE ANNUAL REPORT OF K MART CORPORATION

Turn now to K mart's annual report located in Appendix D. The Balance Sheet (page 32) indicates that K mart's shareholders' equity section consists of Common Stock, Capital in Excess of Par, Retained Earnings, Treasury Shares, and a Foreign Currency Translation Adjustment.[14] Note that Retained Earnings is by far the largest component ($4.345 billion), followed by contributed capital of $792 million ($204 + $588). As of January 25, 1989 total liabilities (excluding Deferred Income Taxes), contributed capital, and Retained Earnings represented 57 percent, 6 percent, and 35 percent of total assets, respectively. When compared to the companies listed in Table 12–1, these percentages show that K mart's reliance on debt financing is average, its reliance on contributed capital is below average, and its reliance on internally generated funds is above average.

K mart has 500 million shares of authorized, $1 par value, common stock of which 204.3 million shares have been issued. Page 27 indicates that "as of January 25, 1989, there were 84,595 shareholders of record . . . [and] K mart Corporation common stock is listed and traded on the New York, Pacific, Midwest, and Tokyo Stock Exchanges." The bottom of page 34 states that "ten million shares of no par value preferred stock with voting and cumulative dividend rights are authorized but unissued. Of these, 500,000 shares have been designated Series A Junior Participating Stock. Currently there are no plans for the issuance of preferred stock."

The cost of treasury shares as of January 25, 1989 was $131 million, which represents only 16 percent of contributed capital. Note on page 26 that "in November 1987, the Board of Directors authorized the repurchase of up to $500 million of the company's common stock. Under this authorization, the company repurchased 1.0 million of the company's common stock for $33 million during 1988 and 2.7 million shares for $75 million during 1987." Thus, while the Board is authorized to make substantial share repurchases, it has opted not to do so. In this respect, K mart is unlike the companies listed in Table 12–3, whose share repurchase programs have created treasury stock accounts exceeding contributed capital. K mart's stock acquisitions are used primarily to support the employee savings and stock option plans described on pages 47 and 48.

The Consolidated Statement of Shareholders' Equity (page 34) summarizes the activity in the equity accounts during 1986, 1987, and 1988. In all three years sizable cash dividends were declared and relatively small amounts of common stock were issued under the employee savings and/or stock option plans. Treasury shares were repurchased in 1987 and 1988, and a three-for-two stock split was declared and distributed in 1986. Events occuring during the three-year period that have not been covered in the text thus far include (1) a common stock issuance for conversion of debentures in 1986 and (2) foreign translation adjustments in each year.

The Statement of Cash Flows (page 33) indicates that stockholders' equity transactions, with the exception of dividend payments, have not represented major financing activities. Common stock issuances, reissuances of treasury shares,

---

14. The Foreign Currency Translation Adjustment pertains to companies that hold substantial investments in foreign subsidiaries and is covered in Chapter 16.

and treasury share purchases have all been relatively small since the beginning of 1987. Dividend payments, on the other hand, have ranged consistently between 35 percent and 40 percent of Income from continuing retail operations (page 14). Note also that the market value, book value, and par value of K mart's common stock are quite different. As of January 25, 1989, for example, the market value was $39 3/8 (page 27), the book value was $25.12 (page 14), and the par value was $1.00 (page 34). Finally, as indicated on page 42 and discussed in Chapter 11, "at January 25, 1989, $2,351 million of consolidated retained earnings were free of [revolving credit agreement] restrictions."

REVIEW PROBLEM

Figure 12-15 refers to the stockholders' equity transactions of Pike Place Corporation over its first three years of operations: 1988, 1989, and 1990. Transactions are described and followed by the appropriate journal entries. The stockholders' equity section of the balance sheet is prepared at the end of each of the three years.

Figure 12–15 Review problem

1988		
(1) The company issues 1000 shares of $1 par value stock for $70 per share.		
Cash (1000 sh × $70/sh)	70,000	
Common Stock (1000 sh × $1 par value/sh)		1,000
Additional Paid-in Capital (C/S)		69,000
(2) The company issues 500 shares of no par value, $5, cumulative preferred stock for $50 per share.		
Cash (500 sh × $50/sh)	25,000	
Preferred Stock		25,000
(3) Net income during the year = $2000		
Dividends = $0		

**Pike Place Corporation
Stockholders' Equity
December 31, 1988**

Preferred stock (500 sh, no par value)	$ 25,000
Common stock (1000 sh @ $1 par value)	1,000
Additional paid-in capital (C/S)	69,000
Retained earnings	2,000
Total stockholders' equity	$ 97,000

Note: Dividends in arrears on cumulative preferred stock = $2500 (500 sh × $5/sh)

Figure 12–15 (continued)

1989

(1) The company purchases 200 treasury (common) shares for $60 per share.

Treasury Stock (200 sh × $60/sh)	$ 12,000	
Cash		12,000

(2) Net income for the year = $20,000

Dividends = $6600: $5000 for preferred stockholders ($2500 dividends in arrears and $2500 [500 sh × $5/sh]) for 1989, and $1600 for the common stockholders (800 outstanding sh × $2/sh). The dividends were declared and paid.

Preferred Dividends	5,000	
Common Dividends	1,600	
Dividends Payable		6,600
To record the declaration of dividends.		
Dividends Payable	6,600	
Cash		6,600
To record the payment of dividends.		

Pike Place Corporation
Stockholders' Equity
December 31, 1989

Preferred stock (500 sh, no par value)	$ 25,000
Common stock (1000 sh @ $1 par value)	1,000
Additional paid-in capital (C/S)	69,000
Retained earnings	15,400*
Less: Treasury stock (200 sh × $60/sh)	12,000
Total stockholders' equity	$ 98,400

*$2000 + $20,000 − $6600

Figure 12–15 (continued)

1990

(1) The company reissued 100 treasury shares for $65 each.

Cash (100 sh × $65/sh)	6,500	
Treasury Stock (100 sh × $60/sh)		6,000
Additional Paid-in Capital (T/S)		500

(2) The company reissued 50 treasury shares for $40 each.

Cash (50 sh × $40/sh)	2,000	
Additional Paid-in Capital (T/S)	500	
Retained Earnings	500	
Treasury Stock (50 sh × $60/sh)		3,000

(3) The company declared a 2:1 stock split in the form of a 100 percent stock dividend. 950 common shares were outstanding at the time of the split.

Stock Dividend (closed to Retained Earnings)	950	
Common Stock (950 sh × $1 par value/sh)		950

(4) The company entered into a debt covenant that required a minimum Retained Earnings balance of $30,000. The board of directors voted to restrict retained earnings of $30,000.

Retained Earnings	30,000	
Restricted Retained Earnings		30,000

(5) Net income at the end of the year = $35,000

Dividends = $6300: $2500 to preferred stockholders and $3800 to common stockholders [1800 sh outstanding × $2/sh]. The dividends were declared but unpaid at year end.

Preferred Dividends	2,500	
Common Dividends	3,800	
Dividends Payable		6,300

Pike Place Corporation
Stockholders' Equity
December 31, 1990

Preferred stock (500 sh, no par value)		$ 25,000
Common stock (1950 sh @ $1 par value)		1,950[a]
Additional paid-in capital (C/S)		69,000[b]
Retained earnings		
Restricted	30,000	
Unrestricted	12,650	42,650[c]
Less: Treasury stock (100 sh × $30/sh)[d]		3,000[e]
Total stockholders' equity		$135,600

    a. $1000 + $950
    b. $69,000 + $500 − $500
    c. $15,400 − $500 − $950 + $35,000 − $6300
    d. 50 sh × $60/sh prior to the 2:1 stock split
    e. $(12,000) + $6000 + $3000

SUMMARY OF LEARNING OBJECTIVES

1 Identify the three forms of financing, and describe the relative importance of each to major U.S. corporations.

Companies can generate assets from three different sources: (1) borrowings, (2) issuing equity securities, and (3) retaining funds generated through profitable operations. Borrowings are represented by liabilities on the balance sheet, equity issuances are represented by contributed capital (preferred stock, common stock, and additional paid-in capital), and retaining funds is represented by earned capital (retained earnings). Major U.S. corporations generally rely more heavily on liabilities as a form of financing than on the combined total of contributed and earned capital. Earned capital is typically more important than contributed capital. The relative importance of each form of financing, however, varies across companies, depending upon a number of factors.

2 Distinguish debt from equity, and explain why such a distinction is important to investors and creditors, managers, and accountants.

Debt involves a contractual relationship with an outsider. The contract usually states a fixed maturity date, interest charges, security in case of default, and additional provisions designed to protect the interests of the debtholders. Interest is an expense on the income statement and is deductible for tax purposes. In case of liquidation, creditors have rights to the company's assets before owners. Creditors do not vote in the annual election of the board of directors.

Equity involves a relationship with an owner. There is no legal contract, no fixed maturity date, and no periodic interest payment. Dividends are at the discretion of the board of directors. They are not considered an expense on the income statement and are not tax deductible. Equityholders have lower asset priority than debtholders in case of liquidation, but they have a direct voice in the operation of the company, primarily through voting power over the board of directors.

Distinguishing debt from equity is important to investors and creditors because equity investments are generally riskier than debt investments but offer the potential for higher returns. From the company's perspective, issuing debt involves the commitment of future cash outflows but interest is tax deductible. Issuing equity, while avoiding fixed contractual cash outflows, dilutes the ownership of the existing shareholders and makes it easier for outside investors to gain significant control. From the accountant's perspective, debt and equity are classified in different sections of the balance sheet and, unlike interest payments and debt redemptions, exchanges of equity are never reflected on the income statement.

3 Explain the economic consequences associated with the methods used to account for stockholders' equity.

The economic consequences associated with accounting for stockholders' equity arise from the effects of financial ratios that include the dollar amount of stockholders' equity or its components on a company's stock prices, credit rating, or any debt covenants that restrict additional borrowings, the payment of dividends, or the repurchase of outstanding equity shares. The dollar amount of stockholders' equity can be found in a number of the financial ratios used by Dun & Bradstreet, for example, to determine a company's credit rating. Such ratios are also commonly used to define restrictions in debt covenants imposed on management. The use of financial ratios in these ways can encourage management, for example, to structure debt financing in a way that resembles equity so that additional debt need not be reported on the balance sheet. Issuing certain forms of preferred stock and other hybrid securities may represent such a strategy.

4   Describe the basic characteristics of the corporate form of organization.

A corporation is a separate legal entity that provides protection from legal liability but imposes constraints on the owners (stockholders). In general, the liability of corporate stockholders is limited to their investments; the corporation is taxed at the corporate tax rate (approximately 34 percent); dividends, which must be declared by the board of directors, are taxed again in the hands of the stockholders; and markets exist where the equity interests of major U.S. corporations can be purchased and sold readily.

5   Describe the rights associated with preferred and common stock and the methods used to account for stock issuances.

Stock that is preferred as to dividends carries the right, if dividends are declared by the board, to receive a certain specified dividend payment before the common stockholders receive a dividend. If the preferred stock is cumulative, when the corporation misses a dividend, dividends in arrears are created in the amount of the missed preferred dividend. In future periods, as dividends are declared, dividends in arrears are paid first to the preferred stockholders, the preferred stockholders are then paid their normal, annual dividend and, finally, the common stockholders are paid from what remains. If the preferred stock carries a participating feature, the preferred stockholders not only receive their initial specified amount but they also share in the remaining dividends with the common stockholders. Stock that is preferred as to assets carries a claim to the corporation's assets, in case of liquidation, that has higher priority than the claim carried by common stock. In many ways preferred stock resembles debt.

Common stock is characterized by three fundamental rights: (1) the right to receive dividends if they are declared by the board, (2) a residual right to the corporation's assets in case of liquidation, and (3) the right to exert control over corporate management, which is exercised primarily by voting in the election of the board at the annual stockholders' meeting.

Preferred and common stock issuances must be authorized in the corporate charter and approved by the board of directors and, in some cases, the stockholders. The number of shares outstanding may differ from the number of shares originally issued because outstanding shares are often repurchased and held in treasury. When stock with no par value is issued for cash, the Cash account is debited for the proceeds, and the Stock account is credited for the entire dollar amount. When stock with a par (or stated) value is issued for cash, the Cash account is debited for the total proceeds, the Stock account is credited for the number of shares issued times the par value per share, and the Additional Paid-in Capital account is credited for the remainder.

6   Distinguish among the market value, book value, par value, and stated value of a share of common stock.

The market value of a share of stock is the price at which the stock can be purchased and sold on the open market. The book value of a share of stock is equal to the book value of the corporation, as indicated on the balance sheet (stockholders' equity or net assets), less preferred capital divided by the number of common shares outstanding.

The par value of a share of stock has no relationship to its market value or book value and, for the most part, has no economic significance. At one time, it represented a legal concept, instituted by some states, that intended to protect creditors by making common stockholders liable for at least the par value of the stock, even if their investments were for amounts that were less than par. Over time, however, the concept of par value proved to be ineffective because corporations simply assigned par values to common shares that were far below their market prices. Many states then attempted to protect corporate creditors by substituting the concept of stated value for par value. This legal concept requires that dividends paid to stockholders cannot reduce stockholders' equity below a certain dollar amount, called the *stated value*. However, in most states corporate law designates the amount of Retained Earnings as the limitation on the dividends that can be declared by a corporation, and many debt covenants restrict dividends even further. These limitations effectively render the concept of stated value legally and economically meaningless, because corporate dividends are constrained by these restrictions more tightly than they are constrained by the stated value restriction.

7 Define treasury stock, explain why corporations acquire it, and summarize the methods used to account for it.

Outstanding common stock is often repurchased by companies. Such stocks are either (1) held in treasury, to be reissued at a later date, or (2) retired. Treasury stock purchases normally must be authorized and approved by the company's board of directors and stockholders. Treasury stock carries none of the usual rights of ownership.

Companies purchase treasury stock to support employee compensation plans, to fend off possible takeover attempts, to prepare for merger activity, to increase the market price of the company's outstanding stock, and to increase the company's earnings per share (net income/outstanding common shares). Retiring treasury shares enables management to return capital to stockholders and thereby reduce the scale of the company's operations.

Under the cost method, when a company purchases its own outstanding common stock, a permanent account, called Treasury Stock, is debited for the cost of the purchase. This account is disclosed below retained earnings in the stockholders' equity section of the balance sheet. If treasury stock is reissued at a price greater than its original cost, the Cash account is debited for the proceeds, the Treasury Stock account is credited for the cost, and the difference is credited to the Additional Paid-in Capital (Treasury Stock) account. If treasury stock is reissued at an amount less than the original cost, the Cash account is debited for the proceeds, the Treasury Stock account is credited for the original cost, and Additional Paid-in Capital (Treasury Stock) is debited for the difference, if there is a sufficient balance in the account to cover the difference. If the difference between the cost and the proceeds exceeds the balance in the Additional Paid-in Capital account, Retained Earnings is debited.

8 Define cash and property dividends, and describe some of the dividend strategies followed by corporations.

Cash dividends represent distributions of cash to the stockholders. Property dividends (dividends in kind) represent distributions of property, usually debt or equity securities in other companies, to the stockholders.

When a cash dividend is declared, a Cash Dividend account is debited and a current liability account, Dividends Payable, is credited on the date of declaration. The dollar amount is equal to the cash dividend per share multiplied times the number of outstanding shares. The dividend account is a temporary account that is closed directly to Retained Earnings at the end of the accounting period. On the date of record, no entry is made in the books of the corporation. The shareholders as of this date are the recipients of the dividends. On the date of payment the cash dividend is paid, and the Dividends Payable liability is removed from the balance sheet.

When a property dividend is declared, the property to be distributed is adjusted to fair market value on the date of declaration. If the fair market value exceeds the balance-sheet value, the asset is debited, and a gain is recognized in the amount of the difference between the balance-sheet value and the fair market value. If the fair market value is less than the balance-sheet value, a loss is recognized. Such gains and losses are disclosed on the income statement. After the property is adjusted to fair market value, property dividends are treated exactly as cash dividends. On the date of declaration, the dividend account is debited, and the associated liability is credited in the amount of the fair market value of the property. On the date of record no entry is made. On the date of payment the property and the liability are removed from the books.

When to declare a dividend, and how much to declare depend on the nature, financial condition, and desired image of the company, as well as legal constraints. If dividends are to be paid in cash, the board of directors must first be certain that the corporation has sufficient cash to meet the payment. Some companies have adopted policies of paying no dividends. Such companies reinvest their earnings primarily to support growth without having to rely too heavily on debt and equity financing. Other companies pay quarterly dividends at the rate of a relatively fixed percentage of net income and also attempt to increase their dividend payments consistently from year to year. Some companies consistently increase dividends from year to year, but the distributions do not represent a consistent percentage of net income.

9 Distinguish among a stock split, a stock split in the form of a dividend, and an ordinary stock dividend. Summarize the methods used to account for each, and briefly explain why corporations declare stock splits and stock dividends.

In a stock split the number of outstanding shares is simply split into smaller units, which requires the corporation to distribute additional shares. In a stock dividend, additional shares, usually expressed as a percentage of the outstanding shares, are issued to the stockholders. Professional accounting standards recommend that relatively large stock dividends (over 25 percent) be referred to as stock splits in the form of dividends, and that relatively small stock dividends (less than 25 percent) be referred to as ordinary stock dividends.

When the board of directors of a corporation declares an ordinary stock dividend (less than 25 percent), a Stock Dividend account is debited for the number of shares to be issued times the fair market value of the shares, the Common Stock account is credited for the number of shares issued times the par value, and Additional Paid-in Capital (Stock Dividend) is credited for the remainder.

When the board of directors of a corporation declares a stock split in the form of dividend (greater than 25 percent), a Stock Dividend account is debited for the number of shares to be issued times the par value of the shares, and the Common Stock account is credited for the same dollar amount. When the board declares a stock split, no entry is recorded in the books. The par value of the stock is simply reduced in proportion to the split.

While the methods described above are recommended under generally accepted accounting principles, not all companies follow them. Accounting practices differ because many accountants believe that stock dividends and stock splits do not represent economic exchanges between a corporation and its shareholders. It is also difficult to justify the use of the market value or par value of the stock to value the distribution.

Stock splits or large stock dividends are often declared to reduce the per-share price of the outstanding shares, so that investors can more easily purchase them. The reasons for ordinary stock dividends are less clear. Such distributions have a relatively small effect on the number of outstanding shares and do little to reduce per-share prices and broaden stock ownership. Corporations that are short of cash may distribute stock, instead of cash, dividends so that the shareholders are at least receiving something. Corporations may also issue stock dividends to capitalize a portion of retained earnings, rendering them unavailable for future dividends.

10 Explain how retained earnings are appropriated and why corporations follow such a practice.

An appropriation of retained earnings is a book entry involving only the Retained Earnings account that serves to restrict a portion of retained earnings from the payment of future dividends. It involves no asset or liability accounts. Such entries are executed either at the discretion of the board of directors or in conformance with the terms of contracts (e.g., debt covenants). In practice, most companies simply disclose the existence, nature, and dollar amount of Restricted Retained Earnings instead of recording a journal entry to appropriate retained earnings.

APPENDIX 12A

Proprietorships and Partnerships

There are three major types of business enterprises: the **individual proprietorship,** the **partnership,** and the corporation. Approximately 70 percent of the business enterprises in the United States are individual proprietorships, 17 percent are partnerships, and 13 percent are corporations. While proprietorships and partnerships tend to be relatively small, a number of large enterprises use the partnership form. Professional firms, for example, such as brokerage houses and public accounting and law firms, which generate hundreds of millions of dollars annually, are normally organized as partnerships. This appendix introduces proprietorships and partnerships, identifies the trade-offs involved in choosing between them and the corporate form, and briefly discusses the methods used to account for the owners' equity section of a partnership or proprietorship.

Individual proprietorships and partnerships are organized in much the same way and differ only in terms of the number of owners. Proprietorships are owned by single parties, while partnerships are owned by two or more parties. In general, proprietorships and partnerships are simply extensions of their owners; unlike corporations, they are not legal entities in and of themselves. In the following discussion a proprietorship is viewed as a simplified partnership: that is, a "partnership" consisting of a single partner. The essence of a partnership is the agreement signed among the partners, but of course such an agreement is not necessary in a proprietorship.

As stated, a partnership is not a separate legal entity. No formal charter or state certificate is required to form a partnership, and the government does not generally recognize a partnership as such. One or more individuals simply establish a business by purchasing or renting equipment or space, acquiring inventory, and obtaining any local operating licenses that might be required. It is usually necessary to have an attorney draw up a **partnership agreement,** which specifies the rights and obligations of the partners (e.g., capital contributions, duties, distribution of profits, and limitations on selling partnership interests), but a partnership agreement is solely for the protection of the partners. It is not required by law. Legally, a partnership is nothing more than an agreement drawn up among the partners. Partnerships are not sued, nor are they taxed. The relevant legal entities are the partners themselves.

LEGAL LIABILITY OF THE PARTNERS: UNLIMITED

In a partnership the individual partners, not the partnership itself, are legally responsible for all obligations of the business. If the enterprise incurs debts, suffers losses, or becomes bankrupt, the partners are jointly and severally responsible for all debts incurred. That is, the partners are not only responsible for their own portions of the enterprise's debts, but are also liable for the portions of the other partners, if they are unable to meet their respective responsibilities. Consequently, a partner's personal assets (e.g., home and automobile) are at risk and might be required to satisfy creditor claims. Unlike a corporation, where the liability of a stockholder is limited to his or her capital contribution, the legal liability faced by a partner is unlimited and may extend well beyond the amount originally contributed to the business.

INCOME TAXES: PERSONAL RATES, AND NO EFFECT FROM WITHDRAWALS

Partnerships are not subject to federal or state income taxes. Instead, the partners must include their shares of the total partnership profits, which are usually specified in the partnership agreement, on their individual income tax returns. Partnership profits, therefore, are taxed at the personal income tax rates of the individual partners, which range from approximately 15 percent to as much as 38 percent in some cases. Recall that corporations, as legal entities, are taxed at the corporate income tax rate (approximately 34 percent).

The amount of taxable partnership profit for each partner is not determined, or even affected by, the assets (usually cash) each partner withdraws from the partnership. This feature differs from a corporation in that corporate dividends are taxed separately in the hands of the shareholders. While it tends to reduce the total income tax liability of partners, this feature can create a problem for partnerships, especially those that finance expansion with internally generated funds.

For example, assume that Bob and Tom form a partnership and agree to share the rights to the profits equally and to limit their cash withdrawals in the early years, so that cash will be available to the partnership for expansion. In the first year of operations, assume that the partnership recognized net income of $50,000, giving Bob and Tom the right to $25,000 each. However, neither partner could withdraw $25,000 in cash because the partnership's cash was used to purchase productive assets during the year. Nonetheless, Bob and Tom are both required to report $25,000 as taxable income on their federal income tax returns which, in turn, increases the income tax they must pay as individuals. A problem arises in this case because the partnership provided the partners no additional cash with which to pay the additional taxes.

RETURNS TO PARTNERS: LIMITED MARKETS, BUT RELATIVELY FREE WITHDRAWALS

Partnership interests are not always easily transferable, and there are no active markets where such interests are readily purchased and sold. It is often difficult, therefore, to place a market value on a given partner's interest, and it is equally difficult to assess a partner's return in terms of capital appreciation. Instead, the return for most partners comes in the form of cash withdrawals.

Cash withdrawals from a partnership are limited only by agreement among the partners. They may be limited, for example, to a percentage of a partner's interest in the partnership, or they may be restricted in some way to provide working capital for operations or funds for expansion. Certainly, operating a partnership efficiently would be difficult if cash withdrawals by the partners were totally unrestricted. However, the partnership itself is not a legal entity, and within the constraints specified by the partnership agreement, withdrawals are relatively unencumbered.

CHOOSING A FORM OF BUSINESS: A SUMMARY

Figure 12A–1 summarizes the trade-offs between choosing the partnership (proprietorship) or corporate form of business. Relative freedom to create the terms of the partnership contract and lower overall tax rates generally favor the partnership form of business, while limited liability is a distinct advantage of corporations. Some companies, which are owned and operated by relatively few individuals and are not in need of large amounts of capital, are generally not organized as corporations. In such situations the owners and managers often work closely together, monitoring each other's activities, which in turn reduces the need for

Figure 12A–1 Trade-offs among the partnership and corporate forms of business

	Partnership (including proprietorship)	Corporation
Owners' Liability	Unlimited (personal assets at risk)	Limited to investment
Federal Income Tax	Personal tax rates of owners; income tax payments unaffected by withdrawals	Corporation is taxed at corporate tax rate (double taxation)
Owner Returns	Limited markets; relatively free withdrawals	Capital appreciation and declared dividends

limited liability. Companies in need of large amounts of capital, on the other hand, have difficulty collecting such funds without offering limited liability to investors. Consequently, such enterprises are usually organized as corporations.

ACCOUNTING FOR PARTNERSHIPS

There are few differences between accounting for partnerships (including proprietorships) and accounting for corporations. The differences relate to the owners' equity section and the balance sheet and are more a matter of form than substance.

Formation, Profit Distribution, and Withdrawals

The owners' equity section of a partnership consists of a Capital account for each individual partner. The Capital account is credited when a partner contributes assets or services to the partnership, credited (debited) when the partner receives his or her proportionate share of the partnership income (loss), and debited when the partner withdraws assets from the enterprise.

Formation of a Partnership
Assume that Buzz and Jeanie decide to form a partnership. Buzz contributes $50,000 cash, and Jeanie contributes a building appraised at $175,000, which has a $75,000 mortgage. If the partnership assumes the mortgage on the building, the following journal entry would record the formation of the partnership.

Cash	50,000	
Building	175,000	
Mortgage Note Payable		75,000
Capital, Buzz		50,000
Capital, Jeanie (175,000 − 75,000)		100,000
To record the formation of a partnership.		

Partnership Profit Distributions
Assume further that Buzz and Jeanie agree to share profits in the same proportion as their capital accounts, in this case 1:2 ($50,000:$100,000), and that during the first year of operations the partnership net income is $30,000 (revenues of

$80,000 less expenses of $50,000). The allocation of the $30,000 profit to the partners' Capital accounts entails two steps: (1) closing the Revenue and Expense accounts into the Income Summary account and (2) closing the Income Summary account into Buzz and Jeanie's respective Capital accounts. To implement these two steps, the following entries would be recorded.

Revenues	80,000	
Expense		50,000
Income Summary		30,000
To close Revenues and Expenses into Income Summary.		
Income Summary	30,000	
Capital, Buzz		10,000
Capital, Jeanie		20,000
To close Income Summary into the Capital accounts at a 1:2 ratio.		

Partnership Withdrawals

Assume that Buzz and Jeanie each withdrew $10,000 in cash during the year. The dollar amount of the withdrawals would reduce the partners' Capital accounts, and the following entry would be recorded.

Capital, Buzz	10,000	
Capital, Jeanie	10,000	
Cash		20,000
To record partner withdrawals.		

Capital Account Summary

The activity in Buzz and Jeanie's Capital accounts during the first year of the partnership operations would appear in ledger form as in Figure 12A–2.

While the journal entries and T-accounts illustrated above are straightforward, several points are important. Note first that the building contributed by Jeanie was recorded on the partnership books at its fair market value ($175,000). This transaction is equivalent to Jeanie contributing $100,000 in cash and the partnership then using the cash and signing a $75,000 mortgage to purchase an identical building. Thus, on the financial statements of the partnership, $175,000 serves as the capitalized cost of the building and is therefore subject to depreciation. The mortgage appears as a $75,000 liability on the financial statements, and Jeanie's Capital account is credited for $100,000.

Figure 12A–2   Partnership capital account ledgers

Capital, Buzz		Capital, Jeanie	
	50,000		100,000
	10,000		20,000
10,000		10,000	
	50,000		110,000

Note also that Buzz and Jeanie agreed to share profits in proportion to their Capital accounts. Such an arrangement is a common way to allocate profits, but it is certainly not the only way. Partners are free to use any mutually agreeable allocation scheme. Under the scheme Buzz and Jeanie have chosen, it is interesting to note that the capital proportion at the end of the first year is no longer 1:2. It is now 1:2.2 ($50,000:$110,000), which, under their agreement, would be used to allocate the net income recognized in the second year.

Finally, if Buzz and Jeanie provided services for the partnership, each partner's Capital account would normally be increased by the fair market value of the service. Payments received for such services would be treated as withdrawals and serve to reduce the Capital account. Consequently, services performed by a partner for a salary would have no effect on the partner's Capital account as long as the salary was equivalent to the market value of the service.

ADDITIONAL PARTNERSHIP ISSUES

We have covered only the basics of partnerships and partnership accounting. More difficult and complex conceptual issues must be addressed, for example, when accounting for the admission of a new partner, the withdrawal of a partner from the partnership, and partnership liquidations. There are a number of reasonable ways to account for these transactions, and generally accepted accounting principles are not completely clear in these areas. In each of these cases the fundamental accounting problem relates to the fact that the fair market value of the partnership is different from the value of the partnership as indicated on the financial statements. Comprehensive coverage of these areas can be found in intermediate or advanced accounting textbooks.

SUMMARY OF LEARNING OBJECTIVE

11 List the basic features of a partnership and briefly describe the methods used to account for its formation, the allocation of partnership profits, and partnership withdrawals.

Partnerships (including proprietorships) are not legal entities. The terms of a partnership are specified by the partnership agreement, which is drawn up among the partners. In general, the partners bear unlimited liability, federal income taxes are paid at the individual rates of each partner, markets for ownership interests are relatively limited, and withdrawals are limited only by the partnership agreement and not taxed in the hands of the partners.

The owners' equity section of a partnership consists of a Capital account for each individual partner. The Capital account is credited when the partner contributes assets or services to the partnership in the amount of the fair market value of the contribution; credited (debited) when the partner is allocated his or her proportionate share of the partnership income (loss), which is specified in the partnership agreement; and debited when the partner withdraws assets from the enterprise.

KEY TERMS

Appropriation of retained earnings (p. 590)
Authorized (shares) (p. 571)
Book value (of company/shares) (pp. 561, 577)
Contributed capital (p. 561)
Corporation (p. 569)
Cumulative preferred stock (p. 572)
Date of declaration, record, and payment (p. 583)
Dilution (p. 565)
Dividends in arrears (p. 572)
Dividends in kind (p. 583)
Double taxation (p. 570)
Earned capital (p. 561)
Hybrid securities (p. 568)
Individual proprietorship (p. 600)
Issued (shares) (p. 571)
Leverage (p. 565)
Market value (of stock) (p. 576)
Net assets (p. 561)

Net worth (p. 561)
Ordinary stock dividend (p. 587)
Outstanding (shares) (p. 571)
Par value (pp. 572, 577)
Participating (preferred stock) (p. 574)
Partnership (p. 600)
Partnership agreement (p. 601)
Preferred stock as to assets (p. 571)
Preferred stock as to dividends (p. 571)
Private placement (p. 569)
Promoters (p. 569)
Public placement (p. 569)
Residual interest (p. 563)
Stated value (p. 577)
Statement of stockholders' equity (p. 591)
Stock dividend (pp. 583, 587)
Stock split (p. 586)
Stock split in the form of a dividend (p. 587)
Takeover (p. 565)
Treasury stock (p. 566)

QUESTIONS FOR DISCUSSION AND REVIEW

1. Distinguish between borrowed capital, contributed capital, and earned capital, and explain why such a distinction is important to creditors and investors, managers, and auditors. How is this distinction depicted on the financial statements?

2. Why might a manager wish to structure a financing transaction as equity instead of debt? What are hybrid securities, and what kinds of problems do they present for accountants?

3. Name and briefly describe the accounts that compose the stockholders' equity section of the balance sheet.

4. Provide several reasons why major U.S. corporations tend to rely on debt more heavily than contributed capital or earned capital as a source of financing.

5. Explain how a debt covenant might impose restrictions on management that are expressed in terms of stockholders' equity accounts.

6. Differentiate debt from equity, and describe why such a differentiation is important to investors and creditors, managers, and accountants.

7. What basic trade-offs does a manager face when deciding to raise capital by issuing either debt or equity?

8. What is a corporate takeover? Explain why managers are concerned by them. What is dilution, and how does it relate to corporate takeovers? How might purchasing outstanding stock help to block a takeover attempt?

9. Distinguish preferred stock from common stock. How do the rights of preferred stockholders differ from those of common stockholders? Why is preferred stock listed at the top of the stockholders' equity section? Should preferred stock always be considered contributed capital?

10. Why would the authorization of new shares be a concern of the existing stockholders? Why does the number of outstanding shares often differ from the number of issued shares?

11. What are dividends in arrears? Are they considered liabilities? Why or why not?

12. Why do large companies tend to be corporations? What is double taxation, and how is it such a disadvantage to the corporate form of business?

13. Explain how corporations both protect and constrain stockholders.

14. Explain how common stockholders have control over management. What is the role of the board of directors?

15. Define and differentiate among the market value, and book value, par value, and stated value of a share of common stock.

16. Why is the book value of a share of stock often below its market value?

17. What is treasury stock, and why do major U.S. corporations purchase so much of it? Why does the purchase of treasury stock usually increase the earnings-per-share ratio?

18. When treasury stock is reissued for a dollar amount less than its original cost, what two accounts can be debited for the difference between the cost and the proceeds? How does this method of accounting often confuse the distinction between contributed capital and earned capital?

19. What is a dividend, and what three dates are relevant when accounting for dividends?

20. Briefly explain some of the different dividend strategies followed by major U.S. companies. Why would an investor ever wish to invest in a company that paid no dividends?

21. Marketable securities are carried on the balance sheet at the lower-of-cost-or-market value. Explain how this accounting convention might affect the method used to account for dividends that are paid in the form of marketable securities.

22. What is the difference between an ordinary stock dividend, a stock split in the form of a dividend, and a stock split? Why do companies split their stock? Why do companies issue ordinary stock dividends? Summarize the methods recommended by generally accepted accounting principles to account for stock splits in the form of dividends and stock splits. Why do many companies not practice these methods?

23. What is an appropriation of retained earnings? Explain how a debt covenant might underlie an appropriation of retained earnings. Are any assets or liabilities affected when retained earnings are appropriated? If not, what purpose does such an action serve?

24. Briefly describe the statement of stockholders' equity, and describe the kind of information that can be found on it that is not found elsewhere in the financial report.

25. Appendix 12A. Describe the trade-offs between organizing a business as a partnership instead of as a corporation.

26. Appendix 12A. Describe how the owners' equity section of a partnership differs from that of a corporation. Why is a partnership agreement so important to the partnership, and how does this agreement help to determine the balances in the partners' Capital accounts?

EXERCISES

E12–1   *(Debt, contributed, and earned capital, and the classification of preferred stock)*   The balance
sheet of Schmitt and Associates, Inc. follows.

Assets		Liabilities and Stockholders' Equity	
Current assets	$ 85,000	Current liabilities	$ 52,000
Noncurrent assets	315,000	Long-term note payable	35,000
		Preferred stock	50,000
		Common stock	80,000
		Additional paid-in capital	
		Preferred stock	50,000
		Common stock	100,000
		Retained earnings	113,000
		Less: Treasury stock	80,000
		Total liabilities and	
Total assets	$400,000	stockholders' equity	$400,000

Required:

a. What portions of Schmitt's assets were provided by debt, contributed capital, and
earned capital? Reduce contributed capital by the cost of the treasury stock.

b. Compute the company's debt/equity ratio. Compute the debt/equity ratio if the preferred
stock issuance was classified as a long-term debt.

c. In most states, to what dollar amount of dividends would the company be limited?

E12–2   *(The effects of transactions on stockholders' equity)*   The following are possible transactions
that affect stockholders' equity.

(1) A company issues common stock above par value for cash.

(2) A company declares a 3-for-1 stock split.

(3) A company repurchases 10,000 shares of its own common stock in exchange for cash.

(4) A company declares and issues an ordinary stock dividend. Assume that the fair market value of the stock is greater than the par value.

(5) A company reissues 1000 shares of treasury stock for $75 per share. The stock was
acquired for $60 per share.

(6) A company pays a cash dividend that had been declared fifteen days earlier.

(7) A company generates net income of $250,000.

(8) A company declares a dividend in kind (i.e., property dividend). The book value of the
asset to be distributed is greater than its market value.

Required: For each transaction above indicate

a. the accounts within the stockholders' equity section that would be affected,

b. whether these accounts would be increased or decreased, and

c. the effect (increase, decrease, or no effect) of the transaction on total stockholders' equity.

E12–3   *(Authorizing and issuing preferred and common stock)*   Deming Contractors was involved in
the following events involving stock during 1991. Prepare entries, if appropriate, for each
event.

(1) Authorized to issue: (a) 100,000 shares of $100 par value, 8 percent preferred stock;
(b) 150,000 shares of no par, $5 preferred stock; and (c) 250,000 shares of $5 par
value, common stock.

(2) Issued 10,000 shares of $5 par value common stock for $20 per share.

(3) Issued 25,000 shares of the $100 par value preferred stock for $200 per share.

(4) Issued 50,000 shares of no par preferred stock for $150 each.

E12–4 *(The effects of treasury stock purchases on important financial ratios)* On December 30, 1990, Washington and Associates purchased 500 of its 5000 outstanding common shares at a price of $25 per share. Before the treasury stock purchase, the company's financial statements appeared as below.

Income Statement

Revenues	$400,000
Expenses	280,000
Net income	$120,000

Balance Sheet

Assets	$880,000
Liabilities	450,000
Stockholders' equity	430,000

Required:

a. Provide the journal entry for the treasury stock purchase.

b. Compute the debt/equity ratio before and after the treasury stock purchase.

c. Compute earnings per share before and after the treasury stock purchase.

E12–5 *(Reissuing treasury stock)* On April 1, 1989, Rivers, Inc. was authorized to issue 100,000 shares of $10 par value common stock and 10,000 shares of $9, no par preferred stock. During the remainder of 1989 the company entered into the following transactions.

(1) Issued 25,000 shares of common stock in exchange for $500,000 in cash.

(2) Issued 5000 shares of preferred stock in exchange for $60,000 in cash.

(3) Purchased 3000 common shares for $15 per share.

(4) Sold 1000 treasury shares for $18 per share on the open market.

(5) Issued 1000 treasury shares to employees for a reduced price of $5 per share.

The company entered into no other transactions that affected stockholders' equity during 1989.

Required:

a. Prepare entries for each of the transactions.

b. Assume that Rivers, Inc. generated $500,000 in net income in 1989 and did not declare any dividends during 1988. Prepare the stockholders' equity section of the balance sheet as of December 31, 1989.

E12–6 *(Reissuing treasury stock)* The stockholders' equity section of Rodman Corporation as of December 31, 1989, follows.

Common stock	$40,000
Additional paid-in capital	5,000
Retained earnings	30,000
Total stockholders' equity	$75,000

During 1990 the company entered into the following transactions.

(1) Purchased 500 shares of treasury stock for $30 per share.

(2) As part of a compensation package, reissued half of the treasury shares to employees for $4 per share.

(3) Reissued the remainder of the treasury stock on the open market for $33 per share.

Required:

a. Provide the journal entries for each transaction, and prepare the stockholders' equity section of the balance sheet as of December 31, 1990.

b. What portion of the Additional Paid-in Capital account is attributed to treasury stock transactions?

E12–7

(Treasury stock exceeds contributed capital) In 1980 AAA Corporation began operations issuing 100,000 shares of $10 par value common stock for $25 per share. Since that time the company has been very profitable. The stockholders' equity section as of December 31, 1989 follows.

Common stock	$1,000,000
Additional paid-in capital (C/S)	1,500,000
Retained earnings	4,000,000
Total stockholders' equity	$6,500,000

In 1990 the company entered into a program of buying back some of the outstanding shares. During the year the company purchased 30,000 outstanding shares at a price of $95 per share.

Required:

a. Prepare the journal entry to record the purchase of the treasury shares.

b. Assuming that net income of $350,000 was earned and dividends of $50,000 were declared during the year, prepare the stockholders' equity section of the balance sheet as of the end of 1990.

c. Explain how the dollar value of the treasury stock account can be larger than the dollar amount of contributed capital.

E12–8

(Book value per share, stock issuances, and treasury stock purchases) The condensed balance sheet of Renton, Inc. follows.

Assets	$200,000	Liabilities	$ 70,000
		Stockholders' equity	130,000
		Total liabilities and	
Total assets	$200,000	stockholders' equity	$200,000

Ten thousand shares of common stock and no preferred stock are presently outstanding.

Required: The following requirements are independent.

a. Compute the book value per common share.

b. Compute the book value per common share if the company issues 5000 shares of common stock at $15 per share.

c. Compute the book value per common share if the company issues 5000 shares of common stock at $10 per share.

d. Compute the book value per outstanding share of common stock if the company purchases 5000 shares of treasury stock at $15 per share.

e. Compute the book value per outstanding share of common stock if the company purchases 5000 shares of treasury stock at $10 per share.

f. What effect does issuing stock have on the value of the outstanding shares? Upon what does this effect depend?

g. What effect does purchasing treasury stock have on the book value of the outstanding shares? Upon what does this effect depend?

E12-9

(Inferring equity transactions from the statement of stockholders' equity)   The information below was taken from the statement of stockholders' equity of Bantam Corporation.

	1989	1988
Preferred stock (no par)	$ 700	$400
Common stock ($1 par value)	1,000	900
Additional paid-in capital		
Common stock	40	20
Treasury stock	10	—
Less: Treasury stock	130	150

Required: Provide the journal entries for the following.

a. The issuance of preferred stock during 1989.

b. The issuance of common stock during 1989.

c. The sale of treasury stock during 1989.

E12-10

(Issuing a property dividend in the form of marketable securities)   The Board of Directors of Worthington Industries declared a property dividend on March 12, 1990. The company will distribute 100,000 shares of IBM—currently selling for $60 per share—to its stockholders. The company reported the IBM securities on its balance sheet as current marketable securities. They were the only marketable securities held by the company, and were purchased on December 31, 1989.

Required:

a. Assume that Worthington Industries paid $45 per share for the IBM stock. Prepare the entries necessary on the

   (1) Date of declaration

   (2) Date of record

   (3) Date of payment.

b. Assume that Worthington Industries paid $80 per share for the IBM stock. Prepare the entries necessary on the

   (1) Date of declaration

   (2) Date of record

   (3) Date of payment.

c. Assume that the company paid $80 per share for the IBM stock, sold the securities prior to declaring the dividend, and declared a cash dividend in the amount of the proceeds. Prepare the entries necessary on the

   (1) Date of declaration

   (2) Date of record

   (3) Date of payment.

E12-11

(Issuing cash and property dividends on outstanding common stock)   The Board of Directors of Enerson Manufacturing is in the process of declaring a dividend. The company is considering two options.

Option 1: Pay a cash dividend of $20 per share.

Option 2: Distribute 50,000 shares of Xerox stock held as a temporary investment. The Xerox stock cost Enerson $45 per share and is currently selling for $55 per share.

Enerson Manufacturing is authorized to issue 500,000 shares of common stock. The company has issued 275,000 shares to date and has reacquired 25,000 shares. These 25,000 shares are held in treasury.

Required:

a. How many shares of common stock are eligible to receive a dividend?
b. Assume that the board selects Option 1. Prepare the appropriate journal entries on the
   (1) Date of declaration
   (2) Date of record
   (3) Date of payment.
c. Assume that the board selects Option 2. Prepare the appropriate journal entries on the
   (1) Date of declaration
   (2) Date of record
   (3) Date of payment.

E12–12   *(Cumulative preferred stock and dividends in arrears)*   The stockholders' equity section of Mayberry Corporation, as of the end of 1990, follows. Mayberry began operations in 1986. The 5000 shares of preferred stock have been outstanding since 1986.

Preferred stock (10,000 sh authorized, 5000 issued, cumulative,	
nonparticipating, $5 dividends, $10 par value)	$ 50,000
Common stock (500,000 sh authorized, 200,000 sh issued, 50,000	
held in treasury, no par value)	1,600,000
Additional paid-in capital (P/S)	140,000
Retained earnings	110,000
Less: Treasury stock	80,000
Total stockholders' equity	$1,820,000

Since 1986 the company has paid the following total cash dividends:

1986	$ 0
1987	40,000
1988	100,000
1989	20,000
1990	20,000

Required:

a. Compute the dividends paid to the preferred and common stockholders for each of the years since 1986.
b. Compute the balance of dividends in arrears as of the end of each year.
c. Should dividends in arrears be considered a liability? Why or why not?

E12–13   *(Stock dividends and stock splits)*   The stockholders' equity section of Pioneer Enterprises as of December 31, 1990 follows.

Common stock (5000 shares issued @ $5 par)	$25,000
Additional paid-in capital (C/S)	50,000
Retained earnings	30,000
Less: Treasury stock (1000 shares @ $12)	12,000
Total stockholders' equity	$93,000

Required: Prepare journal entries for the following independent transactions.

a. The company declares and distributes a 5 percent stock dividend on the outstanding shares. The market price of the stock is $35 per share.
b. The company declares a 3:2 stock split on the outstanding shares in the form of a 50 percent stock dividend.

c. The company declares a 2:1 stock split on the outstanding shares in the form of a 100 percent stock dividend.

d. The company declares a 2:1 stock split on the outstanding shares and decreases the par value of the outstanding stock accordingly.

e. Compute the ratio of contributed capital to earned capital after independently considering each of the four actions listed above. Reduce contributed capital by the cost of the treasury stock. Do not compute the cumulative ratio.

E12–14

(Why do companies declare stock dividends?) The December 31, 1990, balances in Retained Earnings and Additional Paid-in Capital for Railway Shippers Company are $135,000 and $50,000, respectively. Five thousand, $10 par value common shares are outstanding with a market value of $85 each. The company's cash position at year end is lower than usual, so the board of directors is considering issuing a stock dividend instead of the normal cash dividend. They are considering the three options listed below.

Option 1: A 20 percent stock dividend: 1000 new shares would be issued.

Option 2: A 50 percent stock dividend: 2500 new shares would be issued.

Option 3: A 2:1 stock split in the form of a stock dividend: 5000 new shares would be issued.

Required:

a. Prepare the journal entry for Option 1, above and comment on why this alternative may not be attractive. Why do companies issue ordinary stock dividends?

b. Provide journal entries for Options 2 and 3.

c. Why do companies issue large stock dividends or split their stock?

E12–15

(Appropriating retained earnings) Taylor Manufacturing entered into a borrowing arrangement that requires the company to maintain a Retained Earnings balance of $500,000. The company also wishes to finance internally a major plant addition in the not-too-distant future. Accordingly, the board of directors has decided to appropriate $650,000 of the Retained Earnings balance. Prior to the board's action the balance in the Retained Earnings account was $800,000.

Required:

a. Why would the board of directors appropriate retained earnings in the situation described above, and why might an auditor insist that it be done?

b. Prepare the journal entry that would accompany the board's decision.

c. Show how retained earnings would be disclosed on the balance sheet after the appropriation.

d. How large a dividend could the company legally declare after the appropriation?

E12–16

(Appendix 12A: Partnership formation, withdrawals, and profit allocation) Bob and Tom began a partnership on January 1, 1989. Bob contributed $50,000, and Tom contributed land with a fair market value of $60,000 and a building with a fair market value of $40,000. The partners have agreed to divide partnership profits in proportion to their Capital accounts at the end of each year.

Required:

a. Record the journal entries to establish the partnership.

b. Net income at the end of 1989 was $15,000. Provide the journal entry to allocate the profit to the Capital accounts of Bob and Tom.

c. During 1990 Bob withdrew $35,000, and Tom withdrew $30,000 from the partnership. Provide the journal entries to reflect these withdrawals.

d. Net income for 1990 was $30,000. Provide the journal entry to allocate the profit to the Capital accounts of Bob and Tom.

e. Prepare a summary of the balance sheet as of December 31, 1990.

E12–17   *(Appendix 12A: Partnership and corporate tax rates)*   Mike Doyle has operated Doyle Engineering as a sole proprietorship for the past five years. Given the increasing chance of being sued, Mr. Doyle is considering incorporating his company. His personal income tax rate is 28 percent for federal income taxes and 15 percent for state income taxes, while the corporate income tax rate is projected to be 34 percent for federal income taxes and 20 percent for state income taxes.

Doyle Engineering has annual earnings of $850,000 (not including any transactions with Mr. Doyle). Mr. Doyle's only source of cash on which to live has been withdrawals of $95,000 per year, and he wishes to continue this cash flow in the future. If Mr. Doyle incorporates his business, he would be the sole stockholder.

Required:

a. Discuss the benefits of incorporation in case Doyle Engineering is sued. Are there any drawbacks to incorporating?

b. Compute the total tax liability if Mike Doyle does the following.

1. Incorporates his business and withdraws the $95,000 as a dividend

2. Remains a partnership and takes the $95,000 as an owner withdrawal

3. Incorporates his business and pays himself a $95,000 salary.

PROBLEMS

P12–1   *(Hybrid securities and debt covenants)*   Lambert Corporation issued 1000 shares of $100 par value, 8 percent, cumulative, nonparticipating preferred stock for $100 each. The stock is preferred as to assets, redeemable after five years at a prespecified price, and the preferred stockholders do not vote at the annual stockholders' meeting. The condensed balance sheet of Lambert prior to the issuance follows.

Assets	$580,000	Liabilities	$250,000
		Stockholders' equity	330,000
		Total liabilities and	
Total assets	$580,000	stockholders' equity	$580,000

Lambert has entered into a debt agreement that requires the company to maintain a debt/equity ratio of less than 1:1.

Required:

a. Provide the journal entry to record the preferred stock issuance, and compute the resulting debt/equity ratio, assuming that the preferred stock is considered an equity security.

b. Compute the debt/equity ratio, assuming that the preferred stock is considered a debt security.

c. What incentives might the management of Lambert have to classify the issuance as equity instead of debt? Do you think that the issuance should be classified as debt or equity? What might Lambert's external auditors think?

P12–2   *(The effects of treasury stock transactions on important financial ratios)*   The balance sheet of Baker Bros. follows.

Assets	$840,000	Liabilities	$300,000
		Preferred stock	50,000
		Common stock	300,000
		Additional paid-in capital (C/S)	100,000
		Retained earnings	130,000
		Less: Treasury stock	40,000
		Total liabilities and	
Total assets	$840,000	stockholders' equity	$840,000

Of the 200,000 common shares authorized, 50,000 shares were issued for $8 each when the company began operations. There have been no common stock issuances since: 45,000 shares are currently outstanding and 5,000 shares are held in treasury. Net income for the year just ended was $45,000.

Required:

a. Compute the par value of the issued common shares.

b. Compute the book value of each common share.

c. At what average price were the treasury shares purchased?

d. Baker is considering reissuing the 5000 treasury shares at the present market price of $10 per share. What effect would this action have on the company's debt/equity ratio, book value per outstanding share, and earnings-per-share ratio?

e. If Baker chooses to purchase 5000 additional shares of treasury stock at $10 instead, what effect would such an action have on the company's debt/equity ratio, book value per outstanding share, and earnings-per-share ratio?

P12–3   *(The significance of par value)*   Several independent transactions are listed below. Prepare journal entries for each transaction.

(1) 10,000 shares of no-par common stock are issued for $70 per share.

(2) 10,000 shares of $1 par value common stock are issued for $70 per share.

(3) 10,000 shares of $10 par value common stock are issued for $70 per share.

(4) 5,000 shares of no-par preferred stock are issued for $150 per share.

(5) What is the significance of par value from a financial accounting standpoint? Is par value significant in any economic sense?

P12–4   *(Cash, property, and stock dividends)*   Royal Company is currently considering declaring a dividend to its common shareholders, according to one of the following plans:

1. Declare a cash dividend of $15 per share.

2. Declare a dividend in kind. Royal Company would distribute 1 share of marketable securities for every 5 shares of common stock currently held. The marketable securities were originally purchased for $60 per share and are currently selling for $75 per share.

3. Declare a 20 percent stock dividend. Royal Company would distribute 2 shares of common stock for every 10 shares of common stock currently held. The company's common stock is currently selling for $50 per share.

Royal Company is authorized to issue 100,000 shares of $10 par value common stock. To date, the company has issued 75,000 shares and is currently holding 10,000 shares in treasury stock.

Required:

a. How many shares of common stock are eligible to receive a dividend?

b. Prepare the entries necessary on the date of declaration, date of record, and the date of payment for the following.

1. Cash dividend

2. Dividend in kind (property dividend)

c. Prepare the entry to record the stock dividend, assuming that the dividend is declared and issued on the same date.

d. Assume that instead of declaring a dividend in kind, Royal Company sold the marketable securities and used the cash to pay a cash dividend. Prepare the entry for the sale of the securities and the entries necessary on the date of declaration, date of record, and the date of payment. Is there any economic difference between this procedure and paying the dividend in kind? Would these two procedures affect the financial statements differently?

P12–5   *(Dividend payments and preferred stock)*   The following information was extracted from the financial records of Garner Corporation.

> Preferred stock: 15,000 shares outstanding; 10 percent; $50 par value
> Common stock: 50,000 shares outstanding; $15 par value

Garner Corporation began operations on January 1, 1984. The company has paid the following amounts in cash dividends over the past 7 years.

1984	$ 65,000
1985	100,000
1986	70,000
1987	50,000
1988	125,000
1989	110,000
1990	99,000

Required: Prepare a sheet to contain the following schedule.

Year	Total Dividends Declared	Dividends to Preferred	Dividends to Common	Dividend per Share (Preferred)	Dividend per Share (Common)

a. Complete this schedule for each year from 1984 through 1990, assuming that the preferred stock is noncumulative and nonparticipating.

b. Complete this schedule for each year from 1984 through 1990, assuming that the preferred stock is cumulative and nonparticipating.

c. Complete this schedule for each year from 1984 through 1990, assuming that the preferred stock is cumulative and participates at the rate of 1 percent of the par value.

P12–6   *(The maximum dividend)*   The following selected financial information was extracted from the December 31, 1989, financial records of Cotter Company:

	Debit	Credit
Cash	25,000	
Marketable securities (2500 shares of Oreton Corporation)	80,000	
Common stock ($10 par value, 100,000 shares authorized; 50,000 issued)		500,000
Additional paid-in-capital: common stock		100,000
Retained earnings (before closing)		245,000
Income summary (net income for 1989)		43,000

The company's board of directors is currently contemplating declaring a dividend. The marketable securities have a current value of $50 per share. The company's common stock is presently selling for $40 per share.

Required:

a. Given the present financial position of Cotter Company, how large a cash dividend can the board of directors declare?

b. How large an ordinary stock dividend can the board legally declare?

c. Assume that the dividends are declared and issued on the same day. Prepare the journal entry to record the maximum dividend in each case above.

d. If the company sold its marketable securities, how large a cash dividend could it declare and pay?

P12–7

(Stock splits and ordinary stock dividends) Stevenson Enterprises is considering the following items:

(1) The company may declare a 10 percent stock dividend, issuing an additional share of common stock for every 10 shares outstanding; the common stock is currently selling for $25 per share.

(2) The company may issue a 2:1 stock split in the form of a 100 percent stock dividend. If so, the company wishes to maintain the par value of the shares.

Prior to these events Stevenson Enterprises reports the following:

Common stock ($6 par value, 650,000 shares authorized, 70,000 issued, 60,000 outstanding, and 10,000 held as treasury stock)	$ 420,000
Additional paid-in-capital (C/S)	525,000
Retained earnings	695,000
Less: Treasury stock	100,000
Total stockholders' equity	$1,540,000

Required:

a. Assume that Stevenson Enterprises declares the ordinary stock dividend but not the stock split. Prepare the necessary journal entry. Prepare the stockholders' equity section of the balance sheet to reflect the ordinary stock dividend.

b. Assume that Stevenson Enterprises declares the stock split but not the ordinary stock dividend. Prepare the stockholders' equity section of the balance sheet to reflect the stock split.

c. Assume that Stevenson Enterprises declares the ordinary stock dividend and then the stock split. Prepare the necessary journal entries. Prepare the stockholders' equity section of the balance sheet to reflect both actions.

d. Assume that Stevenson Enterprises declares the stock split and then the ordinary stock dividend. Prepare the necessary journal entries. Prepare the stockholders' equity section of the balance sheet to reflect both actions.

P12–8

(Miscellaneous stockholders' equity transactions) The stockholders' equity section of Rudnicki Corp. contained the following balances as of December 31, 1988.

Preferred stock (10%, $100 par value, cumulative)	$1,000,000
Preferred stock (12%, $100 par value, noncumulative)	1,500,000
Common Stock ($20 par value, 500,000 shares authorized, 175,000 issued and 25,000 held in treasury)	3,500,000
Additional paid-in-capital	
Preferred stock (10%)	1,050,000
Preferred stock (12%)	1,275,000
Common stock	2,345,000
Retained earnings	4,256,000
Less: Treasury stock	5,750,000
Total stockholders' equity	$9,176,000

During 1989, Rudnicki Corp. entered into the following transactions affecting stockholders' equity.

(1) On May 13, the company repurchased 1000 shares of its common stock in the open market at $215 per share.

(2) On September 26, the company issued 200 shares of its 10 percent preferred stock at $190 per share.

(3) On October 19, the company reissued 5000 shares of the stock held in treasury. They sold for $225 per share: 500 of the shares reissued had been purchased on May 13, and the remaining 4500 shares had been purchased for $230 per share.

(4) On December 2, the company declared a cash dividend of $750,000, which was paid on December 23. The company has not declared a dividend since 1987. (Rudnicki Corp. uses a separate dividend account for each type of stock.)

(5) On December 27, the company pays the dividend declared on December 2.

(6) On December 29, the company declares a 2:1 stock split on the company's common stock.

Required:

a. Prepare the necessary entries for each transaction.

b. Assume that Rudnicki Corp. earned net income of $899,000 during 1989. Prepare the stockholders' equity section as of December 31, 1989.

P12-9 *(Inferring transactions from the balance sheet)* The stockholders' equity section of Morrel Company's balance sheet reports the following:

	1989	1988
Preferred stock (9%, $100 par value)	$ 200,000	$ 110,000
Common stock ($10 par value, 750,000 shares authorized, 90,000 issued and 5000 held in treasury)	900,000	750,000
Additional paid-in-capital		
Preferred stock	150,000	35,000
Common stock	465,000	298,000
Retained earnings	575,000	495,000
Less: Treasury stock	110,000	—
Total stockholders' equity	$2,180,000	$1,688,000

Required:

a. How many shares of preferred stock were issued during 1989? What was the average issue price?

b. How many shares of common stock were issued during 1989? What was the average issue price?

c. Prepare the entry to record the repurchase of the company's own stock during 1989. What was the average repurchase price?

d. Assume that the treasury shares were purchased on the last day of 1989. Did the purchase increase or decrease the book value of the outstanding shares? By how much?

P12-10 *(Inferring stockholders' equity transactions from information on the balance sheet)* Voce Corporation reports the following in their December 31, 1988 financial report.

	1988	1987
Cumulative preferred stock (10%, $100 par value)	$ 400,000	$ 400,000
Common stock ($10 par value, 11,000 shares authorized, issued, and outstanding)	110,000	70,000
Additional paid-in-capital		
Common stock	625,000	500,000
Treasury stock	124,000	55,000
Retained earnings	975,000	250,000
Less: Treasury stock	84,000	105,000
Total stockholders' equity	$2,150,000	$1,170,000

Required:

a. Compute the number of shares of common stock issued during 1988.

b. Compute the average market price of the common shares issued during 1988.

c. Assume that Voce Corporation earned net income of $2,000,000 during 1988. Compute the amount of dividends that were declared during 1988.

d. If Voce Corporation did not declare or pay any dividends during 1987, and again assuming a net income during 1988 of $2,000,000, compute the amount declared as dividends to common stockholders during 1988.

e. Assume that the total balance in Treasury Stock on December 31, 1987, represents the acquisition of 1500 shares of common stock on March 3, 1986. Prepare the entry that would have been necessary on March 3, 1986.

f. Assume that all shares of treasury stock reissued during 1988 were reissued at the same time and at the same price. Prepare the entry to record the reissuance of the treasury stock.

g. At what per-share price was the treasury stock reissued?

P12–11   *(Stockholders' equity over a four-year period)*   Aspen Industries incorporated in the state of Colorado on March 23, 1987. The company was authorized to issue 1,000,000 shares of $12 par value common stock. Since the date of incorporation, Aspen Industries has entered into the following transactions that contributed and earned capital.

(1) On March 23, 1987, the company issued 50,000 shares of common stock in exchange for $30 per share.

(2) On December 5, 1987, the company issued a 50 percent stock dividend.

(3) On May 6, 1988, the company issued 60,000 shares of common stock in exchange for $45 per share.

(4) On September 24, 1988, the company repurchased 15,000 shares of its own stock for $51 per share.

(5) On December 1, 1988, the company reissued 5000 shares held in treasury for $55 per share.

(6) On February 14, 1989, the company declared a 3:1 stock split and adjusted the par value of the stock. (Hint: Consider the effect of the stock split on treasury stock.)

(7) On August 19, 1989, the company reissued 8000 shares held in treasury for $20 per share.

(8) On December 27, 1989, the company declared a cash dividend of $100,000.

(9) On January 3, 1990, the company paid the dividend declared on December 27, 1989.

(10) On October 31, 1990, the company reissued 2000 shares held in treasury for $30 per share.

Required:

a. Prepare the necessary journal entries to record these transactions.

b. Prepare the stockholders' equity section of Aspen's balance sheet as of December 31, 1990. Assume that Net Income for 1987, 1988, 1989, and 1990 was $400,000, $100,000, $100,000 and $20,000, respectively.

P12–12

(Blocking takeovers and treasury stock purchases)   Five shareholders together own 35 percent of the outstanding stock of Edmonds Industries. The remaining 65% is divided among several thousand stockholders. There are 400,000 shares of Edmonds stock currently outstanding. A condensed balance sheet follows.

Assets		Liabilities and Stockholders' Equity	
Cash	$ 3,150,000	Liabilities	$ 1,250,000
Other current assets	4,200,000	Common stock	8,000,000
Noncurrent assets	8,220,000	Retained earnings	6,320,000
		Total liabilities and	
Total assets	$15,570,000	stockholders' equity	$15,570,000

It has become known that Vadar, Inc., is planning to take over Edmonds by purchasing a controlling interest of the outstanding stock. Vadar hopes to gain enough control to elect a new board of directors and replace Edmonds' current management. The current board of directors, on which the five major stockholders serve, is considering how to block the apparent takeover attempt.

Required:

a. Describe how the company might be able to block the takeover attempt through a program of treasury stock purchases. How many shares would the company need to purchase to concentrate ownership enough to keep Vadar from acquiring a controlling interest? Assume that the other members of the board own no stock.

b. The current market price of the outstanding stock is $45, but the board feels that any major buy-back would have to be at a premium of approximately $5 per share. How much cash would Edmonds need to purchase enough shares to block the takeover attempt?

c. Assume that Edmonds was able to borrow $4,000,000. Prepare the balance sheet of Edmonds after stock had been purchased.

P12–13

(Bankruptcy and protecting the interests of the creditors)   The balance sheet of Natathon International is provided below.

Assets		Liabilities and Stockholders' Equity	
Current assets	$200,000	Liabilities	$400,000
Fixed assets	500,000	Common stock	150,000
		Additional paid-in capital	50,000
		Retained earnings	100,000
		Total liabilities and	
Total assets	$700,000	stockholders' equity	$700,000

Although the balance sheet appears reasonably healthy, Natathon is on the verge of ceasing operations. Appraisers have estimated that, while current assets are worth $200,000, the fixed assets of the company can only be sold for $450,000. There are 1000 outstanding shares of common stock owned by ten stockholders, each with a 10 percent interest (i.e., 100 shares). Before ceasing operations, the board of directors, which is comprised primarily of the major stockholders, is considering several alternative courses of action.

1. Liquidate the assets, declare a $250 per-share dividend, and distribute the remaining assets to the creditors.

2. Liquidate the assets, declare a $400 per-share dividend, and distribute the remaining assets to the creditors.

3. Liquidate the assets, purchase the outstanding shares for $250 each, and distribute the remaining assets to the creditors.

4. Liquidate the assets, and purchase the outstanding shares for $650 each.

Required:

a. Prepare the journal entry to reflect the writedown of the assets.

b. Prepare the journal entry to accompany each of the alternative courses of action.

c. Comment on the legality of each of the board's proposals, and explain how the assets should be distributed after liquidation.

P12–14 *(Appendix 12A: Partnership or corporation; income taxes)* Shannon and Patrick Cummings decided to start a business called the S & P Diaper Service. Shannon contributed $120,000 to the business. Patrick contributed $80,000 and a delivery truck that cost $90,000 two years ago and currently has an appraised value of $50,000. Shannon and Patrick are contemplating the following operations.

1. Form a partnership that allocates profits based upon the proportion of their Capital accounts.

2. Form a corporation and issue common stock with a par value of $20 per share.

3. Form a corporation and issue common stock with a stated value of $15 per share.

4. Form a corporation and issue no par common stock.

If Shannon and Patrick form a corporation, they will issue 10,000 shares of common stock. All shares will be issued to Shannon and Patrick based upon the proportion of their initial investments.

During the first year of operations, S & P Diaper Service generated net income of $45,000.

Required:

a. Prepare the journal entry to record the formation of this business under each of the four options.

b. Prepare the entry to distribute net income to Shannon and Patrick under option (1).

c. Assume that Shannon and Patrick each made a cash withdrawal in the amount of the income allocated to them under option (1). Compute their individual net cash inflows, assuming an individual income tax rate of 33 percent.

d. Prepare the entry to declare a cash dividend equal to net income (after tax) under the second option above. Assume a *corporate* tax rate of 34 percent.

e. Compute their individual net cash inflows, again assuming an *individual* tax rate of 33 percent.

f. Explain the concept of double taxation, and discuss other economic differences among the four options.

CASES

C12–1   *(Initial public offering)* Egghead, Inc., is a software chain with over 120 stores nationwide. Until May, 1988, all the common shares of the company were held by its founders and employees. At that time the company filed for an initial public offering of 3.6 million common shares. The shares were priced at $15 each. After the offering, Egghead will have 15.6 million shares outstanding. Assume that the company holds no treasury stock.

Required:

a. Assume that Egghead's common stock has a $1 par value. Provide the journal entry to record the issuance of the new shares.

b. Assume all the shares originally outstanding were sold for $10 per share. Provide the contributed capital section of Egghead's balance sheet both before and after the sale of the new stock.

c. Do you think that the company's board of directors and existing shareholders had to approve the public issuance before it occurred? Why or why not?

d. Provide several reasons that may have caused the company to raise the $54 million with an equity, instead of a debt, issuance.

C12–2   *(Cash dividends: accounting methods, financial statement effects, and management strategies)* On April 10, 1988, F. W. Woolworth Co., a major retailer, increased its quarterly dividend by 24 percent, from 33¢ to 41¢ per share. The new dividend was payable June 1 to the shareholders of record on May 2. The company cited strong earnings as the reason for the increase.

Required:

a. Assume that Woolworth had 10 million shares of stock outstanding. Provide the journal entries that would be recorded on April 10, May 2, and June 1.

b. Would each entry increase, decrease, or have no effect on the company's current ratio, working capital position, and debt/equity ratio? Assume that the dividend account is closed immediately to Retained Earnings.

c. Like Woolworth, many companies base their dividend payments on earnings. Are dividends actually paid out of profits? Are all profitable companies in a position to pay large dividends? Why or why not?

d. Briefly explain some of the major factors considered by the boards of directors of companies deciding whether or not to pay dividends and how much to pay.

C12–3   *(Issuing stocks to the shareholders)* Information from the Statement of Retained Earnings for the year ended December 31, 1985, of The Interlake Corporation is provided below (dollars in thousands).

Beginning retained earnings balance	$305,133
Net income	32,555
Less: Cash dividends	14,873
Property dividends	131,477
Ending retained earnings balance	$191,338

The notes to the company's financial statements stated, "On June 23, 1986 The Interlake Corporation made a . . . distribution of shares in the Acme Steel Company. . . . Shareholders received one share of the Acme Steel Company for each share of Interlake Corporation common stock owned of record on June 9, 1986. No gain or loss was recorded."

Required:

a. Was the distribution made by Interlake a 2:1 stock split, a 100 percent stock dividend, or a property dividend? Support your answer.

b. Provide the journal entries recorded by Interlake on the date of declaration, the date of record, and the date of payment.

c. What was the balance-sheet value of the stock distributed?

d. What was the fair market value of the stock distributed?

C12–4   *(Do stock dividends represent economic exchanges between a corporation and its shareholders)*   On April 18, Bergen Brunswig, a health service and consumer electronics products distribution concern, declared a 37 percent stock dividend. After the stock dividend, the number of shares outstanding increased to approximately 24.66 million. Assume that the stock dividend was declared and paid on the same day.

Required:

a. How many shares of stock were outstanding prior to the dividend?

b. Assume that the market price of the stock was $15 per share and that the par value was $5 per share on the day the dividend was declared and paid. Provide the journal entry to record the distribution.

c. Compute the value of Bergen Brunswig if all outstanding shares, prior to the stock dividend, could have been sold for $15 each. Using this value, compute the per-share value of the company's outstanding shares after the stock dividend.

d. Assume that Mr. Jones owned .9 million shares prior to the stock dividend. How many shares did Mr. Jones own after the stock dividend? What percent of the company did Mr. Jones own before and after the stock dividend? What was the value of Mr. Jones' total shareholdings before and after the stock dividend?

e. Does a stock dividend actually represent an economic exchange between a corporation and its shareholders? Why or why not?

f. Provide several reasons why a company would issue a stock dividend?

C12–5   *(Stock splits: effects on market prices)*   On July 15, 1988, Walbro Corporation, a maker of automotive components, declared a 3:2 stock split. The split was payable August 26 to shareholders of record July 29.

Required:

a. If a shareholder owned 100 shares before the split, how many shares did he or she own after the split?

b. In May, 1986, the board of directors of Nordstrom, Inc., approved a 2:1 stock split when the stock was priced at $78.75 per share. It fell immediately to slightly over $39 per share, but jumped to $42 the following day. Explain why the price of a stock would be reduced by one half immediately after a 2:1 stock split and then increase the following day.

c. Why do companies split their stock? Briefly explain and justify the methods used to account for such transactions.

C12–6   *(Economic issues involving treasury stock purchases)*   The following extracts are from *The Wall Street Journal.*

> RJR Nabisco Inc. said it plans to buy back as much as 8 percent of its outstanding stock for $52 to $58 dollars per share, or up to $1.2 billion. Analysts said the move probably signals that the tobacco and food giant has decided not to acquire another company. It also is an apparent effort to bolster the price of RJR shares, which like other tobacco stocks, have lagged the market. . . . Earnings [per share] will go up . . . and the fear of dilutive acquisition will be down.
>
> John Hegler, *The Wall Street Journal*, 29 March 1988, p. 8.

Georgia-Pacific Corp.'s Board authorized an ambitious buy-back program that could result in the purchase of as much as 19 percent of the company's stock. The action will boost the forest products giant's debt but is meant to bolster its stock price. . . . To accomodate the buy-back, Georgia-Pacific's Board approved raising the company's debt/equity target ratio of 40 percent to 45 percent from its current 30 percent to 35 percent.

John Hegler, *The Wall Street Journal*, 30 March 1988, p. 25.

Gillette Co. . . . said it will accelerate a stock buy-back program it began in 1986 and purchase as many as 11 million of its shares on the open market during the next few months. . . . Moody's Investors Service said it placed Gillette's. . . long-term debt ratings. . . under review for possible downgrade because of Gillette's stock buy-back acceleration.

David Stuff, *The Wall Street Journal*, 20 April 1988, p. 32.

Required: Explain how a treasury stock purchase could accomplish the following:

a. Bolster a company's stock price and its earnings per share
b. Reduce the threat of a dilutive acquisition
c. Cause a company to boost its debt and increase its debt/equity ratio
d. Cause a credit-rating service to downgrade a company's credit rating.

C12-7 *(Issuing hybrid securities: economic consequences)* Forbes (3 June 1985) points out that companies wishing to protect their credit ratings and unwilling to issue more stock are raising capital by issuing hybrid securities. The article specifically mentions certain kinds of preferred stock issuances.

Required:

a. What is a hybrid security? Explain why certain kinds of preferred stocks are considered to be hybrid securities.
b. How can a company protect its credit rating by issuing hybrid securities instead of bonds?
c. How can a company avoid violating a debt covenant by issuing hybrid securities instead of bonds?
d. How can a company avoid diluting its stock and inviting a takeover by issuing hybrid securities instead of common stocks?

Long-Term Investments

Learning Objectives

1 Define long-term investments, and identify the accounts that are commonly included in the long-term investment section of the balance sheet.

2 Describe the economic consequences associated with reporting long-term investments.

3 Explain how long-term notes receivable arise, and describe the method used to account for them.

4 Explain why companies purchase bonds, and describe the method used to account for bond investments.

5 Explain why companies make long-term investments in equity securities.

6 Distinguish among the lower-of-cost-or-market method, the cost method, and the equity method of accounting for long-term equity investments, and describe the conditions under which each method is used.

7 Define consolidated financial statements, and describe when they are prepared and how they differ from financial statements that account for equity investments using the equity method.

≣ This chapter is devoted to long-term investments: long-term notes receivable, investments in corporate bonds, and investments in stocks. Such investments are entered into by companies to increase interest or dividend income and, in some cases, to exercise influence over the management of the investee company. Long-term investments are those that are not expected to mature or be liquidated in the time period that defines current assets (i.e., one year or the current operating cycle, whichever is longer).

Long-term notes receivable arise when companies provide goods, services, or loans to other parties in exchange for formal promissory notes. For example, Mc-Donnell Douglas indicates in its 1987 financial report that long-term notes receivable, which totaled $1.7 billion at the end of 1987, were "acquired primarily from sales of commercial aircraft." Such notes specify cash interest and principal payments to be received at designated future dates beyond the time period defining current assets.

Long-term investments in **corporate bonds** are normally made on the open market to increase interest income over the long run. Abbott Laboratories, for example, reported $42.4 million invested in long-term corporate bonds as of the end of 1987. Investing in bonds is similar to holding notes receivable: companies that buy bonds are essentially loaning money (or providing financing) in anticipation of receiving contractual future cash inflows.

Unlike holding notes receivable and bonds, which represent investments in debt securities, purchasing outstanding stock in another (investee) company is an *equity investment*. Such investments produce dividend income or, if they represent a large enough portion of the investee company's voting stock, can be used to influence the decisions of the investee company's management. As of December 31, 1987, for example, Chrysler Corporation held a substantial amount of the outstanding stock ($242 million) of Mitsubishi Motors Corporation. Such equity investments are classified as long-term if they are either (1) not marketable or (2) intended to be held beyond the time period that defines current assets.[1]

THE RELATIVE SIZE OF LONG-TERM INVESTMENTS

The relative size of long-term investments, including long-term notes receivable, bond investments, and equity investments, varies widely across major U.S. companies. Table 13–1 shows long-term investments, expressed as absolute dollar amounts and as percentages of total assets, for a selected group of major U.S. companies.

In general, as a percentage of total assets, long-term investments are not particularly large. Many major companies, such as Wendy's International, carry an immaterial amount of long-term investments. A few companies, however, such as Ralston Purina and Chrysler Corporation, carry substantial long-term investments on the balance sheet.

---

1. Two other assets often included in the long-term investment section of the balance sheet are *special funds* and the *cash surrender value of life insurance.* Special funds typically arise when companies periodically put aside cash in separate investment accounts to prepare for such occurrences as paying off long-term debts, plant expansion, or the retirement of outstanding stock. The cash surrender value of a life insurance policy represents the dollar amount for which the policy could be cashed in at a particular point in time. It appears on the balance sheet when a company holds an ordinary life insurance policy on one or more of its officers. The methods used to account for these two long-term assets are normally covered in intermediate accounting textbooks.

Table 13–1 The relative size of long-term investments (selected U.S. companies)

Company	Dollar Amounts of Long-Term Investments (in millions)	Percent of Total Assets
Wendy's International	$ .7	Not material
Delta	55.4	1%
J. C. Penney Company	381.0	4
Arco	898.0	4
Eli Lilly	287.0	5
PepsiCo	581.0	6
Dow Chemical	1,064.0	7
Chrysler Corporation	2,720.0	14
Ralston Purina	681.0	18

Source: 1987 financial reports.

It is also important to realize that the dollar values and percentages in Table 13–1 present an understated measure of the importance of long-term investments. This understatement is due primarily to two factors. First, Table 13–1 is based on data from 1987 financial reports, which were prepared prior to the issuance of Statement of Financial Accounting Standard (SFAS) No. 94, requiring that the assets and liabilities of majority-owned subsidiaries be included on the balance sheets of the parent companies. Before 1988, many companies, such as Chrysler Corporation, McDonnell Douglas, and General Motors, did not report certain long-term receivables and investments on their balance sheets because these assets had been transferred to wholly-owned subsidiaries that were established to handle customer financing requirements. Such assets must now be included on the balance sheet of the parent company, which in turn can significantly increase the relative importance of long-term investments on the parent's balance sheet. For example, if the assets of Chrysler's wholly-owned finance subsidiary, Chrysler Financial Corporation, are included on Chrysler's balance sheet, the dollar amount of long-term investments increases to $25 billion, which is more than 50 percent of Chrysler's total assets. Similarly, had the $74 billion in notes receivable held by General Motors Acceptance Corporation (GMAC) been added to the balance sheet of General Motors, they would have represented approximately 40 percent of the company's total assets.

Table 13–1 also excludes financial institutions (e.g., banks and insurance companies) because in many areas of financial reporting, these companies are subject to specialized financial accounting standards. Short-term investments and receivables, for example, are not distinguished from long-term investments and receivables on the balance sheets of financial institutions. As a result, the relative size of long-term investments cannot easily be ascertained for financial institutions. Nonetheless, it is clear that these companies invest heavily in receivables and debt and equity securities. To illustrate, as of December 31, 1987, the dollar amount of total receivables and investments for three major banks, BankAmerica, Chase Manhattan Bank, and The Bank of New York Company, equalled 73 percent, 64 percent, and 75 percent of total assets, respectively. Approximately 90 percent of these assets were in the form of notes receivable.

THE ECONOMIC CONSEQUENCES OF REPORTING LONG-TERM INVESTMENTS

The economic consequences associated with reporting long-term investments are not as obvious as those related to reporting current assets, long-lived assets, liabilities, and stockholders' equity. None of the common ratios used by creditors and investors to assess a company's financial condition explicitly use long-term investments and debt covenants are rarely expressed in terms of the dollar amount of long-term investments. However, the methods used to account for long-term notes receivable as well as debt and equity investments do affect the reported dollar values of assets, liabilities, and net income, and through this effect, might influence credit ratings, investor and creditor decisions, and compliance with covenants expressed in terms of assets, liabilities, or net income. As a result, while the economic consequences associated with reporting long-term investments may be more subtle than those associated with certain other accounts, they can be significant and, therefore, should not be ignored. We point out cases where economic consequences are significant as they arise throughout the chapter.

ACCOUNTING FOR LONG-TERM INVESTMENTS: TWO IMPORTANT CONCEPTS

Before we present the actual methods used to account for long-term notes receivable and investments in corporate bonds and stocks, you must understand two important concepts, both of which have been discussed in previous chapters. They are (1) the effective-interest method and (2) the distinction between debt and equity.

Understanding the **effective interest method** is important because it is used to account for long-term notes receivable and bond investments. Both assets are characterized by contracts that designate future cash inflows, which are discounted at the effective interest rate to value the assets on the balance sheet at present value. The effective-interest method is discussed in Chapter 11, where the methods used to account for long-term notes payable and bonds payable are covered. Chapter 11 also defines notes payable and bonds, and describes the relationship between the stated interest rate and the effective interest rate, and the determination of bond prices (Appendix 11A). You may wish to review this material before reading the sections in this chapter on long-term notes receivable and bond investments.

Understanding the distinction between debt and equity is important to understanding why the methods used to account for long-term equity investments differ from those used to account for long-term notes receivable and bond investments. Much of Chapter 12 is devoted to the different characteristics of debt and equity, and the discussions here assume that you understand the relevant material in Chapter 12.

LONG-TERM NOTES RECEIVABLE

Long-term notes receivable normally arise when companies loan money, provide goods, or provide services in exchange for formal promissory notes, designating cash payments that extend beyond the time period that defines current assets.

Such notes usually state a principal amount (*face* or *maturity value*), the date at which the principal is to be paid *(maturity date),* and a provision for interest payments, which is usually expressed as an annual percentage of the principal.

Long-term notes receivable are held by many major U.S. companies, and their relative size, compared to total assets, ranges from immaterial to very significant. For example, *Accounting Trends and Techniques* (New York: AICPA, 1988) reports that, of the 600 major U.S. companies surveyed, 167 (28 percent) reported some kind of long-term note receivable.[2] For many companies, such as Coca-Cola Enterprises and RJR Nabisco, there was no indication in their 1987 financial reports that they held any long-term notes receivable. Other companies, such as Dow Chemical, McDonald's Corporation, and Alcoa, either disclosed Long-Term-Notes Receivable as a separate account on the balance sheet or included them with other assets, disclosing the actual dollar amount in the footnotes to the financial statements. For these three companies the dollar amounts of long-term notes receivable represented only 3 percent, 1 percent, and 3 percent of total assets, respectively. As indicated earlier, companies such as McDonnell Douglas, Chrysler Corporation, General Motors, and financial institutions hold substantial investments in long-term notes receivable.

Accounting for Long-Term Notes Receivable

The effective-interest method is used to account for long-term notes receivable. This method bases both the receivable on the balance sheet and the related periodic interest revenue on an estimate of the present value of the receivable's future cash inflows. It consists of the following two general rules:

1. The balance-sheet value of the long-term receivable is determined by the present value of the receivable's future cash inflows, discounted at the effective interest rate at the time the receivable is established. The effective interest rate remains constant over the life of the receivable.

2. The interest revenue recognized during each period of the receivable's life is equal to the effective interest rate multiplied by the balance-sheet value of the receivable as of the beginning of that period. The balance-sheet value of the receivable approaches the maturity value over the life of the receivable.

In practice, notes receivable are commonly issued under either of two conditions: (1) at face value, where the stated interest rate equals the effective interest rate, or (2) at a discount, where the stated interest rate is less than the effective interest rate. If the stated rate is zero, the note is described as non-interest-bearing. The next section demonstrates the methods used to account for notes receivable issued at a discount, where the stated rate (3 percent) is less than the effective rate (10 percent). The methods used to account for notes issued at face value, and for non-interest-bearing notes are described in Chapter 11.

Assume that on January 1, 1990, Citicorp Bank lends $7028 to Rockwell International. The terms of the loan specify that Citicorp will receive $8000 on December 31, 1991, and $240 in interest at the end of each year for two years. In other words, the amount lent is $7028, and the note has a principal of $8000, a

---

2. Descriptions such as *noncurrent receivables* and *other receivables* were often used. Balance-sheet classifications also varied. *Long-term investments, other assets, sundry assets,* and other similar descriptions were used to identify the asset category under which long-term receivables were disclosed.

Figure 13–1   Accounting for long-term notes receivable; effective rate (10%) greater than stated rate (3%)

Cash Flows

1/1/90	$\longrightarrow$	12/31/90	$\longrightarrow$	12/31/91
−$7,028		+$240[a]		+$ 240[a]
				+$8,000

[a] $8,000 × 3%

General Journal

Note Receivable	8,000			Cash	240			Cash	240	
Discount on Note		972		Discount on Note	463			Discount on Note	509	
Cash		7,028		Interest Revenue		703[b]		Interest Revenue		749[c]

To record the receipt of a note.   To record interest revenue and   To record interest revenue and
                                          amortize the discount.   amortize the discount.

Cash	8,000	
Note Receivable		8,000

To record receipt of principal.

[b] $7,028 × 10%
[c] $7,491 × 10%

Balance Sheet Value

Note receivable	8,000			Note receivable	8,000	
Less: Discount on note	972	7,028		Less: Discount on note	509	7,491

General Ledger

Discount on Note Receivable

	972	(1/1/90)
(12/31/90 adjustment) 463		
	509	(12/31/90)
(12/31/91 adjustment) 509		
	0	

time to maturity of two years, and a stated annual interest rate of 3 percent ($240 ÷ $8000). Discounting the future cash inflows (interest and principal payments) at 10 percent results in a present value of $7028, so the effective interest rate on this note is 10 percent. (The method used to determine the effective interest rate is discussed in Chapter 11). Figure 13–1 illustrates the cash flows and the methods Citicorp would use to account for this note over its two-year life.

When Citicorp receives the note on January 1, 1990, the cash payment ($7028) is recorded and the note receivable is established in the amount of the principal ($8000). The cash payment does not equal the principal, so Discount on Note Receivable in the amount of $972 is credited. This contra-asset account is disclosed on the asset side of the balance sheet and is subtracted from the Long-Term Note Receivable account. Thus, the balance-sheet value of the note receivable is equal to $7028: the principal ($8000) less the discount ($972). The $972 discount can be viewed as interest revenue, over and above the amount indicated by the stated rate, waiting to be recognized over the two-year life of the note.

The journal entry on December 31, 1990, records the receipt of $240 cash in interest, amortizes a portion of the discount ($463), and recognizes interest revenue ($703) on the note. Interest revenue exceeds the cash interest received, and the amortization of the discount accounts for the difference. The amount of interest revenue is determined by multiplying the effective rate (10 percent)—the actual interest rate earned by Citicorp—by the balance-sheet value of the note receivable ($7028) at the beginning of the period. The amount of the discount, which is amortized, is determined by subtracting the $240 cash payment from the $703 interest revenue. After this entry is recorded, the balance-sheet value of the note receivable is increased to $7491 because the discount, which is subtracted from the note receivable on the balance sheet, has been reduced to $509.

The journal entry on December 31, 1991, records the second $240 cash interest receipt, amortizes the remainder of the discount ($509), and recognizes the interest revenue ($749) during 1991. Once again, the amount of revenue, which exceeds the cash interest receipt, is determined by multiplying the effective rate (10 percent) by the balance-sheet value of the note receivable ($7491) at the beginning of the period. Again, the amortization of the discount accounts for the difference between the cash receipt and the interest revenue. Note also that the principal amount of the note is received on the maturity date.

Long-term notes receivable are usually carried on the balance sheet at the principal amount, less both unamortized discounts and an allowance for uncollectibles.[3] To illustrate how companies disclose the methods used to account for long-term notes issued at a discount, consider the following excerpt from the 1987 financial report of Bank of America.

Loans are generally carried at the principal amount outstanding [less unamortized discounts]. Interest income on discounted loans is generally accrued based on methods that approximate the [effective] interest method. . . .A provision for credit losses, which is a charge against earnings, is added to bring the allowance to a level which, in management's judgment, is adequate to absorb future losses inherent in the credit portfolio.

The Straight-Line Method

The journal entries and calculations illustrated so far represent the effective-interest method. As shown, this method ensures that the periodic interest revenue reported on the income statement is based on the value of the outstanding note receivable and the effective (actual) interest rate. It also ensures that the note receivable is carried on the balance sheet at the present value of the note's future cash inflows, discounted at the effective interest rate at issuance. In cases where the difference between the stated and the effective rates is small, many companies amortize Discounts on Notes Receivable using the straight-line instead of the effective-interest method. That is, they amortize equal amounts of the discount into

---

3. The methods used to account for uncollectibles on long-term notes receivable are essentially the same as those used to account for uncollectibles on short-term receivables. See Chapter 7 for a discussion of accounting for bad debts. Accounting for uncollectible notes can pose major problems for banks and other financial institutions.

interest revenue during each period of the note's life. Referring to Figure 13–1, for example, under the straight-line method, in both 1990 and 1991 the discount would be amortized in the amount of $486 ($972/2) and interest revenue of $726 ($486 + $240) would be recognized.

According to generally accepted accounting principles, the straight-line method is acceptable only if it results in financial statement numbers (i.e., interest revenue and balance-sheet value of the note receivable) that are not materially different from those produced by the effective-interest method. While the straight-line method may be simpler to apply, it misstates periodic interest revenue as well as the balance sheet value of the note because it fails to reflect the actual interest rate earned by the lender. Furthermore, as computerization reduces the cost of record-keeping, companies are increasingly using the effective-interest method.

INVESTMENTS IN CORPORATE BONDS

Bonds are typically purchased by companies on the open market to provide a relatively low-risk return, primarily in the form of interest receipts and sometimes in the form of price appreciation. Such investments should be classified as long-term if management intends to hold them for longer than the time period of current assets.

The relative size of long-term debt investments (including corporate bonds, government bonds, and in some cases redeemable preferred stocks), compared to total assets, varies significantly across the balance sheets of major U.S. companies. *Accounting Trends and Techniques* (New York: AICPA, 1988) reports that, of the 600 companies surveyed, 118 (20 percent) disclosed material long-term investments in debt securities. Most companies, such as IBM and J. C. Penney, include no description of bond investments in their 1987 financial reports. Others, such as Abbott Laboratories and H&R Block, describe their debt investments in the footnotes; the related dollar amounts are normally included in some general asset category (e.g., investments or other assets) on the balance sheet. For both Abbott and H&R Block, debt investments amounted to 7 percent of total assets. The dollar amounts of debt investments held by insurance companies, on the other hand, are often well over 50 percent of total assets. At the end of 1987, for example, Safeco reported debt investments that accounted for 61 percent of total assets.

The Definition of a Bond and Bond Prices: A Brief Review

Recall from Chapter 11 that bonds represent a contract that entitles the holder to a stream of semiannual interest payments until the maturity date, at which time the holder is paid the face value (usually $1000 per bond). The semiannual interest payment is determined by multiplying the stated interest rate times the face value, and dividing the result by 2.

Bonds can be purchased from the issuing company when they are initially issued or, afterward, from other investors on the open market. The price of a bond, which tends to fluctuate over its life, is basically determined by what investors are willing to pay for the right to receive the semiannual interest payments. Such factors as the credit rating of the issuing company, the interest rate stated on the bond, the provisions of the bond contract, and the market rate of interest have a direct bearing on bond prices and their fluctuations.

The effective interest rate, which often differs from the rate stated on the bond, represents the actual return on the bond. It is that rate which, when used to discount the future interest and principal payments, results in a present value equal to the bond's price. When the price of a bond is greater than its face value (premium), the effective rate is less than the stated rate. When the price of a bond is less than its face value (discount), the effective rate is greater than the stated rate. When the price of a bond is equal to its face value (par), the effective rate is equal to the stated rate.

Accounting for Bond Investments

This section consists of three parts. The first covers the purchase of bonds, the second describes the methods used to account for bond investments from purchase to maturity, and the third describes how to account for bonds that are sold prior to maturity.

Purchasing Bond Investments

Bond purchases are recorded in the Bond Investment account at cost, which includes the purchase price (excluding interest accrued since the last interest payment date) and any incidental costs of acquisition, such as brokerage commissions and taxes. The dollar amount paid for accrued interest should be debited to Interest Receivable, which is written off when the first interest payment is received.[4]

To illustrate, assume that the Quaker Oats Company purchased 10 bonds, each with a face value of $1000, a stated interest rate of 10 percent, and a remaining life of two years. These bonds were purchased as a long-term investment for a total cost (including brokerage commissions and accrued interest) of $10,963: $10,363 plus $600 of accrued interest. At the time of the purchase, Quaker Oats recorded the following journal entry.

Bond Investment	10,363	
Interest Receivable	600	
Cash		10,963

To record the purchase of 10 bonds for $10,363 plus $600 accrued interest.

Premium:
Effective rate
< Stated rate

Discount:
Effective rate
> Stated rate

In the example, the bonds were purchased at a premium: the price of the bonds ($10,363) exceeded the face value ($10,000). Consequently, the effective rate of return provided by the bond investment was less than the stated interest rate. Bonds can also be purchased at a price equal to the face value (effective rate equals stated rate), or at a discount, where the price is less than the face value (effective rate exceeds stated rate). Chapter 11 describes the methods used to account for bonds issued at face value, a discount, and a premium. Because the methods used to account for bond investments are very similar, the next section presents only a bond investment purchased at a premium as an example.

Accounting for Bond Investments from Purchase to Maturity

As in the case of long-term notes receivable, the effective-interest method is used to account for bond investments from the date of purchase to the date of maturity. Note in the following example how the journal entries and calculations used to account for bond investments are very similar to those used to account for

---

4. The methods used to account for accrued interest on issued bonds are discussed in Chapter 11.

Figure 13–2 Accounting for bonds

Annual stated interest rate (10%), annual effective rate of return (8%)
Face value = 10 bonds × $1,000 per bond = $10,000
Semiannual interest payment = ($10,000 × 10%) ÷ 2 = $500

Cash Flows

Purchase date	→ 6 mo.	→ 1 year	→ 6 mo.	→ Maturity date
−$10,363	+$500	+$500	+$500	+$ 500
				+$10,000

Present value of future cash flows discounted at 4% semiannual rate

$10,363	$10,278	$10,189	$10,097	$10,000

General Journal

Bond Inv. 10,363	Cash 500	Cash 500	Cash 500	Cash 500
Cash 10,363	Int. Rev. 415*	Int. Rev. 411*	Int. Rev. 408*	Int. Rev. 403*
To record the purchase	Bond Inv. 85	Bond Inv. 89	Bond Inv. 92	Bond Inv. 97
of bonds.	To record the receipt	To record the receipt	To record the receipt	To record the receipt of
	of interest.	of interest.	of interest.	interest.
				Cash 10,000
				Bond Inv. 10,000
				To record the sale of bonds
				at maturity.

Bond Inv. = Bond Investment
Int. Rev. = Interest Revenue
*4% × balance sheet value at beginning of period

Balance Sheet Value

$10,363	$10,278	$10,189	$10,097	$10,000
	($10,363 − $85)	($10,278 − $89)	($10,189 − $92)	($10,097 − $97)

long-term notes receivable. Keep in mind, however, that the example below involves bonds purchased at a premium, while the example covered earlier (Figure 13–1) involved a note receivable issued at a discount.

Assume that Campbell Soup Company purchases 10 bonds, each with a face value of $1000, a stated interest rate of 10 percent, and a time to maturity of two years. Interest payments of $500 ([10,000 × 10%]÷2) are to be received semiannually. The bonds are purchased at $1036.30 each, causing the effective rate of return (8 percent) to be less than the stated rate (10 percent). Assume also that the bonds are purchased immediately after an interest payment date, indicating that no interest has been accrued as of the date of purchase.

The cash flows associated with the bond investment are shown at the top of Figure 13–2, and three items of interest are provided across all relevant points in time: (1) the present value of the future cash flows, calculated at each date by discounting the remaining cash flows at the 4 percent (8%÷2) effective rate of return;[5] (2) the appropriate journal entries under the effective-interest method; and (3) the balance-sheet value of the bond investment.

---

5. Recall from Chapter 11 that determining the appropriate table factors to use when computing the present value of semi-annual cash payments and the payment at maturity involves dividing the annual effective rate by 2 and using twice as many time periods.

At the date of purchase, the bond investment is recorded at its $10,363 cost, which includes all incidental costs of acquisition. In applying the effective-interest method, interest revenue is calculated each period by multiplying the semiannual effective rate of return (4 percent) by the balance-sheet value of the bond investment at the beginning of that period. At the end of the first six-month period, for example, the $415 interest revenue is computed by multiplying the 4 percent effective rate times $10,363, the balance-sheet value of the bond investment at the beginning of the period. The cash interest receipt is $500, so an $85 debit is required to make the journal entry balance. Crediting the $85 to the Bond Investment account serves to bring its balance-sheet value to the present value ($10,278) of the bond's future cash inflows, discounted at 4 percent, as of the end of the first six-month period. The interest revenue ($415) is less than the cash interest receipt ($500) because the actual semiannual rate of return on the bond (4 percent) is less than the semiannual stated rate (5 percent = 10% ÷ 2). The company purchased a bond for $10,363 that will provide a principal payment of only $10,000 at maturity.

The process described above is repeated every six months throughout the remaining life of the bond and eventually, at the maturity date, the balance-sheet value of the bond investment is reduced to its face value ($10,000). Note, once again, that the effective-interest method keeps the balance-sheet value of the bond investment equal to the present value throughout the life of the bond.

A common way to illustrate the effective-interest method applied to a bond purchase is to prepare a bond investment schedule. Figure 13–3 contains such a schedule using the calculations from the previous example. Review the schedule, and note that it is simply another way to illustrate what is shown in Figure 13–2.

In Figure 13–2 and the bond investment schedule in Figure 13–3, note that the $363 ($10,363 − $10,000) premium was not explicitly recorded when the bonds were purchased and, accordingly, was not amortized over the bond investment's life. In other words, a separate Premium on Bond Investment account was not recognized. At purchase, the Bond Investment account was simply debited for the entire cost, and over the remaining life, the Bond Investment account was decreased as interest revenue was earned.

While this procedure is acceptable and used by virtually all major U.S. companies, explicitly recording and amortizing bond premiums (and discounts) is actually recommended, but not required, under generally accepted accounting princi-

Figure 13–3 Bond investment schedule: bonds purchased at a premium

$10,000 face value: Life = 2 years   Annual Stated Interest Rate = 10%   Annual Effective Interest Rate = 8%

Date	Interest Revenue (4% × Balance Sheet Value)	Interest Receipt (5% × Face Value)	Book Value of Bond Investment
Purchase	—	—	$10,363
6 months	$415	$500	−85
			10,278
1 year	411	500	−89
			10,189
6 months	408	500	−92
			10,097
Maturity	403	500	−97
			$10,000

ples. This policy of allowing either approach is somewhat different than in the case of accounting for bond liabilities. As described in Chapter 11, when bonds are issued at prices that differ from their face values, a discount or premium, if material, must be recognized on the balance sheet and amortized over the life of the bond.

Selling a Bond Investment Before Maturity

When bonds are sold prior to maturity, interest accrued to the date of sale should first be recognized, which also involves updating the balance in the Bond Investment account. Cash is then debited for the proceeds, the amount received for accrued interest is recorded as a credit to Interest Receivable, the Bond Investment account is written off the balance sheet, and a gain or loss is recognized on the transaction. As described in Chapter 14, the gain or loss would normally appear in a special section of the income statement that includes non-operating revenues and expenses.

To illustrate, assume that on June 30 Atlantic Richfield sold a bond investment for a total cash price of $52,000, which included $2000 of accrued interest. When the accrued interest was recorded on June 30, interest revenue of $1600 was recognized, and the Bond Investment account, which had a book value of $49,000, was reduced by $400. The following journal entries would be entered to reflect these facts.

June 30	Interest Receivable	2,000	
	Interest Revenue		1,600
	Bond Investment		400
	To record the recognition of $2000 in accrued interest and update the Bond Investment account.		

June 30	Cash	52,000	
	Bond Investment ($49,000 − $400)		48,600
	Interest Receivable		2,000
	Gain on Sale of Bonds		1,400
	To record the sale of a bond investment prior to maturity.		

In the example, a $1400 gain was recognized. Had the bonds been sold for $48,000 instead of $52,000, a loss in the amount of $2600 would have been recognized with the following entry:

June 30	Cash	48,000	
	Loss on Sale of Bonds	2,600	
	Bond Investment		48,600
	Interest Receivable		2,000
	To record the sale of a bond investment prior to maturity.		

LONG-TERM EQUITY INVESTMENTS

An equity investment occurs when another company's outstanding common stock is purchased. Chapter 6 discusses short-term investments in equity securities and notes that they are defined as such because they meet two criteria: (1) the equity securities are marketable and (2) management intends to liquidate (sell) them within the time period that defines current assets. This section covers equity investments that fail to meet either or both of these two criteria.

Companies make long-term investments in the equity securities of other companies primarily for two reasons: (1) investment income in the form of dividends and stock price appreciation and (2) management influence, where the voting power of the purchased shares allows the investor company to exert some control over the board of directors and management of the investee company. The primary motivation behind the long-term equity investments for most major U.S. companies is reason (2), influence over the investee company's operations and management.

Most large, well-known U.S. companies are constantly involved in acquisitions, whereby they purchase all, or a majority, of the outstanding common stock of another company, and then change the investee company's operations and/or management. In 1986, for example, General Electric (GE) purchased all of the outstanding common stock of RCA Corporation, which at the time owned National Broadcasting Company (NBC), for $6.4 billion. As reported in GE's 1987 financial report, "subsequent to the acquisition, GE sold . . . a number of RCA and NBC operations whose activities were not compatible with GE's long-range strategic plans."

In another example, DuPont stated in its 1987 financial report that in 1986 alone "the company completed six major acquisitions for a total purchase price of $1.2 billion." These investments included majority interests of the outstanding common stock of Inland Steel Coal Company, Sierra Coal Company, and Tau Laboratories, Inc. In each case DuPont made significant changes to either the operations or the management of the acquired companies.

It is also common to exert influence over the operations and management of a company by purchasing a significant portion, but less than a majority (51 percent), of the company's outstanding common stock. *Accounting Trends and Techniques* (New York: AICPA, 1988) reports that, of the 600 major U.S. companies surveyed, well over half reported such investments. As of December 31, 1987, Chrysler Corporation, for example, held a significant portion, but less than 51 percent, of the outstanding common stock of Mitsubishi Motors Corporation, Diamond Star Motors Corporation, and Officine Alfieri Maserati SpA.

Accounting for Long-Term Equity Investments

Unlike long-term investments in debt securities, such as notes receivable and bonds, where the future cash inflows are specified by contract, the future cash inflows related to long-term equity investments are uncertain. Dividend payments, price appreciation, and other returns associated with owning equity securities cannot be predicted with reasonable accuracy. Consequently, using the effective-interest method to account for equity investments violates the principle of objectivity, and other methods must be employed.

Potential to Influence Defines the Appropriate Accounting Method
We have noted that long-term investments in equity securities are commonly made to exert influence over the operations and management of the investee company. Financial accounting standards define the appropriate accounting method in terms of the potential for such influence—specifically, in terms of the percentage of outstanding voting stock owned by the investor company.

Table 13–2   Accounting for long-term investments in equity securities

Percentage of Stock Ownership	Potential to Influence	Accounting Method
Less than 20%	Small	Lower-of-cost-or-market or cost method
20%–50%	Significant	Equity method
Greater than 50%	Control	Consolidated statements

If the investor company owns less than 20 percent of the outstanding voting stock of the investee company, the potential for influence is relatively small, and the two entities can be viewed as independent. The equity investment, therefore, is accounted for using either the lower-of-cost-or-market method or the cost method.

When the percentage of ownership is between 20 percent and 50 percent, the investor company has the potential to exert "significant influence" over the investee company, and the two entities cannot be viewed as completely independent. A method called the equity method is then used to account for the equity investment.

When the percentage of ownership is greater than 50 percent, the investor company has "control" over the investee company, and, for accounting purposes, the two entities are viewed as one, and consolidated financial statements are prepared. The conditions that define the methods used to account for long-term equity investments are summarized in Table 13–2.

The following discussion presents the mechanics involved in applying the lower-of-cost-or-market method, the cost method, and the equity method, and the conditions under which each method is used.[6]

Lower-of-Cost-or-Market Method

The **lower-of-cost-or-market method** is used when a company holds marketable equity securities that amount to less than 20 percent of the outstanding voting stock of the investee company. Chapter 6 describes the lower-of-cost-or-market method as applied to short-term equity securities, and you may wish to review this material now. Applying the lower-of-cost-or-market method to long-term equity securities is almost identical and can be summarized by the following four rules.

1. All purchases of marketable equity securities classified as long-term are recorded at cost, which includes the incidental costs of acquisition.

Investment in Equity Securities	100	
Cash		100
To record the purchase of 10 shares of XYZ stocks at $10 per share (includes brokerage fees) on January 1, 1989.		

Investment in Equity Securities	200	
Cash		200
To record the purchase of 40 shares of ABC stock at $5 per share (includes brokerage fees) on March 1, 1989.		

---

6. Consolidated statements are only briefly introduced in this chapter. More complete discussions can be found in Chapter 16 of this text as well as in intermediate and advanced financial accounting texts.

2. Sales of marketable equity securities classified as long-term result in recognized gains or losses in the amount of the difference between the proceeds of the sale and the acquisition cost of the sold securities.

Cash	39	
Investment in Equity Securities		30
Gain on Sale of Equity Securities		9
To record the sale of 3 shares of XYZ for $13 per share on June 3, 1989.		

Cash	40	
Loss on Sale of Equity Securities	10	
Investment in Equity Securities		50
To record a sale of 10 shares of ABC for $4 per share on November 23, 1989.		

3. Dividends on marketable equity securities classified as long-term are recognized as income at the date of declaration. When the dividends are received, the receivable is removed from the balance sheet.

Dividend Receivable	20	
Dividend Income		20
To record the declaration of a $20 dividend on XYZ securities on December 1, 1989.		

Cash	20	
Dividend Receivable		20
To record the receipt of previously declared dividends on December 21, 1989.		

4. At the end of the accounting period, the *aggregate* original cost of the portfolio of long-term equity securities on hand is compared to the *aggregate* market value of these same securities on that date.

(a) If the aggregate market value is less than the aggregate cost, an allowance account, which is disclosed as a contra to the Long-Term Investments in Equity Securities account, is set equal to the difference between the aggregate market value and the aggregate cost. The corresponding debit or credit entry is to the Unrealized Loss on Long-Term Equity Investments account, which is disclosed as a contra account in the stockholders' equity section.

Assume in the ongoing example that no additional transactions occurred during 1989, and the aggregate market value of the portfolio of XYZ and ABC securities held on December 31, 1989, is equal to $200, $20 below the aggregate cost which is $220 ($300 − $80). The following adjusting journal entry would be recorded on December 31, 1989.

Unrealized Loss on Long-Term Equity Investments*	20	
Allow. for Unrealized loss on Long-Term Equity Investments		20
To recognize an unrealized loss on the portfolio of long-term equity securities.		

*This account does not appear on the income statement. It reduces stockholders' equity directly.

(b) If the aggregate market value of the portfolio of equity securities is equal to or exceeds the aggregate cost at the end of the accounting period, the allowance account should be equal to zero and adjusted if necessary.

Figure 13–4   The lower-of-cost-or-market method for long-term equity investments

Tandem Corporation Balance Sheet Excerpts December 31, 1989		
Long-term investments		
Long-term investments	$10,000	
Less: Allowance for unrealized loss on long-term equity investments	2,000	$8,000
Stockholders' equity		
Common stock		50,000
Additional paid-in capital		30,000
Retained earnings		8,000
Less: Unrealized loss on long-term equity investments		2,000
Total stockholders' equity		$86,000

Assume that no transactions occurred during 1990, and that the aggregate market value of the portfolio of XYZ and ABC securities at year end was $250, which is above the aggregate cost ($220). The following entry would be recorded on December 31, 1990.

```
Allow. for Unrealized Loss on Long-Term Equity Investments        20
     Unrealized Loss on Long-Term Equity Investments                       20
     To recognize a recovery of a previously recognized unrealized loss.
```

Applying the lower-of-cost-or-market (LCM) method to investments in marketable equity securities classified as long-term is the same as applying the LCM method to equity securities classified as short-term, with one important exception. The Unrealized Loss on Long-Term Equity Investments account is not treated as a temporary account that appears on the income statement and is closed to Retained Earnings. Rather, it is treated as a permanent contra account and disclosed as such in the stockholders' equity section of the balance sheet. Also, when previously recognized losses are subsequently recovered, a revenue is not recognized; the Unrealized Loss on Long-Term Equity Investments account is simply credited.

To illustrate, suppose that at the end of its first year of operations, 1989, Tandem Corporation held investments in the marketable equity securities of both Brandley Company and Morton Enterprises (less than 20 percent of the voting stock). These securities were purchased for a total cost of $10,000, and Tandem's management did not intend to sell them within the time period of current assets. As of December 31, 1989, the aggregate market value of these investments had fallen to $8000. Tandem would make the following adjusting journal entry, and its long-term investment and stockholders' equity sections on the balance sheet would appear as in Figure 13–4. In the absence of dividends, there would be no affect on the income statement.

```
Unrealized Loss on Long-Term Equity Investment        2000
     Allow. for Unrealized Loss on Long-Term Equity Invest.        2000
     To record the writedown of marketable equity investments classified as long-term.
```

Assume that during 1990 Tandem continued to hold the marketable equity securities of both companies, and the aggregate market value of the portfolio rose to

Figure 13-5 The lower-of-cost-or-market method for long-term equity investments

Tandem Corporation		
Balance Sheet Excerpts		
December 31, 1990		

Long-term investments		
Long-term investments	$10,000	
Less: Allowance for unrealized loss on long-term equity investments	500	$9,500
Stockholders' equity		
Common stock		50,000
Additional paid-in capital		30,000
Retained earnings		11,000
Less: Unrealized loss on long-term equity investments		500
Total stockholders' equity		$90,500

$9500 as of December 31, 1990, a recovery of $1500 ($9500 − $8000). In this situation, Tandem would record the following adjusting journal entry, and the long-term investment and stockholders' equity sections of the December 31, 1990 balance sheet would appear as in Figure 13-5. Once again, in the absence of dividends, the income statement would be unaffected.

Allowance for Unrealized Loss on Long-Term Equity Investment	1500	
Unrealized Loss on Long-Term Equity Investment		1500
To record the recovery of equity investments classified as long-term.		

The accounting treatment described above ensures that unrealized gains and losses from relatively small (less than 20 percent) long-term investments in marketable equity securities do not affect the investor company's net income. Long-term investments, by definition, are not expected to be liquidated in the near future and, therefore, short-term fluctuations in their market values have little bearing on a company's long-run performance. However, unrealized losses and recoveries on long-term investments in marketable equity securities do affect stockholders' equity; thus, they affect ratios, such as the debt/equity ratio, that are used in debt covenants and to determine a company's credit rating.

The account Unrealized Loss on Long-Term Equity Investments is not frequently found on the balance sheets of major U.S. companies. In many cases the dollar amount of the investment in long-term marketable equity securities subject to the LCM rule is relatively small and often immaterial. However, for insurance companies, where equity investments make up a significant portion of total assets, unrealized changes in the market values of those securities can be substantial. Safeco Insurance Company, for example, reported unrealized losses on market equity securities in the amount of $15.1 million as of December 31, 1987. Furthermore, an Unrealized Loss account does not appear on the balance sheets of other major U.S. companies, like J. C. Penney for example, because these companies adjust the Retained Earnings account directly for unrealized losses and recoveries on marketable equity securities held as long-term investments. While this accounting treatment appears to be inconsistent with generally accepted accounting principles, it is only followed when the dollar amounts of these adjustments are immaterial.

Figure 13–6   The cost method of accounting for long-term equity investments

General Journal

1989		
Jan. 15	Long-Term Investment in Equity Securities	1,000
	Cash	1,000
	To record the purchase of 100 equity shares @ $10 per share.	
Nov. 29	Dividend Receivable	50
	Dividend Income	50
	To record the declaration of a dividend to be received.	
Dec. 15	Cash	50
	Dividend Receivable	50
	To record the receipt of the previously-declared $50 dividend.	

1991		
May 5	Cash	700
	Loss on Sale of Long-Term Equity Securities	300
	Long-Term Investment in Equity Securities	1,000
	To record the sale of 100 equity shares, originally purchased @ $10 each, for $7 per share.	

The Cost Method

Some equity securities have no readily determinable market values. Equity securities in corporations whose securities are not publicly traded (i.e., closely held corporations), for example, may have restrictions on trading and therefore have no public market values. Relatively small investments (less than 20 percent of the outstanding voting stock) in such securities, which by definition cannot easily be liquidated, are accounted for using the **cost method.** It is impossible to apply the LCM method to such securities because their market values cannot be determined.

Applying the cost method is very straightforward. Purchases of equity securities are recorded at cost, including incidental costs of acquisition; dividends are recorded as income when declared; and sales, when they eventually occur, give rise to book gains or losses that are reflected on the income statement.

To illustrate, suppose that on January 15, 1989, Beldon, Inc. purchased 100 equity securities in a closely held corporation for $10 per share. On December 15 Beldon received a $50 dividend that had been declared on November 29. No other activity occured in the account until May 5, 1991, when Beldon sold the securities privately for $7 each. The journal entries contained in Figure 13–6 would reflect these transactions.

The Equity Method

Some companies have the ability to significantly influence the operating decisions and management policies of other companies. Such influence indicates a substantive economic relationship between the two companies and may be evidenced, for example, by representation on the board of directors, the interchange of management personnel between companies, frequent or significant transactions between companies, or the technical dependency of one company on the other. Significant investments in the equity securities (voting stock) of another company may also indicate significant influence and a substantive economic relationship. To achieve a reasonable degree of uniformity, the accounting profession concluded that an investment of 20 percent or more in the voting stock of another company represents a "significant influence," and that equity investments from 20 percent to 50 percent of the voting stock should be accounted for using the **equity method.**

The accounting procedures used to apply the equity method reflect a substantive economic relationship between the investor and the investee companies. The equity investment is originally recorded on the investor's books at cost, but is adjusted each subsequent period for changes in the net assets of the investee. As the balance-sheet value of the investee increases or decreases, so does the Long-Term Equity Investment account of the investor.

Specifically, the carrying value of the long-term investment on the investor's balance sheet is (1) periodically increased (decreased) by the investor's proportionate share of the net income (loss) of the investee and (2) decreased by all dividends transferred to the investor from the investee. In other words, the equity method of accounting acknowledges a close economic link between the two companies. Investee earnings, which indicate net asset growth, and investee dividends, which represent net asset reductions, are reflected proportionately on the balance sheet of the investor.

To illustrate, assume that on January 1, 1989, American Electric Company purchased 40 percent of the outstanding voting stock of Masley Corporation for $40,000. During 1989 Masley recognized net income of $10,000 and declared (Dec. 1) and paid (Dec. 20) dividends of $1500 to American Electric. During 1990 Masley recognized a net loss of $5000 and declared (Dec. 1) and paid (Dec. 20) only a $500 dividend to American Electric. Under the equity method, the journal entries contained in Figure 13−7 would be recorded on the books of American Electric.

It is important to understand how the equity method reflects a significant economic relationship between the investor and investee companies. The net income (loss) of the investee serves to proportionately increase (decrease) the investment account of the investor. Thus the investee's net asset growth or decline is reflected on the investor's balance sheet and income statement. Note also that dividends transferred from the investee to the investor are not treated as revenue on the investor's books. Revenue is recognized when the investor's proportionate share of

Figure 13−7 The equity method of accounting for long-term equity investments

General Journal

1989

Jan. 1 Long-Term Investment in Equity Securities 40,000
      Cash 40,000
    To record the purchase of 40% of Masley's outstanding shares.

Dec. 1 Dividend Receivable 1,500
      Long-Term Investment in Equity Securities 1,500
    To record the declaration of a $1,500 dividend by Masley.

Dec. 20 Cash 1,500
      Dividend Receivable 1,500
    To record the receipt of the dividend declared on December 1.

Dec. 31 Long-Term Investment in Equity Securities 4,000
      Income from Long-Term Equity Investments 4,000
    To record the recognition of 40% of Masley's 1989 net income ($10,000 × 40%).

1990

Dec. 1 Dividend Receivable 500
      Long-Term Investment in Equity Securities 500
    To record the declaration of a dividend by Masley.

Dec. 20 Cash 500
      Dividend Receivable 500
    To record the receipt of the dividend declared on Dec. 1.

Dec. 31 Loss on Long-Term Equity Investment 2,000
      Long-Term Investment in Equity Securities 2,000
    To record the recognition of 40% of Masley's 1990 net loss ($5,000 × 40%).

Table 13-3   The relative importance of investments in affiliate companies (selected U.S. companies)

Company	Dollar Amount of Investment (millions of dollars)	Percentage of Total Assets
Marriott Corporation	$495	9%
McGraw-Hill	98	6
Time, Inc.	164	4
DuPont	541	2
Goodyear Tire and Rubber Co.	107	1

Source: 1987 financial reports.

the investee's net income is recorded, not when the dividends are declared or transferred. Dividends are simply treated as an exchange of assets on the investor's books. The Long-Term Investment account is decreased, Dividends Receivable is increased on the date of declaration, and the receivable is exchanged for cash on the date of payment.

The equity method also provides another reason why a company's net income (loss) rarely reflects its cash flow from operating activities. The income recognized from the investee company rarely equals the cash dividends received from the investee. *Forbes* magazine describes the equity method as "misleading" because "the investor company never really sees any nondividend cash from the investee company" on which it often recognizes substantial income.[7]

Equity investments in the amount of 20–50 percent of an investee company's voting stock are very common for major U.S. companies. *Accounting Trends and Techniques* (New York: AICPA, 1988) reports that, of the 600 companies surveyed, 316 (53 percent) reported using the equity method of accounting. Table 13–3 indicates the importance of investments accounted for under the equity method, relative to total assets, to several major U.S. corporations as of December 31, 1987. Investee companies that are 20–50 percent owned by investor companies are often referred to as *affiliate* or *associated* companies.

Income from equity investments can also represent a material percentage of net income. At the end of 1987, for example, Alcoa, J. C. Penney, and Dow Chemical reported income from affiliate companies (as a percentage of total net income) of 10 percent, 6 percent, and 3 percent, respectively. The following excerpt was taken from the 1987 financial report of Marriott Corporation. It describes how the company accounts for equity investments in affiliate companies: "Investments in 50 percent or less-owned affiliates over which the company has the ability to exercise significant influence are accounted for using the equity method."

Cost, Lower-of-Cost-or-Market, and Equity Methods: A Comparative Example
In Figure 13–8 the journal entries used to apply the cost, LCM and equity methods are compared. Read the given information, and review Figure 13–8 closely, noting how the three methods are both similar and dissimilar.

Hauser Construction Company purchased 500 shares (20 percent of the voting stock) of Minicomputer, Inc. on January 23, 1989, for $5 per share. Hauser held the securities throughout 1989, and on December 31, 1989, when the market price had dropped to $4 per share, Minicomputers recognized a $3000 net loss. At

---

7. Aaron Bernstein, "Reading Between the Lines," *Forbes*, 10 May 1982, p. 78.

Figure 13–8   Accounting for long-term investments in equity securities

	Cost Method		Lower-of-Cost-or-Market Method		Equity Method	
Jan. 23, 1989						
(Purchase of securities)	LT Inv.	2,500	LT Inv.	2,500	LT Inv.	2,500
	Cash	2,500	Cash	2,500	Cash	2,500
Dec. 31, 1989						
Net loss ($3000)	(No entry)		(No entry)		Loss on LT Inv.	600
					LT Inv.	600
					(20% × $3000 net loss)	
Dividend ($1 per share)	Cash	500	Cash	500	Cash	500
	Div. Inc.	500	Div. Inc.	500	LT Inv.	500
Market price ($4 per share)	(No entry)		Unrealized Loss on LT Inv.*	500	(No entry)	
			Allow. for Loss	500		
			(500 × [$5 − $4])			
			*Stockholders' equity account			
Dec. 31, 1990						
Net income ($10,000)	(No entry)		(No entry)		LT Inv.	2,000
					Income from LT Inv.	2,000
					(20% × $10,000 net income)	
Dividends ($2 per share)	Cash	1,000	Cash	1,000	Cash	1,000
	Div. Inc.	1,000	Div. Inc.	1,000	LT Inv.	1,000
Market price ($6 per share)	(No entry)		Allow. for Loss	500	(No entry)	
			Unrealized Loss on LT Inv.	500		
			("recovery" limited to previous loss)			

LT Inv. = Long-Term Investment
Div. Inc. = Dividend Income

the same time, however, Minicomputers declared and paid a dividend of $1 per share. During 1990 Hauser neither bought nor sold any Minicomputer stock, and on December 31, 1990, the market value had risen to $6 per share. On that date Minicomputers reported net income of $10,000 and declared and paid a dividend of $2 per share. To simplify the example, assume that the dividends were declared and paid on the same day.

Business Acquisitions, Mergers, and Consolidated Financial Statements

A **business acquisition** occurs when an investor company acquires a **controlling interest** (more than 50 percent of the voting stock) in another company. If the two companies continue as separate legal entities, the investor company is referred to as the **parent company,** and the investee company is called the **subsidiary.** In 1985, for example, Monsanto acquired the outstanding stock of G. D. Searle and Co., which operates as a Monsanto subsidiary. In such cases **consolidated financial statements** (including the income statement, balance sheet, statement of retained earnings, statement of cash flows, and statement of stockholders' equity) are prepared by the parent. Consolidated statements ignore the fact that the parent and the subsidiary are actually separate legal entities and, for reporting purposes, treat the two companies as a single operating unit.

It is important to realize that consolidated statements are prepared for financial accounting purposes only. The parent and the subsidiary maintain separate legal status. In many respects they may continue to operate as relatively independent entities, and the subsidiary maintains a separate set of financial statements. Only because the parent has a controlling interest over the subsidiary do professional accounting standards require that the financial condition of the two companies be represented to the public as one.

A **merger,** or **business combination,** occurs when two or more companies combine to form a single legal entity. In most cases the assets and liabilities of the smaller company are merged into those of the larger, surviving, company. The stock of at least one company, usually the smaller one, is often retired, and it ceases to exist as a separate entity. In 1987, for example, American Motors Corporation ceased to exist as a separate entity when it was merged into Chrysler Corporation. Technically speaking, consolidated financial statements are not prepared after a merger because there is no parent/subsidiary relationship. At least one of the companies involved in the combination no longer exists. However, the financial statements of the surviving company do reflect the assets and liabilities of the merged entities.

Most business acquisitions and combinations are accomplished when cash and/ or other assets (often stock) of the parent are paid to the stockholders of the subsidiary in exchange for the assets and liabilities of the subsidiary.[8] Such transactions are commonly accounted for under the **purchase method:** the assets and liabilities of the subsidiary are recorded on the balance sheet of the parent at fair market value, and the difference between the purchase price and the net fair market value of the subsidiary's assets and liabilities is recorded as goodwill. As noted in Chapter 9 and Appendix 9A, which cover long-lived assets, goodwill is an intangible asset that must be amortized over a period not to exceed forty years.[9]

For example, on December 18, 1986, Delta Air Lines, Inc. purchased all the outstanding shares of Western Air Lines, Inc. for $787 million, which consisted of $384 million in cash and Delta common stock valued at $403 million. Delta received the assets and liabilities of Western, which at the time of the transaction, had fair market values as described in Figure 13−9.

To record the purchase, Delta made the following journal entry. The assets and liabilities of Western were then included on the 1986 balance sheet of Delta.

Current Assets	349	
Property, Plant, and Equipment	748	
Other Assets	24	
Goodwill	407	
Current Liabilities		310
Long-Term Liabilities		431
Cash		384
Common Stock		403
To record the purchase of Western Air Lines.		

Accounting for business acquisitions and mergers and preparing consolidated financial statements are actually more complex than we have indicated here. Fur-

---

8. In the following discussion we use the terms *parent* and *subsidiary* to denote the investor and investee companies. In the case of business combinations, however, the term *parent* should be interpreted as the survivor company, and the term *subsidiary* as the merged company.

9. Another method used to account for a business combination is called the *pooling-of-interest method:* goodwill is not recognized, and the assets, liabilities, and retained earnings of the subsidiary are recorded on the balance sheet of the parent at cost. This method is discussed in Chapter 16.

Figure 13–9   Computation of goodwill

		Fair Market Value (in millions)
Current assets		$349
Property, plant, and equipment		748
Other assets		24
Less:		
Current liabilities	310	
Long-term debt	431	741
Net fair market value of Western's assets and liabilities		380
Less: Purchase price		787
Goodwill (excess of purchase price over fair market value of net assets)		$407

ther discussion can be found in Chapter 16 of this text and in intermediate and advanced financial accounting texts.

The Equity Method or Consolidated Statements?

Accounting for an equity investment under the equity method can give rise to financial statements that are much different than those prepared as consolidated statements. The following example describes an equity investment, comparing the balance sheet produced under the equity method to a consolidated balance sheet.

Suppose that the December 31, 1990 balance sheets of Megabucks, a large manufacturing company, and Tiny, Inc., a smaller distribution outlet, are as shown in Figure 13–10. Note initially that the debt/equity ratio of Megabucks is 67 percent ($20,000 ÷ $30,000), and assume further that Megabucks purchased the outstanding stock of Tiny, Inc. for $10,000.

Figure 13–10   The balance sheets of Megabucks and Tiny, Inc.

Megabucks Balance Sheet December 31, 1990			
Assets	$50,000	Liabilities	$20,000
		Stockholders' equity	30,000
		Total liabilities and	
Total assets	$50,000	stockholders' equity	$50,000

Tiny Incorporated Balance Sheet December 31, 1990			
Assets	$20,000	Liabilities	$15,000
		Stockholders' equity	5,000
		Total liabilities and	
Total assets	$20,000	stockholders' equity	$20,000

The Equity Method. Under the equity method, Megabucks would record the following journal entry.

Long-Term Investment	10,000	
Cash		10,000
To record the purchase of Tiny, Inc. for $10,000.		

Note that the journal entry to record the investment has no effect on the total assets, total liabilities, total stockholders' equity, or the debt/equity ratio of Megabucks. The transaction is simply recorded as an exchange of two assets, a long-term investment and cash. In future periods under the equity method, Megabucks' total assets will reflect the net incomes (losses) reported by Tiny, Inc., less any dividends.

Consolidated Financial Statements. If Megabucks accounts for this acquisition as a purchase and prepares consolidated financial statements, it would record the transaction with the following journal entry. Assume that Tiny's assets and liabilities are reported on its balance at fair market value.

Assets	20,000	
Goodwill	5,000	
Liabilities		15,000
Cash		10,000
To record the acquisition of Tiny, Inc. for $10,000.		

In this case both the assets and the liabilities of Megabucks would be increased by $15,000. The resulting consolidated balance sheet would appear as in Figure 13–11. Note that the debt/equity ratio is now 1.17 ($35,000 ÷ $30,000). Treating the transaction as a purchase and preparing a consolidated balance sheet, as opposed to using the equity method, increases the debt/equity ratio of Megabucks from .67 to 1.17.

This difference between the equity method and preparing consolidated financial statements has encouraged many companies in the past to choose the equity method when at all possible. Such a choice may come in the form of purchasing slightly less than 50 percent of the investee company's common stock, or purchasing over 50 percent and claiming that "control is temporary or does not rest with the majority owner." In *Forbes* magazine, the national director of accounting and auditing at Seidman & Seidman, a major accounting firm, noted that the eq-

Figure 13–11   Consolidated balance sheet

Megabucks Balance Sheet December 31, 1991			
Assets	$65,000	Liabilities	$35,000
		Stockholders' equity	30,000
		Total liabilities and	
Total assets	$65,000	stockholders' equity	$65,000

uity method can be viewed as a method of off-balance-sheet financing. He pointed out that using the equity method can "present a more favorable impression of debt/equity ratios, working capital ratios, and returns on assets invested in the business."[10] Consequently, financial statement users and auditors should pay special attention to cases where there is some question about whether the equity method should be used or consolidated financial statements should be prepared.

Accounting for Equity Investments: A Summary

This section provides a framework that summarizes the methods used to account for investments in equity securities. Recall that we covered short-term investments in equity securities in Chapter 6, and that such investments are reported on the balance sheet at lower-of-cost-or market value. That chapter points out that for equity investments to be classified as current assets on the balance sheet, they must meet two criteria: they must be (1) marketable and (2) management must intend to liquidate them within the time period of current assets. Equity investments that fail to meet either or both of these criteria must be listed in the long-term investment section of the balance sheet. The proportion of ownership determines the accounting methods used for the equity investments listed as long-term.

Figure 13–12 summarizes the appropriate accounting methods for all (short-term and long-term) investments in equity securities. In general, three questions must be answered before the appropriate accounting method and disclosure can be determined: (1) Is the security marketable? (2) Does management intend to liquidate the security within the time period of current assets? and (3) Is the proportion of ownership less than 20 percent, between 20 percent and 50 percent, or greater than 50 percent?

If the purchased equity securities are marketable, and management intends to liquidate them within the time period of current assets, the investment is considered short-term regardless of the proportion of ownership, and it is carried on the balance sheet at the lower-of-cost-or-market value (Path 1).

If the purchased securities are marketable, but management does not intend to liquidate them within the time period of current assets, the investment is considered long-term. Such long-term investments, where less than 20 percent of the voting shares are held, are carried on the balance sheet at the lower-of-cost-or-market value (Path 2). Long-term investments of between 20 percent and 50 percent of the voting shares are accounted for using the equity method (Path 3). Long-term investments of 50 percent or more of the voting shares give rise to consolidated statements (Path 4).

Equity investments that are not marketable are accounted for using the cost method if they represent less than 20 percent of the voting shares (Path 5), or the equity method if they represent an investment of between 20 percent and 50 percent (Path 6). Consolidated statements should be prepared if such investments represent 50 percent or more of the voting stock (Path 7).

---

10. Anne McGrath, "The Best of Both Worlds," *Forbes,* 26 September 1983, pp. 102, 106.

Figure 13–12   Investments in equity securities

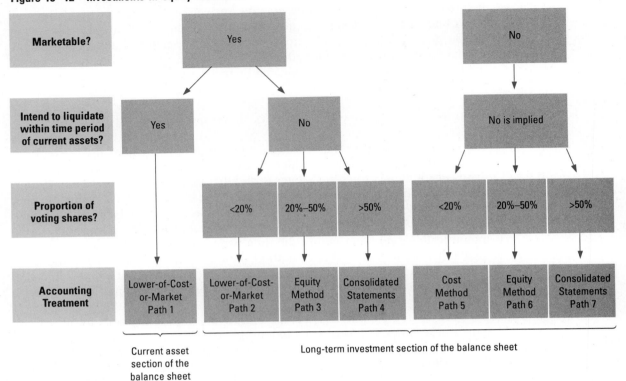

Current asset section of the balance sheet

Long-term investment section of the balance sheet

THE ANNUAL REPORT OF K MART CORPORATION

Turn now to K mart's annual report located in Appendix D. The section entitled Basis for Consolidation (page 35) states that "the company includes all majority owned subsidiaries in the consolidated financial statements." As indicated on pages 19, 45, and 52, K mart's principle subsidiaries include Builders Square, Inc., K mart Apparel Corp., K mart Canada Limited, Makro, Inc., Pay Less Drug Stores, Northwest, Inc., and the Walden Book Company, Inc. Accordingly, K mart's consolidated financial statements include the assets and liabilities of these entities. Any goodwill recognized when these subsidiaries were acquired is included on the balance sheet in the account Other Assets and Deferred Charges.

The section on New Ventures (page 36) indicates that "in March 1988, K mart Corporation purchased a 51 percent ownership interest in Makro Inc. from SHV North America Corporation . . . The Makro acquisition has been accounted for as a purchase. The results of operations have been consolidated with those of the company from the date of acquisition. The excess of cost over fair value of the assets acquired [goodwill], which is not significant, is being amortized over 40 years on a straight-line basis."

The Balance Sheet discloses Investments in Affiliated Retail Companies of $506 million (4 percent of total assets) and $379 million (3 percent of total assets) for 1989 and 1988, respectively. The section entitled Basis for Consolidation (p. 35), states that "investments in affiliate retail companies owned 20 percent or more are accounted for by the equity method using their December financial statements. The equity investments are described on pages 21, 38, and 39. Note that K mart owns 49 percent of Meldisco and 22 percent of Coles Myer Ltd. and that the results of operations (including net income and dividends) for each company are summarized on pages 38 and 39.

Equity income reported on the Income Statement equaled $105 million, $92 million, and $83 million for 1989, 1988, and 1987, respectively. These amounts represented significant portions of K mart's net incomes (between 13 percent and 14 percent) for those years. On the Statement of Cash Flows, Undistributed Equity Income in the amounts of $42 million (1989), $36 million (1988), and $23 million (1987) have been deducted from Income from Continuing Operations in the computation of Net Cash Provided by Operations. These adjustments reflect the fact that the cash receipts from dividends declared by the affiliate companies were less than the equity income reported on the Income Statement.

REVIEW PROBLEM

Trailor Corporation entered into the five transactions listed below on January 1, 1989. Each transaction is described and is immediately followed by the related journal entries that would be recorded over the subsequent two-year period.

(1) Trailor loaned $3986 to Markus Company on January 1, 1989, expecting to receive $5000 on December 31, 1990. The stated interest rate on the loan is 0 percent, and the effective interest rate is 12 percent.

1989

Jan. 1	Note Receivable	5000	
	Cash		3986
	Discount on Note Receivable		1014
	To record the loan to Markus Company.		
Dec. 31	Discount on Note Receivable	478*	
	Interest Revenue		478
	To recognize accrued interest on the note.		
	*($5,000 − $1014) × 12%		

1990

Dec. 31	Discount on Note Receivable	536*	
	Interest Revenue		536
	*($5,000 − [$1014 − $478]) × 12%		
	Cash	5000	
	Note Receivable		5000
	To recognize accrued interest and the receipt of final payment.		

(2) Trailor purchased 10 bonds, each with a face value of $1000, for $10,842 on January 1, 1989, and intended to hold them until maturity on December 31, 1993. The stated interest rate on the bonds was 12 percent (paid semiannually), and the effective interest rate was 10 percent. Interest payment dates are June 30 and December 31. Unexpectedly, Trailor sold the bonds on January 1, 1990, for $11,000.

1989

Jan. 1   Bond Investment   10,842
                Cash   10,842
          To record the purchase of bonds.

June 30   Cash   600ᵃ
                Interest Revenue   542ᵇ
                Bond Investment   58
          To record the receipt of interest.

          ᵃ$10,000 × (12% ÷ 2)
          ᵇ$10,842 × (10% ÷ 2)

Dec. 31   Cash   600ᵃ
                Interest Revenue   539ᵇ
                Bond Investment   61
          To record the receipt of interest.

          ᵃ$10,000 × (12% ÷ 2)
          ᵇ(10,842 − 58) × (10% ÷ 2)

1990

Jan. 1   Cash   11,000
                Bond Investment   10,723*
                Gain on Sale   277
          To record the sale of the bond investment.
          *10,842 − 58 − 61

(3) Trailor purchased 10 percent of the outstanding equity securities (400 shares) of Latent Company for a total of $8000 ($20 per share). Trailor intended to hold the securities as a long-term investment, and held them throughout 1989 and 1990. The per-share market values of the equity securities as of the end of 1989 and 1990 were $17 and $22, respectively.

1989

Jan. 1   Investment in Equity Securities   8000
                Cash   8000
          To record the purchase of Latent equity shares.

Dec. 31   Unrealized loss on Long-Term Equity Investments   1200*
                Allowance for Loss on Equity Investments   1200
          To record the writedown of Latent securities to market value.
          *400 shares × ($20 − $17), a stockholders' equity account.

1990

Dec. 31   Allowance for Unrealized Loss Equity Investments   1200*
                Unrealized Loss on Equity Investments   1200
          To record the recovery of Latent securities.
          *Recovery is limited to the amount of the unrealized loss.

(4) On January 1, 1989, Trailor purchased 30 percent of the outstanding common stocks of Rowers Company for $50,000. Income reported by Rowers during 1989 and 1990 was $15,000 and $8000, respectively. Rower declared and paid dividends to Trailor in the amount of $3000 during each of the two years.

1989

Jan. 1

Investment in Equity Securities	50,000	
Cash		50,000
To record the purchase of Rowers common stock.		

Dec. 31

Investment in Equity Securities	4500*	
Income from Equity Investment		4500

*$15,000 × 30%

Cash	3000	
Investment in Equity Securities		3000
To record 30 percent of Rower's income and all dividends paid in 1989. Assume that dividends were declared and paid on the same day.		

1990

Investment in Equity Securities	2400*	
Income from Equity Investment		2400

*$8000 × 30%

Cash	3000	
Investment in Equity Securities		3000
To record 30 percent of Rower's income and all dividends paid in 1990. Assume that dividends were declared and paid on the same day.		

(5) On January 1, 1989, Trailor purchased 100 percent of the outstanding common stock of Kleece Corporation for $20,000. The fair market values of the individual assets and liabilities of Kleece Corporation, as of the time of the acquisition, were $40,000 and $28,000, respectively. Trailor amortizes goodwill over a forty-year period.

1989

Jan. 1

Assets	40,000	
Goodwill	8,000	
Liabilities		28,000
Cash		20,000
To record the acquisition of Kleece Corporation.		

Dec. 31

Amortization Expense	200*	
Goodwill		200
To record the amortization of goodwill.		

*$8000 ÷ 40 years

1990

Dec. 31

Amortization Expense	200*	
Goodwill		200
To record the amortization of goodwill.		

*$8000 ÷ 40 years

SUMMARY OF LEARNING OBJECTIVES

1   Define long-term investments, and identify the accounts that are commonly included in the long-term investment section of the balance sheet.

Long-term investments represent notes receivable and investments in debt and equity securities that are not expected to mature or be liquidated in the time period that defines current assets. Accounts normally included in the long-term investment section of the balance sheet are notes receivable and investments in (1) bonds and other debt securities, and (2) common stocks of other companies. The cash value of life insurance policies held on company officers and special investment funds are also found in the long-term investment section of the balance sheet, but were not covered in this chapter.

2   Describe the economic consequences associated with reporting long-term investments.

The methods used to account for long-term notes receivable (effective-interest method), bond investments (effective-interest method), and equity investments (lower-of-cost-or-market, cost, equity, consolidated statements) have effects on reported assets, liabilities, and net income, and thus they can influence credit ratings, investor decisions, and compliance with covenants expressed in terms of reported assets, liabilities, or net income.

3   Explain how long-term notes receivable arise, and describe the method used to account for them.

Long-term notes receivable normally arise when companies loan money, provide goods, or provide services that are exchanged for formal promissory notes designating cash payments that extend beyond the time period of current assets. Such notes usually state a principal amount (face or maturity value), the date at which the principal is to be paid (maturity date), and a provision for interest payments, usually expressed as an annual percentage of the principal.

The effective-interest method is used to account for long-term notes receivable. This method bases both the receivable on the balance sheet and the related periodic interest revenue on an estimate of the present value of the note's future cash inflows. It consists of the following two general rules: (1) The balance sheet value of the long-term receivable is determined by the present value of the receivable's future cash inflows, discounted at the effective interest rate at the time the receivable is established. The effective interest rate remains constant over the life of the receivable. (2) The interest revenue recognized during each period of the receivable's life is equal to the effective interest rate multiplied by the balance-sheet value of the receivable as of the beginning of that period. The balance-sheet value of the receivable approaches the maturity value over the life of the receivable.

4   Explain why companies purchase bonds, and describe the method used to account for bond investments.

Bonds are normally purchased to provide a relatively low-risk return, primarily in the form of interest receipts and sometimes in the form of price appreciation. Bond purchases are recorded at cost, which includes the purchase price as well as any incidental costs of acquisition, such as brokerage commissions and taxes. Interest accrued from the last interest payment date to the purchase date is recognized as interest receivable, which is written off when the first interest payment is received. The effective-interest method is then used to account for bond investments over their remaining lives. Under this method, interest revenue is computed each period by multiplying the effective rate of return by the balance-sheet value of the bond investment at the beginning of the period, and the bond investment account is adjusted each period for the difference between the interest revenue and the cash interest received. When bonds are sold prior to maturity, interest is accrued from the last interest payment date to the date of sale, Cash is debited for the proceeds, the bond investment account is written off the balance sheet, and a gain or loss is recognized.

5 **Explain why companies make long-term investments in equity securities.**

Companies make long-term investments in the equity securities of other companies for two primary reasons: (1) investment income in the form of dividends and/or stock price appreciation and (2) management influence, where the voting power of the purchased shares allows the investor company to exert influence or control over the board of directors and management of the investee company. The primary motivation behind the long-term equity investments for most major U.S. companies is reason (2), influence over the investee company's operations and management.

6 **Distinguish among the lower-of-cost-or-market method, the cost method, and the equity method of accounting for long-term equity investments, and describe the conditions under which each method is used.**

Applying the lower-of-cost-or-market method can be summarized by the following four rules: (1) all purchases of marketable equity securities classified as long-term are recorded at cost, which includes the incidental costs of acquisition, (2) sales of marketable equity securities classified as long-term result in recognized gains or losses in the amount of the difference between the proceeds of the sale and the acquisition cost of the sold securities, (3) dividends on marketable equity securities classified as long-term are recognized as income when declared, and (4) at the end of the accounting period, the aggregate original cost of the long-term marketable equity securities on hand is compared to their aggregate market value. If the aggregate market value is less than the aggregate cost, the allowance account is set equal to the difference between the aggregate market value and the aggregate cost. If the aggregate market value of the equity securities is equal to or greater than the aggregate cost, the allowance account should be equal to zero, and it should be adjusted if necessary to make it so.

Under the cost method, purchases of equity securities are recorded at cost, including incidental costs of acquisition, dividends are recorded as income when declared, and sales give rise to book gains or losses in the amount of the difference between the acquisition cost of the securities and the proceeds from the sale.

Under the equity method, the purchase of equity securities is originally recorded at cost, and the carrying value of the long-term investment on the investor's balance sheet is (1) periodically increased (decreased) by the investor's proportionate share of the net income (loss) of the investee and (2) decreased by all dividends transferred to the investor from the investee.

The lower-of-cost-or-market method is used for investments in marketable securities that involve less than 20 percent of the investee company's voting stock. The cost method is used for investments in nonmarketable securities that involve less than 20 percent of the investee company's voting stock. The equity method is used for investments in marketable or nonmarketable securities that involve from 20 to 50 percent of the investee company's voting stock.

7 Define consolidated financial statements, and describe when they are prepared and how they differ from financial statements that account for equity investments using the equity method.

Consolidated financial statements represent the combined financial statements of a parent company and any companies acquired by the parent. Such acquisitions occur when the parent purchases a controlling interest (51 percent of the outstanding voting stock) in another company, or as the result of a merger, where the merged company ceases to exist. Consolidated statements should be prepared when a parent owns 51 percent or more of a subsidiary's outstanding common stock.

When consolidated financial statements are prepared, the assets and liabilities of the subsidiary are included with those of the parent . If the purchase price exceeds the fair market value of the subsidiary's net assets, goodwill, which is subject to amortization, is also recognized on the balance sheet of the parent. Under the equity method, the assets and liabilities of the investee company are not included with those of the parent which in turn can represent a form of off-balance-sheet financing.

KEY TERMS

Business acquisition (p. 645)
Business combination (p. 646)
Consolidated financial statements (p. 645)
Controlling interest (p. 645)
Corporate bond (p. 626)
Cost method (p. 642)
Effective-interest method (p. 628)

Equity method (p. 642)
Long-term notes receivable (p. 626)
Lower-of-cost-or-market method (p. 638)
Merger (p. 646)
Parent company (p. 645)
Purchase method (p. 646)
Subsidiary (p. 645)

QUESTIONS FOR DISCUSSION AND REVIEW

1. List and briefly describe each of the asset categories that are normally included in the long-term investment section of the balance sheet.
2. Differentiate an investment in a debt security from an investment in an equity security. Describe the trade-offs faced by the investing company when purchasing debt or equity securities. How do these differences affect the methods used to account for debt and equity investments?

3. Describe how the methods used to account for a long-term investment could bring about economic consequences in terms of credit ratings, investor and creditor decisions, and debt covenants.

4. List the basic provisions found in contracts underlying long-term promissory notes. What bearing do these provisions have on the methods used to account for such notes on the financial statements?

5. What base is used to value long-term notes receivable on the balance sheet? Describe the procedures used to compute this valuation base.

6. Differentiate between the stated interest rate of a note receivable and the effective interest rate. If the stated rate is equal to the effective rate, what is the relationship between the present value of the note and its face value?

7. Assume that a cash amount of $7000 will be received in two years. Calculate its present value, using a 3 percent discount rate. Take the same cash flow and calculate the present value with a 6 percent discount rate. What can you say about the relationship between the discount rate and the present value? If you were a manager trying to set the value of a given note receivable as high as possible, would you choose a high discount rate or a low discount rate?

8. Explain how the effective interest rate on a note receivable is determined.

9. What is the effective-interest method? What are its two general rules? The effective-interest method serves to amortize Discounts on Notes Receivable over the life of a note. How is this method different from the straight-line method, and which is preferred from a theoretical measurement standpoint? Why?

10. Why would a company accept a note receivable with a stated interest rate that is below the market interest rate for similar notes? Why would a company accept a non-interest-bearing note?

11. Define a bond investment and describe how it is different from a long-term note receivable. In what ways are the two investments similar? In general, what method is used to account for these two investments?

12. How is the effective rate of return on a bond computed? Why is it important from an accounting standpoint to compute the effective rate of return? How is the effective-interest method applied in the case of a bond investment?

13. If the effective rate is greater than the stated rate on a bond, what is the relationship between the price of the bond investment and the face value of the bond? Why would a company purchase a bond at a price greater than its face value?

14. When accounting for a bond investment under the effective-interest method, how is interest revenue computed each period? Under what conditions will the interest revenue be constant from period to period? Under what conditions will it increase? Under what conditions will it decrease?

15. The chapter states that a single effective interest rate is used in the effective-interest method throughout the life of the bond investment even though market interest rates may change over that time period. What bearing will changes in the market rate have on the economic value of the bond? Is this captured on the financial statements?

16. Differentiate a short-term marketable security from a long-term equity investment. Why are long-term equity investments not recorded at present value like long-term debt investments?

17. What bearing does the percentage of stock ownership have on the method used to account for a long-term equity investment? Why?

18. Refer to Figure 13–12, and describe the conditions under which the following four methods are used to account for short- and long-term equity investments: (a) lower-of-cost-or-market, (b) cost, (c) equity, and (d) consolidated statements.

19. Refer to Figure 13–8, and describe the different journal entries used under the cost, lower-of-cost-or-market, and equity methods. How does each of the three methods

treat (a) the purchase of the equity investment, (b) changes in the market value of the equity investment, (c) the recognition of income by the investee company, and (d) the declaration of a dividend by the investee company?

20. Under the equity method, why do dividends declared by the investee company reduce the Long-Term Investment account?

21. What is the difference between a business acquisition and a merger?

22. Describe goodwill, and explain why it is never accrued, but often appears on the balance sheets of major U.S. companies.

23. Explain why a company might prefer the equity method to consolidated statements when accounting for a long-term equity investment.

EXERCISES

E13–1

(Establishing the book value of a note receivable)   Rayalon Company loaned cash to Barner Brothers and received in exchange a two-year note receivable with a face value of $5000, which yielded an effective interest rate of 10 percent.

Required:

a. How much cash was loaned to Barner Brothers, assuming that the stated interest rate on the note was (1) 10 percent, (2) 0 percent, and (3) 6 percent? Interest payments on the note were received annually.

b. Prepare the journal entries on Rayalon's books to record the loan under each of the three stated interest rates in (a).

E13–2

(Present value calculations and recording notes receivable)   Notes receivable with the following terms were exchanged for cash.

Note	Stated Interest Rate	Effective Interest Rate	Face Value	Life
A	0%	10%	$2000	3 years
B	0	8	4000	4 years
C	4	4	7000	4 years
D	6	8	9000	6 years
E	8	8	5000	10 years

Required:

a. Compute the amount of cash exchanged for each note.

b. For each note, prepare the journal entry to record the loan and the recognition of the note receivable.

E13–3

(The movement of book value and interest revenue over a bond investment's life)   Weatherton Enterprises made three bond investments during 1989. The terms of each follow. Interest is received semiannually.

Bond Investment	Face Value	Stated Interest Rate	Effective Interest Rate	Remaining Life
A	$20,000	10%	10%	3 years
B	15,000	8	10	10 years
C	7,000	12	10	5 years

Required:

a. Compute the price of each bond investment.

b. For each investment, indicate whether the book value of the bond investment will increase, decrease, or remain constant over the remaining life of the bond.

c. For each investment, indicate whether the interest revenue recognized each period will increase, decrease, or remain constant over the remaining life of the bond.

E13–4
(The pattern of interest revenue over the life of a note issued at a discount) Fodor Financial Ser-. vices loaned $5674 to Watson, Inc. in exchange for a five-year, non-interest-bearing note with a face value of $10,000. The note was designed to yield a 12 percent effective interest rate.

Required:

a. Prepare the journal entry to record the initial transaction.

b. How much interest revenue should Fodor recognize in the first year?

c. What is the book value of the note receivable at the end of the first year?

d. Will the interest revenue recognized by Fodor in the second year be greater than, equal to, or less than the interest revenue recognized in the first year? Why and by how much?

e. Will the interest revenue recognized by Fodor in the third year be greater than, equal to, or less than the interest revenue recognized in the second year? Why and by how much?

E13–5
(The effective-interest method values a note receivable at present value over the note's life) On January 1, 1990, Bodinger Financial Services lent $4826 to Weyton Industries. In exchange, Bodinger received a note with a maturity date of December 31, 1991, a face value of $5000, and a stated annual interest rate of 8 percent to be paid each December 31 throughout the life of the note.

Required:

a. Compute the present value of the note's future cash outflows at discount rates of 8 percent, 10 percent, and 12 percent.

b. What is the effective rate of interest on the note?

c. Using the effective rate of interest calculated in (b), compute the present value of the note's future cash inflows as of January 1, 1990, and January 1, 1991.

d. Prepare the journal entries to record the transactions on January 1, 1990, December 31, 1990, and December 31, 1991.

e. Compute the net book value of the note receivable as of January 1, 1991. Is this amount greater than, equal to, or less than the present value of the note's future cash inflows calculated in (c)? Why?

E13–6
(Accounting for bond investments) On January 1, 1990, Christie Sohn Company purchased five bonds ($1000 face value) with a stated annual interest rate of 12 percent. The bonds mature in five years, and over that time interest is paid semiannually on June 30 and December 31. The bonds were purchased to yield an annual rate of 12 percent.

Required:

a. Without computing the present value of the bonds, state whether Christie Sohn purchased the bonds at face value, at a premium, or at a discount.

b. Prepare the entry to record the purchase of the bonds.

c. Prepare the entries associated with the bond investment on June 30 and December 31, 1990.

d. Compute the book value of the bond investment as of December 31, 1990.

e. Repeat (a)–(d), assuming that the bonds were purchased to yield 8 percent.

f. Repeat (a)–(d), assuming that the bonds were purchased to yield 16 percent.

E13–7

(Inferring information about a note receivable from the financial statements) An excerpt from the financial statements of Lombardy Services follows. The information refers to a single note receivable.

	1990	1989
Note receivable	$10,000	$10,000
Less: Discount on note receivable	600	800
Interest revenue	$ 828	$ 811

Required:

a. What is the effective interest rate on the note receivable?

b. What is the stated interest rate on the note receivable?

c. Provide the journal entry to record interest revenue during 1990.

d. What is the present value of the note's future cash inflows as of December 31, 1990, using the effective interest rate on the date when the note was issued?

E13–8

(Choosing the appropriate method to account for long-term equity investments) Indicate the answers that would complete the following chart with the appropriate method of accounting for long-term equity investments: (1) lower-of-cost-or-market method, (2) cost method, (3) equity method, (4) consolidated financial statements.

	Are the Securities Marketable?	
Percentage of Ownership in Investee Company	**Yes**	**No**
1. Less than 20%		
2. 20%–50%		
3. Greater than 50%		

E13–9

(Classifying and accounting for equity investments) Hartney Consulting Services is involved in the following investments as of December 31, 1990.

(1) Owns 40 percent of the common stock issued by Doyle Corporation. Doyle Corporation's stock is actively traded, and Hartney Consulting intends to hold this investment for at least five years.

(2) Owns 55 percent of the common stock issued by Jacobs Automotive Parts Manufacturing. This stock is actively traded. Hartney Consulting intends to hold this investment indefinitely.

(3) Owns 10 percent of the common stock issued by Markert Computers. Markert Computers is a closely held company with just two other stockholders.

(4) Owns 45 percent of the common stock issued by Luther Brewery. Luther Brewery has just recently joined the New York Stock Exchange. Hartney intends to sell this investment to raise cash within the next five years.

(5) Owns 15 percent of the common stock of Hartney Farms. Remaining ownership in Hartney Farms is limited to Jeff Hartney, President, and his siblings.

(6) On November 30, 1990, Hartney Consulting owned 18 percent of Whittenbach Industries. During December Hartney Consulting purchased an additional 15 percent of the company. This company's stock is actively traded, and Hartney fully intends to hold this stock for four years.

Required:

a. Indicate whether each investment should be classified as short-term or long-term on the December 31, 1990 balance sheet. Also indicate the appropriate accounting treatment for each investment. Explain your answer.

b. Explain why the nonmarketable equity securities are disclosed in the long-term investment section of the balance sheet and are not carried at lower-of-cost-or-market.

E13–10

(The cost method)   Mystic Lakes Food Company began investing in equity securities for the first time in 1990. During 1990, the company engaged in the following transactions involving equity securities. Assume that the stock of Thayers International and Bayhe Enterprises is not considered marketable and that ownership is less than 20 percent of the equity. Prepare journal entries to record these transactions.

(1) Purchased 10,000 shares of Thayers International for $25 per share.

(2) Purchased 25,000 shares of Bayhe Enterprises for $40 per share.

(3) Thayers International declared a $2 per share dividend.

(4) Sold 5000 shares of Bayhe Enterprises for $30 per share.

(5) Sold 8000 shares of Thayers International for $40 per share.

E13–11

(Applying the lower-of-cost-or-market rule)   Refer to the data provided in E13–10.

Required:

a. Assume that the stock of Thayers International and Bayhe Enterprises is considered marketable. Prepare journal entries to record these transactions.

b. Assume that the market values on December 31, 1990, of Thayers International and Bayhe Enterprises are $27 and $32, respectively. Prepare the entry to adjust the company's long-term investments to the lower-of-cost-or-market value.

E13–12

(Inferring information about the lower-of-cost-or-market rule from the financial statements) Basket-n-Candles Gift Shops reported the following information regarding its long-term marketable equity investments in the company's 1991 financial report.

	1991	1990
Long-term investments in equity securities	$710,000	$580,000
Less: Allowance for unrealized loss on long-term equity investments	40,000	55,000
	$670,000	$525,000

Required:

a. Was the difference between the portfolio market value of the long-term equity investments and the portfolio cost of the long-term equity investments greater in 1990 or 1991? Explain your answer.

b. Prepare the adjusting journal entry that was necessary on December 31, 1991, for the long-term equity investments under the lower-of-cost-or-market rule.

c. What was the effect of the lower-of-cost-or-market rule on net income during 1991?

E13–13

(Purchasing equity and debt securities)   Finny, Inc. currently has $1,000,000 available for long-term investments. The company is considering three different investment opportunities. The investment opportunity selected will be the company's only short-term or long-term investment.

• Investment 1: Purchase 50,000 shares of common stock in Abby Lane Music Company. These shares are currently selling for $20. Finny, Inc. would become the largest stockholder of Abby Lane Music, owning 25 percent of the company's outstanding stock.

• Investment 2: Purchase 1000 bonds (face value = $1000 per bond) issued by Watson Enterprises. Over their fifteen-year life, these bonds will provide a cash inflow from interest of $50,000 every June 30 and December 31. These bonds would cost $975,000.

• Investment 3: Purchase 25,000 shares of common stock in Abby Lane Music Company and 500 bonds issued by Watson Enterprises.

Required:

a. Discuss the general advantages and disadvantages of each investment.

b. Assume that Finny, Inc. selects Investment 1. Prepare the entry to record this investment. What method should Finny, Inc. use to account for this investment? Explain how Finny, Inc. should record dividends declared by Abby Lane Music Company. Why?

c. Assume that Finny, Inc. selects Investment 2. Prepare the entry to record this investment.

d. Assume that Finny, Inc. selects Investment 3. Prepare the entry to record this investment. What method should Finny, Inc. use to account for the equity investment portion of the investment? Why?

E13–14   *(Accounting for long-term equity investments: lower-of-cost or market and cost methods)*   On July 15, 1989, during its first year of operations, Transit Canada purchased 500 shares of Lansing, Inc. common stock for $32 per share and 100 shares of Melmen Company common stock for $12 per share. Both investments represented less than 20 percent of the outstanding shares of the investee companies. Transit has no plans to liquidate the investments in the foreseeable future. As of the end of 1989, the per-share market values of Lansing and Melmen stock were $30 and $13, respectively. Transit Canada has no other long-term investments.

Required:

a. Prepare the journal entry to record the purchase of the equity securities on July 15, 1989.

b. Provide the adjusting journal entry prepared by Transit on December 31, 1989.

c. Assume that Transit held the investments throughout 1990 and, as of December 31, 1990, the per-share market values of Lansing and Melmen common stock were $33 and $6, respectively. Provide the adjusting journal entry prepared by Transit on December 31, 1990.

d. Compute the book value of Transit's long-term investment in equity securities as of December 31, 1990.

e. Repeat (a)–(d), assuming that Lansing and Melmen common stocks are not actively traded.

E13–15   *(The equity method)*   On January 1, 1989, Sonar Solar Systems, purchased 10,000 shares of Reilly Manufacturing for $180,000. The investment represented 30 percent of Reilly's outstanding common stock. Sonar intended to hold the investment indefinitely. During 1989 Reilly earned net income of $40,000, and during 1990 Reilly suffered a net loss of $8000. Reilly paid dividends both years of $1.50 per share.

Required:

a. Prepare all relevant journal entries that would be recorded on Sonar's books during 1989 and 1990.

b. Compute the book value of Sonar's Long-Term Equity investment account as of December 31, 1989, and December 31, 1990.

E13–16

(Inferring information about the equity method from the financial statements)   Mainmont Industries uses the equity method to account for its long-term equity investments. The following information is from the financial statements of Mainmont and refers to an investment in the securities of Tumbleweed Construction, a company that is 40 percent owned by Mainmont.

	1990	1989
Long-term investment in equity securities	$29,000	$25,000
Income from equity securities	12,000	7,000

Mainmont neither purchased nor sold any equity securities during 1990.

Required:

a. How much net income did Tumbleweed Construction earn during 1990?

b. What was the dollar amount of the total dividend declared by Tumbleweed Construction during 1990?

c. Provide the journal entries recorded by Mainmont during 1990 with respect to its investment in Tumbleweed Construction.

E13–17

(Recording an acquisition under the purchase method)   Multiplex purchased 100 percent of the outstanding common stock of Lipley Company for $430,000. At the time of the acquisition, the fair market values of Lipley's individual assets and liabilities were as follows.

Cash	$ 45,000
Accounts receivable	30,000
Inventory	80,000
Plant and equipment	280,000
Payables	120,000

Required:

a. Provide the journal entry recorded by Multiplex at the time of the acquisition.

b. Assume that Multiplex amortizes goodwill over a forty-year period using the straight-line method. Compute the dollar amount of goodwill that was amortized during the year following the acquisition.

c. Assume that the book values of the assets and liabilities on Lipley's balance sheet as of the date of the acquisition were $275,000 and $120,000, respectively. Explain how the net book value of Lipley could be less than the net fair market value of Lipley's assets and liabilities, which in turn is less than the price Multiplex paid for Lipley's common stock.

PROBLEMS

P13–1

(The relationship between the stated rate and the effective rate)   The stated and effective interest rates for several notes follow. Indicate whether each note would sell at a discount, at par value, or at a premium.

Note	Stated Interest Rate	Effective Interest Rate
1	10%	10%
2	6	8
3	12	15
4	8.9	8.1

P13-2   *(Notes receivable: the effective-interest method, the straight-line method, and present value)*   On
January 1, 1989, Barnhiser Brothers lent $8900 to Wentworth Company and received in
exchange a non-interest-bearing, two-year note with a face value of $10,000. The effective
interest rate on the note is 6 percent.

Required:

a. Compute the present value of the note's future cash inflows as of January 1, 1989, and
   December 31, 1989.
b. Prepare the journal entry to record the transaction on January 1, 1989.
c. Use the effective-interest method to amortize the discount, and prepare the adjusting
   journal entry recorded by Barnhiser on December 31, 1989. Compute the book value of
   the note on December 31, 1989.
d. Use the straight-line method to amortize the discount, and prepare the adjusting journal
   entry recorded by Barnhiser on December 31, 1989. Compute the book value of the
   note receivable as of December 31; 1989.
e. Why is the effective-interest method preferred to the straight-line method?

P13-3   *(Interest-bearing notes receivable issued at face value and a discount, and non-interest-bearing
notes)*   Epsom Financial Services loaned cash to West Ore Corporation on January 1,
1990, in exchange for a six-year note with a face value of $5000. Interest is to be paid
every December 31. After a review of West Ore Corporation's credit rating, Epsom determines that an appropriate effective annual interest rate to charge West Ore Corporation
would be 12 percent.

Required:

a. Assume that the annual stated rate on the note is 12 percent. Prepare the entries to do
   the following:
   (1) Record the acquisition of the note (show computations).
   (2) Record the first interest payment received from West Ore.
   (3) Record the payment received from West Ore when the note matures.
b. Assume that the annual stated rate on the note is 6 percent. Prepare the entries to do
   the following:
   (1) Record the acquisition of the note (show computations).
   (2) Record the first interest payment received from West Ore.
   (3) Record the payment received from West Ore when the note matures.
c. Assume that the note is a non-interest-bearing note. Prepare the entries to do the following:
   (1) Record the acquisition of the note (show computations).
   (2) Record the first interest payment received from West Ore.
   (3) Record the payment received from West Ore when the note matures.

P13-4   *(Converting an account receivable to a note receivable)*   Max Lamber currently owes Boulder
Sporting Goods $10,806 on account from a recent purchase. Due to Mr. Lamber's financial
difficulty, Boulder Sporting Goods agrees, on November 1, 1990, to convert the open receivable to a three-year note. The note specifies that interest at an annual rate of 6 percent
is to be paid every October 31. The face value of the note is $12,000.

Required:

a. Compute the present value of the cash inflows associated with the note receivable at 8
   percent, 10 percent, and 12 percent. What is the effective interest rate on this note?
b. Prepare the entry to record the conversion of the account receivable to a note receivable.

c. Prepare the entries that would be necessary to amortize the discount throughout the life of the note. Assume that financial statements are prepared every December 31.

d. Prepare the entry on November 1, 1993, when the note matures.

P13–5   *(Receiving a note in exchange for merchandise)*   Johnson House Supplies sold some merchandise on April 1, 1990, to one of its distributors. Johnson House Supplies received $10,000 in cash and a two-year note with a face value of $100,000. The note has an annual stated rate of 4 percent and states that interest is to be paid every March 31. Johnson's credit department has determined that an acceptable annual effective rate would be 12 percent. Johnson's year end is December 31.

Required:

a. Compute the present value of the note receivable's future cash inflows. Show computations.

b. Prepare the entry to record the sale of the merchandise. The company uses the periodic inventory method.

c. Prepare a schedule that shows the dollar amount of note receivable discount amortization throughout the life of the note. Also prepare the entries that Johnson House Supplies would have to record throughout the life of the note.

d. What amount would Johnson House Supplies have accepted in cash on April 1, 1990, so that they would have been indifferent between accepting this amount of cash and accepting $10,000 cash and the note described above?

P13–6   *(Receiving a note in exchange for a building)*   Sandlman Shoe Company reported the following on its balance sheet as of December 31, 1990.

Building	$500,000
Accumulated depreciation	100,000

On January 1, 1991, Sandlman Shoe Company sold this building in exchange for a three-year, non-interest-bearing note with a face value of $693,000. The market value of the building at the time of the transaction is $550,125.

Required:

a. Compute the present value of the note receivable's future cash inflows at a 6 percent, 8 percent, and 10 percent discount rate. What is the effective interest rate on the note?

b. Prepare the entry to record the sale of the building.

c. Prepare all entries necessary throughout the life of this note. What does the balance, at any point in time, in Discount on Notes Receivable represent?

P13–7   *(Accounting for bond investments purchased at a discount)*   Gidley Enterprises purchased 100 bonds ($1000 face value) on December 31, 1990, that mature in three years. Interest is paid semiannually on June 30 and December 31 at an annual rate of 8 percent. The purchase price of these bonds gave rise to an effective rate of return for Gidley of 12 percent.

Required:

a. Compute the price of these bonds on December 31, 1990.

b. Prepare the entry to record the acquisition of these bonds.

c. Supply the values that would complete the following schedule using the effective interest method.

Date	Cash Received	Interest Earned	Increase in Bond Investment	Bond Investment

    d. Prepare the entries necessary throughout the life of the bond to record collection of interest payments.

    e. Prepare the entry necessary when the bond matures.

P13-8 *(Bond investments: the effective-interest method and present value)* On July 1, 1989, Wanderlust Housing purchased 10 bonds, each with a face value of $1000 and a stated annual interest rate of 6 percent. The bonds matured 1 1/2 years from the date of purchase and paid interest semiannually on June 30 and December 31. The annual effective rate of return is 10 percent.

Required:

a. Compute the present value of the bonds' future cash inflows as of July 1, 1989; December 31, 1989; June 30, 1990; and December 31, 1990.

b. Prepare the journal entry to record the purchase on July 1, 1989.

c. Provide the values to complete the following chart using the effective interest method.

Date	Interest Revenue	Cash Interest Received	Book Value of Bond Investment
June 30, 1989			
December 31, 1989			
June 30, 1990			
December 31, 1990			

d. Under the effective-interest method, at what value is the bond investment carried on the balance sheet?

P13-9 *(Accounting for bond investments purchased at a discount and a premium)* On July 1, 1990, Lawton Corporation purchased bonds as a long-term investment with a total face value of $200,000. The bonds have an annual stated interest rate of 10 percent, and they pay interest semiannually on December 31 and June 30. The bonds mature on June 30, 2000.

Required:

a. Assume that Lawton Corporation purchased these bonds for $177,060.

    (1) Without computing the effective interest rate on these bonds, state whether the annual effective interest rate would be less than, equal to, or greater than the annual coupon (stated) rate. Explain your answer.

    (2) Compute the present value of the bond's future cash flows using discount rates of 8 percent, 10 percent, and 12 percent. What is the effective rate of return on these bonds?

    (3) Prepare the entry to record the acquisition of these bonds.

    (4) Prepare any entries associated with these bonds necessary on December 31, 1990.

b. Assume that these bonds were purchased at a price that produced an effective annual interest rate of 8 percent.

    (1) Compute the price of these bonds.

    (2) Record the acquisition of these bonds.

    (3) Prepare any entries associated with these bonds necessary on December 31, 1990.

P13-10 *(Bond investments and changing market interest rates)* Hussin Import Company invested in 100 bonds (face value = $1000) on July 1, 1989. The bonds have an annual coupon (stated) rate of 14 percent and pay interest semiannually on December 31 and June 30. The bonds were purchased to yield an annual rate of 10 percent (same as the prime interest rate). On July 1, 1990, the prime rate had dropped to 6 percent. The bonds mature in 10 years.

Required:

a. Without computing the present value of the bonds, state whether these bonds were purchased above, at, or below face value. Explain your answer.

b. Prepare the entry to record the investment in these bonds (show computations). Hussin Imports intends to hold the investment for at least two years.

c. Prepare all entries necessary for these bonds from the date they were acquired, excluding the entry in (b), through June 30, 1990.

d. Would you advise Hussin Imports to hold or sell the bonds given the prime rate on July 1, 1990? Explain your answer and include computations. Assume that the bonds are presently at a price that would provide the buyer with a return equal to the prime rate.

e. Assume that Hussin Imports sold these bonds on July 1, 1990. Prepare the entry to record the sale.

f. Assume that the prime interest rate on July 1, 1990, was 12 percent and that Hussin Imports sold the bonds. Prepare the entry to record the sale (show computations). Assume again that the bonds are presently at a price that would provide the buyer with a return equal to the prime rate.

P13–11   *(Inferring information about the lower-of-cost-or-market rule from the financial statements)* Soundsign Enterprises began operations in 1988. The following information was extracted from the company's financial records.

	1990	1989	1988
Long-term investment in equity securities	$410,000	$380,000	$520,000
Allowance for unrealized loss on long-term equity investments	—	50,000	40,000
	$410,000	$330,000	$480,000

Required:

a. Prepare the adjusting journal entry that Soundsign Enterprises recorded to adjust the carrying value of its long-term portfolio to lower-of-cost-or-market value at the end of 1988, 1989, and 1990.

b. Was the aggregate market value of the company's long-term equity investments greater than, less than, or equal to the aggregate cost of the company's long-term equity investments as of December 31, 1990? Explain your answer.

P13–12   *(Inferring the method used to account for long-term equity investments from financial statements)* The following information was taken from the financial statements of Acme Households.

	1990	1989
Long-term investments in equity securities	$25,000	$20,000
Less: Allowance for unrealized losses on long-term equity investments	700	1,200

Required:

a. What method does Acme use to account for its long-term investments in equity securities: the cost method, the lower-of-cost-or-market method, or the equity method?

b. Assume that Acme sold no equity securities during 1990. What dollar amount did Acme invest in long-term equity securities during 1990? Did the price of Acme's portfolio of long-term equity securities in relation to its market value increase or decrease during 1990? By how much?

c. Provide the adjusting journal entry prepared on December 31, 1990, to record the price change. How did this journal entry affect the amount of net income reported by Acme during 1990? How did it affect Acme's debt/equity ratio as of December 31, 1990?

d. Assume that on January 1, 1991, Acme sells its entire portfolio of long-term equity investments for $28,000 and purchases no additional securities during 1991. Provide the journal entry to record the sale and the adjusting journal entry recorded on December 31, 1991.

P13–13 (*Investments in equity securities: the lower-of-cost-or-market method*) The following information was obtained from the long-term investment records of Sparrow Electronics as of January 1, 1990.

Investment	Purchase Date	Percent of Company Owned	Number of Shares Owned	Cost
Beck Enterprises	3/15/87	15%	10,000	$250,000
Moosehead Industries	10/5/88	10	5,000	100,000
Heinekin, Inc.	4/20/88	8	3,000	75,000

During 1990 Sparrow Electronics entered into the following transactions associated with these securities.

(1) February 2: Received a dividend (previously declared) from Moosehead Industries of $1.50 per share.
(2) March 19: Sold 2000 shares of Beck Enterprises for $40 per share.
(3) May 29: Purchased an additional 1000 shares of Heinekin, Inc. for $28 per share.
(4) June 30: Beck Enterprises declared a dividend of $2.00 per share.
(5) July 10: Received the dividend check from Beck Enterprises.
(6) November 27: Purchased an additional 3000 shares of Beck Enterprises for $45 per share.

Additional Information

1. As of December 31, 1990 Sparrow Electronics intends to hold these securities for at least 15 months.
2. The market values (per share) of these securities on December 31, 1990, follows.

Beck Enterprises	$42.50
Moosehead Industries	28.00
Heinekin, Inc.	24.00

Required: Assume that all of these securities can be classified as marketable and that the balance in Allowance for Unrealized Losses on Long-Term Equity Investments was $8000 as of January 1, 1990. Prepare all journal entries necessary during 1990 associated with these securities.

P13–14 (*The lower-of-cost-or-market and cost methods*) Don Harris, the controller of Abbot Industry, has provided you with the following information concerning the company's equity investments.

Investment	Purchase Date	Cost	12/31/90 Market Value	12/31/89 Market Value	Marketable
Langley, Inc.	3/12/86	$110,000	$120,000	$105,000	Yes
Valley Corporation	10/8/87	150,000	125,000	135,000	Yes
Sparry, Limited	7/21/87	175,000	175,000	180,000	No
Boston Celtics	6/30/88	50,000	60,000	75,000	Yes
Enterprise Flights	11/1/88	300,000	250,000	285,000	Yes
Garner Industries	4/17/89	80,000	70,000	75,000	No
Newton Labs	10/4/90	200,000	50,000	55,000	Yes

Additional Information

1. These investments are all considered long-term, and no investment represents more than 20 percent of the investee's outstanding voting stock.
2. The investment in Enterprise Flights was sold for $272,000 on August 17, 1990.
3. During 1990 Abbot Industry earned $20,000 in dividends from investments in long-term marketable equity securities and $8000 in dividends from investments in long-term nonmarketable equity securities. Three thousand dollars of the latter amount had not yet been collected as of December 31, 1990.

Required:

a. Compute the balance in Allowance for Unrealized Losses for Long-Term Equity Investments as of December 31, 1989.
b. Prepare the entry to record the sale of the investment in Enterprise Flights during 1990.
c. Prepare the entry to record the investment in Newton Labs. Also prepare the entries to record the dividends earned by Abbot Industry during 1990.
d. Compute the balance in Allowance for Unrealized Losses for Long-Term Equity Investments as of December 31, 1990. Prepare the necessary entry.
e. Construct the long-term investment section of the balance sheet as of December 31, 1990.

P13–15   *(Long-term equity investments: the lower-of-cost-or-market method versus the equity method)*   A summary of the December 31, 1989 balance sheet of Masonite Tires is provided below.

Assets	$160,000	Liabilities	$ 70,000
		Stockholders' equity	90,000
Total	$160,000	Total	$160,000

On January 1, 1990, Masonite purchased 2000 (25 percent of the outstanding common shares) shares of Bingo Boots for $40,000 and held the investment throughout 1990 and 1991. During 1990 and 1991 Bingo earned net income of $15,000 and $20,000, respectively. Bingo paid total dividends of $10,000 and $15,000 during 1990 and 1991. The per share prices of Bingo common stock as of the end of 1989 and 1990 were $18 and $21, respectively. During 1990 and 1991 Masonite generated revenues (excluding revenues related to the investment in Bingo) of $85,000 and $75,000, respectively, and incurred expenses of $50,000 and $70,000, respectively. Assume that all these revenues and expenses involve cash. Masonite pays no dividends.

Required:

a. Assume that Masonite uses the lower-of-cost-or-market method.
   (1) Prepare a balance sheet as of January 1, 1990.
   (2) Prepare a balance sheet as of December 31, 1990 and income statement for the year ended December 31, 1990.
   (3) Prepare a balance sheet as of December 31, 1991 and income statement for the year ended December 31, 1991.
b. Assume that Masonite uses the equity method.
   (1) Prepare a balance sheet as of January 1, 1990.
   (2) Prepare a balance sheet as of December 31, 1990 and income statement for the year ended December 31, 1990.
   (3) Prepare a balance sheet as of December 31, 1991 and income statement for the year ended December 31, 1991.
c. Identify some reasons why the management of Masonite may wish to use the lower-of-cost-or-market method instead of the equity method. Describe why the equity method

might be preferred. Does holding 20 percent of a company's outstanding common stock necessarily mean that the investor company can exert substantial influence over the investee?

P13-16   *(The lower-of-cost-or-market method and the equity method)*   Rankin Food Corporation entered into the following transactions involving investments during 1990.

(1) January 10: Purchased 10,000 shares of common stock of Wharton, Inc. at $50 per share. These shares represent 10 percent of Wharton's outstanding common stock.

(2) January 28: Reclassified an equity investment in Hamilton Hardware Manufacturers from short-term to long-term. This investment had cost Rankin $100,000 for 4000 shares. On January 28 the market value of the investment equaled the cost of the investment. Rankin owns 2 percent of Hamilton Hardware.

(3) February 5: Purchased 100,000 shares of common stock of St. Clair International at $75 per share. These shares represent 25 percent of St. Clair's outstanding common stock.

(4) April 13: Received a dividend check from Hamilton Hardware for $1.50 per share. No accounting recognition was given when the dividend was declared.

(5) June 26: Sold 1000 shares of the investment in Wharton, Inc. for $55 per share.

(6) July 18: Purchased 150,000 shares of Crozier Limited's common stock at $20 per share. Rankin owns 30 percent of Crozier's outstanding common stock.

(7) August 1: Received a dividend check from Wharton, Inc. for $2.00 per share. The company had been notified on July 25 that Wharton, Inc. had declared this dividend and had made the appropriate entry at that time.

(8) October 9: Sold 20,000 shares of BJR Corporation for $15 per share. This investment had cost $17.50 per share on December 1, 1989 (at which time BJR had 2 million common shares outstanding).

(9) October 10: Received notification that Crozier Limited had declared a dividend of $2.10 per share. The dividend was to be distributed on October 30.

(10) October 30: Received the dividend check from Crozier Limited.

(11) December 20: Purchased an additional 1000 shares in Wharton, Inc. at $48 per share.

Additional Information

1. As of January 1, 1990, the only long-term investment held by Rankin was the investment in BJR Corporation.

2. As of January 1, 1990, the balance in Allowance for Unrealized Loss on Long-Term Investments was $17,000.

3. The management of Rankin intends to hold the remaining equity securities purchased during 1990 for at least two years. All of these investments are considered marketable.

4. As of December 31, 1990, Rankin's controller had obtained the following information.

	12/31/90 Market Value (per share)	1990 Net Income (loss)*
Crozier Limited	$25.00	$1,000,000
Hamilton Hardware	17.50	578,000
Wharton, Inc.	53.00	(250,000)
St. Clair International	78.50	(750,000)

*The Net Income represents only those profits earned by these companies since Rankin invested in them.

Required:

a. Prepare journal entries for each transaction.

b. Prepare all entries necessary on December 31, 1990, associated with these investments.

c. Prepare the long-term investments section that would be reported on the balance sheet as of December 31, 1990. What would be the balance in Unrealized Loss on Long-Term Equity Investments as of December 31, 1990?

P13–17 *(Cost, lower-of-cost-or-market, and equity methods)* Peeples Plastic Industries invested in the equity securities of three companies during 1990 with the intention of holding the investments indefinitely. The transactions follow.

(1) Purchased 10,000 shares of common stock issued by Seely Freight Company for $15 per share.

(2) Purchased 25,000 shares of common stock issued by American Surgical Corporation for $20 per share.

(3) Purchased 20,000 shares of common stock issued by Lambert Athletic Equipment for $18 per share.

(4) Prepared an entry to record a $1.50 per share dividend declaration by Lambert Athletic Equipment.

(5) Sold a previous investment in Bench Restaurant Supply for $354,000.

(6) Received the dividend check from Lambert Athletic Equipment.

(7) Received a dividend check from Seely Freight Company for $2.00 per share. Peeples Plastic had not previously been notified of the dividend.

Additional Information

1. The investment in Bench Restaurant Supply was accounted for using the lower-of-cost-or-market method for long-term investments. The investment had cost $300,000, and on January 1, 1990, the Allowance for Unrealized Losses on Long-Term Equity Securities had a balance of $5000. This investment was Peeples' only long-term investment as of January 1, 1990.

2. The market values (per share) of the three securities on December 31, 1990, follow.

Seely Freight Company	$14.00
American Surgical Corporation	17.50
Lambert Athletic Equipment	18.00

3. The three companies generated the following Net Income (Loss) during 1990.

Seely Freight Company	$ 500,000
American Surgical Corporation	90,000
Lambert Athletic Equipment	(300,000)

Assume that these net income amounts represent the profits earned by these companies since the date that Peeples Plastic invested in them.

Required:

a. Assume that the securities of the three companies acquired during 1990 are not marketable and that Peeples Plastic owns 12 percent of each company. Prepare all the entries necessary for these investments during 1990. Also prepare the long-term investment section of the balance sheet as of December 31, 1990. What is the impact of these transactions on the income statement?

b. Assume that the securities of the three companies acquired during 1990 are marketable and that Peeples Plastic owns 12 percent of each company. Prepare all the entries necessary for these investments during 1990. Also prepare the long-term investment section of the balance sheet as of December 31, 1990. What is the impact of these transactions on the income statement?

c. Assume that the securities of the three companies acquired during 1990 are marketable and that Peeples Plastic owns 25 percent of each company. Prepare all the entries necessary for these investments during 1990. Also prepare the long-term investment section of the balance sheet as of December 31, 1990. What is the impact of these transactions on the income statement?

P13–18   *(Comprehensive problem on long-term equity investments of less than 50 percent and debt investments)* The following investment information was obtained from the internal financial records of Hummel Worldwide Industries as of January 1, 1990. The market values and balance-sheet balances listed are as of January 1, 1990.

Group A: Marketable Long-Term Equity Investments (Ownership < 20%)

Investment	Cost	Market Value
Ricks Construction	$200,000	$175,000
International Machines	250,000	260,000
Ruhe Art Supplies	80,000	75,000
Cotter Can Company	190,000	205,000

Group B: Nonmarketable Long-Term Equity Investments (Ownership < 20%)

Investment	Cost
Greenwell, Inc.	$150,000
Hurst Publishing	225,000
Anderson Paint Company	110,000
Vital Foods	60,000

Group C: Marketable Long-Term Equity Investments (Ownership from 20% to 50%)

Investment	Cost	Market Value	Balance Sheet Balance	Percent Owned
Laidig Research Lab	$650,000	$640,000	$695,000	25%
Lake Smelting	400,000	425,000	395,000	30
Manning Electronics	375,000	450,000	500,000	25

Group D: Nonmarketable Long-Term Equity Investments (Ownership from 20% to 50%)

Investment	Cost	Balance Sheet Balance	Percent Owned
Guyer Drilling Company	$500,000	$540,000	30%
Tallman Fabrics	245,000	330,000	35

Group E: Marketable Long-Term Debt Investments (i.e. bonds and notes)

Investment	Face Value	Book Value	Annual Stated Rate	Annual Effective Rate
Flash Air Freight	$800,000	$823,000	10%	8%

During 1990 Hummel Industries was involved in the following transactions.

(1) Received $10,000 in dividends from Ricks Construction and Ruhe Art Supplies that had been accrued on December 31, 1989.

(2) Purchased 10,000 shares of common stock issued by Rising Moon Cola Company for $20 per share. Rising Moon has 1 million shares of common stock outstanding and is privately held.

(3) Was notified that Hurst Publishing was declaring a dividend. Hummel's portion is $2000.

(4) Sold 1000 shares of Cotter Can Company for $45 per share. On January 1, 1990, Hummel Industries owned 5000 shares of this security.

(5) Sold merchandise to Hahn Broadcasting on May 31 in exchange for a two-year non-interest-bearing note with a face value of $250,000. The effective annual interest rate is 6 percent.

(6) Received the dividend check from Hurst Publishing.

(7) Received a dividend check in the amount of $35,000 from Tallman Fabrics. Hummel Industries had not made any entry regarding this dividend when it had been declared by Tallman Fabrics.

(8) Received the interest payment on the bond from Flash Air Freight on July 1.

(9) Purchased an additional 1000 shares of Ruhe Art Supplies for $50 per share.

(10) Recorded the declaration and receipt of dividends from Ruhe Art Supplies ($1000), Anderson Paint Company ($2500), Laidig Research Lab ($10,000), and Guyer Drilling ($7500)

Additional Information

1. The following information was obtained by Hummel Worldwide Industries at year end.

Investment	12/31/90 Market Value	1990 Net Income (Loss)
Ricks Construction	$190,000	$400,000
International Machines	100,000	(200,000)
Ruhe Art Supplies	140,000	125,000
Cotter Can Company	165,000	354,000
Greenwell, Inc.	NA	50,000
Hurst Publishing	NA	510,000
Anderson Paint Company	NA	(50,000)
Vital Foods	NA	10,000
Rising Moon Cola Co.	195,000	305,000
Laidig Research Lab	700,000	955,000
Lake Smelting	410,000	(250,000)
Manning Electronics	500,000	(60,000)
Guyer Drilling	NA	140,000
Tallman Fabrics	NA	90,000

2. The interest on the bond is due every July 1 and January 1.

Required:

a. Indicate the appropriate accounting treatment for each type of investment.

b. Prepare journal entries to record each of the transactions.

c. Prepare all adjusting journal entries necessary on December 31, 1990, associated with these investments.

d. What is the impact of each investment on the 1990 net income of Hummel Worldwide Industries.

e. Construct the long-term investment section of Hummel Worldwide Industries' balance sheet as of December 31, 1990. Prepare a supporting schedule for any investments grouped together.

P13–19

(The equity method versus consolidated financial statements)   A summary of the 1989 balance sheet of Belden, Ltd. follows.

Assets	$180,000	Liabilities	$ 90,000
		Stockholders' equity	90,000
Total	$180,000	Total	$180,000

On January 1, 1990, Belden acquired 100 percent of the outstanding common stock of Martin Monthly for $62,000 cash. At the time of the acquisition, the fair market values of the assets and liabilities of Martin were $86,000 and $64,000, respectively. During 1990 Martin operated as a subsidiary of Belden; it recognized $15,000 of net income and paid a $10,000 dividend.

Required:

a. Account for the acquisition as a purchase. Provide the journal entry to record the acquisition, and prepare Belden's consolidated balance sheet as of January 1, 1990.

b. How much goodwill will Belden amortize during 1990 if the company amortizes goodwill over forty years using the straight-line method?

c. Account for the acquisition using the equity method. Provide the journal entry to record the acquisition, and prepare Belden's balance sheet as of January 1, 1990.

d. Compute the debt/equity ratios produced by the two methods of accounting for this investment. Explain why Belden's management might wish to use the equity method instead of preparing consolidated financial statements.

CASES

C13–1

(The effective rate of return on bond investments)   In its December 31, 1987 consolidated balance sheet, Sears, Roebuck & Company reported the following.

	1987	1986
Assets (in millions)		
Investments		
Bond investments	$14,204	$11,377

Required:

a. What assumption must be made to ensure that the bonds and other debt investments on Sears' balance sheet are being carried at the present value of the bond investments' contractual future cash inflows? Briefly explain.

b. Assume that the amount disclosed as of the end of 1986 ($11,377) resulted from an investment in bonds with a face value of $10,000 that occurred on January 1, 1986. Was the effective rate of return on the bond investment greater than, less than, or equal to the stated interest rate?

c. In addition to the facts in (b), assume that the annual stated interest rate on the purchased bonds is 12 percent and the annual effective rate of return is 10 percent. Compute the cost of the bond investments made by Sears during 1987. To simplify the problem, assume that interest payments are made annually on December 31 and that no bonds were sold during 1987.

d. Assume that the market price of the bonds on January 1, 1988, was $15,000. Would the effective rate of return earned on the bonds if purchased on that date be greater than, less than, or equal to the effective rate of return experienced by Sears? Briefly explain why the effective rate of return on bonds purchased at different times might be different. Provide the journal entry to record the sale of the bonds on January 1, 1988.

C13-2   *(Accounting for long-term investments in equity securities)*   Norton Company manufactures abrasives, ceramics, plastics, and other products used in chemical processing. Its 1987 financial statements included the following information about its long-term investments in equity securities (in millions).

	1987	1986
Investments in associated companies	$58.1	$56.8

Note:
The . . . statements of Norton Company include the accounts of all subsidiaries of which the company owns in excess of 50 percent of the common stock. . . . Investments of 20 percent to 50 percent . . . are accounted for using the equity method, while investments of less than 20 percent are accounted for using the cost method.

Required:

a. Because Norton shows Investments in Associated Companies on its balance sheet, what must be true about the percent of ownership Norton holds in these companies?

b. Compare Note 1 with Figure 13–12, and assume that all investments referred to are in the form of marketable equity securities. In what way does Norton's accounting treatment depart from generally accepted accounting principles? How could such treatment be justified?

c. Assume that one of the associated companies referred to is used to finance the sales of Norton's products to customers. Explain how such an arrangement might represent off-balance-sheet financing.

C13-3   *(Inferences about marketable security transactions from the information disclosed on the balance sheet)*   The investments in the Long-Term Marketable Equity Securities account of Scope Industries follow (dollars in thousands).

	1986	1985
Marketable securities (market value: $18,052 for 1986 and $23,177 for 1985)	$16,230	$21,090

Note:
The noncurrent portfolio of marketable equity securities is stated at the lower-of-aggregate-cost-or-market value at the balance-sheet date. Dividend income is accrued as earned. Unrealized losses are recorded directly in a separate stockholders' equity account.

Required:

a. What can be ascertained about the percentage of outstanding voting stock held by Scope in each investee company?

b. Assume that the account Unrealized Losses on Long-Term Equity Investments showed a balance of $200,000 on the 1984 balance sheet. Provide the journal entry that would have been recorded with respect to long-term investments in equity securities at the end of 1985.

c. Compute the dollar amount of the unrealized loss recognized by Scope during 1986.

d. Compute the cost of the marketable equity securities sold by Scope during 1986. Provide the aggregate journal entry if the securities were sold for a total of $7 million.

C13-4

(Evaluating the equity method)   Several years ago, Teledyne, a multimillion-dollar conglomerate, reported net income per share of $19.96. Of this amount, $3.49, or approximately $72 million, resulted from the equity method of accounting. In that same year the company received $18 million in dividends from its investee companies. Some accountants have argued that the net income amount reported by Teledyne from the equity method is distorted because the company only received $18 million in cash on its equity investments, yet it recognized $72 million in income.

Required: Comment on this criticism of the equity method. In your answer, explain the accounting procedures that characterize the equity method, and why income is recognized that is not always backed by cash receipts. Explain also why investors and creditors must be careful when analyzing financial statements prepared under the equity method.

C13-5

(The equity method and finance subsidiaries)   A number of large corporations have set up their own finance companies, primarily because the ability to grant credit to customers can significantly increase sales. A well-known example is General Motors Acceptance Corporation (GMAC), which handles much of the credit issued to customers who finance the purchase of GM automobiles. Such finance companies are typically set up as separate corporations, with the parent company holding a significant portion of the stock. In the past the parent corporations often used the equity method to account for the investment in the finance company, instead of consolidating the finance company's assets and liabilities.

Required: Explain why the equity method might be preferred over consolidated financial statements in such cases. Express your answer in terms of important financial ratios, debt covenants, and future levels of reported net income.

The Complete Income Statement

Learning Objectives

1 Describe the economic consequences associated with reporting net income.

2 Differentiate the capital-maintenance view of income from the transaction view, and explain why present-day financial statements follow the transaction view.

3 Describe the difference between an operating transaction and a capital transaction, and indicate how capital transactions are categorized on the capital/operating continuum.

4 Characterize the transactions and events included in each of the five categories that constitute a complete income statement.

5 Define intraperiod tax allocation, and explain how it relates to the income statement.

6 Describe how earnings per share are disclosed on the income statement.

≣ Chapters 6 through 13 consider the accounts that appear on the balance sheet. It is clear from the discussion in these chapters that virtually all balance sheet accounts are linked to at least one account on the income statement. By covering the balance sheet, therefore, we have already implicitly covered much of the income statement, but we have not yet discussed that statement as a coordinated whole by considering such issues as income measurement, the difference between operating and capital transactions, and the disclosure and classification rules specified by generally accepted accounting principles. The objective of this chapter is to bring together into one coordinated discussion the concepts underlying income measurement and the categories that compose the income statement.

This chapter is divided into four sections. The first three sections consider (1) the economic consequences associated with income measurement and disclosure, (2) conceptual issues of income measurement, and (3) the disclosure rules that must be followed when preparing an income statement. The fourth section covers the statement of retained earnings.

THE ECONOMIC CONSEQUENCES ASSOCIATED WITH INCOME MEASUREMENT AND DISCLOSURE

Income is the most common measure of a company's performance. It has been related to stock prices, suggesting that equity investors use income in their decisions to buy and sell equity securities. For example, an article published in the *Journal of Accountancy* states that "[accounting] research . . . has provided some well-established conclusions. Perhaps the most conclusive finding is the importance of accounting income to investors."[1]

Income has also been related to bond prices, which indicates that debt investors use income in their decisions to buy and sell corporate bonds. Credit-rating agencies, such as Standard & Poors, Moody's and Dun & Bradstreet, also use income numbers to establish credit ratings. A recent article in *The Wall Street Journal* (8 June 1988), for example, reported the following:

> *Moody's Investor Services Inc. said it upgraded to AA3 from A1 the deposit rating for BancOhio National Bank. Moody's said the upgrade was in response to improvement in BancOhio's profitability . . . [the bank's] credit card portfolio continues to be weak, but good asset quality and strong profitability elsewhere in the bank have produced a strong balance sheet.*

In addition, three of Dun & Bradstreet's fourteen key business ratios (return on sales, return on assets, and return on net worth) explicitly use a measure of income in the formula, and most of the numbers used in the remaining eleven ratios are indirectly affected by the dollar amount of reported income.

Due to the importance attached to income, periodic public earnings announcements, which appear in newspapers such as *The Wall Street Journal* and in corporate annual reports, are also considered important news items. The following, for example, was published in *The Wall Street Journal* (8 June 1988) and represents a

---

1. James W. Deitrick and Walter T. Harrison, Jr., "EMH, CMR, and the Accounting Profession," *Journal of Accountancy* (February 1984), pp. 88–94.

typical earnings announcement: "Sun Microsystems Inc., Mountain View Calif., expects to post earnings of about $1.60 a share for fiscal 1988, ending June 30, up 44% from a year earlier."

The following excerpt was published in the 1987 financial report of Toys "Я" Us. It appeared in the letter written by the company's chief executive officer to the stockholders: "We are pleased to report that . . . Toys "Я" Us has demonstrated a consistently outstanding growth record. Our net earnings have risen from $17 million in 1978 to almost $204 million in 1987—an annual compounded growth rate of over 31 percent."

In addition to helping investors and creditors make informed investment decisions, various measures of income are also found in contracts written among stockholders, creditors, and managers. As indicated before, such contracts are normally designed either to protect the interests of creditors or to control managers and encourage them to act in the interests of the stockholders.

Loan agreements relating to the outstanding debts of Marriott Corporation, for example, limit the company's annual dividends to a portion of net income. Such covenants serve to protect the investments of corporate creditors by limiting the amount of cash that can be paid to the stockholders in the form of dividends. The Board of Directors of the Pillsbury Company encourages management to act in the stockholders' interests by providing incentive compensation for certain key employees. As reported in the 1987 financial report, the payment of this compensation is based on "the company's cumulative annual growth in earnings per share over the four-year period following the award."

Indeed, the measurement, definition, and disclosure of income is important to investors, creditors, managers, auditors, and the general public in a number of different ways. Students of accounting, therefore, must understand how it is determined and presented.

THE MEASUREMENT OF INCOME: A CONCEPTUAL PERSPECTIVE

There are two fundamental ways to view a company's performance: (1) the capital-maintenance view and (2) the transaction (inflow/outflow) view.

The Capital-Maintenance View

Under the **capital-maintenance view,** performance for a particular period is determined by comparing a company's net book value (assets − liabilities) at the end of a period with its net book value at the beginning of that period. The difference between these two values, minus the proceeds from any equity issuances, and plus dividends paid during the period, is considered income. For example, assume that the 1988 and 1989 balance sheets of Realing Company are as shown in Figure 14−1.

At the beginning of 1989 and 1990 the net book values of the company are $35,000 and $57,000, respectively. If Realing collected $10,000 from an equity issuance during 1989 and paid a $5000 dividend, under the capital maintenance view, income of $17,000 would be computed and disclosed as in Figure 14−2.

Figure 14–1   Balance sheets

Realing Company Balance Sheets December 31, 1989 and December 31, 1988		
	1989	**1988**
Assets	$99,000	$80,000
Liabilities	42,000	45,000
Stockholders' equity (net book value)	$57,000	$35,000

The Transaction (Inflow/Outflow) View

The **transaction (inflow/outflow) view** determines and discloses income by focusing on the individual transactions executed during a period. Each transaction is recorded and classified as capital or operating, and operating transactions are further divided into revenues and expenses. Income is computed by matching expenses against revenues in the proper time period.

To illustrate, consider the Realing Company in the earlier example, and assume that five transactions during 1989 accounted for the $22,000 increase in book values from 1988 ($35,000) to 1989 ($57,000):

(1) Stock was issued for $10,000.

(2) Services were performed for $28,000.

(3) Expenses of $11,000 were incurred.

(4) Long-term liabilities of $8000 were paid.

(5) Dividends of $5000 were declared and paid.

Under the transaction view, Transactions (1), (stock issuance), (4) (payment of long-term liabilities), and (5) (dividend payment) would be classified as capital transactions and would not be included in the measure of net income. Transactions (2) (service performed) and (3) (expenses incurred), the operating transactions, would be matched, and net income would be determined and disclosed as in Figure 14–3.

Although both the capital-maintenance view and the transaction view result in the same dollar amount of net income, present-day financial statements are based on the transaction view of performance. Each independent transaction is represented by a journal entry that records a change in the relevant asset, liability, stockholders' equity, revenue, expense, and dividend accounts. In line with the matching principle, at the end of the accounting period the dollar amounts in the Expense accounts are matched against the dollar amounts in the Revenue accounts to determine net income which, in turn, is closed to Retained Earnings.

Figure 14–2   The capital maintenance view of income (year ended December 31, 1989)

Income	=	Net book value at end of period	−	Net book value at beginning of period	−	Equity issuance	+	Dividends
$17,000	=	$57,000	−	$35,000	−	$10,000	+	$5,000

Figure 14-3   The transaction view of income

Realing Company Income Statement For the Year Ended December 31, 1989	
Fees earned	$28,000
Expenses	11,000
Net income	$17,000

The transaction view is used primarily because it produces a breakdown of those items (revenues and expenses) that indicate performance. When transactions are treated separately, they can be grouped into different categories and disclosed in a way that more fully explains why a company did or did not achieve high performance during a given period. With these categories financial statement users are better able to understand and appreciate the reasons underlying a company's successes and failures.

For example, review the 1985 and 1986 income statements of Coca-Cola Enterprises, Inc. (Figure 14-4). Because revenues and expenses are broken down into separate categories, the reader is able to ascertain that a decrease in net income (from $36 million to $28 million) occurred even though revenues increased from $1.27 billion to $1.95 billion. The breakdown of expenses indicates that an increase in interest expense (from $32 million to $83 million) was one of the primary reasons.

While the transaction view gives rise to account categories that can provide

Figure 14-4   Statements of income

Coca-Cola Enterprises, Inc. Income Statements For the Periods Ending December 31, 1986 and December 31, 1985 (in millions)		
	1986	**1985**
Net operating revenues	$1,951	$1,271
Cost of sales	1,137	755
Gross profit	814	516
Selling, administration, and general expenses	645	431
Operating income	169	85
Interest income	6	5
Interest expense	83	32
Other income (deductions)	(7)	6
Income before income taxes	85	64
Income taxes	57	28
Net income	$ 28	$ 36
Source: 1986 annual report.		

useful information, determining whether a particular exchange is an operating or capital transaction can be difficult and subjective. The following section develops a framework that differentiates capital from operating transactions. Specifically, we divide all transactions into five groups and discuss how each group is classified in the present-day financial accounting system.

Capital and Operating Transactions: A Framework

Figure 14–5 represents a continuum for classifying capital and operating transactions. Note that five categories of transactions are described and that each is placed at a point along the continuum. Category 1 at the extreme left contains purely capital transactions, and Category 5 contains operating transactions. Categories 2, 3, and 4 include events considered to be capital transactions under generally accepted accounting principles, but the categories toward the middle (e.g., Category 4) contain transactions that increasingly resemble operating activities. Later we point out that operating transactions can also be subdivided into categories, based primarily on how germane they are to the normal, everyday operating activities of a company. Review the figure closely; we discuss it in detail in what follows.

Exchanges with Stockholders

Exchanges with owners include (1) issuances of preferred or common stock, (2) purchases, retirements, and reissuances of treasury stock, and (3) cash, property, and stock dividends. This group of financing transactions is located on the far left side of the continuum because these are purely capital transactions, involved exclusively with the formation and dissolution of the company's equity capital and

Figure 14–5 Classifying capital and operating transactions

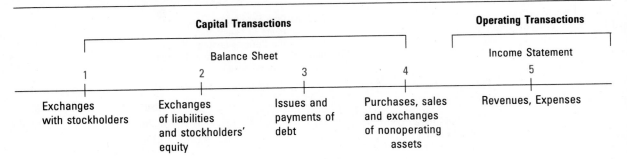

1. Exchanges with stockholders: Stock issuances, stock redemptions, and dividend payments.
2. Exchanges of liabilities and stockholders' equity: Debt refinancing and conversion of convertible bonds and stocks.
3. Issues and payments of debt: Cash borrowings evidenced by notes payable, issuing bonds, and payments on debts, including the redemption of debt.
4. Purchases, sales and exchanges of nonoperating assets: Purchases, sales, and exchanges of assets including marketable securities, receivables, long-term investments, and long-lived assets.
5. Revenues: Inflows of assets (or outflows of liabilities) due to operations.
   Expenses: Outflows of assets (or inflows of liabilities) due to the generation of revenues.

the returns (i.e., dividends) to the company's owners. The most distinctive and important feature about the transactions in this category is that they never affect the income statement. Even when treasury stock is reissued for an amount different than its cost, the dollar amount of the difference is not recognized as a gain or a loss on the income statement.

Exchanges of Liabilities and Stockholders' Equity

Exchanges of liabilities and stockholders' equity refer to transactions in which liabilities are exchanged for other liabilities (debt refinancing arrangements) or converted into stockholders' equity (conversion of convertible bonds or preferred stocks to common stock). Such financing exchanges are considered capital transactions because they deal only with a company's capital structure. Accordingly, they generally do not affect the income statement. However, these transactions are located to the right of exchanges with stockholders because in certain limited circumstances they can give rise to gains or losses that appear on the income statement.[2]

Issues and Payments of Debt

Issues and payments of debt include cash borrowings associated with the issuance of notes or bonds payable as well as the cash payments required to service or retire such liabilities. These transactions involve exchanges with a company's creditors and thus are reflected in the liability section of the balance sheet. They are considered capital transactions because they involve how a company finances its operations through debt. However, these transactions are not completely separate from a company's operations. Interest payments on debt are directly reflected on the income statement through interest expense; book gains and losses are recognized when debt is retired; and premiums and discounts on notes and bonds are amortized to the income statement over the life of the debt. Consequently, this category of transactions is located to the right of exchanges of liabilities and stockholders' equity.

Purchases, Sales, and Exchanges of Nonoperating Assets

Category 4 includes the purchase, sale, or exchange of all noncash assets except accounts receivable and inventory. Such assets include marketable securities, prepaid expenses, long-term investments, and long-lived assets. The acquisition or sale of any of these assets are considered capital transactions because they combine to form the capital base upon which operations are conducted. Marketable securities, prepaid expenses, long-term investments, and long-lived assets, for example, are all *capitalized* when they are purchased.

Note that the definition of this category excludes accounts receivable and inventory. These assets are viewed separately because they involve both capital and operating activities. Specifically, the sale of accounts receivable and the purchase of inventory are considered capital transactions, while the acquisition of a receivable resulting from the sale of inventory is considered an operating transaction.[3]

---

2. The methods used to account for refinancing arrangements and the conversion of convertible bonds and stocks are complex and controversial, and we do not discuss them in this textbook. For our purposes it is sufficient to note that, according to current generally accepted accounting principles, such transactions rarely give rise to income statement gains and losses.

3. Many companies sell outstanding accounts receivable to financial institutions for immediate cash. These transfers accelerate cash collections from sales on account as well as pass on the risks and costs associated with uncollectible accounts to the financial institution. Such exchanges are called *factoring* arrangements. Sales made on credit using major credit cards, such as VISA, American Express, and MasterCard represent factoring arrangements.

Although considered to include capital transactions, this category is located next to the operating section of the continuum because it is only a matter of time before these capitalized costs appear on the income statement. Prepaid expenses and long-lived assets, for example, are amortized, depleted, or depreciated on the income statement over their useful lives. Capitalized inventory costs are matched against revenues when inventories are sold. When the lower-of-cost-or-market rule is applied to marketable securities and inventory, unrealized losses are recognized on the income statement. Income statement gains and losses are recognized when marketable securities, accounts receivable, long-term investments, and long-lived assets are sold.

Revenues and Expenses

The right side of the continuum includes exchanges that are considered operating transactions. As mentioned before, revenues represent inflows of assets (or outflows of liabilities) due to a company's operating activities, and, in line with the matching principle, expenses represent outflows of assets (or inflows of liabilities) associated with the generation of the revenues. **Capital transactions** basically involve setting up a company so that it can conduct operations, while **operating transactions** entail the actual conduct of the operations. Earlier in the text we referred to a company as a fruit tree: capital transactions affect the size and structure of the tree (represented by the balance sheet), and operating transactions reflect the harvest and sale of the fruit (represented by the income statement).

Classifying Operating Transactions

Revenues and expenses, which include gains and losses, range from those that are fundamental and necessary to a company's operations to those that are only marginally related to operations. Figure 14–6 shows three groups of operating transactions, based primarily on how germane the transactions are to the normal operations of a company and how frequently they occur.

Group A contains revenues and expenses that result from transactions that are normal to company operations and occur frequently. Examples include the sale of the company's inventories or services and the payment and recognition of expenses due to such items as wages, utilities, rent, insurance, depreciation, and other administrative and selling activities.

Group B contains revenues and expenses that are much less germane to the normal activities of a company and/or may occur infrequently. Examples include interest earned on bank savings accounts held by manufacturing, retail, and service companies, rent earned from temporarily leasing company property planned to be used later for other purposes, gains and losses recognized on sales of long-lived assets and debt retirements, and gains and losses related to such items as litigation, employee strikes, and natural disasters.

Group C contains gains and losses recognized from such activities as changes in accounting principles (e.g., from LIFO to FIFO, or from double-declining-balance to straight-line depreciation), which reflect very little about the operations occurring during the periods in which such changes were made. They are simply book entries.

In the past there was considerable controversy over the proper classification and disclosure of the transactions contained in Groups B and C. Some accoun-

Figure 14-6   Classifying operating transactions

Unusual and Infrequent ←——————————————————————→ Normal and Recurring

Group C	Group B	Group A
Gains and losses due to changes in accounting principles (5)	Revenues and expenses from activities not germane to a company's primary activity, which may occur infrequently	Normal and recurring operating revenues and expenses (1)

Extraordinary items (4)	Disposals of segments (3)	Other revenues and expenses (e.g., bank interest) (2)

tants argued that transactions from Group C should not enter into the computation of net income. Others took an even more extreme view and suggested that transactions in both Groups B and C were not germane to operations and, accordingly, should not appear on the income statement, which should be limited to operating revenues and expenses in the strictest sense.

In 1966 the accounting profession adopted the position that nonoperating items (Groups B and C) should be included on the income statement, but they must be separately and clearly disclosed in specific categories. Specifically, it was recommended that the income statement consist of five categories: (1) operating revenues and expenses, (2) other revenues and expenses, (3) disposals of business segments, (4) extraordinary items, and (5) changes in accounting principles. In terms of Figure 14-6, Category 1 corresponds to Group A, Categories 2, 3, and 4 come from Group B, and Category 5 corresponds to Group C.

The different categories on the income statement allow users to assess the significance of the items in each category and choose to include or exclude them in the computation of net income as the situation dictates. The next section defines and illustrates the five categories of a complete income statement.

A COMPLETE INCOME STATEMENT: DISCLOSURE AND PRESENTATION

Figure 14-7 provides an income statement that contains each of the five categories introduced in the previous section. Review the statement carefully. The following discussion considers first the income statement in general and then covers each category individually.

The computation of net income on the income statement involves five major components, each representing one of the five categories. In general, as one moves from the top to the bottom of the income statement, the events become increasingly less important to the operations of the business. Net operating income (operating revenues less operating expenses) reflects financial performance resulting from transactions that are both fundamental to a company's normal activities and occur frequently. Other revenues and expenses and disposals of busi-

Figure 14–7 A complete income statement

XYZ Company Income Statement For the Period Ending Dec. 31, 1990			
Gross sales		$325	⎫
Less: Sales discounts and returns		25	⎬ 1. Operating revenues
Net sales		300	⎭
Less: Cost of goods sold			⎫
Beginning inventory	$ 75		⎪
+ Gross purchases	150		⎪
− Purchase discounts and returns	5		⎬
+ Freight-in	20		⎪
− Ending inventory	80	160	⎪
Gross profit		140	⎭
Operating expenses			⎫ 1. Operating expenses
Wages and salaries	30		⎪
Advertising	10		⎪
Insurance	8		⎪
State and local taxes	7		⎬
Depreciation	25		⎪
Utilities	20		⎪
Miscellaneous	15	115	⎭
Net operating income		25	
Other revenues		10	⎫
Less: Other expenses		13	⎬ 2. Other revenues and expenses
Net income from continuing operations before tax		22	
Less: Federal income tax		7	
Net income from continuing operations		15	
Income (loss) on segment up to disposal (net of tax)		(3)	⎫
Gain (loss) on disposal of segment (net of tax)		5	⎬ 3. Disposal of business segment
Net income before extraordinary items		17	
Extraordinary gain (loss) (net of tax)		(5)	⎬ 4. Extraordinary item
Net income before changes in accounting principle		12	
Income effect due to change in accounting principle (net of tax)		7	⎬ 5. Changes in accounting principles
Net income		$ 19	
Earnings per share (100 shares outstanding)			
Net income from continuing operations (after tax)		$ .15	
Disposal of business segment		.02	
Extraordinary items		(.05)	
Change in accounting principle		.07	
Total earnings per share		$ .19	

ness segments reflect the financial effects of events that are either not part of a company's normal operations or do not occur frequently. Extraordinary gains and losses result from events that are both highly unusual and infrequent, and gains and losses due to changes in accounting principles result simply from book entries.

The income statement is divided into these categories to enable users to distinguish revenues and expenses that are due to operations from those due to unusual, infrequent, and sometimes uncontrollable events (e.g., extraordinary items), or simply to changes in accounting principles (e.g., LIFO to FIFO). Presumably, measures of profit disclosed near the top of the income statement (e.g., net operating income) better reflect management's performance and are more indicative of the future than are those disclosed near the bottom of the statement (e.g., net income). The boards of directors of many companies, for example, express their management compensation agreements in terms of net operating income instead of net income. The boards apparently believe that if management acts to increase net operating income, it will increase the long-run earnings of the company and, thus, further the interests of the stockholders. Consider the following excerpt from the 1987 financial report of the Pillsbury Company: "Certain employees of the Company participate in compensation programs which include a base salary plus incentive payments based on the level of operating earnings."

Intraperiod Tax Allocation

Federal income taxes, which do not include state and local taxes, are disclosed in two different ways on the income statement. The first income tax disclosure immediately follows net income from continuing operations (before tax). It represents the tax expense assessed on the company due to net operating income ($25), other revenues ($10), and other expenses ($13). The dollar amount ($7) was computed approximately by multiplying net income from continuing operations before tax ($22) by the company's federal income tax rate (34 percent).

The dollar amounts associated with the remaining items (disposal of business segments, extraordinary items, and changes in accounting principles) are all disclosed *net of tax*. Such presentation means that each of these revenue and expense items is disclosed on the income statement after the related income tax effect has been removed. The practice of including the income tax effect of a particular transaction with the transaction itself on the income statement is known as **intraperiod tax allocation.**

For example, during 1987 CBS Inc. retired long-term debt with a book value of $28.6 million for $29.1 million dollars. A loss of $.5 million was recognized on the transaction with the following journal entry.

Long-term Debt	28.6	
Extraordinary Loss on Early Retirement of Debt	.5	
Cash		29.1
To record the retirement of long-term debt.		

The loss, however, was tax deductible and served to decrease CBS's 1987 tax liability by $.2 million. This tax benefit was recorded in the books with the following journal entry, and a loss on early retirement (net of tax) of $.3 million ($.5 million − $.2 million) was disclosed on CBS's 1987 income statement. This loss was disclosed on the income statement under extraordinary items.

Income Tax Liability	.2	
Extraordinary Loss on Early Retirement of Debt		.2
To record the tax benefit.		

In another example, Ralston Purina Company sold its domestic agricultural products business in 1986 for $545 million. The book value of the sold business was $168 million, and a gain of $377 million was recognized on the transaction with the following journal entry.

Cash		545	
Net Assets of Agricultural Business			168
Gain on Disposal of Segment			377
To record the sale of a business segment.			

The gain, however, was included in Ralston Purina's taxable income and increased the company's 1986 tax liability by $167 million. The increase in tax liability was recorded with the following journal entry, and Ralston Purina disclosed a $210 million ($377 − $167) gain on its 1986 income statement. The gain appeared under disposals of business segments.

Gain on disposal of segment	167	
Income tax liability		167
To record the increase in tax liability.		

The general formula for computing the net-of-tax dollar amount for a revenue or expense item is provided below.

Net-of-tax dollar amount = (Gross revenue or expense) × (1 − tax rate)

If, for example, an extraordinary gain or loss of $10,000 is recognized on a transaction, and the company's federal income tax rate is 34 percent, the net-of-tax dollar amount disclosed on the income statement would be calculated as follows:

$$\text{Net of tax dollar amount} = \$10,000 \times (1 - 34\%)$$
$$= \$6600$$

Earnings-Per-Share Disclosure

Generally accepted accounting principles also require that earnings per share be disclosed on the face of the income statement and that the specific dollar amounts associated with (1) net income from continuing operations (after tax), (2) disposals of business segments, (3) extraordinary items, and (4) changes in accounting principles be disclosed separately. Note the form of this disclosure in Figure 14−7. The earnings per share amount for each category is calculated by dividing the dollar amount of the gain or loss associated with that category by the number of common shares outstanding. The disclosure illustrated in Figure 14−8 is from the 1987 income statement of General Electric Company.

Figure 14−8   Disclosing earnings per share

General Electric Company Earnings Per Share Disclosure For the Year Ended December 31, 1987	
Net earnings per share (in dollars)	
Before extraordinary item and cumulative effect of changes in accounting principles	$2.33
Extraordinary item—loss on early extinguishment of long-term debt	(.07)
Cumulative effect of change in method of accounting for deferred income taxes	.63
Cumulative effect of change in method of accounting for inventory	.31
Net earnings per share	$3.20
Source: 1987 annual report.	

Operating Revenues and Expenses: Usual and Frequent

Operating revenues and expenses refer to asset and liability inflows and outflows related to the acquisition and delivery of the goods or services provided by a company. The term **usual transaction** refers to the normal operations of the business. If a company is in business to sell furniture, for example, *usual* revenues come from the sales of furniture. Automobile dealerships, on the other hand, are in business to sell and service automobiles; for them, revenues generated from selling office furniture would not be considered usual.

The term **frequent transaction** refers to how often the revenue is generated or the expense incurred. Revenues and expenses are considered frequent if they are expected to recur in the foreseeable future. They are not "one-shot," unpredictable events. For many companies the sale of a fixed asset or a long-term investment, for example, which can generate either a gain or a loss, is a transaction that tends to occur infrequently.

Other Revenues and Expenses: Unusual or Infrequent

The section of the income statement headed "Other revenues and expenses" contains revenues and expenses related to a company's secondary or auxiliary activities. The most common examples are interest income and interest expense, which relate to the company's investments and debt financing, respectively. While interest is certainly important and recurring, with the exception of financial institutions, it is not directly a part of the acquisition and selling of a company's goods and services. IBM Corporation and Coca-Cola Enterprises, like many other large U.S. companies, include both interest income and interest expense in this category. Another item commonly disclosed in this section is income (or loss) from long-term investments accounted for under the equity method. Both Sears, Roebuck & Company and the New York Times Company, for example, disclose equity earnings from associated companies in this manner on their 1987 income statements.

Other examples include dividend income from investments, gains and losses from sales of investments and long-lived assets, receivable and inventory write-downs, gains and losses on foreign currency translations, losses due to employee strikes, income from the rental of excess warehouse space, and gains and losses due to litigation.[4] In 1987, for example, MCI Communications Corporation reported gains from an antitrust settlement ($39 million) and the sale of nonoperating assets ($3 million) in this section of the income statement. That same year Johnson & Johnson reported a $140 million loss due to the writedown of inventory in the same manner. This loss resulted from the company's decision to remove Extra-Strength Tylenol capsules from the consumer market in response to a highly publicized criminal tampering case.

The key feature about the items in this section of the income statement is that they are "unusual or infrequent, but not both." Interest and dividend income, for example, are considered unusual because they are not germane to the normal operations of the business. They are secondary to the major activities of most companies. At the same time, however, interest and dividend revenue may be recognized every year and are therefore considered to occur frequently. Receivable and

---

4. Book gains and losses due to foreign currency translations are discussed in Chapter 16.

inventory writedowns and losses from employee strikes, on the other hand, while part of the normal business risks faced by virtually all companies, occur infrequently. They are, therefore, considered to be infrequent but not unusual.

The nature of a particular business and the environment in which it operates must be considered when deciding what is unusual and/or infrequent. Dividend and interest income, for example, are secondary to the operations of manufacturing, retailing, and service companies, yet they represent the primary revenues for financial institutions. Interest income during 1987 for BankAmerica Corporation, for example, represented 80 percent of total revenues generated by the company. Consequently, for BankAmerica interest income is both usual and frequent.

Disposal of a Business Segment

A **business segment** is defined as a separate line of business, product line, or class of customer involving an operation that is independent from a company's other operations. Highly diversified companies consist of many independent segments. DuPont, for example, consists of eight different segments: agriculture, biomedical products, coal, fibers, industrial and consumer products, petroleum exploration, petroleum refining, marketing and transportation, and polymer products. Each of DuPont's segments generates well over $1 billion in revenue each year. The sale or discontinuance of any one of these segments would be referred to as a disposal of a business segment, and the related financial effects would be disclosed separately on the income statement.

In 1987 a number of major U.S. companies sold or discontinued independent segments. Maytag Corporation sold Toastmaster, a wholly-owned subsidiary, for $52 million, Eli Lilly sold its cosmetic segment, Elizabeth Arden, to Fabergé for $557 million, and Greyhound recognized a loss of $51 million when it discontinued Verex, its mortgage insurance subsidiary. In each case the income or loss attributed to the segment's operations up to the time of the disposal, and the gain or loss from the disposal itself were reported on the 1987 income statement under the caption, "disposal of business segments."

The disposal of a business segment is a significant and complex transaction that is subject to a number of detailed rules under generally accepted accounting principles. We do not cover these detailed rules here. For our purposes, it is sufficient to view the disposal of a segment as similar to the sale or retirement of a long-lived asset: more specifically, the sale or retirement of a large piece of equipment that generates revenues and incurs expenses that are independent of the company's other operations.

Note in the complete income statement in Figure 14–7 that two separate disclosures are associated with a disposed business segment, and that each disclosure presents the financial effects net of tax.[5] The first disclosure reflects the income or loss associated with the segment's operations for the time period extending from the previous balance-sheet date to the point when the segment is actually disposed of. Since the segment is an independent entity, the expenses associated with it can be matched against its revenues to provide a net income or loss for

---

5. The following discussion somewhat oversimplifies the two separate disclosures associated with a disposed business segment. More detailed coverage can be found in intermediate or advanced financial accounting texts.

that time period. The second disclosure reflects the gain or loss recognized when the segment is actually disposed of. At that time, the assets and liabilities of the segment are written off the books, the proceeds (if the segment is sold) are recorded, and a gain or loss on the disposal is recognized in the dollar amount of the difference between the book value of the segment and the proceeds.

To illustrate, in March and October, respectively, of 1987 RJR Nabisco, Inc. sold its spirits and wine business and its quick-service restaurant business, essentially Kentucky Fried Chicken, for a combined total of $2.04 billion. These transactions gave rise to the combined journal entries provided below.

Cash and Notes Receivable	2,040	
Liabilities	1,594	
Assets		3,200
Gain on Disposal of Business Segments		434
To record the sales of wine and spirits business and		
Kentucky Fried Chicken (dollars in millions).		
Gain on Sale of Business Segment	219	
Income Tax Liability		219
To record the tax effect.		

A $434 million gain was recognized because segments with a combined book value of $1,606 million ($3,200 − $1,594) were sold for $2,040 million. This gain increased Nabisco's income tax liability by $219 million; as a result, the net-of-tax gain reported on the income statement was $215 million ($434 − $219). Between December 31, 1986, and the disposal dates in March and October, the two business segments generated a combined loss, after taxes, of $7 million. Consequently, the lower portion of the income statement prepared by RJR Nabisco as of the end of 1987 appeared as in Figure 14−9.

Figure 14−9 Accounting for disposal of a business segment

RJR Nabisco
Excerpt from Income Statement
For the Year Ended December 31, 1987
(in millions)

Income from continuing operations	$1,081
Loss from discontinued operations (net of tax)	(7)
Gain on sale of discontinued operations (net of tax)	215
Income before extraordinary items	1,289
Extraordinary item	(80)
Net income	$1,209
Earnings per share	
Continuing operations	$ 4.19
Discontinued operations	0.83
Extraordinary item	(0.32)
Net income per share	$ 4.70

Source: 1987 annual report.

Extraordinary Items: Unusual and Infrequent

Extraordinary items are defined as material events of a character significantly different from the typical, customary business activities of an entity, which are not expected to recur frequently in the ordinary operating activities of a business. In other words, extraordinary items are both unusual and infrequent.

The most common extraordinary items reported by major U.S. companies are gains and losses resulting from early retirements of long-term debts.[6] *Accounting Trends and Techniques* (New York: AICPA, 1987) reports that, of the 600 major U.S. companies surveyed, 107 (18 percent) disclosed at least one extraordinary item on the income statement, and 54 (51 percent) of these resulted from gains or losses recognized on early debt retirements. Dow Chemical, Wendy's International, Monsanto, CBS Inc., and Alcoa, for example, all recognized material gains or losses from early debt retirements in 1987. Each reported the gain or loss as an extraordinary item on the 1987 income statement.

To illustrate the methods used to account for an early debt retirement, consider Federal-Mogul Corporation, which retired debt with a book value of $19.6 million for $22.5 million in 1986. The $2.9 million loss ($22.5 − $19.6) reduced the company's income tax liability by $1.4 million, and the net of tax loss reported as an extraordinary item on the company's income statement was $1.5 million ($2.9 − $1.4). The following journal entries were recorded in the books of Federal-Mogul Corporation.

Long-Term Debt	19.6	
Extraordinary Loss on Early Retirement	2.9	
Cash		22.5
To record the early retirement of debt (dollars in millions).		
Income Tax Liability	1.4	
Extraordinary Loss on Early Retirement		1.4
To record the tax benefit.		

Other examples of extraordinary items include income tax benefits from operating loss carryforwards;[7] gains and losses from terminating pension plans; gains and losses from litigation settlements; losses resulting from casualties like floods, earthquakes, tornados, hurricanes, droughts and volcanoes; and gains and losses resulting from expropriations (forced government takeovers or purchases of company property) and prohibitions under new law.

As in the case of "Other revenues and expenses," the nature of the company in question and the environment in which it operates are critical in determining what is and is not considered extraordinary. A company that operates in a lowland area where floods are common, for example, would not report a flood loss as

---

6. The early retirement of long-term debt is a fairly common transaction for many major U.S. companies. Consequently, it does not always meet the infrequent criterion for an extraordinary item. However, generally accepted accounting principles specifically require that book gains and losses from such transactions be disclosed as extraordinary items.

7. When a company incurs a loss for tax purposes in a given year, it may match that loss against revenues earned in subsequent periods. This procedure serves to reduce the tax liability in those periods. The dollar amount of the tax benefit in each future period is called an *operating loss carryforward* and is disclosed on the income statement of that period as an extraordinary item. Operating loss carryforwards are relatively common. Of the 107 extraordinary items reported in *Accounting Trends and Techniques* (New York: AICPA, 1986, p. 322), 50, (47 percent) were due to operating loss carryforwards.

extraordinary because it would not be infrequent. Similarly, gains and losses from lawsuits may or may not be considered extraordinary. Most large U.S. companies are constantly involved in various forms of litigation, so that gains and losses from lawsuits are considered unusual, but not infrequent. Many smaller companies, on the other hand, are infrequently involved in litigation, so resulting gains or losses would be considered extraordinary. The two examples below illustrate the journal entries involved when recognizing an extraordinary gain and an extraordinary loss, both of which are reported net of tax.

Assume that a flood, which is a very unusual occurrence, completely destroys a warehouse and the inventory stored inside. The tax rate is 34 percent, and the cost of the warehouse and inventory are $40,000 and $10,000, respectively. The loss, reported net of tax as an extraordinary item on the income statement, would be $33,000 ($50,000 − $17,000).

Extraordinary Loss	50,000	
Warehouse		40,000
Inventory		10,000
To record the flood loss.		
Income Tax Liability ($50,000 × 34%)	17,000	
Extraordinary Loss		17,000
To record the tax benefit.		

Assume a company wins a lawsuit in the amount of $30,000. Such a gain is considered extraordinary for this particular company, and the income tax rate is 34 percent. The extraordinary gain reported net of tax on the income statement is $19,800 ($30,000 − $10,200).

Cash	30,000	
Extraordinary Gain		30,000
To record the proceeds from the lawsuit.		
Extraordinary Gain ($30,000 × 34%)	10,200	
Income Tax Liability		10,200
To record the tax effect.		

Changes in Accounting Principles

Chapter 5 defines the concept of consistency, and mentions that once a company chooses an acceptable principle or method of accounting (e.g., straight-line depreciation, FIFO inventory valuation, etc.), it must continue to use that method consistently from one year to the next. Consistency helps to maintain the credibility of accounting reports, enabling investors, creditors, and other interested parties to make more meaningful comparisons and to identify more easily the trends in a company's performance across time.

However, if a company can convince its auditors that the environment in which it operates has changed and another accounting method is now more appropriate than the one currently in place, it can change an accounting method and still be in conformance with generally accepted accounting principles. Such changes can have significant effects on reported income and must be disclosed in three prominent places in the financial report: (1) the auditor's report to the shareholders must mention the change, (2) the footnotes to the financial statements must clearly describe the change, and (3) the cumulative effects of the change on net income must be disclosed (net of tax) separately on the income statement, immediately below extraordinary items.

To illustrate, in 1986 the Timken Company changed its method of depreciating long-lived assets from accelerated to straight-line. According to management (and the auditors agreed,) straight-line depreciation was preferable because it was more consistent with the depreciation methods used by other companies in the industry and thus enhanced financial statement comparability across companies. Timken's accountants ascertained that over the years since the long-lived assets had been acquired, $106 million in depreciation had been charged under the accelerated method over and above the amount that would have been charged under the straight-line method. Consequently, the following journal entry, which reduced the balance in the Accumulated Depreciation account by $106 million and increased net income by the same amount, was recorded. It restates the balance sheet to reflect the straight-line method, and recognizes the cumulative effect of the accounting change as a book gain.

Accumulated Depreciation	106	
Cumulative Gain from Accounting Change		106
To record the cumulative effect of the change from		
accelerated to straight-line depreciation.		

Although somewhat unusual, Timken's management also chose to change to the straight-line method of depreciation for income tax purposes, which increased its 1986 tax liability by $46.6 million. The following journal entry records the increased income tax liability.

Cumulative Gain from Accounting Change	46.6	
Income Tax Liability		46.6
To record the $46.6 million increase in income tax liability.		

The cumulative effect of the accounting change, therefore, increased Timken's 1986 income, net of tax, by $59.4 million ($106 − $46.6). The excerpts contained in Figure 14–10, which were taken from the 1986 financial report of The Timken Company, illustrate the disclosures that normally accompany changes in accounting principles. Note that Timken also changed its method of accounting for its pension plan.[8]

To illustrate the recognition of a book loss due to a change in an accounting principle, assume that Fall Creek Associates decided on January 1, 1989, to change from the straight-line method of computing depreciation on plant assets to the sum-of-the-years'-digits method, for both tax and financial accounting purposes. The decision was approved by the company's external auditors. The assets were originally purchased in 1987 at a cost of $200,000, and were estimated at the time to have a service life of four years. Assuming no salvage value, the relevant comparisons are provided in Figure 14–11.

Had Fall Creek Associates used the sum-of-the-years'-digits method from the time it purchased the assets, it would have recorded $40,000 more of accumulated depreciation as of the beginning of 1989. The adjusting journal entry to

---

8. Note that the auditor's report in Figure 14–10 states that Timken followed "generally accepted accounting principles consistently . . . except for changes, with which [the auditors] concur, in the methods of accounting for depreciation." Since the end of 1986, when this report was written, the wording of the standard audit report has been modified. Nonetheless, changes in accounting principles must still be described, and the audit report should refer the reader to the related information in the footnotes.

Figure 14–10   Disclosing changes in accounting principles

The Timken Company
Excerpts from the Financial Report
For the Year Ended December 31, 1986

Notes to the Financial Statements

Note B. Effective January 1, 1986, the Company changed its method of depreciation for substantially all property, plant, and equipment from accelerated methods (primarily double-declining balance) to the straight-line method. The Company believes the straight-line method is preferable to the method previously used since it is more consistent with depreciation methods used by most similar industrial companies and, therefore, should improve comparability of financial reporting.

Auditor's Report to the Shareholders

In our opinion, the financial statements referred to above present fairly the consolidated financial position of The Timken Company . . . in conformity with generally accepted accounting principles consistently applied during the previous three-year period, *except for changes, with which we concur, in the methods of accounting for depreciation as described in Note B* to the consolidated financial statements.*

1986 Income Statement (dollars in millions)

Income before cumulative effect of accounting change	$(82.7)
Cumulative effect of accounting changes	
Depreciation (net of tax of $46.6)	59.4
Pension plan (net of tax of $22.1)	26.0
Net income	$ 2.7

  *Italics added.

---

record the cumulative effect of the depreciation method change, therefore, requires that $40,000 be added to the Accumulated Depreciation account on Fall Creek's balance sheet. A loss in the amount of $40,000 would also be recognized.

Loss on Change of Accounting Method	40,000	
Accumulated Depreciation		40,000
To record the cumulative effect of a change from straight-line to SYD depreciation.		

The $40,000 loss is deductible for tax purposes and, assuming a 34 percent income tax rate, would produce a tax savings of $13,600 ($40,000 × 34%). As a result, the journal entry on page 696 would be recorded, and the loss (net of tax) disclosed on the income statement would be $26,400 ($40,000 − $13,600).

Figure 14–11   A change from straight-line to sum-of-the-years'-digits

Year	Sum-of-the-Years'-Digits Depreciation	Straight-Line Depreciation	Excess of SYD over SL Depreciation per Year
1987	$80,000	$50,000	$30,000
1988	60,000	50,000	10,000
			$40,000

Income Tax Liability ($40,000 × 34%)	13,600	
Loss on Change in Accounting Principle		13,600
To record the income tax benefit associated with the accounting change.		

As mentioned before, the cumulative effects on net income due to changes in accounting methods are common and can be very significant. In 1986, for example, AT&T and Burlington Northern decreased net income by $175 million and $336 million (net of tax), respectively, when they changed to the units-of-production method of depreciation. In 1987, General Electric increased net income by $858 million by changing its methods of accounting for deferred income taxes and inventories. In each case the change was clearly described in the footnotes, the auditors concurred with and mentioned the change in the opinion letter, and the cumulative effect of the change on net income was separately disclosed on the income statement.

Nonetheless, financial statement users must still be careful not to overlook or be confused by such changes. As reported in *Forbes,* "when a company changes its accounting practices from one year to the next, all but the most diligent readers of annual reports can get lost."[9] General Motors Corporation, for example, changed five different accounting methods in the period of time between 1986 and 1988. In each case the change served to increase net income. A GM spokesman said that "each change brings us more in line with the industry," and that "we're not trying to hide anything at all." An industry analyst, on the other hand, noted that GM's "management is under pressure to show a good financial performance, and these changes serve to make it harder to compare the company's financial results over time."[10]

It is also important to realize that an accounting method differs from an accounting estimate, which is used to implement an accounting method. Straight-line depreciation, for example, is an accounting method, which is implemented by estimating the useful life and salvage value of a long-lived asset. The allowance method of accounting for bad debts is implemented by estimating the amount of bad debts at the end of each year. This section discusses how to account for a change in an accounting method. A section of Chapter 9 and Appendix B at the end of the text describe how to account for revisions in accounting estimates.

Income Statement Categories: Subjective Classifications

The different classifications contained on the income statement provide information that can be used (1) to assess the financial performance of a company and (2) to control and direct the activities of management through contracts. It is also important to realize, however, that many of these classifications are based on subjective, and sometimes biased, interpretations of the terms *usual* and *frequent.* As noted in *Forbes* magazine, "clever accountants can find all sorts of different meanings in those simple sounding words. . . . It all comes down to a judgment."[11]

For example, consider Primerica Corp., a large financial service supplier. In its preliminary *unaudited* financial statements for 1987 the company disclosed $183 million in income from continuing operations, and a $61 million-dollar extraor-

---

9. Laura Rohmann, "Add a Dash of Cumulative Catch-up," *Forbes,* 6 June 1983. p. 98.
10. Jacob M. Schlesinger, "GM Net Rose 18% in Quarter on Special Item," *The Wall Street Journal,* 22 April 1988, p. 18.
11. Penelope Wang, "Dictionary Please," *Forbes,* 7 March 1988 p. 88.

dinary loss. The loss, which the company treated as extraordinary because management considered it both unusual and infrequent, came from investments that decreased in value during the period. However, the company's auditors took the position that investment losses are not an infrequent occurrence for a financial service supplier, and on its audited financial statements Primerica Corp. included the $61 million loss in "Other revenues and expenses." The accounting treatment required by the auditors reduced income from continuing operations by 33 percent to $122 million.

In another case, Western Savings of Phoenix, a savings and loan company, reported $49 million in *operating* income in 1987, almost half of which ($24 million) was due to the sale of one large investment. Many accountants agreed that this particular sale was nonrecurring and that similar gains could not be expected in the future. Consequently, the gain on this transaction should not have been included in the operating section of the income statement. *Forbes* pointed out that this and other accounting practices followed by the company suggested that "Western is a classic case of how reported profits can misrepresent economic reality."[12]

The subjectivity associated with classifying gains and losses in different sections of the income statement affects the different measures of income and, accordingly, can have significant economic consequences. We noted earlier in the chapter, for example, that The Pillsbury Company has instituted a compensation plan that rewards management on the basis of operating income. An important question is whether interest expense is considered an operating or a nonoperating expense in the measurement of operating income as defined by the plan. Including interest as an operating expense could discourage management from borrowing needed funds; including it as a nonoperating expense, on the other hand, could encourage managers to borrow too much. Classifying interest as operating or nonoperating is a subjective decision. Yet, as we illustrate here, it can influence the manner in which a company functions.

Income Statement Format: Single-Step or Multistep

Income statements are presented using either of two formats: (1) a single-step format or (2) a multistep format. The difference between the two relates primarily to the disclosure of operating revenues and expenses and "Other revenue and expense" items. Under both formats, disposals of business segments, extraordinary items, and changes in accounting principles are disclosed separately.

Under the **single-step format,** which is used by slightly over half of the major companies in the United States, all operating and other revenues are grouped in a single category, while all operating and other expenses are grouped in a second category. The 1987 income statement of Goodyear Tire & Rubber Company, which is prepared using the single-step format, appears in Figure 14–12.

The **multistep format** separates cost of goods sold from other operating expenses, highlighting the gross profit dollar amount. This format also separates operating items from "other revenues and expenses." The 1985 income statement of Monsanto, which was prepared using the multistep format, appears in Figure 14–13.

12. Allan Sloan, "Phoenix' Wild West Show," *Forbes*, 31 May 1988, pp. 37–38.

Figure 14–12   Income statement using single-step format

Goodyear Tire & Rubber Company Income Statement For the Year Ended December 31, 1987 (in millions)		
Net sales		$ 9,905
Other income		180
		10,085
Cost and expenses		
Cost of goods sold	$7,375	
Selling, administrative, and general expenses	1,635	
Interest and amortization of debt discount	282	
Unusual items	(135)	
Foreign currency exchange	39	
Minority interest in net income of subsidiaries	17	9,213
Income from continuing operations before tax		872
United States and foreign taxes on income		358
Income from continuing operations		514
Discontinued operations		257
Net income		$ 771
Earnings per share of common stock		
Income from continuing operations	$ 8.49	
Discontinued operations	4.24	
Net income	$12.73	

THE STATEMENT OF RETAINED EARNINGS

As illustrated in Chapter 3, all items on the income statement are eventually closed to Retained Earnings. These items constitute net income, which is disclosed on the statement of retained earnings. The financial effects of other events, such as the declaration of dividends, the appropriation of retained earnings, and the sale of treasury stock for an amount less than its acquisition cost (discussed in Chapter 12) are booked directly to the Retained Earnings account and are often disclosed separately on the statement of retained earnings. A sample statement of retained earnings that includes such items appears in Figure 14–14.[13]

In addition to the items appearing in Figure 14–14, generally accepted accounting principles require that the financial effects of certain other events also be booked directly to Retained Earnings. These events, all of which must have occurred before the beginning of the current accounting period, give rise to book entries called **prior period adjustments.** Similar to disposals of business segments, extraordinary items, and changes in accounting methods, prior period adjustments are reported net of tax. The most common prior period adjustment (the only one discussed in this text) is the correction of an accounting error made in a previous period. The methods used to correct such errors are discussed and illustrated in Appendix B at the end of the text.

---

13. Chapter 12 notes that for many companies the statement of retained earnings is included within the statement of stockholders' equity, which explains the changes in all the stockholders' equity accounts during a period.

Figure 14–13   Income statement using multistep format

Monsanto Income Statement For the Year Ended December 31, 1985 (in millions)	
Net sales	$6,747
Cost of goods sold	4,841
Gross profit	1,906
Marketing and administrative expenses	919
Technological expenses	548
Amortization of intangible assets	88
Restructuring expense	949
Operating loss	(598)
Interest expense	(178)
Interest income	63
Gain from sale of oil and gas operations	392
Other income	23
Loss before income taxes and extraordinary gain	(298)
Income taxes	170
Loss before extraordinary gain	(128)
Extraordinary gain from debt repayment	30
Net loss	$ (98)
Earnings per share	
Before extraordinary gain	$(1.67)
Extraordinary gain	0.40
After extraordinary gain	$(1.27)
Source: 1987 annual report.	

Figure 14–14   Statement of retained earnings

Slayden Company Statement of Retained Earnings For the Period January 1–December 31, 1990	
Beginning retained earnings balance (unappropriated)	$2,300
Less: Sale of treasury stock for amount less than original cost	200
Plus: Net income	890
Less: Cash and property dividends declared	600
Less: Appropriated retained earnings (in accordance with terms of a debt covenant)	1,000
Ending retained earnings balance (unappropriated)	$1,390

THE ANNUAL REPORT OF K MART CORPORATION

Turn now to K mart's annual report located in Appendix D. Note that the Income Statement (page 31) (1) uses a single-step format, (2) discloses for 1987 a gain from discontinued operations and an extraordinary loss, and (3) reports earnings per share and its components on the face.

In the single-step format operating revenues (Sales) are grouped with "other revenues" (License fees and rental income, Equity in income of affiliate retail companies, and Interest income) and operating expenses (Cost of merchandise sold, Selling, general and administrative expenses, and Advertising) are grouped with "other expenses" (Interest expense from debt and capital lease obligations). The resulting number, Income from continuing retail operations before taxes, is reduced by the amount of Income taxes in the computation of Income from continuing operations.

Note B on page 36 describes K mart's program of disposing of its insurance operations. In 1988 "K mart completed the sale of Lone Star Life Insurance Company, terminated the agreement for the operation of store insurance centers and terminated the lease of the former insurance operations' headquarters." Insurance operations are definitely separate and distinct from K mart's normal activities and, accordingly, would classify as a separate segment.

The $28 million gain from discontinued operations reported on the 1987 Income Statement resulted from the December 1986 sale of "Furr's Cafeteria, Inc. and Bishops Buffets, Inc., two cafeteria chains, for $238 million in cash to Calvalcade Foods, Inc." The gain from the sale of these two separate segments is described on page 36 as "net after-tax."

Note J on page 42 indicates that the cash proceeds from the sale of the two cafeteria chains provided funds for the December 1986 "early redemption of all $250 million of [K mart's] 12 3/4% sinking fund debentures due March 1, 2015. The resulting redemption premium [gain] of $16 million, net of applicable income taxes of $16 million, was reported as an extraordinary item."

The components of earnings per share are disclosed on the bottom of the Income Statement. The actual numbers are calculated by dividing the dollar amounts of the net income components by the average number of shares outstanding. For example, in 1987 Income from continuing retail operations ($570 million) is divided by 201.5 million shares to come up with the $2.84 earnings per share amount reported on the Income Statement. The $.14 and $.08 earnings per share amounts associated with Discontinued operations and the Extraordinary item were computed by dividing $28 million and $16 million, respectively, by 201.5 million shares.

The Statement of Retained Earnings can be found on page 34, where it is combined with the other stockholders' equity items on the Statement of Stockholders' Equity. For 1987, 1988, and 1989 the Retained Earnings balance was adjusted only for net income and dividends. K mart paid total dividends of $690 million over the three-year period, which represented approximately 33 percent of net income.

REVIEW PROBLEM

The operating revenues and expenses of Panawin Enterprises for 1990 follow, along with a description of several additional transactions, events, and pieces of information. Review the information provided, including the related journal entries. Assume that income taxes on income from continuing operations are $7000, the effective income tax rate on other items is 34 percent, the balance in Retained Earnings as of December 31, 1989, is $106,000, and that dividends declared during 1990 total $16,000.

Operating revenues	$85,000
Operating expenses	62,000
Net operating income	$23,000

Additional Information

(1) Machinery with an original cost of $14,000 and a book value of $11,000 was sold for $9000. The transaction was considered unusual but not infrequent.

Cash	9000	
Accumulated Depreciation	3000	
Loss on Sale of Machinery	2000	
Machinery		14,000
To record the sale of machinery.		

(2) A separate line of business (segment) was sold on March 14, 1990, for $18,000 cash. The book values of the assets and liabilities of the segment as of the date of the sale were $10,000 and $4000, respectively. The business segment recognized revenues of $18,500 and expenses of $14,000 from January 1, 1990, to March 14, 1990.

Revenues of the Segment	18,500	
Expenses of the Segment		14,000
Income Summary		4,500
To record the income earned by the business segment (closing entry recorded at time of sale).		

Cash	18,000	
Liabilities	4,000	
Assets		10,000
Gain on Sale of Segment		12,000
To record the sale of a business segment.		

Income Summary ($4500 × 34%)	1530	
Income Tax Liability		1530
To record the income tax liability related to the segment's 1990 operations.		

Gain on Sale of Segment (12,000 × 34%)	4080	
Income Tax Liability		4080
To record the income tax liability related to the sale of the segment.		

(3) On September 12, 1990, Panawin retired outstanding bonds with a face value of $120,000 before maturity for a cash payment of $130,000. The bonds were originally issued at a premium, and the unamortized premium as of the date of retirement was $3000. The loss on the retirement is considered extraordinary.

Bond Payable	120,000	
Unamortized Premium	3,000	
Loss on Retirement	7,000	
Cash		130,000
To record the retirement of outstanding bonds.		

Income Tax Liability ($7000 × 34%)	2380	
Loss on Retirement		2380
To record the income tax benefit related to the early retirement.		

(4) The company changed its inventory flow assumption from last-in, first-out (LIFO) to first-in, first-out (FIFO). This change increased the ending inventory balance for 1990 by $8000.

Inventory	8000	
Income from Change in Inventory Valuation		8000
To record the change from LIFO to FIFO.		

Income from Change in Inv. Valuation	2720	
Income Tax Liability ($8000 × 34%)		2720
To record the income tax liability related to the change from LIFO to FIFO.		

Now note how the income statement (Figure 14-15) and statement of retained earnings (Figure 14-16) have been prepared.

Figure 14-15   Income statement for review problem

Panawin Enterprises Income Statement For the Year Ended December 31, 1990		
Operating revenues	$85,000	(given)
Operating expenses	62,000	(given)
Net operating income	23,000	
Loss on sale of machinery	(2,000)	
Net income from continuing operations before tax	21,000	
Less: Federal income tax	7,000	(given)
Net income from continuing operations	14,000	
Income from disposed segment (net of tax)	2,970	($4,500 − $1,530)
Gain on sale of segment (net of tax)	7,920	($12,000 − $4,080)
Net income before extraordinary items	24,890	
Extraordinary loss on retirement of debt (net of tax)	(4,620)	(−$7,000 + 2,380)
Net income before change in accounting principle	20,270	
Income effect from change from LIFO to FIFO (net of tax)	5,280	($8,000 − $2,720)
Net income	$25,550	
Earnings per share (10,000 shares outstanding)		
Net income from continuing operations	$ 1.40	(14,000 ÷ 10,000)
Disposed business segment	1.09	([$2,970 + $7,920] ÷ 10,000)
Extraordinary item	(.46)	($4,620 ÷ 10,000)
Change in accounting principle	.53	($5,280 ÷ 10,000)
Total earnings per share	$ 2.56	($25,550 ÷ 10,000)

Figure 14-16   Statement of retained earnings for review problem

Panawin Enterprises Statement of Retained Earnings For the Year Ended December 31, 1990	
Beginning retained earnings balance	$106,000
Plus: Net income	25,550
Less: Dividends	16,000
Ending retained earnings balance	$115,550

SUMMARY OF LEARNING OBJECTIVES

1   Describe the economic consequences associated with reporting net income.

Income is the most common measure of a company's performance. It has been related to stock prices, suggesting that equity investors use income in their decisions to buy and sell equity securities. It has been related to bond prices, indicating that debt investors use income in their decisions to buy and sell corporate bonds. Income is also used by credit-rating agencies to establish credit ratings.

Various income measures are also found in contracts written among stockholders, creditors, and managers. Such contracts are normally designed either to protect the interests of creditors or to encourage managers to act in the interests of the stockholders.

2 **Differentiate the capital-maintenance view of income from the transaction view, and explain why present-day financial statements follow the transaction view.**

Under the capital-maintenance view, performance for a particular period is determined by comparing a company's net book value (assets − liabilities) at the end of a period with its net book value at the beginning of that period. The difference between these two values, minus the proceeds from any equity issuances, and plus dividends paid during the period, is considered income.

The transaction view determines and discloses income by focusing on the individual transactions executed during a period. Each transaction is recorded and classified as capital or operating, and operating transactions are further divided into revenues and expenses. Income is computed by matching expenses against revenues in the proper time period.

Present-day financial statements are based on the transaction view of performance primarily because it produces a breakdown of those items involved in performance. When transactions are treated separately, they can be grouped into different categories and disclosed in a way that more fully explains why a company did or did not achieve high performance during a given period. With these categories, financial statement users are better able to understand and appreciate the reasons underlying a company's successes and failures. However, determining whether a particular exchange is an operating or capital transaction can be difficult and subjective.

3 **Describe the difference between an operating transaction and a capital transaction, and indicate how capital transactions are categorized on the capital/operating continuum.**

Capital transactions involve setting up a company so that it can conduct operations. Operating transactions entail the actual conduct of the operations. The text identifies five categories of transactions, each of which falls in a different place on the capital/operating continuum. The categories are (1) exchanges with stockholders; (2) exchanges of liabilities and stockholders' equity; (3) issues and payments of debt; (4) purchases, sales, and exchanges of nonoperating assets and (5) operating transactions. Generally accepted accounting principles consider Categories 1−4 as capital transactions.

Exchanges with stockholders are considered purely capital because they are involved exclusively with the formation and dissolution of the company's equity capital and the returns to the company's stockholders.

Exchanges of liabilities and stockholders' equity are considered capital transactions because they deal only with a company's capital structure. These transactions are considered slightly less capital than exchanges with stockholders because in certain limited circumstances they can give rise to gains or losses that appear on the income statement.

Issues and payments of debt involve exchanges with a company's creditors and are reflected in the liability section of the balance sheet. On the capital/operating continuum, this category of transactions is located to the right of exchanges of liabilities and stockholders' equity because interest costs and gains and losses on debt retirements are reflected on the income statement.

Purchases, sales, or exchanges of nonoperating assets are considered capital transactions because these assets represent the capital base upon which operations are conducted. This category is located next to the operating section of the continuum because it is only a matter of time before these capitalized costs are allocated to the income statement.

4 Characterize the transactions and events included in each of the five categories that constitute a complete income statement.

The financial effects of five types of events warrant special disclosure and presentation on the income statement: (1) operating revenues and expenses, (2) other revenues and expenses, (3) disposals of business segments, (4) extraordinary items, and (5) changes in accounting principles.

Operating revenues and expenses refer to asset and liability inflows and outflows related to the acquisition and delivery of the goods or services provided by a company. These items are essential to the company's operations and occur frequently.

Other revenues and expenses are related to a company's secondary activities. The key feature about these items is that they are either not essential to the company's primary activity or occur infrequently.

A business segment is defined as a separate line of business, product line, or class of customer involving an operation that is independent from a company's other operations. If such a segment is disposed of, the income earned by the segment up to the time of disposal and the gain or loss on the disposal itself are disclosed separately on the income statement. Extraordinary items are both not essential to the company's primary operation and infrequent. The effect on income of a change in accounting principle is disclosed in three prominent places in the financial report: (1) the auditor's opinion letter to the shareholders, (2) the footnotes to the financial statements, and (3) as a separate line item at the bottom of the income statement.

5 Define intraperiod tax allocation, and explain how it relates to the income statement.

Federal income taxes are disclosed in two different ways on the income statement. The first income tax disclosure immediately follows net income from continuing operations (before tax). It represents the tax expense recognized by the company due to net operating income and other revenues and expenses.

The dollar amounts associated with the remaining items (disposal of business segments, extraordinary items, and changes in accounting principles) are all disclosed *net of tax*. Such presentation means that each of these revenue and expense items is disclosed on the income statement after the related income tax effect has been removed. The practice of including the income tax effect of a particular transaction with the transaction itself on the income statement is known as *intraperiod tax allocation*.

6 Describe how earnings per share are disclosed on the income statement.

Generally accepted accounting principles require that earnings per share be disclosed on the face of the income statement and that the specific amounts associated with (1) net income from continuing operations (after tax), (2) disposals of business segments, (3) extraordinary items, and (4) changes in accounting principles be disclosed separately. The calculation involves dividing the dollar amounts of each of the four items listed by the average number of shares outstanding during the accounting period.

KEY TERMS

Business segment (p. 690)

Capital-maintenance view (p. 679)

Capital transaction (p. 684)

Extraordinary item (p. 692)

Frequent transaction (p. 689)

Intraperiod tax allocation (p. 687)

Multistep format (p. 697)

Operating transaction (p. 684)

Prior period adjustment (p. 698)

Single-step format (p. 697)

Transaction (inflow/outflow) view (p. 680)

Usual transaction (p. 689)

QUESTIONS FOR DISCUSSION AND REVIEW

1. Why is the amount of income such an important number? Briefly explain how it is used by investors, creditors, and other interested parties.

2. Differentiate between the capital-maintenance view of income and the transaction view. Why is the transaction view used in present-day financial statements, and what is the difficulty associated with implementing the transaction view?

3. What is a capital transaction, and how does it differ from an operating transaction?

4. The text states that all transactions can be placed on a capital/operating continuum. List the five categories of transactions discussed in the chapter, and briefly explain why each is placed where it is on the capital/operating continuum.

5. Define the terms *usual* and *frequent* as they are used in the chapter. Provide an example of (a) a transaction that is both usual and frequent, (b) a transaction that is usual and infrequent, (c) a transaction that is unusual and frequent, and (d) a transaction that is unusual and infrequent.

6. Describe how transactions that fall into each of the four categories identified in (5) are presented on the income statement.

7. Explain the idea of intraperiod tax allocation. List the items that are disclosed net of tax on the income statement and statement of retained earnings.

8. How are earnings per share disclosed on the face of the income statement? Why is it done in this manner?

9. Define a business segment. What two items are disclosed on the income statement when a business segment is sold or discontinued?

10. What is an extraordinary item? Explain how a certain transaction entered into by one company might be considered extraordinary, while the same transaction entered into by another company might be considered as part of normal operations.

11. Is a change in an accounting principle/method inconsistent with the notion of consistency? If management wishes to change an accounting principle, of what must the auditors be convinced?

12. In what three places in the financial report can you find evidence that a company changed a major accounting principle?

13. How can dividing income into its components (i.e., income from operations, income from continuing operations, discontinued operations, extraordinary items, and

changes in accounting methods) give rise to economic consequences. State your answer in terms of the prices of a company's equity securities, its credit ratings, the contracts it has with its creditors, and management compensation systems.

14. Differentiate between the single-step and the multistep formats for the income statement.

15. List the items that are normally disclosed on the statement of retained earnings. Where is the statement of retained earnings found in the financial reports of many major U.S. companies?

16. What are prior period adjustments, and how are they disclosed in the financial statements?

EXERCISES

E14–1   *(Which statement is affected?)*   Listed below are transactions or items that are frequently reported in financial statements.

(1) Income effect due to changing from the double-declining-balance method to the straight-line method of depreciation.

(2) Collection of accounts receivable.

(3) Purchase an insurance policy on December 31 that provides coverage for the following year.

(4) Accrue a liability for wages earned by the employees.

(5) Estimate uncollectible accounts receivable using the aging method.

(6) Recognize a gain on the sale of plant equipment.

(7) Recognize a loss when the government expropriates land for a highway.

(8) Declare a property dividend valued at $100,000.

(9) Under the requirements of a debt covenant, appropriate a portion of retained earnings.

(10) Receive dividends on stocks held as an investment. The dividends were declared and paid on the same day.

(11) Recognize the cost of inventory sold during the year under the periodic method.

(12) Pay rent for the current year.

Required:

a. Indicate whether each item would be included on the company's income statement, statement of retained earnings, or neither, using the following codes:
   IS   Income statement
   SR   Statement of retained earnings
   N   Neither

b. Indicate whether the items you coded IS would be considered

   (1) usual and frequent,

   (2) unusual or infrequent,

   (3) unusual and infrequent, or

   (4) other.

E14–2   *(Capital or operating transactions?)*   A number of transactions are described below.

(1) Declaration of a stock dividend

(2) Purchase of 50 percent of the outstanding stock of another company

(3) Payment of previously accrued interest payable

(4) Accrual of interest expense

(5) Purchase of machinery

(6) Recognition of depreciation on machinery

(7) Purchase of treasury stock

(8) Sale of treasury stock at a price less than its original cost

(9) Conversion of debt to common stock

(10) Receipt of cash on an outstanding receivable

(11) Sale of inventory on account

(12) Purchase of inventory on account

(13) Declaration of dividends

(14) Receipt of dividends on short-term marketable securities

(15) Early retirement of outstanding long-term debt

Required:

a. Refer to Figure 14–5 in the text, and classify each transaction in one of the following categories.

(1) Exchanges with stockholders

(2) Exchanges of liabilities and stockholders' equity

(3) Issues and payments of debt

(4) Purchases, sales, and exchanges of nonoperating assets other than accounts receivable and inventory

(5) Operating transactions

b. Briefly explain why the transactions are considered increasingly operating (or decreasingly capital) as the categories move from 1 to 5.

E14–3 *(Debt covenants expressed in terms of income)* Worthy Manufacturing maintains a credit line with First Bank that allows the company to borrow up to $1 million. A covenant associated with the loan contract limits the company's dividends in any one year to 50 percent of net income. The 1990 income statement of Worthy Manufacturing is provided below.

Net sales	$840,000
Less: Cost of goods sold	570,000
Gross profit	270,000
Selling and administrative expenses	120,000
Net operating income	150,000
Gain on sale of securities	14,000
Interest expense	4,000
Net income from continuing operations before tax	160,000
Less: Income tax	51,200
Net income from continuing operations	108,800
Extraordinary gain (net of tax)	22,000
Net income before change in accounting principle	130,800
Income effect due to change in accounting principle	52,000
Net income	$182,800

Required:

a. Compute the maximum amount of dividends Worthy can pay if the debt covenant is expressed as 50 percent of each of the following:

(1) Net income

(2) Income before change in accounting principle

(3) Income before extraordinary items (from continuing operations)

(4) Net operating income

b. Explain why the bank may wish to state the contractual limitation on dividends in terms of income from operations instead of net income.

E14-4   *(The transaction and capital-maintenance views of income)*   The December 31, 1990 balance sheet of Mayheim Company is provided below.

Assets	$75,000	Liabilities	$20,000
		Stockholders' equity	55,000
		Total liabilities and	
Total assets	$75,000	stockholders equity	$75,000

During 1991 the company entered into the following transactions.

(1) Common stock was issued for $32,000 cash.

(2) Services were performed for $45,000 cash.

(3) Cash expenses of $24,000 were incurred.

(4) Long-term liabilities of $15,000 were paid.

(5) Dividends of $6000 were declared and paid.

Required:

a. Classify each transaction as operating or capital and then prepare an income statement under the transaction view.

b. Prepare an income statement under the capital-maintenance view.

c. What advantage does the transaction view have over the capital-maintenance view?

d. What is the difficulty associated with implementing the transaction view?

E14-5   *(Reconciling the transaction view and capital-maintenance view)*   The income statement for the year ended December 31, 1989, of Bentley Brothers follows.

Operating revenues	$35,000
Operating expenses	20,000
Net operating income	15,000
Loss on sale of marketable securities	3,000
Net income from continuing operations before tax	12,000
Less: Income tax	3,840
Net income from continuing operations	8,160
Extraordinary gain (net of tax)	6,000
Net income before change in accounting principle	14,160
Income effect due to change in accounting principle (net of tax)	8,000
Net income	$22,160

During 1989 Bentley issued common stock for $30,000. The company also declared and paid a $10,000 dividend. The book value of the company on January 1, 1989, was $50,000.

Required:

a. Compute the book value of Bentley Brothers as of December 31, 1989.

b. Provide an income statement under the capital-maintenance view.

E14-6   *(Disposal of a business segment)*   MTM Enterprises consists of four separate divisions: building products, chemicals, mining, and plastics. On March 15, 1989, MTM sold the chemicals division for $785,000 cash. Financial information related to the chemicals division follows.

(1/1/89–3/15/89)		(As of March 15, 1989)	
Sales	$145,000	Assets	$1,850,000
Operating expenses	160,000	Liabilities	1,200,000
Net operating income (loss)	$(15,000)		

Required:

a. Provide the journal entry (or entries) to record the sale of the chemicals division. Assume an income tax rate of 34 percent.

b. Prepare the section of MTM's 1989 income statement that relates to the disposal of the business segment.

E14–7

(Accounting for unusual losses) You are currently auditing the financial records of Paxson Corporation. During the current year, inventories with an original cost of $2,750,000 were destroyed by an earthquake. The company was unsure how to record this loss and is seeking your advice. The loss is deductible for tax purposes, and the company's tax rate is 34 percent.

Required:

a. Prepare the journal entry (or entries) to record the loss of the inventory if the loss is not considered extraordinary.

b. Prepare the journal entry (or entries) to record the loss of the inventory if the loss is considered extraordinary.

c. Should the loss be classified as an extraordinary loss or as an ordinary loss. Explain.

d. Would your answer to (c) change if the plant had been located in San Francisco? Explain.

E14–8

(Earnings-per-share disclosure) The following income statement was reported by Battery Builders for the year ending December 31, 1989.

Sales	$95,000	
Rent revenue	23,000	
Interest income	7,000	
Total revenues		$125,000
Cost of goods sold	52,000	
Operating expenses	24,000	
Interest expense	12,000	
Loss on sale of fixed asset	6,000	
Total expenses		94,000
Income from continuing operations (before tax)		31,000
Less: Income tax		10,000
Income from continuing operations		21,000
Income from disposed segment (net of tax)		3,000
Gain on sale of disposed segment (net of tax)		2,000
Income before extraordinary items		26,000
Extraordinary loss (net of tax)		7,000
Income before change in accounting principle		19,000
Income due to change in accounting principle (net of tax)		6,000
Net income		$ 25,000

Required: Show how Battery Builders would report earnings per share on the face of the income statement assuming the following:

a. An average of 5000 shares of common stock was outstanding during 1989.

b. An average of 10,000 shares of common stock was outstanding during 1989.

c. An average of 20,000 shares of common stock was outstanding during 1989.

E14-9

(Considering an item as extraordinary can have significant economic consequences) The managers of Elton Enterprises share in a bonus that is determined and paid at the end of each year. The amount of the bonus is defined by multiplying net income from continuing operations (after tax) by 10 percent. The bonus is not used in the calculation of income from continuing operations. During 1990 Elton was a defendant in a lawsuit and was required to pay $580,000 over and above the amount covered by insurance. The loss is tax deductible, and the company's tax rate is 34 percent. The company was last involved in a lawsuit five years ago. Net income from continuing operations (before tax), excluding the loss from the lawsuit, for 1990 was $850,000.

Required:

a. Compute management's 1990 bonus, assuming that the lawsuit is considered unusual but not infrequent.

b. Compute management's 1990 bonus, assuming that the lawsuit is considered extraordinary.

c. Repeat (a) and (b) above, assuming that Elton was awarded the $580,000 settlement instead of having to pay it.

d. Explain how the decision to include or not to include an item as extraordinary can have significant economic consequences.

E14-10

(Intraperiod tax allocation and the financial statements) The following information was taken from the financial records of Selmo Consolidated. All items below are pretax.

	Debit	Credit
Operating revenues		87,000
Operating expenses	32,500	
Gain on sale of marketable securities		5,200
Loss on sale of segment	21,000	
Income earned on disposed segment		3,000
Extraordinary loss	5,000	
Income due to change in accounting principle		12,500
Retained earnings (beginning balance)		72,000
Dividends declared	18,000	

The company's income tax rate is 34 percent, and the items above are treated identically for financial reporting and tax purposes.

Required: Prepare the following:

a. An income statement (single-step format).

b. A statement of retained earnings.

E14-11

(Intraperiod tax allocation) The following pretax amounts were obtained from the financial records of Watson Company for 1989.

	Debits	Credits
Retained earnings: 1/1/89		867,000
Sales revenue		1,375,000
Rent revenue		360,000
Cost of goods sold	495,000	
Administrative expenses	100,000	
Depreciation expense	250,000	
Selling expenses	189,000	
Extraordinary loss	202,000	
Loss on sale of fixed assets	105,000	
Dividends declared	450,000	

The company's tax rate is 34 percent.

Required:

a. Prepare an income statement for the year ended December 31, 1989, using the multi-step format.

b. Prepare a statement of retained earnings for the year ended December 31, 1989.

c. What is the income tax effect associated with each item that is reported net of tax? Assuming that no taxes were owed at the beginning of 1989 and no tax payments were made during 1989, what is the total income tax liability at the end of 1989?

PROBLEMS

P14–1   *(Classifying transactions as capital or operating)*   Pinkett Manufacturing produces and sells football equipment. The company was involved in the following transactions or events during 1990.

(1) The company purchased $250,000 worth of materials to be used during 1991 to manufacture helmets and shoulder pads.

(2) The company sold football equipment for a price of $500,000. The inventory associated with the sale cost the company $375,000.

(3) One of the company's plants in San Francisco was damaged by a minor earthquake. The total amount of the damage was $100,000.

(4) The company issued 10 ($1000 face value) bonds at a premium of 785.

(5) The company incurred $143,000 in wage expenses.

(6) The company was sued by a high school football player who was injured while using some of the company's equipment. The football player will probably win the suit, and the amount of the settlement has been estimated at $10,000. This is the sixth lawsuit filed against the company in the past three years.

(7) The company switched from the double-declining-balance depreciation method to the straight-line depreciation method.

(8) The company declared and paid $50,000 in dividends.

(9) The company incurred a loss when it sold some securities it was holding as an investment.

Required:

a. Classify each of these transactions as capital or operating.

b. Refer to Figures 14–5 and 14–6 in the text, and identify the category in which each of the items listed should be placed.

c. Which of these items should be included on the company's income statement? Briefly describe how they should be disclosed.

P14–2   *(Bonus contracts based on income can affect management's business decisions)*   The managers of Trader Supply House are paid a salary and share in a bonus that is determined at the end of each year. The total bonus is determined by multiplying the company's income from operations by 20 percent. The bonus is not considered an operating expense. Interest on borrowed funds is considered an operating expense when computing the bonus.

During 1990 the company decided to expand its plant facility. The estimated cost of the expansion was $1 million. To raise the necessary funds the company could either borrow $1 million at an annual interest rate of 10 percent or issue 50,000 shares of common stock at $20 each. The company raised the funds using one of these two methods, and income from operations (excluding any interest charges) for 1990 was reported as follows.

Operating revenues	$7,800,000
Operating expenses (excluding interest)	6,500,000
Income from operations	$1,300,000

Required:

a. Assume that on January 1, 1990, Trader Supply House borrowed the $1 million. Compute the total bonus shared by the company's managers.

b. Assume that on January 1, 1990, Trader Supply House issued common stock to raise the $1 million. Compute the total bonus shared by the company's managers.

c. Why might the management choose to issue equity instead of borrow the $1 million? Is such a decision necessarily in the best interest of the company's stockholders?

d. Repeat (a) and (b) above, assuming that interest expense is not considered an operating expense when computing the bonus.

P14-3   *(Capital-maintenance and transaction views of income)*   Raleigh Corporation began operations on February 10, 1990. During 1990 the company entered into the following transactions.

(1) Issued $100,000 of common stock and $25,000 of preferred stock.

(2) Performed services for $450,000.

(3) Issued $475,000 in long-term debt for cash.

(4) Incurred expenses: $125,000 for wages, $25,000 for supplies, $50,000 for depreciation, and $75,000 for miscellaneous expenses.

(5) Purchased fixed assets for $200,000 cash.

(6) Declared, but did not pay, cash dividends of $10,000.

(7) Purchased fixed assets in exchange for a long-term note valued at $100,000.

Required:

a. Classify each transaction as either an operating transaction or a capital transaction.

b. Prepare an income statement under the transaction view.

c. Prepare an income statement under the capital-maintenance view.

P14-4   *(Preparing an income statement from the adjusted trial balance)*   Excerpts from Crozier Industries' adjusted trial balance as of December 31, 1990 follow:

	Debit	Credit
Sales		987,000
Sales Returns	9,000	
Cost of Goods Sold	456,000	
Dividends	50,000	
Rent Expense	90,000	
Wage Payable		175,000
Loss on Sale of Food Services Division	2,000	
Loss Incurred by Food Services Division	10,000	
Depreciation Expense	100,000	
Cumulative Effect on Income of Change in Depreciation Methods	135,000	
Gain on Land Appropriated by the Government		97,000
Insurance Expense	12,000	
Inventory	576,000	
Administrative Expenses	109,000	
Prepaid Insurance	48,000	
Gain on Sale of Marketable Securities		142,000

The amounts shown do not include any tax effects. Crozier's tax rate is 34 percent.

Required:

a. Indicate which items should be included on the company's income statement. Classify each item to be included on the income statement as one of the following.
   (1) Usual and frequent
   (2) Unusual or infrequent
   (3) Disposal of business segment
   (4) Unusual and infrequent
   (5) Change in accounting method

b. Prepare an income statement with the single-step format.

P14-5

(Disclosing extraordinary items) In its 1989 financial report Anderson Company reported $750,000 under the line item "Extraordinary losses" on the income statement. The company's tax rate is 34 percent. The footnote pertaining to extraordinary losses indicates that the $750,000 loss, before tax, is comprised of the following items.

(1) A loss of $200,000 incurred on a warehouse in Florida damaged in a hurricane.

(2) A loss of $175,000 incurred when Anderson sold the assets of a business segment.

(3) A loss of $235,000 incurred when a warehouse in Iowa was blown up by a disgruntled employee.

(4) Accounts receivable written off in the amount of $50,000.

(5) A loss of $90,000 incurred when one of the company's distribution centers in Arizona was damaged by a flood.

Required:

a. Discuss how each of these items should be disclosed in the financial statements, including whether or not they should be disclosed net of tax.

b. Show how the "Extraordinary items" section of the income statement should have been reported.

P14-6

(Disclosing net of tax, and the earnings-per-share calculation) Woodland Farm Corporation has the following items to include in its financial statements.

	Debit	Credit
Extraordinary loss from a flood	250,000	
Extraordinary gain from bond retirement		55,000
Sales of inventory		250,000
Loss on disposal of business segment	100,000	
Income effect due to change in accounting method		80,000
Advertising expense	50,000	
Income earned by disposal of business segment		150,000

None of the listed amounts include any income tax effects. The company's tax rate is 34 percent.

Required:

a. Describe how each item above would be disclosed on the income statement or statement of retained earnings.

b. Compute the tax effect of each of the items that should be disclosed net of tax. What dollar amount would be shown on the financial statements for each of these items?

c. Assume that income from continuing operations (after tax) was $400,000, and 100,000 shares of common stock were outstanding during the year. Provide the earnings-per-share calculation.

P14–7

(Intraperiod tax allocation, income tax expense, and income tax liability) The following information has been obtained from the internal financial records of B, J & R Company.

Retained earnings, December 31, 1988	$1,259,000
Dividends declared and paid during 1989	100,000
Dividends declared during 1989 but not paid	75,000
Dividends declared during 1988 and paid in 1989	90,000
1989 income from continuing operations (before taxes)	850,000
Extraordinary losses in 1989 (before tax effect)	135,000

The company's tax rate is 34 percent. Assume that financial accounting income equals income for tax purposes.

Required:

a. What is the company's net income for the year ended December 31, 1989?

b. What is the total income tax expense of B, J & R Company for 1989? Show computations.

c. Prepare a statement of retained earnings for the year ended December 31, 1989.

d. Assume that the Income Tax Liability account had a zero balance on January 1, 1989, and that no income tax payments were made during 1989. What should be the balance in this account on December 31, 1989? Is this amount different than the amount from (b)? Why or why not?

P14–8

(Income effect due to a change in depreciation methods) On January 1, 1985, Glenn Corporation purchased some manufacturing equipment for $750,000. The equipment was estimated to have a salvage value of $50,000 and a useful life of ten years. The company used the straight-line method of depreciation for both book and tax purposes. On December 31, 1989, Glenn Corporation decided that it should use the double-declining-balance method for both book and tax purposes. The company's tax rate is 34 percent.

Required:

a. Compute depreciation expense and accumulated depreciation for 1985, 1986, 1987, and 1988 using both the straight-line method and the double-declining-balance method.

b. Prepare the journal entry (or entries) that would be recorded on December 31, 1989, to record the change from the straight-line method to the double-declining-balance method for both book and tax purposes.

c. Where and how on the financial statements would the income effect of this change be disclosed?

P14–9

(Examine the financial report of K mart Corporation) The following questions might be asked by an individual contemplating investing in or loaning money to a company.

a. Are comparative financial statements presented? For how many years are they presented?

b. Have any extraordinary items been reported recently? What were these items and what were the dollar amounts involved?

c. Has the company changed any accounting methods lately? If so, what were the changes?

d. Did the company report more than one type of revenue? If so, how many types? What was net revenue for the most recent year?

e. What was the total amount of dividends declared during the most recent year? What percentage of income is normally paid out in the form of dividends?

f. Did the company present cost of goods sold as a single line item or in a detailed format?

g. How many different types of expenses did the company report?

h. Have net income and income from continuing operations increased or decreased over the past few years?

i. Has the company disposed of any business segments recently?

j. Did the company experience any unusual or infrequent (but not both) events during the most recent year? What were these events?

k. Did the company have any restricted retained earnings as of the last day of the most recent year? What was the dollar amount?

l. What portion of earnings-per-share dollar amounts in the last three years was due to continuing operations, disposed business segments, extraordinary items, or changes in accounting methods?

Required: Examine the financial report of K mart Corporation in Appendix D of this textbook and answer the questions above.

P14-10 *(Preparing an income statement)* Tom Brown, controller of Microbiology Labs, informs you that the company has sold a segment of its business. Mr. Brown also provides you with the following information for 1989.

	Continuing Operations	Discontinued Segment
Sales	$10,000,000	$1,000,000
Cost of goods sold	2,500,000	600,000
Operating expenses	750,000	100,000
Loss on sale of office equipment	60,000	—
Gain on disposal of the assets of the discontinued segment		400,000

Additional Information

The following information is not reflected in any of the above amounts.

(1) Microbiology Labs is subject to a 34 percent tax rate.

(2) Microbiology Labs switched from the double-declining-balance method to the straight-line method of depreciation. The cumulative effect of this change on continuing operations, before taxes, is an increase of $250,000. The change had no effect on the discontinued operations.

(3) During 1989, Microbiology Labs retired outstanding bonds that were to mature in 1991. The company incurred a loss of $100,000, prior to taxes, on the retirement of the bonds.

(4) Microbiology Labs owns several apple orchards as part of its operations. During 1989 the company's apple crop was destroyed by an infestation of a rare insect. This unusual and infrequent loss, prior to taxes, totaled $800,000.

(5) 1 million shares of common stock were outstanding throughout 1989.

Required: Prepare an income statement for the year ended December 31, 1989, using the multistep format, including the recommended earnings-per-share disclosures.

P14-11 *(Comprehensive problem)* Laidig Industries has prepared the following unadjusted trial balance as of December 31, 1989.

	Debit	**Credit**
Cash	100,000	
Accounts Receivable	350,000	
Allowance for Doubtful Accounts		50,000
Inventory (balance 1/1/89)	467,000	
Prepaid Insurance	60,000	
Fixed Assets	890,000	
Accumulated Depreciation		267,000
Accounts Payable		195,000
Dividends Payable		50,000
Bonds Payable		500,000
Common Stock		100,000
Retained Earnings		673,000
Sales		1,276,000
Gain on Sale of Land		76,000
Extraordinary Loss	32,000	
Income Effect due to Change in Accounting Principle	23,000	
Purchases	750,000	
Administrative Expenses	100,000	
Selling Expenses	255,000	
Interest Expense	25,000	
Dividends	135,000	

Additional Information

(1) A physical count of inventory on December 31, 1989, indicated that the company had $510,000 of inventory on hand.

(2) An aging of accounts receivable indicates that $105,000 is uncollectable.

(3) The company uses straight-line depreciation. The assets have a ten-year life and zero salvage value.

(4) The company used a third of the remaining insurance policy during 1989.

(5) The company pays interest for its bond payable on January 1 of every year. The coupon rate and the effective rate are both 10 percent annum.

(6) The company's tax rate is 34 percent. All income tax charges are recorded at the end of the year.

(7) 500,000 shares of common stock were outstanding during 1989.

Required: Prepare the following:

a. The necessary adjusting, and closing entries on December 31, 1989.

b. An income statement (single-step format), including recommended earnings per share disclosures.

c. A statement of retained earnings.

CASES

C14–1

(Public earnings announcements) The Wall Street Journal disclosed that Atlantic Richfield Company (ARCO) reported record earnings for 1988.* Financial analysts were surprised that earnings were so high and claimed it was the result of a restructuring program begun in 1985, which was not well received at the time. One analyst claimed: "They have been vindicated."

*Frederick Rose, "Arco's earnings set a record; Amoco falls", *The Wall Street Journal*, 24 January 1989, p. PC10.

Required:

a. Why are such announcements made in publications like *The Wall Street Journal?*
b. What effect on the price of ARCO's common stock would you expect from the earnings announcement above? Why?
c. The announcement above refers to the bottom-line net income number reported by ARCO. What additional questions about ARCO's income would an interested investor or creditor have? Why?

C14–2

(Capital-maintenance and transaction views of income) Scott Paper Company is the world's leading manufacturer of tissue paper products. In its December 31, 1987 financial statements, the following was reported (dollars in millions).

	1987	1986
Assets	$4,480.5	$3,939.4
Liabilities	2,906.2	2,580.1
Stockholders' equity	1,574.3	1,359.3

Assume the company issued common stock for $18.8 million during 1987 and declared no dividends.

Required:

a. Compute net income for 1987 under the capital-maintenance view.
b. If the company had *decreased* its common stock outstanding by $12 million (instead of increasing it by $18.8 million), would the net income number you computed in (a) be larger or smaller? By how much?
c. Briefly describe the transaction view of income, and explain why it is used instead of the capital-maintenance view. What problems are associated with implementing the transaction view?

C14–3

(Income statement disclosure and capital/operating transactions) PacifiCorp is a diversified electric utility that derives some of its $2.2 billion in annual revenue from nonelectric sources.

Required:

a. In what section of the income statement would you expect the revenue from nonelectric sources to be disclosed? Support your answer in terms of the usual (or unusual) and frequent (or infrequent) nature of the revenue.
b. In its 1987 annual report, PacifiCorp stated that over $486 million was expended for construction of new facilities and investments in other companies. Would these expenditures be considered capital or operating transactions? Why?
c. Briefly describe the difference between capital and operating transactions, and indicate the category in which the expenditures described in (b) would be placed on the capital/operating continuum in Figure 14–5.

C14–4

(Changing accounting principles/methods) In 1987 General Electric changed its method of accounting for inventories, which increased that year's income by $496 million, reduced by additional income taxes of $215 million.

Required:

a. Provide the two journal entries prepared by General Electric to record the change in inventory method and the related income tax effect.
b. What dollar amount of gain due to the accounting change was reported on the income statement by the company?
c. Where on the income statement was this amount disclosed and in what other places in the financial report could additional information about the change be found?

d. Briefly discuss some of the pros and cons, from management's viewpoint, of changing from one accounting method to another.

C14-5   *(Extraordinary losses)*   Weyerhaeuser Company is principally engaged in the growing and harvesting of timber and the manufacture, distribution, and sale of forest products. When Mount St. Helens, a volcano located in Washington State, erupted in May of 1980, 68,000 acres of the company's standing timber, logs, buildings, and equipment were destroyed. As a result, the company recognized a $36 million (net of tax) extraordinary loss on its income statement.

Required:

a. What must have been true for Weyerhaeuser to classify this event as *extraordinary?*
b. If Mount St. Helens continues to erupt periodically, would future related losses necessarily be classified by Weyerhaeuser as extraordinary? Why or why not?
c. At the time of the eruption, Weyerhaeuser's income tax rate was approximately 48 percent. Compute the entire loss (ignoring the tax effect) incurred by the company and provide the journal entries prepared by the company's accountants to record the loss and the related income tax effect.

C14-6   *(Disclosing nonoperating items on the income statement)*   During 1983 PepsiCo's earnings either rose or fell, depending upon the source of the information. Standard & Poor's reported that PepsiCo experienced a 25 percent earnings gain while Value Line, another investor service, reported that PepsiCo experienced a 7 percent loss. The discrepancy involved a "normal but nonrecurring charge" taken by PepsiCo to write down foreign bottling assets. Standard & Poor's ignored the charge in its earning calculation, while Value Line included the charge.

Required:

a. Provide reasonable arguments that could have been used by Standard & Poor's and Value Line to support the decision either to ignore or include the charge in the calculation of PepsiCo's income.
b. Briefly describe the categories comprising a complete income statement and explain how such charges are usually disclosed.
c. *Forbes* (21 May 1984) reports that "most financial analysts [are not concerned about] the geographic location of such items on the income statement." It is only important that they be disclosed. Explain why financial analysts might take such a position; at the same time, however provide an argument suggesting that the specific location of an item on the income statement is important in an economic sense. State your argument in terms of how income numbers are used in contracts.

The Statement of Cash Flows

Learning Objectives

1 Describe the basic structure and format of the statement of cash flows.

2 Define cash flows from operating, investing, and financing activities.

3 Explain how the statement of cash flows complements the other financial statements and how it can be used by those interested in the financial condition of a company.

4 Identify the important investing and financing transactions that do not appear on the statement of cash flows.

5 Describe the economic consequences associated with the statement of cash flows.

6 Prepare a statement of cash flows from the original journal entries and Cash account in the ledger under both the direct and indirect methods.

7 Convert accrual numbers, which appear on the income statement, to cash flow numbers.

8 Express the statement of cash flows in terms of the basic accounting equation, and understand how to prepare a statement of cash flows from the information contained in two balance sheets, an income statement, and a statement of retained earnings.

≣ The statement of cash flows contains a summary of the transactions entered into by a company over a period of time that involve the Cash account. It is designed to highlight the cash flows associated with three aspects of the company's economic activities: (1) operations, (2) investments, and (3) financing. The basic structure of the statement of cash flows is provided in Figure 15–1. The reported numbers were taken from the 1987 financial report of Amoco Corporation.

Recall that the statement of cash flows has already been presented and briefly discussed. Chapter 1 introduced the statement and provided an example. Chapter 2 discussed the basic nature of the statement and related it to the income statement, balance sheet, and statement of retained earnings. Chapters 3 and 4 briefly explained how a statement of cash flows can be prepared from the cash account in the ledger, and the appendix to Chapter 4 showed how an income statement can be converted to the operating section of the statement of cash flows. Consequently, you have already been exposed to the fundamentals of the statement of cash flows. This chapter provides a more complete discussion of the nature of the statement, how it can be used, and how it is prepared.

The statement of cash flows is a relatively new addition to the set of financial accounting statements required under generally accepted accounting principles. It was established as a standard of financial reporting in 1987 when the Financial Accounting Standards Board decided (in FASB Statement No. 95, *Statement of Cash Flows*) to modify the statement of changes in financial position, which had been required since 1971.[1] Many companies, such as Polaroid, Coca-Cola Enterprises, and Monsanto, immediately adopted the new standard and included a statement of cash flows in their 1987 financial reports. Others, such as Procter & Gamble, Eastman Kodak, and Goodyear Tire and Rubber, waited until 1988, when the standard officially became a requirement.

THE DEFINITION OF CASH

Chapter 6 of this text defines cash for purposes of balance sheet disclosure, and points out that it consists of coin, currency, and available funds on deposit at the bank. Negotiable instruments like money orders, certified checks, cashiers' checks, personal checks, and bank drafts are also considered cash. The total of these items as of the balance sheet date is the cash amount that appears on the balance sheet.

When preparing the statement of cash flows, companies commonly consider as cash the items already mentioned as well as certain **cash equivalents,** which include commercial paper and other debt investments with maturities of less than three months.[2] They do so because these items can be converted to cash immediately; for all intents and purposes, at a particular point in time they are virtually the same as cash. In the remainder of this chapter, where we illustrate the statement of cash flows, we will also treat cash equivalents as cash. The following excerpt, which represents a typical description of these cash equivalents, is from the 1987 financial report of Time Inc.: "Cash Equivalents. Cash equivalents consist of

---

1. Financial Accounting Standards Board, Statement of Financial Accounting Standard No. 95, *The Statement of Cash Flows,* (Stamford, Conn.: FASB, 1987).

2. Some corporations, like McDonnell Douglas, Eli Lilly and Walt Disney, also include short-term investments, such as marketable securities, in the definition of cash for purposes of the statement of cash flows. Such a practice is acceptable under generally accepted accounting principles because marketable securities, by definition, are highly liquid.

Figure 15–1   Sample statement of cash flows

Amoco Corporation Statement of Cash Flows For the Year Ended December 31, 1987 (in millions)	
Cash provided (used) by operating activities	$ 4,012
Cash provided (used) by investing activities	(1,985)
Cash provided (used) by financing activities	(952)
Increase (decrease) in cash	1,075
Cash—beginning of year	441
Cash—end of year	$ 1,516
Source: 1987 annual report.	

commercial paper and other investments that are readily convertible into cash, and generally have original maturities of three months or less."

A GENERAL DESCRIPTION OF THE STATEMENT OF CASH FLOWS

In Figure 15–2 the statement of cash flows is described in terms of the other financial statements. It explains the change in the cash balance from one balance sheet date to the next. A similar figure appears in Chapter 2 (Figure 2–15) and is described there.

Figure 15–3 illustrates the statement of cash flows more completely. This statement is divided into three sections (operating activities, investing activities, and financing activities) and shows the cash inflow and outflow categories that normally comprise each section.

Cash Provided (Used) by Operating Activities

Cash provided (used) by **operating activities** includes those cash inflows and outflows associated directly with the acquisition and sale of the company's inventories and services. This category includes the cash receipts from sales and accounts receivable as well as cash payments for the purchase of inventories, payments on accounts payable, selling and administrative activities, and interest and taxes. In general, the items appearing in this section also appear on the income statement. Keep in mind, however, that the dollar amounts associated with these items on the statement of cash flows usually differ from those on the income statement, which is prepared on an accrual basis.

The Direct Method
The statement of cash flows illustrated in Figure 15–3 was prepared using the **direct method.** It is so called because the computation of cash provided (used) by operating activities ($930) consists of cash inflows and outflows that can be traced *directly* to the Cash account in the ledger. For example, the $7000 collected

Figure 15–2   Interrelationships among the financial statements

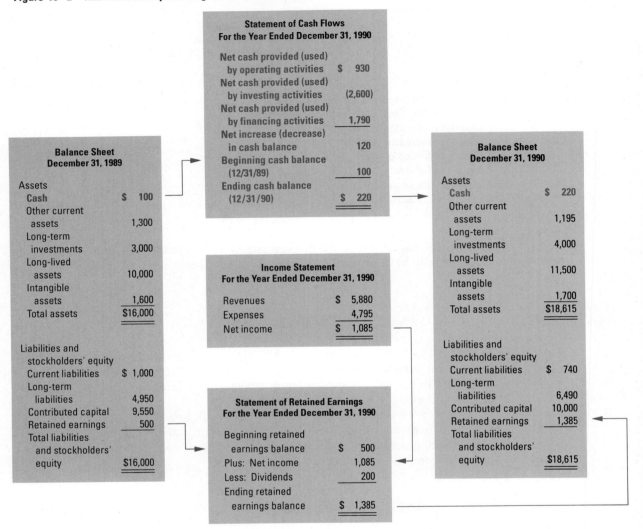

from customers, the $5200 paid for operations, and the $870 used for other operating items all represent aggregate totals of journal entries that were initially recorded in the journal and posted to the Cash account in the ledger.

The Indirect Method

Another method of computing and disclosing cash provided (used) by operating activities that is acceptable under GAAP is called the **indirect method.** Under this method, cash provided (used) by operating activities is computed *indirectly,* by beginning with the net income figure, which appears on the income statement, and adjusting it for the differences between cash flows and accruals. The indirect method of computing cash from operating activities is illustrated in Figure 15–4.

In general, items added back to net income in the computation of cash provided (used) by operating activities (e.g., depreciation, amortization, book losses,

Figure 15-3   Standard statement of cash flows

XYZ Corporation
Statement of Cash Flows
For the Year Ended December 31, 1990

Operating activities		
Cash received from customers	$ 7,000	
Cash paid for operations (suppliers, employees, and others)	(5,200)	
Cash provided (used) by other operating items	(870)	
Net cash provided (used) by operating activities		$ 930
Investing activities		
Cash outflows from the purchase of noncurrent assets	(3,000)	
Cash inflows from sale of noncurrent assets	400	
Net cash provided (used) by investing activities		(2,600)
Financing activities		
Cash inflows from borrowings	3,000	
Cash inflows from stock issuances	2,000	
Cash outflows from debt retirements	(1,460)	
Cash outflows from treasury stock purchases	(1,550)	
Cash outflows from dividend payments	(200)	
Net cash provided (used) by financing activities		1,790
Net increase (decrease) in cash and cash equivalents		120
Cash and cash equivalents at the beginning of the year		100
Cash and cash equivalents at the end of the year		$ 220

and accrued expenses) decrease net income on the income statement, but involve no cash outflows. Items subtracted from net income in this computation (e.g., accounts receivable and inventory buildups, and the recognition of deferred revenues) increase net income on the income statement, but involve no cash inflows. Note also that these adjustments are separated into two categories: (1) noncash charges to the noncurrent accounts and (2) changes in current accounts. The first category includes depreciation and amortization charges as well as book gains and losses recognized on the transfer of long-term assets and liabilities. The second category includes the changes during the period in the current asset and current liability accounts other than cash. On the statements of cash flows prepared by major U.S. companies, the net effects of the adjustments in this second category are often combined into a single number.

The adjustments to net income are explained and illustrated more completely in the appendix to Chapter 4, where we convert an accrual-based income statement to the operating section of the statement of cash flows. We also review these adjustments and the indirect method later in this chapter.

Both the direct and the indirect methods result in the same dollar amount ($930) for cash provided (used) by operating activities; in that respect, they simply represent two different forms of presentation. In fact, when the FASB made the statement of cash flows a requirement, it allowed either the direct or the indirect method. If the direct method is chosen, however, the FASB requires that it be accompanied by a schedule of the adjustments that reconcile net income to cash provided (used) by operating activities. This schedule can appear either in the footnotes to the financial statements or on the face of the statement itself. Since

Figure 15–4   Cash from operating activities: indirect method

Operating activities		
Net income		$1,085
Noncash charges to noncurrent accounts		
Depreciation, amortization, and other noncash charges on		
noncurrent items	$ 400	
Book losses	50	
Book gains	(450)	0
Changes in current accounts other than cash		
Net decreases (increases) in current assets	105	
Net increases (decreases) in current liabilities	(260)	(155)
Net cash provided (used) by operating activities		$ 930

the adjustments on this schedule are the same as those disclosed under the indirect method, the direct method (including the accompanying schedule) discloses more about the changes in the Cash account than the indirect method. To encourage increased disclosure and what the FASB believes to be a more straightforward presentation, it has recommended that companies use the direct method. However, the vast majority of major U.S. companies choose not to follow this recommendation; they use the indirect method probably because it requires fewer disclosures and is less costly to prepare.

Cash Provided (Used) by Investing Activities

Cash provided (used) by **investing activities** includes the cash inflows and outflows associated with the purchase and sale of a company's noncurrent assets. This section includes the cash effects from purchases and sales of long-term investments, long-lived assets, and intangible assets. The statement of cash flows in Figure 15–3, for example, shows that $3000 were used to purchase such items, and $400 were collected from selling noncurrent assets. These cash inflows and outflows can all be traced to entries to the Cash account in the company's ledger.

Cash Provided (Used) by Financing Activities

Cash provided (used) by **financing activities** includes cash inflows and outflows associated with a company's two sources of outside capital: liabilities and contributed capital. This category primarily includes the cash inflows associated with borrowings and equity issuances as well as the cash outflows related to debt repayments, treasury stock purchases, and dividend payments. The statement of cash flows in Figure 15–3 shows that the company borrowed $3000, raised $2000 by issuing stock, made principal payments on debt in the amount of $1460, used $1550 to purchase treasury stock, and paid cash dividends of $200. These cash flows can also be traced to the Cash account in the company's ledger.

Note also that the cash payments associated with interest on the company's outstanding debt are not included in this section, even though they represent a cost of financing. Instead, such payments are included in the operating section of the statement of cash flows. This practice might be questioned because it confuses the distinction between financing and operating activities. Perhaps the FASB chose to classify interest payments as operating activities to preserve the correspondence between the items on the income statement and those comprising the operating section of the statement of cash flows.

Figure 15–5 shows the statement of cash flows, prepared using the direct method, that appears in the 1987 financial report of MCI Communications Corporation. It is followed by a schedule that reconciles net income to the amount of cash provided (used) by operating activities, which was disclosed in the footnotes to the financial statements.

Figure 15–5   Example of statement of cash flows: direct method

<table>
<tr><td colspan="2" align="center">**MCI Communications Corporation**
Statement of Cash Flows
For the Year Ended December 31, 1987
(in millions)</td></tr>
<tr><td>Operating activities</td><td></td></tr>
<tr><td> Cash received from customers</td><td>$3,926</td></tr>
<tr><td> Cash paid to suppliers and employees</td><td>(3,287)</td></tr>
<tr><td> Interest paid</td><td>(131)</td></tr>
<tr><td> Antitrust settlements</td><td>15</td></tr>
<tr><td>Cash provided (used) by operating activities</td><td>523</td></tr>
<tr><td>Investing activities</td><td></td></tr>
<tr><td> Cash outflow for communications system</td><td>(578)</td></tr>
<tr><td> Proceeds from sale of assets</td><td>216</td></tr>
<tr><td>Cash provided (used) by investing activities</td><td>(362)</td></tr>
<tr><td>Financing activities*</td><td></td></tr>
<tr><td> Increases in long-term debt</td><td>209</td></tr>
<tr><td> Retirement of debt</td><td>(210)</td></tr>
<tr><td> Issuance of common stock</td><td>14</td></tr>
<tr><td> Purchase of treasury stock</td><td>(11)</td></tr>
<tr><td>Cash provided (used) by financing activities</td><td>2</td></tr>
<tr><td>Net increase (decrease) in cash and cash equivalents</td><td>163</td></tr>
<tr><td>Cash and cash equivalents at the beginning of the year</td><td>216</td></tr>
<tr><td>Cash and cash equivalents at end of year</td><td>$ 379</td></tr>
<tr><td>**Reconciliation of Net Income to**
Cash from Operating Activities</td><td></td></tr>
<tr><td>Net income</td><td>$88</td></tr>
<tr><td>Adjustments to net income</td><td></td></tr>
<tr><td> Depreciation and amortization</td><td>518</td></tr>
<tr><td> Loss on early retirement of debt</td><td>18</td></tr>
<tr><td> Gain on sale of assets</td><td>(3)</td></tr>
<tr><td> Gain on antitrust settlement</td><td>(24)</td></tr>
<tr><td> Net change in operating accounts other than cash and cash equivalents</td><td>(74)</td></tr>
<tr><td>Cash provided (used) by operating activities</td><td>$ 523</td></tr>
</table>

*MCI's 1987 financial report states: "MCI has not paid dividends on its common stock and has no present plans to do so."

Source: 1987 annual report.

Figure 15–6   Six kinds of useful information

MEASUREMENT BASIS	TYPE OF TRANSACTION		
	Operating	Investing	Financing
Cash	1 (SCF)	2 (SCF)	3 (SCF)
Accrual	4 (IS/BS)	5 (BS)	6 (BS)

SCF = Statement of cash flows   IS = Income statement   BS = Balance sheet

HOW THE STATEMENT OF CASH FLOWS COMPLEMENTS THE INCOME STATEMENT AND BALANCE SHEET

On several occasions we have discussed the important distinction between operating and capital (investing and financing) transactions, and how information about these two activities is useful to investors, creditors, and other interested parties. We also pointed out the usefulness of information prepared on both the accrual and cash basis. As Figure 15–6 illustrates, combining the three types of transactions (operating, investing, and financing) with the two measurement bases (accrual and cash) gives rise to six kinds of potentially useful information.

The income statement provides a summary of a company's operating transactions on an accrual basis (Cell 4). The balance sheet represents the accumulated accruals of the company's operating, investing, and financing transactions as of a particular point in time (Cells 4, 5, and 6). Comparing two balance sheets at different points of time can provide an indication of the company's investing and financing activities during the intervening time period (Cells 5 and 6).

Note that the income statement and balance sheet do not appear in Cells 1, 2, or 3 because these statements indicate little about the cash effects of the company's operating, investing, and financing activities. The statement of cash flows is designed to fill this void. Professor Loyd Heath, whose writings did much to motivate the development of the statement of cash flows, describes it as being *complementary* to the income statement and balance sheet, "reporting a different type of information."[3]

The FASB's move to require the statement of cash flows was primarily a response to a perceived lack of what many considered to be important and useful cash flow information. Diana Kahn, project manager for the FASB, said, "Cash flow is one of the best measures of corporate liquidity," and Pat McConnell, associate director of a major securities firm, commented that the FASB's decision to require the statement of cash flows "will generally be a boon for financial analysts who want to know more about the current cash position of the companies they cover."[4]

---

3. Loyd Heath, "Let's Scrap the Funds Statement," *The Journal of Accounting* (October 1978), pp. 94–103.
4. Lee Berton, "FASB Rule Requires Public Companies to Issue Annual Cash-Flow Statements," *The Wall Street Journal,* 23 November 1987, p. 10.

OF CASH FLOWS CAN BE USED

tement of cash flows is used primarily to assess performance in two basic
1) a company's ability to generate cash and (2) the effectiveness of a com-
cash management. The ability to generate cash is determined by the
1 of the company's operating activities as well as its **financial flexibility,**
reflects the company's capacity to borrow, issue equity, and sell nonoper-
sets (e.g., investments). During 1987, for example, Alcoa generated $1.1
hrough its operating activities, which was sufficient to finance $237 mil-
additional investments as well as reduce a sizable portion of its outstanding
olgate-Palmolive Company, on the other hand, only generated $34 mil-
ough its operations but had enough financial flexibility to finance its $195
expansion by reducing its cash balance and increasing its borrowings.
ive cash management requires that two competing objectives be bal-
n one hand, cash must be available to meet debts as they come due. That
ncy must be maintained. On the other hand, cash must be invested in
ve assets that provide returns. Sources of cash include the sale of inven-
d services, borrowings, equity issuances, and the selling of long-term assets. Uses of cash include purchasing and manufacturing inventories, selling and
administrative costs, debt interest and principal payments, purchasing long-term
assets, purchasing treasury stock, and dividend payments. Effective cash management involves managing these cash sources and uses in a way that provides a
high return without bearing too great a risk of insolvency.

The statement of cash flows provides information about a company's ability to
generate cash and the effectiveness of its cash management by (1) explaining the
change in the cash balance, (2) summarizing the cash effects of operating transactions, and (3) summarizing the cash effects of capital (investing and financing)
transactions.

Explaining the Change in the Cash Balance

It is important for investors, creditors, and other interested parties to know where
a company gets its cash, what it does with its cash, and whether the cash sources
can generate enough in the future to meet existing and future obligations. For example, what portion of a company's cash is generated through operations, the
sale of investments, or debt and equity issuances? Similarly, what portion of a
company's cash payments go toward supporting operations, repayments on debt,
and dividends? Answers to these kinds of questions can provide an overview of a
company's ability to generate cash as well as its cash management policies.

To illustrate, Table 15−1 contains a summary of the statements of cash flows
reported by seventeen major U.S. companies at the end of 1987. Included are the
cash effects of operating activities, investing activities, and financing activities as
well as the net income number and the net change in the cash balance for 1987.
It also indicates whether a company used the direct or indirect method of presentation.

Note first that all of the corporations listed, except MCI, used the indirect
method of presentation. Note also that for most companies (twelve of seventeen)
cash from operations exceeded net income, in several cases by quite a large
amount. For example, cash from operations exceeded net income for Alcoa,

Table 15–1   Summarized statements of cash flows (dollars in millions)

Company	Net Income	Cash from Operations	Cash from Investments	Cash from Financing	Net Cash Change	Method (Dir/Ind)
Alcoa	$ 200	$1,115	$ (237)	$ (936)	$ (58)	Ind
Amoco	1,360	4,012	(1,985)	(952)	1,075	Ind
Apple Computers	217	188	(121)	(77)	(10)	Ind
Colgate-Palmolive	54	34	(195)	52	(109)	Ind
Coca-Cola Enterprises	88	299	(546)	(249)	(496)	Ind
DuPont	1,786	4,139	(2,853)	(1,114)	172	Ind
Eli Lilly & Co.	410	795	196	(492)	499	Ind
Gillette Company	230	213	(217)	29	25	Ind
J. C. Penney Co.	569	733	(359)	(901)	(527)	Ind
McDonnell Douglas	313	85	(505)	385	(35)	Ind
MCI Communications	88	523	(362)	2	163	Dir
Monsanto	436	902	(489)	(464)	(51)	Ind
New York Times Co.	160	262	(328)	115	49	Ind
Polaroid Corp.	116	150	(113)	15	52	Ind
Ralston Purina Co.	526	439	354	(894)	(101)	Ind
Sears, Roebuck & Co.	1,650	5,800	(6,066)	87	(179)	Ind
Time, Inc.	250	492	(535)	(137)	(180)	Ind

Source: 1987 annual reports.

Amoco, DuPont, and Sears by $915 million, $2.6 billion, $2.4 billion, and $4.2 billion, respectively. In general, such differences arise because noncash expenses, such as depreciation, amortization, and other write-offs, are quite large for many companies.

All of the corporations listed in Table 15–1 show a positive dollar value for cash from operations, and all but two show negative dollar values under cash from investments. In other words, most of these companies are expanding their operations by purchasing noncurrent assets and using operating cash, at least partially, to finance it. Eli Lilly and the Ralston Purina Company, the only two companies to show net cash inflows from investing activities, sold major sections of their businesses during 1987. Ralston Purina sold its restaurant operations, and Eli Lilly sold its cosmetic segment, Elizabeth Arden, Inc.

In general, it appears that all the companies listed in Table 15–1 are financially strong and, as already noted, most of them are expanding. However, three relatively distinct categories are evident with respect to how these companies financed their expansion during 1987: (1) Alcoa, Amoco, Apple, DuPont, J. C. Penney, and Monsanto generated enough cash through operations to finance their expansion and reduce their outstanding debts, (2) Gillette, MCI, Polaroid, and Sears, Roebuck & Co. generated enough cash through operations to finance their expansion, but they did not reduce their outstanding debts, and (3) Coca-Cola, Colgate-Palmolive, McDonnell Douglas, The New York Times Company, and Time, Inc. did not generate enough cash through operations to finance their expansion and were required to either borrow or reduce their available cash balances.

Summarizing the Cash Effects of Operating Transactions

The amount of cash generated through operating activities is very important to financial statement users because the successful sale of a company's services or inventories is a prerequisite for a successful business. Also, while cash from operations can vary from one year to the next, operating activities, by definition, are normal and expected to reoccur. Consequently, positive net cash flows from operations, especially across several periods of time, can indicate financial strength. As Table 15–1 shows, operations are a major source of cash for successful companies.

It is generally desirable to finance asset purchases and debt payments with cash generated from operations. Companies able to follow such a strategy consistently tend to have higher credit ratings and are generally viewed as financially more stable than those unable to do so. DuPont, for example, one of the ten largest companies in the world with a AAA credit rating, commented in its 1987 financial report: "Cash provided by operations in 1987 was $4.1 billion, [which was] used to finance the company's capital expenditures (over $3 billion), repurchase 1,968,000 shares of the company's common stock ($172 million), reduce borrowings ($198 million), and pay dividends ($802 million)."

The management of AT&T, the largest communications company in the world, stated in its 1987 financial report: "Strong cash flow from operations during 1987 permitted us to continue efforts toward increased financial flexibility. We redeemed $830 million of preferred stock and retired $417 million of long-term debt. Our external financing was limited to $343 million. Consequently, for the second consecutive year, we have reduced our utilization of external sources of financing."

Keep in mind also that cash provided (used) by operating activities and net income both represent measures of a company's operating performance. It is important to realize that neither measure is better than the other. They provide information that addresses different aspects of financial performance. The accrual basis, which underlies the income statement, measures revenues and expenses in terms of asset and liability flows, which in turn give rise to a relatively long-run measure of a company's earning power. Cash provided (used) by operating activities, on the other hand, has a more short-run orientation, providing an indication of a company's current ability to produce cash from operations that can be used to purchase assets, pay debts, pay dividends, or purchase treasury stock. Both aspects of financial performance are necessary for a company's success; thus, both are relevant to investors, creditors, managers, auditors, and other interested parties. Indeed, a company's long-run performance is important, but it is equally important to realize that long-run performance results from a series of successful short-run decisions.

Summarizing the Cash Effects of Capital Transactions

The investment and financing transactions entered into by a company during a given period can be very important to those interested in a company's economic condition and financial future. The statement of cash flows is the only financial statement that directly provides such information. It allows one to assess, for example, changes in a company's investment policies, indicating the kind of assets in which the company is investing and how these investments affect the company's cash balance.

Similarly, the magnitude and direction of any changes in a company's capital structure are indicated by the statement of cash flows. Is the company relying more on debt or equity financing? Is there a move toward long- or short-term debt? Are the company's investments consistent with the changes in the company's capital structure? Are long-term investments, for example, being financed with short-term debt? Each of these management decisions can have significant effects on a company's future cash flows; accordingly, answers to these kinds of questions can provide an indication of its financial future. Just as a company must operate successfully, it must also develop a strong capital base to support those operations.

The 1987 statement of cash flows of Chrysler Corporation, for example, indicates that the company pursued an aggressive program of expansion during the year. This program involved the purchase of American Motors Corporation ($741 million), the purchase of Electrospace Systems, Inc. ($371.7 million), and expenditures for long-lived assets and special tools of over $1.9 billion. These expenditures were financed primarily through operations, the issuance of common stock, long-term borrowings, and available cash. During 1987 Chrysler's total assets increased by almost 40 percent to $19.9 billion, while its total liabilities increased by over 40 percent to $13.3 billion.

Significant Noncash Transactions Must be Disclosed

The statement of cash flows includes only those transactions that directly affect the Cash account. Many important transactions, however, neither increase nor decrease Cash and, as a result, are excluded from the face of the statement. For example, the purchase of a long-lived asset in exchange for a long-term note payable can be a significant capital transaction, yet, as illustrated by the journal entry below, it has no effect on the Cash account.

Equipment	20,000	
Note Payable		20,000
To record the purchase of equipment financed with a long-term note.		

Similarly, the acquisition of land, the payment of a debt with common stock, and the declaration of a dividend are capital transactions that are not found on the statement of cash flows.

These kinds of capital transactions can be very important to a company's financial condition, and the FASB requires in its standard on cash flows that they be described clearly in the footnotes to the financial statements. It is important that such information be accessible to readers who are interested in examining the financing and investment activities of a company.

For example, in 1986 MCI Communications Corporation acquired Satellite Business Systems (SBS) and selected other assets from IBM. In exchange, MCI issued common stock and signed a note payable. No cash was exchanged in the transaction and, accordingly, neither the acquired assets nor the increases in the Common Stock and Notes Payable accounts appeared on the 1986 statement of

Figure 15-7 Disclosing significant noncash transactions

MCI Communications Corporation Excerpt Following Statement of Cash Flows For the Year Ended December 31, 1986	
Acquisition of SBS (in millions)	
Common stock issued to acquired SBS	$ 376
Communications systems acquired	(428)
Other assets acquired	(52)
Current obligations assumed	104
Cash outflow to acquire SBS	$ 0
Source: 1986 annual report.	

cash flows. However, the transaction was important enough to warrant disclosure, and MCI reported it as shown in Figure 15-7, directly below the statement of cash flows in its 1986 financial report.

Important operating transactions that do not affect cash, like the sale or purchase of inventory on account, also do not appear directly on the statement of cash flows. However, the existence of such transactions can be determined by analyzing the adjustments that reconcile net income with cash flows provided (used) by operating activities. Such adjustments are discussed and illustrated later in the chapter.

THE STATEMENT OF CASH FLOWS: ECONOMIC CONSEQUENCES

The economic consequences associated with the statement of cash flows result primarily from the fact that investors, creditors, and other interested parties use it to assess the investment potential and creditworthiness of companies and the equity and debt securities they issue. *Forbes* magazine reports that "many people feel that cash flow information is important and in some cases even more important than net income."[5] In another article *Forbes* commented that "a number of stock advisers are basing their work in part on cash flow," and that "an investor who ignores cash flow in picking stocks is being deprived of one of the most valuable tools in an arsenal." Furthermore, many writers have claimed that had investors relied more heavily on cash flow numbers, instead of working capital and the current ratio, famous bankruptcies, like W. T. Grant, Penn Central, Sambo's Restaurants, AM International, and Wickes might have been foreseen earlier.[6]

The increasing importance of cash flow information to investors and creditors creates incentives for management to **window dress** the statement of cash flows. Such incentives can be troublesome because in the short run it is relatively easy for management to present a favorable cash position. Delaying payments on short-term payables, for example, can significantly boost the amount of cash pro-

---

5. Richard Greene, "The Missing Number," *Forbes*, 18 June 1984, p. 123.
6. Richard Greene and Paul Bornstein, "A Better Yardstick," *Forbes*, 27 September 1982, pp. 66, 69.

vided (used) by operating activities. Selling investments, even if it is not in the stockholders' long-run interests, can increase cash inflows from investing activities, while delaying debt payments, and dividends can inflate cash from financing activities. Accounting Professors Edward Swanson and Richard Vangermeersch, for example, have stated that "the possibilities for manipulating the cash provided by operations figure, as well as other sources and uses of cash, are endless."[7]

Consequently, those who use the statement of cash flows must be careful not to place too much importance on the cash flows of a particular period, which can be manipulated. However, such manipulation is much less effective when statements are viewed across several periods because payments that are delayed in one period must normally be paid in the next. For this reason the FASB requires that cash flow statements from at least the previous three years be disclosed in the financial report.

From management's standpoint, it is also important to realize that decisions designed to manipulate the disclosures on the statement of cash flows are often counterproductive. While such decisions may improve the appearance of a company's cash position in the current period, in addition to often being unethical they can (1) represent poor business decisions, (2) make the cash position of the company look worse in the future, (3) reduce the credibility of the company and its financial reports in the eyes of investors, creditors, and other interested parties and, if fraudulent, (4) expose management to future lawsuits. Accordingly, the company's external auditors, who are also responsible to financial statement users, must be on the lookout for such manipulations.

An additional economic consequence associated with the statement of cash flows is that, in general, it has raised the record-keeping costs of major U.S. corporations. *The Wall Street Journal* reported that "the FASB rule [requiring cash flow statements] forces many big corporations to issue statements based only on their cash transactions, which will likely raise their financial record-keeping costs."[8] As suggested earlier, such costs may explain why most large U.S. companies use the indirect method of presentation, which requires fewer disclosures than the direct method, and does not require that operating cash flows be traced back to the entries in the Cash account in the ledger.

THE MECHANICS OF PREPARING THE STATEMENT OF CASH FLOWS

The remainder of this chapter is devoted primarily to the mechanics of preparing the statement of cash flows. We provide a set of basic data and then prepare the statement, using both the direct and indirect methods, and using two different procedures. The first procedure assumes that we have access to the original journal entries and that they are not too numerous to analyze individually. The statement of cash flows is then prepared by tracing the effect of each transaction on the Cash account in the ledger. While this procedure is often impractical in real-world settings, it does highlight the source of each of the dollar amounts on the statement of cash flows.

7. Edward P. Swanson and Richard Vangermeersch, "Correspondence Relating to 'Let's Scrap the Funds Statement'," *The Journal of Accountancy* (December, 1979), pp. 88–97.

8. Lee Berton, "FASB Rule Requires Public Companies to Issue Annual Cash-Flow Statements," *The Wall Street Journal*, 23 November 1987, p. 10.

The second procedure invokes the more realistic assumption that the original journal entries are too numerous to analyze individually and that it is impractical to prepare the statement of cash flows from entries in the Cash account in the ledger. We are, therefore, forced to derive the numbers on the statement of cash flows from the information contained in two balance sheets, the income statement, and the statement of retained earnings. Here we explain the change in the Cash balance by analyzing the changes in the other account balances.

We have chosen to illustrate these two procedures to emphasize that the statement of cash flows can be prepared from information at several different points in the accounting cycle (i.e., journal entries, ledger, and final statements). Both procedures produce the same result, and to the extent that you understand both, you will better appreciate the nature of the statement as well as how it relates to the other financial statements.

An Example: Basic Data for ABC Enterprises

The basic data consists of a balance sheet as of December 31, 1990 (Figure 15–8), a set of journal entries that reflect the activities during 1991 (Figure 15–9), a ledger that contains the account balances and posted journal entries (Figure 15–10), and an income statement, statement of retained earnings and balance sheet, which were prepared as of December 31, 1991 (Figure 15–11).

Review the basic data thoroughly. It provides a review of the procedures involved in preparing an income statement, statement of retained earnings, and balance sheet. Once you have examined these statements and are familiar with the transactions contained in the illustrations, it should be much easier to understand the procedures involved in preparing the statement of cash flows.

The cash balance on the December 31, 1990 balance sheet of ABC Enterprises, Inc. is $8000. The other current assets, land, partially depreciated machinery, and patent comprise the remaining assets, bringing the asset total to $58,000. Current liabilities, notes payable issued at a discount, common stock, additional paid-in-capital, and retained earnings, reduced by the treasury stock, constitute the equity side of the balance sheet.

Figure 15–9 contains a record of the transactions (1–16), adjusting journal entries (17–23), and closing journal entries (24–26) recorded by ABC during the period 1991. Note that each transaction is accompanied by a brief description. Review each transaction and make sure that you understand the associated journal entry.

Now that you have reviewed each of the journal entries, note that the general ledger is contained in Figure 15–10. The beginning balance (as of December 31, 1990) for each balance sheet account is contained in the ledger, and each journal entry has been posted in the appropriate T-account. The numbers appearing in front of each ledger entry correspond to the numbers of the journal entries. Trace the accounts involved in each journal entry to the T-accounts in the general ledger.

At this point the preparation of the income statement, statement of retained earnings, and balance sheet is relatively straightforward, and these statements are contained in Figure 15–11. The income statement is simply prepared from Journal Entry 24, which closes the revenue and expense accounts to the income summary. The statement of retained earnings is prepared from the Retained Earnings

Figure 15–8   Balance sheet for ABC Enterprises

ABC Enterprises, Inc. Balance Sheet December 31, 1990			
Assets			
Cash		$ 8,000	
Accounts receivable	$12,000		
Less: Allowance for bad debts	1,000	11,000	
Inventory		3,000	
Prepaid insurance		2,000	
Total current assets			$24,000
Land		20,000	
Machinery	8,000		
Less: Accumulated depreciation	2,000	6,000	
Patent		8,000	
Total noncurrent assets			34,000
Total assets			$58,000
Liabilities and Stockholders' Equity			
Accounts payable		$12,000	
Accrued payables		1,500	
Income taxes payable		500	
Payments in advance		3,000	
Dividends payable		1,000	
Total current liabilities			$18,000
Notes payable	$25,000		
Less: Discount	2,000		
Total long-term liabilities			23,000
Common stock (1,000 sh × $10 par)		10,000	
Additional paid-in capital		2,000	
Retained earnings		6,000	
Less: Treasury stock		1,000	
Total stockholders' equity			17,000
Total liabilities and stockholders' equity			$58,000

T-account in the general ledger. Note that both stock and cash dividends are included on the statement. The final balances in the permanent accounts (asset, liability, and stockholders' equity accounts) make up the balance sheet. The balance sheet in Figure 15–11 is dated December 31, 1991, one year after the balance sheet provided in Figure 15–8.

Focusing on Individual Transactions

As indicated earlier, the statement of cash flows can be prepared using either the direct or the indirect method. We first illustrate the direct method and then the indirect method.

Figure 15–9   General journal entries during 1991 for ABC Enterprises

(1) Issued 1,000 shares of $10 par value capital stock for $15 per share.

Cash (1,000 shares × $15)	15,000	
Common Stock (1,000 shares × $10)		10,000
Additional Paid-in Capital		5,000

(2) Purchased building (20-year life) in exchange for 2000 shares of common stock. The fair market value of the shares at the time of the purchase was $15 per share.*

Building (2,000 shares × $15)	30,000	
Common Stock (2,000 shares × $10)		20,000
Additional Paid-in Capital		10,000

    *The building is valued on the balance sheet at the fair market value of the stock ($15 per share) exchanged for it.

(3) Paid accrued payables and income taxes payable (see balance sheet).

Accrued Payables	1,500	
Income Taxes Payable	500	
Cash		2,000

(4) Paid dividend liability (see balance sheet).

Dividend Payable	1,000	
Cash		1,000

(5) Purchased inventory on account.

Inventory	12,000	
Accounts payable		12,000

(6) Sold inventory which cost $11,000 for $32,000 ($22,000 on account and $10,000 for cash). ABC uses the perpetual inventory method.

a. Cash	10,000	
Accounts Receivable	22,000	
Sales		32,000
b. Cost of Goods Sold	11,000	
Inventory		11,000

(7) Paid miscellaneous expenses (e.g., salaries, rent, utilities) and estimated income taxes.

Miscellaneous Expenses	8,000	
Income Tax Expense	1,000	
Cash		9,000

(8) Sold partially-depreciated machinery (no depreciation taken in year of sale). The original cost of the machinery was $2,000, and accumulated depreciation equaled $500.

Cash	1,400	
Accumulated Depreciation (Machinery)	500	
Loss on Sale of Machinery	100	
Machinery		2,000

(9) Received payments on outstanding accounts receivable.

Cash	10,000	
Accounts Receivable		10,000

Figure 15-9 (continued)

(10) Paid some accounts payable.

Accounts Payable	15,000	
Cash		15,000

(11) Acknowledged and wrote off an $800 bad debt.

Allowance for Bad Debts	800	
Accounts Receivable		800

(12) Purchased land for cash.

Land	10,000	
Cash		10,000

(13) Sold treasury stock, which originally cost $1,000, for $1,300.

Cash	1,300	
Treasury Stock		1,000
Additional Paid-in Capital (T/S)		300

(14) Declared cash dividends.

Cash Dividends	3,000	
Dividends Payable		3,000

(15) Issued a 5% stock dividend (4,000 shares outstanding, fair market value = $20 per share).

Stock dividends ([4,000 × 5%] × $20)	4,000	
Common Stock ([4,000 × 5%] × $10 par)		2,000
Additional Paid-in Capital		2,000

(16) Paid $2,800 ($1,000 principal and $1,800 interest) on the last day of the period for an outstanding note payable. Also amortized the discount. The annual interest rate on the note is 8% on a principal of $25,000.

Notes Payable	1,000	
Interest Expense ($25,000 × 8%)	2,000	
Discount on Notes Payable		200
Cash		2,800

Adjusting Journal Entries at end of 1991

(17) Accrued miscellaneous expenses and income taxes.

Miscellaneous Expenses	3,000	
Accrued Payables		3,000
Income Tax Expense	200	
Income Taxes Payable		200

(18) Depreciated machinery ($6,000 ÷ 6-year life).

Depreciation Expense (Machinery)	1,000	
Accumulated Depreciation (Machinery)		1,000

Figure 15–9   (continued)

(19) Depreciated building ($30,000 ÷ 20-year life).

Depreciation Expense (Building)	1,500	
Accumulated Depreciation (Building)		1,500

(20) Amortized patent ($20,000 ÷ 10-year life).

Amortization Expense (Patent)	2,000	
Patent		2,000

(21) Amortized prepaid insurance ($3,000 ÷ 3-year life).

Insurance Expense	1,000	
Prepaid Insurance		1,000

(22) Provided services on payments in advance (see balance sheet).

Payments in Advance	3,000	
Fees Earned		3,000

(23) Estimated bad debts ($22,000 [credit sales] × 5%).

Bad Debt Expense	1,100	
Allowance for Bad Debts		1,100

Closing Entries at end of 1991

(24) Closed revenue and expense accounts into income summary.

Sales	32,000	
Fees Earned	3,000	
Loss on Sale of Machinery		100
Cost of Goods Sold		11,000
Miscellaneous Expenses		11,000
Interest Expense		2,000
Depreciation Expense (Machinery)		1,000
Depreciation Expense (Building)		1,500
Amortization Expense (Patent)		2,000
Insurance Expense		1,000
Bad Debt Expense		1,100
Income Tax Expense		1,200
Income Summary		3,100

(25) Closed income summary into retained earnings.

Income Summary	3,100	
Retained earnings		3,100

(26) Closed dividend accounts into retained earnings.

Retained Earnings	7,000	
Cash Dividends		3,000
Stock Dividends		4,000

Figure 15–10　General Ledger

Cash			
	8,000		
(1)	15,000	2,000	(3)
(6)	10,000	1,000	(4)
(8)	1,400	9,000	(7)
(9)	10,000	15,000	(10)
(13)	1,300	10,000	(12)
		2,800	(16)
	5,900		

Accounts Receivable			
	12,000		
(6)	22,000	10,000	(9)
		800	(11)
	23,200		

Allowance for Bad Debts			
		1,000	
(11)	800	1,100	(23)
		1,300	

Inventory			
	3,000		
(5)	12,000	11,000	(6)
	4,000		

Prepaid Insurance			
	2000	1000	(21)
	1000		

Land		
	20,000	
(12)	10,000	
	30,000	

Machinery			
	8000		
		2000	(8)
	6000		

Accumulated Depreciation (Machinery)			
		2000	
(8)	500	1000	(18)
		2500	

Building		
(2)	30,000	
	30,000	

Accumulated Depreciation (Building)		
		1,500 (19)
		1,500

Patent		
	8,000	
		2,000 (20)
	6,000	

Accounts Payable			
		12,000	
		12,000	(5)
(10)	15,000		
		9,000	

Accrued Payables			
		1500	
(3)	1500	3000	(17)
		3000	

Payments in Advance		
		3000
(22)	3000	
		0

Income Taxes Payable			
		500	
(3)	500	200	(17)
		200	

Dividends Payable			
		1000	
(4)	1000	3000	(14)
		3000	

Notes Payable		
		25,000
(16)	1,000	
		24,000

Discount on Notes Payable		
	2000	
		200 (16)
	1800	

Common Stock		
		10,000
		10,000 (1)
		20,000 (2)
		2,000 (15)
		42,000

Additional Paid-in Capital		
		2,000
		5,000 (1)
		10,000 (2)
		300 (13)
		2,000 (15)
		19,300

Figure 15–10 (continued)

Treasury Stock			Retained Earnings		
1000				6000	
	1000	(13)		3100	(25)
0			(26) 7000		
				2100	

Sales			Fees Earned		
	32,000	(6)		3000	(22)
(24) 32,000			(24) 3000		
	0			0	

Cost of Goods Sold			Miscellaneous Expenses		
(6) 11,000	11,000	(24)	(7) 8000		
0			(17) 3000	11,000 (24)	
			0		

Depreciation Expense (Machinery)			Depreciation Expense (Building)		
(18) 1000	1000	(24)	(19) 1500	1500	(24)
0			0		

Insurance Expense			Amortization Expense (Patent)		
(21) 1000	1000	(24)	(20) 2000	2000	(24)
0			0		

Bad Debt Expense			Interest Expense			Loss on Sale of Machinery		
(23) 1100	1100	(24)	(16) 2000	2000	(24)	(8) 100	100	(24)
0			0			0		

Stock Dividends			Cash Dividends			Income Summary			Income Tax Expense		
(15) 4000	4000	(26)	(14) 3000	3000	(26)	(25) 3100	3100	(24)	(7) 1000		
0			0			0			(17) 200	1200	(24)
									0		

The Direct Method

Under the direct method, all three sections of the statement of cash flows (operating, investing and financing) are prepared *directly* from the Cash account in the ledger. The process involves three basic steps: (1) the cash inflows and outflows, which were originally entered as debits and credits in the Cash account, are identified, (2) each cash flow is classified as resulting from an operating, investing, or financing transaction, and (3) the cash flows are placed in the appropriate sections of the statement of cash flows.

Identifying Cash Inflows and Outflows.

Refer to the general ledger in Figure 15–10, and note the transactions that affected the Cash account during 1991. They include Transactions (1), (3), (4), (6), (7), (8), (9), (10), (12), (13), and (16). Tracing through the left side of the cash T-account, we see cash sources from (1) the issuance of stock ($15,000), (6) the sale of inventory ($10,000), (8) the sale of machinery ($1400), (9) receipts from accounts receivable payments ($10,000), and (13) the sale of treasury stock ($1300). The right side of the T-account con-

Figure 15–11   Financial statements for ABC Enterprises

ABC Enterprises, Inc.
Income Statement
For the Year Ended December 31, 1991

Sales		$ 32,000
Fees earned		3,000
Cost of goods sold		(11,000)
Gross profit		24,000
Operating expenses		
Miscellaneous expenses	$11,000	
Insurance expense	1,000	
Bad debt expense	1,100	
Depreciation expense (machinery)	1,000	
Depreciation expense (building)	1,500	
Amortization of patent	2,000	17,600
Net operating income		6,400
Nonoperating revenues and expenses		
Loss on sale of machinery	100	
Interest expense	2,000	2,100
Net income from continuing operations before taxes		4,300
Less: Income tax expense		1,200
Net income		$ 3,100

ABC Enterprises, Inc.
Statement of Retained Earnings
For the Year Ended December 31, 1991

Beginning retained earnings balance		$ 6,000
Plus: Net income		3,100
Less: Cash dividends	$3,000	
Stock dividends	4,000	7,000
Ending retained earnings balance		$ 2,100

tains entries that represent cash payments for (3) accrued and income tax payables ($2000), (4) dividends ($1000), (7) miscellaneous and tax expenses ($9000), (10) accounts payable ($15,000), (12) the purchase of land ($10,000), and (16) interest and principal on the outstanding loan ($2800). All of these transactions affect the Cash account and therefore appear on the statement of cash flows.

Classifying Cash Flows as Operating, Investing or Financing. Figure 15–12 describes each of the transactions that affect the Cash account and explains why it is classified as an operating, investing, or financing activity.

Preparing the Statement of Cash Flows. The statement of cash flows can be prepared now by placing each transaction in the appropriate section of the statement. The final statement of cash flows appears in Figure 15–13.

Figure 15–11   (continued)

ABC Enterprises, Inc. Balance Sheet For the Year Ended December 31, 1991			
Assets			
Cash		$ 5,900	
Accounts receivable	$23,200		
Less: Allowance for bad debts	1,300	21,900	
Inventory		4,000	
Prepaid insurance		1,000	
Total current assets			$ 32,800
Land		30,000	
Machinery	6,000		
Less: Accumulated depreciation	2,500	3,500	
Building	30,000		
Less: Accumulated depreciation	1,500	28,500	
Patent		6,000	
Total noncurrent assets			68,000
Total assets			$100,800
Liabilities and Stockholders' Equity			
Accounts payable		$ 9,000	
Accrued payables		3,000	
Income taxes payable		200	
Dividends payable		3,000	
Total current liabilities			$ 15,200
Notes payable	24,000		
Less: Discount	1,800	22,200	
Total long-term liabilities			22,200
Common stock (4,200 sh × $10 par)		42,000	
Additional paid-in capital		19,300	
Retained earnings		2,100	
Total stockholders' equity			63,400
Total liabilities and stockholders' equity			$100,800

Note that each item on the statement is followed by a number in parenthesis, which refers to the related transaction, journal, and ledger entry in the example. These numbers typically do not appear on the statement of cash flows; they are included to help you trace the origin of each item.

Note also that significant noncash transactions, such as the purchase of a building for stock in Transaction (2), do not appear on the statement of cash flows. No cash is exchanged in this transaction; therefore, it is not reflected on the statement. As indicated earlier, professional accounting standards require that such transactions, if material, be clearly disclosed in the footnotes to the financial statements because they reflect both a significant investment and a significant financing decision. Issuing stock for a building is essentially equivalent to issuing stock for cash ($30,000) and then using the cash to purchase the building. Such transactions are normally disclosed in a separate schedule in the footnotes to the financial statements.

Figure 15–12 Classifying transactions as operating, investing, or financing

Journal Entry	Description and Explanation	Amount and Classification
(1)	Cash is received for common stock. An equity issuance is an outside source of capital.	$15,000 financing cash source
(3)	Cash payment for payables. Taxes and accrued payables arise from operating activities.	$ 2,000 operating cash use
(4)	Cash payment for dividends. Dividends are a return of capital to the equity investors.	$ 1,000 financing cash use
(6)	Cash receipts from sales of inventory. Inventory sales, by definition, are operating activities.	$10,000 operating cash source
(7)	Cash payments for salaries, rent, utilities and taxes—all operating expenses.	$ 9,000 operating cash use
(8)	Cash receipt from sale of machinery. Long-lived assets are not sold as part of operations. Such assets make operating activities possible.	$ 1,400 investing cash source
(9)	Cash receipts from accounts receivable. Accounts receivable relate to previous sales.	$10,000 operating cash source
(10)	Cash payments on accounts payable. Accounts payable relate to previous inventory purchases.	$15,000 operating cash use
(12)	Cash payment on land purchase. Land is an investment.	$10,000 investing cash use
(13)	Sale of treasury stock. Treasury stock was originally issued as capital stock, a source of outside capital.	$ 1,300 financing cash source
(16)	Cash payment for interest and principal on note payable. Interest ($1800) is an operating expense and the principal payment ($1000) is a return to outside sources of capital.	$ 1,800 operating cash use $ 1,000 financing cash use

In addition, we have not yet provided a schedule that explains the differences between net income and cash provided (used) by operating activities. Such a schedule, which under the direct method would have to be clearly disclosed in the financial report, consists of the same adjustments that appear on the statement of cash flows prepared under the indirect method which is discussed below.

The Indirect Method

Figure 15–14 contains a statement of cash flows prepared under the indirect method. In many ways it is exactly the same as the statement of cash flows (direct method) in Figure 15–13. The dollar amount of cash provided (used) by operating activities is the same (−$7800), and the sections devoted to investing and financing activities are equivalent. The only difference between the two methods involves the way in which cash provided (used) by operating activities is computed.

Figure 15–13   Statement of cash flows: direct method

ABC Enterprises, Inc.		
Statement of Cash Flows		
For the Year Ended December 31, 1991		
Operating activities		
Cash collections from sales and accounts receivable (6 and 9)	$ 20,000	
Cash paid to suppliers (10)	(15,000)	
Cash paid on miscellaneous expenses and taxes payable (3 and 7)	(11,000)	
Cash paid for interest (16)	(1,800)	
Net cash provided (used) by operating activities		$ (7,800)
Investing activities		
Purchase of land (12)	(10,000)	
Sale of machinery (8)	1,400	
Net cash provided (used) by investing activities		(8,600)
Financing activities		
Proceeds from issuing equity (1)	15,000	
Proceeds from the sale of treasury stock (13)	1,300	
Cash dividends (4)	(1,000)	
Principal payment on outstanding note payable (16)	(1,000)	
Net cash provided (used) by financing activities		14,300
Net increase (decrease) in cash balance		(2,100)
Beginning cash balance		8,000
Ending cash balance		$ 5,900

Under the indirect method, cash provided (used) by operating activities (−$7800) is computed by adjusting net income ($3100), which appears on the income statement, for the timing differences between operating accruals and cash flows. As indicated earlier in the chapter, these adjustments are classified into two categories: (1) noncash charges to noncurrent accounts (e.g., depreciation, amortization, book losses and gains) and (2) changes in current accounts other than Cash (e.g., Accounts Receivable, Inventory, Accounts Payable, Income Tax and Miscellaneous Accruals, Payments in Advance, and Prepaid Insurance). Finally, although not indicated in Figure 15–14, significant noncash transactions would also have to be disclosed clearly in the financial report under the indirect method.

Explaining the Difference Between Net Income and Cash Provided (Used) by Operating Activities

The difference between net income and cash provided (used) by operating activities must be explained under either the direct or the indirect method. Under the direct method, the required adjustments must be included in a separate schedule; under the indirect method, such adjustments appear on the face of the statement. This section explains how these adjustments are determined using the journal entries in Figure 15–9. The adjustments themselves appear in Figure 15–14 in the operating section of the statement of cash flows prepared under the indirect method.

Figure 15-14   Statement of cash flows: indirect method

ABC Enterprises, Inc. Statement of Cash Flows For the Year Ended December 31, 1991			
Operating activities			
Net income		$ 3,100	
Noncash charges to noncurrent accounts			
Depreciation of machinery	$ 1,000		
Depreciation of building	1,500		
Amortization of patent	2,000		
Loss on sale of machinery	100		
Decrease in discount on notes payable	200	4,800	
Changes in current accounts other than cash			
Increase in net accounts receivable	(10,900)		
Increase in inventory	(1,000)		
Decrease in accounts payable	(3,000)		
Increase in miscellaneous expenses and taxes payable	1,200		
Decrease in payments in advance	(3,000)		
Decrease in prepaid insurance	1,000	(15,700)	
Net cash provided (used) by operating activities			$ (7,800)
Investing activities			
Purchase of land		(10,000)	
Sale of machinery		1,400	
Net cash provided (used) by investing activities			(8,600)
Financing activities			
Proceeds from issuing equity		15,000	
Proceeds from the sale of treasury stock		1,300	
Cash dividends to stockholders		(1,000)	
Principal payment on outstanding note payable		(1,000)	
Net cash provided (used) by financing activities			14,300
Net increase (decrease) in cash balance			(2,100)
Beginning cash balance			8,000
Ending cash balance			$ 5,900

Consider first the adjustments that add the depreciation of machinery ($1000), the depreciation of building ($1500), and the amortization of patent ($2000) to net income. In each case an expense was recognized on the income statement that served to decrease net income, but no cash was paid. Refer to Adjusting Journal Entries (18), (19), and (20) in Figure 15-9. The dollar amounts associated with these items, therefore, are added back to net income in the computation of cash provided (used) by operating activities.

Similarly, the loss on the sale of machinery ($100) and the decrease in the discount on the notes payable ($200) are added back to net income. Both represent items that decrease net income but involve no cash outflow. Journal Entry (8) shows that a loss was recognized on a transaction that actually increased cash by $1400, which is indicated in the investing section of the statement. In Journal Entry (16) the amortization of the discount served to increase interest expense from

$1800, which reflects the cash outflow for interest, to $2000. Note also that while book losses and the amortization of discounts are added back to net income in the computation of cash provided (used) by operating activities, book gains and the amortization of premiums are deducted from net income.

Journal Entry (6a) indicates that sales of $32,000 were recognized during the period, and Adjusting Journal Entry (23) indicates that $1100 of these sales were not expected to produce cash. These amounts were disclosed on the income statement and increased net income by a net amount of $30,900 ($32,000 − $1100). However, the sales transaction (6a) only generated $10,000 in cash. Later, when other outstanding receivables were collected (Journal Entry [9]), another $10,000 was generated. In total, therefore, $20,000 were received during the period from inventory sales that occurred either in the current or previous periods. As a result, $10,900 ($30,900 − $20,000) must be subtracted from net income in the computation of cash provided (used) by operating activities. This $10,900 adjustment corresponds to the increase in the balance of net accounts receivable (accounts receivable less allowance for uncollectibles).

Journal Entry (6b) indicates that a cost of goods sold of $11,000 was recognized during the period, which in turn appeared on the income statement and reduced net income. Journal entry (10), which reflects payments on accounts payable, indicates that $15,000 in cash was actually paid for inventory purchases that occurred either in the current or previous periods. Thus, $4000 ($15,000 − $11,000) must be subtracted from net income in the computation of cash provided (used) by operating activities. The addition of the adjustments for the increase in Inventory ($1000) and the decrease in Accounts Payable ($3,000) in Figure 15−14 represent this $4000 adjustment.

Journal Entries (3), (7), and (17) together indicate that tax and miscellaneous expenses of $12,200 ($9000 + $3000 + $200) were recognized during the period, while only $11,000 ($2000 + $9000) were actually paid. Consequently, $1200 ($12,200 − $11,000) were added back to net income in the computation of cash provided (used) by operating activities.

The adjustment for payments in advance ($3000) represents a case where net income was increased during the period, but no cash was received. Adjusting Journal Entry (22) shows that fees earned of $3000 were recognized with no corresponding cash increase. The cash was collected in an earlier period when payments in advance were initially recognized. Accordingly, $3000 are deducted from net income on the statement of cash flows in Figure 15−14.

The $1000 amortization of prepaid insurance (Journal Entry [21]) reduced net income during the period and, similar to other cases of amortization (e.g., long-lived asset depreciation, intangible asset amortization, and amortization of discounts), is added back to net income in the computation of cash provided (used) by operating activities.

The Direct and Indirect Methods: A Reconciliation

The adjustments to reconcile net income with cash provided (used) by operating activities can be viewed as the adjustments necessary to convert an accrual-based income statement to the operating section of the statement of cash flows prepared under the direct method. Such a reconciliation is provided in Figure 15−15. The column on the left represents the income statement (Figure 15−11). The adjustments in the middle can be found on the statement of cash flows prepared under

Figure 15-15   Converting an income statement to a statement of operating cash flows

Income Statement		Adjustments		Operating Cash Flows: Direct Method
Sales	$32,000			
Bad debt expense	(1,100)			
	30,900	Less: Increase in net accounts receivable	$10,900	$20,000
Fees earned	3,000	Less: Decrease in payments in advance	3,000	0
Cost of goods sold	(11,000)	Plus: Increase in inventory	1,000	
		Decrease in accounts payable	3,000	(15,000)
Misc. expenses and tax expense	(12,200)	Less: Net increase in misc. expenses and taxes payable	1,200	(11,000)
Insurance expense	(1,000)	Less: Decrease in prepaid insurance	1,000	0
Depreciation Machinery Building	(1,000) (1,500)	Plus: Add back (no cash effect)	2,500	0
Amortization Patent	(2,000)	Plus: Add back (no cash effect)	2,000	0
Loss on sale of machinery	(100)	Plus: Add back (no cash effect)	100	0
Interest expense	(2,000)	Less: Amortization of discount	200	(1,800)
Net income	$ 3,100	Cash provided (used) by operating activities		$ (7,800)

the indirect method (Figure 15-14). The column on the right represents operating cash flows presented under the direct method (Figure 15-13).

Note that the adjustments required to convert the revenues and expenses on the income statement to operating cash inflows and outflows are expressed in terms of changes in the related balance sheet accounts. The adjustment to sales, for example, is related to the change during the period in the net balance of Accounts Receivable. The adjustment to Fees Earned is expressed in terms of the change in the Payments in Advance account, while the adjustment to Cost of Goods Sold is related to the change in both Inventory and Accounts Payable. Although not indicated in Figure 15-15, the adjustments to depreciation, amortization, and the book loss can all be expressed in terms of changes in such accounts as Accumulated Depreciation, Machinery, and Patent. The main point is that every revenue and expense account is related to one or more accounts on the balance sheet, and that the changes in these balance sheet accounts during a period can be used to determine the corresponding cash inflows and outflows. A more complete discussion of these kinds of adjustments is contained in the following section.

PREPARING THE STATEMENT OF CASH FLOWS FROM TWO BALANCE SHEETS, AN INCOME STATEMENT, AND A STATEMENT OF RETAINED EARNINGS

In the preceding section we prepared the statement of cash flows by focusing on the cash effects of the individual transactions of the period. This section demonstrates how the statement of cash flows can be prepared when the analysis of individual transactions is either impractical or, in some cases, impossible. We show that the statement can be prepared primarily from the information contained in two balance sheets, the income statement, and the statement of retained earnings. This method is followed by most companies and the resulting statements of cash flow are the same as those that result from using the first procedure (see Figures 15–13 and 15–14).

We explain this method by first showing that the change in the cash account during a given period can be explained in terms of changes in the balances of the other accounts on the balance sheet. We then illustrate the procedure using the information contained in the December 31, 1990 balance sheet (Figure 15–8) and the December 31, 1991 financial statements (Figure 15–11) of ABC Enterprises.

Changes in the Cash Account in Terms of Changes in the Other Balance Sheet Accounts

The statement of cash flows can be viewed as one way of explaining how the balance sheet at the beginning of a particular period became the balance sheet at the end of that period. It focuses on Cash, a specific balance sheet account, and consists of a series of line items that summarize how changes in the Cash account can be explained in terms of changes in the other balance sheet accounts.

Recall the basic accounting equation (assets = liabilities + stockholders' equity), which can be stated as follows.

$$A = L + SE$$

Total assets can be divided into cash and noncash assets, and stockholders' equity consists of contributed capital and retained earnings. The accounting equation, therefore, can also be expressed as follows. That is, cash (C) plus noncash assets (NA) is equal to liabilities (L) plus contributed capital (CC), plus retained earnings (RE).

$$C + NA = L + CC + RE$$

Liabilities (L) can be separated into current liabilities (CL) and long-term liabilities (LTL), and noncash assets (NA) can be separated into current noncash assets (CNA) and long-term noncash assets $(LTNA)$. Thus, the equation becomes

$$C + CNA + LTNA = CL + LTL + CC + RE$$

This equation can be rearranged and expressed in terms of cash by adding $-CNA$ and $-LTNA$ to both sides. As a result, cash (C) equals current liabilities (CL), plus long-term liabilities (LTL), plus contributed capital (CC), plus retained earnings (RE), minus current noncash assets (CNA), minus long-term noncash assets $(LTNA)$.

$$C = CL + LTL + CC + RE - CNA - LTNA$$

Changes in cash, therefore, can be expressed in terms of changes in the noncash balance sheet accounts.

$$\Delta C = \Delta CL + \Delta LTL + \Delta CC + \Delta RE - \Delta CNA - \Delta LTNA$$

The change in retained earnings (ΔRE) for a period is equal to revenues (R), less expenses (E), less dividends (D). In addition, changes in long-term liabilities (ΔLTL) can be separated into those affecting cash (ΔLTL_c) and those not affecting cash (ΔLTL_{nc}). In a similar manner, changes in long-term assets ($\Delta LTNA$) can be separated into those affecting cash ($\Delta LTNA_c$) and those not affecting cash ($\Delta LTNA_{nc}$). Inserting these substitutes in the preceding equation gives rise to the following equation, and rearranging the terms produces the equation contained in Figure 15–16.

$$\Delta C = \Delta CL + \Delta LTL_c + \Delta LTL_{nc} + \Delta CC + R - E - D - \Delta CNA - \Delta LTNA_c - \Delta LTNA_{nc}$$

The equation in Figure 15–16 represents a conceptual description of the statement of cash flows, expressed in terms of the changes in the noncash balance sheet accounts. It indicates that increases and decreases in cash due to operating, investing, and financing activities can be determined as described in Figure 15–17.

To illustrate how Figure 15–17 can be interpreted, review the statement of cash flows (indirect method) contained in Figure 15–14. Note that the depreciation and amortization charges are added to net income in the computation of cash provided (used) by operating activities. Each charge represents a decrease to a long-term noncash asset that did not affect Cash ($LTNA_{nc}$). Similarly, the loss on the sale of machinery ($LTNA_{nc}$) and the amortization of the discount (LTL_{nc}) are also added to net income. The changes in the current accounts other than Cash represent changes in noncash current assets (CNA) and current liabilities (CL).

In the computation of cash provided (used) by investing activities, the purchase of land and the sale of machinery represent an increase and decrease, respectively, in a long-term asset account that decrease and increase Cash ($LTNA_c$). In the computation of cash provided (used) by financing activities, the proceeds from the two (common and treasury) stock sales, the payment of dividends, and the payment on the outstanding note payable represent an increase in contributed capital (CC), a dividend payment (D), and a decrease in a long-term liability account (LTL_c), respectively.

Figure 15–16   A conceptual description of the statement of cash flows

	Operating Activities		Investing Activities	Financing Activities
$\Delta C =$	$R - E$ + $\Delta CL - \Delta CNA$	+ $\Delta LTL_{nc} - \Delta LTNA_{nc}$	$- \Delta LTNA_c$	+ $\Delta LTL_c + \Delta CC - D$
	Net income Changes in current accounts	Noncash charges to noncurrent accounts (e.g. depreciation, amortization, gains and losses)	Purchases and sales of long-term assets	Long-term borrowings and repayments, stock issuances and repurchases, and dividends

Figure 15–17 Changes in cash in terms of changes in the noncash balance sheet accounts

---

Cash Provided (Used) by Operating Activities

Net income $(R - E)$	Plus (minus) increases (decreases) in current liability accounts (ΔCL). Examples include short-term payables.
	Minus (plus) increases (decreases) in current asset accounts (ΔCNA). Examples include receivables, inventories, and prepaid expenses.
	Plus (minus) noncash charges that increase (decrease) long-term liability accounts (ΔLTL_{nc}). Examples include discounts and premiums on note, and gains and losses on debt retirements.
	Minus (plus) increases (decreases) in noncash charges that increase (decrease) long-term asset accounts $(\Delta LTNA_{nc})$. Examples include depreciation, amortization, and book gains and losses recognized when long-term assets are transferred.

Cash Provided (Used) by Investing Activities

Cash increases	Decreases in noncash asset accounts $(\Delta LTNA_c)$. Examples include sales of investments, long-lived assets, and intangible assets.
Cash decreases	Increases in noncash asset accounts $(\Delta LTNA_c)$. Examples include purchases of investments, long-lived assets, and intangible assets.

Cash Provided (Used) by Financing Activities

Cash increases	Increases in long-term liability (ΔLTL_c) and contributed capital (ΔCC) accounts. Examples include borrowings and stock issuances.
Cash decreases	Decreases in liability (ΔLTL_c) and contributed capital accounts (ΔCC) and dividends (D). Examples include principal payments on outstanding debts, repurchases of outstanding shares, and dividend payments.

Analyzing Changes in Noncash Balance Sheet Accounts

Figure 15–18 contains the December 31, 1990 and 1991 balance sheets of ABC Enterprises, and the related income statement and statement of retained earnings. Additional information is disclosed in the section that appears below the statements. These statements are the same as those contained in Figures 15–8 and 15–11.

In the following sections we prepare a statement of cash flows (direct method) from the information contained in Figure 15–18. Cash provided (used) by operating activities is derived first, followed by the cash provided (used) by investing activities, and cash provided (used) by financing activities. In the figures that appear throughout these sections, italics are used to indicate dollar amounts taken directly from the information in Figure 15–18. The amounts derived in these figures do not correspond to the original journal and ledger entries given in Figures 15–9 and 15–10. Instead they represent the aggregated amounts debited or credited to the financial statement accounts.

Figure 15–18 The financial statements of ABC Enterprises

ABC Enterprises, Inc. Balance Sheets For December 31, 1990 and 1991		
Account	**1991**	**1990**
Assets		
Cash	$ 5,900	$ 8,000
Accounts receivable	23,200	12,000
Less: Allowance for bad debts	1,300	1,000
Inventory	4,000	3,000
Prepaid Insurance	1,000	2,000
Land	30,000	20,000
Machinery	6,000	8,000
Less: Accumulated depreciation	2,500	2,000
Building	30,000	—
Less: Accumulated depreciation	1,500	—
Patent	6,000	8,000
Total assets	$100,800	$58,000
Liabilities and Stockholders' equity		
Accounts payable	$ 9,000	$12,000
Accrued payables	3,000	1,500
Income taxes payable	200	500
Payments in advance	—	3,000
Dividends payable	3,000	1,000
Notes payable	24,000	25,000
Less: Discount on notes payable	1,800	2,000
Common stock	42,000	10,000
Additional paid-in capital	19,300	2,000
Retained earnings	2,100	6,000
Less: Treasury stock	—	1,000
Total liabilities and stockholders' equity	$100,800	$58,000

Cash Provided (Used) by Operating Activities

This section analyzes the cash flows associated with each income statement account: Sales and Bad Debt Expense, Fees Earned, Cost of Goods Sold, Miscellaneous Expenses, Insurance Expense, Depreciation of Machinery and Building, Amortization of Patent, Loss on the Sale of Machinery, Interest Expense, and Income Tax Expense.

Sales and Bad Debt Expense. The cash inflow from sales can be determined by analyzing the changes in Accounts Receivable and Allowance for Bad Debts. Refer to the T-accounts and related journal entries in Figure 15–19.

The beginning and ending balances in Accounts Receivable and the Allowance for Bad Debts appear on the balance sheets in Figure 15–18. We assume that all sales were made on account; therefore, $32,000 (see income statement) was debited to Accounts Receivable during the year. The $1100 bad debt expense (see in-

Figure 15–18   (continued)

ABC Enterprises, Inc.
Income Statement
For the Year Ended December 31, 1991

Sales		$ 32,000
Fees earned		3,000
Cost of goods sold		(11,000)
Gross profit		24,000
Operating expenses		
Miscellaneous expenses	$11,000	
Insurance expense	1,000	
Bad debt expense	1,100	
Depreciation expense (machinery)	1,000	
Depreciation expense (building)	1,500	
Amortization of patent	2,000	17,600
Net operating income		6,400
Nonoperating revenues and expenses		
Loss on sale of machinery	100	
Interest expense	2,000	2,100
Net income from continuing operations before taxes		4,300
Less: Income tax expense		1,200
Net income		$ 3,100

ABC Enterprises, Inc.
Statement of Retained Earnings
For Period Ending December 31, 1991

Beginning retained earnings balance		$6,000
Plus: Net income		3,100
Less: Cash dividends	$3,000	
Stock dividends	4,000	7,000
Ending retained earnings balance		$2,100

Additional Information
1. Two thousand shares of common stock ($10 par; $15 fair market value) were issued for a building early in 1991.
2. A 5% stock dividend on 4000 outstanding shares was distributed late in 1991 when the fair market value of the $10 par value stock was $20 per share.
3. Reissued treasury stock, originally purchased for $1000, for $1300.

come statement) was credited to the Allowance for Bad Debts at year end, which (when the beginning and ending balances in the allowance account are considered) implies that uncollectibles in the amount of $800 must have been written off and credited to Accounts Receivable. Therefore, an additional credit to Accounts Receivable of $20,000 must have been entered during the year. The corresponding debit represents cash receipts on outstanding accounts during the year.

Cash collections from sales: $20,000

Figure 15-19   Determining cash inflow from sales

Sales	Accounts Receivable	Allowance for Bad Debts	Bad Debt Expense

32,000 (1)	12,000
	(1) 32,000 800 (3)
	          20,000 (4)
		1,000
		   1,100 (2)
		(3) 800
			(2) 1,100

	23,200	1,300	

Effect on Accounts

Transactions	Accounts	Debit (Net)	Credit (Net)
(1)	Accounts Receivable	32,000	
	Sales		32,000
(2)	Bad Debt Expense	1,100	
	Allowance for Bad Debts		1,100
(3)	Allowance for Bad Debts	800	
	Accounts Receivable		800
(4)	Cash	20,000	
	Accounts Receivable		20,000

Fees Earned. The cash inflow related to Fees Earned can be determined by analyzing the change in the Payments in Advance account. Refer to Figure 15-20.

The beginning ($3000) and ending ($0) balances in the Payments in Advance account appear on the balance sheets in Figure 15-18. The recognition of $3000 in Fees Earned (see income statement) involved a $3000 debit to Payments in Advance. This entry accounts for the entire change in the Payments in Advance account, indicating that no cash inflow was associated with fees earned.

Cost of Goods Sold. The cash outflow associated with Cost of Goods Sold can be determined by analyzing the changes in the Inventory and Accounts Payable accounts. Refer to Figure 15-21.

The beginning and ending balances in Inventory and Accounts Payable appear on the balance sheets in Figure 15-18. The $11,000 debit to Cost of Goods Sold (see income statement) was credited to Inventory, which (when the beginning and ending balances in the inventory account are considered) implies that inventory purchases of $12,000 must have been made during the year. Assuming that all inventory purchases were made on account, $12,000 must have been credited to Accounts Payable. Considering the beginning and ending balances in Accounts Payable, an additional debit of $15,000 must have been recognized during the year. The corresponding credit represents cash payments of $15,000 on accounts payable during the year.

Cash paid to suppliers: $15,000

Figure 15-20 Determining cash inflow from fees earned

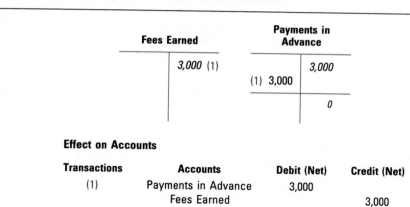

Transactions	Accounts	Debit (Net)	Credit (Net)
(1)	Payments in Advance	3,000	
	Fees Earned		3,000

Figure 15-21 Determining cash outflow from inventory purchases

I/S

Cost of Goods Sold		Inventory		Accounts Payable	
(1) 11,000		3,000	11,000 (1)		12,000
		(2) 12,000		(3) 15,000	12,000 (2)
		4,000			9,000

Effect on Accounts

Transactions	Accounts	Debit (Net)	Credit (Net)
(1)	Cost of Goods Sold	11,000	
	Inventory		11,000
(2)	Inventory	12,000	
	Accounts Payable		12,000
(3)	Accounts Payable	15,000	
	Cash		15,000

Miscellaneous Expenses. The cash outflow related to Miscellaneous Expenses can be determined by analyzing the change in the Accrued Payables account. Refer to Figure 15-22.

The beginning ($1500) and ending ($3000) balances in Accrued Payables appear on the balance sheets in Figure 15-18. Assuming that all miscellaneous expenses were accrued, the debit of $11,000 to Miscellaneous Expenses (see income statement) must have involved a $11,000 credit to Accrued Payables. Considering the beginning and ending balances in accrued payables, a $9500 debit must have been entered in the account. The corresponding credit represents cash payments on accrued payables.

Cash paid on miscellaneous expenses: $9500

Figure 15–22   Determining cash outflows from miscellaneous expenses

Miscellaneous Expenses		Accrued Payables	
(1) *11,000*			*1,500*
			11,000 (1)
		(2) 9,500	
			3,000

Effect on Accounts

Transactions	Accounts	Debit (Net)	Credit (Net)
(1)	Miscellaneous Expenses	11,000	
	Accrued Payables		11,000
(2)	Accrued Payables	9,500	
	Cash		9,500

Figure 15–23   Determining cash outflow related to insurance expense

Insurance Expense		Prepaid Insurance	
(1) *1,000*		*2,000*	
			1,000 (1)
		1,000	

Effect on Accounts

Transactions	Accounts	Debit (Net)	Credit (Net)
(1)	Insurance Expense	1,000	
	Prepaid Insurance		1,000

Insurance Expense. The cash outflow related to Insurance Expense can be determined by analyzing the change in the Prepaid Insurance account. Refer to Figure 15–23.

The beginning ($2000) and ending ($1000) balances in Prepaid Insurance appear on the balance sheets in Figure 15–18. The debit of $1000 to Insurance Expense (see income statement) involved a $1000 credit to Prepaid Insurance. This entry accounts for the entire change in the Prepaid Insurance account, indicating that no cash was paid for insurance during the year.

Depreciation of Machinery, Depreciation of Building, Amortization of Patent, and Loss on Sale of Machinery. There are no cash effects associated with depreciation, amortization, or book gains and losses.

Figure 15-24   Determining cash outflow related to interest expense

Interest Expense		Discount on Notes Payable	
(1) *2,000*		*2,000*	
			200 (1)
		1,800	

Effect on Accounts

Transactions	Accounts	Debit (Net)	Credit (Net)
(1)	Interest Expense	2,000	
	Discount on Notes Payable		200
	Cash		1,800

Interest Expense. The cash outflow related to Interest Expense can be determined by analyzing the change in the Discount on Notes Payable account. Refer to Figure 15-24.

The beginning ($2000) and ending ($1800) balances in the Discount on Notes Payable account appear on the balance sheets in Figure 15-18. The $200 difference between the beginning and ending balances indicates that the discount was amortized in the amount of $200 during the year. Discounts are amortized into Interest Expense as illustrated in Figure 15-24. Thus, $1800 cash must have been paid for interest during the year.

Cash paid for interest: $1800

Income Tax Expense. The cash outflow related to Income Tax Expense can be determined by analyzing the change in the Income Tax Payable account. Refer to Figure 15-25.

The beginning ($500) and ending ($200) balances in the Income Tax Payable account appears on the balance sheets in Figure 15-18. The debit of $1200 to Income Tax Expense (see income statement), assuming that income taxes were accrued, involved a $1200 credit to income tax payable. Considering the beginning and ending balances in Income Tax Payable, $1500 must have been debited to the account during the year. The corresponding credit represents cash payments for income taxes.

Cash paid for income taxes: $1500

Investing Activities

In this section we determine the cash inflows and outflows associated with investing activities by analyzing changes in the long-lived asset accounts. Specifically, we analyze the $10,000 increase in the Land account and the $2000 decrease in the Machinery account. The building was acquired in exchange for stock and involved no cash exchange, while the $2000 decrease in the patent account reflects amortization, which also involved no cash receipt or payment.

Figure 15-25   Determining cash outflow related to income taxes

Income Tax Expense		Income Tax Payable	
(1) *1,200*			*500*
			1,200 (1)
		(2) 1,500	
			200

Effect on Accounts

Transactions	Accounts	Debit (Net)	Credit (Net)
(1)	Income Tax Expense	1,200	
	Income Tax Payable		1,200
(2)	Income Tax Payable	1,500	
	Cash		1,500

Figure 15-26   Determining cash outflow for land purchases

Land	
20,000	
(1) *10,000*	
30,000	

Effect on Accounts

Transaction	Accounts	Debit (Net)	Credit (Net)
(1)	Land	10,000	
	Cash		10,000

Purchase of Land. The $10,000 increase in the Land account (see Figure 15−18) indicates that land was acquired during the period. Since there is no indication that noncash assets were exchanged for the land or a liability was credited, we assume that the land was purchased for a $10,000 cash payment. Refer to Figure 15−26.

Cash payment for land: $10,000

Sale of Machinery. The cash inflow from the sale of machinery can be determined by using the available information to reconstruct the journal entry that recorded the transaction. Refer to Figure 15−27.

The beginning and ending balances in the Machinery and Accumulated Depreciation accounts can be found on the balance sheets in Figure 15−18. Depreciation expense on the machinery in the amount of $1000 (see income statement) was recognized during the period; accordingly, $1000 must have been credited to

Figure 15-27   Determining cash inflow from sale of machinery

Machinery		Accumulated Depreciation		Loss on Sale of Machinery		Depreciation Expense	
8,000	2,000 (2)		2,000	(2) 100		(1) 1,000	
		(2) 500	1,000 (1)				
6,000			2,500				

Effect on Accounts

Transactions	Accounts	Debit (Net)	Credit (Net)
(1)	Depreciation Expense	1,000	
	Accumulated Depreciation		1,000
(2)	Cash	1,400	
	Accumulated Depreciation	500	
	Loss on Sale of Machinery	100	
	Machinery		2,000

Accumulated Depreciation. The Accumulated Depreciation account, therefore, must have been debited for $500 when the machine was sold. Given the $100 loss on the sale (see income statement), the $2000 reduction in the Machinery account, and the $500 debit to Accumulated Depreciation, the journal entry to record the sale can be reconstructed, and the amount of cash received ($1400) can be determined.

Cash receipt from sale of machinery: $1400

Financing Activities

In this section we determine the cash inflows and outflows associated with financing activities by analyzing changes in the long-term liability and stockholders' equity accounts. Specifically, we analyze the $1000 decrease in the Notes Payable account, the increase in the Common Stock and Additional Paid-in Capital accounts, the issuance of treasury stock for $1,300, and the declaration of a $3000 cash dividend.

Principal Payment on Notes Payable. We have no indication that the $1000 decrease in the Notes Payable account (see Figure 15-18) was due to anything other than the payment of cash. Refer to Figure 15-28.

Cash payment on notes payable: $1000

Issuance of Common Stock and Treasury Stock. The cash inflows from the issuance of common stock and treasury stock can be determined by analyzing the changes in the Common Stock, Additional Paid-in Capital, and Treasury Stock accounts. Note that the "Additional Information" section of Figure 15-18 indicates that a building was acquired for common stock, a stock dividend was distributed, and treasury stock was sold for $1300. Refer to Figure 15-29.

Figure 15–28 Determining cash outflow from payments on notes

Notes Payable

		25,000
(1)	1,000	
		24,000

Effect on Accounts

Transaction	Accounts	Debit (Net)	Credit (Net)
(1)	Notes Payable	1,000	
	Cash		1,000

Figure 15–29 Determining cash inflow from stock issuances

Building	Treasury Stock	Stock Dividend
0	1,000	(2) 4,000
(1) 30,000	1,000 (3)	
30,000	0	

Common Stock	Additional Paid-in Capital
10,000	2,000
20,000 (1)	10,000 (1)
2,000 (2)	2,000 (2)
	300 (3)
10,000 (4)	5,000 (4)
42,000	19,300

Effect on Accounts

Transactions	Accounts	Debit (Net)	Credit (Net)
(1)	Building	30,000	
	Common Stock		20,000
	Additional Paid-in Capital		10,000
(2)	Stock Dividend	4,000	
	Common Stock		2,000
	Additional Paid-in Capital		2,000
(3)	Cash	1,300	
	Treasury Stock		1,000
	Additional Paid-in Capital		300
(4)	Cash	15,000	
	Common Stock		10,000
	Additional Paid-in Capital		5,000

Figure 15–30   Determining cash outflow from dividend payments

Cash Dividends		Dividends Payable	
(1) *3,000*			*1,000*
		(2) 1,000	3,000 (1)
			3,000

Effect on Accounts

Transactions	Accounts	Debit (Net)	Credit (Net)
(1)	Cash Dividends	3,000	
	Dividends Payable		3,000
(2)	Dividends Payable	1,000	
	Cash		1,000

The beginning and ending balances in Common Stock, Additional Paid-in Capital, and Treasury Stock appear on the balance sheets in Figure 15–18. The purchase of the $30,000 building increased Common Stock and Additional Paid-in Capital by $20,000 and $10,000, respectively. Common Stock and Additional Paid-in Capital each increased by $2000 when the $4000 stock dividend was distributed. Additional Paid-in Capital increased by $300 when the treasury stock was issued for $1300 cash, which was greater than its $1000 cost. The additional information that follows the financial statements in Figure 15–18 describes these three transactions. Given the ending balances in Common Stock and Additional Paid-in Capital, there must have been a stock issuance for cash in the amount of $15,000 during the year.

Cash receipts from issuance of treasury stock: $1300
Cash receipts from issuance of common stock: $15,000

Cash Dividends. The cash dividend payment can be determined by analyzing the change in the Dividends Payable account. Refer to Figure 15–30.

The beginning ($1000) and ending ($3000) balances in the Dividends Payable account appear on the balance sheets in Figure 15–18. The declaration of the $3000 cash dividend (see statement of retained earnings) created a $3000 dividend payable liability. Therefore, $1000 must have been debited to Dividends Payable during the year, which represents cash payments to the stockholders.

Cash payment for dividends: $1000

The Completed Statement of Cash Flows

We have now completed the preparation of the statement of cash flows (direct method) from the information contained in Figure 15–18. The statement is shown in Figure 15–31 and corresponds exactly to the statement in Figure 15–13. Preparing the statement under the indirect method is accomplished in a similar manner, except that the operating section contains adjustments to net income. These adjustments were described earlier in the chapter.

Figure 15–31   Statement of cash flows for ABC Enterprises: direct method

ABC Enterprises, Inc. Statement of Cash Flows For the Year Ended December 31, 1991			
Operating activities			
Cash collections from sales and accounts receivable		$20,000	
Cash paid to suppliers		(15,000)	
Cash paid on miscellaneous expenses	(11,000)	(9,500)	
Cash paid for income taxes		(1,500)	
Cash paid for interest		(1,800)	
Net cash provided (used) by operating activities			$(7,800)
Investing activities			
Purchase of land		(10,000)	
Sale of machinery		1,400	
Net cash provided (used) by investing activities			(8,600)
Financing activities			
Proceeds from issuing common stock		15,000	
Proceeds from sale of treasury stock		1,300	
Cash dividends		(1,000)	
Principal payment on outstanding note payable		(1,000)	
Net cash provided (used) by financing activities			14,300
Net increase (decrease) in cash balance			(2,100)
Beginning cash balance			8,000
Ending cash balance			$ 5,900

ANALYZING THE STATEMENT OF CASH FLOWS: AN APPLICATION

Now that the statement of cash flows has been prepared, we can use it to assess ABC Enterprises' cash-management policies. Earlier in the chapter we stated that the statement of cash flows can be used to evaluate cash management in three interrelated ways: (1) to explain the change in the Cash balance, (2) to summarize the cash effects of operating transactions, and (3) to summarize the cash effects of capital (investing and financing) transactions.

Explaining the Change in the Cash Balance. ABC's cash position decreased (from $8000 to $5900) during 1991. For the most part this decrease was caused by investing and operating activities, which required $8600 and $7800, respectively. Financing activities, which provided $14,300, almost made up for these cash deficits. While the exact sources and uses of cash in each of these three areas should be examined, the $7800 cash deficit due to operating activities appears to be the most troublesome, and definitely deserves special attention.

Summarizing the Cash Effects of Operating Transactions. ABC's income statement shows that net income for 1991 totaled $3100. At the same time, the operations that produced net income reduced the cash balance by $7800. Interestingly, these two measures produce significantly different numbers that are used to evaluate the same (operating) activities.

Figure 15–32 explains the difference between net income and cash provided (used) by operations. These same adjustments can be found on the statement of cash flows in Figure 15–14 (indirect method).

Four items appear to be the most important: (1) the $10,900 buildup in net accounts receivable, (2) the $3000 decrease in accounts payable, (3) the $3000 decrease in payments in advance, and (4) the depreciation and amortization of the long-lived assets.

The net accounts receivable buildup increased net income, but not cash. Coupled with the decrease in accounts payable, it indicates that ABC paid its suppliers more quickly than it received payments from its customers. Such a strategy can give rise to cash flow problems. The $3000 decrease in payments in advance was reflected in revenues (and thus net income), but produced no cash. Presumably, the $3000 was received some time before December 31, 1990. The depreciation and amortization of long-lived assets reduced net income by a total dollar amount of $4500 ($1000 + $1500 + $2000), but required no cash.

Keep in mind also that the management of ABC could have manipulated cash provided (used) by operating activities. For example, had management chosen to defer the $15,000 cash payment on accounts payable (Transaction [10] in Fig. 15–9), cash provided (used) by operating activities would have been +$7200 instead of −$7800. Note that this particular decision would have had no effect on net income.

Summarizing the Cash Effects of Capital Transactions. ABC Enterprises relied heavily on stock issuances for its cash needs during 1991. The statement of cash flows shows that common stock was issued for cash in the amount of $15,000 and that the sale of treasury stock produced $1300. Both issuances diluted ABC's outstanding stock. The sale of a piece of machinery produced $1400.

Figure 15–32 Reconciling net income and cash provided (used) by operating activities

ABC Enterprises, Inc.			
Statement of Cash Flows (operating activities)			
For the Year Ended December 31, 1991			
Operating activities			
Net income		$ 3,100	
Noncash charges to noncurrent accounts			
Depreciation of machinery	$ 1,000		
Depreciation of building	1,500		
Amortization of patent	2,000		
Loss on sale of machinery	100		
Decrease in discount on notes payable	200	4,800	
Changes in current accounts other than cash			
Increase in net accounts receivable	(10,900)		
Increase in inventory	(1,000)		
Decrease in accounts payable	(3,000)		
Increase in miscellaneous expenses and taxes payable	1,200		
Decrease in payments in advance	(3,000)		
Decrease in prepaid insurance	1,000	(15,700)	
Net cash provided (used) by operating activities			$(7,800)

The cash produced by the financing and investing sources was used primarily to cover the cash deficit from operating activities (−$7800) and to purchase land ($10,000). Dividend and principal payments on outstanding loans amounted to $1000 each.

Note again that ABC Enterprises issued 2000 shares of common stock, valued at $15 each, for a building (see Transaction [2] in Fig. 15−9). While this transaction does not affect ABC's Cash balance and does not appear on the statement of cash flows, it is nonetheless very important, and should be reported in the footnotes to the financial statements. Apparently, ABC relied even more heavily on equity issuances and purchased more long-term assets than the statement of cash flows indicates.

THE ANNUAL REPORT OF K MART CORPORATION

Turn now to K mart's annual report located in Appendix D. A description of cash flow activities, the Statement of Cash Flows, and Supplemental Cash Flow Information can be found on pages 26, 33, and 37, respectively.

The description of cash flow activities includes a discussion of (1) net cash provided by operations, (2) the inventory turnover ratio, (3) the working capital ratio, (4) net cash used for investing, (5) net cash used for financing, (6) dividends, (7) the ratio of income to fixed charges, and (8) the company's capital structure. This section essentially represents management's discussion of K mart's solvency position. Note that information from the three sections of the statement of cash flows plays a prominent role in this discussion.

The Statement of Cash Flows was prepared under the indirect method and the definition of cash includes cash equivalents and temporary investments. Net cash provided by operations is computed by adjusting Income from continuing retail operations for (1) noncash charges (credits) to earnings, (2) Cash provided by (used for) current assets and current liabilities, and (3) Discontinued operations. The first category includes depreciation and amortization, deferred income taxes (see Chapter 10), undistributed equity income (see Chapter 13), increases in other long-term liabilities, and other adjustments. In each of these cases net income was affected without a corresponding effect on cash. The second category includes adjustments to inventories, accounts payable, and other current accounts. The third category reflects the cash inflows and outflows due to the sale of K mart's insurance and cafeteria operations (see Note B on page 36). As discussed in Chapter 14, such transactions closely resemble the sale of a long-term asset and, accordingly, it might be more appropriate to include the related cash effects in the investing section of the statement of cash flows.

The investing section of the Statement of Cash Flows primarily includes investments and sales of long-term assets while the financing section summarizes the cash effects associated with changes in long-term liability and stockholders' equity accounts. Specifically, the financing section includes issuance of long-term debt, payments on long-term debt and capital leases, common and treasury stock issuances, treasury stock purchases, and dividend payments. Note E on page 37 indicates that "in 1986 the company issued $186 million in common stock in exchange for its 6 percent convertible subordinated debentures due July 15, 1999." While this noncash transaction was excluded from the Statement of Cash Flows, it was important enough to warrant separate disclosure in the footnotes.

It is apparent from the Statement of Cash Flows that over the past three years K mart has consistently expanded its operations while paying substantial dividends. Cash provided by operations has been more than adequate to cover these payments as well as either reduce outstanding long-term debts or increase the cash balance. Note that the consistent increase in net cash provided by operations can largely be attributed to a consistent reduction in the increase in inventories. It seems that K mart has been able to support increased sales and profits while controlling its inventory purchases. Note also that the company has made significant payments on its outstanding long-term debt and capital lease obligations during the past three years. Except in the most recent year, these payments have exceeded long-term borrowings by a large amount.

REVIEW PROBLEM

Figure 15–33 contains balance sheets (December 31, 1990 and 1991) for XYZ Enterprises. The income statement and the statement of retained earnings for 1991 are on page 764. Following these statements are several selected pieces of information that more completely describe the activity of XYZ during 1991.

The two forms of the statement of cash flows are contained in Figures 15–34 (direct method) and 15–35 (indirect method). We have included relevant calculations on the statements to explain how the numbers were derived. Examine each cash flow statement closely, and trace the calculations back to the original financial statements and given information in Figure 15–33.

Figure 15–33 **Financial statements for XYZ Enterprises**

	1991	1990
XYZ Enterprises		
Balance Sheets		
For December 31, 1990 and 1991		
Assets		
Cash	$ 3,000	$ 2,500
Accounts receivable	4,500	4,000
Inventory	10,500	8,000
Prepaid rent	3,000	2,000
Fixed assets	40,000	35,000
Less: Accumulated depreciation	12,000	10,000
Patent	8,000	9,000
Total Assets	$57,000	$50,500
Liabilities and stockholders' equity		
Accounts payable	6,500	3,000
Other current payables	7,000	10,000
Bonds payable	19,000	19,000
Plus: Premium on bonds payable	2,500	3,000
Common stock	15,000	10,000
Additional paid-in capital	4,000	3,000
Retained earnings	3,000	2,500
Total liabilities and stockholders' equity	$57,000	$50,500

Figure 15-33   (continued)

XYZ Enterprises Income Statement For the Year Ended Dec. 31, 1991		XYZ Enterprises Statement of Retained Earnings For the Year Ended Dec. 31, 1991	
Sales	$55,000	Beginning balance	$2,500
Less: Cost of goods sold	35,000	Plus: Net income	2,000
Gross profit	20,000	Less: Cash dividends	1,500
Rent expense	2,000	Ending balance	$3,000
Interest expense	2,000		
Miscellaneous expense	9,000		
Depreciation of fixed assets	5,000		
Amortization of patent	1,000		
Gain on sale of machinery	1,000		
Net income	$ 2,000		

Additional Information

1. Purchased $3000 of prepaid rent.
2. Sold a piece of machinery (cost: $5000; accumulated depreciation: $3000) for $3000 cash. Purchased additional machinery for $10,000 cash.
3. Annual interest payment on note payable is $2,500.
4. Issued 500 shares of $10 par value common stock for $12 per share.

Figure 15-34   Statement of cash flows for XYZ Enterprises: direct method

XYZ Enterprises
Statement of Cash Flows
For the Year Ended December 31, 1991

Operating activities
Sales	(55,000 − 500 [increase in accounts receivable])	$ 54,500
COGS	(35,000 + 2,500 [increase in inventory]	
	− 3,500 [increase in accounts payable])	(34,000)
Rent	(2,000 + 1,000 [increase in prepaid rent])	(3,000)
Interest	(2,000 + 500 [decrease in premium])	(2,500)
Misc.	(9,000 + 3,000 [decrease in other current payables])	(12,000)
Depreciation (no cash effect)		0
Amortization (no cash effect)		0
Gain	(no cash effect)	0

Net cash provided (used) by operating activities $ 3,000

Investing activities
Sale of machinery	(see note below)	3,000
Purchase of machinery (see note below)		(10,000)

Net cash provided (used) by investing activities   (7,000)

Financing activities
Issue of common stock (increase in common stock and APIC)	6,000
Cash dividends	(see statement of retained earnings
	and no increase in dividend payable)	(1,500)

Net cash provided (used) by financing activities   4,500
Increase (decrease) in cash balance   500
Beginning cash balance   2,500
Ending cash balance $ 3,000

Note:

	Cost of Fixed Assets		Accumulated Depreciation	
Beginning Balance		$35,000		$10,000
Plus: Increases	(purchases)	10,000	(depreciation expense)	5,000
Less: Decreases	(sales)	5,000	(sold machinery)	3,000
Ending Balance		$40,000		$12,000

Cash	3,000	
Accumulated Depreciation	3,000	
Machinery		5,000
Gain on Sale of Machinery		1,000

Figure 15–35   Statement of cash flows for XYZ Enterprises: indirect method

XYZ Enterprises **Statement of Cash Flows** **For the Year Ended December 31, 1991**		

Operating activities			
Net income		$2,000	
Noncash charges to noncurrent accounts			
Depreciation of fixed assets	$ 5,000		
Amortization of patent	1,000		
Gain on sale of machinery	(1,000)		
Decrease in premium	(500)	4,500	
Changes in current accounts other than cash			
Increase in accounts receivable	(500)		
Increase in inventory	(2,500)		
Increase in prepaid rent	(1,000)		
Decrease in other payables	(3,000)		
Increase in accounts payable	3,500	(3,500)	
Cash provided (used) by operating activities			$ 3,000
Investing activities			
Sale of machinery (see note below)		3,000	
Purchase of machinery (see note below)		(10,000)	
Cash provided (used) by investing activities			(7,000)
Financing activities			
Issue of common stock (increase in common stock and additional paid-in capital)		6,000	
Cash dividends (see statement of retained earnings and no change in dividend payable)		(1,500)	
Net cash provided (used) by financing activities			4,500
Net increase (decrease) in cash balance			500
Beginning cash balance			2,500
Ending cash balance			$ 3,000

Note:

	Cost of Fixed Assets		**Accumulated Depreciation**	
Beginning Balance		$35,000		$10,000
Plus: Increases	(purchases)	10,000	(depreciation expense)	5,000
Less: Decreases	(sales)	5,000	(sold machinery)	3,000
Ending Balance		$40,000		$12,000

SUMMARY OF LEARNING OBJECTIVES

1 Describe the basic structure and format of the statement of cash flows.

The statement of cash flows explains the change in a company's cash account from one accounting period to the next. It is divided into three sections: (1) cash provided (used) by operating activities, (2) cash provided (used) by investing activities, and (3) cash provided (used) by financing activities. Each of these sections contains the cash inflows and outflows of the period that were associated with the indicated activity.

2 Define cash flows from operating, investing, and financing activities.

Cash flows from operating activities include those cash inflows and outflows associated directly with the acquisition and sale of a company's inventories and services. Such activities include the cash receipts from sales and accounts receivable as well as cash payments from the purchase of inventories, payments on accounts payable, selling and administrative expenses, and interest and taxes.

Cash flows from investing activities include the cash inflows and outflows associated with the purchase and sale of a company's noncurrent assets. Such activities include the cash effects from the purchase and sale of long-term investments, long-lived assets, and intangible assets.

Cash flows from financing activities include cash inflows and outflows associated with a company's two sources of outside capital: liabilities and contributed capital. Such activities include the cash inflows associated with borrowings and equity issuances as well as the cash outflows associated with debt repayments, treasury stock purchases, and dividends.

3 Explain how the statement of cash flows complements the other financial statements and how it can be used by those interested in the financial condition of a company.

While the income statement provides a summary of a company's operating transactions on an accrual basis, and the balance sheet represents the accumulated accruals of the company's operating, investing, and financing transactions as of a particular point in time, neither statement indicates much about the cash effects of the company's operating, investing, and financing activities. The statement of cash flows is designed to fill this void by summarizing the cash effects of the company's operating, investing, and financing transactions.

The statement of cash flows is used primarily to evaluate a company's ability to generate cash (i.e., financial flexibility) as well as the effectiveness of its cash-management policies. Financial flexibility reflects a company's ability to generate cash through operations, borrowings, issuing equity, or selling noncurrent assets. Effective cash management involves investing cash to provide a high rate of return while maintaining enough cash to meet debts as they come due (i.e., solvency). The statement of cash flows is helpful to this evaluation in three interrelated ways: (1) it explains the change in the cash balance, (2) it summarizes the cash effects of operating transactions, and (3) it summarizes the cash effects of capital (investing and financing) transactions.

4 Identify the important investing and financing transactions that do not appear on the statement of cash flows.

The statement of cash flows includes only those transactions that either increase or decrease the Cash account. Many important operating and capital transactions do not affect the Cash account and are therefore excluded from the statement. For example, the purchase of machinery in exchange for a long-term note payable, the acquisition of land or the payment of a debt with capital stock, and the declaration of a dividend are all capital transactions that have no effect on the Cash account and are therefore excluded from the statement. The sale or purchase of inventory on account are operating transactions that do not appear on the statement of cash flows.

The Financial Accounting Standards Board requires that capital transactions that do not affect the Cash account be described clearly in the footnotes to the financial statements. No special disclosures are required for operating transactions that do not affect the Cash account, because the effects of such transactions can be inferred from the reconciliation of net income to net cash provided (used) by operating activities.

5 Describe the economic consequences associated with the statement of cash flows.

The economic consequences associated with the statement of cash flows result primarily from the fact that investors, creditors, and other interested parties use it to assess the investment potential and creditworthiness of companies and the equity and debt securities they issue. The rising importance of cash flow information to report users creates incentives for managers to window dress the statement of cash flows. Such incentives can present problems because in the short run it is relatively easy for management to present a favorable cash position. Such manipulation is much less effective, however, when statements are viewed across several periods because payments delayed in one period must normally be paid in the next. For this reason the FASB requires that cash flow statements from at least the previous three years be disclosed in the financial report. An additional economic consequence associated with the statement of cash flows is that, in general, it has raised the record-keeping costs of major U.S. corporations. Such costs may explain why most large U.S. companies use the indirect method of presentation, which is generally less costly than the direct method, because it does not require that operating cash flows be traced back to the original entries.

6 Prepare a statement of cash flows from the original journal entries and Cash account in the ledger under both the direct and the indirect methods.

Preparing a statement of cash flows from the Cash account in the ledger involves three basic steps. First, the cash inflows and outflows, which were originally entered as debits and credits in the Cash account, respectively, are identified. Second, each cash flow is classified as resulting from an operating, investing, or financing transaction. Third, the cash flows are placed in the appropriate sections of the statement of cash flows. Under the direct method, a schedule reconciling net income and cash provided (used) by operating activities must be clearly disclosed in the financial report.

Under the indirect method, the investing and financing sections are prepared from the Cash account, but cash provided (used) by operating activities is computed by adjusting net income for the differences between accruals and cash flows. These adjustments are disclosed in two categories: (1) noncash charges to noncurrent accounts and (2) changes in current accounts other than Cash.

7 Convert accrual numbers, which appear on the income statement, to cash flow numbers.

The revenues and expenses that appear on the income statement can be converted to cash inflows and outflows by adjusting them for changes in the related balance sheet accounts. For example, sales revenue can be converted to cash inflows from sales by examining changes in the Accounts Receivable and the Deferred Revenue accounts. Similarly, Cost of Goods Sold can be converted to cash outflow due to purchases of inventory by examining changes in the Inventory and Accounts Payable accounts. In sum, each revenue and expense is related to one or more accounts on the balance sheet, and changes in these accounts can be used to determine the related cash flows. These kinds of adjustments are illustrated in Figure 15–15 and summarized in the appendix of Chapter 4.

8 Express the statement of cash flows in terms of the basic accounting equation, and understand how to prepare a statement of cash flows from the information contained in two balance sheets, an income statement, and a statement of retained earnings.

The basic accounting equation states that assets equal liabilities plus stockholders' equity:

$$A = L + SE$$

The change in assets is equal to the change in liabilities plus the change in stockholders' equity.

$$\Delta A = \Delta L + \Delta SE$$

Separating the change in assets (ΔA) into changes in cash (ΔC), noncash current assets (ΔCNA), and long-term assets that affect cash ($\Delta LTNA_c$) and do not affect cash ($\Delta LTNA_{nc}$); separating the change in liabilities (ΔL) into changes in current liabilities (ΔCL), and long-term liabilities that affect (ΔLTL_c) and do not affect cash (ΔLTL_{nc}); separating the change in stockholders' equity (ΔSE) into changes in contributed capital (ΔCC) and retained earnings (ΔRE), which is equal to revenues *(R)* plus expenses *(E)*, less dividends *(D)*; and rearranging the entire equation, we have the following equation.

$$\Delta C = \overbrace{R - E + \Delta CL - \Delta CNA + \Delta LTL_{nc} - \Delta LTNA_{nc}}^{\text{Operating Activities}} -$$

$$\overbrace{\Delta LTNA_c}^{\text{Investing Activities}} + \overbrace{\Delta LTL_c + \Delta CC - D}^{\text{Financing Activities}}$$

This equation, which appears in Figure 15–16, represents a conceptual statement of the statement of cash flows, explaining how the change in the Cash balance can be explained in terms of changes in the balance sheet accounts. Figure 15–17 describes how such changes can be used to prepare a statement of cash flows.

KEY TERMS

Cash equivalent (p. 720)   Investing activities (p. 724)
Direct method (p. 721)   Operating activities (p. 721)
Financial flexibility (p. 727)   Solvency (p. 727)
Financing activities (p. 724)   Window dress (p. 731)
Indirect method (p. 722)

QUESTIONS FOR DISCUSSION AND REVIEW

1. The statement of cash flows is divided into three sections. Name these sections and explain how such a division is useful.

2. How is cash defined with respect to the statement of cash flows? Why is this definition used?

3. Define cash provided (used) by operating activities, and differentiate this dollar amount from net income, which appears on the income statement.

4. Cash can be generated by selling inventory or services, selling long-term assets like investments and equipment, and borrowing or issuing equity. How are these various forms of generating cash treated on the statement of cash flows, and why are they treated differently?

5. Of what use is the statement of cash flows to investors, creditors, and other interested in the financial condition of a company?

6. How does the statement of cash flows complement the other financial statements? What kind of information does it provide that the others do not?

7. What is a capital transaction, and how can it be differentiated from an operating transaction? What are investing and financing transactions, and how do they relate to capital transactions?

8. What is financial flexibility, and how does the statement of cash flows provide information about it?

9. What is involved in cash management, and why is it important that a company manage its cash correctly?

10. What is solvency, and of what use is the statement of cash flows in evaluating the solvency position of a company?

11. In what three ways can the statement of cash flows be used to evaluate a company's ability to generate cash and its cash-management policies?

12. Why do managers have incentives to manipulate the dollar amounts on the statement of cash flows? Provide several examples of how managers might window dress the statement of cash flows. What has the Financial Accounting Standards Board done to mitigate this problem?

13. Why is manipulating information on the statement of cash flows often not in the best interest of management?

14. Describe the differences between the income statement, which is prepared on an accrual basis, and the operating section of the statement of cash flows. Do both operating statements provide the same kind of information? If not, how do they differ? Is it possible for a profitable company to go bankrupt? How?

15. Provide several examples of important financing and investment transactions that would not appear on the statement of cash flows. What does the Financial Accounting Standards Board require with respect to such transactions?

16. Explain how one could infer the existence of operating transactions that do not affect the Cash account. For example, how could a reader of a company's financial statements be able to determine if the company made a large inventory purchase on account?

17. Differentiate the direct method from the indirect method in preparing the statement of cash flows. Which method is more straightforward, and why? Which method provides more disclosure?

18. Converting an income statement to a statement of operating cash inflows and outflows (and vice-versa) is very important in understanding the statement of cash flows and how it relates to the income statement. In general, how does one make such conversions, and why might they be useful to financial statement users?

19. When preparing a reconciliation between net income and cash provided (used) by operating activities for purposes of a statement of cash flows under either the direct or indirect method, into what two categories are the required adjustments separated? Provide several examples of the adjustments included in each category.

20. Name an asset account and a liability account that are directly related to the revenue accounts, Sales and Fees Earned. Name asset and/or liability accounts that are directly related to the income statement accounts, Interest Expense, Depreciation Expense, Insurance Expense, Wage Expense, and Cost of Goods Sold.

21. How are book gains and losses, depreciation, and amortization treated when converting accrual numbers to cash-basis numbers? Why?

22. Express the change in the Cash balance during a period in terms of changes in the other balance sheet accounts. Begin with the basic accounting equation, and explain how this expression can be used to prepare a statement of cash flows from the information contained in two balance sheets, an income statement, and a statement of retained earnings.

EXERCISES

E15–1

(Classifying transactions)   Classify each of the following transactions as an operating, investing, or financing activity, even those that would not appear explicitly on the statement of cash flows. Some transactions may be classified in more than one category.

(1) Purchase of machinery for cash
(2) Issuance of common stock for cash
(3) Sale of inventory on account
(4) Purchase of outstanding stock (treasury stock) for cash
(5) Sale of land held as a long-term investment
(6) Purchase of a building for cash and a mortgage payable
(7) Cash payment for principal and interest on an outstanding debt
(8) Cash payment on accounts payable
(9) Payment of a cash dividend
(10) Payment of wages to employees

E15–2

(Operating, investing, or financing activity?)   The following are several activities that Wallingford, Inc. engaged in during 1991.

(1) Wrote off an open receivable as uncollectible.
(2) Purchased a piece of plant equipment.
(3) Reacquired 5000 shares of its common stock.

(4) Sold a building in exchange for a five-year note.

(5) Declared, but did not pay, a cash dividend.

(6) Retired bonds payable by issuing common stock.

(7) Collected on a long-term note receivable.

(8) Issued a stock dividend.

(9) Recorded depreciation on fixed assets.

(10) Paid interest on long-term debt.

(11) Purchased inventory on account.

(12) Collected open accounts receivable.

(13) Exchanged a building for land.

(14) Issued 75,000 shares of preferred stock.

(15) Purchased a two-year fire insurance policy.

Required: Assume that each of these transactions involved cash unless otherwise indicated. Indicate in which section of the statement of cash flows each transaction would be classified. Classify each transaction as one of the following:

a. An operating activity

b. An investing activity

c. A financing activity

d. Not included on the statement of cash flows.

E15-3   *(Cash management policies across companies)* Summaries of the 1991 statements of cash flows for five different companies follow. For each company compute the missing dollar amount, and briefly describe the company's cash-management policy for 1991.

Cash Provided (Used) by				
Company	Operations	Investments	Financing	Net Increase (Decrease)
AAA	$380	?	$(180)	$ (12)
BBB	219	(450)	240	?
CCC	?	(414)	7	(137)
DDD	150	(130)	?	420
EEE	?	(120)	(100)	92

E15-4   *(Journalizing and classifying transactions)* Presented below is a list of transactions entered into by Boyd Manufacturing during 1991.

(1) Recorded depreciation expense of $100,000.

(2) Sold 10,000 shares of common stock ($10 par value) for $25 per share.

(3) Purchased 5000 shares of IBM for $85 per share.

(4) Purchased a three-year insurance policy for $27,000.

(5) Purchased a building with a fair market value of $200,000 in exchange for a twenty-five-year mortgage. The agreement called for a down payment of $10,000.

Required: Assume that each transaction is independent. Provide the journal entry for each transaction, and indicate how the cash effect, if any, would be disclosed on the company's statement of cash flows. That is, provide

a. the dollar amount of the cash effect,

b. whether it increases or decreases cash, and

c. the section of the statement of cash flows in which it would appear.

E15-5   *(Converting accrual to cash numbers)* The following are several account titles that could appear on an income statement.

1. Cost of Goods Sold
2. Insurance Expense
3. Sales Revenue
4. Rent Expense
5. Dividend Revenue

6. Wage Expense
7. Supplies Expense
8. Interest Expense
9. Rent Revenue
10. Depreciation Expense

Several possible balance sheet accounts follow.

a. Cash
b. Merchandise Inventory
c. Retained Earnings
d. Unearned Sales Revenue
e. Interest Payable
f. Dividends Receivable
g. Fixed Assets
h. Rent Payable
i. Accounts Payable
j. Accounts Receivable
k. Premium on Bonds Payable
l. Allowance for Doubtful Accounts

m. Allowance for Unrealized Losses on Marketable Securities
n. Prepaid Rent
o. Wages Payable
p. Common Stock
q. Supplies Inventory
r. Discount on Bonds Payable
s. Unearned Rent
t. Marketable Securities
u. Prepaid Interest
v. Bonds Payable
w. Accumulated Depreciation
x. Prepaid Insurance

Required:

a. Assume that you wish to compute the cash inflow or outflow associated with each income statement account. Match each income statement account with the related balance sheet account (or accounts) you would analyze in this computation.

b. For Sales Revenue, Cost of Goods Sold, and Interest Expense, indicate whether an increase in the related balance sheet accounts (identified in [a]) would be added to or deducted from the income statement item when computing the cash effect.

E15–6 *(Depreciation: a source of cash?)* Your boss asks you to examine the following income statements of Hamilton Hardware, Crozier Craft Supplies, and Watson Glass.

	Hamilton Hardware	Crozier Crafts	Watson Glass
Sales	$900,000	$900,000	$900,000
Cost of goods sold	400,000	400,000	400,000
Depreciation expense	100,000	140,000	200,000
Other expenses	200,000	200,000	200,000
Net income	$200,000	$160,000	$100,000

In the notes to the financial statements you notice that Hamilton Hardware uses the straight-line method of depreciation, that Crozier Craft Supplies uses the sum-of-the-years'-digits method, and that Watson Glass uses the double-declining-balance method.

Required:

a. Compute cash provided (used) by operating activities for each company, assuming that the dollar amounts for sales, cost of goods sold, and other expenses reflect cash flows using each of the following:

(1) The direct method format
(2) The indirect method format.

b. Why is the cash provided (used) by operations different than net income? Which of the two methods shows this more clearly?

c. Would you agree or disagree with the following statement? "Depreciation is an important source of cash for most companies." Explain your answer.

E15–7

(Preparing a statement of cash flows from original transactions)   Steve and Kathy began a small retailing operation on January 1, 1991. During 1991 the following transactions occurred.

(1) Steve and Kathy contributed $10,000 of their own money to the business.

(2) $60,000 was borrowed from the bank.

(3) Long-lived assets were purchased for $20,000 cash.

(4) Inventory was purchased: $30,000 cash and $10,000 on account.

(5) Inventory with a cost of $25,000 was sold for $80,000: $15,000 cash and $65,000 on account.

(6) Cash payments included $20,000 for operating expenses, $5000 for loan principal, and a $2000 dividend.

(7) $10,000 in expenses were accrued at the end of the year.

Required:

a. Prepare journal entries for each economic event.

b. Prepare a balance sheet as of the end of 1991 and an income statement and statement of retained earnings for 1991 for Steve and Kathy's business.

c. Prepare a Cash T-account and a statement of cash flows using the direct method.

d. Prepare a statement of cash flows using the indirect method, but this time prepare it from the company's two balance sheets, the income statement, and the statement of retained earnings. Steve and Kathy's first balance sheet contains all zero balances.

E15–8

(Preparing a statement of cash flows from the cash account in the ledger)   Driftwood Shipbuilders entered into the following transactions during 1991.

(1) Sold $4000 of no par value common stock.

(2) Purchased $6500 of inventory on account.

(3) Purchased new equipment for $3400.

(4) Collections on accounts receivable totaled $10,000.

(5) Made payments to suppliers of $5000.

(6) Declared and paid dividends of $3000.

(7) Paid rent of $12,000 for the last six months of 1991 and the first six months of 1992.

(8) Made sales totaling $100,000: $39,000 on account and the remainder for cash.

(9) Paid $45,000 in cash for miscellaneous expenses.

(10) Sold marketable securities with a cost of $20,000 for $25,000.

Required:

a. Prepare journal entries for each transaction.

b. Prepare a Cash T-account and post all transactions affecting cash to the account. Assume a beginning cash balance of $25,000.

c. Prepare a statement of cash flows (direct method) from the cash T-account.

E15–9

(Computing cash outflows from accrual information)   The following year-end totals were taken from the records of Landau's Supply House. Compute the cash outflows associated with insurance and wages during 1991.

	1991	1990
Prepaid insurance	$7000	$4000
Wages payable	6000	0
Insurance expense	3000	5000
Wage expense	9000	2000

E15-10

(*Reconstructing a transaction and its cash effect*) The following information was taken from the records of Johnson and Daley, Inc.

	1991	1990
Machinery	$ 30,000	$ 20,000
Accumulated depreciation	(15,000)	(12,000)
Depreciation expense	7,000	6,000
Gain on sale of machinery	2,000	500

Additional Information: Machinery with a cost of $5000 was sold during 1991.

Required:

a. How much machinery was purchased during 1991?

b. How much cash was collected on the sale of the machinery during 1991?

c. Provide the journal entry to record the sale of the machinery.

E15-11

(*Computing cash provided by operations from accrual information*) Income statement and balance sheet excerpts of Shevlin and Shores for the period ending December 31, 1990, follow. Compute cash provided (used) by operating activities for the period ending December 31, 1990. Use both the direct and indirect forms of presentation.

Income Statement Excerpts

Sales		$45,000
Cost of goods sold		30,000
Gross profit		15,000
Wage expense	$3,000	
Advertising expense	1,000	
Depreciation expense	2,000	6,000
Net income		$ 9,000

Balance Sheet Excerpts

Account	1990	1989
Accounts receivable	$4,000	$ 6,000
Deferred revenues	0	3,000
Inventory	9,000	12,000
Accounts payable	3,000	4,000
Wages payable	1,800	700
Prepaid advertising	3,000	1,000
Accumulated depreciation	5,000	3,000

E15-12

(*Preparing a statement of cash flows from information contained in two balance sheets, an income statement, and a statement of retained earnings*) The following information was taken from the records of L. L. Corn and Company. Prepare a statement of cash flows (direct method) for the period ending December 31, 1991. Assume that all transactions involve cash.

Account	1991	1990
Cash	$ 5,000	$ 8,000
Noncash operating assets	15,000	13,000
Nonoperating assets	20,000	30,000
Operating liabilities	1,000	8,000
Nonoperating liabilities	6,000	4,000
Contributed capital	25,000	30,000
Retained earnings	8,000	9,000
Revenues	35,000	
Expenses	34,000	
Dividends	2,000	

E15–13

(Preparing a statement of cash flows from information contained in two balance sheets, an income statement, and a statement of retained earnings) The following information was taken from the records of Jones Supply House. Prepare a statement of cash flows (direct method) for the period ending December 31, 1991. Assume that all transactions involve cash.

Account	1991	1990
Cash	$ 9,000	$ 5,000
Noncash operating assets	18,000	25,000
Nonoperating assets	27,000	23,000
Operating liabilities	7,000	2,000
Nonoperating liabilities	6,000	10,000
Contributed capital	35,000	30,000
Retained earnings	6,000	11,000
Revenue	59,000	
Expense	61,000	
Dividends	3,000	

E15–14

(Computing net income from cash provided by operating activities) The operating cash flows and balance sheet excerpts of Schlee and Associates for the period ending December 31, 1990 follow. Compute net income for the period ending December 31, 1990.

Operating Activities

Cash inflows from sales	$ 65,000
Cash payments for inventories	(40,000)
Cash payments for wages	(6,000)
Cash payments for advertising	(1,000)
Cash provided (used) by operating activities	$ 18,000

Balance Sheet Excerpts

Account	1990	1989
Accounts receivable	$ 3,000	$ 9,000
Deferred revenues	4,000	2,000
Inventory	15,000	10,000
Accounts payable	7,000	4,000
Wages payable	2,100	1,300
Prepaid advertising	5,000	8,000
Accumulated depreciation	8,000	3,000

PROBLEMS

P15-1

(Placing transactions on the statement of cash flows) The following events occurred during 1990 for Frames Unlimited.

(1) Purchased inventory for $50,000 in cash.

(2) Recorded $80,000 in insurance expense for the portion of an insurance policy that expired in 1987.

(3) Paid $50,000 for rental space that the company will not use until 1989.

(4) Sold land with a cost of $80,000 for $95,000 cash.

(5) Repaid $90,000 on a long-term note. Included in the $90,000 is $15,000 in interest, $9000 of which was accrued in 1989.

(6) Recorded bad debt expense in the amount of $45,000.

(7) Reissued 5000 shares of treasury stock for $30 per share. The stock was acquired at $20 per share.

(8) Declared and issued a stock dividend. 10,000 shares of common stock ($10 par value) were issued with a fair market value at the time of $25 per share.

(9) Issued $500,000 face value bonds for cash at a total discount of $30,000.

(10) Purchased a building for $100,000 in cash, $50,000 in common stock, and a note with a present value of $217,000.

(11) Recorded $40,000 in sales to customers on account.

Frames Unlimited is in the process of preparing a statement of cash flows under the direct method.

Required: Use a chart like the one shown to indicate the following.

a. The section of the statement of cash flows in which each transaction should be listed. Use the following terms:

(1) Operating—for operating activities

(2) Investing—for investing activities

(3) Financing—for financing activities

(4) N/A—for items that would not be included on the statement of cash flows

b. Whether the transaction would involve an inflow or an outflow of cash

c. The dollar amount, if appropriate, that the company would report on the statement of cash flows.

The first transaction is done for you as an example.

Transaction	Section	Inflow	Outflow	Amount
(1)	Operating		✓	$50,000

P15-2

(Placing transactions on the statement of cash flows) Koppel Enterprises entered into the following transactions during 1987.

(1) Sold merchandise for $50,000 in cash.

(2) Purchased a parcel of land. The company paid $20,000 in cash and issued a note payable for the remainder.

(3) Purchased a three-year insurance policy for $65,000.

(4) Purchased a building in exchange for a long-term note with a face value and present value of $115,000.

(5) Collected $100,000 on a long-term note receivable. Included in the $100,000 is $6000 in interest earned and accrued in the previous period and $4000 in interest earned in the current period.

(6) Collected $30,000 for customers that will not be earned until 1995.

(7) Reacquired 5000 shares of its common stock for $10 per share.

(8) Declared and paid a cash dividend of $70,000.

(9) Paid $25,000 for wages incurred in a prior period.

(10) Retired $500,000 in bonds payable. The company gave the creditor $300,000 in cash and $200,000 in common stock.

(11) Purchased $40,000 of inventory on account.

(12) Wrote off an open account receivable ($5000) as uncollectible.

(13) Recorded $90,000 in depreciation expense for the year.

Koppel Enterprises is in the process of preparing its statement of cash flows under the direct method.

Required: Use the following chart format to indicate the following.

a. The section of the statement of cash flows in which each transaction would be listed. Use the following terms:

(1) Operating—for operating activities

(2) Investing—for investing activities

(3) Financing—for financing activities

(4) N/A—for items that would not be included on the statement of cash flows.

b. Whether the transaction would involve an inflow or an outflow of cash.

c. The dollar amount, if appropriate, that the company would report on the statement of cash flows.

The first transaction is done for you as an example.

Transaction	Section	Inflow	Outflow	Amount
(1)	Operating	✓		$50,000

P15–3   *(Classifying transactions and their cash effects)* MHT Enterprises entered into the following transactions during 1993.

(1) Sold a piece of equipment for $1000 with a book value of $800.

(2) Purchased a parcel of land for $10,000.

(3) Purchased a three-year insurance policy for $9000.

(4) Issued 1000 shares of common stock at $5 per share.

(5) Collected a short-term note, including interest, in the amount of $2500.

(6) Collected $3000 that will not be earned until 1995.

(7) Purchased a building in exchange for a long-term note with a face value of $15,000 (the present value of the note is $12,000).

(8) Declared and paid a dividend in kind valued at $7000.

(9) Paid $500 in wages.

(10) Converted an outstanding receivable into a short-term note receivable that matures in February 1994.

(11) Purchased $4500 of inventory on account.

(12) Wrote off an account ($500) as uncollectible.

(13) Recorded $9000 in depreciation expense for the year.

Required:

a. The controller of MHT Enterprises is trying to explain the change in the company's cash balance from January 1, 1993, to December 31, 1993. The controller has asked you to analyze each of the transactions. You are to indicate whether cash was provided, used, or not affected by each transaction. If the cash balance is affected by the transaction, indicate the dollar amount of the increase or decrease. Unless otherwise indicated, assume that all transactions involve cash.

b. Classify each transaction identified in (a) as affecting cash as one of the following:

    1. An operating activity

    2. An investing activity

    3. A financing activity.

P15–4   *(Classifying transactions and their cash effects)*   Several transactions entered into by Luther Winery during 1993 follow.

(1) Received $50,000 for wine previously sold on account.

(2) Paid $55,000 in wages.

(3) Sold a building for $100,000. The building had cost $170,000 and the related accumulated depreciation at the time of sale was $55,000.

(4) Declared and paid a dividend in kind valued at $500,000.

(5) Repurchased 10,000 shares of outstanding common stock at $50 per share.

(6) Purchased a two-year $100,000 fire and storm insurance policy on June 30.

(7) Purchased some equipment in exchange for 1000 shares of common stock. The stock was currently selling for $75 per share.

(8) Purchased $500,000 in equity securities considered to be long term.

(9) Issued $200,000 face value in bonds. The bonds were sold at 101.

(10) Owed $30,000 in rent as of December 31.

Required: Record each transaction on a chart like the following. Classify the sections of the statement of cash flows as cash flow from operating, investing, or financing activities. Transaction (1) is done as an example. (*Hint:* Some transactions may affect more than one section of the statement. For these transactions allocate the appropriate dollar amount to each section.)

Transaction	Effect on Cash	Section of Statement	Explanation
(1)	+50,000	Operating	Operations is defined in terms of inventory activity.

P15–5   *(A company's cash-management policy across time)*   Ruttman Enterprises began operations in early 1988. Summaries of the statement of cash flows for the years 1988, 1989, and 1990 follow.

	1990	1989	1988
Cash provided (used) by operating activities	?	$(202)	?
Cash provided (used) by investing activities	$ 100	?	$(500)
Cash provided (used) by financing activities	(150)	300	900
Increase (decrease) in cash	?	(2)	88
Cash balance at beginning of year	86	?	0
Cash balance at end of year	176	86	?

Required:

a. Compute the missing dollar amounts.

b. Briefly comment on the company's cash-management policy over the three-year period.

P15-6   *(Deriving the cash effects of investing transactions)*   Webb Industries reported the following information concerning the company's property, plant and equipment in the 1994 financial report.

	1994	1993
Buildings	$ 750,000	$800,000
Accumulated depreciation	(100,000)	(90,000)
Equipment	500,000	400,000
Accumulated depreciation	(75,000)	(85,000)
Land	250,000	250,000
Depreciation expense: buildings	30,000	25,000
Depreciation expense: equipment	10,000	12,000

Listed below are four independent cases involving buildings, equipment, and land during 1994.

(1) The company purchased a building for $200,000.

(2) The company sold equipment in December that was purchased for $50,000 at the beginning of the year. It recorded a gain of $5000 on the sale and also recorded a depreciation expense of $10,000 at the time of sale.

(3) The company sold a piece of land for $300,000 at a gain of $75,000.

(4) The company acquired a building in exchange for land. The land had a book value of $150,000 and a market value of $600,000.

Required:

a. For each case explain the change from 1993 to 1994 in the Buildings, Equipment, and Land accounts. (For example, in Case [1] explain the change in the Building account, the related Accumulated Depreciation account, and the balance in the related Depreciation Expense account.)

b. For each case compute the effect on the cash balance and indicate the appropriate disclosure on the statement of cash flows.

P15-7   *(Deriving the cash generated from a common stock issuance)*   The stockholders' equity section of Merton's Associates is provided below.

	1991	1990
Common stock ($1 par value)	$128,000	$100,000
Additional paid-in capital (C/S)	55,000	12,000
Retained earnings	41,000	35,000
Treasury stock	(5,000)	(10,000)*
Total stockholders' equity	$219,000	$137,000

*4000 shares at $2.50 per share.

Additional Information About Transactions During 1991

(1) 1/1/91: A 20 percent stock dividend was issued. The fair market value of the stock at the time was $3.00 per share.

(2) 5/10/91: Treasury stock with a cost of $5000 was sold for $3000.

(3) 8/25/91: Land was purchased in exchange for 6000 shares of common stock. The fair market value of the stock was $3.00 per share.

(4) 12/31/90: Common stock was issued for cash.

Required: How many shares of common stock did Merton issue during 1991, and how much cash did the issuance generate? Show all calculations clearly. (*Hint:* Calculate the number of shares of common stock issued for cash.)

P15-8

(Converting cash flow numbers to accrual numbers, and vice versa) Wilson, Inc. began operations in 1990. The following selected information was extracted from its financial records.

	1991	1990
Sales returns	$ 25,000	$ 20,000
Cost of goods sold	375,000	280,000
Inventory	110,000	125,000
Accounts receivable	150,000	100,000
Insurance expense	50,000	35,000
Cash collected on sales	500,000	350,000
Accounts payable	115,000	105,000
Cash paid for insurance	80,000	65,000

Required:

a. Compute gross sales (accrual basis) for 1990 and 1991.

b. Calculate the amount of cash paid to suppliers during 1991 for inventory.

c. Compute the balance in the Prepaid Insurance account as of December 31, 1990, and December 31, 1991.

P15-9

(Reconciling the income statement, the direct method, and the indirect method) Battery Builders, Inc. prepared statements of cash flows under both the direct and the indirect methods. The operating sections of each statement under the two methods follow. Prepare an income statement from the information provided.

Direct method

Collections from customers	$ 24,000
Payments to suppliers	(13,000)
Payments for operating expenses	(9,000)
Cash provided (used) by operating activities	$ 2,000

Indirect Method

Net income	$ 6,000
Depreciation	4,000
Gain on sale of equipment	(2,000)
Increase in inventory	(3,000)
Increase in accounts receivable	(3,000)
Increase in accounts payable	2,000
Decrease in accrued payables	(2,000)
Cash provided (used) by operating activities	$ 2,000

P15-10

(Manipulating dollar amounts on the statement of cash flows) Pendleton Enterprises began operations on January 1, 1989. Balance sheet and income statement information for 1989, 1990, and 1991 follow.

	1991	1990	1989
Cash	$ 6,000	$ 9,000	$ 7,000
Accounts receivable	8,000	5,000	4,000
Accounts payable	5,000	3,000	2,000
Revenues	12,000	14,000	8,000
Expenses	14,000	9,000	6,000

Required:

a. Assume that all balance sheet accounts are current. Prepare the operating sections of the statements of cash flows for 1989, 1990, and 1991 under the direct method.

b. Assume that the $4000 of outstanding accounts receivable on December 31, 1989 was actually collected before the end of 1989. Prepare the statements of cash flows under the direct method for all three years.

c. Ignore the assumption on (b), and assume alternatively that the company deferred an additional $3000 on the payment of accounts payable as of December 31, 1989 (i.e., accounts payable equal $5000, and cash equals $10,000 on December 31, 1989). Prepare the operating section of the statements of cash flows for all three periods.

d. How can managers manipulate cash provided (used) by operations, and what usually happens in the subsequent period?

P15–11   *(Preparing the statement of cash flows from two balance sheets and an income statement)*   The 1990 and 1991 balance sheets and related income statement of Watson and Holmes Detective Agency follow. Prepare a statement of cash flows under both the direct and the indirect methods for 1991.

Balance Sheet	1991	1990
Assets		
Cash	$10,000	$ 8,000
Accounts receivable	7,000	4,000
Less: Allowance for doubtful accounts	1,000	500
Inventory	8,000	7,000
Long-lived assets	12,000	10,000
Less: Accumulated depreciation	4,000	2,000
Total assets	$32,000	$26,500
Liabilities and Stockholder's Equity		
Accounts payable	5,000	4,000
Deferred revenues	1,000	2,000
Long-term note payable	10,000	10,000
Less: Discount on note payable	800	1,000
Common stock	12,000	8,000
Retained earnings	4,800	3,500
Total liabilities and stockholders' equity	$32,000	$26,500

Income Statement	
Revenues	$40,000
Cost of goods sold	22,000
Depreciation expense	2,000
Interest expense	4,000
Bad debt expense	2,000
Other expenses	8,000
Net income	$ 2,000

P15–12   *(Paying short-term debts: effects on working capital, the current ratio, and the statement of cash flows)*   Lumbard and Brothers began operations on January 1, 1989. They engaged in the following economic events during 1989.

(1) Issued 5000 shares of no-par common stock for $10 per share.

(2) Purchased on account 20,000 units of inventory for $1 per unit.

(3) Paid and capitalized $6000 for rent covering 1989 and 1990.

(4) Purchased furniture for $30,000, paying $20,000 in cash and signing a long-term note for the remaining balance.

(5) Sold on account 9000 units of inventory for $3.50 per unit.

(6) Paid one half of the outstanding accounts payable.

(7) Received $10,000 from customers on open accounts.

(8) Paid miscellaneous expenses of $9000 for the year.

(9) Depreciation recorded on the furniture totaled $5000.

(10) Accrued interest on the long-term note payable amounted to $1000.

(11) Declared dividends of $3000 at year end to be paid in January, 1990.

(12) Recorded entry for rent expired during 1989.

Required:

a. Prepare journal entries for these events.

b. Prepare an income statement, statement of retained earnings, balance sheet, and statement of cash flows (indirect method).

c. Compute working capital and the current ratio.

d. Assume that the company pays the outstanding accounts payable on the final day of 1989. Recompute working capital, the current ratio, and cash provided (used) by operating activities.

P15–13   *(Preparing the statement of cash flows and reconciling the operating section with the income statement)* Stern Marketing *included the following statements in its 1992 financial report.*

Income Statement

Marketing revenue	$1,000,000
Salary expense	250,000
Office supplies used	175,000
Depreciation expense	100,000
Insurance expense	60,000
Rent expense	120,000
Net income	$ 295,000

Balance Sheets	**1992**	**1991**
Cash	$100,000	$125,000
Accounts receivable	150,000	100,000
Office supply inventory	75,000	100,000
Prepaid insurance	50,000	10,000
Office furniture	500,000	450,000
Less: Accumulated Depreciation	325,000	225,000
Total assets	$550,000	$560,000
Rent payable	$ 20,000	$ —
Common stock ($10 par value)	100,000	100,000
Additional paid-in capital	125,000	125,000
Retained earnings	305,000	335,000
Total liabilities and stockholders' equity	$550,000	$560,000

Required:

a. Convert each of the accrual-basis income statement accounts to a cash basis. Would you classify this method as directly or indirectly computing cash provided (used) by operating activities?

b. Prepare a proof of results. That is, begin with net income and adjust net income to arrive at cash provided (used) by operating activities. Would you classify this method as directly or indirectly computing cash provided (used) by operating activities?

c. Refer to Figure 15−15 in the chapter, and use the same format to reconcile the income statement with operating cash flows.

P15−14   *(Constructing a balance sheet from the statement of cash flows)*   Johnson Vending Company began operations on January 5, 1992. The company's statement of cash flows for the year ended December 31, 1992 follows.

Operating Activities			
Net Income		$1,000,000	
Adjustments to net income			
Depreciation	$ 100,000		
Change in accounts receivable	(75,000)		
Change in accounts payable	50,000		
Change in inventory	(115,000)		
Change in prepaid insurance	(5,000)		
Unrealized loss on marketable securities	10,000		
Change in wages payable	15,000	$ (20,000)	
Net cash provided (used) by operating activities			$ 980,000
Investing Activities			
Acquisition of fixed assets		$ (650,000)	
Purchase of securities		(250,000)	
Net cash provided (used) by investing activities			$(900,000)
Financing Activities			
Issue of common stock ($10 par value, 10,000 shares)		$ 175,000	
Issue of bonds (200 bonds each with $1,000 face value)		195,000	
Payment of cash dividends		(100,000)	
Net cash provided (used) by financing activities			$ 270,000
Net increase (decrease) in cash balance			350,000
Beginning cash balance			0
Ending cash balance			$ 350,000

Required: Assume that all accounts had a balance of zero as of January 5, 1992. Using the statement of cash flows, construct the company's balance sheet as of December 31, 1992.

P15−15   *(Additional questions about Johnson Vending's statement of cash flows)*   Johnson Vending Company began operations on January 5, 1992. The company's statement of cash flows is presented in (P15−14).

Required:

a. Using the company's statement of cash flows, answer the following questions. Provide support for each answer.

   (1) What amount of net income did the company generate during 1992? Was net income more or less than cash from operations?

   (2) What was the market value of short-term marketable securities on December 31, 1992?

   (3) What was the balance in Additional Paid-in Capital (common stock) as of December 31, 1992?

   (4) Why were dividends paid in cash included in the section for "Cash used by financing activities"?

   (5) Why was depreciation added back to net income to arrive at cash provided by operating activities?

(6) Why were the changes in the accounts other than Cash used to adjust net income to arrive at the amount of cash provided by operating activities? Explain each adjustment.

(7) Were cash collections on sales greater than or less than the dollar amount of sales on the income statement?

b. Did Johnson Vending Company use the direct or indirect method in preparing its statement of cash flows? Explain your answer.

P15–16   *(Preparing the statement of cash flows from two balance sheets and an income statement: book losses and amortized discounts)*   The following information was extracted from the financial records of Lewis Manufacturing Industries.

Income Statement

Sales	$200,000
Cost of goods sold	90,000
Depreciation expense	25,000
Interest expense	15,000
Salary expense	12,000
Supplies expense	6,000
Loss on sale of marketable securities	5,000
Loss on sale of fixed assets	10,000
Net income	$ 37,000

Balance Sheets

	1994	1993
Cash	$ 747,000	$ 593,000
Marketable securities	85,000	140,000
Accounts receivable	450,000	400,000
Supplies inventory	10,000	12,000
Inventory	150,000	175,000
Short-term notes receivable	100,000	50,000
Machinery and equipment	550,000	500,000
Accumulated depreciation	90,000	75,000
Total assets	$2,002,000	$1,795,000
Accounts payable	$ 60,000	$ 95,000
Wages payable	10,000	10,000
Bonds payable	500,000	500,000
Discount on bonds payable	5,000	10,000
Common stock ($10 par value)	200,000	100,000
Additional paid-in capital	900,000	800,000
Retained earnings	337,000	300,000
Total liabilities and stockholders' equity	$2,002,000	$1,795,000

Additional Information:

1. The company purchased machinery in exchange for 10,000 shares of common stock. The stock was selling for $20 per share at the time.

2. The short-term receivable was received from a customer in exchange for the sale of merchandise inventory.

Required: Prepare a statement of cash flows for the year ended December 31, 1994, using both the direct and the indirect methods.

P15-17 *(Preparing the statement of cash flows from two balance sheets and an income statement: book gains and amortized premiums)* The following information was extracted from the 1994 financial records of Conlon Restaurant Supply Company.

Income Statement

Sales	$160,000
Cost of goods sold	100,000
Depreciation expense	12,000
Insurance expense	10,000
Interest expense	11,000
Gain on sale of plant equipment	10,000
Net income	$ 37,000

Balance Sheets	**1994**	**1993**
Cash	$173,000	$120,000
Accounts receivable	60,000	65,000
Inventory	210,000	110,000
Prepaid insurance	14,000	24,000
Plant equipment	275,000	350,000
Less: Accumulated depreciation	67,000	75,000
Total assets	$665,000	$594,000
Accounts payable	$ 51,000	$ 45,000
Bonds payable	200,000	200,000
Premium on bonds payable	3,000	5,000
Common stock ($10 par value)	75,000	50,000
Additional paid-in capital	125,000	100,000
Retained earnings	211,000	194,000
Total liabilities and stockholders' equity	$665,000	$594,000

Additional Information:
The company sold a piece of plant equipment for cash that had originally cost $100,000. The accumulated depreciation associated with the equipment at the time of sale was $20,000.

Required: Prepare a statement of cash flows for the year ended December 31, 1994, using both the direct and the indirect methods.

P15-18 *(Preparing the statement of cash flows and using it to set dividend policy)* Rudnicki Engineering Firm provided the following income statement for 1994 in its annual financial report.

	1994		**1993**	
Sales		$5,967,000		$5,590,000
Salary expense	$2,025,000		$1,794,000	
Advertising expense	755,000		710,000	
Bad debt expense	275,000		260,000	
Administrative expenses	898,000		832,000	
Janitorial expense	132,000		120,000	
Supplies expense	281,000		299,000	
Depreciation expense	963,000	5,329,000	978,000	4,993,000
Net income		$ 638,000		$ 597,000

Additional Information:
(1) The company declared and paid a dividend of $550,000 in 1993, but did not declare any dividends in 1994.

(2) 1993

(a) 35 percent of the sales were on account.

(b) The accounts receivable balance decreased by $2,980,000 from January 1 to December 31.

(c) As of December 31, the company still owed $145,000 in wages and $67,000 on the supplies used during the year.

(3) 1994

(a) 75 percent of the sales were on account.

(b) The Accounts Receivable balance increased by $1,671,750 from January 1 to December 31.

(c) As of December 31, the company still owed $25,000 in wages and $50,000 in advertising.

(d) On January 1, 1993, the company had a balance of $13,245 in cash.

(4) The company had no write-offs or recoveries of accounts receivable during 1993 or 1994.

Required:

a. Prepare the operating section of the statement of cash flows for 1993 and 1994, using the direct method.

b. Assume that you are a member of the board of directors of the Rudnicki Engineering Firm. Several influential stockholders have called you and complained that the company generated more net income in 1994 than in 1993, yet chose not to declare a dividend in 1994. How would you explain the board's position on dividends in 1993 versus 1994?

P15–19
(Preparing a complete set of financial statements from a set of original transactions) Adams Photographic Equipment began operations on January 1, 1993. During 1993 the company entered into the following transactions.

(1) Sold $2,050,000 of merchandise in exchange for cash. The related inventory had cost $875,000.

(2) Issued 50,000 shares of $15 par value common stock for $30 per share in exchange for cash. Also issued, for cash, 1000 shares of 10 percent, $100 par value preferred stock for $102 per share.

(3) Purchased $750,000 of fixed assets in exchange for cash.

(4) Sold $880,000 of merchandise on account. The related inventory had a cost of $490,000. $500,000 of the sales made on account were collected during the year.

(5) Purchased $2,000,000 of inventory on account. $1,075,000 were subsequently paid during 1993.

(6) Paid $500,000 in miscellaneous expenses (rent, utilities, and wages).

(7) Purchased a two-year insurance policy for $80,000.

(8) Purchased short-term marketable securities for $250,000.

(9) Issued twenty bonds, each with a face value of $1000, at 146 (annual coupon rate = 16 percent and annual yield rate = 10 percent). The bonds pay interest semiannually on December 31 and June 30.

(10) Declared, but did not pay, a $100,000 dividend.

(11) Purchased land in exchange for 1000 shares of $15 par value common stock. The shares were selling for $40 per share at the time.

(12) Made the first interest payment on the bonds on December 31.

Adjusting entries:

(a) The fixed assets were purchased on January 1 and had an estimated useful life and salvage value of five years and $50,000, respectively. The company uses the straight-line depreciation method.

(b) The company used one-fourth of the insurance policy during 1993.

(c) The market value of the marketable securities on December 31 was $225,000.

(d) As of December 31, the company had incurred, but had not yet paid, $75,000 in miscellaneous expenses.

(e) The company estimates that 8 percent of credit sales will prove uncollectible.

(f) The market value of the inventory was $5000 less than the cost.

Required:

a. Prepare journal entries for each of the original and adjusting transactions. Establish T-accounts for each account. Post the entries to the T-accounts.

b. Prepare the necessary closing entries. Post these entries.

c. Prepare the income statement and balance sheet for Adams Photographic Equipment for the year ended December 31, 1993.

d. Prepare the statement of cash flows for Adams Photographic Equipment for the year ended December 31, 1993, using both the direct and the indirect methods.

P15–20   *(Preparing the financial statements: an advanced example)*   Wallace Corporation included the following balance sheet as of December 31, 1993, in its 1993 financial report.

Cash	$ 57,000	Accounts payable	$ 95,000
Marketable securities	275,000	Rent payable	10,000
Less: Allowance for unrealized losses		Dividends payable	250,000
on marketable securities	5,000	Unearned sales revenue	50,000
Accounts receivable	600,000	Short-term note payable	100,000
Less: Allowance for doubtful accounts	25,000	Bonds payable	500,000
Inventory	475,000	Less: Discount on bonds payable	50,000
Prepaid insurance	15,000	Common stock (100,000 shares,	
Equity investment in Lewis, Inc.	345,000	$10 par value)	1,000,000
Land	399,000	Additional paid-in capital (C/S)	438,000
Building	125,000	Retained earnings	857,000
Less: Accumulated depreciation	24,000	Less: Treasury stock	212,000
Plant and equipment	868,000	Total liabilities and stockholders'	
Less: Accumulated depreciation	82,000	equity	$3,038,000
Patent	15,000		
Total assets	$3,038,000		

During 1994 Wallace Corporation entered into the following transactions.

(1) Sold short-term marketable securities that had originally cost $180,000 for $198,000.

(2) Sold $4,243,000 of merchandise on account. The related inventory had cost $2,476,000.

(3) Repaid the principal on the short-term note payable, and incurred and paid $5000 in interest on the note.

(4) Sold 5000 shares of treasury stock for $30 per share. The shares had been purchased at $25 per share.

(5) Made interest payments on June 30 and December 31 on the bond payable. The annual coupon rate is 10 percent, while the annual yield rate is 12 percent.

(6) Purchased $3,180,000 of inventory. $3,100,000 was purchased on account, and the remainder was purchased for cash.

(7) Purchased a parcel of land for $500,000 in cash.

(8) Received $75,000 in dividends from the investment in Lewis, Inc. (Wallace Corp. owns 25 percent of Lewis, Inc.)

(9) Paid $957,000 in miscellaneous expenses (wages, utilities, and rent), including the rent payable.

(10) Collected $4,550,000 from open accounts.

(11) Paid $2,320,000 to suppliers in settlement of open accounts.

(12) Distributed the dividend payable, and declared and paid an additional dividend of $200,000.

(13) Collected $100,000 in cash for services that would not be rendered until 1996.

(14) Purchased $355,000 in short-term marketable securities.

(15) Sold a piece of fully-depreciated equipment for $7250 that had originally cost $50,000.

(16) Wrote off $18,000 of accounts receivable as uncollectible.

Adjusting Entries (12/31/94):

(a) The market value of short-term marketable securities on December 31 exceeded the cost by $1000.

(b) Historically, 10 percent of ending accounts receivable have proven to be uncollectible.

(c) Lewis, Inc. generated a net loss of $60,000.

(d) The building has an estimated salvage value of $6,000 and an estimated *remaining* life of five years.

(e) The plant and equipment have an estimated salvage value of $86,000 and an estimated *remaining* life of seven years.

(f) The prepaid insurance expires on April 1, 1995.

(g) The patent has a *remaining* useful life of three years.

(h) As of December 31, 1994, Wallace Corporation owes $20,000 in rent.

Required:

a. Ignoring income taxes, prepare journal entries for each of the original and adjusting entries.

b. Prepare the necessary closing entries.

c. Prepare the income statement for Wallace Corporation for the year ended December 31, 1994.

d. Prepare a cash T-account showing all activity affecting cash during 1994.

e. Prepare a statement of cash flows for Wallace Corporation for the year ended December 31, 1994, using both the direct and the indirect methods.

f. Using the December 31, 1993, balance sheet and the statement of cash flows, prepare a balance sheet for Wallace Corporation as of December 31, 1994.

CASES

C15-1

(Are depreciation and amortization sources of cash?) Airborne Express, Inc. provides door-to-door express delivery of small packages and documents throughout the United States. Its December 31, 1987 income statement included the following.

Revenues	$632,303*
Expenses	
Transportation	233,914
Station and ground operations	175,761
Flight operations and maintenance	78,379
General and administrative	75,901
Sales and advertising	25,928
Depreciation and amortization	40,824
Net income	$ 1,596

*Dollars in thousands.

Required: Critique the following statement: On the company's statement of cash flows, the dollar amount of depreciation and amortization was added to net income in the computation of cash provided (used) by operations. It would appear, then, that depreciation and amortization represent sources of cash for Airborne Express.

C15–2

(Classifying cash flows, especially interest and dividends) King's Table operates buffet style restaurants throughout the U.S. In 1986, the company pursued a strategy of remodeling and expansion, using cash from operating activities and bank borrowings.

Required:

a. In which section of the statement of cash flows (operating, investing or financing) would the following items appear?
  (1) Cash borrowed from a bank
  (2) Cash paid for remodeling
  (3) Cash paid to build a new restaurant
b. If the company had issued stock specifically for expansion projects, in which section of the statement of cash flows would the cash proceeds from the sale of stock appear?
c. In which sections of the statement of cash flows would interest paid on the bank borrowings and dividends paid to the stockholders appear? Since interest represents a return to debt capital providers, why is it not disclosed in the same section as dividends, which represent a return to equity capital providers?

C15–3

(Analyzing a statement of cash flows) The statements of cash flows for the years 1986, 1987, and 1988 of The Quaker Oats Company follow (dollars in millions).

	1988	1987	1986
Operating activities			
Net income	$ 255.7	$ 243.9	$ 179.6
Depreciation and amortization	121.9	112.2	76.7
Other noncash charges to noncurrent accounts	(18.0)	60.7	18.1
(Increase) in receivables	(73.1)	(216.0)	(31.8)
(Increase) in inventories	(53.4)	(72.9)	(39.0)
Decrease (increase) in other current assets	201.6	(174.4)	22.2
Increase in accounts payable	16.5	74.6	25.2
(Decrease) increase in other current liabilities	(5.6)	161.0	15.4
Other, net	23.9	36.7	17.7
Cash provided (used) by operating activities	469.5	225.8	284.1
Investing activities			
Additions to property, plant, and equipment	(207.2)	(182.3)	(146.6)
Cost of acquiring other companies	—	(556.9)	—
Decrease (increase) in long-term receivables and investments	(5.9)	43.8	(47.2)
Disposition of businesses	—	74.6	—
Disposals of property, plant, and equipment	32.4	24.1	16.2
Cash provided (used) by investing activities	(180.7)	(596.7)	(177.6)

	1988	1987	1986
Financing activities			
Cash dividends	(79.9)	(63.2)	(57.5)
Change in deferred compensation	1.5	1.1	(20.0)
Net increase (decrease) in debt	(458.9)	634.3	123.1
Issuance of treasury stock	33.4	49.1	20.0
Purchase of treasury stock	(53.6)	—	(116.1)
Redemption of preferred stock	—	—	(34.2)
Cash provided (used) by financing activities	(557.5)	621.3	(84.7)
Net (decrease) increase in cash and short-term investments	$(268.7)	$250.4	$ 21.8

Required: Answer the following questions.

a. The Quaker Oats Company has expanded considerably over the last three years. Explain where the company has generated the funds to finance this expansion.

b. What major transaction did the company enter into in 1987? How did the company generate the funds to finance this transaction?

c. In which two current assets has the company been investing over the past three years? Compute the total net investment in these two current assets.

d. Cash dividends over the past three years have been what percent of net income?

e. In what way did the company use the cash it generated through operating activities during 1988?

f. Summarize the company's cash-management strategy over the past three years.

C15-4
(The statement of changes in financial position and the statement of cash flows) The following statement was included in the 1986 financial report of The Procter & Gamble Company. It is a statement of changes in financial position, which was replaced in 1988 by the statement of cash flows (dollars in millions).

	1986
Sources of funds	
Net earnings	$ 709
Depreciation, depletion, and amortization	491
Other noncash charges to noncurrent accounts	213
Total from operations	1,413
Additions to long-term debt	1,562
Decrease (increase) in accounts receivable	(28)
Increase in payables and accrued liabilities	216
Issuance of preferred stock	250
Other items, net	(91)
Total sources of funds	3,322
Use of Funds	
Capital expenditures	1,069
Dividends to shareholders	445
Reduction of long-term debt	114
Increase in inventories	69
Decrease in short-term debt	6
Acquisitions of other companies	1,532
Total use of funds	3,235
Increase (decrease) in cash and marketable securities	$ 87

Required:

a. Compute cash provided (used) by operating, investing, and financing activities. Assume that "Other items, net" refer to increases in current assets.

b. Prepare a statement of cash flows assuming beginning cash of $100 million.

c. In what way does the present statement of cash flows provide an improved format over the statement of changes in financial position.

d. Discuss the cash-management policies followed by Procter & Gamble during 1986.

C15-5   *(Accrual and cash flow accounting)*   In *Forbes* Loan Officer Jan Blackford commented that cash flow analysis has risen in importance due to a "trend over the past twenty years toward capitalizing and deferring more and more expenses. Although the practice may match revenues and expenses more closely, a laudable intent, it has also made it harder to find the available cash in a company—and easier for lenders to wind up with a loss." The article further stated that "During [a recent recession] a wave of bankruptcies drew attention to the need for better warning signals of the sort cash flow analysis could provide."*

*Jinny St. Goar, "Where's 4th quarter profits reflecting unusual accounting method? *Forbes,* 8 April 1985, p. 120.

Required:

a. Why would the process of capitalizing match revenues and expenses more closely, yet make it harder to find the cash available in a company?

b. Discuss the difference between earning power and solvency, why both are essential for a successful business, and how present-day financial accounting statements provide measures of each.

c. Explain why a wave of bankruptcies would draw attention to cash flow analysis.

PART 3

Additional Important Issues

Consolidated Financial Statements and International Operations

Learning Objectives

1 Distinguish between a business acquisition and a merger.

2 Explain how to account for a business acquisition or merger under the purchase method.

3 Explain how to account for a business acquisition or merger under the pooling-of-interests method.

4 Describe the economic consequences associated with preparing consolidated financial statements.

5 Define an exchange rate, and describe how fluctuating exchange rates give rise to gains and losses.

6 Define hedging, and explain how it can reduce the risks associated with fluctuating exchange rates.

7 List the basic steps involved when preparing consolidated statements for multinationals with foreign subsidiaries.

8 List the four basic kinds of accounting systems used in the world, and describe the efforts by international groups to bring about greater harmony among the accounting practices used in different countries.

≡ Many companies expand by purchasing other companies and/or extending operations into other countries. For example, as of December 31, 1987, Johnson & Johnson, one of the world's largest consumer products companies, owned 28 different U.S. companies as well as 159 companies that operated in 60 different countries throughout the world. In 1986 alone Johnson & Johnson spent $416 million acquiring other domestic and foreign operations. This chapter covers the methods used to account for such acquisitions and the special accounting issues related to transacting with entities operating in foreign countries. It also provides a brief summary of the accounting standards and practices in foreign countries as well as the relatively recent efforts of international accounting standard-setting bodies to develop guidelines for financial reporting, auditing, ethics, and education. These efforts encourage greater uniformity and understanding of the accounting practices used throughout the world.

CONSOLIDATED FINANCIAL STATEMENTS

Chapter 13 covered long-term investments in the equity securities of other companies. There we noted that equity investments of less than 20 percent of the investee company's outstanding voting stock are accounted for under either the lower-of-cost-or-market method or the cost method. Investments between 20 percent and 50 percent of the outstanding voting stock indicate "significant influence" over the operations of the investee company, and are accounted for under the equity method. Investments in excess of 50 percent of the investee company's outstanding voting stock give rise to **consolidated financial statements,** which reflect the combined accounts of both the investor and the investee companies. Virtually all major U.S. corporations prepare financial statements on a consolidated basis. The following excerpt is from the 1987 financial report of IBM and is typical of the disclosures made by other major U.S. companies.

> *The consolidated financial statements include the accounts of International Business Machines Corporation and its U.S. and non-U.S. subsidiary companies. Investments in . . . other companies, in which IBM has a 20–50 percent ownership, are accounted for by the equity method. Investments of less than 20 percent are accounted for by the cost method.*

The remainder of this section distinguishes business acquisitions from mergers and covers the methods used to account for such transactions. The section concludes with a discussion of the economic consequences related to reporting consolidated financial statements.

Business Acquisitions and Mergers Distinguished

A **business acquisition** occurs when an investor company acquires a **controlling interest** (more than 50 percent of the voting stock) in another (investee) company. If the two companies continue as separate legal entities, the investor company is referred to as the **parent,** and the investee company is called the **subsidiary.** In December 1986, for example, Time, Inc. acquired the outstanding stock of

Scott, Foresman and Co., the publisher of this text, which continues to operate as a subsidiary of Time. In such cases consolidated financial statements (including the income statement, balance sheet, statement of retained earnings, statement of cash flows, and statement of stockholders' equity) are prepared by the parent. Consolidated statements ignore the fact that the parent and the subsidiary are actually separate legal entities and, for reporting purposes, treat the two companies as a single operating unit.

Consolidated statements are prepared for financial accounting purposes only. The parent and the subsidiary maintain separate legal status and, in many respects, may continue to operate as relatively independent entities. In addition, the subsidiary prepares a separate set of financial statements, and both the subsidiary and the parent maintain separate sets of accounts. Professional accounting standards require that the financial condition and results of operations of the two companies be presented to the public in a single set of financial statements because the parent has a controlling interest over the subsidiary, and thus has the ability to exert control over its operations.

A **merger** or **business combination** occurs when two or more companies combine to form a single legal entity. In most cases the assets and liabilities of the smaller company are merged into those of the larger, surviving, company. The stock of at least one company, usually the smaller, is often retired, and the merged company ceases to exist as a separate organization. In 1986, for example, Magic Chef, Inc., a manufacturer of home appliances and soft-drink vending equipment, ceased to exist as a separate entity when it was merged into the Maytag Corporation. Technically speaking, consolidated financial statements are not prepared after a merger because there is no parent/subsidiary relationship. At least one of the companies involved in the combination no longer exists. However, the financial statements of the surviving company do reflect the assets, liabilities, and operations of the merged entity.

A business acquisition often precedes a merger. That is, a parent acquires the stock of a subsidiary and then later decides to merge the subsidiary's operations into those of the parent. In December 1986, for example, Delta Airlines purchased all of the outstanding common stock of Western Airlines for $787 million. Western operated as a wholly owned subsidiary until April 1, 1987, when Delta decided to merge Western's operations into its own. At that time Western ceased to exist as an independent entity.

Accounting for Business Acquisitions and Mergers: The Purchase Method

Equity shares in other companies can be acquired by paying cash or other assets, issuing stock, or issuing bonds to the acquired company's shareholders. Often some combination of these forms of payment is used. When Delta Air Lines acquired Western Air Lines, for example, the $787 million payment to Western's shareholders consisted of $383 million in cash and 8.3 million shares of Delta stock, each with a value of $48.75.

For simplicity, in the following examples we assume that cash is paid for the acquired stock. In such cases, and in the overwhelming majority of all cases, the **purchase method** is used to account for acquisitions and mergers. During 1986,

Figure 16–1   Balance sheets for Multi Corporation and Littleton Company (before acquisition)

Multi Corporation Balance Sheet December 31, 1990		Littleton Company Balance Sheet December 31, 1990	
Assets		Assets	
Cash	$ 65,000	Cash	$ 6,000
Accounts receivable	70,000	Accounts receivable	9,000
Notes receivable	35,000	Inventory	10,000
Inventory	120,000	Long-lived assets (net)	35,000
Long-lived assets (net)	230,000		
Total assets	$520,000	Total assets	$60,000
Liabilities and stockholders' equity		Liabilities and stockholders' equity	
Accounts payable	$ 90,000	Accounts payable	$14,000
Long-term note	130,000	Long-term notes payable	16,000
Common stock	200,000	Common stock	22,000
Retained earnings	100,000	Retained earnings	8,000
Total liabilities and stockholders' equity	$520,000	Total liabilities and stockholders' equity	$60,000
		Additional information Common shares outstanding	8,000

for example, McGraw Hill, Inc., a large publishing company, made fourteen acquisitions, all for cash, and all accounted for as purchases. In certain limited situations, however, where a large portion of the payment entails issuing common stock to the subsidiary's shareholders, another method, called pooling-of-interests, can be used. The following discussion covers the purchase method; the pooling-of-interests method is covered later in this section.

To illustrate how the purchase method is used to account for business acquisitions and mergers, assume that on December 31, 1990, Multi Corporation acquired a controlling interest in the equity shares of Littleton Company. The December 31 balance sheets for both companies and some additional information for Littleton Company appear in Figure 16–1.

When a parent company (Multi Corporation) purchases a controlling interest in a subsidiary (Littleton), the parent is essentially purchasing the assets and liabilities of the subsidiary. It is important to realize that the historical costs of the subsidiary's assets, which are included on Littleton's balance sheet in Figure 16–1, are of little consequence to the purchase decision. The parent is actually purchasing the fair market values, not the historical costs, of the assets and liabilities of the subsidiary. An important rule, therefore, in understanding the purchase method of accounting for consolidated financial statements is the following: Under the purchase method, when a parent purchases a controlling interest in a subsidiary, the assets and liabilities of the subsidiary are recorded on the balance sheet of the parent at their fair market values.

Figure 16–2   Fair market values for Littleton Company

Littleton Company Schedule of Fair Market Values of Assets and Liabilities December 31, 1990	
Cash	$ 6,000
Accounts Receivable	9,000
Inventory	15,000
Long-Lived Assets	40,000
Accounts Payable	(14,000)
Long-Term Notes Payable	(16,000)
Fair market value of net assets	$ 40,000

Consequently, from Multi Corporation's standpoint it is more appropriate to view the value of Littleton's net assets as shown in Figure 16–2, where all assets and liabilities have been valued at their individual fair market values. As of December 31, 1990, 8000 shares of Littleton common stock are outstanding. The per-share market value of the net assets, therefore, is $5 ($40,000÷8000 shares).

The following sections account for Multi Corporation's purchase of Littleton shares under four independent cases: (1) purchase 100 percent of the common stock for a price equal to the per-share market value of the net assets, (2) purchase between 50 percent and 100 percent of the common stock for a price equal to the per-share market value of the net assets, (3) purchase 100 percent of the common stock for a price greater than the per-share market value of the net assets, and (4) purchase between 50 percent and 100 percent of the common stock for a price greater than the per-share market value of the net assets.[1]

Case 1: Purchase 100 percent of Littleton Stock at the Per-Share Market Value of the Net Assets

Assume that Multi Corporation purchased all 8000 shares of the outstanding stock of Littleton for $5 per share, a total cost of $40,000. To record the initial acquisition, Multi Corporation would make the following journal entry.

Dec. 31   Investment in Subsidiary   40,000
        Cash   40,000
        To record the purchase of 8000 shares of Littleton common
        stock at $5 per share.

When consolidated financial statements are prepared, Multi Corporation must add Littleton's assets and liabilities, at their *fair market values,* to its balance sheet; at the same time, to avoid double counting, Multi must eliminate the $40,000 originally recognized in the Investment in Subsidiary account. The following adjusting journal entry, therefore, is recorded in the books of Multi Corporation before consolidated statements are prepared.

---

1. It is unusual for a company to be purchased for less than the fair market value of its net assets, and we do not cover such cases in this text. These situations are covered in intermediate or advanced financial accounting texts.

Dec. 31	Cash	6,000	
	Accounts Receivable	9,000	
	Inventory	15,000	
	Long-Lived Assets	40,000	
	Accounts Payable		14,000
	Long-Term Note Payable		16,000
	Investment in Subsidiary		40,000

To add the assets and liabilities of Littleton at fair market value and eliminate the investment account.

These two journal entries simply serve to add the assets and liabilities of Littleton, the subsidiary, to the balance sheet of Multi Corporation, the parent, at their fair market values. Note that recording the assets and liabilities of the subsidiary on the parent's balance sheet at fair market value does not violate the historical cost principle. From the parent's standpoint, these dollar amounts represent the costs of the assets and liabilities purchased in the acquisition. They can be documented by an objectively verifiable transaction.

Note also that under the purchase method, the stockholders' equity accounts of the subsidiary (e.g., Common Stock, Additional Paid-in Capital, and Retained Earnings) are not reflected on the consolidated financial statements of the parent. These accounts represent the ownership interests of Littleton's original stockholders, which now have been transferred to the stockholders of Multi Corporation in the form of Littleton's assets and liabilities. To include both the assets and liabilities of Littleton as well as its stockholders' equity accounts on the consolidated financial statements would essentially be counting the same items twice.

In this case the fair market value of the net assets and liabilities ($40,000) exactly equals the purchase price ($40,000). Such situations, however, are unusual because most companies have accumulated a certain amount of goodwill, which implies that the value of the subsidiary exceeds the fair market value of its net assets. The more common case, where the purchase price exceeds the fair market value of the net assets, is illustrated later in Cases 3 and 4.

The preceding example presented two journal entries that Multi Corporation would record to reflect the acquisition of Littleton in the preparation of consolidated financial statements. An alternative, but equivalent, way to prepare consolidated financial statements involves a worksheet, which is illustrated in Figure 16–3.

To prepare a consolidated balance sheet using a worksheet, the separate balance sheets of Multi Corporation and Littleton Company, after the acquisition, should initially be placed in the first two columns of the worksheet. The adjusting/eliminating entry serves (1) to adjust the inventory ($5000) and long-lived assets ($5000) of Littleton to reflect their fair market values and (2) to eliminate the $40,000 Investment in Subsidiary account as well as Littleton's Common Stock ($22,000) and Retained Earnings ($8000) accounts from the consolidated balance sheet. After recording the adjusting/eliminating entry, the totals for the consolidated balance sheet accounts are prepared simply by adding (or subtracting) across the rows.

The adjusting journal entry illustrated earlier and the worksheet illustrated in Figure 16–3 are equivalent, both accomplishing the same purpose. Each method reflects the fact that the ownership interests of Littleton's original stockholders have been transferred to the stockholders of Multi Corporation in the form of Littleton's assets and liabilities, valued at their fair market values.

Figure 16–3   Worksheet for Multi Corporation: Case 1

			Adjustments and Eliminations		Consolidated Balance Sheet
Accounts	**Multi Corp.**	**Littleton Co.**	**Dr.**	**Cr.**	
		Multi Corporation Consolidated Worksheet December 31, 1990			

Accounts	**Multi Corp.**	**Littleton Co.**	**Dr.**	**Cr.**	**Consolidated Balance Sheet**
Cash	25,000	6,000			31,000
Accounts Receivable	70,000	9,000			79,000
Notes Receivable	35,000	—			35,000
Inventory	120,000	10,000	5,000		135,000
Investment in Subsidiary	40,000	—		40,000	—
Long-Lived Assets	230,000	35,000	5,000		270,000
Total Assets	520,000	60,000	10,000	40,000	550,000
Accounts Payable	90,000	14,000			104,000
Long-Term Note	130,000	16,000			146,000
Common Stock	200,000	22,000	22,000		200,000
Retained Earnings	100,000	8,000	8,000		100,000
Total Liabilities and Stockholders' Equity	520,000	60,000	30,000		550,000

Case 2: Purchase Between 50 Percent and 100 Percent of Stock at the Per-Share Market Value of the Net Assets

Assume that Multi Corporation purchased 6400 shares (80 percent) of Littleton's outstanding stock for $5 per share, a total cost of $32,000. The journal entries to record the transaction, entered on the books of Multi Corporation, are provided in Figure 16–4.

In this case, as in Case 1, the journal entry to record the acquisition serves to add the assets and liabilities of Littleton to the balance sheet of Multi Corporation at their fair market values. However, now the purchase price ($32,000) is less than the fair market value of Littleton's net assets and liabilities ($40,000) because Multi Corporation purchased only 80 percent of Littleton's stock. As a result, $8000 is credited to an account called **Minority Interest,** which represents that portion of the subsidiary's stock owned by individuals or entities other than the parent **(minority stockholders).** The dollar amount of this credit ($8000) is computed by multiplying the net value of Littleton's assets and liabilities ($40,000) by the portion of Littleton's stock that is owned by the minority stockholders (20 percent). The Minority Interest account is necessary because Multi Corporation included all of Littleton's assets and liabilities on the consolidated balance sheet, yet it only owns 80 percent of the outstanding stock.

The economic significance of minority interest is somewhat unclear. It can be interpreted as a liability, in that it represents an interest held by outsiders in a portion of the net assets listed on the consolidated balance sheet. On the other hand, it resembles a stockholders' equity item because the interest held by outsiders is an equity interest held by outside stockholders. Consequently, minority interest is

Figure 16–4 Consolidated journal entries for Multi Corporation: Case 2

Dec. 31	Investment in Subsidiary	32,000	
	Cash		32,000
	To record the purchase of 6,400 shares (80%) of Littleton common stock.		
Dec. 31	Cash	6,000	
	Accounts Receivable	9,000	
	Inventory	15,000	
	Long-Lived Assets	40,000	
	Accounts Payable		14,000
	Long-Term Note Payable		16,000
	Minority Interest (20% × $40,000)		8,000
	Investment in Subsidiary		32,000
	To add the assets and liabilities of Littleton at fair market value and eliminate the investment account.		

normally disclosed on the consolidated balance sheet between the long-term liability and the stockholders' equity sections.[2]

As in Case 1, we prepared the consolidated balance sheet using the worksheet, as illustrated in Figure 16–5. The worksheet in Figure 16–5 differs from that in Figure 16–3 (Case 1) in two basic ways: (1) Multi Corporation's cash position is $8000 higher, because the investment in the subsidiary is $32,000 instead of $40,000 and (2) Minority Interest in the amount of $8000 is recognized on the transaction.

Case 3: Purchase 100 Percent of Stock at a Price Greater than the Per-Share Market Value of the Net Assets

Assume that Multi Corporation purchased all 8000 shares of the outstanding stock of Littleton for $8 per share, a total cost of $64,000. The journal entries to record the transaction appear in Figure 16–6.

The purchase price in this case ($64,000) exceeds the fair market value of Littleton's net assets ($40,000) by $24,000; therefore, goodwill is recognized on the acquisition. Multi Corporation apparently believes that Littleton is worth more than the fair market value of its net assets. It paid $3 per share over and above the $5 ($40,000÷8000) per-share market value of the net assets, resulting in a total payment of $24,000 ($3/sh × 8000 shares) for goodwill, which Littleton had accumulated up to the date of the purchase. Goodwill, an intangible asset, appears on the asset side of the consolidated balance sheet, usually below fixed assets, and is amortized over a period of time not to exceed forty years. (Goodwill is also discussed in Chapter 5, Appendix 9A, and Chapter 13.)

As in Cases 1 and 2, we prepared the consolidated balance sheet using the worksheet, as illustrated in Figure 16–7.

---

2. There are several different views on how to account for purchases where a parent acquires between 50 percent and 100 percent of the subsidiary's outstanding stock. As a result, the appropriate computation of minority interest and its classification as a liability or a stockholders' equity item on the consolidated balance sheet are also somewhat controversial. In this text we have adopted primarily what is called an *entity view* because we believe it to be logical, consistent, and understandable. However, other views, which are discussed in advanced accounting texts, are followed by a significant number of U.S. companies.

Figure 16–5   Worksheet for Multi Corporation: Case 2

<table>
<tr><td colspan="6" align="center">Multi Corporation
Consolidated Worksheet
December 31, 1990</td></tr>
<tr>
<td rowspan="2">Accounts</td>
<td rowspan="2">Multi Corp.</td>
<td rowspan="2">Littleton Co.</td>
<td colspan="2">Adjustments
and Eliminations</td>
<td rowspan="2">Consolidated
Balance Sheet</td>
</tr>
<tr><td>Dr.</td><td>Cr.</td></tr>
<tr><td>Cash</td><td>33,000</td><td>6,000</td><td></td><td></td><td>39,000</td></tr>
<tr><td>Accounts Receivable</td><td>70,000</td><td>9,000</td><td></td><td></td><td>79,000</td></tr>
<tr><td>Notes Receivable</td><td>35,000</td><td>—</td><td></td><td></td><td>35,000</td></tr>
<tr><td>Inventory</td><td>120,000</td><td>10,000</td><td>5,000</td><td></td><td>135,000</td></tr>
<tr><td>Investment in
  Subsidiary</td><td>32,000</td><td>—</td><td></td><td>32,000</td><td>—</td></tr>
<tr><td>Long-Lived Assets</td><td>230,000</td><td>35,000</td><td>5,000</td><td></td><td>270,000</td></tr>
<tr><td>Total Assets</td><td>520,000</td><td>60,000</td><td>10,000</td><td>32,000</td><td>558,000</td></tr>
<tr><td> </td><td></td><td></td><td></td><td></td><td></td></tr>
<tr><td>Accounts Payable</td><td>90,000</td><td>14,000</td><td></td><td></td><td>104,000</td></tr>
<tr><td>Long-Term Note</td><td>130,000</td><td>16,000</td><td></td><td></td><td>146,000</td></tr>
<tr><td>Minority Interest</td><td>—</td><td>—</td><td></td><td>8,000</td><td>8,000</td></tr>
<tr><td>Common Stock</td><td>200,000</td><td>22,000</td><td>22,000</td><td></td><td>200,000</td></tr>
<tr><td>Retained Earnings</td><td>100,000</td><td>8,000</td><td>8,000</td><td></td><td>100,000</td></tr>
<tr><td>Total Liabilities and
  Stockholders' Equity</td><td>520,000</td><td>60,000</td><td>30,000</td><td>8,000</td><td>558,000</td></tr>
</table>

Figure 16–6   Consolidated journal entries for Multi Corporation: Case 3

Dec. 31	Investment in Subsidiary	64,000	
	Cash		64,000
	To record the purchase of 8,000 shares of Littleton common stock at $8 per share.		
Dec. 31	Cash	6,000	
	Accounts Receivable	9,000	
	Inventory	15,000	
	Long-Lived Assets	40,000	
	Goodwill ($3* × 8,000 sh.)	24,000	
	Accounts Payable		14,000
	Long-Term Note Payable		16,000
	Investment in Subsidiary		64,000
	To add the assets and liabilities of Littleton at fair market value and eliminate the investment account.		

*$8 price per share − $5 per share market value of net assets

Figure 16–7 Worksheet for Multi Corporation: Case 3

			Adjustments and Eliminations		Consolidated Balance Sheet
Accounts	**Multi Corp.**	**Littleton Co.**	**Dr.**	**Cr.**	
Cash	1,000	6,000			7,000
Accounts Receivable	70,000	9,000			79,000
Notes Receivable	35,000	—			35,000
Inventory	120,000	10,000	5,000		135,000
Investment in Subsidiary	64,000	—		64,000	—
Long-Lived Assets	230,000	35,000	5,000		270,000
Goodwill	—	—	24,000		24,000
Total Assets	520,000	60,000	34,000	64,000	550,000
Accounts Payable	90,000	14,000			104,000
Long-Term Note	130,000	16,000			146,000
Common Stock	200,000	22,000	22,000		200,000
Retained Earnings	100,000	8,000	8,000		100,000
Total Liabilities and Stockholders' Equity	520,000	60,000	30,000		550,000

Multi Corporation
Consolidated Worksheet
December 31, 1990

Transactions where 100 percent of a subsidiary's stock is purchased at a price that exceeds the per-share market value of the subsidiary's net assets are very common. In 1987 alone, Ralston Purina Company, for example, made four such acquisitions (Eveready Batteries, Drake Bakeries, Continental Baking Company, and Benco Pet Foods, Inc.), each of which was accounted for under the purchase method. The total purchase price of the four acquisitions equaled approximately $2 billion and gave rise to the entries in Figure 16–8.

Case 4: Purchase between 50 Percent and 100 Percent of Stock at a Price Greater than the Per-Share Market Value of the Net Assets

Assume that Multi Corporation purchased 6400 shares (80 percent) of Littleton's outstanding stock for $8 per share, a total cost of $51,200. The journal entries to record the transaction appear in Figure 16–9.

In this case both goodwill and minority interest are recognized. Goodwill is recognized because Multi Corporation paid $8 for each share, which is $3 more than the $5 per-share market value of the net assets. The total goodwill recognized by Multi Corporation on the transaction is $19,200 (6400 shares × $3). Minority interest is recognized because Multi Corporation purchased only 80 percent of Littleton's stock. As in Case 2, the amount of minority interest recognized on the transaction is computed by multiplying the fair value of the Littleton's net assets ($40,000) times the percentage of Littleton's shares owned by the minority stockholders (20 percent).

Figure 16–8   Journal entries to record 1987 purchases by Ralston Purina Company (dollars in millions)

Investment in Subsidiaries	2,005	
Cash		2,005
To record the purchase of subsidiaries during 1987.		
Working Capital*	312	
Fixed Assets	1,138	
Goodwill	604	
Long-Term Liabilities		49
Investment in Subsidiaries		2,005
To add the assets and liabilities of purchased subsidiaries at fair market value and eliminate the investment account.		

*Represents excess of current assets over current liabilities.

Figure 16–9   Consolidated journal entries for Multi Corporation: Case 4

Dec. 31	Investment in Subsidiary	51,200	
	Cash		51,200
	To record the purchase of 6,400 shares (80%) of Littleton common stock at $8 per share.		
Dec. 31	Cash	6,000	
	Accounts Receivable	9,000	
	Inventory	15,000	
	Long-Lived Assets	40,000	
	Goodwill ($3* × 6,400 sh)	19,200	
	Accounts Payable		14,000
	Long-Term Note Payable		16,000
	Minority Interest (20% × $40,000)		8,000
	Investment in Subsidiary		51,200
	To add the assets and liabilities of Littleton at fair market value and eliminate the investment account.		

*$8 price per share − $5 per share market value of net assets.

As in Cases 1, 2, and 3, we prepare the consolidated balance sheet using the worksheet, as illustrated in Figure 16–10.

Acquisitions where both goodwill and minority interest are recognized occur periodically in the United States, but are much less common than those where 100 percent of the subsidiary's stock is purchased. Often, such transactions are followed quite closely by the acquisition of the outstanding minority stock. In 1986, for example, Alcoa acquired approximately 91 percent of the outstanding stock of TRE Corporation for $326 million, of which $239 million were paid in cash. This transaction recognized both goodwill and minority interest, which were included in Alcoa's 1986 balance sheet, an excerpt of which appears in Figure 16–11. In January 1987, shortly after the acquisition, Alcoa acquired the remaining outstanding stock, and TRE became a wholly owned subsidiary of Alcoa.

Figure 16–10   Worksheet for Multi Corporation: Case 4

Accounts	Multi Corp.	Littleton Co.	Adjustments and Eliminations Dr.	Adjustments and Eliminations Cr.	Consolidated Balance Sheet
Multi Corporation					
Consolidated Worksheet					
December 31, 1990					
Cash	13,800	6,000			19,800
Accounts Receivable	70,000	9,000			79,000
Notes Receivable	35,000	—			35,000
Inventory	120,000	10,000	5,000		135,000
Investment in Subsidiary	51,200	—		51,200	—
Long-Lived Assets	230,000	35,000	5,000		270,000
Goodwill	—	—	19,200		19,200
Total Assets	520,000	60,000	29,200	51,200	558,000
Accounts Payable	90,000	14,000			104,000
Long-Term Note	130,000	16,000			146,000
Minority Interest	—	—		8,000	8,000
Common Stock	200,000	22,000	22,000		200,000
Retained Earnings	100,000	8,000	8,000		100,000
Total Liabilities and Stockholders' Equity	520,000	60,000	30,000	8,000	558,000

Figure 16–11   Excerpt from balance sheet for Alcoa

Alcoa
Excerpt from 1986 Consolidated Balance Sheet
December 31, 1986
(dollars in millions)

Current assets	$2,250
Property, plant, and equipment	6,230
Goodwill	230
Other assets	835
Total assets	$9,545
Current liabilities	$1,411
Long-term liabilities	3,622
Minority interests	791
Stockholders' equity	3,721
Total liabilities and stockholders' equity	$9,545

Source: 1986 annual report.

Intercompany Receivables and Payables

When the parent company prepares a consolidated balance sheet, in addition to the adjusting entry to add the assets and liabilities at fair market value and eliminate the investment account, any receivables or payables between the parent and the subsidiary (intercompany receivables and payables) must also be eliminated. Such eliminating entries avoid including receivables and payables that, from the perspective of the consolidated financial statements, do not exist.

The following excerpt from the 1987 financial report of Toys "Я" Us describes how major U.S. companies account for intercompany transactions when preparing consolidated financial statements: "The consolidated financial statements include the accounts of the Company and its subsidiaries [as of] January 31, 1988. All material intercompany balances and transactions have been eliminated."

Suppose, for example, that prior to the acquisition of Littleton, Multi Corporation loaned Littleton $7000. After the loan, the $7000 would appear as a note receivable on Multi Corporation's balance sheet and a note payable on Littleton's. If no eliminating entry is recorded when Multi Corporation acquires Littleton, both the receivable and the payable will appear on Multi Corporation's consolidated financial statement, and it would seem that Multi Corporation owed money to itself. To avoid such a misstatement, Multi Corporation would record the following eliminating entry when preparing its consolidated financial statements.

Dec. 31	Note Payable	7000	
	Note Receivable		7000
	To eliminate a $7000 intercompany receivable and payable.		

To illustrate how such an elimination would appear on the consolidated worksheet, assume the same facts as Case 4 (Figure 16–10), except that Littleton owed Multi Corporation $7000, which gave rise to a receivable and payable that required elimination. The worksheet appears in Figure 16–12.

Consolidated Income Statement

Each of the four cases discussed for the preceding example illustrate how a consolidated balance sheet is prepared under the purchase method for an acquisition made on December 31, 1990, the last day of the year. The revenues and expenses of the subsidiary that were recognized during 1990 are not combined with those of the parent to form a consolidated income statement for 1990. Under the purchase method, only the revenues and expenses of the subsidiary that are recognized *after the date of the acquisition* are consolidated with those of the parent. In the four cases illustrated earlier, for example, the initial consolidated income statement would be prepared for the year 1991, not 1990. Subsidiary revenues and expenses recognized prior to the acquisition are not consolidated because the price paid for the subsidiary's stock by the parent, which appears on the December 31, 1990 consolidated balance sheet in the form of the market value of the subsidiary's net assets and goodwill, should already reflect the subsidiary's operating activities during 1990.

Preparing a consolidated income statement for a period subsequent to an acquisition requires that the revenues and expenses recognized by the subsidiary during that period be combined with those of the parent. As in the case of a consolidated balance sheet, **intercompany transactions** must also be eliminated to prevent double counting. Common intercompany revenues and expenses that must be eliminated when preparing a consolidated income statement include (1)

Figure 16–12 Worksheet for Case 4 with eliminating entries

	Multi Corporation						
	Consolidated Worksheet						
	December 31, 1990						

Accounts	Multi Corp.	Littleton Co.	Adjustments and Eliminations		Consolidated Balance Sheet
			Dr.	Cr.	
Cash	13,800	6,000			19,800
Accounts Receivable	70,000	9,000			79,000
Notes Receivable	35,000	—		7,000	28,000
Inventory	120,000	10,000	5,000		135,000
Investment in					
Subsidiary	51,200			51,200	—
Long-Lived Assets	230,000	35,000	5,000		270,000
Goodwill	—	—	19,200		19,200
Total Assets	520,000	60,000	29,200	58,200	551,000
Accounts Payable	90,000	14,000			104,000
Long-Term Note	130,000	16,000	7,000		139,000
Minority Interest	—	—		8,000	8,000
Common Stock	200,000	22,000	22,000		200,000
Retained Earnings	100,000	8,000	8,000		100,000
Total Liabilities and					
Stockholders' Equity	520,000	60,000	37,000	8,000	551,000

sales and purchases of goods and services between the parent and the subsidiary and (2) interest on receivables and payables between the parent and the subsidiary.[3] The following example illustrates how a consolidated balance sheet and a consolidated income statement can be prepared using a worksheet. Note that the consolidated statements are prepared one year after the date of the acquisition.

Assume that on January 1, 1990, Mammoth Corporation purchased 100 percent of the 10,000 outstanding shares of Small Company for $7 per share, a total price of $70,000. At that time the book value of Small Company was $35,000 ($25,000 in common stock and $10,000 in retained earnings). The book values of Small's inventory and long-lived assets were less than their fair market values by $5000 and $10,000, respectively, and the remaining assets and liabilities approximately reflected their market values. Thus, the fair market value of Small's net assets totaled $50,000 ($35,000 + $5000 + $10,000), and Mammoth paid $20,000 ($70,000 − $50,000) for goodwill.

During 1990 Mammoth loaned $9000 to Small Company, the principal of which was outstanding at year end, and accrued interest owed by Small to Mammoth totaled $600. The $9000 appeared as a note receivable on Mammoth's balance sheet and a note payable on Small's balance sheet. The $600 in accrued interest was recognized as a receivable and a revenue by Mammoth and as a

---

3. Other intercompany transactions that require elimination are not covered in this text. Such transactions are described in intermediate or advanced texts.

payable and an expense by Small. Also during 1990 Mammoth provided a service for Small Company, receiving $12,000 cash in payment, which was recognized as a revenue by Mammoth and an expense by Small. Figure 16–13 shows the consolidated financial statements prepared by Mammoth, as of December 31, 1990.

Mammoth Corporation's consolidated financial statements were prepared in six steps:

(1) The following journal entry was recorded on January 1, 1990, to recognize the purchase of Small's common stock for $70,000.

Investment in Subsidiary	70,000	
Cash		70,000
To record the purchase of Small's stock for $70,000.		

(2) The worksheet was prepared and the financial statements of Mammoth and Small, as of December 31, 1990, were placed in the first two columns. Note that the financial statements are dated one year after the acquisition.

(3) The assets of Small were adjusted to fair market value, the investment account and Small's stockholders' equity section were eliminated, and goodwill was recognized as of the acquisition date. (note *a*).

(4) Intercompany receivables and payables and revenues and expenses were eliminated (notes *b, c,* and *d*). To avoid double counting, the $9000 amount owed by Small to Mammoth (note *b*), the $600 of interest accrued on the loan (notes *c* and *d*), and Mammoth's $12,000 sale to Small (note *e*) were removed from the books of both companies.

(5) The dollar amounts for each balance sheet and income statement account were totaled across the rows of the worksheet. Note that the $18,000 retained earnings balance disclosed by Small consists of the $10,000 beginning of the year balance plus the $8000 net income earned during 1990.

(6) A portion of the goodwill that was recognized on the consolidation was amortized.

Pooling of Interests

We have assumed up to now that the parent acquired the outstanding voting stock of the subsidiary by paying cash to the stockholders of the subsidiary. As indicated earlier, other forms of payment, such as common stock and debt securities, are also common. A special case arises when substantially all the payment (at least 90 percent) is in the form of common stock issued by the parent to the stockholders of the subsidiary. In such a situation the parent has not acquired the subsidiary; instead, the two companies have combined their resources through an exchange of stock. The stockholders of both the parent and the subsidiary become stockholders of the consolidated entity and, therefore, have an interest in the assets and liabilities of that entity. Such an exchange is called a **pooling of interests.**

Pooling of interests is less common than purchase in corporate America, but it does occur occasionally. For example, in 1986 when Magic Chef, Inc. was merged into Maytag Corporation, the transaction was accounted for as a pooling of interests because Maytag received all the outstanding shares of Magic Chef by issuing 32.1 million shares of its common stock. Similarly, in 1985 Wendy's International

Figure 16–13 Worksheet for consolidated financial statements of Mammoth Corporation

Accounts	Mammoth	Small Co.	Adjustments and Eliminations Dr.	Adjustments and Eliminations Cr.	Consolidated Financial Statements
Balance sheet					
Cash	11,000	10,000			21,000
Accounts Receivable	69,000	9,000			78,000
Interest Receivable	1,000	—		600[c]	400
Notes Receivable	35,000	—		9,000[b]	26,000
Inventory	120,000	14,000	5,000[a]		139,000
Investment in Subsidiary	70,000			70,000[a]	—
Long-Lived Assets	230,000	44,000	10,000[a]		284,000
Goodwill	—	—	20,000[a]		20,000*
Total Assets	536,000	77,000	35,000	79,600	568,400
Accounts Payable	96,000	15,000			111,000
Interest Payable	—	3,000	600[c]		2,400
Long-Term Note	140,000	16,000	9,000[b]		147,000
Common Stock	200,000	25,000	25,000[a]		200,000
Retained Earnings	100,000	18,000	10,000[a]		108,000
Total Liabilities and Stockholders' Equity	536,000	77,000	44,600		568,400
Income statement					
Sales	215,000	45,000	12,000[e]		248,000
Interest Income	4,500		600[d]		3,900
Cost of Goods Sold	(120,000)	(23,000)			(143,000)
Selling and Administrative Expenses	(45,000)	(9,000)		12,000[e]	(42,000)
Interest Expenses	(15,000)	(2,000)		600[d]	(16,400)
Taxes	(12,000)	(3,000)			(15,000)
Net Income	27,500	8,000	12,600	12,600	35,500

[a] Entry to adjust assets to fair market value, eliminate investment account and Small's stockholders' equity section, and recognize goodwill.

[b] Entry to eliminate intercompany note receivable/payable of $9,000.

[c] Entry to eliminate intercompany interest receivable/payable of $600.

[d] Entry to eliminate intercompany interest income/expense of $600.

[e] Entry to eliminate intercompany sale/expense of $12,000.

*Note: Although not illustrated in this example, Mammoth should amortize a portion of the dollar amount of goodwill at the end of 1990.

considered it a pooling of interests when it acquired all the outstanding shares of Restaurant Systems, Inc., a franchise owner operating thirty-six restaurants in Georgia and Alabama, by issuing 3.4 million shares of its common stock.

Pooling of Interests: The Accounting Procedures

Two points are important in understanding the procedures used to account for a pooling of interests. First, the financial statements of the parent and the subsidiary, including the assets and liabilities as well as the revenues and expenses of the period in which the exchange occurs, are combined at book value, not fair market value. This accounting treatment reflects the fact that there is no acquisition or purchase by the parent. Instead, the parent and the subsidiary are simply combining resources that have already been accounted for on their individual financial statements.

Second, the total stockholders' equity of the consolidated entity after the combination must equal the stockholders' equity of the parent plus the stockholders' equity of the subsidiary prior to the combination. This equality must be maintained because no additional equity is created by the combination itself. However, the parent issues additional stock during the exchange, which increases the dollar amount of the parent's contributed capital accounts. To maintain the equality indicated above, therefore, this dollar amount must be charged against (reduce) certain capital accounts when consolidated financial statements are prepared. This amount is charged first against the Common Stock account of the subsidiary, second against the Paid-in Capital accounts of the parent and the subsidiary, and third against the Retained Earnings accounts of the parent and the subsidiary. This treatment reflects the fact that, in effect, the additional stock issued by the parent to the subsidiary's stockholders serves to replace the original stock of the subsidiary.

To illustrate the procedures used to account for a pooling of interests, refer to the December 31, 1990, balance sheets of Multi Corporation and Littleton Company in Figure 16–1. Assume that on December 31, 1990, Multi Corporation issued 2000 shares of its own common stock, with a $10 par value, to the shareholders of Littleton in exchange for 100 percent of Littleton's outstanding shares. The journal entry prepared by Multi Corporation follows.

Dec. 31	Investment in Subsidiary	30,000*	
	Common Stock (2000 sh × $10 par)		20,000
	Additional Paid-in Capital		10,000
	To record the exchange of 2000 shares of common stock for all the outstanding stock of Littleton Company.		

*Net book value of Littleton

Note that the investment account is valued at the book value, not the market value, of Littleton's net assets. As indicated earlier, in a pooling of interests the net assets of the subsidiary have not been purchased by the parent. The resources of the two companies have simply been combined. Thus, the fair market values of the subsidiary's assets and liabilities are no longer relevant, and the assets and liabilities of both companies are carried on the consolidated balance sheet at their original book values.

The worksheet containing the entry to eliminate the investment account appears in Figure 16–14. In addition, the worksheet contains the 1990 income statements of both Multi Corporation and Littleton. Recall that in a pooling of interests, in contrast to a purchase, the revenues and expenses of the parent and the subsidiary that are recognized during the period in which the combination occurs are combined in the preparation of consolidated financial statements. To simplify the example, we have assumed no intercompany transactions.

Figure 16–14   Worksheet for Multi Corporation: pooling of interests

Multi Corporation **Consolidated Worksheet** **December 31, 1990**					
Accounts	**Multi Corp.**	**Littleton Co.**	**Adjustments and Eliminations**		**Consolidated Financial Statements**
			Dr.	**Cr.**	
Balance sheet					
Cash	65,000	6,000 ·			71,000
Accounts Receivable	70,000	9,000			79,000
Notes Receivable	35,000	—			35,000
Inventory	120,000	10,000			130,000
Investment in Subsidiary	30,000	—		30,000	—
Long-Lived Assets	230,000	35,000			265,000
Total Assets	550,000	60,000	——	30,000	580,000
Accounts Payable	90,000	14,000			104,000
Long-Term Note	130,000	16,000			146,000
Common Stock	220,000*	22,000	22,000		220,000
Additional Paid-in Capital	10,000*	—	8,000		2,000
Retained Earnings	100,000	8,000			108,000
Total Liabilities and Stockholders' Equity	550,000	60,000	30,000		580,000
Income statement					
Sales	175,000	45,000			220,000
Cost of Goods Sold	(90,000)	(20,000)			(110,000)
Selling and Administrative Expenses	(65,000)	(22,000)			(87,000)
Net Income	20,000	3,000			23,000

*Includes stock issued during the exchange (C/S = $20,000, APIC = $10,000)

The eliminating entry on the worksheet, in addition to eliminating the Investment account ($30,000), serves first to eliminate Littleton's Capital Stock account ($22,000) and, second, to reduce the dollar amount of Paid-in Capital by $8000. In the unlikely case that the entire Paid-in Capital account of both the parent and the subsidiary had been reduced to zero, the remaining dollar amount would have been applied against Retained Earnings.

The stockholders' equity of Multi Corporation prior to the combination ($300,000) plus the stockholders' equity of Littleton ($30,000) equals the total stockholders' equity reported on the consolidated balance sheet ($330,000). The Retained Earnings amount reported on the consolidated balance sheet ($108,000), however, is larger than the retained earnings amount reported by

Figure 16–15 **Journal entries for Multi Corporation's stock issuance and acquisition of Littleton**

Dec. 31	Cash	64,000	
	Common Stock (2,000 sh. × $10 par)		20,000
	Additional Paid-in Capital		44,000
	To record the issuance of common stock for $64,000.		
Dec. 31	Investment in Subsidiary	64,000	
	Cash		64,000
	To record the acquisition of Littleton common stock.		

Multi Corporation ($100,000). In essence, the pooling-of-interests method allowed Multi Corporation to add Littleton's Retained Earnings balance ($8000) to its own. Note also that Littleton's 1990 net income ($3000) was added to that of Multi Corporation ($20,000) in the process of consolidation.

The Pooling-of-Interests Method and the Purchase Method: A Comparison

Assume that on December 31, 1990, Multi Corporation executed the business combination described in the previous section in two separate steps. First, it issued 2000 shares of common stock, each with a market price of $32, for $64,000 cash. Then it used the $64,000 to purchase the 8000 outstanding shares of Littleton at $8 per share. Note that these two transactions lead to the same result as a pooling of interests between Multi Corporation and Littleton. That is, Multi Corporation issued 2000 shares of common stock in exchange for 100 percent of Littleton's outstanding stock. However, as shown in Figure 16–15, the acquisition of Littleton would be accounted for as a purchase.

As with Figure 16–1, assume that the fair market values of Littleton's inventory and long-lived assets exceed their book values by $5000 each. The worksheet used to prepare the consolidated financial statements of Multi Corporation as of December 31, 1990, appears in Figure 16–16.

As discussed earlier, under the purchase method, the eliminating entry serves to eliminate the $64,000 in the Investment account, adjust the Inventory ($5000) and Long-Lived Assets ($5000) to reflect fair market value, and eliminate the Common Stock ($22,000) and Retained Earnings ($8000) of Littleton. In addition, the 1990 income statement accounts of Littleton are not added to those of Multi Corporation in the consolidated process.

Note that although the two transactions described are economically equivalent to a pooling of interests, the resulting consolidated financial statements are quite different (see Figures 16–14 and 16–16). To aid the comparison between pooling-of-interests and purchase accounting, both sets of financial statements are provided in Figure 16–17.

The basic differences between consolidated financial statements prepared under the pooling-of-interests and the purchase methods involve (1) the valuation of inventory and long-lived assets, (2) the recognition of goodwill, (3) the dollar amount of retained earnings, and (4) the treatment of income earned by the subsidiary during the period of, and prior to, the consolidation. These differences are summarized in Table 16–1.

Figure 16-16 Worksheet for Multi Corporation: purchase method using funds from stock issuance

	Multi Corporation Consolidated Worksheet December 31, 1990				

Accounts	Multi Corp.	Littleton Co.	Adjustments and Eliminations		Consolidated Financial Statements
			Dr.	Cr.	
Balance sheet					
Cash	65,000	6,000			71,000
Accounts Receivable	70,000	9,000			79,000
Notes Receivable	35,000	—			35,000
Inventory	120,000	10,000	5,000		135,000
Investment in Subsidiary	64,000	—		64,000	—
Long-Lived Assets	230,000	35,000	5,000		270,000
Goodwill	—	—	24,000		24,000
Total Assets	584,000	60,000	34,000	64,000	614,000
Accounts Payable	90,000	14,000			104,000
Long-Term Note	130,000	16,000			146,000
Common Stock	220,000	22,000	22,000		220,000
Additional Paid-in Capital	44,000	—			44,000
Retained Earnings	100,000	8,000	8,000		100,000
Total Liabilities and Stockholders' Equity	584,000	60,000	30,000		614,000
Income statement					
Sales	175,000	45,000*			175,000
Cost of Goods Sold	(90,000)	(20,000)*			(90,000)
Selling and Administrative Expenses	(65,000)	(22,000)*			(65,000)
Net Income	20,000	3,000*			20,000

*Not included in the consolidated financial statements because these revenues and expenses were recognized before the acquisition on December 31, 1990.

Accounting for Business Acquisitions and Mergers: Economic Consequences

The methods used to account for business acquisitions and mergers (purchase or pooling of interests) lead to economic consequences because the choice of method can affect important accounting numbers and ratios on the consolidated financial statements. These numbers are used by investors and creditors to assess earning power and solvency and to control and direct the actions of management through contracts.

Figure 16–17   Comparison of pooling-of-interests and purchase methods: Multi Corporation financial statements

	Multi Corporation Consolidated Financial Statements December 31, 1990	
Consolidated Financial Statements	**Pooling of Interest**	**Purchase Method**
Balance sheet		
Cash	$ 71,000	$ 71,000
Accounts receivable	79,000	79,000
Notes receivable	35,000	35,000
Inventory	130,000	135,000
Long-lived assets	265,000	270,000
Goodwill	—	24,000
Total assets	$580,000	$614,000
Accounts payable	104,000	104,000
Long-term note	146,000	146,000
Common stock	220,000	220,000
Additional paid-in capital	2,000	44,000
Retained earnings	108,000	100,000
Total liabilities and stockholders' equity	$580,000	$614,000
Income Statement		
Sales	$220,000	$175,000
Cost of goods sold	(110,000)	(90,000)
Selling and administrative expenses	(87,000)	(65,000)
Net income	$ 23,000	$ 20,000

Table 16–1   Differences between the pooling-of-interests and purchase methods

Accounts Affected	Pooling of Interests	Purchase
Assets and liabilities of subsidiary	Historical cost	Fair market value
Goodwill	Not recognized	Excess of cost over fair market value of net assets
Retained earnings of subsidiary	Added to retained earnings of parent	Eliminated
Income of subsidiary recognized in period of, and prior to, consolidation	Added to income of parent	Not recognized

In the 1960s, for example, when companies were relatively free to choose between the pooling-of-interests and purchase methods, the pooling-of-interests method was very popular. Many companies chose it for three basic reasons: (1) to increase their retained earnings' balances; (2) to avoid carrying assets at inflated market values and recognizing goodwill, which increased future depreciation and amortization charges; and (3) to inflate consolidated net income by including the subsidiary's entire earnings for the year on the consolidated income statement, regardless of when during the year the acquisition took place. In 1970 the accounting profession concluded that such practices often misstated the financial statements, and reacted by significantly limiting the conditions under which the pooling-of-interests method was allowed. Among other restrictions, for example, pooling-of-interest accounting can only be used when at least 90 percent of the payment made by the parent is in the form of common stock, and the exchange must occur in a single transaction.

Now that the criteria for allowing the pooling-of-interests method are more restrictive, it is considerably less popular than it was in the 1960s. Still, companies have been known recently to structure acquisitions to meet the pooling-of-interests criteria, often in an effort to inflate retained earnings, current income, and future income. Whether this strategy is in the interest of the stockholders is unclear, but structuring transactions to take advantage of accounting rules can cause management to depart from sound business practices. Such strategies can also reduce the credibility of a company's financial reports in the eyes of the public. Furthermore, the pooling-of-interests method has come under severe criticism for ignoring the fair market value of the subsidiary's net assets as well as its goodwill, both of which are reflected in the exchange price when the shareholders of the parent and the subsidiary negotiate the transaction.

It is also true, however, that the purchase method can enhance certain values reported on the consolidated financial statements. As the example in the previous section illustrates, the purchase method typically shows a higher inventory value which, in turn, results in higher current assets, higher working capital, and a higher current ratio, all of which are used by investors and creditors and in debt covenants. Moreover, when common stock is issued by a parent to raise cash that is in turn used to purchase a subsidiary's stock, the Stock and Additional Paid-in Capital accounts of the parent are valued at the fair market value of the shares issued. This valuation is typically higher than if the pooling-of-interests method is used, giving rise to a lower debt/equity ratio.

Another example of an economic consequence associated with accounting for equity investments was described in Chapter 13, where we compared the equity method to consolidated statements. There we showed that using the equity method instead of preparing consolidated financial statements could be viewed as a method of off-balance-sheet financing. The 1987 annual report of Dow Chemical, for example, states that the company owns a 50 percent interest in three major businesses: Dow Corning Corporation, Dowell Schlumberger Companies, and MT Partnership. By purchasing a 50 percent, instead of a 51 percent, interest in these companies, Dow was able to account for these investments under the equity method, instead of as purchases, which would require that the assets and liabilities of these businesses be included on Dow's consolidated financial statements. As a result, Dow avoided disclosing the liabilities of these three businesses, which totaled $1.46 billion, on its consolidated balance sheet.

ACCOUNTING FOR INTERNATIONAL OPERATIONS

As companies expand, they often search for new sources of supply and new markets in other countries. Most major U.S. companies operate in more than one country, and many have operations in countries throughout the world. IBM, for example, has operations in approximately eighty foreign countries. Such companies are called **multinational** or **transnational corporations.**

Consider, for example, two of the major U.S. companies in the photographic industry, Eastman Kodak and Polaroid, which generated $1.3 and $1 billion in world-wide revenues, respectively, in 1987. As much as 43 percent of the total revenues of both companies was generated from operations in countries other than the United States. Table 16–2 compares the relative importance of foreign operations in the generation of sales, profits, and total assets for three well-known U.S. companies: Goodyear Tire and Rubber Company, McDonald's Corporation, and Reebok International, Ltd.

It is also true that many U.S. investors and creditors do not restrict their investment activities to U.S. securities markets, and a number of major U.S. companies list their stocks and bonds on foreign security exchanges. The securities of The Procter & Gamble Company, for example, are traded on exchanges in New York, Cincinnati, Amsterdam, Paris, Basle, Geneva, Lausanne, Zurich, Frankfort, Antwerp, Brussels, and Tokyo.

The internationalization of business introduces two issues of major concern to accountants. First, most transactions with foreign entities as well as transactions in other countries involve currencies other than the U.S. dollar. For example, when Polaroid makes a sale to a Japanese customer, the receivable is often expressed in Japanese yen. In addition, the financial statements of an IBM subsidiary operating in France are usually expressed in French francs. Such situations present an accounting problem because the financial statements of U.S. companies must be expressed in terms of U.S. dollars, and the exchange rates between the U.S. dollar and other foreign currencies are constantly fluctuating. Accounting for such fluctuations is discussed in this section.

The second major accounting issue introduced by the internationalization of business is that financial statements, financial accounting standards, and financial accounting practices vary significantly across countries. In Switzerland, for example, managers are encouraged to conceal certain important information from the

Table 16–2   The importance of foreign operations in 1987 (dollars in millions)

	Goodyear	McDonald's	Reebok
Total sales	$9,905	$4,893	$1,389
Foreign sales/total	38%	30%	6%
Total operating income (before taxes)	1,077	1,162	165
Foreign operating income/total	43%	24%	24%
Total assets	8,288	6,981	868
Foreign/total	35%	35%	16%

Source: 1987 financial reports.

stockholders and to intentionally understate the value of their assets, while in Holland, only 300 miles away, the accounting standards are based on the U.S. system. Such diversity makes it difficult for international investors and creditors to compare the performances of companies operating in different countries. The final section of this chapter describes some of the accounting practices used in other countries as well as some recent attempts by international groups to encourage greater uniformity in the accounting methods practiced throughout the world.

Exchange Rates Among Currencies

An **exchange rate** is the value of one currency in terms of another currency. For example, as of June 8, 1988, $1.81 could be exchanged for 1 British pound, $.70 could be exchanged for 1 Swiss franc, and $.00768 could be exchanged for 1 Japanese yen. Expressed in another way, as of that same date, $1 (U.S.) could have been exchanged for .55 (1÷1.81) British pounds, 1.43 (1÷.70) Swiss francs, or 130.2 (1÷.00768) Japanese yen. Like the prices of all goods and services, the exchange rates among currencies vary from one day to the next. Table 16−3 shows the rates at which selected foreign currencies could be exchanged for U.S. dollars on two different dates less than one month apart: June 8, 1988, and July 1, 1988. Note especially the percentage changes indicated on the right side of the table.

As the table shows, between June 8 and July 1 the value of most foreign currencies (except the Canadian dollar and the Mexican peso) fell relative to the U.S. dollar. The value of the Swiss franc, for example, fell from $.70 to $.66, a decrease of 6 percent. Fluctuations in exchange rates of this nature can give rise to economic gains and losses for individuals and entities that transact in both U.S. dollars and Swiss francs.

To illustrate, suppose that you paid $700 to purchase 1000 Swiss francs on June 8, and on July 1 you converted the Swiss francs back into dollars. You would have received only $660 dollars in the exchange and, therefore, would have incurred an economic loss of $40 ($700 − $660) on the transactions. In essence, you held 1000 Swiss francs during a period in which the value of the franc fell relative to the U.S. dollar. On the other hand, had you paid 1000 Swiss francs to purchase $700 on June 8, and on July 1 exchanged the dollars back into Swiss francs, you would have collected 1052 Swiss francs, and enjoyed an economic gain of 52 (1052 − 1000) Swiss francs.

Table 16–3   Foreign exchange rates (prices in U.S. dollars)

	June 8, 1988	July 1, 1988	Percent Change
Australia (dollar)	.799	.797	−.2%
Britain (pound)	1.81	1.71	−5
Canada (dollar)	.81	.82	+1
Japan (yen)	.0079	.0075	−5
Mexico (peso)	.0004	.0004	0
Switzerland (franc)	.70	.66	−6
West Germany (mark)	.58	.55	−5

Receivables and Payables Held in Other Currencies

Many U.S. companies engage in transactions with non-U.S. entities that are denominated in foreign currencies. These transactions often give rise to receivables or payables that are denominated in foreign currencies. In 1987, for example, Goodyear Tire and Rubber Company had sales of almost $4 billion to customers in other countries, a large percentage of which gave rise to receivables that were expressed in currencies other than the U.S. dollar.

Suppose that during 1987 Goodyear sold goods to a Japanese company, accepting in return a note promising the payment of 50,000 Japanese yen at some time in the future. When Goodyear prepares its financial statements, which must be expressed in U.S. dollars, this receivable must be translated from Japanese yen into U.S. dollars. Depending on the relative changes in the values of the two currencies between the time of the transaction and the time the financial statements are prepared, a gain or loss will result from the process of translation. Such gains and losses appear on the income statement. Goodyear's 1987 income statement, for example, showed a loss from foreign currency exchange of $38.9 million. The next two sections demonstrate how exchange gains and losses are recognized on the financial statements.[4]

Holding Receivables Expressed in Foreign Currencies

Suppose that International Inc., a U.S. company that prepares financial statements expressed in U.S. dollars, sold inventories to Swiss Airlines and accepted a note receivable in return. The note states that Swiss Airlines is to pay International 5000 Swiss francs. The note was signed on December 1, when 1 U.S. dollar was equivalent to 2 Swiss francs. The value of the transaction in terms of U.S. dollars as of December 1 was $2500 (5000 ÷ 2); accordingly, International recorded a receivable at the time of the transaction in the amount of $2500. The currency conversion calculation and the journal entry to record the sale are provided in Figure 16–18.

Assume further that on December 31, when International prepares financial statements, the rate of exchange between U.S. dollars and Swiss francs changed to 1 U.S. dollar per 1.8 Swiss francs. The note receivable that was recorded on the books at $2500 on December 1 is now worth $2778 (5000 ÷ 1.8 or $2500 × 2.0 ÷ 1.8). Therefore, International has enjoyed an economic gain of $278 ($2788 − $2500) because it held a right to 5000 Swiss francs during a period of time in which Swiss francs increased in value relative to U.S. dollars. In simple terms, 5000 Swiss francs can be exchanged for more U.S. dollars on December 31 than they could on December 1. The currency conversion calculation and the journal entry, that would restate the note receivable and record the gain, an exchange gain, is provided in Figure 16–19. The exchange gain would appear on International's income statement.

An exchange loss will be recognized on International's books if, at a later date, the value of the U.S. dollar rises relative to the Swiss franc. Assume that, as of January 31 of the following year, 1 U.S. dollar could be exchanged for 2.2 Swiss francs. In this case the adjustment would be calculated, and the adjusting journal entry would be recorded by International as in Figure 16–20.

---

4. To make the computations easier, the exchange rates used in these examples are not realistic.

Figure 16–18   Recording a sale in a non-U.S. currency

Conversion of Swiss francs to U.S. dollars:
    $2,500 = 5,000 Swiss francs × (1 dollar ÷ 2 Swiss francs)

Dec. 1	Notes Receivable	2,500	
	Sales		2,500
	To record the sale of inventory for 5,000 Swiss francs.		

Figure 16–19   Recognizing an exchange gain on a receivable

Conversion of Swiss francs to U.S. dollars:

    $2,778 = 5,000 Swiss francs × (1 U.S. dollar ÷ 1.8 Swiss francs)

Adjustment: $2,778 − $2,500 = $278

Dec. 31	Notes Receivable	278	
	Exchange Gain		278
	To record an exchange gain on a receivable expressed in Swiss francs.		

Figure 16–20   Recognizing an exchange loss on a receivable

Conversion of Swiss francs to U.S. dollars:

    $2,272 = 5,000 Swiss francs × (1 U.S. dollar ÷ 2.2 Swiss francs)

Adjustment: $2,272 − $2,778 = −$506

Jan. 31	Exchange Loss	506	
	Notes Receivable		506
	To recognize an exchange loss on a receivable expressed in Swiss francs.		

Holding Payables Expressed in Foreign Currencies

Exchange gains and losses can also occur from holding payables denominated in non-U.S. (foreign) currencies. Assume that on December 1 Cross Cultural, Inc. purchased inventory from a Japanese company, promising to pay 100,000 yen at a later date. At that time 140 Japanese yen could be exchanged for 1 U.S. dollar. As of December 31 and the following January 31, 125 and 160 yen, respectively, could be exchanged for 1 U.S. dollar. Assuming that Cross Cultural, Inc. held the payable throughout the two-month time period and prepared financial statements on December 31 and January 31, the journal entries and related calculations that are shown in Figure 16–21 would have been recorded to reflect these changes in the exchange rates.

Figure 16–21   Recognizing exchange losses and gains on payables

---

December 1: Purchase of Inventory

Conversion of Japanese yen to U.S. dollars:

$$\$714 = 100{,}000 \text{ yen} \times (1 \text{ U.S. dollar} \div 140 \text{ yen})$$

Dec. 1	Inventory	714	
	Accounts Payable		714
	To record the purchase of inventory for 100,000 Japanese yen.		

December 31: Computation and Recognition of Exchange Loss

Conversion of Japanese yen to U.S. dollars:

$$\$800 = 100{,}000 \text{ yen} \times (1 \text{ U.S. dollar} \div 125 \text{ yen})$$

Adjustment: $714 − $800 = −$86

Dec. 31	Exchange Loss	86	
	Accounts Payable		86
	To recognize an exchange loss on holding a payable expressed in Japanese yen.		

January 31: Computation and Recognition of Exchange Gain

Conversion of Japanese yen to U.S. dollars:

$$\$625 = 100{,}000 \text{ yen} \times (1 \text{ U.S. dollar} \div 160 \text{ yen})$$

Adjustment: $800 − $625 = $175

Jan. 31	Accounts Payable	175	
	Exchange Gain		175
	To recognize an exchange gain on holding a payable expressed in Japanese yen.		

Exchange Gains and Losses: Four Possible Combinations

To summarize, the recognition of an exchange gain or loss depends on the combination of two factors: (1) whether the U.S. company holds a receivable or payable that is denominated in a foreign currency, and (2) whether the foreign currency increases or decreases in value relative to the U.S. dollar. Figure 16–22 illustrates the four possible combinations.

If a U.S. company holds a receivable denominated in a foreign currency, and the foreign currency rises in value relative to the U.S. dollar, the U.S. company recognizes an exchange gain on its income statement as illustrated in Cell 1. Holding a receivable in a currency that decreases in value relative to the U.S. dollar, on the other hand, gives rise to an exchange loss as illustrated in Cell 3. Holding a payable expressed in terms of a foreign currency produces exactly the opposite effect: that is, as the foreign currency rises in value, exchange losses are recognized as illustrated in Cell 2. As the foreign currency drops in value, exchange gains accrue as illustrated in Cell 4.

Figure 16-22   Exchange gains and losses

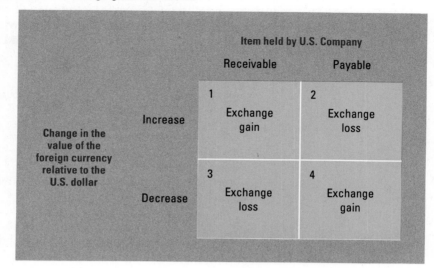

Hedging and the Economic Consequences of Fluctuating Exchange Rates

Exchange-rate fluctuations are constant and often significant. As illustrated in the previous section, such erratic movement can give rise to exchange gains and losses that cause income and other reported values (e.g., receivables and payables) to vary substantially from one period to the next. Variations in exchange rates, as a result, can give rise to economic consequences through their effects on stock prices, credit ratings, management compensation, and debt covenants. Such consequences increase the economic risks associated with engaging in transactions that are denominated in foreign currencies.

While management has very little control over exchange rates, it can reduce some of the risks associated with holding receivables and payables denominated in foreign currencies. Multinational companies commonly use a strategy called **hedging** to reduce the variation in income due to fluctuating exchange rates. This strategy involves taking a position in a foreign currency in an amount that is equal and opposite to a particular receivable or payable expressed in that currency.

To illustrate, assume that on July 1 General Motors (GM) sells a group of automobiles to British Petroleum (BP), receiving in exchange a note stating that BP will pay GM 100,000 British pounds in one year. If the exchange rate as of July 1 is $1.70 per British pound, GM would record the following journal entry.

Conversion of British pounds to U.S. dollars:

$170,000 = 100,000 British pounds × ($1.70 ÷ 1 pound)

July 1	Note Receivable	170,000	
	Sales		170,000
	To record the sale of automobiles in exchange for a note receivable expressed in British pounds.		

If GM chooses not to hedge this receivable, and the exchange rate changes to $1.50 per British pound as of December 31, GM will recognize a $20,000 exchange loss during the period when it records the following adjusting journal entry at the end of the year. This loss would appear on GM's income statement.

Conversion of British pounds to U.S. dollars:

$$\$150,000 = 100,000 \text{ British pounds} \times (\$1.50 \div 1 \text{ pound})$$

Adjustment: $170,000 − $150,000 = $20,000 (loss)

Dec. 31	Exchange Loss	20,000	
	Notes Receivable		20,000
	To recognize an exchange loss on a receivable expressed in British pounds.		

GM could have negated the effect on income of this $20,000 loss if it had chosen to hedge the receivable. That is, GM could have borrowed 100,000 British pounds on July 1 and agreed to pay it back one year later. By doing so, GM would have taken a position in British pounds that was equal and opposite to the outstanding receivable. It would have entered into a payable (100,000 British pounds) that would have balanced the outstanding receivable (100,000 British pounds). Had GM adopted such a strategy, on December 31 it would have recognized a $20,000 exchange gain on the outstanding payable, which would have negated the effect on income of the $20,000 exchange loss recognized on the receivable. The journal entries to record the borrowing and the recognition of the exchange gain are provided in Figure 16−23.

Hedging is commonly practiced by U.S. multinationals to reduce the risks associated with holding receivables and payables in foreign currencies, where exchange rates are constantly fluctuating. General Motors, for example, holds long-term debt that is payable in Canadian dollars, Australian dollars, Swiss francs,

Figure 16−23 Hedging an outstanding receivable

July 1:
Conversion of British pounds to U.S. dollars:

$$\$170,000 = 100,000 \text{ British pounds} \times (\$1.70 \div 1 \text{ pound})$$

July 1	Cash	170,000	
	Note Payable		170,000
	To record the borrowing of 100,000 British pounds.		

December 31:
Conversion of British pounds to U.S. dollars:

$$\$150,000 = 100,000 \text{ British pounds} \times (\$1.50 \div 1 \text{ pound})$$

Adjustment: $170,000 − $150,000 = $20,000

Dec. 31	Note Payable	20,000	
	Exchange Gain		20,000
	To recognize an exchange gain on a payable expressed in British pounds.		

Japanese yen, German marks, Spanish pesatas, Belgian francs, British pounds, and other currencies. Many of these payables were established by GM to hedge the effects on income and reduce the economic risks associated with holding outstanding receivables denominated in these currencies. The following excerpt from the 1987 financial report of the Goodyear Tire & Rubber Company describes long-term debts held by the company that are payable in Japanese yen and Swiss francs. "The Yen bonds due in 1994, 1995, and 1996, and the Swiss franc bonds due in 2000 and 2006, are completely hedged by contract against future fluctuations in the U.S. dollar value of those currencies. At December 31, 1987, $323.9 million associated with these hedged contracts are recorded in long-term accounts and notes receivable on the consolidated balance sheet."

Preparing Consolidated Financial Statements for Multinationals

This chapter began by covering the methods used to prepare consolidated financial statements. The previous section demonstrated how assets and liabilities expressed in foreign currencies are converted to U.S. dollars and how exchange gains and losses are determined. This section discusses how multinational companies prepare consolidated financial statements in cases where their subsidiaries' financial statements are expressed in foreign currencies. The accounting methods used in this area are complex and controversial, and in this section we cover only the basic ideas. More complete coverage can be found in intermediate or advanced financial accounting texts.

Multinational U.S. companies often own subsidiaries that operate in other countries and have financial statements that are expressed in foreign currencies. General Mills, for example, has major subsidiaries in France, Holland, Belgium, Spain, Canada, and Latin America, all of which publish their own financial statements denominated in their own local currencies. When General Mills prepares consolidated financial statements at year end, the financial statements of these subsidiaries must be translated into U.S. dollars and then combined with the accounts of General Mills.

The process of preparing consolidated financial statements for a U.S. multinational basically consists of three steps: (1) classifying the foreign subsidiaries, (2) expressing each subsidiary's financial statements in terms of U.S. dollars, and (3) following the rules of preparing consolidated statements as described earlier in the chapter.

Classifying Foreign Subsidiaries

Foreign subsidiaries fall into two general classes: Type I and Type II. **Type I foreign subsidiaries** operate independently from the parent and are integrated within the country or countries in which they operate. General Electric, for example, owns CGR, a company that manufactures, sells, and services medical equipment in Europe and Latin America. CGR is considered a Type I foreign subsidiary because its operations are largely independent of General Electric.

Type II foreign subsidiaries, on the other hand, are integral parts or extensions of parent companies. Such subsidiaries may act as suppliers for the parents or as channels of marketing and distribution for the parents' products. General Mills, for example, has several Type II foreign subsidiaries in Canada that are involved primarily in the marketing and distribution of food products produced by the parent (e.g., Cheerios breakfast cereal).

All subsidiaries located in countries that experience hyperinflation (i.e., more than 100 percent cumulative inflation over a three-year period) are considered Type II foreign subsidiaries, even if they operate independently from the parent. Brazil, Mexico, and Argentina are examples of hyperinflation economies.

Expressing the Statements of Type I and Type II Subsidiaries in Terms of U.S. Dollars

When the financial statements of Type I foreign subsidiaries are translated into U.S. dollars, any gain or loss due to the translation is referred to as a *translation adjustment*. Such adjustments are not considered part of income and are disclosed in the stockholders' equity section of the consolidated balance sheet. The dollar values of the translation adjustments each year are cumulated, giving rise to a stockholders' equity account called **Cumulative Translation Adjustment.**

Table 16–4 illustrates the disclosure and relative size of the Cumulative Translation Adjustment account. It contains excerpts of the stockholders' equity section taken from the 1987 financial reports of several major U.S. companies.

Note that the cumulative translation adjustment can be significant and either positive or negative. Positive dollar amounts result when the foreign currency of the subsidiary increases in value relative to the U.S. dollar, and negative amounts result when the currency of the subsidiary decreases in value relative to the U.S. dollar.

When the financial statements of Type II foreign subsidiaries are translated to U.S. dollars, gains or losses resulting from the translation process are considered part of consolidated income. Type II foreign subsidiaries are viewed as integral parts of the parent and, therefore, translation gains and losses are included as components of the parent's income. Since subsidiaries located in hyperinflation economies are also included in the Type II category, gains and losses resulting from their restatements are also included in consolidated income.

Exchange gains and losses from the restatement of Type II foreign subsidiaries can also be significant, as shown by the following excerpts from the 1987 financial reports of The Gillette Company and Johnson & Johnson.

The Gillette Company
Included in other charges on the income statement were net exchange losses of $49.8 million . . . primarily relating to translation of the assets and liabilities of subsidiaries in Argentina, Brazil, and Mexico.

Table 16–4   Stockholders' equity and the cumulative translation adjustment (dollars in millions)

	Common Stock	Additional Paid-in Capital	Cumulative Translation Adjustment	Retained Earnings	Treasury Stock	Total
Amoco	$2,114	—	$ (51)	$10,044	—	$12,107
CBS, Inc.	60	$240	37	912	—	1,249
Chevron Corp.	1,026	874	113	13,767	—	15,780
Colgate-Palmolive	84	126	184	1,380	$(477)	1,297
Gillette Co.	137	155	(148)	1,084	(628)	600
Dow Chemical	541	817	95	5,226	(910)	5,769
Monsanto	164	872	100	3,282	(517)	3,901

Source: 1987 financial reports.

Table 16–5 Preparing consolidated financial statements for multinationals with foreign subsidiaries

Step	Type I Subsidiary	Type II Subsidiary
1. Classify foreign subsidiaries.	Independent of parent.	Integral part or extension of parent. Hyperinflation countries.
2. Express financial statements of each subsidiary in U.S. dollars.	Cumulative translation adjustment; stockholders' equity.	Exchange gain or loss; income statement.
3. Prepare consolidated financial statements.	Follow procedures described earlier.	Follow procedures described earlier.

Johnson & Johnson
Net currency transaction and translation gains and losses included in net earnings were losses of $41 million . . . in 1987, incurred principally in Latin America.

Preparing Consolidated Financial Statements

After foreign subsidiaries have been classified as either Type I or Type II, and their statements have been translated to U.S. dollars, consolidated financial statements are prepared by the parent in the manner described earlier in the chapter. Table 16–5 summarizes the general rules covered in this section. Keep in mind that we have only discussed the basic ideas involved in understanding the preparation of consolidated financial statements for multinational companies. The technical rules and the specific procedures can get quite involved.

ACCOUNTING STANDARDS AND PRACTICES THROUGHOUT THE WORLD

Financial accounting standards and the accounting methods used in the countries throughout the world are quite diverse. Just as nations have different histories, economies, cultures, and political systems, they also have different systems of financial accounting. Indeed, accounting systems have evolved in response to the demands of the business environment, and the business environments faced by companies in different parts of the world are vastly dissimilar.

At a very general level, four basic kinds of accounting systems have been identified: (1) the British-American-Dutch model, (2) the Continental model, (3) the South American model, and (4) the Communist model.[5] The countries in each of these four categories tend to have certain environmental characteristics in common. Such characteristics include the nature and development of the domestic capital market, political and economic ties with other countries in the category, the legal system, annual rates of inflation, the size and complexity of the companies operating within the country, the sophistication of management and the financial community, and the general level of education.

The **British-American-Dutch model,** which is based primarily on the generally accepted accounting principles of the United States, is used largely by countries in

5. See Gerhard Mueller, H. Gernon, and G. Meek, *Accounting: an International Perspective* (Homewood, Ill.: Richard D. Irwin, 1987) for a discussion of the different accounting systems used throughout the world.

North America, Australia, and India. These accounting systems tend to be oriented toward the decision needs of investors, and the countries in this category tend to have large, well-developed securities markets, high levels of education, and a number of multinational corporations. A consumer orientation and a legal system that encourages litigation also tend to be more prevalent in these countries.

The **Continental model** includes Japan and most of the countries in Europe. The accounting methods used in these countries are not oriented toward the needs of investors. Rather, they provide information that is used to satisfy government requirements, such as computing income taxes. Banks are very important providers of capital in these economies, and financial accounting practices tend to be largely at the discretion of management and highly conservative, sometimes withholding relevant information from the shareholders.

As the name suggests, the **South American model** includes most of the countries in South America. These countries, with the exception of Brazil which uses Portuguese, share Spanish as their common language as well as a rich cultural heritage. In general, their accounting methods are oriented toward the needs of government planners, and uniform rules are imposed on virtually all business entities. The most distinguishing feature about this system is that it includes periodic adjustments for inflation, a phenomenon that has plagued South America for many years.

The **Communist model** includes the countries in the communist bloc. Since there is limited private ownership in these countries, the accounting rules are rather rigid and oriented primarily to government planners. Financial statements in these countries, for example, are not prepared for outside investors and creditors. Instead, they are submitted to agency administrators and government planners, who implement the tight central economic control characteristic of the communist system. The recent *perestroika* and *glasnost* reforms, which have encouraged greater economic exchange, less restricted markets, and more openness, may influence this system of accounting to provide greater levels of disclosure.

SETTING STANDARDS FOR INTERNATIONAL ACCOUNTING

The fact that so much diversity exists in world-wide accounting standards and practices makes it difficult for investors and creditors to compare the performances of companies operating in different countries. Comparing the performance of a South American textile mill to that of an Australian textile mill, for example, is almost impossible because their financial reports are prepared using different accounting methods. Such differences can lead to a loss of credibility in the financial statements and investment decisions based on misunderstanding. It is also costly and time-consuming for financial statement users to educate themselves about the different accounting practices followed internationally.

A number of efforts have been made to achieve greater international understanding and uniformity of accounting practices. The **International Accounting Standards Committee** (IASC), for example, was formed in 1973 to develop worldwide accounting practices. This private-sector body, which represents over ninety professional accounting bodies in nearly seventy countries, could be viewed as the international counterpart of the FASB. To date, it has issued approximately thirty international accounting standards, each of which can be viewed as an effort to harmonize the world's accounting standards by eliminating differences that cannot be explained by the environment.

Other international groups are also active. The **International Federation of Accountants** (IFAC), for example, was formed in 1977 to develop guidelines for accounting professionals throughout the world. Its membership consists of professional accountants in over sixty-five countries, who deal with such issues as auditing guidelines, educational requirements for professional accountants, and ethics. Another active group is the **United Nations,** which recently reaffirmed recommendations issued in 1977 to encourage multinational companies to provide certain disclosures. Finally, the **Organization for Economic Cooperation and Development** (OECD), which consists of twenty-four governments from the industrialized world, issued a code of conduct in 1976 for multinational companies that includes guidelines for voluntary disclosures of financial information.

In addition to the bodies described above, regional and local organizations are also involved in the effort to enhance the understanding and comparability of world-wide accounting reports by establishing more uniform accounting and auditing practices. The fact that so many groups and resources are involved indicates significant support for the effort. Nonetheless, the environmental and cultural differences across countries are great, and the progress toward harmony has been, and will probably continue to be, slow.

THE ANNUAL REPORT OF K MART CORPORATION

Turn now to K mart's annual report located in Appendix D. The financial statements (pages 31–34) are referred to as *consolidated* because they include the accounts of K mart's domestic and foreign subsidiaries (page 52). K mart's domestic subsidiaries include Builders Square, Inc., K mart Apparel Corp., Makro Inc., Pay Less Drug Stores Northwest, Inc., and Walden Book Company, Inc. K mart's only foreign subsidiary is K mart Canada Limited. The discussion on pages 18–20 provides a description of the activities of these subsidiaries.

Note A on page 35 indicates that "the company includes all majority owned subsidiaries in the consolidated financial statements. . . . All significant intercompany transactions and accounts have been eliminated in consolidation." Note D on page 36 states that "in March 1988, K mart Corporation purchased a 51 percent ownership interest in Makro Inc. from SHV North America Corporation. . . . The Makro acquisition has been accounted for as a purchase. The results of operations have been consolidated with those of the company from the date of acquisition. The excess of cost over fair value of the assets acquired [goodwill], which is not significant, is being amortized over forty years on a straight-line basis."

"In September 1987, K mart Corporation formed a partnership with Bruno's Inc. of Birmingham, Alabama to develop American Fare hypermarket stores in the United States. K mart has a 51 percent ownership interest in the partnership [and] will consolidate the results of American Fare operations in 1989."

The Balance Sheet (page 32) and the Statement of Shareholders' Equity (page 34) disclose relatively small foreign currency translation adjustments. The accumulated balance as of January 25, 1989, was a $3 million credit, preceded by debit balances of $75 million, $101 million, and $105 million as of 1988, 1987, and 1986, respectively. The major reason for the change in the cumulative translation adjustment since 1986 is described on page 39. K mart owns a 22 percent interest in the equity of Coles Myer Ltd., the largest retailer in Australia. The related income and dividends recognized on K mart's books, which are accounted for under the equity method (see Chapter 13), are denominated in Australian dollars that must be converted to U.S. dollars for purposes of preparing financial statements. As noted on page 39, "the average exchange rates from Australian to U.S. dollars were .7847 in 1988, .7016 in 1987 and .6711 in 1986. Note that the rate rose from 1986-1988. The cumulative effect of translating the company's equity in the investment in Coles Myer as of January 25, 1989 was an increase of $3 million." In other words, K mart held an asset (investment) denominated in Australian dollars over a period of time when the Australian dollar rose relative to the U.S. dollar. The economic gain enjoyed by K mart is reflected in the shareholder's equity section, instead of the income statement, because Coles Myer is classified as an independent (Type I) affiliate retail company.

Overall, K mart's international operations are relatively limited. They have only one majority-owned foreign subsidiary, a 22 percent investment in an Australian retail operation, and a cumulative foreign currency translation adjustment of an almost immaterial $3 million. The company's common stock, however, is traded on the Tokyo Stock Exchange (page 27).

REVIEW PROBLEMS

Two review problems are provided in this section. In the first, a set of consolidated statements is prepared using the purchase method. The second problem illustrates a hedging transaction.

Preparing Consolidated Financial Statements Using the Purchase Method

On January 1, 1990, Mega Corporation purchased 100 percent of the 10,000 outstanding common shares of Microfile Company for $120,000 ($12 per share). The payment consists of $50,000 in cash and seventy twenty-year bonds issued at face value ($1000). At the time of the acquisition, the net book value of Microfile was $80,000 (common stock: $55,000, retained earnings: $25,000). The historical cost and fair market value of Microfile's inventory and long-lived assets are provided in Figure 16−24.

During 1990 Microfile provided a consulting service for Mega Corporation for a total price of $13,000, accepting a two-year note as payment. As of December 31, $1000 in interest had accrued on the note. The journal entry to record the purchase on January 1 appears on page 830, and the consolidated worksheet, prepared one year later on December 31, appears in Figure 16−25.

Figure 16−24   Microfile: asset book and market values

January 1, 1990	Historical Cost	Fair Market Value
Inventory	$40,000	$47,000
Long-lived assets	45,000	55,000

Figure 16-25   Worksheet for Mega Corporation

	Mega Corporation Consolidated Worksheet December 31, 1990				

Accounts	Mega Corp.	Microfile Co.	Adjustments and Eliminations		Consolidated Financial Statements
			Dr.	Cr.	
Balance sheet					
Cash	20,000	10,000			30,000
Accounts Receivable	70,000	13,000			83,000
Notes Receivable	35,000	15,000		13,000[c]	37,000
Interest Receivable	—	2,000		1,000[d]	1,000
Inventory	230,000	45,000[a]	7,000[b]		282,000
Investment in Subsidiary	120,000	—		120,000[b]	—
Long-Lived Assets	330,000	55,000[a]	10,000[b]		395,000
Goodwill	—	—	23,000[b]		23,000
Total Assets	805,000	140,000	40,000	134,000	851,000
Accounts Payable	177,000	10,000			187,000
Interest Payable	3,000	—	1,000[d]		2,000
Long-Term Liabilities	250,000	30,000	13,000[c]		267,000
Common Stock	200,000	55,000[a]	55,000[b]		200,000
Retained Earnings	175,000	45,000[a]	25,000[b]		195,000
Total Liabilities and Stockholders' Equity	805,000	140,000	94,000		851,000
Income statement					
Sales	915,000	65,000	13,000[e]		967,000
Interest Revenue	—	2,000	1,000[f]		1,000
Cost of Goods Sold	(450,000)	(20,000)			(470,000)
Selling and Administrative Expenses	(230,000)	(15,000)		13,000[e]	(232,000)
Interest Expense	(25,000)	(3,000)		1,000[f]	(27,000)
Taxes	(105,000)	(9,000)			(114,000)
Net Income	105,000	20,000	14,000	14,000	125,000

[a]The Inventory, Long-Lived Assets, Common Stock, and Retained Earnings amounts are December 31 balances that differ from the balances as of the January 1 acquisition.

[b]Entry to adjust assets to fair market value, eliminate investment account and Microfile's stockholders' equity section, and recognize goodwill.

Purchase price: $12 per share × 10,000 sh. =	$120,000
Less: Book value, $8 per share × 10,000 sh. =	80,000
Less: Market value write up	
Inventory	7,000
Long-lived assets	10,000
Purchased goodwill	$ 23,000

[c]Entry to eliminate intercompany note receivable/payable of $13,000.

[d]Entry to eliminate intercompany interest receivable/payable of $1,000.

[e]Entry to eliminate intercompany sale/expense of $13,000.

[f]Entry to eliminate intercompany interest revenue/expense of $1,000.

Jan. 1	Investment in Subsidiary	120,000	
	Cash		50,000
	Bonds Payable		70,000
	To record the purchase of 100 percent		
	of Microfile's outstanding stock.		

Note that the acquisition occurred on January 1 and that the consolidated financial statements were prepared on December 31, one year later. Thus, the book value of Microfile as of December 31 ($100,000) is different from its book value on January 1 ($80,000) when the acquisition took place. Note also that under the purchase method, the income statement accounts of Microfile for the period January 1 to December 31 are included in the consolidated income statement.

A Hedging Transaction

On January 1, 1989, Multinational Enterprises sold spare parts to Deutschland Auto, an automobile manufacturer located in West Germany. In exchange, Multinational accepted a three-year note receivable in the amount of 500,000 German marks. The exchange rate at the time of the transaction was $1 (U.S.) per 2 German marks. The management of Multinational did not want to bear the risk that the German mark might decrease in value against the U.S. dollar. Accordingly, on January 1, 1989, Multinational borrowed 500,000 marks from a West German bank, signing a three-year note payable. The exchange rate between the U.S. dollar and the German mark as of January 1, 1989, December 31, 1989, and December 31, 1990, and the journal entries recorded by Multinational on these three dates appear in Figure 16–26.

Note that Multinational recognized no net gain or loss from the fluctuating exchange rates in 1989 or 1990. In each year the exchange gain or loss recognized on the outstanding payable exactly counterbalanced the exchange gain or loss recognized on the outstanding receivable. The erratic effects of fluctuating exchange rates on Multinational's net income, therefore, were nullified by the hedging strategy.

SUMMARY OF LEARNING OBJECTIVES

1   Distinguish between a business acquisition and a merger.

A business acquisition occurs when an investor company acquires a controlling interest in an investee company, and the two companies continue as separate legal entities. The investor company is referred to as the *parent*, and the investee company is called the *subsidiary*. A merger or business combination occurs when two or more companies combine to form a single entity. In most cases the assets and liabilities of a smaller company are merged into those of a larger, surviving company. The stock of at least one company, usually the smaller, is retired, and the merged company ceases to exist as a separate organization.

Figure 16-26 Multinational Enterprises: exchange rates and hedging entries

Exchange Rates

	January 1, 1989	December 31, 1989	December 31, 1990
$1 (U.S.)	2.0 marks	2.5 marks	1.5 marks

January 1, 1989
Conversion of German marks to U.S. dollars:

$250,000 = 500,000 German marks $\times$ (1 dollar $\div$ 2 German marks)

Jan. 1	Note Receivable	250,000	
	Sales		250,000
	To record the sale of spare parts for 500,000 German marks.		

Jan. 1	Cash	250,000	
	Note Payable		250,000
	To record the borrowing of 500,000 German marks.		

December 31, 1989
Conversion of German marks to U.S. dollars:

$200,000 = 500,000 German marks $\times$ (1 dollar $\div$ 2.5 German marks)

Adjustment: $250,000 − $200,000 = $50,000

Exchange Loss	50,000	
Note Receivable		50,000
To recognize an exchange loss on the outstanding note receivable.		

Note Payable	50,000	
Exchange Gain		50,000
To recognize an exchange gain on the outstanding note payable.		

December 31, 1990
Conversion of German marks to U.S. dollars:

$333,333 = 500,000 German marks $\times$ (1 dollar $\div$ 1.5 German marks)

Adjustment: $333,333 − $200,000 = $133,000

Note Receivable	133,000	
Exchange Gain		133,000
To recognize an exchange gain on the outstanding note receivable.		

Exchange Loss	133,000	
Note Payable		133,000
To recognize an exchange loss on the outstanding note payable.		

2   Explain how to account for a business acquisition or merger under the purchase method.

Under the purchase method, cash and/or other assets of the parent are used to purchase the assets and liabilities of the subsidiary. The assets and liabilities of the subsidiary are added to those of the parent at their fair market values. If the purchase price exceeds the fair market value of the net assets, goodwill is recognized on the balance sheet of the parent. If the parent purchases between 50 percent and 100 percent of the subsidiary, minority interest is recognized on the books of the parent. Revenues and expenses of the subsidiary recognized prior to the acquisition are not included in the consolidated income statement. All intercompany receivables, payables, revenues, and expenses are eliminated when preparing a consolidated balance sheet and income statement.

3   Explain how to account for a business acquisition or merger under the pooling-of-interests method.

When a parent acquires a subsidiary and substantially all (90 percent) of the payment is made with the parent's common stock, the pooling-of-interests method is used. In such situations the parent has not purchased the subsidiary; instead, the two companies have combined their resources. Under this method, the assets and liabilities of the subsidiary are added to those of the parent at book value, and no goodwill is recognized on the transaction. In addition, the retained earnings of the subsidiary are normally added to that of the parent, and the revenues and expenses of the subsidiary that are recognized during the period in which the combination occurs are included in the consolidated income statement. All intercompany receivables, payables, revenues, and expenses are eliminated when preparing a consolidated balance sheet and income statement.

4   Describe the economic consequences associated with preparing consolidated financial statements.

Preparing consolidated financial statements can have economic consequences because the alternative allowable methods affect important accounting numbers and ratios that investors and creditors use to assess earning power and solvency and to control the actions of managers. Two examples include the differences between the purchase method and the pooling-of-interests method, and the differences between using the equity method and preparing consolidated financial statements.

Compared to the purchase method, the pooling-of-interests method generally gives rise to (1) a greater Retained Earnings' balance, (2) higher levels of current earnings because the earnings of the subsidiary recognized during the period in which the combination occurs are included in consolidated earnings, and (3) higher levels of future earnings because assets are carried at book value, instead of inflated market values, and there is no recognition of goodwill. Future depreciation and amortization charges, therefore, are lower. Even though the criteria to qualify for pooling-of-interests accounting are restrictive, the characteristics of the method motivate many companies to structure acquisitions to meet them. For these reasons, and because it ignores the fair market value of the subsidiary's net assets as well as its goodwill, both of which are reflected in the exchange price when the shareholders of the parent and the subsidiary negotiate the transaction, the pooling-of-interests method has come under severe criticism.

It is also true that the purchase method can enhance certain values reported on the consolidated financial statements. It typically shows a higher inventory value, which in turn results in higher current assets, higher working capital, and a higher current ratio. Moreover, when common stock is issued by the parent to raise cash that is then used to purchase the subsidiary's stock, the Stock and Additional Paid-in Capital accounts of the parent are valued at the fair market value of the shares issued. This valuation is typically higher than if the pooling-of-interests method is used, giving rise to a lower debt/equity ratio.

Using the equity method, as opposed to preparing consolidated financial statements, can be viewed as a form of off-balance-sheet financing because under the equity method, the liabilities of the subsidiary need not be added to those of the parent. This difference can significantly affect the debt/equity ratio of the parent.

5 Define an exchange rate, and describe how fluctuating exchange rates give rise to gains and losses.

An exchange rate is the value of one currency in terms of another. Many U.S. companies engage in transactions with non-U.S. entities that are denominated in foreign currencies. These transactions often give rise to receivables or payables that are denominated in the foreign currency. When a U.S. company prepares financial statements, these receivables and payables must be translated to U.S. dollars. Depending on the relative changes in the values of the two currencies between the time of the transaction and the time the financial statements are prepared, a gain or loss will result from the process of translation. Such gains and losses appear on the income statement of the U.S. company.

6 Define hedging, and explain how it can reduce the risks associated with fluctuating exchange rates.

Exchange-rate fluctuations can create significant swings in income from one period to the next. Such erratic behavior can cause economic consequences because important financial accounting numbers and financial ratios vary from period to period, affecting credit ratings, management compensation, and debt covenants. Such fluctuations, therefore, increase the economic risks associated with transacting in foreign currencies.

Multinational corporations commonly use a strategy called *hedging* to reduce the variation in income due to fluctuating exchange rates. This strategy basically involves taking a position in a foreign currency in an amount that is equal and opposite to particular receivables or payables expressed in that currency.

7 List the basic steps involved when preparing consolidated statements for multinationals with foreign subsidiaries.

Consolidated statements for multinationals with foreign subsidiaries are prepared using three basic steps. First, the subsidiaries are classified as either Type I or Type II. A Type I subsidiary operates independently from the parent and is integrated within the country or countries in which it operates. A Type II subsidiary is an integral part or extension of the parent, often serving as a supplier or channel of marketing or distribution for the parent. Subsidiaries in hyperinflation economies are considered Type II subsidiaries.

Second, the financial statements of subsidiaries are expressed in terms of U.S. dollars using an exchange rate. Converting the financial statements of a Type I subsidiary gives rise to a cumulative translation adjustment, which is disclosed in the stockholders' equity section of the parent's balance sheet. Converting the financial statements of a Type II subsidiary gives rise to exchange gains and losses that are included on the parent's income statement. Third, consolidated statements are prepared by the parent using the procedures described in the first part of the chapter.

8   **List the four basic kinds of accounting systems used in the world, and describe the efforts by international groups to bring about greater harmony among the accounting practices used in different countries.**

Financial accounting standards and the accounting methods used in the countries throughout the world are quite diverse. Four basic kinds of accounting systems have been identified: (1) the British-American-Dutch model, used primarily in North America, Australia, and India; (2) the Continental model, used primarily in Japan and most of Western Europe; (3) the South American model, used primarily in South America; and (4) the Communist model, used primarily in Communist countries. The countries in each of these four categories have certain environmental characteristics in common (e.g., development of capital markets, political and economic ties, legal systems, size and complexity of companies, general level of education).

Because such diversity makes it difficult for investors and creditors to compare the performances of companies operating in different countries, a number of efforts have been made to achieve greater international understanding and uniformity of accounting practices. The International Accounting Standards Committee issues international accounting standards. The International Federation of Accounts develops auditing, educational, and ethical guidelines for accounting professionals throughout the world. The United Nations, the Organization for Economic Cooperation and Development, and many regional and local groups have also been active.

KEY TERMS

British-American-Dutch model (p. 825)
Business acquisition (p. 795)
Business combination (p. 796)
Communist model (p. 826)
Consolidated financial statements (p. 795)
Continental model (p. 826)
Controlling interest (p. 795)
Cumulative translation adjustment (p. 824)
Exchange rate (p. 817)
Hedging (p. 821)
Intercompany transactions (p. 806)
International Accounting Standards Committee (IASC) (p. 826)
International Federation of Accountants (IFAC) (p. 827)

Merger (p. 796)
Minority interest (p. 800)
Minority stockholders (p. 800)
Multinational corporation (p. 816)
Organization for Economic Cooperation and Development (OECD) (p. 827)
Parent (p. 795)
Pooling of interests (p. 808)
Purchase method (p. 796)
South American model (p. 826)
Subsidiary (p. 795)
Transnational corporation (p. 816)
Type I foreign subsidiary (p. 823)
Type II foreign subsidiary (p. 823)
United Nations (p. 827)

QUESTIONS FOR DISCUSSION AND REVIEW

1. Briefly describe the conditions under which the cost method, the lower-of-cost-or-market method, the equity method, and consolidated financial statements are used to account for investments in equity securities.

2. What is a business acquisition, and how does it differ from a merger? Are consolidated financial statements prepared after a merger?

3. Under the purchase method, why is it important to consider the net market value of the subsidiary's assets instead of the book value? Is adding the assets and liabilities of the subsidiary to the balance sheet of the parent a violation of the historical cost principle? Why or why not?

4. Under what conditions is goodwill recognized on the balance sheet of the parent? Why does the recognition of goodwill imply lower future net income numbers?

5. Under what conditions is minority interest recognized on the balance sheet of the parent? What is minority interest? Is it considered a liability or an element of stockholders' equity? Why?

6. How are the values of goodwill and minority interest determined when both are recognized in an acquisition?

7. Why are the revenues and expenses of a subsidiary that are recognized prior to an acquisition not included in consolidated income under the purchase method?

8. Define intercompany receivables, payables, revenues, and expenses, and explain how and why they are eliminated when preparing consolidated financial statements.

9. When a business combination essentially involves an exchange of stock, why is it inappropriate to use the purchase method?

10. Describe the procedures involved in implementing the pooling-of-interests method. How do they differ from those of the purchase method?

11. Explain why a company may wish to structure an acquisition so that it could use the pooling-of-interests method instead of the purchase method.

12. Explain why a company may wish to structure an acquisition so that it could use the equity method instead of preparing consolidated financial statements.

13. What two issues are of major concern to accountants with respect to international operations? Why?

14. Define an exchange rate, and explain how exchange-rate fluctuations give rise to economic gains and losses.

15. Under what conditions are exchange gains recognized by companies that engage in transactions denominated in foreign currencies? Under what conditions are exchange losses recognized by companies that engage in transactions denominated in foreign currencies?

16. What is hedging, and why do so many companies practice it? How could a company hedge an outstanding receivable denominated in Japanese yen?

17. Describe the three basic steps followed by multinationals when they prepare consolidated financial statements.

18. Distinguish between a Type I and a Type II foreign subsidiary. In which category are subsidiaries that operate in hyperinflation countries included? Where on the financial statements are the translation adjustments disclosed for each type of subsidiary?

19. Why are the financial accounting standards and practices used in countries throughout the world so diverse?

20. Identify the four basic kinds of accounting systems used in the world. Describe the countries that use each system and several of the basic characteristics of each system.

21. Explain why the diverse accounting systems used throughout the world create a problem, and describe some of the recent efforts to solve it.

EXERCISES

E16-1   *(100 percent purchases in excess of the net market value of the assets and liabilities)*   The following chart describes six transactions where 100 percent of a subsidiary's voting stock was purchased for cash. Provide the missing values.

	Purchase Price	Net Book Value	Net Fair Market Value in Excess of Book Value	Goodwill
(1)	?	$ 7,000	$1,000	$1,000
(2)	$ 6,000	6,000	?	0
(3)	12,000	?	4,000	3,000
(4)	15,000	10,000	3,000	?
(5)	?	2,000	1,000	3,000
(6)	12,000	4,000	8,000	?

E16-2   *(Per-share book and market value)*   The book value of a share of Mesley common stock on December 31 was $12. The balance-sheet value and the market value of the company's assets and liabilities as of that date follow.

	Balance-Sheet Value	Market Value
Cash	$ 15,000	$ 15,000
Receivables	26,000	26,000
Inventories	15,000	25,000
Fixed assets	40,000	42,000
Liabilities	(60,000)	(60,000)
Net book value	$ 36,000	—
Net market value		$ 48,000

On December 31, Conglomerate, Inc. purchased 100 percent of the outstanding stock of Mesley for $20 per share.

Required:

a. How many shares of common stock did Mesley have outstanding as of December 31, 1990?

b. Compute the per-share net market value of Mesley's common stock.

c. Why would Conglomerate pay more than the per-share market value for a share of Mesley common stock?

d. Record the journal entries made by Conglomerate when the transaction occurred and when the consolidated balance sheet was prepared.

E16-3   *(Computing goodwill and minority interest)*   Maxwell Industries paid $18 per share for 80 percent of the 10,000 outstanding shares of Kendall Hall. The balance sheet of Kendall Hall and additional market-value information follow. Compute the amounts of goodwill and minority interest recognized by Maxwell.

	Historical Cost	Fair Market Value
Current assets	$125,000	$140,000
Noncurrent assets	65,000	75,000
Liabilities	70,000	70,000
Stockholders' equity	120,000	—

E16-4   *(Recognizing 100 percent acquisition and goodwill with journal entries)*   Megaton Enterprises purchased the entire outstanding stock of three companies during 1990. Information about the purchase price of each transaction and information from the financial statements of the three purchased companies follow. All purchases were made for cash.

Purchase	Price	Historical Cost		Fair Market Value	
		Assets	**Liabilities**	**Assets**	**Liabilities**
1	$ 7,000	$20,000	$16,000	$23,000	$16,000
2	33,000	35,000	13,000	43,000	13,000
3	10,000	19,000	16,000	21,000	16,000

Required: Prepare the journal entries that would be recorded on the books of Megaton for each purchase. Record both the entry at purchase and the entry at consolidation for each purchase.

E16–5

(100 percent purchase and the recognition of goodwill) The December 31, 1990, balance sheet of Lassiter Company follows.

Assets		Liabilities and Stockholders' Equity	
Current assets	$20,000	Current liabilities	$10,000
Noncurrent assets	46,000	Long-term liabilities	30,000
Total assets	$66,000	Common stock	20,000
		Retained earnings	6,000
		Total liabilities and	
		stockholders' equity	$66,000

On January 1, 1991, the Acme Brothers purchased 100 percent of the outstanding common stock of Lassiter for $45,000 cash. At the time the fair market values of Lassiter's current and noncurrent assets were $24,000 and $50,000, respectively. The liabilities are reported on the balance sheet at fair market value.

Required:

a. Provide the journal entry that would be recorded by Acme on the date of the purchase.
b. Provide the entry that Acme will record when it prepares a consolidated balance sheet.

E16–6

(Recognizing minority interest but no goodwill) Taylor Sisters purchased a controlling interest in three different companies during 1990. Information about the size of each purchase, the purchase price, and the financial condition of each company follows. All purchases were made for cash.

Purchase	Percent of Shares Purchased	Price	Historical Cost		Fair Market Value	
			Assets	**Liabilities**	**Assets**	**Liabilities**
1	90%	$ 6,300	$20,000	$16,000	$23,000	$16,000
2	80	24,000	35,000	13,000	43,000	13,000
3	70	3,500	19,000	16,000	21,000	16,000

Required: Provide the journal entries recorded on the books of Taylor Sisters for each purchase. Provide both the entry at purchase and the entry to record the consolidation.

E16–7

(Recognizing goodwill and minority interest) The December 31 condensed balance sheet of Weymeier and Company follows.

Assets		Liabilities and Stockholders' Equity	
Current assets	$18,000	Current liabilities	$10,000
Noncurrent assets	52,000	Long-term liabilities	50,000
Total assets	$70,000	Retained earnings	10,000
		Total liabilities and	
		stockholders' equity	$70,000

On January 1 of the following year Tenney Auto Manufacturers purchased 60 percent of the outstanding common stock of Weymeier for a total price of $21,000 cash. At the time the fair market values of Weymeier's current and noncurrent assets were $25,000 and $60,000, respectively. The liabilities are reported on the balance sheet at fair market value.

Required:

a. Provide the journal entry recorded by Tenney on the date of the purchase.
b. Provide the entry that Tenney will record when it prepares its consolidated balance sheet.

E16–8 *(Eliminating intercompany transactions)*   Safeton owns 100 percent of the outstanding stock of Mayliner. When Safeton prepared its consolidated financial statements on December 31, the accountant noticed that Safeton loaned $100,000 to Mayliner on July 1 of that year. Accrued but unpaid interest on the loan as of December 31 totaled $5500.

Required: Provide the journal entry to eliminate the following:

a. The intercompany note receivable/payable
b. The intercompany interest receivable/payable
c. The intercompany revenue/expense.

E16–9 *(Completing a consolidated worksheet)*   Harrison Chemical purchased 100 percent of the outstanding stock of Watson Supply on December 31 for $100,000 cash. As of that date the fair market values of the inventory and fixed assets of Watson equaled $70,000 and $125,000, respectively. Provide the information to complete the following consolidated worksheet, which already reflects the entry recorded at acquisition.

Accounts	Harrison	Watson	Adjustments and Eliminations		Consolidated Balance Sheet
			Dr.	Cr.	
Cash	73,000	10,000			
Accounts Receivable	110,000	40,000			
Inventory	220,000	60,000			
Investment in Subsidiary	100,000	—			
Fixed Assets	615,000	120,000			
Goodwill	30,000	—			
Total assets	1,148,000	230,000			
Accounts Payable	80,000	70,000			
Long-Term Notes	450,000	80,000			
Common Stock	500,000	70,000			
Retained Earnings	118,000	10,000			
Total liabilities and stockholders' equity	1,148,000	230,000			

E16–10 *(Pooling of interests)*   Financial information for Acquisition, Inc., and Sub Company follows.

Accounts	Acquisition	Sub	Fair Market Value (Sub)
Current Assets	$80,000	$10,000	$15,000
Fixed Assets	60,000	22,000	25,000
Long-Term Liabilities	40,000	5,000	5,000
Common Stock	40,000	20,000	
Additional Paid-in Capital (common stock)	10,000	—	
Retained Earnings	50,000	7,000	

On December 31, Acquisition acquired 100 percent of Sub Company's stock by issuing to the shareholders of Sub 400 shares of no-par-value common stock.

Required:

a. Provide the journal entries recorded by Acquisition at the date of the exchange and before the consolidated balance sheet was prepared.

b. Prepare a consolidated balance sheet using the pooling-of-interests method.

E16–11
(Exchange gains/losses on outstanding payables) On January 1, 1988, Trebly Company borrowed 100,000 British pounds from the Royal Bank of Britain, signing a five-year note payable. Exchange rates between the U.S. dollar and the British pound are provided below.

Date	U.S. Dollars per Pound
January 1, 1988	$2.00
December 31, 1988	2.10
December 31, 1989	1.90

Required: Provide the journal entries prepared by Trebly to record the borrowing transaction and the exchange gains/losses recognized on December 31, 1988, and December 31, 1989. Ignore any interest charges on the note.

E16–12
(Exchange gains/losses on outstanding receivables) On January 1, 1988, Outreach, Incorporated, sold services to a Canadian supply company and accepted a three-year note in the amount of 5000 Canadian dollars. Exchange rates between the U.S. dollar and the Canadian dollar are provided below.

Date	U.S. Dollars per Canadian Dollars
January 1, 1988	$.80
December 31, 1988	.85
December 31, 1989	.75

Required: Provide the journal entries prepared by Outreach to record the receipt of the note and the exchange gains/losses recognized on December 31, 1988, and December 31, 1989. Ignore any interest on the note.

E16–13
(Hedging to reduce the risk of currency fluctuations) This exercise refers to (E16–12). Assume that Outreach hedged the 5000 (Canadian dollar) receivable by borrowing 5000 Canadian dollars from a Canadian bank on January 1, 1988. Demonstrate using journal entries how this transaction removes Outreach's exposure to fluctuating exchange rates.

E16–14
(Fluctuating exchange rates, debt covenants, and hedging) International Services entered into a debt covenant requiring it to maintain a current ratio of at least 1.5:1. The company's condensed balance sheet as of December 31 follows.

Assets		Liabilities and Stockholders' Equity	
Current assets	$ 80,000	Current liabilities	$ 50,000
Noncurrent assets	200,000	Long-term liabilities	100,000
Total assets	$280,000	Stockholders' equity	130,000
		Total liabilities and stockholders' equity	$280,000

International's primary customer is Buckingham, Ltd., a company located in Britain, and as of December 31 Buckingham owed International 40,000 British pounds. The exchange rate as of December 31 between U.S. dollars and British pounds was $1.60 per pound.

Required:

a. What dollar amount of International's current assets on the balance sheet is associated with the receivable owed by Buckingham?

b. Assume that all account balances remain the same over the next year. Below what exchange rate (U.S. dollars per British pound) would International be in violation of the debt covenant?

c. Assume that $1600 of Accounts Payable on the balance sheet represent a debt to a British bank of 1000 British pounds. Below what exchange rate would International be in violation of the debt covenant now? Consider both the receivable and the payable.

d. Describe how International could hedge to reduce the risk of being in violation of the debt covenant.

PROBLEMS

Note: The balance sheets and fair market value information provided in P16–1 are also used in P16–2 through P16–5.

P16–1   *(100 percent purchase and the recognition of goodwill)*   The condensed balance sheets as of December 31 for Burns and Associates and Jordan Excavation are provided below.

	Burns	Jordan
Assets		
Cash	$ 156,000	$ 10,000
Accounts receivable	150,000	40,000
Inventory	300,000	40,000
Fixed assets	400,000	130,000
Total assets	$1,006,000	$220,000
Liabilities and stockholders' equity		
Accounts payable	80,000	20,000
Long-term liabilities	300,000	50,000
Common stock	400,000	90,000
Additional paid-in capital		
(common stock)	100,000	10,000
Retained earnings	126,000	50,000
Total liabilities and		
stockholders' equity	$1,006,000	$220,000

As of December 31 the market values of Jordan's inventories and fixed assets were $70,000 and $120,000, respectively. Liabilities are at fair market value on the balance sheet.

On December 31 Burns and Associates purchased Jordan Excavation for $180,000: $120,000 in cash and $60,000 in bonds issued at face value. The preceding balance sheets were prepared immediately prior to the acquisition.

Required:

a. Prepare the journal entries recorded by Burns to recognize the acquisition and the addition of Jordan's assets and liabilities to its balance sheet.

b. Prepare a consolidated worksheet and the consolidated balance sheet.

P16–2   *(Minority interest and no goodwill)*   This problem refers to P16–1. Assume that Burns and Associates purchased 80 percent of the outstanding stock of Jordan for $136,000 cash.

Required:

a. Prepare the journal entries recorded by Burns to recognize the acquisition and the addition of Jordan's assets and liabilities to its balance sheet.

b. Prepare a consolidated worksheet and a consolidated balance sheet.

P16-3

(Minority interest and goodwill) This problem refers to P16-1. Assume that Burns and Associates purchased 80 percent of the 10,000 shares of outstanding stock of Jordan for $140,000 cash.

Required:

a. Prepare the journal entries recorded by Burns to recognize the acquisition and the addition of Jordan's assets and liabilities to its balance sheet.
b. Prepare a consolidated worksheet and a consolidated balance sheet.

P16-4

(Pooling of interests) This problem refers to P16-1. Assume that Burns and Associates acquired 100 percent of the outstanding stock of Jordan in exchange for 2500 shares of common stock with no par value.

Required:

a. Prepare the journal entries recorded by Burns to recognize the acquisition and the addition of Jordan's assets and liabilities to its balance sheet.
b. Prepare a consolidated worksheet and a consolidated balance sheet.

P16-5

(Pooling of interests or purchase?) This problem refers to P16-1. Assume that Burns and Associates acquired 100 percent of the outstanding stock of Jordan first by issuing 2500 shares of no-par-value common stock for $72 per share, and then using the $180,000 cash proceeds to purchase all outstanding common shares of Jordan.

Required:

a. Prepare the journal entries recorded by Burns to recognize the issuance of stock, the acquisition of Jordan's shares, and the addition of Jordan's assets and liabilities to its balance sheet.
b. Prepare a consolidated worksheet and a consolidated balance sheet.
c. How is this series of transactions different from a pooling of interests?

P16-6

(Minority interest and goodwill) Marymount purchased a controlling interest in three companies during 1990. Financial information concerning the three companies follows.

	Company A	Company B	Company C
Assets			
Cash	$ 6,000	$ 4,000	$ 2,000
Accounts receivable	12,000	9,000	7,000
Inventory	30,000	12,000	18,000
Fixed assets	70,000	30,000	15,000
Total assets	$118,000	$55,000	$42,000
Liabilities and Stockholders' Equity			
Current liabilities	7,000	12,000	5,000
Long-term liabilities	25,000	20,000	18,000
Common stock	50,000	10,000	15,000
Retained earnings	36,000	13,000	4,000
Total liabilities and stockholders' equity	$118,000	$55,000	$42,000
Fair market value			
Inventory	$ 45,000	$18,000	$18,000
Fixed assets	75,000	35,000	15,000

All other assets and liabilities on the balance sheet are at fair market value.

Shares of stock outstanding before acquisition	10,000	1,000	2,000

Marymount purchased 8000, 600, and 1500 shares of Company A, Company B, and Company C, respectively. The share prices and cash payments follow.

	Shares Purchased	Price/Share	Cash Payment
Company A	8000	$10.60	$84,800
Company B	600	40.00	24,000
Company C	1500	11.00	16,500

Required: Provide the journal entries recorded by Marymount to recognize the acquisition of the shares and the addition of the assets and liabilities of each subsidiary company to its balance sheet.

P16–7

(Exchange gains and losses)   Hughes International is a U.S. company that conducts business throughout the world. Listed below are selected transactions entered into by the company during 1990.

(1) Sold merchandise to Royal Equipment Company (a United Kingdom company) in exchange for an account receivable in the amount of 240,000 pounds. At the time the exchange rate was .75 British pounds per U.S. dollar.

(2) Sold merchandise to Honda Automobile Company (a Japanese company) in exchange for a note receivable that calls for a payment of 300,000 yen. The exchange rate was 100 yen to the U.S. dollar.

(3) Purchased inventory from Venice Leathers (an Italian company) in exchange for a note payable that calls for a payment of 50 million lira. The exchange rate was 1000 lira to the U.S. dollar.

(4) Purchased inventory from B.C. Lumber (a Canadian company) in exchange for an account payable in the amount of 150,000 Canadian dollars. The exchange rate was 1.50 Canadian dollars per U.S. dollar.

On December 31, 1990, the exchange rates were as follows.

Foreign Currency	Currency per U.S. dollar
British pound	1.20
Japanese yen	75.00
Italian lira	1600.00
Canadian dollar	1.20

Required:

a. Convert each transaction above to the equivalent amount in U.S. dollars.

b. Prepare journal entries to record each transaction.

c. Assume that the receivables and payables are still outstanding as of December 31, 1990. Compute the amount of exchange gain or loss for each transaction. Prepare the appropriate journal entries.

d. Why do fluctuating exchange rates give rise to exchange gains and losses?

P16–8

(Hedging the risks of currency fluctuations)   On January 1, 1989, ITC sold supplies to Katsuo Motors, a Japanese company. In exchange, ITC accepted a four-year note receivable in the amount of 10,000,000 Japanese yen. The exchange rate at the time of the transaction was .008 U.S. dollars per Japanese yen. To reduce the risks of fluctuating exchange rates between the U.S. dollar and the Japanese yen, ITC issued bonds on January 1 at face value, payable in the amount of 10,000,000 Japanese yen. The exchange rates between the U.S. dollar and the Japanese yen for December 31, 1989, and December 31, 1990, are provided below.

	December 31, 1989	December 31, 1990
1 Japanese yen	.006 dollar	.007 dollar

Required: Provide journal entries to accomplish the following:

a. Record the sale of supplies and the bond issuance.

b. Recognize the exchange gains/losses as of December 31, 1989.

c. Recognize the exchange gains/losses as of December 31, 1990.

P16-9

(Consolidated statements, the equity method, and debt covenants) Mammoth Enterprises purchased 50 percent of the outstanding stock of Atom, Inc. on December 31 for $60,000 cash. On that date the book value of Atom's net assets was $70,000. The market value of Atom's assets was $180,000, $20,000 above book value. Mammoth's condensed balance sheet, immediately before the acquisition, follows.

Assets		Liabilities and Stockholders' Equity	
Current assets	$150,000	Current liabilities	$ 30,000
Noncurrent assets	350,000	Long-term liabilities	200,000
Total assets	$500,000	Common stock	100,000
		Retained earnings	170,000
		Total liabilities and	
		stockholders' equity	$500,000

Mammoth entered into a debt covenant earlier in the year that requires the company to maintain a debt/equity ratio of less than 1:1.

Required:

a. Assume that Mammoth treats the transaction as a purchase, and compute Mammoth's debt/equity ratio both before and after the acquisition. Consider minority interest a liability.

b. Under the equity method (covered in Chapter 13), Mammoth would simply record the investment by increasing the Investment account and decreasing Cash by $60,000. Explain why in this situation Mammoth would probably prefer the equity method instead of treating this transaction as a purchase and preparing consolidated financial statements.

P16-10

(Pooling of interests vs. purchase) Financial information for Lampley and Greystoke follow.

Account	Lampley	Greystoke	Fair Market Value (Greystoke)
Current assets	$160,000	$20,000	$30,000
Fixed assets	120,000	44,000	50,000
Current liabilities	80,000	10,000	10,000
Common stock	80,000	40,000	
Additional paid-in capital	20,000	—	
Retained earnings	100,000	14,000	

Required:

a. Assume that on December 31 Lampley acquired 100 percent of Greystoke's stock by issuing to the shareholders of Greystoke 2000 shares of no-par-value common stock. Prepare the consolidated balance sheet for Lampley under the pooling-of-interests method.

b. Assume that on December 31 Lampley issued 2000 shares of no-par common stock for $40 per share, and then used the $80,000 cash proceeds to purchase all of Greystoke's outstanding common stock. Prepare the consolidated balance sheet for Lampley under the purchase method.

c. Compute Lampley's current ratio and debt/equity ratio under both methods. Compare the ratios, and briefly discuss why Lampley might choose one method over the other of acquiring Greystoke. Consider future income effects also.

P16–11

(100 percent pooling of interests: preparing consolidated financial statements)   On December 31 Lake Forest Developers issued 15,000 shares of common stock, each with a fair market value of $10, to the stockholders of Smallville Supply in exchange for 100 percent of Smallville's outstanding stock. The fair market values of Smallville's inventories and fixed assets at the time of the acquisition were $45,000 and $85,000, respectively. As of December 31 Smallville owed Lake Forest $12,000, represented by a short-term note upon which $1000 in interest income (receivable) on Lake Forest's financial statement and $1000 in interest expense (payable) on Smallville's financial statements had been accrued. During the year, Smallville provided a service for Lake Forest for which it earned and collected $20,000 in cash. Lake Forest charged the $20,000 to administrative expenses. The financial statements of the two companies, immediately prior to the exchange, follow.

Account	Lake Forest	Smallville
Balance Sheet		
Assets		
Cash	$170,000	$ 10,000
Accounts receivable	23,000	15,000
Interest receivable	3,000	—
Note receivable	12,000	—
Inventory	100,000	30,000
Fixed assets	300,000	80,000
Total assets	$608,000	$135,000
Liabilities and Stockholders' Equity		
Short-term payables	6,000	13,000
Interest payable	2,000	2,000
Long-term notes payable	100,000	20,000
Common stock	200,000	75,000
Retained earnings	300,000	25,000
Total liabilities and stockholders' equity	$608,000	$135,000
Income Statement		
Sales	$250,000	$ 80,000
Interest income	2,000	—
Costs of goods sold	140,000	40,000
Selling and administrative expenses	50,000	10,000
Interest expense	10,000	2,000
Income taxes	15,000	7,000
Net income	$ 37,000	$ 21,000

Required:

a. Prepare the journal entry to record the acquisition.

b. Use a consolidated worksheet, and prepare the consolidated financial statements.

c. Compute the current ratio, the debt/equity ratio, and earnings per share for Lake Forest after the exchange. Assume that Lake Forest had 25,000 shares of common stock outstanding prior to the exchange.

P16–12

(Purchase accounting)   This problem refers to the information contained in P16–11. Assume that Lake Forest Developers issued 15,000 shares of common stock for $10 each and then used the $150,000 cash proceeds to purchase all of Smallville's outstanding common stock.

Required:

a. Prepare the journal entry (or entries) to record the exchange.

b. Use a consolidated worksheet, and prepare the consolidated financial statements.

c. Compute the current ratio, the debt/equity ratio, and earnings per share for Lake Forest Developers immediately after the acquisition. Assume that Lake Forest had 25,000 shares of common stock outstanding prior to the acquisition.

P16-13 *(80 percent purchase: preparing the consolidated balance sheet)* This problem refers to P16–11. Assume that Lake Forest Developers purchased 80 percent of Smallville's outstanding stock for $120,000 cash.

Required:

a. Prepare the journal entry to record the acquisition.

b. Use a consolidated worksheet, and prepare the consolidated balance sheet.

CASES

C16-1 *(Accounting for business combinations and the politics of standard-setting)* In a lecture presented at Stanford University in 1978, accounting professor Stephen A. Zeff made the following remark.

> *From 1968 through 1970 accounting standard-setters struggled with the accounting methods for business combinations. It was flanked on the one side by the Federal Trade Commission and the Department of Justice, who favored the elimination of pooling-of-interests accounting in order to produce a slowing effect on the merger movement, and on the other side by merger-minded corporations who were fervent supporters of pooling-of-interests accounting.*

Required:

a. Explain why many large U.S. corporations would be in favor of pooling-of-interests accounting, and why its elimination might "produce a slowing effect on the merger movement."

b. Briefly describe how accounting standard-setters responded to the situation described above.

c. Do you think that accounting standards should be used to achieve national and governmental goals such as slowing a merger movement, increasing corporate investment, or controlling inflation? Why or why not?

C16-2 *(Consolidating a finance subsidiary's financial statement: economic consequences)* In 1985 wholly owned finance subsidiaries of major U.S. companies were accounted for by the parent using the equity method. These companies justified the procedure by claiming that the operations of the subsidiaries were so unlike those of the parents that consolidating the subsidiaries' financial statements would distort those of the parents. At the same time, by using the equity method the parents were able to avoid including the subsidiaries' liabilities, which were often quite large, on their consolidated balance sheets. In 1985, for example, adding the liabilities of General Motors Acceptance Company, a finance subsidiary, to those of General Motors (GM), the parent, would have quadrupled GM's debt/equity ratio.

Forbes commented that if the FASB required such companies to consolidate their finance subsidiaries, it "could cause difficulties with bond indenture agreements and loan covenants requiring that certain ratios be maintained."* Others have commented that such problems are of little concern because they can be avoided by writing debt covenants so that all financial ratios are defined in terms of generally accepted accounting principles. Moreover, most financial statement users are reasonably sophisticated and are already aware of the subsidiary's debt. Credit-rating agencies claim, for example, that as long as the debt of the subsidiary is disclosed, it matters little whether it is consolidated or not.

*Jinny St. Goer, "Back to the balance sheet," *Forbes,* 25 February 1985, pp. 122–23.

Required:

a. Briefly explain the difference between using the equity method and preparing consolidated financial statements, and describe how requiring the consolidation of subsidiary financial statements could "cause difficulties with bond indenture agreements."

b. How might the fact that most financial statement users are reasonably sophisticated affect the nature of the accounting standards developed by the FASB?

C16–3

(Accounting for foreign currencies: an economic consequence)   An article in *Forbes* noted that "accounting rules . . . can often change the way companies do business."* Under the accounting rule covering receivables and payables denominated in foreign currencies, for example, "it is very important for companies to monitor their currency dealings." A case in point is R. J. Reynolds Industries, who recently "opened regional treasury offices in London and Hong Kong to keep tabs on world-wide cash flow and direct local borrowings". In that same article a partner from a major accounting firm indicated that "more and more companies are centralizing their treasury-management function. Those that don't may be operating at a disadvantage."

*Christopher Power, "RJR's foreign coup," *Forbes,* 12 September 1983, p. 226.

Required:

a. Explain why the methods of accounting for foreign currencies might cause a company to centralize its treasury-management function, and why those that don't may be operating at a disadvantage.

b. What is one of the main strategies used by U.S. companies to reduce the risks of holding receivables or payables denominated in non-U.S. currencies.

c. Explain how this strategy works—specifically, how it might be used to reduce the possibility of violating a covenant on an outstanding debt.

C16–4

(Accounting practices in different countries: problems and solutions)   Barbara Thomas, in an article published in *Business Law* (August 1983), noted that "The internationalization of capital markets and the dramatic increase in the foreign direct investments of multinational enterprises have increased the need for relevant, timely, and comparable information about the activities of business enterprises having operations in more than one nation." However, this need will be difficult to fulfill "because the various national governments approach accounting measurements and financial disclosure matters differently. The following major items typify these differences."

1. Consolidation practices vary widely. In some countries, for example, it is not customary to present consolidated financial statements at all.

2. In some countries there are practical links between income tax and financial reporting.

3. All leases are treated as operating leases in many countries.

4. Foreign currency translations are measured and reported in a variety of ways.

5. In many parts of the world financial statements are required only on an annual basis.

6. A statement of cash flows is not required in some jurisdictions.

7. The standards governing the qualification of auditors and the role of the audit vary widely across countries.

Required:

a. Explain why differences like those listed exist and why they make it difficult for investors operating in an international environment.

b. Briefly describe what is being done to promote greater uniformity in international accounting practices.

C16–5

(Hidden reserves: do they make economic sense?)   Most of continental Europe allows banks, and certain other financial institutions, to keep special loss provisions off the books or to stockpile hidden cash. For example, "German banks are allowed such reserves, and they are safer and better equipped to take risks than they would be if they didn't have them. The reserves build confidence. They protect against bankruptcy and ensure that banks can cover their losses", says Reinhard Goerdeler, a prominent German accountant.*

Jane Sasseen, "Should banks tell all?" Forbes, 3 December 1984, pp. 214, 216.

Required:

a. Contrast Goerdeler's comments to the basic philosophy underlying generally accepted accounting principles in the United States.

b. Do you think that U.S. disclosure rules should be applied to German banks? Why or why not?

c. Explain why greater uniformity in the accounting practices used in the different countries of the world may be slow in coming.

d. Within the guidelines of generally accepted accounting principles, are there ways that U.S. companies can establish certain kinds of "hidden reserves"? If so, provide several examples, and explain why they might wish to do so.

Using Financial Statement Information

Learning Objectives

1 Explain how financial statement information is used for prediction and control.

2 List and describe the basic steps involved in assessing the earning power and solvency position of a company.

3 List and describe the five categories of financial ratios covered in this chapter. Identify the ratios included in each category.

4 Identify and describe the major limitations of financial accounting information.

≡ The information that appears in the financial statements is used in many ways by a variety of individuals and entities. Investors and creditors use it to evaluate company performance and to predict the amount and timing of the future cash flows associated with their investments. They also use financial information to control, direct, and monitor the activities of management. As representatives of the stockholders, the boards of directors of many companies base executive compensation on various measures of income, while creditors protect their loan investments by writing debt covenants in terms of financial statement numbers such as working capital, the current ratio, the debt/equity ratio, and retained earnings. Public utilities use financial accounting numbers to set customer rates, and labor unions use such information to negotiate with management for higher wages and better working conditions. Credit-rating agencies, such as Standard & Poor's, Moody's, and Dun & Bradstreet, use financial statement information to determine credit ratings. Indeed, financial accounting information plays an important role in a number of different kinds of business decisions.

It is also true, however, that financial accounting information is only one of several alternative sources of information, and in many ways it is quite limited. Financial reports, for example, are typically published several months after the balance-sheet date, enabling many other media to provide more timely financial information. Moreover, generally accepted accounting principles are the result of a political process that gives rise to a wide variety of accceptable accounting methods. Financial statements, as a result, (1) are significantly influenced by the subjective judgments and incentives of the managers who prepare them, (2) are based on historical and conservative information, (3) are not adjusted for inflation, and (4) generally do not reflect market values. Consequently, while financial accounting information is useful, it must be used in both the appropriate situation and the appropriate manner. Understanding how and in what situations to use financial accounting information is the subject of this chapter.

The chapter is divided into four major sections. Section 1 contains a general discussion of the way financial accounting information can be used to predict future cash flows and to control the actions of management. Section 2 begins with a discussion of the importance of the audit opinion, significant transactions, and a company's credit rating. We then analyze a set of comparative financial statements for a fictitous company called Seafair, Inc., using a technique called *ratio analysis.* Section 3 further explains the nature of solvency and how information on the financial statements can be used to assess it. Section 4 focuses on those areas where financial statements provide little or no information. Appendix C at the end of the text discusses how the financial statements can be adjusted to reflect general inflation and current market values.

PREDICTION AND CONTROL

There are two fundamental ways in which financial accounting numbers are useful: (1) they help to predict a company's future cash flows by providing an indication of its earning power and solvency position, and (2) they help investors and creditors to control, direct, and monitor the business decisions of a company's managers.

Financial Accounting Numbers as Prediction Aids

Financial accounting numbers report on past events. In and of themselves they are not predictions, nor are they forecasts. However, to the extent that past events are indicative of the future, financial accounting numbers can be used to make predictions about a company's future cash flows. Indeed, the main objective of financial reporting, as stated by the Financial Accounting Standards Board, is "to help present and potential investors and creditors and other users in assessing the amount, timing, and uncertainty of future cash flows."[1]

Earning power and solvency are important indicators of a company's future cash flows. **Earning power** refers to a company's ability to increase its wealth through operations and generate cash in the future. **Solvency** refers to a company's ability to meet its obligations as they come due; specifically, it refers to how well the timing of a company's cash inflows matches the timing of its cash obligations. Earning power, which essentially refers to future cash flows, is distinct from solvency, which is concerned primarily with day-to-day cash inflows and outflows. Yet, these two concepts are not independent, and one can hardly exist without the other. A company must meet its short-run obligations, for example, to maintain its earning power; by the same token, operations—the source of a company's earning power—provide much of the cash used to meet short-run obligations.

Equity Investments, Earning Power, and Accrual Accounting

An investment in a company's common stock represents an investment in the ownership of that company. Equity investments involve no formal contracts and are not subject to fixed maturity dates (i.e., they have indefinite lives). Returns to owners come either in the form of dividends or stock price appreciation, both of which relate to the earning power of the company or its ability to generate cash in the future. Companies with high earning power either pay higher dividends or are more highly valued in the equity market than are those with low earning power.

Financial accounting numbers based on the accrual concept, which measures a company's operating performance in terms of asset and liability flows, are designed to provide information about earning power. Items on the income statement, especially net income from operations, are particularly relevant in this regard. Equity investors, whose returns are related to the earning powers of the companies they own, are therefore especially interested in accrual-based financial accounting numbers.

Debt Investments, Solvency, and Cash Accounting

Debt investments, on the other hand, have fixed maturities (i.e., they have definite lives) that are explicitly stated in debt contracts. Returns to creditors come in the form of interest and principal payments, which are drawn from a company's available cash reserves over the life of the debt. Creditors, therefore, have a special interest in both a company's solvency position and the finanical accounting numbers that help to form predictions about cash flows over the periods of their outstanding loans. Balance-sheet numbers that reflect short-run cash flows and the statement of cash flows are particularly relevant to the debt investment decision.

---

1. Financial Accounting Standards Board, "Objectives of Financial Reporting by Business Enterprises," *Statement of Financial Concepts No. 1* (Stamford, Conn.: FASB, November 1978).

Once again, be careful not to conclude that creditors are uninterested in earning power and accrual numbers, or that equity investors are not interested in solvency and cash flows. Earning power and solvency are related, and one cannot be assessed without recognizing the importance of the other. As Professor Loyd Heath and Paul Rosenfield note, "Investors and creditors . . . need to evaluate the solvency as well as the profitability of companies in which they have interest.[2]

Furthermore, keep in mind that equity and debt investors are not the only parties interested in a company's earning power and solvency position. Auditors have an important economic stake in the financial performance and condition of their clients; employees are interested in the financial health of their employers; other companies are concerned with the financial state and operations of their suppliers, customers, and competitors; and regulatory bodies need to know the financial condition of companies and industries that are heavily relied upon by the public (e.g., electric utilities).

Financial Accounting Numbers and Control

Another way in which financial accounting numbers are useful is in controlling the business decisions of managers. Investors and creditors, who provide a company with its capital, can control the actions of its managers by requiring that their contracts be written in terms of financial accounting numbers.

Equity Investors and Management Control

Stockholders have incentives to encourage management to act in ways that maximize the present value of future dividend payments. Since such payments depend on a company's earning power and long-run profitability, stockholders want management to make business decisions that maintain high levels of earning power. A common method used to attain such a goal is to base a significant portion of management's compensation on reported profits. Such compensation schemes, which are set by a company's board of directors, can lead to payments either in the form of cash or shares of stock. Exxon Corporation, for example, has implemented a management incentive program that pays eligible employees a percentage of the company's earnings if net income in a given year exceeds 6 percent of invested capital (as defined in the bonus plan). These bonuses have been paid in both cash and shares of Exxon common stock.[3]

Creditors and Management Control

Creditors are also interested in protecting their investments by controlling the business decisions of management. They are concerned that companies may not be able to meet their loan obligations because company assets may have been (1) paid to the shareholders in the form of dividends or purchases of outstanding stock, (2) pledged to other creditors, or (3) mismanaged. To reduce the probability of such events, a creditor may restrict certain business decisions of managers as

---

2. Loyd Heath and Paul Rosenfield, "Solvency: The Forgotten Half of Financial Reporting," *Journal of Accountancy* (January 1979) pp. 48–54.

3. It is unclear that basing management compensation on accounting measures of profit serves to maximize the long-run earning power of major companies in the United States. Some contend that such compensation schemes encourage management to manipulate reported profits and to make operating, investing, and financing decisions that increase profits in the short run. See, for example, "Managing Our Way to Economic Decline" by Robert H. Hayes and William J. Abernathy, which appeared in the *Harvard Business Review* (July–August 1980), pp. 67–77.

a condition of the loan. Such restrictions are written into the loan contract and expressed in terms of financial accounting numbers.

In March of 1987, for example, Alcoa entered into an eight-year, $600 million revolving credit agreement with a group of banks. The agreement requires that during the period of the loan (1) the current ratio be not less than 1:1 and (2) a minimum working capital of $500 million be maintained. In another debt covenant, The Pillsbury Company is restricted with respect to paying dividends and purchasing its own common stock. As of May 31, 1987 retained earnings could not be reduced below $225 million.

In summary, a wide variety of parties, especially equity investors and creditors, are interested in financial accounting numbers because they provide information about earning power and solvency. Such information can be used for purposes of prediction and control. The remainder of the chapter considers how financial information, especially that contained in the financial statements, can be used to assess earning power and solvency.

ANALYZING FINANCIAL INFORMATION: ASSESSING EARNING POWER AND SOLVENCY

Assessing earning power and solvency involves four steps: (1) reviewing the auditor's report, (2) assessing the nature and importance of significant transactions, (3) evaluating a company's credit rating, and (4) analyzing the information contained in the financial report. Each step is explained in the following discussion.

The Auditor's Opinion Letter

From a user's perspective, perhaps the most important section of the financial statements is the opinion letter, written and signed by the external auditor. This letter serves as the accounting profession's "seal of approval," stating whether or not, and to what extent, the information in the financial statements fairly reflects the financial position and operations of the company.

After reviewing the financial records of a company, the auditor usually renders an **unqualified (clean) opinion,** stating that the financial statements fairly reflect the financial position and operations of the company. An unqualified report also states that all necessary tests were conducted in concluding that a company's financial statements conform to generally accepted accounting principles.[4] In such cases the reader can be reasonably assured that the information in the statements is credible and that the company in question is in reasonable financial health.

Accounting Trends and Techniques (New York: AICPA, 1987) reports that, of the 600 major U.S. companies surveyed, 410 (68 percent) received an unqualified opinion in 1986. It follows that 190 (32 percent) of these companies received something other than an unqualified audit report. Auditors depart from the standard report for one or more of the following reasons:

1. The scope of the auditor's examination is affected by conditions that preclude the application of one or more auditing procedures considered necessary.

---

4. Examples of standard, unqualified auditor's reports can be found in Chapter 1 of this text and in Appendix D where the financial report of K mart Corporation is located.

2. The auditor's opinion is based in part on the report of another auditor.
3. The financial statements are affected by a departure from generally accepted accounting principles.
4. Major accounting principles/methods have been changed.
5. The financial statements are affected by uncertainties concerning future events, the outcome of which cannot be estimated as of the date of the auditor's report.
6. There is a question about whether the company can continue as a going concern in the future.

If the auditor departs from the standard report for any of the reasons listed above, the financial statement user should proceed cautiously. Departures due to scope limitations, departures from generally accepted accounting principles, material uncertainties, and going-concern questions can be serious and may raise doubts about a company as a potential investment. Departures due to relying on other auditors and accounting principle/method changes, on the other hand, are usually less worrisome. Figure 17–1 provides excerpts from several recent audit opinions from 1986 financial reports, each of which describes a different reason for departing from the standard report.[5]

The audit report can generally be relied upon because auditors have significant economic incentives to maintain high levels of competence and independence. Legal liability, reputation, and professional standards of quality and ethics all play important roles in encouraging an auditor to conduct a thorough investigation and to report in an independent manner. Keep in mind, however, that management controls the audit fee and has the power to change auditors. Such influence has been used, on occasion, to compromise the quality and integrity of an auditor's work.

Be aware also that not all companies are audited by certified public accountants. Only those whose equity securities are traded on public stock exchanges are legally required to do so. Such publicly-traded companies tend to be the largest in the U.S. (in terms of annual sales or total assets), yet they represent only a small portion of the total number of U.S. companies. These other companies may or may not choose to have their statements audited. Many are required to do so as a condition for private equity issuances or bank loans, but most are not audited at all. A comprehensive audit by a public accounting firm can be very time-consuming and costly, and for many small companies, especially those that do not rely on outside sources of capital, the benefit from the audit simply does not justify the costs. In such cases the financial statement user must proceed with extreme caution.

Significant Transactions

Assessing earning power and solvency also involves reviewing significant transactions entered into by a company or significant recent events that might affect a company's performance. Such items can have an important effect on the future

---

5. These reports were published prior to a rewording of the audit report in 1989. The departures illustrated in Figure 17–1, however, would be largely uneffected by the modification except for the wording of General Electric's accounting principle/method change. Current audit reports simply mention the accounting change and refer the reader to the related footnote to the financial statements. The reference to "consistently applied during the period except for changes, with which we concur" does not appear in current reports.

Figure 17-1 Examples of qualified audit reports

Material Uncertainty

To the Board of Directors and Shareholders of GenCorp:

As described in Note 0 to the consolidated financial statements Aerojet General, a wholly-owned subsidiary of GenCorp . . . has been subject to environmental litigation arising from discharges of chemicals in past years at Aerojet's Sacramento, California facility. Eventual liabilities of Aerojet relating to this matter cannot be reasonably estimated at this time. . . .

Going Concern Question

To the Shareholders and Board of Directors of Allegheny International, Inc.:

As described in Note 6 to the consolidated financial statements, the Company has received waivers from lending institutions suspending the applicability of certain debt covenants while it arranges to keep its current financing in place. . . . The Company's ability to continue as a going concern is contingent upon its ability to maintain adequate financing and attain profitable operations.

Change of Accounting Principle/Method

To Share Owners and Board of Directors of General Electric Company:

In our opinion, the . . . financial statements present fairly the financial position of General Electric Company . . . in conformity with generally accepted accounting principles consistently applied during the period except for the changes, with which we concur, in the methods of accounting for income taxes and overhead recorded in inventory as described in Note 1 to the financial statements.

Source: 1986 annual reports.

---

direction of a company and may distort the financial statements, making it more difficult to assess a company's financial position and operations. Examples include major acquisitions, the discontinuance or disposal of a business segment, unresolved litigation, major writedowns of receivables or inventories, offers to purchase outstanding shares (tender offers), extraordinary gains or losses, and changes of accounting methods. The financial effects of such transactions or events are usually prominently disclosed in the financial report, and if they are significant enough, they are even mentioned in the auditor's report.

To illustrate the importance of these items and where they can be found in the financial report, consider the following examples. In 1987 Eli Lilly sold Elizabeth Arden, the company's cosmetic segment. The transaction produced $561 million in cash, and the gain on the sale, which was disclosed separately on the income statement, increased net income by $233 million (57 percent).

At the end of 1985 a district court in Texas entered judgment for Pennzoil Company against Texaco Inc. in the amount of $11.1 billion, the largest lawsuit in history. Texaco appealed the verdict but filed for relief in 1987 under the bankruptcy laws. As of February 1988, the final judgment had not been rendered, and

Texaco's auditors described the pending settlement in a qualified audit opinion, raising doubts about Texaco's ability to continue as a going concern. Almost three full pages in the notes to the 1988 financial report were devoted to the case.[6]

In November of 1986, The Goodyear Tire & Rubber Company announced an offer to purchase over 40 million of its outstanding shares at $50 per share. At the time, the share price was approximately $33 per share. When the shares were actually purchased in 1987, the number of outstanding shares was reduced from approximately 110 million to 70 million. This purchase was described in the footnotes.

In 1986, Burlington Northern changed the method of depreciating its railroad assets. The change reduced net income by $336 million and increased the company's 1986 loss from $525 million to $861. The financial effect of the change was reported separately on the income statement and the change was mentioned in the auditor's report.

The Credit Rating

Information about a company's credit rating is also of interest to investors, creditors, and others in their evaluations of earning power and solvency. Credit-rating agencies, such as Moody's Investor Service, Dun & Bradstreet, and Standard & Poor's, provide extensive analyses of the operations and financial positions of many companies as well as ratings of the riskiness of their outstanding debts. Such ratings have a direct bearing on a company's ability to issue debt in the future and on the terms of that debt.

The Wall Street Journal, for example, reported that Moody's Investor Service raised its rating on the outstanding debt of Columbia Savings & Loan Association from B1 to Ba-2. The rating concern said the action was "based on Columbia's good core profitability, its improved relative equity levels, and its capable management, as well as the risk profile of its operations."[7]

Procter & Gamble Company reported in its 1987 financial report: "The Company maintained its strong financial position in 1987. Indicative of its strength are cash and securities on hand of $741 million, and an excellent credit rating." That same year Abbott Laboratories reported: "The Company has maintained its favorable bond rating (AA+ by Standard & Poor's Corporation and Aa1 by Moody's Investor Service) and continues to have readily available financial resources, including unused lines of credit of $200 million at December 31, 1987."

Analyzing the Financial Statements Themselves

The final step in the assessment of earning power and solvency consists of analyzing the financial statements themselves. Figure 17–2 contains the income statements, balance sheets, statements of retained earnings, and statements of cash flows of Seafair, Inc. for the years 1988, 1989, and 1990. Assume that the company began operations on January 1, 1988, by issuing 800 shares of common

---

6. In April of 1988, Texaco's auditors amended the 1987 opinion and removed the qualification. This action was taken after Texaco entered a plan of joint reorganization with Pennzoil, and the litigation and bankruptcy proceedings were terminated.

7. *The Wall Street Journal,* 13 June 1988, p. 26.

Figure 17-2   Comparative financial statements

Seafair, Inc. Financial Statements For the Years Ended December 31, 1988-1990			
	1990	**1989**	**1988**
Income Statement			
Sales (net)	$88,000	$75,000	$65,000
Less: Cost of goods sold	35,200	32,000	32,500
Gross profit	52,800	43,000	32,500
Selling expenses	17,000	15,000	13,000
Administrative expenses (includes depreciation)	12,000	11,000	11,000
Net operating income	23,800	17,000	8,500
Less: Interest expense	3,000	3,500	1,000
Net income from continuing operations before tax	20,800	13,500	7,500
Less: Federal income taxes	8,320	5,400	3,000
Net income from continuing operations	12,480	8,100	4,500
Extraordinary (loss) gain—net of tax	(4,000)	—	—
Net income	$ 8,480	$ 8,100	$ 4,500
Balance Sheet			
Assets			
Cash	$ 3,000	$ 4,000	$ 2,000
Accounts receivable	8,000	3,000	3,000
Inventory	12,000	6,000	4,000
Long-term investments	2,000	5,000	—
Long-lived assets (net)	48,000	43,000	23,000
Total assets	$73,000	$61,000	$32,000
Liabilities and stockholders' equity			
Accounts payable	$ 7,000	$ 4,000	$ 2,000
Short-term notes payable	7,000	7,000	2,000
Long-term notes payable	21,920	27,400	7,500
Common stock	25,000	15,000	15,000
Additional paid-in capital	5,000	3,000	3,000
Retained earnings	7,080	4,600	2,500
Total liabilities and stockholders' equity	$73,000	$61,000	$32,000
Statement of Retained Earnings			
Beginning balance	$ 4,600	$ 2,500	$ 0
Plus: Net income	8,480	8,100	4,500
Less: Dividends	6,000	6,000	2,000
Ending balance	$ 7,080	$ 4,600	$ 2,500
Number of common shares outstanding	1,000	800	800
Market price of common shares	$ 60	$ 45	$ 40

Figure 17–2 (continued)

	Seafair, Inc. Financial Statements For the Years Ended December 31, 1988–1990		
	1990	**1989**	**1988**
Statement of Cash Flows (Direct Method)			
Operating activities			
Cash received from customers	$ 83,000	$ 75,000	$ 62,000
Cash paid to suppliers	(38,200)	(32,000)	(34,500)
Cash paid for selling expenses	(17,000)	(15,000)	(13,000)
Cash paid for administrative expenses	(7,200)	(6,700)	(8,700)
Cash paid for interest	(3,000)	(3,500)	(1,000)
Cash paid for taxes	(8,320)	(5,400)	(3,000)
Cash paid for extraordinary loss	(4,000)	—	—
Net cash provided (used) by operating activities	5,280	12,400	1,800
Investing activities			
Purchases of long-lived assets	(9,800)	(24,300)	(25,300)
Purchases of long-term investments	—	(5,000)	—
Sales of long-term investments	3,000	—	—
Net cash provided (used) by investing activities	(6,800)	(29,300)	(25,300)
Financing activities			
Proceeds from short-term notes	—	5,000	2,000
Proceeds from long-term notes	—	19,900	7,500
Payments on long-term notes	(5,480)	—	—
Proceeds from issuing common stock	12,000	—	18,000
Dividends paid	(6,000)	(6,000)	(2,000)
Net cash provided (used) by financing activities	520	18,900	25,500
Net increase (decrease) in cash balance	(1,000)	2,000	2,000
Beginning cash balance	4,000	2,000	0
Ending cash balance	$ 3,000	$ 4,000	$ 2,000
Reconciliation of net income with net cash flow from operating activities			
Net income	$ 8,480	$ 8,100	$ 4,500
Depreciation	4,800	4,300	2,300
Change in accounts receivable	(5,000)	—	(3,000)
Change in inventory	(6,000)	(2,000)	(4,000)
Change in accounts payable	3,000	2,000	2,000
Net cash flow from operations	$ 5,280	$ 12,400	$ 1,800

stock for $18,000. The end-of-year market prices of the company's common stock and the number of common shares outstanding at the end of each year are also disclosed. Take a few moments now to review the information on these statements. As a first pass, use your present knowledge of financial statements to assess the earning power and solvency position of Seafair over the three-year period. Assume that you have already reviewed the auditor's report, any significant transactions entered into recently, and Seafair's credit rating.

When analyzing financial accounting information, keep in mind that accounting numbers are not very meaningful in and of themselves. They become useful when they are compared to other numbers. For example, suppose that you read in *The Wall Street Journal* that Seafair's 1990 net income was $8480. Would you interpret that announcement as favorable or unfavorable news? This question is difficult to answer in the absence of a basis for comparison. Income of $8480 is neither large nor small in an absolute sense. It depends on such factors as the amount of net income reported by Seafair in previous years, the amount of net income reported by other companies in Seafair's industry, and the size of Seafair's operations and capital base. Is $8480 more or less net income than was reported in 1989 and 1988? Is $8480 more or less than the net income amounts reported by the other companies in the industry? Is $8480 a large or small percentage of the company's sales, assets, or stockholders' equity?

Financial accounting numbers are only meaningful when compared to other relevant numbers, and such comparisons can be made in three basic ways: (1) across time, (2) across different companies within the same industry, and (3) within the financial statements of the company at a given point in time. The following discussion describes each of these three methods of comparison and shows how they can be combined in the analysis of Seafair's financial statements.

Comparisons Across Time

Financial accounting numbers can be made more meaningful if they are compared across time. At a minimum, generally accepted accounting principles require that the financial statements of the current and the preceding years be disclosed side-by-side in published financial reports. While this is helpful for identifying changes from one year to the next, many companies provide comparisons of selected items, accounting and nonaccounting, across five- or ten-year periods. Such disclosures can often be used to identify important trends and turning points.

J. C. Penney Company, for example, provides a five-year comparison of most income statement items, selected per-share and balance-sheet items, and the number of its employees. Delta Air Lines provides a ten-year comparison of most income statement items, selected per-share and balance-sheet items, and such nonaccounting information as available seat miles, revenue passenger miles, and passenger load factor. Wendy's International provides a ten-year comparison of selected information about operations financial position, per-share data, financial ratios (e.g., gross margin, current ratio, and debt/equity ratio), restaurant data (e.g., number of U.S. and international restaurants), and other data, including the numbers of shareholders and employees.

Review the comparative income statements of Seafair, and note that sales and the various measures of income (i.e., net operating income, net income from continuing operations, and net income) consistently increased over the three-year period. Despite a $4000 extraordinary loss in 1990, Seafair was still able to increase net income from 1989 to 1990. Also note on the comparative balance sheets that total assets have grown considerably over the time period, especially accounts receivable, inventories, and long-lived assets. Most of the growth in receivables and inventories occurred during 1990, while large investments in long-lived assets were made in 1989. The Cash account remained at approximately the same level throughout the three-year time period.

On the liability and stockholders' equity side of the balance sheet, current liabilities (accounts payable plus short-term notes payable) gradually increased, while long-term liabilities increased substantially during 1989 and were reduced in 1990. An issuance of 200 shares of common stock provided much of Seafair's capital during 1990; note also that dividends were paid in each of the three years.

The statements of cash flows explain the activity in the Long-Term Assets, Long-Term Liabilities, Stockholders' Equity, and Dividend accounts mentioned above. They also show that net cash provided (used) by operating activities was positive throughout the analysis period, and particularly large in 1989. Note also that the market price of Seafair's common stock has increased since 1988.

By comparing financial statement numbers across time, a user can develop a "feel" for a company's activities and its general financial condition and can identify certain trends and turning points. However, users must view such comparisons cautiously. First, there is no assurance that historical trends will continue into the future. Current changes in the nature of the company, the industry in which it operates, or the business environment in general must also be considered.

Second, a user must be aware of the accounting methods used by a company over the period of the comparison. As noted in Chapter 14 and in the preceding discussion, the financial effect of an accounting principle/method change can be significant; it must be disclosed separately on the income statement and mentioned in the auditor's report. When such changes are disclosed, the numbers reported on the statements should be adjusted to achieve a common basis for comparison across the analysis periods.

Comparisons Within the Industry

A second type of comparison that can enhance the meaningfulness of financial accounting numbers is to compare them to those of similar companies. Similar companies are usually found in the same industry; thus, industry-wide statistics are often a useful basis for comparison. Information concerning industry averages is reported by such sources as (1) *Dun & Bradstreet's Key Business Ratios*, (2) *Robert Morris Associates' Annual Statement Studies*, (3) *Moody's Investor Service*, and (4) *Standard & Poor's Industry Surveys*.

Differences in what are considered normal accounting numbers across industries can be very significant. A number of chapters throughout this text have highlighted such differences by reporting industry averages for certain assets and liabilities. Chapter 6, for example, reported that current assets, as a percentage of total assets, varies from an average of 26 percent in the motion picture theater industry to an average of 86 percent in the new and used car industry. Consequently, it is very important that the accounting numbers of a given company in a given industry be evaluated in terms of the norms established in that industry.

However, like comparisons across time, comparisons across an industry must be prepared and interpreted with caution. Companies do not always fall neatly into industry classifications; as a result, it is not always easy to find either the appropriate industry averages or other companies in exactly the same industry. Even when the companies compared are classified in the same industry, they do not necessarily face the same business environment. Such differences can render financial statement comparisons virtually meaningless. Finally, as with comparisons across time, financial statement users must pay special attention to the accounting methods and estimates used by the companies being compared. In the automobile industry, for example, General Motors uses accelerated methods to depreciate its fixed assets, while Chrysler primarily uses the straight-line method.

Comparisons Within the Financial Statements: Common-Size Statements and Ratio Analysis

A third way to analyze financial statement numbers is to compare them to other numbers on the financial statements of the company at a particular point in time. Such comparisons can take two forms: (1) common-size financial statements and (2) ratio analysis.

Common-Size Financial Statements. Financial statement numbers can be expressed as percentages of other numbers on the same statements. On the income statement, expense items and net income are often expressed as percentages of net sales. On the balance sheet, assets and liabilities can be expressed as percentages of total assets (or liabilities plus stockholders' equity). Presenting such information gives rise to **common-size financial statements.** Common-size income statements and balance sheets for Seafair, Inc. from 1988 to 1990 appear in Figure 17–3.

On the income statement, note that net income from continuing operations increased over the analysis period, both in an absolute sense and as a percentage of sales. As a percentage of sales, it increased from 7 percent in 1988 to 11 percent in 1989, and to 14 percent in 1990. This increase was largely due to the gradual decrease in the cost of goods sold as a percentage of sales. Also, the dollar amount of administrative expenses appears to have been almost constant over the three-year period, even as the sales volume increased. As a percentage of sales, therefore, administrative expenses decreased from 1988 to 1990.

On the balance sheet, note how the Cash account represents a relatively small percentage of total assets as of the end of 1990. The 1990 Accounts Receivable and Inventory balances seem to have grown considerably relative to total assets, while Long-Lived Assets, which have increased each year in an absolute sense, have consistently decreased as a percentage of total assets.

The capital structure of Seafair shifted during 1989 when it substantially increased its long-term debt position. As of the end of 1989, Long-Term Notes Payable represented 45 percent of total liabilities plus stockholders' equity, which is significantly higher than the 24 percent of 1988. It appears that the additional long-term debt was used primarily to finance the $20,000 net investment ($43,000 − $23,000) in long-lived assets. The equity issuance in 1990 produced $12,000 and increased Seafair's relative reliance on equity financing. These funds were used primarily to pay off a portion of the long-term notes payable and increase the company's investment in inventories and long-lived assets.

The common-size financial statements in Figure 17–3 are more informative than the simple comparisons in Figure 17–2 for two basic reasons. First, they provide relative instead of absolute comparisons. For example, while the absolute dollar amount of administrative expenses remained approximately level across the three-year period, it decreased significantly as a percentage of net sales. Similarly,

Figure 17–3   Common-size financial statements

Seafair, Inc. Financial Statements For the Years Ended December 31, 1988–1990						
	1990	**Percent**	**1989**	**Percent**	**1988**	**Percent**
Income Statement						
Sales (net)	$88,000	100*	$75,000	100*	$65,000	100*
Less: Cost of goods sold	35,200	40	32,000	43	32,500	50
Gross profit	52,800	60	43,000	57	32,500	50
Selling expenses	17,000	19	15,000	20	13,000	20
Administrative expenses	12,000	14	11,000	15	11,000	17
Net operating income	23,800	27	17,000	23	8,500	13
Less: Interest expense	3,000	3	3,500	5	1,000	2
Net income from continuing operations before tax	20,800	24	13,500	18	7,500	11
Less: Federal income taxes	8,320	9	5,400	7	3,000	5
Net income from continuing operations	12,480	14	8,100	11	4,500	7
Extraordinary (loss) gain—net of tax	(4,000)	5	—		—	—
Net income	$ 8,480	9	$ 8,100	11	$ 4,500	7
Balance Sheet						
Assets						
Cash	$ 3,000	4	$ 4,000	7	$ 2,000	6
Accounts receivable	8,000	11	3,000	5	3,000	9
Inventory	12,000	16	6,000	10	4,000	13
Long-term investments	2,000	3	5,000	8	—	—
Long-lived assets (net)	48,000	66	43,000	70	23,000	72
Total assets	$73,000	100	$61,000	100	$32,000	100
Liabilities and stockholders' equity						
Accounts payable	$ 7,000	10	$ 4,000	7	$ 2,000	6
Short-term notes payable	7,000	10	7,000	11	2,000	6
Long-term notes payable	21,920	30	27,400	45	7,500	24
Common stock	25,000	34	15,000	24	15,000	47
Additional paid-in capital	5,000	7	3,000	5	3,000	9
Retained earnings	7,080	9	4,600	8	2,500	8
Total liabilities and stockholders' equity	$73,000	100	$61,000	100	$32,000	100

*The percentages in these columns do not sum to 100 percent due to rounding.

Seafair's investment in long-lived assets, which increased steadily over the analysis period, actually remained relatively constant as a percentage of total assets.

Second, common-size comparisons can help to identify plausible explanations for important developments such as changes in profit across time. For example, income from continuing operations increased, both in an absolute sense and as a percentage of sales, during the three-year period. The primary reason for this increase is that the cost of goods sold and administrative expenses, while increasing in absolute dollar amounts, actually decreased as percentages of net sales.

Ratio Analysis. Preparing common-size financial statements is simply a matter of computing ratios in which income statements or balance sheet items act as numerators and sales or total assets serve as denominators. Computing additional ratios using two or more financial statement numbers is also a common and useful practice generally known as **ratio analysis.** Previous chapters have mentioned and briefly discussed some of the more popular ratios, including the current ratio (current assets÷current liabilities), the debt-to-equity ratio (total debt÷total stockholders' equity), and earnings per share (net income÷total common shares outstanding). This section describes some widely used ratios and explains what aspects of financial performance or condition they help to assess.

The following discussion divides the ratios into five categories: (1) profitability, (2) solvency, (3) activity, (4) capitalization, and (5) market ratios. **Profitability ratios** compare net income to various other financial statement numbers and, in general, provide information about the earning power of a company. **Solvency ratios** involve comparisons of current assets to current liabilities, providing information about a company's ability to meet its short-term debts as they come due. **Activity ratios** assess the speed of accounts receivable and inventory turnover. This information indicates how quickly receivables, on average, are converted to cash and how long inventory items are carried by a company. **Capitalization ratios** focus primarily on a company's financing sources (i.e., its long-term debt and stockholders' equity position). **Market ratios** involve the market price of a company's common shares and the dividend and price-appreciation returns to the shareholders.

Two general points are particularly important when computing ratios. First, with only a few exceptions, there are no hard and fast rules for the computation of ratios. The ratios discussed here are merely representative of ratios that are widely used. Users can adjust them to fit different situations, and certainly other ratios might be equally or more relevant to a given decision.

Second, in the computation of many ratios income statement numbers are compared to balance-sheet numbers. Since the income statement refers to a period of time and the balance sheet refers to a specific point in time, in calculating these ratios it is usually best to compute an average for the balance-sheet number. Such an average is typically calculated by adding the account balance at the beginning of the period to the account balance at the end of the period, and dividing the result by 2. When calculating return on equity, for example, net income is divided by average stockholders' equity, which is equal to the Stockholders' Equity balance at the beginning of the period plus the Stockholders' Equity balance at the end of the period, divided by 2.

Profitability Ratios. Net income or profit is the primary measure of the overall success of a company. This number is often compared to other measures of financial activity or condition (e.g., sales, assets, stockholders' equity) to assess performance. These comparisons are referred to as *profitability ratios* and are designed to measure earning power.

The income statement includes several different measures of profit. Income from operations, income from continuing operations (before and after taxes), and net income, for example, are all included on Seafair's income statements in Figures 17−2 and 17−3. Under various circumstances, any of these measures may be used appropriately in the computation of the profitability ratios. Whatever profit measure is chosen, it is important that it be used consistently in comparisons across time as well as with similar companies.

Figure 17–4 Profitability ratio: return on equity for Seafair, Inc.

1988	$4,500 ÷ [($20,500ᵃ + $18,000ᵇ) ÷ 2]	= .23
1989	$8,100 ÷ [($22,600 + $20,500) ÷ 2]	= .38
1990	$12,480 ÷ [($37,080 + $22,600) ÷ 2]	= .42

[a]Stockholders' equity is equal to the dollar amounts in Common Stock, Additional Paid-in Capital, and Retained Earnings.
[b]Recall that Seafair, Inc. began operations by issuing 800 shares of common stock for $18,000.

In computing the profitability ratios that follow, we typically use income from net continuing operations because this measure of profit excludes disposals of business segments, extraordinary items (as in the case of Seafair), and the income effects of changes in accounting principles/methods. In general, such items cannot be expected to occur with regularity in the future. We will consider five profitability ratios.

Return on equity. The ratio providing return on equity compares the profits generated by a company to the investment made by the company's stockholders.

Net Income from Continuing Operations ÷ Average Stockholders' Equity

Income from continuing operations, which appears in the numerator, is viewed as the return to the company's owners, while the balance-sheet value of stockholders' equity, which appears in the denominator, represents the amount of resources invested by the stockholders.

This ratio is considered a measure of the efficiency with which the stockholders' investment is being managed. As the ratio increases, management tends to be viewed as more efficient from the owner's perspective. Stockholders often compare this ratio against the returns of other potential investments available to them to determine whether their investment in a company is performing satisfactorily.

The returns on equity for Seafair over the three-year period appear in Figure 17–4. Compared to the returns on most investments, these appear to be reasonably high and have consistently increased since 1988. Apparently, Seafair's profits have increased at a higher rate than the total investment of the company's stockholders.

These returns also compare favorably with those experienced in most industries. The average return on equity for life insurance companies, department stores, TV broadcasting firms, hotels, motion picture theaters, and aircraft manufacturing, for example, are all 10 percent or less. The only industries that provide comparable returns, on average, are professional service firms (e.g., medical, legal, and accounting services) and accident and health insurance companies.

Return on assets. Another measure of return on investment is return on assets. This measure is somewhat broader than return on equity because it compares the returns to both stockholders and creditors to total assets, the total resources provided by stockholders and creditors.

(Net Income from Continuing Operations + Interest Expense) ÷ Average Total Assets

Accordingly, the numerator includes both the return to the stockholders (net income from continuing operations) and the return to the creditors (interest expense), while the denominator consists of the balance-sheet value of total assets, which is equivalent to the investments of both the stockholders (stockholders' eq-

Figure 17–5   Profitability ratio: return on assets for Seafair, Inc.

1988	$4,500 + $1,000 ÷ [($32,000 + $18,000*) ÷ 2] = .22
1989	$8,100 + $3,500 ÷ [($61,000 + $32,000) ÷ 2] = .25
1990	$12,480 + $3,000 ÷ [($73,000 + $61,000) ÷ 2] = .23

*Recall that Seafair, Inc. began operations by issuing 800 shares of common stock for $18,000.

---

uity) and the creditors (total liabilities). Seafair's return on assets is computed in Figure 17–5.

Once again, Seafair's return on assets compares favorably with that of most industries. Average returns above 8 percent are not particularly common. Department stores and hotels, for example, typically provide returns on assets of approximately 4 percent, while the average for restaurants, grocery stores, and retail sporting goods is roughly 7 percent. Professional service firms are among the few industries that normally provide a comparable return on assets.

While Seafair's return on assets is reasonably high, it is consistently below the return on equity. Because return on assets is a broader measure, including the overall return to both creditors and stockholders, the average return received by the creditors must have been less than that received by the stockholders. In essence, Seafair used borrowed funds to produce a return for the stockholders that exceeds the costs of the borrowings. Such a strategy, referred to as using **financial leverage,** is quite common.

Earnings per share. Earnings per share is perhaps the best known of all the ratios, largely because it is often treated by the financial press as the primary measure of a company's performance.

Net Income from Continuing Operations ÷ Average Number of Common Shares Outstanding

According to generally accepted accounting principles, it must appear on the face of the income statement and be calculated in accordance with an elaborate set of complex rules that are beyond the scope of this book. These rules are typically covered in intermediate or advanced financial accounting texts.

Earnings per share is a measure of a company's profitability strictly from the standpoint of the common stockholders. Unlike return on equity or return on assets, which scale profitability by a measure of capital investment, this ratio scales the stockholders' return by the number of common shares outstanding. Seafair's earnings-per-share calculations appear in Figure 17–6.

Earnings per share increased consistently for Seafair during the three-year period, especially from 1988 to 1989. Recall that in 1989 Seafair used borrowed capital to finance the profit increase. Consequently, profits increased without an increase in outstanding common stock, which in turn gave rise to a substantial increase in the earnings-per-share figure.

Figure 17–6   Profitability ratio: earnings per share for Seafair, Inc.

1988	$4,500 ÷ [(800 + 800) ÷ 2]	= $ 5.63
1989	$8,100 ÷ [(800 + 800) ÷ 2]	= $10.13
1990	$12,480 ÷ [(1,000 + 800) ÷ 2]	= $13.87

During 1990, however, Seafair issued common stock, increasing the number of outstanding shares. Without a proportional increase in profits, this action could have diluted the holdings of the original stockholders. However, profits increased sufficiently to more than compensate for the additional outstanding stock, resulting in a further increase in earnings per share. An interesting point here is that potential dilution is an important concern of the existing common stockholders, which serves to discourage a company's managers from raising capital in the equity markets too frequently.

The earnings-per-share amounts for Seafair are high compared to other companies, but there is considerable variation. Companies such as AT&T, Colgate-Palmolive, Polaroid, Chrysler, Nordstrum, Microsoft, and Wendy's International have recently recorded earnings per share of approximately $2.00 or less. RJR Nabisco, GTE Corporation, and J. C. Penney have reported earnings per share in the $3.00–$5,00 range. McDonnell Douglas has consistently reported earnings per share in the $7.00–$8.00 range.

Return on sales, or *profit margin*. Return on sales, or profit margin as it is often called, is simply computed by dividing a measure of profit by net sales.

$$\text{Net Income from Continuing Operations} \div \text{Net Sales}$$

This ratio provides an indication of a company's ability to generate and market profitable products and control its costs, while taking advantage of increases in sales due to increasing prices or increasing the number of units sold. Return on sales calculations for Seafair appear in Figure 17–7.

Seafair's return on sales numbers are generally higher than those in other industries. For example, department stores, grocery stores, hardware stores, and new and used car dealers, which deal in high volume and small markups, average approximately a 2–3 percent return on sales. Companies in the insurance industry average around 6 percent. A return on sales of 10 percent or more is somewhat unusual, except for professional service firms, which commonly return approximately 18 percent.

While Seafair's return on sales has increased consistently over the three-year period, this ratio, in general, must be interpreted cautiously. It ignores, for example, the amount of investment that was required to generate the sales and the related profit. While this is not the case for Seafair, a high return on sales in conjunction with a low return on equity or assets may indicate a relatively unattractive investment opportunity for existing or potential stockholders and creditors.

Focusing on return on sales exclusively may also conceal the importance to the stockholders of maximizing profits. For example, at a given level of investment, a company with a $10,000 income on $100,000 of sales has a higher profit margin (10 percent) than a company with a $20,000 income on $250,000 of sales (8 percent). However, the company with the lower profit margin is providing twice the total return to the stockholders ($20,000 > $10,000). Consequently, expressing a

Figure 17–7 Profitability ratio: return on sales for Seafair, Inc.

1988	$4,500 ÷ $65,000	= .07
1989	$8,100 ÷ $75,000	= .11
1990	$12,480 ÷ $88,000	= .14

Figure 17–8   Profitability ratio: times interest earned for Seafair, Inc.

1988	$7,500 ÷ $1,000	=	7.50
1989	$13,500 ÷ $3,500	=	3.86
1990	$20,800 ÷ $3,000	=	6.93

management bonus contract in terms of profit margin, for example, may encourage management to maximize the profit margin instead of income. Such an incentive may not be in the best interest of the stockholders.

Times-interest-earned ratio. Times-interest-earned ratio measures the extent to which a company's annual profits cover its annual interest expense. While this ratio reflects earning power, it is also of interest to creditors who are concerned about a company's ability to meet its future interest payments as they come due. This ratio provides an example of the significant overlap between earning power and solvency.

Net Income from Continuing Operations before Taxes ÷ Interest Expense

The profit number in the numerator should reflect the primary, recurring business operations of the company, and should be calculated before income taxes because interest is deductible for tax purposes. The denominator, interest expense, can usually be found on the income statement, but keep in mind that accrued interest expense on the income statement can be quite different from the actual cash interest payments made during the period. Such payments are a primary concern of creditors. The times-interest-earned calculations for Seafair appear in Figure 17–8.

In general, Seafair's profits seem adequate to cover its annual interest expense. Note, however, that the ratio dropped temporarily, but significantly, in 1989. This drop could have been caused by fluctuations in the market rates of interest or by the addition (and removal in 1990) of particularly costly debt. In any case, such an abrupt and significant shift warrants further investigation.

Times-interest-earned ratios often vary from one year to the next and across different companies, even within the same industry. Exxon reported times-interest-earned ratios of 3.6 in 1986 and 15.2 in 1987. In 1987 Arco and Amoco, major companies in the oil industry, reported ratios of 2.2 and 6.4, respectively.

Solvency Ratios. Solvency refers to a company's ability to meet its debts as they come due. Two ratios are often used to measure this ability: (1) the current ratio and (2) the quick ratio. Both ratios use balance sheet numbers only, comparing measures of current assets to current liabilities.

Two important points should be made about these ratios. First, the current ratio and the quick ratio are often called *liquidity ratios,* but many accountants believe that this description is inappropriate and confusing. *Liquidity* typically refers to how quickly assets can be converted into cash, while *solvency* refers to whether cash can be produced to meet debts as they come due. Liquidity and solvency may be related, in that liquid assets are helpful in meeting debts, but the two concepts are certainly not the same. A company may have a number of liquid assets but still be unable to meet its debts if, for example, the debts all come due at the same time. Similarly, a company with few liquid assets may be able to meet its debts if the debts are all long-term. The current ratio and the quick ratio provide a measure of a company's ability to meet current obligations with current assets, which is more directly a measure of solvency than of liquidity.

Figure 17–9 Solvency ratio: current ratio for Seafair, Inc.

1988	$9,000 \div $4,000 = 2.25
1989	$13,000 \div $11,000 = 1.18
1990	$23,000 \div $14,000 = 1.64

The second point of interest is that neither ratio provides a very valid measure of solvency. Solvency is a complex phenomenon that is primarily related to the timing of a company's future cash inflows and outflows. Comparing current assets and current liabilities at a particular point in time is rarely a reliable measure of such a dynamic notion. Later in this chapter we devote a special section to solvency and how financial accounting numbers can be used to assess it.

Current ratio. Current ratio compares current assets to current liabilities as of the balance sheet date.

$$\text{Current Assets} \div \text{Current Liabilities}$$

Current ratios for Seafair appear in Figure 17–9.

Average current ratios across industries vary from less than 1.0 (e.g., motion picture theaters) to between 3.0 and 4.0 (e.g., department stores and hardware stores). Seafair seems to have maintained a current ratio of slightly less than 2:1 over the three-year period. At first glance, it seems that the company is reasonably solvent. Note, however, that the buildup in current assets during 1990 ($13,000 to $23,000) is due to large increases in accounts receivable and inventory. There is some question about when and to what extent these assets will be converted to cash that will be available to pay off the current liabilities.

Quick ratio. Quick ratio is similar to the current ratio, except that it provides a more stringent test of a company's solvency position.

$$(\text{Cash} + \text{Marketable Securities}) \div \text{Current Liabilities}$$

Current assets like accounts receivable, inventories, and prepaid expenses, which are not immediately convertible to cash, are excluded from the numerator. Seafair's quick ratios appear in Figure 17–10.

Most major U.S. companies have quick ratios that are less than .50. GTE Corporation, J. C. Penney, Nordstrum, and Colgate-Palmolive, for example, have quick ratios that are less than .05. Thus, the quick ratios disclosed by Seafair seem to be in the normal range.

However, Seafair's quick ratios could suggest a solvency problem. The company is maintaining a level of cash that is not sufficient to meet its existing short-term obligations. While such a position is not unusual, it does put pressure on the receivables and inventories, which have been building up over the three-year pe-

Figure 17–10 Solvency ratio: quick ratio for Seafair, Inc.

1988	$2,000 \div $4,000 = .50
1989	$4,000 \div $11,000 = .36
1990	$3,000 \div $14,000 = .21

Note: Seafair, Inc. carries no investments in marketable securities.

Figure 17–11 Activity ratio: receivables turnover for Seafair, Inc.

Receivables Turnover

1988	$65,000 ÷ $3,000*	= 22
1989	$75,000 ÷ [($3,000 + $3,000) ÷ 2]	= 25
1990	$88,000 ÷ [($3,000 + $8,000) ÷ 2]	= 16

*Even though the beginning balance in accounts receivable in 1988 was zero, we felt that an average outstanding balance of $3,000 during the year was a more reasonable assumption.

Average Days Outstanding (365 ÷ Turnover)

1988	365 ÷ 22	= 17 days
1989	365 ÷ 25	= 15 days
1990	365 ÷ 16	= 23 days

---

riod, to produce cash. Consequently, activity ratios, which measure the turnover of accounts receivable and inventory, take on special importance.

Activity Ratios. Activity ratios measure the speed with which assets move through operations. They involve the calculation of a number called *turnover,* which indicates the number of times during a given period that assets are acquired, disposed of, and replaced. Dividing 365 by the turnover number produces the average number of days during the year that the assets were carried on the balance sheet. Turnover is commonly calculated for accounts receivable and inventory, but is also sometimes computed for long-lived assets and total assets.

Receivables turnover. Receivables turnover reflects the number of times the trade receivables were recorded, collected, and recorded again during the period.

Net Credit Sales ÷ Average Accounts Receivable

It measures the effectiveness of the credit-granting and collection activities of a company. High receivables turnover often suggests effective credit-granting and collection activities, while low turnover can indicate late payments and bad debts, probably due to credit being granted to poor-risk customers and/or to ineffective collection efforts. A very high turnover, however, is not always desirable; it may indicate overly stringent credit terms, leading to missed sales and lost profits.

As suggested earlier, receivables turnover may be particularly relevant to solvency. Recall that Seafair's cash balance is not sufficient to cover its current liabilities. If the receivables tend to turn over quickly, they can produce the additional cash necessary to cover debts that are soon to become due. Seafair's calculations for receivables turnover and number of days outstanding appear in Figure 7–11. (We assume in the calculations that all of Seafair's sales are on credit.)

The average number of days outstanding for receivables varies significantly across industries, usually depending on the extent to which a particular industry relies on credit sales. Grocery stores, for example, average approximately three days because most of their customers pay immediately. Department stores, which rely heavily on credit sales, average approximately thirty days. Professional services, which normally bill their clients after a service is provided, receive payment, on average, in sixty days.

The average number of days that Seafair's receivables were outstanding increased from fifteen in 1989 to twenty-three in 1990. While these calculations may indicate less stringent credit-granting policies, it is not obvious that this increase is a problem. Perhaps in 1988 and 1989 Seafair's credit-granting policies were too stringent. One way to evaluate the number of days outstanding is to compare it to the credit terms issued by Seafair. If Seafair sells merchandise on account with credit terms of 2/10, net 30, for example, most customers are paying within the thirty-day credit period, but are not paying quickly enough to receive the cash discount. Such a situation seems reasonable, suggesting that Seafair's receivables turnover is not cause for serious concern at this time.

However, further investigation may still be warranted for several reasons. First, the receivables turnover number is an overall average. The Accounts Receivable balance may consist of some accounts that are typically paid off very quickly and others that are either being paid off slowly or are uncollectible and have not yet been written off. Second, the slower turnover experienced in 1990 could indicate a trend that may continue into the future. Finally, in line with the concern about Seafair's solvency position, it is still not clear whether the receivables are turning over quickly enough to provide enough cash to meet current obligations.

Inventory turnover. Inventory turnover ratio measures the speed with which inventories move through operations.

$$\text{Cost of Goods Sold} \div \text{Average Inventory}$$

It compares the amount of inventory carried by a company to the volume of goods sold during the period, reflecting how quickly, in general, inventories are sold. Because profit (and often cash) is usually realized each time inventory is sold and substantial costs are often associated with carrying inventories, an increase in the inventory turnover ratio is normally desirable. However, high inventory turnovers can indicate that inventory levels are too low, giving rise to lost sales and profits due to items being out of stock. Like receivables turnover, this ratio is often converted to a time-basis expression by dividing it into 365 days. The inventory turnover and average-days'-supply calculations for Seafair appear in Figure 17–12.

The average number of days it takes companies to turn over their inventories

Figure 17–12   Activity ratio: inventory turnover for Seafair, Inc.

Inventory Turnover

1988	$32,500 ÷ $4,000*	= 8.1
1989	$32,000 ÷ [($6,000 + $4,000) ÷ 2]	= 6.4
1990	$35,200 ÷ [($12,000 + $6,000) ÷ 2]	= 3.9

*Even though the beginning balance in inventory in 1988 was zero, we felt that an average outstanding balance of $4,000 during the year was a more reasonable assumption.

Average Days Supply in Inventory (365 ÷ Turnover)

1988	365 ÷ 8.1 = 45 days
1989	365 ÷ 6.4 = 57 days
1990	365 ÷ 3.9 = 94 days

Figure 17–13   Capitalization ratio: cost of debt for Seafair, Inc.

1988	$1,000 (1 − .4) ÷ [($9,500 + 0) ÷ 2]	= .13
1989	$3,500 (1 − .4) ÷ [($34,400 + $9,500) ÷ 2]	= .10
1990	$3,000 (1 − .4) ÷ [($28,920 + $34,400) ÷ 2]	= .06

Note: Interest paying liabilities include short- and long-term notes payable.

varies across industries. Grocery stores and restaurants, which carry perishable foods, turn their inventories over every week or two. Department stores, new and used car dealers, and many manufacturing operations turn their inventories, on average, every 60–70 days. Seasonal operations, like retail sporting goods and clothing stores, replace their inventories every season, or every 90–100 days.

Seafair's inventories seem to be moving more slowly each year. In 1988 Seafair held a forty-five-day supply of inventory; by 1990, it held a ninety-four-day supply. Such a trend may indicate that (1) Seafair's inventory is gradually becoming less sellable, (2) Seafair is increasingly incurring higher inventory carrying costs and is becoming less efficient, or (3) there are a number of obsolete items in inventory that should be written off the books. An individual analyzing Seafair would certainly want to investigate further the reason for the decreasing inventory turnover. Similar to receivables turnover, the inventory turnover ratio represents a broad average. Some inventory items may be moving very quickly while others may not be moving at all.

Capitalization Ratios. Capitalization ratios help users to evaluate the capital structure of a company or, in general, the composition of the liability and stockholders' equity side of the balance sheet. Ratios like cost of debt, financial leverage, and debt/equity address questions such as: What are the relative returns to creditors and stockholders, and from what sources does a company finance its operations? The cost of debt and the debt/equity ratios provide an indication of a company's future cash requirements and, accordingly, its solvency position. Financial leverage is more a measure of earning power.

Cost of debt ratio. Cost of debt ratio is computed by dividing the after-tax interest cost by the amount of outstanding interest-paying liabilities.

(Interest Expense [1 − Tax Rate]) ÷ Average Interest-Paying Liabilities

This ratio provides an estimate of the average annual cost of carrying contractual debt. The cost of debt calculations for Seafair appear in Figure 17–13.

Seafair's cost of debt consistently decreased from 1988 to 1990. Such a trend seems reasonable; as companies develop and become more stable, they are generally better able to negotiate for improved terms on their borrowings. Maturing companies represent increasingly lower risks to creditors, who in turn are willing to charge lower interest rates.

A company strives to lower its cost of debt by paying as low an interest rate as possible. However, the interest rate is only one of many terms in most debt contracts; other terms, like security or collateral arrangements, may be equally relevant. Financial statement users can also review the footnotes for more specific information about the terms of a company's outstanding debt.

Financial leverage. Financial leverage involves borrowing funds and investing them in assets that provide returns in excess of the tax-deductible cost of the borrowings. One way to measure this concept is to compare two previously-discussed ratios: return on equity and return on assets.

Return on Equity − Return on Assets

Earlier we noted that return on equity reflects only the return to the stockholders, while return on assets reflects the overall return to both stockholders and creditors. To the extent that return on equity exceeds return on assets, the return to stockholders will exceed the return to creditors. In such cases a company is managing its debt effectively and is thereby reaping the benefits of financial leverage for its stockholders. However, leverage can work to the detriment of the stockholders if the cost of debt exceeds the return generated from the borrowed funds. Seafair's financial leverage ratios for 1988, 1989, and 1990 appear in Figure 17−14.

The financial leverage ratios of major industries vary from approximately 3 percent to around 15 percent. Life insurance and many heavy manufacturing companies experience financial leverage of about 3−4 percent, while hotels operate at approximately 6 percent, new and used car dealerships at 11 percent, and professional services at 14 percent.

Seafair appears to be managing its debt effectively; it has financial leverage ratios in the upper portion of the normal ranges. For the three-year period return on equity has been consistently above return on assets, especially in more recent years. Recall that Seafair's cost of debt, which was relatively high in 1988, has decreased consistently since that time.

Debt/equity ratio. The debt/equity ratio relates the capital provided by creditors to that supplied by stockholders.

Total Liabilities ÷ Total Stockholders' Equity

While there are a number of different ways to calculate this ratio, we have chosen what is probably the most common form: total liabilities (both current and noncurrent) divided by the balance of all stockholders' equity accounts.

The debt/equity ratio indicates the extent to which a company can sustain losses without jeopardizing the interests of its creditors. Recall that creditors have priority claims over stockholders; in case of liquidation the creditors have first right to a company's assets. From an individual creditor's standpoint, therefore, the amount of equity in the company's capital structure can be viewed as a buffer, helping to ensure that there are sufficient assets to cover individual claims. A high debt/equity ratio may concern an individual creditor because it indicates that the

Figure 17−14   Capitalization ratio: financial leverage for Seafair, Inc.

1988	.23 − .22 = .01
1989	.38 − .25 = .13
1990	.42 − .23 = .19

Note: See previous calculations of return on equity (Figure 17−4) and return on assets (Figure 17−5).

Figure 17–15   Capitalization ratio: debt ÷ equity for Seafair, Inc.

1988	$11,500 ÷ $20,500 =	.56
1989	$38,400 ÷ $22,600 =	1.70
1990	$35,920 ÷ $37,080 =	.97

claims of the other creditors are large relative to the available assets, increasing the chance that certain creditor claims may not be completely satisfied in the event of liquidation. In general, a high debt/equity ratio also suggests a risky and highly leveraged position, requiring large future cash outflows (interest and principal payments). This in turn raises questions about a company's ability to remain solvent. Seafair's debt/equity ratios appear in Figure 17–15.

Normal debt/equity ratios of major U.S. companies, with the exception of financial institutions, range from approximately .40 to about 2.5. Wendy's International, for example, carries a debt/equity ratio of about .40–.50. Polaroid Corporation and IBM carry debt/equity ratios of .50–.70. J. C. Penney, Chevron, General Motors, and the Boeing Company maintain ratios above 1.0 but usually below 1.5. The debt/equity ratio of McDonnell Douglas borders around 2.0. Financial institutions, such as American Express Company and BankAmerica Corporation, can have debt/equity ratios of as much as 25 to 30 to 1.

Seafair's debt/equity ratio, which seems to be well within a normal range, has been somewhat unstable over the past three years. The company began in 1988 with relatively little debt in its capital structure, perhaps because debt terms were not particularly attractive at that time. Seafair borrowed significantly during 1989 and became much more highly leveraged. Then, by issuing stock and paying off debt in 1990, it moved back to a more moderate position. This inconsistent pattern may introduce uncertainty about Seafair's financing policies and future plans.

Market Ratios. Market ratios measure returns to common stockholders that are due to changes in the market price of the common stock and the receipt of dividends. Three such ratios are discussed below: the price/earnings ratio, dividend yield, and return on investments.

Price/earnings ratio. The price/earnings ratio is used by many financial statement analysts to assess the investment potential of common stocks.

Market Price per Share ÷ Earnings per Share

Specifically, by relating the price of a company's common stock to its earnings, this ratio provides a measure of how the stock price reacts to changes in net income. The higher the price/earnings ratio, the more sensitive the stock price. For example, a 10:1 price/earnings ratio suggests that a $1 per share increase in earnings would bring about a $10 increase in the stock price. A 20:1 ratio suggests that a $1 per share earnings increase would generate a $20 increase in stock price. The price/earnings ratios for Seafair appear in Figure 17–16.

In calculating earnings per share, we used income from continuing operations, which excludes the $4000 extraordinary loss in 1990. Had this loss been included, the price/earnings ratio at the end of 1990 would have been 6.4 ($60 ÷ 9.42) instead of 4.3.

Price/earnings ratios vary widely from one company to the next. They can even change significantly from one year to the next for a single company. The price/

Figure 17–16   Market ratio: price/earnings ratio for Seafair, Inc.

1988	$40 ÷ $5.63	= 7.1
1989	$45 ÷ $10.13	= 4.4
1990	$60 ÷ $13.87	= 4.3

Note: See previous calculations
for earnings per share (Figure 17–6).

earnings ratio of Procter & Gamble Company, for example, went from approximately 17:1 at the end of 1986 to nearly 60:1 at the end of 1987. Normally, such ratios range between 10:1 and 25:1. However, some companies have price/earnings ratios as low as 4:1, and others can be as high as 60 or 70:1.

The price/earnings ratios of Seafair seem to be somewhat below the normal range. It is difficult, however, to explain why because there are so many factors that determine the price of a company's common stock. Stock analysts sometimes attempt to predict common stock prices by first predicting earnings per share and then multiplying the result by the price/earnings ratio. Unfortunately, the instability of the price/earnings ratio renders this method unreliable.

Dividend yield ratio. The dividend yield ratio relates the dividends paid on the share of common stock to its market price.

Dividends per Share ÷ Market Price per Share

It indicates the cash return on the stockholder's investment. Seafair's dividend yields appear in Figure 17–17.

The dividend yields of most major U.S. companies are below .05. The 1987 yields of IBM, The Boeing Company, Goodyear Tire & Rubber, McDonald's Corporation, and General Electric, for example, all ranged from .01 to .05.

The increased dividend yield experienced by Seafair in 1989 occurred because dividends tripled to $7.50 per share, while the price of outstanding common stocks increased by only $5 (12 percent). In the following year, dividends were reduced to $6 per share, while the price of common stock increased substantially. As with the price/earnings ratio, it is often difficult to interpret the dividend yield because stock prices are affected by such a wide variety of factors, only one of which is the current cash dividend payment.

Annual return on investment. The annual return on investment provided by a share of common stock is computed by subtracting the market price at the beginning of the year (Market Price$_0$) from the market price at the end of the year (Market Price$_1$), adding the dividends per share paid during the year, and dividing the result by the market price at the beginning of the year.

(Market Price$_1$ − Market Price$_0$ + Dividends) ÷ Market Price$_0$

The numerator reflects the pretax return to the stockholder, and the denominator

Figure 17–17   Market ratio: dividend yield for Seafair, Inc.

1988	($2,000 ÷ 800) ÷ $40	= .06
1989	($6,000 ÷ 800) ÷ $45	= .17
1990	($6,000 ÷ 1,000) ÷ $60	= .10

Figure 17–18   Market ratio: annual return on investment for Seafair, Inc.

1988	($40 − $22.50* + $2.50) ÷ $22.50* = .89
1989	($45 − $40 + $7.50) ÷ $40 = .31
1990	($60 − $45 + $6.00) ÷ $45 = .47

*Market price at the beginning of 1988 ($18,000 ÷ 800 shares).

reflects the amount of the stockholder's investment. This ratio provides a measure of the pretax performance of a share of common stock. The annual returns for Seafair's shares appear in Figure 17–18.

Returns on common stock investments vary significantly among companies and across time. Over the past few years, in general, returns of 10 percent to 20 percent could be considered reasonable. With that as a benchmark, investments in Seafair's common shares have provided far more than a reasonable annual return. However, returns can only be evaluated in terms of how much risk an investor is required to bear. Investments in highly leveraged, risky companies, where stock price fluctuations are great, should provide higher rates of return, on average, than companies with small amounts of debt and less stock price variation. In the case of Seafair, while it is difficult to assess exactly how much risk the stockholders are bearing, it seems from our analysis that the level of risk is not unreasonable.

Summary and Overview of Financial Ratios. Figure 17–19 shows all of the ratios discussed in this section and provides the formula and a brief description for each ratio.

SOLVENCY ASSESSMENT

We pointed out earlier that the solvency ratios provide a limited picture of a company's solvency position. This section describes the nature of solvency more completely and explains how financial accounting numbers can be used to assess it. In so doing, we assess Seafair's solvency position.

Solvency is the ability to meet debts as they come due. Assessing solvency, therefore, essentially involves estimating future cash flows, determining whether the future inflows are timed so that adequate cash is available to cover future cash obligations as they mature. If the inflows provide adequate cash to cover the outflows, the company is considered solvent.

In evaluating the timing of a company's future cash flows, three basic factors should be considered: (1) operating performance, (2) financial flexibility, and (3) liquidity. Figure 17–20 depicts how these three factors relate to solvency.

Note the general flow of the diagram. Solvency is broken down into two fundamental components: the ability to generate cash, which leads to the timing of cash inflows, and cash requirements, which lead to the timing of cash outflows. Operating performance, financial flexibility, and liquidity all affect the timing and amount of these cash flows.

Figure 17–19   Financial accounting ratios

Ratio	Formula	Description
Profitability Ratios		
Return on equity	Net Income from Continuing Operations ÷ Average Stockholders' Equity	Effectiveness at managing capital provided by owners.
Return on assets	(Net Income from Continuing Operations + Interest Expense) ÷ Average Total Assets	Effectiveness at managing capital provided by all investors.
Earnings per share	Net Income from Continuing Operations ÷ Average Number of Common Shares Outstanding	Profits generated per share of common stock.
Return on sales	Net Income from Continuing Operations ÷ Net Sales	Ability to create profits from operating activities.
Times interest earned	Net Income from Continuing Operations before Taxes ÷ Interest Expense	Ability to meet fixed interest charges with profits from operations.
Solvency Ratios		
Current ratio	Current Assets ÷ Current Liabilities	Ability to cover current debts with current assets.
Quick ratio	(Cash + Marketable Securities) ÷ Current Liabilities	Ability to cover current debts with cash-like assets.
Activity Ratios		
Receivables turnover	Net Credit Sales ÷ Average Accounts Receivable	Number of times receivables are collected each year.
Inventory turnover	Cost of Goods Sold ÷ Average Inventory	Number of times inventories are replaced each year.
Capitalization Ratios		
Cost of debt	(Interest Expense $(1 -$ Tax Rate)$)$ ÷ Average Interest-Paying Liabilities	Average cost of interest-paying debt.
Financial leverage	Return on Equity $-$ Return on Assets	Use of debt to produce returns for owners.
Debt/equity	Total Liabilities ÷ Total Stockholders' Equity	Relative importance of debt and equity in the capital structure.
Market Ratios		
Price/earnings	Market Price per Share ÷ Earnings per Share	Sensitivity of stock price to changes in earnings.
Dividend yield	Dividends per Share ÷ Market Price per Share	Cash return on stockholders' investment.
Return on investment	(Market Price$_1$ $-$ Market Price$_0$ + Dividends) ÷ Market Price$_0$	Annual rate of return on common shares for period (1).

Figure 17–20   Important factors in predicting solvency

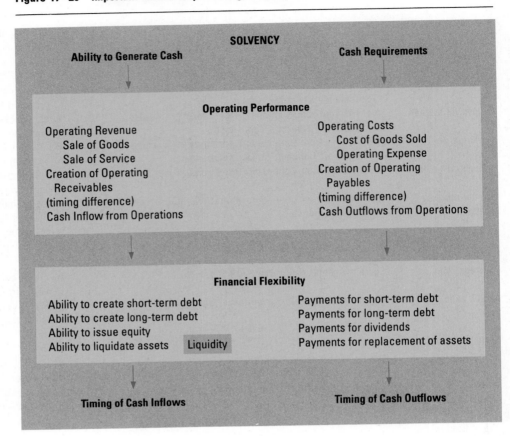

Operating Performance

Operating performance, an indication of earning power, represents a company's ability to increase its net assets (assets minus liabilities) through operations. The sale of goods or services leads to the inflow (outflow) of assets (liabilities), while operating expenses, such as the cost of goods sold and selling and administrative expenses, lead to the outflow (inflow) of assets (liabilities). The extent to which these asset and liability flows change a company's net asset position from one period to the next is referred to as *operating performance*.

Operating performance is very important in the assessment of solvency. It provides perhaps the most important source of cash inflows and outflows. However, operating performance, as measured by the income statement and the profitability ratios, is the result of an accrual process. There is often a significant timing difference between the creation of a receivable or payable and the corresponding cash inflow or outflow. This timing difference can be critical in the assessment of solvency, especially when liabilities are due in the short run.

The operating section of the statement of cash flows provides an explanation of the cash generated from operations. Also, the activity ratios, such as receivables and inventory turnover, include how quickly inventories are converted into receivables and how quickly receivables, in turn, are converted into cash.

Seafair's profitability ratios suggest that the company has strong potential earning power. The statement of cash flows (see Figure 17–2) also shows that cash from operating activities has been an important source of cash throughout the three-year period. Consequently, Seafair has demonstrated an ability to generate cash through operations, an essential element of solvency. However, this conclusion is based on past information, and Seafair's ability to meet *future* debt payments is the most important concern. Moreover, the activity ratios, especially inventory turnover, could indicate a potential problem. As observed earlier, accounts receivable and inventory have been turning over more slowly with each passing year.

Financial Flexibility

Financial flexibility refers to a company's ability to produce cash through means other than operations. For example, can a company produce cash through available credit lines or by issuing additional current or long-term debt, or has it exhausted its borrowing capacity? Is there a market for equity issuances, or has the value of the outstanding stock been diluted recently? Does the company maintain a portfolio of marketable securities, and is there a market where the company's long-term investments and assets can be sold? Companies capable of generating cash through a number of these options are considered financially flexible.

The following excerpt from the 1987 financial report of The Gillette Company illustrates the importance of financial flexibility.

> *Gillette continues to have access to substantial sources of capital in world financial markets. The Company's ability to generate funds internally and its substantial unused lines of credit are ample to cover all anticipated needs.*

Both the cash inflow and outflow components of financial flexibility are important when assessing solvency. Additional debt, which produces an immediate cash inflow, also gives rise to future periodic cash outflows in the form of principal and interest payments. Equity issuances produce cash but, at the same time, bring about the expectation of future dividend payments. The liquidation of long-lived assets normally leads to the need for replacement. Further, growing companies must continually invest in new assets, which means there will be significant future cash requirements. While financial flexibility is an indication of a company's ability to generate cash, utilizing it creates future cash obligations.

Financial flexibility can be assessed by examining financial ratios like the current ratio, the quick ratio, the debt/equity ratio, and financial leverage. Each provides information about a company's **borrowing capacity.** The current ratio and the quick ratio provide information about a company's short-term debt position. The debt/equity ratio indicates the relative importance of liabilities in a company's capital structure, and the financial leverage ratio suggests whether a company has been able to use debt to create a return for the stockholders.

A review of the footnotes to the financial statements, and especially of the long-term debt section, can also be useful in assessing financial flexibility. Among other things, it can indicate which assets are presently being used as security for outstanding loans. Finally, market ratios and earnings per share can help to determine whether equity issuances are feasible. Examining such ratios over time can indicate if, and to what extent, issuing additional equity will dilute the value of the outstanding common stock.

Seafair's quick ratio indicates that the Cash balance is not presently sufficient to cover currently maturing liabilities, but the current ratio shows that current assets exceed current liabilities by almost 2:1. In addition, receivables and inventories, which can be used as security on future loans, are both at relatively high levels, and the debt/equity ratio appears to be well within acceptable limits. As a result, Seafair can probably issue more debt, if such debt is necessary to pay off current loans as they come due. However, note that Seafair's main cash sources over the past three years have been borrowings and equity issuances, as shown on the statements of cash flows. Also, the equity issuances in 1988 and 1990 have diluted Seafair's common stock. These activities have used up a portion of the company's financial flexibility.

Liquidity

Liquidity is part of financial flexibility. It represents the ability of a company to convert its existing assets to cash. Certain assets may be very marketable (e.g., marketable securities) and thus easily converted to cash, while others may be obsolete or useful only within the operations of a specific company (e.g., certain long-lived assets). Asset liquidity is important in the assessment of solvency because it represents another potential source of cash that can be used to meet maturing obligations. In addition, highly liquid assets can often be used as security on outstanding loans.

Liquidity can be assessed by reviewing the order of the assets listed on the balance sheet. In general, as one goes up the balance sheet, the assets are more liquid. A large percentage of current relative to total assets can indicate high liquidity. Also, the receivables and inventory turnover ratios are an indication of liquidity. High turnovers tend to indicate high liquidity.

In 1990 current assets made up approximately 32 percent of Seafair's total assets. This percentage is considerably higher than in both 1989 (21 percent) and 1988 (28 percent). However, Seafair's current assets consist primarily of receivables and inventories, which are turning over more slowly and seem to be increasingly less liquid. Furthermore, the statement of cash flows indicates that a long-term investment was sold in 1990, which produced $3000. This amount accounts for the company's entire ending Cash balance.

Operating Performance, Financial Flexibility, and Liquidity: Relationships

The relationships among operating performance, financial flexibility, and liquidity are also important in the assessment of solvency. Fast growing companies, for example, often issue large amounts of debt and equity to expand operations and maximize operating performance. This strategy, while often creating high profits, can render a company financially inflexible. Since profits and cash are not synonymous, these highly profitable companies may become insolvent because they cannot raise cash quickly enough to cover their short-term debts. Conversely, a company wishing to maximize its financial flexibility and liquidity may be severely limiting its future operating performance because it fails to take advantage of available sources of capital and leverage.

Liquidity and operating performance are also related. The liquidity of assets that are not essential to operations (e.g., marketable securities) should be assessed separately from the liquidity of assets that are essential to operations (e.g., long-lived assets). While both kinds of assets produce cash that can be used to pay off debts, each has a different implication for the company's future operating performance. Liquidating marketable securities, for example, has a limited impact on company operations, while selling off long-lived assets can cut operations back significantly.

LIMITATIONS OF FINANCIAL ACCOUNTING INFORMATION

While financial accounting information can be used to assess a company's earning power and solvency position, it still suffers from a number of significant limitations that must be understood before it can be used appropriately. The following discussion presents some of the major limitations.

Much Relevant Information Is Ignored

Financial statements are only one of many sources of information relevant to the financial performance and condition of a particular company. Virtually all macroeconomic information, for example, such as the general rate of inflation, the rate of unemployment, and movements in the rate of interest, influences the financial well-beings of many companies and is relevant to many investment decisions, yet is not included in financial statements. Investors and creditors must rely on other sources for such information.

In addition, much relevant microeconomic (company-specific) information is absent from the financial statements. The principle of objectivity, for example, prevents much relevant and potentially useful information from appearing on the financial statements. Several examples follow.

No Human Resources
Estimates of the value of a company's human resources are not included on the balance sheet. For many companies, especially those in the fast-growing service sector, **human capital** is the most important "asset." How can one assess the value of a professional basketball team, for example, without considering the value of its players, or the value of a law or public accounting firm without considering the value of the professional staff? Certainly, estimating the value of human capital is difficult and subjective, and it is not surprising that such valuations do not fall within the scope of generally accepted accounting principles. Nonetheless, there is little doubt that human capital is an important part of successful operations for many companies.

No Goodwill
Goodwill is another "asset" that is not accrued on the financial statements. It represents the value of a company as a working unit—the way a company's assets interact to produce a product or service that has been used and relied upon, often

for years, by customers or clients. Consider, for example, the reputation for service and quality that a company like IBM has built up over the past years. This intangible factor is an important part of future sales, customer, supplier, and employee relationships and, in general, IBM's overall future success.

Despite its value, internally-generated goodwill is not explicitly recognized anywhere on the financial statements. Like human resources, estimating the value of goodwill is difficult and subjective; therefore, it is not covered within the framework of generally accepted accounting principles. However, it can be an important part of a company's value and should not be ignored by anyone interested in a company's financial condition and future.[8]

Few Market Values

Several chapters in this text have discussed how market values are relevant to the decisions of investors and creditors. Yet because market values are difficult to measure objectively, they are disclosed on the financial statements in only a few cases. For the most part, historical costs are found on the balance sheet, and (as mentioned before) there is some question about the usefulness of historical cost for decision-making purposes.

Individuals who are interested in assessing a company's financial condition and performance should consider estimating and incorporating into the financial statements the replacement costs and the fair market values of the company's assets. These procedures are discussed in Appendix C at the end of the text.

No Inflation Adjustments

One of the assumptions that provides a basis for preparing the financial statements is that the value (i.e., purchasing power) of the dollar is stable. This assumption ignores inflation and causes the numbers on the financial statements to be expressed in dollars that have different levels of purchasing power. It is questionable whether comparing these numbers, or adding and subtracting them, gives rise to meaningful amounts. Total assets and net income, for example, are the result of adding and/or subtracting numbers that are expressed in dollars of different purchasing power.

Individuals interested in assessing the financial performance of a company should adjust the financial statements for the effects of general inflation. These procedures are discussed and illustrated in Appendix C at the end of the text.

Management Biases and Incentives

Another important limitation of the information on the financial statements is that it is prepared by managers who are affected by the reported numbers. Managers are not inherently unethical, and they do not attempt at every opportunity to exploit the investors and creditors who provide the company's capital. Indeed, we have argued on several occasions in this text that it is in the manager's long-run best interest to report truthfully. However, it is well-known that managers choose those accounting methods and estimates that report the results of their actions in ways that protect and further their own interests. They are fully aware that the financial statements are used by outsiders to evaluate and control their actions, and that their future levels of wealth are often directly tied to the financial accounting numbers. To the extent that they are able, therefore, they will in-

---

8. Recall that goodwill that has been purchased in an acquisition is recognized on the financial statements. In such cases the value of the goodwill has been objectively determined by a documented transaction.

fluence those numbers. Such influence may come in the form of a choice of a particular accounting method (e.g., LIFO vs. FIFO), the estimates used to apply the chosen accounting methods (e.g., bad debt estimate or estimated useful life of a fixed asset), or any of a number of other subjective operating and reporting decisions.

Financial statement users should be aware that the statements are being prepared by managers who have an economic stake in what the statements report. Accordingly, they should examine the footnotes closely to identify the accounting methods that have been chosen, while being particularly aware of those areas in the statements that are most sensitive to the subjective estimates and judgmental reporting decisions of management. Certainly, the auditor and the audit opinion provide some control over management's choices, but even within the framework of generally accepted accounting principles, the manager can exercise discretion in a number of areas. Throughout this text we have made a special effort to identify such areas.

Financial Statement Information Cannot Be Used to Identify Undervalued, Publicly-Traded Securities

The financial reports of major U.S. companies are published annually, and important numbers, such as net income, are publicly available almost as soon as they are determined. Consequently, it is difficult, if not impossible, for investors to use financial accounting information to identify undervalued stocks or bonds that are traded on the public security markets.

Consider, for example, an investor who is deciding whether to purchase General Motors (GM) common stock by analyzing the company's financial statements. Assume that the investor conducts a complete earning power and solvency analysis, similar to that described in the chapter, and concludes that GM stocks, which are presently trading at $80 each, are actually worth $100. Believing that the stocks are worth more than their market price, the investor decides to purchase the shares, expecting the price to rise as the stock market learns of the undervaluation.

Unfortunately, such a strategy would probably not be very productive. The problem is that the major security markets have been found to be efficient with respect to public information. That is, the prices of the securities traded in these markets adjust almost instantaneously to reflect the public release of new information. Financial accounting information, therefore, is impounded in the price of a security when it is made public. In other words, the $80 market price for GM stock already reflects the information contained in the financial report, and it is unlikely that the investor can use that information to make a profit on the stock. The investor must look elsewhere for such information.

While financial statement analysis may not be particularly helpful in identifying undervalued publicly-traded securities, this certainly does not mean that it is useless. Analyzing GM's financial statements may help one to decide whether the risk and return associated with GM's stock are consistent with his or her preferences. Banks use financial statement analysis to guide loan decisions and to determine the terms of the loans they grant. Financial statement ratios have been used to predict bankruptcy. Financial statement analysis can be useful when deciding whether to purchase equity and debt interests in companies that are not traded on the public exchanges. And finally, as mentioned before, financial statement numbers can be used in contracts to control, direct, and monitor the actions of managers.

USING RATIOS TO ASSESS EARNING POWER AND SOLVENCY: K MART CORPORATION AND WAL-MART, INC.

In this section financial ratios are used to assess the earning power and solvency positions of K mart and Wal-Mart, Inc. Table 17-1 compares the two companies on the financial ratios covered in the chapter. Each ratio was computed from information contained in the 1989 annual report (K mart's annual report is located in Appendix D), and the analysis is conducted for fiscal years 1989 and 1988. In several cases, indicated by N/A (not available), the annual report does not contain the necessary information.

Both K mart and Wal-Mart are national discount department store chains that offer a wide variety of general merchandise to customers. Wal-Mart stores operate in 25 states and the company's total assets ($6.4 billion) and 1989 revenues ($20.1 billion) are approximately 50 percent and 75 percent, respectively, of K mart's total assets and revenues. The retail operations of the two companies are very similar and their major accounting policies are virtually the same. Both K mart and Wal-Mart received standard, unqualified audit reports from major U.S. accounting firms in 1989 and 1988; neither company entered into any significant transactions during that time period, and both companies have high credit ratings.

The profitability ratios indicate that both companies have demonstrated earning power. Wal-Mart experienced extremely high returns on equity and assets, compared to both K mart and the average for the industry, which approximate .14 (ROE) and .07 (ROA). Such returns result from Wal-Mart's ability to earn high levels of net income on relatively low levels of shareholder and total asset investment. Wal-Mart also shows an unusual ability to cover interest payments with earnings. K mart's returns on equity and assets and times interest earned ratio, while less impressive than Wal-Mart's, are certainly adequate as they too exceed industry averages.

While return on sales is roughly the same for both companies, K mart's earning per share amounts significantly exceed those of Wal-Mart, both companies showing improvement from 1988 to 1989. Further review of the annual reports indicates that Wal-Mart has 565 million common shares outstanding while K mart has only 200 million. Wal-Mart's ownership appears to be much more diluted than K mart's, indicating that the benefits from Wal-Mart's strong earning power are spread across almost three times as many shares of common stock. The price of Wal-mart's common stock fluctuates over approximately the same range (between $25 and $35) as the price of K mart's.

The current ratios of the two companies are very close and approximate those of the industry. Wal-Mart's quick ratio, however, appears to be quite low. For the past two years the company has carried a relatively small cash balance brought about by large investments in long-term assets in 1988 that were not completely covered by operating cash flows and borrowings. The low cash balance makes inventory turnover, which is discussed next, much more important because cash generated from inventory sales will be needed to cover current liabilities as they come due.

The receivables turnover ratios for K mart and Wal-Mart are not particularly important because neither company relies heavily on credit sales. Inventory turnover, however, is crucial because both companies carry large amounts of merchandise. As of the end of fiscal 1989, K mart and Wal-Mart had $5.671 billion (80 percent of current assets) and $3.351 billion (92 percent of current assets) in-

Table 17–1   1989 and 1988 financial ratios of K mart and Wal-Mart

	K mart		Wal-Mart	
Profitability Ratios	**1989**	**1988**	**1989**	**1988**
Return on equity	.17	.17	.32	.32
Return on assets	.10	.09	.17	.16
Earnings per share ($)	4.00	3.40	1.48	1.11
Return on sales	.03	.03	.04	.04
Times interest earned	3.60	3.60	9.80	9.35
Solvency Ratios				
Current ratio	2.00	1.90	1.80	1.70
Quick ratio	.27	.13	.01	.01
Activity Ratios				
Receivables turnover (days)	5.9[a]	N/A	1.97	2.0
Inventory turnover (days)	103.0	N/A	68.00	69.0
Capitalization Ratios				
Cost of debt	.06	N/A	.07	N/A
Financial leverage	.07	.08	.15	.16
Debt/equity[b]	1.40	1.50	1.10	1.20
Market Ratios				
Price/earnings				
High	9.9	14.2	22.8	38.6
Low	7.3	6.4	16.9	18.0
Dividend yield				
High	.044	.052	.006	.006
Low	.032	.023	.005	.003
Return on investment				
High	.88	N/A	.70	N/A
Low	−.15	N/A	−.007	N/A

Source: 1989 annual reports.

[a]Receivables were included with other current assets on the balance sheet, making this amount an overstatement of receivables turnover.

[b]Deferred income taxes were excluded from debt.

vested in inventories, respectively. Wal-Mart's inventory turnover, which approximates the industry average, is much quicker than that of K mart. While not indicated on Table 17–1, K mart's inventory turnover has improved over the past few years, attributed largely to the POS system described on page 17 of the annual report. However, this area is one that K mart still needs to improve.

The cost of debt experienced by K mart and Wal-Mart seems to be reasonable and both companies, especially Wal-Mart, have shown an ability to use financial leverage. K mart's financial leverage ratio approximates that of the industry and Wal-Mart's is much higher. Wal-Mart's strong earning power is the main reason for its success in this area. K mart's debt/equity ratio is higher than Wal-Mart's, which is similar to that of the industry. As indicated on page 14 of K mart's annual report, the company has been working to reduce its reliance on debt over the past several years.

The market ratios are somewhat difficult to interpret because they depend on common stock prices which fluctuate throughout the year. Note that in each case we indicate the range over which the ratio varied. Wal-Mart's common stock trades at a much higher multiple of earnings (18.0–38.6) than does K mart's (6.4–14.2). That is, a relatively small change in Wal-Mart's earnings has been followed by a relatively large change in its common stock price. K mart shows a substantially higher dividend yield primarily because it pays higher dividends than Wal-Mart. K mart pays dividends of approximately 32 percent of earnings while Wal-Mart pays dividends of only 11 percent of earnings.

The return on investment ratios indicates that investors purchasing common stock in either company during fiscal 1988 would have experienced widely different returns depending on the exact date of the purchase. Investors purchasing at the lowest 1988 price and selling at the highest 1989 price would have earned 88 percent and 70 percent returns on K mart and Wal-Mart stock, respectively. Investors purchasing at the highest 1988 price and selling at the lowest 1989 price, on the other hand, would have had −15 percent and −.7 percent returns on K mart and Wal-Mart stock, respectively. Thus, investing in either company during 1988 could have resulted in a substantial gain or a substantial loss, depending on when the stock was purchased and sold.

In summary, the analysis indicates that Wal-Mart has demonstrated stronger earning power, faster inventory turnover, and less reliance on debt. K mart, on the other hand, shows higher earnings per share because its stock is less diluted, a greater cash balance, and a higher dividend yield. It is also apparent that K mart should focus on improving inventory turnover and reducing its reliance on debt. While the analysis has provided some insights, it is still difficult to draw any definite conclusions. Financial statement numbers provide a very limited and subjective view of the operations and financial condition of a company.

SUMMARY OF LEARNING OBJECTIVES

1 Explain how financial statement information is used for prediction and control.

Financial accounting numbers can be used in two fundamental ways: (1) they help to predict a company's future cash flows by providing an indication of its earning power and solvency position, and (2) they help investors, creditors, and other interested parties control, direct, and monitor the business decisions of a company's managers.

Financial accounting numbers report on past events, and to the extent that past events are indicative of the future, financial accounting numbers can be used in making predictions about a company's future cash flows. Earning power and solvency are important indicators of a company's future cash flows. Earning power refers to a company's ability to increase its wealth through operations and generate cash in the future. Solvency refers to a company's ability to meet its obligations as they come due. Financial accounting numbers based on the accrual concept are designed to provide information about earning power. Balance sheet numbers, which reflect short-run cash flows, and the statement of cash flows are particularly relevant in the assessment of solvency.

Investors and creditors can use financial accounting numbers to control the actions of managers by requiring that they enter into contracts that are written in terms of financial accounting numbers. Stockholders can encourage management to act in their interests by basing management's compensation on profits. Creditors can constrain the actions of managers and protect their own interests by writing restrictions, expressed in terms of financial accounting numbers, into loan contracts.

2 List and describe the basic steps involved in assessing the earning power and solvency position of a company.

When assessing earning power and solvency, a financial statement user should (1) review the audit report, (2) look for significant transactions, (3) review the company's credit rating, and (4) analyze the financial statements.

The audit report states whether, and to what extent, the information in the financial statements conforms to generally accepted accounting principles. In most cases an auditor renders an unqualified opinion, but occasionally an auditor departs from the standard report for any of a number of reasons, some of which can be quite serious. Most small companies do not have their financial statements audited.

Users should also look for significant transactions entered into by a company or significant events that might have taken place recently. Such items can have an important effect on the future direction of a company and may distort the financial statements, making it more difficult to assess a company's financial health. Examples include major acquisitions, the discontinuance or disposal of a business segment, unresolved litigation, major writedowns of receivables or inventories, offers to purchase outstanding shares (tender offers), extraordinary gains or losses, and changes in accounting methods.

Information about a company's credit rating is also of interest to users. Credit-rating agencies, such as Moody's Investor Service, Dun & Bradstreet, and Standard & Poor's, provide extensive analyses of the operations and financial positions of many companies as well as ratings of the riskiness of their outstanding debts. Such ratings have a direct bearing on a company's ability to issue debt in the future and on the terms of that debt.

Users should also perform ratio and solvency analyses on the financial statements. Such examinations involve computing a number of financial ratios and comparing them to other relevant numbers. These comparisons can be made in three basic ways: (1) across time, (2) across different companies within the same industry, and (3) within the financial statements of the company at a given point in time. A solvency analysis involves assessing the operating performance and financial flexibility of a company as well as the liquidity of its assets.

3 List and describe the five categories of financial ratios covered in this chapter. Identify the ratios included in each category.

Financial ratios can be divided into five categories: (1) profitability, (2) solvency, (3) activity, (4) capitalization, and (5) market ratios. Profitability ratios compare net income to various other financial statement numbers and, in general, provide information about the earning power of a company. Profitability ratios include return on equity, return on assets, earnings per share, return on sales, and the times-interest-earned ratio.

Solvency ratios involve comparisons of current assets to current liabilities, providing information about a company's ability to meet its short-term debts as they come due. Solvency ratios include the current ratio and the quick ratio. Many have noted, however, that solvency is quite complex and cannot be adequately captured by these ratios.

Activity ratios assess the speed of accounts receivable and inventory turnover. This information indicates how quickly receivables, on average, are converted to cash and how long inventory items are carried by a company. Activity ratios include receivables turnover and inventory turnover.

Capitalization ratios focus primarily on a company's financing sources (i.e., its long-term debt and stockholders' equity positions). Capitalization ratios include cost of debt, financial leverage, and the debt/equity ratio.

Market ratios involve the market price of a company's common shares and the dividend and price-appreciation returns to shareholders. Market ratios include the price/earnings ratio, dividend yield, and return on investment.

4   Identify and describe the major limitations of financial accounting information.

The information contained in the financial reports is limited in a number of significant ways. It is not particularly timely because financial reports are published several months after year-end. It excludes macroeconomic information; estimates of the value of a company's human resources; goodwill, which represents the value of a company as a working unit; and a number of relevant market values (replacement cost and fair market value). The information in the financial statements is not adjusted for the effects of inflation, is prepared by managers who have an economic stake in what the statements report, and cannot be used to identify undervalued stocks or bonds that are traded on the public security markets.

KEY TERMS

Activity ratios (p. 862)   Liquidity (p. 878)
Borrowing capacity (p. 877)   Market ratios (p. 862)
Capitalization ratios (p. 862)   Operating performance (p. 876)
Common-size financial statements (p. 860)   Profitability ratios (p. 862)
Earning power (p. 850)   Ratio analysis (p. 862)
Financial flexibility (p. 877)   Solvency (p. 850)
Financial leverage (p. 864)   Solvency ratios (p. 862)
Human capital (p. 879)   Unqualified (clean) opinion (p. 852)

QUESTIONS FOR DISCUSSION AND REVIEW

1. In what two fundamental ways are financial accounting numbers used? Provide three examples of each.

2. Discuss the concept of earning power, and differentiate it from the concept of solvency. How are they related? How can financial accounting numbers be used to assess each?

3. What are the basic differences between equity and debt investments, and why would equity and debt investors be interested in both earning power and solvency? Would equity investors tend to be more interested in earning power or solvency? Would debt investors tend to be more interested in earning power or solvency? Why?

4. Why might a company's stockholders want its managers to be paid bonuses in the form of cash or shares of stock instead of a straight salary? How might such a compensation scheme be implemented?

5. Why do debt covenants often restrict the borrowing company to a certain minimum ratio of current assets to current liabilities? Why might the same covenant contain a provision that limits the annual payment of dividends to a percentage of net income?

6. Describe how audit reports may deviate from "clean" opinions. Explain why financial statement users should review them closely.

7. Do most U.S. companies have their financial statements audited? Why or why not? If you were the manager of a small business, under what conditions would you have your financial statements audited?

8. Why are comparisons of financial statement numbers important to financial statement analysis? In what three ways can such comparisons be made?

9. Why is it helpful to compare financial accounting numbers across time? Why must such comparisons be viewed cautiously?

10. Where can industry-wide statistics be found? Of what use are they to the financial statement analyst, and how can they be misleading?

11. Explain the nature of common-size financial statements and how they can be used in conjunction with comparisons across time to provide useful information.

12. Identify and briefly define the five categories of financial statement ratios discussed in this chapter. Discuss each category in terms of how it relates to the assessment of earning power and solvency.

13. Why is the return on assets ratio considered a broader measure of financial performance than the return on equity ratio? Why must one be careful when using the return on sales ratio?

14. How can the activity ratios be used to complement the solvency ratios?

15. What is financial leverage, and is it generally a measure of earning power or solvency? Why is the debt/equity ratio of interest to a company's debtholders?

16. How do financial analysts often use the price/earnings ratio? Why must this be done cautiously?

17. What is solvency, and what three factors must be considered in its assessment? Define these factors, and explain how they are related.

18. Identify and briefly describe the three limitations of financial accounting numbers described in the chapter. What kind of relevant information is ignored on financial accounting statements? Why is it ignored?

19. Name five ways in which managers can bias financial statements and still remain within the guidelines of generally accepted accounting principles.

20. Why can't financial accounting numbers be used to identify undervalued securities that are traded on the major U.S. exchanges? In what other ways and situations can financial accounting numbers be used?

EXERCISES

E17–1

(Defining and categorizing ratios)   Listed below are various financial accounting ratios that a potential investor or creditor might use to analyze a company.

1. Return on sales	9. Receivables turnover
2. Quick ratio	10. Financial leverage
3. Cost of debt	11. Earnings per share
4. Debt/equity ratio	12. Return on investment
5. Current ratio	13. Inventory turnover
6. Dividend yield	14. Return on equity
7. Return on assets	15. Price/earnings ratio
8. Times interest earned	

Required:

a. State the formula for each ratio.
b. Classify each ratio as a (1) profitability ratio, (2) capitalization ratio, (3) solvency ratio, (4) activity ratio, or (5) market ratio.

E17–2

(Computing ratios and preparing common-size financial statements)   The 1989 and 1990 financial statements of Ken's Sportswear follow.

	1990	1989
Balance Sheet		
Assets		
Cash	$ 9,000	$ 7,000
Accounts receivable	12,000	9,000
Inventory	18,000	15,000
Long-lived assets (net)	60,000	50,000
Total assets	$99,000	$81,000
Liabilities and stockholders' equity		
Accounts payable	16,500	12,000
Long-term liabilities	46,000	40,000
Common stock ($10 par value)	20,000	20,000
Additional paid-in capital	5,000	5,000
Retained earnings	11,500	4,000
Total liabilities and stockholders' equity	$99,000	$81,000
Income Statement		
Sales (all on credit)	$72,000	
Less: Cost of goods sold	30,000	
Gross profit	42,000	
Operating expenses	12,000	
Net income from operations	30,000	
Interest expense	5,000	
Net income from continuing operations before tax	25,000	
Income taxes	8,500	
Net income	$16,500	
Dividends	$ 9,000	
Per-share market price	$ 36	$ 30
Outstanding common shares	2,000	2,000

Required:

a. Compute all ratios described in Figure 17–19 for 1990. Assume a tax rate of 34 percent. Only long-term liabilities are interest-paying.

b. Prepare common-size financial statements.

E17–3 *(Solvency and the role of the activity ratios)* Financial information from the records of Blanchard Masonry follows. The company began operations in 1987. Assume that the year-end 1987 balances are the average balances during 1987.

Account	1990	1989	1988	1987
Cash	$ 7,000	$ 7,000	$ 5,000	$ 5,000
Accounts receivable	20,000	14,000	8,000	7,000
Inventory	15,000	14,000	12,000	12,000
Total current assets	$42,000	$35,000	$25,000	$24,000
Current liabilities	$14,000	$12,000	$10,000	$10,000
Sales (all on credit)	50,000	45,000	40,000	35,000
Less: Cost of goods sold	28,000	25,000	22,000	20,000
Gross profit	$22,000	$20,000	$18,000	$15,000

Required:

a. Compute the current ratio for each year.

b. Compute gross margin for each year.

c. Compute inventory turnover and average days supply in inventory.

d. Compute receivables turnover and average number of days outstanding.

e. Comment on the company's solvency position over the four-year period.

E17–4 *(Solvency and the statement of cash flows)* Beecham Limited began operations in early 1988. Summaries of the statements of cash flows for 1988, 1989, and 1990 follow.

	1990	1989	1988
Net cash provided (used) by operating activities	?	$(252)	?
Net cash provided (used) by investing activities	$ 150	?	$(400)
Net cash provided (used) by financing activities	(200)	400	800
Net increase (decrease) in cash balance	?	(2)	78
Beginning cash balance	76	?	0
Ending cash balance	$ 156	$ 76	?

Required:

a. Compute the missing dollar amounts, and briefly comment on the company's cash-management policies during the three-year period.

b. Does the company appear to have faced any solvency problems during the period? Explain your answer.

E17–5 *(The effects of transactions on financial ratios)* Conlon Travel Supplies entered into the following transactions during 1990.

(1) Purchased inventory on account.

(2) Purchased plant machinery by issuing long-term debt.

(3) Recorded the estimate for bad debt expense for the year.

(4) Paid wages that were accrued on December 31, 1989.

(5) Sold inventory on account for 20 percent over cost.

(6) Purchased an insurance policy on December 31, 1990, in exchange for cash. The policy covers 1991.

Required: Fill in a chart like the one that follows by indicating whether each transaction would increase (+), decrease (−), or have no effect (NE) on the following:

a. The quick ratio
b. The current ratio
c. The debt/equity ratio.

Treat each transaction independently, and assume that prior to each transaction the company's balance sheet appeared as follows.

Assets		Liabilities and stockholders' equity	
Cash and marketable securities	$100	Current liabilities	$ 60
Other current assets	100	Long-term liabilities	190
Long-lived assets	150	Stockholders' equity	100
		Total liabilities and	
Total assets	$350	stockholders' equity	$350

Transaction	Quick Ratio	Current Ratio	Debt/Equity Ratio
(1)			
(2)			
(3)			
(4)			
(5)			
(6)			

E17–6   *(Using solvency and activity ratios together)*   The following information was extracted from the 1990 financial report of the Generic Clothing Company.

	1990	1989
Current assets		
Cash	$ 15,000	$ 30,000
Short-term marketable securities	225,000	10,000
Accounts receivable (net)	90,000	95,000
Inventory	50,000	225,000
Prepaid insurance	20,000	25,000
Total current assets	$400,000	$385,000
Current liabilities		
Accounts payable	$ 75,000	$ 60,000
Wages payable	10,000	10,000
Current portion of long-term debt	375,000	100,000
Total current liabilities	$460,000	$170,000

Required:

a. Based upon the above data, compute the following for Generic Clothing Company for both 1989 and 1990.
   (1) The current ratio
   (2) The quick ratio
b. Assume that net credit sales for the years ended December 31, 1989 and 1990, were $780,000 and $800,000, respectively, and that the balance of Accounts Receivable as of January 1, 1989, was $100,000. Compute the receivables turnover for both years. Also compute the number of days outstanding.

c. Does it appear that the solvency position of the company improved or worsened from 1989 to 1990? Explain.

E17–7

(Explaining return on equity with inventory turnover) PLP Corporation began operations on January 1, 1987. The initial investment by the owners was $100,000. The following information was extracted from the company's records.

	Net Income	December 31 Stockholders' Equity	December 31 Inventory	Cost of Goods Sold
1987	$510,000	$100,000	$200,000	$1,200,000
1988	490,000	290,000	255,000	1,350,000
1989	515,000	315,000	320,000	1,395,000
1990	505,000	510,000	365,000	1,400,000

Required:

a. Compute the return on equity for each year. Has the company been effective at managing the capital provided by the equity owners?

b. Does the information about inventory and the cost of goods sold indicate any reason for the trend in return on equity? Support your answer with any relevant ratios.

E17–8

(Debt covenants can limit additional debt and dividend payments) At the end of 1989, Montvale Associates borrowed $120,000 from the Bayliner Bank. The debt covenant specified that Montvale's debt/equity ratio could not exceed 1.5:1 during the period of the loan. A summary of Montvale's balance sheet after the loan follows.

	1989
Assets	
Current assets	$130,000
Noncurrent assets	350,000
Total assets	$480,000
Liabilities and stockholders' equity	
Current liabilities	130,000
Long-term liabilities	150,000
Stockholders' equity	200,000
Total liabilities and stockholders' equity	$480,000

Required:

a. Compute Montvale's debt/equity ratio as of December 31, 1989.

b. How much additional debt can the company incur without violating the debt covenant?

c. How large a dividend can the company declare at the end of 1989 without violating the debt covenant?

d. If Montvale had declared, but not yet paid, a $20,000 dividend before it took out the loan, could the company pay the dividend afterwards without violating the debt covenant? Why or why not?

E17–9

(Examining market ratios over time) The information below refers to the financial records of Morrissey Brothers over a five-year period.

	1990	1989	1988	1987	1986
Net income	$60,000	$50,000	$40,000	$24,000	$20,000
Dividends declared	$24,000	$15,000	$16,000	$10,000	$12,000
Closing per-share price	$ 42	$ 37	$ 30	$ 35	$ 30
Number of shares outstanding	18,000[b]	20,000	20,000[a]	10,000	10,000

[a]The stock was issued on January 1, 1988.
[b]The treasury shares were purchased on January 1, 1990.

Required:

a. Compute dividends declared as a percentage of net income during each of the five years.

b. Compute the price/earnings ratio, dividend yield, and return on investment for 1987, 1988, 1989, and 1990.

c. Comment on the performance of an investment in Morrissey Brothers stock from 1987 to 1990.

E17-10   *(Debt covenants can limit investments and dividends)*   A summary of the 1989 balance sheet of Mayberry Services and Investments follows.

	1989
Assets	
Current assets	$12,000
Land investments	55,000
Total assets	$67,000
Liabilities and stockholders' equity	
Accounts payable	$ 9,000
Long-term liabilities	30,000
Stockholders' equity	28,000
Total liabilities and stockholders' equity	$67,000

On January 1, 1990, the company borrowed $40,000 (long-term debt) to purchase additional land. The debt covenant states that Mayberry must maintain a current ratio of at least 2:1 over the period of the loan.

Required:

a. As of January 1, 1990, how much of the $40,000 can Mayberry invest in land without violating the debt covenant?

b. Assume that Mayberry invested the maximum allowable amount in land. Prepare Mayberry's balance sheet as of January 1, 1990. Compute the current ratio and debt/equity ratio.

c. Assume that Mayberry invested the maximum allowable in land on January 1, 1990. During 1990 Mayberry generated $150,000 in revenues (all cash), paid off the accounts payable outstanding as of December 31, 1989, and incurred $130,000 in expenses, of which $123,000 were paid in cash. The company neither purchased nor sold any of its long-term land investments, made no principal payments on the long-term debt, and issued no equity during 1989. How large a dividend can the company declare, but not pay, at the end of 1990 without violating the debt covenant? Compute the resulting debt/equity ratio if the company declares the maximum allowable dividend.

E17-11   *(Using ratios and the statement of cash flows to assess solvency and earning power)*   The financial information below was taken from the records of Lotechnic Enterprises. The company pays no dividends.

	1990	1989	1988	1987
Current assets	$ 35,000	$ 31,000	$ 24,000	$ 20,000
Noncurrent assets	93,000	86,000	64,000	33,000
Total assets	128,000	117,000	88,000	53,000
Current liabilities	$ 30,000	$ 25,000	$ 13,000	$ 8,000
Long-term liabilities	40,000	40,000	35,000	15,000
Capital stock	20,000	20,000	20,000	20,000
Retained earnings	38,000	32,000	20,000	10,000
Total liabilities and				
stockholders' equity	$128,000	$117,000	$ 88,000	$ 53,000

	1990	1989	1988	1987
Net cash provided (used) by operating activities	$ (2,000)	$ 3,000	$ 6,000	$ 7,000
Net cash provided (used) by investing activities	(10,000)	(20,000)	(31,000)	(12,000)
Net cash provided (used) by financing activities	15,000	15,000	25,000	8,000
Net increase (decrease) in cash	$ 3,000	$ (2,000)	0	$ 3,000
Interest expense	$ 5,000	$ 5,000	$ 4,000	$ 2,000
Income from continuing operations	24,000	21,000	14,000	13,000

Required:

a. Compute the current ratio, the debt/equity ratio, and return on assets for each of the four years. Assume that the year-end balances in 1987 reflect the average balances during the year.

b. Prepare a common-size balance sheet for each of the four years.

c. Use the statement of cash flows, and analyze the earning power and solvency positions of Lotechnic.

PROBLEMS

P17-1

(Computing ratios and the role of market values)   Avery Corporation reported the following selected items as part of its 1990 financial report.

Cash	$ 15,000
Short-term marketable securities (at cost)	150,000
Accounts receivable	100,000
Inventory	100,000
Total assets	970,000
Accounts payable	95,000
Interest payable	50,000
Mortgage payable[a]	300,000
Common stock (at par value of $10 per share)	200,000
Additional paid-in capital	125,000
Retained earnings (after closing entries)	200,000
Net sales	2,000,000
Cost of goods sold	900,000
Interest expense	100,000
Net income before taxes	757,575
Net income	500,000

[a]$50,000 of the mortgage payable is due within the next year.

Required:

a. Compute the following ratios. Where necessary assume that year-end balances are equal to average balances during the year.

(1) Current ratio

(2) Quick ratio

(3) Earnings per share

(4) Times-interest-earned ratio

(5) Return on assets

(6) Inventory turnover

(7) Return on equity

b. Assume that the market value of the portfolio of short-term marketable securities is $200,000. Recompute the ratios in (a) that would be affected if the ratios were based on market values instead of historical cost. Assume that the appreciation of the securities would be included in income (ignore income tax effects). Would basing the ratios on the cost or market value of items be more useful in determining the earning power and solvency of the company? Explain.

P17-2   *(Computing ratios and the effect of transactions on return on equity)* Kinney Conglomerates generated the following amounts for the year ended December 31, 1990.

Net income from continuing operations before taxes	$2,250,000
Less: Income taxes	765,000
Extraordinary gain	100,000
Net income	1,585,000

Additional Information

(1) During 1990 the company declared and paid $1,500,000 in dividends.

(2) The stock of Kinney Conglomerates increased to $35 per share during 1990 from $30 as of January 1, 1990.

(3) The company incurred $80,000 in interest expense during 1990. The total debt that is subject to interest is $800,000.

(4) As of January 1, the company had 100,000 shares of common stock outstanding. During 1993 the company issued 50,000 additional shares. Assume that the additional shares were issued evenly throughout the year.

Required:

a. Compute the following ratios:

   (1) Earnings per share

   (2) Cost of debt

   (3) Price/earnings

   (4) Dividend yield

   (5) Return on investment.

b. What effect (increase, decrease, or no effect) did each of the items listed under additional information above have on Kinney's return on equity ratio?

P17-3   *(Comparing companies on earning power)* The following information was obtained from the 1990 financial reports of Hathaway Toy Company and Yakima Manufacturing.

	Hathaway Toy	Yakima Mfg.
Net operating income	$1,455,000	$1,455,000
Less: Interest expense	—	195,000
Net income from continuing operations before tax	1,455,000	1,260,000
Less: Income taxes	580,000	505,000
Net income	$ 875,000	$ 755,000
Current liabilities	$ 240,000	$ 25,000
Mortgage payable	—	1,950,000
Common stock ($10 par value)	800,000	350,000
Additional paid-in capital	915,000	150,000
Retained earnings	745,000	225,000
Total liabilities and stockholders' equity	$2,700,000	$2,700,000

Assume that the only change to stockholders' equity is due to net income earned in 1990.

Required:

a. Which company is more effective at managing the capital provided by the owners?

b. Which company is more effective at managing capital provided by all investors?

c. Compute the earnings per share for each company.

d. Is Yakima Manufacturing using its debt effectively for the equity owners?

P17–4 *(Extraordinary items and financial ratios)* The following condensed income statements were obtained from the financial reports of Robotronics, Inc. and Technology, Limited for 1990.

	Robotronics, Inc.	Technology, Ltd.
Net operating income	$975,000	$ 850,000
Less: Interest expense	100,000	175,000
Net income from continuing operations before taxes	875,000	675,000
Less: Income taxes	265,000	300,000
Net income from continuing operations	610,000	375,000
Extraordinary gain (net of taxes of $320,000)	—	1,300,000
Net income	$610,000	$1,675,000

The following selected information was obtained from the companies' balance sheets as of December 31, 1990.

	Robotronics, Inc.	Technology, Ltd.
Current liabilities	$ 140,000	$ 25,000
Bonds payable	725,000	0
Mortgage payable	1,490,000	405,000
Common stock	500,000	600,000
Additional paid-in capital	215,000	325,000
Retained earnings	290,000	515,000
Total liabilities and stockholders' equity	$3,360,000	$1,870,000

The only difference in stockholders' equity was due to income earned in 1990.

Required:

a. Assume that you are considering purchasing the common stock of one of these companies. Which company has a higher return on equity? Would your conclusion be different if the impact of the extraordinary item had been considered? Why should or should not extraordinary items be considered?

b. Which company uses leverage more effectively? Does your answer change if you consider the impact of the extraordinary item?

P17–5 *(Adjusting the financial statements for the effects of different accounting methods)* The financial statements as of December 31, 1990 for Williams Company and Warner Services follow.

	Williams Company		Warner Services	
	1990	1989	1990	1989
Assets				
Current assets	$15,000	$ 8,000	$15,000	$ 8,000
Fixed assets (net)	80,000	90,000	64,000	80,000
Total assets	$95,000	$98,000	$79,000	$88,000
Liabilities and stockholders' equity				
Current liabilities	$ 7,000	$ 6,000	$ 7,000	$ 6,000
Long-term liabilities	25,000	37,000	25,000	37,000
Stockholders' equity	63,000	55,000	47,000	45,000
Total liabilities and stockholders' equity	$95,000	$98,000	$79,000	$88,000

	Williams Company		Warner Services	
	1990	1989	1990	1989
Revenues	$81,000	$52,000	$81,000	$52,000
Expenses	58,000	35,000	64,000	45,000
Net income	$23,000	$17,000	$17,000	$ 7,000

Both companies began operations on January 1, 1989, and purchased fixed assets at a cost of $100,000 at that time. Williams Company depreciated its fixed assets over a ten-year period, using the straight-line rate and assuming no salvage value. Warner Services also estimated a ten-year life and no salvage value, but used the double-declining-balance method. Assume that net income is equal to net income from continuing operations.

Required:

a. Compute return on equity, return on sales, the current ratio, and the debt/equity ratio for each company for 1989 and 1990. Do not adjust the statements for the different depreciation methods. From these ratios, which company appears to have the greatest earning power?

b. Adjust Warner's books assuming that it used the straight-line method of depreciation. Compute return on equity, return on sales, the current ratio, and the debt/equity ratio for 1989 and 1990. After the adjustment, which company appears to have the greatest earning power?

P17-6   *(Borrow or issue equity: effects on financial ratios)*   Edgemont Repairs began operations on January 1, 1988. The 1988, 1989, and 1990 financial statements follow.

	1990	1989	1988
Assets			
Current assets	$ 30,000	$10,000	$ 8,000
Noncurrent assets	83,000	45,000	41,000
Total assets	$113,000	$55,000	$49,000
Liabilities and stockholders' equity			
Current liabilities	$ 12,000	$ 7,000	$ 5,000
Long-term liabilities	50,000	10,000	10,000
Stockholders' equity	51,000	38,000	34,000
Total liabilities and			
stockholders' equity	$113,000	$55,000	$49,000
Revenues	$ 70,000	$45,000	$37,000
Operating expenses	27,000	24,000	24,000
Interest expense	5,000	1,000	1,000
Income taxes	13,000	6,000	6,000
Net income	$ 25,000	$14,000	$ 6,000
Dividends	$ 12,000	$10,000	$ 2,000
Number of shares outstanding	10,000	10,000	10,000

On January 1, 1990, the company expanded operations by taking out a $40,000 long-term loan at a 10 percent annual interest rate.

Required:

a. Assume net income equals income from continuing operations. Compute return on equity, return on assets, return on sales, the times-interest-earned ratio, financial leverage, and the debt/equity ratio for 1989 and 1990.

b. On January 1, 1990, the company's common stock was selling for $20 per share. Assume that Edgemont issued 2000 shares of stock, instead of borrowing the $40,000, to raise the cash needed to pay for the January 1 expansion. Recompute the ratios in (a) for 1990. Ignore any tax effects.

c. Should the company have issued the equity instead of borrowing the funds? Explain.

P17–7   *(Percentage changes and common-size financial statements)* You are considering investing in Gidley Electronics. As part of your investigation of Gidley Electronics, you obtained the following balance sheets for the years ended December 31, 1989 and 1990.

	1990	1989
Assets		
Current assets		
Cash	$ 110,000	$ 115,000
Short-term marketable securities	175,000	220,000
Accounts receivable	350,000	400,000
Inventory	290,000	240,000
Prepaid expenses	55,000	35,000
Total current assets	980,000	1,010,000
Property, plant, and equipment	650,000	590,000
Less: Accumulated depreciation	165,000	130,000
Total assets	$1,465,000	$1,470,000
Liabilities and stockholders' equity		
Current liabilities		
Accounts payable	$ 60,000	$ 50,000
Wages payable	15,000	20,000
Unearned revenue	50,000	35,000
Income taxes payable	55,000	35,000
Current portion of long-term debt	110,000	135,000
Total current liabilities	290,000	275,000
Bonds payable	380,000	440,000
Common stock ($10 par value)	220,000	170,000
Additional paid-in capital	145,000	115,000
Retained earnings	430,000	470,000
Total liabilities and stockholders' equity	$1,465,000	$1,470,000

Required:

a. Compute the dollar change in each account from 1989 to 1990. Also compute the percentage change in each account from 1989 to 1990.

b. Convert the balance sheets to common-size balance sheets. Also compute the percentage change in the common-size numbers of each account from 1989 to 1990.

c. Does the information provided in (b) provide any additional information to that contained in (a)? Explain.

P17–8   *(Comprehensive ratio analysis)* (This problem relates to Problem P17–7). You have just been hired as a stock analyst for a large stock brokerage company. Your first assignment is to analyze the performance of Gidley Electronics. Presented below are the company's income statement and statement of retained earnings for the years ended December 31, 1989 and 1990. The company's balance sheet for these years is presented as part of Problem P17–7.

	1990		**1989**	
Income Statement				
Revenue				
Net cash sales	$1,405,000		$1,255,000	
Net credit sales	2,450,000		3,010,000	
Total revenue		$3,855,000		$4,265,000
Less: Cost of goods sold				
Beginning inventory	240,000		300,000	
Net purchases	1,755,000		2,005,000	
Cost of goods available for sale	1,995,000		2,305,000	
Less: Ending inventory	290,000		240,000	
Cost of goods sold		1,705,000		2,065,000
Gross profit		2,150,000		2,200,000
Selling and administrative expenses				
Depreciation expense	95,000		100,000	
General selling expenses	470,000		450,000	
General administrative expenses	580,000	1,145,000	620,000	1,170,000
Net operating income		1,005,000		1,030,000
Interest expense		150,000		165,000
Net income from continuing operations				
before taxes		855,000		865,000
Less: Income taxes		345,000		350,000
Net income		$ 510,000		$ 515,000

	1990	**1989**
Statement of Retained Earnings		
Beginning retained earnings balance	$ 470,000	$ 165,000
Plus: Net income	510,000	515,000
Less: Dividends	550,000	210,000
Ending retained earnings balance	$ 430,000	$ 470,000

The market prices of the company's stock as of January 1, 1989, December 31, 1989, and December 31, 1990, were $65, $69, and $54 per share, respectively. The January 1, 1989 balance in stockholders' equity was $450,000, there were no changes in accounts receivable during 1989, and the income tax rate was 40 percent for 1989 and 1990.

Required: Answer the following questions (including any relevant ratios in your answers) for both 1989 and 1990. Unless the December 31, 1988 balance is provided, assume that the December 31, 1989 balance reflects the average balance during 1989.

(1) How much, on average, is the company paying for its debt? Do income taxes increase or decrease the cost of debt? Explain.

(2) How effective is the company at managing investments made by the equity owners?

(3) Is the company using debt to the best interests of the equity owners?

(4) Will the company be able to meet its current obligations using current assets? Using cash-like assets?

(5) How sensitive are stock prices to changes in earnings?

(6) How many days is the average account receivable outstanding? Are the days outstanding increasing or decreasing?

P17-9

(Preparing the financial statements from financial ratios)   Tumwater Canyon Campsites began operations on January 1, 1990. The following information is available at year end. Assume that all sales were on credit.

Net income from continuing operations	$ 25,000
Receivables turnover	8
Inventory turnover	5
Return on sales	8%
Gross margin	40%
Quick ratio	50%
Accounts payable	$150,000

Required: Prepare an income statement and the current asset and liability portion of the balance sheet for 1990. Current assets consist of cash, accounts receivable, and inventory. Accounts payable is Tumwater's only current liability. (*Hint:* Begin by using return on sales to compute net sales.)

P17-10

(Common-size financial statements)   Bob Cleary, the controller of Mountain-Pacific Railroad, has prepared the following financial statements for 1989 and 1990.

	1990	1989
Balance Sheet		
Assets		
Current Assets		
Cash	$ 10,000	$ 312,000
Short-term marketable securities	125,000	120,000
Accounts receivable	500,000	150,000
Inventory	200,000	210,000
Prepaid expenses	50,000	75,000
Total current assets	885,000	867,000
Long-term investments	225,000	225,000
Property, plant, and equipment	430,000	540,000
Less: accumulated depreciation	65,000	100,000
Total Assets	$1,475,000	$1,532,000
Liabilities and stockholders' equity		
Current liabilities		
Accounts payable	$ 10,000	$ 50,000
Wages payable	5,000	2,000
Dividends payable	125,000	5,000
Income taxes payable	50,000	35,000
Current portion of long-term debt	100,000	175,000
Total current liabilities	290,000	267,000
Mortgage payable	350,000	450,000
Common stock ($10 par value)	200,000	110,000
Additional paid-in capital	135,000	95,000
Retained earnings	500,000	610,000
Total liabilities and stockholders' equity	$1,475,000	$1,532,000

	1990		1989	
Income Statement				
Revenue				
Net cash sales	$1,955,000		$2,775,000	
Net credit sales	4,150,000		1,410,000	
Total revenue		$6,105,000		$4,185,000
Less: Cost of goods sold				
Beginning inventory	210,000		300,000	
Net purchases	4,005,000		2,475,000	
Cost of goods available for sale	4,215,000		2,775,000	
Less: ending inventory	200,000		210,000	
Cost of goods sold		4,015,000		2,565,000
Gross profit		2,090,000		1,620,000
Selling and administrative expenses				
Depreciation expense	75,000		90,000	
General selling expenses	575,000		600,000	
General administrative expenses	480,000	1,130,000	420,000	1,110,000
Net operating income		960,000		510,000
Interest expense		50,000		65,000
Net income from continuing operations				
before taxes		910,000		445,000
Less: Income taxes		365,000		175,000
Net income before extraordinary				
items		545,000		270,000
Extraordinary loss—net of				
tax benefit of $40,000		60,000		—
Net income		$ 485,000		$ 270,000

	1990	1989
Statement of Retained Earnings		
Beginning retained earnings balance	$ 610,000	$ 350,000
Plus: Net income	485,000	270,000
Less: Dividends	595,000	10,000
Ending retained earnings balance	$ 500,000	$ 610,000

The market prices of the company's stock as of January 1, 1989, December 31, 1989, and December 31, 1990, were $50, $45, and $70 per share, respectively. Assume an income tax rate of 40 percent and assume that interest expense was incurred only on long-term debt (including the current maturities of long-term debt).

Required:

a. Prepare common-size balance sheets and income statements for 1989 and 1990.

b. Which income statement account experienced the largest shift from 1989 to 1990? Did this shift appear to have any impact on the balance sheet? Explain.

c. What benefits do common-size financial statements provide over standard financial statements?

P17–11   *(Comparing ratios to industry averages)* (This problem is related to Problem P17–10.) Mountain-Pacific Railroad is interested in comparing itself to the rest of the industry. Bob Cleary, the controller, has obtained the following industry averages from a trade journal. (The industry averages were the same for 1989 and 1990.)

Return on equity	.50
Current ratio	3.10
Quick ratio	1.85
Return on assets	.30
Cost of debt	.0855
Receivables turnover	8.15
Earnings per share ($)	41.15
Price/earnings ratio	.451
Debt/equity ratio	.77
Return on sales	.072
Financial leverage	.20
Dividend yield	.375
Return on investment	.102
Times-interest-earned ratio	9.89
Inventory turnover	21.7

Required:

a. Compute these ratios for Mountain-Pacific Railroad for both 1989 (using year-end balances) and 1990 (using average balances where appropriate). Identify significant trends. Could the company experience solvency problems? Explain.

b. Compare the ratios of Mountain-Pacific Railroad to the industry averages. Do you think that Mountain-Pacific Railroad is doing better, worse, or the same as the industry? Explain your answer, and be as specific as possible.

P17-12   *(Assessing the loan risk of a potential bank customer)*   You have just been hired as a loan officer for Washington Mutual Savings. Selig Equipment and Mountain Bike, Inc., have both applied for $125,000 nine-month loans to acquire additional plant equipment. Neither company offered any collateral for the loans. It is the strict policy of the bank to have only $1,350,000 outstanding in uncollateralized loans at any point in time. Since the bank currently has $1,210,000 in uncollateralized loans outstanding, it will be unable to grant loans to both companies. The bank president has given you the following selected information from the companies' loan applications.

	Selig Equipment	Mountain Bike, Inc.
Cash	$ 15,000	$ 160,000
Accounts receivable	215,000	470,000
Inventory	305,000	195,000
Prepaid expenses	180,000	10,000
Total current assets	715,000	835,000
Noncurrent assets	1,455,000	1,875,000
Total assets	$2,170,000	$2,710,000
Current liabilities	$ 285,000	$ 325,000
Long-term liabilities	950,000	875,000
Contributed capital	790,000	910,000
Retained earnings	145,000	600,000
Total liabilities and stockholders' equity	$2,170,000	$2,710,000
Net credit sales	$1,005,000	$1,625,000
Cost of goods sold	755,000	960,000

Required: Assume that all account balances on the balance sheet are representative of the entire year. Based upon this limited information, which company would you recommend to the bank president as the better risk for an uncollateralized loan? Support your answer with any relevant analysis.

P17–13   *(Issuing debt or equity: effects on ratios and owners)*   Watson Metal Products is planning to expand its operations to France in response to increased demand from the French for quality metal products to use in production processes. Ben Watson, president of Watson Metal Products, and his consultants have estimated that the expansion will require an investment of $5 million. They have also estimated that this expansion will cause income from operations to increase by $1,500,000. The company is considering financing the expansion through one of the following alternatives.

Alternative 1: Issue 200,000 shares of common stock for $25 per share.

Alternative 2: Issue long-term debt at an annual interest cost of 15 percent. The principal would be payable in ten years.

Alternative 3: Issue 100,000 shares of common stock for $25 per share and finance the remainder by issuing long-term debt at an annual interest rate of 15 percent. The principal would be payable in ten years.

The income statement for the year ended December 31, 1989 of Watson Metal Products was as follows:

Sales	$150,000,000
Cost of goods sold	90,000,000
Other expenses	45,000,000
Net operating income	15,000,000
Interest expense	4,000,000
Net income from continuing operations before taxes	11,000,000
Less: Income taxes	4,400,000
Net income from continuing operations	$ 6,600,000
Earnings per share	$3.30

The common stock of Watson Metal Products has a par value of $10 per share. Prior to the expansion, the total debt of the company was $35 million, and total stockholders' equity was $45 million. There were no changes in total debt and total stockholders' equity other than those due to net income and the expansion project.

Required:

a. Assume that the company's net income from non-French operations in 1990 equals the income earned in 1989, and that the estimated income from operations on the expansion is realized in 1990. Compute earnings per share, return on equity, return on assets, financial leverage, and the debt/equity ratios as of December 31, 1990, if the company finances the expansion through the following:

   (1) Alternative 1

   (2) Alternative 2

   (3) Alternative 3.

   Assume that the December 31, 1990, balances equal average balances during 1990.

b. Assume that you are currently a stockholder in Watson Metal Products. Which expansion alternative would you prefer? Explain your answer.

c. What amount of income from continuing operations would Watson Metal Products have to generate from the expansion project so that earnings per share would be the same before and after the expansion under each alternative?

P17–14

(Preparing financial statement data from financial ratios) The following relationships were obtained for Boulder Mineral Company for 1990.

Current ratio	3:1
Inventory turnover (average days supply)	12.167
Quick ratio	1.5:1
Debt/equity	.4:1
Return on equity	.75:1
Return on assets	.65:1
Return on sales	.2:1
Receivables turnover	25
Earnings per share	$16.00

Additional Information

1. Boulder Mineral Company recognized $450,000 in income from continuing operations after taxes for 1990.
2. Credit sales comprise 80 percent of net sales.
3. Cost of goods sold is 55 percent of net sales.
4. Current liabilities are 35 percent of total liabilities.
5. The balance in the Cash account is $68,000.
6. The only difference between income from operations and income from continuing operations before taxes is interest expense.
7. The par value of common stock is $10 per share.
8. Assume that the balances as of December 31, 1990, were representative of the account balances throughout the year.
9. The income tax rate was 34 percent.

Use year-end balances to compute all ratios.

Required: Using the above information compute the following items.

a. Stockholders' equity
b. Total liabilities
c. Total assets
d. Interest expense
e. Income from continuing operations before taxes
f. Net sales
g. Credit sales
h. Accounts receivable
i. Cost of goods sold
j. Inventory turnover
k. Inventory
l. Current liabilities
m. Current assets
n. Marketable securities
o. Noncurrent assets
p. The number of shares of common stock outstanding
q. The total par value of common stock outstanding

CASES

C17–1   *(Financial performance objectives in terms of earning power and solvency)*   The following quote was taken from the 1988 financial report of the Quaker Oats Company:

> *Any review of Quaker's financial performance over the last six years must be seen in the context of the financial objectives we set in fiscal 1981. The financial objectives, which commit us to achieving a balance of returns and growth and thus measure our success in providing value to the stockholders, are to:*
>
> *1. achieve a return on equity at 20 percent or above,*
> *2. achieve "real" earnings per share growth averaging 5 percent or better,*
> *3. increase Quaker's dividend, consistent with "real" earnings growth, and*
> *4. maintain a strong financial position, as represented by Quaker's current bond and commercial paper ratings.*

Required:

a. Define return on equity and explain why Quaker Oats might express a financial objective in terms of it.

b. Objectives 2 and 3 above refer to "real" earnings per share and "real" earnings growth. Normally, designating a performance measure as "real" indicates that the effect of inflation has been removed from it. Why would Quaker Oats want to remove the effect of inflation from reported earnings numbers in its statement of objectives?

c. Which of the objectives above refer to measures of earning power and which refer to measures of solvency? Define and differentiate these two concepts and explain how each objective above relates to either earning power or solvency.

C17–2   *(A going concern qualification)*   The December 28, 1986, auditor's report for Allegheny International, Inc., an airline company, contained the following excerpt:

> *As described in Note 6 to the consolidated financial statements, the Company has received waivers from lending institutions suspending the applicability of certain debt covenants while it arranges to keep its current financing in place to the consummation of the merger described in Note 2. The Company's ability to continue as a going concern is contingent upon its ability to maintain adequate financing and attain profitable operations. The consolidated financial statements do not include any adjustments relating to the recoverability or classification of recorded asset amounts or the amounts and classification of liabilities that might be necessary should the Company be unable to continue as a going concern.*

Required:

a. Explain the meaning of this excerpt and why the auditors would include such a statement in the auditor's report.

b. Briefly describe how such a report would affect the way in which an investor, creditor, or other interested party would analyze Allegheny's financial statements.

C17–3   *(Changing accounting methods)*   In 1980 electrical equipment manufacturer RTE Corporation more than doubled its reported earnings per share by changing depreciation methods. The company's controller commented in *Forbes* (22 November 1982) that "We realize that compared to our competitors, our conservative methods of depreciation might have hurt us with investors because of its negative impact on earnings." Similarly, Inland Steel's controller was quoted as saying: "Why should we put ourselves at a disadvantage by depreciating more conservatively than other steel companies do?"

In that same article a partner in charge of accounting standards at a major U.S. accounting firm noted: "Some people would view a company that uses accelerated depreciation as being more conservative in its financial reporting and thus having higher quality earnings.

IBM, for example, is still using the so-called sum-of-the-years' digits method, which raises depreciation charges dramatically in the early years of an asset's life and then slows down as time goes by. A company changing from accelerated to straight-line might be viewed by some people as reporting at the time lower quality earnings."

Required:

a. Do you believe that a company is putting itself at a disadvantage relative to the other companies in its industry by using a more conservative depreciation method? Why or why not?

b. Do you believe that credit rating agencies would give lower ratings to companies using conservative depreciation methods because their reported net income numbers tend to be lower than their competitors who use less conservative methods? Why or why not?

c. Explain how a change to a less conservative depreciation method may be favored by management which is paid on an income bonus plan and is restricted by the terms of covenants written on outstanding debt.

d. Provide the rationale for why companies that use conservative depreciation methods might be viewed more favorably by investors, creditors, and other interested parties.

C17–4   *(Human capital and the financial statements)* In *The Accounting Review* (January 1971) Baruch Lev and Aba Schwartz noted that "The dichotomy in accounting between human capital and nonhuman capital is fundamental; the latter is recognized as an asset and therefore is recorded in the books and reported on the financial statements, whereas the former is totally ignored by accountants." Most economists, on the other hand, have a different view on this issue. Milton Freidman, for example, states: "From the broadest and most general point of view, total wealth includes all sources of 'income' of consumable services. One such source is the productive capacity of human beings, and accordingly this is one form in which wealth can be held."

Required:

a. Explain why human capital is treated differently by accountants and economists.

b. From the auditor's perspective explain why human resources are not accounted for on the balance sheet.

c. Because human resources are ignored, the financial statements of what kinds of companies (i.e., manufacturers, retailers, services, or financial institutions) tend to be misstated by the greatest amount? Why?

d. Briefly explain some of the other major items of information that are ignored by financial accounting statements.

C17–5   *(Financial accounting information in an efficient market)*   In an article published in the *Journal of Accountancy* (February 1984) James Deitrick and Walter Harrison noted that the major markets for common stocks (e.g., the New York Stock Exchange, the American Stock Exchange) have been found to be efficient. That is, "common stock prices behave as if they fully incorporate all existing information quickly and without bias. This implies that information, old and new, has been impounded into security prices as a result of the analysis and collective wisdom of investors and their advisors." This finding has encouraged many accountants to contend that the information contained in financial reports cannot be used to identify undervalued common stocks in an efficient market.

Required:

a. Provide the rationale for why the information contained in financial reports cannot be used to identify undervalued securities.

b. Explain how financial accounting information can be useful even though it may not be helpful in identifying undervalued securities that are traded in efficient markets.

The Time Value of Money

≡ Financial accounting information is useful because it provides investors, creditors, and other interested parties with measures of solvency and earning power. In developing these measures, the valuation of the transactions in which the company participates, and ultimately the valuation of a company's assets and liabilities are very important. It is essential, therefore, that investors, creditors, managers, auditors, and others understand the concepts of valuation.

The economic value of an asset or liability is its present value. In computing present value, the future cash inflows and outflows associated with an asset or liability are predicted and then adjusted in a way that reflects the **time values of money** (i.e., a dollar in the future is worth less than a dollar at present). Financial accounting statements rely extensively on the concept of present value; in theory, providing measures of present value is the ultimate goal of financial accounting.

This appendix covers the time value of money and, specifically, the concept of present value. We first point out that money has a price (interest). The price of money gives it a time value; it ensures that money held today has a greater value than money received tomorrow. We then introduce the notion of compound interest and proceed to work a number of examples that equate future cash flows to present values. We conclude by discussing how present value fits into the financial accounting system.

INTEREST: THE PRICE OF MONEY

Money, like any other scarce resource, has a price. Individuals wishing to borrow money must pay this price, and those who lend it receive this price. The price of money is called *interest* and is usually expressed as a percentage rate over a certain time period (usually per year, but sometimes per month). The dollar amount of interest is the result of multiplying the percentage rate by the amount of money borrowed or lent *(principal)*. For example, a 10 percent interest rate per year on a principal of $100 will produce $10 (10% × $100) of interest after one year.

TIME VALUE

In an environment that charges interest for the use of money, would you rather have one dollar now or would you rather receive one dollar one year from now? If you chose to receive the dollar immediately, you could lend it, and it would grow to some amount greater than one dollar after a year had passed. Someone, perhaps a bank, would be willing to pay you interest for the use of that dollar. Therefore, in a world where money has a price, a dollar today is worth more than a dollar at some time in the future. The difference between the value of a dollar today and the value of a dollar in the future is called the time value of money. For example, if the interest rate is 10%, $1 placed in a bank today will grow to $1.10 ($1 × 1.10) in one year. In this example the time value of a dollar is $.10.

Size of Time Value

Let's go one step further and explore the factors that determine the size of the time value of money. That is, what factors determine whether the time value of money is large or small? The first factor is obviously the price of money, or the interest rate. If there were no interest rate, the time value of money would be zero. Accordingly, as the interest rate gets larger, so does the difference between the value of a dollar today and the value of a dollar in the future. The higher the interest rate, the greater the time value of money. In the example above, a 20 percent interest rate would give rise to a time value of money equal to $.20.

The second factor determining the magnitude of the time value of money is the length of the time period. Which do you think is larger, the difference in value between a dollar today and a dollar tomorrow or the difference in value between a dollar today and a dollar ten years from now? Clearly, a dollar will grow much more in ten years than it will in one day. Thus, the longer the time period, the greater the time value of money.

Inflation

One additional important point should also be noted. We have assumed in the dicussion so far that the interest rate is simply the price of money. You might view this price as a rental fee for the use of money. Just as you pay rent for the use of someone's apartment, you must also pay rent for the use of someone's money.

However, in addition to the rental price of money, there is another reason why someone would prefer a dollar today to a dollar in the future. In times of rising prices (inflation), for example, one would definitely prefer a dollar today to a dollar in the future because today's dollar will buy more goods than the future dollar. In inflation, the prices of today's goods are less than the prices for the same goods in the future. Thus, in an inflationary environment there are actually two reasons why one would prefer a dollar today to a dollar in the future: (1) the rental price charged for using the dollar and (2) the erosion of the purchasing power of the dollar in the future.

In the real world, interest rates are set so that they reflect both factors. A 10% interest rate, for example, might be viewed as 6% rental fee and 4% inflation factor. Unfortunately, when using an interest rate to compute the time value of money, it is quite difficult to clearly separate the rental factor from the inflation factor. As a practical matter, there is little one can do other than to realize that both factors exist and that they are nearly impossible to separate accurately. As indicated in Chapter 5 and again in Appendix C, financial accounting ignores this problem by assuming that inflation does not exist.

TIME VALUE COMPUTATIONS

Computations involving the time value of money can be viewed from either of two perspectives: (1) The future value of a sum of money received today or (2) the present value of a sum of money received in the future. The following sections discuss these two perspectives.

Future Value

In our discussion of the time value of money, we stated that $1 invested at a given interest rate for a period of time will grow to an amount greater than $1. This dollar amount is called the **future value.**

Simple Interest

As in the example above, $1 invested at a 10% per year interest rate will grow to $1.10 ($1 × 1.10) at the end of one year. This $1.10 is referred to as the future value in one year of $1, given a 10% interest rate. In such a situation an individual would be indifferent between receiving $1 now or $1.10 in one year. A simple interest calculation for one period is illustrated below.

Compound Interest

If we wish to compute the future value of $1 at the end of more than one period (say, two years), given a 10 percent interest rate, we use the notion of **compound interest.** That is, in the second year the 10 percent interest rate is applied to both the original $1 principal and the $.10 interest earned in the first year. Here, the future value of $1 at the end of two years, given a 10 percent interest rate compounded annually, is equal to $1.21. An individual would be indifferent between receiving $1 now, $1.10 in one year, or $1.21 in two years, given a 10 percent interest rate compounded annually. The computation is depicted below.

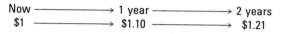

Table Factors

This same basic procedure could be used to calculate the future value of $1 for any number of periods in the future. After very many periods, though, this computation becomes quite time-consuming. Try, for example, to compute the future value of $1 in forty years, given an 8 percent interest rate compounded annually. Fortunately, tables have been developed that expedite these calculations considerably. Turn now to Table A-1, which follows this appendix. (The factors in this table and in Tables A-2, A-3, A-4, A-5, and A-6 are carried out to five digits beyond the decimal point. In our discussions however, we round the factors to two or three digits beyond the decimal point to simplify calculations.) This is a future value table. It enables you to quickly compute the future value of any amount for any number of periods in the future. To compute a future value, first, find the intersection of the interest rate and the number of periods. This amount is called the **table factor.** Then simply multiply this table factor times the dollar amount. For example, find the table factor for a 10 percent interest rate and two periods. It equals 1.21. Multiplying this factor times $1 gives you the future value in two years of $1 invested at a 10 percent annual interest rate. Multiplying this factor times $20 gives you the future value in two years of $20 invested at a 10 percent annual interest rate.

Note that the table factor in this example (1.21) is equal to 1.10 × 1.10 or $(1.10)^2$. In general, the formula for the future value calculation is as follows:

$$\text{Future Value} = A(1 + i)^n$$
$$\text{where} \quad A = \text{money amount}$$
$$i = \text{annual interest rate}$$
$$n = \text{number of periods}$$

Figure A−1 illustrates the future value calculation of $100 invested at 8 percent, 10 percent, and 12 percent for one, two, and three periods.

Figure A-1   Future value

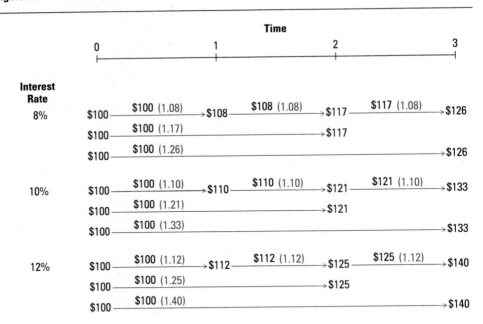

The chart demonstrates three important points. First, it shows that the factors found on the future value table are nothing more than the individual interest factors $(1 + i)$ multiplied by themselves for the number of periods $(1 + i)^n$. For example, the table factor for $n = 3$, $i = 12\%$ is 1.40 ($1.12 \times 1.12 \times 1.12$). Can you find the table factor for three periods and an 8 percent interest rate on the future value table? Can you derive it?

Note also in Figure A-1 that in each of the three time periods, as the interest rate gets higher, the time value of money is larger. In Period 3, for example, the time value of money at an 8 percent interest rate is $26 ($126 − $100). At 10 percent, it is $33 ($133 − $100) and at 12% it is $40 ($140 − $100). And finally, as the time period becomes longer, the time value of money becomes greater. These last two points illustrate the idea mentioned earlier that the magnitude of the time value of money is determined by the size of the interest rate and the length of the time period.

Future Value of Ordinary Annuities

It often happens in business transactions that cash payments of equal amounts are made periodically throughout a period of time. Installment payments on loans, for example, are typically set up in this manner. A flow of cash payments of equal amounts paid at periodic intervals is called an **annuity.** If these payments are made at the end of each period, the flow of payments is called an **ordinary annuity,** or an *annuity in arrears*. An ordinary annuity is illustrated below. This five-year ordinary annuity shows $100 payments made at the end of each year for five years.

Now	→	1	→	2	→	3	→	4	→	5
		$100		$100		$100		$100		$100

How would one go about computing the future value of this entire ordinary annuity? What would an ordinary five-year annuity of $100 grow to at the end of five years, given a 10 percent interest rate compounded annually? There are basically three ways to approach this problem, and they are illustrated in Figure A–2: (1) you can view each payment separately and compute its growth over each individual time period, (2) you can view each payment separately and use the table for future value (Table A–1), or (3) you can use the table for future value of an ordinary annuity (Table A–2). Both tables appear at the end of this appendix.

As is evident from the illustration, all three methods bring you to the correct solution ($610). However, method (3), the use of Table A–2 requires by far the fewest computations. The table factor for five periods and a 10 percent interest rate (6.10) is simply multiplied by the amount of the periodic annuity payment ($100). Note that this table factor is simply the addition of all the individual table

Figure A–2 Future value of ordinary annuities

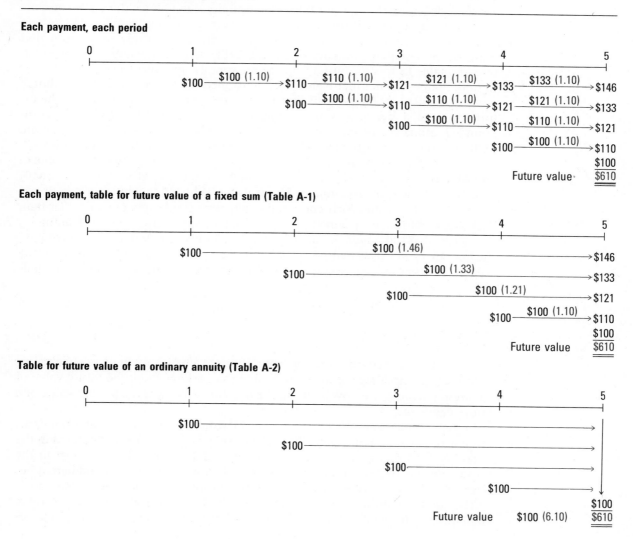

factors used in method (2) (6.10 = 1.46 + 1.33 + 1.21 + 1.10 + 1.00). Thus, the factor in Table A−2 for a given time period is simply the summation of the individual time period factors in Table A−1. Table A−2 is merely a short cut that makes it easier to compute the future values for ordinary annuities.

Think for a moment now about the simple interest factor $(1 + i)$. As we have discussed, the factors in Table A−1 are the simple interest factors compounded, or $(1 + i)^n$. A given factor in Table A−2 for a specified length of time is the result of adding together the compound factors for each component time period $[(1 + i)^n]$. Thus, the simple interest calculation underlies the factors in both Table A−1 and Table A−2. In each we have built upon the very fundamental notion of simple interest.

Future Value of an Annuity Due

Annuities are often paid at the beginning of each period rather than at the end. Such a series of equal cash payments is referred to as an **annuity due** and is frequently observed when, for example, lease agreements require payments in advance. Calculating the future value of an annuity due follows the same concepts as those for an ordinary annuity. The only difference comes from the obvious fact that annuity due payments come one period earlier and, thus, earn one period more of interest than ordinary annuities. Table A−3, following this appendix, provides table factors for future value of an annuity due calculations.

In the same manner that Figure A−2 illustrated the future value of an ordinary annuity calculation, Figure A−3 illustrates three approaches to computing the future value of a five-year annuity due, given a 10 percent interest rate compounded annually. Again, while all three methods come to the correct solution, Method 3, which uses the factor found on Table 3 (6.71), is by far the easiest.

Compare the computations on this chart to those illustrating the future value of an ordinary annuity on Figure A−2. The future value here is $61 ($671 − $610) greater than the ordinary annuity future value. Why? This difference can be explained by the fact that each annuity due payment comes one period earlier than each ordinary annuity payment and thus earns more interest over the annuity's life. The fifth $100 payment earns an extra $10 over one period, the fourth payment an extra $11 over two periods, the third an extra $12 over three periods, the second an extra $13 over four periods, and the first an extra $15 over five periods (61 = 10 + 11 + 12 + 13 + 15).

Present Value

Now that we have covered the concept of future value it should be relatively easy to look at the other side of the coin. Rather than asking about the future value of a current payment, we now focus on the question, "What is the present value of a future payment?"

In the original example, we stated that $1 would grow to $1.10 after one year, given a 10 percent interest rate. This relationship can just as easily be stated in the opposite way. That is, $1 is the present value of $1.10 received one year in the future, given a 10 percent interest rate. As investors, we would be indifferent between $1 now (the present value) or $1.10 (future value) one year in the future.

The computation of present value is exactly the reciprocal of the future value computation. Recall that the simple interest factor for the future value in one pe-

Figure A-3 Future value of an annuity due

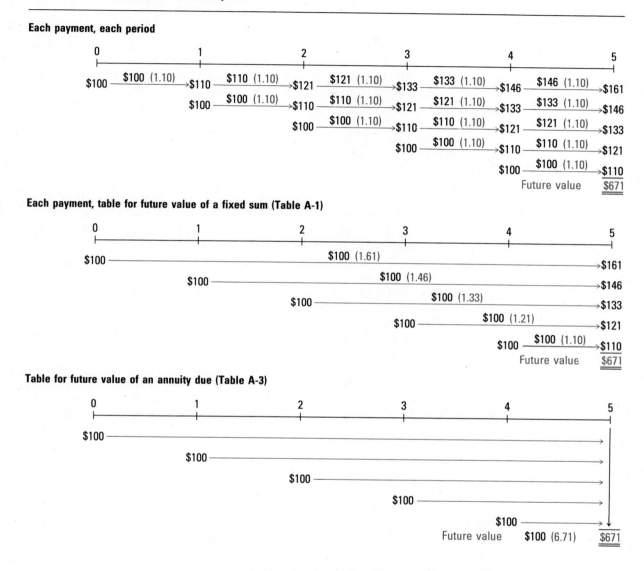

Each payment, each period

Each payment, table for future value of a fixed sum (Table A-1)

Table for future value of an annuity due (Table A-3)

riod at 10 percent interest is $(1 + i)$. The simple interest factor for present value is the reciprocal, $1 \div (1 + i)$. In the future value example presented earlier $\$1 \times (1 + .10)$ equaled $\$1.10$, the future value. To compute the present value, we simply multiply $\$1.10$ by $1 \div (1 + .10)$ to arrive at $\$1$. The present value computation is illustrated as follows.

Now ⟵——————— 1 year
$1 ⟵——————— $1.10

If the present value computation involves more than one period, just as in the future value case, the notion of compounding must be considered. The present value factor, once again, is simply the reciprocal of the future value factor, $1 \div (1 + i)^n$. A two-period, 10 percent interest rate example follows.

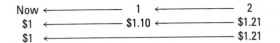

This example demonstrates that the present values of both $1.21 in two years and $1.10 in one year are equal to $1, given a 10 percent interest rate compounded annually. In such a case, an investor would be indifferent among having $1 now, receiving $1.10 in one year, or receiving $1.21 in two years. The example also shows that the present value of a future payment can be calculated in several different ways.

As for future values, there are tables (Tables A−4, A−5, and A−6 following this appendix) designed to expedite the computations required to calculate present values. The factors contained in these tables are the reciprocals of the corresponding factors in the future value tables. Table A−4 contains the table factors for the present values of single payments in the future. In the illustration above one could use the table by multiplying $1.21 by .826 (Table A−4, $n = 2$, $i = 10\%$) to arrive at the $1 present value. Obviously, as the number of time periods increases, the time savings from using the tables also increases.

Present values for ordinary annuities and annuities due must also be computed from time to time, and Table A−5 (ordinary annuity) and Table A−6 (annuity due) are designed for that purpose. As with future values, there are basically three ways to compute the present value of ordinary annuity and annuity due payment streams; they are depicted in Figures A−4 (ordinary annuity) and A−5 (annuity due). In both cases a $100, five-year annuity at a 10 percent interest rate is illustrated.

Again compare the two charts, and note that the present value of an annuity due is $38 ($417 − $379) greater than the present value of the ordinary annuity. The fact that each of the five payments in the annuity due is one period earlier than the corresponding ordinary annuity payment accounts for this difference.

An Illustration

Students often quickly grasp the general concepts of future and present value yet still have difficulty making the appropriate computations for a specific problem. We have designed the following example to demonstrate how straightforward future and present value computations can be, and also how many different ways one can approach the same problem. We also introduce a concept we call **equivalent value.** It can be useful in understanding the notion of time value.

Assume a $500, five-year ordinary annuity at a 12 percent interest rate compounded annually. The cash flows are illustrated below. Let's see how many different ways we can compute the future and present value of this payment stream. Five such examples are shown in Figure A−6.

Can you follow each of the five methods shown? Note that each method brings you to a future value of $3176 and a present value of $1804. No matter how many different ways one tackles this problem, the same future and present values emerge.

Figure A–4 Present value of an ordinary annuity

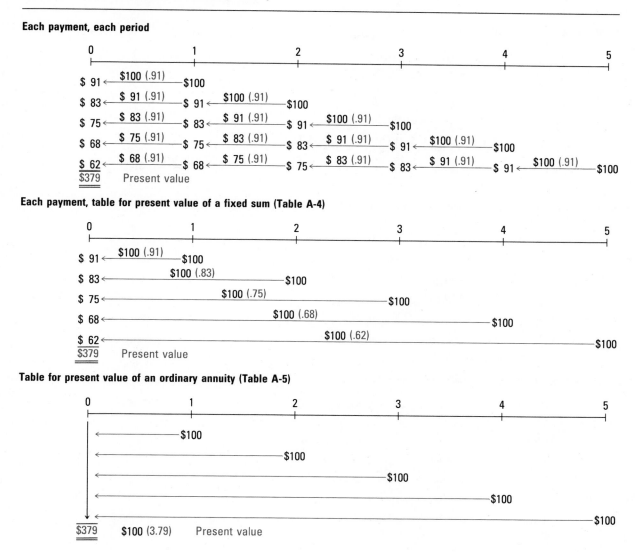

Each payment, each period

Each payment, table for present value of a fixed sum (Table A-4)

Table for present value of an ordinary annuity (Table A-5)

Equivalent Value

To understand the concept of equivalent value, view the $500 annuity payments, the present value, and the future value as being indifference amounts. That is, in this example an investor would be indifferent among a five-year, $500 ordinary annuity, $1804 now, or $3176 five years from now. These three payments are, in other words, equivalent in value.

The idea of equivalent value is further illustrated in the fifth computation in Figure A–6. It involves two steps. We first compute the amount that would be equivalent to the five-year ordinary annuity if one lump sum were received at the end of Period 3 ($2533). This amount is the equivalent value of this particular annuity at the end of Period 3. We then adjust this amount to present or future

Figure A–5   Present value of an annuity due

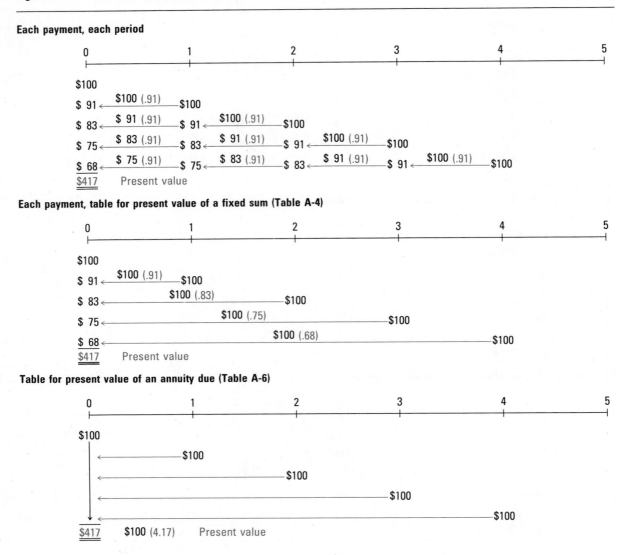

value by multiplying it by the appropriate table factor. Figure A–7 illustrates the equivalent values of the five-year ordinary annuity if lump-sum payments were made at the end of each of the five periods.

Figure A–7 demonstrates that given a 12 percent interest rate compounded annually, an investor would be indifferent among the following seven payments. Can you derive these amounts?

1. a five-year, $500 ordinary annuity
2. $1804 now (present value)
3. $2021 at the end of one year

Figure A–6 Example calculations

Future Value	Present Value

Future Value

1. Each payment, each period

$500 (1.12) (1.12) (1.12) (1.12) =	$ 787
$500 (1.12) (1.12) (1.12) =	702
$500 (1.12) (1.12) =	627
$500 (1.12) =	560
$500 =	500
Future value	$3,176

2. Each payment individually

$500 (1.574) =	$ 787
500 (1.405) =	702
500 (1.254) =	627
500 (1.120) =	560
500 (1.000) =	500
Future value	$3,176

3. Ordinary annuity table

Future value $500 (6.353) = $3,176

4. Compute present value and then compute future value of present value

A. Present value

$500 (3.604) = $1,802

B. Future value

$1,802 (1.7623)   = $3,176

5. Compute equivalent value at Period 3 and then compute future value of that number

A. Value at Period 3

$ 500 (1.254) =	$ 627
500 (1.120) =	560
500 (1.000) =	500
500 (.893) =	447
500 (.797) =	399
	$2,533

B. Future value

$2,533 (1.254)   = $3,176

*Rounding difference

Present Value

Each payment, each period

500 (.893) (.893) (.893) (.893) (.893) =	$ 284
500 (.893) (.893) (.893) (.893) =	318
500 (.893) (.893) (.893) =	356
500 (.893) (.893) =	399
500 (.893) =	447
Present value	$1,804

Each payment individually

$500 (.567) =	$ 284
500 (.636) =	318
500 (.712) =	356
500 (.797) =	399
500 (.893) =	447
Present value	$1,804

Ordinary annuity table

Present value $500 (3.604) = $1,802*

Compute future value and then compute present value of future value

A. Future value

$ 500 (6.353) = $3,176

B. Present value

$3,176 (.5674)   = $1,802*

Compute equivalent value at Period 3 and then compute present value of that number

A. Value at Period 3

$500 (1.12) (1.12) =	$ 627
$500 (1.12) =	560
500 (1.00) =	500
500 (.893) =	447
500 (.893) (.893) =	399
	$2,533

B. Present value

$2,533 (.712)   = $1,804

4. $2262 at the end of two years
5. $2533 at the end of three years
6. $2839 at the end of four years
7. $3176 at the end of five years (future value)

Figure A-7   Equivalent values

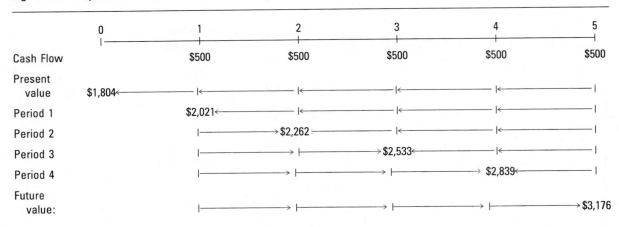

PRESENT VALUE AND FINANCIAL ACCOUNTING

We stated earlier that present value is the economic form of valuation. Investors, creditors, and managers use it to compare the values of alternative investments. Bankers, lawyers, and other business decision makers use it to derive the terms of contracts like mortgages, leases, pensions, and life insurance. Virtually any transaction that can be broken down into periodic cash flows utilizes the time value of money concept and can be reduced to present value, future value, and other equivalent values. The time value of money is covered in finance, economics, accounting, and other business courses. You may have already studied present value in previous courses, and you will probably see it again in the future. The uses of present value in business decision making are almost limitless.

The study of financial accounting in its reliance on the time value of money concept is no exception. As you already know, financial accounting information is useful because it helps investors, creditors, and other interested parties evaluate and control the business decisions of management. In other words, financial accounting is used to assess value: the value of entire companies, the value of individual assets and liabilities, and the value of specific transactions. Since present value is the economic form of valuation, financial accounting information must reflect present value if it is to be useful.

However, a critical problem is associated with using present value on the financial statements. The present value calculation requires that both future cash flows and future interest rates be predicted. In the vast majority of cases, predicting the future cash flows associated with a particular asset or liability with a reasonable degree of confidence is almost impossible. For example, how would one go about predicting the future cash inflows and outflows associated with the purchase of a specific piece of equipment like an automobile? Moreover, accurately predicting interest rates has for years eluded even the best economists. The predictions that management must make to apply present value are simply too subjective for financial statements that are to be used by those outside the company. Auditors are unwilling and unable to verify such subjective judgments. The legal liability faced by both managers and auditors makes such verification potentially very costly.

For these reasons, although present value remains the goal of financial measurement, most of the valuation bases on the financial statements represent surrogate (substitute) measures of present value. Historical cost, fair market value, replacement cost, and net realizable value can all be viewed as surrogate measures of present value. These valuation bases are used primarily because present value is simply too subjective and unreliable for a system that requires auditors to verify financial statements prepared by management for stockholders and other outside interested parties. Present value calculations, in general, violate the principle of objectivity.

In some cases, however, the future cash flows associated with an asset or a liability are predictable enough to allow for sufficiently objective present value calculations. As discussed in Chapters 5, 11, and 13, contractual agreements like notes receivable and payable meet the criterion of objectivity. Mortgages, bonds, leases, and pensions are other examples of contracts that underlie cash flows and thus remove much of the subjectivity associated with cash flow prediction. In these cases present values are incorporated into the financial statements.

In summary, there are two reasons why accounting students must understand present value. First, present value is the economic form of valuation and is therefore the ultimate goal of accounting measurement. It is the standard against which all financial accounting measurements must be compared and evaluated. Second, in those cases where cash flow prediction is sufficiently objective (e.g., contracts), present value methods are used, and present values are actually incorporated into the financial statements. The balance-sheet valuation base of the assets and liabilities arising from such contracts is present value.

EXERCISES

EA–1

(Future values) Ben Watson found $20,000 lying on the sidewalk and decided to invest the money. He believes that he can earn a 10 percent rate (compounded annually) on his investment for the first four years, 12 percent for the following three years, and 15 percent for the following five years.

Required: How much money will Ben have at the end of the following time periods?

a. 4 years

b. 7 years

c. 12 years

EA–2

(Present value of future bond payments—ordinary annuity and annuity due) Rudnicki Corporation raises money by issuing bonds. The bond agreement states that Rudnicki must make interest payments in the amount of $50,000 at the end of each year for ten years and make a $500,000 payment at the end of the tenth year. Assume that the discount rate is 12 percent.

Required:

a. What amount, as a lump sum, would the company have to invest today to meet the $50,000 annual interest payments and the $500,000 principal payment at the end of the tenth year?

b. What amount would have to be invested if the bond agreement stated that the interest payments were to be made at the beginning of each of the ten years?

EA-3

(The highest present value?) Congratulations! You have just won the lottery. The lottery board offers you three different options for collecting your winnings:

1. You will receive payments of $500,000 at the end of each year for twenty years.
2. You will receive a lump-sum payment of $4,500,000 today.
3. You will receive a lump-sum payment of $1 million today and payments of $2,100,000 at the end of Years 5, 6, and 7.

Assume that all earnings can be invested at a 10 percent annual rate.

Required: Determine which option has the highest present value.

EA-4

(Comparing ordinary annuities and annuities due) Consider a three-year $800 ordinary annuity (the first payment is one year from now) and a three-year $800 annuity due (the first payment is now). Assume a discount rate of 10 percent.

Required: For each of the two annuities compute the equivalent value as of the following points in time.

a. Now
b. The end of Period 1.
c. The end of Period 2.
d. The end of Period 3.
e. Which of the above is referred to as the present value?
f. Which of the above is referred to as the future value?

EA-5

(Different terms of financing) Dunn Drafting Company is considering expanding its business. Because of constraints on how much the company can spend for new equipment, the president wants to make sure that the company enters into the best possible deal. Dunn Drafting has four options for paying for the new equipment.

1. Make a lump-sum payment of $240,000 today.
2. Make a lump-sum payment of $500,000 eight years from now.
3. Make a lump-sum payment of $600,000 ten years from now.
4. Make payments of $50,000 at the beginning of each year for six years. The first payment is due now.

Required:

a. Compute the present value of each option. Assume the relevant interest rate is 12 percent.
b. If you were the president of Dunn Drafting Company, which option would you select?
c. Would your answer to (b) change if the annual interest rate was 8 percent? If so, which option would you now prefer?

EA-6

(Saving for a college education—future value) The Croziers have a three-year-old son named Ryan, and they want to provide for Ryan's college education. They estimate that it will cost $35,000 per year for four years when Ryan enters college fifteen years from now. Assume that all investments can earn a 10 percent annual interest rate, and that the four annual payments will be made at the end of each year.

Required:

a. How much would the Croziers have to invest today to meet Ryan's college expenses?
b. How much would the Croziers have to invest at the end of each year for fifteen years to meet Ryan's college expenses?
c. Answer questions (a) and (b) above assuming an 8 percent annual interest rate.

PROBLEMS

PA–1

(The value of common stocks)   Christie Bauer is contemplating investing in South Bend Iron-works. She estimates that the company will pay the following dividends per share over the next four years, and that the current price of the company's common stock ($100) will remain unchanged.

Year 1	Year 2	Year 3	Year 4
$5	$6	$7	$8

Christie wants to earn 15 percent on her investment.

Required: Assume that Christie plans to sell the investment at the end of the fourth year. How much would she be willing to pay for one share of common stock in South Bend Iron-works?

PA–2

(Computing future value, present value, and equivalent value)   Wharton Company is planning to make the following investments.

(1) $1000 at the end of each year for five years at a 10 percent annual rate. Wharton Company will leave the accumulated principal and earnings in the bank for another five years at a 12 percent annual rate.

(2) $3000 at the end of each year for seven years at a 15 percent annual rate. Wharton will not make the first $3000 payment until 4 years from now.

Required:

a. How much money will Wharton have at the end of ten years?

b. How much would Wharton have to invest in a lump sum today to have an equivalent amount at the end of ten years, given a 12 percent annual rate of return?

PA–3

(Computing present value and equivalent value of contracted cash flows)   The terms of three different contracts follow.

1. $8000 received at the beginning of each year for ten years, compounded at a 6 percent annual rate.

2. $8000 received today and $20,000 received ten years from today. The relevant interest rate is 12 percent.

3. $8000 received at the end of Years 4, 5, and 6. The relevant annual interest rate is 10 percent.

Required:

a. Compute the present value of each contract.

b. Compute the equivalent value of each contract at the end of Years 5 and 10.

PA–4

(The highest present value?)   J. Hartney, president of Doyle Industries, has a choice of three bonus contracts. The first option is to receive an immediate cash payment of $25,000. The second option is a deferred payment of $60,000, to be received in eight years. The final option is to receive an immediate cash payment of $5000, a deferred payment of $27,000 to be received in three years, and a deferred payment of $20,000 to be received in twenty years. Assume that the relevant interest rate is 9 percent. Which bonus option has the highest present value?

PA–5

(Computing equivalent values)   Boulder Wilderness Adventures purchased rafting and kay-aking equipment by issuing a note to Recreational Co-op, the seller of the equipment. The note required a down payment of $5000, annual payments of $10,000 at the end of each year for five years (the first payment to be one year from now), and a final payment of

$15,000 at the end of the fifth year (this payment is in addition to the $10,000 annual payments). Assume that 8 percent is the relevant annual interest rate.

Required: Recreational Co-op is indifferent between receiving the cash flows described above or any other cash flow that represents an equivalent value. Compute equivalent values as of the following points in time.

a. Today
b. At the end of two years
c. At the end of four years
d. At the end of five years

PA–6   *(Present and future values)*   Assume an annual interest rate of 12 percent for each of the following independent cases. Compute the value at time 0 and the value at the end of the investment period for all the cash flows described.

a. $10,000 is invested and held for four years.
b. $2000 is invested at the end of each year for eight years.
c. $5000 is invested at the beginning of each year for three years.
d. $3000 is invested at the end of each year for five years. The balance is left to accumulate interest for an additional five years.
e. A company will receive $25,000 at the end of seven years.
f. A company will receive $3000 at the end of each year for two years.
g. A company will receive $4000 at the beginning of each year for three years.

PA–7   *(Present value of a note receivable and inferring the effective interest rate)*   Joy Don Corp. sells a building to Trifle and Life in exchange for a note. The note specifies a lump-sum payment of $300,000 ten years in the future and annual payments (beginning today) of $2000 at the beginning of each year for ten years. Assume an annual interest rate of 10 percent.

Required:

a. Would Joy Don be wise to accept $110,000 now instead of the note?
b. At what interest rate, to the nearest integer, would Joy Don be wise to accept the $110,000 instead of the note? (*Hint:* Use a trial and error approach. The answer is an integer.)

Table A–1   Future value of $1 (future amount of single sum)

Periods (n)	2%	3%	4%	5%	6%	7%	8%
1	1.02000	1.03000	1.04000	1.05000	1.06000	1.07000	1.08000
2	1.04040	1.06090	1.08160	1.10250	1.12360	1.14490	1.16640
3	1.06121	1.09273	1.12486	1.15763	1.19102	1.22504	1.25971
4	1.08243	1.12551	1.16986	1.21551	1.26248	1.31080	1.36049
5	1.10408	1.15927	1.21665	1.27628	1.33823	1.40255	1.46933
6	1.12616	1.19405	1.26532	1.34010	1.41852	1.50073	1.58687
7	1.14869	1.22987	1.31593	1.40710	1.50363	1.60578	1.71382
8	1.17166	1.26677	1.36857	1.47746	1.59385	1.71819	1.85093
9	1.19509	1.30477	1.42331	1.55133	1.68948	1.83846	1.99900
10	1.21899	1.34392	1.48024	1.62889	1.79085	1.96715	2.15892
11	1.24337	1.38423	1.53945	1.71034	1.89830	2.10485	2.33164
12	1.26824	1.42576	1.60103	1.79586	2.01220	2.25219	2.51817
15	1.34587	1.55797	1.80094	2.07893	2.39656	2.75903	3.17217
20	1.48595	1.80611	2.19112	2.65330	3.20714	3.86968	4.66096
30	1.81136	2.42726	3.24340	4.32194	5.74349	7.61226	10.06266
40	2.20804	3.26204	4.80102	7.03999	10.28572	14.97446	21.72452

Periods (n)	9%	10%	11%	12%	14%	15%
1	1.09000	1.10000	1.11000	1.12000	1.14000	1.15000
2	1.18810	1.21000	1.23210	1.25440	1.29960	1.32250
3	1.29503	1.33100	1.36763	1.40493	1.48154	1.52088
4	1.41158	1.46410	1.51807	1.57352	1.68896	1.74901
5	1.53862	1.61051	1.68506	1.76234	1.92541	2.01136
6	1.67710	1.77156	1.87041	1.97382	2.19497	2.31306
7	1.82804	1.94872	2.07616	2.21068	2.50227	2.66002
8	1.99256	2.14359	2.30454	2.47596	2.85259	3.05902
9	2.17189	2.35795	2.55804	2.77308	3.25195	3.51788
10	2.36736	2.59374	2.83942	3.10585	3.70722	4.04556
11	2.58043	2.85312	3.15176	3.47855	4.22623	4.65239
12	2.81266	3.13843	3.49845	3.89598	4.81790	5.35025
15	3.64248	4.17725	4.78459	5.47357	7.13794	8.13706
20	5.60441	6.72750	8.06231	9.64629	13.74349	16.36654
30	13.26768	17.44940	22.89230	29.95992	50.95016	66.21177
40	31.40942	45.25926	65.00087	93.05097	188.88351	267.86355

Table A-2   Future value of an ordinary annuity of $1

Periods (n)	2%	3%	4%	5%	6%	7%	8%
1	1.00000	1.00000	1.00000	1.00000	1.00000	1.00000	1.00000
2	2.02000	2.03000	2.04000	2.05000	2.06000	2.07000	2.08000
3	3.06040	3.09090	3.12160	3.15250	3.18360	3.21490	3.24640
4	4.12161	4.18363	4.24646	4.31013	4.37462	4.43994	4.50611
5	5.20404	5.30914	5.41632	5.52563	5.63709	5.75074	5.86660
6	6.30812	6.46841	6.63298	6.80191	6.97532	7.15329	7.33593
7	7.43428	7.66246	7.89829	8.14201	8.39384	8.65402	8.92280
8	8.58297	8.89234	9.21423	9.54911	9.89747	10.25980	10.63663
9	9.75463	10.15911	10.58280	11.02656	11.49132	11.97799	12.48756
10	10.94972	11.46388	12.00611	12.57789	13.18079	13.81645	14.48656
11	12.16872	12.80780	13.48635	14.20679	14.97164	15.78360	16.64549
12	13.41209	14.19203	15.02581	15.91713	16.86994	17.88845	18.97713
15	17.29342	18.59891	20.02359	21.57856	23.27597	25.12902	27.15211
20	24.29737	26.87037	29.77808	33.06595	36.78559	40.99549	45.76196
30	40.56808	47.57542	56.08494	66.43885	79.05819	94.46079	113.28321
40	60.40198	75.40126	95.02552	120.79977	154.76197	199.63511	259.05652

Periods (n)	9%	10%	11%	12%	14%	15%
1	1.00000	1.00000	1.00000	1.00000	1.00000	1.00000
2	2.09000	2.10000	2.11000	2.12000	2.14000	2.15000
3	3.27810	3.31000	3.34210	3.37440	3.43960	3.47250
4	4.57313	4.64100	4.70973	4.77933	4.92114	4.99338
5	5.98471	6.10510	6.22780	6.35285	6.61010	6.74238
6	7.52333	7.71561	7.91286	8.11519	8.53552	8.75374
7	9.20043	9.48717	9.78327	10.08901	10.73049	11.06680
8	11.02847	11.43589	11.85943	12.29969	13.23276	13.72682
9	13.02104	13.57948	14.16397	14.77566	16.08535	16.78584
10	15.19293	15.93742	16.72201	17.54874	19.33730	20.30372
11	17.56029	18.53117	19.56143	20.65458	23.04452	24.34928
12	20.14072	21.38428	22.71319	24.13313	27.27075	29.00167
15	29.36092	31.77248	34.40536	37.27971	43.84241	47.58041
20	51.16012	57.27500	64.20283	72.05244	91.02493	102.44358
30	136.30754	164.49402	199.02088	241.33268	356.78685	434.74515
40	337.88245	442.59256	581.82607	767.09142	1342.02510	1779.09031

Table A–3 Future value of an annuity due of $1

Periods (n)	2%	3%	4%	5%	6%	7%	8%
1	1.02000	1.03000	1.04000	1.05000	1.06000	1.07000	1.08000
2	2.06040	2.09090	2.12160	2.15250	2.18360	2.21490	2.24640
3	3.12161	3.18363	3.24646	3.31013	3.37462	3.43994	3.50611
4	4.20404	4.30914	4.41632	4.52563	4.63709	4.75074	4.86660
5	5.30812	5.46841	5.63298	5.80191	5.97532	6.15329	6.33593
6	6.43428	6.66246	6.89829	7.14201	7.39384	7.65402	7.92280
7	7.58297	7.89234	8.21423	8.54911	8.89747	9.25980	9.63663
8	8.75463	9.15911	9.58280	10.02656	10.49132	10.97799	11.48756
9	9.94972	10.46388	11.00611	11.57789	12.18079	12.81645	13.48656
10	11.16872	11.80780	12.48635	13.20679	13.97164	14.78360	15.64549
11	12.41209	13.19203	14.02581	14.91713	15.86994	16.88845	17.97713
12	13.68033	14.61779	15.62684	16.71298	17.88214	19.14064	20.49530
15	17.63929	19.15688	20.82453	22.65749	24.67253	26.88805	29.32428
20	24.78332	27.67649	30.96920	34.71925	38.99273	43.86518	49.42292
30	41.37944	49.00268	58.32834	69.76079	83.80168	101.07304	122.34587
40	61.61002	77.66330	98.82654	126.83976	164.04768	213.60957	279.78104

Periods (n)	9%	10%	11%	12%	14%	15%
1	1.09000	1.10000	1.11000	1.12000	1.14000	1.15000
2	2.27810	2.31000	2.34210	2.37440	2.43960	2.47250
3	3.57313	3.64100	3.70973	3.77933	3.92114	3.99338
4	4.98471	5.10510	5.22780	5.35285	5.61010	5.74238
5	6.52333	6.71561	6.91286	7.11519	7.53552	7.75374
6	8.20043	8.48717	8.78327	9.08901	9.73049	10.06680
7	10.02847	10.43589	10.85943	11.29969	12.23276	12.72682
8	12.02104	12.57948	13.16397	13.77566	15.08535	15.78584
9	14.19293	14.93742	15.72201	16.54874	18.33730	19.30372
10	16.56029	17.53117	18.56143	19.65458	22.04452	23.34928
11	19.14072	20.38428	21.71319	23.13313	26.27075	28.00167
12	21.95338	23.52271	25.21164	27.02911	31.08865	33.35192
15	32.00340	34.94973	38.18995	41.75328	49.98035	54.71747
20	55.76453	63.00250	71.26514	80.69874	103.76842	117.81012
30	148.57522	180.94342	220.91317	270.29261	406.73701	499.95692
40	368.29187	486.85181	645.82693	859.14239	1529.90861	2045.95385

Table A–4 Present value of $1 (present value of a single sum)

Periods (n)	2%	3%	4%	5%	6%	7%	8%
1	0.98039	0.97087	0.96154	0.95238	0.94340	0.93458	0.92593
2	0.96117	0.94260	0.92456	0.90703	0.89000	0.87344	0.85734
3	0.94232	0.91514	0.88900	0.86384	0.83962	0.81630	0.79383
4	0.92385	0.88849	0.85480	0.82270	0.79209	0.76290	0.73503
5	0.90573	0.86261	0.82193	0.78353	0.74726	0.71299	0.68058
6	0.88797	0.83748	0.79031	0.74622	0.70496	0.66634	0.63017
7	0.87056	0.81309	0.75992	0.71068	0.66506	0.62275	0.58349
8	0.85349	0.78941	0.73069	0.67684	0.62741	0.58201	0.54027
9	0.83676	0.76642	0.70259	0.64461	0.59190	0.54393	0.50025
10	0.82035	0.74409	0.67556	0.61391	0.55839	0.50835	0.46319
11	0.80426	0.72242	0.64958	0.58468	0.52679	0.47509	0.42888
12	0.78849	0.70138	0.62460	0.55684	0.49697	0.44401	0.39711
15	0.74301	0.64186	0.55526	0.48102	0.41727	0.36245	0.31524
20	0.67297	0.55368	0.45639	0.37689	0.31180	0.25842	0.21455
30	0.55207	0.41199	0.30832	0.23138	0.17411	0.13137	0.09938
40	0.45289	0.30656	0.20829	0.14205	0.09722	0.06678	0.04603
50	0.37153	0.22811	0.14071	0.08720	0.05429	0.03395	0.02132
60	0.30478	0.16973	0.09506	0.05354	0.03031	0.01726	0.00988

Periods (n)	9%	10%	11%	12%	14%	15%
1	0.91743	0.90909	0.90090	0.89286	0.87719	0.86957
2	0.84168	0.82645	0.81162	0.79719	0.76947	0.75614
3	0.77218	0.75131	0.73119	0.71178	0.67497	0.65752
4	0.70843	0.68301	0.65873	0.63552	0.59208	0.57175
5	0.64993	0.62092	0.59345	0.56743	0.51937	0.49718
6	0.59627	0.56447	0.53464	0.50663	0.45559	0.43233
7	0.54703	0.51316	0.48166	0.45235	0.39964	0.37594
8	0.50187	0.46651	0.43393	0.40388	0.35056	0.32690
9	0.46043	0.42410	0.39092	0.36061	0.30751	0.28426
10	0.42241	0.38554	0.35218	0.32197	0.26974	0.24718
11	0.38753	0.35049	0.31728	0.28748	0.23662	0.21494
12	0.35553	0.31863	0.28584	0.25668	0.20756	0.18691
15	0.27454	0.23939	0.20900	0.18270	0.14010	0.12289
20	0.17843	0.14864	0.12403	0.10367	0.07276	0.06110
30	0.07537	0.05731	0.04368	0.03338	0.01963	0.01510
40	0.03184	0.02209	0.01538	0.01075	0.00529	0.00373
50	0.01345	0.00852	0.00542	0.00346	0.00143	0.00092
60	0.00568	0.00328	0.00191	0.00111	0.00039	0.00023

Table A–5 Present value of an ordinary annuity of $1

Periods (n)	2%	3%	4%	5%	6%	7%	8%
1	0.98039	0.97087	0.96154	0.95238	0.94340	0.93458	0.92593
2	1.94156	1.91347	1.88609	1.85941	1.83339	1.80802	1.78326
3	2.88388	2.82861	2.77509	2.72325	2.67301	2.62432	2.57710
4	3.80773	3.71710	3.62990	3.54595	3.46511	3.38721	3.31213
5	4.71346	4.57971	4.45182	4.32948	4.21236	4.10020	3.99271
6	5.60143	5.41719	5.24214	5.07569	4.91732	4.76654	4.62288
7	6.47199	6.23028	6.00205	5.78637	5.58238	5.38929	5.20637
8	7.32548	7.01969	6.73274	6.46321	6.20979	5.97130	5.74664
9	8.16224	7.78611	7.43533	7.10782	6.80169	6.51523	6.24689
10	8.98259	8.53020	8.11090	7.72173	7.36009	7.02358	6.71008
11	9.78685	9.25262	8.76048	8.30641	7.88687	7.49867	7.13896
12	10.57534	9.95400	9.38507	8.86325	8.38384	7.94269	7.53608
15	12.84926	11.93794	11.11839	10.37966	9.71225	9.10791	8.55948
20	16.35143	14.87747	13.59033	12.46221	11.46992	10.59401	9.81815
30	22.39646	19.60044	17.29203	15.37245	13.76483	12.40904	11.25778
40	27.35548	23.11477	19.79277	17.15909	15.04630	13.33171	11.92461
50	31.42361	25.72976	21.48218	18.25593	15.76186	13.80075	12.23348
60	34.76089	27.67556	22.62349	18.92929	16.16143	14.03918	12.37655

Periods (n)	9%	10%	11%	12%	14%	15%
1	0.91743	0.90909	0.90090	0.89286	0.87719	0.86957
2	1.75911	1.73554	1.71252	1.69005	1.64666	1.62571
3	2.53129	2.48685	2.44371	2.40183	2.32163	2.28323
4	3.23972	3.16987	3.10245	3.03735	2.91371	2.85498
5	3.88965	3.79079	3.69590	3.60478	3.43308	3.35216
6	4.48592	4.35526	4.23054	4.11141	3.88867	3.78448
7	5.03295	4.86842	4.71220	4.56376	4.28830	4.16042
8	5.53482	5.33493	5.14612	4.96764	4.63886	4.48732
9	5.99525	5.75902	5.53705	5.32825	4.94637	4.77158
10	6.41766	6.14457	5.88923	5.65022	5.21612	5.01877
11	6.80519	6.49506	6.20652	5.93770	5.45273	5.23371
12	7.16073	6.81369	6.49236	6.19437	5.66029	5.42062
15	8.06069	7.60608	7.19087	6.81086	6.14217	5.84737
20	9.12855	8.51356	7.96333	7.46944	6.62313	6.25933
30	10.27365	9.42691	8.69379	8.05518	7.00266	6.56598
40	10.75736	9.77905	8.95105	8.24378	7.10504	6.64178
50	10.96168	9.91481	9.04165	8.30450	7.13266	6.66051
60	11.04799	9.96716	9.07356	8.32405	7.14011	6.66515

Table A–6   Present value of an annuity due of $1

Periods (n)	2%	3%	4%	5%	6%	7%	8%
1	1.00000	1.00000	1.00000	1.00000	1.00000	1.00000	1.00000
2	1.98039	1.97087	1.96154	1.95238	1.94340	1.93458	1.92593
3	2.94156	2.91347	2.88609	2.85941	2.83339	2.80802	2.78326
4	3.88388	3.82861	3.77509	3.72325	3.67301	3.62432	3.57710
5	4.80773	4.71710	4.62990	4.54595	4.46511	4.38721	4.31213
6	5.71346	5.57971	5.45182	5.32948	5.21236	5.10020	4.99271
7	6.60143	6.41719	6.24214	6.07569	5.91732	5.76654	5.62288
8	7.47199	7.23028	7.00205	6.78637	6.58238	6.38929	6.20637
9	8.32548	8.01969	7.73274	7.46321	7.20979	6.97130	6.74664
10	9.16224	8.78611	8.43533	8.10782	7.80169	7.51523	7.24689
11	9.98259	9.53020	9.11090	8.72173	8.36009	8.02358	7.71008
12	10.78685	10.25262	9.76048	9.30641	8.88687	8.49867	8.13896
15	13.10625	12.29607	11.56312	10.89864	10.29498	9.74547	9.24424
20	16.67846	15.32380	14.13394	13.08532	12.15812	11.33560	10.60360
30	22.84438	20.18845	17.98371	16.14107	14.59072	13.27767	12.15841
40	27.90259	23.80822	20.58448	18.01704	19.94907	14.26493	12.87858
50	32.05208	26.50166	22.34147	19.16872	16.70757	14.76680	13.21216
60	35.45610	28.50583	23.52843	19.87575	17.13111	15.02192	13.36668

Periods (n)	9%	10%	11%	12%	14%	15%
1	1.00000	1.00000	1.00000	1.00000	1.00000	1.00000
2	1.91743	1.90909	1.90090	1.89286	1.87719	1.86957
3	2.75911	2.73554	2.71252	2.69005	2.64666	2.62571
4	3.53129	3.48685	3.44371	3.40183	3.32163	3.28323
5	4.23972	4.16987	4.10245	4.03735	3.91371	3.85498
6	4.88965	4.79079	4.69590	4.60478	4.43308	4.35216
7	5.48592	5.35526	5.23054	5.11141	4.88867	4.78448
8	6.03295	5.86842	5.71220	5.56376	5.28830	5.16042
9	6.53482	6.33493	6.14612	5.96764	5.63886	5.48732
10	6.99525	6.75902	6.53705	6.32825	5.94637	5.77158
11	7.41766	7.14457	6.88923	6.65022	6.21612	6.01877
12	7.80519	7.49506	7.20652	6.93770	6.45273	6.23371
15	8.78615	8.36669	7.98187	7.62817	7.00207	6.72448
20	9.95011	9.36492	8.83929	8.36578	7.55037	7.19823
30	11.19828	10.36961	9.65011	9.02181	7.98304	7.55088
40	11.72552	10.75696	9.93567	9.23303	8.09975	7.63805
50	11.94823	10.90630	10.03624	9.30104	8.13123	7.65959
60	12.04231	10.96387	10.07165	9.32294	8.13972	7.66492

Error Corrections

≡ **Errors** are inappropriate applications of information that is available at the time the error is committed. Included within the definition of errors are miscalculations (e.g., mathematical mistakes), oversights (e.g., failure to accrue or defer certain assets or liabilities), and the use of improper accounting methods (e.g., expensing what should have been capitalized). Totaling inventory account sheets incorrectly, failing to accrue interest payable on long-term loans, and expensing the costs of acquiring long-lived assets, for example, all represent accounting errors.

Most accounting errors give rise to the recognition of expenses or revenues in improper time periods. Such errors tend to correct themselves over time. To illustrate, assume that on January 1, 1986, FMC Corporation paid $3000 for insurance coverage to extend over the following three-year period. Mistakenly, management expensed the entire $3000 payment instead of capitalizing the cost and amortizing it over the life of the policy. Figure B−1 shows the journal entries representing (1) what FMC did, (2) what FMC should have done, and (3) the correcting entries that would be necessary if the error was discovered at different points in time (December 31, 1987, or December 31, 1988) during the three-year period.

Focus first on the journal entries *actually* recorded by FMC and the journal entries that *should* have been recorded by FMC. For the time being, ignore the correcting entries. Because of FMC's error, the entire $3000 of insurance expense is recognized in 1986, when $1000 should have been recognized in each of the three periods. Expenses are therefore overstated by $2000 in 1986 and understated by $1000 in both 1987 and 1988. Note, however, that the misstatements across the three-year period exactly counterbalance each other. The $2000 expense overstatement in 1986 is counterbalanced by the two $1000 expense understatements in 1987 and 1988. The total amount of expense recognized over

Figure B−1   Counterbalancing error

	January 1, 1986	December 31, 1986	December 31, 1987	December 31, 1988

What FMC did.	Insurance Exp. 3,000
	   Cash 3,000
	To record payment for
	  insurance coverage.
		No entry	No entry	No entry

What FMC should have done.	Prepaid Ins. 3,000
	   Cash 3,000
	To record payment for
	  insurance coverage.
		Insurance Exp. 1,000
		   Prepaid Ins. 1,000
		To amortize prepaid
		  insurance.
			Insurance Exp. 1,000
			   Prepaid Ins. 1,000
			To amortize prepaid
			  insurance.
				Insurance Exp. 1,000
				   Prepaid Ins. 1,000
				To amortize prepaid
				  insurance.

Correcting entry required if error is discovered at this time before closing.			Prepaid Ins. 1,000
			Insurance Exp. 1,000
			   Retained Earn. 2,000
			To correct error.
			  (If discovered before
			  closing on 12/31/87.)
				Insurance Exp. 1,000
				   Retained Earn. 1,000
				To correct error.
				  (If discovered before
				  closing on 12/31/88.)

Note: Insurance Exp. = Insurance Expense; Prepaid Ins. = Prepaid Insurance; Retained Earn. = Retained Earnings

the three-year period ($3000) is the same under either approach. Only the timing of the expense recognition differs.

Recall that expenses are closed into Retained Earnings at the end of each accounting period. It follows then that FMC's Retained Earnings balance is understated by $2000 after closing at the end of 1986, understated by $1000 after closing at the end of 1987, and stated correctly after closing at the end of 1988. Similarly, the asset account, Prepaid Insurance, is understated by $2000 as of the end of 1986, understated by $1000 as of the end of 1987, and stated correctly as of 1988. With respect to both the income statement and the balance sheet, therefore, FMC's error completely corrected itself after closing at the end of the third year.

Generally accepted accounting principles require that if an error is discovered before it corrects itself, a correcting journal entry must be recorded to recognize the cumulative effect of the error and to restate the current financial statements to reflect the existing facts. Figure B−1 shows two such correcting entries: (a) if the error is discovered before closing on December 31, 1987 and (b) if the error is discovered before closing on December 31, 1988. These journal entries represent two independent cases.

If the error is discovered before closing at the end of 1987, the Retained Earnings account is credited for $2000 to correct the Retained Earnings understatement as of the end of 1986. Prepaid Insurance is debited for $1000 to reflect the fact that one year still remains on the insurance policy. This $1000 will be amortized during 1988. Insurance expense of $1000 is debited to recognize the amount of insurance that expired during 1987.[1]

If the error is not discovered until the end of 1988 (prior to closing), only Retained Earnings and Insurance Expense are adjusted. Retained Earnings is credited for $1000, to correct the understatement as of the end of 1987, and Insurance Expense of $1000 is recognized to reflect the amount of insurance that expired during 1988. If the error is not discovered until after it has corrected itself (after December 31, 1988), no correcting entry is necessary.

As briefly discussed in Chapter 14, correcting entries that adjust the Retained Earnings balance are known as *prior period adjustments*. Prior period adjustments are placed on the statement of retained earnings as adjustments to the beginning balance of Retained Earnings. An example of the financial statement disclosure of the December 31, 1987, correcting entry (see Figure B−1) on the statement of retained earnings appears in Figure B−2. Assume that FMC Corporation earned net income of $6000 and declared dividends of $5000 during 1987.

It is important to understand how and when errors correct themselves, because the answers to such questions have a bearing on the appropriate correcting journal entry. Errors discovered before they correct themselves, for example, require a correcting entry that can be prepared by following the three-step process shown in Figure B−3. Errors discovered after they correct themselves, on the other hand, require no entry.

The following section describes several different kinds of errors and demonstrates how they should be corrected. Study each example thoroughly. Correcting errors can be a challenging exercise that tests your understanding of how the financial statements relate to each other from one period to the next.

---

1. If the error is discovered after the books are closed on December 31, 1987, or shortly thereafter, Prepaid Insurance is debited, and Retained Earnings is credited for $1000 each.

Figure B-2   Example of correcting entry on statement of retained earnings

FMC Corporation Statement of Retained Earnings For the Year Ended December 31, 1987	
Beginning balance in retained earnings	$4,000
Plus: Prior period adjustment due to error correction	2,000
Restated beginning balance of retained earnings	6,000
Plus: Net income	6,000
Less: Cash dividends	5,000
Ending balance in retained earnings	$7,000

CORRECTING ERRORS: THREE EXAMPLES

Suppose that Acme Company began operations on January 1, 1988. You are the company's auditor, and on December 31, 1989, before the books are closed, you discover a series of accounting errors. The company prepares financial statements at the end of each year. The errors follow.

1. Ending inventory was miscounted at the end of 1988. It was overstated by $2000. Acme uses the periodic inventory method, and inventory at the end of 1989 was correctly counted.

2. On January 1, 1988, Acme borrowed $54,000 from a bank, agreeing to repay $60,000 one year later. In line with the contract, Acme made the $60,000 cash payment on January 1, 1989, and the outstanding loan was retired. However, Acme neglected to accrue interest on December 31, 1988. Interest expense of $6000 was incorrectly recognized when the cash payment was made on January 1.

3. On January 1, 1988, Acme expensed two assets that should have been capitalized: (1) a $1000 insurance policy that was prepaid for two years and (2) a $5000 piece of equipment with a five-year useful life (assume no salvage value and that the equipment should have been depreciated using the straight-line method).

Figure B-3   Correcting an error: a three-step process

1. Retained earnings must be adjusted so that the effect of the error on the retained earnings account at the beginning of the period is corrected. This adjustment corrects the income statement effects of the error, which have accumulated in the retained earnings account from the time when the error was committed to the time of its discovery and correction.

2. The effects of the error on the income statement accounts of the current period must be corrected by adjusting the revenue and/or expense accounts affected.

3. The balance sheet accounts, other than retained earnings, must be adjusted so that they disclose the proper ending balance at the end of the current period.

Inventory Error

Recall the formulas for cost of goods sold and net income:

Net Sales
Less: Cost of Goods Sold (Beginning Inventory + Net Purchases − Ending Inventory)
Less: <u>Expenses</u>
Net Income

In view of the formula, the $2000 ending inventory overstatement at the end of 1988 resulted in an understatement of the cost of goods sold. This misstatement, in turn, caused a $2000 overstatement of net income. Net income was subsequently closed to Retained Earnings at the end of 1988, so Retained Earnings as of December 31, 1988 was also overstated by $2000. Ending inventory of 1988 represents beginning inventory of 1989. The $2000 error at the end of 1988, therefore, resulted in an overstatement of beginning inventory and an overstatement of the cost of goods sold for 1989.

Consequently, both Retained Earnings as of December 31, 1988, and Cost of Goods Sold for 1989 are misstated. The following correcting entry, recorded as of the end of 1989, restates Cost of Goods Sold and the beginning balance of Retained Earnings. The Inventory account need not be adjusted because ending inventory for 1989 was correctly counted.

Retained Earnings	2000	
Cost of Goods Sold		2000
To correct Cost of Goods Sold and the beginning balance in Retained Earnings.		

This correcting entry is required if the error is discovered before the books are closed on December 31, 1989. Had the error been discovered after closing on that date, during 1990 for example, no correcting entry would have been necessary. Net income for 1989 would have been understated by $2000. This understated amount would have been closed to Retained Earnings, which in turn would have counterbalanced the overstatement in Retained Earnings from 1988. With respect to retained earnings, the error would have corrected itself.

Accrued Interest Neglected

Acme ignored accrued interest on December 31, 1988, and you discover this error on December 31, 1989. To determine the appropriate correcting entry, it is helpful to compare what Acme actually did with what it should have done. Figure B−4 shows the sequence of journal entries that Acme recorded (indicated as "What Acme did.") and the sequence of journal entries that should have been recorded (indicated as "What Acme should have done.").

The fundamental difference between the two approaches illustrated in Figure B−4 is the timing of the $6000 interest expense. Acme actually recognized the interest expense incorrectly in 1989, when it should have been recognized in 1988. As a result, Interest Expense for 1989 must be reduced by $6000 and the beginning balance of Retained Earnings must be restated to correct the failure to record interest expense in 1988. The correcting entry follows.

Retained Earnings	6000	
Interest Expense		6000
To correct Interest Expense and the beginning balance in Retained Earnings.		

Figure B-4 Correcting an accrual error: Acme

	December 31, 1988	January 1, 1989

What Acme did.

No entry

Note Payable	54,000	
Interest Expense	6,000	
Cash		60,000

To record interest expense and principal payment on outstanding note payable.

What Acme should have done.

Interest Expense	6,000	
Interest Payable		6,000

To record interest expense on outstanding note payable.

Note Payable	54,000	
Interest Payable	6,000	
Cash		60,000

To record principal payment on outstanding note payable.

As with the preceding inventory error, had this error been discovered after closing in 1989, no correcting entry would have been necessary. The $6000 overstatement of net income in 1988 would have been counterbalanced by the $6000 understatement of net income in 1989.

Improper Expensing

On January 1, 1988, Acme expensed the costs of two assets that should have been capitalized and amortized: prepaid insurance and machinery. The $1000 cost of the insurance policy should have been capitalized and amortized at a rate of $500 during 1988 and 1989.[2] Acme's error, therefore, caused a $500 overstatement of insurance expense in 1988 and no insurance expense recognition in 1989. The following journal entry serves to correct the misstatement. Once again, had the error been discovered after closing on December 31, 1989, no correcting entry would have been necessary.

Insurance Expense	500	
Retained Earnings		500

To correct Insurance Expense and the beginning balance in Retained Earnings.

The $5000 piece of equipment should have been depreciated over its five-year useful life at a rate of $1000 per year. In error, Acme expensed the entire $5000 in the first year and allocated no expenses to later periods. Expenses are, therefore, overstated by $4000 in 1988 and, if left uncorrected, will be understated by $1000 in each of the four subsequent years. However, at the end of 1989, before the error had corrected itself, it was discovered. According to generally accepted

---

2. Acme expensed the entire cost of the insurance policy and made no adjusting entry at the end of the period to recognize the unexpired portion.

accounting principles, the error should be corrected as of December 31, 1989. The appropriate entry, which gives rise to a prior period adjustment, follows.

Equipment	5000	
Depreciation Expense	1000	
Accumulated Depreciation		2000
Retained Earnings		4000

To correct Depreciation Expense, the balance-sheet value of the machinery account, and the beginning balance in Retained Earnings.

The debit to Equipment for $5000 records the original cost of the equipment on the balance sheet. The debit to Depreciation Expense for $1000 recognizes the appropriate amount of depreciation for the second period ($5000/5 years). The $2000 credit to Accumulated Depreciation records on the balance sheet the amount of accumulated depreciation that would have been on the books had Acme originally capitalized the cost of the equipment and depreciated it at a rate of $1000 per year (2 years × $1000 per year). The $4000 credit to Retained Earnings is necessary because $5000 of expenses were closed to Retained Earnings in 1988 when only $1000 should have been. Future depreciation will be at the rate of $1000 per year ($5000/5 years).

CORRECTING ERRORS AND REVISING ESTIMATES DISTINGUISHED

Do not confuse errors with inexact estimates, which are an important part of the financial accounting process. Indeed, much of the information in the financial statements is the result of approximations and judgments about the future. The role and importance of estimates in accounting for accounts receivable (i.e., bad debt estimate), long-lived assets (i.e., estimated life and salvage value), and liabilities (e.g., warranty estimates) has already been discussed.

Estimates, by definition, are rarely correct. Almost without exception they turn out to be a little too high or a little too low. Occasionally, in light of new information, estimates need to be revised. Unlike correcting an error, however, revising an estimate does not require a correcting journal entry. Instead, estimates are revised prospectively. That is, the accounting methods currently in use are simply continued and applied in accordance with the new information. An example of an estimate revision appears in Chapter 9, where we illustrate the accounting procedures involved when the estimated useful life of a long-lived asset is revised.

Although the revision of an estimate does not involve a correcting entry, generally accepted accounting principles require that its effect on income be disclosed in the footnotes to the financial statements. The excerpt below, which illustrates such a disclosure, is from the 1987 financial report of Time, Inc.

Change in Estimate: In the first quarter of 1986 the Company changed the rate of amortization of its pay-TV programming costs to more closely reflect audience viewing patterns. The effect of this change was to reduce [reported] programming costs by $58 million and $57 million, resulting in increased net income of $35 million and $31 million, or $.58 per share and $.49 per share during 1987 and 1986, respectively.

EXERCISES

EB-1

(Misstatements due to accounting errors)   Wetzel Real Estate, Inc., owns several buildings and rents out office space. On January 1, 1990, the company collected $450,000 in cash from one of its tenants. The $450,000 represents the tenant's rent for the period of time from January 1, 1990 to December 31, 1992. Wetzel's bookkeeper made the following entry.

Cash	450,000	
Rent Revenue		450,000
To record the receipt of a rent payment.		

Wetzel Real Estate, Inc., did not make any adjusting entries related to the rent in 1990, 1991, or 1992. Ignore any tax effects of the error.

Required:

a. Complete a chart like the following.

	Rent Revenue per Company's Books	Correct Rent Revenue	Annual Difference	Cumulative Difference
1990				
1991				
1992				
Total				

b. In what direction and by how much will the rent revenue be misstated for 1992?

c. In what direction and by how much will the account Collections of Rent in Advance (Deferred Revenue) be misstated as of December 31, 1991?

d. In what direction and by how much will Retained Earnings be misstated after closing entries on December 31, 1991?

e. In what direction and by how much will Retained Earnings be misstated prior to the closing entries on December 31, 1991?

f. Is there some point at which the company's books will no longer be misstated? If so, when and why?

EB-2

(Correcting an expense that should have been capitalized)   On January 1, 1988, the accountant for Wetzel Corporation mistakenly expensed a $12,000 payment for an insurance policy that provided coverage for 1988, 1989, and 1990. Assume no income tax effect and that no adjusting entries were recorded relating to the policy in 1988, 1989, and 1990.

Required: Provide the correcting journal entries if the error is discovered before the books are closed on the following dates.

a. December 31, 1988

b. December 31, 1989

c. December 31, 1990

d. December 31, 1991

EB-3

(Different accounting treatments for errors and estimate revisions)   McDaniel International uses the straight-line method to depreciate its fixed assets. The company purchased an assembly-line workstation on January 1, 1988, for $500,000. The workstation's estimated useful life and salvage value were six years and $20,000, respectively. As of January 1, 1991, the balance in Accumulated Depreciation for this workstation equaled $240,000. During 1991 the company decided that the original estimate of the workstation's life was inaccurate and that it has a remaining useful life of five years (i.e., until 1996) with no change in the estimated salvage value.

Required:

a. Assume that the company treats this revision as an error. Prepare the appropriate entry (or entries) to correct the books and to record depreciation expense for 1991. Ignore any tax effects.

b. Assume that the company treats this revision as an estimate revision. Prepare the appropriate entry to record depreciation expense for 1991.

c. Which of the two accounting treatments is appropriate, and why?

EB–4

(Revision of estimate or accounting error?) Seger Distributors began operations in 1986 and has used the allowance method to account for bad debts. Each year bad debts have been estimated at 2 percent of credit sales.

	1986	1987	1988	1989
Credit sales	$24,000	$31,000	$35,000	$47,000
Account written off	700	500	750	1,000

At the end of 1989 the company's accountants, on the basis of past experience, decided that the annual bad debt estimate should be changed to 2.5 percent of credit sales.

Required:

a. Prepare a schedule of the activity in the Allowance for Uncollectibles account for 1986, 1987, and 1988.

b. Assume that the change to 2.5 percent is treated as the revision of an estimate. Provide the journal entry that would be recorded on December 31, 1989, to recognize the bad debt expense for that year.

c. Prepare a schedule of the activity in the Allowance for Uncollectibles account for 1986, 1987, and 1988, assuming that the 2.5 percent rate had been used since the company's inception. Assume no income tax effect.

d. Assume that the change to 2.5 percent is treated as the correction of an error. Provide the correcting entry that would be recorded on December 31, 1989.

e. Should the change to 2.5 percent be considered a revision of an estimate or the correction of an error? Explain.

EB–5

(Preparing the financial statements from an unadjusted trial balance) Clements, Inc. presents you with the following partial unadjusted trial balance as of December 31, 1988.

	Dr.	Cr.
Cash	1,205,000	
Inventory	900,000	
Fixed Assets	800,000	
Accumulated Depreciation		240,000
Dividends Payable		75,000
Common Stock		2,000,000
Retained Earnings		895,000
Sales		760,000
Sales Discounts	50,000	
Purchases	450,000	
Selling Expenses	225,000	
Purchase Returns		40,000
Loss from Flood (extraordinary)	565,000	
Gain on Sale of Marketable Securities		320,000
Dividends	200,000	
Adj. to Re. Earn. Due to Error made in a Prior Period		175,000
Administrative Expenses	110,000	
Total	4,505,000	4,505,000

Additional Information

1. All of the amounts shown are before taxes, and the company's tax rate is 34 percent.
2. The inventory balance above represents the inventory on hand as of January 1, 1988.
3. A count of inventory at the close of business on December 31, 1988 revealed that the company had $795,000 of inventory on hand.
4. The balance in Accumulated Depreciation represents the January 1, 1988 balance. The company uses straight-line depreciation and has depreciated its fixed assets at a rate of 10 percent of the cost per year. However, at the end of 1988 the company's accountants, on the basis of recent developments in the industry, decided to revise the depreciation rate to 12 percent of the cost.

Required:

a. Prepare an income statement (multistep format) for the year ended December 31, 1988.
b. Prepare a statement of retained earnings for the year ended December 31, 1988.

EB-6   *(Correcting errors due to inventory miscounts)*   Milton Enterprises included the following income statements in its 1991 financial report.

	1991	1990
Net sales	$800,000	$700,000
Less: Cost of goods sold	350,000	300,000
Gross profit	450,000	400,000
Operating expenses	300,000	275,000
Net income	$150,000	$125,000

In reviewing the company's inventory records, the following errors were discovered on January 1, 1992. Assume that the company had not closed its books for 1991.

1. The physical count on December 31, 1990, was overstated by $25,000.
2. The physical count on December 31, 1991, was understated by $40,000.

Required:

a. Prepare the entry necessary on January 1, 1992, to correct only the December 31, 1990 inventory error.
b. Prepare the entry necessary on January 1, 1992, to correct only the December 31, 1991 inventory error.
c. Prepare the entry necessary on January 1, 1992, to correct both the December 31, 1990, inventory error and the December 31, 1991 inventory error.
d. Compute corrected net income amounts for 1990 and 1991.

PROBLEMS

PB-1   *(Correcting a revenue that should have been deferred)*   On January 1, 1988, the accountant of Mayberry Township recorded as revenue a $16,000 cash receipt for services yet to be performed. On December 31, 1989, before the books are closed, you discover the error and note that 75 percent of the services had been performed as of that date: 25 percent in 1988 and 50 percent in 1989. Assume no income tax effect and that mistakenly no adjusting entries were recorded related to the service in 1988 and 1989. Prepare the correcting journal entry that would be recorded on December 31, 1989, before Mayberry's books are closed.

PB-2

(Misstatements due to accounting errors)   Data Analysis, Inc., purchased several computers on January 1, 1990, for a total cost of $500,000. The company's bookkeeper made the following entry to record the acquisition of the computers.

Depreciation Expense	500,000	
Cash		500,000
To record the purchase of computers.		

The computers have an estimated useful life of five years and an estimated salvage value of $75,000. Data Analysis, Inc., did not make any adjusting entry on December 31, 1990. Furthermore, the company never discovered the error. Ignore any tax effects of the error.

Required:

a. Assume that Data Analysis, Inc., uses the straight-line method to depreciate its fixed assets. Complete a chart like the following:

	Depreciation Expense per Company's Books	Correct Depreciation Expense	Annual Difference	Cumulative Difference
1990				
1991				
1992				
1993				
1994				
Total				

b. In what direction and by how much will Accumulated Depreciation be misstated as of December 31, 1993?

c. In what direction and by how much will Retained Earnings be misstated prior to closing entries on December 31, 1993?

d. In what direction and by how much will Retained Earnings be misstated after closing entries on December 31, 1993?

e. Is there some point at which the company's books will no longer be misstated? If so, when and why?

PB-3

(Revision of an accounting estimate)   Teledyne Communications purchased fixed assets in early 1984 for $500,000. At that time the company estimated the useful life and salvage value of the assets to be 20 years and $50,000, respectively. At the beginning of 1989, in view of recent technological developments, the company decided that the assets would be useful only an additional five years (i.e., until 12/31/93). The salvage value estimate was unchanged. The company uses the straight-line method of depreciation.

Required:

a. Prepare a schedule of Depreciation Expense and Accumulated Depreciation for 1984 through 1988.

b. How much Depreciation Expense will be recognized on December 31, 1989?

c. How much Depreciation Expense will be recognized during 1990?

d. Assume that the estimate revision is accounted for as an error, and provide the correcting cumulative journal entry that would be recorded on December 31, 1989. Assume no income tax effect.

e. Why is the situation described considered an estimate revision instead of an error, and why are estimate revisions accounted for prospectively?

PB-4

(Correcting errors)   The income statements for 1987, 1988, and 1989 of Wehylings Nursery follow.

	1989	1988	1987
Net sales	$46,000	$38,000	$35,000
Less: Cost of goods sold	30,000	25,000	21,000
Gross profit	16,000	13,000	14,000
Operating expenses	12,000	10,000	8,000
Net income	$ 4,000	$ 3,000	$ 6,000

A review of the records before the books are closed on December 31, 1989, uncovered the following errors.

1. Ending inventories on December 31, 1986, and December 31, 1988, were overstated by $3000. Ending inventories on December 31, 1987, and December 31, 1989, were correctly stated.

2. Cash received in 1988 in the amount of $4000 was incorrectly recorded as revenue. The revenue should have been recognized in 1989 when the company performed the contracted service.

3. Accrued interest expense in the amount of $1500 was ignored at the end of 1987. It was incorrectly recognized in 1988 when the interest payment was made. The same error, also in the amount of $1500, was committed at the end of 1988.

Required:

a. Prepare corrected income statements for 1987, 1988, and 1989.

b. Provide any correcting entries that should be recorded on December 31, 1989 (prior to closing entries) as the errors are discovered. Ignore income tax effects.

Accounting for Changing Prices: Inflation and Market Values

≡ The usefulness of financial statements is limited because (1) they are not adjusted for the effects of general inflation and (2) assets, especially inventories and long-lived assets, are normally carried at historical cost instead of current market value. Astute financial statement users can improve their assessments of earning power and solvency by adjusting the statements to reflect these two factors. This appendix covers such adjustments and discusses how they might lead to more meaningful financial statements.

GENERAL INFLATION: THE PROBLEM AND ADJUSTMENTS TO THE FINANCIAL STATEMENTS

Chapter 5 introduced the **stable dollar assumption** and noted that measuring a company's financial condition and performance requires a constant unit of measurement. Since the dollar is the unit of measurement in the United States, we are forced to assume that the **purchasing power** of the dollar, the amount of goods and services it can buy, is constant across time. The purchasing power of the dollar, however, is not stable.

The Extent of General Inflation

Inflation is a fact of life. Each year a dollar buys less and less as its purchasing power continues to erode. The U.S. government publishes statistics periodically that measure the extent of general inflation. These statistics are expressed in the form of general price-level indexes. One such index is called the **Consumer Price Index (CPI),** which expresses the prices of a general basket of consumer goods and services each year as a percentage of the price of the same goods and services from a selected base year that is chosen arbitrarily. The price level of the base year (1967) is set at 100, and the price level of each subsequent year is expressed as a percentage of the base. The CPI for selected years is provided in Figure C–1.

While inflation has calmed somewhat in recent years, it is clear from Figure C–1 that inflation is a significant economic phenomenon. Between 1967 (100) and 1984 (311), for example, the general price level in the United States more than tripled. That is, a dollar spent in 1984 purchased, on average, one-third as many goods and services as a dollar spent in 1967. From 1984 to 1988 the general price level increased by approximately 12 percent ([347 − 311]÷311).

Conventional Financial Statements Are Misstated

Because present-day, conventional financial statements are based on the stable dollar assumption, they ignore the effects of inflation. Such statements are measured in terms of **nominal dollars,** dollars of different levels of purchasing power. On a conventional balance sheet, for example, the costs of individual assets are added together in the computation of total assets, even though these assets were purchased in different time periods with dollars of different purchasing power. Such a practice leads to misstatements. Does it make sense, for example, to add the $10,000 cost of a fixed asset purchased in 1967 to the $10,000 cost of a fixed

Figure C–1 Selected consumer price indexes

Year	Consumer Price Index
1940	42
1950	72
1960	89
1967	100
1970	116
1980	247
1984	311
1985	322
1986	328
1987	334
1988	347*

Source: U.S. Department of Commerce, *Statistical Abstracts of the United States* (1988).
*Estimate based on the first nine months of 1988.

asset purchased in 1988, and come up with a $20,000 total? Of what economic meaning is this $20,000 total?

Consider for the moment what it would be like if the definition of a foot, another unit of measure, were to change from year to year. Suppose, for example, that 1 foot was 12 inches long as of the end of 1989, but was declared by the government to be only 10 inches long at the end of 1990. Assume further that a tree is measured at 1 foot as of the end of 1989 and grows 1 foot, as defined by the new government proclamation, during 1990. Is the tree 2 feet tall at the end of 1990? If you handled this question in the same way as it is treated in conventional (nominal dollar) financial statements, you would answer yes. However, in actuality the foot as a unit of measurement would have lost much of its meaning. A distinction now needs to be made between a 1989 foot and a 1990 foot. The tree is not 2 feet tall in terms of either measurement unit. It is 22 inches tall: 1.83 feet in terms of the 1989 unit of measurement and 2.2 feet in terms of the 1990 measure.

As a foot is important only in terms of the length it represents, a dollar is important only in terms of what it can buy—its purchasing power. Because the dollar's purchasing power varies from year to year, without an adjustment for inflation, conventional (nominal dollar) financial statements are misstated. Such misstatements which include misstatements of net income, assets, liabilities, and the related financial ratios, result from applying mathematical rules to nominal dollar amounts, which are not subject to valid mathematical analysis (i.e., addition, subtraction, multiplication, and division) because they do not share a common denominator. They reflect many different levels of purchasing power.

For example, the matching principle states that the cost of equipment purchased in 1984 should be capitalized and depreciated over the equipment's useful life. This process produces a measure of net income that is the result of subtracting expenses (depreciation), which are measured in dollars of 1984 purchasing power, from revenues, which are measured in dollars from later time periods with different levels of purchasing power. Net income is misstated because dollars of different purchasing power cannot validly be subtracted from one another. The revenue and expense measurements lack a common denominator.

Inflation Adjustments: An Overview

The objective of adjusting the financial statements for inflation is to find a common denominator that makes valid mathematical analysis possible. This objective is achieved by converting the nominal dollar values on conventional financial statements to dollar values that all reflect the purchasing power of the same year. The resulting, inflation-adjusted financial statements are expressed in dollars of the same purchasing power and, accordingly, are subject to valid mathematical analysis. Such statements are called **constant-dollar financial statements.**

The dollar amount of an item on a conventional financial statement can be adjusted to reflect the purchasing power of a given year by multiplying it by a ratio that relates the Consumer Price Index (CPI) of that year to the CPI of the year in which the item was originally acquired and recorded.[1] The result of this multiplication is an amount for the item that is restated in terms of dollars of that particular year. To illustrate this process, assume that you wish to restate the balance-sheet value of a tract of land that was purchased for $15,000 in 1980, when the price-level index was 247, to 1984 dollars (price-level index = 311). This restatement requires the computations in Figure C−2.

The dollar amount at which the land was originally recorded ($15,000) is multiplied times the ratio that divides the index in 1984 (311) by the index associated with the period (1980) when the land was acquired (247). The resulting number ($18,887) represents the balance-sheet (historical cost) value of the land in terms of 1984 dollars. Applying this same procedure to the items on a set of conventional financial statements would give rise to financial statements expressed in terms of constant 1984 dollars. The dollar amounts appearing on these inflation-adjusted statements could then more meaningfully be mathematically analyzed because they all share a common denominator: 1984 purchasing power. Net income, current assets, current liabilities, total assets, total liabilities, and the financial ratios would therefore be the result of valid mathematical operations.

This example describes, in general, how conventional financial statements can be restated in terms of constant 1984 dollars. Note that by changing the numerator of the conversion ratio to the purchasing power of any other year, this process can be used to restate conventional financial statements in terms of dollars of any time period. The remainder of this appendix restates the numbers on conventional financial statements to dollars as of the date of the most recent balance sheet. Financial statements as of December 31, 1988, for example, will be restated to constant 1988 dollars. Thus, land purchased in 1980 for $15,000 that appears on a conventional balance sheet dated December 31, 1988, will be restated to $21,073 ($15,000 × [347 ÷ 247]) in terms of 1988 dollars, the most recent common denominator.

Note also that the balance-sheet value of the land expressed in 1988 dollars ($21,073) is greater than its value expressed in 1980 dollars ($15,000). This difference arises from inflation: it took $21,073 in 1988 to buy the same basket of goods and services that $15,000 purchased in 1980. The restated dollar amount does not, however, represent the market value of the land in 1988. The $21,073 is still a measure of historical cost, expressed in 1988 dollars instead of 1980 dol-

---

1. This appendix uses the consumer price index (CPI) in the price-level adjustments primarily because in the past the FASB approved its use. However, other indexes, such as the Wholesale Price Index or the GNP Deflator, could also be used, and in certain cases these other indexes may be more appropriate.

Figure C–2 Restating land purchased in 1980 to 1984 dollars

Amount in 1980 Dollars		Conversion Ratio		Amount in 1984 Dollars
$15,000	×	(311 ÷ 247)	=	$18,887

lars, and it still suffers from the limitations associated with historical costs. Market values are determined by forces of supply and demand, which are not captured by simply adjusting the purchasing power of the measuring unit. Adjusting the financial statements to reflect market values is a different process and is discussed later in this appendix.

When restating the dollar amounts on conventional financial statements to reflect the purchasing power of the most recent year, balance sheet and income statement items should be adjusted separately. These adjustments are discussed in the following sections.

Adjusting Balance Sheet Items

When adjusting balance sheet items for general inflation, monetary items must be distinguished from nonmonetary items. This distinction and the methods used to adjust monetary and nonmonetary items for the effects of inflation are explained in the following discussion.

Monetary Items Distinguished from Nonmonetary Items

Monetary items are balance sheet assets and liabilities that are expressed (often by formal contract) in terms of a fixed number of dollars, regardless of price changes. Cash, accounts receivable, notes receivable, and bond investments are monetary items (i.e., monetary assets) because they are valued on the balance sheet at amounts that reflect *fixed* future cash receipts. These cash receipts are not affected by inflation because they are fixed dollar amounts. They do not change as prices rise or fall. Similarly, almost all payables on the balance sheet are considered monetary items (i.e., monetary liabilities) because they are valued at amounts that reflect future cash payments that are often *fixed* by contract. As in the case of monetary assets, these cash payments are unaffected by inflation.

Nonmonetary items, on the other hand, are *not* valued on the balance sheet at amounts reflecting fixed future cash receipts or payments. These items, which include marketable equity securities, inventories, long-term investments in equity securities, and long-lived assets, are typically valued at historical cost or the lower of cost or market. Changes in the prices of these items are reflected in the inflation rate. In general, in times of inflation the prices of marketable securities, inventories, long-term investments in equity securities, and long-lived assets tend to increase.

When preparing a balance sheet expressed in constant dollars, monetary and nonmonetary items are treated differently. The balance sheet dollar amounts of monetary items are not adjusted because they reflect fixed cash inflows or outflows that are unaffected by inflation. However, holding monetary items during periods of inflation gives rise to economic losses and gains, known as **purchasing-**

Figure C-3   Monetary and nonmonetary item and constant-dollar financial statements

	Constant-dollar Balance Sheet	Constant-dollar Income Statement

Monetary items
  Cash, receivables, debt
  investments, and payables
	No adjustment	Purchasing power losses and gains

Nonmonetary items
  Equity investments,
  inventories, and long-lived
  assets
	Restate to constant dollars	No adjustment

power losses and gains, that are recognized on an inflation-adjusted (constant-dollar) income statement. The balance sheet dollar amounts of nonmonetary items, on the other hand, are restated to constant dollars because the prices of these items are reflected in changes in the price level. However, these restatements are not reflected on an inflation-adjusted (constant-dollar) income statement. The treatment of monetary and nonmonetary items on constant dollar financial statements is summarized in Figure C-3.

Purchasing-Power Losses from Holding Monetary Assets

Holding a monetary asset during a period of inflation gives rise to a purchasing-power loss because the cash that will be received from it in the future will have less purchasing power than is indicated by the dollar value of the asset on the conventional balance sheet. It is economically unwise, for example, to hold large amounts of cash during inflationary periods because the amount of goods and services that it can purchase is continually decreasing.

Assume that Lakers and Sons received $5000 cash and held it for an entire year. If the inflation rate during that year was 8 percent (e.g., the CPI changed from 300 to 324), the purchasing-power loss experienced by Lakers and Sons from holding the cash would be computed as follows.

Purchasing-Power Loss: $5000 × (324 ÷ 300) = $5400 − $5000 = $400

Note in the calculation that the $5000 cash amount is multiplied by a ratio (324 ÷ 300) that represents the relative rise in the general price level since the cash was received. This multiplication gives rise to $5400, the amount of cash required at the end of the year to purchase the same goods and services that $5000 would purchase at the beginning of the year. By simply holding the $5000 cash, therefore, Lakers and Sons experienced a decrease in purchasing power during the year of $400 ($5400 − $5000). This decrease in purchasing power represents an economic loss for the company, which would be reflected on a constant-dollar income statement.

Purchasing-Power Gains from Holding Monetary Liabilities

Holding a monetary liability during a period of inflation gives rise to a purchasing-power gain. The cash that must be paid in the future will have less purchasing power than is indicated by the dollar amount of the liability on the conventional balance sheet.

Assume, for example, that on January 1 Sonics Sisters purchased inventory in the amount of $1000 on account and did not pay the account payable for an entire year, during which time the general inflation rate was 6 percent (e.g., the CPI changed from 285 to 302). The purchasing-power gain associated with holding the payable during this inflationary period would be calculated as follows.

$$\text{Purchasing-Power Gain: } \$1000 \times (302 \div 285) = \$1060 - \$1000 = \$60$$

The original amount of the payable ($1000) is multiplied by a ratio (302 ÷ 285) that represents the relative rise in the general price level since the payable was created. This multiplication gives rise to $1060, the amount to which the payable would have to be increased if an equal amount of purchasing power were to be given up when the liability is paid. Since the payable remains at $1000, Sonics Sisters enjoys a $60 purchasing-power gain. An economic gain accrues to the company because dollars with less purchasing power than those originally borrowed will be repaid. Purchasing-power gains also are reflected on constant-dollar income statements.

Net Purchasing-Power Losses and Gains: An Illustration

The information in Figure C−4, concerning monetary assets and liabilities, is from the financial records of Beringer Company for December 31, 1988, 1989, and 1990. End-of-period price indexes are also provided. Assume that the average price indexes during 1989 and 1990 were 350 and 370, respectively. The purchasing-power loss and gain experienced by Beringer during 1989 and 1990, respectively, are calculated in Figure C−5.

In 1989 the net monetary asset position at the beginning of the period ($300) is multiplied by the ratio of the end-of-period index (360) divided by the beginning-of-period index (340). Subtracting the $300 from the result gives rise to an $18 purchasing-power loss, which is due to holding net monetary assets during the period. However, during 1989 monetary liabilities built up by more than monetary assets ($500). This amount is multiplied by the ratio of the end-of-period index divided by the average index during 1989, assuming that the buildup occurred evenly throughout the year. Subtracting the $500 from the result gives rise to a $14 purchasing-power gain during the year. The net purchasing-power loss, consequently, is $4 ($18 − $14). This loss would appear on an income statement stated in terms of constant 1989 dollars.

The computations for 1990 are similar. In this case, however, the period began with a net monetary liability position of $200, and the buildup of monetary assets during the period exceeded monetary liabilities by $300. The net monetary liability position at the beginning of the period gave rise to an $11 purchasing-power

Figure C−4 Beringer Company monetary items

Monetary Item	1990	1989	1988
Cash	$700	$ 400	$500
Accounts receivable	300	600	200
Less: Payables	900	1,200	400
Net monetary assets (liabilities)	$100	$ (200)	$300
End-of-period price index	380	360	340

Figure C-5 Calculating purchasing-power losses and gains

Net purchasing-power loss during 1989

Net monetary assets (1/1/89)	$300 × (360 ÷ 340) − $300 = $18 loss
Net increase in monetary liabilities	$500 × (360 ÷ 350) − $500 = $14 gain
Net purchasing-power loss	$ 4 loss

Net purchasing-power gain during 1990

Net monetary liabilities (1/1/90)	$200 × (380 ÷ 360) − $200 = $11 gain
Net increase in monetary assets	$300 × (380 ÷ 370) − $300 = $ 8 loss
Net purchasing-power gain	$ 3 gain

gain, while the buildup in monetary assets generated an $8 purchasing-power loss during the period. The net result is a $3 purchasing-power gain for 1990. This gain would be reported on an income statement stated in terms of constant 1990 dollars.

Restating Nonmonetary Items to Constant Dollars

Restating the dollar amounts of nonmonetary items (equity investments, inventories, and long-lived assets) to constant dollars of the current year is fairly straightforward. As discussed earlier, the reported dollar amount of each item is simply multiplied by a ratio that relates the CPI of the current year to the CPI of the year in which the item was originally acquired and recorded. For example, assume that a conventional balance sheet (December 31, 1988) of Martin Enterprises contained inventories and land reported at $30,000 and $50,000, respectively. Assume further that the land was purchased in 1985 (CPI = 322), the inventories were acquired evenly throughout 1990 (average CPI = 340), and the 1988 year-end CPI is 347. The calculations to restate the Inventory and Land accounts to constant 1988 dollars appear in Figure C-6.

The restated dollar amounts for inventory ($30,618) and land ($53,882) would appear on a constant-dollar (1988) balance sheet. There is no adjustment, however, to the constant-dollar income statement because price changes of nonmonetary items, which result entirely from inflation, do not create economic gains and losses.

Suppose, for example, that the Celtic Company paid $1000 for a tract of land (a nonmonetary item) on January 1, and as of December 31, one year later, the price of the land had increased to $1050. The inflation rate during the year was 5 percent (e.g., CPI changed from 300 to 315). In this case the cost of the land at the end of the year would be restated to year-end (December 31) dollars in the following way.

Cost of land restated to December 31 dollars: $1000 × (315 ÷ 300) = $1050

While the $1050, which is $50 greater than $1000, would appear on the December 31 constant-dollar balance sheet, the company would not have enjoyed a $50 economic gain during the year. The $1050 would buy exactly the same amount of goods and services on December 31 that $1000 could have purchased on January 1.

Figure C-6   Restating nonmonetary items

Account	Nominal Dollar Amount		Conversion Ratio		Constant 1988 Dollar Amount
Inventory	$30,000	×	(347 ÷ 340)	=	$30,618
Land	$50,000	×	(347 ÷ 322)	=	$53,882

To show why there is no economic gain, assume that there is only one consumable commodity (corn) and that on January 1 its price was $1.00 per bushel. If at that time the Celtic Company used the $1000 to buy corn instead of land, it could have purchased 1000 bushels. If the price of corn moves with the 5 percent inflation rate, on December 31 it will cost $1.05 per bushel. At that time, if the company sells the land for $1,050, it could use the proceeds to purchase 1000 bushels of corn. Consequently, the land could be traded for 1000 bushels of corn at both January 1 and December 31. If the Celtic Company sells the land on December 31, it may have an additional $50, but that extra $50 would simply enable it to maintain (not increase) its purchasing power.

This example also illustrates how conventional financial statements can misstate net income by ignoring inflation. Under generally accepted accounting principles, if the Celtic Company sells the land for $1050 on December 31, it recognizes a gain of $50 ($1050 − $1000), which would appear on the income statement and increase net income. However, as we discussed above, the Celtic Company is actually no better off at the end of the year.

Adjusting Income Statement Items

The revenue and expense accounts on conventional income statements are adjusted to constant dollars in the same way as the nonmonetary balance sheet items. The dollar amount of each account is multiplied by a ratio that relates the CPI of the income statement year to the CPI of the year in which the item was originally recorded. Constant-dollar net income is then computed by subtracting the inflation-adjusted expenses from the inflation-adjusted revenues and adding or subtracting the net purchasing-power gain or loss from holding monetary items.

When restating a conventional income statement, it is important to keep in mind that each revenue and expense must be related to the transaction from which it arose. The denominator of the conversion ratio must represent the price index at the time the original transaction was recorded. The dollar amount of depreciation expense, for example, which is related to the acquisition of a fixed asset, is adjusted for inflation by multiplying it by the ratio of the current value of the price index divided by the price index at the time the fixed asset was acquired. Similarly, the cost of goods sold, which arises from the purchase of merchandise inventory, must be adjusted by taking into account the dates when the inventories were acquired.

To illustrate how income statement items are restated to constant dollars, review the 1989 income statement of Price Rise, Inc. which appears in Figure C-7.

Figure C-7   Conventional income statement

<table>
<tr><td colspan="3" align="center">Price Rise, Inc.
Income Statement
For the Year Ended December 31, 1989</td></tr>
<tr><td>Sales</td><td></td><td>$480,000</td></tr>
<tr><td>Less: Cost of goods sold</td><td></td><td></td></tr>
<tr><td>   Inventory (1/1/89)</td><td>$ 45,000</td><td></td></tr>
<tr><td>   Plus: Purchases</td><td>320,000</td><td></td></tr>
<tr><td>   Less: Inventory (12/31/89)</td><td>65,000</td><td>300,000</td></tr>
<tr><td>Gross profit</td><td></td><td>180,000</td></tr>
<tr><td>Depreciation expense</td><td></td><td>20,000</td></tr>
<tr><td>Miscellaneous expenses</td><td></td><td>100,000</td></tr>
<tr><td>Net income</td><td></td><td>$ 60,000</td></tr>
</table>

Assume:

(1) CPI (1/1/89).   320

(2) CPI (12/31/89).   340

(3) Average CPI during 1989.   330

(4) CPI when fixed assets were acquired.   300

(5) Sales, inventory purchases, and miscellaneous expenses occurred evenly throughout 1989.

(6) Purchasing power loss from holding net monetary assets during the year. $540

The computations in Figure C-8 convert this conventional income statement to an income statement expressed in constant 1989 dollars.

Sales and miscellaneous expenses were assumed to occur evenly throughout the year; therefore, the denominator of the conversion ratio (330) is the average price index for 1989. Depreciation expense is adjusted by the price index in effect at the time the fixed assets were acquired (300). The calculation to adjust Cost of Goods Sold, which is equal to beginning inventory plus purchases less ending inventory, involves adjusting each of these three numbers separately. Beginning inventory is converted by relating its value to the price index in effect at the beginning of the year (320). Purchases are assumed to be made evenly throughout the year, so the purchase number is converted by referring to the average index during the year (330). Ending inventory, which is assumed to have been purchased near the end of the year (i.e., FIFO assumption), is already stated in terms of current dollars. Note further that a purchasing-power loss, which must have come about because Price Rise, Inc. held net monetary assets during the year, is also included in the computation of constant-dollar net income.

A Comprehensive Illustration

Marymount Corporation began operations on January 1. During the year the company entered into the transactions described in Figure C-9. Each transaction is followed by a journal entry and information about the consumer price index at the time of the transaction. The financial statements as of December 31, both conventional and constant-dollar, are contained in Figure C-10.

Figure C–8 Restating a conventional income statement to constant 1989 dollars

	Conventional Amount		Conversion Ratio	Adjusted Amount (12/31/89 dollars)
Sales		$480,000	340 ÷ 330	$494,545
Less: Cost of goods sold				
Inventory (1/1/89)	$ 45,000		340 ÷ 320	$ 47,813
Plus: Purchases	320,000		340 ÷ 330	329,697
Less: Inventory (12/31/89)	65,000	300,000	340 ÷ 340	65,000	312,510
Depreciation expense		20,000	340 ÷ 300		22,667
Miscellaneous expenses		100,000	340 ÷ 330		103,030
Conventional net income		$ 60,000			—
Purchasing power (loss)					(540)
Constant-dollar (1989) net income					$ 55,798

Figure C–9 Transactions of Marymount Corporation

General Journal

Jan. 1   Cash   35,000
          Capital Stock   35,000
        To record the issuance of capital stock for $35,000 (CPI = 300).

Jan. 1   Long-Lived Asset   10,000
          Cash   10,000
        To record the purchase of a long-lived asset for $10,000 (10-year life, no salvage value, and straight-line method of depreciation; CPI = 300).

Jan. 1   Inventory   16,000
          Cash   16,000
        To record the purchase of 2,000 units of inventory at $8 per unit (CPI = 300).

Evenly throughout the year (average CPI = 312)

       Accounts Receivable   24,000
          Sales   24,000
       Cost of Goods Sold   8,000
          Inventory   8,000
        To record sales of $1,000 units of inventory on account for $24 per unit.

       Expenses   6,000
          Cash   4,000
          Short-Term Payables   2,000
        To record total expenses incurred evenly throughout the year.

Dec. 31   Depreciation Expense   1,000
          Accumulated Depreciation   1,000
        To record depreciation for the year (12/31 CPI = 324).

Figure C-10   Restating conventional financial statements to constant-dollar financial statements: Marymount Corporation

	Conventional		Adjustment	Constant dollar
Income statement				
Sales	$24,000	×	(324 ÷ 312)	$24,923
Less: Cost of goods sold	8,000	×	(324 ÷ 300)	8,640
Expenses	6,000	×	(324 ÷ 312)	6,231
Depreciation expense	1,000	×	(324 ÷ 300)	1,080
Purchasing power (loss)	—			(1,412)[a]
Net income	$ 9,000			$ 7,560
Balance sheet				
Assets				
Cash	$ 5,000		No adjustment needed	$ 5,000
Accounts receivable	24,000		No adjustment needed	24,000
Inventory	8,000	×	324 ÷ 300	8,640
Long-lived asset	10,000	×	324 ÷ 300	10,800
Less: Accumulated depreciation	1,000	×	324 ÷ 300	1,080
Total assets	$46,000			$47,360
Liabilities and stockholders' equity				
Short-term payables	2,000		No adjustment needed	$ 2,000
Contributed capital[b]	35,000	×	324 ÷ 300	37,800
Retained earnings	9,000		See explanation below	7,560[c]
Total liabilities and stockholders' equity	$46,000			$47,360

[a]Purchasing-power loss:

$$\begin{array}{lrl}
\text{Net monetary assets (1/1)*} & \$\,9,000 \times (324 \div 300) - 9,000 = & \$\ \ 720 \text{ loss} \\
\text{Buildup of monetary assets**} & \$18,000 \times (324 \div 312) - 18,000 = & \underline{692} \text{ loss} \\
& \text{Purchasing-power loss} & \underline{\$1,412} \text{ loss}
\end{array}$$

$$*9,000 = 35,000 - 10,000 - 16,000$$
$$**18,000 = \ 5,000 + 24,000 - \ 2,000 - 9,000$$

12/31 net monetary assets

[b]Contributed capital is treated like a nonmonetary item.
[c]Beginning balance ($0) + constant-dollar income ($7,560) − dividends ($0)

ADJUSTING FINANCIAL STATEMENTS TO REFLECT MARKET VALUES: CURRENT COSTS AND EXIT VALUES

The prices of assets—inventories and long-lived assets in particular—are simultaneously affected by two independent forces: general inflation and supply and demand factors. The previous section described how financial accounting statements can be restated in constant dollars to control for the effects of general inflation. This section discusses changes in market values and factors of supply and demand, and how they can be reflected in the financial statements.

The Difference Between Market-Value Changes and Inflation

Changes in the market prices of individual assets must be distinguished from inflation. A change in the market price of an asset reflects a shift in the supply of or demand for that specific asset. Inflation, on the other hand, is a measure of the average increase in the market prices of all assets and services in the economy. While market-price changes are used in computing an inflation index (e.g., CPI), the index itself is a broad average that does not represent the price changes of individual assets.

Suppose, for example, that an inflation index was computed by taking an average of the price changes of two assets: Asset A, which increased in price by 10 percent, and Asset B, which decreased in price by 4 percent. While the index would reflect an overall inflation rate of 3 percent ([10% − 4%] ÷ 2), it would represent the market-price change of neither of the assets used to compute it.

The financial effects of changes in the market prices of individual assets and of inflation should be treated separately on the financial statements. Price changes due to market-value shifts reflect changes in wealth and should be considered part of income. Inflation adjustments to restate the values of inventories and long-lived assets to constant dollars do not reflect changes in wealth and should be excluded from income.

To illustrate, consider a tract of land that was purchased by Jones and Associates on January 1 for a price of $1000. One year later, on December 31, the company receives, but does not accept, an offer to sell the land for $1500. Given an inflation rate during the year of 10 percent (e.g., CPI changed from 310 to 341), by how much did the company's wealth increase due to holding the land?

Based primarily on the principle of objectivity and the concept of conservatism, conventional financial statements would recognize no increase in the company's wealth. The offer to sell was not accepted, so there was no transaction on which to recognize a gain. A conventional balance sheet would carry the land at historical cost ($1000), and the income statement would not reflect the appreciation of the land.

Nonetheless, it is fairly clear that Jones and Associates is economically better off at the end the year than it was at the beginning. The question is, by how much? Your first reaction might be to compute the increase in wealth by simply subtracting $1000 from $1500, arriving at a $500 holding gain, the increase in price that occurred while the company held the land. However, there was 10 percent inflation during the year, and on December 31 it took $1.10 to purchase what $1.00 could purchase on January 1. As a result, the actual increase in wealth enjoyed by the company during the year was only $400, as calculated in Figure C−11.

Figure C−11   Differentiating inflation from a change in market value

Market price of land (1/1/89)	$1,500
Less: Inflation-adjusted cost of land [$1,000 × (341 ÷ 310)]	1,100
Increase in wealth	$ 400

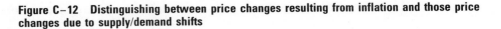

Figure C-12   Distinguishing between price changes resulting from inflation and those price changes due to supply/demand shifts

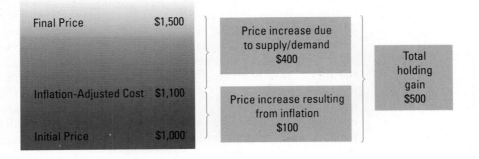

The price of the land purchased by Jones and Associates increased during the year for two separate reasons: (1) the general rate of inflation and (2) a change in the supply of and/or demand for land in the area. Roughly speaking, as indicated in Figure C-12, the inflation rate pushed the price of the land from $1000 to $1100, and shifts in the supply and demand of the land increased the price from $1100 to $1500.

The following sections explain how conventional financial statements can be adjusted to reflect changes in market values. You will note that gains and losses from holding inventories and long-lived assets, which change in price, are recognized on the income statement. To simplify the computations, we assume no inflation and therefore ignore the problem of distinguishing between price changes due to supply and demand shifts and price changes due to inflation. However, keep in mind that this is a simplification; in reality, such a distinction should be made. To repeat, price changes due to supply and demand shifts should be reflected in income, while price changes due to inflation should not.

Current Input or Output Market Values?

The market price of an inventory item or long-lived asset depends on the market in which the asset is traded. Such assets can be valued in either the **input market,** the market in which a company purchases its inputs, or the **output market,** the market in which the company sells its outputs. The current input price is called either the **current cost** or **replacement cost.** The current output price is called either the **exit value** or **fair market value.**

For example, a car dealer purchases cars from the manufacturer (input market) and sells them to customers (output market). Assume that on January 1, the dealer purchases a Toyota for $9000 from the manufacturer. On January 30 the Toyota could be sold for $10,000 and replaced with an equivalent model for $9500. As of January 30, the historical cost of the Toyota is $9000, the current (replacement) cost is $9500, and the fair market (exit) value is $10,000.

Conventional financial statements value inventory and long-lived assets on the balance sheet primarily in terms of historical costs and, for the most part, recognize revenues and expenses on the income statement only when they are realized.

Current-cost financial statements and **exit-value financial statements,** on the other hand, value inventory and long-lived assets on the balance sheet in terms of current input costs and fair market values, respectively. In addition, both current-cost and exit-value accounting recognize gains (losses) on the income statement as the respective market prices of inventories and long-lived assets increase (decrease), whether or not they are realized. These gains (losses) are called **holding gains (losses)** because they accrue to a company while the inventories or long-lived assets are being held. The rationale underlying their recognition on the income statement is that they reflect increases (decreases) in economic wealth. The following section presents an example to illustrate the basic differences among conventional financial statements, current-cost financial statements, and exit-value financial statements.

Adjusting Financial Statements for Changes in Market Values: An Example

Sargon Company began operations on January 1, 1990. On that date, the company borrowed $20,000 in exchange for a long-term note and raised $30,000 by issuing common stock. Inventory was immediately purchased for $15,000, and long-lived assets were purchased for $25,000. The financial statements for January 1, 1990, and December 31, 1990, are provided in Figure C−13.

Current-Cost Financial Statements
Expressing Sargon's financial statements in terms of current costs involves three basic adjustments: (1) inventory and cost of goods sold are restated to reflect current cost, (2) long-lived assets and depreciation expense are restated to reflect current cost, and (3) gains or losses on holding the inventory and long-lived assets are recognized.

Restating inventory to reflect current cost involves increasing the Inventory account on the December 31 balance sheet to $20,000. Restating the cost of goods sold to reflect current cost involves increasing the Cost of Goods Sold account on the income statement to $55,000, the current cost of the sold inventory at the time of sale (given in Figure C−13). Restating long-lived assets to reflect current cost involves increasing the Long-Lived Assets account on the December 31 balance sheet to $30,000, which, if depreciated at a rate of 12 percent per year, increases Depreciation Expenses to $3600.

The holding gains experienced by Sargon during the year fall into two categories: (1) realized holding gains and (2) unrealized holding gains. **Realized holding gains** refer to market-value increases of inventory that was sold or long-lived assets that expired during the year. The realized holding gain on sold inventory was $5000, the $55,000 current cost of the sold inventory less the $50,000 cost of the sold inventory (the cost of goods sold). The realized holding gain on long-lived assets was $600, the $3600 of current-cost depreciation less the $3000 of historical-cost depreciation. The total realized holding gain, therefore, was $5600 ($5000 + $600).

Unrealized holding gains refer to market-value increases of inventory and long-lived assets that were on hand at year end. The unrealized holding gain on inventory on hand at year end was $2000, the difference between the cost of the

Figure C-13   Financial statements for Sargon Company

	December 31	January 1
Balance sheet		
Assets		
Cash	$12,000	$10,000
Accounts receivable	15,000	—
Inventory	18,000	15,000
Long-lived assets	25,000	25,000
Less: Accumulated depreciation	3,000	—
Total assets	$67,000	$50,000
Liabilities and stockholders' equity		
Accounts payable	$13,000	—
Long-term note payable	19,000	20,000
Common stock	30,000	30,000
Retained earnings	5,000	—
Total liabilities and stockholders' equity	$67,000	$50,000

Income statement

Revenues		$75,000
Less: Cost of goods sold		
Beginning inventory	$15,000	
Purchases	53,000	
Less: Ending inventory	18,000	
		50,000
Gross profit		25,000
Expenses (including interest and taxes)		13,000
Depreciation expense		3,000
Net income		$ 9,000

Statement of retained earnings

Beginning retained earnings	$ 0
Plus: Net income	9,000
Less: Dividends	4,000
Ending retained earnings	$ 5,000

Additional information

1. Depreciation on long-lived assets is taken at a rate of 12% per year and no long-lived assets were purchased or sold during 1990.
2. December 31 market values:

	Current costs	Exit values
Inventory	$20,000[a]	$27,000[b]
Long-lived assets	$30,000	$20,000

[a]The current cost of the sold inventory at time of sale: $55,000.
[b]The exit value of inventory remained at 150% of cost throughout 1990.

Figure C–14   Conversion to current-cost financial statements: Sargon Company

	Conventional	Adjustment	Current Costs
Balance sheet (Dec. 31, 1990)			
Assets			
Cash	$12,000	—	$12,000
Accounts receivable	15,000	—	15,000
Inventory	18,000	+$2,000	20,000
Long-lived assets	25,000	+ 5,000	30,000
Less: Accumulated depreciation	3,000	+ 600	3,600
Total assets	$67,000		$73,400
Liabilities and stockholders' equity			
Accounts payable	$13,000	—	$13,000
Long-term note payable	19,000	—	$19,000
Common stock	30,000	—	30,000
Retained earnings	5,000		11,400*
Total liabilities and stockholders' equity	$67,000		$73,400
*See statement of retained earnings.			
Income Statement (1990)			
Revenues	$75,000	—	$75,000
Less: Cost of goods sold	50,000	+ 5,000	55,000
Gross profit	25,000		20,000
Expenses (include interest and taxes)	13,000	—	13,000
Depreciation expense	3,000	+ 600	3,600
Realized holding gain	—		5,600
Net income	$ 9,000		9,000
Unrealized holding gain			6,400
Current-cost income			$15,400
Statement of Retained Earnings (1990)			
Beginning retained earnings balance	$ 0		$ 0
Plus: Net income	9,000		15,400
Less: Dividends	4,000		4,000
Ending retained earnings balance	$ 5,000		$11,400

inventory on the conventional balance sheet ($18,000) and its year-end current cost ($20,000). The unrealized holding gain on unexpired long-lived assets was $4400, the difference between the cost of the long-lived assets on the conventional balance sheet ($25,000) and their year-end current cost ($30,000), less the excess of current-cost depreciation ($600). The adjustments to restate the conventional financial statements of Sargon Company to current-cost financial statements are shown in Figure C–14.

Note that current-cost income ($15,400) less the unrealized holding gain ($6400) is equal to conventional net income ($9000). The additional cost of goods sold ($5000) and depreciation expense ($600) recognized on the current-cost income statement is exactly offset by the realized holding gain ($5600). Consequently, the main difference between current-cost income and conventional net income is the increase in the current costs of the inventories and long-lived assets on hand at year end.

Exit-Value Financial Statements

Expressing Sargon's financial statements in terms of exit values also involves three basic adjustments: (1) inventory is restated to reflect exit value, (2) long-lived assets are restated to reflect exit value, and (3) gain or losses on holding the inventory and long-lived assets are recognized.

Restating inventory to reflect exit value involves increasing the Inventory account on the December 31 balance sheet to $27,000. Restating long-lived assets to reflect exit value involves decreasing the Long-Lived Asset account on the December 31 balance sheet to $20,000.

Under exit-value accounting, because inventories and long-lived assets are carried at selling price, a distinction is not made between realized and unrealized holding gains/losses. A holding gain of $34,000 was recognized on the $68,000 ($15,000 + $53,000) of inventory purchased during the year. This gain was computed in the following way.

$$(\$68,000 \times 150\%) - \$68,000 = \$34,000 \text{ inventory holding gain}$$

A $5000 holding loss was recognized on long-lived assets, which decreased in fair market value from $25,000 to $20,000. The adjustments to restate the conventional financial statements of Sargon Company to reflect exit values are shown in Figure C−15.

Under exit-value accounting, gross profit is not meaningful because inventories are carried at selling price, and holding gains are recognized without regard to the date of sale. Similarly, depreciation is not meaningful because long-lived assets are carried at fair market value instead of historical or current cost. As a result, the income statement consists of only three items: (1) the expenses incurred during the year, (2) the holding gain/loss due to changes in the fair market values of the long-lived assets, and (3) the holding gain/loss due to changes in the selling prices of inventories.

Note that the difference between exit-value income ($16,000) and conventional net income ($9000) is $7000. This difference is explained by the fact that exit-value accounting recognized (1) a $9000 holding gain on year-end inventory, which was ignored on the conventional statements, and (2) a $5000 holding loss on long-lived assets, which exceeded conventional depreciation by $2000: thus the $7000 difference ($9000 − $2000). Exit-value income is based on the assumption that all assets are sold and all liabilities are paid off at year end.

Why Adjust Conventional Financial Statements to Reflect Current Costs and Exit Values?

Adjusting conventional financial statements to reflect market values can be useful in evaluating a company's performance. Indeed, many accountants argue that current-cost and exit-value income better reflect the performance of management

Figure C-15   Conversion to exit-value financial statements: Sargon Company

	Conventional	Adjustment	Exit Value
Balance Sheet (Dec. 31, 1990)			
Assets			
Cash	$12,000	—	$12,000
Accounts receivable	15,000	—	15,000
Inventory	18,000	+ $9,000	27,000
Long-lived assets	25,000	−5,000	20,000
Less: Accumulated depreciation	3,000		—
Total assets	$67,000		$74,000
Liabilities and stockholders' equity			
Accounts payable	$13,000	—	$13,000
Long-term note payable	19,000	—	19,000
Common stock	30,000	—	30,000
Retained earnings	5,000		12,000*
Total liabilities and stockholders' equity	$67,000		$74,000
*See statement of retained earnings.			
Income Statement (1990)			
Revenues	$75,000		—
Less: Cost of goods sold	50,000		—
Gross profit	25,000		—
Expenses (include interest and taxes)	$13,000		$13,000
Depreciation expense	3,000		—
Net income	$ 9,000		
Holding (loss) on long-lived assets			(5,000)
Holding gain on inventory			34,000
Exit-value income			$16,000
Statement of Retained Earnings (1990)			
Beginning retained earnings balance	$ 0		$ 0
Plus: Net income	9,000		16,000
Less: Dividends	4,000		4,000
Ending retained earnings balance	$ 5,000		$12,000

than conventional net income. Current costs and exit values measure the opportunity costs of using and holding assets and, accordingly, should be considered by management when selling or exchanging assets and in evaluating the returns earned on the assets used in a business. It is also very difficult for investors, creditors, and other interested parties to reliably evaluate the performance of a company and its management without some knowledge of the market values of the company's assets.

To illustrate, suppose a particular manager purchased an asset two years ago for $8000, and it is expected to produce $1000 in net cash inflows over each of the next five years. The asset could be sold for $3000 (exit value), and it would require $4500 (current cost) to replace it with an equivalent asset. Ignoring tax considerations, which of the following alternatives should the manager choose:

(1) continue to use the asset, (2) sell the asset and not replace it, or (3) sell the asset and replace it? Managers constantly face such decisions.

The value of Alternative 1, continuing to use the asset, is the present value of the future net cash inflows. Assuming an 8 percent discount rate, the value to the company of this alternative is $3993 ($1000 × 3.993). The value of Alternative 2, sell and not replace, is $3000, the exit value of the asset. The value of Alternative 3 is $2493, the proceeds from selling the asset ($3000), less the cost of replacing it ($4500), plus the present value of using it ($3993). In this case the appropriate decision for the manager is to continue to use the asset (Alternative 1) because that provides the highest value of the three choices.

This example illustrates two important points. First, the values of the three alternatives could not have been determined without knowledge of the present value, current cost, and exit value of the asset. The manager could not reliably make the decision, nor could the decision be reliably evaluated by investors, creditors and others unless all three market values were known. Consequently, current costs and exit values are important to those who manage a company as well as those who wish to evaluate management.

The second point of this example is that the historical cost of the asset ($8000) had no bearing on the manager's decision. The cost of the asset could have been $1 or it could have been $50,000; it did not affect the manager's choice. The $8000 had already been paid, and nothing could be done about it. It represents what is called a **sunk cost,** and such costs are irrelevant to these kinds of decisions. Consequently, historical cost is of limited use when evaluating a company's operating performance.

THE ECONOMIC CONSEQUENCES OF ADJUSTING FOR PRICE CHANGES

According to generally accepted accounting principles, companies in the United States are not presently required to adjust their financial statements for the effects of inflation and changes in market values. Some companies, however, provide brief descriptions in their financial reports of the effects of price changes on operations. The following excerpt, for example, was taken from the 1987 financial report of the Ralston Purina Company.

> *Management recognizes that inflationary pressures may have an adverse effect on the Company through higher asset replacement costs and related depreciation and higher material costs. The Company attempts to minimize these effects through cost reductions and profit margins. However, it is management's view that inflation has not had a significant impact on operations in the three years ended September 30, 1987.*

Nonetheless, the effects of inflation and market-value changes can be quite large. In 1981, for example, when the conventional net income numbers of the thirty Dow Jones Industrial companies were adjusted for current costs, total operating earnings for the group dropped from $31 billion to approximately $14 billion. Table C–1 shows the 1982 income numbers of twelve major U.S. companies under three conditions: (1) as reported on the financial statements, (2) adjusted for general inflation (constant-dollar), and (3) adjusted for current (replacement) costs.

Table C–1 The effects of inflation and current-cost adjustments on the financial statements of selected U.S. companies

Company	1982 Net Income (in millions)		
	As Reported	Constant Dollars	Current Costs
American Tel & Tel	$6,992	$ 50	$ 1,418
Standard Oil (Ohio)	1,879	1,448	$ 1,356
Standard Oil (Indiana)	1,826	1,214	990
General Electric	1,817	1,066	1,179
Atlantic Richfield	1,676	915	789
Shell Oil	1,605	730	424
Mobil Oil	1,380	−71	−50
Standard Oil (Calif.)	1,377	318	−668
Texaco	1,281	33	−905
Eastman Kodak	1,162	983	1,022
General Motors	963	112	207
DuPont	894	413	554

Source: Janet Bamford, "Out of Sight, Out of Mind?" *Forbes,* 4 July 1983, p. 133.

In each case in Table C−1 the income numbers adjusted for inflation and current costs are lower than the reported amounts and, in most cases, the differences are substantial. Note, in particular, Mobil, Standard Oil (Calif.), and Texaco, where the adjustments produce negative income amounts. Note also that these companies are all heavy manufacturing concerns, which carry large amounts of inventory and long-lived assets. The dollar amounts of Cost of Goods Sold and Depreciation on the adjusted statements, therefore, are considerably higher than those reported on conventional statements.

Adjustments for inflation and market values can have significant economic consequences because they alter the measures of income and important financial ratios and, accordingly, can change the earning power and solvency assessments of financial statement users. If used in executive compensation plans and debt covenants, these adjustments could have an important effect on management's decisions. Many analysts and managers claim that using constant-dollar financial statements can lead to improved decision making. Consider FMC Corporation, for example, which has required its operating managers to use inflation-adjusted numbers for internal reporting purposes since 1980. David Harmer, director of financial control, was quoted in *Forbes* as saying, "We figure that in the first four years of using this system we have turned about $75 million worth of under-utilized assets into cash."[2]

Recently, the inflation rate in the United States has calmed somewhat, and adjusting financial statements for inflation and market values is less of a concern than it was in the 1970s, when inflation raged at double-digit levels. In fact, in 1985 *Forbes* commented that inflation-adjusted accounting "ranks about fifty-seventh on the burning-issue list—somewhere after the danger of invasion by crazed Canadian geese."[3] However, inflation has not been eliminated and could

---

2. Jinny St. Goar, "Experiment Abandoned?" *Forbes,* 18 November 1985, p. 218.
3. Ibid.

return to previous levels; market values are constantly changing; and investors, creditors, and managers can still benefit from considering such issues when using financial accounting numbers.

ACCOUNTING FOR CHANGING PRICES AND MARKET VALUES: THE CURRENT SITUATION

Accounting for inflation and changing market prices has been a controversial topic since the early 1900s. Many different procedures for adjusting for inflation and incorporating current costs and exit values into the financial statements have been proposed and debated. Indeed, in 1979 the FASB passed Statement No. 33, which required certain large U.S. companies to provide supplementary disclosures of the effects of inflation and current costs, only to rescind the standard several years later. Most of these proposals have been based on the premise that adjusting financial statements for the effects of inflation and changing market values provides more relevant information than can be found on conventional statements, which are based on nominal dollars and rely heavily on historical costs. Few accountants argue with this premise, yet conventional historical costs continue to represent the cornerstone of present-day financial statements. Why?

The problems with incorporating inflation adjustments, current costs, and exit values into present-day financial statements revolve primarily around the principle of objectivity, the concept of conservatism, and the costs associated with implementing such procedures. Current costs and exit values are normally very difficult to estimate objectively and accurately. Auditors, therefore, are largely unable or unwilling to audit inflation adjustments and market values. It is also quite costly for managers to generate the information (e.g., market-value estimates) necessary for constant-dollar and current-cost reports.

Moreover, it is not clear that investors even used the information required by Statement No. 33. In a survey conducted by a major U.S. accounting firm, which asked financial analysts about the usefulness of the required disclosures, only half of the respondents reported that they found them to be useful. Many accountants believe that analysts make their own adjustments for inflation and market values, based primarily on their particular knowledge of the company under consideration and the industry in which it operates. Statement No. 33, for example, required companies to prepare constant-dollar statements using the Consumer Price Index, yet it is well-known that no general index is relevant to all companies or industries.

Conventional historical cost statements are the cornerstone of the financial accounting system, and it appears that they will remain so indefinitely. Yet, adjustments for inflation, current costs, and exit values can still be used to improve the usefulness of financial statements, and nothing prevents users from doing so. As stated in *Forbes*, "No doubt there are technical problems with [the methods] for showing the effects of inflation [and market values] on companies, but . . . any system that measures [such effects] reasonably well is closer to reality than one that ignores them altogether."[4]

---

4. Janet Bamford, "Out of Sight, Out of Mind?" *Forbes*, 4 July 1983, p. 133.

EXERCISES

EC–1   *(Classifying monetary and nonmonetary items)*   The adjusted trial balance of Jacobs Industries, Inc. as of December 31, 1990, contained the following selected accounts. Classify each account as either monetary or nonmonetary. Justify each of your choices.

Cash
Accounts Receivable
Office Equipment
Accumulated Depreciation—Office Equipment
Bonds Payable
Inventory
Accounts Payable
Discount on Bonds Payable
Long-Term Marketable Equity Securities
Building
Land
Mortgage Payable
Wages Payable

EC–2   *(Sales increases unadjusted for inflation can be deceptive)*   The following information was taken from the financial records of Dickerson Motors.

	1990	1989	1988	1987	1986
Sales	$60,000	$45,000	$40,000	$25,000	$20,000

At the company's annual stockholders' meeting, the president commented that sales doubled from 1986 to 1988 and tripled from 1986 to 1990. The Consumer Price Index numbers for the years 1986 through 1990 are provided below.

	1990	1989	1988	1987	1986
CPI	400	380	360	340	320

Required:

a. Comment on the accuracy of the president's statement.

b. Compute the percentage increases in sales from 1986 to 1988 and 1986 to 1990 if the sales figures are adjusted for inflation.

EC–3   *(Computing purchasing-power gains and losses)*   Roberts Company had monetary assets and liabilities of the following for the period 1988–90. Compute the purchasing-power gains or losses for 1989 and 1990. Assume average CPIs for 1989 and 1990 to be 350 and 370 respectively.

	1990	1989	1988
Cash	$5,000	$ 4,000	$ 7,000
Accounts Receivable	8,000	7,000	9,000
Notes Receivable	3,000	4,000	4,000
Accounts Payable	3,000	12,000	10,000
Notes Payable	5,000	7,000	6,000
Consumer Price Index	380	360	340

EC–4   *(Dividing profit as measured under conventional accounting into the portion due to inflation and the portion due to market-value changes)*   Coral Gable Jewelery Wholesalers purchased ten 1-karat diamond rings on April 3, 1990, for $5000 each. On this date the Consumer Price Index was 400. Due to problems in South Africa, diamonds were soon in short supply. Several of the company's customers entered into bidding wars to acquire these rings. On December 31, 1990, Coral Gable Jewelry sold each of these rings for the $15,000 bid price. On this date the Consumer Price Index was 500.

Required:

a. Compute the following:

  (1) The gain on the sale as measured under generally accepted accounting principles
  (2) The portion of the gain due to inflation
  (3) The portion of the gain due to changes in the supply and demand for diamond rings.

b. Which of the three measures of profit indicates the company's increase in wealth? Why?

EC-5   *(The basic difference between conventional accounting and current-cost accounting)*   Montlake Furniture purchased two dining room tables for $500 each on March 1. On August 4 the company sold one of the tables for $850, at which time its replacement cost was $600. As of December 31, the replacement cost of the remaining table had risen to $650. On January 12 of the following year Montlake sold the second table for $850. The replacement cost at that time was $700.

Required:

a. Compute the profit recognized in each year under conventional accounting and current-cost accounting.

b. Compute the total profit over the two-year period recognized under each method. What is the basic difference between conventional accounting and current-cost accounting?

EC-6   *(The differences among conventional, current-cost, and exit-value inventory accounting)*   The information below refers to the inventory activity for Carson's Supply House during the year.

	Units	Per-Unit Cost	Current Cost	Selling Price
Beginning inventory	0			
Purchases	40,000	$2	$2	$6
Less: Sales	35,000		$3	$6
Ending inventory	5,000		$4	$6

All purchases and sales are made in cash.

Required: Compute the amount of profit (including holding gains where appropriate) recognized under the following:

a. Conventional accounting

b. Current-cost accounting (realized and unrealized)

c. Exit-value accounting.

EC-7   *(The basic differences among conventional, constant-dollar, and exit-value accounting)*   Mary Letterman purchased a tract of land for $15,000 on January 1, 1988. On December 31, 1988, she received an offer to sell the land for $25,000, but did not accept it. On December 31, 1989, she sold the land for $30,000.

Consumer Price Index information follows.

January 1, 1988	400
December 31, 1988	450
December 31, 1989	480

Required: Compute the income (include holding gains where appropriate) from the activities above for 1988 and 1989 under the following:

a. Conventional accounting   c. Exit-value accounting.

b. Constant-dollar accounting

EC-8

(Adjusting for the current costs of inventory and long-lived assets)   Avery Enterprises purchased 5000 units of inventory for $8 per unit, and a building for $300,000 on January 1, 1990. The company sold 1500 units for $35 per unit on April 10, and 3000 units for $40 per unit on September 24. Avery Enterprises uses the straight-line depreciation method. The building has an estimated useful life of ten years with a salvage value of $10,000.

Required:

a. Prepare an income statement that reflects these activities under generally accepted accounting principles.

b. Assume that the cost to replace the inventory and the building throughout 1990 was $20 per unit and $275,000, respectively. Prepare a current-cost income statement.

c. Assume that the cost to replace the inventory and the building throughout 1990 was $5 per unit and $375,000, respectively. Prepare a current-cost income statement.

EC-9

(Choosing to hold, sell, or replace an asset)   Greg Miller, president of Kingsman Company, is trying to decide whether to continue to hold, to sell, or to replace some productive equipment. Mr. Miller has the following information at his disposal.

1. The equipment could be sold for $504,000.
2. The equipment will generate cash inflows of $50,000 over the next fifteen years.
3. New equipment would cost $875,000.
4. The new equipment would generate cash inflows of $50,000 over the next twenty years.
5. The discount rate is 10 percent.

Required:

a. What is the value of selling the equipment?
b. What is the value of holding the equipment?
c. What is the value of selling and replacing the equipment?
d. Which option should Mr. Miller select?

PROBLEMS

PC-1

(Adjusting monetary and nonmonetary items for inflation)   Puget Sound Shipyard is currently preparing its inflation-adjusted financial statements for 1990. As of December 31, 1990, the Consumer Price Index is 400. Selected accounts from the company's general ledger, and the Consumer Price Index at the time that the amount in the account was first recorded on the books appear in the following chart.

Account	Consumer Price Index
Accounts Payable	350
Plant Equipment	312
Accounts Receivable	345
Bonds Payable	425
Investment in Bonds	200
Inventory	438

Required:

a. Classify each account as either a monetary item or a nonmonetary item.

b. Indicate which accounts would be increased, decreased, or unchanged for inflation-adjusted financial statements as compared to conventional financial statements. Explain why the accounts are treated differently.

c. For those accounts in (b) that you indicated would be increased or decreased, compute the magnitude of the adjustment. Assume that all accounts are valued at $1000 on the December 31, 1990 balance sheet.

PC–2
(Adjusting nonmonetary items for the effects of inflation)   On January 1, 1990, Tracey Production Company entered into the following transactions.

(1) Purchased plant equipment for cash in the amount of $200,000. This equipment has an estimated useful life of ten years and no salvage value.

(2) Purchased office furniture and equipment for cash in the amount of $150,000. These items have an estimated life of five years and an estimated salvage value of $25,000.

(3) Purchased 25,000 units of inventory for $10 per unit. All 25,000 units are still on hand at the end of the year.

Required:

a. Prepare entries to record each of these transactions.

b. For each transaction indicate whether Tracey Production Company acquired a monetary item or a nonmonetary item.

c. Assume that the Consumer Price Index changed from 300 to 390 during 1990. Compute the inflation-adjusted amounts for each nonmonetary item as of December 31, 1990.

d. Assume that the Consumer Price Index changed from 500 to 450 during 1990. Compute the inflation-adjusted amounts for each nonmonetary item as of December 31, 1990.

e. Why do nonmonetary items have no impact on the income statement during periods of inflation or deflation under constant-dollar accounting?

PC–3
(Preparing a constant-dollar income statement)   Elliot Book Company included the following income statement in its 1990 financial report.

Sales		$1,550,000
Less: Cost of goods sold		
Beginning inventory	$380,000	
Net purchases	995,000	
Less: Ending inventory	410,000	965,000
Gross profit		585,000
Less: Expenses		
Depreciation	50,000	
Selling and administrative	305,000	
Interest	100,000	455,000
Net income		$ 130,000

Assume the following:

1. The Consumer Price Indexes as of January 1 and December 31 were 400 and 450, respectively. The average CPI for the year was 425.

2. The depreciation expense is related to a fixed asset purchased on January 1, 1990.

3. Sales, inventory purchases, selling and administrative expenses, and interest expense occurred evenly throughout the year.

4. The company experienced a net purchasing-power gain of $450 during 1990.

5. The company follows the periodic FIFO inventory cost flow assumption.

Required: Prepare a constant-dollar income statement for the year ended December 31, 1990.

PC-4

(Separating the impacts of inflation from the impacts of changes in market values) Anderson Ranch raises beef cattle. In order to increase the size of its herd, Anderson purchased 750 acres of land for $500,000 on December 31, 1989. During 1990 the state decided to build a highway through the middle of these 750 acres and offered Anderson $750,000 for the entire 750 acres. On December 31, 1990, Anderson accepted the offer.

Required:

a. For each of the following three cases, compute the price increase due to inflation and the price increase due to changes in the land's exit value.

  (1) Assume that during 1990 the Consumer Price Index remained constant at 340.

  (2) Assume that during 1990 the Consumer Price Index changed from 340 to 425.

  (3) Assume that during 1990 the Consumer Price Index changed from 340 to 595.

b. Which of the cases in (a) is assumed under conventional accounting?

c. Why should the impact of inflation be separated from the impact of shifts in supply and demand for inventory and long-lived assets?

PC-5

(The irrelevance of historical cost) Steve Rice manages the fixed assets of Rettman and Sons, Inc. He has collected the following information about three different assets that are presently in operation.

Asset	Historical Cost	Present Value	Fair Market Value	Replacement Cost
A	$17,000	$32,000	$28,000	$30,000
B	35,000	26,000	30,000	25,000
C	8,000	21,000	23,000	22,000

Required:

Assume that the present value of the old asset is equal to the present value of the replacement assets, and answer the following questions.

a. In each case, should Steve hold, sell, or sell and replace the asset? Ignore the effect of income taxes.

b. In each case, double the dollar amount of historical cost and see if that changes Steve's decision.

PC-6

(Is depreciation a method of saving cash for the replacement of assets?) Buckingham Enterprises purchased a machine for $50,000 on January 1, 1985, to produce a product that can be readily sold. The machine was estimated to have a five-year useful life and no salvage value. Buckingham uses the straight-line method of depreciation. The following information refers to the activity of the machine for 1985 through 1989.

	1989	1988	1987	1986	1985
Cash sales	$80,000	$70,000	$65,000	$62,000	$50,000
Cash expenses	55,000	50,000	48,000	45,000	35,000
Cash income	$25,000	$20,000	$17,000	$17,000	$15,000
Less: Depreciation	10,000	10,000	10,000	10,000	10,000
Net income	$15,000	$10,000	$ 7,000	$ 7,000	$ 5,000
Beginning cash	$40,000	$30,000	$20,000	$10,000	0
Cash income	25,000	20,000	17,000	17,000	15,000
Less: Dividends	15,000	10,000	7,000	7,000	5,000
Ending cash	$50,000	$40,000	$30,000	$20,000	$10,000

The company's policy has been to pay dividends each year in the amount of net income. The president felt that such a policy would allow enough cash to accumulate so that a new machine could be purchased when the old one wore out at the end of 1989. However, as of December 31, 1989, the company has only accumulated $50,000 cash and the new machine costs $75,000. The president is wondering what went wrong.

Required:

a. Is depreciation a method of saving cash for the replacement of assets? Explain to the president why the company is short of the required cash.

b. Assume that the replacement cost of the machine during the five-year period was as shown below.

	1989	1988	1987	1986	1985
Replacement cost	$75,000	$70,000	$65,000	$60,000	$55,000

Assume that Buckingham based its depreciation on current cost instead of historical cost over the five-year period. How much cash would they have saved if they had maintained the same policy of paying dividends in the amount of income?

c. Is depreciation based on current cost a method of saving cash for the replacement of assets? Explain.

PC–7   *(Dividends based on conventional income can reduce a company's capital)*   Selected financial information for Amandie Villages follows for a given year.

	December 31	January 1
Cash	$20,000	$15,000
Accounts receivable	15,000	10,000
Accounts payable	2,000	8,000
Revenues	40,000	
Expenses	30,000	
Dividends	9,000	

The company pays dividends in the amount of 90 percent of net income each year. The company has been profitable over the past several years and has held large cash balances during that time. It has also been company policy to pay off payables as soon as they arise.

Consumer Price Index information follows.

January 1	270
Average during the year	300
December 31	330

Assume that revenues and expenses occur evenly throughout the year and that dividends are paid on the last day of the year.

Required:

a. Compute constant-dollar income for the year.

b. Comment on the company's policy to pay dividends in the amount of 90 percent of conventional income, hold large cash balances, and pay off payables as soon as they arise.

PC–8   *(Debt covenants and constant-dollar accounting)*   Temple Industries has signed a debt covenant specifying that retained earnings must be maintained at or above $10,000 throughout the period of the loan. At year end the company's board of directors is contemplating paying a dividend. Financial information for the year follows.

	December 31	January 1
Monetary assets	$25,000	$20,000
Long-lived assets	38,000	40,000
Total assets	$63,000	$60,000
Monetary liabilities	$ 5,000	$15,000
Common stock	30,000	30,000
Retained earnings	28,000	15,000
Total liabilities and stockholders' equity	$63,000	$60,000

Additional Information

1. The long-lived assets were purchased on January 1 and no additional long-lived assets were purchased or sold during the year.
2. Sales and expenses occurred evenly throughout the year.
3. Consumer Price Index: January 1 (375), Average (400), December 31 (425).

Required:

a. How large a dividend could be paid without violating the debt covenant, if retained earnings are measured under generally accepted accounting principles?
b. How large a dividend could be paid without violating the debt covenant, if retained earnings are measured under constant-dollar accounting?
c. Why might borrowers prefer to write debt covenants in terms of accounting numbers computed under constant-dollar accounting? What problems might arise when using such numbers?

CASES

CC–1

(Capital intensive industries and constant dollar and current-cost financial statements) In a study conducted by the FASB, companies in capital-intensive industries, such as utilities and chemical manufacturers, showed much lower profits after their income statements had been adjusted to constant dollars. When these same statements were adjusted for current costs, the resulting profit numbers were even lower. The same phenomenon was also true for companies in the mining and construction industries, which relied heavily on large amounts of relatively old equipment.

Required: Explain why the profits of capital-intensive companies would be reduced significantly when their financial statements were adjusted for inflation and current costs. Suggest why such a phenomenon would not be as prominent in the service industry and for financial institutions.

CC–2

(Maintaining capital and paying dividends) A noted economist, Sir John Hicks, commented that income is the maximum value which can be consumed during a period of time and still be as well off at the end of the period as at the beginning. With that in mind, note that a number of companies pay dividends, which are less than the net income amounts indicated on their conventional income statement, but considerably greater than constant-dollar or current-cost net income. In 1979, for example, Ford Motor Company paid dividends of almost $4 per share, reported conventional net income of $9.75 per share, and reported current-cost income of $1.78 per share. At that time certain major U.S. companies were required to report current-cost income.

Required:

a. Explain why conventional net income may not be a reliable measure of income in the terms of Hicks' definition and how constant-dollar income and current-cost income might represent improvements.

b. In terms of Hicks' definition of income explain why companies which pay dividends in excess of constant-dollar or current-cost income could be asking for trouble in the future.

CC-3

(Purchasing-power gains and interest rates)   In an article published in the *Financial Analysts Journal* (May-June, 1981) Larry Revsine argued that a company does not enjoy a purchasing-power gain on its outstanding debt unless the interest rate paid on the debt fails to cover the inflation rate over the period of the loan. He points out that the interest rates charged borrowers are comprised of two components: (1) a real component, which reflects the cost of borrowing in the absence of inflation and (2) a component corresponding to the anticipated rate of inflation over the period of the debt. As he points out: "The lender seeks protection from purchasing-power losses by negotiating an additional interest component equal to the anticipated rate of inflation." In other words, when high rates of inflation are anticipated borrowers are charged higher interest rates.

Required:

a. Define purchasing-power gains and explain how holding outstanding debt gives rise to them.

b. Differentiate between a monetary and nonmonetary item and explain why purchasing-power gains and losses are only recognized on monetary items.

c. Provide the rationale for the argument that a company does not experience a purchasing-power loss on outstanding debt unless the interest rate fails to cover the inflation rate. Would that same rationale apply to purchasing-power losses held on outstanding notes receivable? Explain.

d. Consider the fact that a purchasing-power gain from holding an outstanding debt would be reported on a constant-dollar income statement. That same income statement would also report inflation-adjusted interest expense, which would reflect any additional cost associated with the inflation factor charged by the creditor. Would constant-dollar net income be overstated, understated, or correctly stated if the inflation factor (1) exactly equaled the actual inflation rate, (2) was below the actual inflation rate, or (3) was greater than the actual inflation rate?

The Annual Report of K Mart Corporation

11-YEAR FINANCIAL SUMMARY

	1988	1987	1986
SUMMARY OF OPERATIONS *(Millions)*			
Sales	$27,301	$25,627	$23,812
Cost of merchandise sold	$19,914	$18,564	$17,258
Selling, general and administrative expenses	$ 6,184	$ 5,913	$ 5,517
Interest expense–net	$ 313	$ 308	$ 326
Income from continuing retail operations before income taxes	$ 1,244	$ 1,171	$ 1,028
Income from continuing retail operations	$ 803	$ 692	$ 570
PER-SHARE DATA *(Dollars)*			
Earnings per common and common equivalent share from continuing retail operations	$ 4.00	$ 3.40	$ 2.84
Cash dividends declared	$ 1.32	$ 1.16	$ 1.00
Book value	$ 25.12	$ 22.08	$ 19.66
FINANCIAL DATA *(Millions)*			
Working capital	$ 3,654	$ 3,003	$ 2,533
Total assets	$12,126	$11,106	$10,578
Long-term obligations–Debt	$ 1,358	$ 1,191	$ 1,011
—Capital leases	$ 1,588	$ 1,557	$ 1,600
Shareholders' equity	$ 5,009	$ 4,409	$ 3,939
Capital expenditures–Owned property	$ 570	$ 542	$ 552
Depreciation and amortization–Owned property	$ 337	$ 304	$ 280
Weighted average shares outstanding	200	202	199
FINANCIAL RATIOS			
Return on sales–Income from continuing retail operations before income taxes	4.6%	4.6%	4.3%
—Income from continuing retail operations	2.9%	2.7%	2.4%
Return on beginning assets from continuing retail operations	7.2%	6.5%	5.7%
Return on beginning shareholders' equity from continuing retail operations	18.2%	17.6%	17.4%
Debt and equivalent as a % of total capitalization	38.0%	39.4%	43.2%
Employee compensation and benefits, per sales dollar	14.7%	14.9%	15.1%
Working capital ratio	2.0	1.9	1.7

1985	1984	1983	1982	1981	1980	1979	1978
$22,035	$20,762	$18,380	$16,611	$16,394	$14,118	$12,731	$11,696
$15,987	$15,095	$13,354	$12,237	$12,308	$10,380	$ 9,283	$ 8,566
$ 5,227	$ 4,811	$ 4,188	$ 3,969	$ 3,744	$ 3,284	$ 2,839	$ 2,503
$ 363	$ 292	$ 228	$ 220	$ 230	$ 200	$ 149	$ 132
$ 757	$ 835	$ 859	$ 408	$ 311	$ 429	$ 625	$ 634
$ 472	$ 503	$ 491	$ 255	$ 211	$ 252	$ 355	$ 342
$ 2.42	$ 2.58	$ 2.53	$ 1.34	$ 1.12	$ 1.34	$ 1.88	$ 1.82
$ .92	$ .84	$ .72	$ .68	$ .64	$ .60	$ .56	$ .48
$ 17.32	$ 17.24	$ 15.57	$ 13.93	$ 13.20	$ 12.66	$ 11.86	$ 10.46
$ 2,437	$ 2,422	$ 2,268	$ 1,827	$ 1,473	$ 1,552	$ 1,403	$ 1,308
$ 9,991	$ 9,262	$ 8,183	$ 7,344	$ 6,657	$ 6,089	$ 5,635	$ 4,836
$ 1,456	$ 1,107	$ 711	$ 596	$ 415	$ 419	$ 209	$ 209
$ 1,713	$ 1,780	$ 1,822	$ 1,824	$ 1,752	$ 1,618	$ 1,422	$ 1,294
$ 3,273	$ 3,234	$ 2,940	$ 2,601	$ 2,456	$ 2,343	$ 2,185	$ 1,916
$ 547	$ 622	$ 368	$ 306	$ 361	$ 302	$ 292	$ 217
$ 246	$ 192	$ 161	$ 152	$ 136	$ 116	$ 93	$ 77
188	188	187	186	186	185	184	183
3.4%	4.0%	4.7%	2.5%	1.9%	3.0%	4.9%	5.4%
2.1%	2.4%	2.7%	1.5%	1.3%	1.8%	2.8%	2.9%
5.2%	6.2%	6.8%	3.9%	3.5%	4.5%	7.4%	7.7%
14.6%	17.1%	18.9%	10.4%	9.0%	11.6%	18.5%	20.7%
50.8%	49.8%	47.0%	48.7%	47.2%	46.8%	43.1%	44.4%
15.2%	15.0%	15.4%	16.4%	15.7%	15.8%	15.2%	14.6%
1.8	1.8	1.9	1.8	1.8	2.0	1.8	1.9

1988 OPERATIONS AND FINANCIAL REVIEW

MANAGEMENT DISCUSSION & ANALYSIS

Overview of 1988

Fiscal 1988 was a record year for K mart Corporation. Consolidated sales were $27.3 billion, an increase of 6.5% over 1987. Consolidated sales in comparable stores –those stores open throughout both fiscal years–increased 2.8% over 1987. Income from continuing retail operations in 1988 was $803 million, compared with $692 million in 1987, an increase of 16.0%.

A strong performance by the general-merchandise group was primarily responsible for the record results in 1988. The group's sales and earnings growth was principally due to continued refinement of and innovation in advertising and merchandising programs, increased emphasis on competitive pricing and price leadership, implementation of retail automation programs in additional stores, continued cost control measures and the favorable impact of a declining corporate income tax rate.

During 1988, the company opened 64 new K mart stores in the United States and Canada, compared with 36 openings in 1987. In addition, the company began a major store enlargement and relocation program in 1988, designed to expand or relocate smaller locations into full-size K mart stores. During 1988, the company expanded 22 locations and relocated an additional 16 stores as a result of this program.

The growth of the specialty retail group continued during 1988 with 154 store openings, compared with 258 in 1987 and 195 in 1986. The specialty group recorded increased sales in 1988 mainly due to this continued expansion.

Growth, innovation and progress have been key factors in the success of K mart Corporation. Management recognizes that to enhance the market presence and customer franchise the company has achieved, K mart must continue to explore new retail concepts. It was with this goal in mind that in 1988 K mart entered into several new retail ventures, including Makro warehouse clubs and the American Fare hypermarket concept store.

Fiscal 1988 marked the 24th consecutive year that K mart Corporation increased the cash dividends declared to its shareholders. Dividends declared in 1988 were $1.32 per share, compared with $1.16 per share in 1987, an increase of 13.8%.

During 1988, the company issued $300 million of medium-term notes at varying fixed interest rates and maturities under a shelf registration filed in February 1988. Additionally, through the end of fiscal 1988, the company had purchased 3.7 million shares of its common stock for $108 million under authorization granted by the Board of Directors in 1987 for the repurchase of up to $500 million of the company's common stock.

Analysis of General Merchandise Operations

The general-merchandise group primarily includes U.S. and Canadian K mart stores and, in 1988, Makro warehouse clubs. A three-year summary of the general-merchandise group's sales and operating income follows:

CASH DIVIDENDS DECLARED PER SHARE

(Dollars)
$1.50
1.25
1.00
.75
.50
.25

1979 1980 1981 1982 1983 1984 1985 1986 1987 1988

(Millions U.S. $)	1988	% Change	1987	% Change	1986
Sales					
United States	$22,177	4.5	$21,228	3.6	$20,481
Canada	1,010	10.8	912	10.3	827
Total Sales	$23,187	4.7	$22,140	3.9	$21,308
Operating Income	$ 1,436	3.7	$ 1,384	5.6	$ 1,311

The general-merchandise group's increased sales in 1988 were principally due to increased emphasis on lower everyday shelf prices, K mart's continued merchandise enhancement and store refurbishment programs, and inflation. K mart sales in comparable stores—those domestic and Canadian stores open throughout both fiscal years—increased 2.5% in 1988 and 3.6% in 1987. The lower comparable store increase in 1988 was primarily due to an increasingly competitive retail environment and the change in weekly advertising from the twice-a-week circulars to the once-a-week advertisements. Sales per square foot (including unconsolidated K mart store licensee sales) were $188 in 1988, compared with $183 in 1987, an increase of 2.4%.

Adjusted for the sale of domestic Kresge and Jupiter stores during 1987, the general-merchandise group's sales increased 4.4% as compared with 1986, primarily due to new advertising and merchandising programs, increased emphasis on competitive pricing and inflation.

Included in the U. S. general-merchandise group in 1988 was Makro Inc. In March 1988, K mart purchased a 51% interest in Makro, previously a wholly owned subsidiary of SHV North America Corporation. Makro warehouse clubs carry a broad assortment of general merchandise and food products. Originally, four stores located in Cincinnati, Washington, D.C., Philadelphia and Atlanta, each occupying from 150,000 to 200,000 square feet, were in operation. During 1988, three additional stores were opened and the store in Atlanta was closed, leaving six Makro stores at year end. Up to four additional Makro stores are scheduled to open in 1989.

K mart Canada Limited's (including Canadian K mart, Kresge and Jupiter stores) general merchandise sales in U.S. dollars increased 10.8% and 10.3% in 1988 and 1987, respectively. The 1988 sales increase in U.S. dollars reflected an 8.1% improvement in the average Canadian dollar, compared with a 4.9% improvement in 1987. K mart Canada's sales in Canadian dollars increased 2.5%, compared with a 5.2% increase in 1987. The 1988 results in Canadian dollars were attributable to a strong Christmas selling season and improved merchandising strategies. The 1987 increase was primarily a result of enhanced merchandising strategies and a favorable Canadian economy.

Operating income measures the group's performance before interest, corporate expenses and income taxes. Operating income for the general-merchandise group increased 3.7% to $1,436 million in 1988, compared with $1,384 million in 1987 and $1,311 million in 1986. The 1988 increase is primarily the result of improved sales and expense control programs achieved by K mart stores, partially offset by lower gross profit margins due to a highly competitive retail environment and an increased emphasis on lower everyday shelf prices. The results for 1987 improved despite additional pension expense due to a voluntary early retirement program and an increase in store closing expense as compared with 1986.

A significant factor in improved expense control during 1988 was the continued expansion of the retail automation program. During 1988, an additional 421 point-of-sale (POS) systems were installed in domestic K mart stores, bringing the total number to 1,180. The company plans to install an additional 503 POS systems in existing stores and equip all new K mart stores with POS systems in 1989.

In addition to POS, other aspects of the retail automation program also contributed to the efficiency and reduced cost of store operations. These include an improved merchandise receiving system which enhances the speed of merchandise processing, computerized pharmacy and layaway systems, and the satellite communications network.

In conjunction with the retail automation program, K mart continued development of the centralized merchandising functions during 1988. By reducing the decision-making layers between customer and vendor, centralization allows quicker response to changing fashions and consumer spending patterns. Using information provided by POS scanning and the satellite network, centralized buying will result in better in-stock positions in K mart stores, improved inventory control and turnover, and increased sales volume.

The general-merchandise group's store opening program was accelerated in 1988. During the year, 64 K mart stores opened in the United States and Canada, compared with 36 openings in 1987. An additional 70 stores are expected to open in 1989. The company also embarked on a store enlargement program in 1988, converting 22 smaller locations into full-size K mart stores. This program is aimed at improving the company's competitive advantage in more markets. For stores where expansion is not possible, the company is opening new, larger stores. Of the 23 K mart stores that closed in 1988, 16 were relocated to larger stores in the same market and four were converted to Builders Square stores.

The following table highlights the general-merchandise group's store activity during 1988:

| | End 1986 | End 1987 | 1988 Activity | | | |
			Acquired	Opened	Closed	End
K mart						
U.S.	2,086	2,105	–	63	23	**2,145**
Canada	118	118	–	1	–	**119**
Kresge and Jupiter						
U.S.	86	1	–	–	1	–
Canada	52	49	–	–	12	37
Makro	–	–	4	3	1	6
Total General Merchandise	**2,342**	**2,273**	**4**	**67**	**37**	**2,307**
K mart Retail Square Feet (Millions)	**126**	**128**				**131**
K mart Store Sales per Square Foot	**$ 177**	**$ 183**				**$ 188**

In addition to the store expansion program, K mart Corporation continues to modernize and refurbish stores, creating a more appealing and convenient shopping atmosphere. The company is concentrating efforts on allocating more space to apparel departments and updating home care centers, Kitchen Korners, electronics and domestic centers. During 1988, 163 K mart stores were completely refurbished, including an updated floor plan emphasizing apparel, a better merchandise mix and new fixturing.

Refer to Note (M) of the accompanying Notes to Consolidated Financial Statements for further information regarding the company's business groups.

Analysis of Specialty Retail Operations

The company's specialty retail group operates warehouse home improvement centers, super drug stores and retail book stores in the domestic retail market and special purchase discount stores in Canada. The following is a brief description of specialty retail operations:

- *Builders Square, Inc.*—A typical Builders Square warehouse home improvement store occupies 80,000 square feet and carries a wide selection of low-priced do-it-yourself merchandise displayed in a warehouse-style format. Builders Square operating results continued to improve in 1988 despite a significantly higher LIFO charge.

- *Pay Less Drug Stores Northwest, Inc.*—Pay Less operates super drug stores which occupy from 25,000 to 80,000 square feet and offer a variety of merchandise ranging from traditional drug store offerings to cameras and film developing, automotive, lawn and garden items, and sporting goods merchandise. During 1988, Pay Less implemented new pricing and advertising programs which resulted in increased gross margins because of the elimination of many promotional and food products. The net result for 1988 was a lower inventory investment, higher inventory turnover and an improvement in operating profit as compared with 1987.

- *Walden Book Company, Inc.*—A Waldenbooks store usually occupies 3,000 square feet in a regional or local shopping mall and offers video and audio tapes and computer software as well as books. In addition to its own stores, Waldenbooks now operates 225 book departments in K mart stores and the American Fare store. Waldenbooks also continues to develop specialty store concepts targeted at specific consumer markets such as Waldensoftware, Waldenbooks and More, and Brentanos. The 1988 operating results for Waldenbooks were lower than 1987 primarily due to a significantly higher LIFO charge.

- *Bargain Harold's Discount Limited*—Bargain Harold's stores offer exceptionally sharp pricing on special purchase merchandise and are designed to serve numerous Canadian communities too small to support traditional variety stores. The 1988 results for Bargain Harold's were improved over 1987 principally due to an improved merchandise mix.

In 1988, K mart introduced two new specialty concepts, Office Square and Sports Giant. Office Square stores occupy approximately 25,000 square feet and carry mainly office supplies, office furniture and business equipment. The first two Office Square stores opened during 1988 in the Chicago area. Sports Giant stores will be approximately 50,000 square feet and will sell sporting goods, footwear and apparel merchandise. The first Sports Giant stores are planned to open in early 1989 in the Detroit area.

A three-year summary of the specialty retail group's sales and operating income follows:

(Millions)	1988	% Change	1987	% Change	1986
Sales	$4,114	18.0	$3,487	39.2	$2,504
Operating Income	$ 72	(4.1)	$ 75	103.6	$ 37

The specialty retail group's 18.0% sales increase in 1988 resulted in part from the group's store expansion program. Additionally, the group achieved a 4.3% comparable store sales increase in 1988, despite a slight decline in comparable store sales of Pay Less resulting from a change in merchandising strategy that eliminated many lower-margin products including promotional items. The 1987 sales increase in the specialty group was principally the result of 258 store openings during the year.

The specialty retail group's operating income decreased 4.1% to $72 million in 1988 from $75 million in 1987. The decrease in operating income was mainly the result of a significantly higher LIFO charge for the group and higher store closing expense, primarily due to the closing of the Wonder World division of Pay Less, which more than offset improvements in operating income for the group. The group's 1987 operating income was significantly higher than 1986 mainly due to improved operating results at Builders Square and Pay Less.

The specialty group continues to expand as illustrated in the following store summary:

STORES OPEN AT END OF YEAR BY BUSINESS GROUP

GENERAL MERCHANDISE STORES   SPECIALTY RETAIL STORES

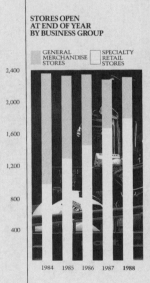

1984 1985 1986 1987 **1988**

	End 1986	End 1987	1988 Activity Opened	Closed	End	Planned End 1989
Builders Square	86	118	15	–	133	142
Pay Less Drug Stores	218	254	26	11	269	309
Waldenbooks	994	1,139	106	27	1,218	1,274
Bargain Harold's	142	150	5	2	153	154
Office Square	–	–	2	–	2	2
Sports Giant	–	–	–	–	–	2
Total Specialty Retail	1,440	1,661	154	40	1,775	1,883
Specialty Retail Square Feet (Millions)	16	20			22	

Refer to Note (M) of the accompanying Notes to Consolidated Financial Statements for additional information regarding the company's business groups.

Licensee Operations and Equity Investments

Meldisco

The company's domestic K mart footwear departments are operated by the Meldisco subsidiaries of Melville Corporation. Substantially all departments are owned 49% by the company and 51% by Melville. Sales of the licensee footwear departments increased 4.8% to $1,063 million in 1988 and increased .7% to $1,013 million in 1987. The sales increase in 1988 was primarily due to a successful Christmas selling season and increased emphasis on brand name athletic footwear and workboots. Equity in income was unchanged in 1988 as compared with 1987. Equity in income in 1987 was below 1986 due to flat sales and a decline in the gross profit margin. The lower 1987 gross margin was a result of increased price competition and the higher cost of imported merchandise as a result of a weaker U.S. dollar.

Late in 1988, Pay Less entered into a license agreement with Meldisco whereby the footwear departments in most Pay Less stores will be operated by Meldisco. Pay Less will receive licensee fees from the operation of these departments beginning in 1989.

Refer to Note (H) of the accompanying Notes to Consolidated Financial Statements for further information regarding the company's investment in Meldisco.

Coles Myer Ltd.

K mart's income from Australian operations, which consisted primarily of equity in income of Coles Myer Ltd., Australia's largest retailer, was $61 million in U.S. dollars in 1988, compared with $49 million and $35 million in 1987 and 1986, respectively. The increase in 1988 equity income was mainly due to strong operating results, lower Australian income tax rates and an 11.8% improvement in the average Australian dollar versus the U.S. dollar. Coles Myer's 1988 sales increased 17.3% in Australian dollars. This sales growth was achieved mainly through strong comparable store sales increases and the acquisition of new enterprises. Equity in income in 1987 increased due to higher operating income, one-time gains on the sale of certain property and investments, and the extinguishment of debt. The average Australian dollar exchange rates were .7847 in 1988, .7016 in 1987 and .6711 in 1986.

At December 27, 1988, Coles Myer operated 758 supermarket, food service and liquor stores, 439 discount stores (including 133 K mart stores), 78 department stores and 161 specialty retail stores across Australia and New Zealand. Fiscal 1988 marks the first year K mart stores operated in New Zealand.

For additional information regarding the company's investment in Coles Myer, refer to Note (H) of the accompanying Notes to Consolidated Financial Statements.

Income from Continuing Retail Operations

Income from continuing retail operations before income taxes was $1,244 million for 1988, an increase of 6.3% from 1987. Income from continuing retail operations before income taxes in 1987 was $1,171 million, an increase of 13.8% from 1986.

Earnings per share from continuing retail operations were $4.00, $3.40 and $2.84 for 1988, 1987 and 1986, respectively.

The effective income tax rate on income from continuing retail operations in 1988 was 35.5%, compared with 40.9% in 1987 and 44.6% in 1986. The decline in the company's effective income tax rate in 1988 and 1987 was primarily a result of the Tax Reform Act of 1986 which reduced the federal statutory corporate income tax rate to 34% in 1988 from 39% in 1987 and 46% in 1986.

Financial Accounting Standard No. 96 "Accounting for Income Taxes" (FAS 96) was issued in December 1987. The standard requires adjustment of deferred tax liabilities for enacted changes in the statutory federal tax rate. During 1988, the standard was amended by Financial Accounting Standard No. 100 "Accounting for Income Taxes–Deferral of the Effective Date of FASB No. 96" which delays required implementation of FAS 96 until fiscal years beginning after December 15, 1989. Had K mart adopted FAS 96 in 1988, the company would have recognized additional income, which was not considered material, due to a reduction in deferred tax liabilities.

Refer to Note (I) of the accompanying Notes to Consolidated Financial Statements for further information regarding income taxes.

Cost of Merchandise Sold

Cost of merchandise sold, including buying and occupancy costs, as a percent of sales was 72.9% in 1988, compared with 72.4% in 1987 and 72.5% in 1986. This increase in 1988 was attributable to an increased emphasis by the general-merchandise group on competitive pricing and price leadership, the inclusion of the lower-margined Makro stores in 1988 results and an increased LIFO charge. The improvement in cost of merchandise sold as a percent of sales in 1987 was attributable to better gross margin management in the general-merchandise group, partially offset by a higher proportion of specialty retail group sales which have a lower gross margin than the general-merchandise group.

Substantially all of the company's domestic inventories are measured using the last-in, first-out (LIFO) method of inventory valuation. LIFO provides a more accurate matching of current costs with current revenues and measures the impact of inflation on inventories during periods of rising prices. Based on the U.S. Department of Labor's Department Store Price Index for the year ended January 25, 1989, the inflationary impact on inventories resulted in a pretax charge to income of $160 million in 1988, compared with pretax charges of $98 million and $75 million in 1987 and 1986, respectively. The higher LIFO charge in 1988 is primarily due to higher inflation than in 1987 and lower gross profit margins. The higher LIFO charge in 1987 was mainly due to greater inflationary pressures during the year.

Operating Expenses

Selling, general and administrative expenses, including advertising, were 22.7% of sales in 1988, compared with 23.1% and 23.2% of sales in 1987 and 1986, respectively.

The following factors influenced operating expenses in 1988:

Employee compensation and benefits increased 5.4% in 1988 to $4,016 million and 6.0% in 1987 to $3,809 million. As in 1987, the 1988 increase was primarily attributable to salary increases for existing employees and the company's store opening programs. Employee compensation and benefits as a percent of sales was 14.7% in 1988, compared with 14.9% in 1987 and 15.1% in 1986. The decreases in both 1988 and 1987 were attributed to careful management of store hours and increased utilization of retail automation systems to improve productivity. Also contributing to the decline in 1988 was the inclusion of Makro, which has a lower expense structure than that of traditional K mart stores.

Pension expense was $35 million in both 1988 and 1987 and $9 million in 1986. The 1987 pension expense included a $12 million charge for the company's voluntary early retirement program.

For additional information regarding the company's pension plans refer to Note (O) of the accompanying Notes to Consolidated Financial Statements.

Advertising expense decreased to $581 million in 1988, compared with $617 million in 1987 and $581 million in 1986. The company realized a substantial cost savings by changing the domestic K mart store weekly advertising program to comprehensive once-a-week circulars from the previous program of twice-a-week advertisements. Other new advertising programs in 1988 included the Martha Stewart home furnishings promotion designed to make consumers aware of the extensive line of home furnishings available at K mart stores, the Betsy McCall magazine promotion which is aimed at girls age 6 through 12, and K mart's sponsorship of the 1988 winter and summer Olympic Games.

Interest Expense

A schedule of the components of net interest expense on debt follows:

(Millions)	1988	1987	1986
Interest Expense on Debt	$172	$156	$171
Interest Income	33	22	23
Net Interest Expense on Debt	$139	$134	$148

The increase in net interest expense on debt in 1988 was principally a result of additional higher cost, fixed-rate borrowings during the year. The decrease in 1987 net interest expense resulted primarily from reduced levels of borrowings net of short-term investments and the retirement of high-cost 12¾% debt in 1986. The company's weighted average interest rates on total debt were 9.5% in 1988, 8.9% in 1987 and 9.2% in 1986. Weighted average interest rates for short-term borrowings were 7.5%, 6.8% and 6.6% for 1988, 1987 and 1986, respectively.

Discontinued Operations

During 1988, the company completed the sale of the Lone Star Life Insurance Company, terminated the agreement for the operation of store insurance centers, terminated the lease of the former insurance operations headquarters and negotiated the sale of the two remaining insurance companies, KM Insurance Company and Victoria Lloyds Insurance Company, pending regulatory approval. Management believes that the remaining reserves for discontinued insurance operations are adequate at January 25, 1989.

Refer to Note (B) of the accompanying Notes to Consolidated Financial Statements for further information regarding discontinued operations.

Net Income

Net income for the year was $803 million, an increase of 16.0% over 1987 net income of $692 million. Improved 1988 net income was primarily the result of higher operating income and a lower income tax rate in 1988 than in 1987. Net income in 1986 was $582 million and included a $28 million net after-tax gain on the disposal of Furr's Cafeterias, Inc., Bishop Buffets, Inc. and the company's Designer Depot division, partially offset by a $16 million net charge due to redemption of the company's 12¾% sinking fund debentures. Earnings per share were $4.00, $3.40 and $2.90 for 1988, 1987 and 1986, respectively.

New Ventures

In 1987, K mart entered into a partnership with Bruno's Inc., a leading food retailer in the Southeast, to develop American Fare hypermarket concept stores. The first store opened on January 29, 1989 in Atlanta, Georgia and occupies approx-imately 244,000 square feet. A second American Fare is scheduled to open later in 1989 in the Charlotte, North Carolina area. These stores offer a broad assortment of general merchandise and food products as well as specialty shops and services.

Refer to Note (D) of the accompanying Notes to Consolidated Financial Statements for further information regarding new ventures.

Effects of Inflation

The financial statements of K mart Corporation were prepared on a historical cost basis under generally accepted accounting principles. K mart Corporation, like most non-food retailers, uses the LIFO method of inventory valuation in its historical financial statements. Thus, the cost of merchandise sold approximates current cost. In addition, because the company is continually refurbishing existing stores and opening new stores, depreciation and amortization expense more closely approximates current cost. The company's rental expense is generally fixed and is not affected by inflation although percentage rentals do account for some of the impact of inflation.

Financial Condition

Financial Objectives

K mart Corporation's financial policy is designed to provide the company and its shareholders an optimum return on investment, a solid capital structure and a high degree of financial flexibility. Obtaining optimum return on investment requires deployment of the company's assets and resources where they will provide the best return. In seeking optimum return, K mart management continues to review potential retail investment opportunities in addition to funding an improved merchandise mix, the refurbishment and expansion of existing K mart stores, and the expansion of the company's specialty retail operations. In addition, K mart management sold or closed K mart and specialty stores which did not generate sufficient returns. The company expects that funds required to finance refurbishment of existing stores, future expansion, acquisitions and the repurchase of the company's common stock will be provided primarily by internally generated funds, additional debt offerings, the sale and leaseback of owned properties and the leasing of land and buildings.

Return on Investment

Return on investment (ROI) is an important measure of the company's effective use of its resources. ROI measures the relationship of income from continuing retail operations to invested capital. Income from continuing retail operations is adjusted for after-tax interest expense. Invested capital or total capitalization consists mainly of shareholders' equity, interest bearing liabilities and debt equivalent lease obligations. The company's objective is to maximize ROI without eroding its competitive position.

The following analysis shows the computation of ROI:

(Millions)	1988	1987	1986
Income from continuing retail operations	$ 803	$ 692	$ 570
Interest expense net of taxes	228	201	188
Income from continuing retail operations before financing costs	$1,031	$ 893	$ 758
Total beginning capitalization from continuing retail operations	$7,607	$7,254	$6,793
Return on beginning investment from continuing retail operations	13.6%	12.3%	11.2%

Improved ROI in both 1988 and 1987 was primarily the result of increased operating income in the general-merchandise group and a lower corporate income tax rate.

Cash Flow

Company funds generated by operations, investing and financing activities as reported in the Consolidated Statements of Cash Flows on page 33, as well as the company's capitalization structure, are summarized below. Note (E) of the accompanying Notes to Consolidated Financial Statements contains additional information regarding the Consolidated Statements of Cash Flows.

Net cash provided by operations was $1,211 million in 1988, $908 million in 1987 and $770 million in 1986. Increased cash provided by operations in 1988 was primarily the result of higher income from continuing retail operations, increased depreciation and amortization expense, and a lower rate of increase in inventories net of accounts payable. Depreciation and amortization expenses are recognized in determining income from continuing retail operations but do not require cash outlays. These expenses have been steadily rising each year due to capital expenditures for the K mart store refurbishment and expansion programs, the retail automation program and the specialty retail group's store opening program. Inventory, net of accounts payable, is also an important component of cash provided by continuing retail operations. Inventory, net of accounts payable, was 2.3% higher at January 25, 1989 than at January 27, 1988.

The inventory turnover ratio, using replacement cost as measured by the first-in, first-out (FIFO) method of inventory valuation, was 3.0 in both 1988 and 1987 and 3.1 in 1986.

Refer to Note (F) of the accompanying Notes to Consolidated Financial Statements for further information regarding merchandise inventories.

The working capital ratio demonstrates the company's ability to meet short-term obligations. The company's working capital ratio was 2.0 in 1988, 1.9 in 1987 and 1.7 in 1986. The improvement in 1988 is primarily due to increased cash and investments partially offset by a slight increase in accounts payable. The improvement in 1987 was due to an increase in inventory and a decrease in short-term borrowings.

Net cash used for investing was $505 million in 1988, compared with $539 million in 1987 and $583 million in 1986. Capital expenditures for owned property of $459 million, $379 million and $343 million in the general-merchandise group in 1988, 1987 and 1986, respectively, included refurbishments, expansions, retail automation and store openings. The specialty retail group's capital expenditures for owned property of $111 million in 1988, $163 million in 1987 and $209 million in 1986 were principally the result of new store openings. Offsetting the net cash used for investing in 1988 was $69 million received from sale and leaseback transactions entered into during the year.

Net cash used for financing was $207 million in 1988, $441 million in 1987 and $293 million in 1986. The decrease in cash used for financing was mainly a result of the issuance of $300 million of medium-term notes, offset by the company's stock repurchase program and increased dividends paid. In November 1987, the Board of Directors authorized the repurchase of up to $500 million of the company's common stock. Under this authorization, the company repurchased 1.0 million shares of its common stock for $33 million during 1988 and 2.7 million shares for $75 million during 1987. K mart's stock repurchase program is designed to enhance shareholder value and improve return on shareholders' equity.

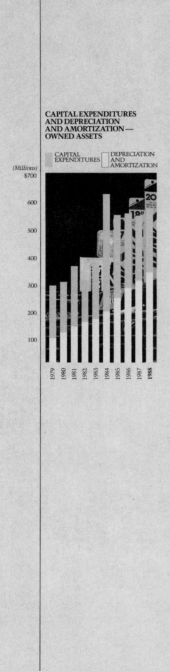

CAPITAL EXPENDITURES AND DEPRECIATION AND AMORTIZATION— OWNED ASSETS

CAPITAL EXPENDITURES / DEPRECIATION AND AMORTIZATION

(Millions)

$700, 600, 500, 400, 300, 200, 100

1979 1980 1981 1982 1983 1984 1985 1986 1987 1988

In February 1988, the company filed a shelf registration covering debt offerings up to $500 million. Under this shelf registration, K mart issued $300 million of medium-term notes at varying interest rates and maturities throughout the year. The company has no immediate plans for issuance of the $200 million remaining under this shelf registration.

During 1987, K mart issued $200 million of 10½% debentures due in 2017. This was the final $200 million of debt covered by the May 1986 shelf registration.

In January 1987, the company redeemed $250 million of 12¾% sinking fund debentures due in 2015 primarily with the proceeds from the sale of its cafeteria operations.

For additional information regarding these financing activities refer to Note (J) of the accompanying Notes to Consolidated Financial Statements.

Dividends paid during 1988 were $256 million, compared with $225 million in 1987 and $187 million in 1986. Dividends paid per share were $1.28, $1.12 and $.98 in 1988, 1987 and 1986, respectively.

The following table provides additional information regarding dividends paid and common stock prices in 1988 and 1987:

| | Fiscal Quarters Dividends Paid | | Calendar Quarters Market Prices | | | |
	1988	1987	1988 High	1988 Low	1987 High	1987 Low
First	$ .29	$ .25	$36⅝	$29	$44⅝	$29⅜
Second	.33	.29	37	30¼	45⅜	38⅛
Third	.33	.29	39¾	31¼	48⅜	38⅞
Fourth	.33	.29	39⅜	33¾	41¼	21⅝
Total Year	$1.28	$1.12	$39¾	$29	$48⅜	$21⅝

As of January 25, 1989, there were 84,595 K mart Corporation shareholders of record, compared with 86,847 at fiscal year end 1987. K mart Corporation common stock is listed and traded on the New York, Pacific, Midwest and Tokyo Stock Exchanges (trading symbol KM).

The ratio of income to fixed charges demonstrates the company's ability to cover charges of a fixed nature, consisting primarily of interest expense, in relation to income from continuing retail operations. The ratio of income to fixed charges was 3.6 in 1988, 3.5 in 1987 and 3.2 in 1986. The increases in both 1988 and 1987 were principally due to higher earnings, partially offset in 1988 by increased interest expense.

The following three-year analysis of the company's *capital structure* indicates K mart's long-term financial flexibility by comparing total debt and equivalent with total capitalization:

CAPITALIZATION

(Millions)	1988	%	1987	%	1986	%
Long-term debt due within one year	$ 1	–	$ 2	–	$ 4	.1
Capital lease obligations due within one year	89	1.1	85	1.1	79	1.1
Notes payable	–	–	–	–	296	4.1
Long-term debt	1,358	16.1	1,191	15.7	1,011	13.9
Capital lease obligations	1,588	18.8	1,557	20.5	1,600	22.0
Other	165	2.0	163	2.1	143	2.0
Total debt and equivalent	3,201	38.0	2,998	39.4	3,133	43.2
Deferred income taxes	220	2.6	200	2.6	182	2.5
Shareholders' equity	5,009	59.4	4,409	58.0	3,939	54.3
Total capitalization	$8,430	100.0	$7,607	100.0	$7,254	100.0

Total debt and equivalent as a percent of total capitalization was 38.0% in 1988, 39.4% in 1987 and 43.2% in 1986. The decreases in both 1988 and 1987 were primarily a result of higher shareholders' equity resulting from the company's increased profitability.

Due to the seasonal nature of the retail industry, the company continues to utilize commercial paper and revolving credit to cover peak working capital requirements. The approximate average short-term borrowings outstanding during 1988, 1987 and 1986 were $401 million, $671 million and $487 million, respectively. The maximum amounts of aggregate short-term borrowings outstanding during 1988 were $808 million, compared with $1,047 million and $947 million in 1987 and 1986, respectively. Total short-term lines of credit available and unused were $595 million, $695 million and $712 million at the end of 1988, 1987 and 1986, respectively. The amount of short-term borrowings during 1988 was lower than 1987 primarily as a result of the issuance of $300 million of medium-term notes.

CORPORATE RESPONSIBILITY

Charitable Contributions

Each and every day K mart Corporation and its associates share in the responsibility of providing personal and economic support in the communities where we do business. They support the non-profit organizations and service agencies which are a vital part of our communities' ability to grow and prosper.

During 1988, our charitable contributions totaled $9 million. Our grants included scholarships for 46 pharmacy schools across the nation, a two-year pledge to Read America, Win America to help fight illiteracy, merchandise for Armenian relief, and programs benefitting local as well as national agencies. We also began a two-year partnership with the Invent America! program, which will reach hundreds of thousands of elementary school students across America.

Community Involvement

K mart associates continue the commitment to their communities with many Good News activities. The visibility and strength of their programs resulted in a trademark registration for the Good News Committees. The national Good News Holiday Programs provided food baskets for more than 80,000 families and helped more than 40,000 children with their Christmas shopping. The Children's Tree program garnered an award from the Presidential Citation Program for Private Sector Initiative. Nearly one thousand of our K mart stores participated in this program, which provided Christmas gifts for thousands of needy children.

Responding to the issues surrounding our country's ability to be innovative and competitive, K mart became the official retail sponsor for Invent America!. Invent America! is an education program and invention competition developed by the United States Patent Model Foundation to teach children critical problem-solving and analytical skills. The Foundation provides schools with classroom guides that encourage students to solve everyday problems they encounter. Children develop models of their inventions and submit them in local, state, regional and national competitions sponsored by Invent America!. We look forward to becoming involved with our local schools and students in promoting this program and the values it represents. Many retailers have buy American programs. We think this program is the best way to ensure there are American products to buy.

Minority Affairs

Growth of our minority vendor base for goods and services continued during 1988. Purchases from minority- and female-owned business firms increased 46% to $374 million in 1988. Advertising in minority trade media exceeded $4 million and we banked with 40 minority- and female-owned banks. Our efforts to further relationships will continue as K mart Chairman Joseph E. Antonini has been elected Chairman of the National Minority Supplier Development Council. Ronald R. Dejaeghere, Vice President of Community Affairs, is coordinating the minority purchasing program for K mart.

Corporate Ethics

The reputation of the company is one of our most valuable assets. To preserve and protect that asset, K mart prepared a booklet setting forth a general statement of the standards by which the company conducts its business. The booklet, entitled "Standards of Business Conduct", is available to employees, customers, suppliers and shareholders. To obtain a copy of the booklet, contact the Public Affairs department at K mart International Headquarters.

REPORTS BY MANAGEMENT AND INDEPENDENT ACCOUNTANTS

K mart Responsibility for Financial Statements

K mart Corporation management is responsible for the integrity of the information and representations contained in this annual report. This responsibility includes making informed estimates and judgments in selecting the appropriate accounting principles in the circumstances. Management believes the financial statements conform with generally accepted accounting principles and have been prepared on a consistent basis.

To assist management in fulfilling these obligations, the company utilizes several tools, which include the following:

- The company maintains a system of internal accounting controls to provide for the integrity of information for purposes of preparing financial statements and to assure that assets are properly accounted for and safeguarded. This concept of reasonable assurance is based on the recognition that the cost of the system must be related to the benefits to be derived. Management believes its system provides this appropriate balance.

- An Internal Audit Department is maintained to evaluate, test and report on the application of internal accounting controls in conformity with standards of the practice of internal auditing.

- The Board of Directors appoints the independent accountants to perform an examination of the company's financial statements. This examination includes, among other things, a review of the system of internal controls as required by generally accepted auditing standards.

- The Audit Committee of the Board of Directors, consisting solely of outside directors, meets regularly with management, internal auditors and the independent accountants to assure that each is carrying out its responsibilities. The internal auditors and independent accountants both have full and free access to the Audit Committee, with and without the presence of management.

J. E. ANTONINI
Chairman of the Board, President
and Chief Executive Officer

T. F. MURASKY
Vice President and
Chief Financial Officer

Report of Independent Accountants

To the Shareholders and Board of Directors of K mart Corporation

In our opinion, the accompanying consolidated balance sheets and the related consolidated statements of income, shareholders' equity and of cash flows present fairly, in all material respects, the financial position of K mart Corporation and its subsidiaries at January 25, 1989 and January 27, 1988, and the results of their operations and their cash flows for each of the three years in the period ended January 25, 1989, in conformity with generally accepted accounting principles. These financial statements are the responsibility of the company's management; our responsibility is to express an opinion on these financial statements based on our audits. We conducted our audits of these statements in accordance with generally accepted auditing standards which require that we plan and perform the audit to obtain reasonable assurance about whether the financial statements are free of material misstatement. An audit includes examining, on a test basis, evidence supporting the amounts and disclosures in the financial statements, assessing the accounting principles used and significant estimates made by management, and evaluating the overall financial statement presentation. We believe that our audits provide a reasonable basis for the opinion expressed above.

Price Waterhouse

200 Renaissance Center
Detroit, Michigan
March 8, 1989

CONSOLIDATED STATEMENTS OF INCOME

(Millions, except per-share data)	January 25, 1989	January 27, 1988	January 28, 1987
	Fiscal Year Ended		
Sales	$27,301	$25,627	$23,812
Licensee fees and rental income	249	237	234
Equity in income of affiliated retail companies	105	92	83
Interest income	33	22	23
	27,688	25,978	24,152
Cost of merchandise sold (including buying and occupancy costs)	19,914	18,564	17,258
Selling, general and administrative expenses	5,603	5,296	4,936
Advertising	581	617	581
Interest expense:			
Debt	172	156	171
Capital lease obligations	174	174	178
	26,444	24,807	23,124
Income from continuing retail operations before income taxes	1,244	1,171	1,028
Income taxes	441	479	458
Income from continuing retail operations	803	692	570
Discontinued operations (Note B)	–	–	28
Extraordinary item (Note J)	–	–	(16)
Net income for the year	$ 803	$ 692	$ 582
Earnings per common and common equivalent share:			
Continuing retail operations	$ 4.00	$ 3.40	$ 2.84
Discontinued operations	–	–	.14
Extraordinary item	–	–	(.08)
Net income	$ 4.00	$ 3.40	$ 2.90
Weighted average shares	200.6	203.5	201.5

See accompanying Notes to Consolidated Financial Statements.

CONSOLIDATED BALANCE SHEETS

($ Millions)	January 25, 1989	January 27, 1988
Assets		
Current Assets:		
Cash (includes temporary investments of $594 and $134, respectively)	$ 948	$ 449
Merchandise inventories	5,671	5,571
Accounts receivable and other current assets	527	353
Total current assets	7,146	6,373
Investments in Affiliated Retail Companies	506	379
Property and Equipment—net	3,896	3,744
Other Assets and Deferred Charges	578	610
	$12,126	$11,106
Liabilities and Shareholders' Equity		
Current Liabilities:		
Accounts payable—trade	$ 2,334	$ 2,309
Accrued payrolls and other liabilities	650	608
Taxes other than income taxes	282	242
Income taxes	226	211
Total current liabilities	3,492	3,370
Capital Lease Obligations	1,588	1,557
Long-Term Debt	1,358	1,191
Other Long-Term Liabilities	459	379
Deferred Income Taxes	220	200
Shareholders' Equity:		
Common stock, 500,000,000 shares authorized; shares issued 204,293,757 and 203,512,539, respectively.	204	204
Capital in excess of par value	588	572
Retained earnings	4,345	3,806
Treasury shares	(131)	(98)
Foreign currency translation adjustment	3	(75)
Total shareholders' equity	5,009	4,409
	$12,126	$11,106

See accompanying Notes to Consolidated Financial Statements.

CONSOLIDATED STATEMENTS OF CASH FLOWS

(Millions)	Fiscal Year Ended		
	January 25, 1989	January 27, 1988	January 28, 1987
Cash Provided by (Used for):			
Operations			
Income from continuing retail operations	$ 803	$ 692	$ 570
Noncash charges (credits) to earnings:			
Depreciation and amortization	437	401	377
Deferred income taxes	8	12	58
Undistributed equity income	(42)	(36)	(23)
Increase in other long-term liabilities	97	67	52
Other–net	53	56	13
Cash provided by (used for) current assets and current liabilities:			
(Increase) in inventories	(86)	(418)	(677)
Increase in accounts payable	19	102	312
Other–net	(73)	90	(59)
Total provided by continuing retail operations	1,216	966	623
Discontinued operations			
Gain from discontinued operations	–	–	28
Items not affecting cash–net	–	–	(95)
Cash provided by (used for) discontinued operations	(5)	(58)	214
Total provided by (used for) discontinued operations	(5)	(58)	147
Net cash provided by operations	1,211	908	770
Investing			
Additions to owned property	(570)	(542)	(552)
Proceeds from the sale of property	117	30	36
Other–net	(52)	(27)	(67)
Net cash used for investing	(505)	(539)	(583)
Financing			
Proceeds from issuance of long-term debt and notes payable	346	200	169
Reduction in long-term debt and notes payable	(184)	(318)	(266)
Extraordinary item–premium on debt redemption	–	–	(16)
Reduction in capital lease obligations	(96)	(83)	(80)
Common stock issued	16	46	73
Reissuance of treasury shares	–	14	14
Purchase of treasury shares	(33)	(75)	–
Dividends paid	(256)	(225)	(187)
Net cash used for financing	(207)	(441)	(293)
Net Increase (Decrease) in Cash and Equivalents	499	(72)	(106)
Cash and Equivalents at Beginning of Year	449	521	627
Cash and Equivalents at End of Year	$ 948	$ 449	$ 521

See accompanying Notes to Consolidated Financial Statements.

CONSOLIDATED STATEMENTS OF SHAREHOLDERS' EQUITY

($ Millions)	Common Stock $1 par value		Capital in Excess of Par Value	Retained Earnings	Treasury Shares	Foreign Currency Translation Adjustment	Total Shareholders' Equity
	Shares	Amount					
Balance at January 29, 1986	**191,522,481**	**$128**	**$343**	**$2,958**	**$(51)**	**$(105)**	**$3,273**
Net income for the year				582			582
Cash dividends declared, $1.00 per share				(193)			(193)
Three-for-two stock split		67	(67)				–
Common stock sold under stock option and employees' savings plans	2,792,834	2	63				65
Common stock issued for conversion of debentures	7,867,995	5	181				186
Reissue of 666,328 treasury shares for employees' savings plan			8		14		22
Foreign currency translation adjustment						4	4
Balance at January 28, 1987	**202,183,310**	**202**	**528**	**3,347**	**(37)**	**(101)**	**3,939**
Net income for the year				692			692
Cash dividends declared, $1.16 per share				(233)			(233)
Common stock sold under stock option plans	1,329,229	2	29				31
Purchase of 2,679,200 treasury shares, at cost					(75)		(75)
Reissue of 723,360 treasury shares for employees' savings plan			15		14		29
Foreign currency translation adjustment						26	26
Balance at January 27, 1988	**203,512,539**	**204**	**572**	**3,806**	**(98)**	**(75)**	**4,409**
Net income for the year				803			803
Cash dividends declared, $1.32 per share				(264)			(264)
Common stock sold under stock option plans	781,218		16				16
Purchase of 1,054,600 treasury shares, at cost					(33)		(33)
Foreign currency translation adjustment						78	78
Balance at January 25, 1989	**204,293,757**	**$204**	**$588**	**$4,345**	**$(131)**	**$ 3**	**$5,009**

Ten million shares of no par value preferred stock with voting and cumulative dividend rights are authorized but unissued. Of these, 500,000 shares have been designated Series A Junior Participating Preferred Stock. Currently there are no plans for the issuance of preferred stock.

In May 1988, the company distributed a stock purchase right as a dividend on each outstanding share of K mart common stock. Each right entitles the shareholder to purchase one one-thousandth of a share of newly designated Series A Junior Participating Preferred Stock at an exercise price of $110, or to purchase, at the right's then-current exercise price, common shares of K mart having a value twice the right's exercise price. The rights are exercisable only if a person or group acquires, or attempts to acquire, ownership of 20% or more of the company's common stock, or, if the person or group acquires 10% of the company's common stock and the Board of Directors of the company determines that such ownership is adverse to the long-term interests of the company and its shareholders.

See accompanying Notes to Consolidated Financial Statements.

NOTES TO CONSOLIDATED FINANCIAL STATEMENTS

(A) Summary of Significant Accounting Policies

Fiscal Year: The company's fiscal year ends on the last Wednesday in January. Fiscal years 1988, 1987 and 1986 consisted of 52 weeks and ended on January 25, 1989, January 27, 1988 and January 28, 1987, respectively.

Basis of Consolidation: The company includes all majority owned subsidiaries in the consolidated financial statements. Investments in affiliated retail companies owned 20% or more are accounted for by the equity method using their December financial statements. All significant intercompany transactions and accounts have been eliminated in consolidation.

Foreign Operations: Foreign currency assets and liabilities are translated into U.S. dollars at the exchange rates in effect at the balance sheet date. Results of operations are translated at average exchange rates during the period for revenues and expenses. Translation gains and losses resulting from fluctuations in the exchange rates are accumulated as a separate component of shareholders' equity.

Inventories: Merchandise inventories are valued at the lower of cost or market, using the retail method, on the last-in, first-out basis for substantially all domestic inventories and the first-in, first-out basis for the remainder.

Property Owned: Land, buildings, leasehold improvements and equipment are recorded at cost. Major replacements and refurbishings are charged to the property accounts while replacements, maintenance and repairs that do not improve or extend the life of the respective assets are expensed currently. The company capitalizes interest cost as part of the cost of constructing capital assets. The cost of all properties retired and the accumulated depreciation thereon are eliminated from the accounts and the resulting gain or loss is taken into income.

Depreciation: The company computes depreciation on owned property principally on the straight-line method for financial statement purposes and on accelerated methods for income tax purposes. Most store properties are leased and improvements are amortized over the term of the lease but not more than 25 years. Other annual rates used in computing depreciation for financial statement purposes are 2% to 4% for buildings, 10% to 14% for store fixtures and 5% to 33% for other fixtures and equipment.

Leased Property under Capital Leases: The company accounts for capital leases, which transfer substantially all of the benefits and risks incident to the ownership of property, as the acquisition of an asset and the incurrence of an obligation. Under this method of accounting for leases, the asset is amortized using the straight-line method and the obligation, including interest thereon, is liquidated over the life of the lease. All other leases (operating leases) are accounted for by recording periodic rental expense over the life of the lease.

Licensee Sales: The company's policy is to exclude sales of licensed departments from total sales. Sales from licensed departments are primarily comprised of sales from the Meldisco subsidiaries of Melville Corporation. See Note (H) for further information regarding licensee sales from Meldisco.

Pre-Opening and Closing Costs: The company follows the practice of treating store operating costs incurred prior to opening a new retail unit as current period expenses. When the decision to close a retail unit is made, the company provides for future net lease obligations, nonrecoverable investments in fixed assets, other expenses directly related to discontinuance of operations and estimated operating losses through expected closing dates.

Income Taxes: Deferred income taxes are provided on nonpermanent differences between financial statement and taxable income. The company accrues appropriate U.S. and foreign taxes payable on all of the earnings of subsidiaries and affiliates, except with respect to earnings that are intended to be permanently reinvested, or are expected to be distributed free of additional tax by operation of relevant statutes currently in effect and by utilization of available tax credits and deductions.

(B) Discontinued Operations

During 1988, the company continued disposing of its discontinued insurance operations. K mart completed the sale of Lone Star Life Insurance Company, terminated the agreement for the operation of store insurance centers and terminated the lease of the former insurance operations' headquarters. The company also negotiated the sale of the two remaining insurance companies, KM Insurance Company and Victoria Lloyds Insurance Company, pending regulatory approval. The reserve for the disposition of the company's discontinued insurance operations is considered adequate at January 25, 1989.

In December 1986, the company sold Furr's Cafeterias, Inc. and Bishop Buffets, Inc., two cafeteria chains, for $238 million in cash to Cavalcade Foods, Inc., a subsidiary of Cavalcade Holdings, Inc. Although the cafeteria operations had been consistently profitable, they did not fit into corporate growth plans. Concurrent with the sale of its cafeteria operations, K mart decided to reduce certain high-cost, long-term debt (see Note J) with the proceeds and divest itself of the unprofitable Designer Depot operation. As a result, the company established at January 28, 1987, a reserve which includes all anticipated losses subsequent to January 28, 1987. The $28 million net after-tax gain from discontinued operations included a tax benefit of $7 million which resulted from taxes provided at capital gains rates offset by tax benefits provided at ordinary income tax rates.

The company and Cavalcade Foods have guaranteed indebtedness related to certain cafeteria properties on a joint and several basis. Cavalcade Foods subsequently indemnified K mart Corporation from any liability pursuant to its guarantees. As of January 25, 1989, the amount guaranteed was $64 million.

(C) Contingency

In a lawsuit resulting from a dispute with Fashion House, Inc., a judgment was rendered against K mart Corporation in the amount of $59 million plus interest, a total of $79 million at January 25, 1989. The dispute involved Fashion House acting as a buying agent with respect to acquiring certain types of apparel merchandise for K mart. K mart plans to appeal the judgment. While management and legal counsel are presently unable to predict the outcome or to estimate the amount of any liability the company may have with respect to this lawsuit, it is not expected that this matter will have a material adverse effect on the company.

(D) New Ventures

In March 1988, K mart Corporation purchased a 51% ownership interest in Makro Inc. from SHV North America Corporation. Makro currently operates six warehouse clubs, each occupying from 150,000 to 200,000 square feet, offering both groceries and general merchandise.

The Makro acquisition has been accounted for as a purchase. The results of operations have been consolidated with those of the company from the date of acquisition. The excess of cost over the fair value of the assets acquired, which is not significant, is being amortized over 40 years on a straight-line basis.

In September 1987, K mart Corporation formed a partnership with Bruno's Inc. of Birmingham, Alabama to develop American Fare hypermarket stores in the United States. K mart has a 51% ownership interest in the partnership and Bruno's owns 49%. Each company is equally represented in management of the partnership. The first American Fare hypermarket opened January 29, 1989, in Atlanta, Georgia. The store is 244,000 square feet and offers both groceries and general merchandise. K mart will consolidate the results of American Fare operations in 1989.

(E) Supplemental Cash Flow Information

The company incurred capital lease obligations to obtain store facilities and equipment of $124 million, $42 million and $31 million in 1988, 1987 and 1986, respectively. In 1986, the company issued $186 million in common stock in exchange for its 6% convertible subordinated debentures due July 15, 1999. These noncash transactions have been excluded from the Consolidated Statements of Cash Flows. Further information regarding the 1986 debt conversion is included in Note (J).

The company considers cash on hand in stores, deposits in banks, certificates of deposit and short-term marketable securities as cash and cash equivalents for the purposes of the statement of cash flows. The effect of changes in foreign exchange rates on cash balances is not material.

Cash paid for interest and income taxes follows:

(Millions)	1988	1987	1986
Interest (net of amounts capitalized)	$330	$329	$385
Income taxes	$423	$386	$456

(F) Merchandise Inventories

A summary of inventories by method of pricing and the excess of current cost over stated LIFO value follows:

(Millions)	January 25, 1989	January 27, 1988
Last-in, first-out (cost not in excess of market)	$5,090	$5,104
Lower of cost (first-in, first-out) or market	581	467
Total	$5,671	$5,571
Excess of current cost over stated LIFO value	$ 898	$ 738

(G) Property and Equipment

The components of property and equipment are:

(Millions)	January 25, 1989	January 27, 1988
Property owned:		
Land	$ 127	$ 148
Buildings	381	370
Leasehold improvements	689	606
Furniture and fixtures	3,353	3,015
Construction in progress	68	62
Property under capital leases	2,416	2,336
	7,034	6,537
Less—accumulated depreciation and amortization:		
Property owned	(2,033)	(1,756)
Property under capital leases	(1,105)	(1,037)
Total	$3,896	$3,744

(H) Investments in Affiliated Retail Companies

Meldisco Subsidiaries of Melville Corporation

All U.S. K mart footwear departments are operated under license agreements with the Meldisco subsidiaries of the Melville Corporation, substantially all of which are 49% owned by the company and 51% owned by Melville. Fees and income earned under the license agreements in 1988, 1987 and 1986 of $166 million, $159 million and $164 million, respectively, are included in licensee fees and rental income. The company's equity in the income of these operations and dividends received in 1988, 1987 and 1986 were as follows:

(Millions)	1988	1987	1986
Equity in income of Meldisco operations	$ 43	$ 43	$ 48
Dividends	$ 35	$ 40	$ 47

Meldisco subsidiaries' summarized financial information follows:

	Year Ended December 31,		
(Millions)	1988	1987	1986
Net sales	$1,063	$1,013	$1,006
Gross profit	$ 449	$ 428	$ 442
Net income	$ 89	$ 88	$ 99

	December 31,		
(Millions)	1988	1987	1986
Inventory	$ 134	$ 126	$ 124
Other current assets	96	80	90
Noncurrent assets	1	1	1
Total assets	231	207	215
Current liabilities	31	26	39
Net assets	$ 200	$ 181	$ 176
Equity of K mart Corporation	$ 97	$ 88	$ 85

Coles Myer Ltd.

The company has a 22.0% equity interest in Coles Myer Ltd., the largest retailer in Australia.

Income earned under the K mart license agreement of $4 million in 1988 and $3 million in both 1987 and 1986 is included in licensee fees and rental income. The company's equity in the income of Coles Myer's operations, dividends, year-end investment in Coles Myer and the market value of Coles Myer's common stock owned by the company follows:

(Millions U.S. $)	1988	1987	1986
Equity in income	$ 61	$ 49	$ 35
Dividends	$ 29	$ 16	$ 13
Equity of K mart Corporation	$406	$288	$231
Market value of Coles Myer's common stock	$830	$432	$379

Equity in income increased in both 1988 and 1987 due to higher operating income and one-time gains on the sale of certain property and investments, and, in 1987, the extinguishment of debt. The average exchange rates from Australian to U.S. dollars were .7847 in 1988, .7016 in 1987 and .6711 in 1986.

The cumulative effect of translating the company's equity in the investment in Coles Myer as of January 25, 1989, was an increase of $3 million, and as of January 27, 1988 and January 28, 1987 was a reduction of $57 million and $73 million, respectively.

Summarized financial information adjusted for conformity with U.S. generally accepted accounting principles for Coles Myer's most recent fiscal years follows:

	Fiscal Year Ended		
(Millions U.S. $)	July 31, 1988	July 26, 1987	July 27, 1986
Net sales	$9,442	$7,602	$7,222
Net income	$ 205	$ 170	$ 153

(Millions U.S. $)	July 31, 1988	July 26, 1987	July 27, 1986
Current assets	$1,378	$1,131	$ 842
Noncurrent assets	2,297	1,614	1,387
Total assets	$3,675	$2,745	$2,229
Current liabilities	$1,295	$1,023	$ 815
Noncurrent liabilities	913	535	482
Equity	1,467	1,187	932
Total liabilities and equity	$3,675	$2,745	$2,229

The company and Coles Myer have guaranteed indebtedness related to certain properties in Australia on a joint and several basis. Coles Myer subsequently indemnified K mart Corporation from any liability incurred pursuant to its guarantees. As of January 25, 1989, the amount guaranteed was $25 million.

Unremitted earnings of unconsolidated affiliates included in consolidated retained earnings were $241 million at January 25, 1989.

(I) Income Taxes

Components of income from continuing retail operations before income taxes follows:

(Millions)	1988	1987	1986
U.S.	$1,139	$1,082	$ 951
Foreign	105	89	77
Total	$1,244	$1,171	$1,028

The provision for income taxes consists of:

(Millions)	1988	1987	1986
Current:			
Federal	$330	$371	$320
State and local	81	71	57
Foreign	22	25	23
Deferred:			
Excess of tax over book depreciation	43	38	46
LIFO inventory	1	11	(4)
Lease capitalization	(5)	(7)	(10)
Other	(31)	(30)	26
Total income taxes	$441	$479	$458

A reconciliation of the company's effective tax rate for continuing retail operations to the federal statutory rate follows:

(Millions)	1988	1987	1986	1988	1987	1986
Federal statutory rate	$423	$457	$473	34.0%	39.0%	46.0%
State and local taxes, net of federal tax benefit	53	43	31	4.3	3.7	3.0
Tax credits	(10)	(4)	(15)	(.8)	(.3)	(1.4)
Equity in income of affiliated retail companies subject to lower tax rates	(31)	(31)	(31)	(2.5)	(2.6)	(3.0)
Other	6	14	—	.5	1.1	—
Total income taxes	$441	$479	$458	35.5%	40.9%	44.6%

The amounts shown on the consolidated balance sheets for deferred income taxes result principally from the difference between financial statement and income tax depreciation, reduced by the effect of accounting for certain leases as capital leases.

Tax credits were higher in 1988 as a result of increased Targeted Jobs Tax credits. Tax credits were lower in 1987 due to the repeal of investment credits under the Tax Reform Act of 1986.

Undistributed earnings of subsidiaries, which are intended to be permanently reinvested, totaled $219 million at January 25, 1989.

Financial Accounting Standard No. 96 (FAS 96) "Accounting for Income Taxes" was issued in December 1987 and was effective for fiscal years beginning after December 15, 1988. Financial Accounting Standard No. 100 (FAS 100) was issued in December 1988 and delayed the mandatory date of implementation for FAS 96 to fiscal years beginning after December 15, 1989. K mart did not elect application in 1988. The provisions of FAS 96 generally follow the liability method of accounting for income taxes. Accordingly, the statement requires adjustment of a deferred tax liability or asset for the effect of a change in tax law or rates. The effect shall be included in income from continuing operations for the period that includes the enactment date. Had K mart adopted FAS 96 in 1988, the company would have recognized additional income, which was not considered material, due to a reduction in deferred tax liabilities.

(J) Long-Term Debt

(Millions)	January 25, 1989	January 27, 1988
8⅜% debentures due 2017 (net of unamortized discount of $11)	$ 289	$ 289
10½% debentures due 2017	200	200
8⅛% debentures due 1997 (net of unamortized discount of $1)	199	198
12⅛% notes due 1995 (net of unamortized discount of $1)	149	149
Medium-term notes	300	—
12½% debentures due 2005	100	100
Commercial paper	—	182
Other	122	75
Total	1,359	1,193
Portion due within one year	1	2
Long-term debt	$1,358	$1,191

In February 1988, K mart Corporation filed a shelf registration statement with the Securities and Exchange Commission covering a proposed offering of up to $500 million principal amount of debt securities. As of January 25, 1989, the company had issued $300 million fixed-rate medium-term notes maturing from two to 10 years from the date of issue. The average coupon rate of these notes is 9.25% and the average term of the notes is 6.2 years.

In December 1987, the company issued $200 million of 10½% debentures due December 1, 2017. The debentures are redeemable at 100% of the principal amount through annual sinking fund payments on December 1, 1998 through 2016 of not less than $10 million or more than $30 million. Prior to December 1, 1997, the company may not redeem any debentures from or in anticipation of borrowed funds having an interest cost to the company of less than 10.5% per year. The debentures are otherwise redeemable in whole or in part, at any time at the option of the company, at prices declining from 110.5% to 100% of the principal amount. Interest is payable semi-annually on June 1 and December 1 of each year.

(J) Long-Term Debt continued

In January 1987, the company issued $300 million of 8⅜% debentures due January 15, 2017. The debentures are redeemable at 100% of the principal amount through annual sinking fund payments on January 15, 1998 through 2016 of not less than $15 million or more than $45 million. Prior to January 15, 1997, the company may not redeem any debentures from or in anticipation of borrowed funds having an interest cost to the company of less than 8.7% per year. The debentures are otherwise redeemable, in whole or in part, at any time at the option of the company, at prices declining from 108.4% to 100% of the principal amount. Interest is payable semi-annually on January 15 and July 15 of each year.

In July 1986, the company issued $200 million of 8⅛% debentures due January 1, 1997. The debentures are not redeemable prior to July 1, 1993. On or after that date the debentures may be redeemed, at the option of the company, in whole or in part, at any time at 100% of the principal amount plus interest accrued to the date of redemption. Interest is payable semi-annually on January 1 and July 1 of each year.

The $150 million of 12⅛% notes are due March 1, 1995 and the $100 million of 12½% debentures are due March 1, 2005. The respective notes and debentures are not redeemable prior to maturity. Interest is payable semi-annually with respect to each of these issues on March 1 and September 1 of each year.

Extraordinary Item—In December 1986, the company called for early redemption all $250 million of its 12¾% sinking fund debentures due March 1, 2015. The resulting redemption premium of $16 million net of applicable taxes of $16 million was reported as an extraordinary item in 1986. Proceeds from the sale of the company's cafeteria operations were the primary source of funds for the redemption.

In November 1986, the company called for redemption all of its outstanding 6% convertible subordinated debentures due July 15, 1999. Under terms of the original indenture agreement, holders were entitled to convert their debentures to common stock at $23.67 per share. As a result of the call and the tender of debentures for conversion at other times during 1986, the company retired $186 million outstanding principal amount in exchange for the issuance of 7,867,995 shares of common stock. The remaining principal amount of less than $2 million was redeemed for cash.

The company has entered into revolving credit agreements with various banks in the aggregate amount of $340 million as of January 25, 1989, and $585 million as of January 27, 1988. The agreements provide for borrowings at an interest rate based on the prime rate, "CD-based rate" or "LIBOR-based rate" at the company's election. As of January 25, 1989, the company had no outstanding borrowings under these agreements. The revolving credit agreements contain certain restrictive provisions regarding the maintenance of net worth, working capital, coverage ratios and payment of cash dividends. At January 25, 1989, $2,351 million of consolidated retained earnings were free of such restrictions.

Principal payments on long-term debt for five years subsequent to 1988, in millions, are: 1989-$1; 1990-$6; 1991-$31; 1992-$31; 1993-$133.

(K) Compensating Balances

At January 25, 1989, the company had bank lines of credit aggregating $599 million which provide for interest rates not exceeding the "prime" lending rate on any borrowings thereunder. In support of certain lines of credit, it is expected that compensating balances will be maintained on deposit with the banks, which will average 10% of the line to the extent that it is not in use and an additional 10% on the portion in use, whereas other lines require fees in lieu of compensating balances. The company is free to withdraw the entire balance in its accounts at any time.

(L) Leases

Description of Leasing Arrangements: The company conducts operations primarily in leased facilities. K mart store leases are generally for terms of 25 years with multiple five-year renewal options which allow the company the option to extend the life of the lease up to 50 years beyond the initial noncancellable term. Substantially all specialty retail units are leased, generally for terms varying from five to 25 years with varying renewal options.

Certain leases provide for additional rental payments based on a percent of sales in excess of a specified base. Also, certain leases provide for the payment by the lessee of executory costs (taxes, maintenance and insurance). Some selling space has been sublet to other retailers in certain of the company's leased facilities.

Lease Commitments: Future minimum lease payments with respect to capital and operating leases are:

	Minimum Lease Payments	
(Millions)	Capital	Operating
Fiscal Year:		
1989	$ 345	$ 404
1990	341	394
1991	337	378
1992	329	357
1993	319	333
Later years	3,060	3,055
Total minimum lease payments	4,731	4,921
Less—minimum sublease rental income	—	(271)
Net minimum lease payments	4,731	4,650
Less:		
Estimated executory costs	(1,447)	(521)
Amount representing interest	(1,607)	(2,196)
	1,677	1,933
Portion due within one year	89	128
Long-term obligations under leases	$1,588	$1,805

The company has guaranteed indebtedness related to certain leased properties financed by industrial revenue bonds. As of January 25, 1989, the total amount of such guaranteed indebtedness is $256 million, of which $111 million is included in capital lease obligations.

(L) Leases continued

Rental Expense: A summary of operating lease rental expense and short-term rentals follows:

(Millions)	1988	1987	1986
Minimum rentals	$402	$372	$332
Percentage rentals	57	55	54
Less—sublease rentals	(54)	(42)	(47)
Total	$405	$385	$339

Reconciliation of Capital Lease Information: The impact of recording amortization and interest expense versus rent expense on capital leases is as follows:

(Millions)	1988	1987	1986
Amortization of capital lease property	$100	$ 97	$ 97
Interest expense related to obligations under capital leases	174	174	178
Amounts charged to earnings	274	271	275
Related minimum lease payments net of executory costs	(261)	(254)	(254)
Excess of amounts charged over related minimum lease payments	$ 13	$ 17	$ 21

Related minimum lease payments above exclude executory costs for 1988, 1987 and 1986 in the amounts of $82 million, $79 million and $80 million, respectively.

(M) Business Group Information

The dominant portion of the company's business is general merchandise retailing through the operation of a chain of K mart discount department stores and six Makro warehouse clubs. Operations identified as specialty retailing include Pay Less Drug Stores, Waldenbooks, Builders Square and Bargain Harold's Canada. Business group information follows:

(Millions)	1988	1987	1986
Sales			
General merchandise	$23,187	$22,140	$21,308
Specialty retail	4,114	3,487	2,504
Total	27,301	25,627	23,812
Licensee fees and other income			
General merchandise	273	252	249
Specialty retail	9	7	8
Total	282	259	257
Equity in income of affiliated retail companies	105	92	83
Total revenues from continuing retail operations	$27,688	$25,978	$24,152
Operating income			
General merchandise	$ 1,436	$ 1,384	$ 1,311
Specialty retail	72	75	37
Total	1,508	1,459	1,348
Equity in income of affiliated retail companies	105	92	83
Interest expense—Debt	(172)	(156)	(171)
—Capital lease obligations	(174)	(174)	(178)
Corporate expense	(23)	(50)	(54)
Income from continuing retail operations before income taxes	1,244	1,171	1,028
Income taxes	441	479	458
Income from continuing retail operations	$ 803	$ 692	$ 570
Identifiable assets			
General merchandise	$ 9,108	$ 8,254	$ 8,137
Specialty retail	2,426	2,364	1,996
Total	11,534	10,618	10,133
Investments in affiliated retail companies	506	379	317
Assets of discontinued operations	86	109	128
Total assets	$12,126	$11,106	$10,578
Capital expenditures—Owned and leased			
General merchandise	$ 583	$ 421	$ 374
Specialty retail	111	163	209
Total capital expenditures	$ 694	$ 584	$ 583
Depreciation and amortization expense			
General merchandise	$ 374	$ 349	$ 341
Specialty retail	63	52	36
Total depreciation and amortization expense	$ 437	$ 401	$ 377

Identifiable assets are those assets of the company associated with a specific business group or discontinued operations. Corporate and foreign assets are insignificant. Other investments in affiliated retail companies include the company's investments in Coles Myer and Meldisco.

(N) Earnings Per Common and Common Equivalent Share

Earnings per common and common equivalent share were computed by dividing net income by the weighted average number of shares of common stock and dilutive common stock equivalents outstanding during each year. Common shares at the beginning of 1986 were increased by the number of shares issued or issuable on conversion of the 6% convertible debentures (issued in 1974), and net income was adjusted for interest expense net of the related tax effect. The number of common shares was increased by the number of shares issuable under the Stock Option Plans, less the number of shares that were assumed to have been purchased at average market prices with the proceeds of sales under the plans.

(O) Pension Plans

The company and its domestic subsidiaries have noncontributory pension plans covering most employees who meet certain requirements of age, length of service and hours worked per year. Benefits paid to retirees are based upon age at retirement, years of credited service and average earnings. K mart Canada Ltd. employees are covered by a defined contribution plan.

The company's policy is to fund at least the minimum amounts required by the Employee Retirement Income Security Act of 1974. The plans' assets consist primarily of equity securities, fixed income securities, guaranteed insurance contracts and real estate. The company made no contribution to its principal pension plan in fiscal 1988, 1987 or 1986.

Pension expense was $35 million in both 1988 and 1987, and $9 million in 1986. The assumed discount rate for the company's primary pension plan was 9.0% for 1988, 8.5% for 1987 and 9.0% for 1986. Pension expense for 1987 included a one-time charge of $12 million resulting from terms of an early retirement program offered to certain employees in 1987.

In 1987, the company adopted Financial Accounting Standard No. 87 (FAS 87) "Employers' Accounting for Pensions", which did not have a material effect on the company's pension expense.

For the company's principal pension plans, the following tables summarize the funded status, components of pension cost and actuarial assumptions under FAS No. 87:

(Millions)	January 25, 1989	January 27, 1988
Actuarial value of benefit obligations:		
Estimated present value of vested benefits	$(597)	$(428)
Estimated present value of non-vested benefits	(97)	(148)
Accumulated benefit obligation	(694)	(576)
Value of future pay increases	(177)	(186)
Projected benefit obligation	(871)	(762)
Estimated market value of plan assets	986	897
Plan assets in excess of projected benefit obligation	115	135
Unrecognized net asset	(144)	(152)
Unrecognized prior service cost	20	–
Unrecognized net gain	(47)	(6)
Accrued pension costs	$ (56)	$ (23)

($ Millions)	Fiscal 1988	Fiscal 1987
Components of pension expense:		
Normal service cost	$ 44	$ 44
Interest cost on projected benefit obligation	72	65
Return on plan assets	(126)	(40)
Net amortization and deferral of other components	35	(53)
Total	$ 25	$ 16
Actuarial assumptions:		
Discount rates	9.0%	8.5%
Expected return on plan assets	9.5%	9.5%
Salary increases	5.0%	5.0%
Amortization periods	16.3	19.4

(P) Employees' Savings Plan

The Employees' Savings Plan provides that employees of the company and certain subsidiaries who have completed two "Years of Service" can invest from 2% to 16% of their earnings in the employee's choice of a diversified common stock fund, a guaranteed investment fund or a K mart common stock fund. For each dollar the employee invests up to 6% of his or her earnings, the company will contribute an additional 50 cents which is invested in the K mart common stock fund.

Company contributions to the K mart common stock fund may be remitted to the Trustee in cash or in the form of company common stock. Contributions remitted to the Trustee in cash may be used to acquire K mart common stock on the open market or directly from the company by subscription or purchase.

As of June 17, 1986, 5,517,750 shares of K mart common stock were made available for issuance or sale to the Trustee, consisting of 2,517,750 treasury shares and 3,000,000 authorized but unissued shares. As of January 25, 1989, 4,128,062 shares remained available. The company's expense related to the Employees' Savings Plan was $37 million in both 1988 and 1987, and $36 million in 1986.

(Q) Stock Option Plans

Under the company's 1973 Stock Option Plan, as most recently amended in 1987, options to acquire up to 10,500,000 shares of common stock may be granted to officers and key employees at no less than 100% of the fair market value on the date of grant.

The 1973 Plan also provides for stock appreciation rights (SARs) in tandem with nonqualified stock options (NQSOs) for officers and eligible directors who are limited under the Securities Exchange Act of 1934 in transactions involving shares of the company's stock. Such an optionee may request that the Compensation and Incentives Committee permit the optionee to surrender all or part of an exercisable option in return for stock, cash or a combination of both equal to any appreciation in the value of the surrendered shares over the option price. In 1988, fluctuations in the market price of the company's common stock relative to the grant price resulted in a $1 million credit to compensation expense. Compensation expense of $9 million in 1987 and $17 million in 1986 was recorded for the excess of the market price of the option over the grant price.

Under the terms of the 1981 Stock Option Plan, options to acquire up to 12,000,000 shares of common stock may be granted to officers and other key employees of the company at no less than 100% of the fair market value on the date of grant. Options under the 1981 Plan may be either incentive stock options (ISOs) pursuant to Section 422A of the Internal Revenue Code or NQSOs.

Such options under the 1973 and 1981 plans may have a maximum term of 10 years as to an ISO and a maximum term of 10 years and two days as to an NQSO and are exercisable two years after the date of grant, except that an ISO granted prior to 1987 shall not be exercised by an optionee who has a prior ISO outstanding. The two-year limitation does not apply if employment terminates due to total and permanent disability or death, in the event of a change of control of the company or if and to the extent the Compensation and Incentives Committee may so determine in its discretion. Payment upon exercise of an option may be made in cash, already owned shares or a combination of both. Such shares will be valued at their fair market value as of the date of exercise. SARs do not apply to options under the 1981 Plan.

Pertinent information covering the plans follows:

	1988		1987	
	Number of Shares	Option Price Per Share	Number of Shares	Option Price Per Share
Outstanding at beginning of year	6,871,323	$12.87-$43.88	7,076,822	$12.87-$35.96
Granted	2,341,800	34.31	2,148,900	43.88
Exercised	(850,781)	12.87- 35.96	(1,408,849)	12.87- 35.96
Cancelled	(438,200)	12.87- 43.88	(945,550)	12.87- 43.88
Outstanding at end of year	7,924,142	12.87- 43.88	6,871,323	12.87- 43.88
Exercisable at end of year	3,626,342	$12.87-$35.96	2,788,573	$12.87-$23.09
Available for grant at end of year	8,256,731		10,178,967	

(R) Quarterly Financial Information (Unaudited)

Each of the quarters includes 13 weeks.

(Millions, except per-share data)			Quarter		
1988	**First**	**Second**	**Third**	**Fourth**	**Total**
Gross revenue from continuing retail operations	$5,902	$6,763	$6,435	$8,555	$27,655
Cost of merchandise sold	$4,193	$4,887	$4,647	$6,187	$19,914
Net income	$ 121	$ 163	$ 126	$ 393	$ 803
Earnings per common and common equivalent share	$ .60	$ .81	$ .63	$ 1.96	$ 4.00

(Millions, except per-share data)			Quarter		
1987	**First**	**Second**	**Third**	**Fourth**	**Total**
Gross revenue from continuing retail operations	$5,651	$6,381	$6,042	$7,882	$25,956
Cost of merchandise sold	$3,985	$4,588	$4,339	$5,652	$18,564
Net income	$ 116	$ 145	$ 110	$ 321	$ 692
Earnings per common and common equivalent share	$ .57	$ .71	$ .54	$ 1.58	$ 3.40

Accelerated depreciation (p. 411) Methods used to depreciate fixed assets under which greater costs are allocated to earlier periods than are allocated to later periods.

Accounting cycle (p. 96) The procedures leading from an exchange transaction to the preparation of the financial statements, including journal entries, posting to the ledger, and preparing the worksheet.

Accounting equation (p. 47) Assets equal liabilities plus stockholders' equity: the equation upon which the balance sheet and all other financial statements are based.

Accounting period (p. 110) The period of time between the preparation of the financial statements. Statements are often prepared monthly, quarterly, semiannually, or annually.

Accounting Principles Board (p. 33) The accounting standard-setting body that operated from 1959 to 1971 and issued thirty-one accounting opinions.

Accounting Research Bulletins (p. 32) The 51 standards of accounting issued between 1939 and 1959 by the Committee on Accounting Procedures.

Accounts Payable (p. 60) A balance sheet account indicating the dollar amount owed to suppliers from purchases (usually of inventory) made on open account.

Accounts Receivable (p. 57) A balance sheet account indicating the dollar amount due from customers from sales made on open account.

Accrual accounting (p. 157) A system of accounting that recognizes revenues and expenses when assets and liabilities are created or discharged because of operating activities. The revenues and expenses are not necessarily recognized when cash is received or paid. The income statement is prepared on an accrual basis.

Accruals (p. 166) Adjusting journal entries designed to ensure that assets and liabilities that are created or discharged because of operating activities of the current period are recognized as revenues and expenses in that period. Examples include accrued wages and accrued interest.

Accumulated amortization (p. 59) The amount of amortization that has accumulated on an intangible asset since it was placed into service. Intangible assets are reported at their net book values (original cost less accumulated amortization) on the balance sheet.

Accumulated depreciation (p. 58) The amount of depreciation that has accumulated on a fixed asset since it was placed into service. Fixed assets are reported at their net book values (original cost less accumulated depreciation) on the balance sheet.

Activity method (p. 418) A method of amortizing the cost of long-lived assets that allocates costs to accounting periods on the basis of the asset's activity during that period. This method is used primarily to amortize natural resource costs.

Activity ratios (p. 862) Financial statement ratios that assess the speed with which inventories, accounts receivable, and sometimes fixed assets turn over.

Actuary (p. 487) A statistician who specializes in such areas as assessing insurance risks and setting insurance premiums. Actuaries are used to estimate future pension costs.

Additional Paid-in Capital (p. 570) An account that often appears in the contributed capital section of the balance sheet of a corporation. It represents capital contributed by the stockholders over and above the stated, or par, value of capital stock. It is often referred to as Capital in Excess of Par or Stated Value.

Adjusted trial balance (p. 114) The trial balance that is listed on the worksheet after the adjusting entries are added to the unadjusted trial balance.

Adjusting journal entries (p. 166) Journal entries recorded at the end of the accounting period to ensure that all assets and liabilities created or discharged during that period are recognized in that period. The three kinds of adjusting journal entries are accruals, cost expirations, and revaluation adjustments.

Adjustments (p. 114) Entries on the worksheet that capture certain relevant phenomena that did not involve exchange transactions during the accounting period. Adjustments are added to the unadjusted trial balance to produce the adjusted trial balance. *See* **Adjusting journal entries.**

Aging schedule (p. 308) A method of estimating bad debts and analyzing outstanding accounts receivable that categorizes individual accounts on the basis of the amount of time each has been outstanding. Each category is then multiplied by a different uncollectible percentage, under the assumption that older accounts are more likely than new accounts to be uncollectible.

Allowance method (p. 304) A method used to account for bad debts that estimates the dollar amount of bad debts at the end of each accounting period; records an adjusting journal entry to recognize bad debt expense and reduce the net accounts receivable balance; and writes off actual bad debts into an allowance account when they occur.

American Accounting Association (p. 27) The principal association of accounting educators.

American Institute of Certified Public Accountants (AICPA) (p. 19) The official organization of certified public accountants in the United States. This organization sets the standards of performance and ethics for practicing certified public accountants.

Amortization (p. 172) The systematic allocation of a deferred charge over its life. It is often used with specific reference to intangible assets, but prepaid expenses are amortized and so are discounts and premiums on long-term receivables and payables. Depreciation is the amortization of a fixed asset.

Amortization base (p. 402) The amount of an intangible asset's cost that is subject to amortization. It equals capitalized cost less estimated salvage value.

Amortization schedule (p. 524) A schedule that shows a note receivable or payable's (investment) book value, interest expense (revenue), and unamortized discount or premium throughout its life. Amortization schedules are also prepared for bonds and capital leases.

Annual interest (p. 12) A periodic charge on a borrowing or debt investment, usually determined by multiplying the annual interest rate times the principal of the debt.

Annual report (p. 21) A document that a company publishes each year, containing the financial statements, a description of the company and its operations, an audit report, a management letter, footnotes to the financial statements, and other financial and nonfinancial information.

Annuity (p. 910) Periodic cash payments of equal amounts.

Annuity due (p. 912) An annuity for which each periodic payment is made at the beginning of each period.

Appropriation of retained earnings (p. 590) A book entry involving only the Retained Earnings account that serves to restrict a portion of Retained Earnings from the payment of dividends. Such restrictions can be imposed contractually or voluntarily.

Asset (p. 10) An item listed on the left side of the balance sheet that has been acquired by the company in an objectively measurable transaction and has future economic benefit. Assets include cash, securities, receivables, inventory, prepaid expenses, long-term investments, property, plant, equipment, and intangibles.

Asset Depreciation Range (p. 916) Guidelines published by the Internal Revenue Service that define the minimum allowable useful lives for various kinds of long-lived assets. These lives are used in the depreciation of long-lived assets for purposes of computing taxable income.

Association of Government Accountants (p. 27) The principal association of accountants working in federal government positions.

Audit committee (p. 17) A subcommittee of the board of directors that works with management to choose the external auditor and monitor the audit so that it is conducted in a thorough, objective, and independent manner.

Audit report (p. 6) A letter written and signed by a CPA that indicates the extent of the audit and whether or not the financial statements fairly reflect the financial position and operations of a company and have been prepared in conformance with generally accepted accounting principles.

Authorized shares (p. 571) The number of shares a company is entitled to issue, as stated in the corporate charter.

Averaging assumption (p. 344) A method of determining the cost of goods sold and the ending inventory by computing a weighted average cost of the items sold and the items remaining.

Balance sheet (p. 10) A financial statement that indicates the financial condition of a business as of a given point in time. It includes assets, liabilities, and stockholders' equity, and represents a statement of the basic accounting equation.

Bank loan officer (p. 22) An individual who works for a bank and is responsible for loans granted by the bank.

Batch processing (p. 124) An approach to processing transactions that involves the periodic processing of data in similar groups.

Betterment (p. 402) A postacquisition expenditure that improves a fixed asset by increasing its life, increasing the quality or quantity of its output, or decreasing the cost of operating it. The cost of a betterment is included in the capitalized cost of the asset and amortized over its remaining life.

Board of directors (p. 12) A group of individuals who are elected by the stockholders of a corporation and have the power to declare dividends, set executive compensation, hire and fire management, and set corporate policy. The board also appoints the audit committee.

Bond (p. 632) A debt security usually issued by a corporation to a large number of investors to raise a large amount of cash. A bond involves a formal commitment that requires the issuing company to make cash interest payments to the bondholder and a principal payment when the bond matures, usually between five and thirty years after the bond is issued.

Bond discount (p. 519) The amount by which a bond's price is under its face value. The bond discount is recognized at issuance and amortized into Interest Expense over the life of the bond.

Bond market (p. 516) The market in which corporate bonds are purchased and sold.

Bond premium (p. 519) The amount of a bond's issuance price in excess of the face value. The bond premium is recognized at issuance and amortized over the life of the bond.

Bonds Payable (p. 60) A balance sheet long-term liability account indicating the total face amount of outstanding bonds.

Bonus system (p. 465) A method of compensating the management of a company that links compensation to some measure of the company's performance, often net income. The payments are normally made in the form of cash or corporate common stock.

Book value of company/shares (p. 562) The book value of a company is equal to the balance-sheet value of stockholders' equity, which is sometimes referred to as *net assets* or *net worth*. The book value of a share of outstanding stock is the book value of the company divided by the number of outstanding shares.

Borrowing capacity (p. 877) The ability of a company to raise capital by issuing debt securities or other borrowings.

British-American-Dutch model (p. 825) The system of financial accounting in North America, the United Kingdom, Australia, India, and Holland. It is based primarily on the generally accepted accounting principles of the United States.

Business acquisition (p. 645) An event by which an investor company acquires a controlling interest (51 percent or more of the voting stock) in another (investee) company. The investor company is called the *parent* and the investee company is called the *subsidiary*.

Business combination (p. 646) See **Merger.**

Business segment (p. 690) A separate line of business, production line, or class of customer representing an operation that is independent of a company's other operations.

Business transaction (p. 48) Asset and liability exchanges that are entered into by a company in the course of conducting business.

Call provision (p. 518) A provision in a debt contract that allows the issuing company to repurchase outstanding bonds after a specified date for a specified price.

Capital lease (p. 531) A lease that is treated as a purchase for the purposes of financial accounting. In a capital lease the lessee is considered to have purchased the leased asset and financed it through the periodic lease payments. Capital leases give rise to both the recognition of balance sheet assets and liabilities.

Capital maintenance view of performance (p. 679) A performance measure that compares an entity's book value at the end of a period with the entity's book value at the beginning of the period. The measure is also adjusted for dividends and equity issuances during the period.

Capital Stock (p. 61) An account in the contributed capital section of the balance sheet of a corporation. It indicates the par or stated value of the issued and outstanding shares and encompasses both common stock and preferred stock. However, common and preferred stock are usually disclosed separately, and a Capital Stock account is not necessary.

Capital transaction (p. 72) A business transaction that involves building or financing the productive capacity of the company. These transactions are not reflected on the income statement and are represented on the statement of cash flows under the sections that list the company's investing and financing activities.

Capitalization (p. 171) The process of recording the cost of an expenditure as an asset. Capitalized assets are placed on the balance sheet and then matched against revenues as the benefits associated with the asset are realized.

Capitalization ratios (p. 862) Financial statement ratios that focus primarily on a company's sources of financing. Examples include the debt/equity ratio, cost of debt, and the financial leverage ratio.

Capitalize (p. 172) To place the cost of an expenditure on the balance sheet.

Cash budget (p. 258) An accounting report, prepared and used internally, that projects future cash inflows and outflows, and thereby helps to assess a company's future cash needs.

Cash discount (p. 299) Usually attached to a sale or purchase on open account, a cash discount is an offer to receive or pay less than the gross price if payment is made within a designated discount period.

Cash disbursements journal (p. 136) A special-purpose journal specifically designed to keep a record of cash payments.

Cash equivalent (p. 720) Commercial paper and other debt instruments with maturities of less than three months. Such items are often included in the definition of cash for purposes of the balance sheet and the statement of cash flows.

Cash flow accounting (p. 157) A system of accounting that simply keeps a balance of cash and a record of cash inflows and outflows. The statement of cash flows is based on cash flow accounting.

Cash flow from financing activities (p. 69) A section on the statement of cash flows that reflects the cash inflows and outflows associated with a company's two sources of outside capital: liabilities and contributed capital.

Cash flow from investing activities (p. 69) A section of the statement of cash flows that reflects the cash inflows and outflows associated with the purchase and sale of assets other than inventory and short-term receivables.

Cash flow from operating activities (p. 69) A section of the statement of cash flows that reflects the cash inflows and outflows associated with the acquisition and sale of a company's products and services.

Cash receipts journal (p. 133) A special-purpose journal designed specifically to keep a record of cash receipts.

Cash value of life insurance (p. 58) The dollar amount for which a life insurance policy can be cashed in. This amount often appears in the long-term investment section of the balance sheet.

Central processor (p. 124) The equipment that performs the processing in a computer. It directs the internal processes of the computer, including arithmetic computations, logic, and memory storage.

Certificate of deposit (p. 541) A short-term obligation of a bank that pays a specified rate of interest for a specified period of time. Often interest penalties are assessed in the case of early withdrawal.

Certified internal auditors (p. 28) Those internal auditors who have passed the certification exam developed and administered by the Institute of Internal Auditors.

Certified management accountants (p. 28) Those management accountants who have passed the certification exam developed and overseen by the National Association of Accountants.

Certified public accountants (p. 5) Those individuals, designated on a state-by-state basis, who have passed the certification exam developed by the American Institute of Certified Public Accountants and who have the requisite amount of public accounting experience. Individuals who render opinions on financial statements must be certified public accountants.

Chief financial officer (p. 28) An executive who heads the financial activities of a company. This individual is often responsible for the preparation of the financial statements.

Class-action lawsuit (p. 229) A legal action taken against a defendant by a group of individuals who have suffered damages. Class-action suits are often filed by stockholders and creditors who have incurred losses against a company's management and auditors.

Classified balance sheet (p. 54) A balance sheet divided into classifications, including current assets, long-term investments, fixed assets, intangible assets, current liabilities, long-term liabilities, and stockholders' equity.

Clean audit opinion (p. 852) *See* **Unqualified audit opinion.**

Closing entries (p. 116) The entries to the worksheet, journal, and ledger that transfer the end-of-period balances in the temporary (Revenue, Expense, and Dividend) accounts to Retained Earnings. Revenue and Expense accounts are first closed into the Income Summary.

Closing process (p. 115) The process that closes the temporary accounts to Retained Earnings at the end of the accounting period. It involves four steps: (1) create an Income Summary account, (2) close the Revenue and Expense accounts to Income Summary, (3) close the Income Summary account to Retained Earnings, and (4) close the Dividend accounts to Retained Earnings.

Collateral (p. 511) Assets designated to be paid to a creditor in case of default on a loan by a debtor. Often referred to as *security* on the loan.

Collection period (p. 317) A financial ratio indicating how many days, on average, the short-term receivables of a given company are outstanding: (Accounts Receivable ÷ Sales) × 365 days.

Commercial paper (p. 458) Short-term notes issued by companies with high credit ratings in exchange for cash from other companies.

Committee on Accounting Procedures (p. 32) The accounting standard-setting body that operated between 1939 and 1959 and issued 51 accounting research bulletins.

Common-size financial statements (p. 860) Financial statements in which income statement items are expressed as percentages of net sales and balance sheet items are expressed as percentages of total assets.

Common stock (p. 10) An ownership interest in a corporation. Holding a common stock certificate usually carries with it the right to receive dividends if they are declared and the right to vote for the corporation's board of directors.

Communist model (p. 826) The system of financial accounting used in countries in the Communist bloc. This system produces information that is required by and primarily oriented toward government planners.

Compensating balance (p. 257) Minimum cash balances that must be maintained in savings or checking accounts until certain loan obligations are satisfied.

Compensation (p. 16) Salary, wages, and bonuses paid to company employees, management, and executives.

Compound interest (p. 909) Interest that is earned on previously earned interest. When a dollar amount is left to earn interest over two periods, interest is earned during the second period on both the principal and the interest earned in the first period.

Compound journal entry (p. 102) A journal entry involving more than two accounts.

Computerized accounting system (p. 121) An accounting system in which the steps of the accounting cycle are performed with the aid of a computer. Computerized systems consist of hardware, software, procedures, and personnel.

Conceptual framework (p. 33) An ongoing project conducted by accounting standard setters that is designed to guide policymakers as they set accounting standards. It includes a statement of objectives, the desirable characteristics of accounting information, and the definitions of important accounting terms.

Conditional liability (p. 464) A liability that cannot be determined until year end because it is based on net income, which cannot be computed until that time. Examples include income tax and bonus liabilities.

Conservatism (p. 228) An exception to the principles of financial accounting; it holds the following: "When in doubt, understate rather than overstate an entity's value."

Consignment (p. 345) An agreement by which a consignor (owner) transfers inventory to a consignee (receiver) who takes physical possession and places the items up for sale. When the inventory is sold, the consignee collects the sales proceeds, keeps a percentage, and returns the remainder to the consignor.

Consistency (p. 225) A principle of financial accounting holding that business entities should use the same accounting methods from one period to the next.

Consolidated financial statements (p. 22) Financial statements of a company that include its assets and liabilities as well as the assets and liabilities of its majority-owned subsidiaries.

Constant-dollar financial statements (p. 944) Financial statements expressed in terms of dollars with equivalent purchasing power.

Consumer Price Index (CPI) (p. 942) An index that expresses the price of a general basket of goods and services each year as a percentage of the price of the same basket of goods and services from a selected base year. This index represents a measure of inflation.

Consumption (p. 4) Expenditures made on goods and services that are consumed immediately and bring about immediate gratification.

Continental model (p. 826) The system of financial accounting used in Japan and most of the Western European countries. This system is not oriented toward the needs of investors; it provides information primarily to meet government requirements.

Contingency (p. 466) An existing condition that can lead to either a positive or negative outcome, depending upon the occurrence of a future event.

Contra account (p. 177) A balance sheet account that offsets another balance sheet account. Examples include Accumulated Depreciation, Allowance for Uncollectibles, and Bond Discounts and Premiums.

Contributed capital (p. 48) That portion of the stockholders' equity section of the balance sheet of a corporation that indicates contributions from stockholders.

Control accounts (p. 132) The accounts appearing in the general ledger that contain the overall balance of related subsidiary accounts. For example, the Accounts Receivable control account contains the overall balance of the individual customer subsidiary accounts.

Controller (p. 27) The chief accounting officer of a company.

Controlling interest (p. 645) Ownership of more than 50 percent of outstanding voting stock of a company.

Corporate bond (p. 626) A bond issued by a corporation. *See* **Bond.**

Corporate form of business (p. 31) *See* **Corporation.**

Corporation (p. 61) A legal entity separate and distinct from its owners. Corporations are taxed and can be sued and provide legal liability protection for their owners. The owners of a corporation are referred to as stockholders or shareholders.

Cost expiration (p. 169) The process of converting a capitalized cost to an expense. Adjusting journal entries are often used to expire previously capitalized costs. Depreciation of fixed assets and amortization of intangible assets are examples.

Cost of Goods Sold (p. 66) An account on the income statement that indicates the cost of the inventory sold during the period.

Cost method (p. 642) A method used to account for equity investments with no ready market. Under this method, the balance-sheet value of the investment is carried at its historical cost.

Covenant (p. 518) An agreement between a company's creditors and its managers that often restricts the managers' behavior in some way. These restrictions are usually designed to protect the creditor's investment, and they are often written in terms of accounting numbers and ratios.

Credit (p. 102) The right side of a journal entry, indicating a decrease in an asset account or an increase in a liability or stockholders' equity account.

Credit analyst (p. 22) An individual who is employed, usually by a bank, to assess the ability of a potential debtor to pay back debts as they come due.

Credit rating (p. 74) An assessment of the risk associated with a company and its outstanding debts. Credit ratings are usually expressed in alphabetical and/or numerical grades (e.g., AA1). Credit rating agencies include Standard & Poor's, Dun & Bradstreet, and Moody Investor's Service.

Credit sales (p. 57) Sales of products or inventories in exchange for accounts receivable.

Creditor (p. 10) An individual or entity to which a company has an outstanding debt.

Cumulative preferred stock (p. 572) When a company misses a dividend on preferred stock with a cumulative feature, the missed dividend becomes a *dividend in arrears*, which must be paid when and if the company issues a dividend in the future.

Cumulative translation adjustments (p. 824) Book adjustments recognized when the financial statement of a Type I foreign subsidiary are translated to U.S. dollars. Such adjustments are not considered part of income and are disclosed in the stockholders' equity section of the consolidated balance sheet.

Current assets (p. 56) Assets on the balance sheet that are expected to be converted to cash or expired in one year or the operating cycle, whichever is longer.

Current cost (p. 954) The cost to replace inventory or long-lived assets with equivalent assets as of the date of the balance sheet.

Current-cost financial statements (p. 955) Financial statements that carry inventory and long-lived assets on the balance sheet at current cost. Gains or losses from holding these assets while their current costs increase or decrease (holding gains and losses) are recognized on a current-cost income statement.

Current liability (p. 60) Obligations on the balance sheet that are expected to be paid with the use of assets presently listed as current on the balance sheet.

Current Maturity of Long-Term Debt (p. 60) A balance sheet current liability account representing that portion of a long-term liability that is due in the current period.

Current ratio (p. 73) Current assets divided by current liabilities. This ratio is often used to assess the solvency position of a company.

Customers (p. 3) Individuals or entities that purchase goods from a firm.

Date of declaration, record, and payment (p. 583) The board of directors of a corporation declares a dividend on the date of declaration, which is paid on the date of payment to the shareholders who own the stock on the date of record.

Debentures (p. 518) Unsecured bonds.

Debit (p. 102) The left side of the journal entry, indicating an increase in an asset account or a decrease in a liability or stockholders' equity account.

Debt covenant (p. 568) A loan contract that often contains terms that restrict managers, protecting the investment of the debtholders. *See* **Covenant.**

Debt/equity ratio (p. 73) Total liabilities divided by total stockholders' equity. This ratio indicates the extent to which a company relies on debt financing.

Debt investment (p. 11) The purchase of a debt security by a company or a loan of goods or services to another entity.

Debt ratio (p. 452) Total debt divided by total assets; a measure of the proportion of assets generated through borrowings.

Debt restriction (p. 12) A term written into a debt contract or covenant that restricts the behavior of the company's managers. Such restrictions are often written in terms of accounting numbers. *See* **Covenant.**

Debtholders (p. 562) Individuals or entities who own debt securities that carry rights to receive interest and principal payments in the future from a company.

Default (p. 12) To fail to make a contractual payment on a debt.

Deferred Cost (p. 397) A miscellaneous category of assets that often includes prepaid expenses extending beyond the current accounting period, and intangible assets such as organizational costs and other start-up costs.

Deferred Income Taxes (p. 482) An account usually listed in the long-term liabilities section of the balance sheet that is associated with income tax benefits expected to reverse in future periods. This book liability usually arises in the latter periods of a fixed asset's life when a company has used straight-line depreciation for book purposes and accelerated depreciation for income tax purposes. There is some question about whether this account actually represents a liability, because companies are often able to defer the reversal of the tax benefit by purchasing additional fixed assets.

Deferred Revenue (p. 60) A balance sheet liability that will be converted to a revenue when the related service is performed or product is delivered (e.g., payments in advance). *See* **Unearned revenues.**

Defined benefit plan (p. 486) A pension plan in which the employer promises to provide each employee with a specified benefit at retirement.

Defined contribution plan (p. 486) A pension plan where the employer promises only to make a series of contributions of a specified amount to a pension fund.

Depletion (p. 402) The process of amortizing the costs of acquiring and extracting natural resources.

Deposits in transit (p. 260) Bank deposits that have been entered in the books of a company but not yet processed by a bank and reflected on a bank statement.

Depreciation (p. 172) The periodic allocation of the cost of a fixed asset to the income statement over the asset's useful life. It loosely approximates the reduction in the asset's usefulness.

Depreciation base (p. 410) The portion of the cost of a long-lived asset that is subject to depreciation: capitalized cost less estimated salvage value.

Determinable current liability (p. 456) A current liability that can be precisely measured, for which the amount of cash required to satisfy the obligation and the date of payment are reasonably certain.

Dilution (p. 565) A reduction in the relative ownership of a stockholder due to the issuance of additional stock to other stockholders.

Direct method (p. 161) A method of preparing the statement of cash flows where the cash inflows and outflows can be traced directly to the Cash account in the ledger. Under the direct method, net cash flow from operating activities is computed by adjusting each income statement item for its cash effect.

Direct writeoff (p. 310) A method of accounting for bad debts that recognizes bad debt expense and removes an outstanding receivable from the books when the specific account is deemed uncollectible. This method of accounting for bad debts is normally considered unacceptable under generally accepted accounting principles.

Discount on Notes Receivable/Payable (p. 512) A financial statement account with a credit (debit) balance, which is established when a note receivable (payable) is issued for an amount different from its face value. Discounts are amortized into Interest Revenue (Expense) over the life of the note.

Discount rate (p. 542) The lending rate charged to banks by the Federal Reserve Board. Also used to describe the rate used in present-value computations.

Discussion Memorandum (p. 34) A document published by an FASB task force that highlights the alternative accounting treatments in a given area and discusses the pros and cons of each. Sixty days after the Discussion Memorandum is published, a public comment period is conducted.

Dissimilar assets (p. 423) Long-lived assets of different general types that perform different functions and are employed in different lines of business. The methods used to account for exchanges of similar assets are different from those used to account for exchanges of dissimilar assets.

Dividends (p. 10) Payments made to the stockholders of a corporation as returns on their equity investments. Dividends are declared by the board of directors.

Dividends in arrears (p. 572) Missed dividends on preferred stock with a cumulative feature. Dividends in arrears are not liabilities, but they must be paid when and if the company declares a dividend.

Dividends in kind (p. 583) Dividends paid in the form of property other than cash.

Double-declining-balance (p. 412) The most extreme form of accelerated depreciation. Each period the book value of the fixed asset is multiplied by two times the straight-line rate. This method is very popular for tax purposes. *See* **Accelerated depreciation.**

Double-entry system (p. 103) The cornerstone of financial accounting, which specifies that all transactions involve exchanges where something is received and something is given up. Transactions are recorded with journal entries, consisting of at least one debit and one credit, which measure the increase and decrease in the affected accounts in a way that maintains the equality of the accounting equation.

Double taxation (p. 576) A phenomenon that occurs in a corporation where both corporate profits and dividends received by the shareholders are separately subject to federal income taxes.

Earned capital (p. 561) A measure of a company's assets that have been generated through profitable operations and not paid out in the form of dividends. On the balance sheet, earned capital is represented by the Retained Earnings balance.

Earning power (p. 11) The ability of a company to generate profits and net assets in the long-run future. Net income is considered an indication of earning power.

Earnings per share (p. 75) Net income divided by the number of common shares outstanding. A very popular ratio for evaluating the performance and earning power of a company.

Economic consequences (p. 23) The costs and benefits to investors, managers, auditors, and consumers associated with establishing, changing, or implementing accounting standards.

Economic entity (p. 19) A firm, business, or company that conducts operations to achieve an economic objective.

Economic entity assumption (p. 211) An assumption of financial accounting holding that a company is a separate economic entity that can be identified and that its performance can be measured.

Economic event (p. 98) Any occurrence that involves a transfer of resources from one party to another.

Effective-interest method (p. 628) The accounting method used to value long-term liabilities and long-term notes receivable, and the related interest charges, so that the book value of such a note represents an estimate of the present value of the note's future cash flows, assuming that the discount rate is constant over the life of the note.

Effective interest rate (p. 508) The actual rate of interest on an obligation or receivable. It is that rate which, when used to discount the future cash payments associated with the obligation or receivable, results in a present value that is equal to the initial proceeds provided by the obligation or receivable.

Efficient security markets (p. 863) A market for debt or equity securities where the prices of the securities almost instantaneously reflect publicly available information.

Employment Retirement Income Security Act (ERISA) (p. 487) Act passed by Congress in 1974 which requires employers to fund their pension plans at specified minimum levels and provides other safeguards designed to protect employees.

Equipment (p. 58) A long-lived or fixed asset account on the balance sheet that includes machinery, vehicles, furniture, and similar items.

Equity (p. 11) An ownership interest.

Equity investment (p. 626) The purchase of an ownership interest (e.g., common stock) in a company.

Equity method (p. 642) A method used to account for equity investments in the amount of 20 percent to 50 percent of the investee company's outstanding voting stock. The accounting procedures of this method reflect a substantial economic relationship between the investee and investor companies.

Equityholders (p. 563) Individuals or entities that hold ownership interests (e.g., common stock) in a company. Often referred to as *stockholders* or *shareholders* in the case of a corporation and *partners* in the case of a partnership.

Equivalent value (p. 914) Dollar amounts paid in different time periods that are equivalent in value.

Error (p. 930) A miscalculation or mathematical error where readily available facts were not considered in the implementation of an accounting method. Correcting errors discovered in subsequent time periods involves accounting adjustments to the Retained Earnings balance, called *prior period adjustments*.

Error of overstatement (p. 229) An error that leads financial statement users to believe that an entity is in better financial condition than it actually is.

Error of understatement (p. 229) An error that leads financial statement users to believe that an entity is in worse financial condition than it actually is.

Escrow (p. 257) The state of an item (e.g., cash) that has been put into the custody of a third party until certain conditions are fulfilled.

Estimate (p. 935) Judgments and predictions involved in applying certain accounting methods. Estimates are rarely correct and often need to be revised, but such revisions do not require correcting journal entries.

Exchange gains/losses (p. 818) Gains and losses recognized on the income statement due to changes in the exchange rates of outstanding receivables and payables denominated in foreign currencies.

Exchange rate (p. 817) The value of one currency expressed in terms of another currency.

Exchange transaction (p. 99) Transactions backed by documented evidence in which assets and/or liabilities are actually exchanged between parties.

Exit value (p. 954) The current selling price of an asset, usually inventories or long-lived assets. Often referred to as *fair market value*.

Exit-value financial statements (p. 955) Financial statements in which the balance sheet reflects the exit values of inventories and long-lived assets, and the income statement reflects gains or losses from holding these assets as their exit values increase or decrease (holding gains and losses).

Expense (p. 10) Asset outflows or liabilities that are created in an effort to generate revenues for a company. Examples include cost of goods sold, salaries, interest, advertising, taxes, utilities, depreciation, and others. Revenues less expenses is equal to net income.

Expensed (p. 170) To treat an expenditure as an expense by running the account through the income statement and closing it to Retained Earnings.

Exposure Draft (p. 34) A document, published by the Financial Accounting Standards Board, that proposes a financial accounting standard. Exposure drafts are often revised before they become official standards, and sometimes they are rejected.

Extraordinary item (p. 692) An event of a character significantly different from the typical, customary business activities of an entity, which is not expected to recur frequently in the ordinary activities of the business. Book gains or losses resulting from extraordinary items are disclosed separately in the income statement.

Face value (p. 216) The value printed on the face of an item (e.g., cash). The face value of an account receivable is the total dollar amount of the outstanding account. When used in the context of notes or bonds, the face value is the amount that is written on the face of the note or bond certificate and paid to the holder at maturity

Fair market value (p. 216) The sale price of an item in the output market.

Fees earned (p. 66) Revenues earned by a company for services to its clients.

Final trial balance (p. 118) The trial balance that results from the completion of the worksheet. It contains the end-of-period balances of the permanent accounts: assets, liabilities, and stockholders' equities.

Financial accounting (p. 3) A process through which managers report financial information about an economic entity to a variety of individuals who use this information in a variety of different decisions.

Financial accounting standard (p. 34) A standard of financial accounting that has been passed by the Financial Accounting Standards Board or another body that has been given authoritative support by the Securities and Exchange Commission.

Financial Accounting Standards Board (p. 33) The professional body that is currently responsible for establishing financial accounting standards.

Financial analyst (p. 22) An individual who is employed to analyze the investment potential of business firms.

Financial Executive Institute (p. 28) An organization consisting primarily of chief financial officers, controllers, and treasurers.

Financial flexibility (p. 727) A company's capacity to raise cash through methods other than operations. Examples include borrowings, issuing equity, or selling assets.

Financial leverage (p. 871) A strategy used by management that involves borrowing funds and investing them in assets that produce returns exceeding the after-tax cost of the borrowing.

Financial ratios (p. 73) Ratios that use numbers appearing on the financial statements.

Financial report (p. 3) A document published annually for the stockholders of a corporation. In addition to the financial statements, the financial report often includes a letter from the president, a letter from the management, summary financial data, and other information about the company. *See* **Annual report.**

Financial statements (p. 7) The statements that indicate the financial position and performance of a company. Included are the balance sheet, income statement, statement of retained earnings or statement of stockholders' equity, statement of cash flows, footnotes, and the audit report (if present).

Financing activities (p. 11) The activities of a company by which it generates capital to pay for its operations. The financial effects of the financing activities of a given period are summarized on the statement of cash flows and typically involve the management of borrowings and equity issuances.

First-in, first-out (p. 344) A method for valuing cost of goods sold and ending inventory; it assumes that the first items purchased are the first items sold.

Fiscal period assumptions (p. 211) An assumption of financial accounting holding that an entity's life can be divided into individual fiscal periods.

Fiscal year (p. 212) A year ending on a date other than December 31. Many U.S. companies have accounting periods that are fiscal years.

Fixed assets (p. 397) A category of long-lived assets including buildings, machinery, and equipment.

FOB destination (p. 346) Freight terms indicating that the seller is responsible for the freight until it is received by the buyer.

FOB shipping point (p. 346) Freight terms indicating that the seller is responsible for the freight only to the point from which it is shipped.

Footnotes to the financial statements (p. 6) Descriptions and schedules included in the financial report that further explain the numbers on the balance sheet, income statement, statement of retained earnings or statement of stockholders' equity, and statement of cash flows.

Freight-in (p. 347) An income statement account indicating the freight costs of purchased inventory. Also called *Transportation-in.*

Frequent transactions (p. 689) Operating transactions that are expected to recur repeatedly in the foreseeable future.

Future value (p. 908) The monetary amount to which an invested or given sum will grow as of a specified future date at a given interest rate.

Gain contingency (p. 466) A contingency where the possible future outcome is an increase in assets or a decrease in liabilities. Gain contingencies are rarely disclosed on the financial statements.

General journal (p. 105) The journal containing all journal entries except those recorded in the special-purpose journals. In the absence of special-purpose journals, the general journal contains all the journal entries.

General ledger (p. 108) The ledger that contains an account and a dollar balance for each account appearing on the financial statements. The general ledger contains the control accounts for those accounts with related subsidiary ledgers.

Generally Accepted Accounting Principles (GAAP) (p. 4) The current standards of financial reporting. They include the principles established by the Committee on Accounting Procedures, the Accounting Principles Board, and the Financial Accounting Standards Board, those bodies that have been given authoritative support by the Securities and Exchange Commission. The auditor states in the auditor's report whether the company's financial statements are prepared in conformance with these standards.

Going concern assumption (p. 213) An assumption of financial accounting holding that the life of an economic entity is indefinite. That is, the entity will not be discontinued in the current period.

Goods in transit (p. 345) Goods that are in transit between the buyer and the seller as of the end of an accounting period.

Goodwill (p. 59) The value of an entity over and above the fair market value of its assets less its liabilities. It reflects a company's reputation, clients, and a number of other intangible factors. Goodwill is not accrued on the financial statements, but it is recognized by a parent company when it purchases a subsidiary for a dollar amount that exceeds the fair market value of the subsidiary's net assets.

Government Accounting Office (p. 26) The government organization that audits the operations of the federal govenment and reports to Congress.

Government Accounting Standards Board (p. 27) A private-sector agency that establishes guidelines for accounting in government organizations.

Gross method (p. 300) A method of accounting for cash discounts that recognizes the initial sale or purchase at the gross sales price, and recognizes a cash discount only if payment is received within the discount period.

Hardware (p. 123) The physical equipment needed to operate a computer system.

Hedging (p. 821) A strategy used by management to reduce the risks associated with transacting in foreign currencies (i.e., fluctuating income due to exchange gains and losses). This strategy involves taking a position in a foreign currency that is equal in amount and opposite to currently outstanding receivables or payables that are expressed in that foreign currency.

Historical cost (p. 12) The dollar amount paid for an asset when it was acquired. Many assets on the balance sheet are carried at historical cost.

Holding gain/loss (p. 955) Increases or decreases in wealth associated with holding assets that increase or decrease in market value. Current-cost and exit-value financial statements recognize holding gains and losses.

Human capital (p. 879) The value of a company's human resources. Such valuations do not fall within the scope of generally accepted accounting principles and accordingly, are not reflected on the financial statements.

Hybrid security (p. 568) A security that has some characteristics of debt and some characteristics of equity.

Imprest system (p. 259) A set of procedures designed to control activities involving frequent cash disbursements (e.g., petty cash and payroll).

Incidental acquisition costs (p. 266) Costs associated with purchasing an asset in addition to the purchase price of the asset. Examples include brokerage commissions, insurance, and taxes.

Income statement (p. 10) A financial statement, prepared on an accrual basis, that indicates the performance of a company during a particular period. The income statement contains revenues and expenses, and highlights the net income number.

Income Summary (p. 116) A ledger account created specifically for the purpose of closing the Revenue and Expense accounts. In the closing process, the Revenue and Expense accounts are closed into the Income Summary account, which in turn is closed into the Retained Earnings account. The dollar amount of the difference between revenues and expenses is equal to the net income of the period, which is highlighted in the Income Summary account during this process.

Income tax payable (p. 60) The dollar amount owed to the federal government for taxes assessed against taxable income; usually disclosed on the balance sheet as a current liability.

Independent audit (p. 5) The examination conducted by an individual or entity having no financial interest in the company, which determines whether the financial statements of the company fairly reflect its financial condition, and whether the statements have been prepared in conformance with generally accepted accounting principles.

Independent certified public accountant (p. 16) An indvidual with a CPA certificate who has no financial interest in a company and has the power to attest publicly to the fairness of its financial statements.

Indirect method (p. 188) A method of preparing the statement of cash flows that computes cash flows from operating activities by adjusting net income for the differences between cash flows and accruals.

Individual proprietorship (p. 600) *See* **Proprietorship.**

Inflation (p. 942) Loss in purchasing power of currency over time.

Inflow/outflow view of performance (p. 263) A measure of entity performance that matches the inflows of a given period with the outflows. The income statement exemplifies this view of performance.

Input market (p. 215) The market where an entity purchases the inputs for its operations.

Institute of Internal Auditors (p. 28) The principal organization of internal auditors. This organization administers a professional examination and confers upon those who pass it the designation of Certified Internal Auditor.

Intangible asset (p. 59) Balance sheet assets that have no physical substance. They usually represent legal rights to the use or sale of valuable names, items, processes, or information. Patents, trademarks, and goodwill on acquired companies are examples.

Intention to convert (p. 265) A phrase that describes one of the criteria by which an investment in a security is classified in the current asset section of the balance sheet. Management must intend to convert the investment into cash within the time period for current assets.

Intercompany transactions (p. 806) Transactions between a parent and subsidiary that must be eliminated when preparing consolidated financial statements.

Interest (p. 907) The price, usually expressed as an annual rate, associated with transferring (borrowing or lending) money for a period of time.

Interest Payable (p. 60) A balance sheet acount that indicates an obligation to pay interest that is owed, usually considered a current liability.

Interest payment on a bond (p. 516) The periodic cash interest payment made by the issuing company to the bondholders. It is equal to the stated interest rate times the face value. Bond interest payments are usually made semiannually.

Internal auditor (p. 27) Company accountants who examine and evaluate the company's accounting system to ensure that it operates efficiently and that all internal controls are adequate.

Internal control system (p. 7) Procedures and records designed to ensure that (1) a company's assets are adequately protected from loss or misappropriation, and that (2) all relevant and measurable economic events are accurately reflected in the company's financial statements.

Internal information system (p. 25) The system of information developed and used within a company to support the business decisions of the company's management.

Internal Revenue Code (p. 25) The book prepared by the Internal Revenue Service that contains the official federal income tax laws.

Internal Revenue Service (IRS) (p. 27) The government body that issues regulations that govern the determination of income for purposes of federal income taxation.

International Accounting Standards Committee (p. 826) A private-sector body founded in 1973 that works to develop and encourage uniform worldwide accounting practices.

International Federation of Accountants (p. 826) A group of professional accountants in over 65 countries that sets practice and ethical guidelines for accounting professionals throughout the world.

Intraperiod tax allocation (p. 687) The practice of disclosing the income tax effect of a particular income statement or statement of retained earnings item with the item itself. Such items (e.g., disposals of segments, extraordinary items, changes in accounting principles, and prior period adjustments) are disclosed net of their income tax effects.

Inventory (p. 56) Items or products on hand that a company intends to sell to its customers.

Inventory turnover (p. 369) A financial ratio indicating how many times, on average, a company's inventory is sold and replaced in a given year: Cost of Goods Sold ÷ average Inventory.

Investing activities (p. 11) The activities of a company by which it manages its long-term assets. The investment activities of a given period are summarized on the statement of cash flows, and typically involve the purchases and sales of long-term assets.

Investment (p. 3) A purchase that trades off current consumption for future consumption. Examples include investing in stocks and bonds, real estate, rare art objects, or simply placing money in the bank.

Issued shares of stock (p. 571) Shares of stock that have been issued to stockholders and may or may not be currently outstanding. Some previously issued shares, for example, may have been repurchased by the company and held in the form of treasury stock.

Journal (p. 105) The original book of record that contains a chronological list of the transactions entered into by a company, usually in journal-entry form. The journal consists of the general journal and all special-purpose journals.

Journal entry (p. 102) The form in which transactions are initially recorded in the financial records. Such an entry consists of three components: (1) the accounts affected (asset, liability, stockholders' equity, revenue, expense, or dividend), (2) the direction of the effect (debit or credit), and (3) the dollar amount of the effect. The left side of the journal entry is referred to as the debit, and the right side is referred to as the credit.

Journal entry box (p. 104) The instructional aid, illustrated in Figure 3–4, that shows how journal entries are prepared and how they maintain the equality of the accounting equation.

Journalizing (p. 105) The process of recording a journal entry in the journal.

Labor unions (p. 23) Organizations that represent the interests of a company's employees in their negotiations with management.

Land (p. 397) Real estate held for investment purposes, usually appearing in the long-term investment section of the balance sheet. Land used in the operations of a business is considered a long-lived asset and is normally referred to as *property*.

Last-in, first-out (p. 344) A method of valuing the cost of goods sold and ending inventory, which assumes that the most recent items purchased are the first items sold.

Lease (p. 530) A contract granting use or occupation of property during a specified period of time in exchange for specified rent payments.

Leasehold obligation (p. 504) The present value of the future payments associated with a capital lease, long-term liability on the balance sheet.

Ledger (p. 107) The book of record where a running balance for each asset, liability, stockholders' equity, revenue, expense, and dividend account is maintained. It consists of both the general ledger and all subsidiary ledgers.

Ledger account form (p. 109) The form of the ledger accounts that is used in practice. It contains an account title and a reference number as well as columns for the date, a description of the entries, a posting reference, and four columns for the dollar amounts.

Leverage (p. 565) *See* **Financial leverage.**

Liabilities (p. 10) Financial obligations that must be met in the future by a company, listed on the right side of the balance sheet.

Life of a bond (p. 517) The period of time from the issuance of a bond to the maturity date, when the face value is paid to the bondholders.

Line of credit (p. 458) The credit granted to a company by a bank or group of banks, allowing it to borrow up to a certain maximum dollar amount, with interest being charged only on the outstanding balance.

Liquidity (p. 878) The speed with which an asset can be converted into a cash inflow or a liability becomes a cash outflow. Highly liquid assets can be converted to cash almost immediately.

Listed companies (p. 32) Companies whose debt or equity securities are traded on the public security exchanges.

Loan contracts (p. 11) The contracts that underlie the borrowings of a company. Loan contracts typically contain a provision for interest, a maturity date, security arrangments in case of default, and restrictions on the behavior of management.

Long-lived assets (p. 397) A section of the balance sheet that includes assets acquired for use in the day-to-day operations of the company. They include property, plant, and equipment as well as intangible assets.

Long-term investments (p. 57) A section on the asset side of the balance sheet that includes investments in equity securities, debt securities, real estate, life insurance, and other special funds. These investments are intended to be held, and provide benefits for a period of time beyond that of current assets.

Long-term liabilities (p. 60) A section of the balance sheet that includes obligations that will require the use of assets in a period of time beyond that which defines current assets.

Long-Term Notes Payable (p. 60) A balance sheet account that refers to obligations on loans that are due in a period of time beyond that which defines current assets. These obligations are backed by formal contracts.

Long-Term Notes Receivable (p. 626) A balance sheet account that refers to receivables evidenced by formal contracts. These receivables are due in a period of time beyond that which defines current assets.

Loss contingency (p. 466) A contingency where the possible future outcome leads to a reduction in assets or an increase in liabilities. *See* **Contingency.**

Lower-of-cost-or-market rule (p. 216) The rule underlying accounting for security investments and inventories stating that the balance-sheet value of such items will be the item's historical cost or its market value, whichever is lower.

Maintenance expenditure (p. 402) A postacquisition cost that serves to repair or maintain a long-lived asset in its present operating condition. Maintenance expenditures are immediately expensed.

Management consulting service (p. 28) A service offered by public accounting firms that is designed to assist a company's management in operating the business. Recently, much of such consulting is concerned with the design and implementation of computer-based accounting systems.

Management letter (p. 6) A letter in the financial report stating primarily that management is responsible for the preparation and integrity of the financial statements. Management letters differ from one company to the next and often contain a number of statements referring to management's responsibilities.

Managerial accounting (p. 25) The accounting system used by managers to direct their internal business decisions.

Managers (p. 16) Individuals, supplied with capital by a company's equity owners (stockholders), who are compensated through wages, salaries, and bonuses to earn returns for the owners. *Manager* is also used to describe an individual who has a management position in a public accounting firm.

Manufacturing company (p. 348) A company that acquires raw materials and, through a process that combines labor and overhead, manufactures inventory.

Markdown (p. 300) A reduction in sales price normally due to decreased demand for an item.

Marketable Securities (p. 56) A balance sheet account that includes stocks and bonds that are both readily marketable and intended to be sold within the time period of current assets.

Market ratios (p. 862) Financial statement ratios that involve the market price of a company's common shares and the returns to shareholders from dividends and price appreciation.

Market value of stock (p. 576) The price at which a share of stock can be exchanged in the open market as of a particular point in time.

Matching principle (p. 158) The principle stating that performance is measured by matching efforts against benefits in the time period in which the benefits are realized. Net income is the result of matching expenses against revenues in the time period in which the revenues are realized.

Materiality (p. 227) An exception to the principles of financial accounting stating that only those transactions dealing with dollar amounts large enough to make a difference to financial statement users need be accounted for in a manner consistent with the principles of financial accounting.

Maturity date (p. 58) The date when a loan agreement ends. As of the maturity date, if the payments are made on the loan, the associated debt is satisfied. Normally, the face value of the note is paid to the holder on the maturity date.

Merchandise inventory (p. 339) Items or products on hand that a company intends to sell to its customers.

Merger (p. 646) A business combination whereby two or more companies combine to form a single legal entity. In most cases the assets and liabilities of the smaller company are merged into those of the larger company, and the stock of the smaller, merged company is retired.

Minority interest (p. 801) An account on the consolidated balance sheet of a parent corporation representing that portion of the subsidiary's stock owned by individuals other than the parent.

Minority stockholders (p. 801) Stockholders of a subsidiary who own that portion of the subsidiary not owned by the parent.

Modified Accelerated Cost-Recovery System (MACRS) (p. 416) The tax law covering the acceptable methods of depreciating fixed assets.

Monetary item (p. 945) Balance sheet assets and liabilities expressed in terms of a fixed number of dollars (often by contract) that are unaffected by inflation. Examples include cash, debt investments, receivables, and payables.

Mortgage Payable (p. 60) A balance sheet account that refers to long-term obligations secured by real estate.

Moving average (p. 357) Description of the combination of the averaging assumption and the perpetual inventory method.

Multinational corporation (p. 816) A corporation with operations or subsidiaries in foreign countries, often called a *transnational corporation.*

Multistep income statement (p. 697) An income statement format that separates the cost of goods sold from operating expenses, highlighting gross profit. This format also separates operating items from other revenues and expenses.

Municipal Finance Officer's Association (p. 27) The principal organization of accountants working in state and local governments.

Natural resource cost (p. 397) The cost of acquiring the rights to and extracting natural resources.

Net assets (p. 561) Total balance sheet assets less liabilities, equal to stockholders' equity. Often referred to as *net worth*.

Net book value (p. 59) The dollar value assigned to an item on the balance sheet. The net book value of a company (i.e., stockholders' equity) is equal to total assets less total liabilities.

Net income/loss (p. 10) The difference between the revenues generated by a company in a particular time period and the expenses required to generate those revenues. Often referred to as *profit* or earnings.

Net method (p. 300) A method of accounting for cash discounts that recognizes a sale (purchase) on an open account at the net sales price, and recognizes a contra revenue (cost reduction) if payment is made after the discount period.

Net present value (p. 216) The difference between discounted future cash inflows and discounted future cash outflows.

Net realizable value (p. 216) The net cash amount expected from the sale of an item, usually equal to the selling price of an item less the cost to complete the item and the cost to sell the item.

Net worth (p. 561) *See* **Stockholders' equity** or **Net assets.**

Nominal dollars (p. 942) Dollars of differing purchasing power. Conventional financial statements are expressed in terms of nominal dollars.

Non-interest-bearing note (p. 508) A note receivable or payable with a stated interest rate of zero.

Nonmonetary items (p. 945) Balance sheet assets that are not valued in terms of fixed numbers of dollars to be received in the future. Instead, they are valued at historical cost or lower-of-cost-or-market value. The prices of these items (equity investments, inventories, and long-lived assets) are usually affected by inflation.

Nonprofit entity (p. 22) An organization that is not designed to make a profit. Rather, most nonprofit entities generate funds through contributions, user fees, or taxes, and use these funds to achieve some organizational or social purpose.

Nonsufficient fund (NSF) penalty (p. 260) An assessment charged by banks against their customers for writing checks that are not backed by adequate funds.

Note receivable (p. 58) A receivable that is backed by a formal promissory note. The promissory note states an interest rate, a principal amount, a maturity date, and often designates security or collateral.

Notes payable (p. 504) Obligations evidenced by formal notes. They normally involve direct borrowings from financial institutions or arrangements to finance the purchase of assets.

Not-for-profit accounting (p. 24) The system of accounting used to record the financial activities of nonprofit entities. It is often called *fund accounting,* and it differs from financial accounting primarily because it is not designed to measure profit.

Objectively measurable events (p. 98) Exchange transactions backed by evidence that documents that the dollar values of the exchanges are considered objectively measurable. In general, dollar values are considered objectively measurable if they result from exchanges involving two parties with differing incentives.

Objectivity (p. 219–20) A principle of financial accounting stating that the values of transactions and the assets and liabilities created by them must be objectively determined.

Off-balance-sheet financing (p. 76) The structuring or reporting of transactions by management so that debt need not be reported in the liability section of the balance sheet or, in some cases, on the balance sheet at all.

Open accounts (p. 297) Informal credit trade agreements; the term is usually used to describe accounts receivable or accounts payable.

Operating activities (p. 11) The activities of a company that involve the provision of a service to its clients or the buying and selling of its product. The financial effects of the operating activities of a given period are summarized on both the income statement and the statement of cash flows.

Operating cycle (p. 250) The time it takes, in general, for a company to begin with cash, convert the cash to inventory, sell the inventory, and receive cash payment. Operating cycles vary greatly across different companies.

Operating expenses (p. 66) A section on the income statement that includes the periodic and usual expenses a company incurs to generate revenues.

Operating lease (p. 530) A rental arrangement in which an owner (lessor) transfers property to a lessee for a specified period of time for a specified price. After the lease expires, the property reverts to the lessor. For financial accounting purposes, operating leases are treated as simple rentals.

Operating performance (p. 876) A company's ability to increase its net assets through operating activities.

Operating transactions (p. 72) Business exchanges directly involving the acquisition and sale of a company's inventories or services.

Ordinary annuity (p. 910) An annuity that specifies periodic payments to be made at the end of each period.

Ordinary stock dividend (p. 587) A relatively small stock dividend; the number of shares issued represents less than 25 percent of the number of shares outstanding before the issuance.

Organizational costs (p. 434) Costs incurred prior to the start of a company's operations. Typically included are fees for underwriting, legal and accounting services, licenses, titles, and promotional expenditures.

Organization for Economic Cooperation and Development (p. 827) A group of twenty-four countries in the industrialized world, which (among a number of activities) issued a code of conduct in 1986 for multinational companies. The code includes guidelines for voluntary disclosures on financial reports.

Other expenses (p. 67) A section of the income statement that includes expenses associated with activities that are not central to the primary activities of a company. These expenses are either unusual or infrequent, but not both.

Other revenues (p. 66) A section on the income statement that includes revenues generated from activities that are not central to the primary operations of a company. These revenues are either unusual or infrequent, but not both.

Output market (p. 215) The market where an entity sells the outputs that result from its operations.

Outstanding checks (p. 260) Checks that have been written but have not yet been processed by a bank.

Outstanding shares of stock (p. 571) Issued shares that are presently held by shareholders.

Overhead (p. 348) Manufacturing costs that cannot be directly linked to particular products. Overhead costs include indirect materials, indirect labor, utility, taxes, insurance costs, and depreciation charges.

Owners' equity (p. 62) The section of the right side of the balance sheet that measures the portion of a company's assets that has either been contributed by the company's owners or generated through profitable operations and not distributed to or withdrawn by the owners. Owners' equity is usually used in the context of partnerships or proprietorships.

Par value (p. 572) In the context of preferred stock, par value is often used in the determination of the amount of the annual preferred dividend payment. It also determines the dollar amount disclosed in the Preferred Stock account on the balance sheet. In the context of common stock, par value has little economic significance, but it is used to determine the dollar amount disclosed in the Common Stock account on the balance sheet.

Parent company (p. 645) A company that owns a controlling interest (more than 50 percent of the voting stock) in another (subsidiary) company.

Participating preferred stock (p. 574) Stocks preferred as to dividends, which have the right, if dividends are declared, not only to an annual dividend amount (determined by the dividend percentage) but also a right to a portion of the additional dividend paid to the common stockholders.

Partnership (p. 61) A form of business organization in which the owners (partners) share the profits and bear the legal responsibility for the actions of the business.

Partnership agreement (p. 601) A contract written among the partners of a partnership that specifies the rights and obligations of the partners.

Patent (p. 59) A grant made by the government that gives an inventor the sole right to make, use, and sell the invention. The cost of acquiring a patent is listed as an intangible asset on the balance sheet.

Payments in Advance (p. 120) A liability account representing services yet to be performed by a company for which cash payments have already been collected. Also referred to as *Deferred Revenues* or *Unearned Revenues*.

Pension (p. 471) A sum of money paid to a retired or disabled employee, the amount of which is usually determined by the employee's years of service.

Percentage-of-credit-sales approach (p. 305) A method of estimating bad debts that multiplies a given percentage by the credit sales of a given accounting period.

Periodic inventory method (p. 344) A method of carrying inventory on the books that records each purchase as it occurs, and takes an inventory count to determine ending inventory at the end of the accounting period.

Permanent accounts (p. 115) Financial statement accounts that accumulate from one accounting period to the next. Included are asset, liability, and stockholders' equity accounts.

Perpetual inventory method (p. 344) A method of carrying inventory on the books that maintains an up-to-date record, recording each purchase as it occurs and recording an inventory outflow at each sale.

Petty cash (p. 257) Small amounts of cash kept on a company's premises to cover the day-to-day cash needs of office operations.

Physical controls (p. 259) The procedures and records designed to safeguard assets from loss or theft.

Physical obsolescence (p. 408) The state of an asset when repairs are not economically feasible.

Plant (p. 58) A long-lived asset account that includes such items as factories, office buildings, and warehouses.

Policymakers (p. 7) The individuals or groups that are directly involved in the setting of accounting standards. Included are the Financial Accounting Standards Board and the Securities and Exchange Commision.

Pooling of interests (p. 808) A business combination in which a company acquires a controlling interest (more than 50 percent of the voting stock) in another company by issuing shares to the stockholders of the company. In such situations the stockholders of the two companies combine their resources in the form of an exchange of stock shares.

Portfolio (p. 268) A group of securities held by an individual or company.

Postacquisition expenditures (p. 402) Costs incurred to improve or maintain long-lived assets after they have been acquired.

Post-retirement health care costs (p. 472) Health care costs of retired employees that are paid by the employer firm.

Preferred stock as to assets/dividends (p. 571) Stock preferred as to assets carries a claim to corporate assets in the case of liquidation that has a higher priority than the residual claim held by the common stockholders. Stock preferred as to dividends carries the right to receive dividends of a specified amount before dividends are distributed to the common stockholders.

Premium on Bonds Payable (p. 504) A financial statement account representing the amount by which the proceeds of a bond issuance exceed the face value. Bond premiums are amortized over the life of the bonds into interest expense.

Prepaid Expenses (p. 57) A balance sheet account representing expenses that have been paid before the corresponding service or right is actually used.

Present value (p. 216) The current monetary amount that is equivalent in value to a future cash payment.

Price/earnings ratio (p. 75) The price of a share of stock divided by net income per share. This ratio indicates how sensitive the price of a common share is to a change in earnings.

Prime interest rate (p. 542) The interest rate charged by a bank to its best (lowest risk) customers.

Principal (p. 511) The sum of money owed as a debt, upon which interest is calculated.

Prior period adjustment (p. 698) The financial effects of certain transactions (usually error corrections) that result in direct adjustments to the Retained Earnings account. All prior period adjustments occurred prior to the beginning of the current accounting period and are disclosed on the statement of retained earnings.

Private placement (p. 569) A stock issuance that is made available only to specific parties.

Proceeds (p. 576) The amount of cash collected on a sale, a borrowing, a bond issuance, or a stock issuance.

Profit (p. 10) The difference between the revenues generated by a firm in a particular time period and the expenses required to generate those revenues. Often referred to as *net income* or *earnings*.

Profit-seeking entities (p. 3) Companies, firms, or businesses that provide a service or a product in an effort to make a profit for the owners.

Profit-sharing plan (p. 465) A method of compensating company employees or managers that pays them a portion of the company's profits at the end of the year.

Profitability ratios (p. 862) Financial statement ratios that compare net income to various other financial statement numbers, providing a measure of earning power.

Programmer (p. 124) An individual who writes *programs,* which are the software used in a computer system.

Promissory note (p. 57) A contract that states the face value of an obligation, the date when the face value is due, and the periodic interest payments to be made while the obligation is outstanding.

Promoters (p. 569) Individuals who organize a corporation, apply for a charter, and establish the corporate bylaws. They often contribute assets in exchange for equity interest and arrange for additional equity issuances if necessary.

Property (p. 58) A long-lived asset account representing the real estate upon which a company conducts its operations.

Proprietorship (p. 61) A form of business with a single owner. A proprietorship is not a legal entity.

Providers of capital (p. 15) Individuals or entities that invest capital in a company. Included are debt and equity investors.

Public accountants (p. 28) Accountants who offer their services to the general public. Public accounting firms offer auditing, tax, and management consulting services to their clients.

Public input (p. 36) The lobbying efforts conducted by interested parties who wish to influence the accounting standard-setting process.

Public placement (p. 569) A stock issuance that is made available to the general public.

Purchase journal (p. 133) A special-purpose journal designed specifically to maintain a record of a company's inventory purchases.

Purchase method (p. 646) A method of accounting for a business acquisition by which the assets and liabilities of the subsidiary are added to those of the parent at fair market value, and the difference between the purchase price and the fair market value of the subsidiary's net assets is recorded as goodwill.

Purchasing power (p. 214) The amount of goods and services a monetary amount can buy at a given point in time.

Purchasing-power gain/loss (p. 942) Increases or decreases in a company's wealth due to holding monetary items in a period of inflation. Such gains and losses are recognized on constant-dollar income statements.

Qualified auditor's opinion (p. 853) An auditor's report stating that for some reason a company's financial statements do not fairly reflect its financial condition or performance, or that the statements were not prepared in accordance with generally accepted accounting principles.

Quantity discount (p. 300) A reduction in the per-unit price of an item if a certain number of items are purchased.

Quick ratio (p. 251) Cash plus marketable securities, divided by current liabilities; often used as an indication of a company's solvency position.

Ratio analysis (p. 862) Analyzing the financial statements by computing and examining financial ratios.

Readily marketable (p. 265) Able to be sold immediately. This expression is usually used to describe marketable securities listed as current assets.

Realized gain or loss (p. 268) To "cash in" a gain or loss by selling a security or other investment.

Realized holding gain/loss (p. 955) Market value increases or decreases of inventory that is sold or long-lived assets that expire during an accounting period. Such gains and losses are recognized separately on current-cost financial statements.

Recognized gain or loss (p. 268) To record a gain or loss in the books so that it is reflected on the financial statements.

Record control (p. 258) The procedures and records designed to ensure that all relevant and measurable economic events are accurately reflected in a company's financial statements.

Redemption (p. 529) The repurchase of outstanding debt (e.g., bonds), either before or at the maturity date.

Relevant events (p. 98) Any event having economic significance to a company. Events that affect a company's future cash flows are considered to be economically significant.

Reliability (p. 225) The extent to which a financial statement actually represents that which it purports to represent.

Replacement cost (p. 216) The current price that an entity would pay in the input market to replace an existing asset. *See* **Current cost.**

Research and development costs (p. 434) Costs incurred in the development of new products and processes.

Residual interest (p. 563) The right of common stockholders to receive corporate assets in the case of liquidation, after the creditors and preferred stockholders have received their share.

Retail company (p. 347) A company that simply purchases inventory and sells it for a price greater than its cost. Retailers provide primarily a distribution service, doing little to change or improve the products.

Retained Earnings (p. 10) The account on the right side of the balance sheet that represents the amount of the company's assets that have been generated through profitable operations and not paid out in the form of dividends.

Retirement (p. 402) To discontinue the use of an asset or to buy back outstanding bonds.

Returnable deposits (p. 461) Deposits paid by customers to guarantee performance or to cover expected future obligations.

Return on equity (p. 75) Net income divided by stockholders' equity. This ratio is often used to assess the earning power of a company.

Revaluation adjustments (p. 180) Adjusting journal entries designed to bring the dollar amounts of certain accounts in line with the existing facts. Examples include bad debt estimates, adjustments due to bank reconciliations, revaluations of marketable securities and inventories to apply the lower-of-cost-or-market rule, and the accrual of contingent liabilities.

Revenues (p. 10) Asset inflows or liability reductions associated with the operating activities of a company. Examples include sales, fees earned, service revenues, interest income, and various book gains.

Revenue recognition (p. 224) A principle of financial accounting stating that revenue cannot be recognized until the following four criteria have been met: (1) the earning process must be substantially complete, (2) the revenue must be objectively measurable, (3) the future cost associated with the sale must be estimable, and (4) the cash collection must be assured.

Risk-free return (p. 541) The return associated with a riskless security (e.g., certificates of deposit and treasury notes).

Risk premium (p. 542) The return over and above the risk-free rate that reflects the level of risk associated with a debtor company. The risk-free rate plus the risk premium equals the required rate of return.

Sales (p. 402) A revenue associated with the sale of a good or product.

Sales journal (p. 132) A special-purpose journal designed specifically to maintain a record of inventory sales.

Sales on account (p. 57) Sales of inventories or services in exchange for accounts receivable.

Sales returns (p. 311) Previously sold items that are returned in exchange for cash or credit.

Salvage value (p. 408) The value of a long-lived asset at retirement.

Secured notes (p. 511) Formal promissory notes backed by assets (collateral) that are distributed to creditors in the event of default.

Securities and Exchange Commission (p. 32) The government body that is responsible for the information available on the public security markets. The Securities and Exchange Commission delegated the authority to set accounting standards to the accounting profession, but still takes a very active role.

Security analyst (p. 22) An individual employed to analyze the investment potential of debt and equity securities.

Segregation of duties (p. 138) An important principle of internal control specifying that recordkeeping should be separated from the administration of operations, transactions, and assets.

Senior accountant (p. 29) The second level in the management hierarchy of a public accounting firm. Senior accountants are usually responsible for several staff accountants.

Service charges (p. 260) Assessments charged by banks to their customers for services like printing and processing checks and collecting receivables.

Service revenue (p. 66) Revenues earned on services provided. *See* **Fees earned.**

Shareholders (p. 61) Individuals or entities that hold ownership interests in a corporation; often referred to as *stockholders*.

Short-term Notes Receivable/Payable (p. 311) Balance sheet assets (obligations) that are backed by formal contracts and expected to provide (use) assets in the current period.

Single-step income statement (p. 697) An income statement format in which all operating and other revenues are included in a single category, while all operating and other expenses are grouped together in a separate category.

Smooth income (p. 507) A strategy used by management to avoid wide variations from one year to the next in reported net income. This strategy can be pursued by making certain operating decisions or using certain accounting methods. Using conservative accounting estimates in successful years and liberal accounting estimates in unsuccessful years would smooth income over time.

Software (p. 124) The programs, instructions, and routines for using the hardware of a computer system.

Solvency (p. 11) The ability of a company to meet its cash obligations as they come due. The statement of cash flows and other solvency ratios are used to assess a company's solvency position.

Solvency ratios (p. 862) Financial statement ratios that rely primarily on comparisons of various current assets and current liabilities, providing information about a company's ability to meet debt payments as they come due.

South American model (p. 826) A system of financial accounting used primarily in South America. This system is oriented toward the needs of government planners, and its rules are imposed on virtually all entities.

Special-purpose journals (p. 132) Journals designed to maintain records of frequently repeated transactions. Cash receipts, cash disbursements, inventory purchase, and inventory sales are often recorded in special-purpose journals.

Specific identification (p. 344) A procedure used to value the cost of goods sold and ending inventory that allocates actual costs to items sold and items remaining.

Stable dollar assumption (p. 213) An assumption of financial accounting stating that the value of the monetary unit used to measure an entity's performance is stable across time and across entities.

Staff accountant (p. 29) The entry-level position in a public accounting firm.

Stated interest rate (p. 508) The annual rate of interest stated on the face of a formal promissory note or bond certificate. The stated interest rate times the face value determines the periodic interest payments.

Stated value (p. 577) A dollar amount attached to a share of stock, which at one time served to limit corporate dividends and other forms of distribution to shareholders. Recent changes in the law to protect the interests of corporate creditors have rendered this constraint largely meaningless.

Statement of cash flows (p. 67) This financial statement traces the cash inflows and outflows of a company during a given period. It is divided into three areas of cash flow: operating activities, financing activities, and investment activities.

Statement of retained earnings (p. 10) This financial statement reconciles the balance in the Retained Earnings account from one period to the next. The beginning balance in Retained Earnings, plus net income, less dividends is usually equal to the ending balance in Retained Earnings.

Statement of stockholders' equity (p. 591) A financial statement normally included in the annual reports of major U.S. companies that explains the changes in the Stockholders' Equity accounts during an accounting period. Generally accepted accounting principles require that these changes be described somewhere in the annual report.

Stock dividend (p. 587) A dividend paid to a corporation's stockholders in the form of the corporation's stock.

Stock market (p. 31) The markets where equity securities are publicly traded.

Stock split (p. 586) An action taken by a corporation's board of directors to divide the number of outstanding shares into a larger number of less valuable units.

Stock split in the form of a stock dividend (p. 587) A relatively large stock dividend; the number of outstanding shares is increased by 25 percent or more.

Stockbrokers (p. 22) Individuals hired by others to buy and sell securities for them. These individuals often provide advice about the investment potential of the securities and are paid commissions on the security purchases and sales they execute.

Stockholders (p. 12) Individuals or entities that hold ownership interests (common stocks) in a corporation; often referred to as *shareholders*.

Stockholders' equity (p. 10) The section of a corporate balance sheet that represents the stockholders' interests in the corporation. It consists primarily of contributed capital and retained earnings.

Straight-line depreciation (p. 179) A procedure for depreciating long-lived assets (or amortizing intangibles) that recognizes equal amounts of depreciation (or amortization) in each year of an asset's useful life. Straight line is also used to amortize premiums and discounts on notes or bonds, if the results do not differ materially from those produced by the effective-interest method.

Subsidiary (p. 59) A company with the majority of its outstanding stock owned by another company, called the *parent*.

Subsidiary ledgers (p. 108) Ledgers that tie directly to control accounts and provide further breakdowns of the balances in those control accounts.

Sum-of-the-years'-digits (p. 411) A method of accelerated depreciation that is less extreme than the double-declining-balance method. Each period the depreciation base is multiplied by a ratio relating the remaining life to the sum of the life's digits.

Sunk cost (p. 960) A previously incurred cost that has no bearing on a current decision.

Suppliers (p. 3) Individuals or entities that provide goods or services to a company.

Supplies inventory (p. 57) Items used to support a company's operations, including, for example, office supplies or spare parts.

T-account (p. 107) A useful way to think about the accounts contained in the ledger. Each account is in the form of a T. The left side of the T represents the debit, while the right side represents the credit.

Table factors (p. 909) The numbers found in the present and future value tables.

Take a bath (p. 507) An expression used to describe a company that chooses to record an additional large writeoff in an unsuccessful year to improve reported net income in future years.

Takeover (p. 565) A situation where another company, investor, or group of investors purchases enough of the outstanding stock to gain a controlling interest (50 percent or more of the voting stock) in a purchased company

Tax accounting (p. 25) The area of accounting that deals specifically with determining (and usually minimizing) an individual's or entity's tax liability.

Tax deductible (p. 565) An expense that, according to the Internal Revenue Code, can be subtracted from revenues in the computation of taxable income.

Taxable income (p. 25) The amount of income that is subject to federal or state income taxes. Taxable income is measured by tax law and is often not the same as net income or profit.

Technical obsolescence (p. 408) The state of an asset when technical advances have rendered the asset's services no longer useful.

Temporary accounts (p. 115) Financial statement accounts that are set to zero through the closing process at the end of each accounting period. Included are revenue, expense, and dividend accounts.

Third-party collections (p. 462) Situations where companies act as collecting agencies for government or other entities. Examples include income and social security tax withholdings, sales taxes, and union dues.

Timeliness (p. 212) How quickly and how often financial reports are prepared. Timely reports are prepared soon enough to provide information for a given decision.

Time value of money (p. 907) A dollar today is worth more than a dollar in the future because money has a price, called *interest.*

Trade-in (p. 402) A transaction in which an old asset and usually cash are exchanged for a new asset.

Trademark (p. 432) An intangible asset representing a name, symbol, or other device identifying a product, legally restricted to the use of the owner or manufacturer.

Transactions (p. 48) Exchanges that are entered into by a company in the course of conducting business.

Transaction view of performance (p. 680) A method of determining and disclosing income that focuses on the individual transactions executed during a period. Each transaction is recorded and classified as operating or capital, and the operating transactions are further divided into revenues and expenses in the computation of net income.

Transportation-in (p. 347) An income statement account indicating the freight costs of purchased inventory, also called *freight-in.*

Treasurer (p. 27) The individual who oversees the financial resources of a company and is responsible for managing the company's cash position.

Treasury notes (p. 541) Obligations of the federal government that pay interest at a specified rate for a specified period of time, usually less than six months.

Treasury stock (p. 566) Previously issued stock that has been repurchased by the issuing company and held in treasury. Treasury stock is often reissued at a later date.

Type I foreign subsidiary (p. 823) A foreign subsidiary that operates independently from the parent and is integrated within the country or countries in which it operates.

Type II foreign subsidiary (p. 823) A foreign subsidiary that is an integral part of the parent's operations. Such subsidiaries may act as suppliers, or *channels*, of marketing and distribution for the parent.

Unadjusted trial balance (p. 111) The list of accounts and end-of-period account balances copied from the ledger to the worksheet. Preparing the unadjusted trial balance represents the first step in completing the worksheet.

Uncollectibles (p. 57) Outstanding receivables that are not expected to be collected.

Unearned Revenues (p. 176) A liability account that reflects the receipt of an asset before the associated service has been performed. Also referred to as *Payments in Advance* or *Deferred Revenues.*

Uniformity (p. 226) The extent to which all business entities use the same accounting methods.

United Nations (p. 827) An organization of countries designed to promote world peace and economic exchange. This organization recently reaffirmed a 1977 recommendation to encourage multinational corporations to provide certain public disclosures.

Unqualified audit opinion (p. 852) An auditor's report stating that the financial statements fairly reflect the financial condition and operations of a business and have been prepared in accordance with generally accepted accounting principles, also referred to as a *clean opinion.*

Unrealized gains and losses (p. 268) Gains and losses represented by price changes of held securities. These gains and losses have not been cashed in.

Unrealized holding gains/losses (p. 955) Increases or decreases during an accounting period in the market prices of inventory or long-lived assets that are held by a company at year end. Such gains and losses are separately disclosed on current-cost income statements.

Unsecured notes (p. 511) Formal promissory notes that are not backed by collateral, also called *debentures.*

Usual transaction (p. 689) An operating transaction that reflects the normal and customary activities of a company.

Valuation bases (p. 216) The values (e.g., historical cost, replacement cost, fair market value, present value) used to determine the dollar amount of an entity's assets and liabilities on the balance sheet.

Wages Payable (p. 60) A balance sheet account representing obligations that are owed to employees for services already performed.

Warranty (p. 470) An agreement by which a seller promises to remove deficiencies in the quantity, quality, or performance of a product sold to a buyer.

Went private (p. 566) Term used to describe a company that has purchased all of its publicly-traded outstanding stock.

Window dressing (p. 255) A phrase used to describe the activity of managers who use accounting methods or make operating decisions purely to make the financial statements appear more attractive to financial statement users.

Withdrawals (p. 62) Assets withdrawn from a partnership by the partners as a return on previously made contributions.

Working capital (p. 73) Current assets less current liabilities.

Worksheet (p. 111) A document used at the end of an accounting period to systematically transfer the balances in the ledger to the financial statements.